THOMSON REUTERS
CHECKPOINT™

P9-DTT-306

WG&L Tax Series

FEDERAL TAXATION OF PARTNERSHIPS AND PARTNERS

FOURTH EDITION

Revised Chapters 5, 8, 10A, 12, 17, 22, 23, 24, and 26 (replacing student main volume chapters)

2021 ABRIDGED EDITION
FOR STUDENT USE ONLY

WILLIAM S. McKEE
Member of the Virginia and District of Columbia Bars

WILLIAM F. NELSON
Member of the Georgia and District of Columbia Bars

ROBERT L. WHITMIRE
Member of the California Bar

GARY R. HUFFMAN
Member of the Texas and District of Columbia Bars

JAMES P. WHITMIRE
Member of the Colorado and Virginia Bars

With the assistance of Ronald L. Buch, Jr. on Chapter 10

THOMSON REUTERS™

How to Use the Main Volume Portion of the Student Supplement

Revised Chapters 5, 8, 10A, 12, 17, 22, 23, 24, and 26 of *Federal Taxation of Partnerships and Partners, Fourth Edition*, are included in this student supplement in their entirety. These chapters in the current student main volume should no longer be consulted.

The supplement begins after these chapters.

CHAPTER 5

Transfer of a Partnership Interest in Exchange for Services

¶ 5.01 OVERVIEW OF AN UNSETTLED AREA

[1] In General

The issuance of partnership interests to individuals in connection with the performance of services, past or anticipated, is a common event. Surprisingly, the tax consequences of these types of transactions are among the most unsettled in the partnership area. Over a quarter of a century ago, beginning in 1993, the Service acted to reduce this confusion by issuing guidance in the form of Revenue Procedures[1] that provide taxpayer-favorable certainty in many common situations. Unfortunately, Proposed Regulations were issued in 2005 that would prospectively modify, in very substantial ways, the guidance in these Revenue Procedures.[2] These Proposed Regulations apply only to interests is-

---

[1] Rev. Proc. 93-27, 1993-2 CB 343, modified by Rev. Proc. 2001-43, 2001-2 CB 191. See generally ¶ 5.02[2].

[2] REG-105346-03 (May 24, 2005). See Notice 2005-43, 2005-1 CB 1221 (draft of new Revenue Procedure to reflect 2005 Proposed Regulations and replace Revenue Procedure 93-27 and Revenue Procedure 2001-43). In addition to changes in the § 721 Regulations, the 2005 proposals include related changes and additions in Regulations §§ 1.83-3, 1.83-6, 1.704-1(b), 1.706-3, 1.707-1(c), and 1.761-1(b). The effective date of these proposed changes and additions is deferred pending publication of final regulations. A decade later, in 2015, the Treasury modified the still-outstanding 2005 proposals in a very minor way by modifying and finalizing the proposed § 1.706-3 changes as Regulations §§ 1.706-6(a) and 1.706-6(b).

sued on or after the date final regulations are published. To date, they have not been finalized, creating an ongoing aura of uncertainty.

It is important to keep in mind that the rules and concepts discussed in this Chapter are only applicable to interests issued to a partner acting in his capacity as a member of the partnership.[3] Section 707(a)(2)(A) gives the Service the authority to issue Regulations defining the circumstances under which a partner who performs services for a partnership and receives "a related direct or indirect allocation and distribution" should be viewed as acting "other than in his capacity as a member of the partnership." The Service responded to this invitation by issuing Proposed Regulations § 1.707-2 in 2015.[4] These Proposed Regulations (which are effective only on finalization) would require that distributions made pursuant to any partnership interest received in exchange for services must satisfy a multi-factor test (the most important of which is the presence of significant entrepreneurial risk) in order to avoid treatment as "disguised payments for services" issued to the recipient other than in his capacity as a partner.[5]

[2] Difficulties Created By the Enactment of Section 83

Another major source of uncertainty is § 83. Enacted in 1969 and focused primarily on corporate issuances of restricted stock for services, § 83 generally applies to all service-connected transfers of property.[6] It applies to any (1) "transfer"[7] (2) of "property" (3) "in connection with the performance of services."[8] It encompasses unrestricted transfers as well as transfers of property subject to restrictions. Under § 83(a), the service provider's income is equal to the excess of the fair market value[9] of the transferred property over any amount paid by the service provider for the property. Both the taxable event

---

[3] See § 707(a)(1), discussed in Chapter 14 of this treatise.

[4] See Notice of Proposed Rulemaking, REG-115452-14, 80 Fed. Reg. 43,652 (July 23, 2015), discussed at ¶ 14.02[4][d].

[5] In the preamble to these Proposed Regulations, the Treasury announced its intent to issue a revenue procedure providing an additional exception to the safe harbor in Revenue Procedure 93-27, 1993-2 CB 343, that would apply to profits interests issued in conjunction with a partner foregoing payment of an amount that is substantially fixed. See Notice of Proposed Rulemaking, REG-115452-14, 80 Fed. Reg. 43,652, 43,654 (July 23, 2015). To date, no such exception has been formalized.

[6] § 83(a)(1). Regulations § 1.61-2(d)(6) makes it clear that in the case of any overlap, § 83 trumps § 61 for transfers after June 30, 1969.

[7] See generally ¶ 5.04[1].

[8] See generally ¶ 5.04[2].

[9] See generally ¶ 5.06.

and the determination of the fair market value of the property occur at the time the property is "transferred."

In the context of § 83, the word "transfer" does not have its usual meaning. Instead, it means a transaction or event that causes the putative owner to have "substantially vested"[10] beneficial ownership of the property that is free of any substantial risk of forfeiture[11] or is "transferable."[12]

For purposes of § 83, "the term 'property' includes real and personal property other than money or an unfunded and unsecured promise to pay money or property in the future."[13] A partnership interest (whether a profits interest or a capital interest) is intangible personal property,[14] and generally is not equivalent to an unfunded and unsecured promise to pay money or property in the future.[15] Consequently, transfers of partnership interests are transfers of property subject to § 83. Unfortunately, the timing and valuation rules in § 83 do not interact well with the general scheme of Subchapter K.

In the absence of a § 83(b) election, a service provider is not treated as the owner of a restricted interest until the interest is substantially vested. So, pending substantial vesting of her interest, there has not been a "transfer" of the interest to the service provider; the service provider is not treated as the tax owner of the interest, cannot be a partner for purposes of Subchapter K, cannot be allocated partnership income, loss, or other partnership items, and cannot be treated as receiving partnership distributions or making contributions.

The deferral of partner status under § 83 creates a number of issues, including the following:

1. By deferring the time the transfer of an interest is deemed to occur, § 83 creates a variety of distortions with regard to the treatment of con-

---

[10] Ownership of property is substantially vested if the property is transferable or not subject to a substantial risk of forfeiture. Reg. § 1.83-3(b).

[11] Reg. § 1.83-3(c).

[12] For this purpose, property subject to a substantial risk of forfeiture is "transferable" only if the owner has the right to transfer it to a transferee free of substantial risk of forfeiture. Reg. § 1.83-3(d).

[13] Reg. § 1.83-3(e).

[14] Uniform Partnership Act (UPA) § 26. Interests in limited liability companies are also intangible personal property. See Uniform Limited Liability Company Act §§ 501, 102(24); C. Bishop & D. Kleinberger, Limited Liability Companies: Tax and Business Law ¶ 5.04[2][c][iii] (Thomson Reuters/Tax & Accounting 1994).

[15] Unfunded and unsecured rights to future payment were excluded from the § 83 definition of "property" to prevent § 83 from swallowing the cash method of accounting and thereby subjecting traditional nonqualified deferred compensation arrangements to immediate taxation. As broadly applicable as it is, § 83 was not intended to supplant the substantial body of law governing deferred compensation arrangements. See generally Reg. §§ 1.451-1(a), 1.451-2(a); Rev. Rul. 60-31, 1960-1 CB 174. See also TD 9659, 2014-1 CB 653 ("Summary of Comments," second paragraph).

tributions with respect to the restricted interest while it remains subject to a substantial risk of forfeiture; and distributions to the interest
holder during this period will be treated as ordinary compensation income to the recipient, without regard to the character or existence of
partnership income;

2. If the compensation payments are not immediately deductible by the
   partnership, unfavorable timing consequences will follow for the partners as a group;

3. The inability of the partnership to allocate profits to the holder of an
   unvested interest creates a vacuum for such allocations, is likely to
   upset the economic arrangement intended by the partners, and may
   invalidate partnership allocations under § 704(b);

4. In the event of an actual forfeiture, there are flaws and uncertainties
   as to the amount and character of the service provider's income or
   loss on the forfeiture; and

5. The § 83 timing rules relating to restricted interests are inconsistent
   with the long-standing timing rules in Regulations § 1.721.[16]

Under § 83(b), any recipient of restricted property may elect to include the
unrestricted value of the property in income at the time of the transfer even if
the property is not substantially vested when received. Given the issues summarized above, recipients of partnership interests should carefully consider the
merits of this election. Unfortunately, a § 83(b) election is not without its own
disadvantages, not the least of which is an immediate tax on the service provider for compensation she may never receive.

One of the difficulties inherent in determining the consequences of an issuance of a partnership interest in exchange for services is the inherent conflict
between some (but not all) of the answers that seem intuitively correct and
those that seem dictated by the law. Intuitively, it seems that a transfer of a
mere right to share in future partnership appreciation and income should not be
taxed upon receipt. While this intuitive expectation is consistent with the Treasury's long-standing administrative position, it is not supported by the language of § 83,[17] even though it is informed by experience: Admissions to
professional partnerships have never been treated as taxable events.[18] It also reflects practical considerations: (1) valuing a mere expectancy is difficult to do
in practice and even more difficult to deal with administratively; (2) if this expectancy is to be taxed, the difficulties inherent in the other side of the transaction must be considered: should the transferor be taxed on the excess of the
value of the expectant interest over its basis (presumably zero) and be entitled

---

[16] The § 721 timing rules would be amended by the 2005 Proposed Regulations. See
¶ 5.02[3][c].

[17] A contrary interpretation of the existing law is set forth in ¶ 5.02[4].

[18] See discussion at ¶ 5.02[4].

to either a deduction or some sort of tax-recognized asset that will have future tax benefits?; and (3) the transferee's share of future partnership income and appreciation will be included in his distributive share of partnership income when realized by the partnership; certainly, service providers should not be taxed twice on the same income. Although the intuitive notion that no tax results from the receipt of a partnership profits interest for services is difficult to derive analytically, it continues, in large measure by administrative fiat, to be reality, at least pending finalization of the 2005 Proposed Regulations.

[3] Compensatory Transfers of Partnership Interests: Summary

At the time of this writing, ignoring the long-outstanding but not yet finalized 2005 Proposed Regulations,[19] the tax consequences of compensatory transfers of partnership interests may be summarized as follows:

1. The receipt of an interest in partnership capital in connection with the performance of past or future services for the issuing partnership or another person is a taxable event under § 61 and is subject to the timing rules of § 83.[20]

2. By administrative decree, the receipt of an interest in partnership profits for past or future services rendered "to or for the benefit of" the issuing partnership is not treated as a taxable event unless (a) the profits interest relates to a "substantially certain and predictable stream of income from partnership assets"; (b) within two years of receipt, the partner disposes of the profits interest; or (c) the profits interest is a limited partnership interest in a § 7704(b) publicly traded partnership.[21] The determination of whether a partnership interest is a profits interest within this safe harbor is made at the time of the grant of the interest. The interest is not retested when it vests, and neither the granting or vesting of such interests are taxable events for the partnership or the service partner. Accordingly, the recipient partner does not need to make a § 83(b) election.[22] This administrative position is both practical and justifiable as a policy matter, but is impossible to square with § 83.

3. For purposes of distinguishing capital and profits interests, a capital interest is any partnership interest that would entitle the recipient to a

---

[19] Discussed in ¶ 5.02[3]. Whatever happens to these Proposed Regulations is unlikely to resolve the conundrum noted in the prior paragraph in any event.

[20] Crescent Holdings, LLC, 141 TC 477, 493 (2013) (§ 83 applies to nonvested capital interest). See generally ¶ 5.02[3][f].

[21] Rev. Proc. 93-27, 1993-2 CB 343.

[22] Rev. Proc. 2001-43, 2001-2 CB 191, discussed at ¶ 5.02[2].

share of liquidation proceeds if the partnership sold its assets for their fair market value and liquidated immediately after the recipient receives the interest. A profits interest is an interest that entitles the recipient only to a share of future profits and appreciation.[23]

4. The receipt of a profits interest may or may not be a taxable event in any situation not within the safe harbor created by the revenue procedures. For example, transfers of profits interests for services not rendered to or for the benefit of the issuing partnership may be taxable, but that result is not certain.

5. In cases falling outside the safe harbor, the Service is likely to treat the issuance of any profits or capital interest that is subject to a substantial risk of forfeiture and is related to the performance of services as a taxable event subject to the timing rules of § 83. Consequently, if a service provider receives such an interest and does not make an election under § 83(b),[24] the interest will be valued and taxed to the owner at the time the interest becomes substantially vested. The service provider will *not* be recognized as a partner prior to the time the interest becomes substantially vested.

6. With regard to the consequences of forfeitures, the § 83(b) Regulations provide a simple rule, obviously focused on corporate stock rather than partnership interests, to the effect that a recipient of nonvested property who makes a § 83(b) election and subsequently forfeits the nonvested property is entitled to deduct a loss (generally a capital loss) equal to the excess of the amount (if any) paid for the property over the amount realized, if any, as a consequence of the forfeiture.[25] This simple formulation does not work well for two reasons: (1) it fails to credit the service provider with basis for any income realized as a consequence of the § 83(b) election, and (2) in the partnership context, it fails to take into account any basis adjustments related to pre-forfeiture partnership contributions and distributions and allocations of partnership profits .

7. In the absence of a § 83(b) election, the Regulations set forth a substantially identical defective rule for the computation of gain or loss

---

[23] Rev. Proc. 93-27, 1993-2 CB 343; Rev. Proc. 2001-43, 2001-2 CB 191; Crescent Holdings, LLC, 141 TC 477, 493 (2013) (adopting the definition in Rev. Proc. 93-27).

[24] If there is any sort of question as to whether the safe harbor applies to a transaction, it generally will be prudent to make the § 83(b) election. If it is not made and the Service challenges the availability of the safe harbor, the differences in the consequences to both the partnership and the service partner are too severe to risk a foot-fault.

[25] Reg. § 1.83-2(a).

but explicitly dictate ordinary loss treatment upon forfeitures of nonvested property.[26]

¶ 5.02 SERVICE-CONNECTED TRANSFERS OF PARTNERSHIP INTERESTS

[1] Historical Overview: Pre-1993

The starting point in the Code is the nonrecognition rule in § 721(a) which clearly and broadly provides (with very few exceptions, none of which are relevant here) for nonrecognition of gain or loss by a partnership or any partner on a contribution of property to a partnership in exchange for a partnership interest. However, the scope of § 721(a) does not explicitly encompass the issuance of partnership interests for services. Section 83, on the other hand, provides a comprehensive scheme for taxing compensatory transfers of "property." Prior to the addition of § 83 to the Code in 1969, a number of earlier cases held, without the aid of this provision, that a compensatory transfer of an interest in partnership *capital* was a taxable event.[27] Moreover, Regulations under § 61 have long provided that gross income includes the fair market value of property received as compensation for services,[28] and long-standing Regulations under § 721 provide as follows:

> To the extent that any of the partners gives up any part of his right to be repaid his contributions (*as distinguished from a share in partnership profits*) in favor of another partner as compensation for services (or in satisfaction of an obligation), section 721 does not apply. The value of an interest in such partnership capital so transferred to a partner as compensation for services constitutes income to the partner under section 61.[29]

---

[26] Reg. § 1.83-1(b)(2). The Regulations also confer an ordinary loss deduction (to the extent the basis of the property has been increased by the recognition of income to the service provider under § 83(a)) on any service provider in connection with forfeitures of vested properties. Reg. § 1.83-1(e).

[27] See, e.g., United States v. Frazell, 335 F2d 487 (5th Cir. 1964) (cert. denied); F.C. McDougal, 62 TC 720 (1974) (acq.); Glenn E. Edgar, 56 TC 717, 747 (1971); Leonard A. Farris, 22 TC 104 (1954) (acq.), rev'd, 222 F2d 320 (10th Cir. 1955); Harry W. Lehman, 19 TC 659 (1953). The reversal in *Farris* was apparently based, not on a conclusion that a compensatory shift in partnership capital is not a taxable event, but on a difference of opinion between the Tax Court and the Fifth Circuit as to exactly when the shift occurred.

[28] See Reg. § 1.61-2(d).

[29] Reg. § 1.721-1(b)(1) (emphasis added).

The scope of Regulations § 1.721-1(b)(1) is uncertain in two respects. First, and most importantly, by distinguishing transfers of interests in "contributions" from interests in a "share in partnership profits," it could be read to imply that a transfer of an interest in partnership profits is not a taxable event. However, in *Sol Diamond*,[30] the full Tax Court (in a reviewed opinion) and the Seventh Circuit held that the receipt of a profits interest is a taxable event, with the Tax Court expressly holding that the parenthetical clause does not shelter the receipt of a profits interest from tax under § 61.[31] Perhaps the most significant aspect of the Seventh Circuit's affirming opinion is the repeated references to the fact that the value of Diamond's profits interest was readily determinable at the time of its receipt. Thus, the opinion strongly suggests that a profits interest is not subject to tax on receipt unless it "has a market value capable of determination."[32] Subsequently, in *William G. Campbell*, the Tax Court effectively rejected the Seventh Circuit's administratively convenient approach and chose to "reaffirm [its] holding that section 721(a) and the Regulations thereunder are simply inapplicable where, as in the *Diamond* case and the instant case, a partner receives his partnership interest in exchange for services he has rendered to the partnership."[33] Finding no available nonrecognition provision, the court determined that the transactions in question were taxable and governed by § 83.[34] The Tax Court then turned to the issue of valuation. While it acknowledged the implication in the Seventh Circuit's affirming opinion in *Diamond* that profits interests with speculative value should not be taxed on receipt, it proceeded to value Campbell's interests based on expert testimony and its own analysis of the facts.

Campbell was reversed by the Eighth Circuit in an oddly benign decision.[35] The Eighth Circuit held that Campbell owed no tax upon receipt of his partnership profits interests because the interests had no fair market value due to the speculative nature of the projected tax benefits and revenue of the partnerships. This aspect of the Eighth Circuit's opinion is reminiscent of the Seventh Circuit's efforts to hedge its affirming opinion in *Diamond*.[36] Perhaps more significantly, the Eighth Circuit also indicated—but did not specifically hold—that Campbell's receipt of profits interests for services was not a taxa-

---

[30] Sol Diamond, 56 TC 530 (1971), aff'd, 492 F2d 286 (7th Cir. 1974).

[31] Sol Diamond, 56 TC 530, 545.

[32] Sol Diamond v. Commissioner, 492 F2d 286, 290 (7th Cir. 1974).

[33] William G. Campbell, 59 TCM 236, 249 (1990), rev'd, 943 F2d 815 (8th Cir. 1991).

[34] The court rejected Campbell's alternative argument that the interests should not be treated as § 83 property because they were analogous to unfunded, unsecured promises to pay, which are not § 83 property. William G. Campbell, 59 TCM 236, 250 (1990).

[35] Campbell v. Commissioner, 943 F2d 815 (8th Cir. 1991).

[36] Diamond v. Commissioner, 492 F2d 286, 290 (7th Cir. 1974).

ble event under fundamental principles of partnership tax law, without regard to valuation issues.[37]

The second basic uncertainty in Regulations § 1.721-1(b)(1) is created by its puzzling reference to a partner's "contributions." From this, one could easily draw the negative implication that the receipt of an interest in partnership capital appreciation could somehow fall within the purview of § 721, and thus the receipt of such an interest would not be a taxable event.[38] The Regulations, however, seem to be internally inconsistent in this respect because they provide that the "value" of an interest in "partnership capital" (from whatever source, one might think) transferred to a partner for services constitutes taxable income to him under § 61. They go on to further provide that "[t]he value of an interest in such partnership capital so transferred to a partner as compensation for services constitutes income to the partner under section 61. The amount of such income is the *fair market value* of the interest in capital so transferred ...."[39]

In practice, the purview of this provision of the Regulations has never been limited to transfers of rights to "contributions." Instead, even prior to the enactment of § 83, a partner who received a compensatory transfer of an interest in partnership capital was taxed on the fair market value of the interest so transferred, without regard to the Regulations' reference to "contributions."[40] Nevertheless, the extent to which a partnership interest is property for § 83 purposes is somewhat clouded by the § 721 Regulations, which can be read to

---

[37] The court "ma[d]e short work" of the government's argument, raised for the first time on appeal, that Campbell should be taxed on receipt of the profits interests in question because his services were performed for his employer (a sponsor of the partnership) and not the partnership itself. Campbell v. Commissioner, 943 F2d 815, 818 (8th Cir. 1991). The Eighth Circuit declined to address the issue and noted that contrary to the government's protestations, the Tax Court had *not* specifically held that Campbell performed only employee capacity services.

[38] For example, assume that *A* and *B* each contribute $50,000 to a partnership for the purchase of land, and at a time when the land has appreciated in value to $150,000, they admit *C* as an equal partner. Subsequent to *C*'s admission, each partner has a fair market value capital account of $50,000. *A* and *B* have thus not surrendered their claim for a return of their initial contributions, and the Regulations may be read to imply that no taxable transfer occurs. There is simply no way to justify this result under the Code or the Regulations.

[39] Reg. § 1.721-1(b)(1) (emphasis added). For a historical perspective on this Regulation, see ¶ 5.02[4][c].

[40] See Glenn E. Edgar, 56 TC 717, 747 (1971); cf. F.C. McDougal, 62 TC 720 (1974) (acq.). In Robert Johnston, 69 TCM 2283 (1995), the Tax Court held that a service partner realized income equal to the fair market value of an interest in partnership capital that was shifted to him upon the admission of limited partners to his partnership. Even though the case was decided decades after the enactment of § 83, the court relied on Regulations § 1.721-1(b)(1), noting that the result would be the same under "sec. 83, if applicable here." Id. at 2290 n.15. Although it is not entirely clear why the court did not apply § 83 directly, it may be because both parties failed to rely on it.

draw a distinction between an interest in partnership capital, which is clearly property, and an interest in future partnership profits, which arguably is not property for §§ 61 and 83 purposes. Faced with the uncertain interaction between the long-standing § 721 Regulations and the unforgiving language in § 83, the Service decided to retreat by issuing Revenue Procedure 93-27.[41]

[2] An Uneasy Administrative Truce: 1993 to Date

The publication of Revenue Procedure 93-27 marked the beginning of a new era of relative certainty for many service partners. Cutting through the prior legislative and judicial confusion by administrative fiat, this Revenue Procedure creates a broad, taxpayer-friendly safe harbor that has now been in existence for over a quarter of a century and has served both taxpayers and the tax system well, as demonstrated by the relative lack of litigation during this era. The safe harbor is based on what is now the commonly accepted definition of a "profits interest"—a partnership interest that would not entitle the holder to a share of the proceeds if all partnership assets were sold for their fair market value and the net sale proceeds were distributed to the partners in liquidation of the partnership, all as of the time the interest in question is received.[42] Generally, this Revenue Procedure provides that if a person receives a profits interest in exchange for providing services to or for the benefit of a partnership, either in a partner capacity or in anticipation of becoming a partner, the Service will not treat the receipt of the interest as a taxable event as to either the partner or the partnership. There are only three exceptions to this safe harbor:

1. If the profits interest relates to a substantially certain and predictable stream of income from partnership assets, such as income from high-quality debt securities or a high-quality net lease;
2. If the partner disposes of the profits interest within two years of receipt; or
3. If the profits interest is a limited partnership interest in a "publicly traded partnership" within the meaning of § 7704(b).[43]

Thus, Revenue Procedure 93-27 creates a broad safe zone, subject only to these three tightly defined exceptions, within which profits interests are not taxable upon receipt. The exceptions attempt to isolate for further review and possible litigation those interests that are relatively easy to value.

---

[41] Rev. Proc. 93-27, 1993-2 CB 343.

[42] Rev. Proc. 93-27, § 2.01, 1993-2 CB 343, clarified in Rev. Proc. 2001-43, § 3, 2001-2 CB 191 (substantially nonvested interests).

[43] Rev. Proc. 93-27, § 4, 1993-2 CB 343, 344.

Revenue Procedure 93-27 applies to interests transferred for services provided "to or for the benefit of" the issuing partnership. The words "for the benefit of" seem to leave open the possibility that a profits interest transferred for services to a person or entity other than the partnership may qualify for the safe harbor.[44] These situations may arise, for example, if key employees of an organization in the business of organizing and managing investment and development partnerships are admitted as "profits interest" partners in all such partnerships, whether or not they perform services for each partnership.

This revenue procedure does not represent the Service's position on the substance of the law;[45] rather, it assures taxpayers that the Service will not attempt to tax transfers of partnership profits interests in most, but not all, typical situations in which partnership interests are transferred for services.[46]

Revenue Procedure 93-27 has been amplified by Revenue Procedure 2001-43,[47] which applies only to partnership interests described in Revenue Procedure 93-27. Revenue Procedure 2001-43 acknowledges the timing and valuation rules in § 83 and rationalizes their application to substantially nonvested safe harbor interests. It expands the language of Revenue Procedure 93-27 to the effect that the determination of the existence and value of a capital interest "generally is made at the time of receipt"[48] and to encompass all safe harbor interests, whether or not restricted.[49] It specifically provides that the determination of whether a safe harbor partnership interest is a capital interest or a profits interest is made at the time the interest is received even if the interest is substantially nonvested at that time, and no taxable event or additional valuation is required when the interest vests. The Service will not treat

---

[44] Prop. Reg. § 1.721-1(b)(3) (2005). See REG-105346-03, Preamble, Explanation of Provisions § 1 (last paragraph), 70 Fed. Reg. 29675, 29678 (May 24, 2005) (requesting comments on this approach).

[45] Revenue Procedure 93-27, 1993-2 CB 343, states as "background" that in *Campbell* the Eighth Circuit

> suggested that the taxpayer's receipt of a partnership profits interest received for services was not taxable, but decided the case on valuation. Other courts have determined that in certain circumstances the receipt of a partnership profits interest for services is a taxable event under section 83 of the Internal Revenue Code. [Citations omitted.] The courts have also found that typically the profits interest received has speculative or no determinable value at the time of receipt.

[46] The issuance of Revenue Procedure 93-27, 1993-2 CB 343, has led to more than two decades of relative calm on the partnership interest for services battlefield. As discussed later, the likely end of that era has been foreshadowed by the promulgation of the 2005 Proposed Regulations. See ¶ 5.02[3].

[47] Rev. Proc. 2001-43, 2001-2 CB 191.

[48] Rev. Proc. 93-27, § 2.01, 1993-2 CB 343. Neither Revenue Procedure mentions the § 83(a) rules deferring the valuation and taxation of "transfers" of restricted property until the restriction ends.

[49] Rev. Proc. 2001-43, § 3, 2001-2 CB 191, 192.

the grant of the interest or the event that causes the interest to become substantially vested as a taxable event for the partner or the partnership. Thus, "[t]axpayers to which this revenue procedure applies need not file an election under section 83(b) of the Code."

In order to qualify for this largess, the following requirements must be met:

1. The partnership and the service partner must treat the service partner as the owner of the interest from the date of its grant and the service provider must take into account the distributive share associated with the interest for the entire period during which the service partner holds the interest;

2. Neither the partnership nor any partner can deduct any amount (as wages, compensation, or otherwise) based on the fair market value of the interest at the time of grant or vesting; and

3. All other conditions of Revenue Procedure 93-27 must be satisfied.

These two revenue procedures effectively create an extra-statutory regime that obviates most of the generally applicable § 83 rules for nonvested property. The usual rule that nonvested property is valued and taxed when it vests is turned on its head for nonvested profits interests, even in the absence of a § 83(b) election, and the recipient of the nonvested property is treated as the owner of the property from the date it is received, contrary to the generally applicable § 83 rules and regardless of whether a § 83(b) election is made.

For partners who receive nonvested interests, this regime creates a peculiar dichotomy between (1) a partner who pays a small price for an interest with an equally small liquidation value, and (2) a partner who pays nothing for an interest that has no current liquidation value. The former can elect to make or not make a § 83(b) election, whereas the latter apparently can only choose between § 83(b) treatment and something similar to § 83(b) treatment, whether he wants it or not. Most individuals will, of course, prefer something like § 83(b) treatment in any event, but this may not always be the case.

The consequences of forfeitures of nonvested interests are not addressed by these revenue procedures. The § 83(b) Regulations provide a simple rule, obviously focused on corporate stock rather than partnership interests, to the effect that a recipient of nonvested property who makes a § 83(b) election and subsequently forfeits the nonvested property is entitled to deduct a loss (generally a capital loss) equal to the excess of the amount (if any) paid for the property over the amount realized, if any, as a consequence of the forfeiture.[50] This simple formulation does not work well for two reasons: (1) it fails to credit the service provider with basis for any income realized as a consequence of the § 83(b) election, and (2) in the partnership context it fails to take into account

---

[50] Reg. § 1.83-2(a).

any basis adjustments related to pre-forfeiture partnership contributions and distributions and allocations of partnership profits and losses.

Literally, the § 83(b) Regulations do not apply to interests covered by the revenue procedures unless the service partner makes an otherwise irrelevant § 83(b) election. In the absence of a § 83(b) election, the Regulations set forth a substantially identical deficient computation of gain or loss but explicitly dictate ordinary loss treatment upon forfeitures of nonvested property.[51]

[3] Omens of Change: The 2005 Proposed (But Not Yet Finalized) Regulations

The armistice declared by the Service in Revenue Procedure 93-27 has been threatened, but not yet ended, by the publication of Proposed Regulations in 2005. These Proposed (but not yet finalized) Regulations explicitly reject the theory that the receipt of a partnership interest in connection with services is not a realization event, and thereby reopen the debate over the proper taxation of partnership profits interests received for services. In conjunction with the issuance of these Proposed Regulations, the Service issued a Notice relating to a proposed revenue procedure that provides additional rules relating to an elective safe harbor contained in the Proposed Regulations. The 2005 Proposed Regulations and Notice 2005-43 (collectively, the "2005 Proposed Regulations") apply only to transfers on or after the date final regulations are published.[52]

Under the 2005 proposals, a safe harbor would be available for transfers of eligible partnership interests[53] if a partnership and all of its partners affirmatively elect into it. For electing partnerships, the primary impact of the safe

---

[51] Reg. § 1.83-1(b)(2). The Regulations also confer an ordinary loss deduction but only (to the extent the basis of the property has been increased by the recognition of income to the service provider under § 83(a)) on any service provider in connection with forfeitures of vested properties.

[52] REG-105346-03, 70 Fed. Reg. 29675 (May 24, 2005); Notice 2005-43, 2005-1 CB 1221 (proposed Revenue Procedure reflecting 2005 Proposed Regulations and replacing Revenue Procedures 93-27 and 2001-43). In addition to changes in the § 721 regulations, the 2005 package included related proposed changes and additions in Regulations §§ 1.83-3, 1.83-6, 1.704-1(b), 1.706-3, 1.707-1(c), and 1.761-1(b). All of these proposed changes and additions are deferred pending publication of final regulations. A decade later, in 2015, the Treasury modified the then still outstanding 2005 package in a very minor way by modifying and finalizing the § 1.706-3 changes as Reg. §§ 1.706-6(a) and 1.706-6(b).

[53] Pursuant to Section 3.02(1) of the proposed Revenue Procedure in Notice 2005-43, 2005-1 CB 1221, an interest is not eligible for the safe harbor if it is "(a) related to a substantially certain and predictable stream of income from partnership assets, such as income from high-quality debt securities or a high-quality net lease, (b) transferred in anticipation of a subsequent disposition, or (c) an interest in a publicly traded partnership within the

harbor would be to mandate the use of "liquidation value" instead of fair market value whenever it is necessary to value a partnership interest under § 83. With this exception, the usual § 83 rules would apply. For example, service providers receiving safe harbor profits interests that are not substantially vested would have to file § 83(b) elections to ensure that the interest is valued prior to vesting. This approach, while consistent with the general § 83 scheme, stands in marked contrast to the administrative practice under Revenue Procedure 93-27, as supplemented by Revenue Procedure 2001-43,[54] pursuant to which the receipt of a safe harbor profits interest is treated as a nontaxable event without further action on the part of the recipient of the interest or the partnership.

Another significant departure from the prior administrative practice is the scope of the 2005 Proposed Regulations: They are broadly applicable to all types of partnership interests regardless of whether the interest is a profits interest or a capital interest, and also regardless of whether the interest is substantially vested.[55] However, they are explicitly limited to interests transferred in consideration of services performed for the issuing partnership,[56] whereas the prior Revenue Procedures were ambiguous on this point.

A representative of the Treasury Department has stated publicly that Treasury is awaiting the outcome of the "carried interest" legislation first proposed in early 2009 before acting to finalize the 2005 Proposed Regulations.[57] As originally conceived, the carried interest legislation would generally tax as ordinary income all gain from the disposition of certain partnership interests (including certain distributions with respect thereto) received in exchange for the provision of services. Although the 2017 Tax Cuts and Jobs Act made some adjustments to the treatment of carried interests,[58] the larger issue of comprehensive ordinary income treatment remains very much alive, and finalization of the 2005 Proposed Regulations is not currently slated for action.

---

meaning of § 7704(b)." These exceptions are a slightly reworked version of the exceptions listed in Revenue Procedure 93-27, 1993-2 CB 343.

[54] Rev. Proc. 2001-43, 2001-2 CB 191. See ¶ 5.02[2].

[55] REG-105346-03, Preamble, Explanation of Provisions § 1, 70 Fed. Reg. 29675 (May 24, 2005). See, e.g., Prop. Reg. §§ 1.83-3(l)(1), 1.721-1(b)(3) (2005).

[56] REG-105346-03, Preamble, Explanation of Provisions § 1 (last paragraph), 70 Fed. Reg. 29675, 29678 (May 24, 2005) (requesting comments on this approach). See Prop. Reg. § 1.721-1(b)(3) (2005).

[57] Tax Notes Today, "Partnership Guidance on Hold Pending Legislative Action, Treasury Officials Say," 2009 TNT 100-3 (May 27, 2009).

[58] See ¶ 9.02[1][d].

[a] Application of Section 83 Under the 2005 Proposed Regulations

The 2005 Proposed Regulations expressly reject the nonrealization theory espoused by the taxpayer in *Campbell*. Instead, they explicitly provide that the realization and timing rules of § 83 are applicable to all transfers of partnership capital and profits interests in connection with the performance of services to the partnership, whether by existing or newly admitted partners.[59]

[b] Valuation of Partnership Interests

Under § 83(a), a person receiving property in exchange for services is required to include the fair market value of such property in income when his or her rights in the property become "substantially vested" within the meaning of Regulations § 1.83-3(b). As part of the 2005 proposals, Proposed Regulations § 1.83-3(e) would provide a special rule for determining the fair market value of an eligible partnership interest received in exchange for services. Under that rule (which would be subject to such additional rules, conditions, and procedures as may be prescribed in any future guidance), a partnership and all of its partners would be allowed to elect a safe harbor under which the fair market value of any eligible partnership interest transferred in connection with the performance of services would be treated as being equal to the "liquidation value" of that interest. The proposed Revenue Procedure included in the 2005 proposals provides that an interest is not eligible for the safe harbor if it is "(a) related to a substantially certain and predictable stream of income from partnership assets, such as income from high-quality debt securities or a high-quality net lease, (b) transferred in anticipation of a subsequent disposition, or (c) an interest in a publicly traded partnership within the meaning of § 7704(b)."[60]

"Liquidation value" would be defined, consistently with generally accepted notions, to be the amount of cash the owner of the partnership interest would receive if the partnership sold all of its assets (including goodwill, going concern value, and any other intangibles associated with the partnership's operations) for cash equal to the fair market value of those assets and then liquidated.[61]

---

[59] Prop. Reg. §§ 1.721-1(b)(1) and 1.83-3(e) (2005). The preamble to the 2005 Proposed Regulations states that "[t]he proposed regulations apply section 83 to all partnership interests, without distinguishing between partnership capital interests and partnership profits interests." REG-105346-03, Preamble, Explanation of Provisions § 1, 70 Fed. Reg. 29675 (May 24, 2005).

[60] Notice 2005-43, § 3.02(1), 2005-1 CB 1221. These exclusions are a slightly more detailed version of the exceptions listed in Revenue Procedure 93-27, 1993-2 CB 343.

[61] "Liquidation value" is not defined in the Proposed Regulations; instead, the definition is found in the accompanying proposed Revenue Procedure. Notice 2005-43, § 4.02, 2005-1 CB 1221. This definition is virtually identical to the formulation used in Revenue

An election to apply the safe harbor would require satisfaction of the following detailed set of conditions:

1. The partnership must attach an election document, executed by a partner who has responsibility for federal income tax reporting by the partnership, to the partnership tax return for the taxable year that includes the effective date of the election, stating that the partnership is electing, on behalf of the partnership and each of its partners, to have the safe harbor apply irrevocably with respect to all eligible partnership interests transferred in connection with the performance of services while the safe harbor election remains in effect. The safe harbor election must specify an effective date, which may not be prior to the date the election is executed.

2. Except as otherwise specifically provided, the partnership agreement must contain provisions binding on all partners providing that (a) the partnership is authorized and directed to elect the safe harbor, and (b) the partnership and each of its partners (including any person to whom an eligible partnership interest is transferred in connection with the performance of services) agrees to comply with all requirements of the safe harbor with respect to all eligible partnership interests transferred in connection with performance of services while the election remains in effect. If a partner that is bound by such provisions transfers an eligible interest to another person, the requirement that each partner be bound by such provisions is satisfied only if the transferee assumes the transferor's obligations under the partnership agreement. If an amendment to the partnership agreement is required to bind the transferee, the amendment must be effective before the date on which a transfer occurs for the safe harbor to apply to the transfer.

3. If the partnership agreement does not contain all of these provisions or the provisions are not legally binding on all of the partners, then each partner must execute a document containing provisions that are legally binding on such person stating that (a) the partnership is authorized and directed to elect the safe harbor and (b) the partner agrees to comply with all requirements of the safe harbor with respect to all eligible interests transferred in connection with the performance of services while the election remains effective. Each person classified as a partner must execute this document, which must be effective

---

Procedure 93-27 to distinguish between capital and profits interests. In this regard, it is not entirely clear why the drafters chose to limit the inclusion of intangibles in the parenthetical phrase to those "associated with the partnership's operations." It would seem that all intangibles owned by the partnership should be treated as assets regardless of whether they are related to operations.

before the date on which a transfer occurs for the safe harbor to apply to the transfer. If a partner who has submitted the required document transfers an eligible interest to another person, the condition that each partner submit the necessary document is satisfied only if the transferee either submits the required document or assumes the transferor's obligations under a document previously submitted with respect to the transferred interest.

Treatment of a compensatory interest as a safe harbor interest modifies the generally applicable § 83 rules in only two ways: (1) most importantly, it replaces the usual fair market value standard with the liquidation value rule whenever the valuation of a safe harbor interest is required under the § 83 rules; and (2) it modifies the § 83 vesting concept slightly by making it a little easier for interests that are contingent on the performance of services to be treated as substantially vested.[62] Apart from these changes, the full panoply of the § 83 rules applies to transfers of all types of partnership interests to service providers.

Section 5 of the proposed Revenue Procedure in Notice 2005-43[63] summarizes the application of the safe harbor to service providers and service recipients as follows: Service providers (1) recognize compensation income upon receipt of the interest equal to the liquidation value of the interest at that time less any amount paid for the interest if the interest is vested or a § 83(b) election is made; or (2) if the interest is not substantially vested and no § 83(b) election is made, and the service provider holds the interest until it vests, the service provider recognizes compensation income on the vested interest based on the liquidation value of the interest at that time less any amount paid for the interest.

Service recipients (1) are entitled to a deduction equal to the amount included in gross income by the service provider if the requirements of § 162 or § 212 are met;[64] and (2) generally, the deduction is allowed for the tax year of the service recipient that includes the last day of the provider's tax year in which the compensation income is included (if the deduction relates to the transfer of a vested interest, the timing of the deduction is based on the service recipient's method of accounting).

[c] Timing of Income and Deductions

The approach taken by the 2005 proposals creates an irreconcilable conflict between the timing rules of § 83 and the existing § 707(c) Regulations.

---

[62] Notice 2005-43, § 4.03, 2005-1 CB 1221. See ¶ 5.02[3][d].

[63] Notice 2005-43, 2005-1 CB 1221.

[64] If these requirements are not satisfied, presumably the service recipient would be entitled to increase the basis of its assets by this amount.

Under § 83, a service provider includes the value of property in income when the property becomes "substantially vested" and the service recipient claims a corresponding deduction for its taxable year that includes the same date.[65] In contrast, § 707(c) guaranteed payments to a partner are included in the partner's taxable year that includes the end of the partnership year in which the partnership deducts the payments.[66] The 2005 Proposed Regulations would reconcile this conflict by providing that partnership interests issued to partners for services rendered are treated as guaranteed payments, but that the § 83 timing rules override the timing rules of § 707(c) to the extent that they are inconsistent.[67]

Pending finalization of the 2005 Proposed Regulations (or some other action that resolves this conflict), partners and partnerships must make potentially uncomfortable decisions as to which of the current conflicting sets of timing rules to follow. Presumably, the statutory timing rules in § 83(h) should trump the § 707(c) timing rules, which are entirely a creature of the Regulations. On the other hand, it may be difficult for the Service to successfully challenge partnerships that rely on and are in full compliance with the existing § 707(c) Regulations as long as they are in force. Arguably, taxpayers have a fielder's choice to do what suits them best as long as this conflict continues.

Under the existing § 83(b) Regulations, an interest in property is substantially vested when it either is not subject to a substantial risk of forfeiture or is transferable.[68] A substantial risk of forfeiture exists if rights in property are conditioned, directly or indirectly, upon the future performance (or refraining from performance) of substantial services by any person.[69] The rights of a person in property are "transferable" for this purpose only if such person can transfer the property to a transferee whose rights are not subject to a substantial risk of forfeiture.[70]

[d] Special Vesting Rule for Safe Harbor Interests

A special rule in Section 4.03 of Notice 2005-43 provides that a safe harbor interest that would otherwise be treated as substantially nonvested is transformed into a vested interest (thereby confirming the owner as a partner) under

---

[65] Reg. § 1.83-1(a); § 83(h).

[66] Reg. § 1.707-1(c).

[67] Prop. Reg. § 1.721-1(b)(4) (2005); Prop. Reg. § 1.707-1(c) (2005).

[68] Reg. § 1.83-3(b).

[69] Reg. § 1.83-3(c). For property transferred after 2012, the Regulations have been clarified to indicate there is no substantial risk of forfeiture if, at the time of the transfer, the forfeiture condition is unlikely to be enforced. Only certain enumerated transfer restrictions (see Reg. §§ 1.83-3(j) and 1.83-3(k)) can create a substantial risk of forfeiture. See Reg. § 1.83-3(c)(1) (last two sentences, as added in 2014).

[70] Reg. § 1.83-3(d).

certain circumstances. Under this rule, even if the entire interest is not vested under the general § 83 rules, it is treated as vested if the right to the "capital account balance equivalent" associated with the interest is not subject to a substantial risk of forfeiture or the interest is transferable.

"Capital account balance equivalent" is generally defined as the liquidation value of the interest immediately prior to a forfeiture (i.e., the amount of cash that the holder of the interest would receive if, immediately prior to the forfeiture, the interest vested and the partnership sold all of its assets (including goodwill, going concern value, or any other intangibles associated with the partnership's operations) for cash equal to the fair market value of those assets and then liquidated).[71] A small cushion is built into this relatively high bar by an exception in the Notice: The potential forfeiture of a portion of the capital account balance equivalent will not cause an interest to be nonvested "if the sole portion of the capital account balance equivalent forfeited is the excess of the capital account balance equivalent at the date of termination of services over the capital account balance equivalent at the end of the prior partnership tax year or any later date before the date of termination of services." In other words, if a forfeiture is triggered by a termination of services during a tax year, only the capital account balance equivalent at the end of the preceding tax year need be protected to bring the special vesting rule into play.[72]

Under this definition, a partnership interest would not be treated as subject to a substantial risk of forfeiture if, upon the occurrence of a forfeiture, the holder of the interest were entitled to receive a distribution of all previously allocated but undistributed profits, including any gains that would be allocated to the partner under the terms of the partnership agreement if the partnership sold all of its assets at fair market value.

EXAMPLE 5-1: *PRS* has two partners, *A* and *B*, each with a 50 percent interest in *PRS*. On March 1, 2005, *SP* agrees to perform services for the partnership in exchange for a partnership interest. Under the terms of the partnership agreement, *SP* is entitled to 10 percent of the future profits of *PRS*, but is not entitled to any of the partnership's capital as of the date of transfer. Although *SP* must surrender the partnership interest upon termination of services to the partnership, *SP* is not required to surrender any share of profits accumulated through the end of the partnership taxable year preceding the partnership taxable year in which *SP* terminates services. Under the special vesting rule in Notice 2005-43, *SP*'s interest

---

[71] Notice 2005-43, § 4.03, 2005-1 CB 1221.

[72] There is no explanation of this modification in the Notice or elsewhere in the 2005 proposals. Based solely on the language quoted in the text, there is no reason to think the same grace would be afforded upon a forfeiture triggered by anything other than a cessation of services.

in *PRS* would be treated as substantially vested at the time of the transfer if a safe harbor election were made.[73]

[e] Recognition of Gain or Loss by Partnership

One area of uncertainty under the existing Revenue Procedure 93-27 regime is whether a partnership recognizes gain or loss on a compensatory transfer of an interest in partnership capital. Under general federal income tax principles, when appreciated property is used to pay an obligation of the transferor, gain is recognized by the transferor. The 2005 proposals explicitly provide that no gain or loss would be recognized by a partnership upon the transfer or substantial vesting of a compensatory partnership interest.[74] A "compensatory partnership interest" is defined by the 2005 proposals as a partnership interest transferred in connection with the performance of services for the partnership (either before or after the formation of the partnership), including an interest that is transferred upon the exercise of a compensatory partnership option, without regard to whether the interest is a safe harbor interest.[75]

The preamble to the 2005 Proposed Regulations states that "[t]he rule providing for the nonrecognition of gain or loss does not apply to the transfer or substantial vesting of an interest in an eligible entity ... that becomes a partnership under § 301.7701-3(f)(2) as a result of the transfer or substantial vest-

---

[73] Notice 2005-43, 2005-1 CB 1221 (Section 6, Example 1).

[74] Prop. Reg. §§ 1.83-6(b) (2005), 1.721-1(b)(2) (2005). The preamble to the 2005 Proposed Regulations states that

> [s]uch a rule is more consistent with the policies underlying section 721—to defer recognition of gain and loss when persons join together to conduct a business—than would be a rule requiring the partnership to recognize gain on the transfer of these types of interests.... Under [Regulations] § 1.704-1(b)(4)(i) (reverse section 704(c) principles), the historic partners generally will be required to recognize any income or loss attributable to the partnership's assets as those assets are sold, depreciated, or amortized.

REG-105346-03, Preamble, Explanation of Provisions § 6, 70 Fed. Reg. 29675, 29678 (May 24, 2005). See Example 5-6 in ¶ 5.03[5].

[75] Prop. Reg. § 1.721-1(b)(3) (2005).

ing of the interest."[76] Thus, a Revenue Ruling 99-5[77] transaction is not protected by the 2005 Proposed Regulations.

[f] Partner Status of Service Provider

Consistent with the principles of § 83, the 2005 proposals provide that if (1) a partnership interest is transferred in connection with the performance of services, and (2) an election under § 83(b) is not made, the holder of the partnership interest would not be treated as a partner until the interest becomes substantially vested.[78] If a § 83(b) election is made, the service provider would be treated as a partner upon the initial transfer of the interest.[79]

The notion that transferred property is not treated as owned by the transferee until it is substantially vested may work tolerably well if the property is stock in a C corporation but can have surprising and largely unintended consequences when applied to interests in partnerships and other pass-through entities, as illustrated below.

> **EXAMPLE 5-2:** Individuals *A*, *B*, and *C* form partnership *ABC* to develop and operate an office building. *A* and *B* each contribute $60,000 to the capital of the partnership in exchange for a one-third interest in capital and profits. *C* contributes no capital but agrees to manage the construction and operation of the partnership's office building for the remaining one-third interest in the partnership capital and profits. Thus, at the outset, *C* has a capital account on the partnership's books of $40,000. *C*'s interest, however, is subject to the restriction that he will forfeit his entire interest if he leaves the partnership's service prior to the time the office building is completed and 90 percent leased. Since this is a "substantial risk of forfeiture," *A* and *B* are considered the only partners until the substantial risk of forfeiture on *C*'s interest lapses.[80]

The failure to recognize *C* as a partner from the outset produces substantial distortions. Operating losses and depreciation during the lease-up period

---

[76] The preamble cites F.C. McDougal, 62 TC 720 (1974) (service recipient recognizes gain on transfer of half interest in appreciated property to service provider immediately prior to the contribution by the service recipient and the service provider of their respective interests in the property to a newly formed partnership). REG-105346-03, Preamble, Explanation of Provisions § 6, 70 Fed. Reg. 29675, 29679 (May 24, 2005). No explanation is given for this exception to the general nonrecognition rule for transferors in the 2005 proposals. See Example 5-7 in ¶ 5.03[5].

[77] Rev. Rul. 99-5, 1999-1 CB 434 (Situation 1) (gain recognized on sale of 50 percent interest in assets).

[78] Prop. Reg. § 1.761-1(b) (2005). See Crescent Holdings LLC, 141 TC 477, 500-505 (2013).

[79] Prop. Reg. § 1.761-1(b) (2005).

[80] Reg. § 1.83-1(a).

would be allocable entirely to *A* and *B*,[81] even though *C* may share joint and several liability for the partnership's indebtedness. Partnership cash flow distributed to *C* would be taxable to him as ordinary compensation income even though such cash flow would be completely sheltered by partnership depreciation deductions if *C* were recognized as a partner for tax purposes. The amounts taxed to *C* under this rule are either deductible by the partnership or capitalized as a part of the cost of the office building.[82]

Assume that the office building is successfully completed and 90 percent leased, so that *C*'s interest ceases to be subject to a substantial risk of forfeiture, and that the value of his interest at that time is $80,000. *C* is then taxable on $80,000 of ordinary compensation income under § 83(a)(1), and the partnership is entitled to a deduction or capital expenditure of $80,000 (the amount of income received by *C*) which must be allocated to *A* and *B*.[83]

The allocation of partnership liabilities must be adjusted under §§ 721 and 752 at the time *C* becomes a partner. Thus, if the partnership has liabilities, *A* and *B* are deemed to have received a distribution under § 752(b) as a result of the "admission" of *C* upon the vesting of *C*'s interest, and *C* is deemed to have made equivalent contributions under § 752(a). Prior to the lapse of *C*'s substantial risk, *A* and *B* are the only partners for tax purposes.

The partners may avoid all of these consequences if *C* elects under § 83(b) to be taxed on the value of his interest at the inception of the partnership, thus immediately confirming himself as a partner. The cost would be current recognition of income by *C* equal to the liquidation value of the interest at that time (presumably $40,000, one third of the partnership's capital), determined without regard to any restrictions other than nonlapse restrictions. *A* and *B* collectively are entitled to a deduction or capital expenditure at the same time and in the same amount.

If a service partner makes a significant capital contribution, failure to make a § 83(b) election can prove worthy.

> **EXAMPLE 5-3:** In the *ABC* partnership (described in Example 5-2), partner *C* contributes $40,000, one third of the partnership's initial capital, but his interest is nevertheless subject to the substantial risk of forfeiture described in Example 5-2. *A* and *B* each contribute one third of the initial capital, subject to no restrictions.
>
> Because *C* has contributed full value for his interest, it might be assumed that the receipt of his interest is not compensatory and that § 83 does not apply. Section 83, however, does not require that a transfer be compensatory to fall within its purview. Instead, it applies to all transfers

---

[81] Crescent Holdings, LLC, 141 TC 477, 500–505 (2013).

[82] See ¶ 5.02[3][b].

[83] § 83(h); see ¶ 5.02[3][g][ii].

of property "in connection with the performance of services."[84] Thus, even if a service provider receives no bargain in the purchase price, he may be subject to tax under § 83 when the property becomes vested.

If § 83(a) applies to *C*'s interest, the results would be the same as those outlined in Example 5-2, except that *C*'s income upon the lapse of the risk of forfeiture would be the liquidation value of his interest at that time less his initial contribution of $40,000.

C can, and generally should, avoid the adverse consequences of § 83(a) in situations of this sort by electing to be taxed immediately under § 83(b). This election has no cost, because the liquidation value of *C*'s interest in the year the partnership is formed is the same as his contribution to the partnership.

Treating unvested service providers as non-partners can, in some situations involving professional service partnerships, lead to the awkward possibility that no partnership may exist for tax purposes. In most professional services firms (such as law firms and accounting firms), each partner's right to a share of future profits is dependent upon such partner continuing to provide services in furtherance of the partnership business. Thus, it could be difficult to conclude that the profits interest of a partner in a professional services firm is ever substantially vested for § 83 purposes.[85] Therefore, unless more than one of the partners makes a § 83(b) election, no partnership would exist under the 2005 proposals.

[g] Capital Account Maintenance

[i] Capital account adjustments upon issuance of a compensatory interest. The 2005 proposals would increase the capital account of the recipient of a compensatory partnership interest by the amount included in the partner's compensation income under § 83.[86] If the partnership has elected the safe harbor, this rule would produce an appropriate result because the fair market value of the transferred interest is equal its liquidation value. In other cases, an appropriate result might not be achieved if the fair market value of the interest

---

[84] § 83(a); see Lawrence J. Alves, 79 TC 864 (1982), aff'd, 734 F2d 478 (9th Cir. 1984).

[85] If a safe harbor election is made under the 2005 proposals, a different conclusion regarding vesting may be reached under the special vesting rule included in § 4.03 of Notice 2005-43. See ¶ 5.02[3][d]. Under this rule, vesting would occur immediately if the right to the associated capital account balance equivalent of a service provider is not subject to a substantial risk of forfeiture. In most professional service partnerships, a withdrawing partner is entitled to receive a distribution of contributed capital plus previously allocated but undistributed profits, thus meeting this vesting requirement. The discussion in the text is thus relevant largely to those partnerships that do not elect the safe harbor provisions of the 2005 proposals.

[86] Prop. Reg. § 1.704-1(b)(2)(iv)(b)(1) (2005).

conveyed does not correspond to the amount of capital, if any, that the partners have agreed to attribute to the service provider. This may make it difficult for the partnership to comply with the economic effect safe harbor of the § 704(b) Regulations, which requires liquidation in accordance with capital account balances.[87]

The 2005 proposals would provide that the transfer or vesting of a compensatory partnership interest is an event that triggers a revaluation of the capital accounts of the existing partners, but only if the transfer or vesting results in the service provider recognizing income under § 83 (or would result in such recognition if the interest had a fair market value other than zero).[88] As discussed earlier, the results of the revaluation will generally produce results consistent with the expectations of the partners if the safe harbor is elected. If the safe harbor is not elected, the results may be more problematic.

> **EXAMPLE 5-4:** As compensation for services, *C* receives a substantially vested 10 percent interest in the future profits of equal partnership *AB*, which owns property with a tax basis and § 704(b) book value of $100 and a market value of $200. Partnership *AB* does not elect the safe harbor. Under Proposed Regulations § 1.704-1(b)(2)(iv)(f)(5)(iii) (2005), *AB* revalues its assets immediately prior to issuing the compensatory interest, increasing the § 704(b) book value to $200 and each of *A*'s and *B*'s capital accounts to $100. While neither *A* nor *B* has agreed that *C* would receive any capital in an immediate liquidation of *AB*, assume *C*'s profits interest has a fair market value of $10. Under the 2005 Proposed Regulations, *AB* would be required to credit *C* with a capital account of $10; *A* and *B* would each be allocated $5 of *AB*'s $10 deduction, reducing their respective capital accounts to $95 each. If *A* and *B* do not agree to liquidate in accordance with these capital account balances, future allocations of income and loss to the partners will not satisfy the economic effect safe harbor of the § 704(b) Regulations.[89]

[ii] Allocation of the partnership's deduction. Under the 2005 proposals, a partnership issuing an interest in exchange for services would be treated

---

[87] The preamble to the 2005 Proposed Regulations notes this problem but concludes that § 83 dictates the amount of capital that must be attributed to the service provider. See REG-105346-03, Preamble, Explanation of Provisions § 4.A, 70 Fed. Reg. 29675, 29677 (May 24, 2005). This issue alone will likely drive most partnerships issuing profits interests to service partners to elect the safe harbor if these regulations are adopted in the form proposed.

[88] Prop. Reg. § 1.704-1(b)(2)(iv)(f)(5)(iii) (2005).

[89] Presumably, *A* and *B* would not enter into the transaction unless they anticipated *C*'s services would increase the value of the partnership by at least $10. Hence, it might be reasonable to "book up" the partnership assets to $210 and the capital accounts of *A* and *B* to $105 each to reflect this and assure the correct economic results. Alternatively, the partnership agreement could be amended to provide that the first $10 of gain from the

as making a § 707(c) guaranteed payment for services, deductible by the partnership under the timing rules of § 83(h).[90] While the economic burden of this payment seems clearly to be borne by the historic partners, there is no special rule under the 2005 proposals that would require this deduction to be allocated to partners other than the service provider. Instead, the preamble to the 2005 proposed regulations states that Treasury and the Service "believe that section 706(d)(1) adequately ensures that partnership deductions that are attributable to the portion of the partnership's taxable year prior to a new partner's entry into the partnership are allocated to the historic partners."[91]

Section 706(d)(1) provides generally that "if during any taxable year of the partnership there is a change in any partner's interest in the partnership, each partner's distributive share of any item of income, gain, loss, deduction, or credit of the partnership for such taxable year shall be determined by the use of any method prescribed by ... regulations which takes into account the varying interests of the partners in the partnership during such taxable year."

The Service's belief, as stated in 2005, that § 706(d)(1) would mandate the right results effectively assumed that there would be a "closing of the books" immediately prior to the admission of the service provider as a partner. This assumption might have seemed somewhat optimistic (or, perhaps, prescient) under the Regulations as they then existed. The subsequent issuance ten years later, in 2015, of final and proposed § 706(d) Regulations provide clear support for this assumption.[92]

There is also a potential issue under § 706(d)(2), which limits use of the closing of the books method with respect to certain items. Under § 706(d)(2)(B), payments of compensation for services made by a partnership using the cash method of accounting are treated as "allocable cash basis items."[93] Under § 706(d)(2)(A), each partner's distributive share of any allocable cash basis item must be determined under a daily, pro-rata method of accounting. The 2005 proposals would address this difficulty head-on by adding Proposed Regulations § 1.706-3(a) (2005) as follows: "The transfer of property subject to section 83 in connection with the performance of services is not an allocable cash basis item within the meaning of section 706(d)(2)(B)."[94]

---

property is allocable to *A* and *B* (thus potentially restoring each of their capital accounts to $100).

[90] Prop. Reg. §§ 1.721-1(b)(4) (2005), 1.707-1(c) (2005).

[91] REG-105346-03, 70 Fed. Reg. 29675, 29677 (May 24, 2005).

[92] Reg. § 1.706-4, Prop. Reg. § 1.706-4(e)(2)(x) (2015) (compensation deduction related to transfer of interest to service provider treated as extraordinary item occurring prior to the transfer or vesting of the interest), as discussed in TD 9728, 80 Fed. Reg. 45865, 45874 (Aug. 3, 2015), REG-109370-10, 80 Fed. Reg. 45905, 45910 (Aug. 3, 2015). See ¶ 12.03[1].

[93] See ¶ 12.03[2].

[94] Prop. Reg. § 1.706-3(a) (2005).

[h] Forfeitures

There are two circumstances under which a service provider may be recognized as a partner for tax purposes upon the issuance of a substantially nonvested partnership interest that is subsequently forfeited: (1) if the interest is subject to a § 83(b) election; or (2) if the interest is within the safe harbor. What are the tax consequences to the partnership and the service partner if the interest is eventually forfeited?

Regulations § 1.83-6(c) generally provides that if a deduction, reduction in gross income, or increase in basis was allowable upon the transfer of the interest, the person to whom it was allowable (the issuing partnership, in this instance) is required to include the same amount in its income for the year during which the forfeiture occurs. If no § 83(b) election applies, no gain or loss would be recognized by the partnership either on the transfer of a compensatory partnership interest or the subsequent vesting or forfeiture of the interest under the 2005 proposals[95] and therefore no income inclusion is required because of the forfeiture. However, if the forfeited interest was subject to a § 83(b) election, Regulations § 1.83-2(a) provides that the service provider will be treated as entering into a sale or exchange and realizing a capital loss (if the property is a capital asset) equal to the excess of any amount paid for the forfeited property over any amount realized on the forfeiture.

Because the owner of an interest that is subject to a § 83(b) election is treated as a partner for tax purposes, she can be allocated partnership items that are later forfeited. These allocations may not have economic effect if a forfeiture actually occurs. The 2005 proposals contain proposed amendments to the § 704(b) Regulations to deal with this situation. Under these Proposed Regulations, if a § 83(b) election has been made with respect to a nonvested interest, allocations of partnership items would be deemed to be in accordance with the partners' interests in the partnership if the following conditions are met:

1. The partnership agreement requires that the partnership make "forfeiture allocations" for the year during which the forfeiture occurs if the interest is later forfeited; and
2. All material allocations and capital account adjustments under the partnership agreement not pertaining to the interest are recognized under § 704(b).[96]

"Forfeiture allocations" are allocations to the owner of the forfeited interest consisting of a pro-rata portion of each item of gross income and gain or gross deduction and loss (to the extent such items are available) for the taxable year of the forfeiture in a positive or negative amount equal to:

---

[95] Prop. Reg. § 1.721-1(b)(2) (2005).
[96] Prop. Reg. § 1.704-1(b)(4)(xii)(b) (2005).

(1) The excess (not less than zero) of the—

(i) Amount of distributions (including deemed distributions under § 752(b) and the adjusted basis of any property so distributed) to the partner with respect to the forfeited partnership interest (to the extent such distributions are not taxable under section 731); over

(ii) Amounts paid for the interest and the adjusted tax basis of property contributed by the partner (including deemed contributions under section 752(a)) to the partnership with respect to the forfeited interest; minus

(2) The cumulative net income (or loss) allocated to the partner with respect to the forfeited partnership interest.[97]

While this formula may appear complicated, the concept is not: To the extent an allocation in a prior year does not have an effect on the amount the service provider ultimately receives from the partnership, the allocation should be reversed upon forfeiture of the interest. To maximize the likelihood of prior allocations being reversed in full, forfeiture allocations would be made from all of the partnership's properly signed partnership items for the entire taxable year of the forfeiture, even if the interest is forfeited prior to the end of the year.[98] Unfortunately, the success of this approach is dependent on the existence of sufficient properly signed partnership items in the year of the forfeiture. A better solution, modeled on the remedial allocation method under § 704(c) (see Regulations § 1.704-3(d)) would be to create additional remedial items of income, gain, loss, or deduction in the forfeiture year to assure the service provider is allocated the correct amount and character, with offsetting remedial items in the same amount and character (and the opposite sign) being allocated to the other partners.[99]

If the safe harbor is elected, a service partner may be treated as having a substantially vested interest under the special vesting rule discussed in ¶ 5.02[3][d] even though the interest would not otherwise be treated as substantially vested under § 83. Like any interest with respect to which a § 83(b) election is made, such an interest could be forfeited in the future. However, because the special vesting rule only applies where the right to at least a portion of the "associated capital account balance equivalent" is not subject to a substantial risk of forfeiture, it may be possible to argue in some situations that forfeiture allocations are not necessary. However, from a practical point of

---

[97] Prop. Reg. § 1.704-1(b)(4)(xii)(c) (2005). This rule does not apply if, at the time a § 83(b) election is made, there is a plan that the interest will be forfeited. In such a case, the partner's distributive shares will be determined in accordance with the partner's interest in the partnership. Prop. Reg. § 1.704-1(b)(4)(xii)(e) (2005).

[98] Prop. Reg. §§ 1.704-1(b)(4)(xii)(f) (2005), 1.706-3(b) (2005).

[99] See REG-105346-03, Preamble, Explanation of Provisions § 4, 70 Fed. Reg. 29675, 29678 (May 24, 2005) (requesting comments on this approach).

view, it may be more prudent to include unnecessary allocation provisions than to risk dealing with their absence on audit.

In a case where the safe harbor is elected and a § 83(b) election is also made, Section 4.04 of the proposed Revenue Procedure in Notice 2005-43[100] would provide that, in addition to forfeiture allocations, a service provider forfeiting an interest must also include as ordinary income in the taxable year of the forfeiture an amount equal to the excess, if any, of (1) the amount of income or gain that the partnership would be required to allocate to the service provider as forfeiture allocations over (2) the amount of forfeiture allocations actually made.[101]

[i] Effective Date

The 2005 proposals, including the proposed Revenue Procedure in Notice 2005-43,[102] will apply to transfers of property on or after the date the Regulations are finalized.

[j] Conclusions

At this writing, it appears the Treasury has decided the presently applicable rules are simply too generous to service providers and should be tightened up. While the ongoing carried interest discussion has extended the lifespan of the current regime, it would not be wise to assume this extension will continue indefinitely.

It would be tempting to ignore all of this and simply carry on under the current rules as if they were going to stay in place indefinitely. In some respects, that is all that is actually required. There is no reason to modify current issuances of compensatory partnership interests prior to the effective date of these rules. However, consideration of the likelihood that the 2005 proposals will be finalized in substantially the form proposed should affect the drafting of agreements for newly created partnerships and limited liability companies, may influence the choice of entity for new businesses, and may dictate the need for amendments to existing agreements, depending in large part on the likely appetite of the business for the issuance of future compensatory interests.

The questions that should drive this process include: (1) Does the business anticipate the issuance of significant compensatory interests to service

---

[100] Notice 2005-43, 2005-1 CB 1221.

[101] The most likely circumstance in which this rule might apply is when there have been prior allocations of loss to the forfeiting partner.

[102] Notice 2005-43, 2005-1 CB 1221. Revenue Procedures 93-27 and 2001-43 will be obsoleted at the same time.

providers? (2) Will it be feasible to structure the issuance of such interests to come within the safe harbor contained in the 2005 proposals? (3) Is the business willing to live with the downstream consequences of electing to be within the safe harbor created under the 2005 proposals and/or making the § 83(b) election? Generally, most businesses contemplating partnership status will be able to come within the 2005 safe harbor rules. Further, most of those businesses will conclude rather quickly that the § 83(b) election is the best option. That leads directly to consideration of the probability of forfeitures and the impact of the proposed rules relating to forfeitures on both the partnership and any forfeiting service partners, as discussed earlier in ¶ 5.02[3][h].

[4] Profits Interests: The Case for Nonrealization

[a] In general

The primal articulated foundation for Treasury's approach in the 2005 Proposed Regulations is that a compensatory transfer of a partnership interest is subject to § 83 because the interest is "property" within the meaning § 83. This approach is fundamentally flawed because it skips a necessary first step in the analysis: Has there been a taxable event that is subject to the timing rules in § 83? In other words, is the issuance of a partnership profits interest in exchange for services a transaction that triggers the realization of gross income within the meaning of § 61?[103] As discussed below in this ¶ 5.02[4], there are significant arguments that the issuance of a profits interest for services should not result in the realization of any income, and therefore the timing rules of § 83 are entirely irrelevant.

The realization requirement is not a new or novel concept in the Code or Subchapter K, particularly as it relates to § 721. Nor is it a concept the Treasury or the courts seemed to dispute prior to 2005. Returning to the case law discussed in ¶ 5.02[1], the taxpayer in *Campbell* advanced, on appeal to the Eighth Circuit, a nonrealization theory (based in part on § 707) for the proposition that no income is realized upon receipt of a profits interest for services if the relevant services are rendered to or for the benefit of the issuing partnership. Somewhat surprisingly, the government did not "quarrel" with this nonrealization argument,[104] but argued, before the Eighth Circuit, that Campbell's services were rendered to Campbell's employer, the sponsor of the issuing partnerships, rather than to the issuing partnerships. While the circuit court expressed support for the nonrealization argument, it did not ground its hold-

---

[103] See § 61(a); Reg. § 1.61-1(a): "Gross income includes income *realized* in any form ...." (emphasis added).

[104] Campbell v. Commissioner, 943 F2d 815, 818 (8th Cir. 1991).

ing on this approach, opting instead to base its reversal on a determination that the interests in question could not be taxed on receipt because their value was speculative.

While the circuit court's determination that the interests transferred to Campbell had only speculative value provided a valid basis for resolving the case at hand, the nonrealization approach would provide a generally applicable and arguably sounder grounding for resolving cases involving the receipt of profits interests. That approach is considered below in this ¶ 5.02[4].

The Tax Court in *Campbell* and *Diamond* erred primarily because the court addressed the issue only through the prism of §§ 61 and 83, without coming to grips with the impact of the partnership taxation rules in Subchapter K of the Code. These rules, which are premised on nonrealization concepts, should arguably render both §§ 61 and 83 inapplicable to the receipt of a profits interest for services.

[b] Case Law Prior to the 1954 Code

In *Campbell*, the Tax Court based its analysis on the assumption that the receipt of a partnership interest in exchange for a contribution (whether of property or services) must be a taxable event in the absence of an applicable nonrecognition provision. As noted earlier, this assumption is incorrect because it skips a step in the analysis: A nonrecognition provision is not necessary in the absence of a realization event. Under the pre-1954 law (which has not been materially affected by subsequent changes), such transactions did not result in the "realization" of income.

The pre-1954 case law uniformly refused to treat purported "salary" payments by partnerships to partners as realized "compensation"; instead, such payments were treated as distributive shares of partnership income to the extent thereof.[105] These authorities concluded that payments by partnerships to partners for services *cannot* be "compensation."

The rationale for this nonrealization treatment was that, under the aggregate theory, the partner and the partnership were treated as one: "[A]n individual cannot be his own employee, nor can a partner be an employee of his own partnership."[106] A partner could no more *realize* income from the receipt of "compensation" from the partnership than he could if he paid himself a salary. Because a partner could not realize compensation income from the receipt of

---

[105] Commissioner v. Moran, 236 F2d 595 (8th Cir. 1956); Armstrong v. Phinney, 394 F2d 661 (5th Cir. 1968); Commissioner v. Doak, 234 F2d 704 (4th Cir. 1956); Foster v. United States, 221 F. Supp. 291 (SDNY 1963), aff'd, 329 F2d 717 (2d Cir. 1964); Andrew O. Miller, Jr., 52 TC 752 (1969) (acq.); Augustine M. Lloyd, 15 BTA 82 (1929) (acq.); Estate of Tilton, 8 BTA 914 (1927) (acq.). See HR Rep. No. 1337, 83d Cong., 2d Sess. 68 (1954).

[106] Commissioner v. Moran, 236 F2d 595, 598 (8th Cir. 1956).

actual cash payments denominated as salary, it seems beyond cavil that the partner could not realize income upon "receipt" of a mere intangible right to future partnership income.

Under pre-1954 case law, the only exception to this rule was that the receipt of an interest in the existing value of partnership *capital* for services was taxable.[107] The cases establishing this exception are consistent with the rule that a partnership could not pay compensation to a partner. The capital shifts in these cases reflect payments by the other partners, rather than the partnership.[108] Clearly, a compensatory payment from one partner to another is a realization event.

Treating the receipt of a partnership profits interest for services as a non-realization event also is consistent with the pre-1954 rule that no income was realized upon a contribution of *property* to a partnership. Before the § 721 nonrecognition provision was added in 1954, there was no statutory nonrecognition provision protecting a partner from recognizing income upon a contribution of property to a partnership in exchange for an interest in partnership capital. Nevertheless, Congress, the courts, and the Bureau of Internal Revenue all agreed that the contribution of property to a partnership was not a taxable event. This was the result even though a contributing partner has, as an economic matter, effectively exchanged an interest in the property she contributed for an interest in other property (or cash) that theretofore had belonged to other partners.[109] If a transaction that has the economic result of giving a partner an interest in the value of other property (or cash) does not result in income realization, it seems obvious that a transaction that gives a partner only an interest in future income and appreciation from such other property should not result in income realization.

[c] Enactment of Sections 707 and 721 in 1954

Section 61(a)(1) of the 1954 Code defines "gross income" to include "compensation for services." The legislative history confirms that § 61 is merely a restatement, with minor modifications not relevant here, of the defini-

---

[107] Farris v. Commissioner, 222 F2d 320 (10th Cir. 1955), rev'g 22 TC 104 (1954); Harry W. Lehman, 19 TC 659 (1953).

[108] See, e.g., Augustine M. Lloyd, 15 BTA 82, 88–89 (1929) (acq.).

[109] See, e.g., Hearings on HR 7835 Before the Senate Comm. on Finance, 73d Cong., 2d Sess. 77 (Mar. 6, 1934) (statement of Mr. Bartholow); Helvering v. Walbridge, 70 F2d 683 (2d Cir. 1934); Flannery v. United States, 25 F. Supp. 677 (D. Md.), aff'd, 106 F2d 315 (4th Cir. 1939); Edward B. Archbald, 27 BTA 837 (1933), aff'd, 70 F2d 720 (2d Cir. 1934); GCM 10092, XI-1 CB 58, revoked on other grounds by GCM 26379, 1950-1 CB 58; Sol. Op. 42, 3 CB 61 (1920), obsoleted by Rev. Rul. 69-31, 1969-1 CB 307, 308; TBR 34, 1 CB 46 (1919), obsoleted by Rev. Rul. 69-31, 1969-1 CB 307, 308.

tion of "gross income" under § 22(a) of the 1939 Code. Thus, § 61 imports the historic concepts of realization from the 1939 Code to the 1954 Code.[110]

The 1954 Code added Subchapter K as the first comprehensive codification of the rules of partnership taxation. Subchapter K includes two provisions, §§ 721 and 707, that bear on the question of whether the receipt of a profits interest for services is a taxable event.

Section 721(a) (formerly § 721 of the 1954 Code) provides for the nonrecognition of gain or loss to the partnership and the partners upon a contribution of property for a partnership interest. The legislative history states that "[c]ontributions to a partnership will have the same effect under the proposed provisions as under present practice,"[111] and that § 721 "codifies existing case law."[112] No particular reference was made to the tax consequences of the receipt of a partnership interest for services. This omission suggests that Congress did not intend to change established law concerning the taxation of service partners. Accordingly, no negative inference should be drawn from the fact that § 721 does not deal with contributions of services.

The pre-1954 rule that a partnership could not pay compensation to its partners was justified by more than abstract notions of realization and aggregation. Partnerships normally do not "pay" partners for property or services; instead, the core notion of partnership taxation is that partners receive an "allocation" or "distributive share" of income jointly derived from pooled labor and capital. Paying and sharing are two entirely different concepts. If normal allocations to service partners could be treated as paid compensation, the sharing concept of partnership taxation would be rendered ineffectual. The blanket "no compensation" rule of prior law, however, proved to be "unrealistic and unnecessarily complicated" when applied to "salary" payments that exceeded partnership income.[113] Accordingly, in 1954 Congress enacted § 707 to permit, for the first time, certain transactions between partnerships and partners to be taxed under an entity-based approach.

Sections 707(a) and 707(c) provide two limited exceptions to the general rule that a partner cannot receive compensation from a partnership. These provisions are exclusive: A partner cannot receive "compensation" from a partnership unless the transaction is described in § 707(a) or § 707(c). In the words of the Fifth Circuit:

---

[110] See HR Rep. No. 1337, 83d Cong., 2d Sess. A18–A19 (1954); S. Rep. No. 1622, 83d Cong., 2d Sess. 168–169 (1954).

[111] HR Rep. No. 1337, 83d Cong., 2d Sess. 68 (1954); S. Rep. No. 1622, 83d Cong., 2d Sess. 94 (1954) (substantially similar language).

[112] HR Rep. No. 1337, 83d Cong., 2d Sess. A227 (1954); S. Rep. No. 1622, 83d Cong., 2d Sess. 388 (1954).

[113] HR Rep. No. 1337, 83d Cong., 2d Sess. 68 (1954); S. Rep. No. 1622, 83d Cong., 2d Sess. 92 (1954).

Bearing in mind, that the general statutory policy for treating partnerships for tax purposes contemplated that the income of a partnership would flow through to the individual partners, *it is not difficult to envision the purpose of Congress when it created an exception to this general rule to limit the excepted activities to those specifically outlined.* In doing so, Congress determined that in order for the partnership to deal with one of its partners as an "outsider" the transaction dealt with must be something outside the scope of the partnership. If, on the other hand, the activities constituting the "transaction" were activities which the partnership itself was engaged in, compensation for such transaction must be treated merely as a rearrangement between the partners of their distributive shares in the partnership income.[114]

The question then becomes whether the receipt of a profits interest for services is described in § 707(a) or § 707(c).

Section 707(a) of the 1954 Code (now § 707(a)(1) of the 1986 Code) provides, contrary to prior law, that transactions between a partnership and a partner *who is not acting in his capacity as a partner in the transaction* "shall be treated as occurring between the partnership and one who is not a partner." Of course, any property or services that can be "sold" to a partnership by a partner acting in a nonpartner capacity can also be "contributed" by that partner in a partner capacity. Accordingly, whether property or services are "contributed" in a partner capacity or "sold" in a nonpartner capacity necessarily depends on the nature or quality of the consideration received by the partner, rather than on the nature or quality of the services transferred or performed.[115] If the consideration received is an entrepreneurial-type sharing interest in the partnership's income, it should not be treated as received in a nonpartner capacity under § 707(a).[116]

The 1954 Code also added § 707(c) to deal with the tax consequences of payments of fixed compensation, or "guaranteed payments," by partnerships to partners for services rendered in their partner capacity. Section 707(c) applies

---

[114] Pratt v. Commissioner, 550 F2d 1023, 1026 (5th Cir. 1977) (emphasis added). See Foster v. United States, 329 F2d 717, 718 (2d Cir. 1964); Andrew O. Miller, Jr., 52 TC 752, 759 (1969).

[115] For example, if an associate lawyer becomes a partner of a law firm, the nature of his services to the firm may not change. It is, rather, the change in the way the lawyer is compensated for his services that confirms that the lawyer acts in a partner capacity after being admitted to the firm.

[116] See Reg. § 1.721-1(b)(2) (treating transfer to partner of capital interest for services as § 707(c) guaranteed payment to partner in partner capacity, as distinguished from § 707(a) payment to nonpartner). A partner who receives an entrepreneurial share of partnership profits for services necessarily receives such consideration in a partner capacity not subject to § 707(a), but the converse is not always true: Even if the consideration for services is a fixed, nonentrepreneurial payment, it may be received in a partner capacity. As discussed later, nonentrepreneurial consideration for services rendered in a partner capacity is taxed under § 707(c), not § 707(a).

only to payments for services rendered in a partner capacity that are determined without regard to partnership income. Such payments are income to the recipient partner under § 61 and are deductible (or capital) expenditures by the partnership, but are otherwise treated as distributive shares of partnership income. Because a payment to a partner pursuant to a partnership profits interest cannot be determined "without regard to the income of the partnership," such payment cannot, by definition, be a § 707(c) guaranteed payment.

Thus, except for payments described in § 707(a) or § 707(c), § 707 did not change the historic rule that a partner cannot receive compensation from a partnership; indeed, it confirmed this rule. A transaction in which a partner receives an entrepreneurial interest in partnership profits for services is not described in § 707(a) or § 707(c). The Tax Court in *Diamond* and *Campbell* failed to consider the applicability of § 707—the statutory authority that should have controlled the case.

In the context of this historical statutory analysis, it is easier to understand the language currently in Regulations § 1.721-1(b). Regulations § 1.721-1(a) reiterates the basic statutory rule that no gain is recognized when property is contributed for a partnership interest. Regulations § 1.721-1(b)(1) provides, in relevant part, that "[t]o the extent that any of the partners gives up any part of his right to be repaid his contributions (*as distinguished from a share in partnership profits*) in favor of another partner as compensation for services ... section 721 does not apply" (emphasis added). Finally, Regulations § 1.721-1(b)(2) provides that such a capital transfer for services rendered to the partnership (i.e., a "capital shift") is "a guaranteed payment for services under section 707(c)." The Tax Court in *Diamond* found the parenthetical emphasized above to be "obscure" and the product of "opaque draftsmanship in the Regulations."[117]

However, when properly viewed in this context, the Regulation is neither obscure nor opaque. It adapts the law, as it existed before the 1954 Code, to the provisions of the new Subchapter K. First, it provides that capital shifts are taxable, in recognition of the fact that such shifts were taxable under prior law and were not rendered tax-free by the enactment of § 721. Second, the Regulations provide that the tax consequences of capital shifts will be determined under § 707(c), rather than § 707(a) or the general rules of § 61. This is proper because, as discussed above, partnership payments to partners cannot be § 61 compensation unless they are described in § 707, and § 707(c), rather than § 707(a), applies to payments that are determined without regard to partnership income and made for services rendered in a partner capacity. Finally, through the parenthetical clause, the Regulations properly exclude profits interest transfers from their purview because (1) such transactions were not taxable

---

[117] Sol Diamond, 56 TC 530, 546 (1971), aff'd, 492 F2d 286 (7th Cir. 1974).

under pre-1954 law and (2) the only provision of the 1954 Code that could have made them taxable was § 707, which did not do so.[118]

[d] Effect of Section 83

Because § 83, relied on by the Tax Court in *Campbell*, was not enacted until 1969, it is necessary to consider whether it changed the rule that the receipt of a profits interest for services is not taxable. Section 83 by its terms applies broadly to "property" transferred "in connection with the performance of services." Its sole stated purpose, however, is to rationalize the timing rules that previously applied to compensatory transfers of property (particularly stock) to employees subject to restrictions that, at the time of receipt, depress the value of the transferred property.[119] Because § 61 already defined "income" in the broadest permissible constitutional manner, encompassing all realized income, it is hard to see how the enactment of § 83 could have broadened the concept of *what* constitutes income (as opposed to *when* income is recognized). Further, there is no indication in the statute or its legislative history that the word "property" means anything more under § 83 than it does under § 61.[120] Finally, neither the legislative history nor the statutory language of § 83 refers to partners, partnerships, or partnership interests—an unlikely omission if Congress intended § 83 to affect significantly the structural integrity of Subchapter K.

The conclusion that the enactment of § 83 did not change the tax treatment of the receipt of a profits interest for services is confirmed by the § 83 Regulations, which provide that § 83 only applies to transfers to "employees and independent contractors."[121] A partner cannot be an employee or independent contractor of a partnership unless the partner is treated as a nonpartner

---

[118] See Hearings on Advisory Group Recommendations on Subchapters C, J, and K of the Internal Revenue Code Before the House Comm. on Ways and Means, 86th Cong., 1st Sess. 53 (1959) (testimony of Mr. Willis, chairman of the advisory group), cited in Sol Diamond, 492 F2d 286, 290 (7th Cir. 1974). See also Cowan, "Receipt of an Interest in Partnership Profits Consideration for Services: The *Diamond* Case," 27 Tax L. Rev. 161, 178–183 (1972) (compilation of extensive contemporaneous evidence—e.g., testimony, articles, legislative history of proposed legislation—that documents consensus view that receipt of a profits interest for services was not a taxable event).

[119] See HR Rep. No. 413, 91st Cong., 1st Sess. 86 (1969); S. Rep. No. 552, 91st Cong., 1st Sess. 119 (1969); HR Conf. Rep. No. 782, 91st Cong., 1st Sess. 303 (1969).

[120] Cf. Reg. § 1.61-2(d).

[121] Reg. §§ 1.83-1(a)(1), 1.83-5(b)(1), 1.83-7(a), 1.83-8(b)(2). These Regulations presumably are based on § 83(a), which provides that § 83 does not apply to property received by "the person for whom [the] services are performed." Under the aggregate, nonrealization theory that applies to the partnership-partner transactions not covered by § 707, a partner receiving property in a partner capacity for services is also the "person for whom such services are performed."

with respect to the transaction under § 707(a).[122] As discussed previously, the transfer of an entrepreneurial interest in future profits in exchange for services cannot be within the scope of § 707(a).

The view that the receipt of a profits interest for services is not subject to § 83 is also confirmed by proposed changes to the § 721 Regulations issued in 1971 in conjunction with the proposal of the initial set of § 83 Regulations. These Proposed Regulations, which were outstanding for more than thirty years before being withdrawn, expressly retained the parenthetical of the existing § 721 Regulations, which carves out transfers of a "share in partnership profits." Thus, like the drafters of the existing § 721 Regulations, the drafters of the Proposed § 721 Regulations (who also wrote the § 83 Regulations) apparently believed that the receipt of a partnership profits interest for services is not a taxable event.

[e] Summary

The receipt of a partnership profits interest for services was not a taxable event prior to the enactment of the 1954 Code, and nothing in the 1954 Code or § 83 changed this result. As a matter of statutory construction, the tax-free nature of such transactions is established by the fact that § 707 provides the exclusive circumstances in which partnership-to-partner transactions can be taxed outside the confines of Subchapter K, as if they occurred between unrelated parties, and by the fact that the receipt of a profits interest for services is not described in § 707. Instead, tax on a partner's entrepreneurial share of partnership profits should be imposed under the framework of Subchapter K when the partnership realizes actual profits that are included in the partner's distributive share.

---

[122] Even if a transfer of a profits interest were treated as a § 707(c) transaction, § 83 could not apply for two additional reasons. First, § 707(c) expressly states that guaranteed payments are treated as made to one who is not a partner only for purposes of §§ 61, 162, and 263; there is no mention of § 83. Second, because §§ 83 and 707(c) prescribe specific timing rules that are inconsistent with each other, the sections cannot both apply to the same transfer of property. Compare HR Rep. No. 1337, 83d Cong., 2d Sess. 94 (1954), and Reg. § 1.707-1(c) (second sentence) with § 83(a). Thus, applying § 83 to § 707(c) payments would effectively repeal the timing rule of § 707(c) any time a guaranteed payment obligation is satisfied in "property," but would leave it intact if the obligation is satisfied in money. Section 83 simply cannot be read to achieve such a partial repeal of another express statutory provision. These problems offer one explanation as to why Proposed Regulations § 1.721-1(b)(1) (1971) (withdrawn and replaced by REG-105346-03, May 24, 2005) was outstanding without being finalized for more than thirty years. But cf. Hensel Phelps Constr. Co., 74 TC 939 (1980), aff'd, 703 F2d 485 (10th Cir. 1983) (§ 83 applies to transfer of partnership capital interest for services; applicability of § 83 assumed without discussion); Thomas E. Larson, 55 TCM 1637 (1988) (same).

[5] Compensatory Transfers of Interests Outside the Safe Harbor

Revenue Procedure 93-27[123] and its companion, Revenue Procedure 2001-43,[124] only provide amnesty for certain "profits interests," as discussed earlier in ¶ 5.02[2]. The safe harbor in the 2005 Proposed Regulations would encompass both profits and capital interests, as discussed earlier in ¶ 5.02[3]. Both regimes exclude certain types of interests, generally those that are readily subject to valuation and, under Revenue Procedure 93-27, capital interests.

While there is relatively little authority regarding the treatment of compensatory interests outside the current safe harbor, it is not difficult to predict Treasury's likely position based on the § 83 approach espoused by the 2005 Proposed Regulations. Unless the Treasury modifies this approach or the courts adopt the nonrealization approach (discussed in ¶ 5.02[4]) to negate it, the likely rules are as follows:

1. *Vested capital interests.* Historically, the owner of a capital interest in a partnership in which capital is a material income-producing factor has generally been recognized as a partner for tax purposes.[125] Under this approach, a person who receives a service-connected transfer of an unrestricted capital interest should generally be treated as a partner under §§ 61 and 83, be taxed on receipt of the interest in an amount equal to the excess of its fair market value over the amount, if any, he pays for the interest, and thereafter be taxed on his distributive share of partnership income under § 702. If he later sells the interest, the tax consequences should be determined under § 741. There is no apparent authority for treating the owner of a capital interest in a partnership in which capital is not a material income-producing factor any differently.

2. *Unvested capital interests.* If a service partner receives a capital interest that is not "substantially vested" within the meaning of Regulations § 1.83-1(a)(1), and does not make an election under § 83(b), the unrestricted fair market value of the interest will be determined and taxed at the time the interest becomes substantially vested and the service provider will not be recognized as a partner prior to that time.

---

[123] Rev. Proc. 93-27, 1993-2 CB 343.

[124] Rev. Proc. 2001-43, 2001-2 CB 191.

[125] Former § 704(e)(1), which was the primary support for this proposition, was repealed in 2015 by the Bipartisan Budget Act of 2015, § 1102(c), Pub. L. No. 114-74 (Nov. 2, 2015). Concurrently, the following sentence was added to the definition of partner in § 761(b): "In the case of a capital interest in a partnership in which capital is a material income-producing factor, whether a person is a partner with respect to such interest shall be determined without regard to whether such interest was derived by gift from any other person." Whether these changes were intended to modify the historical approach described in this sentence seems very unlikely. See generally Chapter 3.

If he makes a § 83(b) election, he will be taxed on the current unrestricted fair market value of the interest and be recognized as a partner upon receipt of the interest.

3. *Vested profits interests.* A service provider who receives a non-safe harbor vested profits interest will be taxed on the unrestricted fair market value of the interest upon receipt regardless of whether he makes a § 83(b) election.

4. *Unvested profits interests.* A service provider who receives a non-safe harbor interest that is not substantially vested will be treated as receiving property subject to § 83 and will be taxed on the current unrestricted fair market value (if any) if he makes a § 83(b) election. Otherwise, the service provider will not be recognized as a partner until the interest substantially vests, at which time the holder of the interest will be taxed on the then-unrestricted fair market value of the interest.

5. *Non-property interests.* The § 83 Regulations recognize a type of profit-sharing arrangement that is not "property" for purposes of § 83: an unfunded and unsecured promise to pay money or property in the future.[126] There may be some advantages in utilizing this type of arrangement in certain circumstances, but a major disadvantage is the loss of the opportunity for the service provider to make a § 83(b) election and be recognized as a partner at little or no up-front tax cost.

Acceptance of the nonrealization analysis discussed in ¶ 5.02[4] would not change the expected results in items 1, 2, or 5 above. However, with regard to both vested and unvested profits interests, as described in items 3 and 4 above, there should not be any realization of income upon the receipt or vesting of the interest. It is unclear whether a service provider holding an interest that is not substantially vested would be recognized as a partner prior to vesting, but the overall scheme of Subchapter K would favor recognition from the date of receipt under most circumstances with mandatory allocation chargebacks in the event of a forfeiture.

Additional issues raised by the application of § 83 are explored in ¶ 5.03.

---

[126] Reg. § 1.83-3(e).

¶ 5.03 APPLICATION OF SECTION 83 TO COMPENSATORY TRANSFERS OF PARTNERSHIP INTERESTS

[1] Transfers

For § 83 purposes, "a transfer of property occurs when a person acquires a beneficial ownership interest in such property (disregarding any lapse restriction, as defined by Regulations § 1.83-3(i))."[127] Not every ostensible transfer of a partnership interest in connection with the performance of services constitutes a "transfer" for § 83 purposes. Thus, for example, Regulations § 1.83-3(a)(2) provides that the grant of an option to acquire property is not a transfer of property.[128] Accordingly, if a service provider "purchases" an interest in partnership capital, giving a nonrecourse note for the full price, he may be treated as acquiring no more than the equivalent of an option to buy the interest, rather than actual ownership of the interest.[129]

Similarly, if a service provider purchases an interest in partnership capital for its fair market value, but the partnership is obligated to buy the interest back for the same price when the service provider ceases to work for the partnership, the interest may not be treated as having been transferred to the service provider because he has not assumed any risk of loss with respect to the interest.[130]

[2] In Connection With the Performance of Services

Section 83 applies only to transfers of property "in connection with the performance of services." Under the Regulations, a transfer is service-connected if it is made "in recognition of the performance of, or the refraining from the performance of, services."[131] The Regulations also state that "[t]he existence of other persons entitled to buy [property] on the same terms and conditions as an employee ... may ... indicate that ... a transfer to the employee is not in recognition of the performance of, or the refraining from the performance of, services."[132] However, a transfer may be service-connected even if others acquire

---

[127] Reg. § 1.83-3(a)(1).

[128] Regulations § 1.83-3(a)(4) further provides that "an indication that no transfer has occurred is the extent to which the conditions relating to the transfer are similar to an option."

[129] Cf. Reg. § 1.83-3(a)(6) Example (2).

[130] See Reg. § 1.83-3(a)(6).

[131] Reg. § 1.83-3(f).

[132] Reg. § 1.83-3(f).

similar property at the same time and on the same terms as a service provider.[133]

The consequences of this rule are critically important to any person who acquires a partnership interest in anticipation of performing future services for the partnership. Even if the person pays full value for his interest and even if his purchase price matches the price paid by others for their interests, the acquisition of the interest may be subject to § 83. If the interest is "substantially vested"[134] at the time it is acquired, the fact that the transaction is subject to § 83 should be of little concern because (1) the taxable event under § 83 occurs immediately[135] and (2) the value of the interest that is included in income is reduced by the amount paid for the interest. If, however, the interest is not substantially vested when it is acquired, because it is subject to a substantial risk of forfeiture and is not transferable, no taxable event will occur until the interest becomes substantially vested, at which time the partner will be required to include in income the excess of the then-value of the interest over the price he paid for it. If the value of the interest has increased substantially, the resulting tax may also be substantial. Moreover, any income realized under § 83 is ordinary compensation income.

In view of the foregoing, it generally makes sense for a person who acquires a partnership interest, especially where he pays full value for it, to make a § 83(b) election if there is even a remote chance that the interest is not substantially vested when received. Where an election is made under § 83(b), the § 83 event will occur at the time of receipt even if the interest is not substantially vested when received, rather than later when it finally vests.

[3] Time of Transfer and Valuation

If property is substantially vested at the time it is transferred, it is required to be valued at the time of the transfer.[136] Otherwise, it is generally valued when or as it becomes substantially vested. Property becomes substantially vested "when it is either transferable or not subject to a substantial risk of forfeiture."[137] Under § 83(b), even if property is not substantially vested at the time it is transferred, the recipient of the property can elect to value the property and include it in income at the time of the transfer.

---

[133] See Lawrence J. Alves, 79 TC 864 (1982), aff'd, 734 F2d 478 (9th Cir. 1984).

[134] Reg. § 1.83-3(b).

[135] Reg. § 1.83-1(a)(1).

[136] Reg. § 1.83-1(a); see Hensel Phelps Constr. Co., 74 TC 939, 954 n.6 (1980), aff'd, 703 F2d 485 (10th Cir. 1983).

[137] Reg. § 1.83-3(b).

The generally applicable § 83 scheme controls the time at which a person who receives a compensatory transfer of a partnership interest must value the interest and include such value in income.[138] Factual questions may occur concerning the time at which an interest is actually acquired. These questions are most likely to occur at the commencement of a partnership and relate primarily to when the partnership actually comes into existence. Thus, for example, in *Hensel Phelps Construction Co.*,[139] the Tax Court determined that a partnership came into existence and a service partner acquired an interest in the partnership on the date the partnership agreement was executed and the partnership was capitalized by a contribution of real estate, rather than at an earlier time when the partners agreed to form the partnership and began to act in concert with a view to its eventual formation.

The 2005 Proposed Regulations would provide for the use of liquidation value instead of fair market value any time a safe harbor partnership interest is required to be valued under § 83, regardless of whether it is upon receipt of a vested interest, the vesting of a nonvested interest, or pursuant to a § 83(b) election.[140]

[4] Valuing Property for Section 83 Purposes: Lapse and Nonlapse Restrictions

Generally, the recipient of a compensatory transfer of property is required to include in income the excess of the fair market value of such property at the time it becomes substantially vested, over any amount paid by the recipient for the property. This fair market value amount is determined with regard to any "nonlapse restriction," but without regard to any "lapse restriction."[141]

Accordingly, the starting point for valuing property is its unrestricted fair market value. The classic definition of "fair market value" is the price a willing buyer would pay to a willing seller, neither being under any compulsion to

---

[138] Regulations § 1.721-1(b)(2) treats the compensatory grant of a partnership interest as a guaranteed payment, which is includible in income for the taxable year of a partner "within or with which" ends the taxable year in which the partnership deducts the payment. This timing rule is inconsistent with the § 83 scheme (partner's year of receipt controls) and is likely to be amended. See Prop. Reg. §§ 1.707-1(c), 1.721-1(b)(2) (2005).

[139] Hensel Phelps Constr. Co., 74 TC 939, 954 n.6 (1980), aff'd, 703 F2d 485 (10th Cir. 1983).

[140] Notice 2005-43, § 5, 2005-1 CB 1221. See ¶ 5.02[3][b].

[141] § 83(a); Reg. § 1.83-1(a)(1). Regulations § 1.61-2(d)(6) provides that the rules of Regulations §§ 1.61-2(d)(1), 1.61-2(d)(2), and 1.61-2(d)(4) apply to the determination of the value of property transferred in a § 83 transaction, if "the property is not subject to a restriction that has a significant effect on the fair market value of such property." As they apply to compensatory transfers of partnership interests, the § 61 Regulations simply require that property be valued at fair market value.

buy or sell, and both having full knowledge of all relevant facts.[142] While the fair market value of a partnership interest may be determined by reference to the value of the assets and business held by the partnership, the fair market value as so determined should usually be discounted to reflect the fact that a partnership interest is generally worth proportionately less than an equivalent direct ownership interest in the partnership's assets or business.[143]

In *Hensel Phelps Construction Co.*,[144] the Tax Court applied § 83 to the transfer of a partnership capital interest and resolved difficulties in valuing the interest under § 83 by examining the value of the services performed for the partnership by the transferee. The taxpayer, a construction company, received an interest in partnership capital and profits in exchange for its agreement to build a hotel on behalf of the partnership. For unexplained reasons, the taxpayer apparently did not offer any evidence as to the value of the interest. Thus, the court acceded to the government's request that, under the "exchange-equivalency" principle established by the Supreme Court in *United States v. Davis*,[145] the interest was worth the amount the taxpayer would normally charge for constructing a hotel.

The fair market value of property for § 83 purposes is determined "without regard to any restriction other than a restriction which by its terms will never lapse."[146] The Regulations refer to a restriction that will never lapse as a "nonlapse restriction,"[147] while all other restrictions are considered "lapse restrictions."[148] Only nonlapse restrictions are taken into account in valuing property for § 83 purposes; all lapse restrictions are ignored.

The Regulations define a "nonlapse restriction" as a permanent limitation on the transferability of property that will (1) require the transferee of the property to sell, or offer to sell, such property at a price determined by a formula, and (2) continue to apply to and be enforced against the transferee or any subsequent holder (other than the transferor).[149]

The Regulations further state that a "limitation subjecting the property to a permanent right of first refusal in a particular person at a price determined under a formula is a permanent nonlapse restriction," but provide that an obli-

---

[142] United States v. Cartwright, 411 US 546, 551 (1973); Reg. § 20.2031-1(b).

[143] See ¶ 23.07[1].

[144] Hensel Phelps Constr. Co., 74 TC 939 (1980), aff'd, 703 F2d 485 (10th Cir. 1983).

[145] United States v. Davis, 370 US 65 (1962).

[146] § 83(a)(1).

[147] Reg. § 1.83-3(h).

[148] Reg. § 1.83-3(i).

[149] Reg. § 1.83-3(h).

gation to resell property at its then fair market value is *not* a nonlapse restriction.[150]

Generally, under Regulations § 1.83-5(a), if property acquired in a § 83 transfer is subject to a nonlapse restriction, "the price determined under the formula price will be considered to be the fair market value of the property unless established to the contrary by the Commissioner." In practice, many interests in service partnerships, particularly professional service partnerships, are subject to nonlapse restrictions. For example, if a partner in a law firm is generally precluded from selling his interest and the partnership is required to redeem the interest for a formula price upon his retirement, the restriction will normally constitute a nonlapse restriction. Consequently, the upper limit on its fair market value for § 83 purposes should be the amount that the partner would receive for his partnership interest applying this formula on the date the interest is acquired.

While nonlapse restrictions are taken into account in valuing property transferred in § 83 transactions, lapse restrictions, which are any restrictions other than nonlapse restrictions,[151] are ignored. One type of lapse restriction is a "substantial risk of forfeiture."[152] A substantial risk of forfeiture exists where rights in the transferred property are conditioned, directly or indirectly, upon (1) the future performance (or refraining from performance) of substantial services by any person or (2) the occurrence of a condition related to a purpose of the transfer, and the possibility of forfeiture is substantial if such service-related performance requirement or such condition is not satisfied.[153]

Substantial risks of forfeiture are not the only category of lapse restrictions, however. For example, assume that a person receives a partnership interest as compensation for past services. The person is not required to perform any future services for the partnership; thus, the interest is not subject to a substantial risk of forfeiture and is "substantially vested."[154] However, the interest is subject to the requirement that it may not be sold or transferred for a period of ten years unless the owner first offers to sell it to the transferor for its then book value. This restriction is a lapse restriction and is ignored in valuing the interest for § 83 purposes. If this type of restriction is permanent, rather than for a fixed period only, it is a nonlapse restriction.

The 2005 Proposed Regulations would provide for the use of liquidation value instead of fair market value any time a safe harbor partnership interest is required to be valued under § 83, regardless of whether it is upon receipt of a vested interest, the vesting of a nonvested interest, or pursuant to a § 83(b)

---

[150] Reg. § 1.83-3(h).
[151] Reg. § 1.83-3(i).
[152] Reg. § 1.83-3(i).
[153] Reg. § 1.83-3(c)(1).
[154] Reg. § 1.83-3(b).

election.[155] If these regulations are adopted in substantially the form proposed, the discussion in this ¶ 5.03[4] will only be relevant to non-safe harbor interests.

[5] Basis Consequences

In general, if a service provider realizes income under § 83(a) as a result of a compensatory transfer of property, § 83(h) allows an equal § 162 deduction to the person for whom the services are provided.[156] While § 83(h) is unqualified in its allowance of a § 162 deduction, Regulations § 1.83-6(a)(4) provides that "[n]o deduction is allowed under section 83(h) to the extent that the transfer of property constitutes a capital expenditure, an item of deferred expense, or an amount properly includible in the value of inventory items." In these cases, the Regulations require the person for whom the services are performed to capitalize the amount that would otherwise be deductible.[157]

Regulations § 1.83-6(a)(1) provides that any deduction or other tax benefit allowable to the service recipient is taken into account in its taxable year "in which or with which ends the taxable year of the service provider in which such amount is includible as compensation." Thus, if property is not substantially vested at the time it is transferred, the § 83(h) deduction is deferred until the property substantially vests and the transferee is required to include it in income under § 83(a).[158]

Regulations § 1.83-6(b) provides that the transferor of property in a § 83 transaction recognizes gain or loss as a result of the transfer. This rule reflects the generally applicable notion that a taxpayer recognizes gain or loss on the transfer of property in satisfaction of an obligation.[159] Under Regulations § 1.83-6(b), the amount realized by a person who makes a § 83 transfer of property is divided into two components: (1) the amount actually paid by the transferee for the property and (2) the amount of gross income realized by the transferee under § 83(a). If the transferred property is not substantially vested

---

[155] Notice 2005-43, § 5, 2005-1 CB 1221. See ¶ 5.02[3][b].

[156] The Regulations condition any § 83(h) deduction on the service recipient's performance of its withholding obligation under § 3402. Reg. § 1.83-6(a)(2).

[157] Reg. § 1.83-6(a)(4). The validity of this Regulation has been upheld. Saul P. Steinberg, 46 TCM 1238 (1983), aff'd sub nom., Pulte Home Corp. v. Commissioner, 771 F2d 183 (6th Cir. 1985) (per curiam); Louis S. Rotolo, 88 TC 1500 (1987). Presumably, § 709 organization and syndication fees are within the ambit of this Regulation.

[158] If property is substantially vested when it is transferred, the service recipient determines the taxable year of the § 83(h) deduction under its normal method of accounting. Reg. § 1.83-6(a)(3); Rev. Rul. 80-96, 1980-2 CB 32.

[159] See, e.g., United States v. Davis, 370 US 65 (1962); International Freighting Corp. v. Commissioner, 135 F2d 310 (2d Cir. 1943).

at the time of the transfer, the transferor must recognize gain (but not loss) in an amount equal to the excess, if any, of the amount paid for the property by the transferee over the basis of the property. When the property substantially vests in the transferee and a deduction or other benefit is allowed under § 83(h), the transferor realizes an additional amount equal to the § 83(h) deduction or benefit. At this point, the transferor may recognize either gain or loss.

> EXAMPLE 5-5: Employer owns 100 shares of X Corporation with a basis of $600 and value of $800. Employer sells the shares to Employee for a cash payment of $700 subject to a substantial risk of forfeiture. Employee does not make a § 83(b) election. Since the shares are not substantially vested at the time of the transfer, Employee is not taxed on the excess of the value of the shares over his purchase price. Nevertheless, at the time of the transfer, Employer receives $700 for shares having a basis of $600 and must recognize gain of $100. At a later date, when the value of the shares has increased to $850, the substantial risk lapses and the shares become substantially vested. Accordingly, under § 83(a), Employee has $150 of gross income ($850 fair market value of the shares at the time they become substantially vested, less $700 amount paid for the shares), and correlatively, Employer is entitled to a deduction of $150 under § 83(h). In addition, under Regulations § 1.83-6(c), Employer recognizes $150 of additional gain with respect to the shares ($700 amount received in cash on the sale of the shares, plus $150 § 83(h) deduction, minus $600 basis in stock and $100 gain recognized at the time the shares were transferred).

Under Regulations § 1.1032-1(a), a corporation does not recognize gain on the issuance of its shares as compensation for services. The gain recognition requirement of Regulations § 1.83-6(c) expressly does not apply to stock transfers that are not taxable to the corporate issuers under § 1032, but no other exception is provided by the Regulations.

Any income realized by a partner as a result of the acquisition of a partnership interest is added to the basis of his interest under Regulations § 1.722-1. If a service partner is taxed on the value of a partnership interest received as compensation, the basis of the interest is equal to its value at the time of the transfer.

If the transfer involves a capital interest and the value of the interest exceeds its basis in the hands of the partnership, a question arises as to whether the transferee's cost basis in his partnership interest should be reflected in an increase in the basis of the partnership's assets. A transfer by a partnership of a capital interest in exchange for services could be viewed as a taxable transfer by the partnership of an undivided interest in its property in exchange for services, followed by a recontribution of the undivided interest to the partnership by the transferee in exchange for his partnership interest. Under this analysis, the transferee acquires a "cost" basis in his share of partnership capital, and then the partnership "reacquires" the capital at a basis, determined under §

723, equal to the transferee's cost basis. Section 704(c) principles should apply to give the service partner the benefit of the basis increase attributable to the capital "contributed" by him.[160]

> **EXAMPLE 5-6:** As compensation for services, *C* receives a 50 percent interest in the capital and profits of partnership *AB*, which owns property with a basis of $100 and a value of $200. Viewing the transaction as if (1) *AB* transferred a 50 percent undivided interest in its property (with a basis of $50 and a value of $100) to *C* as compensation for his services in a taxable transfer, and (2) *C* then contributed his 50 percent interest to the partnership, gives rise to the following tax consequences. The partnership recognizes $50 of gain on the payment to *C*, which is allocated to *A* and *B* equally and increases their book and tax capital accounts by the same amount. The partnership also has a compensation deduction of $100, which is allocated to *A* and *B* equally, decreasing their book and tax capital accounts by the same amount. *C* realizes compensation income of $100 (i.e., the value of his 50 percent interest in the property), and, as a result, is entitled to a $100 cost basis in his interest in the property. Upon *C*'s "contribution" of his interest to the partnership, the partnership accedes to *C*'s $100 basis therein. Thus, subsequent to the transaction, the partnership has property with a $200 value and a $150 basis. When the partnership revalues its assets upon *C*'s admission under Regulations § 1.704-1(b)(3)(iv)(f), the benefit of the resulting $50 increase in the book value of the partnership's assets inures equally to *A* and *B*, and those partners will bear equally the tax consequences of the $50 difference between the book basis and tax basis under the principles of § 704(c).[161]

While the approach described above is consistent with general federal income tax principles and produces a logical result, the only potential authority addressing this approach is the 2005 Proposed Regulations, which state that no gain or loss is recognized by a partnership upon the transfer or vesting of a compensatory partnership interest. If these regulations are adopted in substantially the form proposed, the result in Example 5-6 would be that the basis of the property to partnership *AB* would be unchanged because *C* is not viewed as having received (as a distribution) any portion of the partnership property as compensation for services. The capital accounts of *A* and *B* would be increased to total $200 immediately before the transfer of the interest to *C*. *C* would recognize $100 of income and would thus have a $100 tax basis in his partnership interest. *A* and *B* would share the partnership's corresponding compensation deduction of $100, reducing their total capital accounts to $100. The net result is that *A* and *B* have aggregate book capital accounts of $100 and tax capital accounts of $0, and *C* has a book capital account and a tax basis of $100. Under reverse § 704(c) principles, *A* and *B* will ultimately bear

---

[160] See generally ¶ 11.04.
[161] See ¶ 11.02[2][c][ii].

the tax consequence associated with the $100 difference between the $200 §
704(b) book value and the $100 tax basis of the partnership property.

If the recipient of a partnership interest has rendered services to a partner
of the partnership, rather than the partnership itself, the foregoing analysis
should be modified in several respects. Under these circumstances, the transaction is properly viewed as a taxable transfer of a partnership interest from the
benefited partner to the service partner. The transferee's basis in the interest is
its value because that is the amount of income the transferee realizes.[162] If the
transferee's basis in his partnership interest exceeds his proportionate share of
the partnership's basis in its assets, the transferee may benefit from a § 754
election to adjust the basis of partnership assets under § 743(b).[163] However, in
the absence of a § 754 election, the basis of partnership assets would be unaffected by this type of transaction.

If, in consideration of past services, property is contributed to a new partnership in which the compensated person obtains a capital interest as compensation for those past services, the transaction should be treated as if the
compensated person acquired an undivided interest in such property and then
contributed his interest in such property to the new partnership.[164]

> **EXAMPLE 5-7:** In consideration of services rendered by D to E, E trans-
> fers property with a value of $100,000 and a basis of $50,000 to a new
> equal partnership DE. The transaction is treated as if (1) E transferred an
> undivided interest in property worth $50,000 to D and (2) D and E then
> contributed their undivided interests in the property to the partnership.
> Thus, D realizes $50,000 of ordinary income (assuming his partnership
> interest has a value equal to his share of the contributed capital) and ac-
> quires a corresponding basis in his 50 percent interest in the property. The
> new partnership has an initial basis of $75,000 in the property ($25,000
> for E's interest and $50,000 for D's interest). Future income, gain, loss,
> and deduction with respect to the contributed property are allocated be-
> tween the partners under § 704(c).

¶ 5.04 COMPENSATORY PARTNERSHIP INTERESTS AS INCOME IN RESPECT OF A DECEDENT

If an interest in partnership capital representing compensation for services rendered by a deceased partner prior to his death is transferred to the deceased
partner's successor in interest after his death, Regulations § 1.721-1(b)(1) pro-

---

[162] § 742.

[163] See generally Chapter 24.

[164] See F.C. McDougal, 62 TC 720 (1974) (acq.). See ¶ 5.02[3][e].

vides that "the fair market value of such interest is income in respect of a decedent under section 691." Although this provision of the Regulations does not refer to interests in partnership profits received for services, it appears that profits interests should also be treated as income in respect of a decedent if they are transferred to a deceased partner's successor after his death.

If the deceased partner's interest is not "substantially vested" at the time of his death within the meaning of Regulations § 1.83-3(b), § 83 should also be taken into account in applying the income-in-respect-of-a-decedent rules. As a practical matter, most "substantial risks of forfeiture" either lapse or are violated upon a partner's death. If a substantial risk lapses and causes the deceased partner's interest to vest upon his death, it appears the resulting income should be included in the decedent's final return, and, hence, it is not income in respect of a decedent.[165]

Any restrictions that do not lapse upon the decedent's death should be taken into account in valuing the decedent's partnership interest for estate tax purposes. Upon a subsequent post-mortem lapse of the restrictions, the decedent's successor will have income in respect of a decedent under § 691.

---

[165] Cf. Reg. § 1.421-6(d)(2)(ii) Example (2).

CHAPTER **8**

Determining a Partner's Share of Partnership Liabilities for Basis Purposes

¶ 8.01 OVERVIEW OF THE LIABILITY-SHARING RULES

[1] General

Sections 752(a) and 752(b) speak in terms of increases or decreases "in a partner's share of the liabilities of a partnership," yet nowhere in the statute is any attempt made to indicate the manner in which a partner's "share" of liabilities is to be determined. That task is left entirely to Treasury Regulations. The original liability-sharing rules, which were promulgated in 1956 as Regulations § 1.752-1(e), were a mere two paragraphs in length. While the 1956 Regulations may have exemplified the virtue of brevity, they were ambiguous and unhelpful in resolving even simple liability-sharing questions in the context of modern complex partnerships. The 1956 Regulations were replaced in late

1988 by comprehensive Proposed and Temporary Regulations,[1] which were amended in the fall of 1989.[2] While the Temporary Regulations provided a logical and comprehensive approach to allocating partnership liabilities for § 752 purposes, they were widely criticized for their length and turgidity. In response to this criticism, the Treasury promulgated substantially revised final Regulations generally applicable to liabilities incurred or assumed by partnerships after December 28, 1991.[3]

The various iterations and amendments of the § 752 Regulations generally are effective based on the dates individual partnership liabilities are incurred or assumed.[4] Thus, a single partnership may have liabilities subject to several different versions of these Regulations. Reference should be made to the Fourth Edition of this Treatise for the rules applicable to liabilities that predate the effective date of the 1991 Regulations.

Despite the many changes over the last several decades, all versions of these Regulations share a common theoretical underpinning: Partnership liabilities are divided into two (and only two) categories: recourse and nonrecourse. Recourse liabilities are allocated among the partners in the manner in which the partners share partnership losses, while nonrecourse liabilities are allocated in the manner in which the partners share profits.[5] Recourse liabilities are discussed in ¶ 8.02 of this Chapter; nonrecourse liabilities are discussed in ¶ 8.03.

¶ 8.02 SHARING RECOURSE LIABILITIES

[1] Background: The *Raphan* Case and Section 79 of the Deficit Reduction Act of 1984

In *Raphan v. United States*,[6] the U.S. Claims Court considered whether a limited partnership liability was recourse or nonrecourse for purposes of applying

---

[1] TD 8237, 1989-1 CB 180 (Dec. 30, 1988). For a discussion and analysis of these Regulations, see Abrams, "Long-Awaited Regulations Under Section 752 Provide Wrong Answers," 44 Tax L. Rev. 627 (1989).

[2] TD 8274, 1989-2 CB 101 (Nov. 21, 1989).

[3] TD 8380, 56 FR 66,348 (Dec. 23, 1991), 1992-1 CB 218.

[4] Of course, this generalization is subject to a dazzling array of elections, exceptions, special rules, and transition conventions. See, e.g., Reg. § 1.752-2(l).

[5] The current articulation of this dichotomy is in Regulations § 1.752-1(a), which defines liabilities as recourse liabilities to the extent any partner or related person bears the "economic risk of loss" for the liability, and otherwise as nonrecourse.

[6] Raphan v. United States, 3 Cl. Ct. 457 (1983), rev'd on this issue, 759 F2d 879 (Fed. Cir. 1985).

the 1956 Regulations. The debt in question was secured by partnership assets and the terms of the debt imposed no liability on the partnership or its partners beyond the value of the collateral; however, the limited partnership's general partner personally guaranteed the debt. The Claims Court held that the guarantee did not cause the general partner to be personally liable for the debt within the meaning of the Regulations. Accordingly, the court held that the debt was a nonrecourse liability that could be included in the limited partners' bases. Prodded by the Treasury, which feared a massive raid on the fisc following *Raphan*, Congress concluded that the Claims Court's holding was "inappropriate,"[7] and directed, in § 79(a) of the Deficit Reduction Act of 1984 (the "1984 Act"), that § 752 (and the 1956 Regulations) should be applied without regard to the result reached in *Raphan*.[8] In addition, § 79(b) of the 1984 Act directed the Treasury to amend the 1956 Regulations to address the basis effects of "guarantees, assumptions, indemnity agreements, and similar arrangements." The amended Regulations were to be based "largely on the manner in which the partners, and persons related to the partners, share the economic risk of loss with respect to partnership debt (other than bona fide nonrecourse debt, as defined by [the amended Regulations])."[9]

[2] The Economic Risk of Loss Concept

A partnership liability is a recourse liability only to the extent that one or more partners (or related persons) bear the "economic risk of loss" with respect to the liability.[10] A partner's share of a partnership recourse liability "equals that portion of that liability, if any, for which the partner or related person bears the economic risk of loss."[11] Thus, under the § 752 Regulations, the economic risk of loss concept is critical both in determining whether liabilities are recourse and in allocating recourse liabilities among the partners.

　　The concept of economic risk of loss is explicated in detail in the following text, but it is important to understand one fundamental concept at the outset: A liability that is treated as a nonrecourse liability for other tax and business purposes may nonetheless constitute a recourse liability under the § 752 Regulations. For example, a partner is treated as bearing the economic risk of loss for a liability (and therefore the liability is treated as recourse for

---

[7] HR Rep. No. 432, 98th Cong., 2d Sess. 1235 (1984).

[8] The reversal of the U.S. Claims Court decision in *Raphan* occurred after the 1984 Act was enacted.

[9] HR Rep. No. 861, 98th Cong., 2d Sess. 869 (1984).

[10] Reg. § 1.752-1(a)(1). See Priv. Ltr. Rul. 200050032 (Sept. 15, 2000) (LLC member guarantees debt and waives subrogation rights; recourse debt, allocated to guaranteeing member).

[11] Reg. § 1.752-2(a).

§ 752 purposes)[12] to the extent that the partner (or a related person) holds or guarantees the liability,[13] even if the liability would be treated as nonrecourse for purposes of Regulations § 1.1001-2 or for nontax purposes. Conversely, a debt that is explicitly a full recourse obligation of a limited liability company is nonetheless a nonrecourse liability under these Regulations unless a partner or related person holds or guarantees the debt.[14]

The underlying theme of the "economic risk of loss" concept can be summarized as follows: At any time, a partner bears the economic risk of loss for a partnership liability to the extent that the partner (or a related person) would be legally obligated to make net payments, directly or indirectly, to satisfy the liability out of his nonpartnership assets if, at such time, the partnership had no assets and all its liabilities were due.

The § 752 Regulations phrase the economic risk of loss concept as follows:

> [A] partner bears the economic risk of loss for a partnership liability to the extent that, if the partnership constructively liquidated, the partner or related person would be obligated to make a payment to any person (or a contribution to the partnership) because that liability becomes due and payable and the partner or related person would not be entitled to reimbursement from another partner or person that is a related person to another partner.[15]

Six aspects of the test for economic risk of loss merit emphasis. First, the test takes into account all statutory and contractual obligations relating to partnership liabilities and partner contributions of capital, between the partners and the partnership, between the partnership and its creditors, and between the partners and the partnership's creditors.[16] Thus, guarantees, indemnifications, and other obligations (including obligations created by operation of law) running to creditors, other partners, or the partnership are relevant, even if they are not included in the partnership agreement.

Second, any obligation of a partner to make a payment or a contribution is offset by any right of that partner (or a person related to that partner) to be

---

[12] Reg. § 1.752-1(a)(1).

[13] Reg. § 1.752-2(b)(3)(i)(A). However, the guarantor partner's economic risk of loss may be reduced to the extent the guarantor is subrogated to the rights of the lender under state law. See Reg. § 1.752-2(f) Example (4), discussed later in ¶ 8.02[5][c].

[14] See Reg. § 1.752-2(j)(4)(i).

[15] Reg. § 1.752-2(b)(1).

[16] Reg. § 1.752-2(b)(3); cf. Reg. § 1.704-1(b)(2)(ii)(h) (broadly defining the term "partnership agreement" for purposes of the allocation rules of § 704(b)). See infra ¶ 8.02[4][b]. Under the 1956 Regulations, it was not clear whether indemnities and the like would be taken into account in determining a limited partner's obligation to make an additional contribution.

reimbursed or indemnified by any other partner (or a person related to any other partner) for any such payment or contribution.[17] Thus, for example, even though a limited partner's separate guarantee of a recourse partnership liability is taken into account in determining whether he bears the economic risk of loss for the liability, any economic risk of loss that would otherwise result from the guarantee is reduced to the extent that, upon performance of the guarantee, the guarantor/limited partner would be subrogated to the creditor's claim against the partnership's general partner.[18]

Third, for purposes of determining economic risk of loss, obligations and rights of persons related to a partner can cause the partner to bear the economic risk of loss with respect to a liability.[19]

Fourth, in measuring economic risk of loss, the § 752 Regulations assume that the partnership, all partners, and all persons related to partners will actually discharge their contractual obligations to make payments unless (a) the facts and circumstances indicate a plan to circumvent or avoid an obligation, or (b) there is not a commercially reasonable expectation that the payment obligor will have the ability to make the required payments.[20] This "commercially reasonable" exception is a significant departure from the basic economic risk of loss construct and is arguably inconsistent with the anti-*Raphan* legislation discussed earlier at ¶ 8.02[1].

Fifth, the regulations attempt to police efforts to game the economic risk of loss concept by ignoring "bottom dollar guarantees"[21] and other structures identified as abusive.[22]

Finally, and perhaps most importantly, at any given time, a partner's economic risk of loss for partnership liabilities is determined by assuming (regardless of the partnership's actual financial situation) that the partnership's assets, including any money it holds, are worthless and that the partnership is liquidated.[23]

Even to those accustomed to the conflicting twists of federal tax law, it may seem strange that the § 752 Regulations require a prosperous, ongoing partnership to allocate its recourse liabilities among its partners on the assumption that its assets become instantly worthless and that it liquidates. Most partnerships pay their liabilities out of profits; even those that fall on hard times generally satisfy their obligations by liquidating existing partnership assets,

---

[17] Reg. § 1.752-2(b)(5).

[18] See Reg. § 1.752-2(f) Example (4); ¶ 8.02[4][c].

[19] Reg. § 1.752-2(b)(1). "Related person" is defined in Regulations § 1.752-4(b). See ¶ 8.04.

[20] Reg. §§ 1.752-2(b)(6), 1.752-2(j)(3), 1.752-2(k); see ¶ 8.02[5].

[21] See ¶ 8.02[4][b][v].

[22] See ¶ 8.02[10].

[23] Reg. § 1.752-2(b)(1). See ¶ 8.02[3].

without the necessity of calling on their partners. Even in the direst case, a partnership can be expected to have some asset value remaining to mitigate the amount that its partners must contribute or pay to satisfy its liabilities. Why, then, are the § 752 Regulations based on an assumption that is almost never true?

The answer lies in the simple fact that, with respect to any type of liability, the partnership itself bears the economic risk of loss unless its assets become worthless. The only time a partner will be called upon to come out of pocket with respect to a partnership liability is when the partnership is unable to pay all or a portion of that liability. Thus, any examination of the partners' obligations at a time when the partnership's assets have value would necessarily produce an artificial and potentially skewed analysis as to how the partners bear the economic risk of loss. By crediting partners with outside basis attributable to a liability to the extent the partners would be obligated to make payments in the event of a total loss of value in the partnership's assets, the § 752 Regulations duplicate the consequences of the worst-case hypothetical situation. Where the situation is less catastrophic, no artificial distortions are created by this approach.

[3] Constructive Liquidation: The Condition Precedent to Determining Economic Risk of Loss

A partner bears the economic risk of loss for a partnership liability only to the extent he would be obligated to satisfy the obligation out of his nonpartnership assets if the partnership were wholly unable to pay the liability. Therefore, as a condition precedent to determining who bears the economic risk of loss for partnership liabilities under the § 752 Regulations, it is necessary to hypothesize a situation in which, simultaneously, (1) the partnership's assets become wholly worthless, (2) the partners' capital accounts are adjusted to reflect a loss of the entire book value of the partnership's assets, (3) all contractual and statutory obligations of the partners relating to the partnership and its liabilities are triggered and performed, and (4) the partnership liquidates. The § 752 Regulations understatedly refer to this hypothetical cataclysm as a "constructive liquidation."

The following events are deemed to occur in connection with a constructive liquidation:

    1. *Liabilities become due.* "All of the partnership's liabilities become due and payable."[24] Such liabilities include any "wrapped indebted-

---

[24] Reg. § 1.752-2(b)(1)(i).

ness" owed by a partner or related person to a third party that is treated as a separate liability of the partnership.[25]

2. *Assets become worthless.* With one exception, all partnership assets (including cash) become wholly worthless.[26]

3. *Partnership disposes of assets.* The partnership disposes of all of its assets in a fully taxable transaction for no consideration, except that the partnership is treated as realizing an amount equal to the sum of all liabilities for which the creditor's right to repayment is limited to the assets of the partnership.[27]

4. *All items are allocated.* On the date of the constructive liquidation, all items of partnership income, gain, loss, or deduction are allocated to the partners in accordance with the partnership agreement.[28]

5. *Liquidation.* The partners' interests in the partnership are liquidated.[29]

The net effect of Steps 1 through 4 is to create a hypothetical balance sheet. The asset side of this balance sheet will always be zero. The only liabilities remaining on the other side of the balance sheet will be those with respect to which partners or related persons bear the economic risk of loss. The partners' capital accounts will be fully adjusted to reflect the disposition of all of the partnership's assets and will, in the aggregate, have a net deficit balance exactly equal to the remaining liabilities. The final step is to utilize this balance sheet to determine the extent to which each partner would bear the economic risk of loss with respect to each partnership liability.[30] Before turning to this final step, however, it is helpful to consider an example of the mechanics of a constructive liquidation:

EXAMPLE 8-1: *A* and *B* form the *AB* general partnership to invest in real estate. Each contributes $100,000 cash. In addition, *B* contributes marketable securities that have a fair market value and a basis of $100,000 at all relevant times. All profits and losses are to be allocated equally to the partners, except that any gain or loss with respect to the securities is to be allocated 100 percent to *B*. The partnership agreement provides that capital accounts will be maintained in accordance with the § 704(b) Regulations, liquidating distributions will be based on capital accounts, and any partner with a deficit capital account balance on liquidation must make it up. The partnership buys (1) building *X* for $300,000, consisting of a

---

[25] Reg. § 1.752-2(c)(2).

[26] Reg. § 1.752-2(b)(1)(ii). The exception relates to property contributed to the partnership solely to secure a partnership liability. This is known as the indirect pledge rule, discussed at ¶ 8.02[4][b][iii][B]. See Reg. § 1.752-2(h)(2).

[27] Reg. § 1.752-2(b)(1)(iii).

[28] Reg. § 1.752-2(b)(1)(iv).

[29] Reg. § 1.752-2(b)(1)(iv).

[30] See discussion at ¶ 8.02[4].

$100,000 cash down payment and a $200,000 full recourse note to the seller, and (2) building Y for $400,000, consisting of a $50,000 cash down payment and a $350,000 nonrecourse loan to the seller that is secured by a mortgage on building Y and a pledge of the marketable securities contributed by B. The remaining $50,000 of cash is retained for future needs. After these transactions, the balance sheet of AB is as follows:

Assets		Liabilities and Capital		
Cash	$ 50,000	Recourse loan	$200,000	
Securities	100,000	Nonrecourse loan	350,000	
		Total liabilities		$550,000
		Capital accounts		
Building X	300,000	A	$100,000	
Building Y	400,000	B	200,000	
		Total capital		$300,000
Total assets	$850,000	Total liabilities		
		and capital		$850,000

Upon a constructive liquidation of the partnership immediately after these transactions, the cash and both buildings are treated as worthless; however, the value of the securities is respected because they serve as security for a partnership liability under the indirect pledge rule.[31] Both the recourse and nonrecourse loans are treated as due and payable. The partnership is treated as receiving consideration in the form of relief from liability upon the hypothetical disposition of its assets to the extent that the nonrecourse loan is a liability for which the creditor's repayment rights are limited to one or more partnership assets.[32] Under the indirect pledge rule, B is treated as bearing the economic risk of loss with respect to the nonrecourse loan, but only to the extent of the value of the securities securing the loan. Thus, only $250,000 of the $350,000 nonrecourse loan is a liability with respect to which the creditor's rights are limited to partnership assets, and the partnership is deemed to receive consideration of $250,000 in relief from such liability in exchange for building Y, which has a basis of $400,000, thus generating a $150,000 loss. The cash and building X are treated as being worthless and disposed of in a taxable transaction, generating an additional $350,000 loss. Total losses of $500,000 are therefore allocated equally between A and B, producing the following balance sheet:

Assets		Liabilities and Capital	
	$0	Recourse loan	$200,000
		Capital accounts	

---

[31] Reg. §§ 1.752-2(b)(1)(ii), 1.752-2(h)(2).
[32] Reg. § 1.752-2(b)(1)(iii).

		A	($150,000)
		B	(50,000)
		Total capital	($200,000)
Total assets	$0	Total liabilities and capital	$ 0

This balance sheet demonstrates that A and B have contribution obligations of $150,000 and $50,000, respectively, with respect to the $200,000 recourse loan. Accordingly, $150,000 of the recourse liability is allocated to A, increasing his outside basis by $150,000, and $50,000 of the recourse liability is allocated to B, increasing his outside basis correspondingly. The $100,000 portion of the "nonrecourse" loan that is secured by the securities contributed by B is allocated entirely to B,[33] and the remaining $250,000 of this loan is treated as a nonrecourse liability that is allocated in accordance with the nonrecourse sharing rules discussed at ¶ 8.03.

[4] Payment Obligations

[a] General

The constructive liquidation analysis hypothetically strips the partnership of all its assets and nonrecourse liabilities and establishes the effects that these transactions would have on the partners' capital accounts. The next step in allocating partnership liabilities is to determine how the partners would be required to satisfy the remaining recourse liabilities out of their separate assets. Regulations § 1.752-2(b)(1) provides that

> a partner bears the economic risk of loss for a partnership liability to the extent that, if the partnership constructively liquidated, the partner or related person would be obligated to make a payment to any person (or a contribution to the partnership) because that liability becomes due and payable and the partner or related person would not be entitled to reimbursement from another partner or person that is a related person to another partner.

In determining whether a partner has a payment obligation with respect to a partnership liability, "[a]ll statutory and contractual obligations relating to the partnership liability are taken into account."[34] A partner's obligation to make a payment is reduced by his right to receive reimbursement of the payment from

---

[33] If B had merely retained the securities and pledged them to secure the nonrecourse loan, the same results would occur. Reg. § 1.752-2(h)(1).

[34] Reg. § 1.752-2(b)(3).

another partner or a person related to another partner.[35] Moreover, subject to two anti-abuse rules,[36] "it is assumed that all partners and related persons who have obligations to make payments actually perform those obligations, irrespective of their actual net worth."[37]

In appropriate circumstances, the economic risk of loss for a particular partnership liability may be borne by more than one partner. To illustrate: Assume that (1) a two-member LLC, classified as a partnership for tax purposes, borrows $1,000 from a bank and (2) though neither member has personal liability for the loan in his or her capacity as a member, each guarantees the loan and waives any right of subrogation or substitution against the LLC or the other member. In this situation, the lender has a fielder's choice as to which member to pursue in the event of the LLC's default, and, under the rules explained below, each member literally bears the entire $1,000 economic risk of loss for loan. The existing regulations do not provide a rule to allocate a partnership liability when the associated economic risk of loss overlaps, as it does in this situation.

The Treasury has moved to fill this gap by issuing Proposed Regulations that would provide a formula for the allocation of the economic risk of loss among the risk-bearing partners if there is overlapping risk of loss. Each risk-bearing partner's share of the liability would equal the amount of the liability multiplied by a fraction, the numerator of which is the amount of economic risk such partner is determined to bear with respect to such liability (determined without regard to this rule) and the denominator of which is the sum of such amounts for all risk-bearing partners.[38] Thus, in the preceding illustration, each LLC member would have a risk of loss of $500 with respect to the $1,000 bank loan: that is, the amount of the loan (i.e., $1,000), multiplied by a fraction, the numerator of which is each such member's risk of loss (i.e., $1,000), and the denominator of which is the total risk of loss for all members (i.e., $2,000).

[b] Obligations Taken Into Account

[i] In general. Regulations § 1.752-2(b)(3)(i) sets forth the general rule that "[t]he determination of the extent to which a partner or related person has

---

[35] Reg. § 1.752-2(b)(5). See ¶ 8.02[4][c].

[36] The "plan to circumvent or avoid" rule in Reg. § 1.752-2(j)(3) and the "no reasonable expectation of repayment" rule in Reg. § 1.752-2(k). See ¶ 8.02[10].

[37] Reg. § 1.752-2(b)(6).

[38] Prop. Reg. §§ 1.752-2(a)(2), 1.752-2(f) Example 9, 1.752-2(l) (2014); see REG 136984-12, 78 Fed. Reg. 76,092 (Dec. 16, 2013), 2014-2 IRB 378, corrected at 79 Fed. Reg. 29,701 (May 23, 2014). These Proposed Regulations would apply to liabilities incurred or assumed after the date on which they are published as final regulations.

an obligation to make a payment ... is based on the facts and circumstances at the time of the determination." To the extent an obligation to make a payment is not recognized under this rule because of the relevant facts and circumstances, it is entirely disregarded both for purpose of determining whether a partnership liability is a recourse or nonrecourse liability obligation as well as allocating the economic risk of loss among the partners.[39]

The clarity of this timing rule (specifically, the use of the phrase "at the time of the determination") seems to leave little room for confusion. Consideration of the facts and circumstances existing as of the moment of the constructive liquidation seems to be all that is required, without regard to possible future events. If a contingency that would create an obligation has not occurred at the time of the constructive liquidation, it would seem that the obligation should not be taken into account under this timing rule regardless of the likelihood (or lack thereof) that it might occur in the future. However, as discussed later in this ¶ 8.02[4][b][i], the provisions of Regulations § 1.752-2(b)(4), relating to contingent liabilities, indicate this simplistic analysis is not exactly what is intended and that some future events should be taken into account if they are "likely" to occur.

The payment obligations to be taken into account in determining economic risk of loss are broadly defined by the Regulations to include the following:

1. Contractual obligations outside the partnership agreement, such as guarantees, indemnifications, reimbursement agreements, and other obligations running directly to creditors, to other partners, or to the partnership;[40]

2. Obligations to the partnership that are imposed by the partnership agreement, including the obligation to make a capital contribution or to restore a deficit capital account upon liquidation of the partnership; and

3. Payment obligations (whether in the form of direct remittances to another partner or a contribution to the partnership) imposed by state law, including the governing state partnership statute.

Certain types of contingent payment obligations recognized under Regulations § 1.752-2(b)(3) may be disregarded under Regulations § 1.752-2(b)(4), which identifies two categories of contingent payment obligations:

---

[39] There is only one explicit exception to this general rule: Regulations § 1.752-2(b)(3)(ii), relating to "bottom dollar payment obligations," which are disregarded for all purposes regardless of the general rule. See generally ¶ 8.02[4][b][iv].

[40] See FSA 1993-293 (Dec. 15, 1993) (assumption agreements executed by partners shift economic risk of loss to assuming partners).

    Category 1. The first sentence of Regulations § 1.752-2(b)(4) provides that a payment obligation is disregarded if, taking into account all the facts and circumstances, the obligation is subject to contingencies that make it unlikely the obligation will ever be discharged; and

    Category 2. The second sentence of Regulations § 1.752-2(b)(4) provides that a payment obligation that would arise (a "springing obligation") upon the future occurrence of an event that is not determinable with reasonable accuracy is disregarded until the event occurs.

There are other types of contingent obligations that are not mentioned in this Regulation. Most obviously, a current payment obligation that may cease to exist without any payment by the obligor upon the occurrence of some future event may be contingent in some sense but is not within the ambit of Regulations § 1.752-2(b)(4). Common examples would include obligations that terminate upon the completion of construction, the achievement of various economic goals (90 percent tenant occupancy, gross or net rent levels, etc.), or the retirement of a construction loan. Because these types of contingencies are not covered by Regulations § 1.752-2(b)(4), the general rule in Regulations § 1.752-2(b)(3)(i) applies to these types of obligations based on the facts as they exist on the date of the constructive liquidation: If an event that would cause the obligation to end has not occurred on that date, the obligation should be given effect regardless of the likelihood it may eventually occur (but subject to the anti-abuse rules in Regulations § 1.752-2(j)).[41]

    There are no examples of Category 1 obligations in the Regulations. A single example is offered up regarding Category 2. Example (8) of Regulations § 1.752-2(f) describes an otherwise nonrecourse partnership real estate loan that provides it will become recourse to the extent of any diminution in the value of the encumbered property resulting from the partnership's failure to properly maintain it. The Example states there are no facts (presumably as of the time of the constructive liquidation) to establish any liability under this provision. Therefore, no partner bears any economic risk of loss under the loan, which remains entirely nonrecourse for purposes of § 752.[42]

---

    [41] See ¶ 8.02[10]. In comparison to the "springing obligations" covered by § 1.752-2(b)(4) in Category 2, it may be helpful to think of this type of obligation as a Category 3 "disappearing obligation" that is not covered by § 1.752-2(b)(4).

    [42] Another example of a Category 2 obligation that should be disregarded under the Regulations is the type of "bad boy" guarantee commonly found in commercial real estate loan documents and triple-net lease agreements, pursuant to which owners who engage in certain types of "bad" behaviors (fraud, other types of felonies, certain bankruptcy actions or approvals, etc.) may become personally liable for otherwise nonrecourse obligations. In the absence of actual bad boy actions, a conventional bad boy guarantee should be disregarded under Regulations § 1.752-2(b)(4). The Service has briefly flirted with the notion

It is difficult to reconcile the text in the second sentence of Regulations § 1.752-2(b)(4) and the analysis in Example (8) with the overarching timing rule set forth in Regulations § 1.752-2(b)(3)(i). If a Category 2 obligation is properly viewed as a "springing" obligation that has not actually come into being at the time of the constructive liquidation, the basic timing rule in § 1.752-2(b)(3)(i) would seem to preclude it from being taken into account regardless of how likely or unlikely it is to come into being in the near future. A transaction structured to assure (or virtually assure) that an obligation will "spring" into existence would seem to have little commercial purpose as well as a high likelihood of running afoul of the anti-abuse rules in Regulations § 1.752-2(j).

Category 1 obligations described in the first sentence of Regulations § 1.752-2(b)(4) are conceptually different. They may be characterized as existing (as opposed to "springing") obligations that are subject to future contingencies that make it unlikely "the obligation will ever be discharged." While the language is a bit opaque, presumably "discharged" in this context refers to the likelihood that the partner (or related person) may be required to personally pay the obligation. If this is correct, it seems highly likely the obligation should be ignored under the basic rule in § 1.752-2(b)(3) or the anti-abuse rule of § 1.752-2(j)(3) in any event.

Thus, it seems both sentences in Regulations § 1.752-2(b)(4) are entirely redundant. This may cause unnecessary confusion that could be avoided if Treasury were to either delete this provision from the Regulations or provide a clearer articulation of its intended effect and relationship with Regulations § 1.752-2(b)(3).

Where a payment obligation is not recognized under these rules, the partners' payment obligations are determined by ignoring that obligation.[43]

[ii] Arrangements tantamount to a guarantee. There are many types of contractual arrangements that are not direct payment or contribution obligations but that effectively shift the economic risk of loss with respect to partnership liabilities. The Regulations include an anti-abuse rule that describes these types of contracts as "arrangements tantamount to a guarantee" and provides

---

that a bad boy guarantee should cause a debt to be treated as recourse for purposes of § 752. See CCA 201606027 (Feb. 5, 2016) (promise not to declare insolvency converts nonrecourse loan to recourse), effectively reversed in GLAM 2016-001 (Apr. 15, 2016) (extensive "nonrecourse carve-out" provision does not convert liability to recourse until action actually occurs). The promptness of the Service's reversal of position is testimony to both the political clout of the real estate industry and how strongly the industry felt about the issue.

[43] Reg. § 1.752-2(b)(3)(i) (second sentence).

that they will be treated as shifting the economic risk of loss under certain circumstances.[44]

Regardless of the form of the obligation, a partner is treated as bearing the economic risk of loss with respect to all or a portion of a partnership liability to the extent that:

1. The partner or a related person undertakes the obligation so that the partnership can obtain or retain a loan;
2. The obligation significantly reduces the lender's default risk on the loan; and
3. Either (a) one of the principal purposes of using the obligation is to enable partners who are not directly liable on the loan to include a portion of the loan in the basis of their partnership interest, or (b) a principal purpose of using the obligation is to cause the payment obligations of other partners to be disregarded.

This is an odd sort of anti-abuse rule. It applies only to loss-shifting transactions that have both significant business purpose (elements 1 and 2) and a principal purpose of tax avoidance (element 3). Accordingly, it gives tax effect to the substance of the obligation itself but modifies its consequences under the risk of loss rules to prevent abusive results among the partners. It is also very narrowly targeted—it applies only to loans, as opposed to obligations in general.

To satisfy element 2, the obligation must significantly reduce the risk that a partnership liability will not be satisfied under the facts of a constructive liquidation. For example, a partner's guarantee that the partnership will complete a building should not cause the guarantor-partner to bear the economic risk of loss with respect to an otherwise nonrecourse liability secured by the building, even if the completion guarantee is given to obtain the loan. While the creditor clearly benefits from the completion guarantee, the guarantee does not significantly reduce the risk that the partnership will default on the liability or that the completed building will have insufficient value to satisfy the liability.[45] On the other hand, a guarantee that collateral will have a specified value would effectively eliminate the creditor's risk to the extent of the guaranteed value.[46]

---

[44] Reg. § 1.752-2(j)(2). This rule was modified in 2019 with respect to transactions entered into on or after October 5, 2016 (subject to a pre-existing binding contract exception); partnerships had an option to elect to apply the new rule to all partnership liabilities as of the beginning of the first partnership year ending on or after October 5, 2016. See Reg. § 1.752-2(l)(2).

[45] This example was in Temporary Regulations § 1.752-1T(k) Example (17) (prior to removal by TD 8380 (Dec. 20, 1991)). The unexplained deletion of the example should not create a negative inference; most likely, it fell victim to the general effort to simplify and shorten the § 752 Regulations.

[46] In applying these rules, a single liability may be bifurcated into a recourse liability and a nonrecourse liability. Reg. § 1.752-2(f) Example (5). If a partner guarantees that

Similarly, a lease of property from a partnership to a partner that is not on commercially reasonable terms may be tantamount to a guarantee by the lessee partner, as illustrated by the following example.[47]

> **EXAMPLE 8-2:** *A* and *B* form a partnership for the purposes of buying and leasing computer equipment. *A* invested in this partnership, in part, to obtain the tax benefits arising from partnership losses. The partnership borrows money on a nonrecourse basis to acquire a computer that is subject to an existing two-year lease. In order to induce the creditor to make the loan, *B* agrees to lease the computer from the partnership under a "hell or high water" master lease arrangement that requires *B* to maintain the computer and to continue making lease payments even if the computer is damaged or destroyed. The rental payments under the master lease are sufficient to fully amortize all amounts due under the loan and the master lease agreement is pledged to the lender.
>
> *A* will have sufficient basis in its partnership interest to take full advantage of its share of partnership losses only if the loan is treated as a nonrecourse liability (which would be shared among partners in accordance with their partnership profits interests). Under the anti-abuse rule, however, the master lease may be treated as tantamount to a guarantee, with the result that the partnership liability will be treated as a recourse liability allocable only to *B*, the partner who, because of the master lease, may be treated as having the economic risk of loss for the entire liability.[48]

[iii] Obligations limited to the value of property: direct and indirect pledges.

[A] *Direct pledges.* It is not necessary that an obligation be a general liability obligation of a partner (or a related person) in order to be taken into account in determining who bears the economic risk of loss for a partnership liability. To the contrary, an obligation that is secured only by the obligor's

---

collateral for an otherwise nonrecourse liability will have a minimum value that is less than the full amount of the liability, the portion of the liability equal to the guaranteed value may be treated as a recourse liability and the remainder as a nonrecourse liability. An obligation that eliminates the creditor's risk for a period of time that is less than the entire term of the liability should be treated as tantamount to a guarantee during the time that the obligation is effective. The relevant question is whether, at the particular time the liability is being tested, the obligation would eliminate the creditor's risk under the facts of a constructive liquidation occurring at that time. Reg. § 1.752-2(b)(3)(i).

[47] Reg. § 1.752-2(j)(2)(ii) (second sentence).

[48] This example is based on Temporary Regulations § 1.752-1T(k) Example (20) (prior to removal by TD 8380 (Dec. 20, 1991)). The existing § 752 Regulations contain no examples illustrating the "tantamount to a guarantee rule." Despite the unexplained deletion of Example (20) in the final § 752 Regulations, Example (20) still aptly illustrates the application of this rule.

nonpartnership property (or is otherwise limited to the value of such property) is taken into account as a payment or contribution obligation.[49] Thus, while a partnership liability that is secured only by partnership property is a nonrecourse liability (because no partner bears individually any economic risk of loss), a partnership liability that is secured only by a partner's nonpartnership property may be a recourse liability as to which the partner bears some or all of the economic risk of loss.

"Property" for this purpose does not include a direct or indirect interest in the partnership[50] or a promissory note of the partner (or related person) unless it is "readily tradeable on an established securities market."[51]

If a partner (or related person) pledges nonpartnership property as security for a partnership liability, the partner bears the economic risk of loss for that liability only to the extent of the fair market value of the property as of the time of the pledge or contribution.[52]

[B] Indirect pledges. Under the "indirect pledge rule," a partner is treated as having a payment obligation with respect to a partnership liability to the extent of the value of any property that the partner contributes to the partnership *solely* for the purpose of securing the liability.[53] Regardless of purpose, however, the indirect pledge rule does not apply "unless substantially all of the items of income, gain, loss, and deduction attributable to the contributed property are allocated to the contributing partner, and this allocation is generally greater than the partner's share of other significant items of partnership income, gain, loss, or deduction."[54]

Thus, the § 752 Regulations effectively treat a partner as continuing to own any pledged property contributed solely for the purpose of securing a partnership liability if the contributing partner retains substantially all of the benefits and burdens of owning the property. Application of the indirect pledge rule does not mandate that pledged property cannot be partnership property for purposes other than § 752. However, the Service has ruled that securities owned by a partnership, but selected and traded by a partner entirely for his

---

[49] Reg. § 1.752-2(h)(1).

[50] Reg. § 1.752-2(h)(1).

[51] Reg. § 1.752-2(h)(4).

[52] Reg. § 1.752-2(h)(3). Under the Temporary Regulations, fair market value was required to be determined at certain specified times if the pledged property had a readily ascertainable fair market value or was "of a type that by its terms increases or decreases in value (e.g., a debt instrument on which principal payments are made during its term)" and less regularly for other types of property. Temp. Reg. § 1.752-1T(d)(3)(ii)(F)(*1*)(*i*) (1988). The final Regulations contain no revaluation provisions, although in extreme cases the Service might be able to rely on the anti-abuse rule of Regulations § 1.752-2(j)(3) to force revaluations.

[53] Reg. § 1.752-2(h)(2). See ¶ 8.02[3], Example 8-1.

[54] Reg. § 1.752-2(h)(2).

own account, are property of the partner rather than the partnership, even though they are subject to the claims of partnership creditors.[55]

Like pledged property, indirectly pledged property is valued at the time of the pledge or contribution.[56]

[iv] Obligations to pay interest. The drafters of the § 752 Regulations were concerned that partnerships might attempt to manipulate the economic risk of loss rules by incurring long-term liabilities that are nonrecourse as to principal, but recourse as to interest. If the partnership's nonrecourse obligation to pay principal is substantially deferred, while the guaranteed interest payments are required to be paid currently, the present value of the nonrecourse obligation to pay deferred principal may be nominal in comparison to the present value of the guaranteed interest payments. However, without a special rule, the entire loan would be treated as nonrecourse. Regulations § 1.752-2(e)(1), which is designed to eliminate this perceived potential for abuse, provides:

> [I]f one or more partners or related persons have guaranteed the payment of more than 25 percent of the total interest that will accrue on a partnership nonrecourse liability over its remaining term, and it is reasonable to expect that the guarantor will be required to pay substantially all of the guaranteed future interest if the partnership fails to do so, then the liability is treated as two separate partnership liabilities. If this rule applies, the partner or related person that has guaranteed the payment of interest is treated as bearing the economic risk of loss for the partnership liability to the extent of the present value of the guaranteed future interest payments.

This rule is subject to several significant provisions that narrowly restrict its purview. First, the rule states that it is generally "reasonable to expect that the guarantor will be required to pay substantially all of the guaranteed future interest if, upon a default in payment by the partnership, the lender can enforce the interest guaranty without foreclosing on the property and thereby extinguishing the underlying debt."[57] By negative implication, it would generally be unreasonable to expect an interest guarantor to pay interest that will accrue over the life of the loan if the lender cannot enforce the interest guarantee separately from the loan. It is an odd loan under which the holder can keep the loan outstanding indefinitely in a defaulted state and sue the guarantor for defaulted interest. Second, the rule does not apply unless the term of the guarantee exceeds the shorter of one third of the term of the loan or five years.[58] Finally, the rule does not apply if the guarantor (1) is a partner whose direct

---

[55] Rev. Rul. 55-39, 1955-1 CB 403.

[56] Reg. § 1.752-2(h)(3).

[57] Reg. § 1.752-2(e)(1).

[58] Reg. § 1.752-2(e)(3).

and indirect interest in each item of partnership income, gain, loss, and deduction[59] is 10 percent or less, and (2) the loan constitutes qualified nonrecourse financing within the meaning of § 465(b)(6) (determined without regard to the type of activity financed).[60]

The present value of the future interest payments is determined on the basis of the interest rate stated in the loan documents or, if interest is imputed under either § 483 or § 1274, the applicable federal rate, compounded semiannually.[61] If the guaranteed interest is more than 25 percent of the total interest expected to accrue on a loan, at a time when none of the exceptions apply, this rule applies and will continue to apply even if the guaranteed interest later falls below 25 percent, for example, as a result of future principal amortization.[62]

[v] **Bottom dollar payment obligations.** Section 1.752-2(b)(3)(ii) of the Regulations sets forth special rules for disregarding certain types of guarantees colloquially known as "bottom dollar" guarantees.

[A] *General rule.* As defined by the Regulations, a "bottom dollar payment obligation" is any payment obligation that is the same as or similar to any of the following:

"*(i)* With respect to a guarantee or similar arrangement, any payment obligation other than one in which the partner or related person is or would be liable up to the full amount of such partner's or related person's payment obligation if, and to the extent that, any amount of the partnership liability is not otherwise satisfied.

(ii) With respect to an indemnity or similar arrangement, any payment obligation other than one in which the partner or related person is or would be liable up to the full amount of such partner's or related person's payment obligation, if, and to the extent that, any amount of the indemnitee's or benefited party's payment obligation that is recognized under this paragraph (b)(3) is satisfied.

(iii) With respect to an obligation to make a capital contribution or to restore a deficit capital account upon liquidation of the partnership as described in §1.704-1(b)(2)(ii)(*b*)(*3*) (taking into account §1.704-1(b)(2)(ii)(*c*)), any payment obligation other than one in which the partner is or would be required to make the full amount of the partner's capital contribution or to restore the full amount of the partner's deficit capital account.

---

[59] An indirect interest is one that is held "through one or more partnerships including the interest of any related person." Reg. § 1.752-2(e)(4).

[60] Reg. § 1.752-2(e)(4).

[61] Reg. § 1.752-2(e)(2).

[62] Reg. § 1.752-2(e)(2) (last sentence).

(iv) An arrangement with respect to a partnership liability that uses tiered partnerships, intermediaries, senior and subordinate liabilities, or similar arrangements to convert what would otherwise be a single liability into multiple liabilities if, based on the facts and circumstances, the liabilities were incurred pursuant to a common plan, as part of a single transaction or arrangement, or as part of a series of related transactions or arrangements, and with a principal purpose of avoiding having at least one of such liabilities or payment obligations with respect to such liabilities being treated as a bottom dollar payment obligation as described in paragraph (b)(3)(ii)(C)(*1*)(*i*), (*ii*), or (*iii*) of this section."[63]

Prior to the addition of the bottom dollar prohibition to the Regulation in 2016, some partners endeavored to take advantage of the economic risk of loss concept by guaranteeing the "safest" (or, "bottom") part of an otherwise nonrecourse partnership liability. Thus, for example, a 10 percent partner seeking to increase the basis of its partnership interest might agree to guarantee 100 percent of a 500x nonrecourse debt to the extent the lender would otherwise recover less than 200x. If respected, this guarantee would increase the partner's share of the liability from 50x (10 percent of 500x) to 230x (200x guarantee plus 10 percent of the 300x nonrecourse balance).[64]

The Regulations seek to address this strategy by creating an extraordinarily broad definition of the term "bottom dollar payment obligation" in § 1.752-2(b)(3)(ii)(C)(1). Standing alone, this definition would encompass every guarantee, indemnity, capital contribution, deficit restoration obligation, or similar arrangement that does not require payment of the "full amount" of the guaranteed or indemnified obligation or the obligor's entire capital contribution obligation or deficit restoration obligation. Perhaps in recognition of the excessive breadth of this definition, the Regulations create three carve-outs (described later in ¶ 8.02[4][b][v][B]) to reduce its scope to something more appropriate.

If an arrangement is treated as a bottom dollar payment obligation and disregarded under this rule, the consequence is that it is not given effect in identifying and allocating partnership recourse liabilities under § 752.

Before digging further into the details of the bottom dollar payment obligation rules, it is worth making a few general observations:

1. These rules are a fundamental departure from the overall approach of the § 752 liability sharing rules, which generally create a two-class system of recourse and nonrecourse liabilities and make no attempt to subdivide or grade the actual economic risks associated with different types of recourse debts. Prior to the advent of the bottom dollar rules,

---

[63] Reg. § 1.752-2(b)(3)(ii)(C)(1).

[64] The recourse aspect of this guarantee might also confer advantages on the guarantor under the § 465 at-risk rules. See generally ¶ 11.06[2][b].

all recourse debts were treated the same regardless of their risk profile. While these rules may represent an entirely reasonable effort to harvest "low hanging fruit" in the sense that the mechanics and analytics of separating a bottom dollar guarantee from a top dollar guarantee or a conventional whole dollar guarantee are relatively simple to administer, it is difficult to rationalize (in real economic terms) a rule that ignores all bottom dollar guarantees but respects, for example, a whole dollar guarantee of a well-secured senior debt of a partnership engaged in a prosperous, low-risk business.

2. Prior to the adoption of the 1991 Regulation under § 752, a bottom dollar guarantee was a relatively unknown creature in the financial (or any other) world. It has very little commercial use. It is not at all likely to result in more favorable terms for the borrower or induce the lender to increase the amount of its loan. This suggests that a simple requirement that any guarantee or similar arrangement have a meaningful and demonstrable business purpose might have been a far simpler and administrable approach for the Regulation writers.

[B] *Exceptions.* There are several carve-outs from the bottom dollar payment obligation definition. First, protection for up to 10 percent of the liability is permitted. If a partner has a payment obligation that would otherwise be recognized under Regulations § 1.752-2(b)(3) (the "initial payment obligation") but for the effect of an indemnity, reimbursement agreement, or similar arrangement, it will still be respected as long as the indemnity, reimbursement, or similar arrangement protects no more than 10 percent of the initial payment obligation.[65]

In addition, the Regulations carve out exceptions for (1) payment obligations that are limited to a maximum amount ("top dollar obligations"); (2) payment obligations that are stated as a fixed percentage of an entire liability ("vertical slice obligations"); and (3) proportionate contribution rights.[66]

[C] *Examples.* A few examples may be helpful in exploring some of the intricacies of the carve-outs in the bottom dollar rules. Examples 8-3 and 8-4 are based on examples in the Regulations; Examples 8-5 and 8-6 extend the regulatory examples.

EXAMPLE 8-3: *A, B,* and *C* are equal members of *ABC, LLC. ABC* borrows $1,000 from Bank. *A* guarantees payment of up to $300 of the loan

---

[65] Reg. § 1.752-2(b)(3)(ii)(B).

[66] Reg. § 1.752-2(b)(3)(ii)(C)(2). Rights of proportionate contribution among partners and related persons who are co-obligors with respect to a payment obligation for which each of them is jointly and severally liable are permitted. However, allocations among co-obligors with overlapping risks of loss are problematic, as discussed in ¶ 8.02[4][a].

if any part of the full liability is not recovered by Bank. *B* guarantees payment of up to $200, but only if the Bank otherwise recovers less than $200. Both *A* and *B* waive their rights of contribution against each other.

Because *A* is obligated to pay up to $300 to the extent that any amount of the loan is not recovered by Bank, *A*'s guarantee qualifies under the carve-out for top dollar obligations and therefore is recognized as a payment obligation in the amount of $300.

B is obligated to pay up to $200 only to the extent the Bank otherwise recovers less than $200 of the $1,000 loan. *B*'s guarantee is a classic bottom dollar payment obligation and is not recognized as a payment obligation.

In sum, $300 of the loan is a recourse liability allocated to *A*. The $700 balance of the loan is a nonrecourse liability allocated equally to *A*, *B*, and *C*.[67]

EXAMPLE 8-4: The facts are the same as in Example 8-3 except that, in addition, *C* agrees to indemnify *A* up to $100 for amounts that *A* pays with respect to its guarantee and agrees to fully indemnify *B* with respect to its guarantee.

The determination of whether *C*'s indemnity is recognized is made without regard to whether it would cause *A*'s guarantee not to be recognized.[68] Because *A*'s obligation would be recognized but for the effect of *C*'s indemnity and *C* is obligated to pay *A* up to the full amount of *C*'s indemnity if *A* pays any amount on its guarantee, *C*'s indemnity of *A*'s guarantee qualifies under the carve-out for top dollar obligations and therefore is recognized in the amount of $100.

Because *C*'s indemnity is recognized, *A* is treated as liable for $200 only to the extent any amount in excess of the first $100 of the partnership liability is not satisfied. Thus, *A* does not share in the first dollar of loss on the loan. Accordingly, *A*'s guarantee is a bottom dollar payment obligation and is not recognized.

Because *B*'s obligation is a bottom dollar payment obligation and is not recognized independent of *C*'s indemnity, *C*'s indemnity of *B* is not recognized.

In sum, $100 of *ABC*'s liability is a recourse liability allocated to *C* and the remaining $900 liability is a nonrecourse liability allocated equally to *A*, *B*, and *C*.[69]

EXAMPLE 8-5: The facts are the same as in Example 8-4 except that the amount of *C*'s indemnity to *A* is for up to $30 (not $100) for amounts that *A* pays with respect to its $300 guarantee.

As in Example 8-4, *C*'s guarantee is within the carve-out for top dollar obligations and therefore is recognized in the amount of $30.

---

[67] Reg. § 1.752-2(f)(10) Example 10.

[68] See Reg. § 1.752-2(b)(3)(iii).

[69] Reg. § 1.752-2(f)(11) Example 11.

Because *C*'s indemnity is recognized, *A* is treated as liable for $270 only to the extent any amount beyond $30 of the partnership liability is not satisfied. Thus, *A* is protected against loss with respect to only 10 percent of its $300 "initial payment obligation" and the 10 percent exception in Regulations § 1.752-2(b)(3)(ii)(B) applies to prevent *A*'s guarantee from being treated as a bottom dollar payment obligation. Instead, the net amount is recognized.

As in Example 8-4, both *B*'s guarantee and *C*'s indemnity of it are bottom dollar payment obligations and are not recognized.

In sum, $30 of *ABC*'s liability is a recourse liability allocated to *C*, $270 is a recourse liability allocated to *A*, and the remaining $700 liability is a nonrecourse liability allocated equally to *A*, *B*, and *C*.

EXAMPLE 8-6: The facts are the same as in Example 8-3 except that instead of *A* indemnifying the Bank for $300 of the $1,000 loan, *A* and *B* agree to jointly and severally indemnify the Bank for any loss on the loan up to $300.

The mere fact that the indemnity is joint and several does not cause it to be treated as a bottom dollar payment obligation. It is protected by the co-obligor carve-out in Regulations § 1.752-2(b)(3)(ii)(C)(2). Accordingly, it is recognized as a payment obligation and probably should be shared equally by *A* and *B*.[70]

As in Example 8-3, *C*'s indemnity is a bottom dollar payment obligation and is not recognized.

In sum, $300 of *ABC*'s liability is a recourse liability allocated $150 to *A* and $150 to *B* and the remaining $700 liability is a nonrecourse liability allocated equally to *A*, *B*, and *C*.

Among other things, these Examples illustrate the following points:

1. If an obligation does not require the obligor to bear 100 percent of the relevant loss, it is a bottom dollar payment obligation unless it comes within one of the exceptions (10 percent rule, top dollar obligation, vertical slice obligations, or co-obligor obligation).
2. An obligation that would otherwise qualify under one of these exceptions is disqualified if the obligor is protected against loss by other arrangements. In other words, other relevant arrangements must be taken into account in determining the obligor's net responsibility for losses, and the obligor's net responsibility must qualify under one of the exceptions.

---

[70] While the co-obligor carve-out in § 1.752-2(b)(3)(ii)(C)(2) sanctions the recognition of joint and several liabilities, it does not provide for the allocation of the overlapping risk of loss. As discussed in ¶ 8.02[4][a], Proposed Regulations would correct this deficiency. Example 8-6 assumes the approach of the Proposed Regulations is adopted. See Prop. Reg. §§ 1.752-2(a)(2), 1.752-2(f) Example 9, 1.752-2(l) (2014).

3. The 10 percent exception can be used to protect an obligor against first dollar loss. For example, an obligor who guarantees the entirety of a $100 obligation can come within the 10 percent exception even if another party indemnifies the obligor against the first $10 of loss.

4. An obligation of an obligor who has liability for a portion of a bottom dollar payment obligation is always a bottom dollar payment obligation.

5. Pending finalization of Proposed Regulations,[71] there is some inherent uncertainty as to the proper sharing of any joint and several guarantee, indemnity, or other obligation.

[D] *A fundamental conceptual problem.* Tying the bottom dollar rule to a deficit capital account restoration obligation is conceptually flawed. The purpose of the capital account rules in the § 704(b) regulations is to match the economics of the partnership's activities to the economics of the partners. An expense economically tied to the "bottom dollar" of a partnership liability is nevertheless economically born by a partner and appropriately charged to that partner's capital account. Failure to match tax basis computations with economics is problematic because it is likely to cause unintended distortions that will trap unwary taxpayers or be exploited by their better advised kin. Moreover, the regulations make no attempt to match the deficit restoration obligation to any particular portion of the partnership's liabilities (bottom or top), potentially yielding wildly inappropriate results. Conversely, careful draftsmanship should allow taxpayers to circumvent the bottom dollar rules in other cases, as illustrated in the following example.

EXAMPLE 8-7: *A* and *B* each contribute $100 to the equal *AB* partnership (an LLC), which borrows $800 and buys Equipment *Y*. *AB* elects to expense Equipment *Y*, and has no other income or loss in the first year. *A* guarantees the "top" $400 of the loan, and *B* guarantees the "bottom" $400. *B*'s guarantee is a bottom dollar guarantee and is thus ignored for § 752 purposes, so that the portion of the debt guaranteed by *B* is treated as nonrecourse. *A*'s initial basis in her interest is $700 ($100 capital contribution plus $400 of recourse liability plus $200 share of nonrecourse liability).

 B's initial basis in his interest is $300 ($100 capital contribution plus $200 share of nonrecourse liability). The $1,000 Year 1 loss is shared equally by the partners ($500 each). The partners' bases in their partnership interests do not match their shares of the loss—in contravention of the essential thrust of the § 752 regulatory scheme. *B* is unable to deduct $200 of his $500 allocable loss share.

---

[71] Prop. Reg. §§ 1.752-2(a)(2), 1.752-2(f) Example 9, 1.752-2(l) (2014).

It is relatively easy for *A* and *B* to make this problem go away, if *A* and *B* are willing to accept some additional risk. Instead of guaranteeing the $800 debt, *A* and *B* can each agree to be liable for their deficit capital account. The *AB* partnership agreement could allocate the first $200 of loss equally, the next $400 of loss to *A*, and the last $400 of loss to *B*. Income and gain is first allocated to *B* to reverse losses allocated to him in the last tier of loss allocation, then to *A* to reverse the second tier, and then equally to *A* and *B*. Since *A* and *B* are fully liable for their deficit capital accounts, there are no bottom dollar payment obligations. Yet the economics of this allocation scheme are similar to the guarantee approach set forth in the example: *A* is liable for the "top" $400 of loss on the $800 loan, and *B* for the "bottom" $400. The commercial difference between the two approaches is that a deficit capital account restoration obligation is not limited to a single liability, even if it is limited in amount. In adopting this alternative approach, *A* and *B* must consider other losses the *AB* business may incur. If the business is subject to tort liabilities or other catastrophic risks, the tax benefits of using a deficit restoration obligation may not be worth additional commercial risk.

The purpose of the § 704(b) regulatory scheme is to allocate losses to the partners that may bear them economically, regardless of the likelihood of the loss occurring. The purpose of the bottom dollar rule is to deny basis to a partner if that partner's economic exposure is deemed too remote. These two sets of rules cannot be reconciled. The regulatory attempt to integrate them produces a system that exalts form over substance, and strongly suggests that the bottom dollar path adopted by the Regulations is one that should have been avoided at the outset.[72]

[E] *Effective dates and transition rules.* Limited transition relief from the bottom dollar rules is provided for partners who bore the economic risk of loss for a liability immediately prior to October 5, 2016. These "Transition Partners" are protected from having the bottom dollar rules trigger § 752(b) gain (as measured on October 5, 2016) for a subsequent seven-year period.[73] This transition relief is largely superfluous. The conversion of recourse debt to nonrecourse status generates minimum gain to the partners equal to their defi-

---

[72] Another example of the uncomfortable interface between the §§ 704 and 752 regimes lies in the rules dealing with deductions attributable to nonrecourse debt. As discussed at ¶ 11.02[4][f][v], these deductions are economically born by the lender, but nevertheless reduce the partners' capital accounts. Reg. § 1.704-2(f)(7) Example 1. While the partners' capital accounts are generally restored via a "minimum gain chargeback," there will not always be enough gain or income to offset the initial capital account reduction. The requirement of the "bottom dollar" rules that a partner be required to restore the entire amount of his or her deficit capital account balance apparently requires a partner to be obligated to contribute funds to the partnership attributable to nonrecourse deductions in these circumstances. A clearly nonsensical and unintended result.

[73] See Reg. § 1.752-2(b)(3).

cit capital account balance for which they are no longer liable.[74] Since nonrecourse debt is first allocated in accordance with the partners' shares of minimum gain,[75] the conversion generally should have no impact on the allocation of the liability for § 752 purposes.[76]

The bottom dollar rules are effective for liabilities incurred or assumed by a partnership and payment obligations imposed or undertaken with respect to a partnership liability on or after October 5, 2016, subject to the standard binding contract exception.[77]

[F] *Disclosure requirements.* A partnership is obligated to disclose to the Service the existence of any bottom dollar obligation with respect to a partnership liability on Form 8275 for the taxable year in which the bottom dollar obligation is undertaken.[78]

[c] Offset for Reimbursement Rights

If a partner (or related person) obligated to make a contribution or payment upon a constructive liquidation of the partnership is entitled to be reimbursed by another partner (or related person) for all or a portion of such contribution or payment, then the amount of the reimbursement right reduces the contributing or paying partner's contribution or payment obligation.[79] Correlatively, the reimbursement obligation is treated as a payment obligation that is taken into account in determining the reimbursing partner's share of partnership liabilities.[80]

> **EXAMPLE 8-8:** A limited partner guarantees a portion of a recourse partnership liability. Under the guarantee agreement or state law, the limited partner would be subrogated to the lender's claim against the partnership with respect to any payments made under the guarantee. The limited partner's guarantee is a payment obligation that is taken into account in determining his share of partnership liabilities; however, this obligation is fully offset by the subrogation arrangement under which the limited partner would become a subrogated recourse creditor of the partnership with full rights against the separate assets of the general partners, who are gener-

---

[74] Reg. § 1.704-2(l)(3).

[75] Reg. § 1.752-3(a)(1).

[76] See Preamble to TD 9877, Summary of Comments and Explanations of Revisions at 1.D. (discussing rare cases where results may differ).

[77] Reg. § 1.752-2(l)(2).

[78] Reg. § 1.752-2(b)(3)(ii)(D).

[79] Reg. § 1.752-2(b)(5).

[80] Reg. § 1.752-2(b)(3)(i)(A).

ally liable for partnership obligations. Thus, no part of the guaranteed re-course liability is allocated to the limited partner under § 752.[81]

Even without a right of subrogation, a guarantee of a recourse liability of a general partnership is generally offset by the presumption that the general partners, in their capacity as such, will satisfy their deficit capital account res-toration obligations and thereby prevent the guarantee from being called.[82]

[5] Presumption That Obligations Will Be Satisfied

The § 752 Regulations require the partners' economic risk of loss to be deter-mined by assuming that "all partners and related persons who have obligations to make payments (a payment obligor) actually perform those obligations, irre-spective of their actual net worth, unless the facts and circumstances indi-cate—(i) A plan to circumvent or avoid the obligation under paragraph (j) of this section, or (ii) That there is not a commercially reasonable expectation that the payment obligor will have the ability to make the required payments ...."[83]

The "plan to circumvent or avoid" limitation on the payment presumption has been in the Regulations for many years. It is explicated as part of the gen-eral set of anti-abuse rules in Regulations § 1.752-2(j)(3) and is discussed later at ¶ 8.02[10]. The "commercially reasonable expectation" limitation to the payment presumption was added to the Regulations in 2019 and is further ex-plicated in Regulations § 1.752-(2)(k).[84] Both the new "commercially reasona-ble expectation" Regulations and an expanded version of the "plan to circumvent or avoid" Regulations are included in TD 9877[85] and are applicable to liabilities incurred or assumed on or after October 9, 2019.

A payment obligation is not recognized under Regulations § 1.752-2(k) if the facts and circumstances indicate, at the time the partnership must deter-mine a partner's share of partnership liabilities, that there is not a commer-cially reasonable expectation that the payment obligor will have the ability to make the required payments. The general standard is to apply the factors that a third-party creditor would take into account. Payment obligors include disre-garded entities.

The commercially reasonable standard is not a pure net worth test; if all the partnership's assets become worthless, the payment obligor does not need to have enough assets to fully repay the partnership's loan. Rather, the overall

---

[81] Reg. § 1.752-2(f) Example (4).

[82] Reg. § 1.752-2(f) Example (3).

[83] Reg. § 1.752-2(b)(6).

[84] Former Reg. § 1.752-2(k) dealt with abusive uses of disregarded entities.

[85] TD 9877, 84 Fed. Reg. 54014 (Oct. 9, 2019).

situation, including (perhaps) that of the partnership itself, must be analyzed from the perspective of a third-party creditor. The two examples in the Regulations[86] posit a disregarded LLC that is a general partner in a partnership with $300,000 of equity that borrows another $300,000 to purchase property for $600,000. Both examples are focused on the ability (or inability) of the LLC to satisfy its deficit capital account restoration obligation. If the LLC has no assets other than its partnership interest, the LLC's complete inability, as a general partner, to satisfy any part of a $300,000 liability flunks the commercially reasonable standard and is treated as nonrecourse. But if the LLC has substantial other assets, albeit worth less than $300,000, the debt is classified as recourse and allocated to the LLC. Drawing the "commercially reasonable" line may well prove to be subject to dispute, at least in part because it is not the loan itself that is being tested (both examples involve a loan apparently approved by a "bank" that is presumably a reasonable commercial lender). Rather, the partner's ability to satisfy a possible claim is the focus of the analysis. This seems like the proper focus, but it compounds the difficulty of analyzing the commercial reasonableness issue.[87] It also strongly suggests that the ability of the partnership to pay should be entirely irrelevant to the analysis, at least in part because it is inconsistent with the basic constructive liquidation methodology of the Regulations.

Moreover, it is unclear whether this is a "cliff" rule (all or nothing) or whether the liability can be bifurcated into a "commercially reasonable" recourse portion and the remainder nonrecourse. While the literal language of the Regulation (and the conclusions in the Examples) appears to require a "cliff" approach, Regulations § 1.752-1(i) would support bifurcation where a partner bears part, but not all of the economic risk of loss, albeit in a more benign context (presumably involving a clear dividing line). Again, thoughtful tax planning may mitigate this problem (assuming there is one) by limiting the partner's economic risk of loss to the portion of the liability that it is commercially reasonable to believe the partner can pay. In structuring any limitation of this kind, care should be taken to avoid violating the prohibition on bottom dollar payment obligations.[88]

---

[86] Reg. § 1.752-2(k)(2) Example 1, 1.752-2(k)(2) Example 2.

[87] The potential for confusion regarding this distinction is highlighted by the following ill-conceived sentence in Regulations § 1.752-2(k)(1): "Facts and circumstances to consider in determining a commercially reasonable expectation of payment include factors a third party creditor would take into account when determining whether to grant a loan." Granting a loan is not the appropriate standard, unless by "loan" the Regulations mean the hypothetical liability of a partner following a default by the partnership. This is not a common commercial transaction.

[88] See ¶ 8.02[4][b][5]. In structuring the limitation, the carve-out for "vertical slice obligations" and the allowance of proportionate contributions rights among co-obligors may be particularly useful. See ¶¶ 8.02[4][b][5][B], 8.02[4][b][5][C] Example 8-6.

Liabilities incurred or assumed by a partnership prior to October 9, 2019, are subject to a much more favorable set of rules. The presumption of payment is limited by the general anti-abuse rule in Regulations § 1.752-2(j)(1) and the "circumvent or avoid" standard is considerably less rigorous than that applicable to October 9, 2019, and subsequent liabilities.[89]

[6] Period During Which Payment Obligations Must Be Satisfied; Effect on Recognition of Obligations

If a partner's obligation to make a payment or contribution is unreasonably delayed, the amount of the obligation is adjusted to reflect the time value of the deferral. Specifically, a partner's obligation to make a contribution must be time-value adjusted if it is not required to be made "before the later of—(i) The end of the year in which the partner's interest is liquidated, or (ii) 90 days after the liquidation."[90] A partner's obligation to make a payment other than a contribution is time-value adjusted if it is not required to be satisfied within a reasonable time after the liability to which it relates comes due.[91]

The detailed timing rules of Regulations § 1.752-2(g) are premised on the principle that delayed performance of an obligation does not result in it being completely ignored; rather, the delay causes the obligation to be valued at less than its face amount. Thus, if a limited partner guarantees an otherwise nonrecourse partnership liability, but the guarantee cannot be exercised until five years after the creditor has exhausted its remedies against the partnership, the guarantor-limited partner is treated as bearing the economic risk of loss with respect to the liability only to the extent of the face amount of the liability discounted for a five-year performance delay. The detailed time-value principles of Regulations § 1.752-2(g) are applicable to both obligations to make payments and obligations to make contributions. Curiously, the anti-abuse Regulations in § 1.752-2(j) speak entirely in terms of obligations to make payments. A regulatory example illustrating the time-value rule flatly states that a partner whose payment obligation is delayed for two years following the date of liquidation of the partnership bears the economic risk of loss for the partnership liability.[92] All of this suggests Regulations § 1.752-2(j) does not apply to obligations to make contributions, and the time-value rules and the § 1.752-2(k) requirement of a commercially reasonable expectation of payment are intended to be the exclusive restraints on aggressive planning for delays in

---

[89] The prior version of Regulations § 1.752-2(k) is focused entirely on disregarded entity abuses.

[90] Reg. § 1.752-2(g)(1).

[91] Reg. § 1.752-2(g)(1).

[92] Reg. § 1.752-2(g)(4).

contribution obligations.[93] If this is not the intention of Treasury, a clarification of the Regulations may be in order.

No clear guidance is provided as to what is a reasonable period for performing obligations that are not contribution obligations. In general, however, commercially reasonable prerequisites to performance of a payment obligation should not trigger the discount rules. For example, a condition that performance under a guarantee or indemnity agreement is not required until the creditor exhausts its remedies against the partnership's assets should not be viewed as imposing an unreasonable delay in the performance of the guarantor's obligation.

The issue of what is an unreasonable delay in the time prescribed for performing a payment obligation is clouded by the fact that the constructive liquidation rules assume that at the time of a constructive liquidation "all of the partnership liabilities become payable in full,"[94] whether or not the liabilities would be accelerated upon an actual liquidation of the partnership. For example, assume that (1) a partnership has a liability that will become due in ten years (or upon an earlier default), but that an earlier liquidation of the partnership will not accelerate maturity under the terms of the debt instrument, and (2) a partner has guaranteed the liability. Because the liability is treated as due and payable on the day of the constructive liquidation, it seems the partner's guarantee should be treated as enforceable at the same time. The § 752 Regulations, however, are not clear on this point.[95]

Moreover, the § 752 Regulations do not contain specific rules dealing with when a partner's interest is deemed liquidated; presumably, the rules of Regulations § 1.761-1(d) (liquidation of partner's interest) and § 708(b)(1) (termination of partnership) apply. Thus, a partnership should be treated as liquidated on the earlier of (1) the date on which it terminates under § 708(b)(1)[96] or (2) the date on which it ceases to be a going concern even though its existence is continued for purposes of winding up its affairs, paying its debts, and distributing its remaining assets.

In applying these concepts in the context of a constructive liquidation, the time at which a partner would be required to perform a contribution obligation is determined by ascertaining the time at which he would have to perform under the partnership agreement or applicable law if the partnership actually

---

[93] Of course, business purpose, substance over form, and other general tax law concepts should be applicable in extreme cases.

[94] Reg. § 1.752-2(b)(1)(i).

[95] In this kind of unusual situation (unusual in the sense that most long-term obligations would accelerate on a partnership liquidation), perhaps the constructive liquidation hypothetical construct should be interpreted to treat the partners as making constructive payments (or otherwise satisfying their deficit restoration obligations) in connection with constructive assumptions (as opposed to payment) of the liability.

[96] See ¶ 13.02.

liquidated on the date of the constructive liquidation. For example, assume that (1) a partner is obligated to make an additional contribution five years after the date on which his interest in partnership liabilities is being determined (and, therefore, five years after the date on which a constructive liquidation is deemed to occur) and (2) the obligation would not be accelerated if the partnership is liquidated sooner. Under these circumstances, the contribution obligation would not become payable within the prescribed time period, and thus the obligation would be discounted to its present value.

A contribution or payment obligation is not treated as satisfied by delivery of a promissory note where the maker of the note is either (1) the person required to make the contribution or payment or (2) a related person, unless the note is readily tradeable on an established securities market.[97] However, interest accruing on the note could offset the discount applied in determining the present value of the deferred payment obligation.

If a payment or contribution obligation fails to meet the prescribed timing requirements, the obligation is recognized to the extent of its discounted present value as of the date of the constructive liquidation.[98] Under the § 752 Regulations, a deferred obligation is treated as having a value equal to its principal amount if it bears interest at a rate that equals or exceeds the applicable federal rate (under § 1274(d)) at the time of valuation.[99] If the obligation does not bear adequate interest, its value is the imputed principal amount that it would have under § 1274(b) at the time of valuation.[100]

[7] Nonrecourse Partnership Liabilities Held by a Partner or Related Person

[a] General

If a partner (or a person related to that partner) holds a partnership liability that would otherwise be treated as a nonrecourse liability under the § 752 Regulations, a special rule transmutes that liability into a recourse liability and then allocates the entire risk of loss to that partner.[101] This rule has no application to a liability owed to a partner where the liability is otherwise a recourse partnership liability (i.e., a liability as to which the partners have the economic

---

[97] See Reg. § 1.752-2(g)(3).

[98] Reg. § 1.752-2(g)(2).

[99] Reg. § 1.752-2(g)(2). A contribution obligation must bear interest from the date of liquidation of the partner's interest.

[100] Reg. § 1.752-2(g)(2).

[101] See Reg. § 1.752-2(c)(1).

risk of loss under the general net payment and net contribution rules discussed previously).

The scope of this special rule is considerably broadened by the fact that it applies to nonrecourse partnership liabilities held by "related persons" to partners.[102]

[b] De Minimis Rule

The § 752 Regulations include a significant de minimis rule, under which a partner is not treated as bearing the economic risk of loss for an otherwise nonrecourse partnership liability held by such partner (or a related person), if a

> partner or related person whose interest (directly or indirectly through one or more partnerships including the interest of any related person) in each item of partnership income, gain, loss, deduction, or credit for every taxable year that the partner is a partner in the partnership is 10 percent or less, makes a loan to the partnership which constitutes qualified nonrecourse financing within the meaning of section 465(b)(6) (determined without regard to the type of activity financed).[103]

While this exception does not apply to lenders other than those engaged in the lending business, it does permit an otherwise nonrecourse loan from an institutional lender to a partnership to be treated as a nonrecourse loan (i.e., the lender or a person related to the lender will not be treated as having the economic risk of loss for such loan) even if the lender (or related person) is a partner, as long as the aggregate interest of the lender (and all related persons) in each partnership item is 10 percent or less. If the lending partner (or related person) holds an indirect interest in the borrowing partnership through another partnership, this 10 percent rule applies to the borrowing partnership and includes all interests in the borrower held by the lender (or related persons) directly or indirectly through other partnerships.

The de minimis rule is very helpful in structuring participating loans in connection with real estate transactions. A pervasive concern in structuring such loans is the risk that the putative lender will be treated as a partner, rather than as a creditor, for tax purposes.[104] If the "lender" is treated as a partner, the tax benefits anticipated by the "borrower" are likely to be substantially diminished; the lender may also have adverse tax consequences. The concern that the lender may be treated as a partner is usually exacerbated by the lender's desire to have management rights and powers in excess of those normally held by a conventional lender in order to protect its participation rights.

---

[102] See ¶ 8.04.

[103] Reg. § 1.752-2(d)(1). See ¶ 8.04.

[104] See ¶ 3.04[4].

The de minimis rule provides a tool to minimize the risk that the lender will be treated as a partner in this type of situation, provided that the lender is a qualified lender for purposes of § 465(b)(6).[105] Instead of simply structuring the deal as a participating loan, the lender's position may be bifurcated as follows:

1. (a) The lender (or a related person) forms a partnership with the would-be borrower; (b) this partnership becomes the borrower and owner of the property that is to be encumbered by the loan; (c) the partnership agreement gives the lender (or a related person), in his capacity as a partner, the management rights and powers desired by the lender; and (d) a portion (not in excess of a 10 percent interest) of the lender's participation rights are built into the partnership agreement;[106] and

2. (a) The lender makes a participating, commercially reasonable[107] nonrecourse loan to the partnership that is secured by the partnership's property; (b) the loan documents do not give the lender any control or management rights other than those normally included in conventional nonparticipating loans; and (c) the lender's participation rights under the loan are reduced as necessary to reflect the economic rights held by the lender (or a related person) through the partnership.

By separating the management rights and powers from the loan, this structure should significantly reduce the likelihood that the lender will be treated as a partner with respect to the loan portion of the transaction.

---

[105] See §§ 465(b)(6)(D), 49(a)(1)(D)(iv). The lender must be "actively and regularly engaged in the business of lending money."

[106] This structure can also be used to reduce debt/equity concerns (see ¶ 7.05[1]) by funneling a portion of the funds supplied by the lender into the partnership as a capital contribution.

[107] A "related person" within the meaning of § 49(a)(1)(D)(iv) cannot be a qualified lender for purposes of § 465(b)(6) unless the loan is "commercially reasonable and on substantially the same terms as loans involving unrelated persons." § 465(b)(6)(D)(ii). The relevant "related person" rules are in § 465(b)(3)(C), which generally is based on §§ 267(b) and 707(b)(1), modified to reduce "50%" to "10%." Since the lender (or a related person) will not have more than a 10 percent interest in the borrower-partnership, it will not be a related person to that partnership within the meaning of § 707(b)(1). Additionally, while § 267(e)(1) provides that a person who owns (directly or indirectly) *any* capital or profits interest in a partnership is a related person to the partnership, the provision is designed to operate only for purposes of applying § 267(a)(2). Temporary Regulations § 1.267(a)-2T(b) Q&A-6 confirms that references in other sections to "persons described in section 267(b)" relate to § 267(b) as amended by the Tax Reform Act of 1984 but "without modification by section 267(e)(1)." Accordingly, it should not be necessary to comply with the "commercially reasonable" standard in § 465(b)(6)(D)(ii) in order to negate related-party concerns.

The de minimis rule also applies where a third party holds a nonrecourse partnership liability that is guaranteed by a partner (or a person related to such partner) who holds a 10 percent or smaller interest in each item of partnership income, gain, loss, deduction, or credit for every year that the partner is a partner in the partnership.[108]

[c] Wrapped Indebtedness

An otherwise nonrecourse partnership liability that is held by a partner (or related person) may include or reflect an underlying obligation ("wrapped indebtedness") owed by that partner (or related person) to another creditor. In this situation, if the wrapped indebtedness encumbers partnership property, the partnership is treated as having two liabilities: (1) a debt directly to the holder of the wrapped indebtedness and (2) a debt to the partner (or related person) who holds the "wrapping" indebtedness in an amount equal to the excess of the amount of the wrapping indebtedness over the amount of the wrapped indebtedness.[109]

EXAMPLE 8-9: *Non-wrapped indebtedness.* A partner owns property that is encumbered by a $200,000 nonrecourse liability to an unrelated third party. The partner sells the property to the partnership for $300,000 receiving a down payment of $60,000. The partnership pays the $240,000 balance of the purchase price by taking the property subject to the existing $200,000 first mortgage (the partnership will directly service the $200,000 mortgage) and giving the selling partner a nonrecourse note of the partnership for the remaining $40,000, secured by a second mortgage on the property.

Under these circumstances, there is no wrapped indebtedness. The partnership has two obligations, one to the holder of the $200,000 note, secured by the first mortgage, and one to the selling partner for $40,000, secured by the second mortgage. No partner has any economic risk of loss for the $200,000 liability, which is therefore a nonrecourse liability of the partnership. The $40,000 liability is a partner nonrecourse debt owed to the selling partner. The selling partner bears the economic risk of loss for this liability.

EXAMPLE 8-10: *Wrapped indebtedness.* The facts are the same as in Example 8-9, except that the partnership does not agree to directly service the first mortgage. Instead, the partnership gives the selling partner a nonrecourse note for $240,000 that is secured by an "all-inclusive" mortgage that is junior to the first mortgage. The selling partner is required to service the first mortgage note of $200,000 out of the payments received

---

[108] Reg. § 1.752-2(d)(2).
[109] Reg. § 1.752-2(c)(2).

from the partnership. Under these circumstances, the $240,000 partnership note "wraps" the $200,000 first mortgage note. Thus, the $200,000 first mortgage note is a wrapped indebtedness.

Because the partnership is treated as having a direct obligation to the holder of the wrapped indebtedness, the results in Example 8-10 are the same as in Example 8-9. No partner (including the selling partner) has any economic risk of loss for the $200,000 wrapped indebtedness, even though the wrapped indebtedness is "reflected in" the $240,000 partnership liability to the selling partner. The $40,000 portion of the $240,000 liability to the selling partner that is in excess of the wrapped indebtedness is a partner-held nonrecourse liability of the partnership, as to which the selling partner bears the economic risk of loss.[110]

[8] Special Disregarded Entity Rules (Liabilities Incurred or Assumed Between October 11, 2006, and October 9, 2019)

Well before the adoption of the 2019 wholesale modifications to the rules for allocating recourse liabilities among partners, the Treasury adopted a very detailed and complex set of special rules applicable to partnership interests owned by disregarded entities (DREs). These rules were set forth in Regulations § 1.752-2(k) prior to its amendment in 2019 and apply to liabilities incurred or assumed on or after October 11, 2006, and before October 9, 2019.[111] Accordingly, they will remain relevant for many years.

The impetus for the adoption of the special rules for DREs was the Treasury's concern that DREs could be used to contravene the presumption, in

---

[110] See Reg. § 1.752-2(f) Example (6). The result in both of the text examples would change if the $200,000 first mortgage were a recourse obligation of the selling partner that was not assumed by the partnership. In such a case, whether the partnership took the property "subject to" the first mortgage (as in Example 8-9), or the first mortgage liability were a wrapped indebtedness included in a $240,000 nonrecourse note (as in Example 8-10), the selling partner would have a net payment obligation and the economic risk of loss for the first mortgage liability. In Example 8-10, if the wrapping indebtedness were a recourse obligation, the wrapped indebtedness would be ignored and the entire wrapping indebtedness would be treated as a single recourse partnership liability.

[111] See Reg. §§ 1.752-2(l) (prior law, with a binding contract exception), 1.752-2(l)(1). The 2019 amendments allow taxpayers to elect to apply several of the new provisions (including new Reg. § 1.752-2(k)) retroactively to the beginning of their first tax year beginning after October 5, 2016. See Reg. § 1.752-2(i)(1). For taxpayers hamstrung by the DRE rules discussed in this ¶ 8.02[8], this election may provide miraculous relief.

Treasury's decision to replace the pre-2019 DRE rule in Reg. § 1.752 -2(k) with the new "no reasonable expectation of payment" rule will likely cause a certain amount of confusion for as long as the DRE rule (which no longer appears in the current Code of Federal Regulations) is relevant.

Regulations § 1.752-2(b)(6), that payment obligations of partners will be satisfied. DREs generally shield their owners from liability for DRE obligations, while otherwise being ignored as separate tax entities. This tantalizing combination of characteristics could provide an irresistible temptation for tax planners intent upon passing partnership tax losses to partners while avoiding any real economic risk of loss. There are (and were) other aspects of the allocation Regulations that generally discourage blatant use of DREs for this purpose.[112] Nevertheless, in 2006 the Treasury decided these general rules were insufficient to address the threat posed by DREs, leading to the creation of the 2006 version of Regulations § 1.752-2(k).

The pre-2019 version of Regulations § 1.752-2(k) provides that if a partner owns a partnership interest through a disregarded entity, the partner is treated as bearing the economic risk of loss for a partnership liability only to the extent of the "net value" of the disregarded entity's assets as of the "allocation date." These rules, however, do not apply to an obligation of a disregarded entity to the extent that its owner is otherwise required to make a payment with respect to the obligation.[113] For purposes of applying this rule, the net value of a disregarded entity is equal to:

1. The fair market value of all assets owned by the entity that may be subject to creditors' claims under local law, including the entity's enforceable rights to contributions from its owner and the value of any interests in the partnerships other than the partnership for which net value is being determined, but excluding the entity's interest in the partnership (if any) for which net value is being determined and the fair market value of property pledged to secure a partnership liability under Regulations § 1.752-2(h)(1), less

2. Obligations of the disregarded entity, regardless of priority, that do not constitute obligations for which the disregarded entity is treated as bearing the economic risk of loss under Regulations § 1.752-2(b)(1); such obligations can include liabilities that are unrelated to the partnership interest.[114]

The initial determination of the net value of a disregarded entity is made as of the last day of the partnership's taxable year during which the requirement to determine net value first arises or, if earlier, the first day during such year on which it is necessary to determine the disregarded entity's share of partnership liabilities for basis purposes. After the net value of a disregarded entity is initially determined, it is not later redetermined unless (1) there is

---

[112] By its terms, the Reg. § 1.752-2(b)(6) presumption does not apply if the "facts and circumstances indicate a plan to circumvent or evade the obligation." In addition, the general anti-abuse rule in Reg. § 1-752-2(j)(1) could apply here.

[113] Reg. § 1.752-2(k)(1) (prior law).

[114] Reg. § 1.752-2(k)(2)(i) (prior law).

more than a *de minimis* contribution to or distribution from the disregarded entity of property other than property pledged to secure a partnership liability,[115] unless the contribution is immediately followed by a contribution of equal net value from the disregarded entity to the partnership or the distribution immediately follows a distribution of equal net value from the partnership to the disregarded entity; (2) there is a change in the obligation of the owner of the disregarded entity to make contributions to the disregarded entity; (3) the disregarded entity incurs, refinances, or assumes any obligation other than a Regulations § 1.752-2(b)(1) payment obligation; or (4) a non-*de minimis* asset of the disregarded entity is sold or exchanged other than in the ordinary course of business, in which case net value is only adjusted for the difference between the fair market value of the asset at the time of sale and its value as of the last time the net value of the disregarded entity was determined.

Additionally, under an anti-abuse rule, the net value of a disregarded entity is determined by taking into account a subsequent reduction in the net value of the disregarded entity if, at the time the net value of the disregarded entity is determined, it is anticipated that (1) the net value of the disregarded entity will subsequently be reduced and (2) the reduction is part of a plan that has as one of its principal purposes creating the appearance that a partner bears the economic risk of loss for a partnership liability.[116]

Under former Regulations § 1.752-2(k)(3), if one or more disregarded entities have obligations that may be taken into account with respect to one or more partnership liabilities, the partnership must allocate the net value of each disregarded entity among partnership liabilities in a reasonable and consistent manner, taking into account priorities among partnership liabilities. The Regulations indicate that one reasonable method would be to allocate net value between two liabilities based on the respective seniority of the debts.[117] Oddly, the Regulations allow the entire net value of a single disregarded entity to support allocations of liabilities from several different partnerships without requiring any allocations or apportionments, thus providing potentially significant planning opportunities.[118]

The owner of a disregarded entity is required to provide information to each partnership with respect to which the entity may have any risk of loss re-

---

[115] Reg. §§ 1.752-2(k)(2)(ii)−1.752-2(k)(2)(iv) (prior law).

[116] Reg. § 1.752-2(k)(4) (prior law).

[117] Reg. § 1.752-2(k)(6) Example (3) (prior law).

[118] See Reg. § 1.752-2(k)(6) Example (4) (prior law). The preamble to TD 9289 (Oct. 11, 2006) describes the mechanics for determining the net worth of a disregarded entity, and then states: "That net value is then reported by the owner [of the disregarded entity] to each partnership for which the disregarded entity may have one or more section 1.752-2(b)(1) payment obligations. Each such partnership independently takes the net value of the disregarded entity into account...." The obligation of the owner to report net worth to the partnerships is set forth in Regulations § 1.752-2(k)(5) (prior law).

lating to the entity's classification and the net value of the entity that is to be taken into account by the partnership.[119] If an owner makes the egregious mistake of identifying the entity as a disregarded entity and then failing to provide net value information, the likely (although unstated) consequence may be liability allocations based on a net value of zero. However, if the owner fails to provide any information whatsoever, the partnership presumably should allocate its liabilities without regard to these rules. It is unclear what, if any, consequences the owner's failure will have in this situation.

The disregarded entity rules of former Regulations § 1.752-2(k) were both complex and ineffective (they applied only to disregarded entities, while any pass-through entity that limits the liability of its owners achieved the same result). Their demise will not be mourned.

[9] Tiered Partnerships

Two special rules bear on the determination of economic risk of loss in situations involving partnerships in which other partnerships are partners ("tiered partnerships"). First, where a partnership that is an "upper-tier partnership" (UTP) holds an interest in a "lower-tier partnership" (LTP), the UTP's liabilities include its share of the LTP's liabilities (other than any LTP liability owed to the UTP).[120] Thus, partners of the UTP include their allocable portions of the LTP's liabilities in the outside bases of their UTP interests.

Second, the UTP's share of the economic risk of loss for an LTP's liabilities is determined under a two-step approach. The normal rules are first applied to determine what the UTP's economic risk of loss for LTP liabilities would be if the special tiered partnership rules were inapplicable.[121] The UTP is then treated as bearing the economic risk of loss for any of the LTP's liabilities that are not allocated to it under the normal rules to the extent the partners of the UTP bear the economic risk of loss.[122]

---

[119] Reg. § 1.752-2(k)(5) (prior law).

[120] Reg. § 1.752-4(a); cf. Rev. Rul. 77-309, 1977-2 CB 216 (under the 1956 Regulations, a limited partner's basis for its interest in a UTP includes his share of UTP's share of the LTP's nonrecourse liabilities).

[121] Reg. § 1.752-2(i)(1). In making this determination, any liability of the *LTP* that is owed to the *UTP* is ignored: a *UTP* cannot have a share of liabilities as to which it is the creditor. Reg. § 1.752-4(a).

[122] Reg. § 1.752-2(i)(2). Proposed Regulations, issued on December 16, 2013, would eliminate the approach of funneling LTP liabilities through the UTP to the extent the risk of loss is borne by LTP partners who are also UTP partners. Instead, the UTP's share of LTP liabilities would equal the sum of (1) the share of LTP liabilities with respect to which the UTP has the payment obligation or is the lender under Regulations § 1.752-2(c), plus (2) the amount of any other LTP liabilities with respect to which partners of the UTP bear the economic risk of loss, *provided such UTP partners are not partners in*

EXAMPLE 8-11: *UTP* is the sole general partner of *LTP*, a state law limited partnership. No limited partner of *LTP* is obligated to make any additional contributions to *LTP* or to make any payment with respect to *LTP*'s liabilities. *LTP* has two liabilities: (1) a full recourse liability of $100 and (2) a liability of $200 for which *LTP* has pledged property, but has not assumed general liability. A 10 percent partner of *UTP* has guaranteed both of *LTP*'s liabilities and has waived all subrogation rights.

Applying the basic economic risk of loss rules, *UTP* has a net contribution obligation for, and directly bears the economic risk of loss with respect to, the $100 full recourse liability. Under the normal rules, however, *UTP* would not bear the economic risk of loss for *LTP*'s $200 liability that is secured only by a pledge of *LTP*'s assets and a guarantee by a 10 percent *UTP* partner, because *UTP* and the 10 percent partner are not "related persons." However, if the $200 liability were a *UTP* liability, the partner who guaranteed it would have a payment obligation with respect to the liability, and, therefore, would bear the economic risk of loss for it. Accordingly, under the special tier partnership rules, *UTP* has the economic risk of loss for both of *LTP*'s liabilities.

The § 752 Regulations generally provide that a liability can be taken into account only once for § 752 purposes.[123] However, under the tiered partnership rules, any liability of an LTP that is included in the LTP basis of a person who is a partner in both the LTP and the UTP may also be included in his UTP basis under the two-step approach in Regulations § 1.752-2(i). To avoid double counting in this type of situation, some basis reduction is necessary. The unanswered question is how that reduction should be apportioned between the basis of the common partner's UTP and LTP interests.

EXAMPLE 8-12: *A*, a limited partner in *LTP*, owns a 20 percent interest as a limited partner in *UTP*, a limited partnership that serves as the 10 percent general partner of *LTP*. *LTP* owns property with a value of $200,000 that secures a $100,000 liability. *A* has guaranteed 60 percent of this liability. Despite the fact that *A*, a partner of *UTP*, has guaranteed the debt, the allocation of *LTP* debt is made as if *A* were not a partner in *UTP*. Thus, *A*, in his capacity as a limited partner of *LTP*, is allocated the $60,000 of *LTP* debt that he guaranteed. The remaining $40,000 of this debt is allocated to *UTP* as a recourse liability as a result of *UTP*'s contribution obligation as the general partner of *LTP*.

Under Regulations § 1.752-2(i)(1), *UTP* is allocated the $40,000 part of the liability for which it bears the economic risk of loss, and under Regulations § 1.752-2(i)(2) *UTP* is also allocated the $60,000 portion of

---

the LTP. These Proposed Regulations would apply to liabilities incurred or assumed after the date on which the Proposed Regulations are published as final regulations. Prop. Reg. §§ 1.752-2(i), 1.752-2(l) (2014); see REG 136984-12, 78 Fed. Reg. 76,092 (Dec. 16, 2013), 2014-2 IRB 378, corrected at 79 Fed. Reg. 29,701 (May 23, 2014).

[123] Reg. § 1.752-4(c).

the liability for which its partner *A* bears the economic risk of loss, a total of $100,000. Of this amount, the $60,000 with respect to which *A* bears the risk of loss should be allocated to *A*. The $40,000 balance should be allocated to *UTP*'s general partner under its contribution obligation to *UTP*.

In this analysis, it appears *A* is entitled to total basis increases of $120,000, that is, $60,000 with respect to his interest in *UTP* and $60,000 with respect to his interest in *LTP*. *This cannot be the right result*, because it would violate § 752's "only once" rule.

Proposed Regulations issued in 2013 would resolve this conundrum by modifying the tiered partnership liability sharing rule. As modified, *UTP*'s share of *LTP* liabilities would equal the sum of (1) the share of *LTP* liabilities with respect to which the *UTP* has the payment obligation or is the lender under Regulations § 1.752-2(c), plus (2) the amount of any other *LTP* liabilities with respect to which partners of the *UTP* bear the economic risk of loss, provided such *UTP* partners are not partners in the *LTP*.[124] Prior to the finalization of these Proposed Regulations, there is no clear outcome in Example 8-12, although making the allocation in a manner that reaches the same result as that dictated by the Proposed Regulations ($60,000 to *A* as a partner in *LTP* and $40,000 to *A* as a partner in *UTP*, or the entire $100,000 for which *A* bears the economic risk of loss) seems reasonable.

[10] Anti-Abuse Rules Relating to Recourse Liabilities

[a] Protecting the Performance Premise

The capstone of the recourse liability allocation scheme under the § 752 Regulations is the "performance premise." Buried in Regulations § 1.752-2(b)(6), this premise is that

> all partners and related persons who have obligations to make payments (a payment obligor) actually perform those obligations, irrespective of their actual net worth, unless the facts and circumstances indicate –
> (i) A plan to circumvent or avoid the obligation ..., or
> (ii) That there is not a commercially reasonable expectation that the payment obligor will have to make the required payments ....

---

[124] These Proposed Regulations would apply to liabilities incurred or assumed after the date on which they are published as final regulations. Prop. Reg. §§ 1.752-2(i), 1.752-2(l) (2014); see REG 136984-12, 78 Fed. Reg. 76,092 (Dec. 16, 2013), 2014-2 CB 378, corrected at 79 Fed. Reg. 29,701 (May 23, 2014).

This wildly optimistic assumption is critical to the structure and operation of the economic risk of loss rules. It is the fundamental basis for the entire allocation scheme. As such, it is carefully hedged in a number of ways, two of which are embedded in the performance premise itself:

1. The "*plan to circumvent or avoid*" limitation now in § 1.752-2(b)(6)(i) has been built into the Regulations for many years. It is explicated as part of a recently expanded (in 2019) set of anti-abuse rules in Regulations § 1.752-2(j)(3) and is discussed later in ¶ 8.02[10][b].

2. The "*commercially reasonable expectation*" limitation now in § 1.752-2(b)(6)(ii) is of more recent vintage: It was added to the Regulations in 2019, is further explicated in Regulations § 1.752-2(k),[125] and is discussed in ¶ 8.02[5].

Both the new "commercially reasonable expectation" Regulations and the expanded "plan to circumvent or avoid" Regulations are included in TD 9877[126] and are applicable to liabilities incurred or assumed on or after October 9, 2019. In addition, the anti-abuse package in Regulations § 1.752-2(j) now contains a general anti-abuse rule in § 1.752-2(j)(1), a prohibition against "arrangements tantamount to a guarantee" in § 1.752-2(j)(2) (discussed in ¶ 8.02[4][b][ii]), and the commercially reasonable expectation requirement in § 1.752-2(j)(3).

Regulations § 1.752-2(j)(1) provides generally that an obligation of a partner or related person to make a payment

> may be disregarded or treated as an obligation of another person ... if facts and circumstances indicate that a principal purpose of the arrangement between the parties is to eliminate the partner's economic risk of loss with respect to that obligation or create the appearance of the partner or related person bearing the economic risk of loss when, in fact, the substance of the arrangement is otherwise.

This anti-abuse rule was the touchstone of the Tax Court's seminal *Canal* decision,[127] which involved a highly leveraged distribution to a "seller" LLC member who ostensibly contributed highly appreciated property to a partnership. The creditworthy "buyer" LLC member guaranteed the partnership debt but, in an effort to shift the debt basis to the "seller," it indemnified the "buyer." The Tax Court held the indemnification ran afoul of the anti-abuse rule, finding that the indemnification lacked "economic substance." The

---

[125] Former Reg. § 1.752-2(k) dealt with abusive uses of disregarded entities. It was discarded as part of the 2019 amendments to the Regulations.

[126] TD 9877, 84 Fed. Reg. 54014 (Oct. 9, 2019).

[127] Canal Corp., 135 TC 199 (2010). See also ILM 200246014 (Aug. 8, 2002).

"seller's" principal asset was an intercompany note, whose cancellation was not prevented by the indemnity agreement (and which was indeed subsequently cancelled). Any structure resembling a *Canal*-type transaction is even more problematic under the current regulatory scheme.

[b] Plan to Circumvent or Avoid

Regulations § 1.752-2(j)(3) provides little insight into the application of the "plan to circumvent or avoid requirement" beyond an unhelpful Example and the following nonexclusive list of factors indicative of a prohibited plan to circumvent or avoid an obligation:

1. The partner (or related person) is not subject to commercially reasonable contractual protections that protect the likelihood of payment;
2. The partner (or related person) is not required to provide commercially reasonable documentation regarding the obligor's financial condition to the benefited party;
3. The term of the payment obligation ends before the term of the partnership liability, or the partner or related person has a right to terminate its payment obligation, if the purpose of the limited duration is to terminate the payment obligation before an event occurs that increases the risk of economic loss with respect to the liability;
4. There exists a plan or arrangement in which the primary obligor with respect to the partnership liability directly or indirectly holds money or other liquid assets in an amount that exceeds its reasonably foreseeable needs;
5. The creditor is not entitled to promptly pursue payment from the obligor in the event of a payment default on the partnership liability;
6. In the case of a guarantee, the terms of the partnership liability would have been substantially the same without the guarantee; and
7. Executed documentation of the relevant obligation was not provided to the creditor or other party benefiting from the obligation before, or within a commercially reasonable period of time after, the creation of the obligation.

An Example in § 1.752-2(j)(4) illustrates the application of these factors in a situation in which an LLC obtains a nonrecourse loan in 2020. Subsequently, one of its members guarantees the loan in 2022. The lender did not request the guarantee, the terms of the loan were unchanged in connection with the issuance of the guarantee, the guarantor partner provided no documents to the lender, and the lender imposed no restrictions on asset transfers by the guarantor partner. The Example concludes that absent other countervailing facts, the guarantee is not respected, and the loan continues to be nonrecourse.

The facts in the Example are so extreme that it is not particularly helpful for those seeking guidance as to where the line should be drawn between the existence of a plan to circumvent or avoid and the absence of such a plan. When structuring a guarantee to be respected under this Regulation, it would be prudent to document compliance with all of the enumerated factors other than those not relevant to the transaction at hand. At a minimum, written evidence of the active involvement of the creditor in the structure and terms of the guarantee seems essential.

¶ 8.03 SHARING NONRECOURSE LIABILITIES

[1] General

The § 752 Regulations define "nonrecourse liability" by exclusion. A nonrecourse liability is any liability of the partnership "to the extent that no partner or related person bears the economic risk of loss for that liability."[128] By adopting this definitional approach, the § 752 Regulations ensure that all partnership liabilities will be allocated among the partners under either the recourse sharing rules discussed previously[129] or the nonrecourse sharing rules discussed in this subsection.

The nonrecourse liability-sharing regulations allocate the nonrecourse liabilities of a partnership in three separate tiers. In general, each partner's share of partnership nonrecourse liabilities is the sum of his interest in these three tiers:

1. In tier 1, nonrecourse liabilities of the partnership are allocated to each partner to the extent of his share of partnership "minimum gain";[130]

2. In tier 2, nonrecourse liabilities are allocated to each partner to the extent that each partner would be allocated gain under § 704(c)[131] (or in the same manner as § 704(c) in connection with revaluations of partnership property[132]) if the partnership made a taxable disposition of all partnership property subject to nonrecourse liabilities in ex-

---

[128] Reg. § 1.752-1(a)(2).

[129] See ¶ 8.02.

[130] "Partnership minimum gain" is defined by Regulations § 1.704-2(d) and a "partner's share of minimum gain" is defined by Regulations § 1.704-2(g)(1). See ¶¶ 11.02[4][f][iii], 11.02[4][f][iv].

[131] See ¶ 11.04.

[132] These allocations are described in Regulations § 1.704-1(b)(2)(iv)(f) and are sometimes referred to as reverse § 704(c) allocations.

change for no consideration other than relief of the nonrecourse liabilities; and

3. In tier 3, the partnership's remaining nonrecourse liabilities are allocated to each partner in accordance with that partner's share of partnership profits. The partners may use a variety of methods to
determine profits shares for this purpose.

The general thrust of the nonrecourse allocation rules is to allocate nonrecourse liabilities so as to reflect the manner in which the partners share partnership "profits." This general approach stands in sharp contrast to the overall
approach for allocations of recourse liabilities, which reflects the partners'
sharing of the economic risk of loss. In this context, "economic risk of loss" is
a proxy for loss allocations.

The fundamental difference between the two sets of allocation rules is
firmly rooted in economic reality: the partners bear the real economic risks of
recourse liabilities (and hence should be allocated recourse liabilities in the
manner they share losses), whereas the lenders (rather than the partners) bear
the economic risks associated with nonrecourse liabilities. Although partners
do not have economic exposure with respect to nonrecourse liabilities, they
may receive tax benefits—generally in the form of enhanced credits, depreciation, or other deductions—as a consequence of nonrecourse liabilities. Allocations of nonrecourse liabilities under the § 752 Regulations mimic the manner
in which such benefits are allocated. Again, however, a proxy is used: instead
of focusing directly on loss or expense allocations, the Regulations rely on the
allocations of future gain that may occur upon satisfaction of the nonrecourse
debt (tiers 1 and 2) or, in the absence of any direct link with gain recognition,
the allocations of overall profits or some significant component thereof (tier 3).

[2] Coordinating Shares of Nonrecourse Deductions With Shares of Minimum Gain (Tier 1)

A partner's share of partnership minimum gain generally is determined in accordance with the § 704(b) Regulations.[133] In general, partnership minimum
gain is the excess of partnership nonrecourse liabilities over the § 704(b) book
value of the partnership assets that they encumber.[134]

> **EXAMPLE 8-13:** *A* and *B* form partnership *PRS*. *A* contributes deprecia-
> ble property subject to a nonrecourse liability of $6,000. The property has
> a basis of $4,000 and value of $10,000. *B* contributes $4,000 in cash. The
> initial § 704(b) book value of the property is $10,000 even though its ba-

---

[133] Reg. § 1.704-2(g). See ¶ 11.02[4][f][iv].
[134] Reg. § 1.704-2(d)(3).

sis is \$4,000. Thus, the initial capital accounts of *A* and *B* are equal and *A* and *B* agree to share § 704(b) "book" profits and losses equally.[135]

Under these circumstances, immediately after the transfer there is no partnership minimum gain, even though the partnership's nonrecourse liabilities (\$6,000) exceed the basis of the encumbered property (\$4,000). This is because the § 704(b) book value of the property (\$10,000) is greater than its nonrecourse liabilities and it is book value, not adjusted basis, that is used to compute minimum gain. Thus, initially, none of the nonrecourse liability is allocated under tier 1.

Assuming that the liability continues to be \$6,000, minimum gain will be created to the extent that the § 704(b) book value of the property is depreciated below \$6,000. The creation of such minimum gain will attract and cause the reallocation of nonrecourse liabilities that were previously allocated under tiers 2 and 3.[136]

[3] Effect of Section 704(c)–Type Built-In Gain (Tier 2)

[a] General Rules

Just as a partner's share of minimum gain attracts an equal share of partnership nonrecourse liabilities, the § 752 Regulations provide that a portion of a partner's share of built-in gain under § 704(c)[137] (and the "reverse § 704(c)" rules of the § 704(b) Regulations[138]) attracts partnership nonrecourse liabilities. Specifically, under tier 2 of Regulations § 1.752-3(a), a partner is allocated nonrecourse liabilities in an amount equal to the gain that he would realize under § 704(c) (and the reverse § 704(c) rules) if the partnership sold the assets encumbered by the nonrecourse liabilities for no consideration other than those liabilities.

The tier 2 rules generally make sense because they further the objective of allocating nonrecourse liabilities to the partners who will recognize partnership income upon settlement of those liabilities. These rules also have the salutary effect of minimizing the instances in which gain is recognized on contributions (or revaluations) of appreciated property. Unfortunately, the complex mechanics of § 704(c) and the application of nontraditional allocation

---

[135] The facts of this example and those that follow are based on Revenue Ruling 95-41, 1995-1 CB 132.

[136] This shifting of liabilities (based on Regulations § 1.752-3(a)(1)) is not addressed by Revenue Ruling 95-41, 1995-1 CB 132, which does not consider the impact of depreciating the contributed property.

[137] Reg. § 1.752-3(a)(2); see generally ¶ 11.04.

[138] See Reg. §§ 1.704-1(b)(2)(iv)(*f*), 1.704-1(b)(2)(iv)(*r*), 1.704-3(a)(6). See generally ¶ 11.02[2][c][iii].

methods under § 704(c) can create some surprises in actual operation. The following examples explore the application of these rules and some of the possible issues.

EXAMPLE 8-14: The facts are the same as in Example 8-13. *A* contributed property subject to a $6,000 nonrecourse liability, having a basis of $4,000 and a value of $10,000. There is no tier 1 allocation (book value of $10,000 is in excess of the $6,000 debt). The $6,000 difference between the initial book value of the property ($10,000) and its initial basis to the *PRS* partnership ($4,000) must be accounted for under § 704(c) using one of three methods: the "traditional" method, the traditional method with "curative" allocations, or the "remedial" allocation method.[139] Under Revenue Ruling 95-41,[140] the amount of nonrecourse liabilities allocated to *A* under tier 2 depends on the § 704(c) method used by *PRS* with respect to the property.

Under the traditional method, if the property were disposed of immediately after its contribution for no consideration other than the $6,000 nonrecourse liability, *PRS* would recognize a § 704(b) book loss of $4,000 and a tax gain of $2,000. This $2,000 tax gain would be allocated solely to *A* under § 704(c) and would be treated as a tier 2 allocation to *A*. A book-tax difference of $2,000 for each partner would remain unresolved (*A*'s book capital account would be $2,000 but his tax basis for his interest would be zero; *B* would have a $2,000 book capital account but a $4,000 tax basis).[141]

On the other hand, under the remedial method, if *PRS* disposed of the property for the nonrecourse liability, *A* would be allocated $4,000 of gain under § 704(c), computed as follows: First, $2,000 of gain would be allocated to *A* as in the traditional method; second, *A* would be allocated $2,000 as an additional "remedial" gain allocation to offset a $2,000 § 704(b) loss that would be created and allocated to *B* under the remedial method. Accordingly, under Regulations § 1.752-3(a)(2), use of the remedial method for § 704(c) purposes would cause *A* to be allocated $4,000 of nonrecourse liabilities under tier 2. This, of course, is $2,000 more nonrecourse liabilities than would be allocated to *A* if *PRS* used the traditional method.

As a final option, if the partnership elects to use the traditional method with curative allocations for § 704(c) purposes, Revenue Ruling 95-41 concludes that only $2,000 of the nonrecourse liabilities are allocated to *A* under tier 2 because it is not certain whether there will be any items of income available to "cure" the $4,000 ceiling rule distortion that results from the application of the traditional method alone.[142]

---

[139] Reg. § 1.704-3; see ¶ 11.04.

[140] Rev. Rul. 95-41, 1995-1 CB 132, 133.

[141] Under the traditional method, the "ceiling" rule would prevent the remaining $4,000 of potential § 704(c) gain from ever being allocated to *A*.

[142] Rev. Rul. 95-41, 1995-1 CB 132, 133.

On the facts set forth in the ruling, the Service's approach appears to work reasonably well as long as the contributed property is not depreciable. However, if contributed property is subject to depreciation or amortization, minimum gain may be created by reductions in the book value of the contributed property. The resultant creation of tier 1 allocations may eventually impinge on tier 2 allocations, as illustrated in Example 8-15 below. This issue is not addressed in Revenue Ruling 95-41.

> **EXAMPLE 8-15:** The facts are the same as in Example 8-13. *PRS* elects to comply with § 704(c) by using the traditional method with curative allocations to be made only out of tax gain recognized on disposition of the property. Further, the property is held until it is fully depreciated for both § 704(b) book and tax purposes, but the nonrecourse liabilities remain $6,000. As a result, *B* is allocated $5,000 of book depreciation deductions, but only $4,000 of tax depreciation. The remaining $1,000 unresolved difference results from the effect of the ceiling rule on the § 704(c) depreciation allocations under the traditional method.
>
> If *PRS* disposed of the fully depreciated property solely in satisfaction of the nonrecourse liabilities, it would recognize book and tax gain of $6,000. The book gain, which would be allocated equally to *A* and *B*, would be "minimum gain" because the nonrecourse liabilities of $6,000 exceed the book value of the property (zero) by $6,000, and the entire $6,000 nonrecourse liability would be allocated equally between *A* and *B* under tier 1. However, $4,000 of tax gain will be allocated to *A* and only $2,000 to *B* because of the partners' agreement to eliminate remaining ceiling rule differences out of curative gain allocations on sale. The $1,000 excess of *A*'s tax gain over his book gain results from this curative allocation. If both minimum gain and § 704(c) allocations are taken into account, the total to be allocated appears to exceed the amount of the $6,000 nonrecourse liability to be allocated. Revenue Ruling 95-41 does not explicitly consider the consequences of post-contribution depreciation, but neatly (if inaccurately) "solves" the problem by simply ignoring all curative allocations.[143]

One possible interpretation of Regulations § 1.752-3(a) is that since the entire liability is absorbed by the tier 1 allocation of minimum gain, no allocation can be made under tier 2, simply because there is no liability left to allocate and tier 1 must be satisfied before tier 2. While mathematically simple, this interpretation has the unfortunate (from a policy standpoint) consequence of severing the connection between the allocation of nonrecourse liabilities and the manner in which gain will flow when the liability is settled. Disregarding

---

[143] Revenue Ruling 95-41, 1995-1 CB 132, ignores curative allocations because of a concern regarding the availability of sufficient items to allocate. This concern is inapplicable if the property is fully depreciated, because there clearly will be sufficient gain upon disposition to cure any remaining book-tax differences.

the curative allocations, the nonrecourse liabilities will be allocated $3,000 to each partner under tier 1, but gain recognized by the partnership upon a disposition of the property solely in exchange for relief of indebtedness will be allocated $4,000 to A and $2,000 to B.

A close examination of Regulations § 1.752-3(a) suggests a different interpretation that would make more sense in policy terms without doing violence to the structure of the § 752 Regulations. As written, the § 752 Regulations call for the computation of each partner's share of a nonrecourse liability as the sum of the partner's share of minimum gain (tier 1), the partner's share of taxable § 704(c) gain (tier 2), and the partner's share of any excess nonrecourse liabilities (tier 3). In Example 8-15, A's share of tier 1 is $3,000 and his share of tier 2 is $1,000, a total of $4,000. B's share of tier 1 is $3,000 and his share of tier 2 is a *loss* of $1,000, a net total of $2,000. These results, of course, coincide with the tax allocations to the partners, including the consequences of the curative allocations on sale of the property. The only real issue with this interpretation of the § 752 Regulations is the need to allocate the equivalent of a "loss" to B under tier 2, while the § 752 Regulations speak only in terms of "taxable gain" that would be allocated under § 704(c).[144] If this part of the § 752 Regulations is interpreted literally, then B cannot be allocated a loss under tier 2 and the Regulations would require $7,000 of allocations relative to $6,000 of liabilities. This nonsensical result should be rejected in favor of interpreting the reference to "taxable gain" in Regulations § 1.752-3(a)(2) to mean "taxable gain or loss."[145]

[b] Liabilities Encumbering Multiple Properties

Occasionally, a single nonrecourse obligation will encumber multiple properties. In order to apply the tier 2 rules, this type of liability must be divided among the encumbered properties. The § 752 Regulations permit this to be done using any "reasonable method."[146] A method cannot be reasonable if it allocates to any property an amount of the liability that, when combined with

---

[144] This "loss" is not a real net tax loss in any event, but rather a reduction of B's share of the gain that would otherwise be allocated to him under § 704(b) in the absence of a curative allocation agreement.

[145] The Treasury clearly was not concerned about the impact of curative allocations on tier 2 allocations when it promulgated Regulations § 1.752-3(a)(2). This regulation provision was finalized in 1991, a full year before the concept of a traditional method with curative allocations first appeared as a Proposed Regulations provision. PS-164-84, 57 Fed. Reg. 61,345 (Dec. 24, 1992). While Revenue Ruling 95-41 may be viewed as an attempt to correct this problem, it cannot be reconciled with the existing Regulations. The Treasury should consider amending Regulations § 1.752-3(a)(2) to address situations in which curative allocations overlap partnership minimum gain.

[146] See Reg. § 1.752-3(b). These rules are applicable to liabilities assumed (or incurred) on or after October 31, 2000. Taxpayers may rely on these rules for ear-

any other liability allocated to the property, exceeds the fair market value of that property at the time the liability is incurred. Once allocated, the liability is treated as separate loans encumbering single properties. After a liability is allocated among properties, a partnership may not change the method for allocating the liability. However, if an encumbered property ceases to be encumbered, the portion of the liability then allocated to it must be reallocated to the other encumbered properties in a way that does not violate the fair market value limit. Subsequent reductions in principal must be allocated among the various properties in the same proportions that the liability was originally allocated.[147]

[4] Excess Nonrecourse Liabilities (Tier 3)

As discussed, the allocation rules relating to nonrecourse liabilities generally attempt to ensure consistency with the economics of the partnership by requiring that the basis attributable to nonrecourse liabilities inures to partners in the same manner that those partners will be allocated partnership profits. The first two tiers of Regulations § 1.752-3(a) allocate nonrecourse liabilities directly to the partners to whom gain would be allocated under § 704 if the partnership sold the encumbered property for an amount equal to the liability. The linkage in tier 3 is much less direct, since this tier is composed of "excess" liabilities—liabilities not directly related to any specific gain allocation, and hence not allocated pursuant to tier 1 or tier 2. Accordingly, the § 752 Regulations give the partners considerable latitude in allocating tier 3 liabilities, requiring only that they must be allocated among the partners in accordance with the partners' share of partnership profits.[148]

The Regulations identify four permissible methods of allocating excess nonrecourse deductions to reflect the partners' shares of profits. A partnership is not locked into its selection of method, and may change it from year to year.[149]

First, the Regulations allow a partnership to simply allocate excess nonrecourse liabilities under an amorphous "facts and circumstances" analysis, where the economic arrangement of the partners is scrutinized to determine the manner in which they share partnership profits. Because Regulations § 1.752-3(a)(3) refers to all the facts and circumstances relating to "the eco-

---

lier-incurred liabilities for taxable years ending on or after October 31, 2000. Reg. § 1.752-5(a).

[147] Reg. § 1.752-3(b)(2). See Priv. Ltr. Ruls. 200120020 (Feb. 13, 2001) (requiring allocations of reductions in principal in the same proportion as the liability was originally allocated among the properties), 200340024 (Apr. 10, 2003) (to the same effect).

[148] See Reg. § 1.752-3(a)(3).

[149] Reg. § 1.752-3(a)(3).

nomic arrangement of the partners" and to significant items of income or gain that "have substantial economic effect," one would expect § 704(c) and § 704(c) equivalent allocations under § 704(b) to be ignored because they do not reflect economics or substantial economic effect. The Service, however, has taken the questionable position that § 704(c) allocations must be taken into account in allocating excess nonrecourse deductions to the extent that they are not taken into account in allocating nonrecourse liabilities under tier 2.[150]

> **EXAMPLE 8-16:** *A* and *B* form partnership *PRS*. As in Example 8-13, *A* contributes depreciable property subject to a nonrecourse liability of $6,000. The property has a basis of $4,000 and value of $10,000. *B* contributes $4,000 in cash. The initial § 704(b) book value of the property is $10,000 even though its basis is $4,000. Thus, the initial capital accounts of *A* and *B* are equal and *A* and *B* agree to share § 704(b) "book" profits and losses equally.
>
> Assume that *PRS* uses the traditional method for § 704(c) purposes. Thus, initially no nonrecourse liabilities are allocated to *A* and *B* under tier 1 (the minimum gain tier) and $2,000 of nonrecourse liabilities are allocated to *A* under tier 2 (the § 704(c) tier). This leaves $4,000 of excess nonrecourse liabilities to be allocated under tier 3.
>
> Even though the partners share economic and § 704(b) gain equally, the Service takes the position that under the facts and circumstances test, the $4,000 of potential § 704(c) gain that was *not* taken into account in tier 2 must be given some weight. Thus, under the first method for allocating excess nonrecourse liabilities, *A* must be allocated more than one half of the excess nonrecourse liabilities even though *A* and *B* share all § 704(b) items equally.

Under the second method of allocating excess nonrecourse liabilities, the partnership agreement may specify shares for the partners that are "reasonably consistent with allocations (that have substantial economic effect under the section 704(b) Regulations) of some other significant item of partnership income or gain."[151] Such an allocation ties a partner's share of excess nonrecourse liabilities to at least some portion of his share of partnership profits.[152]

---

[150] Rev. Rul. 95-41, 1995-1 CB 132, 133–134; TD 8906, 2000-2 CB 470 (Oct. 31, 2000).

[151] See Reg. § 1.752-3(a)(3). See CCA 200246014 (Aug. 8, 2002) (percentage specified in agreement ignored as "not consistent with any significant partnership allocation of profits or losses").

[152] Pronouncements from the Service indicate their belief that a "significant item of partnership income" does not include a preferential return with respect to only a portion of an item of income, but only an "allocation percentage that reflects the overall economic relationship between the parties." Tech. Adv. Mem. 200436011 (Apr. 30, 2004) (allocation of liability in accord with 100 percent preferred return up to specified dollar amount rejected). See also ILM 200513022 (Nov. 15, 2004) (same). See ¶ 11.02[4][f][i] note 292.

Third, the partners may allocate excess nonrecourse liabilities in "the manner in which it is reasonably expected that the deductions attributable to those nonrecourse liabilities will be allocated."[153] In effect, this method allows the partners to anticipate future allocations under tier 1 that will result when nonrecourse deductions create minimum gain. A partnership expecting significant nonrecourse deductions can avoid fluctuations in its partners' shares of nonrecourse liabilities by selecting this method of allocating excess nonrecourse liabilities. As with excess nonrecourse liability allocations made pursuant to the first method, care should be taken in making any allocation under the nonrecourse deduction method; the Service has taken the position that partnerships must take into account any excess § 704(c) gain in allocating excess nonrecourse liabilities under this method.

> **EXAMPLE 8-17:** The facts are the same as in Example 8-16. *PRS* uses the traditional method for § 704(c) purposes. It also elects to allocate excess nonrecourse deductions in the manner that deductions attributable to the nonrecourse liabilities will be allocated. Thus, no nonrecourse liabilities are allocated under tier 1 (there is no minimum gain). $2,000 of nonrecourse liabilities are allocated under tier 2 to *A*. This leaves $4,000 of excess nonrecourse liabilities to be allocated under tier 3. Since minimum gain under § 704(b) will be allocated equally to *A* and *B*, it seems logical to assume that excess nonrecourse liabilities should also be allocated equally. However, the Service takes the position that all excess nonrecourse liabilities must be allocated to *B* because, under § 704(c), depreciation of *PRS*'s $4,000 of tax basis in the property must be allocated solely to *B*.[154]

While the Service's position makes sense from a tax policy basis (it matches the allocation of excess nonrecourse liabilities with the manner in which gain could be allocated when recognized), such an approach is inconsistent with the § 752 Regulations. The Service's position focuses on tax deductions rather than § 704(b) book deductions, even though nonrecourse deductions and minimum gain are defined under the § 704(b) Regulations by reference to § 704(b) book value.[155] The presence or absence of § 704(c) gain should have no impact on the manner in which nonrecourse deductions are allocated.

In addition to being facially inconsistent with the language of the § 752 Regulations, determining a partner's share of profits by reference to noneconomic allocations under § 704(c) seems to be a trap for the unwary. Equal partners, for example, expect to share equally and are unlikely to think

---

[153] Reg. § 1.752-3(a)(3).

[154] Rev. Rul. 95-41, 1995-1 CB 132, 134.

[155] Reg. § 1.704-2(d)(3).

that they must make a special election to share excess nonrecourse liabilities equally.

The fourth permissible method (added to the Regulations in 2000[156]) provides that if nonrecourse debt is secured by property that is § 704(c) property, the partnership may allocate excess nonrecourse liabilities first to the contributing partner to the extent that any built-in gain with respect to that property exceeds the amount allocated to the contributing partner under tier 2.[157] If excess nonrecourse liabilities remain unallocated after an allocation pursuant to this fourth option, the remainder may then be allocated pursuant to one of the three options discussed above. Where tier 3 allocations are first made pursuant to excess § 704(c) gain and subsequently in accordance with the manner in which the partners share nonrecourse deductions, the allocations corresponding to the nonrecourse deductions are not impacted by the already considered § 704(c) gain. This method of allocating tier 3 liabilities allows a partnership to accurately track the manner in which gain would be allocated upon disposition of the encumbered property by first taking into account § 704(c) gain.

[5] Tiered Partnerships

The § 752 Regulations provide that a UTP's share of an LTP's liabilities (other than liabilities owed to the UTP) is treated as a UTP liability for purposes of determining the bases of the UTP partners in their UTP interests.[158] The § 752 Regulations also provide special rules for the allocation of recourse liabilities in tiered partnership situations.[159] However, the Regulations contain no guidance for determining a UTP's share of LTP nonrecourse liabilities.

It appears that the procedures for dealing with nonrecourse liabilities in tiered partnership situations are as follows: First, determine the extent to which any LTP partner bears the economic risk of loss for the LTP's liabilities. In making this determination, apply the special tiered partnership rules to determine the UTP's economic risk of loss for such liabilities.[160] Second, as to any

---

[156] TD 8906 (Nov. 13, 2000), 2000-2 CB 470.

[157] See Reg. § 1.752-3(a)(3). The § 704(c) allocation method of excess nonrecourse liabilities is applicable to liabilities assumed (or incurred) on or after October 31, 2000. Taxpayers may rely on these rules for earlier-incurred liabilities for taxable years ending on or after October 31, 2000. Reg. § 1.752-5(a). The fourth allocation option appears to be quite flexible. The built-in gain includes gain attributable to reverse § 704(c) allocations. Thus, it appears that tier 3 debt allocations can be made to *any* partner with a § 704(c) gain account to the extent his or her § 704(c) gain exceeds the amount used to satisfy tier 2 debt allocations, so long as the asset with the § 704(c) gain is subject to the nonrecourse liability.

[158] Reg. § 1.752-4(a).

[159] See Reg. § 1.752-2(i); ¶ 8.02[9].

[160] Reg. § 1.752-2(i).

of the LTP's liabilities for which no partner (including the UTP) bears the economic risk of loss (and which are, therefore, LTP nonrecourse liabilities), apply the normal rules for allocating nonrecourse liabilities as if the UTP were not itself a partnership. The UTP's share of the LTP's nonrecourse liabilities, as so determined, is treated as nonrecourse liabilities of the UTP for purposes of applying § 752 to the UTP partners. The interests of UTP partners in the LTP's minimum gain are controlled by the special tiered partnership rules contained in the § 704(b) Regulations.[161]

¶ 8.04 RELATED PERSONS

Under the § 752 Regulations, a partner shares recourse partnership liabilities to the extent the partner (or a person related to the partner) bears the economic risk of loss for the liabilities.[162] Additionally, the § 752 definitions of economic risk of loss (with all its references to related persons) and nonrecourse liability are imported to the § 704(b) Regulations.[163] Thus, the concept of "related persons" has a significant impact on the application of both § 752 and § 704(b).

For these purposes, a person is related to a partner "if such person and the partner bear a relationship to each other that is specified in section 267(b) or section 707(b)(1)."[164] The potential breadth of this definition is considerably narrowed by the following modifications:

1. "Eighty percent or more" is substituted for "more than 50 percent" each place it appears in § 267(b) and § 707(b)(1);
2. Brothers and sisters are not treated as members of a person's family; and
3. Sections 267(e)(1) and 267(f)(1)(A) are disregarded.[165]

Under Regulations § 1.752-4(b)(1), if a partnership owns the stock of a corporation that makes a loan to the partnership, a partner who owns 80 percent or more of the partnership is considered to be related to the corporation. Thus, any economic risk borne by the corporation with respect to the loan could be attributed to this 80-percent partner even if the partner actually bears no risk. Proposed Regulations § 1.752-4(b)(1)(iv) (2013), if adopted, would "disregard section 267(c)(1) in determining whether stock of a corporation owned, directly or indirectly, by or for a partnership is considered as being

---

[161] Reg. § 1.704-2(k).
[162] Reg. § 1.752-2(a).
[163] See Reg. §§ 1.704-2(b)(3), 1.704-2(b)(4).
[164] Reg. § 1.752-4(b).
[165] Reg. § 1.752-4(b)(1).

owned proportionately by or for its partners if the corporation is a lender as provided in § 1.752-2(c) or has a payment obligation with respect to a liability of the partnership." According to the preamble to these Proposed Regulations: "The IRS and the Treasury Department believe that partners in a partnership, where that partnership owns stock in a corporation that is a lender to the partnership..., should not be treated as related, through ownership of the partnership, to the corporation. A partner's economic risk of loss that is limited to the partner's equity investment in the partnership should be treated differently than the risk of loss beyond that investment."[166]

The § 752 Regulations provide generally that if a person is related to more than one partner, that person will be treated as related to the partner to whom such person has the "highest percentage of related ownership."[167] In those cases in which a person has an equal percentage of related ownership to more than one partner (and no other partner has a greater percentage of relationship), such person's payment obligation or interest in a partner nonrecourse liability, as the case may be, would be allocated equally to all such equally related partners.[168] Under Proposed Regulations § 1.752-4(b)(3) (2013), if a non-partner bears the economic risk of loss for a partnership liability and is related to more than one partner, the liability would be allocated equally to the related partners (rather than to the partner who has the highest degree of relatedness, as provided under the current rule).[169]

For this purpose, the § 752 Regulations provide that all natural persons who are related by virtue of being members of the same family are treated as having a percentage relationship of 100 percent.[170]

To reduce double counting, the § 752 Regulations articulate a "related partner" exception, under which direct or indirect partners in a partnership are not treated as related persons to each other "for purposes of determining the economic risk of loss borne by each," other than for purposes of applying the de minimis rules in Regulations §§ 1.752-2(d) and 1.752-2(e).[171] Thus, if a mother and daughter are both general partners in a partnership, the economic risk of loss of each (determined without attribution) is not augmented by their family relationship.

In *IPO II*,[172] the Tax Court held that the related partner exception is broad enough to sever the relationships between partners and all non-partners who would otherwise be treated as related parties for all purposes.

---

[166] REG-136984-12, 78 Fed. Reg. 76,092 (Dec. 16, 2013).

[167] Reg. § 1.752-4(b)(2)(i).

[168] Reg. § 1.752-4(b)(2)(i).

[169] REG-136984-12, 78 Fed. Reg. 76,092 (Dec. 16, 2013).

[170] See Reg. § 1.752-4(b)(2)(ii).

[171] Reg. § 1.752-4(b)(2)(iii).

[172] IPO II, 122 TC 295 (2004).

EXAMPLE 8-18: Partner A, an individual, owns one percent of partnership AB. Partner B, an S corporation 100 percent owned by A, owns 99 percent of AB. AB borrows \$10,000 from a third party. The debt is guaranteed by A and another S corporation, C, that is 70 percent owned by A and 30 percent by his children. Partner A, as a direct guarantor, clearly bears the economic risk of loss with respect to the loan. Partners A and B are related partners under § 267(b)(2) because A owns 100 percent of B. Therefore, the related partner exception may apply. Ignoring the related partner exception, partner B would be related to the other direct guarantor, C, under § 267(b)(11), as modified by Regulations § 1.752-4(b)(1)(i), because both are more than 80 percent owned by the same person (partner A, taking into account the 30 percent owned by his children and attributed to him under § 267(c)(2)), and therefore partner B would also be treated as bearing the risk of loss with respect to the loan. In *IPO II*, on substantially these facts, the Tax Court concluded that the relationship between partners A and B should be ignored in assessing partner B's relationship with non-partner guarantor C under the related partner exception, and therefore partner B was not treated as bearing any part of the economic risk of loss.

Regardless of how one might feel about the merits of the Tax Court's interpretation of the related partner exception in *IPO II*, it is clear that the decision has the potential to expand the scope of this exception and produce results that are inconsistent with the purpose of the related party rules, the apparent intent of the related party exception, as well as rational tax policy. Consider the following example:

EXAMPLE 8-19: Assume a tiered corporate structure in which parent corporation C owns 100 percent of corporation $S1$, and $S1$ owns 100 percent of corporation $S2$. $S1$ and $S2$ are equal partners in a partnership. Corporation C makes a loan to the partnership. Under § 267, $S1$ and $S2$ are related because one wholly owns the other, so the related partner exception applies. But how exactly should the exception be applied under *IPO II*? If the relationship between $S1$ and $S2$ is ignored, lender C is related to $S1$ (through direct ownership) but not to $S2$ (because the relationship between $S1$ and $S2$ must be ignored). Therefore, $S1$ has the risk of loss but $S2$ does not. Does that make any sense?

The Proposed Regulations issued in 2013 would amend Regulations § 1.752-4(b)(2)(iii) (redesignated as § 1.752-4(b)(2)) so that its provisions would only apply if a person who is a direct or indirect partner in a partnership is also either a lender to the partnership or has a payment obligation with respect to a partnership liability. The effect of the amended version of the exception would be that other direct or indirect partners would not be treated as related to such partner for purposes of determining the economic risk of loss borne by them for such liabilities.[173]

The proposed revision would make the related partner exception inapplicable under the facts of *IPO II* as well as Examples 8-18 and 8-19. That is certainly a good start toward resolving the problems described above. Whether it is a complete solution remains to be seen.

The § 752 Regulations include an anti-abuse rule which provides that if a partnership liability is owed to or guaranteed by a corporation, partnership, or trust for the principal purpose of avoiding the application of the related party rules with respect to a partner (or related party) who is an owner (shareholder, partner, or beneficial owner) of more than 20 percent of the corporation, partnership, or trust, the partner or related party is treated as holding a portion of the entity's interest as a creditor or guarantor.[174] For this purpose, a person's interest in

1. A partnership equals the partner's highest percentage interest in any item of loss or deduction for any taxable year;
2. An S corporation equals the percentage of the outstanding stock in the S corporation owned by the shareholder;
3. A C corporation equals the percentage of the fair market value of the issued and outstanding stock owned by the shareholder; and
4. A trust equals the percentage of the actuarial interests owned by the beneficial owner of the trust.[175]

---

[173] Prop. Reg. § 1.752-4(b)(2) (2013), effective for liabilities incurred or assumed after date of finalization. See REG 136984-12, 78 Fed. Reg. 76,092 (Dec. 16, 2013).

[174] Reg. § 1.752-4(b)(2)(iv)(A).

[175] Reg. § 1.752-4(b)(2)(iv)(B).

CHAPTER **10A**

Centralized Partnership Audit Regime

¶ 10A.01 OVERVIEW

Prior to 1983, there was no specialized regime for examining partnership income tax returns. Instead, partnership issues were examined and litigated at the individual partner level. This partner-by-partner approach was administratively unwieldy, cumbersome, and often produced inconsistent results.

In the Tax Equity and Fiscal Responsibility Act of 1982 (TEFRA), Congress enacted an entirely new regime for centralizing the examination and litigation of "partnership items," and then applying the results of the partnership proceeding to partner-level "affected items," thus assuring uniform treatment of partnership items, while also assuring that partnership item adjustments resulted in bespoke changes to tax liabilities of individual partners. TEFRA also provided all partners with significant participation and opt-out rights. The TEFRA rules are the subject of Chapter 10.

The TEFRA rules generally assured both that adjustments to partnership items would be applied uniformly to all partners and that the effects of those adjustments were tailored to each partner's situation, but the Service continued to be burdened with the task of applying the results of TEFRA proceedings on a partner-by-partner basis and then assessing and collecting any amounts due partner-by-partner. While TEFRA centralized the examination of partnership items, the extensive participation rights accorded to partners favored due process and fairness over efficiency.

In 2015, Congress abruptly[1] abandoned TEFRA, effectively giving up due process and fairness in favor of revenue and administrative convenience, when it enacted the centralized partnership audit regime (CPAR) as part of the Bipartisan Budget Act of 2015. Oddly, for such a major change, there is virtually no meaningful legislative history (House, Senate, or committee reports[2]) of any

---

[1] With little or no legislative review, the CPAR provisions that replaced TEFRA were hastily inserted into an entirely unrelated tax measure (HR 1314, originally entitled the "Ensuring Tax Exempt Organizations the Right to Appeal Act"). Prior to the addition of CPAR, this Act was reported out of the House Ways and Means Committee on March 25, 2015, and passed by the House on April 15, 2015. In the Senate it was entirely rewritten, renamed the "Trade Act of 2015," and passed by the Senate on May 22, 2015. It was then "reconciled" in the House, which added the new CPAR provisions for the first time on or about October 27, 2015, passed by the House on October 28, 2015, agreed to by the Senate on October 30, 2015, and then signed into law by the president on November 2, 2015, as the "Bipartisan Budget Act of 2015." In short, within a seven-day span, the House, Senate, and the president all gave due consideration to and approved this enormously consequential piece of tax legislation. A possible explanation for this alacrity may be the substantial revenue estimate ($9.325 billion for 2016–2025) for CPAR. Joint Comm. on Taxation (JCX-135-15) (Oct. 28, 2015). Other than the Joint Committee annual "blue book," referenced in note 2 below, there are no committee reports relating to the reconciled act.

[2] CPAR is described in the 2015 annual report of the Staff of the Joint Committee. See Staff of Joint Comm. on Taxation, 114th Cong., 2d Sess., JCS-1-16, General Explana-

kind for CPAR. Fortunately, it was enacted with a delayed effective date—tax years commencing on or after January 1, 2018—thereby giving all interested parties some time to react and adjust to its radically different approach to partnership audits. The haste with which CPAR was enacted is evidenced not just by the lack of detail in certain areas and the complexity of the statutory language in others, but also by the enormous grants of regulatory authority to the Treasury and the two sets of technical corrections that have already been enacted to deal with discovered flaws (there should be more): These corrections are included in the Protecting Americans From Tax Hikes Act of 2015 (PATH), and the Consolidated Appropriations Act of 2018 (CAA).

The absence of legislative history and the haste with which CPAR was put together particularly unfortunate because it mandates a number of major changes in the ways in which partnerships are audited and deficiencies are calculated and collected. Very few of these changes are favorable to taxpayers. The statute is clearly intended and designed to make life easier for the tax collector, a bias that is also evident in the Regulations that have been issued to date. This bias, as well as the complexity of the new provisions, is substantial enough that the enactment of CPAR is now a factor that should be taken into account in selecting a form of organization for many new and existing businesses, particularly those that do not or will not qualify to elect out of CPAR.[3]

The exquisitely detailed, complex, and sometimes confusing provisions of CPAR and the Regulations under it are examined at length in the pages that follow. A brief overview will at least provide a sense of the scope and impact of some of the fundamental changes wrought by CPAR and suggest some of the possible reasons for choosing a different form of business entity or electing out[4] of the CPAR regime:

1. *Tax paid by partnership.* For the first time in the history of partnership taxation, the default process under CPAR is based on computing and collecting income tax deficiencies at the partnership level without

---

tion of Tax Legislation Enacted in 2015, at 57–83 (Comm. Print 2016). However, "General Explanations" produced post-enactment by the Staff as "blue books" are given little respect by the courts as legitimate expressions of legislative history (see, e.g. James E. Redlark, 106 TC 31, 45–46 (1996), rev'd and remanded, 141 F3d 936 (9th Cir. 1998) (staff report may be "instructive" if statute is "facially ambiguous"). Worse yet, this particular explanation is not particularly helpful in dealing with the deficiencies in the statute and gives little or no insight into Congress' "intent" as to any aspect of the legislation.

[3] The Service granted some relief to partnerships subjected to the CPAR regime for their 2018 returns by giving partnerships who timely filed their returns an additional period of six months beyond the unextended partnership return due date to file a superseding return without needing to file an administrative adjustment request (AAR). Rev. Proc. 2019-32; 2019-33 IRB 659. See also Rev. Proc. 2020-23, 2020-18 IRB 749 (waiving AAR requirement for 2018 and 2019 return amendments claiming Coronavirus Aid, Relief, and Economic Security Act (CARES Act) benefits).

[4] § 6221(b).

regard to the nature or characteristics of the partners. This is a profound departure from the historical pass-through nature of partnership taxation and creates a very odd and unique situation in which the required reporting of the tax consequences of a partnership's activities must be done on a pass-through basis but a very different, entity focused set of rules is applied on audit. The centerpiece of this change is a complex set of baseline rules in § 6225 providing for the computation of an "imputed underpayment" that must be paid by the partnership, not the partners, unless an election is made to either "push out" or "pull in" audit adjustments from the partnership to the partners. Moreover, the tax is payable for the partnership tax year in which it is finally determined, which is likely to be many years *after* the year of the events creating the underpayment. Thus, the tax may fall on partners who were nowhere to be seen when the activities giving rise to the underpayment occurred.

2. *Underpayment computations.* The methodology of the § 6225 computational rules for the calculation of imputed underpayments are consistently and sometimes virulently anti-taxpayer. They assume the worst case for the application of virtually all taxpayer adverse provisions in the Code: If a deduction could be limited, create a preference, be subject to a limitation, or not allowed for any reason as a deduction against ordinary income with respect to any category of taxpayer, it may be effectively disallowed in computing imputed underpayments.[5]

3. *Tax rate.* The tax rate assumed in determining the imputed underpayment is the highest rate under § 1 or § 11.[6] Under current law, that means partnership ordinary income allocable to corporate partners is heavily overtaxed in computing imputed underpayments, as is partnership long-term capital gain income allocable to individual partners. This rule also effectively ignores the graduated rate structures built into the Code.

4. *Deferral of taxpayer-favorable adjustments.* The adverse taxpayer impact of the rate assumption is magnified by the grouping, subgrouping, and netting rules applicable in computing imputed underpayments. These rules effectively separate and defer most taxpayer-favorable adjustments to the adjustment year under § 6225(a)(2), leaving only the remaining taxpayer-adverse adjustments in the reviewed year.[7] This deferral of taxpayer-favorable adjustments

---

[5] § 6225(b)(4); Reg. § 301.6225-1(d)(3)(i). The largely unexplored potential scope of this rule, as discussed in ¶¶ 10A.02[3] and 10A.06[1], is extremely far-reaching.

[6] § 6225(b)(1)(B).

[7] See ¶ 10A.06[1].

can have a variety of negative effects on taxpayers, the most predictable and prevalent of which is the accrual of interest over the period between the reviewed year and the adjustment year.[8]

5. *Election out.* Under § 6221(b), partnerships with 100 or fewer partners may elect out of CPAR. Unfortunately, no partnership is eligible to elect out if it has a partner that is not an individual, a C corporation (or foreign entity that would be treated as a C corporation if it were domestic), an S corporation, or an estate of a deceased partner. If any partner is a partnership, a trust, an ineligible foreign entity, a disregarded entity, an estate of anyone other than a deceased partner, or any person holding an interest on behalf of someone else, the partnership cannot elect out.[9] These limitations severely limit the availability of the 100-partner exemption and magnify the importance of long-term planning for partnerships that may want to avail themselves of the exemption.

6. *Authority of partnership representative.* Unlike "tax matters partners" under TEFRA, partnership representatives (PRs) have almost unfettered control over the partnership during CPAR audits.[10] This may or may not be viewed as desirable by some or all of the partners (it certainly makes life easier for the Service) and it magnifies the importance of selecting the PR and considering and defining the scope and extent of the authority of the PR by agreement among the partners and the PR outside the Code provisions.

7. *Mitigating the impact of the § 6225 computational rules.* The vast majority of the partnerships that are unable (or unwilling) to elect out of CPAR are not likely to be satisfied with the amount of the imputed underpayment if the partnership is audited. The Code provides several ways to mitigate the most egregious aspects of the imputed underpayment computational mechanics, but none is perfect from the point of view of the partnership and the partners:

   a. *Modifications.* The modification process provides opportunities to correct many of the most taxpayer-adverse consequences of the § 6225 computational rules. However, the rules for collecting information, calculating modifications, and approving modifications

---

[8] The projected revenue in the form of interest likely was a major component in the $9.325 billion revenue estimate for CPAR for 2016–2025. See Joint Comm. on Taxation, JCX-135-15 (Oct. 28, 2015). Several examples exploring the impact of interest costs are included in ¶ 10A.10.

[9] Reg. §§ 301.6221(b)-1(b)(3)(ii), 301.6221(b)-1(b)(3)(iv). The regulatory prohibition against partnerships and disregarded entities as partners is entirely a creation of the Regulations and is difficult to square with the statutory inclusion of S corporations. In policy terms, if one form of pass-through entity is not a disqualifier, why is another form?

[10] § 6223.

give the Service enormous discretion.[11] Relying on the Service to fully reverse the basic pro-fisc approach of CPAR in general and § 6225 in particular would not seem to be a prudent approach.

b. *Pull-in elections.* As part of the modification process, reviewed-year partners can individually elect to file amended returns (or the equivalent) for the reviewed year (and all other affected years) reflecting their shares of the adjustments underlying the imputed adjustments. If all reviewed-year partners elect to "pull-in" their shares of the adjustments by filing such amended returns, the entire imputed underpayment and all the resulting partnership-level tax burden is eliminated. Instead, the partners bear the burden of the proposed adjustments and the after-tax results to all parties should approximate the results that would have been produced if the partnership had not been subject to CPAR, thereby largely obviating the adverse consequences of the § 6225 computational rules. Unfortunately, this way out of the § 6225 quagmire comes with its own problems: (1) it is voluntary in the absence of pre-existing external agreements among the partners (continuing partners who do not file amended returns effectively become free-riders); (2) if the partners' interests vary between the reviewed year and the adjustment year, electing reviewed-year partners whose interests have decreased may find themselves economically subsidizing the adjustment-year partners whose interests are new or increased; and (3) pull-ins may prevent pull-in partners from challenging (or benefitting from a partnership challenge of) the substantive merits of the Service's proposed partnership-level adjustments.[12] Regulations proposed in 2018 would eliminate the free-rider and subsidy issues described in clauses (1) and (2) in many (but not all) situations.[13]

c. *Push-out elections.* After a final partnership adjustment (FPA) is issued, the partnership may elect under § 6226 to "push-out" the reviewed-year adjustments to the reviewed-year partners, thereby

---

[11] See ¶ 10A.06[2].

[12] See discussion in ¶ 10A.06[2][d][iii].

[13] Prop. Reg. §§ 1.704-1(b)(2)(iii)(f) (2018), 1.6225-4(c) (2018), as discussed in ¶ 10A.06[3]. The Proposed Regulations would take into account pull-in elections in allocating expenditures for imputed underpayments to reviewed-year partners or their successors based on their reviewed-year (rather than adjustment-year) interests. However, if the partnership's assets in the adjustment year are insufficient to both pay the tax on the underpayment and satisfy the economic entitlement of pull-in partners, pull-in partners may find themselves shortchanged. Conversely, the Proposed Regulations will generally protect new (or increased) adjustment-year partners from subsidizing reviewed-year partners provided the partnership's assets are sufficient.

relieving the partnership of any liability for the imputed liability.[14] Although this election involves some disadvantages, it is likely to prove popular for partnerships seeking to mitigate the impact of the § 6225 computational rules. Like the pull-in election, the net results of a § 6226 election should reflect the particular characteristics of each partner.

8. *Different years/different partners.* Significant changes in the ownership of a partnership between the reviewed year and the adjustment year create fundamental fairness issues among the partners that did not exist under TEFRA. This problem is accentuated by the bias of the § 6225 computational rules to push pro-taxpayer adjustments from the reviewed year into the future adjustment year as well as delays (new and old) built into the audit procedure itself. In all but the simplest situations, there is almost certainly going to be a lengthy delay between finalization of the reviewed-year and the adjustment-year audits. The 2018 proposed regulations attempt to ameliorate this issue by tracking the adjustments to the partners (or their successors) economically responsible for them, but this remedy may not always be successful.[15]

9. *Reallocation and recharacterization adjustments.* The grouping rules assure that the pro-taxpayer side of any adjustment that changes the character of an item or that allocates or reallocates partnership items among partners is deferred to the adjustment year. The modification rules do not appear to provide any relief for partners trapped in this particular aspect of the § 6225 rules. Among other things, this aspect of the rules is likely to be a significant deterrent for anyone considering aggressive uses of special allocations under § 704(b).

As noted in list items 7.b and 8 above and as discussed later in ¶ 10A.06[3], detailed rules creating a safe harbor for the allocation of the tax on imputed underpayments among reviewed-year partners and adjustment-year partners are articulated in a set of Proposed Regulations published in 2018 but not finalized as of this writing. Significantly these Proposed Regulations are proposed to be retroactively effective for all CPAR partnerships for tax years beginning after 2017.

The authors believe these Proposed Regulations are technically sound, are likely to produce economic results that are rational and consistent with the reasonable expectations of the partners, and are reflective of the overall approach and policy of CPAR. No fundamental objections have been voiced since their

---

[14] See ¶ 10A.08.

[15] Prop. Reg. §§ 1.6225-4(a)(6), 1.6225-4(b) (2018) (rules "must be interpreted in a manner that reflects the economic arrangement of the parties"). See generally ¶ 10A.06[3].

publication in early 2018. It is highly likely they will eventually be finalized in substantially the form proposed. Therefore, we strongly recommend that drafters of partnership agreements and limited liability company operating agreements include consistent allocation provisions in the controlling documents for all entities subject to CPAR.[16]

[1] CPAR Procedures

Partners as such have no right to participate in CPAR proceedings, to approve settlements, or to participate in litigation resulting from a CPAR examination. Instead, all aspects of the conduct of a CPAR administrative proceeding, its settlement, and any ensuing litigation are controlled by the PR selected by the partnership (or by the Service if the partnership does not properly designate a PR).[17] The partners may, by contract, impose restrictions, limitations, and procedures on the PR, but they cannot bind the Service, which is entitled (indeed, required) to rely only on the PR.

Unless a partnership can and does elect out of CPAR, with limited exceptions, any adjustment to a "partnership-related item" must be determined at the partnership level, and any resulting taxes, penalties, and additions to tax, as well as interest, must be assessed against and collected from the partnership, as it is comprised at the time the CPAR proceeding becomes final in the adjustment year.[18] Under CPAR, the centralized partnership administrative procedure begins with the issuance to the partnership of a notice of selection for examination (Examination Notice).[19] The Examination Notice is sent to the partnership, not the PR. It allows the partnership at least thirty days to change its PR before the examination begins. More importantly, it allows the PR to file an administrative adjustment request (AAR) (the CPAR equivalent of an amended

---

[16] There is no real downside in including such allocations even if the Proposed Regulations are not finalized, since they are very likely to produce expected economic consequences in any event.

[17] § 6223.

[18] § 6221; Reg. § 301.6221-1.

[19] There is no mention of an Examination Notice in the statute or the Regulations under § 6231. This requirement has been self-imposed by the Service primarily to assist taxpayers desiring to change PRs in reaction to a pending audit, as discussed in TD 9839, 83 Fed. Reg. 39331, 39336–39339 (Aug. 9, 2018). While mentioned, but not explicitly required, by Regulations § 301.6223-1(e)(2), interim guidance issued under 4.31.9 of the Internal Revenue Manual makes clear that an Examination Notice must precede the issuance of a NAP by at least thirty days. See LB&I-04-1019-010, p. 39 (Oct. 24, 2019) (instructions to auditors to mail NAP no earlier than thirty days but no later than sixty days after issuance of Letter 2205-D). Letter 2205-D is the current template for the Examination Notice.

return) and avoid some of the more draconian aspects of the CPAR system.[20] No sooner than thirty days after the issuance of an Examination Notice, the PR generally will receive a notice of administrative proceeding (NAP),[21] after which the Service will examine the partnership's returns for all years covered by the NAP (the "reviewed years").[22] Section 6225(a) provides that any resulting imputed underpayments for the reviewed year and any affected years must be paid by the partnership (with interest) in the partnership year during which the CPAR proceeding becomes final (the "adjustment year").[23] Any other (aka, taxpayer-favorable) adjustments (e.g., decreases in income, increase in losses) that do not result in imputed underpayments are taken into account by the partnership in the adjustment year.[24] In effect, absent agreements among the partners or elections to involve reviewed-year partners,[25] the reviewed-year partners are affected only if they are partners in the adjustment year.

The rules for adjustments that result in imputed underpayments, and the rules for those that do not, both reference the adjustment year, the year in which a final determination of tax liability is made.[26] This articulation, while technically correct in the context of the statute, is somewhat deceptive without a close examination of the two different activities that are scheduled to occur with respect to the adjustment year. The first is a *payment* of an imputed underpayment for the reviewed year that (1) is computed entirely on the basis of the partnership return for the reviewed year as adjusted by the Service, and (2) bears interest from the due date of the return for the reviewed year until paid.[27] The second is the inclusion of the (generally taxpayer-favorable) *adjustments* that have not contributed to an imputed understatement and have been deferred to the adjustment year. Each of the adjustments in this second category must be "taken into account" by the partnership in the adjustment year "as a reduction in non-separately stated income or as an increase in non-separately stated loss for the adjustment year."[28] Effectively, these taxpayer-favorable adjust-

---

[20] See ¶ 10A.09.

[21] § 6231(a)(1).

[22] § 6225(d)(1).

[23] §§ 6225(a)(1), 6225(d)(2).

[24] § 6225(a)(2).

[25] See §§ 6225(c)(2)(A), 6225(c)(2)(B), 6226.

[26] The adjustment year is the partnership year in which (1) a court decision relating to the adjustment becomes final, (2) an administrative adjustment request (AAR) is made under § 6227, or (3) in any other case, an FPA is mailed or the partnership waives the § 6232(b) limitation on assessments. § 6225(d)(2); Reg. § 301.6241-1(a)(1).

[27] §§ 6233(a)(2), 6233(b)(2); Reg. §§ 301.6233(a)-1(b), 301.6233(b)-1(b).

[28] Reg. § 301.6225-3(b). The general treatment of these adjustments as "non-separately stated" is subject to a host of exceptions that effectively relegate the general rule to a minor role, as discussed in ¶ 10A.07.

ments are merged with the partnership's other income and loss items for the adjustment year. Refunds related to these adjustments do not bear interest.

After parsing through all this, there are effectively two different impacts on the adjustment year tax: (1) a separate imputed underpayment is created consisting of a tax at the highest possible rate on taxpayer-unfavorable adjustments from the reviewed year, which must be paid along with interest on the partnership's adjusted-year return; and (2) taxpayer-favorable item (and credit) adjustments to the partnership's other items of income, loss, and credit for the adjustment year, which are allocated among the adjustment-year partners, and do not include any interest.

After the Service issues a NAP, the initial phase of a CPAR examination involves the examination of, and possible adjustments to, "partnership-related items"[29] for each reviewed year. An adjustment to a partnership-related item is referred to as a "partnership adjustment."[30] Section 6225 and its accompanying regulations provide complex rules for taking partnership adjustments into account to determine an "imputed understatement" for each reviewed year, which is then used to compute an "imputed underpayment" with respect to the year. An imputed underpayment includes taxes, penalties, additions to tax, and interest resulting from adjustments to reviewed-year partnership-related items. The default rule is that the partnership, as constituted in the adjustment year, is liable for any imputed underpayment.

The partnership examination phase concludes with the issuance of either a "no change" letter or a "notice of proposed partnership adjustment" (NOPPA).[31] The NOPPA does not consider whether, or to what extent, any reviewed-year partner's actual tax liability would have changed if partnership-related items had been reported correctly.[32] Instead, the NOPPA determines an imputed understatement[33] for the partnership for each reviewed year and then applies the highest marginal rate of tax in effect for each reviewed year (without regard to the tax attributes of the partners) to determine an imputed underpayment for the year.

After the Service issues a NOPPA that sets out adjustments to partnership-related items and computes one (or more) imputed underpayments for each reviewed year, the proceeding shifts to a "modification" phase. In the modification phase, the PR is allowed to request modifications to the imputed

---

[29] § 6241(2)(B), discussed in ¶ 10A.02[3].

[30] Reg. § 301.6241-1(a)(6).

[31] The issuance of a NOPPA is required by § 6231(a)(2).

[32] Under the prior TEFRA procedures, the application of "partnership item" adjustments to "affected items" was made through computational adjustments or deficiency proceedings following the close of the TEFRA proceeding.

[33] To compute an imputed understatement, adjustments to partnership-related items are separately determined and netted by "category" and then placed in groups and subgroups of similar items. § 6225(a); Reg. § 301.6225-1(c). See ¶ 10A.06[1].

underpayments to take into account partner-level factors, which, if allowed, would reduce the imputed underpayment.[34] The Code and regulations provide for two main categories of modifications:

1. The first category reflects partner-specific attributes, such as partners eligible for a lower rate, tax-exempt partners, and partners eligible for the benefits of tax treaties. These modifications can either (a) reduce the rate of tax used to compute a portion of the imputed underpayment, or (b) remove items from the computation in whole or in part (for example, to reflect the shares of tax-exempt partners).

2. The second category reflects pull-in elections by individual reviewed-year partners to file amended returns (or the equivalent) for the reviewed years and all years affected by reviewed-year adjustments. If such amended returns (or the equivalent) are filed and all amounts due are paid, the imputed underpayment is recomputed by excluding the pull-in partners' shares of the adjusted items; filing amended returns (or the equivalent) is one way to shift the burden of CPAR adjustments to reviewed-year partners and so achieve after-tax results that approximate the results that would be produced from an examination of a partnership that is not subject to CPAR.

Following completion of the modification phase, the Service may issue a notice of "final partnership adjustment" (FPA)[35] imposing imputed underpayments on the partnership for reviewed years. Following the issuance of an FPA, the partnership may shift the burden of the imputed underpayment to its reviewed-year partners by electing under § 6226 to "push out" all of the underlying adjustments to its partners. This election must be made within forty-five days of the FPA date. The effect of the push-out election is to require reviewed-year partners to include their shares of the underlying adjustments, set forth in the FPA, on their own returns.

If the partnership does not challenge the adjustments by filing a petition for judicial review, the adjustments become final on expiration of the normal ninety-day post-FPA period during which the partnership could file a petition. If the partnership challenges the FPA in court, the adjustments become final when the court's decision becomes final. While a § 6226 election must be

---

[34] § 6225(c); Reg. § 301.6225-2. These categories, as well as several other less pervasive types of modifications, are discussed in ¶ 10A.06[2].

[35] Section 6231(a)(3) requires the Service to issue an FPA, which is the jurisdictional document. Regardless of whether it makes a push-out election (see Reg. § 301.6234-1(a)), the partnership (but not any partner) has ninety days from the date of the FPA to challenge it in court. In the absence of a timely petition, both the partnership and the partners have exhausted their rights to challenge the adjustments in the FPA and the Service can assess and collect the imputed underpayment from the partnership (or the partners, if the partnership has elected to push out the adjustments under § 6226(b)). §§ 6226, 6232(b).

made within forty-five days of the FPA, the reviewed-year partners are not required to include the adjustments on their own returns until the later of the end of the ninety-day period or a court challenge is complete. A cost of the push-out election is that interest is computed from each reviewed year to the payment date at a rate that is 2 percentage points higher than the normal underpayment rate under § 6226(c)(2)(C). Unlike the pull-in approach, the § 6226 push-out election does not require the cooperation of the reviewed-year partners and has the benefit, unlike the pull-in approach, of relieving the partnership of liability without requiring proof of actual payment by the reviewed-year partners.

An FPA can be challenged in the U.S. Tax Court, a district court, or the Court of Federal Claims. The reviewing court has "jurisdiction to determine all partnership-related items for the partnership taxable year ..., the proper allocation of such items among the partners, and the applicability of any penalty, addition to tax, or additional amount for which the partnership may be liable ...."[36] Unfortunately, a court's ability to allow a modification that the Service has rejected may be circumscribed to some extent because § 6225(c)(8) provides that "[a]ny modification of the imputed underpayment amount under this subsection shall be made only upon approval of such modification by the Secretary." All CPAR examinations are subject to review by the Service's Office of Appeals.[37]

The PR is allowed to file administrative adjustment requests (AARs) for any year prior to the time the Service issues a NAP for the year.[38] An AAR may result in positive or negative adjustments to partnership-related items. Grouping, subgrouping, and netting rules similar to those in § 6225 apply. Thus, net positive adjustments to a group or subgroup of items produce one or more imputed underpayments for the years covered by the AAR, and net negative adjustments are deferred and taken into account by the partnership and the adjustment-year partners on their returns for the adjustment year. The partnership may also elect, under rules similar to § 6226, to push out adjustments that result from an AAR.

---

[36] § 6234(c).

[37] See IRM 8.19.14: Memorandum for Appeal Employees from Appeals Director (Oct. 18, 2019). All CPAR proceedings are Appeals Coordinated Issues and must be referred for Technical Guidance. IRM 8.19.14.2.2.

[38] § 6227, discussed in ¶ 10A.09. Under CPAR, an AAR is the only method available to modify a filed partnership return.

[2] Recommended Partner Agreements Under CPAR

The CPAR rules effectively force significant changes in the drafting of partnership and limited liability company (LLC) agreements and ancillary documents, including the following:

1. Detailed qualification requirements for original owners and robust transfer restrictions should be created for partnerships and LLCs intending to elect out of CPAR;

2. There should be a detailed engagement agreement between the PR and the entity or its owners. This agreement should give the owners contractual control over specified actions and elections of the PR. Such an agreement will not be binding on the Service or invalidate elections or other actions by the PR but may give aggrieved owners some recourse against the PR in case of violations. Conversely, PRs may insist on this sort of agreement to minimize their exposure;

3. Provision should be made for the application of the 2018 Proposed Regulations[39] detailing the adjustments to certain partnership tax attributes necessitated by CPAR adjustments, including rules for the allocation of these adjustments among partners and their transferees; and

4. The addition of provisions for post-audit contributions and distributions that may be necessary to preserve the partners' economic expectations should be considered.[40]

¶ 10A.02 SCOPE OF CPAR

[1] Arrangements to Which CPAR Applies

As explained in Chapter 3, a partnership may exist for tax purposes whether or not it is a partnership, LLC, or other entity recognized by applicable non-tax law. Instead, §§ 761(a) and 7701(a)(2) provide that the term "partnership" includes a "syndicate, group, pool, joint venture, or other unincorporated organization through or by means of which any business, financial operation, or venture is carried on, and which is not, within the meaning of this title, a corporation or a trust or estate." Thus, "partnership" is a catch-all or residual clas-

---

[39] Prop. Reg. §§ 1.704-1(b)(2)(iii)(f) (2018), 1.6225-4(c) (2018), as discussed in ¶ 10A.06[3].

[40] See R. Whitmire, W. Nelson & W. McKee, Structuring and Drafting Partnership Agreements: Including LLC Agreements ¶ 2.10 (Thomson Reuters/Tax & Accounting, 3d ed. 2003).

sification, defined by exclusion. It is anything involving more than a single taxpayer that is not defined as something else. CPAR applies to any partnership, as so broadly defined for any taxable year beginning after 2017, with few exceptions. Even if an arrangement is not a partnership under this definition, it is treated as a CPAR partnership if it files a partnership return,[41] and even if, after examination, the Service determines that an arrangement that filed a partnership return is not a partnership at all.[42]

In general, CPAR does not apply to partnerships that validly elect under § 761(a) to be excluded from Subchapter K[43] or under § 6221(b) to be excluded from CPAR.[44] However, under limited circumstances, if a partnership has elected out of CPAR but is a "partnership-partner" in a partnership that is subject to audit under CPAR, the partnership-partner may be subject to CPAR vis-à-vis its share of adjustments from the audited partnership.[45]

Going forward, the enactment of CPAR appears to have created a vacuum of sorts for partnerships that elect out of CPAR under § 6221(b). Neither CPAR nor TEFRA apply to these partnerships. Somewhat oddly, it also appears that the consistency requirement in § 6222 does not apply to these partnerships.[46]

[2] Taxes to Which CPAR Applies

While CPAR applies only for purposes of taxes imposed by Chapter 1 of the Code (income tax), to the extent that a determination made in a CPAR proceeding is relevant in determining tax under other chapters, the CPAR determination applies.[47] Chapter 3 of the Code imposes withholding requirements on certain payments to nonresident aliens and foreign corporations. Under § 1446, a partnership must withhold on a foreign partner's distributive share of a partnership's income that is effectively connected with the conduct of a U.S. trade or business. If a CPAR proceeding results in an adjustment to partnership in-

---

[41] § 6241(8); Reg. § 301.6241-5(a).

[42] Reg. § 301.6241-5(b).

[43] Reg. § 301.6241-5(c)(2).

[44] See ¶ 10A.04.

[45] Reg. § 301.6241-3(e)(4)

[46] Section 6222 (the consistency rule) is in Subchapter C of Chapter 63. Section 6221(b) (the election out), which is also in Subchapter C, provides that "this subchapter shall not apply" to partnerships that elect out. See Reg. § 301.6221(b)-1(a): "The provisions of subchapter C ... do not apply for any partnership taxable year for which an eligible partnership ... makes a valid [election out] in accordance with paragraph (c) of this section." See ¶ 10A.04.

[47] Reg. §§ 301.6241-6(a), 301.6241-6(a)(2) Example 2. No provision is made for communicating these adjustments to the partners.

come that is subject to withholding, the withholding tax burden falls on the partnership for the adjustment year.[48] Similar concepts apply to the withholding rules relating to withholdable payments to certain foreign financial institutions and other foreign entities in Chapter 4 of the Code (§§ 1471 through 1476).[49]

[3] Partnership-Related Items: In General

Section 6221(a) requires that

> [a]ny adjustment to a partnership-related item shall be determined, and any tax attributable thereto shall be assessed and collected, and the applicability of any penalty, addition to tax, or additional amount which relates to an adjustment to any such item shall be determined, at the partnership level, except to the extent otherwise provided in this subchapter.[50]

Under § 6221(a), the definition of "partnership-related item" is critical to the scope of CPAR. Under the computational rules in § 6225, it is also critical to the computation of any "imputed underpayment," which is the starting point for most tax computations under CPAR.[51]

Section 6241(2)(B) defines "partnership-related item" broadly as

> (i) any item or amount with respect to the partnership (without regard to whether or not such item or amount appears on the partnership's return and including an imputed underpayment and any item or amount relating to any transaction with, basis in, or liability of, the partnership) which is *relevant* (determined without regard to this subchapter) *in determining the tax liability of any person* under Chapter 1, and (ii) any partner's distributive share of any item or amount described in clause (i). [Emphasis added.]

The key phrase in this definition is "relevant ... in determining the tax liability of any person." The Regulations take a very expansive view of this lan-

---

[48] Reg. § 301.6241-6(b). However, an increase in the withholding rate, as opposed to the amount of income subject to withholding, is not subject to CPAR. Reg. § 301.6241-6(a)(2) Example 1.

[49] Reg. § 301.6241-6(b)(2)(iii).

[50] While all adjustments to partnership-related items have to be determined in a partnership proceeding, items that are not partnership-related items cannot be directly adjusted at the partnership level, although certain partner-level considerations can be taken into account in a "modification" process that occurs under § 6225(c) after the Service has examined and proposed adjustments to partnership-related items. The purpose of the modification process is to allow partner-level consideration to reduce the amount of imputed underpayments. See ¶ 10A.06[2].

[51] See ¶ 10A.06[1].

guage. Effectively, they interpret this phrase generically to mean any item or amount that, under any circumstances, could be relevant in determining the income tax liability of any person. The possible impact on any person's tax liability does not need to be certain or even likely; nor does the impacted person need to be a partner. The impact does not need to be immediate or direct.

The definitions of "partnership adjustment" and "partnership-related item" are in Regulations § 301.6241-1(a)(6). Regulations § 301.6241-1(a)(6)(i) defines a partnership adjustment as the whole or any portion of any adjustment to a *partnership-related item*. Regulations § 301.6241-1(a)(6)(ii) hews closely to the statutory language: It defines a "partnership-related item" as any "item or amount with respect to the partnership ... which is *relevant in determining the tax liability of any person under chapter 1 of the Code chapter 1) (as defined in paragraph (a)(6)(iv) of this section)*; ... [a]ny partner's distributive share of any such item or amount; and ... [a]ny imputed underpayment ...."[52]

Regulations § 301.6241-1(a)(6)(iii) provides more detail: For this purpose, an

> item or amount is with respect to the partnership if the item or amount is shown or reflected, or required to be shown or reflected, on a return of the partnership under section 6031 or the forms and instructions prescribed by the Internal Revenue Service (IRS) for the partnership's taxable year or is required to be maintained in the partnership's books or records.

Regulations § 301.6241-1(a)(6)(iii) also provides the following constraint on the scope of the "partnership-related item" definition:

> An item or amount shown or required to be shown on a return of a person other than the partnership (or in that person's books and records) that results after application of the Code to a partnership-related item based upon the person's specific facts and circumstances, including an incorrect application of the Code or taking into account erroneous facts and circumstances of the partner, is not an item or amount with respect to the partnership.

This important constraint is clearly consistent with one of the basic objectives of CPAR: to increase administrative efficiency by avoiding entanglement with the facts and circumstances of individual partners. In doing so, it high-

---

[52] The italicized language in the quoted material merits some discussion. Chapter 1 is the income tax provisions of the Code (§§ 1 through 1400). The use of the word "person" in this clause contrasts with the reference to "partner" in the next clause. Presumably, the class of persons subject to the first clause is broader than "partners." How much broader? Hopefully, the intent is to include only persons who are indirect partners as opposed to all persons regardless of whether they have any interest in the partnership. However, the text itself does not support any such limitation.

lights an underlying tension between this objective (which is served by narrowing the scope of the definition) and another basic goal of CPAR: to provide a pervasive unified system for the resolution of partnership income tax disputes (which is served by broadening the scope of the definition).

Because of this constraint, it seems any limitation that might come into play based on any individual partner's facts and circumstances is not a partnership-related item and therefore is ignored in computing the partnership's adjustments. The Regulations illustrate the application of this exclusion with a few examples:

- If a partnership-level deduction is subject to a limitation (such as the percentage limitations on charitable deductions of individuals in § 170(b)) at the partner level, the limitation is not a partnership-related item and is not taken into account in determining the partnership adjustment.
- The basis of a partner's partnership interest is not "an item or amount with respect to the partnership" because it is an item or amount shown in the partner's books or records that results after application of the Code to partnership-related items taking into account the facts and circumstances specific to that partner.

The line drawn by this constraint may be helpful in applying the basic computational rules regarding imputed underpayments in § 6225. In addition to the examples in the Regulation, it seems that none of the following items should be taken into account in determining the existence or amount of partnership-related items: (1) the at-risk limitation in § 465, (2) the passive activity loss limitation in § 469, and (3) the application of § 1231 to partners who have both individual § 1231 gains and shares of partnership § 1231 losses (or vice versa).[53] Thus, valid partnership losses that may not be fully deductible at the partner level due to the basis limitation in § 704(d), the at-risk limitation in § 465, or the passive activity loss limitation in § 469 should nevertheless be fully allowed for purposes of computing partnership adjustments under § 6225. All of these limitations are based on the partner's "specific facts and circumstances."

Even as so constrained, Regulations § 301.6241-1(a)(6)(iii) can easily be read to encompass a great many items that *might* (but also might not, in many situations) have an impact on the current taxable income of anyone, whether it

---

[53] The adjustments subject to this limitation bear a strong resemblance to the adjustments treated as "affected items" under former Code § 6231(a)(5) and Regulations § 301.6231(a)(5)-1 of TEFRA. See ¶ 10.02[5]. The case law regarding TEFRA affected items will no doubt play a role (as it should) as the law develops regarding this limitation under CPAR. See the extensive discussion of the interplay of these concepts between TEFRA and CPAR in TD 9844, Preamble, Summary of Comments and Explanation of Revisions 1.B, 84 FR 6468, 6472–6473 (Feb. 27, 2019).

be the partnership, a partner, or any other person. This interpretation is confirmed by Regulations § 301.6241-1(a)(6)(iv), which explicitly provides that an item or amount is "relevant" for this purpose "without regard to whether such item or amount, or an adjustment to such item or amount, has an effect on the *tax liability of any particular person under Chapter 1*." (Emphasis added.) Further color is provided by the Preamble to the Regulation package that provided the bulk of the existing final Regulations, which in this context refers to any items that could be relevant to "someone's" income tax liability.[54]

Regulations § 301.6241-1(a)(6)(v) proffers the following nonexclusive list of examples of partnership-related items:

(A) The character, timing, source, and amount of the partnership's income, gain, loss, deductions, and credits;

(B) The character, timing, and source of the partnership's activities;

(C) The character, timing, source, value, and amount of any contributions to, and distributions from, the partnership;

(D) The partnership's basis in its assets, the character and type of the assets, and the value (or revaluation such as under § 1.704-1(b)(2)(iv)(f) or (s) of this chapter) of the assets;

(E) The amount and character of partnership liabilities and any changes to those liabilities from the preceding tax year;

(F) The category, timing, and amount of the partnership's creditable expenditures;

(G) Any item or amount resulting from a partnership termination;

(H) Any item or amount of the partnership resulting from an election under section 754;

(I) Partnership allocations and any special allocations; and

(J) The identity of a person as a partner in the partnership.

Regulations § 301.6241-1(a)(6)(vi) provides further elucidation in the form of four examples:

Example 1: Partnership buys widgets from *A*. Any deduction or expense of Partnership with respect to the widgets is a partnership-related item, but *A*'s income is not. No indication is given as to whether *A* is a partner or related to a partner, indicating that *A*'s relationship is irrelevant to the analysis, as it should be.

Example 2: Partnership borrows from *B* and pays interest to *B*. Partnership's treatment of the transaction as a loan and the payment as interest ex-

---

[54] TD 9844, Preamble, Summary of Comments and Explanation of Revisions, 84 FR 6468, 6470 (Feb. 27, 2019). The Service has announced its intention to propose Regulations that will carve out certain partnership-related items in connection with audits of the non-partnership returns of a partner or a small group of partners and allow adjustments of such items without the need for CPAR proceedings. Notice 2019-06, § 3, 2019-3 IRB 8.

pense are partnership-related items, but *B*'s treatment of these items is not. By implication, it is not relevant whether *B* is a partner or related to a partner.

Examples 3 and 4: Both of these examples deal with a Partnership non-cash charitable contribution that is improperly treated by partners on their individual returns. Partner *C* reports it as a non-cash contribution, consistent with the Partnership return, but fails to take the 50 percent limit into account, whereas partner *D* reports it as a cash contribution thereby avoiding the limitation of his charitable deduction under the 50 percent rule. The amount and character of the charitable contribution reported by the Partnership is a partnership-related item. However, the amounts of the deductions claimed by the partners are not. *C* is subject to personal audit and assessment of a deficiency under the normal rules in § 6212. However, because *D* has treated his share of the deduction as a cash instead of a non-cash contribution without filing a notice of inconsistent treatment with the Service, the Service may assess *D*'s deficiency directly against *D* as a mathematical or clerical error without issuing a § 6212 deficiency notice, thereby denying *D* the right to contest the deficiency in the Tax Court and forcing him to pursue any further disagreement by paying the tax and filing a refund claim.[55]

The broad reach of the partnership-related item definition is illustrated by Example 7 in Regulations § 301.6225-1(h)(7). This Example involves a nonrecourse liability that is incorrectly reported by a partnership as a recourse liability. Because "such recharacterization could result in ... income if taken into account by any person," Example 7 concludes it produces a positive adjustment that is multiplied by the highest possible tax rate to produce an imputed underpayment for the partnership. While the conclusion in this Example is supported by the text of the Regulations, including Item (E) in Regulations § 301.6241-1(a)(6)(v), the stated rationale is not. A more appropriate technical rationale would be that the amounts of partnership recourse and nonrecourse liabilities are partnership-related items simply because they are required to be "shown or reflected, or required to be shown or reflected, on a return of the partnership."[56]

---

[55] These last two examples do not illustrate the scope of the partnership-related item rules as much as they demonstrate that differences in the exact ways a partner improperly reports an item can have a major effect under the inconsistent treatment rules in § 6222.

[56] Reg. § 301.6241-1(a)(6)(iii); see Reg. § 301.6241-1(a)(6)(v)(E). Partnership Form K-1 requires each partner's share of nonrecourse, qualified nonrecourse, and recourse liabilities to be separately set forth each year, and the partnership balance sheet included in the Partnership Return (Form 1065) as Schedule L requires separate entries for "nonrecourse loans." This rationale is also supported by the partnership's access to the background information necessary to correctly characterize the liability as recourse or nonrecourse. For more insight into the Treasury's articulation of the policy considerations, see TD 9844, Preamble, Summary of Comments and Explanation of Revisions 1.B, 84 FR 6468, 6472–6473 (Feb. 27, 2019).

The Example does not address how the recharacterization of the liability could result in income to any person without regard to that person's specific facts and circumstances. A mere change in the nature of a partnership liability, standing alone, does not create income or gain to anyone. That can only happen if there are other circumstances, most likely a loss allocation or a constructive distribution to a partner who has inadequate basis, that trigger realization of income or gain. However, the last sentence of Regulations § 301.6241-1(a)(6)(iii) explicitly provides that "a partner's adjusted basis is *not* with respect to the partnership because it is an item or amount shown in the partner's books or records that results after application of the Code to partnership-related items taking into account the facts and circumstances specific to that partner." (Emphasis added.) Thus, the Example affirms that even though the amount of a partner's basis for its partnership interest is "not with respect to the partnership" (i.e., is not a partnership-related item), it can be taken into consideration on a worst-case basis in determining whether an adjustment to a partnership-related item could result in income to any person.[57]

Because the adjustment in this Example does not relate to a decrease in an item of partnership income or credit, it cannot be a negative adjustment.[58] By definition, all other partnership adjustments are positive adjustments.[59] Thus, this adjustment is necessarily a positive adjustment.

There is no readily apparent offsetting negative adjustment in this type of situation. The absence of an offsetting adjustment means that the consequences of this type of adjustment are comparable to those associated with a substantive adjustment for a wholly fictitious deduction item: The cost to the partnership and its partners is not merely interest and a present value cost, it is interest plus the entire amount of the positive adjustment multiplied by the highest tax rate. These types of positive adjustments that are not associated with a specific identifiable offsetting tax-recognized item of income, gain, loss,

---

[57] This analysis of Example 7 is consistent with Example 5 of Proposed Regulations § 301.6225-4(e) (2018), in which A and B each have a zero basis in their partnership interests. AB has a $200 liability that it treats as nonrecourse, allocable $100 to each partner. The Service determines that the liability is recourse and none of it should be allocated to A. A's share of AB's liabilities is thus reduced by $100, triggering $100 of imputed income to AB and an imputed underpayment of $40. Unlike Example 7 where the recharacterization triggers income equal to the entire amount of the liability, the recharacterization of the $200 liability produces only $100 of imputed income (the amount by which A's basis is reduced). The different consequences reflect the fact that a liability recharacterization from recourse to nonrecourse can trigger dollar-for-dollar § 465, at-risk consequence. Example 5, on the other hand, has no at-risk implications, so the potential imputed income increase is limited to partner A's liability reduction.

[58] Reg. § 301.6225-1(d)(2)(ii).

[59] Reg. § 301.6225-1(d)(2)(iii). See explanations in the Preamble to REG-123652-18, 227 Fed. Reg. 74940, 74945 (Nov. 24, 2020).

or deduction[60] are sometimes referred to as "one-sided adjustments" and are discussed in detail in ¶ 10A.10[3].

Proposed Regulations issued in 2020 seem to offer a glimmer of hope for those who find themselves caught in the one-sided adjustment trap. These Proposed Regulations would create a bold new special rule for "non-income items" by adding the following sentence at the end of Regulations § 301.6224-1(b)(4):

> If an adjustment to an item of income, gain, loss, deduction, or credit is related to, or results from, an adjustment to an item that is not an item of income, gain, loss, deduction, or credit, the adjustment to the item that is not an item of income, gain, loss, deduction, or credit will generally be treated as zero solely for purposes of calculating the imputed underpayment unless the IRS determines that the adjustment should be included in the imputed underpayment.[61]

Presumably, the adjustment in Example 7 would qualify to be treated as "zero" under this proposal since it relates to a liability, rather than an item of income, loss, deduction, or credit. However, the Preamble to these Proposed Regulations does not even mention Example 7, much less propose to modify it to be consistent with the proposal.[62] Another troubling aspect of the proposed language is that it does not offer any guidance as to the circumstance under which the Service might determine to include the adjustment in the imputed understatement, thereby seeming to confer complete discretion on the Service. On a more positive note, the effective date of these proposed changes is November 24, 2020, the day they were printed in the Federal Register.

---

[60] In a very broad sense, every positive partnership adjustment (even one triggered by the denial of a wholly fictitious deduction) can be viewed as inevitably creating an offsetting adjustment upon the ultimate liquidation of the partners' interests. This view is not likely to be of great solace to those who bear the tax cost of the positive adjustment. Further, the idea of an inevitable offset is not truly universal. For example, consider the application of § 751(a), which requires a seller of a partnership interest to treat as ordinary income her distributive share of the ordinary income that would be generated by a hypothetical sale by the partnership of all of its assets for fair market value. See ¶ 17.02[3]. Since this determination depends on the partnership's books and records, it is a partnership-related item. Accordingly, the sale of a partnership interest can give rise to a partnership imputed underpayment. The Proposed Regulations discussed in ¶ 10A.06[3] would place the burden of this tax on the purchaser of the interest, as it should be. Purchasers should seek contractual protection from this exposure.

[61] Prop. Reg. § 301.6225-1(b)(4) (2020).

[62] See Preamble to REG-123652-18, 227 Fed. Reg. 74940, 74945 (Nov. 24, 2020). The Preamble extends this concept to allow partnerships filing administrative adjustment requests (AARs) to treat non-income item adjustments as zero, subject, of course, to subsequent contrary determinations by the Service.

[4] Partnership-Related Items: The Fundamental Definitional Tension

The expansiveness of the definition of partnership-related item serves well to protect the intended pervasive scope of CPAR, but poorly in the way it interacts with CPAR's operational mechanics. Section 6225 mechanically converts adjustments to partnership-related items into imputed underpayments that are generally taxed to the partnership at the highest tax rate. Because the scope of the partnership-related item definition is intentionally broad, and covers many items and amounts that lack any direct connection to taxable income, it can easily create positive partnership-related item adjustments that are entirely fictional in terms of any likely current taxable income consequences and yet create imputed underpayments (and tax deficiencies) that are entirely real.[63] These types of adjustments create a variety of other nettlesome issues in the application of § 6225, as illustrated in ¶ 10A.10[3].

The drafters of the Regulations were fully aware of the potential for this sort of thing to happen and provided an example that highlights the type of absurdity that can result. As discussed earlier in ¶ 10A.02[3], Regulations § 301.6225-1(h)(7) Example 7 involves a nonrecourse liability that is incorrectly reported by a partnership as a recourse liability. Because "such recharacterization could result in ... income if taken into account by any person," it produces a positive adjustment that is multiplied by the highest possible tax rate to produce an imputed underpayment. In reality, although this type of recharacterization *could* produce income or gain to someone, it is *unlikely* to generate income to anyone. A mere change in the character of a liability, standing alone, does not create income or gain. That can only happen if there are other circumstances, most likely a loss allocation or constructive distribution to a partner who has inadequate basis, that trigger the realization of income or gain.

This approach effectively turns the tax system on its head in computing imputed underpayments. Instead of determining partnership taxable income or loss or items thereof by applying the detailed rules, conditions, limitations, and exceptions provided so voluminously for each specific income or deduction item, CPAR mandates that a partnership's imputed underpayment (which is simply another way of saying "tax deficiency") must be determined, not by looking at the myriad of actual facts and circumstances dictated by the Code, but by assuming the worst possible facts and circumstances and then applying the highest tax rate. Although disguised as a "mere" procedural change for partnership audits, CPAR has the potential to turn partnerships into the most highly taxed form of business organization in the country.[64] Under § 6225, the

---

[63] Among other thoughts, this may inspire some reflection on the relevance of the annual accounting concept in this type of situation.

[64] Partnerships were not generally income taxpayers *at all* prior to the advent of CPAR. Ironically, in the dark of the night, they may have become the most highly taxed

taxable income or loss of a partnership subject to CPAR can, on audit, effectively be determined under a previously unknown set of "worst case" rules, with the resultant partnership tax liability determined by applying the highest tax rate to this inflated and fictional taxable income amount.[65] This aspect of CPAR is so extreme it may raise constitutional issues because of its potential to impose a tax in the absence of any kind of discernible income.[66]

What is needed, but is entirely lacking under the Code and the CPAR Regulations, is a filter between the broad jurisdictional concept of a "partnership-related item" and a subcategory of such items that should reasonably be taken into account in determining imputed underpayments under § 6225.[67] It seems clear that every partnership-related item within the jurisdictional scope of CPAR does not need to create an immediate partnership understatement to protect the administrability of CPAR, and yet that is the blunt way § 6225 operates. The lack of any filter may reflect the difficulties inherent in creating and applying one without running afoul of the CPAR goal of administrative convenience. Alternatively, it may reflect Treasury's unwillingness to embark upon a difficult project that might create administrability issues with no revenue potential.

A less ambitious approach might be to delete Regulations § 301.6241-1(a)(6)(v)(E) and add an exception setting forth the opposite conclusion. Item (E) is significant because of its pervasiveness in the preparation of partnership returns, the burden it creates for return preparers,[68] and the absurdity of the results it can produce, as illustrated by Regulations § 301.6225-1(h)(7) Example 7. It is difficult to imagine a situation in which this change would significantly diminish the jurisdictional scope of CPAR and very easy to demonstrate the issues and unfairness that will result under § 6225 if it is not deleted.[69]

In any event, this problem lays bare a fundamental tension in CPAR. Failure to address it in some way will increase the anxiety and cost of preparing

---

form of business entity. This may explain, in part, why the revenue estimate attached to the enactment of CPAR was so high: $9.325 billion for 2016–2025. See Joint Comm. on Taxation, JCX-135-15 (Oct. 28, 2015).

[65] The impact of the "worst case" approach is compounded because it is also embedded in the subgrouping methodology under § 6225(b)(3), as discussed in ¶ 10A.06[1][c].

[66] Commissioner v. Glenshaw Glass, 348 US 426 (1955).

[67] An alternative type of filter may be presaged by Proposed Regulations § 301.6225-1(b)(4) (2020), which may produce similar results by treating the adjustment amounts for a variety of "non-income items" as zero for purposes of computing imputed understatements, as discussed in ¶ 10A.02[3].

[68] Virtually all partnerships have liabilities. Many return preparers are ill equipped and unaccustomed to evaluating the proper classification of liabilities. Anecdotally, little attention has been given to these entries on Form K-1s because they generally have no current tax impact.

[69] See ¶ 10A.10[3].

partnership tax returns and create more chaos in the tax system, particularly if the Service actually begins to audit significant numbers of partnerships and attempts to apply the rules as currently written.

[5] Partnership-Related Items: The TEFRA Affected Item Approach

In the interests of audit efficiency, CPAR deliberately refuses to burden the Service with the need to look beyond the boundaries of the partnership in determining and assessing a partnership's imputed underpayment. If the animating policy of CPAR is the escalation of administrative efficiency, the wisdom of this approach is difficult to question: TEFRA put the onus on the Service to take into consideration "affected items" (that is, partner-level items whose character or amount is affected, but not determined, by "partnership items") before any tax could be assessed. The result was an audit process that proved fatally cumbersome. This contrast between the two systems is succinctly stated by a single sentence in Regulations § 301.6241-1(a)(6)(iii):

> An item or amount shown or required to be shown on a return of a person other than the partnership (or in that person's books and records) that results after application of the Code to a partnership-related item based upon the person's specific facts and circumstances, including an incorrect application of the Code or taking into account erroneous facts and circumstances of the partner, is not an item or amount with respect to the partnership.

In a broad sense, this single sentence summarizes CPAR's antidote to the quagmire of the TEFRA-affected item system. Under CPAR, in the absence of proactive intervention by the PR, imputed underpayments are determined and *assessed* against the partnership without considering partner-level items. The imputed underpayment can be adjusted to reflect partner-level considerations only if, in the § 6225(c) modification process, the partnership, through its PR, requests that the Service consider partner-level (and, in some cases, indirect partner-level) factors and provides all substantiation requested by the Service. For example, while a partnership distribution is a partnership-related item, the regulations specifically provide that the basis of a partner's interest is not a partnership-related item.[70] Therefore, an increase in a partnership distribution for a reviewed year results in an imputed underpayment based on the worst-case assumption that the partners' bases are all zero. If the partnership

---

[70] Reg. § 301.6241-1(a)(6)(iii).

does not like that result, it must obtain modification under § 6225[71] or elect under § 6226 to push out the results of the partnership proceeding to the reviewed-year partners.

¶ 10A.03 ELECTION OUT

Partnerships with 100 or fewer eligible partners, none of which is a partnership or disregarded entity, may elect out of CPAR. In order to elect out, every partner must be either an individual, a C corporation, a foreign entity that would be treated as a C corporation if it were domestic,[72] an S corporation,[73] or an estate of a deceased partner.[74] The election must be made annually on a timely filed return.[75] Arrangements taking the position that they are not partnerships cannot elect out simply because they do not file returns.

---

[71] Possible modifications include compliant pull-in amended returns (or the equivalent) by partners or a modification approved by the Service under Regulations § 301.6225-2(d)(10) ("Other Modifications").

[72] The scope of this category of entities is uncertain. A foreign entity that is classified as a corporation under the check-a-box regulations is a C corporation. § 1361(a)(2); Reg. §§ 301.7701-2(b)(2)−301.7701-2(b)(8) (corporation defined). Foreign entities that are not per se corporations default to corporate status if all members have limited liability, and domestic entities generally default to pass-through status. See ¶ 3.06[5][a]. So, this class of foreign entities encompasses those that are not C corporations but would be if they were domestic entities—a class that has no obvious members. Regulations § 301.6221(b)-1(b)(3)(iii) defines an "eligible foreign entity" as one that is classified as a C corporation under the check-a-box regulations, which also appears to be an eligible partner under Regulations § 301.6221(b)-1(b)(3)(i).

[73] S corporation shareholders count in determining whether the partnership has more than 100 partners, and their names and taxpayer identification numbers must be disclosed. § 6221(b)(2)(A); Reg. § 301.6221(b)-1(b)(2)(ii). If a qualified subchapter S subsidiary (Q sub) is a partner, the Service has announced its intention to propose regulations under which the election out generally is unavailable unless the S corporation parent of the Q sub has a limited number of owners (consistent with the general 100 partner limit) and agrees to comply with certain reporting requirements. Notice 2019-06, § 3, 2019-3 IRB 8.

[74] Regulations § 301.6221(b)-1(b)(3)(ii) denies election-out privileges if any partner is a partnership (even one that has validly elected out of CPAR, Reg. § 301.6221(b)-1(d)), trust, ineligible foreign entity (Reg. § 301.6221(b)-1(b)(3)(iii)), disregarded entity, estate of an individual other than a deceased partner, or any person (nominee) holding an interest on behalf of another person. Oddly, if any of these types of entities is a valid shareholder of an S corporation that is a partner, the election out *is* available. Reg. § 301.6221(b)-1(b)(3)(iv) Example 2. These restrictions are far more extensive than those indicated by the Joint Committee explanation, which condones elections out by partnerships having disregarded entities, trusts, and other partnerships as partners. Staff of Joint Comm. on Taxation, JCS-1-16, 114th Cong., 2d Sess., General Explanation of the Tax Legislation Enacted in 2015, at 60 (Comm. Print 2016).

[75] § 6221(b)(1)(D)(i); Reg. § 301.6221(b)-1(c).

The exclusions from the list of eligible partners is surprising in many respects. Most significant are the exclusions of partnerships and disregarded entities. The statute excludes partnerships by not including them in the list of eligible partners in § 6221(b)(1)(C), an exclusion that stands in stark contrast to the inclusion of Subchapter S corporations in the approved list. Because both are flow-through tax vehicles, partnerships and Subchapter S corporations pose very similar audit administration problems by compelling the creation and application of rules flexible enough to deal with multi-tier ownership structures. From a policy perspective, given the bias of the CPAR rules in favor of administrability, this distinction is hard to justify. Commentators and others have pointed this out while attempting to convince Treasury to use its authority under § 6221(b)(2)(C) to include partnerships in the list of eligible partners. Treasury has demurred "in the interests of efficient tax administration."[76]

Efforts to persuade Treasury to change its position regarding the possible inclusion of disregarded entities have been based in part on the Joint Committee report for the 2015 tax legislation, which includes several examples of the types of ways Treasury might use its authority to expand the list of eligible partners under § 6221(b)(2)(C), including single-member LLCs, trusts, and partnerships.[77] Treasury has also rejected these entreaties.[78]

In applying the 100-partner limit, the number of partners is based entirely on the number of K-1s the partnership is required to issue for the year, with one exception: If an S corporation is a partner, the partnership must count the K-1 issued to the S corporation itself as well as each K-1 the S corporation is required to issue to its shareholders for the S corporation tax year that ends with or within the partnership's tax year.[79] If an interest is transferred during the year, the partnership must count both the transferor and the transferee (both of whom are issued K-1s) toward the 100-partner limit. Thus, even a partnership with well under 100 partners at any given time during a year may exceed the 100-partner limit if interests are routinely sold or exchanged.

---

[76] TD 9829, Supplementary Information, 1.B "Eligible Partners," 83 Fed. Reg. 24, 26−28 (Jan. 2, 2018).

[77] See Staff of Joint Comm. on Taxation, 114th Cong., 2d Sess., JCS-1-16, General Explanation of Tax Legislation Enacted in 2015, at 60−61 (Comm. Print 2016).

[78] TD 9829, Supplementary Information, 1.B "Eligible Partners," 83 Fed. Reg. 24, 26−28 (Jan. 2, 2018).

[79] Reg. § 301.6221(b)-1(b)(2)(ii). Treasury Decision 9829 indicates very clearly that the Service has no interest in expanding the availability of the election out or deviating from existing rules relating to the issuance of K-1s. TD 9829, Supplementary Information, 1.A.i "Determining the Number of Statements Required To Be Furnished," 83 Fed. Reg. 24, 25−26 (Jan. 2, 2018).

¶ 10A.04 CONSISTENT REPORTING

Partners must report partnership-related items consistently with the final partnership return actually filed by a partnership, including any valid amendments or supplements, any § 6227 administrative adjustment requests (AARs), and any statements furnished to the partner in connection with § 6226 push-out elections.[80] Any failure to do so will result in a correction that is assessed and collected as a mathematical error.[81] If a partnership does not file a return, a partner's treatment of all partnership-related items is deemed to be inconsistent with the partnership return.[82]

A partner may take a position inconsistent with that of the partnership if it files a statement identifying the inconsistency,[83] but any resolution of the issue at the partner level will not be binding on the partnership.[84] However, in general, a notice of inconsistent treatment may not be filed after the Service initiates a partnership proceeding by sending a § 6231 notice of administrative proceeding (NAP).[85]

Somewhat surprisingly, both the Code and the Regulations clearly provide that the consistency requirement does not apply to a partnership that elects out of CPAR pursuant to § 6221(b).[86] However, in a tiered partnership structure,

---

[80] § 6222(a); Reg. §§ 301.6222-1(a)(1), 301.6222-1(a)(4). It is the partnership *return* that governs, not the K-1 furnished to the partner. If the Service notifies the partner of an inconsistency, the partner can elect to report the inconsistency under § 6222(c)(1) in which event the correction will be assessed and collected as a mathematical error. Reg. § 301.6222-1(d). If the partnership files an administrative adjustment request under § 6227 (see ¶ 10A.09) and validly elects to push out taxpayer-adverse adjustments to its partners, any partner who fails to take into account its share of the adjustments will be in violation of the consistency rules. Reg. § 301.6222-1(a)(5) Example 4.

[81] § 6222(b); Reg. § 301.6222-1(b).

[82] Reg. § 301.6222-1(a)(3).

[83] § 6222(c)(1); Reg. § 301.6222-1(c)(1). Because an AAR is treated as part of the partnership return, it seems a partner who disagrees with an AAR filed by a partnership should be able to file a notice of inconsistent treatment (unless a NAP has been issued, see Reg. § 301.6222-1(c)(5)). However, a partner is not permitted to file an inconsistent treatment notice with regard to items reflected in a final decision in a CPAR decision or in a § 6226 push-out statement filed by a partnership with the Service. Reg. §§ 301.6222-1(c)(2), 301.6226-1(e).

[84] § 6222(d); Reg. § 301.6222-1(c)(4)(ii).

[85] Reg. § 301.6222-1(c)(5); see Reg. § 301.6231-1(f) (inconsistent notice allowed if NAP or NOPPA withdrawn by Service).

[86] Section 6222 (the consistency rule) is in Subchapter C of Chapter 63. Section 6221(b) (the election out), which is also in Subchapter C, provides that "this subchapter shall not apply" to partnerships that elect out. See Reg. § 301.6221(b)-1(a): "The provisions of subchapter C ... do not apply for any partnership taxable year for which an eligible partnership ... makes a valid election [the election out] in accordance with paragraph (c) of this section."

an upper-tier partnership (a "partnership-partner" in the vernacular of the Regulations) that has elected out under § 6221(b) is subject to the consistency requirement with respect to its interest in any lower-tier partnership that has not elected out,[87] thereby exposing the upper-tier partnership to tax as though the adjustment were a mathematical or clerical error.[88]

¶ 10A.05 PARTNERSHIP REPRESENTATIVE

In lieu of the tax matters partner of the TEFRA era, under CPAR each partnership must annually designate a person (who need not be a partner) with substantial presence in the United States to be its representative.[89] The partnership representative (PR) has the sole authority to bind the partnership. In the absence of designation by the partnership, the government selects the representative.[90]

A partnership may designate an entity as a PR.[91] If an entity is designated, the partnership must also designate an individual to represent the entity in its role as the PR.[92] To ease the Service's administrative burden of keeping up with resignations by PRs and changes of PR designations by partnerships, the Regulations provide elaborate and restrictive rules to regulate resignations, revocations, and substitutions.[93] The rules applicable to PRs and designated individuals are generally the same, so there is no apparent advantage in using an entity (as opposed to an individual) as the PR.

---

[87] See Reg. §§ 301.6221(b)-1(d), 301.6222-1(a)(2), 301.6222-1(a)(5) Example 6.

[88] § 6222(d)(1)(B); Reg. § 301.6222-1(b)(3).

[89] The designation must be made for each year on the partnership return for that year. Reg. § 301.6223-1(c). Substantial presence requires that the person be available to meet with the Service in the United States at a reasonable time and place, have a United States street address and phone number, and a taxpayer identification number. Reg. § 301.6223-1(b)(2). If an entity is the partnership representative, an individual who meets the substantial presence requirements must be designated to represent the entity. The regulations go to great lengths to assure there is one, and only one, partnership representative, providing detailed rules regarding resignations of the representative (see Reg. § 301.6223-1(d)) and revocations of the designation by the partnership (see Reg. § 301.6223-1(e)). Resignations and revocations may only be made at the time of filing an Administrative Adjustment Request (AAR) under § 6227 (an AAR cannot relate solely to a resignation or revocation) or after receipt of an Examination Notice or NAP.

[90] § 6223(a); Reg. § 301.6223-1(f). The Service will not designate a current employee, agent, or contractor of the Service unless that employee, agent, or contractor was a reviewed-year partner or current-year partner in the partnership. Reg. § 301.6223-1(f)(5).

[91] Reg. § 301.6223-1(b)(3).

[92] Reg. § 301.6223-1(b)(3)(ii).

[93] Reg. §§ 301.6223-1(d), 301.6223-1(e), 301.6223-1(f).

¶ 10A.06 PARTNERSHIP-LEVEL ADJUSTMENTS; IMPUTED UNDERPAYMENTS

The heart of CPAR is the imputed underpayment rules in § 6225. If the Service determines adjustments should be made to any partnership-related item for a reviewed year, § 6225(a)(1) provides that the partnership must pay any resultant "imputed underpayment" for the reviewed year. Any adjustments that do not produce an imputed underpayment for the reviewed year must be taken into account by the partnership in the adjustment year pursuant to § 6225(a)(2). The lynchpin (and hammer) of CPAR is § 6225(b)(1), which provides that the partnership's imputed underpayment for the reviewed year is computed by appropriately netting all partnership adjustments and then "applying the highest rate of tax in effect for the reviewed year under section 1 or 11." The adverse taxpayer impact of this rate assumption is magnified by the grouping and netting rules, which effectively defer many taxpayer-favorable adjustments to the adjustment year under § 6225(a)(2).

Example 4 in Regulations § 301.6225-1(h)(4) illustrates one aspect of this unfavorable impact. A partnership reports $125 of long-term capital gain on its 2019 return. A NOPPA for 2019 recharacterizes this as ordinary income of $125. This produces two adjustments under the netting rules: a $125 ordinary income *increase* in 2019, resulting in an imputed underpayment of $50, and a $125 long-term capital *loss* in the adjustment year, rather than 2019. This means the total tax on this $125 income item for 2019 is $50, 40 percent of the disputed adjustment. Of course, the partners may recover some of this tax when the deferred capital loss is eventually reported on their returns for the adjustment year, but the availability and amount of this recovery is far from certain. As discussed in ¶ 10A.10[2], even more draconian results are likely in the event of a reallocation adjustment, as illustrated by Example 12 in Regulations § 301.6225-1(h)(12).

There is another unfairness inherent in this type of recharacterization adjustment that is not addressed or even acknowledged by the statute or the Regulations: Presumably, the partners paid tax on their shares of the $125 capital gain reported for 2019. Assuming they are still partners in the adjustment year, they *may* be able to recover an equivalent tax for the adjustment year if they can effectively utilize the artificial capital loss created for that year, but that is far from certain. Viewed this way, the total tax cost of the recharacterization of the $125 gain is not just the $50 (plus interest) imputed underpayment paid by the partnership but also any tax paid by the partners on this gain in 2019 less the present value of whatever savings the partners eventually glean from the capital loss in the adjustment year.

The statute also provides that adjustments for the reviewed year "shall first be separately determined (and netted as appropriate) within each category of items that are required to be taken into account separately under section

702(a) or any other provision of this title."[94] Any adjustment that could decrease the amount of the imputed adjustment but is potentially subject to a limitation (or disallowed in whole or in part as a deduction against ordinary income) with respect to any person cannot be taken into account except to the extent otherwise provided by the Treasury.[95]

In general, any imputed underpayment is assessed and collected as if it were a tax imposed for the adjustment year.[96] Interest runs from the return due date for the reviewed year and any penalties, additions to tax, and additional amounts related to the imputed underpayment are determined as if the partnership were an individual and the imputed underpayment were an actual underpayment (or understatement) for the reviewed year.[97]

The Code provides little or no detail as to the computation of imputed underpayments[98] or the allocation of the economic burden of underpayments (or the adjustments underlying such underpayments) among the partners. The little guidance found in the statute both acknowledges the gaps in the Code and confirm the Treasury's authority to fill in the blanks.[99] This ¶ 10A.06 reflects the existing Regulations regarding the basic computational scheme (¶ 10A.06[1]) and the modification process (¶ 10A.06[2]) and well as Proposed Regulations dealing with partner allocations (¶ 10A.06[3]).

[1] Computations

[a] General

Section 301.6225-1(b)(1) of the Regulations provides that the imputed underpayment for any reviewed year of the partnership is equal to:

---

[94] § 6225(b)(3).

[95] § 6225(b)(4). See discussion in ¶ 10A.02[3].

[96] § 6232(a).

[97] § 6233(a).

[98] As discussed in ¶ 10A.06[1], §§ 6225(c) and 6225(d) give partners a limited right to move an imputed understatement from the partnership return for a reviewed year to their personal returns, address a number of other special situations, and provide some definitions but contain little or no guidance as to exactly how to compute an imputed understatement.

[99] See §§ 6225(b)(1) ("appropriately" netting), 6225(b)(3) ("netted as appropriate"), 6225(b)(4) ("to the extent otherwise provided by the Secretary"), 6225(c)(1), 6225(c)(9). In the complete absence of relevant legislative history, invocation of an "appropriate" standard provides great latitude for regulation writers and auditors.

1. The "total netted partnership adjustment," which is the sum of all net positive partnership adjustments in the "reallocation grouping" and the "residual grouping";[100]
2. Multiplied by the highest rate of federal income tax in effect for the reviewed year under § 1 or § 11;
3. Increased by any net positive adjustments in a credit grouping;[101] and
4. Decreased by any net negative adjustments in a credit grouping, but only if the Service determines the adjustment should be taken into account.[102]

Positive "partnership adjustments" (adjustments to partnership-related items) are those adverse to taxpayers (e.g., increases to income or gain items, decreases to credits or deduction items), while negative adjustments are those potentially favorable to taxpayers (e.g., decreases to income or gain items, increases to credits or deduction items).[103] Regulations proposed in 2020 would generally treat the amount of any positive adjustment for "non-income items" as zero for purposes of these computations.[104]

Negative adjustments excluded from the reviewed year imputed underpayment calculation do not disappear; instead, they are taken into account by the partnership in the adjustment year.[105]

---

[100] Reg. § 301.6225-1(b)(2); see ¶ 10A.06[1][b].

[101] Reg. §§ 301.6225-1(b)(1)(v)(A), 301.6225-1(e)(3)(ii); see ¶ 10A.06[1][b].

[102] Reg. §§ 301.6225-1(b)(1)(v)(B), 301.6225-1(e)(3)(ii); see ¶ 10A.06[1][b]. The Regulations also give the Service discretion to subdivide an imputed underpayment into a general imputed underpayment and multiple "specific" imputed underpayments. Reg. § 301.6225-1(g); see Reg. § 301.6225-1(h)(6) Example 6 (general and specific imputed underpayments created by the Service to reflect special item allocations). The Service seems to have complete discretion and control over this process. There is no apparent basis for taxpayers to invoke, object, or participate in the process or challenge any decisions by the Service. Whether this aspect of the Regulations is entirely benign remains to be seen, but it does not appear to have been intended to benefit taxpayers. A possible safeguard is provided by the Treasury's decision to designate all CPAR proceedings as Appeals Coordinated Issues that must be referred for Technical Guidance. IRM IRM 8.19.14.2.2. See generally IRM 8.19.14: Memorandum for Appeals Employees from Appeals Director (Oct. 18, 2019). Taxpayers unduly aggrieved can expect to have a second chance to be heard by different ears.

[103] Reg. § 301.6225-1(d)(2).

[104] Prop. Reg. § 301.6225-1(b)(4) (2020), as discussed in ¶ 10A.02[3].

[105] Reg. §§ 301.6225-1(f)(2), 301.6225-3. See ¶ 10A.07.

[b] Groupings

All partnership adjustments for a year are placed in one of four groupings: (1) the reallocation grouping, (2) the credit grouping, (3) the creditable expenditure grouping, and (4) the residual grouping.[106]

For many partnerships, application of these grouping rules as well as the complex subgrouping and netting rules discussed in ¶¶ 10A.06[1][c] and 10A.06[1][d] will be greatly simplified by certain characteristics of these rules:

1. All adjustments to partnership income or loss must be placed in one of two groups. Of these, the reallocation grouping will only come into play if the Service determines partnership-related items (other than credits or creditable expenditures) should be reallocated among the partners.[107] All other adjustments to items of partnership income or loss (including any adjustments to partnership-related items that would not have been required to be allocated to any reviewed-year partner under § 704(b)) are placed in the residual grouping.[108] Thus, for many partnerships, the residual group will be the only relevant group.

2. If all adjustments are positive, subgrouping is not required, and the "total netted partnership adjustment" is simply the sum of the positive adjustments in the residual group unless there are also reallocation adjustments.

3. If there are reallocation adjustments, each will generally consist of at least two opposite signed adjustments: at least one to reverse the effect of the improper allocation and at least one to effectuate the proper allocation.[109] The "total netted partnership adjustment" is simply the sum of the positive adjustments in the reallocation group and residual group.[110] Any negative adjustments in these groups are taken

---

[106] Reg. § 301.6225-1(c)(1). The Service has the power to modify the groupings whenever, in its view, modified groupings would "appropriately reflect the facts and circumstances." Taxpayers may "request" modifications. See Reg. § 301.6225-2(d)(6). No standards for evaluating or approving taxpayer requests are set forth.

[107] Reg. § 301.6225-1(c)(2). Allocations and reallocations of credits and creditable expenditures are included in the credit and the creditable expenditure groupings.

[108] Reg. § 301.6225-1(c)(5). The parenthetical clause is intended to include adjustments to partnership-related items that do not impact the § 704(b) capital accounts of the partners. See, e.g., Reg. § 301.6225-1(h)(7) Example 7.

[109] Reg. § 301.6225-1(c)(2)(ii). If the reallocation involves multiple income or loss items that must be separately stated under § 702(a) (or for any other reason), then each such item creates two opposite-signed adjustments that are placed in separate subgroupings. See Reg. §§ 301.6225-1(d)(3)(ii), 301.6225-1(h)(12) Example 12.

[110] Reg. § 301.6225-1(b)(2).

into account in the adjustment year as set forth in Regulations § 301.6225-3.[111]

4. All credits are placed in the credit grouping and all creditable expenditures are placed in the creditable expenditures grouping.[112]

Special rules are provided for "recharacterization allocations," which are adjustments (generally in the residual grouping) that change the character of a partnership-related item.[113] Each recharacterization allocation necessarily involves at least two opposite signed adjustments: One reverses the improper characterization of the item and the other effectuates the proper characterization. For example, if income reported as long-term capital gain is recharacterized as ordinary income, there is an increase in ordinary income (a positive adjustment) and a corresponding decrease in long-term capital gain (a negative adjustment). If an expenditure reported as an ordinary deduction is recharacterized as a capital cost, there is an increase in ordinary income (a positive adjustment) and an increase in capitalized costs (a negative adjustment). In either event, the positive adjustment creates an imputed underpayment in the reviewed year while the negative adjustment is deferred and only given effect on the adjustment year return.[114]

[c] Subgroupings

Subgrouping of adjustments is required unless all adjustments within a grouping are positive.[115] If subgrouping is required, it is based on the way the adjusted items would be required to be separately reported under § 702(a) (or for any other reason).[116]

Generally, adjustments that relate to items that would be aggregated for purposes of § 702(a) are aggregated and placed in the same subgrouping and netted regardless of whether they are positive or negative. However, the Regulations create several exceptions to this general aggregation rule:

---

[111] Reg. § 301.6225-1(f)(2).

[112] Reg. §§ 301.6225-1(c)(3), 301.6225-1(c)(4).

[113] Reg. §§ 301.6225-1(c)(6), 301.6225-1(d)(2).

[114] See Reg. § 301.6225-1(h)(4) Example 4 (long-term capital gain converted to ordinary income generates imputed underpayment and tax equal to 40 percent of ordinary income for the reviewed year; long-term capital loss (subject to the usual limits on deductibility) placed in the adjustment year).

[115] Reg. § 301.6225-1(d)(1). See Reg. § 301.6225-1(h)(3) Example 3 (all positive adjustments in residual group; no subgrouping).

[116] Reg. § 301.6225-1(d)(3)(i): subgroup based on "how the adjustment would be required to be taken into account separately under section 702(a) or any other provision of the Code, regulations, forms, instructions, or other guidance prescribed by the IRS applicable to the adjusted partnership-related item."

1. Within all subgroupings, any adjustments to items that may be subject to a preference, limitation, or restriction (or not allowed as a deduction against ordinary income by any person) are placed in separate subgroupings;[117]

2. Within the reallocation grouping, each positive and negative adjustment is placed in a separate subgrouping unless the adjustments are allocated to the same partner or group of partners and would be aggregated under the general aggregation rule;[118]

3. Within the credit grouping and the creditable expenditure grouping, each positive and negative adjustment is placed in its own separate subgrouping;[119] and

4. Within the residual grouping, each adjustment resulting from a recharacterization adjustment is placed in a separate subgrouping unless the adjustments are allocated to the same partner or group of partners and would be subgrouped and netted under the generally applicable rules.[120]

Under these subgrouping rules, adjustments to items that may be subject to a preference, limitation, or restriction (or not allowed as a deduction against ordinary income by any person) are placed in separate subgroupings. This extends the general "worst case" approach of the imputed underpayment rules to the most granular level of the subgrouping rules. It means that any net deduction increase, income decrease, or any other taxpayer-favorable ("negative") subgroup adjustment must be examined against the panoply of the entire Code to determine if there is any rule that *might* restrict the ability of anyone to benefit from the adjustment. Section 704(d) generally limits the deductibility of partnership losses by every partner to the adjusted basis of its partnership

---

[117] Reg. § 301.6225-1(d)(3)(i).

[118] Reg. § 301.6225-1(d)(3)(ii)(A).

[119] Reg. §§ 301.6225-1(d)(3)(ii)(B), 301.6225-1(d)(3)(iii)(A). Special rules are provided for adjustments to creditable foreign tax expenditures, which are separately stated and aggregated in subgroupings based on § 904(d) income categories. Reg. § 301.6225-1(d)(3)(iii)(A). See Reg. § 301.6225-1(h)(8) Example 8 (reduction of creditable foreign tax expenditure (CFTE) produces dollar-for-dollar imputed underpayment for reviewed year); Reg. § 301.6225-1(h)(9) Example 9 (recharacterization of CFTE from passive category to general category under § 904(d); dollar-for-dollar imputed underpayment due to decrease in passive CFTE for reviewed year; no discussion of treatment of increased general CFTE—should be taken into account in adjustment year); Reg. § 301.6225-1(h)(10) Example 10 (reallocation of CFTE among partners; adjustment is in credit grouping, not reallocation grouping; imputed underpayment increased by amount of reallocated credit in reviewed year; same amount of credit deferred to adjustment year); Reg. § 301.6225-1(h)(11) Example 11 (adjustments to CFTEs allocated to partners in different proportions; imputed underpayment equal to gross reduction in CFTE in reviewed year; increase in CTFE deferred to adjustment year).

[120] Reg. § 301.6225-1(d)(3)(iv).

interest.[121] Therefore, any net deduction increase that would be separately reported under § 702(a) must be reduced to zero and cannot be netted against positive increases in other § 702(a) categories because it may not be deductible under some circumstances.[122] On the other hand, if a deduction increase is in the same § 702(a) category as a positive adjustment, it can be used to offset the positive adjustment to produce a net adjustment of zero in that subgroup.[123] In both of these examples, the "excess" (unused) portion of the deduction increase is taken into account in the adjustment year pursuant to Regulations § 301.6225-3.[124]

This result is unsurprising in the reviewed year with respect to negative adjustments that generate net negative adjustments in a particular § 702(a) category. The allowance of negative adjustments that reduce positive adjustments in a § 702(a) category warrants a bit more explanation. This type of negative adjustment indirectly reduces the basis of the partners' interests in the partnership, a reduction that could limit the allowance of losses in other subgroups. Does that mean they should also be disregarded? Clearly not: (1) Example 1 in Regulations § 301.6225-1(h)(1) allows negative adjustments of this sort, at least to the extent of positive adjustments in the same subgroup; and (2) on a more conceptual level, the Regulations speak in terms or limitations, etc. on the deductibility of the item itself, not other items.

[d] Netting Rules

Within each subgrouping, all positive and negative adjustments for a tax year are aggregated and netted to produce a net positive or negative adjustment for that year for the subgrouping.[125] However, within a grouping, if there are positive and negative adjustments with respect to different subgroupings, they cannot be netted in determining the net positive or negative adjustment for the grouping.[126] Further, positive and negative adjustments of different groupings

---

[121] See generally ¶ 11.05[1].

[122] See Reg. § 301.6225-1(h)(1) Example 1 (determination that ordinary deduction claimed in reviewed year should be increased does not reduce imputed underpayment in reviewed year because it would not have been treated as part of the same § 702(a) item as an ordinary income increase and "might be limited if taken into account by any person"; can be taken into account in adjustment year).

[123] See Reg. § 301.6225-1(h)(2) Example 2 (same as Example 1 except increased deduction is part of same § 702(a) item as a smaller ordinary income increase; there is a net negative adjustment in this category; in the absence of other adjustments, no imputed underpayment).

[124] Example 1 explicitly acknowledges this result, Example 2 does not. There is no basis for any difference in treatment. See Reg. § 301.6625-1(f)(2).

[125] Reg. §§ 301.6225-1(e)(1), 301.6225-1(e)(2).

[126] Reg. § 301.6225-1(e)(2); see Reg. § 301.6225-1(h)(1) Example 1.

cannot be netted.[127] Adjustments for each taxable year are computed separately: Adjustments for one taxable year cannot be netted against adjustments from another.[128]

The total netted partnership adjustment is the total of the net positive adjustments in the reallocation grouping and the residual grouping. If either (or both) groupings have a net negative adjustment, it is not taken into account in computing the total netted partnership adjustment.[129]

If there is a net positive adjustment in the credit grouping, it is taken into account in computing the imputed underpayment; a net negative adjustment in this grouping is not taken into account. The only identified item in the creditable expenditure grouping is the creditable foreign tax expenditure (CFTE), which may have several subgroupings. If there is a net decrease in any CFTE subgroup, it is treated as a net positive adjustment and included in the computation of the net credit grouping adjustment; a net increase creates a net negative adjustment and is excluded from the computation of the total netted partnership adjustment.[130]

The following Examples illustrate the operation of some of these rules:

EXAMPLE 10A-1: *Computation of an imputed underpayment.* A partnership is subject to CPAR. The Service determines the following adjustments should be made for 2019: (a) ordinary income should be increased by 50x; (b) trade and business deductions should be increased by 20x; (c) long-term capital gain should be increased by 100x; short-term capital loss should be increased by 20x; (d) new markets tax credits (NMTCs) should be reduced by 10x; (e) the rehabilitation tax credit should be increased by 3x; and (f) the general foreign tax credit should be reduced by 4x. The highest rate of tax for 2019 is 40 percent. The imputed underpayment for 2019 is computed as follows:

1. There are no adjustments in the reallocation grouping.
2. In the residual grouping there is (a) a net positive adjustment of 30x in the § 702(a) ordinary income subgrouping (50x positive adjustment for additional ordinary income net of the 20x negative adjustment for additional deductions); and (b) a net positive adjustment of 100x in the long-term capital gain subgrouping (positive adjustment for increased long-term capital gain of 100x). The negative adjustment of 20x for additional capital loss is in a different subgrouping (the short-term capital gain grouping) and cannot

---

[127] Reg. § 301.6225-1(e)(2).

[128] Reg. § 301.6225-1(e)(2). See Reg. § 301.6225-1(h)(5) Example 5 (no netting between years even as part of a multi-year audit).

[129] Reg. § 301.6225-1(e)(3)(i) (penultimate sentence),

[130] Reg. § 301.6225-1(e)(3)(iii)(A).

be netted.[131] Instead, it is deferred and taken into account as a short-term capital loss in the adjustment year.[132]

3. The net positive adjustment in the residual group is 130x (30x plus 100x).

4. In the credit grouping, there are two subgroupings, with a positive adjustment of 10x in the NMTC group and a negative adjustment of 3x in the rehabilitation subgrouping. These cannot be netted so there is a preliminary net positive adjustment of 10x in the credit grouping.

5. In the creditable expenditure grouping, there is a positive adjustment of 4x, which is included in the credit grouping, so that the final net positive adjustment in the creditable expenditure grouping is 4x.

6. The total netted partnership adjustment is 130x. When this amount is multiplied by 40 percent the result is 52x, which is increased by the net positive adjustment of 10x in the credit grouping and the positive adjustment of 4x in the creditable expenditure grouping, so the imputed underpayment is 66x.[133]

EXAMPLE 10A-2: *Alternative Partner-level Computation.* If the partners in the partnership in Example 10A-1 were individuals subject to a capital gains rate of 20 percent, a rough approximation of their collective deficiency would be:

1. Increased ordinary income of 30x for an additional tax of 12x at 40 percent.

2. Additional net capital gain of 80x for an additional tax of 16x at 20 percent.

3. If credit changes are effectively netted, a net decrease in credits of 11x.

4. A total deficiency of 39x, or about one third less than the partnership imputed deficiency.

CPAR provides three ways for taxpayers to mitigate the potential impact of these draconian rules: (1) the "election out" of CPAR under § 6221(b);[134] (2) pull-in elections by partners who file amended returns (or the equivalent) to transfer imputed underpayments from the partnership to their individual re-

---

[131] Long-term and short-term losses are in separate categories under § 702(a). Therefore, the long-term gain adjustment and the short-term loss adjustment are in different subgroupings and cannot be netted even though they would be netted if recognized directly on the returns of individual or corporate partners. While dictated by the statute (§ 6225(b)(3)), there is no apparent policy basis (in terms of administrability or otherwise) for not netting these adjustments in this situation.

[132] Reg. § 301.6225-3.

[133] See Reg. § 301.6225-1(b)(1).

[134] See ¶ 10A.03.

turns as part of the modification process set forth in §§ 6225(c)(2)(A) and 6225(c)(2)(B);[135] and (3) push-out elections by partnerships to move the entire imputed underpayment from the partnership to the partners' returns.[136] Unfortunately, each of these elections comes with its own limitations and disadvantages.

[2] Modifications

[a] General

Under CPAR, the first phase of a partnership proceeding is an examination that focuses solely on adjustments to partnership-related items. There is no effort to determine how the liability or attributes of reviewed-year partners would have changed if the partnership return for the reviewed year had reflected all partnership-related items as adjusted in the examination.

Once all partnership items have been adjusted and resulting imputed underpayments have been provisionally calculated, the Service is required to include the adjustments and provisional calculations in a Notice of Proposed Partnership Adjustment (NOPPA). After a NOPPA is issued to the partnership, Regulations § 301.6225-2 provides a procedure under which the partnership representative (PR) may request that the Service modify the calculation of imputed underpayments and other partnership-related item adjustments in the NOPPA. Modifications must be requested within 270 days of the NOPPA.[137]

The focus of the modification phase is on adjusting the imputed underpayments to reflect mitigating partner-level facts—for example, giving effect to tax-exempt or corporate partners and the lower long-term capital gain rates for individuals. It is not intended (and is not supposed to be used) as an opportunity for the partnership or the partners to challenge or correct the partnership-related adjustments in the NOPPA.[138]

---

[135] See ¶¶ 10A.06[2][d][i], 10A.06[2][d][ii].

[136] See ¶ 10.08.

[137] Reg. § 301.6225-2(c)(3). The Service may grant an extension of this period and the partnership can agree to shorten it.

[138] "The statutory modification procedures are designed to allow the partnership to modify the amount of the imputed underpayment, not adjust the substance of the partnership adjustments that underlie the imputed underpayment." TD 9844, Preamble, Summary of Comments and Explanation of Provisions, 3.B.i, 84 Fed. Reg. 6468, 6487 (Feb. 27, 2019).

[b] The Modification Process

With limited exceptions, the partnership can request "any type of modification," including modification of a partnership adjustment that does not result in an underpayment (e.g., a net negative adjustment that is treated as a § 702(a) reduction in the adjustment year). However, as indicated in ¶ 10.06[2][a], the modification process is not intended to provide the partnership with an opportunity to challenge the substance of partnership adjustments that underlie the imputed underpayment, presumably because those matters were (in the view of the Service) adequately considered prior to the issuance of the NOPPA. The absence of such an opportunity effectively forces the partnership and the partners to make a variety of decisions (most prominently, pull-in and push-out decisions) prior to any judicial determination as to the validity of the proposed Service audit adjustments. Worse yet, as discussed in ¶ 10.06[2][d], partners who elect to pull in by filing amended returns may find themselves unable to claim refunds if the courts subsequently find the audit adjustments to be incorrect.

Only the PR can request a modification. Partners have no direct right to seek modification. Nevertheless, the modification process may involve requesting modifications based on partner-level facts that could reduce the imputed underpayment. In effect, the modification process is designed to recognize that imputed underpayments assume the worst-case partner-level facts. For example, if partnership adjustments increase reviewed year distributions to the partners, the default assumption is that the partners' outside bases for their interest are zero, and therefore the distribution is fully taxable. A modification request may be appropriate under Regulations § 301.6225-2(d)(10) ("other modifications") if the partners have enough outside basis to absorb some or all of the distribution under § 731.[139]

For purposes of modifications, Regulations § 301.6225-2(a) introduces the term "relevant partner." A relevant partner is any reviewed-year partner, including pass-through partners and indirect partners.[140] A modification may be requested with respect to any relevant partner. As discussed in detail in ¶ 10A.06[3], Proposed Regulations[141] would provide that the benefit of each modification will, in large measure, inure to the benefit of the partners whose non-partnership attributes give rise to the modification.

---

[139] Neither this nor any other type of modification is specifically identified in Regulations § 301.6225-2(d)(10), which speaks in general terms of any modification that the Service determines "is accurate and appropriate in accordance with" Regulations § 301.6225-2(c)(4) ("relevant information" to be provided to Service).

[140] "Pass-through partner" is defined by Regulations § 301.6241-1(a)(5), and "indirect partner" is defined by Regulations § 301.6241-1(a)(4). See Reg. § 301.6225-2(f)(1) Example 1. Disregarded entities are not relevant partners.

[141] See Prop. Reg. §§ 1.704-1(b)(2)(iii)(f) (2018), 1.6225-4(c) (2018).

The Regulations identify several specific types of modifications:

1. Modifications to take into account amended pull-in returns by relevant partners;[142]
2. Modifications to take into account partner-level adjustments under an "alternative procedure" that mimics the results of amended partner pull-in returns;[143]
3. Modifications to take into account a partner's tax-exempt status;[144]
4. Modifications based on a rate of tax lower than the highest applicable rate;[145]
5. Modifications with respect to certain passive activity losses of publicly traded partnerships;[146]
6. Modifications with respect to qualified investment entities (RICs and REITs);[147]
7. Modifications attributable to closing agreements (Reg. § 301.6225-2(d)(8));
8. Modifications to apply treaty provisions (Reg. § 301.6225-2(d)(9)); and
9. Any other modification approved by the Service.[148]

A modification may also change the number and composition of the imputed understatements included in a NOPPA.[149]

If the Service approves a modification of the tax rate applied to a partnership adjustment, the modification only affects the tax rate applied to a portion or all of the total netted partnership adjustment; it does not change the amount of the total netted partnership adjustment to which the changed rate applies.[150]

Section 6625(a)(2) provides that adjustments that do not result in an imputed understatement in a reviewed year are deferred and taken into account in the adjustment year. Regulations § 1.301.6625-2(e) allows partnerships to seek modification of such deferred adjustments pursuant to the regulatory provisions relating to the filing of amended returns by partners, the alternative procedure to the filing of amended returns, changes in the number or composition of an

---

[142] § 6225(c)(2)(A); Reg. §§ 301.6225-2(d)(2)(i)−301.6225-2(d)(2)(ix).

[143] § 6225(c)(2)(B); Reg. § 301.6225-2(d)(2)(x).

[144] § 6225(c)(3); Reg. § 301.6225-2(d)(3).

[145] § 6225(c)(4); Reg. § 301.6225-2(d)(4).

[146] § 6225(c)(5); Reg. § 301.6225-2(d)(3).

[147] Reg. § 301.6225-2(d)(7) (deficiency dividend distributions).

[148] See Reg. § 301.6225-2(d)(10).

[149] See Reg. § 301.6225-2(d)(6).

[150] Reg. § 301.6225-2(b)(3)(i); see Reg. § 301.6225-2(b)(3)(iii) (calculation of rate-modified netted partnership adjustment).

imputed underpayment, closing agreements, and any other modifications approved by the Service.

[c] Modification Requests

In the absence of an extension granted by the Service, a partnership has 270 days from the date the NOPPA is mailed to request a modification and provide all required information to support the request.[151] The Service is barred from issuing a final partnership adjustment (FPA) during this period.[152]

The Service has very broad discretion to demand information to support modification requests, to determine the amounts of modifications, and to decide when everything required to be submitted has been provided. If all information to support a modification is submitted, the information submitted supports the modification, and all other requirements are met (for example, amounts due with respect to amended returns have been paid), the Service is theoretically required to approve the modification. However, § 6225(c)(8) provides that: "Any modification of the imputed underpayment amount under this subsection shall be made only upon approval of such modification by the Secretary." This extraordinarily broad grant of authority to the Service to determine modifications may severely restrict the scope of judicial review.

[d] Pull-In Modifications

To the extent relevant partners elect to "pull-in" their shares of an imputed underpayment, the partnership-level imputed underpayment is recomputed by excluding the electing partners' shares of the partnership adjustment. The requirements to implement the pull-in procedure are stringent. Within 270 days of the issuance of the NOPPA: (1) each electing partner must file amended returns ("compliant returns") for the reviewed year and all other affected years;[153] (2) the compliant returns must take into account all changes in partnership-related items as set forth in the NOPPA;[154] and (3) each electing partner must pay all tax, penalties, additions to tax, and interest due on the

---

[151] § 6225(c)(7); Reg. § 301.6225-2(c)(3). This period may be extended by mutual agreement, Reg. § 301.6225-2(c)(3)(ii), or shortened with the partnership's consent, Reg. § 301.6225-2(c)(3)(iii).

[152] § 6231(b)(2).

[153] Reg. §§ 301.6225-2(d)(2)(ii)(B), 301.6225-2(d)(2)(iii). These amended returns can be filed regardless of whether the statute of limitations under §§ 6511 and 7422 has otherwise run. § 6225(c)(2)(D); Reg. § 301.6225-2(d)(2)(iv).

[154] Changes in non-partnership items are not permitted. Reg. § 301.6225-2(d)(2) (second sentence).

compliant returns.[155] Generally, any relevant partner can determine independently whether to file compliant returns; however, if the modification relates to a "reallocation adjustment," all partners affected by the adjustment must elect to pull-in and participate fully.[156]

The Code and Regulations also provide an "alternative procedure" to filing full-blown amended returns. The effect of the alternative procedure is to change the same items and require the same payments as the amended return procedure.[157]

[i] **Adjustments to be taken into account.** With regard to exactly what is to be "taken into account" by electing partners on their compliant returns, § 6225(c)(2)(A)(ii) simply requires the returns to "take into account all adjustments ... properly allocable to such partners (and the effect of such adjustments on any tax attributes) ...."[158] Neither the rules or the examples in the relevant Regulations add anything meaningful to this explanation.[159] However, the overall sense of the pull-in scheme is to impose the same tax on the electing partners that they would have paid if their original K-1s had included their shares of the adjustments set forth in the NOPPA. In the words of the 2019 Preamble to this part of the Regulations:

> [T]he amended return procedure and the alternative procedure to filing amended returns provide an opportunity for the partnership to request modification to reflect how an item was actually taken into account by its partners and to account for offsetting reductions permitted under generally applicable law. *When a partner files an amended return including his share of the partnership adjustments, the amended return reflects a tax amount based on how the partner originally reported the partnership-related item prior to adjustment compared to how the partnership adjustment affects the partner's original return. This tax amount is the correct amount of tax for that partner after taking into account the partnership adjustment and includes any allowable reductions that may offset any additional income determined at the partnership level.*[160]

To achieve the results contemplated by the Preamble, the gross partnership adjustment must be pulled apart on as granular a level as is needed to preserve the nature and character of each component of the adjustment. While the

---

[155] § 6225(c)(2)(A); Reg. §§ 301.6225-2(d)(2), 301.6225-2(f)(2) Example 2, 301.6225-2(f)(6) Example 6.

[156] 6225(c)(2)(C); Reg. § 301.6225-2(d)(2)(ii)(C). See generally ¶ 10A.06[1][a].

[157] § 6225(c)(2)(B); Reg. § 301.6225-2(d)(2)(x). See ¶ 10A.06[2][e][i].

[158] A "tax attribute" is anything that can affect the amount or timing of a partnership-related item or the amount of tax due for any year. Reg. § 301.6241-1(a)(10).

[159] Reg. §§ 301.6225-2(d)(2), 301.6225-2(f).

[160] TD 9844, Preamble, Summary of Comments and Explanation of Revisions 3.B.i, 84 FR 6468, 6487 (Feb. 27, 2019) (emphasis added).

CPAR Regulations are silent on this point, a reasonable reference point for this process would be the well-developed and familiar "separately stated item" concept in § 702(a), which requires a large number of specific items of partnership income, gain, loss, deduction, and credit to be segregated and included as separate items on the returns of the partners.[161] Thus, for example, assume a NOPPA issued to the *ABCD* partnership asserts an imputed underpayment of $400, based on a net positive partnership adjustment of $1,000. The adjustment includes an increase in long-term capital gain of $300, an increase in short-term capital gain of $200, a decrease in § 179 deductions of $360, and a decrease in cash charitable contribution deductions of $140. Partner *A* elects to pull in her 25 percent share of the $1,000 adjustment. The *ABCD* partnership's adjustment is reduced from $1,000 to $750, its imputed underpayment is reduced from $400 to $300, and *A*'s amended return should reflect a $75 increase in the long-term capital gain previously reported, a $50 increase in the short-term capital gain, a $90 decrease in her § 179 deduction, and a $35 decrease in her cash charitable contribution.

[ii] Penalties, additions to tax, and additional amounts. For purposes of filing a compliant amended return, penalties, additions to tax, and additional amounts are determined at the partnership level. The actual amount of penalties, additions to tax, and additional amounts that a partner must pay with its amended returns is based on the underpayment or understatement of tax reflected on the partner's amended returns.[162] Echoing the TEFRA rules articulated in *United States v. Woods*,[163] the Regulations affirm that the amending partner can raise partner-level penalty defenses after filing the amended return by paying the penalty, addition to tax, or additional amount and thereafter filing a refund claim asserting partner-level defenses.

[iii] Planning pull-in elections. "Pull-in" modifications shift the burden of adjustments to the partners who were partners in the reviewed year (as opposed to the adjustment year) and eliminate items included in the amended returns (or covered by the alternative procedure) from the calculation of the partnership imputed underpayment. Proposed Regulations[164] would allocate the benefits of this reduction to the pull-in partners, as discussed in ¶ 10A.06[3].

---

[161] See generally ¶ 9.01[3]. There are six types of items explicitly specified in §§ 702(a)(1) through 702(a)(6), a catch-all category in § 702(a)(7) of "other items" as set forth in the Regulations, and a residual category, consisting of all items that are not accorded any special treatment under the Code, that has come to be known as "bottom line" taxable income or loss, in § 702(a)(8). The list of separately stated items created by the Regulations under § 702(a)(7) is extensive and always expanding as the complexity of the Code increases.

[162] Reg. § 301.6225-2(d)(2)(viii).

[163] United States v. Woods, 571 US 31 (2013) (TEFRA case).

[164] Prop. Reg. §§ 1.704-1(b)(2)(iii)(f) (2018), 1.6225-4(c) (2018).

However, possible concerns about the creditworthiness of the partnership in the adjustment year (the imputed underpayment plus interest and penalties may leave the partnership's assets insufficient to satisfy the economic entitlement of the pull-in partners) may make some partners wary of using the pull-in election.

The most significant problem with pull-ins is that the process may deprive pull-in partners of any opportunity to challenge the substance of the adjustments set forth in the NOPPA.[165] The amended returns filed by pull-in partners are required to reflect the adjustments set forth in the NOPPA.[166] The partnership, but not any partner, has the right to contest the substance of the adjustments set forth in the final partnership adjustment (FPA) based on the NOPPA by filing a petition for readjustment in any of the usual three courts within ninety days of the mailing of the FPA.[167] The Regulations generally provide that an "FPA will include the amount of any imputed underpayment, as modified under § 301.6225-2 if applicable ...."[168] All modifications are subject to approval by the Service.[169] If the Service has approved modifications relating to amended pull-in returns, such modifications should be given effect under the FPA, which should only reflect the modified balance of the imputed underpayment reflected in the NOPPA. If the partnership successfully contests the substance of the adjustments underlying the balance of the imputed underpayment in a court proceeding, the court decision will necessarily be limited to the balance of the imputed underpayment and will only affect the partnership, which is the only party over whom the court has jurisdiction. The pull-in partners' ability to share in the partnership's victory will be dependent on their ability to file refund claims for the *reviewed* tax years, the years of their pull-in returns.

Unfortunately, the existing Regulations create a series of obstacles for pull-in partners seeking refunds reflecting the partnership's victory. Consider the following example:

EXAMPLE 10A-3: *PRST* has four equal partners. It receives a NOPPA that asserts a $1 million imputed underpayment. Three of the four partners file approved pull-in returns and pay their shares of taxes, including penalties and interest, based on 75 percent of the adjustments underlying the imputed underpayment. There are no other approved modifications. An FPA is issued relating to the remaining 25 percent ($250,000) of the

---

[165] See ¶ 10A.06[2][b]; TD 9844, Supplementary Information, Summary of Comments and Explanation of Revisions, 3.B.i, 84 Fed. Reg. 6468, 6487 (Feb. 27, 2019).

[166] § 6225(c)(2)(A); Reg. § 301.6225-2(d)(2); see Reg. §§ 301.6225-2(f)(2) Example 2, 301.6225-2(f)(6) Example 6.

[167] § 6234(a); Reg. § 301.6234-1(a).

[168] Reg. § 301.6225-1(a)(2).

[169] Reg. § 301.6225-2(b)(1).

NOPPA adjustments. *PRST* contests the substance of the proposed adjustments in the Tax Court and is partially vindicated by a decision eliminating 90 percent of the imputed understatement. The Tax Court has no jurisdiction over the partners, only the partnership, and the Tax Court decision is limited to 25 percent of the contested adjustments included in the modified imputed underpayment.

Conceptually, it would make sense for pull-in partners to automatically receive refunds (including interest) to the extent the amounts they paid in connection with their amended returns would be reduced by any subsequent court decision favorable to the partnership. Unfortunately, neither the Code nor the Regulations contains any hint of the existence of any such automatic refund process for pull-in partners.

Therefore, it appears the pull-in partners must act affirmatively to file refund claims based on a partnership-favorable decision. Do they have the right to further amend their pull-in amended returns to claim such refunds? Regulations § 301.6225-2(d)(2)(vii)(B) speaks directly to this question. This Regulation states generally that a pull-in partner who has filed an approved amended return or satisfied the alternative procedure "may not file a subsequent amended return or claim for refund to change the treatment of partnership adjustments taken into account through amended return or the alternate procedure" except as otherwise described in Regulations § 301.6225-2(d)(2)(vii)(C). It is not difficult to understand the purpose and need for this general prohibition. The Service relied on the original pull-in return to approve modification of the partnership's imputed understatement. It would make mockery of the entire modification process to allow pull-in partners to file amendments in most cases.

Turning expectantly to the exception in Regulations § 301.6225-2(d)(2)(vii)(C), we find that it provides that a pull-in partner may file "a subsequent return or claim for refund if a determination is made by a court or by the IRS that results in a change to the partnership adjustments taken into account in modification ... or a denial of modification by the IRS ...." There has been no "denial of modification" in the situation at hand, so the relevant language is "a change to the partnership adjustments taken into account in modification." While this language may seem a bit opaque, it apparently is intended to refer to the "partnership adjustments" underlying the imputed understatement to the extent they have been taken into account in the modification process. In the situation at hand, that would seem to include the modifications related to the filing of the pull-in returns. This interpretation is confirmed by the Preamble to these Regulations, which states that

> the final regulations under §301.6225-2(d)(2)(vii) now clarify that *partners* may file additional amended returns with respect to *partnership adjustments or imputed underpayments*, including in the case of denied modification or *court readjustment*. To file a subsequent amended return, the

partners must do so in accordance with forms, instructions, and other guidance prescribed by the IRS.[170]

Based on this part of the Preamble, it seems that pull-in partners have the right to file amended returns and claim refunds based on subsequent favorable court decisions (or Service concessions). However, it is clear that any amended returns by pull-in partners must comply with the generally applicable three years from filing/two years from payment statute of limitations in § 6511.[171] Pull-in returns must be filed and approved prior to the issuance of an FPA (perhaps, well in advance). Any court proceeding is unlikely to be completed within three years of the date the FPA is issued. Consequently, in the absence of an agreement to extend the statute of limitations, the statute is likely to expire before the pull-in partners can file amended return or refund claims. Perhaps the Service will routinely grant extensions to partners savvy enough to ask for them, but it would be far more sensible (and more easily administrable) for such extensions to be automatic without any action by pull-in partners under either the Code or the Regulations.

If all of the partners elect to pull-in, they may forfeit any ability to challenge the proposed adjustments.

> EXAMPLE 10A-4: Same facts as Example 10A-3, except all of the partners file approved pull-in returns. After modification, *PRST*'s imputed underpayment should be zero, and it is unclear why or whether the Service can (or should) even issue an FPA. In the absence of an FPA or a resultant court decision, there does not seem to be any basis for the pull-in partners to challenge the substantive adjustments they have been required to take into account on their amended pull-in returns.

This seems like an odd and likely unintended result. It certainly does not reflect best administrative practices or further the cause of efficient tax administration. Whether Treasury has the authority or the will to correct it is another question.

[e]　Other Modifications

[i]　Pull-in modifications: the alternative procedure. Regulations § 301.6225-2(d)(2)(x)(A) provides for a modification that produces results simi-

---

[170] TD 9844, Supplementary Information, Summary of Comments and Explanation of Revisions, 3.B.iii, 84 Fed. Reg. 6468, 6492 (Feb. 27, 2019) (emphasis added).

[171] See Reg. § 301.6225-2(d)(2)(vii)(C): "Any amended return or claim for refund filed under this paragraph (d)(2)(vii) is subject to the period of limitations under section 6511." While one might reasonably expect pull-in partners to benefit from any automatic or agreed-upon partnership-level extensions, there is no such provision in the statute or the Regulations.

lar to the amended return procedure. A major drawback of this alternative procedure is that it does not allow participating partners to obtain refunds in the event of a subsequent favorable result in a judicial proceeding.[172] The alternative procedure will be implemented by to-be-issued forms, instructions, and guidance that are intended to apply partnership adjustments to relevant partners without the requirement that they file full-blown amended returns. The Preamble to the Regulations makes it clear that use of the alternative procedure should not create any meaningful differences (other than the lack of refund rights) compared to filing an amended return.[173]

[ii] **Modifications with respect to tax-exempt partners.** A partnership may request a modification that recomputes an imputed underpayment (as set out in the NOPPA) by eliminating the shares of adjustments that are allocable to relevant tax-exempt partners.[174]

[iii] **Modifications based on less-than-the-highest applicable tax rate.** Unless modified, the rate of tax applied in determining an imputed understatement is the highest rate in effect under § 1 or § 11.[175] Consequently, under current law, to the extent any portion of an understatement is allocable to corporate partners, significant reductions of the partnership tax should be available through a rate-based modification request. This reduction should be more or less automatic; hopefully, the extraordinary level of discretion afforded the Service in the modification procedures, coupled with the apparent lack of effective judicial review of these procedures, will not lead to abuses, subtle or otherwise.[176] The Regulations also provide for the application of lower tax rates that apply to certain types of income (specifically, capital gains and qualified dividends of individuals).[177]

---

[172] See TD 9844, Supplementary Information, Summary of Comments and Explanation of Revisions, 3.B.iv, 84 Fed. Reg. 6468, 6496 (Feb. 27, 2019).

[173] TD 9844, Supplementary Information, Summary of Comments and Explanation of Revisions, 3.B.iv, 84 Fed. Reg. 6468, 6495−6496 (Feb. 27, 2019).

[174] § 6225(c)(3); Reg. § 301.6225-2(d)(3). To the extent a tax-exempt partner's share of the adjustment would be unrelated business taxable income to the partner, it is excluded from the modification amount. See Reg. §§ 301.6225-2(f)(3) Example 3, 301.6225-2(f)(4) Example 4.

[175] § 6225(c)(4); Reg. § 301.6225-2(d)(4).

[176] "Power tends to corrupt, and absolute power corrupts absolutely." Attributed to Lord Acton, British historian (1834−1902).

[177] Reg. § 301.6225-2(d)(4). Regulations § 301.6225-2(f)(7) Example 7 involves a positive adjustment of long-term capital gain income to an individual partner and computes an underpayment based on the "standard" highest rate used in these examples rather than a lower capital gain rate. Hopefully, this aspect of the Example simply reflects a failure of the modification request to ask for a rate reduction with respect to this item.

If an imputed underpayment is modified as a result of both pull-in elections and a rate reduction, it seems obvious that the modified rate reduction should reflect the rates of only the partners who do not pull in.

> **EXAMPLE 10A-5:** Same facts as Example 10A-3, except that all of the pull-in partners are corporations and the only partner who does not pull in is an individual. The modified rate should not reflect the corporate rate.

A similar approach should apply if there are tax-exempt partners.

[iv] Modification of number and composition of imputed underpayments. The ability to request changes in the composition of a grouping, or to create or change the composition of a subgrouping, may be especially helpful because such modifications may make it easier to modify imputed underpayments to align more closely with the terms of the partnership agreement or partner-level factors.[178]

Even if the partnership expects to elect under § 6226 to push out all adjustments, requesting a modification that adds or tailors subgroups may be helpful because the § 6226 push-out election can be made separately for each imputed underpayment.[179]

[v] Other modifications. The statute also provides for modifications with respect to certain passive losses of publicly traded partnerships[180] and "such other factors as the Secretary determines."[181] The Regulations exercise this grant of authority to create additional categories of modifications with respect to (1) partners that are qualified investment entities to account for deficiency dividends under § 860,[182] (2) any closing agreements that have been entered into by the partnership or any relevant partners,[183] (3) treaty provisions,[184] and (4) any other type of modification requested by the partnership or prescribed by the Service in other guidance.[185]

[f] Pull-Ins Involving Pass-Through Partners and Indirect Partners

Partnerships can obtain modifications related to amended returns (or alternative procedure filings) filed by indirect partners that could be taxed on a

---

[178] Reg. §§ 301.6225-2(d)(6), Reg. §§ 301.6225-2(f)(7) Example 7.

[179] Reg. § 301.6226-1(c)(3)(ii)(D).

[180] § 6225(c)(5).

[181] § 6225(c)(6).

[182] Reg. § 301.6225-2(d)(7).

[183] Reg. § 301.6225-2(d)(8).

[184] Reg. § 301.6225-2(d)(9).

[185] Reg. § 301.6225-2(d)(10). The Service has broad discretion to refuse partnership requests for modifications.

share of the partnership's adjustments if either (1) the partnership establishes that the pass-through partner through which the indirect partners holds its interest is not subject to income tax on the adjustments allocated to it, or (2) the partnership requests modification for the imputed underpayment allocable to the pass-through partner, including full payment of all income taxes for the first affected year and all modification years.[186] Solely for purposes of modification, any relevant partner that is a pass-through partner and that has elected out of CPAR under § 6221(b) may take into account its share of partnership adjustments and pay an amount calculated in the same way as an imputed underpayment.[187] The procedures for this election have yet to be established, but the objective is to compute an imputed underpayment at the pass-through partner level by adjusting the pass-through partner's return for the reviewed year. Under yet-to-be-established procedures, a pass-through partner may take into account modifications with respect to its direct and indirect partners.[188]

If a partnership expects to elect under § 6226 to push out a partnership adjustment to its reviewed-year partners, it generally will be important for each pass-through partner of the audited partnership to seek modifications with respect to any of its partners who are indirect partners of the audited partnership. A pass-through partner has no ability to obtain modifications to reduce any adjustment pushed to it under § 6226.

[g] Final Partnership Adjustments Notices

The Service has yet to publish a standard form of FPA notice. In most ways, because CPAR generally views the partnership as the taxpayer, an FPA is likely to resemble the typical statutory deficiency notice for other categories of taxpayers, rather than the old form of TEFRA notice. While the obvious starting point for preparation of a specific FPA is the NOPPA that preceded it, a cluster of major unresolved substantive issues revolve around how (and whether) the modification process will be reflected in the notice. It seems that most agreed-upon modifications should be reflected in the FPA, in part to minimize duplication of efforts by both the Service and taxpayers. In that case:

1. Pull-in adjustments should be taken into account so that the FPA reflects the net amount of each partnership item adjustment after giving effect to all pull-ins by relevant partners;
2. The net amount of each partnership item adjustment should be adjusted to reflect the shares of all tax-exempt partners;
3. Modifications with respect to certain passive activity losses of publicly traded partnerships, qualified investment entities, closing agree-

---

[186] Reg. § 301.6225-2(d)(2)(v).
[187] Reg. § 301.6225-2(d)(2)(vi)(A).
[188] Reg. § 301.6225-2(d)(2)(vi)(B).

ments, treaty provisions, and any other modification approved by the Service should be given effect on an item-by-item basis as appropriate;

4. The very nature of reallocation modifications generally precludes any net impact on the aggregate amount of any partnership item.[189] They may, however, impact the modified tax rate used in computing an imputed understatement if the reallocation moves income between partners in different taxpayer classes and the Service agrees it is appropriate to take rate differences into account in computing the imputed understatement, as discussed in item 5 below. How these matters may be reflected in an FPA is presently unclear.

5. Modifications relating to applicable tax rates for specific classes of partners or types of income, loss, or credit obviously cannot directly affect the aggregate amount of any item adjustment. To the extent partnership requests for such modifications are agreeable to the Service, there is no apparent need to repeat this process and the FPA should take such agreed-rate modifications into account in determining the imputed underpayment reflected in the FPA.

Whether the Service will choose an approach reasonably similar to the one suggested above is currently unclear.

[h] Judicial Review of Modifications

Inconsistencies in the statute create uncertainty as to the likely scope of judicial review of the Service's modification determinations. The text of § 6225(c)(1) mandates that the Service establish procedures for the modification of imputed understatements "consistent with the requirements" of § 6225(c).[190] Several subparagraphs in § 6225(c) contain imperative statements requiring that such procedures "shall provide" specific rules for specific situations.[191] However, § 6225(c)(8) generally provides that "[a]ny modification of an imputed underpayment amount under this subsection shall be made only upon approval of such modification by the Secretary."

Section 6234(c) gives jurisdiction to the courts to "determine all partnership-related items ..., the proper allocation of such items among the partners, and the applicability of any penalty, addition to tax, or additional amount for which the partnership may be liable ...." Arguably this means the courts have jurisdiction to review and redetermine the propriety and amount of the modifications to be taken into account in computing the imputed underpayment. Sec-

---

[189] See § 6225(c)(2)(C).

[190] See also § 6225(c)(9) (procedures to be established for adjustments that do not create an imputed underpayment).

[191] See, e.g., §§ 6225(c)(2)(A), 6225(c)(2)(B), 6225(c)(3), 6225(c)(4), 6225(c)(5).

tion 6225(c)(8), however, suggests that the task before a reviewing court may not be a conventional de novo review of a requested modification, but rather a review of whether the Service abused its discretion in addressing the requested modifications. If the courts adopt an "abuse of discretion" approach, such questions as whether the partnership representative provided all required information to the Service in the modification process may be relevant.

If the courts decide to limit their review of modifications under the "abuse of discretion" standard, partners may be able to obtain a more thorough review by either (1) claiming modifications using either amended pull-in returns or the alternative procedure, or (2) electing to "push out" partnership-related item adjustments under § 6226.[192] Under either of these approaches, the determination of the effect of partnership-level adjustments on each reviewed-year partner is made at the partner level. Normal deficiency procedures and judicial review rights apply in resolving disagreements about how changes made in the CPAR proceeding interact with partner-level items.[193]

[3] Partner Allocations

The payment of an imputed underpayment has an economic effect on the partnership and reduces both the partnership's basis in its assets and the partners' bases in their interests under § 705(b)(2)(B), even though the payment is not a deductible expense.[194] Similarly, if an imputed underpayment results in partnership withholding obligations under § 1446, the withheld amounts are not deductible. However, the portion of the imputed underpayment allocable to foreign partners is applied to the partnership's withholding obligation.[195]

The imputed underpayment rules under CPAR are unique not only in terms of the collection point (the partnership, not the partners, under the default rule in § 6225) but also in terms of the potential economic inequities that can arise as a direct consequence of that collection point. The tax is imposed on the partnership for the "adjustment year," a year that is likely to be many

---

[192] See ¶ 10A.08.

[193] A pull-in partner is required to pay a portion of the tax resulting from partnership-related item adjustments before they are final. A subsequent determination that the partner has overpaid will require a refund claim that generally must be filed within two years of the time the payment is made or within three years of the time the return is filed, whichever is later. See § 6511(a). The partner's own statute (not the partnership's) must be open to make the refund claim so the protections normally afforded by § 6511(c) in connection with agreements to extend the statute may not be helpful. If a partner's statute has run, a determination that he or she overpaid will be a Pyrrhic victory. Reg. § 301.6225-2(d)(2)(vii)(C). See generally ¶ 10A.06[2][d][iii].

[194] Reg. § 301.6241-4(a).

[195] Reg. § 301.6241-6(b)(3).

years after the reviewed year. The reviewed-year partners, not the adjust-ment-year partners, bear the benefits (or burdens) of the events that transpired during the reviewed year; were responsible for the manner in which those events were reported on the tax return for the reviewed year; and were liable for payment of their shares of the taxes on the income (or reaped the benefits of the losses) reported on such return. However, the reviewed-year partners do not bear the consequences of their actions (i.e., the reviewed year imputed un-derpayment) unless they happen to still be partners in the adjustment year. The most extreme illustration of this disconnect and the potential unfairness created by it is a situation in which there is a 100 percent change in the ownership of the partnership between the reviewed year and the adjustment year, so that whatever deficiencies were created by the reviewed-year partners will be borne entirely by the adjustment-year partners.

As discussed below, there are some opportunities for self-help on the part of the adjustment-year partners. One is to cause the partnership to make a push-out election under § 6226 to push the partnership adjustments to the re-viewed-year partners. This is a potentially perfect solution to resolve any un-fairness between the adjustment year and the reviewed-year partners, but has its own costs and disadvantages, as discussed in ¶ 10A.08. Another is the use of reimbursement and similar contract provisions in connection with any trans-actions that shift the interests of partners in CPAR partnerships, so that re-viewed-year partners will be contractually obligated to reimburse their successors for the costs of their shares of any future imputed underpayments relating to reviewed years. Again, a potentially perfect solution, but one that requires perfect foresight, relatively sophisticated professional advice, and comprehensive management of solvency risks to protect the adjustment-year partners.

Despite the obvious culpability of the reviewed-year partners, the statute makes no attempt to address any aspect of this situation. This failure creates a large vacuum to be filled by the Treasury with Regulations, a process that be-gan with the issuance of Proposed Regulations in 2018.[196] The 2018 proposals will create a complex, technically elegant, and fundamentally sound interface between the primary CPAR adjustment and payment rules in §§ 6225 and 6226 and the existing § 705 basis rules,[197] as well as the partnership allocation rules in § 704(b) (the "substantial economic effect" rules) and § 704(c) (con-

---

[196] Notice of Proposed Rulemaking, REG-118067-17, 83 Fed. Reg. 4868 (Feb. 2, 2018) (with conforming changes in Aug. 2018). These Proposed Regulations attempt to effectuate the policy identified in the 2015 Bluebook, which states that the "flowthrough nature of the partnership under subchapter K of the Code is unchanged, but the partner-ship is treated as a point of collection of underpayments that would otherwise be the re-sponsibility of partners." Joint Comm. on Taxation, JCS-1-16, General Explanation of Tax Legislation Enacted in 2015, at 57 (2016), as quoted in the Preamble to REG-118067-17.

[197] See generally Chapter 6.

tributed properties).[198] Much of the complexity arises not from the interface it-self but from the details of the audit, payment, and substantive Subchapter K provisions it is designed to intermediate.

When adopted, the proposals will be retroactively effective and apply to all tax years subject to CPAR (generally tax years beginning after 2017). The thoughtfulness and soundness of the proposals, as well as the lack of critical substantive comments following their publication, makes it highly likely they will eventually be adopted in substantially the form proposed. Accordingly, practitioners should begin the process of amending existing partnership agree-ments to eliminate conflicts with the proposals and should incorporate them into all agreements for new partnerships that anticipate being subject to CPAR.[199]

The proposed interface reflects three foundational policy decisions by the drafters:

1. One is adoption of the basic goal to assure that the economic burden of any reviewed-year adjustments will fall on the reviewed-year part-ners, to the extent possible within the statutory framework. The 2018 Proposed Regulations expand this notion to include not only the re-viewed-year partners but also their "successors," as defined in some detail in the Proposed Regulations. This means, among other things, that anyone involved in structuring or documenting transactions that change the interests of partners in CPAR partnerships should be aware of the shifting of potential tax liabilities from reviewed-year partners to their successors and should, to the extent possible, docu-ment the agreement of the parties if it deviates from the results that would otherwise occur under the proposals. Most obviously, if the buyer of an interest in a CPAR partnership does not want to assume its seller's share of the tax consequences of ongoing *or future* tax au-dits, it should insist on including reimbursement rights in the purchase documentation.[200]

   The need for this kind of protection will be relatively obvious if there is an ongoing partnership audit. However, the lack of an ongo-ing audit does not eliminate the need for buyers to protect themselves contractually: A CPAR Examination Notice could be in the mail at any time as long as the statute of limitations is open for pre-transfer partnership tax years.

---

[198] See generally Chapter 11.

[199] See R. Whitmire, W. Nelson & W. McKee, Structuring and Drafting Partnership Agreements: Including LLC Agreements ¶ 2.10 (Thomson Reuters/Tax & Accounting, 3d ed. 2003).

[200] See Prop. Reg. § 301.6225-4(e) Example 3 (2018).

2. The second policy decision is to create "notional adjustments" that are layered onto the § 704 allocation rules to allocate adjustments to the partners' tax attributes. These rules were inspired by, and are similar to, the tax-only notional item provisions already in use under the § 704(c) remedial allocation method.[201] As is the case under § 704(c), these types of notional adjustments generally have the best chance of getting mathematically correct results without regard to specific future events.

3. Finally, subject to future comments, Treasury made a policy decision that not all partnership adjustment should be taken into account under the proposal. Instead, only "specified tax attributes" are adjusted. The list of attributes to be adjusted is "basis-centric" in the sense that it includes only adjustments relating to the tax basis and book value of partnership property, amounts determined under § 704(c), adjustment-year partners' bases in their partnership interests, and adjustment-year partners' capital accounts as determined and maintained in accordance with Regulations § 1.704-1(b)(2).[202]

[a] Successors Defined

The Proposed Regulations recognize that the reviewed-year partners (and their successors) should bear the net economic cost of any tax changes flowing from reviewed-year adjustments. To implement this, the Proposed Regulations provide an elaborate definition of "successor" partners:[203]

1. An "identifiable transferee partner" is a transferee of all or a portion of a reviewed-year partner's interest to the extent the transferor's capital carries over (or would carry over if the partnership maintained capital account) to the transferee.

2. If, after exercising reasonable diligence, the partnership cannot identify an identifiable transferee, each partner in the adjustment year that is not an identifiable transferee partner or a reviewed-year partner is an unidentifiable transferee partner "to the extent of the portion of its interest in the partnership to the total interests of unidentifiable transferee partners in the partnership."[204]

3. If a partner's entire reviewed-year interest is liquidated during or following the reviewed year, the successors to the liquidated interest are

---

[201] See Reg. § 1.704-3(d), discussed in ¶ 11.06[3][b].

[202] Prop. Reg. § 301.6225-4(a)(2) (2018).

[203] Prop. Reg. § 1.704-1(b)(1)(viii)(*b*) (2018).

[204] Prop. Reg. § 1.704-1(b)(1)(viii)(*b*)(*3*) (2018). This permission will be of great comfort to publicly traded partnerships.

those adjustment-year partners whose interests increase as a result of the liquidating distribution.

4. In the event of a transfer or liquidation of an interest after the reviewed year, "successors" means any identifiable transferee partner, any unidentifiable transferee partner, and any successor to a liquidated interest, as well as all of their subsequent transferees.

5. If there are subsequent transfers of a successor's interest, the same principles apply to all new successors.[205]

[b] Notional Adjustments

[i] No imputed underpayment. If a partnership adjustment does not create an imputed underpayment, partnership adjustments are implemented by the partnership in accordance with the prevailing rules of Subchapter K.[206] For instance, if a partnership adjustment results in a reduction in income during a reviewed year, that reduction adjusts the partnership's § 702 income in the adjustment year.[207] The allocation of the adjustment does not have substantial economic effect under the § 704(b) Regulations, but will be deemed to be in accordance with the partners' interests in the partnership if it is allocated in the manner in which the item would have been allocated in the reviewed year, treating successor partners as reviewed-year partners (assuming such reviewed-year allocation would have had substantial economic effect).[208]

[ii] Imputed underpayment. Similar concepts apply in the case of adjustments that lead to imputed underpayments. However, because an imputed underpayment effectively blocks the flow-through of some or all of the adjusted items, the 2018 Proposed Regulations create notional items of income, gain, loss, deduction, or credit in the adjustment year[209] to adjust "specified tax attributes" of the partnership and partners to reflect the blocked adjusted items.[210] Specified tax attributes are (1) the tax basis and book value of partnership property; (2) any amounts determined under § 704(c); (3) the adjust-

---

[205] Prop. Reg. § 1.704-1(b)(1)(viii)(*b*)(*1*) (2018).

[206] Reg. § 301.6225-3.

[207] Reg. § 301.6225-3(b).

[208] Prop. Reg. § 1.704-1(b)(4)(xiii) (2018).

[209] Prop. Reg. § 301.6225-4(b)(3) (2018).

[210] Prop. Reg. § 301.6225-4(a)(3) (2018). The impact of each partnership adjustment (whether positive or negative) is evaluated separately. See Prop. Reg. § 301.6225-4(b)(1) (2018). If the creation of a notional item is inappropriate (say, in the event of a partner's failure to report a § 731 distribution), some specified tax attributes can be adjusted without notional items. Prop. Reg. §§ 301.6225-4(b)(4), 1.704-1(b)(2)(iii)(*f*)(*4*) (2018).

ment-year partners' bases in their partnership interests;[211] and (4) the adjustment-year partners' § 704(b) capital accounts.[212]

Notional items (which can be positive or negative, as appropriate) created under the Proposed Regulations impact only these specified tax attributes and are otherwise disregarded for purposes of Subchapter K.[213] Any allocation of these notional items necessarily would lack economic effect, but an allocation of such items will be deemed to be in accordance with the partners' interests in the partnership if made in the manner that the underlying item would have been allocated in the reviewed year, taking successor partners into account as if they held their partnership interests during the reviewed year.[214]

> **EXAMPLE 10A-6 (No Modifications):**[215] The *ABC* partnership has three equal partners. *A* contributes unimproved land Whiteacre with a value of $1,000 and a basis of $400. *B* and *C* each contribute $1,000 cash. *ABC* buys Asset for $120 and deducts the entire purchase price. The Service disallows the deduction, creating a $120 imputed understatement for the reviewed year. *ABC* does not seek modification and pays the resultant $48 (40 percent of $120) imputed underpayment in the adjustment year.
>
> Payment of the imputed underpayment blocks the increases in income and the increases to the book value and basis of Asset that would otherwise result from the disallowance. To replicate these missing adjustments, notional items of income ($120 under Proposed Regulations § 301.6225-4(b)(3) (2018)) and notional increases in the basis and book value of Asset ($120) under Proposed Regulations § 301.6225-4(b)(2) (2018) are created, allocated equally to the partners, and deemed to be in accordance with their interest in the partnership under Proposed Regula-

---

[211] A notional item cannot reduce a partner's outside basis below zero. Prop. Reg. § 301.6225-4(b)(6)(iii)(A) (2018). Prop. Reg. § 301.6225-4(b)(6)(iii)(B) (2018) prevents outside basis adjustments in two very specific situations: (1) a partner that is not tax-exempt is the successor to a tax-exempt partner for whom the Service has approved a rate modification; and (2) a successor partner acquires its interest from a related (under § 267(b) or § 707(b)) reviewed-year partner in a transaction or transactions in which all gain or loss was not recognized if a principal purpose of the transfer is to shift the burden of the imputed underpayment among the related parties.

[212] Prop. Reg. § 301.6225-4(a)(2) (2018). No basis adjustments are made with respect to partnership property held in the reviewed year but no longer held in the adjustment year. Prop. Reg. § 1.6225-4(b)(2) (2018). This rule can lead to distortions between the partnership's inside basis and the aggregate of the partners' outside bases, which potentially can be cured by having the partnership make a § 754 election and transferring partners' interests in nonrecognition transactions. See ¶ 24.04[1][b].

[213] Notice of Proposed Rulemaking, REG-118067-17, 83 Fed. Reg. 4868 (Feb. 2, 2018), Explanation of Provisions. 2.B.ii.

[214] Prop. Reg. § 1.704-1(b)(4)(xi) (2018).

[215] See Prop. Reg. § 301.6225-4(e) Example 1 (2018). Example 10A-7 in ¶ 10A.06[3][c] illustrates the impact of modifications on the allocation of imputed underpayment expenditures among the partners.

tions § 1.704-1(b)(4)(xi) (2018). The capital account and the outside basis of each partner is increased by its share ($40 each) of the notional adjustments under Proposed Regulations §§ 301.6225-4(b)(6)(ii) and 301.6225-4(b)(6)(iii)(A) (2018).[216]

The $48 imputed underpayment by *ABC* is a nondeductible expenditure under § 705(b)(1)(B). It is allocated among the partners in the same proportions as the notional income item to which it relates ($16, or one third each) and this allocation is deemed to be in accordance with the partners' interests in the partnership pursuant to Proposed Regulations § 1.704-1(b)(4)(ii)(2018). This payment is also reflected in equal decreases in the capital accounts and outside bases of the partners under Proposed Regulations § 1.704-1(b)(4)(xii) (2018). All of these adjustments occur in the adjustment year.

Notional items are not created for all partnership adjustments; for example, notional items are not created for adjustments related to § 705(a)(2)(B) expenditures, tax-exempt income, or items that would not have been allocated under § 704(b).[217] If a partnership adjustment involves a change in a credit, related notional items of income, gain, loss, or deduction may be created.[218]

[c] Allocations of Tax Expenditures

Under CPAR, expenditures for taxes and related items (interest, penalties, additions to tax, and additional amounts) are, in the absence of an election to the contrary, paid by the partnership for the adjustment year.[219] These expenditures are nondeductible but must be taken into account and allocated among the partners in the adjustment year pursuant to § 704(b).[220] They reduce the partners' § 704(b) capital accounts and the bases of their partnership interests under § 705(a)(2)(B). Some or all of potential partnership tax expenditures may be shifted to the reviewed-year partners as a consequence of pull-in elections by partners pursuant to § 6225 or push-out elections by partnerships pursuant to § 6226.

Partnership expenditures for imputed underpayments do not create notional items. They are taken into account in the adjustment year as § 705(a)(2)(B) expenditures but must be allocated among the reviewed-year partners (or their successors) in proportion to the manner in which such partners were allocated the notional items related to the underpayment, taking into ac-

---

[216] There are several obvious typographical errors in the cross references in the current version of Example 1.

[217] Prop. Reg. § 301.6225-4(b)(4) (2018).

[218] Prop. Reg. § 301.6225-4(b)(3)(vi) (2018).

[219] § 6225(a)(1).

[220] Prop. Reg. § 301.6225-4(c) (2018).

count any modifications to the underpayment amount approved by the Service.[221]

>**EXAMPLE 10A-7 (Modifications):**[222] The facts with respect to the *ABC* partnership are the same as in Example 10A-6, except the Service approves rate modifications with regard to partner *A*, a tax-exempt entity, and partner *C*, a corporation subject to a tax rate of 35 percent. The pre-modification imputed underpayment is $48 (40 percent of $120). The modifications approved by the Service reduce the imputed underpayment to $30 ($16 with respect to *B*'s $40 of increased income, $14 with respect to *C*'s $40 of increased income, and $0 with respect to *A*'s $40 of increased income).
>
>The underlying partnership adjustment in unaffected by the rate modifications, so there is still a $120 notional item of income to be allocated in the manner in which the $120 of income would have been allocated among the partners ($40 to each of *A*, *B*, and *C*) in the reviewed year. Each partner's capital account is increased by $40, as are their outside tax bases in their partnership interests. The partnership's basis and book value of the Asset *X* are restored to its cost of $120.
>
>*ABC*'s $30 expenditure with respect to the imputed underpayment is treated as a § 705(a)(2)(B) expenditure in the adjusted year. Because of the rate modification approved by the Service, the expenditure is allocated $16 to *B*, $14 to *C*, and $0 to *A*, reducing their capital accounts and outside bases accordingly.

Proposed Regulations § 301.6225-4(e) (2018) Example 5 illustrates the allocation of an imputed underpayment expenditure in connection with a partnership adjustment that creates an imputed underpayment but no § 704(b) allocation.

>**EXAMPLE 10A-8 (No § 704(b) Adjustment):** Equal partners *A* and *B* each have a zero basis in their interest in the *AB* partnership. The partnership has a $200 liability that is treated as nonrecourse on its reviewed-year return. On audit, the Service determines the liability is a recourse liability and should be allocated entirely to partner *B*, with the result that partner *A* has a $100 decrease in its liability share, triggering a $100 taxable distribution to it. The partnership does not seek modification and pays the $40 imputed underpayment. In the absence of a § 704(b) allocation, there is no notional item and no specified tax attributes are adjusted.[223] However, because *A* would have borne the entire burden of the tax imposed if the partnership had originally reported in a manner consis-

---

[221] Prop. Reg. §§ 1.704-1(b)(2)(iii)(f)(2), 301.6225-4(e) Example 3 (2018). See Reg. § 301.6225-2 for the modification rules.

[222] See Prop. Reg. § 301.6225-4(e) Example 2 (2018).

[223] See Prop. Reg. § 301.6225-4(b)(4) (2018).

tent with the partnership adjustment, the entire imputed underpayment expenditure is allocated to *A*.[224]

¶ 10A.07 ADJUSTMENTS THAT DO NOT RESULT IN IMPUTED UNDERPAYMENTS

Generally, partnership adjustments in net negative groupings and subgroupings do not result in imputed underpayments and are not taken into account by the partnership in the reviewed year. Instead, these net negative groupings are taken into account subsequently as "negative items"[225] (decreases in partnership income or credit increases) in the adjustment year.[226] While the general rule is that these adjustments are treated as adjustments to partnership "non-separately stated" income or loss for the adjustment year,[227] there are six exceptions to this general rule that collectively almost swallow it. The exceptions are as follows:

1. *Separately stated items.* An adjustment to a partnership-related item that is required to be separately stated under § 702(a) is taken into account as a reduction in the same separately stated category or as an increase in the same category in the adjustment year (depending on whether the adjustment is a reduction or an increase).[228]

2. *Credits.* An adjustment to a partnership-related item that is reported or could be reported by a partnership as a credit on the partnership's return for the reviewed year is taken into account as a separately stated item in the adjustment year.[229]

3. *Reallocation adjustments.* Reallocation adjustments among partners generally create both positive and negative adjustments in equal

---

[224] See Prop. Reg. § 1.704-1(b)(2)(iii)(f)(4) (2018).

[225] In the argot of the Regulations, "negative items" are taxpayer-favorable items that decrease partnership income or increase loss or credits. Reg. § 301.6225-1(d)(2).

[226] § 6225(a)(2); Reg. § 301.6225-3(a). The adjustment year is the partnership year in which (1) a court decision relating to the adjustment becomes final, (2) an administrative adjustment request (AAR) is made under § 6227, or (3) in any other case, an FPA is mailed or the partnership waives the § 6232(b) limitation on assessments. § 6225(d)(2); Reg. § 301.6241-1(a)(1).

[227] Reg. § 301.6225-3(b)(1). An income adjustment from the reviewed year is treated as a reduction of non-separately stated income for the adjustment year and a loss adjustment is treated as an increase in non-separately stated loss for the adjustment year.

[228] Reg. § 301.6225-3(b)(2). See § 301.6225-3(d)(1) Example 1 (character of item preserved).

[229] Reg. § 301.6225-3(b)(3).

amounts. In the absence of other significant reviewed-year adjustments, the positive adjustments will be included in the computation of imputed underpayments in the reviewed years and the negative adjustments will be taken into account by the partnership in the adjustment year under § 702(a) as separately stated items or as non-separately stated items. To the extent possible, the negative side of the positive reviewed-year adjustments is allocated among the adjustment-year partners who were the reviewed-year partners impacted by the original reallocation.[230]

4. *Modification adjustments.* If, as part of a modification approved by the Service, a direct or indirect partner takes into account an adjustment that does not result in an imputed underpayment, the adjustment is not taken into account in the adjustment year.[231]

5. *Effect of § 6226 push-out election.* If a partnership makes a valid push-out election, all partnership adjustments are taken into account by the reviewed-year partners in accordance with § 6226(b) rather than being taken into account in the adjustment year.[232]

6. *Previous adjustments by a partner.* If a partner has taken into account, prior to the issuance of the partnership notice of administrative proceeding (NAP), an adjustment that does not result in an imputed underpayment and that would have been taken into account under this provision, the adjustment is not taken into account by such partner in the adjustment year.[233]

¶ 10A.08 SECTION 6226 PUSH-OUTS

During the forty-five-day period after the date an FPA is issued for a reviewed year, the partnership representative (PR) may cause the partnership to make a "push-out" election that relieves it of the obligation to pay the imputed underpayment set forth in the FPA.[234] If a valid election is made, "section 6225 shall not apply with respect to the underpayment," and no assessment or col-

---

[230] Reg. § 301.6225-3(b)(4). See § 301.6225-3(d)(2) Example 2 (direct single-partner tracing).

[231] Reg. § 301.6225-3(b)(5).

[232] Reg. § 301.6225-3(b)(6). This election does not avoid the § 6225 proceeding; it comes at the end of that proceeding, following the issuance of an FPA. See generally ¶ 10A.08.

[233] Reg. § 301.6225-3(b)(7).

[234] § 6226(a). This election cannot be revoked without the consent of the Service. The details of the election are discussed in ¶ 10A.08[2].

lection can be made against the partnership.[235] Instead, the entire burden for reporting the adjustments to partnership-related items set forth in the FPA, as
well as the obligation to pay taxes, interest, penalties, additions to tax, and additional amounts related to those adjustments, shifts to the reviewed-year partners: "If a partnership makes a valid election ... with respect to any imputed
underpayment, the reviewed year partners ... must take into account their share
of the partnership adjustments ... that are associated with that imputed underpayment and are liable for any tax, penalties, additions to tax, additional
amounts, and interest ...."[236] Despite the push-out election, the partnership retains the right to judicially challenge the FPA by filing a petition in one of the
usual three forums within ninety days of the FPA.[237]

The sweeping absolution of the partnership from virtually all[238] potential
tax liability in connection with push-out elections has far-reaching implications
and enormous potential to produce unintended consequences in both the tax
and non-tax worlds. It will be many years before all the possibilities are un-
covered and explored. In the meantime, the following possibilities may warrant
some consideration:

1. While the statute and the Regulations attempt to address potential
   abuses with regard to partnership insolvencies and the like,[239] there
   are no comparable provisions for partners. Consider the *ABCDE* partnership, in which *A* has a 90 percent interest; her four children own
   the other 10 percent. The partnership runs a successful business and
   has substantial assets. *A* has been driven into bankruptcy by some unrelated business misfortunes and is facing creditor claims in excess of
   the value of her partnership interest. Can a § 6226 push-out election
   render 90 percent of an imputed underpayment wholly or partially un-
   collectible?[240] Do *A*'s other creditors have any say in whether the
   push-out election is made?

2. The absolution of the partnership from potential tax liability is likely
   to encourage lenders to request (or demand) contractual assurances in
   loan agreement that mandate push-out elections for the borrower.
   Widespread adoption of this approach by lenders may effectively con-

---

[235] § 6226(a); Reg. § 301.6226-1(a)(2).

[236] Reg. § 301.6226-1(b)(1); see § 6226(b).

[237] § 6226(d); Reg. § 301.6226-1(f).

[238] If the election allocates adjustments to reviewed-year foreign partners, the partnership is not absolved of withholding obligations under § 1446 relating to the foreign partners. Reg. § 301.6241-6(b)(4).

[239] See ¶ 10A.11[4].

[240] Prior to the advent of CPAR, this is the position the government would have been
faced with. Perhaps the use of a push-out election is an acceptable way to replicate the
historical result.

vert the push-out "election" into de facto reality for partnerships that are borrowers.

To assist partners in making these computations and paying taxes on their shares of the partnership adjustments, § 6226(a)(2) requires the electing partnership to furnish each reviewed-year partner a statement for each reviewed year setting forth the partner's share of adjustments to partnership-related items set forth in the FPA as finally adjusted. The Regulations require this statement to generally report adjustments in the "same manner as *each adjusted partnership-related item* was originally allocated" to the partners on the return under audit.[241] The italicized reference confirms that the level of granularity involved in the determination of the tax liabilities of § 6225 pull-in partners should also apply to the preparation of push-out statements and the computation of correction amounts under § 6226.[242] Consistency between the application of these two provisions reflects the overarching regulatory scheme of computing partner-level tax liabilities by taking into account the specific nature and character of each adjusted item and the interaction between that item and the rest of the return originally filed by the partner. Simply stated, in most cases, the sum of the correction amount and the tax originally reported on the return of a pushed-out partner should be equal to the tax the partner would have paid if its original K-1 had reflected its share of the adjustments set forth in the FPA.

While the election notice must be filed within forty-five days after the FPA is received, the electing partnership is not required to furnish the partner statements until sixty days "after the date all of the partnership adjustments ... are finally determined."[243] For this purpose, "finally determined" means the later of (1) the expiration of the time for the partnership to file a petition contesting the FPA; or (2) if a petition is filed, the date on which a court decision becomes final.[244] Thus, if a petition is filed, there is likely to be a multi-year delay in the filing of the partner statements.[245]

Despite the transfer of income tax liabilities from the partnership to the partners if a push-out election is made, any partnership that wants to contest the FPA in a district court or the Court of Federal Claims must comply with

---

[241] Reg. § 301.6226-2(f)(1)(i) (emphasis added).

[242] See ¶ 10A.06[2][d][i]. The reference point for this process should be the "separately stated items" rules in § 702(a), as discussed in ¶ 9.01[3].

[243] Reg. § 301.6226-2(b)(1). The partnership is required to also file these statements electronically with the Service. Reg. § 301.6226-2(d)(1).

[244] Reg. § 301.6226-2(b)(1).

[245] For many partners receiving push-out notices, the experience may be somewhat akin to being handed a ticking time bomb with no way to know when (or even if) it will go off or how extensive the damage will be.

the deposit requirements in § 6234(b)(1).[246] The amount of the deposit is based on the imputed underpayment, as modified (as well as penalties, additions to tax, and additional amounts) despite the lack of any meaningful correlation between the imputed underpayment and the likely aggregate tax liability of the partners if the FPA is sustained. Since no tax can be assessed against the partnership if a push-out election is made, the partnership may obtain a return of the entire deposit (with interest) by making a request in writing in accordance with rules to be promulgated by the Service.[247] In many situations, these rules are likely to significantly inhibit a partnership's choice of a forum to contest an FPA.[248]

If a partnership contests an FPA judicially, many years may elapse between the time the reviewed-year partners are notified of the push-out election and the time they receive statements of the final adjustments and are required to take their shares of the adjustments into account and pay taxes, interest, and penalties. During this potentially lengthy period, a great variety of life-changing events may occur with regard to the partnership as well as the reviewed-year partners ranging from the mundane (address changes, changes of ownership) to the extreme (death, liquidation, termination, bankruptcy), considerably complicating the application and administration of these provisions.

Mechanically, the statute imposes an additional tax on each reviewed-year partner for the partner's tax year (the "reporting year") in which a § 6226 statement is furnished to the partner.[249] As more fully explained in ¶ 10A.08[3], this tax (the "additional reporting year tax") is the sum of the "correction amounts" for all tax years of the partner that are affected by the adjustments in the statements it receives, beginning with the partner's tax year that includes the last day of the reviewed year (the "first affected year") and including each subsequent "intervening year" prior to the reporting year.[250] The correction amount for the partner's first affected year is the amount by which the partner's income tax would increase or decrease for the year as a consequence of the inclusion of the partner's share of the partnership adjustments as

---

[246] Reg. § 301.6234-1(b). See TD 9844, Preamble, Summary of Comments and Explanation of Revisions 9, 84 FR 6468, 6526 (Feb. 27, 2019).

[247] Reg. § 301.6234-1(c). While jurisdictional deposits generally are *not* treated as payments of tax under the Code, they are treated as payments of tax for purposes of the payment of interest under § 6611. It is a striking testimony to the strange contortions lurking in the shadows of CPAR that in this situation the partnership, which has no possible tax liability, may be required to make a jurisdictional deposit that bears interest as if it were a tax overpayment.

[248] Any partnership that is being audited under CPAR and is considering a possible push-out election would do well to focus on all possible modifications that may be available to reduce the nominal amount of the imputed understatement and thereby reduce the amount of the jurisdictional deposit if a forum other than the Tax Court may be advisable.

[249] § 6226(b)(1).

[250] § 6226(b)(1).

finally determined; for each subsequent intervening year, it is the amount (if any) by which the tax for the year would increase or decrease by reason of adjustments to the partner's "tax attributes"[251] for the first affected year and all prior intervening years.[252]

There are many notable aspects of § 6226 push-out elections. First, and most obviously, the election absolves the partnership of almost all liabilities relating to imputed underpayments. Second, the election does *not* require the partnership to give up the right to challenge FPA adjustments in the courts under § 6234. Despite the push-out election, the no-longer-liable partnership is the only petitioner with the right to challenge the substantive changes underlying the pushed-out adjustments.[253] Third, any dispute regarding a reporting-year return filed by a reviewed-year partner is resolved in normal deficiency proceedings involving that partner only. Fourth, a direct cost is attached to the push-out election: The interest rate on underpayments under § 6621(a)(2) is increased by 2 full percentage points so that it is equal to the short-term rate plus 5 percentage points instead of the short-term rate plus 3 percentage points.[254] Because of the delays and time periods built into the audit system in general and the push-out mechanics in particular, the additional cost of this increased interest rate can be significant, particularly if the audit leads to litigation.

Section 301.6226-3(h) of the Regulations includes several helpful Examples illustrating the operation of the push-out rules. In Example 1, the Service mails an FPA to Partnership in 2023 denying a charitable deduction on Partnership's 2020 return and asserting a 20 percent accuracy penalty. Partnership makes a timely election under § 6226, and files a petition in Tax Court challenging the adjustment. A Tax Court decision sustaining the adjustments becomes final on December 15, 2025. Partnership files the required statements with the Service and its partners on February 2, 2026. Partner A determines his "correction amount" for his first affected year (2020) by determining the increase in his Chapter 1 tax due to his share of the lost charitable deduction. There is no impact on intervening years. A's tax for the 2016 year is the correction amount plus interest from April 15, 2021 (the due date for A's 2020

---

[251] A "tax attribute" is anything that can affect the amount or timing of a partnership-related item or the amount of tax due for any year. Reg. § 301.6241-1(a)(10).

[252] §§ 6226(b)(2)(B), 6226(b)(3); Reg. § 301.6226-3(b)(3)(ii).

[253] Reg. § 301.6226-1(e). Every reviewed-year partner is bound by the partnership-level adjustments as finally determined; the partners do not have the right to challenge the substance of those adjustments. In the absence of agreements to the contrary, this means the costs of litigation will be borne by the adjustment-year partners whereas the results of the litigation will afflict the reviewed-year partners, a potentially serious source of conflict if there are significant ownership changes.

[254] Reg. § 301.6226-3(c)(3).

return), until the date *A* pays the tax, plus the penalty on the correction amount as well as interest on the penalty.

In addition to placing the onus of payment on the partners, the Section 6226 push-out election simplifies the tax attribute adjustments for the electing partnership and its partners. Under the 2018 Proposed Regulations, the pushed-out items simply flow through to the partners in accordance with their respective shares of such items, while the partnership alters its tax attributes affected by such pushed-out items in the adjustment year;[255] the pushed-out items are allocated among the partners in the same manner they would have been allocated under § 704(b) in the reviewed year (and any subsequent years affected by the adjustment).[256]

[1] Push-Out Election Mechanics

To be valid, a push-out election under § 6226 must be filed within the forty-five-day period following the issuance of an FPA. It must be signed by the partnership representative,[257] and contain specified information, including the name, taxpayer identification number, and the current or last known address of each reviewed-year partner.[258] If the FPA includes more than one imputed underpayment, the election must specify the imputed underpayments to which it applies.[259]

The ability to limit the election to specified imputed underpayments can provide significant benefits that may not be available if the FPA includes only one imputed underpayment. This suggests that during the modification phase of the § 6225 proceeding it may be worthwhile to encourage the Service to tailor separate imputed underpayments.

There is, however, a possible dark side to multiple imputed underpayments if the identity or shares of the partners in the adjustment year differ greatly from those in the reviewed year. To the extent the partners have contractual control over the actions of the PR, that control is likely to be exercisable by the adjustment-year partners, not the former reviewed-year partners. The adjustment-year partners may be tempted to use any control they have to encourage the PR to try to structure separate imputed underpayments in a way that results in highly adverse consequences to be pushed out to reviewed-year partners while maximizing the adjustment-year benefits that flow to the adjust-

---

[255] Prop. Reg. § 301.6226-4(a)(3) (2018).

[256] Prop. Reg. § 1.704-1(b)(4)(xiv) (2018).

[257] Reg. § 301.6226-1(c)(3)(i).

[258] Reg. § 301.6226-1(c)(3)(ii).

[259] Reg. § 301.6226-1(c)(3)(ii)(D).

ment-year partners. Partners who sell their interests should be aware of this possibility and consider contractual protection to minimize their exposure.

An election under § 6226(a) "is valid until the IRS determines that the election is invalid."[260] "The Service may determine an election to be invalid without first notifying the partnership or providing the partnership an opportunity to correct any failure to satisfy all of the [election requirements]."[261] If an election is invalid, the partnership's liability for the imputed underpayment is resurrected and the partners' liabilities disappear.

The Service may decide that the election is invalid when made or later if it determines that the partnership has not complied with the requirements to provide statements to partners. The Regulations provide extensive provisions for the correction of statements furnished to partners,[262] but do not specifically address the correction of errors in the original election.

[2] Partnership Statements to Reviewed-Year Partners

A partnership that makes a push-out election must furnish each reviewed-year partner a separate statement ("6226 Statement") containing specified information with respect to the partner's share of the adjustments underlying the imputed underpayment the partnership has elected to push out.[263] 6226 Statements must be furnished to reviewed-year partners no later than sixty days after the end of either the ninety-day period during which the partnership may file a petition challenging the FPA in court, or, if a timely petition is filed, the date of the final court decision.[264] Even though partners are required to take adjustments on their 6226 Statements into account in computing the additional reporting-year tax included on their reporting-year returns, 6226 Statements cannot be included in or conflated with Forms K-1 that the partnership furnishes for the same year.[265] The partnership is required to furnish electronic

---

[260] Reg. § 301.6226-1(c)(1).

[261] Reg. § 301.6226-1(d). If the Service decides that an election is invalid, it is required to notify the partnership within thirty days.

[262] Reg. § 301.6226-2(d).

[263] Reg. § 301.6226-2(a). Failure to provide a correct 6226 Statement is subject to penalty under § 6722. Reg. § 301.6226-2(a). Statements must be furnished in accordance with yet-to-be-issued forms, instructions, and guidance. However, if the partnership mails the statement, it must use the current or last address known to the partnership. If it is returned undeliverable, the partnership must undertake "reasonable diligence to identify the correct address and mail the statement to the correct address." Reg. § 301.6226-1(b)(2). The Regulations also provide for correction of errors. Reg. § 301.6226-1(d).

[264] Reg. § 301.6226-2(b). Section 6234(a) provides that a petition must be filed within ninety days of the FPA.

[265] Reg. § 301.6226-2(a) (second sentence).

copies of all 6226 Statements to the Service within sixty days after the date partnership adjustments are finally determined.[266]

Following receipt of a 6226 statement, each reviewed-year partner computes its "additional reporting year tax," which is equal to the net amount of all increases and decreases in its tax (each, a "correction amount") for the first affected years and all subsequent intervening years. The additional reporting-year tax is then reported and paid as an additional tax (or claimed as a refund) on the partner's return for the year (the "reporting year") in which the statement is furnished.[267]

In general, the Regulations provide that modifications that were approved in the modification phase are disregarded in determining each partner's share of reviewed-year adjustments under § 6226.[268] Thus, for example, modifications resulting from the filing of amended "pull-in" returns by a reviewed-year partner are ignored, and the partner's 6226 Statement will include items that were corrected on those returns. However, if a partner filed a pull-in return that was accepted as a modification, this should not be problematic: The correction amounts[269] required to be included in the partner's return should net to zero in any event.

Regulations § 301.6226-1(e) prescribes the contents of partner 6226 Statements. In addition to identifying details, the statements must include the partner's share of partnership adjustments, modifications (under § 6225(c)) that the Service approved with respect to the recipient partner, and information regarding applicable penalties, etc.

Regulations § 301.6226-2(f) prescribes rules to determine each reviewed-year partner's share of partnership adjustments. Generally, adjustments must be allocated in the same manner as the adjusted partnership-related item was originally allocated.[270]

[3] Additional Reporting-Year Tax

A reviewed-year partner's additional reporting-year tax is based on its share of the partnership adjustments as finally adjusted.[271] The additional reporting-year tax is the aggregate of the positive and negative "correction amounts" applica-

---

[266] Reg. § 301.6226-2(c).

[267] Reg. § 301.6226-3.

[268] Reg. § 301.6226-2(f)(2).

[269] See ¶ 10A.06[2][d][i].

[270] Reg. § 301.6226-2(f)(1). See also Prop. Reg. §§ 1.704-1(b)(4)(xiv), 301.6226-4(a)(3) (2018).

[271] § 6226(b); Reg. § 301.6226-3.

ble to the partner for the "first affected year"[272] and each "intervening year."[273] Positive and negative correction amounts for all years are netted to produce an "additional reporting year tax" that must be paid, together with any related penalties, additions to tax, and additional amounts (and interest) with the partner's return for the reporting year (the year that includes the statement date). The netted amount may be less than zero, but "cannot produce a refund to which the partner is not entitled."[274]

[a] Correction Amounts

In general, the correction amount for the first affected year is the income tax that a partner would have reported for that year if the adjusted partnership items had been correctly reported on the partner's return for that year, *minus* the tax shown to be due on the partner's return for the year, *minus* other tax amounts previously paid with respect to the year, and *minus* any applicable rebates.[275] The correction amount for each intervening year is computed similarly on a year-by-year basis, and reflects the additional income tax that would have been reported for such year if the adjusted partnership items had been properly reported for such year as well as the first affected year and any prior intervening years.[276]

[b] Interest

Each reviewed-year partner must pay interest on the correction amount for the first affected year and each intervening year in which there is a correction amount greater than zero.[277] Interest must also be paid on any penalties, additions to tax, and additional amounts for these years.[278] Negative annual

---

[272] Reg. § 301.6226-3(b)(2)(i).

[273] Reg. § 301.6226-3(b)(3)(i).

[274] Reg. § 301.6226-3(b)(1). In other words, the refund cannot exceed any "overpayment," which cannot exceed the net amount of tax already paid for the reporting year under the generally applicable Code rules. See TD 9844, 84 Fed. Reg. 6465, 6521 (Feb. 27, 2019) (relating to AAR refunds). Tax attributes are apparently adjusted anyway (see ¶ 10A.06[1]), a potentially harsh result.

[275] § 6226(b)(2); Reg. § 301.6226-3(b)(2)(ii).

[276] Reg. § 301.6226-3(b)(3).

[277] § 6226(c)(2); Reg. § 301.6226-3(c)(1). Interest is calculated from the due date of the return for the year (without extension) until paid.

[278] Reg. § 301.6226-3(c)(2). Interest is calculated from the due date of the return for the year (*including* any extensions) until paid.

correction amounts are ignored in determining interest and are *not* netted against positive annual correction amounts for any other years.[279]

The interest rate on amounts payable by reviewed-year partners is 5 percentage points above the applicable federal rate (AFR), rather than the normal underpayment rate of 3 percentage points above the AFR.[280] Avoiding this enhanced interest rate, the impact of which may be compounded by the lack of an offset for negative correction amounts, may be a good reason not to make a push-out election or to seek other ways to limit the interest due, particularly if the underlying substantive adjustment is a timing adjustment that is likely to produce a positive correction amount in the first reviewed year and a roughly equal negative adjustment in the next year. See Example 10A-10 in ¶ 10A.10[1] for a detailed illustration of the impact of these rules.

[c] Penalties, Etc.

If a partnership makes a push-out election, the applicability of penalties, additions to tax, and additional amounts relating to partnership adjustments continue to be determined at the partnership level.[281] Only the obligation to pay shifts to the partners.

The amount of any penalty, addition to tax, or additional amount that a partner must pay is calculated as if the correction amount were an underpayment or understatement in the first affected year or intervening year, based on the characteristics of, and facts and circumstances of, the partner for each such year, after taking into account the partnership adjustments reflected on the partner's 6226 Statement for the year.[282] No penalty, addition to tax, or additional amount applies if this calculation yields no underpayment or the understatement falls below applicable penalty thresholds.

Partner-level defenses (those that are personal to a specific partner, including any reasonable cause and good faith defense under § 6664(c)) can only be raised through a refund claim after a partner has filed its amended return and paid the penalty.[283]

---

[279] Reg. § 301.6226-3(c)(1) (final sentence). Thus, the computational rules for interest are less favorable to taxpayers than the general rule for computing the additional reporting-year tax in Regulations § 301.6226-3(b)(1) (second sentence) which states that "any correction amount that is less than zero can reduce any other correction amount."

[280] § 6226(c)(2)(C).

[281] Reg. § 301.6226-3(d)(1).

[282] Reg. § 301.6226-3(d)(2).

[283] Reg. § 301.6226-3(d)(3).

[d] Pass-Through Partners

Each of the pass-through partners of a partnership (an "audited partnership") that makes a push-out election can elect to either (1) bear the consequences of the push-out and pay the tax on its share of the push-out, or (2) make its own push-out election.[284] This process is designed to be infinitely iterative through as many layers of pass-through owners as elect to make push-out elections.[285] While the push-out process is essentially the same at every layer, there is one significant difference: Modifications can only be taken into account with respect to a pass-through owner's share of the adjustments from the audited partnership. With one likely exception, they are not permitted with respect to any other ownership level.[286]

Regardless of whether a pass-through partner elects to push out, it must comply with two requirements: (1) provide the Service with a "partnership adjustment tracking report," and (2) either pay the pushed-out tax or file (with the Service) and provide (to each "affected partner" of the pass-through partner) a statement similar to the 6226 Statements generally required in connection with push-out elections by audited partnerships.[287] An "affected partner" of a pass-through partner is a "partner that held an interest in the pass-through partner at any time during the taxable year of the pass-through partner to which the adjustments in the statement [from the audited partnership] to the pass-through partner relate ...."[288]

If a pass-through partner fails to furnish the required statements, it must compute and pay an imputed underpayment under rules similar to the rules of § 6225.[289] Unlike a push-out election by the audited partnership itself, there is no independent push-out election by a pass-through partner: It either furnishes

---

[284] Reg. § 301.6226-3(e). Pass-through partners include partnerships, S corporations, and most estates and trusts. Reg. § 301.6226-3(e)(5). S corporation shareholders and beneficiaries of trusts and estates are treated as if they were partners for this purpose. A disregarded entity or a grantor trust that is treated as wholly owned by one person is effectively disregarded: Section 6226 applies directly to the owner of the disregarded entity or trust as if the owner were the reviewed-year partner. Reg. § 301.6226-3(g).

[285] Reg. § 301.6226-3(e)(3)(iv).

[286] Reg. § 301.6226-3(e)(4)(iii). The likely exception is for a modification of an imputed underpayment of the audited partnership that was approved with respect to a pass-through partner or its owners. This modification should be allowed in computing the imputed underpayment of the pass-through partner and, presumably, its owners with respect to their shares of the adjustment, although the Regulations are not explicit on this point. See generally Preamble, Summary of Comments and Explanation of Revisions 4.C.iii.II, 84 FR 6468, 6516 (Feb. 27, 2019).

[287] § 6226(b)(4)(A); Reg. § 301.6226-3(e)(3). See generally ¶ 10A.08[2]. The tracking report and the statements must be filed no later than the extended due date for the audited partnership's adjustment year. § 6226(b)(4)(B); Reg. § 301.6226-3(e)(3)(ii).

[288] Reg. § 301.6226-3(e)(3)(i).

[289] Reg. § 301.6226-3(e)(3).

the required statements (thereby making the election) or it must pay the tax. Superficially, this seems like a simple and efficient system. But what happens if the furnished statements are less than perfect? Do minor foot-faults in furnishing the statements invalidate the push-out election? There is no indication of any potential leniency in the Code or Regulations.

A tracking report is required of every pass-through partner regardless of whether it elects to push out under § 6226.[290] If a pass-through partner elects to push out by furnishing statements to affected partners, each affected partner must take into account the items included in its statement in the same way that direct partners of the audited partnership must take into account the items included in statements from the audited partnership. Each owner of a pass-through partner that is also a pass-through partner can independently choose to pay or push.[291] Thus, audited partnership adjustments can be pushed all the way through a chain of tiered pass-through entities.

¶ 10A.09 ADMINISTRATIVE ADJUSTMENT REQUESTS

Partnerships subject to CPAR cannot file amended returns as such. Instead, § 6227 provides for the filing of administrative adjustment requests (AARs) by CPAR partnerships. Only the partnership representative can file an AAR.[292] Reviewed-year partners are subject to the consistency requirements with regard to AAR adjustments for reviewed years if (1) the partnership makes a push-out election under § 6226,[293] or (2) the adjustments do not result in an imputed underpayment, as set forth in Regulations § 301.6227-3.

A partnership may not file an AAR more than three years after the later of the filing date of the partnership return for the year to which the AAR relates (the "reviewed year") or the due date for filing such return (determined without extensions).[294] Further, a partnership may not file an AAR solely to change its partnership representative (PR) or change the individual designated by the PR.[295] A partnership that is being audited cannot file an AAR for a reviewed year included in the audit after a notice of administrative proceedings

---

[290] Failure to file tracking reports is subject to monetary penalties but does not invalidate an otherwise valid push-out election. Reg. § 301.6226-3(e)(2)(ii).

[291] Reg. § 301.6226-3(e)(3)(iv).

[292] Reg. § 301.6227-1(a). A partner in its capacity as such cannot file an AAR.

[293] Reg. § 301.6222-1(a)(5)(iv) Example 4. See generally ¶¶ 10A.04 and ¶ 10A.08.

[294] § 6227(c); Reg. § 301.6227-1(b).

[295] Reg. § 301.6227-1(a).

(NAP) is mailed by the Service under § 6231.[296] The Service may initiate a review of any AAR up to three years after the AAR is filed.[297]

The Service has recognized the post-NAP prohibition on the filing of AARs can cause unintended problems for some partnerships and has created a self-imposed administrative requirement that the issuance of a NAP must be preceded (by at least thirty days) by the mailing of an Examination Notice to the partnership.[298] The receipt of an Examination Notice thus gives a partnership a brief opportunity to change its PR, modify any aggressive return positions, and undertake any other appropriate clean-up activities before a NAP is issued and the statutory CPAR process formally starts.

An AAR must set forth the adjustments requested, and must include any statements required to be furnished to reviewed-year partners who will be subject to the adjustments requested in the AAR and any other information prescribed by the Service from time to time.[299] If the AAR results in imputed underpayments for any reviewed year, the underpayments must be paid by the partnership concurrently with the filing of the AAR unless the partnership makes a valid election to push out the adjustments to the partners under § 6226.

[1] Adjustments That Create Imputed Underpayments: No Push-Out Election

If an AAR results in an imputed underpayment for a reviewed year,[300] the partnership can elect to pay it[301] or push it out to its reviewed-year partners under rules similar to § 6226.[302] Payment in full or a valid push-out election must accompany every AAR filing that reflects an imputed underpayment for a reviewed year.

---

[296] § 6227(c); Reg. § 301.6227-1(b) (last sentence). Section 6227(d) authorizes Treasury to issue guidance relating to the coordination of § 6227 and the rules of § 905, relating to redeterminations of foreign taxes. Proposed Regulations § 1.905-4(b)(2)(ii) (2019) would implement § 6227(d) by creating an exception for foreign tax redeterminations that impact creditable foreign taxes. Partnerships would be required to file AARs to reflect certain redeterminations without regard to the time restrictions contained in § 6227(c).

[297] Reg. § 301.6227-1(f).

[298] See discussion in ¶ 10A.01[1].

[299] Reg. § 301.6227-1(c)(2). If a partnership fails to provide the required information, the Service may (but is not required to) invalidate the AAR or readjust any adjustments in the AAR.

[300] Computed under rules similar to § 6225. Reg. § 301.6227-1(a).

[301] § 6227(b)(1); Reg. § 301.6227-2(b).

[302] § 6227(b)(2); Reg. § 301.6227-2(c).

The computation of an imputed underpayment in an AAR is similar to the determination of an imputed underpayment under § 6225. However, there are a few restrictions on the types of modifications permitted in an AAR: It cannot (1) modify the imputed underpayment by reducing it for items reported by partners who file conforming amended returns (or use the alternative procedure); (2) modify the grouping or subgrouping rules except as permitted by Regulations § 301.6225-2(d)(6)(ii); or (3) take into account closing agreements (Regulations § 301.6225-2(d)(8)), or "catch-all" modifications (Regulations § 301.6225-2(d)(10)). With these exceptions, modifications are permitted in an AAR and do not require the Service's approval even if approval would be required under § 6225.[303]

Proposed Regulations § 301.6225-1(b)(3) (2020) (discussed in ¶ 10A.02[3]) would generally treat the amount of any positive adjustment for "non-income items" as zero for purposes of imputed underpayment computations. The Preamble to this proposal (REG-123652-18, 227 Fed. Reg. 74940, 74945 (Nov. 24, 2020)) indicates this concept would also apply to AARs, subject, of course, to subsequent contrary determinations by the Service.

In the absence of a push-out election, the partnership filing the AAR is required to pay any resulting imputed underpayment of Chapter 1 income tax (as well as interest, penalties, additions to tax, and additional amounts) concurrently with the filing of the AAR.[304] The partnership tax year in which the AAR is filed is the "reporting year." Accordingly, the reporting-year partners will bear the economic burden of this payment. The 2018 Proposed Regulations would allocate this burden among the reporting-year partners (or their successors) in proportion to their reporting-year interests.[305]

[2] Imputed Underpayments With Push-Out Elections

If a partnership files an AAR and elects to push out an imputed underpayment under § 6226, it must furnish (concurrently with the filing of the AAR) 6226 Statements to the reviewed-year partners that include their shares of adjust-

---

[303] Reg. § 301.6227-2(a)(2)(i). The partnership is required to provide the Service with information about any modifications. Reg. § 301.6227-2(a)(2)(ii). Ultimately, the Service retains the right to challenge any of these modifications (and any other changes to partnership-related items) by initiating its own administrative procedure pursuant to Regulations § 301.6227-1(f).

[304] Reg. §§ 301.6227-2(b)(1), 301.6227-2(b)(2). A portion of this payment may be treated as payment of required foreign withholding taxes under Code Chapters 3 and 4. Reg. § 301.6227-2(b)(3).

[305] Prop. Reg. §§ 1.704-1(b)(2)(iii)(f) (2018), 1.6225-4(c) (2018), as discussed in ¶ 10A.06[3].

ments to partnership-related items.[306] Each reviewed-year partner (other than a pass-through partner that makes its own push-out election) is required to take its share of the adjustments requested in the 6226 Statement into account as part of its additional reporting-year tax as if the 6226 Statement "were issued under section 6226(a)(2) [the general push-out procedure for underpayments] and, on or before the due date for the reporting year must report and pay the additional reporting year tax (as defined in § 301.6226-3(a)), if any ...."[307] In general, the additional reporting-year tax is the amount by which a partner's income tax liability for the reviewed year would have increased if its taxable income was recomputed taking into account its share of the requested adjustments.[308] In addition to the additional reporting-year tax, the reviewed-year partners are liable for interest as well as penalties, additions to tax, and additional amounts with respect to the tax, although the additional 2 percentage point increase in the interest rate imposed by Regulations § 301.6226-3(c)(3) is waived in this situation.[309] If a reviewed-year partner is a pass-through partner, it may elect to push out its share of the adjustments to its partners.[310] The "reporting year" for each reviewed-year partner is the partner's taxable year that includes the date the 6226 Statement is furnished to the partner.[311]

[3] No Imputed Understatement; Mandatory Push-Out

An AAR that does not create an imputed underpayment for the reviewed year can be the functional equivalent of a refund request. If there is no imputed underpayment, the push-out is mandatory: No election is needed. Each reviewed-year partner is required to take into account its share of the requested adjustments in the reporting year as if a 6226 Statement had been issued under § 6226.[312] Every partner (other than a pass-through partner that makes a valid push-out election) receiving such a statement must take into account adjustments reflected in the statement in its reporting year (*not* in its reviewed year)

---

[306] Reg. §§ 301.6227-1(c)(2)(ii), 301.6227-1(d), 301.6227-1(e).

[307] Reg. § 301.6227-3(b)(1).

[308] Reg. § 301.6227-3(b)(2). This nomenclature can be a bit confusing. The additional reporting-year tax is determined with regard to the adjusted income for the reviewed year (and possibly other affected years), not the reporting year, but is payable for the reporting year as if it were a tax for the reporting year.

[309] Reg. § 301.6227-3(b)(1). Affected partners are also spared if reviewed-year pass-through partners also elect to push out. Reg. § 301.6227-3(c)(4) (last sentence).

[310] Reg. § 301.6227-3(c); see discussion in ¶ 10A.08.

[311] Reg. § 301.6227-3(a). The reporting year is likely to be at least a few years after the reviewed year.

[312] Each reviewed-year partner must be furnished the equivalent of a 6226 Statement on the date the AAR is mailed to the Service. Reg. § 301.6227-1(d).

and (1) may reduce its income tax for the reporting year if its additional reporting year tax is less than zero, and (2) may claim refunds created by such reductions.[313] There are two examples in the Regulations, both involving increases in ordinary loss: In Example 1 the tax on a partner's reporting-year return is reduced to a smaller positive amount, and in Example 2 there is a negative tax amount for the year after taking the reduction into account.[314]

As in other contexts, the CPAR deferral of the tax and related economic benefits of taxpayer-favorable adjustments from the reviewed year to a later year (the "reporting" year in this case) carries a significant cost, in present value terms, for taxpayers.

> **EXAMPLE 10A-9:** In 2024, a year after filing its 2022 return, Partnership discovers it overstated its 2022 income by $5 million due to a failure to take into account last-minute changes in Forms K-1 received from lower-tier partnerships. In 2025, Partnership files an AAR for 2022 reflecting no imputed understatement and a $5 million negative adjustment to non-separately stated income that is pushed out to its reviewed-year (2022) partners. The additional reporting-year tax for 2022 is negative $1.75 million (based on a weighted average 2022 actual tax rate of 35 percent for the partners). All the partners have calendar-tax years. The partners' shares of this reporting-year tax are included on their 2025 returns and may result in income-tax reductions or refunds for 2025. Thus, Partnership's error in 2022 has created a delay of approximately three years in the realization of a $1.75 million non-interest-bearing refund. Applying an after-tax annual discount rate of 6 percent to this amount produces an estimated present value of the cost of this delay of about $280,000.

[4] Comparison

It may be helpful to summarize the differences between the treatment of Service-initiated adjustments to partnership-related items set forth in NOPPAs and FPAs and adjustments initiated by partnerships filing AARs. In general, if the Service initiates adjustments:

---

[313] Reg. § 301.6227-3(b)(1) (partner cannot claim a refund to which it "is not entitled").

[314] Reg. § 301.6227-3(b)(2). Example 2 explicitly states the partner may make a refund claim with respect to any overpayment. Example 1 is oddly silent on this point, although it seems the partner should be entitled to a refund for any overpayment in either case.

1. The partners have the ability to elect to pull in and thereby tailor their shares of the adjustments to their individual returns for each reviewed year;

2. The partnership has the ability to shift the adjustments to the partners by electing to push out the adjustments to the partners under § 6226, subject to certain costs and detriments (taxpayer-favorable adjustments deferred to the adjustment year, possible statute of limitations issues for partners attempting to obtain refunds for the adjustment year, additional 2 percent rate of interest on unfavorable adjustments); and

3. To the extent the adjustments are not pulled in or pushed out to the partners, taxpayer-favorable adjustments are deferred to the adjustment year; taxpayer-adverse adjustments are likely to be taxed at rates that are higher than the rates the partners would otherwise have been subject to.

If the partnership initiates adjustments with an AAR:

1. Individual reviewed-year partners cannot pull in their shares of the adjustments to their individual returns;

2. The partnership has the ability to shift the adjustments to the partners by electing to push out the adjustments to the partners under § 6226, subject to certain costs and detriments (taxpayer-favorable adjustments deferred to the *reporting* year, there are no unusual statute of limitations issues for partners attempting to obtain refunds for the reporting year, and there is no increased rate of interest on unfavorable adjustments); and

3. Tax rates are likely to be higher than appropriate on unfavorable adjustments; taxpayer-favorable adjustments will be pushed out and deferred to the reporting year.

This summary assumes the Service does not challenge the AAR under Regulations § 301.6227-1(f). If the Service initiates an administrative proceeding with respect to any partnership year (regardless of whether the year is subject to an AAR), the Service-initiated aspects summarized above are back in play.

¶ 10A.10 COMPUTATIONAL QUIRKS AND WORSE

There are a number of underlying CPAR rules and concepts that are novel to the tax system and hence prone to producing unanticipated and sometimes painfully unfair results. A few of these are explored below, including (1) the pervasive impact of the general timing rule that defers taxpayer-favorable adjustments to a future adjustment year,[315] (2) the application of a very broad definition of partnership-related item to create "one-sided"[316] tax-payer-unfavorable adjustments in the current year (the reviewed year) that may be wholly unrelated to any real income item,[317] (3) the additional delays built into CPAR that tend to delay the final resolution of disputes,[318] and (4) the imposition of a higher rate of interest on most pushed-out taxpayer-adverse adjustments.[319] These concepts can interact and compound with one another in decidedly unfavorable ways for taxpayers.

Much of the following discussion is based in part on the *time value of money* concept. Simply stated, this concept realizes that a dollar available currently is worth more than a dollar received in the future because you have the immediate use of it and hence the ability to invest it and earn a return on it or to use it to reduce your debts and avoid interest costs. The key question is: "How do you determine how much more it is worth?" Generally accepted techniques of financial analysis attempt to answer this question by applying a specifiç annual discount rate to future payments to determine their "present value." For example, at a 6 percent discount rate, a dollar to be received a year in the future has a present value of $0.9434 ($1.00/1.06).

Use of this analytical technique requires selection of an appropriate discount rate. There are a great many factors commonly used to makes this selection (including, for example, the availability and cost of borrowing, expected rates of return, payment risks, duration of deferrals). In the Examples in this chapter, the selection of an appropriate discount rate is somewhat simplified because we can begin with a few basis assumptions, largely reflecting the nature of the payments involved and the creditworthiness of the counterparty (the fisc). Thus, a fair assumption is that there are no significant payment risks in-

---

[315] § 6225(a). See generally ¶ 10A.06.

[316] "One-sided" in the sense there is no required connection to an otherwise recognizable taxable event.

[317] § 6241(2)(B)(i). See generally ¶ 10A.02[4].

[318] Audit cycles have gradually lengthened over several decades, particularly for large and complex cases. Under CPAR, this general trend is exacerbated by (1) the 270-day period set aside for the submission of modification requests after a NOPPA is mailed, and (2) the time (limited only by the taxpayer's willingness to refuse extension requests) for the Service to respond to modification requests. This further interlude in the march toward settlement or the issuance of an FPA is likely to add well over an additional year to the process even without extensions (for example, to allow mandatory review by the IRS Appeals Office). Thereafter, if the partnership elects to push out FPA adjustments pursuant to § 6226(b), and assuming no court challenge by the partnership, the period is further extended by the sixty-day period within which the partnership is required to furnish statements to the partners, plus the time that elapses prior to the partners filing their returns for the year in which they receive their statements (the reporting year). If the partnership files a court petition challenging the FPA, the process will be further attenuated while interest continues to accrue.

[319] § 6226(c)(2)(C). See generally ¶ 10A.08[3][b].

volved because neither the taxpayer or the government is likely to default on the payment of taxes or the issuance of refunds. It is also reasonable to assume that the duration of most deferrals will be for a period of between three and ten years. Beyond these basics, there is still room for a wide range of discount rates across an equally broad spectrum of taxpayers.

While it is not within the scope of this treatise to address the selection of an appropriate discount rate, a few basic observations can be made:

- Many of the costs involved in the Examples involve the timing of tax payments. Under § 6621(a)(2), the interest rate associated with most tax underpayments is the short-term applicable federal rate (AFR) plus 3 percentage points (5 percentage points following § 6226 push-outs under § 6226(c)(2)(C)), compounded daily. Although the short-term AFR for June 2020 was 0.18 percent,[320] the Examples are based on an assumed interest rate of 5 percent (7 percent under § 6226(c)(2)(C)), compounded annually, reflecting a short-term AFR of 2.00 percent. Based on historical data, the authors believe this is more representative of the likely rates going forward.
- Cash flows that are not directly tied to tax payments are assumed to earn interest at a rate of 6 percent. In some cases, the Examples illustrate the results if a higher 12 percent rate is used.

[1] One Year Timing Adjustments

Many tax disputes involve the timing of income and deduction items. Not infrequently, the issue is simply whether an income item should have been reported a year before, or a deduction item a year after, the year it was actually reported. If the Service raises this sort of issue in connection with a CPAR audit, the reviewed-year adjustment will result in an imputed underpayment reflecting the amount of the item and the highest possible tax rate, with a reversal in the form of some sort of reduction of partnership income by the amount of the item in the adjustment year. In this sort of dispute, the deck is stacked against the taxpayers, largely because of the delay in getting the benefits of the reversal. Outside the CPAR world, the stakes are generally limited to a year of interest on the item at the taxpayer's tax rate. Matters are quite different under CPAR.

> **EXAMPLE 10A-10:** The Service raises a timing issue in connection with a CPAR audit of Partnership and determines there is a $10 million positive adjustment in the form of an increase to sales revenue in 2021, the reviewed year, producing an imputed underpayment of $4 million (40 per-

---

[320] Rev. Rul. 2020-12, 2020-24 IRB 928.

cent of $10 million). The Service also audits 2022[321] and, based on the deferral from 2021, concludes Partnership is entitled to a $10 million negative adjustment for 2022, so there is no imputed underpayment for the 2022 reviewed year. Partnership is entitled to claim this adjustment as a decrease in non-separately stated income in the adjustment year (assume 2026).[322] There are no modifications. Partnership concedes the $10 million increase following the issuance of an FPA for 2021. In summary:

- For 2021, there is an imputed underpayment of tax of $4 million for Partnership plus interest at the regular rate of 5 percent, compounded daily for five years (about $1.14 million), a total of $5.14 million, that must be paid in connection with the filing of Partnership's 2026 return.
- For 2022, there is no change for Partnership; the partners have paid tax on $10 million of excessive ordinary income for 2022 and are not entitled to a refund.
- For 2026, there is a reduction (non-separately stated) of $10 million in Partnership taxable income (related to the 2022 adjustment) that will be allocated to the 2026 partners, and a partnership tax of $5.14 million (including interest) related to the 2021 adjustment.

The aggregate cost to Partnership and its partners from this garden-variety timing adjustment under CPAR can be quantified in rough terms by considering four components:

1. The excess (if any) of (a) the additional tax of $4 million for 2021, over (b) the tax that would have been paid by the 2021 partners if an additional $10 million of income had been allocated to them by Partnership in 2021 (assume this excess is $200,000[323]); plus
2. The interest on the $4 million imputed underpayment from 2021 paid with the 2026 return (approximately $1.14 million); plus (or minus)
3. Any increase (or decrease) in the actual tax benefits to the partners as a consequence of realizing the offsetting $10 million tax benefit from 2022 on their 2026 return instead of their 2022 return (assume this amount is zero); plus
4. The decrease, in present-value terms, of the value of the tax savings to the partners from a $10 million taxable income reduction in 2026

---

[321] If the Service does not audit 2022, all is not lost: As long as the statute of limitations is open, Partnership can initiate the adjustment process for 2022 by filing an AAR for 2022 under § 6227. See generally ¶ 10A.09.

[322] Reg. § 301.6225-3(b).

[323] This figure serves as a placeholder and is an entirely arbitrary amount. The inclusion of this component in the suggested methodology reflects the likelihood that the calculated imputed underpayment is greater than the actual tax that would be paid by partners. It serves as a reminder not to ignore this factor.

instead of 2022. At an annual after-tax discount rate of 6 percent, $3.8 million (40 percent of $10 million, less $200,000[324]) received in four years is equivalent to $3 million received immediately, a loss (in present-value terms) of about $800,000.[325]

Viewed in terms of present values and interest accruals, this Example lays bare the "double whammy" imposed on taxpayers by the CPAR timing rules: Unfavorable adjustments are allocated to the year in which they occur and bear interest *from the return date for that year until paid* in the adjustment year, but taxpayer-favorable adjustments, which are deferred to the same year, *do not bear interest*.

This aggregate cost of $2.14 million ($200,000 plus $1.14 million plus $800,000) can be compared to the aggregate benefit that would have been realized if the 2021 and 2022 returns had been accepted as filed. In other words, how much would have been saved by deferring $10 million of sales revenue from 2021 to 2022? In rough terms, using the same after-tax discount rate, that would have been about $240,000 (6 percent of $4 million). The original decision to defer the $10 million of sales revenue can now be second-guessed with perfect hindsight using an analysis along the following lines: Was it worth taking a $2.14 million or more risk to save $240,000? The answer, ignoring litigation costs, is that Partnership should only take this risk (1) if it can afford to, and (2) it thinks there is greater than a 90 percent or so probability that the deferral either will not be challenged or will be sustained if challenged.

Obviously, many variables and assumptions go into this rudimentary analysis of a simple example, but a few conclusions are evident that are not obvious on the face of the statute:

- The risk analysis for planning year-to-year timing decisions for partnerships under CPAR is starkly different and more complex than it is for any other category of taxpayer.
- Timing delays are very detrimental to taxpayers under CPAR. The more years that elapse between the reviewed year and the adjustment year, the more the taxpayer is disadvantaged. CPAR partnerships are hugely incentivized to shorten this period as much as possible. Example 10A-10 is based on the optimistic assumption that only five years will separate the end of the first reviewed year from end of the adjustment year. If that period is doubled, the risk question posed above becomes: "Is it worth risking over $4.3 million to save $240,000?" Worse yet,

---

[324] As discussed in the preceding footnote, this amount is simply a placeholder, a reminder that the actual tax liability of the partners on the income originally reported is likely to be less than 40 percent of the amount of the negative adjustment.

[325] At a 12 percent discount rate, the loss would be $1.385 million ($3.8 million minus $2.415 million) instead of $800,000.

there generally is no way to accurately estimate (or control) the length of this period in advance.

- Once an FPA is received, settlement options for CPAR partnerships should be evaluated not just in terms of the merits of the taxpayer's position and the costs of litigation, but also the costs of delay.
- A § 6226 push-out election is unlikely to improve matters. This Example assumes the actual tax for 2021 would be less than the imputed underpayment by $200,000. While the push-out election captures this savings, the 2 percentage-point increase in the interest rate charged on the $3.8 million balance will likely exceed this savings in most cases.

[2] Reallocation Adjustments

Under § 6225, a reallocation adjustment occurs when the Service determines an allocation of a partnership-related item among the partners should be changed.[326] In the aggregate, allocations adjustments are a zero-sum event for the partnership: There is no change in any item on the partnership's Schedule K. However, every reallocation adjustment creates two or more opposite-signed adjustments for partners or groups of partners. Prior to the advent of CPAR, this was also a zero-sum game for the Treasury unless the affected partners were subject to different rates of tax. Under CPAR, reallocations can have a large positive revenue impact even if all partners are subject to the same tax rates simply because the taxpayer-favorable side of each adjustment is deferred to the adjustment year whereas the taxpayer-adverse side of the adjustment stays in the reviewed year and bears interest until paid in the adjustment year.

> **EXAMPLE 10A-11:** For the 2019 tax year, the *AB* partnership allocated $70,000 of long-term capital loss and $30,000 of ordinary income to *B*. In a CPAR administrative proceeding, the Service determines both of these items should be allocated to *A*. Based on this determination, there are four subgroupings in the reallocation grouping: (1) a $30,000 increase in ordinary income allocated to *A*; (2) a $70,000 decrease in long-term capital loss allocated to *B*; (3) a $30,000 decrease in ordinary income allocated to *B*; (4) a $70,000 increase in long-term capital loss allocated to *A*. Under the general rules, subgroups (1) and (2) are positive adjustments that are added together to create a total netted positive adjustment of $100,000, which is multiplied by 40 percent to produce an imputed underpayment of $40,000. The PR of *AB* obtains a modification to reflect *B*'s capital gain rate of 20 percent, reducing the imputed underpayment by $14,000 (20 percent of $70,000) to a total of $26,000. The $30,000

---

[326] See Reg. § 301.6225-1(c)(2).

decrease in ordinary income allocated to *B* and the $70,000 increase in long-term capital loss allocated to *A* are both negative adjustments that do not create an imputed underpayment and that are taken into account in the adjustment year pursuant to Regulations § 301.6625-3.[327]

The adjustment year is 2025. There is an imputed underpayment of $26,000 for partnership *AB* plus interest at 5 percent, compounded daily for six years (about $9,100), a total of $35,100, that must be paid in connection with the filing of partnership *AB*'s 2025 return. *A* and *B* are both still partners in the adjustment year. The $30,000 decrease in ordinary income is allocated entirely to *B* and $70,000 of long-term capital loss is allocated entirely to *A*.[328] Assume that both of these adjustments can be fully taken into account by each partner on its 2025 return and that their tax savings from these adjustments are $12,000 for *B* (40 percent of $30,000) and $14,000 for *A* (20 percent of $70,000), a total of $26,000. The net "profit" to the fisc is the interest of $9,100 on the underpayment ($35,100 less $26,000). Under Proposed Regulations § 1.704-1(b)(2)(iii)(f) (2018), *A* would be charged with $12,000 of the imputed underpayment, plus interest, and *B* with $14,000, plus interest. Assuming both *A* and *B* can fully tax effect the 2025 adjustments, the only cost to the partners is interest. If *B* cannot utilize a large capital loss in 2025, the cost may be much greater.

The partners could elect to either pull-in or push-out the 2019 adjustments, which might reduce their net cash costs, although a push-out would increase the assumed interest rate from 5 percent to 7 percent at a cost of some $3,600. The point here, though, is that reallocations are a potentially substantial profit center for the Service that is likely to provide a catalyst for a significant increase in the attention and resources devoted to allocation issues by the Service.[329]

[3] One-Sided Adjustments

"One-sided adjustments" is a term that can be used to refer to adjustments that are treated as positive partnership-related items but are not linked to any specific offsetting item of partnership income, gain, loss, or deduction and are not allocated under § 704(b).[330] The severe threats to taxpayers posed by these types of adjustments are discussed and illustrated in this ¶ 10A.10[3] and later

---

[327] See Reg. § 301.6225-1(h)(12) Example 12.

[328] See Reg. §§ 301.6225-3(b)(4), 301.6225-1(d)(2) Example 2.

[329] This is an embarrassingly easy prediction to make, largely because the Service has historically given almost no audit attention to allocation issues and has limited staff expertise in the field to identify and address allocation issues.

[330] The Regulations provide for adjustments that are not allocated under § 704(b) to be included in the residual grouping (Regulations § 301.6225-1(c)(5)(ii)) and to be

in ¶ 10A.10[4]. Fortunately, Regulations proposed in 2020 may eliminate this threat for most (if not all) types of one-sided adjustments by treating the amount of the adjustment as zero and thereby effectively neutralizing it in terms of the computation of imputed underpayments. Proposed Regulations § 301.6225-1(b)(4) (2020) (discussed more extensively in ¶ 10A.02[3]) would generally treat the amount of any positive adjustment for "non-income items" as zero. The proposed definition of non-income items seems to broadly encompass assets, liabilities, and other common balance sheet items, rendering the following discussion and illustrations largely moot.

Pending finalization of this Proposed Regulation, the posterchild for the one-sided adjustment is Example 7 in Regulations § 301.6225-1(h)(7) (improper reporting of nonrecourse liability as recourse liability produces an imputed underpayment equal to the amount of the liability in the reviewed year). While less explicit, Example 1 in Regulations § 301.6225-1(h)(1) (unidentified non-netted deduction deferred to adjustment year) may be another. These types of adjustments are potentially very costly for CPAR partnerships because neither the statute nor the Regulations create any sort of offsetting negative adjustment in the adjustment (or any other) year.[331] Accordingly, it seems any partnership that is subject to a one-sided adjustment in connection with a CPAR audit will bear the full amount of the related imputed underpayment (plus interest) unless it reduces or eliminates the one-sided adjustment through negotiation, litigation, pull-in elections under § 6225, or a push-out election under § 6226. Generally, there is *no* potential offsetting benefit for the partnership or the partners if this type of adjustment is made, just a cost, which grows larger every year until it is paid.

> **EXAMPLE 10A-12:** During the course of a CPAR audit of Partnership for 2022, the Service finds that a $10 million nonrecourse liability has been erroneously reported as a recourse liability on the Form K-1s that Partnership issued to its partners. Partnership is advised of this adjustment after a NAP is issued in 2026. The audit is completed and an FPA is issued in 2029 setting forth only an imputed underpayment of $3.7 million relating to this $10 million adjustment. Partnership has no basis to contest the FPA and quickly agrees to pay it, with the result that there is a final resolution in 2029. Consequently, for tax year 2022, there is an imputed underpayment of $3.7 million, with interest of about $1.55 million (at 5 percent, compounded daily for seven years), for a total of $5.25 million payable with Partnership's 2029 return.

"treated, to the extent appropriate, either as a positive adjustment to income or to a credit." Reg. § 301.6225-1(d)(2)(iii)(B). Most one-sided adjustments are in this category.

[331] After describing the positive adjustment relating to the recharacterization of the liability, Example 7 simply states: "There are no other adjustments for the 2020 partnership taxable year [the reviewed year]." Reg. § 301.6225-1(h)(7) Example 7.

While it might seem appropriate for the Partnership to be entitled to a non-separately stated reduction of $10 million to be taken into account on its 2029 return and passed through to its partners, there does not seem to be any basis for such a reduction.

If a partnership becomes aware of this kind of error before receiving a NAP for the year (or years) during which it occurs, it should be able to eliminate the problem by filing amended returns (and corrected K-1s) as long as it does so before the Service issues a NAP. The Service's creation of a minimum thirty-day "fair warning" period between the issuance of an Examination Notice to a partnership and the mailing of a NAP creates a short window of opportunity for partnerships to head off this kind of problem. However, a partnership must move quickly to take advantage of this opportunity, which requires identifying any issues lurking in its already-filed (and presumably carefully reviewed) returns for the years to be audited, deciding whether and how to address them, and then executing any required steps, likely including the preparation, review, and filing of AARs.[332]

Upon the issuance of a NAP, the partnership and the partners lose all rights to amend any return or take any position inconsistent with the returns previously filed for the years included in the NAP.[333] As set forth in the preamble to the Treasury Decision promulgating the relevant final CPAR regulations:

> [O]nce the IRS initiates an administrative proceeding with respect to a partnership taxable year, any adjustment to a partnership-related item for that year must be determined exclusively within that partnership-level proceeding in accordance with section 6221(a). Neither the partnership, through filing an AAR, nor a partner, by taking an inconsistent position, may adjust a partnership-related item outside of that proceeding.[334]

Within the partnership proceeding, partners have a limited right to make pull-in elections by filing compliant amended returns pursuant to § 6225(c)(2)(A) in modification of an adjustment set forth in a NOPPA.[335] In

---

[332] See LB&I-04-1019-010, p. 39 (Oct. 24, 2019) (instructions to auditors to mail NAP no earlier than thirty days but no later than sixty days after issuance of Letter 2205-D), discussed in ¶ 10A.01[1]. Letter 2205-D is the current template for the Examination Notice. While there is no formal procedure for extending the thirty- to sixty-day period, there is certainly an opportunity to plead for mercy in the form of a delay in the issuance for the NAP during this period.

[333] See § 6227(c) (no partnership AAR after NAP mailed); Reg. § 301.6222-1(c)(5) (partners may not notify Service of inconsistent position after NAP mailed).

[334] TD 9844, Preamble, Summary of Comments and Explanation of Revisions 2.A.i, 84 FR 6468, 6474−6475 (Feb. 27, 2019).

[335] See generally ¶ 10A.06[2][d].

many one-sided situations, pull-in or push-out elections may be the only ways to reduce or eliminate the adverse consequences of a one-sided adjustment.

> **EXAMPLE 10A-13:** The facts are the same as in Example 10A-12. However, after the Service issues a NOPPA, partner Y, who has a 25 percent interest in Partnership, elects to pull-in her share of the adjustment by filing a compliant amended return. The proposed recharacterization of Partnership's $10 million liability can impact Y in one of three ways: It may increase her share of the liability, not change her share of the liability, or decrease her share of the liability. An increase or no change in her share of the liability cannot create any increase in the tax liability shown on her 2022 return as filed, and therefore there would be no change in her tax liability for the year as a consequence of her election.[336] If there is a $2.5 million decrease in her share of the liability, it may generate gain to her in the event the decrease exceeds the year-end basis she would otherwise have in her interest. While this would be unfortunate, it would not be an unexpected result under the generally applicable Subchapter K rules.

Thus, for all partners who can make pull-in elections and file compliant amended returns under § 6225 at no tax cost, the proposed adjustment causes no real tax cost or problems other than those inherent in the modification process in general, as discussed earlier in ¶ 10A.06[2][d][iii]. Even partners who would recognize immediate income as a consequence of decreases in their liability share should be willing to file a compliant return, since they will be obligated to pay the resultant tax in any case, assuming the partnership agreement complies with the 2018 Proposed Regulations discussed earlier in ¶ 10A.06[3].

Alternatively, a push-out election can be used to achieve essentially the same results, except for the imposition of a higher interest rate on the deficiency of any partner who owes taxes as a result. The gross pushed-out adjustment should be segregated at the same level of granularity as a pulled-in adjustment under § 6225,[337] so that only partners whose partnership interest bases would be reduced to an amount less than zero would be adversely affected. However, if the adjustment involves an issue the partnership would like to challenge in a forum other than the Tax Court, there can be significant issues relating to the amount of the deposit requirement, which is likely to be wildly excessive in this type of situation.[338]

---

[336] Any increase in her share of the liability would affect a "tax attribute" (a "tax attribute" is anything that can affect the amount or timing of a partnership-related item or the amount of tax due for any year; see Regulations § 301.6241-1(a)(10)) by increasing the basis of her interest, but any such increase would be exactly offset by the increase in her liability share upon disposition of her interest.

[337] See ¶ 10A.08.

[338] See § 6234(b)(1), discussed in ¶ 10A.08.

[4] One-Sided Adjustments Combined with Other Adjustments

The analysis of the risks and rewards of litigation are likely to be more complicated and less favorable for taxpayers if a CPAR audit involves both one-sided and other adjustments that a partnership wants to contest. Fundamentally, the continuing accretion of interest on the one-sided adjustment is likely to be at odds with the taxpayer's efforts to resolve other contested issues on an equitable basis. In many of these situations, the best solution is likely to be § 6225 pull-in elections by the partners or a § 6226 push-out election by the partnership. It may be easier to deal with these situations if the Service can be persuaded to issue separate NOPPAs or FPAs separating the one-sided modification from the other modifications.

¶ 10A.11 PROCEDURAL MATTERS: REQUIRED NOTICES; STATUTE OF LIMITATIONS; ASSESSMENT AND COLLECTION

[1] Required Notices

Section 6231 requires that the Service issue three notices in connection with CPAR proceedings. All of these notices must be mailed to the partnership and the partnership representative.[339] Section 6231(a) provides that a notice "shall be sufficient if mailed to the last known address of the partnership representative or partnership (even if the partnership has terminated its existence)."

Prior to commencing the formal audit process set forth in § 6231, the Service has created an administrative process that requires it to issue an Examination Notice giving the partnership at least thirty-days advance warning of the impending audit.[340] Thereafter, the audit proceedings formally begin with the issuance to the partnership of a notice of administrative proceeding (NAP). The NAP triggers the examination phase during which the Service examines and proposes adjustments to partnership-related items. If the Service proposes to adjust partnership-related items, it must mail the second required notice—a notice of proposed partnership adjustment (NOPPA).[341] The NOPPA communicates the Service's computation of one or more imputed underpayments and

---

[339] Reg. § 301.6231-1(a).

[340] See LB&I-04-1019-010, p. 39 (Oct. 24, 2019) (instructions to auditors to mail NAP no earlier than thirty days but no later than sixty days after issuance of Letter 2205-D). Letter 2205-D is the current template for the Examination Notice. See generally ¶ 10A.01[1].

[341] § 6231(a)(2).

commences the modification process provided by § 6225(c). During the modification process, the partnership representative may request modifications to the imputed underpayment.

If the partnership and the Service do not settle disagreements over the proposed adjustments, the Service mails the third statutorily required notice—a final partnership adjustment (FPA).[342] To allow time for the modification process in § 6225(c) to take place, an FPA cannot be mailed earlier than 270 days after the NOPPA is mailed unless the partnership agrees to waive the 270-day requirement. After the FPA is mailed, the partnership has ninety days to file a petition challenging the FPA in court. If no petition is timely filed, the partnership becomes liable for the imputed underpayment. It cannot thereafter challenge the FPA or file an administrative adjustment request or refund claim to recover amounts paid pursuant to the FPA.

If the partnership files a timely petition, the Service generally cannot issue an additional FPA;[343] however, in the absence of a petition, it can issue multiple FPAs. The Service may also rescind (with the consent of the partnership) an FPA, in which case the Service thereafter can issue a new FPA unless the statute of limitations has expired. The partnership cannot file a petition challenging a rescinded FPA.[344]

[2] Statute of Limitations and Other Timing Requirements

Under § 6235(a)(1), the Service is barred from adjusting partnership-related items after the date that is three years after the latest of (1) the date on which the partnership return for the reviewed-year taxable year was filed; (2) the return due date for the taxable year; or (3) the date on which the partnership filed an administrative adjustment request with respect to such year under § 6227. The last listed date is significant; it means that filing an AAR starts a new three-year limitations period during which the Service may adjust all partnership-related items.

The date determined under § 6235(a)(1) can be further extended by two special rules that reflect specific aspects of the CPAR audit process. The first is in § 6235(a)(2), which provides that in the case of any modification of an imputed underpayment the statute is extended to the date that is 270 days after the date on which everything required to be submitted by the partnership to the Service pursuant to § 6225(c) has been submitted.[345] Generally, the partnership

---

[342] § 6231(a)(3).

[343] § 6231(c).

[344] § 6231(d).

[345] The text of § 6235(a)(2) obscures its meaning, as interpreted by the Regulations. The statutory language is that, in the case of § 6225(c) modifications, the limitations period will not end before "the date that is 270 days (plus the number of days of any exten-

has 270 days after the NOPPA date to request modification and submit sup-porting information,[346] and the Service cannot send an FPA during that 270-day period. The effect of § 6235(a)(2) is to prevent the adjustment limita-tions period from expiring until 270 days after the 270-day request-and-submit period if there is any modification of an imputed underpayment. The purpose of this extension is to give the Service time to process approved modifications. Thus, unless the partnership waives the 270-day post-NOPPA bar on making adjustments, or there are no approved modifications, the limitations period on adjustments cannot expire before 540 days after the NOPPA. Both 270-day pe-riods can be extended by agreement of the Service and the partnership.[347]

The second special rule is in § 6235(a)(3), which provides that the statute of limitations on the issuance of FPAs cannot expire prior to the date that is 330 days after the mailing date of the NOPPA.[348] However, a NOPPA must be mailed within the generally applicable three-year period. In other words, a NOPPA can extend but cannot resuscitate an expired limitations period.

If a partnership is a debtor in a Chapter 11 bankruptcy proceeding, the statute of limitations is suspended during the period in which the Service is barred from making adjustments, assessments, or collections plus (1) sixty days for adjustments and assessments, and (2) six months for collections.[349] However, the tolling of the statute of limitations does not preclude the Service from moving forward with the administrative process of commencing and con-ducting a CPAR proceeding.[350]

[3] Assessment and Collection of Imputed Underpayments

Imputed underpayments are not assessed under generally applicable deficiency procedures, which, among other things, bar assessments until after the Service

---

sion consented to by the Secretary under paragraph (7) thereof) after the date on which everything required to be submitted to the Secretary pursuant to such section is so submit-ted." The Regulations clearly provide that the phrase whether "everything that is required to be submitted ... is submitted" has nothing to do with the quality or completeness of in-formation submitted by the partnership in the modification process. Reg. § 301.6235-1(b)(2)(ii). Instead, they confirm that the focus is on the 270-day period during which the Service is barred from making adjustments while the partnership requests modi-fications and is permitted to submit supporting information.

[346] Reg. § 301.6225-2(c)(3).

[347] Reg. § 301.6235-1(d).

[348] § 6235(a)(3). The second rule is essentially a back-up to the first rule in the event the partnership does not engage in modification. It gives the Service a reasonable period after expiration of the 270-day post-NOPPA lockdown period to issue an FPA.

[349] § 6241(6)(A); Reg. § 301.6241-2.

[350] Reg. § 301.6241-2(a)(4) (including mailing notices, making demands, and assess-ing taxes).

has mailed a § 6212 notice of deficiency to the taxpayer.[351] Instead, once an imputed underpayment has become final, either by the expiration of the partnership's ninety-day period to file a petition challenging an FPA or, if a court petition is filed, the time that the court's decision becomes final, the Service can move directly to assess and collect the imputed underpayment from the partnership.[352]

Section 6232(f) provides robust provisions to enable the Service to collect imputed underpayments and to encourage partnerships (and their partners) to make prompt and full payment. Payment must be made within ten days after the Service provides notice and demand. If not, interest starts to accrue at the federal short-term rate plus 5 percent, rather than the normal additional 3 percent rate.[353] Further, the Service may proceed directly against each partner of the partnership (as of the close of the adjustment year) to collect from that partner its "proportionate share" of any amount owed by the partnership.[354]

[4] Partners Liability if Partnership Does Not Pay

While the partnership is liable for any imputed underpayment, the adjustment-year partners are effectively guarantors of payment. As stated, under § 6232(f), if a partnership fails to pay amounts due within ten days of a notice and demand for payment, the Service can proceed against each adjustment-year partner for such partner's proportionate share of the unpaid amounts.

In addition, if a partnership ceases to exist, liability shifts to the partners under § 6241(7). Regulations § 301.6241-3 provides that the Service may decide that a partnership has ceased to exist because, under § 708(b)(1), "no part of any business, financial operation, or venture of the partnership continues to be carried on by any of its partners in a partnership."[355] Alternatively, the Service may determine that the partnership has ceased to exist because, based on the information available to it, the Service believes that the partnership does not have the ability to pay amounts that are due or may later become due.[356] The Service cannot determine that a partnership has ceased to exist solely because the partnership has failed to pay an amount due; the question is whether the partnership can pay, not whether it has paid. Further, the Service cannot

---

[351] See § 6232(a).

[352] Section 6232(b) bars assessment until the later of ninety days after the FPA or the date a court decision becomes final.

[353] § 6232(f)(1)(A).

[354] §§ 6232(f)(1)(B), 6232(f)(3).

[355] Reg. § 301.6241-3(b)(2)(i).

[356] Reg. § 301.6241-3(b)(2)(ii).

determine that a partnership has ceased to exist solely because it has made an election under § 6226 to push the imputed liability out to its partners.[357]

If the Service determines that a partnership has ceased to exist, its "former partners" must take into account partnership adjustments as if the partnership had made a push-out election under § 6226. In this circumstance, the Service may provide statements to each former partner of such partner's share of the adjustments. A former partner is a person who was a partner during the adjustment year that corresponds to the reviewed year to which the adjustment relates.[358] If the Service determines that a partnership-partner of an audited partnership has ceased to exist, its partners in the adjustment year become former partners. Finally, if before the end of the adjustment year, a partnership ceases to exist (e.g., by dissolving and filing a final return), there may be no adjustment-year partners to assume liability for the partnership's obligation. In such a case, the former partners who become liable are the persons who were partners during the partnership's last taxable year.[359]

---

[357] Reg. §§ 301.6241-3(b)(2)(ii), 301.6241-3(b)(2)(iii).
[358] Reg. § 301.6241-3(d)(1)(i).
[359] Reg. § 301.6241-3(d)(2).

CHAPTER **12**

Distributive Share Allocations in Connection With Shifts in the Partners' Interests

12-1

¶ 12.01 OVERVIEW OF ALLOCATIONS IN CONNECTION WITH SHIFTS

The partners' interests in profits and losses may be altered or shifted in a number of ways during the course of a partnership's taxable year. For example, all or a portion of a partner's interest may be sold, exchanged, transferred at death, given away, or contributed to a trust, a corporation, or another partnership. Partnership interests held by partnerships, corporations, or trusts may be distributed to partners, shareholders, or beneficiaries. Shifts may also result from the admission of a new partner, the retirement of an old partner, or an agreement among the partners to alter their interests in profits and losses.

In connection with shifts in the partners' interests in profits and losses, §§ 706(c) and 706(d) set forth a series of rules that control (1) the circumstances under which shifts in the partners' interests cause the partnership's taxable year to close with respect to partners involved in the shifts, and (2) the determination of the partners' distributive shares for the partnership taxable year during which shifts occur.

Closing a partnership's year with respect to a partner under § 706(c) is important primarily because it controls *when* the affected partner must take its distributive share of partnership items into account. Prior to 2018, shifts in partners' interests could also cause a termination of the partnership itself under § 708(b)(1)(B), but that provision has been repealed.[1] In general, § 706(c) provides as follows:

---

[1] See Chapter 13 of this treatise.

1. Under § 706(c)(1),[2] shifts in the partners' interests do not close the partnership year unless there is a termination of the partnership.[3]
2. Under § 706(c)(2)(A), the taxable year of a partnership closes "with respect to a partner whose entire interest in the partnership terminates (whether by reason of death, liquidation, or otherwise)."
3. Under § 706(c)(2)(B), the partnership's taxable year does not close with respect to a partner who sells or exchanges less than his entire interest or "whose interest is reduced (whether by entry of a new partner, partial liquidation of a partner's interest, gift, or otherwise)."

If there is a shift in the partners' interests, § 706(d) governs the computation of the partners' distributive shares, regardless of whether there has been a closing of any partner's tax year under § 706(c). In general, § 706(d)(1) provides that if a change occurs in any partner's interest during the partnership's taxable year, all partners' distributive shares are determined by taking into account their varying interests in the partnership during the year. The distributive share rules under § 706(d)(1) apply not only to partners whose interests are transferred, liquidated, or reduced, but also to any other partner whose interest is acquired or increased as a consequence.

¶ 12.02 SHIFTS THAT CLOSE THE PARTNERSHIP'S TAXABLE YEAR

[1] Partnership Year Closes With Respect to All Partners

Section 706(c)(1) sets forth the general rule that unless the partnership terminates under § 708(b), its taxable year does not close with respect to all partners as a consequence of "the death of a partner, the entry of a new partner, the liquidation of a partner's interest in the partnership, or the sale or exchange of a partner's interest in the partnership."[4] Section 708(b)(1) provides that the

---

[2] The original enactment of § 706(c)(1) in 1954 was intended to make clear that various events, such as the death of a partner, that may cause partnership dissolutions under state law do *not* cause a termination of the partnership for tax purposes. See HR Rep. No. 1337, 83d Cong., 2d Sess. 67 (1954); S. Rep. No. 1622, 83d Cong., 2d Sess. 91 (1954).

[3] Subsequent to the repeal of § 708(b)(1)(B) in 2017, a partnership terminates only if "no part of any business, financial operation, or venture of the partnership continues to be carried on by any of its partners in a partnership." See ¶ 13.02.

[4] Section 708(a) provides that a partnership is "considered as continuing if it is not terminated." Under § 708(b), a number of events that may cause the dissolution of the partnership under state law, such as the death or bankruptcy of a partner or the sale of a partnership interest, do not terminate the partnership for tax purposes. See generally ¶ 13.01.

only circumstances under which a partnership terminates (after 2017) is if "no part of any business, financial operation, or venture of the partnership continues to be carried on by any of its partners in a partnership." In the case of a two-person partnership, the complete liquidation of one partner's interest, or the sale by a partner of his interest to his co-partner, causes the termination of the partnership under § 708(b)(1).[5] Prior to 2018, under former § 708(b)(1)(B), shifts in the partners' interests terminated the partnership for tax purposes if "within a 12-month period there is a sale or exchange of 50 percent or more of the total interest in partnership capital and profits." Post 2017, § 708(b)(1) is strongly biased against partnership terminations.

If the partnership terminates and its taxable year closes with respect to all partners under § 708(b)(1), allocation problems are generally not present. Each partner reports his distributive share of partnership income or loss through the closing date of the partnership's taxable year on his return for the taxable year that includes such closing date.

[2] Partnership Year Closes With Respect to Individual Partners

Regardless of whether a partnership is terminated under § 708(b), § 706(c)(2)(A) provides that the taxable year of a partnership closes "with respect to a partner whose entire interest in the partnership terminates (whether by reason of death, liquidation, or otherwise)." Prior to amendment for tax years beginning after 1997, § 706(c)(2)(A) provided that the taxable year of a partnership closed with respect to any partner who sold or exchanged his entire partnership interest, or whose interest was liquidated, but that the death of a partner did not close the taxable year of the partnership. The legislative history of the 1997 change indicates that its narrow purpose was to reverse the historical "no-closing" rule for deceased partners.[6] Although it is not entirely certain,

---

The enumeration in § 706(c)(1) of events that do not close the partnership year in the absence of a § 708(b) termination may be read to suggest that there are other events that close the partnership year even though the partnership itself does not terminate for tax purposes. In Estate of Guy B. Panero, 48 TC 147 (1967), the Tax Court rejected on factual grounds an argument that a state law dissolution, caused by an event other than one of those enumerated in § 706(c)(1), closed the partnership year. The tone of the *Panero* opinion suggests that the Tax Court may not be overly sympathetic to this argument regardless of the factual context. Rejection of this argument seems consistent with the overall statutory pattern and the apparent purposes of § 708(b), notwithstanding the arguably artless wording of § 706(c)(1).

[5] See ¶ 13.04[2].

[6] HR Rep. No. 220, 105th Cong., 1st Sess. 688–689 (1997). The legislative history also makes clear that the amendment is not intended to disturb the rule in § 1398(f), under which transfers to and from the bankruptcy estate of a partner are not treated as dispositions for any tax purposes. See also Aron B. Katz, 116 TC 5 (2001), rev'd and remanded

it appears fairly clear that, aside from the addition of the death of a partner, the scope of § 706(c)(2)(A) was not changed by the 1997 amendment. Sales or exchanges subject to § 706(c)(2)(A) should encompass (1) traditional sales, (2) transfers of partnership interests in most corporate reorganizations,[7] and (3) contributions of partnership interests either to controlled corporations in exchange for corporate stock under § 351[8] or to other partnerships pursuant to § 721.[9] Gifts of partnership interests and distributions of partnership interests from estates to beneficiaries do not cause the partnership year to close with respect to the transferor under § 706(c)(2)(A).[10] It also seems relatively clear that transfers of partnership interests to or from the bankruptcy estates of partners should not cause the partnership tax year to close with respect to such partners.[11] Moreover, neither the admission of a new partner nor an agreement among existing partners to change their interests in partnership profits or losses causes the partnership year to close with respect to any partner.[12]

The subsections that follow discuss the application of § 706(c)(2)(A) to specific types of transfers.

---

as to other issues, 335 F3d 1121 (10th Cir. 2003); Michael H. Gulley, 79 TCM 2171 (2001); Luther E. Smith, 70 TCM 483 (1995).

[7] See Rev. Rul. 87-110, 1987-2 CB 159. This ruling states that no exchange occurs for purposes of former § 708(b)(1)(B) in a § 368(a)(1)(F) reorganization. Presumably, the same analysis is applicable to § 706(c)(2)(A).

[8] See ¶ 16.07[1]. Cf. Rev. Rul. 81-38, 1981-1 CB 386 (§ 351 transfer to corporation is an exchange for purposes of former § 708(b)(1)(B)).

[9] See ¶ 16.07[3]. In Revenue Ruling 86-101, 1986-2 CB 94, the Service ruled that the conversion of a general partner's interest into a limited partnership interest upon his death does not close the partnership taxable year with respect to the deceased partner under § 706(c)(2)(A). Pursuant to Revenue Ruling 84-52, 1984-1 CB 157, this type of conversion is viewed by the Service as a contribution of the old general partnership interest to the partnership in exchange for the new limited partnership interest. See ¶ 16.04[2][b]. Revenue Ruling 86-101 states that although the conversion is treated as an exchange for purposes of § 721, it is "not an exchange ... for purposes of section 706(c)(2)(A) ...."

[10] Reg. § 1.706-1(c)(5) (gift does not close year with respect to donor; allocate income under § 704(e)(1) (former § 704(e)(2))); Reg. § 1.706-1(c)(2)(i) (transfer occurring at death as a result of inheritance or testamentary disposition not a sale or exchange). Although this Regulation is effective for partnership taxable years beginning on or after August 3, 2015, prior law was to be same effect. See Reg. § 1.706-1(c)(4) Example (3) (prior law).

[11] § 1398(f). See HR Rep. No. 220, 105th Cong., 1st Sess. 688–689 (1997). See also Aron B. Katz, 116 TC 5 (2001), rev'd and remanded as to other issues, 335 F3d 1121 (10th Cir. 2003); Michael H. Gulley, 79 TCM 2171 (2000); Luther E. Smith, 70 TCM 483 (1995).

[12] § 706(c)(2)(B). See Priv. Ltr. Rul. 8542044 (July 23, 1985) (entry of new partner in connection with conversion of general to limited partnership; partnership year does not close with respect to the partnership or any partner).

[a] Transactions With Trusts

Prior to the enactment of § 761(e) in 1984 the Service ruled, without explanation, that the distribution of a partnership interest to a trust beneficiary upon termination of a trust closes the partnership year with respect to the trust.[13] Section 761(e) now provides that a distribution of a partnership interest is generally treated as an exchange of the interest under §§ 708, 743, and any other provisions specified by Regulations. Although the ruling may have been questionable at the time it was issued,[14] it seems likely it will eventually be confirmed when Regulations are eventually issued under § 761(e).

Prior to the enactment of § 761(e), the Service ruled privately that transfers of partnership interests to a trust did not close the partnership year with respect to the transferors.[15] This position seems correct even after the enactment of § 761(e), which applies only to distributions; it is difficult to justify applying § 706(c)(2)(A) to these transfers, which generally are either gifts (specifically exempted from § 706(c)(2)(A) by the Regulations) or do not involve any change in beneficial ownership of the interest.

[b] Charitable Contributions

Charitable contributions seemingly should be treated in the same fashion as other gifts, but neither the § 706(c) Regulations nor the Regulations dealing with transfers under former § 708(b)(1)(B)[16] are explicit as to the treatment of partners who make charitable contributions of their interests. While the apparent position of the Service with respect to trust distributions makes prognostication hazardous, it seems that § 706(c) should not close the partnership year upon a charitable contribution of a partnership interest.[17]

---

[13] Rev. Rul. 72-352, 1972-2 CB 395.

[14] Trust distributions are not "sales or exchanges" in the traditional sense. Such distributions strongly resemble distributions from estates to beneficiaries, which are exempted from § 706(c)(2)(A) by Regulations § 1.706-1(c)(2)(i).

[15] Priv. Ltr. Rul. 7952159 (Sept. 27, 1979) (pursuant to Regulations § 1.706-1(c)(5), gifts of partnership interests to irrevocable "split-interest" trusts for benefit of children and charities do not close partnership year with respect to donor; income for year of transfer allocated between donor and trusts pursuant to § 704(e)(1) (former § 704(e)(2))).

[16] See Reg. § 1.708-1(b)(2).

[17] See Priv. Ltr. Rul. 7952159 (Sept. 27, 1979) (gifts of partnership interests to "split-interest" trusts for benefit of charities and children do not close partnership year with respect to donor; income for year of transfer allocated between donor and trusts pursuant to § 704(e)(1) (former § 704(e)(2)).

[c] Distributions by Corporations and Partnerships

Section 761(e) provides that any "distribution" of a partnership interest is treated as an "exchange" for purposes of §§ 708 and 743, as well as any other provisions of Subchapter K designated by Regulations. Given the Service's historical position with respect to trust distributions,[18] it seems likely that Regulations will eventually be promulgated adding § 706 to the list of sections set forth in § 761(e), so that all distributions of partnership interests by corporations and other partnerships will be treated as exchanges for purposes of § 706. Even in the absence of such Regulations, the Service is likely to assert that a distribution of a partnership interest by a corporation or partnership closes the partnership year with respect to the transferor under § 706(c)(2)(A).

[d] Abandonments and Forfeitures

Historically, it has been thought that a "pure" abandonment of property is not treated as a "sale or exchange" for certain purposes.[19] Whether this historical view remains valid is currently clouded by some ongoing uncertainty as to the intent and scope of § 1234A. This provision, in pertinent part, provides that gain or loss from the "cancellation, lapse, expiration or other termination of ... a right or obligation ... with respect to property which is (or on acquisition would be) a capital asset" is treated as gain or loss from the sale of a capital asset. The question that has arisen is whether this language is intended to encompass ownership of the capital asset itself as well as "rights" (option, puts, calls, straddles, etc.) with respect to the asset. The position of the Tax Court is that § 1234A covers ownership as well as other rights, a position that it has held firm on despite a reversal by the Fifth Circuit, which takes the position § 1234A is limited to "rights" and that if Congress had intended it to include direct ownership it would have said so.[20] Under the Tax Court's interpretation, the abandonment of a partnership interest will be treated as a sale or exchange and will close the partnership year as to the abandoning partner under § 706(c).[21]

---

[18] See Rev. Rul. 72-352, 1972-2 CB 395.

[19] See, e.g., Stokes v. Commissioner, 124 F2d 335 (3d Cir. 1941); William H. Jamison, 8 TC 173 (1947) (acq.); Rev. Rul. 93-80, 1993-2 CB 239; cf. Rev. Rul. 57-503, 1957-2 CB 139.

[20] Pilgrim's Pride Corp., 141 TC 533 (2013), rev'd, 779 F3d 311 (5th Cir. 2015); see CRI-Leslie, LLC, 147 TC 217 (2016) (rejecting Fifth Circuit approach.

[21] See ¶ 16.06. See also Robert B. Weiss, 60 TCM 746 (1990) (partner forfeits interest as a result of failure to make required capital contribution; partner not entitled to share of post-forfeiture losses), vacated and remanded on another issue, 956 F2d 242 (11th Cir. 1992).

[e] Subchapter S Terminations

If (1) a corporation's S status terminates other than on the first day of its year, (2) the corporation elects not to prorate its income under § 1362(e)(2), and (3) any taxable year of a partnership ends with or within the successor C corporation's ensuing short taxable year, then, for purposes of § 706(c), the termination of the S election is treated as a sale or exchange of the partnership interest on the last day of the S corporation's short year.[22] Similarly, if a shareholder terminates her entire interest in an S corporation during the taxable year and the affected shareholders and the corporation elect, under § 1377(a)(2), to consider the year as two taxable years, any partnership interest held by the S corporation is treated as sold or exchanged.[23]

[f] Consolidated Returns

If a corporate partner becomes or ceases to be a member of a consolidated group, any partnership interest it holds is deemed to be sold or exchanged for purposes of § 706.[24] Special rules governing the application of the "varying interests" rule in these situations are discussed later in ¶ 12.03[1][c].

[3] Consequences of Closing the Partnership Year

Upon a premature closing of the partnership year under § 706(c)(2)(A), any partner with respect to whom the year closes is required to include in his return for the tax year within which the closing occurs his distributive share of partnership income, gain, loss, deduction, or credit, as well as any guaranteed payments under § 707(c), for the short partnership year.[25] If the partnership's regular taxable year differs from the partner's taxable year, a premature closing of the partnership year may result in the "bunching" of more than twelve months of partnership income on the partner's return for a single year. For example, if the taxable year of a partnership using a January 31 fiscal year closes with respect to a calendar-year partner on December 31, 2020, the partner will be required to include, on his 2020 return, partnership income for both the twelve-month period ending January 31, 2020, and the eleven-month period ending December 31, 2020—a total of twenty-three months of partnership income. Bunching problems of this sort are, however, no longer common, primarily because § 706(b) generally requires a partnership's taxable year to

---

[22] Reg. §§ 1.1362-3(c)(1), 1.706-1(c)(iii).

[23] Reg. §§ 1.1377-1(b)(3)(iv), 1.706-1(c)(2)(iii).

[24] Reg. §§ 1.706-1(c)(2)(iii), 1.1502-76(b)(2)(vi)(A).

[25] See Reg. § 1.706-1(c)(2)(ii) Example; cf. F.A. Falconer, 40 TC 1011, 1016–1017 (1963) (acq.).

coincide with that of a majority of its partners.[26] If the partnership and its partners all use the same taxable year, a premature closing of the partnership's year cannot cause a bunching of partnership income on a partner's return.

[4] Determining the Date the Partnership Year Closes

[a] Sales or Exchanges of Partners' Interests

If a partner sells or exchanges his entire partnership interest, the partnership taxable year closes with respect to him on the date of the sale or exchange. Generally, the date of a sale or exchange is the date selected by the parties, provided the benefits and burdens of ownership of the interest actually shift on that date.[27] If these two factors align, other flaws and technical failures are likely to be ignored by the courts and the Service, including failures to comply with the requirements of the partnership or operating agreement.[28] In a case under the 1939 Code, a sale by a calendar-year partner of his partnership interest on January 2, 1951, was treated as occurring in 1951 notwithstanding the execution during 1950 of an instrument in which he "proposed" to sell the interest.[29] While recognizing the "tax avoidance" motive of the seller, the District Court nevertheless found the date selected by the parties to be the date on which their rights and obligations were altered, and hence the date on which the sale occurred for tax purposes.

The willingness of the courts to permit a sale of a partnership interest to be divided into two sales can be helpful for various purposes. The first sale, standing alone, does not prematurely close the partnership year as to the seller under § 706(c)(2)(A), because it involves less than his entire interest in the partnership. If a partner's tax year differs from that of the partnership, this

---

[26] See ¶ 9.04[1].

[27] Generally, a variety of factual circumstances are taken into account in determining when the benefits and burdens of ownership actually pass from transferor to transferee, including passage of title, transfer of possession, and substantial performance of conditions precedent. See, e.g., Case v. United States, 633 F2d 1240 (6th Cir. 1980); Dettmers v. Commissioner, 430 F2d 1019, 1023 (6th Cir. 1970); Clodfelter v. Commissioner, 426 F2d 1391, 1393–1394 (9th Cir. 1970); LeSage v. Commissioner, 173 F2d 826 (5th Cir. 1949); Commissioner v. Segall, 114 F2d 706, 709–710 (6th Cir. 1940) (cert. denied); Gordon J. Harmston, 61 TC 216 (1973), aff'd per curiam, 528 F2d 55 (9th Cir. 1976); Ted F. Merrill, 40 TC 66, 74 (1963), aff'd per curiam, 336 F2d 771 (9th Cir. 1964).

[28] See, e.g., Evans v. Commissioner, 447 F2d 547 (7th Cir. 1971) (transferee of partnership interest taxable on distributive share even though other partner unaware of transfer and transferee not formally substituted as a partner); Life Care Communities of Am., Ltd., 87 TCM 799 (2004); Rev. Rul. 77-137, 1977-1 CB 178 (unadmitted assignee of limited partnership interest treated as a partner); cf. Rupple v. Kuhl, 177 F2d 823 (7th Cir. 1949).

[29] See Grant v. McCrory, 163 F. Supp. 210 (D. Neb. 1958).

technique should be effective to postpone the closing date and defer the seller's realization of his distributive share, provided (1) the sale of the second portion of the interest is in fact deferred and (2) the second portion is not a de minimis part of the seller's interest.[30]

[b] Liquidations of Partners' Interests

If a partner's interest is liquidated by the partnership, he remains a partner for tax purposes until he has received all payments in liquidation of his interest.[31] Accordingly, while a partnership interest that is being liquidated may be treated as "reduced" (within the meaning of § 706(c)(2)(B)) at an earlier date, the partnership's taxable year does not close, under § 706(c)(2)(A), with respect to the holder of the interest until it is fully liquidated. Again, a de minimis rule is likely to apply if only an inconsequential portion of the total liquidating payment is deferred.

[c] Death of a Partner

Section 706(c)(2)(A) provides that the taxable year of the partnership closes with respect to a deceased partner on the date of the partner's death.

¶ 12.03 ALLOCATIONS OF PARTNERSHIP INCOME WHEN PARTNERS' INTERESTS CHANGE

Section 706(d)(1) provides that if there is a change in any partner's interest during any taxable year of the partnership, each partner's distributive share of any partnership item is determined, pursuant to the Regulations, by taking into account the "varying interests" of the partners in the partnership during the year. The "varying interests" standard dates back to the enactment of the 1954 Code. As explored in this ¶ 12.03, there has been considerable embroidery since that time.

---

[30] See Priv. Ltr. Rul. 7902086 (Oct. 16, 1978) (no closure of partnership year under § 706(c)(2)(A) upon transfer of 90 percent of partner's interest to wholly owned corporation under § 351, even though 10 percent interest apparently retained solely to avoid application of § 706(c)(2)(A)).

[31] See Reg. §§ 1.736-1(a)(6), 1.761-1(d).

[1] The "Varying Interests" Regime

The Regulations contain an excruciatingly precise set of rules for determining a partner's varying interests in partnership items. At their heart, they provide that the partners' distributive shares are determined either by (1) closing the partnership's books as of the date of a sale, exchange, or liquidation of any interest, or (2) prorating the partnership's income for the entire year between the pre- and post-sale, -exchange, or -liquidation periods. It is helpful to keep these basic ideas in mind when navigating the complexities of the rules themselves.

The current Regulations are generally effective for partnership taxable years that begin on or after August 3, 2015.[32] They apply when a partner's interest varies as a result of the disposition of part or all of her interest or the reduction of the interest, whether by the entry of a new partner or otherwise. They are inapplicable to certain allocations among contemporaneous partners (see ¶ 12.04[1]), allocable cash-basis items (see ¶ 12.03[2]), allocations involving tier partnerships (see ¶ 12.03[3]), and certain other special situations.[33]

Every variance in the partners' interests during a taxable year constitutes a "variation" that is treated as a separate portion of the taxable year. Different allocation methods can be used for different variations during a year, subject to the issuance of future guidance restricting such flexibility.[34] The interim-closing-of-the-books method is the default method for allocating items in connection with variations in the partners' interests. The partnership is authorized, however, upon agreement by its partners, to use the proration method in some circumstances.[35]

Entirely apart from § 706(d), there are various circumstances in which partnerships may be compelled or find it useful to use the interim closing method. For example, if an election to adjust the basis of partnership assets is in effect under § 754, an interim closing is generally necessary to compute the basis adjustments with respect to a transferee-partner under §§ 743(b) and 755 (see Chapter 24 of this treatise), and may also be necessary in connection with

---

[32] See Reg. § 1.706-4(g), with some relief for pre-April 14, 2009, publicly traded partnerships. The pre-2015 rules for varying interests were far less precise, as discussed in the Fourth Edition of this treatise.

[33] Reg. § 1.706-4(a)(2) (discharge of indebtedness income, § 704(c) allocations, and allocations governed by book-ups in connection with property reevaluations).

[34] Reg. § 1.706-4(a)(3)(iii).

[35] Reg. § 1.706-4(a)(3)(iii). Regulations § 1.706-4(f) provides that for this purpose, the term "agreement of the partners" means "a dated, written statement maintained with the partnership's books and records" no later than the due date, including any extension, of the partnership's tax return. These requirements also apply to partner agreements relating to the selection of the semi-monthly or monthly convention (¶ 12.03[1][b]), performance of regular monthly or semi-monthly interim closings (¶ 12.03[1][b]), and selection of additional extraordinary items (¶ 12.03[1][d]).

the liquidation of a partner's interest if adjustments to the bases of partnership assets are triggered under §§ 734(b) and 755 (see Chapter 25). Even in the absence of a § 754 election, the lack of an interim closing may make it difficult to apply § 732(d) to subsequent distributions to a transferee (See Chapter 26).

In addition, the interim closing method may be useful to avoid reporting problems that may arise if a partner's tax return for the period during which his interest is sold or liquidated is due before the partnership's income for its entire year is determined. For example, assume a calendar year individual who is a partner in a June 30 fiscal year partnership sells his entire partnership interest on September 30, 2020. He will be required to report his share of partnership income for the three-month period ending on September 30, 2020, on his individual return for 2020, which is due April 15, 2021. Since the partnership taxable year that includes this three-month period does not end until June 30, 2021, the selling or retiring partner must either obtain an extension for filing his 2020 return or file an amended return when the partnership's income for the year is determined if the proration method applies. However, under the interim closing method, the partnership will be able to determine his share of the income for the period ending September 30, 2020, without waiting for the end of its June 30, 2021, fiscal year.

[a] Step-by-Step Approach

Section 1.706-4(a)(3) of the Regulations (the "4(a)(3) Rules") lays out the following step-by-step approach for allocating partnership items related to a taxable year in which there are variations:

1. Determine whether the exceptions for (a) contemporaneous partners,[36] or (b) partnerships in which capital is not a material income-producing factor apply. In either case, the partnership is not subject to the 4(a)(3) Rules;[37]
2. Determine whether any "extraordinary items" arose during the partnership's taxable year. These items are not subject to the 4(a)(3) Rules;[38]
3. Elect either the interim closing method or the proration method for each variation;
4. Determine the date on which each variation occurs utilizing the conventions (calendar day, semi-monthly, or monthly) authorized by § 1.706-4(c) of the Regulations;

---

[36] Reg. §§ 1.706-4(a)(3)(i), 1.706-4(b)(1). See ¶ 12.04[1].

[37] Reg. §§ 1.706-4(a)(3)(i), 1.706-4(b)(2).

[38] Reg. § 1.706-4(a)(3)(ii). Reg. § 1.706-4(e) prohibits proration of extraordinary items.

5. Separate the partnership's taxable year into "segments" reflecting any interim closings during the year. The segments commence with the beginning of the partnership's taxable year and the dates of any subsequent interim closings, and end at the time of the next interim closing or the close of the partnership's taxable year;[39]

6. Apportion the partnership's tax items for the year among the segments based upon the interim closings;[40]

7. Divide each segment into any "proration periods," which are periods within a segment created by a variation for which the partnership chooses to apply the proration method; if there are no such variations, each segment constitutes a single proration period;[41]

8. Prorate all partnership tax items in each segment among the proration periods within the segment;[42] and

9. Determine each partner's distributive share of tax items for the year by taking into account the partner's interests in such items during each segment and proration period.[43]

A helpful Example in Regulations § 1.706-4(a)(4) illustrates the application of these concepts to a taxable year in which there are two variations, one on April 16 and another on August 6, but only one interim closing, on August 6, because the partners agree to apply the proration method to the April 16 variation. Consequently, the end of the first segment of the year is not triggered until the August 6 variation and causes an interim closing on July 31 because the partnership has elected the semi-monthly convention. The items attributable to this seven-month segment are determined based on the July 31 interim closing and are then divided between the two proration periods in the segment based on the number of days in the segment before and after the April 16 variation. The balances of all items for the year are included in the second five-month segment of the year and allocated among the partners in accordance with their respective interests after the August 6 variation.

An unresolved tension exists between the interim closing concept and the bonus depreciation rules in § 168(k) as well as the computation of first-year depreciation under the modified accelerated cost recovery system (MACRS) rules in § 168. Under both sets of rules, most property (other than real prop-

---

[39] Reg. § 1.706-4(a)(3)(vi). The number of segments during any taxable year will be equal to the number of variation dates with respect to which the interim closing method has been chosen plus one.

[40] Reg. § 1.706-4(a)(3)(vii). Items subject to limitations applicable to the partnership year as a whole, such as the annual limitation on property subject to expensing under § 179(b), can be apportioned among the segments by the partnership using any reasonable method.

[41] Reg. § 1.706-4(a)(3)(viii).

[42] Reg. § 1.706-4(a)(3)(ix).

[43] Reg. § 1.706-4(a)(3)(x).

erty) is treated as placed in service at the midpoint of the taxable year, regardless of when the property is in fact placed in service (§ 168(d)(4)(A)). If the partnership's books are closed in connection with a variation before property is treated as placed in service, *all* related depreciation deductions seemingly should be taken into account during the post-closing period, which, under the interim closing concept, is a separate accounting period. However, proposed MACRS regulations that have been outstanding since 1984 take the position that depreciation accrues ratably over the year and include an example that denies late-entering partners more than a pro-rata share of depreciation on property acquired by the partnership after their admission.[44] Significantly, the example reaches this conclusion under the varying interests rule without stating whether the partnership uses the interim closing method or the proration method.[45] Accordingly, the Treasury seems to be of the view that a partnership's election to utilize the interim closing method produces no benefits for late-entering partners.[46] More recent MACRS regulations under § 168(k) are generally consistent with this approach.[47]

[b] Interim Closing Conventions

Partnerships that select the interim closing method with respect to a variation are generally allowed to choose between the following conventions:

1. The calendar-day convention (i.e., a segment ends at the close of any day on which a variation occurs and the next segment begins at the open of the next day);
2. The semi-monthly convention (i.e., any variation that occurs between the first and the fifteenth of the month is deemed to close at the end of the last day of the preceding month with the new segment beginning on the first of the month, otherwise the variance is deemed to occur at the close of the fifteenth, with the next segment beginning on the sixteenth of the month); or

---

[44] Prop. Reg. § 1.168-2(k) (1984).

[45] Prop. Reg. § 1.168-2(k)(2) (1984).

[46] The § 168 Regulations were proposed in 1984, at which time the midyear convention was subsumed within the statutory cost recovery rates. See HR Rep. No. 841, 99th Cong., 2d Sess. II-45 (1986). The Tax Reform Act of 1986 moved the midyear convention into § 168(d) of the statute. The Treasury's view of the relationship between those accounting conventions and the ability of a partnership to allocate depreciation disproportionately to late-entering partners is only likely to be strengthened by this change.

[47] See Reg. § 1.168(d)-1(b)(7) (depreciation prorated in § 168(i)(7)(B)(i) nonrecognition transactions); Reg. § 1.168(k)-2(g)(1)(iii) (third sentence) (same, bonus depreciation). But cf. Reg. § 1.168(k)-2(g)(1)(iii) (sixth sentence) (all bonus depreciation allocated to contributing partner and not partnership if another partner held a depreciable interest in contributed property in same taxable year).

3. The monthly convention (i.e., any variation that occurs between the first and fifteenth days of the month is deemed to occur at the end of the last day of the preceding month; otherwise, the variance is deemed to occur at the end of the last day of the current month).[48]

For all variations in a taxable year with respect to which the interim closing method is selected, a partnership must be consistent in the convention it uses.[49] A partnership utilizing the proration method with respect to a variance is required to use the calendar-day convention.[50]

[c] Partners in Consolidated Groups

The flexibility to choose between the proration and interim closing methods may be constrained in the consolidated return context. A consolidated return must include each subsidiary's tax items for the portion of the consolidated return year for which it is a member of the consolidated group.[51] Unless an irrevocable election to apply a proration method is made, the allocation of items for the periods before and after a subsidiary's status changes is done on an interim closing basis.[52]

When an entering or departing subsidiary is a partner in a partnership, it is treated, solely for purposes of determining the period to which the partnership's items are allocated, as a deemed disposition of its entire interest in the partnership immediately before its change in status.[53] If the subsidiary (together with other members of the group) owns at least 50 percent of the capital and profits of the partnership, then the method used to allocate the partnership's items must be the same as the method (proration or interim closing) used to determine the inclusion of the subsidiary's items in the consolidated or separate return.

---

[48] Reg. § 1.706-4(c)(1). Under no circumstances, however, can a variation within a taxable year be deemed to occur prior to the beginning of such taxable year. See Reg. § 1.706-4(c)(2)(i). Similarly, the conventions cannot result in two variations occurring on the same day; in such cases, the actual dates of each variation must be used. Reg. §§ 1.706-4(c)(2)(ii)), 1.706- 4(c)(4) Example 2. The selection of a convention and the performance of interim closings require the "agreement of the partners" as defined in Reg. § 1.706-4(f).

[49] Reg. § 1.706-4(c)(3)(i). A partnership may elect to perform regular monthly or semi-monthly interim closing of its books, regardless of whether any variation occurs. Reg. § 706-4(d)(1).

[50] Reg. § 1.706-4(c)(3)(i).

[51] Reg. § 1.1502-76(b)(1).

[52] Reg. § 1.1502-76(b)(2)(ii). Under the Regulations, even if a ratable allocation method is elected, certain "extraordinary items" must still be apportioned between the periods on an interim closing basis.

[53] Reg. § 1.1502-76(b)(2)(vi)(A). See Reg. § 1.706-1(c)(2)(iii).

> **EXAMPLE 12-1:** *P*, the parent of a consolidated group, sells all the stock of its subsidiary *T* to *X*, and *T* ceases to be a member of *P*'s consolidated group on June 30 of calendar year 1. *T* has a 10 percent interest in the capital and profits of a calendar-year partnership. Because *T* is deemed to have sold its partnership interest for this purpose, *T*'s distributive share of partnership items for the portion of the partnership year ending on June 30 is included in determining *P*'s calendar year 1 taxable income. Under § 706(c)(2), the partnership's tax year is treated as closing with respect to *T* for this purpose as of the date of *P*'s sale of *T* stock.

Because *T* does not own 50 percent or more of the partnership capital and profits, *T*'s share of the partnership income can be determined under either the proration or interim closing method. However, if the members of the *P* consolidated group in the aggregate "control" the partnership, the method used by the partnership must be the same as the method used for allocating nonpartnership items between *P* and *T*.[54]

[d] Extraordinary Items

"Extraordinary items" of the partnership cannot be prorated, and must be allocated among the partners based on their interests at the precise time of the day[55] on which the extraordinary item occurs, regardless of the method or convention otherwise used by the partnership.[56] Subject to a "small item exception,"[57] the term "extraordinary items" includes items arising from dispositions of assets, § 481 adjustments, discharges of indebtedness, settlements of torts or similar third-party liabilities, credits that arise from non-ratably allocated activities or items, or other items that in the opinion of the Commissioner would, if ratably allocated, result in a substantial distortion of income in any return in

---

[54] Reg. § 1.1502-76(b)(5) Example (6)(c) (*T* owns 75 percent interest in capital and profits of partnership). As stated in Regulations § 1.1502-76(b)(2)(vi)(B), this consistency rule applies if the group members "would be treated under section 318(a)(2) as owning an aggregate of at least 50% of any stock owned by the passthrough entity ...."

[55] Example 5 in Regulations § 1.706-4(e)(4) confirms that same-day transfers of interests before or after the exact time of an extraordinary event are given full effect, so that early sellers and late buyers have no share of the item in question.

[56] Reg. § 1.706-4(e)(1). Publicly traded partnerships are permitted to apply their selected convention in determining who held their interests at the time of the event.

[57] "Small items" are generally items that would otherwise qualify as extraordinary items, except that the total of all items in a particular class of such items (e.g., § 481 adjustments) comprises less than 5 percent of a partnership's gross income (in the case of income or gain items) or gross expenses and losses (in the case of loss or expense items), subject to a $10 million total cap (treating all extraordinary items, whether gain or loss, as positive). Reg. §§ 1.706-4(e)(3), 1.706-4(e)(4) Examples 5, 6.

which the item is included.[58] Further, upon agreement of the partners,[59] a partnership is authorized to treat non-enumerated items as extraordinary items for a taxable year if the partnership consistently treats such items as extraordinary for the taxable year and such treatment does not result in a substantial distortion of income.

The extraordinary item rule may have been based on (or at least inspired by) an earlier Tax Court decision in *Sam J. Vecchio*,[60] which involved the allocation of gain from a sale of partnership property. Pursuant to a state court order resolving certain differences among the partners, the petitioner became obligated to purchase the interest of a 49 percent partner ("Equity") for a fixed purchase price. Petitioner subsequently arranged an installment sale of the partnership's main asset. Based on the court order and the partnership agreement, the Tax Court was called upon to allocate the gain from the sale of the property. It found that the partnership terminated and dissolved and petitioner was obligated to close the purchase of Equity's partnership interest upon the sale of the property. For the year of the sale, the court allocated to Equity an amount of gain equal to its deficit capital account, on the grounds that the gain should first be allocated to offset tax losses previously allocated to Equity. The court then allocated the remainder of the year-of-sale gain to the buyer of the partnership interest, on the grounds that the buyer would be entitled to a cash distribution from the partnership with respect to the purchased interest in an amount that exceeded the remaining gain. *Vecchio* appears to still be good law, as reflected in Regulations § 1.706-4(e)(4) Example 1 (allocation of gain from extraordinary item based on partners' interests at exact time of sale generating gain) and Regulations § 1.706-4(a)(4) Example (partnership's books deemed to close at the end of day on which sale occurs).

[2] Allocable Cash Basis Items

Section 706(d)(2) governs the allocation of certain cash-method items that are economically accrued before, but paid or received after, a change in the partners' interests. In essence, § 706(d)(2) places a cash-method partnership on an

---

[58] Reg. § 1.706-4(e)(2). Under Proposed Regulations § 1.706-4(e)(2)(x) (2015), any deduction for the transfer of a partnership interest for services would be treated as an extraordinary item occurring immediately before the transfer, thus preventing the deduction from being allocated to the service provider. It appears that this restriction may generally be avoided through the use of special allocations. See ¶ 12.04[2]. In addition, special rules would be provided for publicly traded partnerships subject to § 1441 withholding. Prop. Reg. §§ 1.706-4(e)(2)(ix), 1.706-4(f) (2015).

[59] For this purpose, "agreement of the partners" is defined in Regulations § 1.706-4(f).

[60] Sam J. Vecchio, 103 TC 170 (1994).

economic accrual method for the purpose of allocating these items, even though they are not taken into income or are not deductible until actually received or paid. Except as provided in Regulations, the partnership must assign an appropriate portion of each "allocable cash basis item" to each day of its taxable year. The portion assigned to each day is then allocated among the partners in proportion to their interests in the partnership at the close of the day.[61] The term "allocable cash basis item" includes interest, taxes, payments for services or the use of property, and any other items set forth in the Regulations as appropriate to avoid any significant misstatement of the partners' income.[62]

If a cash basis item is economically accrued in a taxable year prior to the year in which it is paid, the item is assigned to the first day of the year during which it is paid.[63] This rule is applicable regardless of whether any change in the partners' interests occurs.[64] Deductible cash basis items that are assigned to the first day of a taxable year under this rule must be allocated to the partners in accordance with their varying interests during the period that the deduction accrued economically, rather than their interests on the first day of a subsequent year.[65] To the extent a deductible cash basis item is allocated to a person who is no longer a partner under this rule, the item must be capitalized and added to the basis of the partnership's assets using the allocation rules in § 755.[66]

> EXAMPLE 12-2: On July 1, equal calendar-year partnership AB incurs a $120,000 obligation bearing simple interest at the rate of 10 percent per annum. On December 1, C is admitted as a one-third partner. On December 31, A sells his interest to D. If the partnership pays $6,000 of economically accrued interest on December 31, five sixths of the payment ($5,000) is allocated equally between A and B (who were the only partners from July through November) and one sixth ($1,000) is allocated equally among A, B, and C. Thus, A and B each have an allocable share of $2,833.33, and C has a $333.33 share of the interest deduction.
>
> The results are the same with respect to B and C if the payment is delayed until January 1 of the next year, except that the deduction is deferred until the year of payment.[67] However, because A is no longer a partner on January 1 of the next year, A's share of the payment is not de-

---

[61] § 706(d)(2)(A). See Prop. Reg. § 1.706-2(a)(1) (2015).

[62] § 704(d)(2)(B). See Prop. Reg. § 1.706-2(a)(2) (2015).

[63] § 706(d)(2)(C)(i). See Prop. Reg. § 1.706-2(a)(3)(i) (2015).

[64] S. Rep. No. 313, 99th Cong., 2d Sess. 922 (1986).

[65] § 706(d)(2)(D)(i). See Prop. Reg. § 1.706-2(a)(4)(i) (2015).

[66] § 706(d)(2)(D)(ii). See Prop. Reg. § 1.706-2(a)(4)(ii) (2015).

[67] See § 706(c)(2)(A). See Prop. Reg. § 1.706-2(b) Example 1 (2015).

ductible by *A* or by any other partner, but instead must be added to the basis of the partnership's assets under § 755.[68]

Section 706(d)(2) also provides a special rule for those relatively rare situations in which prepayments by cash basis partnerships are deductible before economic accrual occurs. In general, these items are assigned to the last day of the year of prepayment.[69] For example, if a December 31 prepayment of January rent is deductible when paid, it would be allocated according to the partners' interests on December 31.

The application of § 706(d)(2) to cash basis income items is unclear. The focus of both the statute and the accompanying legislative history clearly is on deduction items, and the enumeration of specific "allocable cash basis items" in § 706(d)(2)(B) is limited to expense items. However, the grant of authority to issue Regulations under § 706(d)(2)(B)(iv) is arguably broad enough to allow the Treasury to create income items that are "allocable cash basis items."[70]

If § 706(d)(2) is applicable to income items, several questions arise. First, what is the relationship between § 706(d)(2) and § 751, which provides rules governing shifts in the partners' interests in unrealized receivables? Second, what is a cash basis income item? For example, does it include installment receivables under §§ 453 and 453A? Third, what are the mechanical rules for assigning an "appropriate portion" of a cash basis income item to each day in the period to which it is attributable? Suppose, for example, that a law partnership accepts a case and receives a retainer on January 1, performs services at various times through the following December, and renders a statement for its fee (net of the retainer) on January 1 of the following year. To which days is the fee allocable? Is it necessary to account for the services rendered on a daily basis? Are the rules different where the fee eventually charged is result-oriented or wholly contingent? Would Treasury be better advised to simply exempt all income items in Regulations issued pursuant to the authority granted in § 706(d)?

The application of § 706(d)(2) to service partnerships can be extremely complex, especially if there are partnership liabilities, as the following example demonstrates.

---

[68] See § 706(d)(2)(D)(ii). See Prop. Reg. § 1.706-2(b) Example 2 (2015) (treating *D* as having a § 743(b) adjustment).

[69] § 706(d)(2)(C)(ii).

[70] The only Regulations issued to date under this grant of authority provide that an otherwise deductible amount that is deferred under § 267(a)(2) is an allocable cash basis item in the year the deduction is allowed. Temp. Reg. § 1.706-2T (1984). Proposed Regulations issued in 2015 make clear that income items are "allocable cash basis items," but provide no guidance on the issues raised in the text below. Prop. Reg. § 1.706-2(a)(2) (2015) ("income" items).

EXAMPLE 12-3: *ABCX* is an equal accounting partnership that computes its income on the cash method. *X* retires from the partnership on December 31, 2020, in exchange for a distribution equal to his capital account (computed on the cash method), and the partnership admits *D* as an equal partner on January 1, 2021. On January 1, *ABCD* has $100 of receivables and $50 of payables attributable to the last half of 2020, which are collected and paid in 2021. If the partnership has any liabilities, the $100 of 2020 receivables should be allocated entirely to *A*, *B*, and *C* to avoid entanglement with § 751(b).[71] As a consequence, in order to avoid doing violence to the economic arrangement with *D*, a special allocation of $33.33 of 2021 income to *D* is necessary. With respect to the payables, $12.50 must be capitalized pursuant to § 706(d)(2)(D) and added to the partnership's basis in its assets under § 755.[72] The remaining $37.50 must be allocated equally among *A*, *B*, and *C*. Another special allocation to *D* (consisting of $12.50 of 2021 deductions) seems necessary to properly reflect the partners' economic arrangements. Since all partners will share equally in the benefit of the $12.50 § 755 basis adjustment, all partners should share equally the burden of the resulting 2021 overstatement of taxable income ($12.50 divided by four equals $3.12). That the suggested special allocations to *D* are necessary and sufficient to produce the desired economic results may be seen by assuming that *ABCD* has only $33.33 of income and $12.50 of deductions in 2021:

	A	B	C	D
Income:				
$100 receivables from 2020	$33.33	$33.33	$33.33	—
2021 income	—	—	—	$33.33
Deductions:				
$50 payables from 2020	($12.50)	($12.50)	($12.50)	—
2021 deductions	—	—	—	($12.50)
Net Income	$20.83	$20.83	$20.83	$20.83

If *ABCD* distributes all of its cash at the end of 2021, each partner will receive $17.71 ($50 net cash from 2020 activity plus net cash of $20.83 from 2021 divided by four). Each partner's $3.12 share of the § 755 basis adjustment plus his or her share of the cash distributions will equal $20.83, which is his 2021 distributive share of the *ABCD* taxable income.

As Example 12-3 suggests, the level of complexity inherent in § 706(d)(2) brings into serious question the need for its existence, especially in light of the minimal potential for abuse under current law.[73]

---

[71] See Chapter 21.

[72] See ¶ 24.04.

[73] Proposed Regulations contain a de minimis rule if the total allocable cash basis items are less than $10 million and the particular class is less than 5 percent of the part-

[3] Allocations Involving Tier Partnerships

Section 706(d)(3) is designed to eliminate the use of tier partnerships to avoid restrictions on retroactive allocations.[74] It provides that the daily allocation method for cash basis items is applicable to all items (not merely cash basis items) of a lower-tier partnership (LTP) if there is any change in the partners' interests in the upper-tier partnership (UTP).

Proposed Regulations issued in 2015 would apply a pure look-through daily allocation method to tiered partnership structures with a significant de minimis exception.[75] De minimis UTPs would not be subject to this requirement. UTPs are de minimis if each individually owns less than 10 percent of the LTP profits and capital *and* in the aggregate own less than 30 percent of the LTP profits and capital.[76]

> **EXAMPLE 12-4:** *A, B,* and *C* are equal partners in *UTP. UTP* owns a 15 percent interest in *LTP.* In 2015, *LTP* has no extraordinary items and $100,000 of ordinary deductions during the six-month period from the beginning of the year through July 1. *A* sells her *UTP* interest to *D* on August 1, 2015. Under Regulations § 1.706-3(a), *UTP* would be required to assign its entire $15,000 share of *LTP*'s deduction pro rata to each day in the period ending on July 1 and, consequently, allocate it equally among *A, B,* and *C. D* cannot be allocated any part of the deduction.[77]

> **EXAMPLE 12-5:** Same facts as Example 12-4, except *UTP* owns a 9 percent interest in *LTP;* none of the other *LTP* partners own less than 10 percent. *UTP* would be able, but would not be required, to apply Regulations § 1.706-3(a). Under Regulations § 1.706-4, *UTP*'s application of the interim closing method would produce the same allocations of *UTP*'s $9,000 share of *LTP*'s deduction as Regulations § 1.706-3(a), whereas *UTP*'s application of the pro-rata method would allocate the $9,000 as

---

nership's gross income or gross expense items, as the case may be. Prop. Reg. § 1.706-2(c) (2015).

[74] See HR Rep. No. 861, 98th Cong., 2d Sess. 858 (1984); 1 Senate Comm. on Finance, 98th Cong., 2d Sess., Deficit Reduction Act of 1984, S. Prt. No. 169, at 221 (Comm. Print 1984). If the UTP and LTP are on different taxable years, the Senate Finance Committee Explanation suggests that the Treasury may provide, by Regulations, for an interim closing of the LTP's taxable year at the time the UTP's taxable year closes. To date, Treasury has not adopted or proposed this requirement.

[75] Prop. Reg. § 1.706-3(a) (2015). This is not a new or novel concept. See Rev. Rul. 77-311, 1977-2 CB 218 (extending the principles of § 706(c)(2)(B) to tiered partnerships by adopting a look-through approach to effectively ignore the existence of a UTP).

[76] Prop. Reg. § 1.706-3(b) (2015). The de minimis rule does not apply if any of the partnerships are created for the purpose of avoiding the tiered partnership rules.

[77] Prop. Reg. § 1.706-3(c) Example 1 (2015).

follows: $3,000 to *B*, $3,000 to *C*, and the remaining $3,000 would be divided $1,751 (213/365) to *A* and $1,249 (152/365) to *D*.[78]

¶ 12.04 THE EFFECT OF SECTION 706(D) ON THE POWER OF PARTNERS TO CHANGE THEIR DISTRIBUTIVE SHARES BY AGREEMENT

[1] Contemporaneous Partners

Standing alone, §§ 704(a) and 761(c) appear to give persons who are partners during a particular period the right to allocate partnership income or loss for the period among themselves by agreement, without reference to the § 706 varying interests rules, provided only that the agreed allocations (1) satisfy the requirements of §§ 704(b) through 704(e), and (2) are entered into before the due date of the partnership return for the period.[79] Conversely, § 706(d) provides that if there is a change of any partner's interest in the partnership during the partnership year, each partner's distributive share must take into account the varying interests of the partners during the year.

These statutory concepts are appropriately reflected in Regulations § 1.706-4(b)(1), which provides that the variance rules in Regulations § 1.706-4(a)(3) do "not preclude changes in the allocations of the distributive share of [partnership] items" among contemporaneous partners for an entire year (or any segment thereof if the item is entirely attributable to the segment) provided that the allocations are valid under § 704(b) and do not reflect variances attributable to contributions to or distributions from the partnership.

A somewhat related question is whether partners may reallocate their indirect interests in appreciation in partnership assets prior to its realization by the partnership. For example, suppose that equal partnership *AB* purchases an asset for $100 and then, when the asset has appreciated in value to $300 (while its book value for § 704(b) purposes remains $100), the partnership agreement is amended to allocate partnership gain 75 percent to *A* and 25 percent to *B*. Has *A* received a $50 taxable capital shift from *B*? Although the § 704 Regulations contain a vague hint that, in certain circumstances, a failure to

---

[78] Prop. Reg. § 1.706-3(c) Examples 2 & 3 (2015).

[79] S. Rep. No. 938, 94th Cong., 2d Sess. 98 (1976); accord HR Rep. No. 658, 94th Cong., 1st Sess. 124 (1975). See Danny Curtis, 70 TCM 205 (1995) (effort retroactively to allocate to one member of equal two-person partnership income of partnership that was unreported owing to actions of such partner; attempt made after partnership's tax returns examined; retroactive allocation not respected because not timely under § 761(c); "innocent" partner liable for tax on his share of unreported income).

restate capital to prevent a shift in unrealized appreciation may be taxable,[80] it seems quite clear that no taxable shift results when existing partners agree to adjust their interests in unrealized appreciation in partnership assets. Otherwise, any reallocation of profits by an existing partnership, for example, an accounting firm, would result in a taxable capital shift with respect to partnership assets if their fair market values differ from their book values. This conclusion is confirmed by a Private Letter Ruling in which the Service ruled that no tax consequences resulted from an amendment to a partnership agreement that fixed the partners' interests in certain appreciated partnership assets.[81]

Conversely, the Service has concluded that a state court's retroactive award, in a divorce proceeding, of a spouse's community property rights in a partnership interest should not be given effect for tax purposes.[82] The court's order purported to be retroactive, thus giving the spouse an interest in the partnership commencing in a taxable year prior to the date of the award. The Field Service Advice states that the Service does "not believe that the ... order should be given retroactive tax effect," because "state court orders that retroactively change the rights of the parties or the status of payments are not given retroactive effect for federal tax purposes." For this proposition, the Service did not cite § 704 or § 706, but relied instead on *Arthur Z. Gordon*,[83] in which the Tax Court held that state court orders redesignating divorce-related payments as alimony (and not child support)—or vice versa—are disregarded for federal income tax purposes even if the order retroactively changes the rights of the parties or the legal status of the payments. The Service also determined that the tax benefit rule could not be applied on these facts to achieve the same effect as the retroactive reallocation.

[2] Using Section 704(b) Allocations to Achieve the Effect of Retroactive Allocations

In some situations, it may be possible to achieve the economic effect of a retroactive allocation through the use of disproportionate special allocations of post-admission income or losses (or items thereof) under § 704(b).[84]

---

[80] See Reg. § 1.704-1(b)(2)(iv)(f). The existing Regulations do not permit restatement of capital accounts in these circumstances. However, Prop. Reg. § 1.704-1(b)(2)(iv)(F)(5)(v) (2014) would allow it. See ¶ 10.02[2][c].

[81] Priv. Ltr. Rul. 9821051 (Feb. 23, 1998).

[82] FSA 200128031 (Apr. 12, 2001).

[83] Arthur Z. Gordon, 70 TC 525 (1978).

[84] See Mary K.S. Ogden, 84 TC 871 (1984), aff'd per curiam, 788 F2d 252 (5th Cir. 1986). Although the allocations in *Ogden* were held invalid under § 704(b), the Commissioner conceded that, if the allocations had passed muster under the § 704(b) substantial

EXAMPLE 12-6: A calendar-year partnership receives $10,000 per month of gross income and its only expense is an $11,000 per month depreciation deduction. For 2020, the partnership realizes a net taxable loss of $12,000. A new partner is admitted as a 25 percent partner on November 1, 2020. Under § 706(d), the new partner is allocated a $500 share of partnership losses for 2020 (25 percent of two months' post-admission loss of $2,000), rather than a $3,000 share of the full $12,000 loss for the year.

If the agreement provides for the allocation to the new partner of the entire partnership loss for November and December 2020, and if this allocation of post-admission losses satisfies the requirements of § 704(b),[85] it should not be proscribed by § 706(d). Although the new partner would not be allocated a "full" 25 percent ($3,000) share of the 2020 loss, it appears this technique would allow him to be allocated $2,000, rather than $500, of the 2020 loss.

Alternatively, to increase the late-entering partner's share of the 2020 loss to a full $3,000 share for the year, the partners might consider specifically allocating $4,000 per month of November and December depreciation to the new partner, so that his share of total depreciation for two months ($8,000) would exceed his 25 percent share ($5,000) of income for these months by $3,000. The result would be a net allocation to the new partner of $3,000, or 25 percent of the total loss for 2020.

Of course, compliance with § 704(b) requires the new partner to bear the economic burden of any allocated losses, which may make any of these approaches less appetizing.

---

economic effect test, they would have been valid under § 706(c) of prior law, which encompassed the varying-interests standard.

[85] See ¶ 11.02.

CHAPTER 17

Transfers of Interests in Collapsible Partnerships

¶ 17.01 THE COLLAPSIBLE PARTNERSHIP PROVISION: SECTION 751(a)

Section 741 states the general rule that gain or loss on the sale or exchange of a partnership interest is treated as gain or loss from the sale of a capital asset.[1] A major exception to this general rule is set forth in § 751(a), the "collapsible partnership" provision. Section 751(a) provides that amounts received in exchange for all or a portion of a partnership interest are treated as realized in connection with the sale of a noncapital asset to the extent attributable to "unrealized receivables"[2] or "inventory items"[3] of the partnership.

---

[1] See Chapter 16.

[2] See ¶ 17.03.

[3] See ¶ 17.04. For transfers on or before August 5, 1997, § 751(a) only applied to partnership inventory items if they were "substantially appreciated." Section 751 was amended by the Tax Relief Act of 1997 to delete the "substantial appreciation" requirement with respect to transfers of partnership interests but not partnership distributions.

[1] Pre-1954 Judicial Doctrines

An understanding of § 751(a), as well as the abuse that it was intended to curb, begins with a review of the judicial doctrines that developed prior to the enactment of §§ 741 and 751(a) as part of the 1954 Code. Prior statutes contained no counterpart to either section.

Without benefit of statutory guidance, the case law dealing with transfers of partnership interests focused initially on whether the transferred interest should be fragmented into transfers of co-ownership interests in specific partnership assets or treated as a single transfer of an interest in the partnership entity.[4] The Service generally found it expedient to argue for fragmentation, thereby subjecting the transaction to ordinary income treatment to the extent the amount realized by the transferor-partner was attributable to ordinary income assets of the partnership. The Service was quite properly concerned that the allowance of capital gain treatment on the sale of an interest in a partnership holding appreciated ordinary income property might result in the conversion of ordinary income into capital gain if the sale were followed by a "collapse" of the partnership.[5] Conversely, taxpayers realizing gains on sales of

---

[4] See Helvering v. Smith, 90 F2d 590 (2d Cir. 1937) (Judge L. Hand) (partnership not an "independent juristic entity," therefore must examine character of partnership assets); Stilgenbauer v. United States, 115 F2d 283 (9th Cir. 1940) (treated as sale of interest in partnership assets under state law); cf. City Bank Farmers Trust Co. v. United States, 47 F. Supp. 98 (Ct. Cl. 1942) (holding period for partnership interest based on holding period of partnership assets). But see Dudley T. Humphrey, 32 BTA 280 (1935) (partnership interest is a capital asset "separate and distinct from" any ownership interest in partnership assets); McClellan v. Commissioner, 117 F2d 988 (2d Cir. 1941) (per curiam) (distinguishing *Helvering v. Smith*); Commissioner v. Shapiro, 125 F2d 532 (6th Cir. 1942) (capital gain on sale of interest in the entire partnership business, including going concern value); cf. Williams v. McGowan, 152 F2d 570, 572 (2d Cir. 1945) (Judge L. Hand) (dictum) (sale of partnership interest is sale of a capital asset). Judge Hand's preoccupation with the subtleties of state partnership law and disregard for the realities of income taxation contributed materially to the early confusion in this area.

[5] Upon termination of the partnership, the purchasers obtained bases in the former partnership assets equal to the cost of the partnership interests. The tax savings could be spectacular. For example, assume the *AB* partnership is engaged in the construction and sale of a tract of homes. Following substantial completion of construction, but before the realization of substantial income from sales, *A* and *B* sell their interests to *C*, who completes the marketing of the tract. Instead of paying ordinary income tax on the entire profit from the tract, the only income subject to ordinary income tax rates is the difference between the amount paid by *C* and *C*'s proceeds from the sale of the tract. The profits realized by *A* and *B* would be subject only to capital gain tax. See John W. Lenney, 38 TC 287 (1962) (nonacq.). The tax abuse is particularly acute if *C* is a corporation controlled by *A* and/or *B*. See Ed Krist, 12 TCM 801 (1953), aff'd on another issue, 231 F2d 548 (9th Cir. 1956). See generally Jackson et al., "The Internal Revenue Code of 1954: Partnerships," 54 Colum. L. Rev. 1183, 1216 (1954); Taylor, "Tax Problems in the Purchase and Sale of Partnership Interests," 1953 Major Tax Problems 235.

partnership interests were inclined to view the transactions as dispositions of interests in entities.[6]

After numerous setbacks,[7] the Service conceded, in 1950, that "the sale of a partnership interest should be treated as the sale of a capital asset," rather than a sale of undivided interests in partnership assets.[8] This concession was, however, carefully hedged: It was "limited to those cases in which the transaction in substance and effect, as distinguished from form and appearance, is essentially the sale of a partnership interest," and it excluded "payments made to a retiring partner which represent his distributive share of earnings for past services."[9]

Notwithstanding the Service's conditional surrender on the basic capital asset issue, the availability of capital gain treatment to selling partners remained constrained by a number of judicially forged doctrines that continued to develop after 1950. The major themes of these doctrines may be summarized as follows:

1. It was firmly established that a partner could not escape taxation on his share of current partnership income by the simple expedient of selling his interest prior to the end of the partnership taxable year.[10]

2. Relying on assignment-of-income principles, the courts generally rejected attempts to convert personal services income into capital gain through sales of interests in cash basis partnerships holding unrealized accounts receivable and work in process.[11]

---

[6] If the selling partner realized a loss, the adversaries reversed their positions. See, e.g., McClellan v. Commissioner, 117 F2d 988 (2d Cir. 1941) (per curiam).

[7] See, e.g., United States v. Shapiro, 178 F2d 459 (8th Cir. 1949); Long v. Commissioner, 173 F2d 471 (5th Cir. 1949) (cert. denied); Commissioner v. Smith, 173 F2d 470 (5th Cir. 1949) (cert. denied); United States v. Landreth, 164 F2d 340 (5th Cir. 1947); Thornley v. Commissioner, 147 F2d 416 (3d Cir. 1945); Joseph Pursglove, Jr., 20 TC 68 (1953); Estate of Gartling, 6 TCM 879 (1947), aff'd per curiam, 170 F2d 73 (9th Cir. 1948).

[8] GCM 26379, 1950-1 CB 58, 59, declared obsolete by Rev. Rul. 67-406, 1967-2 CB 420.

[9] GCM 26379, 1950-1 CB 58, 59, declared obsolete by Rev. Rul. 67-406, 1967-2 CB 420.

[10] See Leff v. Commissioner, 235 F2d 439 (2d Cir. 1956); Hulbert v. Commissioner, 227 F2d 399 (7th Cir. 1955); United States v. Snow, 223 F2d 103 (9th Cir. 1955) (cert. denied); Le Sage v. Commissioner, 173 F2d 826 (5th Cir. 1949); George F. Johnson, 21 TC 733 (1954); Louis Karsch, 8 TC 1327 (1947). Contra Meyer v. United States, 213 F2d 278 (7th Cir. 1954). In 1954, this rule was codified in § 706(c)(2).

[11] See Tunnell v. United States, 259 F2d 916 (3d Cir. 1958) (lawyer); Helvering v. Smith, 90 F2d 590 (2d Cir. 1937) (lawyer); B. Howard Spicker, 26 TC 91 (1956) (accountant). Contra United States v. Donoho, 275 F2d 489 (8th Cir. 1960) (doctor); Swiren v. Commissioner, 183 F2d 656 (7th Cir. 1950) (cert. denied) (lawyer).

3. Taxpayers who delayed the sale of their partnership interests until the partnership's business activities were substantially complete sometimes found themselves taxed as though the partnership had dissolved prior to the putative sales of their interests.[12]

4. Finally, there was some evidence that the Service might be able to apply its power to require a taxpayer's accounting method to clearly reflect income in order to upset an effort to achieve capital gain treatment through a combination of the completed contract method of accounting and a pre-completion sale of a partnership interest.[13]

Many of these doctrines were not fully developed in 1954. Consequently, Congress coupled the general rule of § 741 with the prophylactic provisions of § 751 "to prevent the conversion of potential ordinary income into capital gain by virtue of transfers of partnership interests."[14] In view of the subsequent development of these protective judicial doctrines, and the apparent ability of the courts to cope with flagrant abuses of the collapsible partnership device without legislative assistance, the enactment of § 751 might have been avoided (and both Subchapter K and this book simplified considerably) if the timing of judicial and legislative developments had been somewhat different. However, as hindsight (and this chapter) demonstrate, enactment of this provision greatly reduced the litigation in this arena. Effectively, Congress created a new set of rules that, although complex, are clearly limited in scope and scale relative to the problem addressed, produce clearly definable and arguably rational results, and minimize the friction and costs in the system. We have come to view favorably changes that meet these minimum standards as we find ourselves working in a world of § 163(j) Regulations and the like.

---

[12] See Haggard v. Wood, 298 F2d 24 (9th Cir. 1961) (sale in form of transfer of partnership interests in substance sale of underlying asset, a cotton crop); Trousdale v. Commissioner, 219 F2d 563 (9th Cir. 1955) (partnership in "state of liquidation"; in substance, sale of liquidation proceeds rather than partnership interest); cf. Bull v. United States, 295 US 247 (1935) (payments to estate of deceased partner characterized as share of partnership income); Doyle v. Commissioner, 102 F2d 86 (4th Cir. 1939) (sale occurred after liquidation of partnership); James Wesley McAfee, 9 TC 720 (1947) (payment to withdrawing partner constituted share of partnership income). However, if substantial work needed to be done to complete the earning of the partnership income, or if the income was contingent or not definitely ascertainable, selling partners sometimes achieved capital gain treatment. See Berry v. United States, 267 F2d 298 (6th Cir. 1959); John W. Lenney, 38 TC 287 (1962) (nonacq.); Ed Krist, 12 TCM 801 (1953), aff'd on another issue, 231 F2d 548 (9th Cir. 1956). But cf. Virgil L. Beavers, 31 TC 336 (1958) (payments were share of liquidation proceeds rather than sale proceeds).

[13] Cf. Standard Paving Co. v. Commissioner, 190 F2d 330 (10th Cir. 1951) (cert. denied).

[14] S. Rep. No. 1622, 83d Cong., 2d Sess. 98 (1954). See Francis E. Holman, 66 TC 809 (1976), aff'd, 564 F2d 283 (9th Cir. 1977) (discussion of the purpose of § 751(a)).

[2] Continuing Vitality of Pre-1954 Judicial Doctrines

The question of whether the pre-1954 Code judicial doctrines have continuing viability under the 1986 Code is rendered moot, in large part, by the breadth of § 751. Very few partnerships will escape the net of § 751 only to fall prey to these judicial snares. As a practical matter, the potential application of the nonstatutory doctrines is probably limited to transfers prior to August 5, 1997, of interests in partnerships holding inventory items that are not substantially appreciated within the meaning of § 751(d)(1).[15] After that date, § 751(a) applies to the sale of an interest in a partnership that owns any inventory.

A somewhat analogous question, involving the viability of the *Kimbell-Diamond* rule[16] following enactment of § 334(b)(2) of the 1954 Code (which treated as an asset acquisition certain stock purchases followed by a liquidation of the purchased corporation), was resolved by the U.S. Court of Claims in favor of the continued effectiveness of the judicial doctrine, relying in part on the absence of any express legislative intent to attribute exclusivity to § 334(b)(2).[17] Other courts considering this question, however, concluded that *Kimbell-Diamond* was preempted by § 334(b)(2).[18] The legislative history of § 751 is similarly devoid of any intent to preempt the field, and thus the U.S. Court of Claims presumably would conclude that the assignment-of-income doctrine and other judicial exceptions have continued vitality under § 741, whereas the Tax Court and at least three of the federal courts of appeals might come to the opposite conclusion.

Further, a few cases and rulings applying the 1954 Code contain language and reasoning reminiscent of the pre-1954 case law. Thus, in *Herman M. Hale*,[19] the Tax Court taxed a portion of the proceeds from the transfer of a partnership interest as ordinary income, relying on various assignment-of-income cases and without referring to § 751.[20] The Service also has is-

---

[15] See ¶ 17.04.

[16] Kimbell-Diamond Milling Co. v. Commissioner, 187 F2d 718 (5th Cir. 1951) (cert. denied) (purchase of stock followed closely by liquidation gives corporate purchaser a cost basis in assets acquired under step-transaction approach).

[17] American Potash & Chem. Corp. v. United States, 399 F2d 194 (Ct. Cl. 1968).

[18] See, e.g., Broadview Lumber Co. v. United States, 561 F2d 698 (7th Cir. 1977); Pacific Transp. Co. v. Commissioner, 483 F2d 209 (9th Cir. 1973); Supreme Inv. Co. v. United States, 468 F2d 370 (5th Cir. 1972); International State Bank, 70 TC 173 (1978).

[19] Herman M. Hale, 24 TCM 1497 (1965) (issue 1).

[20] Cf. George D. Seyburn, 51 TC 578 (1969), in which the donor of a partnership interest to two charities was taxed on rents subsequently received by the partnership under assignment-of-income principles. The court characterized the partnership as "in the process of liquidation" at the time of the transfers and relied heavily on Paul W. Trousdale, 16 TC 1056 (1951), aff'd, 219 F2d 563 (9th Cir. 1955). See note 12. Although the *Seyburn* holding is not an alternative to the application of § 751(a), the court's approval of *Trousdale* suggests that the pre-1954 case law is alive and well.

sued a few rulings under the 1954 Code containing assignment-of-income discussions and little or no reference to § 751.[21]

While all of these cases and rulings are over sixty years old, they suggest that fancy schemes to avoid the mechanics of § 751 may be ensnared by the judicial doctrines described earlier.[22]

[3] Section 751(a) and Transfers of Partnership Interests

The balance of this chapter is devoted to a detailed examination of the application of § 751 to sales or exchanges of partnership interests. The sections that follow deal with the operational provision, § 751(a);[23] the definitions of "unrealized receivables" and "inventory items" contained in §§ 751(c) and 751(d);[24] and certain problems arising in connection with installment sales of interests in collapsible partnerships and sales of interests in collapsible tier partnerships.[25]

Under current law, all inventory items are potentially subject to § 751(a) in connection with transfers, but only these that are substantially appreciated under what is now § 751(b)(3) are taken into account under § 751(b).

The operation of § 751(b) in connection with distributions from partnerships owning § 751 property is discussed in Chapter 21.

¶ 17.02 OPERATION OF SECTION 751(a)

The complexities of § 751(a) are masked by the outward simplicity of the provision, which currently reads in full as follows:

> The amount of any money, or the fair market value of any property, received by a transferor partner in exchange for all or a part of his interest in the partnership attributable to—
>
> (1) unrealized receivables of the partnership, or
> (2) inventory items of the partnership,
>
> shall be considered as an amount realized from the sale or exchange of property other than a capital asset.

---

[21] See Rev. Rul. 60-352, 1960-2 CB 208; Rev. Rul. 58-394, 1958-2 CB 374.
[22] See ¶ 17.01[1].
[23] See ¶ 17.02.
[24] See ¶¶ 17.03, 17.04.
[25] See ¶¶ 17.05, 17.06.

In the discussion that follows, the term "§ 751 property" refers to a partnership's unrealized receivables and inventory items subject to § 751(a).

[1] Transactions Subject to Section 751(a)

Although § 751(a) does not employ the "sale or exchange" language found elsewhere in the Code, the legislative history of the provision indicates that its reach corresponds to that of § 741, which is expressly applicable to any "sale or exchange" of a partnership interest.[26] Section 751(a) is applicable regardless of whether the transfer involves all or part of the transferor's interest,[27] and also regardless of whether the transferee is an outsider or a partner prior to the transfer.[28] It is not, however, applicable to amounts received as distributions from a partnership: The legislative history,[29] the language of § 751(b), and the sense of the overall statutory scheme make it abundantly clear that § 751(b), rather than § 751(a), is the controlling provision with respect to both current and liquidating distributions.

Whether a particular transaction is a transfer (subject to § 751(a)) or a distribution (subject to § 751(b)) can be a perplexing question, particularly where no outsiders are involved and the interests of other partners are increased pro rata as a consequence of the transaction. The issue frequently arises in connection with terminations of two-person partnerships: Did the partner who continues the business purchase his former partner's interest, or was the former partner's interest retired in exchange for a distribution from the partnership? The absence of meaningful economic differences between the two methods of structuring the transaction may contribute to incomplete or ambiguous documentation and consequent difficulties in categorizing the transaction for tax purposes.

These classification problems are discussed at length in Chapter 16.[30] The consequences of classifying a transaction as a transfer subject to § 751(a) are discussed below. The consequences of distribution classification and the application of § 751(b), which can produce substantially different results in certain circumstances, are discussed in Chapter 21.

---

[26] The legislative history supports the proposition that § 751(a) is intended to apply to the same type of transactions as § 741, while § 751(b) is intended to correspond to § 731. See HR Rep. No. 1337, 83d Cong., 2d Sess. 7071 (1954); S. Rep. No. 1622, 83d Cong., 2d Sess. 401 (1954).

[27] Rev. Rul. 59-109, 1959-1 CB 168.

[28] See, e.g., Frank A. Logan, 51 TC 482 (1968).

[29] See note 26.

[30] See ¶ 16.02[3].

[2] The Mechanics of Section 751(a)

The Regulations[31] bifurcate the determination of a transferor-partner's realized gain upon the transfer of a partnership interest as follows:

1. The transferor-partner's § 751(a) income or loss equals the net amount of income or loss that would have been allocated to the transferor with respect to the transferred interest from the partnership's disposition of § 751 property (including any remedial allocations under Regulations § 1.704-3(d)) in a fully taxable transaction for fair market value (taking into account § 7701(g)) immediately prior to the sale of the transferor's interest.
2. The balance of the transferor-partner's realized gain or loss is capital gain or loss.[32]

Under these rules, any premium (i.e., excess of the selling price for the partnership interest over the selling partner's share of partnership asset value) received by the selling partner will be capital gain. Perhaps more likely, any discount (e.g., reflecting a minority interest or lack of liquidity) will reduce the selling partner's capital gain (or create or increase his capital loss) from the transaction. Under the Regulations in effect prior to December 14, 1999, the computational rules were somewhat more convoluted.[33]

Transfers of partnership interests subject to § 751(a) can generate both ordinary income and capital loss (or vice versa). For example, if a hypothetical sale of partnership property would generate $7,000 of ordinary income from § 751 property allocable to the transferred interest, but the transferor has a re-

---

[31] TD 8847, 1999-2 CB 701, 64 Fed. Reg. 69,903–69,922 (Dec. 15, 1999), as modified by TD 9137, 69 Fed. Reg. 42,551–42,559 (July 16, 2004). The current § 751(a) Regulations were part of a larger package that included substantial changes in the Regulations under §§ 732, 734, 743, and 755. They apply to all transfers on or after December 15, 1999.

[32] Reg. § 1.751-1(a)(2).

[33] Under the pre-1999 Regulations, the transferor of an interest in a partnership that held § 751 property was required to perform the following five sequential steps: (1) determine the portion of the amount realized by the transferor that is attributable to the partnership's § 751 property; (2) determine the basis that the transferor's share of the partnership's § 751 property would have had in his hands if distributed to him in a current distribution under § 732 immediately prior to the transfer of his interest; (3) compute the ordinary income or loss under § 751(a) as the difference between the amount realized and the basis determined in the first and second steps above; (4) compute the transferor's capital gain or loss subject to § 741 as the difference between the balance of the amount realized and the balance of his basis in the partnership; and (5) pursuant to § 743(a), do not adjust the basis of partnership assets, including § 751 property, unless the partnership elects under § 754, in which case the basis of all partnership assets, including § 751 property, is adjusted with respect to the transferee as set forth in §§ 743(b) and 755.

alized gain of only $6,000, the transferor must report both ordinary income of $7,000 under § 751(a) and a capital loss of $1,000 under § 741.[34]

A transferor may also realize ordinary income under § 751(a) despite realizing a net loss on the transaction as a whole.[35] For example, in the preceding example, even if the transferor had realized a $2,000 overall *loss* on the transaction, it nevertheless would be required to report $7,000 of ordinary income under § 751(a) while being entitled to claim a $9,000 capital loss under § 741.

[3] Income or Loss From Section 751 Property

[a] General Principles

A transferor-partner's § 751 income or loss from the transfer of a partnership interest is equal to the income or loss from § 751 property that would be allocated to the transferor with respect to the transferred interest upon a hypothetical sale, occurring immediately prior to the transfer, of all partnership property for cash equal to its fair market value.[36] The balance of the transferor-partner's gain or loss is capital under § 741. Section 7701(g), which provides that, for purposes of determining gain or loss, the fair market value of property "shall be treated as being not less than the amount of any nonrecourse

---

[34] Reg. § 1.751-1(g) Example (1).

[35] Notwithstanding the apparent clarity of § 751(a) on this point, Congress, in 1960, attempted to add a new sentence to the statute specifically sanctioning the realization of ordinary income in a net loss sale, stating that this result is "not clear" under the existing statute. See HR Rep. No. 1231, 86th Cong., 2d Sess. 28 (1960). See generally Anderson & Coffee, "Proposed Revision of Partner and Partnership Taxation: Analysis of the Report of the Advisory Group on Subchapter K (Second Installment)," 15 Tax L. Rev. 497, 513–516 (1960). This clarification died in the Senate along with the rest of the 1960 legislation.

Whatever ambiguity there may be in the statute is a product not of § 751(a) itself, but of the second sentence of § 741, which can be read to provide for the recognition of a single gain or loss upon a sale or exchange of a partnership interest, to be treated as capital gain or loss except to the extent provided by § 751(a). Arguably, therefore, the amount treated as ordinary income under § 751(a) cannot exceed the amount of the total gain recognized under § 741. This possible reading should be rejected. It is inconsistent with the legislative history accompanying the enactment of §§ 741 and 751 as part of the 1954 Code. See HR Rep. No. 1337, 83d Cong., 2d Sess. 70 ("In effect, the partner is treated as though he disposed of such item [§ 751 property] independently of the rest of his partnership interest."), 71 (1954) (§ 751(a) "regards the income rights as severable from the partnership interest"); S. Rep. No. 1622, 83d Cong., 2d Sess. 98, 99 (1954) (to the same effect). Further, it is inconsistent with sound tax policy: why should a partner recognize ordinary income with respect to § 751 property if the partnership has no other assets, but not if it has other assets with built-in capital losses? See Prop. Reg. §§ 1.751-1(a)(2), 1.751-1(g) Example 1 (2014).

[36] See ¶ 17.02[3][c].

indebtedness to which such property is subject," is specifically made applicable to this hypothetical sale of all partnership property. Additionally, any remedial allocations under Regulations § 1.704-3(c) are taken into account.

The "hypothetical sale" approach of these rules is based on a sale of assets by the partnership, not a sale by a partner of his interest in the partnership. Consequently, the starting point is the fair market value of the § 751 assets to the partnership, rather than the fair market value of the transferor-partner's share of these assets. This regulatory scheme maximizes the amount of ordinary income and minimizes the capital gain (or increases the capital loss) realized on a typical sale of a partnership interest, since most such sales reflect a discount from fair market value for lack of liquidity or minority status. Under the current Regulations, the entire amount of any such discounts is diverted entirely away from the § 751(a) transaction and funneled into the § 741 portion of the transaction (thus, as noted above, decreasing the amount of the transferor-partner's capital gain or creating or increasing such partner's capital loss).

Allocation of the total amount realized in a simple factual situation is illustrated as follows:

> EXAMPLE 17-1: *A*, a 50 percent partner in *AB*, sells his interest for its market value at a time when the partnership's only item of § 751 property is a zero-basis unrealized receivable that has a market value of $12,000. In this situation, *A*'s 50 percent interest in the unrealized receivable has a market value of $6,000 (50 percent of $12,000). If *AB* sold all of its assets for cash at their fair market value, *A* would be allocated $6,000 of ordinary income, and hence the amount realized for purposes of § 751(a) is $6,000 regardless of the gain realized by *A* on the sale.[37]

The existence of partnership liabilities affects a partner's amount realized upon the disposition of its partnership interest, but generally does not affect a partner's calculation of income or loss from § 751 property.

> EXAMPLE 17-2: The equal *CDE* general partnership's balance sheet is as follows:

	Adjusted Basis	Fair Market Value
Assets:		
Cash	$10,000	$10,000
Unrealized receivables	0	15,000
Capital assets	20,000	35,000
Total Assets	$30,000	$60,000
Liabilities and Capital:		
Liabilities	$12,000	$12,000
Capital:		

[37] See Reg. § 1.751-1(g) Example (1).

C	6,000	16,000
D	6,000	16,000
E	6,000	16,000
Total Liabilities and Capital	$30,000	$60,000

C sells his equal one-third interest in *CDE* to *F* for a cash payment of $16,000. The total amount realized by *C* on the sale is $20,000: cash of $16,000 plus, under § 752(d), one third of the partnership's $12,000 of liabilities. Assume *C*'s basis in his interest is $10,000 ($6,000 capital account plus one-third share of liabilities of $12,000). *C*'s gain is thus $10,000. If *CDE* sold all of its assets for cash at their fair market value, *C* would be allocated $5,000 of the ordinary income from the sale of the receivables (one third of $15,000)—the same amount *C* would be allocated if no partnership liabilities existed. Accordingly, *C* recognizes $5,000 of ordinary income under § 751(a) and the balance of his gain, $5,000, is capital gain under § 741.

In Example 17-2, because *C* is selling his interest for an amount realized that is exactly equal to his share of the value of all partnership assets, the capital gain realized by *C* is equal to his share of the capital gain that would be realized by the partnership if it sold its non-§ 751 property for fair market value. This result is clearly not mandated, or even encouraged, by the computational mechanics, which are designed to force any premium or discount on the sale away from § 751(a) and into the capital gain or loss computation under § 741. *Caveat venditor.*

[b] Selling Partner Has Different Interests in Capital, Profit, and Loss

The measure of a transferor's § 751 income is the share of income (or loss) from § 751 property that would be allocated to the transferred interest upon a hypothetical sale of all partnership property at its fair market value.[38] The application of this seemingly straightforward rule is illustrated as follows:

EXAMPLE 17-3: *G* has a 50 percent interest in the capital of partnership *GH*, is required to bear 50 percent of partnership losses, and is entitled to 75 percent of partnership profits. *G* sells his interest to *I* for $65,000 at a time when his basis is $20,000, the partnership has not realized any net profit or loss, and the current balance sheet of the partnership is as follows:

	Adjusted Basis	Fair Market Value
Assets:		
Cash	$10,000	$ 10,000

---

[38] Reg. § 1.751-1(a)(2).

Capital asset X	30,000	50,000
Unrealized receivables	0	40,000
Total Assets	$40,000	$100,000
Capital:		
G	$20,000	$ 65,000
H	20,000	35,000
Total Capital	$40,000	$100,000

The market value of G's interest is greater than H's because he is entitled to a greater percentage of the unrealized appreciation in partnership assets: Upon a hypothetical sale of the partnership's receivables, G would be entitled to $30,000 of the $40,000 proceeds, and upon a hypothetical sale of capital asset X, G would be entitled to $30,000 of the $50,000 realized (50 percent of $30,000 basis plus 75 percent of $20,000 appreciation). G's interest in partnership cash is $5,000 (50 percent of $10,000). Hence, the market value of G's total partnership interest is $65,000 ($30,000 plus $30,000 plus $5,000).

Upon the sale of G's entire interest for $65,000 cash, G has a gain of $45,000 (amount realized of $65,000 less basis of $20,000). G is allocated § 751(a) income of $30,000, the amount of the income (75 percent of $40,000) that would be allocated to his interest upon the sale of the partnership's unrealized receivables for their fair market value.[39] The remainder of G's realized gain, $15,000, is capital gain under § 741.

The analysis may be more difficult where the partnership owns both appreciated and depreciated assets and the partnership agreement simply allocates net profit and net loss on an annual basis.

EXAMPLE 17-4: The facts are the same as in Example 17-3 except that the market value of capital asset X is $10,000, rather than $50,000; thus, the partnership has an unrealized capital loss of $20,000 in capital asset X. The fact that G's interest in profits differs from his interest in partnership losses makes it difficult to compute his share of the income from § 751 receivables for purposes of applying § 751(a). If the partnership realizes at least $20,000 of income from its receivables in the same year it realizes the loss with respect to capital asset X, G's partnership interest is worth $35,000 ($20,000 interest in partnership capital plus 75 percent of the net gain of $20,000 on disposition of capital asset X and the receivables). However, if the receivables are collected entirely in years other than the year in which the loss on disposition of capital asset X is realized, the value of G's interest is $40,000 ($20,000 capital interest less 50

---

[39] Reg. § 1.751-1(a)(2). See HR Rep. No. 1337, 83d Cong., 2d Sess. 71 (1954).

percent of the $20,000 loss on capital asset X, plus 75 percent of the $40,000 gain on collection of receivables).[40]

This is a relatively simple example of the kind of complex problems that can result from the use of disproportionate profit- and loss-sharing ratios if the partnership agreement is not drafted with extreme care.[41] If G persuades his purchaser that his interest is actually worth $40,000, this economic judgment should probably be given effect in allocating the purchase price under § 751(a), with the result that $30,000 of the $40,000 price is allocable to G's interest in unrealized receivables.[42] However, if G sells his interest for $35,000, it seems appropriate to reduce the allocation to receivables to $25,000.[43] If the partnership agreement is drafted so the loss on the sale of capital asset X is borne equally, regardless of whether the partnership has income items in the same year, the language of the agreement should be given effect under § 751(a), and $30,000 of the $40,000 price should be allocated to G's interest in unrealized receivables.

If partners have contributed property that remains subject to the § 704(c) allocation rules at the time of the sale of a partner's interest, the § 704(c) rules, including any remedial allocations under Regulations § 1.704-3(d), are taken into account in ascertaining the selling partner's share of the income from § 751 property.[44]

> **EXAMPLE 17-5:** Partner A contributes asset X, with a basis of $50 and a market value of $100, to the equal ABC partnership, and is credited with a $100 contribution on the partnership's books. Under § 704(c), the first $50 of gain realized on the sale of asset X must be allocated to A. The three partners agree to share gain in excess of $50 equally. If asset X is § 751 property and has a market value of $160 when A sells his entire

---

[40] The $5,000 increase in proceeds allocable to G results because the $20,000 capital loss, which is borne 50 percent by G, does not reduce income in which G has a 75 percent interest in this example.

[41] In most instances, a properly drafted partnership agreement should, to the extent possible, attempt to ensure the same economic consequences to each partner regardless of whether profits and losses are realized in the same year or in different years, and also regardless of the order in which profits and losses are realized if they are realized in different years. Suggested drafting techniques are discussed and illustrated in R. Whitmire, W. Nelson, W. McKee & S. Brodie, Structuring and Drafting Partnership and LLC Agreements (Thomson Reuters/Tax & Accounting, 4th ed. 2021).

[42] Because GH has an unrealized capital loss in asset X, G's ordinary income of $30,000 under § 751(a) (i.e., $30,000 less zero basis) exceeds his total gain on the sale ($20,000).

[43] This is the sum of 50 percent of $20,000 (the portion of the receivables that may be offset by the unrealized loss in asset X) and 75 percent of $20,000 (the balance of the receivables).

[44] See Prop. Reg. § 1.751-1(g) Example 1(ii) (2014) and the general discussion of § 704(c) in ¶ 11.04.

one-third interest in *ABC*, *A*'s share of the gain from asset *X* is $70 (the sum of 100 percent of the $50 of built-in gain with respect to asset *X*, and one third of the remaining $60 of unrealized gain).

[c] Amount Realized Not Equal to Market Value

If a partnership interest is sold for a purchase price that does not reflect its fair market value, any premium or discount is allocated to the capital portion of the transaction, thereby guaranteeing that the seller's § 751 income or loss will accurately reflect his share of the fair market value of the partnership's § 751 property. The consequences of a sale for more or less than market value can be analyzed using the facts in Example 17-3, in which *G*'s share of the market values of the partnership assets is $65,000.

> **EXAMPLE 17-6:** The facts are the same as in Example 17-3, except that *G* sells his interest in partnership *GH* to *I* for $75,000 (namely, for $10,000 more than the $65,000 stated market value of *G*'s partnership interest, as shown in his capital account). The *GH* partnership's affairs should first be scrutinized carefully to ascertain whether all partnership assets are accurately valued and included on the partnership's balance sheet. If there are items of § 751 property that have been omitted from the balance sheet, or undervalued on the balance sheet, *G*'s § 751 income may be understated. Additionally, there may be intangible assets, such as goodwill, that do not appear on the balance sheet.[45] However, because goodwill is not § 751(a) property, its inclusion or exclusion from the balance sheet will not affect the computation of *G*'s § 751 income.[46]

If, under the facts of Example 17-6, no intangible or other assets account for the extra $10,000 paid by *I*, so that *I* has simply overpaid for *G*'s partnership interest, the computational mechanics of Regulations § 1.751-1(a)(2) effectively allocate this $10,000 premium to the partnership's non−§ 751 property. Under these circumstances, the amount of § 751 income recognized by *G* is unchanged and the entire $10,000 premium increases *G*'s capital gain (or decreases his capital loss).

---

[45] Numerous other types of assets may be present that are not reflected on the partnership's balance sheet. See, e.g., G. Ralph Bartolme, 62 TC 821 (1974) (prepaid interest treated as a partnership asset for purposes of § 743(b)).

[46] The line between "goodwill" and the right to receive income for services "to be rendered" (§ 751(c)(2)) is not always marked with neon lights. See ¶ 17.03[1]. If an election under § 754 to adjust the basis of partnership assets is in effect, *I* is likely to be better off if he can allocate the $10,000 "premium" to work-in-process rather than goodwill. See Reg. § 1.755-1(a)(5); ¶ 24.04[3].

[d] Allocation Agreements

The current Regulations give no credence to attempts by the parties to allocate the purchase price of § 751 property.[47] Nevertheless, such allocation agreements continue to be good practice because they reduce the likelihood of disputes arising with the Service as a result of the parties taking inconsistent positions.

From the seller's viewpoint, an optimum allocation agreement should include:

1. A specific allocation to each "item" of potential recapture property owned by the partnership[48] and
2. An allocation to other "unrealized receivables" and "inventory items" as a group.

A careful buyer, interested in establishing his position with certainty for purposes of the basis adjustments set forth in §§ 732(d) and 743(b), will seek a breakdown of the purchase price that is no less, and perhaps more,[49] detailed, although a buyer's reasons are likely to be different from the seller's and the consequences less immediate in most cases.[50]

An allocation of the purchase price should be part of almost every agreement for the sale of a partnership interest. Failure to agree to an allocation is not only a refusal to take advantage of an easy solution to some difficult legal and factual problems, but is also an invitation for the parties to take inconsistent positions, thereby increasing the chances of scrutiny by the Service. In some situations, it may be argued that negotiation of the detailed allocations required at the time of sale will complicate and impede negotiation of the sale itself, and may even cause the transaction to fail. Nevertheless, if valuation conflicts exist, it is generally advisable to face them before the sale is completed, rather than later when the Service will act as a hostile arbiter and the parties are forced to contend with a completed transaction.

---

[47] TD 8847, 1999-2 CB 701, 64 Fed. Reg. 69,903 (Dec. 15, 1999) (allocation agreement approach is "inconsistent with the hypothetical sale approach of the regulations"). Prior Regulations provided that allocation agreements "generally" would be controlling. See Reg. § 1.751-1(a)(2) (prior to amendment in 1999). This provision was removed in 1999.

[48] See Reg. § 1.751-1(c)(4).

[49] For example, a careful buyer would be interested in having an allocation made to the remaining capital assets of the partnership; such an allocation would impact the buyer's residual allocation to § 197 intangibles under § 755. An allocation to capital gain items would be irrelevant to the seller, whose capital gain or loss is determined under the residual method. Reg. § 1.751-1(a)(2).

[50] For example, the purchaser may be interested in a high allocation to inventory with a view toward reducing his share of partnership ordinary income on the sale of the inventory as a result of his § 743(b) basis adjustment.

[4] Reporting Requirements

If a partnership has any § 751 property, Regulations § 1.751-1(a)(3) requires any transferor-partner to file a statement with his tax return for the taxable year in which the sale or exchange occurs, setting forth (1) the date of the transfer; (2) the amount of gain or loss attributable to § 751 property; and (3) the amount of capital gain or loss.[51]

¶ 17.03 UNREALIZED RECEIVABLES: SECTION 751(c)

Section 751(c) defines the term "unrealized receivables" for purposes of Subchapter K. This definition is relevant not only in the application of § 751, but also in connection with such diverse provisions as § 724(a), relating to the character of gain or loss on the sale of property contributed to a partnership;[52] § 731(a)(2), dealing with the recognition of loss upon certain distributions in liquidation of a partner's interest;[53] § 732(c), providing for the allocation of basis to distributed property;[54] § 735(a), relating to the character of gain or loss on the sale of distributed property;[55] and § 736(b)(2), relating to payments in liquidation of the interest of a retiring or deceased partner.[56]

As originally enacted in 1954, § 751(c) included two classes of potential ordinary income in the definition of "unrealized receivables":

> For purposes of this subchapter, the term "unrealized receivables" includes, to the extent not previously includible in income under the method of accounting used by the partnership, any rights (contractual or otherwise) to payment for—
>
> > (1) goods delivered, or to be delivered, to the extent the proceeds therefrom would be treated as amounts received from the sale or exchange of property other than a capital asset, or
> >
> > (2) services rendered, or to be rendered.

---

[51] In addition, if the transfer triggers a § 743(b) basis adjustment, Regulations § 1.743-1(k) requires the transferee to provide identification and basis information to the partnership, and the partnership to include a statement with its tax return for the year of the transfer identifying the transferee, computing the basis adjustment, and allocating the adjustment to partnership properties.

[52] See ¶ 4.05[6].

[53] See ¶ 19.05.

[54] See ¶ 19.04.

[55] See ¶ 20.02.

[56] See ¶ 22.02.

As the years passed and Congress carved a number of exceptions out of the 1954 capital gain definition, two sentences reflecting these exceptions were added to the definition of "unrealized receivables" and successively expanded. These sentences now provide a sort of mini-history of the unending struggle between Congress and taxpayers on the capital gain front. Solely for purposes of §§ 731, 732, 741, and 751, these exceptions create a third class of "unrealized receivables" that presently includes (1) depreciation recapture under § 1245 (added in 1962); (2) excess depreciation recapture under § 1250 (1964); (3) mining exploration expenditure recapture under § 617(d) (1966); (4) recapture of soil and water conservation expenditures with respect to farm land under § 1252 (1969); (5) accumulated domestic international sales corporation (DISC) income recapture under § 995(c) (1976); (6) recapture of accumulated earnings and profits with respect to stock of certain controlled foreign corporations under § 1248(a) (1976); (7) gain treated as ordinary income upon the transfer of a franchise, trademark, or trade name under § 1253(a) (1976); (8) recapture with respect to oil, gas, geothermal, or other mineral properties under § 1254(a) (1976, 1978); (9) accrued market discount under § 1276 on market discount bonds, as defined in § 1278 (1984); and (10) the ordinary income inherent in any short-term obligation, as defined in § 1283 (1984). In each case, the amount of recapture is determined as if the recapture property had been sold by the partnership at its fair market value.

Additionally, the statutory definition of "unrealized receivables" does not purport to be exclusive.[57] Section 751(c) merely states that the term "includes" the three classes of potential ordinary income described above, thus leaving open the possibility that additional classes may exist. However, to date, the Service has not found it expedient to explore expansion of § 751(c) along these lines.

[1] Payments for Services

One branch of the tripartite definition of "unrealized receivables" is "any rights (contractual or otherwise) to payment for … services rendered, or to be rendered" to the extent not previously includible in income under the partnership's method of accounting. The inspiration for this branch of the definition was a series of pre-1954 cases that bestowed capital gain treatment on sellers of interests in cash-method service partnerships holding zero-basis accounts receivable as their principal appreciated assets.[58] However, this rudimentary

---

[57] Cf. Frank A. Logan, 51 TC 482, 486 (1968) (relying in part on the "includes" language to broadly construe the definition of "unrealized receivables").

[58] See Swiren v. Commissioner, 183 F2d 656 (7th Cir. 1950) (cert. denied); Meyer v. United States, 213 F2d 278 (7th Cir. 1954). See generally Jackson et al., "The Internal Revenue Code of 1954: Partnerships," 54 Colum. L. Rev. 1183, 1216 (1954).

abuse of the capital gain concept did not constrain the drafters of § 751, with the result that the statutory language encompasses substantially more than the problem that inspired it.

The obvious breadth of the statutory language has been given full effect by the courts, which have had little difficulty in holding that the definition includes a wide variety of rights to fees generated in the context of the traditional professional-client service relationship,[59] regardless of whether fully or partially earned[60] and regardless of whether the right to collect the fee is contractual or based on quantum meruit.[61] Application of the definition to nontraditional contractual relationships has proven more difficult in some circumstances. If the partnership has a service agreement that is not cancelable by the party for whom the services are to be performed, it is now settled that payments with respect thereto are unrealized receivables.[62] However, payments attributable to the value of service contracts that are cancelable at will or upon thirty or sixty days' notice have been excluded from the definition of "unrealized receivables."[63] Such payments have been likened to payments for "good-

---

[59] See, e.g., Ware v. Commissioner, 906 F2d 62 (2d Cir. 1990) (finder's fee); Barnes v. United States, 253 F. Supp. 116 (SD Ill. 1966) (doctor); Fred Frankfort, Jr., 52 TC 163 (1969) (acq.) (real estate broker); Frank A. Logan, 51 TC 482 (1968) (lawyer); John Winthrop Wolcott, 39 TC 538 (1962) (architect).

[60] See John W. Ledoux, 77 TC 293 (1981), aff'd per curiam, 695 F2d 1320 (11th Cir. 1983); John Winthrop Wolcott, 39 TC 538 (1962).

[61] See Frank A. Logan, 51 TC 482 (1968).

[62] See Reg. § 1.751-1(a)(2) (unrealized receivables include, with respect to a partnership contract accounted for on the completed contract method, the amount of ordinary income or loss that the partnership would take into account under the constructive completion rules if the partnership disposed of the contract in a taxable transaction at its fair market value); United States v. Woolsey, 326 F2d 287 (5th Cir. 1963) (twenty-five-year contract to manage mutual insurance company); Blacketor v. United States, 204 Ct. Cl. 897 (1974) (alternate holding) (commission agreement to sell output of plywood manufacturer); John W. Ledoux, 77 TC 293 (1981), aff'd per curiam, 695 F2d 1320 (11th Cir. 1983) (dog track management agreement); Rev. Rul. 79-51, 1979-1 CB 225 (amounts earned or to be earned under long-term construction contract by partnership utilizing completed contract method of accounting are unrealized receivables); cf. Roth v. Commissioner, 321 F2d 607 (9th Cir. 1963) (alternate holding) (ten-year exclusive distribution agreement for motion picture treated as unrealized receivable from the sale of goods). However, in Revenue Ruling 58-394, 1958-2 CB 374, the Service ruled that the sale of interests in a partnership holding a nonassignable ten-year contract to manage a mutual insurance company was ordinary income because "relinquishment" of the contract rights did not qualify as the sale or exchange of a capital asset. The ruling quotes, but does not seem to rely on, § 751. In fact, it states: "There are no receivables realized or otherwise as defined by section 751(c)...." Id. at 375.

[63] See Charles F. Phillips, 40 TC 157 (1963) (nonacq.) (contract to act as sales representative, cancelable at will); Harlan E. Baxter, 28 TCM 487 (1969), aff'd, 433 F2d 757 (9th Cir. 1970) (commission sales agreements, cancelable by manufacturers on thirty or sixty days' notice); cf. Miller v. United States, 181 Ct. Cl. 331 (1967) (payments in *Phillips* are for goodwill, deductible under § 736(a)).

will," and thus the courts concluded that capital gain treatment should be accorded to the selling partner.[64] If the notice period under a service agreement is substantial (e.g., a year), an allocation between the "goodwill" and unrealized receivable portions of the agreement may be appropriate, although the reported cases have not dealt with agreements of this sort.

The distinction between terminable and nonterminable service agreements is easy to justify in terms of the statutory language, which speaks of "rights" to payment. If the partnership's right to perform services is terminable at will by the other party to the agreement, there is obviously no "right" to payment in any sense. Theoretical justification for this distinction, however, is a bit more difficult. If the partnership has a "right" to receive payments that will constitute ordinary income, § 751(a) views the proceeds from the sale of a partnership interest as a "substitute" for ordinary income, and, hence, imposes ordinary income tax on the seller.[65] On the other hand, if the partnership has a mere expectancy (rather than a right) to future ordinary income under a terminable agreement, amounts received by a selling partner attributable to such agreement are no less a substitute for ordinary income. The purchaser's willingness to pay a premium with respect to the agreement obviously reflects his expectation that the agreement will not be terminated immediately and that the partnership will receive ordinary income payments under the agreement. Perhaps this distinction can be justified as mirroring the dichotomy, outside the partnership area, between sellers who are paid for goodwill (capital gain) and those who are paid for receivables or work-in-process (ordinary income).

In valuing rights to payment for services rendered or to be rendered, the Regulations provide that the "estimated cost of completing performance" of the contract is taken into account together with "the time between the sale [of the partnership interest subject to § 751(a)] ... and the time of payment."[66] Thus, the amount of the sale price attributable to the contract will ordinarily be the discounted present value of the net profits to be earned under the con-

---

[64] But cf. Securities-Intermountain, Inc. v. United States, 460 F2d 261 (9th Cir. 1972), in which the Ninth Circuit found that a nonpartnership sale of a mortgage service business did not involve the purchase of nondepreciable "goodwill," even though the contractual rights transferred were terminable, and the court allowed the purchaser to depreciate his entire cost. Other courts have found elements of goodwill in these transactions. See, e.g., Bisbee-Baldwin Corp. v. Tomlinson, 320 F2d 929 (5th Cir. 1963); Western Mortgage Corp. v. United States, 308 F. Supp. 333 (CD Cal. 1969). In the partnership context, the terminable nature of these rights should preclude their characterization as unrealized receivables regardless of the presence of goodwill. They may, however, constitute inventory items under § 751(d)(2). See ¶ 17.04[1][b].

[65] See S. Rep. No. 1622, 83d Cong., 2d Sess. 99 (1954).

[66] Reg. § 1.751-1(c)(3).

tract.[67] It may be considerably easier to state this formula than to apply it: Consider, for example, computation of the present value of an agreement to render legal services on a contingent-fee basis.[68] Some guidance will, of course, be furnished by the total purchase price agreed upon by the parties, but this guidance may be less than perfect if other assets of the partnership also pose valuation difficulties or if the price paid does not reflect the market value of the interest transferred.[69] The parties generally can minimize these difficulties by agreeing on an allocation of the price paid for the interest.[70]

The "cost of completing performance" of an agreement should include an allowance for services to be rendered by partners, even though such services may not represent a "cost" to the partnership in the conventional sense. Failure to make allowance for the "cost" of partner-performed services would distort the allocation process by inflating the value of unrealized receivables that involve the performance of substantial future services by partners.

> **EXAMPLE 17-7:** *D* is considering the purchase of *A*'s interest in *ABC*. *ABC* is a law partnership that has recently agreed to handle a large case for a fixed fee. The partners, including *D*, will perform all services related to the case. In valuing the unrealized receivables attributable to *A*'s interest, *D* would not give effect to a full one third of the gross fee to be received in this matter, since handling the case will require a substantial amount of *D*'s time. Instead, *D* would place a value on the receivable equal to the excess, if any, of the present value of his share of the fee less the value he places on the time he estimates he will be required to devote to the case and his share of the other costs of handling the matter. Tax results consistent with this entirely rational economic analysis cannot be accomplished under the Regulations unless services to be rendered by

---

[67] Costs paid or accrued prior to the sales but not previously taken into account under the partnership's accounting method are included in the basis of the receivable. See Reg. § 1.751-1(c)(2).

[68] A contingent-fee case is includible in the definition of "unrealized receivables," notwithstanding the contingency, which relates to the amount of the fee rather than to the "right" of the partnership to collect it. But cf. Berry v. United States, 267 F2d 298 (6th Cir. 1959) (under 1939 Code, capital gain treatment on sale of partnership interest: the partnership's profit under a 76 percent completed construction contract "could not have been determined" at the time of the sale). *Berry* is not good law under § 751(c), which contains no requirement that profit be earned or definitely ascertainable to bring § 751 into play. See Rev. Rul. 79-51, 1979-1 CB 225 (amounts earned or to be earned under long-term construction contract by partnership utilizing completed contract method of accounting are unrealized receivables).

[69] See Muserlian v. Commissioner, 932 F2d 109 (2d Cir. 1991); United States v. Cornish, 348 F2d 175 (9th Cir. 1965); ¶ 24.04[3] (application of § 1060 to § 743(b) basis adjustment of purchaser).

[70] Although not a panacea, allocations agreements are nonetheless recommended for the reasons described in ¶ 17.02[3][d].

partners (including purchasing partners) are treated as a cost of completing performance of unrealized receivables.

[2] Payments for Goods

The second branch of the § 751(c) definition of "unrealized receivables" includes "any rights (contractual or otherwise) to payment for ... goods delivered, or to be delivered" to the extent the proceeds (1) were not previously includible in the partnership's income and (2) would be treated as amounts received from the sale or exchange of property other than a capital asset. Several elements of this definition are identical to those in the definition of "payments for services" as "unrealized receivables." Thus, the definition includes rights to payment for goods to be delivered as well as those previously delivered, provided the partnership has an enforceable right to payment for the goods and the payment was not previously includible in income under the partnership's accounting method.

One aspect of the definition that is unique to payments for goods is the limitation to payments that "would be treated as amounts received from the sale or exchange of property other than a capital asset." This limitation is consistent with the underlying purpose of § 751 to prevent the conversion of ordinary income into capital gain: If the "goods" in question are capital assets, failure to exclude them from the definition of "unrealized receivables" would have the reverse effect, converting capital gain into ordinary income.[71] A comparable exclusion is not necessary in connection with payments for services because all such payments result in ordinary income to the partnership.

The exclusion applies to all payments the partnership has the right to receive in connection with sales of capital assets within the meaning of § 1221, regardless of the holding period of such assets in the hands of the partnership. This exclusion of short-term capital gain and loss from the definition of "unrealized receivables" may allow a partner to convert potential short-term capital gain at the partnership level into long-term capital gain upon a sale of his interest.[72]

---

[71] The Service has ruled privately that a long-term power purchase agreement is not an unrealized receivable, because a sale of the *contract* would generate capital gain, even though the sale of electricity (the "goods") generates ordinary income. Priv. Ltr. Ruls. 9845012 (Aug. 6, 1998), as revised by 199910033 (Dec. 12, 1998), 9848033 (Aug. 31, 1998), as revised by 199910029 (Dec. 12, 1998), 199903013 (Oct. 22, 1998), as revised by 199910056 (Dec. 12, 1998).

[72] However, if property with a short-term holding period is contributed with respect to a partnership interest that has been held for the long-term period, the Regulations create a divided holding period for the partnership interest. See Reg. § 1.1223-3; ¶ 4.01[2][a].

The treatment of rights to payments with respect to § 1231(b) assets is less clear. Under § 702(a)(3), § 1231 gains and losses are netted at the partnership level, and each partner's share of the net partnership § 1231 gain or loss is then netted against his nonpartnership § 1231 gains and losses.[73] If the partner realizes a net § 1231 gain during the year, his net gain generally is capital;[74] otherwise, the net § 1231 loss is an ordinary loss. Thus, whether the proceeds from the sale of partnership § 1231(b) assets "would be treated" as amounts received from the sale of a capital asset seemingly requires an analysis of other partnership § 1231 transactions, as well as each individual partner's other § 1231 gains and losses for each taxable year during which such proceeds will be received. The nightmarish problems inherent in this interpretation of the statute are ignored by the Regulations, which do not refer to § 1231 in defining unrealized receivables.[75] A workable, but technically incorrect, resolution of this problem would be to treat each § 1231 gain as a capital gain without regard to the effects of "netting" at either the partnership or partner level or application of the § 1231(c) recapture rule.[76]

One aspect of § 1231 that is often overlooked in the § 751 context is that § 1231 only applies to assets that have been held for at least the minimum long-term gain period. Depreciable property held for less than the minimum long-term gain period (currently one year) does not qualify for § 1231 treatment.[77] Consequently, the right to receive payments with respect to such "short-term" property is automatically an unrealized receivable.

The term "goods" is not defined. However, there is nothing in the statute or the case law to suggest that the definition is any narrower than the general concept of "property" under the Code.[78]

As in the case of payments for services, the Regulations include in the basis of payments for goods all costs or expenses paid or accrued that have not

---

[73] See Reg. § 1.702-1(a)(3). The application of § 1231(a) may require "double netting" where gains or losses are realized in connection with casualties or thefts; a refinement added by the Tax Reform Act of 1969 and not adequately reflected in § 702(a). See ¶ 9.01[3][a][ii].

[74] Even if a partner has a net § 1231 gain for the year, it may be treated as ordinary income under § 1231(c) to the extent the partner has "non-recaptured net section 1231 losses."

[75] See Reg. § 1.751-1(c)(1).

[76] The reporting requirements in Schedule K-1 (Form 1065) are also not very informative regarding any nuances of the netting rules. Box 10 generally requires a partner's share of partnership net § 1231 gain or loss to be reported, while Code AB for Box 20 is captioned "Section 751 gain (loss)" and is required to set forth a "partner's share of gain or loss on the sale of the partnership interest subject to taxation at ordinary income tax rates."

[77] § 1231(b)(1).

[78] See, e.g., Roth v. Commissioner, 321 F2d 607 (9th Cir. 1963) (alternate holding) (motion picture); Herman Glazer, 44 TC 541 (1965) (alternate holding) (tract homes).

been taken into account under the partnership's accounting method.[79] This rule is a logical adjunct to, and should be construed in conjunction with, Regulations § 1.751-1(c)(3), which allows the cost of completing the goods to offset the payments for the goods.

[3] Recapture Items

The third category of unrealized receivables—the recapture items listed in the second and third sentences of § 751(c)—is fundamentally different from the first two categories. It does not involve the "right" to receive payments that, when received, will be ordinary income. Instead, it involves the computation of the amount of ordinary income that would be realized under the recapture sections upon a hypothetical sale of certain types of recapture property at fair market value. Because this third category relates to hypothetical rather than actual sales, it is conceptually similar to the types of ordinary income items included in the § 751(d) definition of "inventory items."[80] By treating recapture items as unrealized receivables instead of inventory items, Congress originally ensured that they would be treated as § 751 property in connection with both transfers and distributions regardless of whether the "substantial appreciation" test set forth in former § 751(b)(3) was satisfied.[81]

Section 751(c) provides that recapture items are unrealized receivables for purposes of § 751 as well as §§ 731, 732,[82] and 741, but not for purposes of § 736. The inclusion of § 731 in this list seems to be a nullity.[83] The exclusion

---

[79] Reg. § 1.751-1(c)(2).

[80] See ¶ 17.04[1].

[81] See ¶ 21.01[4]. Although the "substantial appreciation" test no longer applies to transfers of partnership interests under § 751(a), it is still relevant with regard to § 751(b) distributions.

[82] Prior to 1997, basis was allocated under § 732(c) first to § 751 assets in an amount up to the adjusted basis of such assets in the hands of the partnership, and second to the remaining assets proportionately based on their relative adjusted basis. Because § 751(c) recapture items all have a zero basis, it was irrelevant under these provisions whether such items were treated as unrealized receivables or as non–§ 751 property for purposes of § 732; either way these items had a zero basis in the hands of the distributee-partner. These allocation rules were substantially modified in 1997 to take into account market value as well as basis. Pursuant to the same legislation, § 751(c) was correspondingly, and appropriately, modified to include recapture items as unrealized receivables for purposes of § 732(c).

[83] The definition of "unrealized receivables" is significant under § 731 only in connection with the application of § 731(a)(2), which provides for the recognition of loss by the recipient of a liquidating distribution only if the distribution consists solely of money, unrealized receivables, and inventory. Because a distribution of an unrealized receivable in the form of potential depreciation recapture necessarily involves distribution of the underlying asset to which the potential recapture attaches, § 731(a)(2) is inapplicable by its

of § 736 prevents partnerships from deducting payments to retiring partners for the value of recapture items.[84]

The statute does not specifically provide that recapture items are not un- realized receivables for purposes of §§ 724(a) and 735(a)(1), which freeze the ordinary income character of contributed and distributed unrealized receivables in the hands of transferee-partnerships and distributee-partners, respectively. However, the Regulations under §§ 735 and 751 mandate this result.[85]

In determining the portion of the purchase price attributable to the selling partner's interest in recapture items, the first step is to determine the fair mar- ket value of each item of potential recapture property held by the partnership. The amount of recapture income that would be realized upon a hypothetical sale of each item at its market value is then computed under the various recap- ture provisions and is treated, for purposes of § 751, as an unrealized receiva- ble with a basis of zero.[86] The selling partner's share of the hypothetical recapture is determined as if the property had actually been sold by the part- nership at that market value.

Prior to December 15, 1999, an arm's-length agreement between the buyer and seller of a partnership interest generally established the fair market value of recapture property, and hence the amount of potential recapture in- come treated as an unrealized receivable.[87] Although this provision has been

---

terms, regardless of how the depreciation recapture element is categorized. Similar reason- ing applies to the other types of statutory recapture items.

[84] See Chapter 22.

[85] See Reg. §§ 1.735-1(a)(1) (reference to Regulations § 1.751-1(c)(1) for definition of "unrealized receivables" effectively excludes recapture items), 1.751-1(c)(4) (definition of "unrealized receivables" includes recapture items for purposes of enumerated sections; no mention of § 724 or § 735). Although Regulations have not been issued under § 724, which was enacted in 1984, there is no reason to expect a different result.

[86] See Reg. § 1.751-1(c)(5). The statutory formula for measuring potential recapture is couched in terms of a hypothetical sale of the recapture property "at its fair market value." If the property is subject to liabilities in excess of value, the amount realized on the hypothetical sale equals the nonrecourse liabilities encumbering the property. Reg. § 1.751-1(a)(2); see Commissioner v. Tufts, 461 US 300 (1983) (amount realized on dis- position of property includes the entire amount of any nonrecourse liability encumbering the property, without regard to the value of the property). The enactment of § 7701(g) as part of the Deficit Reduction Act of 1984, seems to be properly reflected in the current Regulations. Some potential for controversy may still exist, however, because the Confer- ence Report accompanying § 7701(g) states that it does not apply to § 751(c). HR Rep. No. 861, 98th Cong., 2d Sess. 864 (1984). Notwithstanding this statement, which appears to be a typographical error, it is hazardous to take the position that § 7701(g) does not ap- ply to § 751(c), particularly in the face of the addition of the reference to § 7701(g) in Regulations § 1.751-1(a)(2). See Staff of Joint Comm. on Taxation, 98th Cong., 2d Sess., General Explanation of the Revenue Provisions of the Deficit Reduction Act of 1984, at 239 n.15 (Comm. Print 1984) (reference in Conference Report intended to be made to § 752(c)).

[87] See Reg. § 1.751-1(c)(4)(x) (prior to revision in 1999).

deleted from the Regulations, allocation agreements are still advisable in most situations.[88] Because recapture is generally computed on an item-by-item basis,[89] an allocation agreement should set forth the fair market value of each item of the partnership's recapture property for maximum effectiveness.

All, or a portion of, the partnership recapture items that cause the transferor of a partnership interest to be taxed at ordinary income tax rates may subsequently generate ordinary income to the purchaser of the interest if the purchase does not result in adjustment of the basis of partnership assets under § 743(b) as a consequence of both the lack of a § 754 election and the absence of a partnership § 743(d) substantial built-in loss (see ¶ 24.01[4]). If the basis of partnership assets is adjusted under § 743(b), any increase in the basis of partnership recapture property with respect to the transferee under § 743(b) will reduce his share of any gain recognized on the disposition of such assets. Because amounts subject to recapture are generally limited to gain recognized, this reduction is likely to reduce the potential recapture as well. More importantly, at least with respect to *depreciation* recapture, Regulations §§ 1.1245-1(e)(3)(ii) and 1.1250-1(f) eliminate all recapture of pre-transfer depreciation with respect to transferees if a § 754 election is in effect.[90] Regulations under § 1254 eliminate natural resource recapture regardless of whether the partnership has a § 754 election in effect where the transferee-partner determines his basis by reference to cost under § 1012.[91] Other recapture provisions are not so clear. Presumably, similar special provisions will be included when (and if) Regulations are ever issued under §§ 1252, 1278, and 1283.[92] However, the Regulations governing the recapture of mining exploration expenses under § 617(d) do not contain a comparable special rule, nor do the Regulations with respect to partnership-owned DISC stock subject to § 995(c) or stock in controlled foreign corporations subject to § 1248(a). Furthermore, no such protection seems likely in connection with § 1253(a) income on franchises, trademarks, and trade names.

---

[88] See ¶ 17.02[3][d].

[89] See Reg. § 1.751-1(c)(4).

[90] These Regulations do not apply to nonrecognition exchanges, such as those governed by §§ 721 and 351. The result—depreciation recapture is eliminated while gain is deferred—is surprising, to say the least. The Treasury has noted but taken no steps to correct this issue, declaring that Regulations § 1.1245-1(e)(3) is "out of date." Notice of Proposed Rulemaking, Preamble, REG-151416-06, 79 Fed. Reg. 65151, 65158 (Nov. 3, 2014). Taxpayers may observe that both §§ 721 and 351 predate the 1962 enactment of § 1245 and the subsequent promulgation of these long-standing Regulations and question why they should not be given full effect.

[91] Reg. § 1.1254-5(c)(2).

[92] The treatment of partnerships is "reserved" in Regulations §§ 1.1252-1(c), 1.1252-2(e).

[a] Depreciation Recapture Under Section 1245

Section 1245 property generally includes any depreciable property other than buildings and their structural components.[93] Gain realized on a sale of § 1245 property is treated as ordinary income to the extent of depreciation and amortization deductions taken with respect to the property. A selling partner's share of § 1245 gain with respect to an item of § 1245 property is the lesser of the partner's share of the gain from a hypothetical sale of the property for its fair market value or the partner's share of the depreciation claimed with respect to the property.[94]

The interaction of §§ 751(a) and 1245 is illustrated by the following example.

> **EXAMPLE 17-8:** Partnership *ABC* holds two machines, *X* and *Y*, both of which were acquired after 1961. Machine *X* cost $1,000, has been the subject of depreciation deductions of $600 so that its adjusted basis is $400, and has a market value of $500. Machine *Y* cost $800, has been subject to $150 of depreciation (adjusted basis $650), and has a market value of $900. If *X* and *Y* are sold for $1,400, allocable $500 to *X* and $900 to *Y*, the depreciation recapture with respect to machine *X* will be $100 (the entire gain realized, since it is less than prior depreciation with respect to *X*), while the recapture with respect to machine *Y* will be $150 (the portion of the $250 gain realized that is not in excess of prior depreciation with respect to *Y*). If, instead of *ABC* selling machines *X* and *Y*, *A* sells his one-third interest in *ABC*, *A*'s interest in "unrealized receivables" is one third of $250, or $83 ($33 with respect to machine *X* and $50 with respect to machine *Y*).

Unfortunately, real life examples of the application of §§ 751 and 1245 are rarely as simple as the foregoing. A few basic points should be noted, however: If a partnership holds any item of § 1245 property that has a market value in excess of basis, the sale of a partnership interest will trigger ordinary

---

[93] See § 1245(a)(3). Section 1245 property also includes (1) real property that has been subject to amortization under §§ 169, 179, 179A (prior to its repeal), 185 (prior to its repeal), 188 (prior to its repeal), 190, 193, or 194; (2) single-purpose agricultural and horticultural structures; (3) certain petroleum storage facilities; and (4) any railroad grading or tunnel bore. In addition, nonresidential real property depreciated at accelerated rates under the accelerated cost recovery system rules in effect during 1981 through 1986 constitutes § 1245 property. See § 1245(a)(5) (as in effect prior to the Tax Reform Act of 1986).

[94] Reg. § 1.1245-1(e)(2); see Reg. § 1.751-1(c)(4)(iii). See generally ¶ 11.03[2][c]. Full effect is given to curative and remedial allocations under § 704(c). See Reg. §§ 1.1245-1(e)(2)(ii)(C)(*2*), 1.1245-1(e)(2)(ii)(C)(*3*). If the selling partner is entitled to a § 743(b) basis adjustment with respect to partnership recapture property, this adjustment is taken into account in computing its share of the § 1245 recapture. See Reg. §§ 1.1245-1(e)(3), 1.1245-1(e)(4).

income under § 751(a) even though (1) the interest is sold at a loss or (2) the aggregate value of partnership § 1245 property is less than its aggregate adjusted basis. The breadth of § 1245 gives an equally broad scope to § 751(a) in this context. Few sales of partnership interests will completely escape its reach.

[b] Depreciation Recapture Under Sections 1250 and 291

Section 1250 property is any depreciable real property that is not § 1245 property.[95] Upon the disposition of § 1250 property, gain recognized is characterized as ordinary income to the extent of the "applicable percentage" of the "additional depreciation" attributable to the property. The term "additional depreciation" generally refers to the excess of the depreciation adjustments made with respect to a property over the depreciation adjustments that would have been made with respect to a property under the straight-line method of adjustment.[96] If § 1250 property has been held for one year or less, the term simply refers to the depreciation adjustments taken with respect to the property.

The applicable percentage is generally 100 percent unless the property is government assisted, insured, or subsidized in one of the ways described in § 1250(a)(1)(B), or is subject to rapid amortization under § 167(k), in which case the applicable percentage is 100 less one percent for each full month in excess of 100 that the property is held.[97]

Like § 1245, § 1250 is applicable on an item-by-item basis, and hence it is necessary to apportion the sale price to each item of the partnership's § 1250 property in order to determine the portion of the seller's gain subject to § 1250(a). This facet of § 1250 further enhances the desirability of an agreement between the parties allocating the purchase price to specific items of § 1250 property.

A partner's share of partnership § 1250 gain from this hypothetical sale of the partnership's § 1250 property is determined in a manner consistent with the § 1245 Regulations.[98] If the partnership has a § 754 election in effect,

---

[95] § 1250(c).

[96] § 1250(b)(1). Under the general rule in § 168(b)(3), the straight-line method has been the applicable depreciation method for most residential and non-residential real estate since 1986. Consequently, the significance of § 1250 is not as great as in prior times. For property with respect to which the depreciation or amortization deduction for rehabilitation expenditures was allowed under former § 167(k), additional depreciation also refers to the excess of such adjustments over the adjustments that would have been made under the straight-line method of adjustment without regard to the useful life permitted under former § 167(k). § 1250(b)(4).

[97] § 1250(a)(1)(B). For property placed in service prior to 1976, different (and now largely irrelevant) recapture rules are provided in §§ 1250(a)(2) and 1250(a)(3).

[98] Reg. § 1.1250-1(f), referring to Reg. § 1.1245-1(e).

transferees who acquire their interests in sales or exchanges start with initial additional depreciation of zero.[99] If no § 754 election is in effect, each trans- feree apparently takes on the additional depreciation associated with the trans- ferred interest.[100]

The operation of § 1250 in the context of § 751 is illustrated by the fol- lowing example, which deals with property held for less than one year:

> EXAMPLE 17-9: On January 1, 2021, *A* sells his one-third interest in the *ABC* partnership for $600,000. *ABC* owns residential rental property *X*, which was acquired by the partnership on January 31, 2020, has a market value of $650,000, and an adjusted basis of $640,000 at the time of the sale. The partnership's additional depreciation with respect to rental prop- erty *X* is $15,000 and the applicable percentage is 100 percent.
>
> The computations are as follows: Since the gain of $10,000 that would be realized by the partnership on a hypothetical sale of rental prop- erty *X* for $650,000 would be less than the $15,000 of additional depreci- ation with respect to *X*, the § 1250(a) gain is 100 percent of $10,000, one third of which is attributable to *A*'s interest in the partnership. Hence, *A* is treated as receiving $3,333 in exchange for his interest in partnership unrealized receivables. His basis in this unrealized receivable is zero; and, therefore, he realizes ordinary income of $3,333 under § 751(a) upon the sale of his partnership interest.[101] The balance of his gain (or loss) is capi- tal.

Corporate partners are subject to additional recapture on the sale or other disposition of an interest in a partnership owning § 1250 property. Under § 291(a)(1), 20 percent of the excess of the amount that would be treated as ordinary income if the property were § 1245 property over the amount treated as ordinary income under § 1250 must be recognized and treated as ordinary income. This ordinary income amount is apparently treated as a zero-basis un- realized receivable under § 751(c).[102]

For individuals, the maximum rate of tax on long-term capital gains is currently 20 percent.[103] In the case of § 1250 property, however, an amount of

---

[99] Reg. § 1.1250-1(f). This Regulation suffers from the same defect as Regulations § 1.1245-1(e)(3)—it apparently applies to nonrecognition exchanges—as discussed at note 90.

[100] See Reg. § 1.1245-1(e)(2)(ii)(B).

[101] The partnership's basis is zero under Regulations § 1.751-1(c)(5).

[102] See HR Rep. No. 432, 98th Cong., 2d Sess., pt. 2, at 1612 (1984). See also ¶ 9.03[1][d].

[103] § 1(h)(1)(C). For tax years beginning before January 1, 2013, the maximum rate was 15 percent for net long-term capital gains excluding 28 percent rate gain and unrecap- tured § 1250 gain. For tax years ending after December 31, 2012, the maximum rate was increased to 20 percent. However, lower-income taxpayers may continue to enjoy the 15 percent rate for some or all of their net long-term capital gains.

gain equal to the unrecaptured depreciation previously taken with respect to the property ("unrecaptured § 1250 gain") is taxed at a 25 percent rate.[104] Pursuant to authority granted by § 1(h)(9), the Treasury has issued Regulations treating a portion of the transferor's § 741 gain as subject to tax at the 25 percent maximum rate based on the transferor's share of the partnership's unrecaptured § 1250 gain.[105]

[c] Recapture of Mining Exploration Expenses Under Section 617(d)

Under § 617(a), a taxpayer may elect to deduct "hard-mineral" exploration expenditures. If this election is made, the deductions are recaptured when the mine with respect to which the expenditures were made either reaches the producing stage (§ 617(b)) or is disposed of (§ 617(d)), whichever occurs first. If the recapture provisions of § 1254 also apply to a disposition, § 1254 overrides § 617.[106] The amount recaptured under § 617(d) as ordinary income on a sale of mineral property is the lesser of (1) the total amount deducted under § 617(a) that would have been capitalized but for the election, less an adjustment for certain depletion (§ 617(f)), or (2) the gain realized.

Like the depreciation recapture provisions, § 617(d) is applicable on a property-by-property basis. Therefore, it is necessary to determine the market value of each item of the partnership's mining property on a sale of a partnership interest. The recapture with respect to each mining property is then computed as if the property had been sold for its fair market value, and the selling partner's share of the amounts recaptured is treated as a zero-basis unrealized receivable.[107]

The election to deduct exploration expenditures is made at the partner, rather than the partnership, level.[108] Accordingly, different partners may have different "shares" of potential partnership § 617(d) recapture income, depending on whether they have made a § 617(a) election and, if so, when that election was made.[109]

[d] Recapture of Soil and Water Conservation Deductions Under Section 1252

Section 175 permits farmers to elect to deduct soil and water conservation expenses. Section 1252 provides for the recapture of a portion of any deduc-

---

[104] §§ 1(h)(1)(D)(i), 1(h)(6)(A).

[105] Reg. § 1.1(h)-1(b)(3)(ii), discussed at ¶ 16.08[6].

[106] § 617(d)(5).

[107] Reg. §§ 1.751-1(c)(4)(i), 1.751-1(c)(5).

[108] § 703(b).

[109] See ¶ 11.03[2][h].

tions claimed under § 175 with respect to farmland disposed of within ten years of its acquisition. The amount recaptured is the lesser of (1) the applicable percentage (100 percent if the farmland is disposed of within five years of its acquisition, 80 percent if disposed of during the sixth year, and so forth) of the deductions allowed under § 175 or (2) the gain realized in the case of a sale or exchange of the farmland.[110] Section 1252 does not contain special rules for partnerships, but generally authorizes the Secretary to provide by Regulations rules similar to those in § 1245 with respect to matters not covered by the statute. The incorporation of a declining "applicable percentage" into § 1252 raises technical problems similar to those encountered under § 1250 rather than § 1245, a fact that the Regulations may take into account when (and if) they are ever issued. To date, Regulations concerning partnerships have not been proposed.[111]

[e] DISC Recapture

Under § 995(c), a shareholder who disposes of stock in a DISC must include in income, as a dividend, any gain recognized to the extent of the tax-deferred DISC income that is both (1) attributable to the stock disposed of and (2) accumulated during the period such shareholder held the stock. The amount of potential dividend income under § 995(c) is treated as a zero-basis unrealized receivable within the meaning of § 751(c).[112]

[f] Recapture of Accumulated Earnings and Profits of Certain Controlled Foreign Corporations

Section 1248 provides that gains recognized on sales or exchanges of stock in certain controlled foreign corporations (CFCs) are taxable as dividends to the extent of the CFC's earnings and profits (1) attributable to the transferred stock and (2) accumulated during the period the selling shareholder owned the stock. If the transferor is an individual and the stock is a capital asset with a holding period of greater than one year, § 1248(b) limits the § 1248 tax to a pro rata share of (1) the U.S. taxes that the CFC would have paid as a

---

[110] See Reg. § 1.751-1(c)(4)(vii) (hypothetical sale at fair market value).

[111] See Reg. § 1.1252-2(e) (reserved for partnerships).

[112] Reg. §§ 1.751-1(c)(4)(ii), 1.751-1(c)(5). DISCs were generally phased out as of December 31, 1984, although DISC treatment remains available and allows a DISC to defer most of its income attributable to up to $10 million of qualified export receipts if its shareholders pay an interest charge on the deferred tax liability. § 995(f). Since this is not a particularly attractive tax-planning opportunity, DISCs are of relatively little continuing significance. One area of continuing significance is the use of a DISC to circumvent contribution limits for Roth IRAs. See, e.g., Summa Holdings, Inc. v. Commissioner, 848 F3d 779 (6th Cir. 2017).

domestic corporation (less the foreign and domestic taxes actually paid), plus (2) the taxes the shareholder would have paid at capital gains rates on the earnings that would have remained after the payment of corporate taxes.[113]

In connection with transfers of stock in CFCs, the Service has ruled, in Revenue Ruling 90-31,[114] that the CFC's earnings and profits are not reduced at the time the transferor recognizes dividend income under § 1248(a). Instead, an account is established on behalf of the transferee in the amount of the dividend taxed to the transferor, and this previously taxed amount is not taxed again when an actual distribution is made to the transferee.[115]

If stock in a CFC is owned by a domestic partnership, the amount of potential § 1248(a) dividend income is treated as a zero-basis unrealized receivable under § 751(c).[116] Regulations treat CFC stock held by foreign partnerships as owned proportionately by the partners for purposes of § 1248(a); on a sale of the stock by the partnership, the partners are treated as selling their proportionate shares of the stock.[117] This aggregate approach should not affect the treatment of potential § 1248(a) dividend income as an unrealized receivable under § 751(c) upon sales of partners' interests in foreign partnerships.

Section 751(e) provides that, in the case of an individual partner, the amount of the § 1248(a) tax is limited by § 1248(b). In order to emulate the holding of Revenue Ruling 90-31 in connection with transfers of interests in partnerships holding CFC stock, the special account established for transferees of CFC stock under the ruling must be established on behalf of the partnership. Further, it seems that this account, as well as any downward basis adjustment to the stock of the CFC occasioned by a subsequent tax-free receipt of the amount in this account, should be visited upon the transferee-partner. Unfortunately, the methodologies and mechanics for accomplishing these results under Subchapter K are far from clear.[118]

An actual sale by a partnership of stock in a CFC brings into play the § 245A dividends received deduction for domestic corporate partners, which is quite helpful to such taxpayers.[119] A hypothetical sale of partnership-owned

---

[113] See generally J. Kuntz, R. Peroni & J. Bogdanski, U.S. International Taxation ¶ B6.03[6][f] (Thomson Reuters/Tax & Accounting 2013).

[114] Rev. Rul. 90-31, 1990-1 CB 147.

[115] See § 959(d).

[116] Reg. §§ 1.751-1(c)(4)(iv), 1.751-1(c)(5). A domestic partnership is treated as a person for purposes of § 1248. See § 7701(a)(30)(B); Reg. § 1.1248-1(a)(1).

[117] Reg. §§ 1.1248-1(a)(4), 1.1248-1(a)(5) Example (4).

[118] See generally Farmer, Huffman, Jackel & Hintmann, "Partnership Dispositions of Stock in Controlled Foreign Corporations," 110 Tax Notes 1319 (Mar. 20, 2006).

[119] The conference report accompanying the enactment of § 245A provides that the meaning of "dividend received" is intended to be interpreted broadly and consistent with §§ 243 and 245. It says,

CFC stock occasioned by the sale or exchange of a partnership interest apparently does not, however, bring this provision into play.[120]

[g] Franchises, Trademarks, and Trade Names

Under § 1253, gain on the transfer of a franchise, trademark, or trade name is treated as ordinary income where the transferor retains any significant power, right, or continuing interest with respect to the subject matter of the transferred property. In connection with transfers of partnership interests and distributions of partnership assets, any gain with respect to partnership property that would be subject to § 1253(a) if the property had been sold at its fair market value is treated as a zero-basis unrealized receivable for purposes of § 751(c).[121]

Although the statutory language is far from clear, the legislative history of this addition to § 751(c) suggests that potential § 1253(a) income is an unrealized receivable only if the partner potentially subject to tax under § 751 retains rights, with respect to his transferred or liquidated partnership interest, that would bring § 1253(a) into play if the rights were retained on a direct sale of a

---

[f]or example, if a domestic corporation indirectly owns stock of a foreign corporation through a partnership and the domestic corporation would qualify for the participation DRD with respect to dividends from the foreign corporation if the domestic corporation owned such stock directly, the domestic corporation would be allowed a participation DRD with respect to its distributive share of the partnership's dividend from the foreign corporation.

HR Conf. Rep. No. 466, 115th Cong., 2d Sess. at 609 (2017). Section 245A(g) provides regulatory authority to address the treatment of U.S. shareholders owning stock of a specified 10 percent-owned foreign corporation through a partnership.

Some uncertainty as to the application of § 245A to dividends created by § 1248 stems from § 1248(j), which provides that § 245A applies to § 1248 dividends "[i]n the case of the sale or exchange by a domestic corporation of stock in a foreign corporation..." Regulations issued under § 245A(g) will hopefully eliminate any uncertainty caused by the language limiting access to § 245A to sales by corporations (versus partnerships with corporate partners). In this regard, it is helpful that the § 1248 Regulations adopt an aggregate approach to sales by foreign partnerships (which are not U.S. persons, and thus potentially not covered by § 1248). See Reg. § 1.1248-1(a)(4). Such an aggregate approach is entirely appropriate in interfacing § 1248 with § 245A.

[120] See § 1248(g)(2)(B); Reg. § 1.1248-1(e)(3). See also HR Rep. No. 658, 94th Cong., 1st Sess. 248 (1975); S. Rep. No. 94-938, pt. 1, at 271 (1976), 94th Cong., 2d Sess. 266 (1976). But see Technical Corrections Act of 1977, § 2(t)(13); HR Rep. No. 700, 95th Cong., 1st Sess. 44 (1977): "The 1976 Act provides that if a partnership holds stock in a foreign corporation which would be subject to dividend treatment [under § 1248] if sold directly, any gains to a partner ... selling his interest in the partnership will be treated as a dividend."

[121] Reg. §§ 1.751-1(c)(4)(viii), 1.751-1(c)(5).

franchise, trademark, or trade name.[122] Thus, a partner who retains no "strings" on the sale or liquidation of his partnership interest should not be subject to § 751(c) and § 1253(a), even if the partnership holds appreciated franchises, trademarks, or trade names.

[h] Recapture: Oil and Gas, Geothermal, and Other Mineral Properties

If a mine, well, or other natural deposit that constitutes "property" for purposes of § 614 is disposed of, the following are recaptured as ordinary income under § 1254(a): (1) expenditures with respect to the property that have been deducted as intangible drilling and development costs under § 263(c); (2) certain deductions allowed by §§ 616 and 617 that, but for being deducted, would have increased the basis of the property; and (3) deductions for depletion under § 611.[123] The amount so recaptured is limited to the gain realized on the disposition (or the excess of the fair market value of the property over its adjusted basis, where the disposition is not a sale, exchange, or involuntary conversion). This potential recapture is a zero-basis unrealized receivable under § 751(c).[124]

[i] Market Discount Bonds and Short-Term Obligations

Market discount bonds (as defined by § 1278) and short-term obligations (as defined by § 1283) are treated as unrealized receivables, but only to the extent of the amount that would be treated as ordinary income if the bond or obligation had been sold by the partnership.

Section 1276 provides that gain from the disposition of a market discount bond is treated as ordinary income to the extent it does not exceed the accrued market discount on the bond. The recognition of ordinary income on dispositions of certain short-term obligations[125] is governed by § 1271. Under § 1271(a)(3), gain realized on a sale or exchange of a "short-term Government obligation" is treated as ordinary income to the extent it does not exceed a ratable share of the acquisition discount with respect to the obligation. Section 1271(a)(4) provides a similar rule with respect to certain short-term nongovernment obligations.

---

[122] See S. Rep. No. 938, 94th Cong., 2d Sess. 414 (1976); Reg. § 1.751-1(c)(4)(viii) (potential gain is gain to which § 1253(a) would apply if items sold by partnership). The language of the Regulations is ambiguous; it is unclear whether any rights retained upon the transfer of an interest in the partnership are attributed to the hypothetical sale by the partnership.

[123] Reg. § 1.1254-1(a).

[124] Reg. §§ 1.751-1(c)(4)(ix), 1.751-1(c)(5).

[125] See § 1283.

[j] Recapture of Prior Understated Rental Income

Section 467(c) generally applies to dispositions of leased tangible property where the relevant rental agreement has the effect of deferring the payment of economically accrued rent. A cash-method lessor/transferor must recapture, as ordinary income, that portion of the proceeds that are attributable to the economically accrued, but deferred, rent. For purposes of § 751(c), any § 467 recapture to which partnership property is subject is treated as § 1245 or § 1250 recapture.[126] Consequently, potential recapture under § 467(c) with respect to partnership property constitutes a § 751 unrealized receivable for purposes of §§ 731, 732, 741, and 751, but not § 736.

¶ 17.04 INVENTORY ITEMS: SECTION 751(d)

All "inventory items" are treated as § 751 property in connection with transfers of partnership interests. If a partnership's inventory items are, in the aggregate, "substantially appreciated," they also are treated as § 751 property in connection with partnership distributions.[127]

Section 751(d) sets forth the following three categories of inventory items:[128]

1. Stock-in-trade, inventory, and property held primarily for sale to customers in the ordinary course of the partnership's business within the meaning of § 1221(a)(1);[129]
2. Any other property that, upon sale or exchange, would be considered "property other than a capital asset and other than property described in section 1231;"[130] and

---

[126] § 467(c)(5)(C). See Reg. § 1.467-7(c)(7).

[127] In connection with transfers of partnership interests after August 5, 1997, the Taxpayer Relief Act of 1997 amended § 751 to provide that inventory items are treated as § 751 property regardless of whether they are substantially appreciated. In conjunction with this change, the definition of "substantial appreciation," which now only applies in connection with distributions, was moved from § 751(d)(1) to § 751(b)(3).

[128] Prior to 2004, there was a fourth, very narrow, category of inventory items: shares of foreign investment companies, to the extent gain from sales would be taxed as ordinary income under § 1246(a). This category was eliminated in connection with the repeal of the foreign investment company rules in 2004. See American Jobs Creation Act of 2004, Pub. L. 108-357, § 413 (Oct. 22, 2004).

[129] § 751(d)(1).

[130] § 751(d)(2).

3. Any other property that, if held by the selling or distributee-partner, would be considered property of the type described in one of the first two categories.[131]

[1] Section 1221(a)(1) Property (Section 751(d)(1))

The first statutory category of inventory items consists of "true" inventory items that are stock-in-trade, includible in inventory, or held primarily for sale to customers. The justification for the inclusion of these items under § 751 is clear: If sold by the partnership, gain or loss on these items will not qualify for capital gain treatment. Consequently, their inclusion under § 751 is necessary to prevent the conversion of ordinary income to capital gain through sales of partnership interests.[132]

Most of the problems that arise in connection with this category of inventory relate to the familiar factual question of whether a particular asset is held primarily for sale to customers in the ordinary course of business.[133] Resolution of this question in the context of § 751 is controlled by the vast body of case law that has developed under § 1221(a)(1).[134]

[2] Other Ordinary Income Property (Section 751(d)(2))

The breadth of the second category of inventory items is so great that it is a wonder that the drafters of the 1954 Code bothered to specify any other categories of inventory items. It includes "any other property" that, upon sale by the partnership, would be considered property other than a capital asset and other than § 1231 property. This category seems to carry the collapsible partnership concept to its logical extreme: To the extent a selling partner's interest

---

[131] § 751(d)(3).

[132] Several cases decided under the 1939 Code involved partnerships holding inventory property. See, e.g., John W. Lenney, 38 TC 287 (1962) (nonacq.); Ed Krist, 12 TCM 801 (1953), aff'd, 231 F2d 548 (9th Cir. 1956).

[133] See, e.g., Estate of Freeland v. Commissioner, 393 F2d 573 (9th Cir. 1968) (cert. denied) (partnership property held primarily for sale); Ginsburg v. United States, 396 F2d 983 (Ct. Cl. 1968) (subsequent sale of interest in partnership addressed in *Estate of Freeland*; same property *not* held primarily for sale); Morse v. United States, 371 F2d 474 (Ct. Cl. 1967) (per curiam) (same partnership; sale at same time as *Ginsburg*; property *not* held primarily for sale); see also Martin v. United States, 330 F. Supp. 681 (MD Ga. 1971); J. Thomas Requard, 25 TCM 732 (1966).

[134] See generally B. Bittker & L. Lokken, Federal Income Taxation of Income, Estates and Gifts ¶ 47.2.1 (Thomson Reuters/Tax & Accounting, 2d/3d ed. 1993–2019).

is attributable to partnership assets that would produce ordinary income if sold by the partnership, the partner is subject to tax at ordinary income tax rates.[135]

The Regulations give full effect to the breadth of this category by providing: "Thus, accounts receivable acquired in the ordinary course of business for services or from the sale of stock in trade constitute inventory items (see section 1221(4)), as do any unrealized receivables."[136] Although the inclusion of *realized* accounts receivable may be justified under the statutory language, this inclusion was apparently not intended by Congress.[137] In any event, the inclusion of realized receivables in the definition of "inventory items" appears to be of no consequence in connection with the application of § 751(a).

The inclusion of unrealized receivables raises different questions. If correct, it means that the § 751(d) definition of "inventory items" completely encompasses the § 751(c) definition of "unrealized receivables." This proposition seems inconsistent with the structure of § 751 (for example, it would render the references to unrealized receivables in §§ 751(a)(1) and 751(b)(1)(A)(i) surplusage), as well as the disparate treatment accorded inventory items and unrealized receivables under §§ 724 and 735(a), which provide that inventory items lose their ordinary income taint if held for more than five years by a transferee-partnership or by a distributee-partner, respectively, while unrealized receivables do not. Further, under this definitional pattern, the inclusion of unrealized receivables along with inventory items in §§ 731(a)(2)(B) and 732(c)(1) would be redundant: The references to unrealized receivables in these provisions could be deleted without changing their meaning. It is readily apparent from an examination of these provisions that the drafters of the 1954 Code did not contemplate that all unrealized receivables would also be treated as inventory items.[138]

A review of the different types of unrealized receivables also indicates that their blanket inclusion as inventory items is questionable under the literal

---

[135] See Priv. Ltr. Rul. 9845012 (Aug. 6, 1998), revised by Priv. Ltr. Rul. 199910033 (Dec. 12, 1998) (long-term power purchase contract is not an inventory item; sale of the contract would generate capital gain).

[136] Reg. § 1.751-1(d)(2)(ii).

[137] See S. Rep. No. 1622, 83d Cong., 2d Sess. 404 (1954), which includes an example in which a partnership holds "realized" receivables with a basis of $15,000 and a market value of $15,000, "inventory" with a basis of $30,000 and a market value of $39,000, and other assets (other than money) that have a basis of $40,000 and a market value of $46,000. In applying the predecessor of the "substantial appreciation" test, currently found in § 751(b)(3), the example concludes that this test is met because the market value of the "inventory" is more than 120 percent of its basis. The Senate Report excludes the "realized" receivables from this calculation, thus casting doubt on the validity of the Regulations. If the receivables are treated as inventory, the 120 percent test is not met (120 percent of $45,000 is exactly equal to $54,000), and the conclusion in the example is incorrect.

[138] See note 137.

language of § 751(d), which only applies to "property" of the partnership. Un-realized receivables in the form of receivables of a cash-method partnership for services performed or goods delivered are "property." However, the right to re-ceive payment for services to be performed or goods to be delivered in the fu-ture does not constitute "property" in the usual tax-sense of the word.[139]

Further, by referring to "unrealized receivables," the Regulations seem to require inclusion of the recapture items, as well as market discount bonds and short-term obligations described in the second and third sentences of § 751(c), as inventory items.[140] Blanket inclusion of these items is problematic for an-other reason: seven of the eight recapture items specified in the second sen-tence (the only exception is § 1253(a)) and both of the types of financial instruments described in the third sentence are not "property other than capital assets and other than property described in section 1231." The relevant recap-ture and other provisions operate by characterizing certain gains as ordinary in-come, not by excluding the property itself from the definition of capital assets and § 1231 property.

Although the second category of inventory items may be overly broad as it relates to unrealized receivables, it may not be broad enough to include cer-tain other types of ordinary income assets. These potential exclusions may be of greater consequence than the arguable over-inclusion of receivables: The latter generally affects only the computation of substantial appreciation under § 751(b)(3) in connection with distributions, whereas the former may result in the complete exclusion of assets under § 751. The most noteworthy problem area relates to the issue discussed above in connection with the recapture items and financial instruments detailed in the last two sentences of § 751(c). A number of Code provisions recharacterize all or a portion of the gain realized on the sale or exchange of otherwise capital assets as "ordinary income." Sec-tion 306(a), dealing with certain dispositions of preferred stock, is an example of this sort of provision, as are §§ 707(b)(2), 988, 1239, and 1249.[141] These provisions recharacterize the transferor's gain rather than the nature of the as-set with respect to which the gain is realized. Consequently, they literally do not trigger § 751(d)(2), which is limited to "property ... which ... would be considered property other than a capital asset and other than property described

---

[139] See, e.g., Vaaler v. United States, 454 F2d 1120 (8th Cir. 1972) (termination pay-ments to insurance agent, partially in exchange for right to earn renewal commissions, are ordinary income); Robert E. Foxe, 53 TC 21 (1969) (same); Thurlow E. McFall, 34 BTA 108 (1936) (sale of contract right to perform services results in ordinary income). But cf. Realty Loan Corp., 54 TC 1083 (1970), aff'd, 478 F2d 1049 (9th Cir. 1973).

[140] It is not entirely clear that the Treasury intended to include these amounts as in-ventory items. The Regulations in question, Regulations § 1.751-1(d)(2)(ii), was adopted in 1956, prior to the addition of the last two sentences to § 751(c).

[141] Compare § 1248, which characterizes a portion of the gain on the sale of stock in certain CFCs as a dividend. See Rothschild, "Effect of Post-1954 Legislation on Taxation of Partnerships," 22 NYU Inst. on Fed. Tax'n 593, 607–610 (1964).

in § 1231."[142] Perhaps the courts will forgive this linguistic inelegance in order to further the legislative objectives of § 751, but the issue is still in doubt.[143]

The appropriate application of § 751(d)(2) requires careful analysis of the partnership's assets, not all of which may appear on the balance sheet. The need for care is illustrated by *G. Ralph Bartolme*,[144] a case involving the sale of an interest in a partnership that had made a substantial interest prepayment.[145] The selling partner, who had previously deducted his distributive share of the prepayment, thereby reducing his ordinary income from other sources, successfully claimed capital gain treatment on the sale of his partnership interest.[146] The buyer, Mr. Bartolme, was allowed to allocate a portion of his purchase price to "unamortized prepaid interest" under § 743(b) and to amortize the amount so allocated over the term of the prepayment, thereby effectively obtaining a second deduction for the interest prepayment.

With the benefit of hindsight, the Service's failure to pursue Bartolme's seller under §§ 751(a) and 751(d)(2) (formerly § 751(d)(2)(B)) may have been a mistake. The Tax Court opinion in *Bartolme* characterizes the interest prepayment as an "asset with no tax basis," and cites *Spitalny v. United States*[147] in discussing the Service's treatment of the seller.[148] In *Spitalny*, the tax-benefit rule was applied to tax a corporate seller of previously expensed feed and supplies on the amount realized on the sale notwithstanding the nonrecognition provisions of § 337 (as in effect before the Tax Reform Act of 1986). The reference to *Spitalny* suggests that the seller of an expensed "prepaid interest" asset may be vulnerable to ordinary income treatment on a tax-benefit theory

---

[142] The legislative history of § 751 is as clear and unequivocal on this point as the statute. See S. Rep. No. 1622, 83d Cong., 2d Sess. 403 (1954) (treatment as inventory based on nature of the asset; no mention of the character of the income or gain from the asset). Compare § 1253(a), which provides that certain transfers of franchises, trademarks, and trade names shall not be treated as sales or exchanges of capital assets. To the same effect is § 582(c)(1), dealing with certain debt instruments held by financial institutions. See also § 64 (definition of "ordinary income").

[143] The argument that the statutory language should be stretched to include these types of items was undermined considerably by the addition of former § 751(d)(3) (including § 1246(a) "ordinary income" as an inventory item) to the statute in 1962. See note 128. The perceived need to include § 1246(a) income specifically suggests that the omission of the other items discussed in the text was not inadvertent.

[144] G. Ralph Bartolme, 62 TC 821 (1974).

[145] *Bartolme* arose prior to the 1976 enactment of § 461(g), which generally requires interest prepaid by a cash-method taxpayer to be capitalized and deducted as it accrues economically.

[146] See G. Ralph Bartolme, 62 TC 821, 826, 831 (1974) (Tax Court case involving sellers closed by stipulation of no deficiency).

[147] Spitalny v. United States, 430 F2d 195 (9th Cir. 1970).

[148] G. Ralph Bartolme, 62 TC 821, 830–831 (1974).

outside the partnership context.[149] If this is correct, the interposition of a partnership should not change the result: Section 751(d)(2) is clearly broad enough to encompass this type of asset, assuming only that it would be treated as a noncapital/non−§ 1231 asset if sold by the partnership. Thus, § 751(d)(2) seems to ensure that, whatever conversion potential may exist in situations of this sort, it is the same regardless of whether the asset is held directly or by a partnership. The potential difficulty, of course, is recognizing that a § 751(d)(2) asset exists.

[3] Ordinary Income Property in the Hands of the Seller or Distributee (Section 751(d)(3))

Finally, partnership assets that would fall into one of the first three categories "if held by the selling or distributee partner" are also treated as inventory items. Although the legislative history does not indicate the purpose of this particular provision, it was apparently intended to preclude the use of partnerships by dealers seeking to obtain capital gain treatment with respect to property that, if held by them directly, would yield ordinary income upon disposition.[150]

The major difficulties in the application of § 751(d)(3) are addressed in the following subsections.

[a] Property "Held Primarily for Sale"

Whether property is held primarily for sale to customers in the ordinary course of business is a factual question involving the subjective intent of the holder of the property. After extensive litigation, the courts have identified a number of factors to be considered in making this factual determination.[151] While a detailed examination of each of these factors is beyond the scope of this discussion, one aspect is of considerable importance: The primary purpose for which property is held is determined on a property-by-property basis, examining the taxpayer's activities and attempting to determine his intent with respect to each particular property. It is the character of the property sold, rather than that of the taxpayer selling it, that is controlling.[152]

---

[149] See Robert F. Weyher, 66 TC 825 (1976).

[150] See Alexander, "Collapsible Partnerships," 19 NYU Inst. on Fed. Tax'n 257, 262−263 (1961).

[151] See generally B. Bittker & L. Lokken, Federal Income Taxation of Income, Estates and Gifts ¶ 47.2.1 (Thomson Reuters/Tax & Accounting, 2d/3d ed. 1993−2019).

[152] The Code explicitly provides for the segregation of investment and dealer property of securities dealers (see § 1236), but not of other dealers. Nevertheless, it is clear that a

This is not to say that a taxpayer's other activities are not important: They are, and a taxpayer who is a "dealer," in the sense that he regularly buys and sells property of the kind in question, has a much more difficult time demonstrating his investment intent than a taxpayer who has never before bought or sold the type of property involved. Nevertheless, the taxpayer's other activities constitute only one of several factors considered, and it is well established that a dealer may hold, for investment, property of the kind in which he regularly deals.[153]

This focus on the owner's intent with respect to each property held is particularly troublesome in the application of the dual-level test imposed by § 751(d)(3). By requiring that both the intent of the partnership and the intent of the selling partner be examined, this subsection presupposes that the intent of one may differ from that of the other with respect to the same property. An already difficult factual determination is thus elevated to a metaphysical level. The Regulations make no attempt to grapple with this matter, nor has any court been forced to deal with it.[154]

[b] Dealers as Sellers and Distributees

The application of § 751(d)(3) to dealers who are sellers of partnership interests makes at least a certain amount of sense in that it is the dealer who may be subject to an increased ordinary income tax under § 751(a). If the dealer receives an actual distribution of the property, however, literal application of § 751(b) could cause ordinary income tax to be imposed on his nondealer partners. The Regulations avoid this completely irrational result by

---

"dealer" in other types of property may hold property of the same type for investment under certain circumstances. See note 153.

[153] See, e.g., William B. Howell, 57 TC 546, 557 (1972) (acq.); Real Estate Corp., 35 TC 610, 615 (1961), aff'd, 301 F2d 423 (10th Cir. 1962) (cert. denied); Charles E. Mieg, 32 TC 1314, 1321 (1959) (acq.); Rev. Rul. 57-565, 1957-2 CB 546. Compare David Taylor Enters., Inc., 89 TCM 1369 (2005) (vintage cars bought and sold by dealership were held for sale to customers in ordinary course of business; losses deductible against ordinary income) with Graham D. Williford, 64 TCM 422 (1992) (finding that art collection was not held for sale to customers in ordinary course of business; gains taxable as capital gains).

[154] Under former § 341(e), Regulations § 1.341-6(b)(4) provided that where property held by a corporation was "similar" to property that a substantial shareholder held primarily for sale to customers, it was treated as held primarily for sale by the corporation for certain purposes. This provision of the Regulations was subject to serious criticism because it failed to take into account the purpose for which the particular property was held, thereby ignoring the cases cited note 153.

limiting the application of § 751(d)(3) to property retained by the partner-ship.[155]

[c] Technical Problems

Outside the dealer area, some intricate and as yet unexplored technical problems may arise under § 751(d)(3). For example, assume that (1) a partner sells his partnership interest to a "controlled entity" within the meaning of § 1239(c) and (2) the partnership holds depreciable property.[156] If the seller owned the depreciable property directly, any gain on the sale would be ordinary income under § 1239, and thus the property might be viewed as inventory under § 751(d)(3).[157] Similar problems may arise under § 1236 or § 1249, to name just two examples.

¶ 17.05 DEFERRED PAYMENT SALES OF INTERESTS IN COLLAPSIBLE PARTNERSHIPS

A number of interrelated and largely unresolved problems arise where a partner in a partnership holding § 751 property attempts to report gain from the sale of his partnership interest on a deferred basis. The rules generally applicable to installment sales (and other deferred payment sales) of partnership interests are discussed in Chapter 16.[158] Most of the problems encountered where the partnership owns § 751 property relate to installment sales under § 453, and, consequently, the focus of the discussion that follows is the interaction between §§ 453 and 751.

---

[155] Reg. § 1.751-1(d)(2)(iii); see Alexander, "Collapsible Partnerships," 19 NYU Inst. on Fed. Tax'n 257, 263 (1961).

[156] Cf. Rev. Rul. 72-172, 1972-1 CB 265 (sale of 100 percent of partnership interests by husband and wife to controlled corporation is subject to § 1239).

[157] This assumes the questions discussed at ¶ 17.04[1][b] are resolved in favor of the inclusion of § 306 stock and the like as inventory items under § 751(d)(2). Even if these problems are resolved against inclusion, issues arise in the context of Code provisions, such as § 582(c)(1), which deem certain sales of debt instruments by a financial institution to "not be considered a sale or exchange of a capital asset." Presumably, a contribution of such a debt instrument would cause it to be "inventory" to the partnership with respect to the contributing partner. Section 724, which "freezes" the character of contributed inventory to the contributee partnership, should not come into play, since the debt instrument is not "inventory" in the hands of the contributing partner.

[158] See ¶ 16.04[1].

[1] Fragmentation of Partnership Interests Under Section 453

Sales of certain types of property are not eligible for installment reporting.[159] In applying the installment reporting rules to sales of partnership interests, a threshold question is the extent to which the selling partner can use installment reporting where the partnership owns property of the type that would not be eligible for installment reporting if sold by the partnership. Under the general entity approach adopted by § 741, a partnership interest is treated as a capital asset, separate and apart from the assets of the partnership, and, consequently, a sale of the interest should generally be eligible for § 453 treatment in its entirety. However, a certain degree of fragmentation of a partnership interest is clearly required for purposes of § 453; § 453(i)(2) denies installment treatment to "the aggregate amount which would be treated as ordinary income under section 1245 or 1250 (or so much of section 751 as relates to section 1245 or 1250)" and § 453A(e)(2) authorizes the promulgation of Regulations that treat the sale of a partnership interest as the sale of the seller's proportionate share of the partnership assets in order to carry out the interest charge and pledging rules of § 453A.[160] Moreover, the legislative history of § 751(a)[161] and, more recently, § 751(f) (dealing with tiered partnerships)[162] supports fragmentation of the interest for § 453 purposes to the extent the partnership holds § 751 property. Of course, if fragmentation is generally required with respect to § 751 property, the amendments to §§ 453, 453A, and 751(f) were technically unnecessary; hence, the requisite degree of fragmentation with respect to § 751 property must be regarded as uncertain.

---

[159] See ¶ 16.04[1][a].

[160] See ¶ 16.04[1][b]. Additionally, § 453(k) authorizes Regulations preventing the avoidance of § 453(k) through the use of related parties, pass-thru entities, or intermediaries. The legislative history of § 453(k) states that installment sale treatment should be denied only if the seller of the interest could have caused the partnership to sell its publicly traded stock and securities directly. S. Rep. No. 313, 99th Cong., 2d Sess. 131 (1986).

[161] See HR Rep. No. 1337, 83d Cong., 2d Sess. 71 (1954); S. Rep. No. 1622, 83d Cong., 2d Sess. 99 (1954): "The statutory treatment proposed, in general, regards the income rights as severable from the partnership interest and as subject to the same tax consequences which would be accorded an individual entrepreneur." Indeed, the Service originally took the position that a purchaser of a partnership interest was entitled to a cost basis for his share of partnership § 751 property, even if the partnership had not made a § 754 election. See GCM 36329 (July 3, 1975). This position was reversed in GCM 38186 (Nov. 30, 1979).

[162] HR Rep. No. 432, 98th Cong., 2d Sess., pt. 2, at 1229 (1984); 1 Senate Comm. on Finance, 98th Cong., 2d Sess., Deficit Reduction Act of 1984, S. Prt. No. 169, at 240 (Comm. Print 1984) ("[s]ection 751 will be applied by regarding income rights, as section 751 does under present law, as severable from the partnership interest. Under this approach, a partner will be treated as disposing of such items independently of the rest of his partnership interest.").

If § 751 is the basis for fragmenting a partnership interest, the interest should be divided into two parts: (1) one part representing the partner's indirect interest in various items of partnership § 751 property and (2) the other part representing the balance of that partner's partnership interest. Based on this degree of fragmentation, only the selling partner's interest in the partnership's § 751 property would be potentially ineligible for § 453 treatment because of the exclusions discussed in Chapter 16;[163] the balance of the interest should qualify regardless of the nature of the non–§ 751 property held by the partnership. On the other hand, complete fragmentation of the interest might be required under a pure aggregate approach, with the seller's interest in each item of partnership property subject to separate scrutiny under § 453. Complete fragmentation is, however, inconsistent with the general entity approach of § 741 and has been rejected by the Service in favor of partial fragmentation based on § 751. Revenue Ruling 89-108[164] takes the position that payments for a partnership interest are not eligible for installment sale reporting to the extent they are attributable to substantially appreciated inventory that would not be eligible for installment sale reporting if sold directly. Under this ruling, payments that are not attributable to § 751 property apparently qualify for installment reporting regardless of the nature of the underlying partnership assets.

In any event, there is considerable overlap between the categories of assets ineligible for installment sale treatment and those that fall within the definition of § 751 property. Thus, most gain treated as ordinary income under § 751(a) will not be eligible for installment reporting. Property that is inventory for purposes of § 1221(a)(1) is a collapsible asset within the meaning of § 751(d)(1) and is also within the inventory exclusion of § 453(b)(1)(B). Many "unrealized receivables" under § 751(c)(2), relating to services rendered or to be rendered, fall within the judicial exclusion from § 453 of service-related property rights. The overlap is far from complete, however. Some items that fall within the definition of § 751 property are not excluded from § 453 (e.g., the recapture items listed in the second sentence of § 751(c) other than recapture pursuant to §§ 1245 and 1250[165]). Conversely, certain items excluded from § 453 may not be treated as collapsible property (e.g., stock or securities held for investment that are traded on an established securities market). This imperfect overlap apparently allows a selling partner to obtain the benefits of § 453 with respect to payments for property that is included in the portion of his

---

[163] See ¶ 16.04[1][a].

[164] Rev. Rul. 89-108, 1989-2 CB 100, discussed at ¶ 16.04[1][b]. The elimination of the "substantial appreciation" test from § 751(a) by the Taxpayer Relief Act of 1997 should have no effect on this ruling. Revenue Ruling 89-108 was followed in Lori M. Mingo, 105 TCM 1857 (2013), aff'd, 773 F3d 629 (5th Cir. 2014) (§ 751(a) applies to deny installment sale treatment to payments for a partnership interest to the extent attributable to the partnership's cash-method accounts receivable).

[165] § 453(i)(2).

partnership interest that is not fragmented under § 751 but that would not be eligible for § 453 treatment if sold directly by the partner, at least until Regulations to the contrary are issued.[166]

[2] Characterization of Individual Installment Payments

If sales of interests in partnerships holding § 751 property are fragmented as suggested above, additional questions arise in connection with the characterization of individual payments. These questions fall into two subcategories:

1. How are individual payments fragmented in the absence of an agreement between the parties?
2. What is the effect of an agreement between buyer and seller specifically fragmenting the payments?

In the absence of an agreement to the contrary, each installment payment received for the partnership interest is apparently allocated among the partnership assets in proportion to their fair market values.[167]

The fact that some assets may qualify for installment sale treatment and some may not can provide selling partners with an incentive to allocate a disproportionately large part of the year-of-sale payments to nonqualifying assets, thus maximizing the seller's tax deferral with respect to qualifying assets. Assets sold at a loss and inventory assets seem to be the most popular choices for excessive year-of-sale allocations. Surprisingly, the courts have generally given effect to self-serving allocations of this sort if expressly agreed to by buyer and seller.[168] However, sellers lacking the foresight to obtain express allocations from their buyers have fared poorly in their efforts to convince the courts that a disproportionate allocation of year-of-sale payments was intended.[169]

The courts' willingness to give effect to agreed-upon allocations is surprising because such allocations generally have no effect[170] on the buyer. The

---

[166] Section 453(k), which prohibits the use of the installment method in reporting the sale of stock or securities traded on an established market, specifically authorizes the Secretary to promulgate regulations preventing the avoidance of this prohibition through the use of related parties, pass-thru entities, or intermediaries. To date, Treasury has not exercised this grant of regulatory authority. See ¶ 16.04[1][b].

[167] See Veenkant v. Commissioner, 416 F2d 93 (6th Cir. 1969) (per curiam) (cert. denied); Rev. Rul. 68-13, 1968-1 CB 195; Rev. Rul. 57-434, 1957-2 CB 300.

[168] See Charles A. Collins, 48 TC 45 (1967) (acq.); Andrew A. Monaghan, 40 TC 680 (1963) (acq.) Lubken v. United States, 1961-2 USTC ¶ 9537 (SD Cal. 1961); Rev. Rul. 68-13, 1968-1 CB 195; Rev. Rul. 57-434, 1957-2 CB 300.

[169] See, e.g., Blackstone Realty Co. v. Commissioner, 398 F2d 991 (5th Cir. 1968); James A. Johnson, 49 TC 324 (1968).

[170] The buyer is affected only in certain very limited circumstances. For example, payments for a covenant not to compete generally are amortizable over fifteen years under

opposed interests of the parties may be adequate to protect the fisc with respect to allocation of the entire purchase price,[171] but the buyer's lack of either tax or economic interest in the allocation of specific payments affords scant protection against overreaching allocations conceived by knowledgeable sellers and agreed to by indifferent buyers. A more difficult test for the seller to meet is at least suggested by some of the decided cases: that an allocation of specific payments be given effect for tax purposes only if it has economic consequences.[172] However, the Service apparently does not intend to pursue this approach.[173]

If the parties can control the allocation of year-of-sale payments, there is no reason to think subsequent payments cannot also be allocated by agreement

---

§ 197. See ¶ 9.02[3][k]. However, amounts paid or incurred after the taxable year in which the covenant is entered into are amortized over the remaining months in the fifteen-year amortization period, starting with the month in which the amount is paid. See HR Rep. No. 213, 103d Cong., 1st Sess. 327 (1993).

[171] See ¶ 17.02[3][d].

[172] See, e.g., Charles A. Collins, 48 TC 45 (1967) (acq.) (allocation given effect in connection with sale of a single parcel of land: at the buyer's request, only part of the land encumbered by the buyer's obligation); Lubken v. United States, 1961-2 USTC ¶ 9537 (SD Cal. 1961) (cattle and cash allocable thereto excluded in computing 30 percent limit on year-of-sale payments under § 453(b)(2)(B), prior to deletion of this requirement in 1980; cattle not subject to seller's lien); Veenkant v. Commissioner, 416 F2d 93 (6th Cir. 1969) (per curiam) (cert. denied) (sale of motel and adjacent residence integrated: both secured buyer's obligation); Richard H. Pritchett, 63 TC 149, 168–173 (1974) (acq.) (on facts, sales of contiguous parcels of real estate not integrated; mortgages not cross-collateralized). For a case in which tax advisors appear to have had second thoughts about specifically allocating consideration in a single, integrated transaction, see Williams Cos. v. Energy Transfer Equity, L.P., 159 A3d 264 (Del. 2017).

[173] See Revenue Ruling 68-13, 1968-1 CB 195, 198, Example 3, which considered the sale of a business for $8,000, with a $4,000 down payment allocated $3,000 to inventory. Prior to its amendment in 1980, installment sale treatment was not available if year-of-sale payments exceeded 30 percent of the selling price of the property. The Service concluded that the noninventory property qualified for § 453 treatment, noting that the balance of the down payment ($1,000) was less than 30 percent of the $5,000 selling price of the noninventory property, and reciting that the portion of the down payment attributable to inventory was "based upon relative values and arm's-length bargaining." The quoted phrase seems only to mean that the down payment for the inventory must not exceed its value established through arm's-length bargaining. The "relative value" language should not be read as requiring the total down payment to be allocated in proportion to the relative values of the assets sold, since the allocation given effect in Example (3) of the ruling does not comply with this requirement. There are, however, a few subsequent cases involving sales of corporate stock suggesting a less benign approach by the Service. See, e.g., Clarence J. Monson, 79 TC 827 (1982) (holding redemption and subsequent sale to a third party are treated as separate sales for purposes of § 453(b), and the gain on the sale of stock to the third party properly reported on the installment sale method); Chick M. Farha, 58 TC 526 (1972) (purported sale of stock followed shortly by redemption at vastly different price integrated as single sale; installment treatment denied), aff'd, 483 F2d 18 (10th Cir. 1973).

between the parties. However, there is little authority on this point. The seller's objective is to control the timing of the receipt of different types of taxable income. In most cases, this is likely to translate directly into attempts to defer the receipt of payments attributable to high-profit or ordinary income property, while accelerating the receipt of payments for low-profit or capital gain property.

One reported case seems to lend some support to the foregoing analysis. In *Frank A. Logan*,[174] the buyer and seller of a partnership interest agreed that the first ten equal monthly payments by the buyer would be allocated to unrealized receivables, and the remaining eight payments to other partnership assets. The parties' agreement as to the timing of the payments was not challenged by the Service and was accepted by the Tax Court without comment.[175] By allocating earlier payments entirely to partnership receivables and later payments to other partnership assets, the parties to the *Logan* sale accelerated the realization of ordinary income by the seller.[176]

The only apparent restriction on the seller's ability to completely control the timing of the types of income realized is the "recapture first" rule with respect to payments allocable to § 1252 recapture property. The Regulations provide that gain attributable to an item of property subject to recapture under § 1252 (dealing with farmland) must be treated first as ordinary recapture income until all recapture income with respect to that item of property has been reported, and only thereafter as capital gain.[177] Thus, in connection with multiple-asset sales, each payment is first allocated among the assets sold, and the gain portion of payments allocable to each item of § 1252 recapture property is treated as ordinary recapture income until all recapture with respect to that item is reported. Even this restriction can be largely negated in many cases if the parties agree to allocate the last payments received to assets subject to this recapture provision.

---

[174] Frank A. Logan, 51 TC 482 (1968).

[175] Frank A. Logan, 51 TC 482, 484−485 (1968). The seller's deferral of gain in *Logan* was based on the cash basis method of accounting rather than § 453.

[176] There are a number of possible explanations for the unconventional allocation in *Logan*. For example, the seller may have had an expiring net operating loss carryforward or may have expected to be subject to higher marginal tax rates in later years.

[177] Reg. § 1.1252-1(d)(3). Prior to the enactment of § 453(i)(2), denying installment sale treatment to § 1245 and § 1250 recapture, this rule applied to depreciation recapture as well. See Reg. §§ 1.1245-6(d), 1.1250-1(c)(6). The validity of Regulations § 1.1245-6(d) has been upheld by a district court. Dunn Constr. Co. v. United States, 323 F. Supp. 440 (ND Ala. 1971).

¶ 17.06 COLLAPSIBLE TIER PARTNERSHIPS

Tiered partnership structures, in which a parent partnership or upper-tier partnership (UTP) holds interests in one or more tiers of subpartnerships or lower-tier partnerships (LTPs), may raise difficult problems under § 751. These problems generally arise in connection with transfers of interests in the UTP at a time when the LTPs hold § 751 property. Section 751(f) provides that, in determining whether partnership property is an unrealized receivable or an inventory item, a UTP is treated as owning its proportionate share of the property held by any LTP. The purpose of this provision is to ensure that the collapsible partnership rules will be applied evenly without regard to whether property is held directly by a partnership or indirectly through LTPs.

The application of § 751(f) to the simple situation in which a UTP's only significant asset is its interest in an LTP should not pose any material difficulties. In this context, an LTP's activities, trade or business, intent, and so forth should presumably be attributed directly to the UTP along with the ownership of the LTP's assets.

However, matters may become more difficult where the UTP is engaged in its own trade or business. In this situation, should the character of an LTP's assets be determined in its hands and then attributed to the UTP along with the ownership of its share of the LTP's assets? In keeping with the apparent legislative purpose to neutralize the significance of tier partnership arrangements, it seems that this question and all similar questions should be resolved by completely ignoring the separate existence of any LTPs. Accordingly, the UTP should be viewed as owning a share of an LTP's assets and engaging directly in the LTP's business for purposes of determining the character of its share of the LTP's assets. Neither the statute nor the legislative history is particularly helpful in resolving questions of this type, however, so the outcome is not entirely certain.

¶ 17.07 REPORTING REQUIREMENTS

Section 6050K imposes various reporting requirements on certain partnerships and transferors of partnership interests. These requirements apply to sales or exchanges in which the transferor receives money or other property in exchange for an interest in the partnership's § 751 property.[178] Generally, a partnership is required to make a separate return on Form 8308 with respect to each such sale or exchange of which it has notice, setting forth the following information: (1) names, addresses, and identification numbers of the transferor,

---

[178] Reg. § 1.6050K-1(a)(1).

the transferee, and the partnership; (2) the date of the sale or exchange; and (3) any other information required by Form 8308.[179] If twenty-five or more Forms 8308 are required to be filed by a partnership under this rule, the Service may allow the partnership to elect to file a single or a composite document in lieu of separate forms.[180] Forms 8308 (or the optional alternate report) for transfers during each calendar year must be filed with the partnership's income tax return for the taxable year with or within which the calendar year ends.

Any partnership that is required to file a Form 8308 with the Service must supply a copy of the form to the transferor- and transferee-partners prior to January 31 of the calendar year following the year during which the transfer occurs (or, if later, within thirty days after it receives notice of the transfer). If the partnership files a composite report, it must furnish statements to transferors and transferees containing information similar to that set forth on Form 8308.[181]

Any partner who transfers an interest subject to § 6050K must notify the partnership within thirty days of the transfer (or, if earlier, by January 15 of the year following the year of the transfer). The notice must be in writing and must include the names and addresses of the transferor- and transferee-partners, the identification number of the transferor and, if known, the transferee, and the date of the transfer.

For purposes of these rules, a partnership is treated as having notice of a transfer if it receives a notice from the transferor or if it has knowledge that a transfer has occurred that is subject to § 6050K.[182]

The following special rules are provided to facilitate compliance by large partnerships, particularly those that are publicly traded.

1. Sales or exchanges of partnership interests with respect to which a return is required to be filed by a broker under § 6045 (currently, Form 1099-B) are excluded from the reporting requirements of § 6050K.[183]
2. If a partnership has knowledge that a transfer has occurred, it may treat the record holder of the interest as the transferor or transferee of the interest even if it knows the record holder is not the beneficial owner unless it has knowledge of the identity of the beneficial owner. However, the transferor is still required to furnish the normal information to the partnership regarding the transfer.[184]

---

[179] See § 6050K(a); Reg. § 1.6050K-1(b).
[180] Reg. § 1.6050K-1(a)(3).
[181] Reg. § 1.6050K-1(c).
[182] Reg. § 1.6050K-1(e).
[183] Reg. §§ 1.6050K-1(a)(2), 1.6050K-1(d)(2).
[184] Reg. § 1.6050K-1(a)(4)(iii).

CHAPTER **22**

Payments in Liquidation of the Interest of a Retired or Deceased Partner

¶ 22.01 APPLICATION OF SECTION 736 TO LIQUIDATING DISTRIBUTIONS BY CONTINUING PARTNERSHIPS

Section 736 was enacted as part of the 1954 Code to rectify the pre-1954 confusion and uncertainty surrounding the taxation of payments in retirement of a partner's interest. With the exception of a major amendment in 1993, it has survived virtually unscathed since enactment.

The sole purpose and function of § 736 is to segregate liquidating payments from partnerships to retiring partners into several categories for the purpose of applying the relevant operating rules found elsewhere in Subchapter K. The relevant operating rules are among the most complex in Subchapter K. It is the complexity of these rules, rather than any complexity inherent in the relatively simple two-step categorization rules of § 736 itself, that creates most of the difficulties encountered in analyzing and planning for liquidating payments.

Somewhat oddly, § 736(b) (not § 736(a)) is the first step in the process. It divides liquidating payments into two categories: (1) payments for the retiring partner's interest in partnership property, which, under § 736(b), are treated as received under the distribution rules set forth in §§ 731, 732(b), and 751(b); and (2) all other payments, which are taxed as set forth in § 736(a).[1] The second step is § 736(a), which subdivides § 736(b) payments into two categories: (1) those determined "with regard to the income of the partnership," which are treated under § 736(a)(1) as a distributive share of partnership income; and (2) those determined "without regard to the income of the partnership," which are treated under § 736(a)(2) as § 707(c) "guaranteed payments."

The application and consequences of these categorization rules can be expressed as two relatively simple questions and answers:

Question (1): *Is the payment made in exchange for the retiring partner's interest in partnership property*? If the answer is "yes," the payment is a distribution under § 736(b)(1), the applicable operating rules are found in §§ 731, 732(b), and 751(b), and Question (2) is not relevant.

Question (2): *Is the payment determined "with regard to the income of the partnership"*? Answering this question is only necessary for payments that are not in exchange for partnership property. The answer requires consideration (and possibly application) of the "guaranteed payment" categorization rules developed under § 707(c).[2] If the answer is "yes," then the payment is considered a "distributive share" of partnership income under § 736(a)(1) and is treated as a distribution (under the rules of § 731, etc.) accompanied by an allocation of partnership income. If it is *not* determined with regard to partner-

---

[1] Thus, "§ 736(a) payments" are defined by exclusion: They are any payments in retirement of a partner's interest that are not § 736(b) payments for the retiring partner's "interest in partnership property."

[2] See ¶ 14.03[1][a].

ship income, then it is a guaranteed payment under § 736(a)(2) and is subject to § 707(c).

Prior to the 1993 amendment, § 736(b)(2) provided that payments for the retiring partner's interest in § 751(c) unrealized receivables and, except as otherwise provided by the partnership agreement, partnership goodwill were not treated as payments for partnership property. This was a very pro-taxpayer provision:

1. The general definition of § 751(c) unrealized receivables includes both "traditional" receivables (rights to payments for goods and services) of cash-method taxpayers and a lengthy list of recapture items.[3] Prior to 1993, exclusion of these assets from the definition of partnership property in § 736(b) generally ensured rough tax neutrality: The retiree's ordinary income under § 736(a) generally would be counterbalanced by equal reductions in the ordinary income of the continuing partners. Treatment of these assets as partnership property subject to § 736(b) and the resultant application of § 751 would have produced the same ordinary income result for the retiring partner but would not have automatically produced an equal and immediate reduction in the ordinary income of the continuing partners, particularly with regard to recapture items.[4]

2. By giving the partners the option to treat payments for goodwill as either (a) gain (generally capital) to the retiring partner with no immediate impact on other partners, or (b) ordinary income to the retiring partner and a concurrent deduction to the other partners, this aspect of § 736(b)(2)(B) effectively guaranteed there would be little or no net tax on such payments.

Congress curbed these benefits in 1993. The Revenue Reconciliation Act of 1993 (the 1993 Act) added new § 736(b)(3) to limit the availability of § 736(b)(2) to retiring general partners in partnerships where capital is not a material income-producing factor. In all other situations, payments for § 751(c) receivables and goodwill are treated as payments for partnership property. Concurrently, the 1993 Act narrowed the § 751(c) definition of "unrealized receivables" *solely for purposes of § 736* to eliminate the treatment of recapture items as unrealized receivables. The resultant inclusion of recapture items in the § 736(b) definition of property generally means that the remaining partners are no longer able to capture the immediate tax benefits previously available to them under § 736(a) with respect to such items.

---

[3] See ¶ 17.03[3].

[4] The operation of § 751(b) gives the partnership a basis step-up in the retiree's share of unrealized receivables, a benefit that may be effectively equivalent to a near-term income reduction if the unrealized receivables are traditional receivables but may be deferred for many years if they are recapture items.

[1] Transactions Subject to Section 736

Section 736 applies only to payments made by a partnership to a retired partner or a deceased partner's successor in interest in liquidation of his entire interest in the partnership.[5] A partner is treated as a retired partner only when he ceases to be a partner under local law.[6] Under the Regulations, the term "liquidation of a partner's interest" means the termination of a partner's entire interest in the partnership by means of a distribution (or a series of distributions) from the partnership to the partner.[7]

Section 736 does not apply to distributions made to a continuing partner,[8] nor does it apply to distributions in the course of the liquidation of the partnership, as distinguished from the liquidation of a single partner's interest.[9] Moreover, § 736 does not apply to payments received in consideration of the sale or exchange, as opposed to the liquidation, of a retired or deceased partner's interest.[10]

The Regulations state clearly that § 736 may apply to the liquidation of the interest of one partner of a two-person partnership,[11] even though there may be no substantive difference between the "liquidation" of the interest and its sale to the other partner. Thus, the same planning opportunities generally

---

[5] Reg. § 1.736-1(a)(1)(i).

[6] Reg. § 1.736-1(a)(1)(ii); see Francis E. Holman, 66 TC 809, 814–815 (1976), aff'd, 564 F2d 283 (9th Cir. 1977) (expelled partner who ceases to be partner under local law is retired partner for purposes of § 736); Elwood R. Milliken, 72 TC 256 (1979), aff'd unpub. opinion (1st Cir. 1980) (same). Since a partner is not considered a retired partner until he ceases to be a partner under local law, a distribution to a continuing partner that reduces his interest in anticipation of his eventual retirement does not fall within the purview of § 736.

[7] Reg. § 1.761-1(d). The term includes a series of distributions spanning a period of more than one year, provided the series of distributions culminates in the complete termination of the retired partner's economic interest in the partnership. When liquidation occurs through a series of distributions, the interest is not considered liquidated until the final distribution has been made. Id. Payments in "partial liquidation" of a partner's interest are not subject to § 736. Id.

[8] See Reg. § 1.736-1(a)(1)(i).

[9] A distribution of cash or other nonbusiness assets to one partner coupled with a distribution of the partnership's business assets to other partners who continue the partnership's business is not treated as a liquidation of the partnership; rather, the transaction is treated as a § 736 liquidation of the interest of the partner receiving the nonbusiness assets, and a continuation of the partnership by the other partners. Cf. Rev. Rul. 66-264, 1966-2 CB 248.

[10] See ¶ 16.02[3] for a discussion of the characteristics that distinguish the sale of a partnership interest from the liquidation of a partnership interest, and ¶ 16.02[2] for a comparison of the differences in tax consequences between sales and liquidations of partnership interests.

[11] Reg. § 1.736-1(a)(6).

available to partnerships with more than two partners are equally available to two-person partnerships.[12]

Section 736 may apply, even though no actual distribution of cash or property is made, as a consequence of the elimination of the retiring partner's share of partnership liabilities upon a surrender of his interest.[13] Under § 752(b), a reduction in a partner's share of liabilities is treated as a cash distribution.

[2] Application of Section 736 Upon the Death of a Partner

A partnership does not terminate for tax purposes upon the death of a partner,[14] and the decedent's successor in interest is recognized as a continuing partner until the decedent's interest is sold or liquidated.[15] Thus, if a decedent partner's interest is liquidated as a result of his death, the successor to his interest is treated in the same manner as a retired partner for § 736 purposes.[16]

[3] Status of a Retired Partner During the Liquidation Process

For tax purposes, a retired partner is treated as a continuing partner until the § 736 liquidation process is complete.[17] Accordingly, the taxable year of a partnership does not terminate prematurely with respect to a retired partner until such time as all § 736 payments have been received.[18]

Furthermore, even though a retired partner is entitled to receive only fixed liquidating distributions and is not entitled to any distributive share of partnership income, the fact that the retiree is still treated as a partner means that cer-

---

[12] See Priv. Ltr. Rul. 7808071 (Nov. 28, 1977) (former two-person partnership does not terminate if new partner is admitted before last payment for interest of deceased partner).

[13] See Andrew O. Stilwell, 46 TC 247 (1966); cf. Edward H. Pietz, 59 TC 207 (1972).

[14] § 708(b); see ¶¶ 13.04, 23.01.

[15] See Reg. §§ 1.706-1(c)(3)(i), 1.736-1(a)(1)(ii). The death of a partner does, however, close the partnership's tax year with respect to the decedent. § 706(c)(2); see ¶¶ 13.04, 23.01.

[16] See Reg. § 1.736-1(a)(1)(i).

[17] Reg. §§ 1.736-1(a)(1)(ii), 1.736-1(a)(6); cf. Raymond W. Schmitz, 37 TCM 1323, 1324 n.4 (1978); Priv. Ltr. Rul. 8304059 (Oct. 25, 1982) (cash and promissory notes; partners remained partners until all payments received); Priv. Ltr. Rul. 8032053 (May 13, 1980) (two-person partnership; no termination until final payment made to partner receiving cash).

[18] Reg. § 1.736-1(a)(6). See Stephan F. Brennan, 104 TCM 100 (2012), aff'd, 621 Fed. Appx. 408 (9th Cir. 2015).

tain provisions, such as § 704 and § 751, continue to apply to him. Thus, for example, if at the time a partner retires the partnership retains property contributed by the retired partner, § 704(c) will continue to apply with respect to the property and the retiree. Any unresolved § 704(c) book/tax difference will be taxed to the retiree either on sale of the property by the partnership or annually as the § 704(c) book/tax difference is amortized under the convention used by the partnership. As a result, partners who retire under § 736 will continue to have a keen interest in the way the partnership deals with property that they have contributed.[19]

Some or all of any income recognized by retiring partners under § 736 during tax years beginning after 2012 may be subject to the 3.8% Medicare contribution tax on "net investment income" in § 1411.[20]

[4] Categorizing Liquidation Payments

The interaction of the categorization mechanics in § 736 and the operating rules found elsewhere in Subchapter K produces the following pattern of taxation for cash liquidating payments:

1. If the retiring or deceased partner was a general partner in a partnership in which capital was not a material income-producing factor:

   a. Payments with respect to partnership property are taxed under § 731 and produce capital gain or loss to the distributee under § 741. For this purpose, partnership property includes goodwill (if explicit provision is made for goodwill payments) but excludes all § 751(c) unrealized receivables and § 751(d) inventory items that are substantially appreciated within the meaning of § 751(b)(3).

   b. Payments for § 751(c) receivables that are recapture items and substantially appreciated inventory are treated as payments for partnership property and generate ordinary income to the recipient under § 751(b).

   c. All other payments, including payments for § 751(c) receivables (other than recapture items), are taxed as distributive shares of partnership income under § 736(a)(1) or guaranteed payments under § 736(a)(2).

---

[19] Section 704(c) is discussed in detail at ¶ 11.04. The textual discussion applies equally to "book/tax" disparities created by revaluations of partnership property. See Reg. § 1.704-1(b)(2)(iv)(*g*)(*2*); ¶ 11.02[2].

[20] See ¶ 22.01[6].

    2. With respect to all other retiring and deceased partners (i.e., general partners in partnerships in which capital is a material income-producing factor and all limited partners):

      a. Payments with respect to partnership property (including goodwill but excluding all forms of unrealized receivables and substantially appreciated inventory) are taxed under § 731 and produce capital gain or loss to the retiring partner under § 741.

      b. Payments for all forms of unrealized receivables and substantially appreciated inventory generate ordinary income to the retiring partner under § 751(b).

      c. All other payments are taxed as distributive shares of partnership income under § 736(a)(1) or guaranteed payments under § 736(a)(2).

If property is distributed in kind in liquidation of the interest of a retiring partner, the taxation pattern is considerably more complex, as discussed in ¶ 22.06.

[a] Overview of Section 736(b) Payments

Generally, § 736(b) payments include all payments for a retired partner's interest in partnership property. There is one express limitation on items that constitute partnership "property" for § 736(b) purposes. If the retiring partner is a general partner and capital is not a material income-producing factor, § 736(b) property does not include § 751(c) unrealized receivables (other than recapture items)[21] and, unless the partnership agreement provides to the contrary, payments for a retired *general* partner's share of the goodwill of a partnership.

Because § 736(b) payments are treated as distributions by the partnership, they generally result in capital gain or loss to the distributee under §§ 731(a) and 741, except to the extent § 751(b) is applicable. Section 736(b) payments are not deductible by the partnership, and § 734(a) precludes any adjustment to the basis of remaining partnership assets unless (1) the partnership elects under § 754 to adjust the basis of its assets under § 734(b) (or is required to adjust basis because the otherwise avoided downward adjustment exceeds $250,000) or (2) a portion of the distribution is recast as a sale or exchange under § 751(b).[22]

---

[21] See generally ¶¶ 17.03[1], 17.03[2].

[22] See generally Chapters 21 (discussing § 751(b)) and 25 (discussing § 734(b)).

[b] Overview of Section 736(a) Payments

All payments that are not § 736(b) payments are § 736(a) payments.[23] Because § 736(a) payments are defined by exclusion, such payments generally include (1) all excess amounts (whether fixed or contingent) to compensate the retiree for accepting deferred liquidating distributions;[24] (2) if capital is not a material income-producing factor, payments for a retiring general partner's interest in § 751(c) unrealized receivables (other than recapture items) and the goodwill of service partnerships; and (3) payments in the nature of mutual insurance.[25] Because § 736(a) payments are taxable to the recipient either as distributive shares of partnership income[26] or as § 707(c) guaranteed payments,[27] they generally result in ordinary income to the recipient and a reduction in the ordinary income of the other partners.[28]

[5] Flexibility in Planning for the Retirement of a Partner

Considerable flexibility is afforded to partners in planning for the retirement of a partner's interest. Initially, they may choose either to liquidate the retiring partner's interest under § 736 or to effect essentially the same economic result by means of a purchase of the retiring partner's interest proportionately by the continuing partners. Although the economic consequences of a liquidation and a pro rata purchase of a retiring partner's interest by continuing partners may be identical, the tax consequences of the two alternatives may differ considerably.[29]

Even within the confines of the § 736 liquidation procedure, partners are afforded considerable flexibility in allocating tax benefits and burdens between

---

[23] Reg. § 1.736-1(a)(2).

[24] Section § 736(a) payments are not interest and no interest is imputed or required to be paid on deferred § 736 distributions.

[25] Reg. § 1.736-1(a)(2).

[26] § 736(a)(1).

[27] § 736(a)(2); see ¶ 14.03 for a discussion of § 707(c).

[28] A § 736(a)(2) guaranteed payment is always ordinary income to the retired partner and, apparently, is always deductible against ordinary income by the partnership. Reg. § 1.736-1(a)(4); see HR Rep. No. 658, 94th Cong., 1st Sess. 121 n.5 (1975); see also Jackson E. Cagle, Jr., 63 TC 86, 96 (1974), aff'd, 539 F2d 409 (5th Cir. 1976) (holding that § 707(c) guaranteed payments are deductible or capitalizable in accordance with the general rules of §§ 162 and 263, but expressly reserving judgment as to whether § 736(a)(2) guaranteed payments are automatically deductible). If a § 736(a)(1) distributive share includes a distributive share of partnership capital gain, the effect of the payment to the continuing partners resembles that of a capital loss deduction, because their distributive shares of partnership capital gain are reduced.

[29] These differences are analyzed in ¶ 16.02[2].

the partnership and the retiring partner. Thus, the partners have substantial latitude in determining what portion of total liquidating payments is attributable to § 736(b) property and what portion is taxable under § 736(a).[30] Additionally, if the liquidation is effected through a series of payments, the partners by agreement may apportion each installment between § 736(a) and § 736(b) amounts.[31] Finally, the partners may determine whether payments for a retiring general partner's interest in the goodwill of a service partnership are taxed as § 736(b) property payments or as § 736(a) payments.[32]

[6] Medicare Contribution Tax on Section 736 Payments

Some or all of the income recognized by retiring partners may be subject to the 3.8 percent Medicare contribution tax imposed on net investment income (NII) during tax years beginning after 2012. In general, the Medicare contribution tax is 3.8 percent of the lesser of NII or modified adjusted gross income over the applicable threshold amount ($250,000 for joint filers and surviving spouses, $125,000 for married filing separately, $200,000 for all others).[33] Generally, NII encompasses all types of passive income and is equal to the excess of:

1. The sum of (a) gross income from interest, dividends, annuities, royalties, and rents, other than such income derived in the ordinary course of a qualified trade or business; (b) all other gross income from a disqualified trade or business; and (c) taxable net gain attributable to the disposition of property that is not held in a qualified trade or business; over

---

[30] Relying on the inherent adversity of interest that historically has existed between retiring and continuing partners, the Regulations provide that the partners' valuation of the retired partner's interest in § 736(b) property generally will be regarded as correct if the partners act at arm's length. Reg. § 1.736-1(b)(1). But cf. Francis E. Holman, 66 TC 809 (1976), aff'd, 564 F2d 283 (9th Cir. 1977) (payments for retired partners' interests in unrealized receivables not § 736(b) payments). The significance of this adversity diminishes, however, as the marginal rate on a retiring partner's capital gains approaches his rate on ordinary income. If capital gain and ordinary income rates are equal, the retiring partner is generally indifferent as to the character of income, unless he has otherwise unusable capital losses to offset capital gain. Thus, unless there is a substantial difference between his marginal ordinary income and capital gain rates, a retiring partner will have little incentive to argue for a higher valuation for partnership property (payments for which are taxed under § 736(b)), and may be willing to accept inflated § 736(a) payments to provide tax benefits to the continuing partners.

[31] Reg. § 1.736-1(b)(5)(iii).

[32] §§ 736(b)(2)(B), 736(b)(3).

[33] § 1411; Reg. § 1.1411. See generally ¶ 9.01[3][b].

2. The allowable deductions allocable to such gross income.[34]

Sections 1411(c)(4)(A) and 1411(c)(4)(B) provide that gains and losses from "dispositions" of partnership interests are included in net gain to the extent of the net gain that would have been taken into account by the transferor if the partnership had sold all of its assets for fair market value immediately before the disposition. Despite the somewhat inelegant use of the word "disposition," it appears this look-through approach is intended to apply to taxable distributions under § 731. After a few false starts, the Treasury reissued Proposed Regulations in 2013 that would, among other things, specifically address the § 1411 treatment of § 707(c) guaranteed payments in general and each type of § 736 payment specifically.[35] To date, these Proposed Regulations have not been finalized.

Section 707(c) guaranteed payments.[36] Generally, § 707(c) guaranteed payments would be viewed as a substitute for interest and hence included in NII unless they are payment for services, in which case they would be excluded from NII.

Section 736(a)(1) distributive share payments.[37] The Proposed Regulations would characterize § 736(a)(1) payments based on their treatment as passive or nonpassive under § 469;[38] only passive payments would be included in NII. If a retiring partner was materially participating in an active business (other than the business of trading in financial instruments or commodities, see § 1411(c)(2)(B)) of a partnership at the time of retirement, subsequent § 736(a)(1) payments that do not exceed the value of the retiree's interest in partnership unrealized receivables would not be NII.[39]

Section 736(a)(2) guaranteed payments.[40] Section 736(a)(2) payments for goodwill and unrealized receivables would be viewed as gain from the disposition of a partnership interest and therefore treated as NII. All other guaranteed payments would be excluded from NII if related to the performance of services or included in NII if for the use of capital.

---

[34] § 1411(c)(1).

[35] REG-130843-13 (published Dec. 2, 2013, as corrected Feb. 24, 2014). An overarching concept in the Proposed Regulations relating to § 736 payments is that any portion of a § 736 payment that is taken into account in determining an individual's net earnings from self-employment is not included in NII. Prop. Reg. § 1.1411-4(g)(11)(i)(2014), citing § 1411(c)(6).

[36] Prop. Reg. § 1.1411-4(g)(10) (2014).

[37] Prop. Reg. § 1.1411-4(g)(11)(ii) (2014).

[38] See Reg. § 1.469-2(e)(2)(iii).

[39] Prop. Reg. § 1.1411-4(g)(11)(ii)(B) (2014). Excess payments could be NII.

[40] Prop. Reg. § 1.1411-4(g)(11)(iii) (2014).

Section 736(b) payments.[41] Gain or loss with respect to § 736(b) payment would be included in NII.

¶ 22.02 PAYMENTS IN RESPECT OF INTERESTS IN PARTNERSHIP PROPERTY: SECTION 736(b)

[1] Definitions and Tax Pattern

Section 736(b) controls the consequences of all liquidating payments for a retired partner's interest in partnership property. If capital is not a material income-producing factor for a partnership (e.g., a professional services partnership), a retiring general partner's interest in § 736(b) property is determined by excluding both (1) his share of goodwill (unless the partnership agreement provides for goodwill payments) and (2) certain traditional types of "unrealized receivables."[42]

The term "unrealized receivables" is defined in § 751(c) and consists of two distinctly different types of receivables: (1) "traditional" receivables such as accounts receivable, work-in-process, and other rights to "ordinary income payments" for goods and services to the extent not previously included in income under the partnership's accounting method; and (2) an extensive laundry list of recapture items under §§ 617, 995, 1245, 1248, 1250, 1252, 1253, 1271, and 1276.[43] The limited exclusion of traditional unrealized receivables from the § 736(b) definition of "partnership property" applies only to the value of the receivables in excess of their basis in the hands of the partnership, including any special basis adjustments under § 743(b) with respect to the retired partner's interest.[44] The basis of unrealized receivables also includes all costs and expenses attributable to the receivables that have not been taken into account under the partnership's accounting method.[45] Thus, for example, expenses incurred but not paid by a cash-method partnership in generating accounts re-

---

[41] Prop. Reg. § 1.1411-4(g)(11)(iv) (2014).

[42] *A word of warning:* Even if payments for a retiring partner's interest in certain unrealized receivables are not taxed under § 736(b), all unrealized receivables, including traditional types, are included in the definition of § 751(d) "inventory items." See Reg. § 1.751-1(d)(2)(ii). Accordingly, it seems unrealized receivables should be taken into account in determining whether inventory is "substantially appreciated" for purposes of applying §§ 736(b) and 751(b), even in cases where payment for unrealized receivables is taxed under § 736(a). See generally ¶ 21.03.

[43] See § 751(c) (second sentence: "(but not for purposes of section 736)").

[44] Reg. § 1.736-1(b)(2).

[45] Reg. § 1.751-1(c)(2).

ceivable are included in the basis of the receivables, and, to the extent of such basis, the receivables are treated as § 736(b) property.

Similarly, even though payments for a retiring general partner's interest in the goodwill of a service partnership generally are not treated as § 736(b) distributions, goodwill is § 736(b) property to the extent of its basis, even in the absence of a specific provision in the partnership agreement concerning goodwill payments.[46] In determining whether a partnership has a basis in goodwill, special basis adjustments under § 743(b) are taken into account.

[2] Valuing a Partner's Interest in Section 736(b) Property

For purposes of applying § 736(b), a retired partner's interest in partnership property is valued at gross, rather than net, value.[47] Valuing property at gross value is consistent with the treatment of partnership liabilities—that is, under § 752(b), a partner whose interest is liquidated is treated as receiving a constructive cash distribution equal to his pre-liquidation share of partnership liabilities.[48]

For purposes of valuing a retired partner's interest in partnership property, the Regulations provide that "[g]enerally, the valuation placed by the partners upon a partner's interest in partnership property in an arm's length agreement will be regarded as correct."[49] This provision of the Regulations was written when the normal rate of tax on capital gain was considerably less than the generally applicable rate on ordinary income. Thus, the drafters of this provision were willing to assume that, in most cases, the continuing partners' interest in minimizing amounts paid for the retiring partner's interest in property under § 736(b) and maximizing deductible or excludable payments under § 736(a) would be counterbalanced by the retiring partner's desire to avoid the ordinary income consequences of § 736(a) payments. When ordinary income

---

[46] Reg. § 1.736-1(b)(3).

[47] See Reg. § 1.736-1(b)(1).

[48] See Edward H. Pietz, 59 TC 207 (1972); Andrew O. Stilwell, 46 TC 247 (1966); Estate of Thomas P. Quirk, 55 TCM 1188 (1988), aff'd on this issue, remanded on other issues, 928 F2d 751 (6th Cir. 1991); cf. Reg. § 1.736-1(b)(7) Example (1); Mayer S. Tapper, 52 TCM 1230 (1986) (capital loss on constructive cash distribution in connection with partnership termination). In *Pietz* and *Stilwell*, no actual distributions were made to the retiring partners, and § 736 applied solely because the partnerships assumed the retiring partners' shares of partnership liabilities.

[49] Reg. § 1.736-1(b)(1); see Elwood R. Milliken, 72 TC 256 (1979), aff'd unpub. opinion (1st Cir. 1980) (taxpayer's interest in § 736(b) property limited to his share of cash, absent proof as to his interest in other partnership property). Compare Reg. § 1.736-1(b)(1) (in allocating annual payments between § 736(a) and § 736(b), the total amount allocated to § 736(b) property may not exceed the fair market value of the property).

and capital gains rates are equal or nearly so, the assumed adversity may not exist and both the Service and the courts may be more willing to look behind an agreement as to the value of partnership property that is not the result of negotiations between partners with adverse interests.

In any event, if the partners fail to agree as to the value of partnership property, the Service and courts can be expected to value the property based on all the facts and circumstances.[50]

[3] Adjustments to Basis of Partnership Assets

Even though a § 736(b) distribution is "made in exchange for the interest of [a retiring] partner in partnership property," the transaction is treated as a normal partnership distribution subject to the basis adjustment provisions of § 734, and not as a purchase entitling the partnership to a § 1012 cost basis in the retired partner's share of partnership property. Generally, § 734(a) provides that the basis of partnership property is not adjusted as a result of distributions to partners. There are, however, two exceptions to this rule:

1. If a § 754 election is in effect or if there is a substantial basis reduction within the meaning of § 734(d), the basis adjustment rules of § 734(b) require the partnership to adjust the basis of its assets in certain situations.[51]

2. If a portion of the distribution falls within § 751(b), a basis adjustment may result from the fictional taxable exchange created by that section.[52]

[4] Deferred Section 736(b) Payments: Timing Issues

[a] General

Commonly, a retiring partner's interest in partnership § 736(b) property is liquidated in a series of payments spanning several years. For example, when a partner retires from a professional firm, she may receive deferred distributions of capital over a period of years. With two exceptions noted below, the timing of the recognition of gain or loss with respect to such payments is determined

---

[50] See A.O. Champlin, 36 TCM 802, 809 (1977), aff'd unpub. opinion (9th Cir. 1980).

[51] See generally Chapter 25.

[52] See generally Chapter 21.

under § 731,[53] which generally defers the reporting of gain until the distribu-tee's entire basis has been recovered[54] and defers the recognition of loss at least until all distributions have been made.[55] Thus, the general rule is that § 736(b) payments are reported according to a cash basis, cost recovery method of accounting, regardless of the method of accounting of the partner-ship or of the retiring partner receiving the payments.

A significant exception to this general timing rule involves payments sub-ject to § 751(b).[56] Under the fiction created by § 751(b), the retired partner's interest in § 751 property is treated as distributed to him in kind and then sold back to the partnership. Thus, gain or loss attributable to § 736(b) liquidating payments with respect to partnership § 751 property is reported in accordance with the general principles relating to the reporting of gain or loss on sales or exchanges of property.[57]

A second exception to the cost recovery approach to reporting deferred § 736(b) payments is elective. The Regulations provide that if the total amount of § 736(b) installment payments is fixed, a retired partner may elect to appor-tion a part of the total gain or loss under § 736(b) among the installment pay-ments by allocating to each installment that portion of the basis of the liquidated partnership interest that bears the same ratio to his total basis as the amount of the installment bears to the total amount payable under § 736(b).[58]

> **EXAMPLE 22-1:** A retired partner is to receive $400 in four annual in-stallments of $100 each in liquidation of his interest in § 736(b) property, none of which is § 751 property. The partner's basis in his partnership in-terest is $100. Under the general cost recovery rule, the retired partner re-covers his entire basis with the first $100 installment, and the remaining three installments constitute taxable gain in their entirety. If, on the other hand, he elects to apportion the gain among the installments, $25 of each liquidating installment is treated as basis recovery, computed as follows: $100 (the amount of each installment) divided by $400 (the total amount payable for § 736(b) property), multiplied by $100 (the retiring partner's total basis in his partnership interest). The $75 balance of each installment is taxable gain.

---

[53] Reg. § 1.736-1(b)(6).

[54] Reg. § 1.731-1(a)(1).

[55] § 731(a)(2); Reg. § 1.731-1(a)(2). Loss is not recognized to any extent if the liqui-dating payments include *any* property other than cash, § 751(c) unrealized receivables (traditional or otherwise), and § 751(d) inventory (regardless of whether it is substantially appreciated).

[56] Reg. § 1.736-1(b)(6).

[57] See generally ¶ 21.03[6][c].

[58] Reg. § 1.736-1(b)(6). The election must be made in the retiring partner's tax return for the first taxable year in which he receives a § 736(b) payment.

[b] Section 752 Distributions

Under § 752(b), a partner is treated as receiving a distribution of money to the extent of any reduction in his share of partnership liabilities.[59] Therefore, in addition to actual distributions of money and property, the § 736 distributions to a retired partner include any deemed distributions to him under § 752(b).[60]

Because a retired partner continues to be treated as a partner for tax purposes until his interest in the partnership has been completely liquidated,[61] the retired partner's share of partnership liabilities should continue to be determined under the normal rules of § 752 and the Regulations thereunder.[62] Thus, to the extent a retired partner continues to bear the economic risk of loss for a partnership recourse liability, the liability should continue to be included in his basis under § 752(a) until his interest is completely liquidated and he ceases to be treated as a partner for Subchapter K purposes.[63] Any intervening reductions of the liability, of course, trigger § 752(b) distributions to the retired partner that must be taken into account under § 736. Further, after the retired partner receives his final liquidation payment, and, therefore, ceases to be a partner for Subchapter K purposes, no partnership liabilities can continue to be allocated to him. Accordingly, contemporaneously with receiving the final payment, the retired partner will receive a § 752(b) distribution of his remaining share of partnership recourse liabilities.

Similarly, a retired partner should be able to continue to include a share of partnership nonrecourse liabilities in his basis until the liquidation of his interest is complete. In general, partnership nonrecourse liabilities are allocated among partners in three tiers.[64] First, nonrecourse liabilities are allocated to partners to the extent of their interests in partnership minimum gain.[65] Next, a partner is allocated nonrecourse partnership liabilities in an amount equal to any taxable gain that would be allocated to him (1) under § 704(c) (relating to the allocation of "built-in" gain with respect to property contributed by the partner) or (2) under the § 704(c) equivalent rules (relating to the allocation of gain on property that has been revalued for book purposes), if the partnership disposes of all its property that is encumbered by nonrecourse liabilities for no

---

[59] See generally ¶ 7.02.

[60] Reg. § 1.736-1(a)(2).

[61] Reg. § 1.736-1(a)(1)(ii).

[62] See generally Chapter 8.

[63] See Reg. § 1.752-2; ¶ 8.02.

[64] Reg. § 1.752-3. See generally ¶ 8.03.

[65] Reg. § 1.752-3(a)(1); see ¶ 8.04[2]. In general, a partner's share of minimum gain is determined under Regulations § 1.704-2(g).

consideration other than relief from such nonrecourse liabilities.[66] Finally, in the third tier, any remaining partnership nonrecourse liabilities, which are referred to as "excess nonrecourse liabilities," are allocated among the partners according to their percentage interests in partnership profits.[67]

The interaction of these rules for sharing nonrecourse liabilities in the context of § 736 distributions is illustrated by the following example.

EXAMPLE 22-2: Partnership *ABR* is an equal partnership, whose balance sheet is as follows:

	Adjusted Basis	Fair Market Value
Assets:		
Property[68]	$ 300	$900
Liabilities and Capital:		
Nonrecourse liability	$ 600	$600
Capital accounts:		
A	(100)	100
B	(100)	100
R	(100)	100
Total Liabilities and Capital	$ 300	$900

Each partner's share of partnership minimum gain is $100.[69] Accordingly, each partner's share of the partnership nonrecourse liability is $200 (an amount equal to his $100 share of minimum gain, plus a $100 share of the $300 excess nonrecourse liability), and each partner's basis in his partnership interest is $100 ($200 share of partnership liability, less $100 deficit capital account).

R ceases to be a partner for state law purposes on December 1 and is entitled to receive a single cash liquidating payment of $100 (the value of his interest) on the following June 1. After December 1, however, *R* is not entitled to share in general partnership profits.

Since *R* has no interest in general partnership profits after December 1, his interest in partnership excess nonrecourse liabilities terminates on that day. Thus, he receives a § 752(b) distribution on December 1 of

---

[66] Reg. § 1.752-3(a)(2). Section 704 is discussed at ¶ 11.04. The § 704(c) equivalent rules are discussed at ¶¶ 11.02[2][c][ii] and 11.02[2][c][iii]. See generally ¶ 8.03[4] for the interrelationship of these rules and the nonrecourse liability allocation rules.

[67] Reg. § 1.752-3(a)(3); see ¶ 8.04[3].

[68] The property is neither an unrealized receivable, as defined by § 751(c), nor an inventory item, as defined by § 751(d).

[69] The example is based on the assumption that the partnership generated $300 of nonrecourse deductions (Reg. § 1.704-2(b)(1)), which were allocated equally among the partners. Thus, the partnership's minimum gain is $300 (Reg. § 1.704-2(d)) and each partner's share is $100 (Reg. § 1.704-2(g)).

$100. This distribution is a § 736(b) distribution that reduces the basis of R's interest from $100 to zero. However, assuming that the partnership's property is not revalued to its fair market value as a result of his retirement, R's share of partnership minimum gain apparently is not affected. Accordingly, it appears that his basis continues to include that portion of the nonrecourse liability ($100) that equals his share of minimum gain. On the following June 1, when R receives a cash distribution of $100 in final payment for his interest, he ceases to be a partner for Subchapter K purposes and, as a result, also receives a § 752(b) distribution of $100 (representing his share of the nonrecourse liability).[70] Thus, on June 1, R recognizes § 731(a) gain of $200.

[c] Interest on Deferred Section 736(b) Payments

In general, amounts that are computed like interest and paid to a partner for the use of partnership capital constitute guaranteed payments under § 707(c).[71] Because a retired partner who receives post-retirement liquidation distributions is treated as a continuing partner (and not as a partnership creditor) for Subchapter K purposes until his interest is completely liquidated,[72] it seems that any "interest" paid with respect to deferred § 736(b) distributions should be treated as guaranteed payments to the retired partner for the use of his unreturned capital. This notion is buttressed by the fact that § 736(a)(2) treats all payments "made in liquidation of the interest of a retiring partner" as § 707 guaranteed payments if they are determined without regard to partnership income and are not paid for the retiring partner's interest in partnership property under § 736(b).[73]

---

[70] Under Regulations § 1.704-1(b)(2)(iv)(f), a partnership may revalue its property for book purposes in connection with a distribution of money to a retiring partner. If the partnership elects to revalue its property in connection with R's retirement, the results to R should be the same under § 752. As a result of the revaluation, the book value of the property would be increased from $300 to $900. If the partnership then disposed of the property for no consideration other than the $600 nonrecourse liability, it would realize a book loss of $300 and a tax gain of $300 ($600 amount realized, less $300 basis). Under Regulations § 1.704-1(b)(4)(i), $100 of this tax gain would be allocated to R. Under Regulations § 1.752-3(a)(2), R would be allocated an amount ($100) of the nonrecourse liability that equals the gain he would be allocated under Regulations § 1.704-1(b)(4)(i).

[71] See GCM 38133 (Oct. 10, 1979) (fixed payments to partners for use of capital are not interest and cannot be deducted as interest by partnership under § 163; deduction allowed only if the payments are ordinary and necessary business expenses under § 162); GCM 36072 (Apr. 12, 1976) (same as to partnership; however, recipient partner treats guaranteed payment as interest income under § 61(a)(4)). See generally ¶ 13.03.

[72] Reg. § 1.736-1(a)(1)(ii).

[73] See Reg. § 1.736-1(a)(2). While not referring to interest or amounts in the nature of interest on deferred redemption payments for the interest of a retired partner, the Regulations treat § 736 as applying to all payments "made to a withdrawing partner." More-

If deferred liquidation payments cannot bear tax-recognized interest, it follows that the imputed interest rules of §§ 483, 1272, and 7872 do not apply to deferred liquidation distributions under § 736. From a policy perspective, inapplicability of these rules may not be as offensive as might first appear, since the timing of any tax benefits and burdens of deferred liquidation payments under § 736 are matched. Thus, because deferred liquidation payments are not treated as liabilities, the continuing partners cannot increase the bases of their partnership interests by the amount of deferred payments under § 752(a). In addition, the partnership is entitled to adjust the basis of its assets under § 734(b) only when the deferred payments are actually made and the retired partner actually recognizes gain or loss. Finally, if amounts payable to a retired partner include interest-like payments, such payments constitute § 736(a)(2) payments that will be included in the income of the retired partner at the same time that they are deducted by the partnership under the matched timing rules of § 707(c).

[d] Deferred Liquidating Payments Under Section 736(b) Compared to Installment Sale of Partnership Interest

The scheme for taxing deferred liquidating payments for a retired partner's interest in partnership property under § 736(b) differs materially from the scheme for taxing installment sales of property (including partnership interests). The following summarizes some of the significant differences.[74]

[i] **Basis consequences to the acquirer.** If a buyer gives an installment obligation as consideration for the purchase of property, the buyer's initial basis in the property includes the principal amount of the installment obligation even though the seller may not be required to include the deferred payments in income until they are actually made.

By contrast, under § 736(b), a partnership that agrees to make deferred liquidating payments for a retired partner's interest in appreciated partnership

---

over, the Regulations provide detailed rules and examples relating to the application of § 736 to deferred liquidation payments, but make no reference to actual or imputed interest on the deferred amounts. See Reg. §§ 1.736-1(b)(5), 1.736-1(b)(7). Nevertheless, the Service may attempt to treat stated interest on deferred liquidation payments as interest paid under § 707(a), rather than as a guaranteed payment under § 707(c). See Priv. Ltr. Rul. 8304059 (Oct. 25, 1982). This private letter ruling involved a redemption of the interests of limited partners in exchange for notes bearing interest at a specified rate. The ruling treats the retired limited partners as continuing partners until all payments under the notes are satisfied, citing Regulations § 1.736-1(a)(1)(ii). Nevertheless, it concludes that interest paid on the deferred redemption price, pursuant to the notes, constitutes interest paid to a partner not acting in his capacity as a partner under § 707(a), because the deferred redemption price represents indebtedness of the partnership.

[74] See generally ¶ 16.02[2][b].

property may not be entitled to any basis adjustment. If a basis adjustment is available (either because of a § 754 election or the application of § 751(b)), the partnership generally is not entitled to adjust the basis of its property to reflect the liquidation "price" until the retired partner includes the payments in income. Where the deferred payments are taxable under the normal rules of §§ 736(b) and 731, a partnership that makes a § 754 election is not entitled to any adjustment to the basis of its property under § 734(b) until the retired partner recognizes gain from such payments.[75] To the extent payments are taxable under § 751(b), the partnership receives a basis adjustment as a result of the fictional purchase from the retired partner of his interest in § 751 property. In this fictional purchase and sale, the retired partner usually is required to recognize income immediately.[76] However, in the unusual situation in which the retired partner is entitled to report his § 751(b) income under the installment method, the partnership is entitled to an immediate basis adjustment notwithstanding the deferral of income to the retired partner.[77]

[ii] Timing of gain recognition by the transferor. While the basis consequences of the § 736(b) scheme are less favorable to a partnership than the basis consequences to a purchaser in an installment sale, the timing consequences to a retired partner are more favorable under § 736(b) than are the consequences of an installment sale to a seller. In an installment sale, a seller must recognize a ratable portion of the deferred gain with each payment,[78] he may be required to pay interest on the deferred tax,[79] and, if he pledges the installment obligation to obtain a loan, he must treat the loan proceeds as a payment.[80] By contrast, a retired partner may apply all non−§ 751(b) distributions against the basis of his partnership interest before recognizing any taxable gain, no interest is accrued on the taxes on deferred distributions, and pledging his right to future distributions does not trigger gain recognition.

[iii] Imputation of interest. In general, if installment obligations do not bear adequate stated interest, interest is imputed under § 483 or § 1272. Although the matter is not entirely free from doubt, it appears that no interest is imputed on deferred distributions under § 736(b).[81]

[iv] Recognition of liabilities. In general, when encumbered property is sold on the installment method, the seller recognizes the encumbrance as an

---

[75] See ¶ 25.02[8].
[76] See ¶ 21.03[6][c].
[77] See ¶ 21.03[6][c].
[78] § 453(c).
[79] § 453A(c).
[80] § 453A(d).
[81] See ¶ 22.02[4][c].

amount paid at the time of sale and, to the extent the seller has basis, is entitled to treat the assumed liability as a recovery of basis.[82] As discussed previously,[83] when a partner retires and his interest is liquidated under § 736, he may be entitled to defer any § 752 distribution of his share of partnership liabilities until he receives the final liquidating payment.

[5] Examples of the Tax Consequences of Section 736(b) Payments

The following examples illustrate the application of § 736(b) in three typical situations: (1) the liquidation of an interest that was not acquired by purchase or inheritance (Example 22-3); (2) the liquidation of an interest acquired by purchase or inheritance when no § 754 election was applicable to the acquisition of the interest (Example 22-4); and (3) the liquidation of an interest acquired by purchase or inheritance when a § 754 election was applicable to the acquisition of the interest (Example 22-5).

[a] Liquidation of Interest Not Acquired by Purchase/Inheritance

EXAMPLE 22-3: Individual *A*, who did not acquire his interest by purchase or inheritance, is an equal partner in partnership *ABC*. *ABC*'s balance sheet is as follows:

	Adjusted Basis	Fair Market Value
Assets:		
Cash	$135	$135
Inventory	90	150
Capital assets	120	150
Total	$345	$435
Liabilities and Capital:		
Liabilities	$ 90	$ 90
Capital:		
A	85	115
B	85	115
C	85	115
Total	$345	$435

A retires and his partnership interest is liquidated in exchange for a total payment of $145, the gross value of his one-third interest in partnership § 736(b) property. Of this amount, $115 is received in cash and $30

---

[82] Reg. §§ 15A.453-1(b)(2)(ii), 15A.453-1(b)(3)(iii), 15A.453-1(b)(5) Example (2), 15A.453-1(b)(5) Example (3).

[83] See supra ¶ 22.02[4][b].

is "received" under § 752(b), through the reduction of *A*'s proportionate share of partnership liabilities.

Commentary on Example 22-3. Since the partnership's inventory is substantially appreciated within the meaning of § 751(b)(3), the partnership is deemed, under § 751(b), to have made a nonliquidating distribution to *A* of his one-third interest in inventory with a value of $50.[84] *A* takes a carryover basis of $30 in the inventory hypothetically received from the partnership.[85] Immediately after this hypothetical distribution, the partnership is treated as purchasing the distributed inventory for its value of $50, resulting in the recognition of $20 of ordinary income by *A* under § 751(b). The $95 balance of the amount distributed to *A* (total distribution of $145, less $50 deemed paid for *A*'s interest in substantially appreciated inventory) is treated as a distribution under § 731(a) in exchange for *A*'s partnership interest. Since *A*'s remaining basis in his partnership interest is $85 ($115, less $30 attributable to the hypothetical distribution of inventory), *A* recognizes an additional $10 of capital gain.

The partnership is entitled to a $20 increase in the basis of its inventory as a consequence of its hypothetical § 751(b) purchase of inventory from *A*,[86] but in the absence of a § 754 election to adjust the basis of partnership assets under § 734(b), it receives no basis adjustment to reflect the $10 capital gain recognized by *A*.[87] If a § 754 election is in effect, the partnership may also increase the basis of its capital assets from $120 to $130 to reflect the $10 in § 731(a) gain recognized by *A*, thereby obtaining the equivalent of a cost basis in *A*'s share of partnership assets.[88]

[b] Liquidation of Purchased/Inherited Interest—No Section 754 Election in Effect

If a retired partner acquired his interest by purchase or inheritance in a transaction to which no § 754 election was applicable, the tax consequences of § 736(b) distributions differ from those described in Example 22-3. The differences are caused by the disparity between the retired partner's basis in his partnership interest and his proportionate share of the partnership's basis in its assets.[89] If the basis of the retired partner's interest exceeds his share of the basis of partnership assets (and § 732(d) is not applicable to the liquidation of his interest), the differences are twofold:

---

[84] See Reg. § 1.751-1(b)(3).

[85] See § 732(a)(1); Reg. § 1.751-1(b)(3)(iii).

[86] See Reg. § 1.751-1(g) Example (2)(e)(1).

[87] § 734(a).

[88] § 734(b)(1)(A).

[89] For a discussion of basis adjustments upon the death of a partner, see ¶ 23.04.

1. If the partnership holds substantially appreciated inventory, the inter-action of § 751(b) and § 731 may cause the retiring partner to recog-nize more ordinary income and less capital gain (or more capital loss) than is indicated by the economics of the transaction; and

2. The partnership's basis in its assets (other than substantially appreci-ated inventory) cannot be adjusted to reflect the full amount distrib-uted to the retired partner in exchange for his interest in such assets.

EXAMPLE 22-4: The facts are the same as in Example 22-3, except A ac-quired his interest by purchase. No § 754 election was in effect at the time he acquired his interest. At the time his interest is liquidated, A's ba-sis in his interest is $145, or $30 more than his $115 share of the basis of partnership assets. Upon liquidation of the purchased interest, A is treated as receiving a nonliquidating distribution of inventory under § 751(b) and as reselling this inventory to the partnership for its fair market value of $50. Under § 732(c)(1), A's basis in the inventory hypothetically received from the partnership is $30, and he recognizes ordinary income of $20 as a result of the hypothetical distribution and resale of inventory. The $95 balance of the liquidating payment ($145, less $50 attributable to the hy-pothetical sale of inventory) is taxed under § 731(a). Since A's remaining basis in the partnership interest is $115 ($145, less $30 attributable to the hypothetical distribution of inventory), he recognizes a $20 capital loss with respect to the remaining distribution. Thus, A recognizes $20 of or-dinary income and $20 of capital loss.

Commentary on Example 22-4. As in Example 22-3, the partnership is entitled to a $20 increase in the basis of its inventory as a consequence of its hypothetical § 751(b) purchase of A's interest in partnership inventory and, if no § 754 election is applicable to the liquidating distribution to A, the basis of its other assets is unaffected leaving the continuing partners to deal with an unfavorable $10 distortion (the unresolved balance of the pre-retirement differ-ence between A's inside and outside basis in *ABC*). While B and C may find it reasonably simple to avoid any unpleasant consequences from this distortion (for example, by liquidating *BC* before selling the capital asset) in this particu-lar fact pattern, that may not always be the case in more complex situations, even if the continuing partners are aware of the problem.

Unfortunately, a misguided § 754 election for the year of the retirement may actually magnify *BC*'s problem. In this example, an ill-advised § 754 election would not produce a $10 basis increase to wipe out A's $10 share of the unrealized $30 capital gain. Instead, it would generate a $20 basis *decrease* under § 734(b)(2)(A), which would *increase* the distortion from $10 to $30.[90] Thus, a § 754 election can have unexpected repercussions where a distributee's

---

[90] See Reg. § 1.755-1(c)(1)(ii).

basis in his partnership interest is not equal to his share of the basis of partnership assets.[91]

[c] Liquidation of Purchased/Inherited Interest—Section 754 in Effect

The difficulties for the partnership and the retiring partner illustrated in Example 22-4 can be averted if a § 754 election applied to the retired partner's acquisition of his interest. In addition, the adverse consequences to the retired partner (but not the partnership) may be averted if § 732(d) applies to the hypothetical § 751(b) inventory distribution embedded in this transaction.

> **EXAMPLE 22-5:** The facts are the same as in Example 22-4, except that a § 754 election was in effect with respect to A's purchase of his interest. As a result of the election, the basis of A's share of the partnership's inventory is increased to $50. Thus, A's basis in the inventory hypothetically distributed to him under § 751(b) is $50,[92] and he realizes no gain or loss under § 751(b) upon the hypothetical sale of inventory to the partnership for $50. The $95 balance of the $145 liquidating distribution is equal to A's remaining basis in the partnership interest and, accordingly, he realizes no gain or loss with respect to this aspect of the transaction. Thus, if a § 754 election applies to A's purchase of his interest, the specter of artificial ordinary income accompanied by artificial capital loss upon subsequent liquidation of the interest is avoided.

Commentary on Example 22-5. As in Example 22-3 and Example 22-4, the partnership receives a $20 increase in the basis of its inventory as a consequence of its hypothetical § 751(b) purchase of A's share of the inventory. Furthermore, if a § 754 election was applicable to A's purchase of his interest, A's $10 special basis adjustment under § 743(b), with respect to his share of the noninventory property, shifts to the partnership on liquidation of his interest.[93] Thus, if a § 754 election was applicable to A's purchase of his interest, the partnership obtains the equivalent of a cost basis in A's share of all noninventory property.

If a § 754 election did not apply to the acquisition of his interest, A can obtain the same results by making a § 732(d) election, provided the liquidation occurs within two years of the purchase of his interest.[94] Under § 732(d), if (1) a partner acquires his interest in a transfer to which a § 754 election does not apply and (2) a distribution of property is made to such partner within two

---

[91] For a discussion of these repercussions, see ¶ 25.01[3].

[92] Reg. § 1.732-2(b).

[93] Reg. § 1.734-2(b)(1); see ¶ 24.05.

[94] Under certain circumstances, § 732(d) also applies on a nonelective basis, regardless of whether the distribution occurs within two years of the transfer. See ¶ 26.03.

years of such transfer, the distributee may elect to compute the partnership's adjusted basis of the distributed property under § 743(b), as if a § 754 election had been in effect.[95] Thus, the basis of the inventory hypothetically distributed to A under § 751(b) is $50, and, as in the previous variant, he realizes no gain or loss upon the hypothetical resale of the inventory to the partnership or upon the balance of the liquidating distribution.[96]

While a § 732(d) election places A in the same position as if a § 754 election had applied to his acquisition of the interest, the partnership is apparently not so fortunate. Section 732(d) does not seem to entitle the partnership to the $10 increase in the basis of its noninventory property that it would have received if a § 754 election had applied to A's purchase of his interest. The difficulty is that § 732(d), by its terms, gives a distributee a special basis adjustment only in assets that are actually or constructively distributed and does not accord him a special basis adjustment in undistributed assets. Because the distributee does not have a special basis adjustment in the undistributed capital assets, there is nothing to shift to the partnership under Regulations § 1.734-2(b)(1). Though this result is technically correct, its inequity and illogic might lead a sympathetic court to treat § 732(d) as giving the distributee an adjustment in all partnership assets, and thereby permit the partnership to succeed to the distributee's unused adjustment in the undistributed assets.

[6] Adverse Basis Adjustments Resulting From the Failure to Make a Section 754 Election Applicable to the Purchase or Inheritance of a Retired Partner's Interest

There is a danger lurking in the pattern for taxing liquidating distributions of partners who acquired their interests by purchase or inheritance that should be well noted: Where no § 754 election was applicable to the retired partner's purchase or inheritance of his interest, the partnership may suffer adverse basis adjustment consequences if it makes a § 754 election applicable to the subsequent liquidation of the retired partner's interest. As illustrated by Example 22-4, if a § 754 election were applicable to the liquidation payment to A, the partnership would be required to decrease the basis of its noninventory property under § 734(b)(2)(A) by the $20 loss recognized by A. The basis reduction may be avoided in this situation if § 732(d) applies to the distribution because § 732(d) prevents A from recognizing the loss upon liquidation (see Example 22-5) that triggers a reduction in the basis of partnership assets under § 734(b)(2)(A).

---

[95] See Reg. § 1.732-1(d). See generally Chapter 26.
[96] Reg. § 1.751-1(b)(3)(iii); see Reg. § 1.732-1(e).

Similar reductions in the basis of partnership assets may be triggered under § 734(b)(2)(B) where the partnership makes liquidating distributions of property (other than cash) to a partner who acquired his interest by purchase or inheritance in a transfer to which a § 754 election was not applicable. Application of § 732(d) generally should prevent this basis reduction, provided that the property actually distributed is the subject of a special basis adjustment under § 732(d).

In summary, where a § 754 election was not applicable to the purchase or inheritance of a partnership interest but is applicable to the later liquidation of the interest, the partnership may be required to reduce the basis of its assets under § 734(b)(2) as a result of the liquidation. While application of § 732(d) may prevent this reduction, it apparently will not give the partnership the equivalent of a cost basis for the amount it pays for the successor's interest in assets.

On the other hand, where (1) the transaction is structured as a purchase of the retired partner's interest by the continuing partners[97] and (2) a § 754 election is applicable to such purchases, each continuing partner is entitled to basis adjustments under § 743(b), which have the effect of giving each continuing partner a cost basis in the share of partnership assets that he acquires by purchase.

¶ 22.03 SECTION 736(a) PAYMENTS

[1] Defining "Section 736(a) Payments"

Section 736(a) is a "catch-all" provision: All liquidating payments in excess of the value of a retired partner's interest in partnership property, other than certain types of unrealized receivables and goodwill (under certain circumstances), are § 736(a) payments.[98] Section 736(a) thus applies to liquidating payments unrelated to a retired partner's interest in partnership property. For example, § 736(a) applies to payments in the nature of mutual insurance to a

---

[97] See ¶ 16.02[3] for a discussion of the differences between a sale transaction and a redemption or retirement transaction.

[98] Reg. § 1.736-1(a)(2). See Francis E. Holman, 66 TC 809 (1976), aff'd, 564 F2d 283 (9th Cir. 1977) (liquidating payments for partner's interest in unrealized receivables are § 736(a)(2) guaranteed payments); Herman M. Hale, 24 TCM 1497 (1965) (no § 736(a) payments in absence of evidence that total payments exceeded the value of § 736(b) property interest).

retired partner or to a deceased partner's successor in interest.[99] As another example, some professional firms provide for continuing payments to retired partners that may be fixed in amounts or variable (e.g., a continuing share of partnership "points" or "units") for a period of years. While the statute imposes no explicit ceiling on the amount of liquidating payments that may be made under § 736(a), limits probably will be judicially imposed in connection with continuing § 736(a) payments that shift income from high-bracket taxpayers to low-bracket taxpayers in the same family.[100] However, if tax avoidance motives are not so palpable and the parties are dealing at arm's length, continuing § 736(a) payments should generally be given effect.

[2] Taxation of Section 736(a) Payments

Section 736(a) payments come in two flavors: (1) those determined without regard to partnership income, which are treated under § 736(a)(2) as § 707(c) "guaranteed payments"[101] and (2) those determined with regard to partnership income, which are treated under § 736(a)(1) as distributive shares of partnership income.

[a] Section 736(a)(2) Guaranteed Payments

Guaranteed payments are ordinary income to the distributee and are deductible by the partnership under § 162.[102] A guaranteed payment is includible in the income of the distributee for his taxable year with or within which ends the partnership year in which the partnership is entitled to deduct the payment.[103] This timing rule sometimes produces surprising results. For example, assume that A, a cash-method, calendar-year taxpayer, retires from an accrual-method, calendar-year partnership and becomes entitled to a § 736(a)(2) payment of $10,000 on December 31 of year 1. Even if the payment is not made until the following January 1, A must include the payment on his return

---

[99] Reg. § 1.736-1(a)(2). See Donald W. Wallis, 98 TCM 364 (2009) (law firm's retirement payments analyzed; treated as guaranteed payments), aff'd 391 Fed. Appx. 826 (11th Cir. 2010).

[100] But cf. Fred Frankfort, Jr., 52 TC 163 (1969) (acq.). Section 736(a)(2) payments are treated as Section 707(c) guaranteed payments for the purpose of applying the § 1411 Medicare tax on net investment income. See ¶ 22.01[6].

[101] See Reg. § 1.736-1(a)(3)(ii).

[102] Reg. § 1.736-1(a)(4); see supra note 32.

[103] Reg. § 1.736-1(a)(5).

for year 1 because that is the year in which the partnership accrues and deducts the payment.[104]

A retired partner may be treated as receiving a guaranteed payment under § 736(a)(2) even though he receives no actual distribution from the partnership because § 752(b) provides that any decrease in a partner's share of the partnership liabilities is considered "a distribution of money to the partner by the partnership."

> **EXAMPLE 22-6:** The sole asset of partnership *DEF* is a building. The building is encumbered by a $900,000 nonrecourse mortgage, but has an adjusted basis of $600,000 and a fair market value of only $450,000. *D*, a one-third partner, retires at a time when the basis of his partnership interest is $200,000, all of which is attributable to partnership liabilities included in his basis under § 752(a). As the sole consideration for the liquidation of his interest, the partnership takes *D*'s interest, subject to his share of partnership liabilities. *D* thus realizes an immediate hypothetical cash distribution under § 752(b) of $300,000 (his one-third share of the partnership's $900,000 liability),[105] but only $150,000 of this amount is a § 736(b) payment because the value of *D*'s interest in the partnership's § 736(b) property (the building) is only $150,000. Therefore, $150,000 of the total $300,000 "distribution" is apparently a § 736(a)(2) guaranteed payment, includible as ordinary income in *D*'s return for the partnership year with or within which the liability is assumed. The $150,000 guaranteed payment is apparently deductible by the partnership, even though it has not yet paid (and may never pay) the assumed obligation.[106]

[b] Section 736(a)(1) Distributive Share Payments

The second class of § 736(a) payments—those determined with regard to the income of the partnership—is treated under § 736(a)(1) as distributive

---

[104] The retiring partner must be a partner during the year the partnership claims the deduction. In Whitman & Ransom, 90 TCM 37 (2005), several partners withdrew from a law partnership in 1994. At the end of 1994, their capital accounts were negative. On its 1996 partnership tax return, the partnership attempted to eliminate these negative balances by treating the retired partners as receiving guaranteed payments, deductible by the partnership, which in turn were contributed to the partnership to satisfy the negative capital account balances. This ploy was rejected by the court; since the withdrawn partners were not partners in 1996, they could not receive guaranteed payments in that year.

[105] See ¶ 7.02.

[106] As a result of *D*'s retirement, his share of partnership liabilities is shifted to *E* and *F*. It is unclear whether the aggregate basis of the partnership interests of *E* and *F* are increased under § 752(a) by $300,000, the full amount of *D*'s share of liabilities, or whether the fair market value limitation of § 752(c) restricts the amount of the increase in the bases of *E* and *F*. See ¶ 7.06. The basis consequences at the partnership level are also uncertain.

shares of partnership income.[107] A § 736(a)(1) distributive share is taken into account by the distributee-partner under the general rules of § 702 and, accordingly, reduces the distributive shares of the continuing partners.[108] Under the distributive share rules of § 702(b), a § 736(a)(1) distributive share may include capital gain or other tax-favored income, as well as ordinary income.

> **EXAMPLE 22-7:** Retired partner G is entitled to a § 736(a)(1) payment of 10 percent of partnership net income for the year following his retirement. During the year, the partnership recognizes a $1,000 long-term capital gain and incurs $500 of deductible expenses, so that G is entitled to a $50 distribution. G has a $100 (10 percent) distributive share of partnership long-term capital gain under §§ 704 and 702(a)(2), and a $50 (10 percent) distributive share of the partnership's § 702(a)(8) loss. G's basis in his partnership interest is increased from zero to $50 under § 705(a) and, under § 731(a), the distribution of $50 to him results in no further gain or loss.[109]

The § 736(a)(1) distributive share rule applies only to payments "determined with regard to the income of the partnership," while all other § 736(a) payments are taxed under § 736(a)(2) as § 707 guaranteed payments. It is unclear, however, whether payments determined with regard to partnership *gross* income constitute guaranteed payments.[110] Regardless of whether a § 736(a) payment determined with regard to gross income is treated as a guaranteed payment or a distributive share, the distributee receives no benefit from partnership deductions and the full amount of the payment is included in his income. If § 736(a)(2) applies, the payment is ordinary income in its entirety, but, if § 736(a)(1) applies, the nature of the payment is characterized at the partnership level, and thus may include capital gain or other tax-favored income.

As to timing, the Regulations require a retiring partner to include a § 736(a)(1) distributive share in his return for his taxable year with or within which ends the partnership taxable year for which the payment is a distributive share,[111] regardless of when actual distributions are made to the retiring partner.

---

[107] See Reg. § 1.736-1(a)(3)(i). The Service has permitted partners to convert a § 736(a)(1) distributive share payment into a § 736(a)(2) guaranteed payment. See Priv. Ltr. Rul. 7814026 (Jan. 5, 1978) (withdrawing partner agrees to accept lump-sum payment in lieu of continuing share of income, as provided in partnership agreement).

[108] Reg. § 1.736-1(a)(4).

[109] See Priv. Ltr. Rul. 9649007 (Aug. 21, 1996) (withdrawing partner's § 736(a)(1) distributive share is U.S. and foreign source in same proportions as income of partnership).

[110] See ¶ 14.03[1][b].

[111] Reg. § 1.736-1(a)(5).

[3] Deduction of Section 736(a)(2) Payments by Successors

If the partnership's business is discontinued prior to the time that the partnership's liability for § 736(a)(2) guaranteed payments to a previously retired partner has been discharged, the partnership nevertheless terminates under § 708(b)(1). If the liability for continuing § 736(a)(2) payments to the previously retired partner is assumed by the other partners, they may deduct the payments under § 162.[112]

Similarly, if a partnership's business is incorporated or transferred to a new partnership, which assumes the transferor-partnership's liability for continuing § 736(a)(2) payments, the transferee-corporation or partnership may deduct the payments.[113]

¶ 22.04 GOODWILL PAYMENTS

[1] General

The partners can bargain over whether payments that are economically consideration for partnership goodwill are deductible by the continuing partners and ordinary income to the retiring partner, or treated as payments for an interest in a partnership property under § 736(b), if (1) the retiring or deceased partner is a general partner[114] and (2) capital is *not* a material income-producing factor for the partnership.[115] If the partnership agreement specifically provides for goodwill payments, § 736(b) treatment applies; otherwise, § 736(a) governs. In all other instances, payments identified as payments for goodwill *must* be treated as payments for partnership property, and thus taxed under the normal distribution rules (i.e., usually as capital gain to the distributee and nondeductible by the ongoing partners).

Whether capital is a "material income-producing factor" is determined on the basis of the principles applicable under the other Code sections employing similar terminology—that is, §§ 401(c)(2) and 911(d), as well as former § 1348(b)(1)(A).[116] For this purpose, capital is not a material income-producing factor if substantially all of the income of a business consists of fees, commissions, or other compensation for personal services performed by an individual,

---

[112] See Rev. Rul. 75-154, 1975-1 CB 186.

[113] Rev. Rul. 83-155, 1983-2 CB 38.

[114] It is unclear whether any member of a limited liability company can qualify as a general partner for this purpose.

[115] § 736(b)(3).

[116] HR Rep. No. 213, 103d Cong., 1st Sess. 241 (1993).

even though the service provider may have a substantial investment in equipment or a physical plant, as long as the capital investment is incidental to the provision of services.[117] Thus, capital is not a material income-producing factor for most professional partnerships.

When applicable, the mandatory treatment of goodwill as property for purposes of § 736(b) may increase the net tax cost of redeeming the interests of retiring and deceased partners and may tempt partners to recast goodwill payments in some other form so as to obtain current deductions for the ongoing partners. However, the historical incentives to take this approach are reduced somewhat by the fact that goodwill is amortizable pursuant to § 197.[118]

Assuming analysis of the individual partners' tax situations indicates net tax savings can be achieved if the payments are not treated as goodwill payments, there are several possible approaches for creating deductible payments. First, the Regulations have long made it clear that payments in the nature of "mutual insurance" are § 736(a) payments.[119] Second, the legislative history of the 1993 Act notes that the Act "does not affect the deductibility of compensation paid to a retiring partner for past services."[120] Finally, deductible payments may be made to a retiring partner for post-retirement consulting services.[121] All of these approaches raise essentially the same valuation issue: Is the retiring or deceased partner being adequately compensated for his or her interest in partnership goodwill independent of these payments, or does a portion of these payments represent a disguised goodwill payment that should be treated as a § 736(b) payment?

---

[117] HR Rep. No. 213, 103d Cong., 1st Sess. 241 (1993).

[118] The § 197 rules relating to the amortization of goodwill and other intangibles are discussed in ¶ 9.02[3][j].

[119] See Reg. § 1.736-1(a)(2).

[120] HR Rep. No. 213, 103d Cong., 1st Sess. 241 (1993).

[121] The hazards associated with the use of consulting contracts that provide for few, if any, real services actually to be performed are aggravated by the legislative history of § 197, which states:

> [A]n arrangement that requires the former owner of an interest in a trade or business to continue to perform services ... is considered to have substantially the same effect as a covenant not to compete to the extent that the amount paid to the former owner under the arrangement exceeds the amount that represents compensation for the services actually rendered ... by the former owner.

HR Rep. No. 213, 103d Cong., 1st Sess. 216 (1993). If payments under a consulting agreement are recast as payments for a covenant not to compete, the parties may stumble into the worst of all possible outcomes unless the partnership has a § 754 election in effect: ordinary income and self-employment taxes for the former partner, and no tax deductions for the ongoing partners under § 197 (a covenant not to compete is a "section 197 intangible" under § 197(d)(1)(E)) in the absence of a § 754 election.

[2] Interpreting the Partnership Agreement

Payments for a retired *general* partner's interest in partnership goodwill are treated as § 736(a) payments if (1) capital is not a material income-producing factor in the partnership's business and (2) the partnership agreement does not provide for goodwill payments.

The failure of the partnership agreement of a service partnership to be explicit can create problems, as illustrated by cases decided under the pre-1993 version of § 736, under which no goodwill distributions were treated as § 736(b) payments in the absence of express provision in the partnership agreement.[122]

[3] Valuing Goodwill

Lurking beneath the surface question of whether the partners have agreed on a payment for partnership goodwill is the potentially more troublesome question of whether the agreement must accurately reflect the value of partnership goodwill to achieve § 736(b) treatment. Regulations § 1.736-1(b)(3) provides that "[g]enerally, the valuation placed upon goodwill by an arm's length agreement of the partners, whether specific in amount or determined by formula, shall be regarded as correct."[123] While seemingly granting the partners considerable latitude in valuing goodwill, this provision also implies that some relationship to economic reality is necessary to bring a goodwill payment within § 736(b).

In an early case decided under the 1954 Code, the Tax Court suggested, in dicta, that if a partnership agreement provides for a goodwill payment, "the statute would oblige [the court] to determine if the payment in fact was for 'good will of the partnership.'"[124] Subsequently, however, the Tax Court seems

---

[122] See, e.g., V. Zay Smith, 37 TC 1033, aff'd, 313 F2d 16 (10th Cir. 1962) (absent a specific provision providing for goodwill payments, all payments for a retiring partner's interest in goodwill are § 736(a) payments). See also Miller v. United States, 181 Ct. Cl. 331 (1967) (liquidating payment found to represent value of retiring partner's interest in partnership goodwill, but nevertheless treated as § 736(a) payment because agreement failed to provide for payment for goodwill); Michael J. Esler, 56 TCM 41 (1988) (same); see also William J. Cooney, 65 TC 101 (1975). See Milton Tolmach, 62 TCM 1102 (1991) (guaranteed payment treatment despite state court finding that 77 percent of value of withdrawing partner's interest attributable to goodwill). Even where a partnership agreement provides for goodwill payments, ambiguity in drafting may create problems. See Jackson Inv. Co., 41 TC 675 (1964), rev'd on other grounds, 346 F2d 187 (9th Cir. 1965) (ambiguous provision in partnership agreement interpreted through parole evidence of intent). See also Julian E. Jacobs, 33 TCM 848 (1974) (interpretation of another ambiguous agreement).

[123] Note that § 1060 does not apply to valuation issues arising under § 736.

[124] V. Zay Smith, 37 TC 1033, 1038 n.8, aff'd, 313 F2d 16 (10th Cir. 1962).

to have ignored this self-imposed burden by according § 736(b) status to a goodwill payment even though the recipient received no § 736(a) payment for his substantial interest in partnership unrealized receivables.[125]

¶ 22.05 ALLOCATION OF DEFERRED PAYMENTS BETWEEN SECTIONS 736(a) AND 736(b)

If a partnership interest is liquidated by a series of installments spanning two or more taxable years of the partnership or the retiring partner, it is necessary to determine what portion of each installment is taxed under § 736(b) and what portion is taxed under § 736(a). Section 1.736-1(b)(5) of the Regulations provides detailed rules for such allocations with respect to fixed payments and contingent payments, as well as partially fixed/partially contingent payments. The Regulations also permit the prescribed allocation methods to be varied, within certain limits, by agreement of the partners.

[1] Fixed Payments

If a retiring partner is to receive a fixed amount (whether or not supplemented by any additional amounts) in installments over several taxable years, the total fixed § 736(b) payments for a year are that amount that bears "the same ratio to the total fixed agreed payments for such year (as distinguished from the amount actually received) as the total fixed payments under section 736(b) bear to the total fixed agreed payments under sections 736(a) and (b)."[126] The balance of the payment received during the year is taxed under § 736(a).

> **EXAMPLE 22-8:** A partner retires at a time when the agreed value of his interest in § 736(b) property is $60,000. In liquidation of his interest, he is to receive $90,000 in ten equal annual installments. Of each $9,000 installment, $6,000 is a § 736(b) payment and $3,000 is a § 736(a)(2) guar-

---

[125] See Julian E. Jacobs, 33 TCM 848 (1974). In *Jacobs*, the Tax Court found that the partnership had goodwill, but did not seriously examine the value placed on goodwill by the partners, notwithstanding the absence of a payment for receivables.

[126] Reg. § 1.736-1(b)(5)(i); see Estate of Thomas P. Quirk, 55 TCM 1188 (1988), aff'd on this issue, remanded on other issues, 928 F2d 751 (6th Cir. 1991) (fixed payment apportioned between § 736(b) payments for property and § 736(a)(2) payments for unrealized receivables; payments not contingent even though amount and timing in dispute); Elwood R. Milliken, 72 TC 256 (1979), aff'd unpub. opinion (1st Cir. 1980) (Reg. § 1.736-1(b)(5)(i) applied; payments fixed even though amount payable by partnership set off against amount owed to partnership by retiring partner).

anteed payment.[127] If, contrary to the agreement, the retiring partner is paid only $3,500 in one year, the entire amount is treated as a § 736(b) payment. If, in the next year, the partnership pays $10,000 to the retiring partner, $8,500 is a § 736(b) payment ($6,000 plus $2,500 carried over from the previous year) and only $1,500 is a § 736(a)(2) guaranteed payment.[128]

[2] Contingent Payments

If the retiring partner is to receive liquidating payments that are not fixed in amount, such payments are treated first as § 736(b) payments to the full extent of the value of the retiring partner's interest in § 736(b) property, and, thereafter, all payments are § 736(a) payments.[129]

[3] Partially Fixed/Partially Contingent Payments

Not uncommonly, a retiring partner's interest is liquidated in exchange for both fixed and contingent payments. Regulations § 1.736-1(b)(5)(i)[130] is applicable whenever a "fixed amount (whether or not supplemented by any additional amount)" is to be received by a retiring partner. The parenthetical indicates that fixed payments are allocated first. If fixed payments exceed the value of a retiring partner's interest in § 736(b) property, a portion of each fixed payment and all contingent payments are treated as § 736(a) payments. If, on the other hand, the value of § 736(b) property exceeds the aggregate fixed payments, all fixed payments are treated as § 736(b) payments, and contingent payments are allocated first to the balance of the value of the retiring partner's interest in § 736(b) property and then to § 736(a) payments.

---

[127] See Reg. § 1.736-1(b)(5)(i).

[128] Reg. § 1.736-1(b)(5)(i). The Regulations from which Example 22-8 is extracted do not indicate whether the results would be the same if the partnership were an accrual taxpayer. An accrual-method partnership might be required to accrue the $3,000 guaranteed payment annually, regardless of whether it is actually made, if the normal timing rules of § 707 are applied. If accrual were required, then the retiring partner would presumably have to report the $3,000 guaranteed payment annually, whether or not he actually received it, at least in the absence of significant collection issues. See generally ¶ 14.03[2].

[129] Reg. § 1.736-1(b)(5)(ii).

[130] Quoted in ¶ 22.05[1].

[4] The Elective Allocation Method

As an alternative to the foregoing methods of apportioning liquidating payments between § 736(a) and § 736(b) amounts, the Regulations provide that the allocation may be made "in any manner to which all the remaining partners and the withdrawing partner or his successor in interest agree, provided that the total amount allocated to property under section 736(b) does not exceed the fair market value of such property at the date of death or retirement."[131] This flexibility in allocating liquidating payments between § 736(a) and § 736(b) amounts is available only if all of the partners "agree" to such allocation. Presumably, the consistent reporting of the payments by the continuing and withdrawing partners constitutes an effective agreement for this purpose; however, to avoid misunderstanding (and future changes of heart), the agreement should be set out in writing at the time of withdrawal or, preferably, well in advance.

¶ 22.06 SPECIAL PROBLEMS OF PROPERTY DISTRIBUTIONS

The application of § 736 to liquidating distributions that include property other than cash is an unexplored area of Subchapter K. Although the statutory language is amply broad to cover "in-kind" as well as cash liquidating distributions,[132] neither the legislative history, the Regulations, the case law, nor published revenue rulings give any guidance for the application of § 736 to noncash payments. As discussed in the following sections, there is no apparent reason to imbue the word "payment" with any more meaning in the context of noncash distributions than distributions of cash. Accordingly, a distribution of cash or noncash pursuant to §§ 736(b) or 736(a)(1) is simply a distribution subject to the usual distribution rules in Subchapter K. As discussed below, guaranteed payments are another matter entirely.

---

[131] Reg. § 1.736-1(b)(5)(iii).

[132] As originally proposed, Regulations § 1.736-1(a)(2) limited the applicability of § 736 to cash liquidating payments. See Prop. Reg. § 1.736-1(a)(2) (Aug. 12, 1955). The final Regulations, however, deleted any reference to cash payments, thus indicating that § 736 applies to both cash and property payments.

[1] Distributions by Partnerships That Do Not Own Unrealized Receivables

If the partnership has no unrealized receivables, the principal uncertainty created by property distributions under § 736 involves the allocation of distributed property among the §§ 736(a)(1), 736(a)(2), and 736(b) portions of the distribution. The balance sheet in the following example is used in the subsections that follow to illustrate the questions concerning noncash property distributions by partnerships that do not own unrealized receivables.

EXAMPLE 22-9: Equal partner C retires from the ABC partnership when its balance sheet is as follows:

	Adjusted Basis	Fair Market Value
Assets:		
Cash	$45,000	$45,000
Capital assets:		
X	7,000	10,000
Y	5,000	5,000
Z	3,000	15,000
Total	$60,000	$75,000
Capital:		
A	$20,000	$25,000
B	20,000	25,000
C	20,000	25,000
Total	$60,000	$75,000

[a] Property Distributions Resulting in No Section 736(a) Payments

Generally, liquidating distributions consisting in whole or in part of property other than cash to a retiring partner create no problems where the partnership has no unrealized receivables and the distribution does not trigger a § 736(a) payment. Assume C, in Example 22-9, receives $15,000 in cash and capital asset X (market value $10,000) in complete liquidation of his interest. Because the value of these distributions does not exceed the value of C's interest in the partnership's § 736(b) property (one third of $75,000, or $25,000), the entire distribution is governed by § 736(b) and the normal distribution rules apply. Accordingly, C recognizes neither gain nor loss on the distribution (§ 731(a)), and asset X takes a basis of $5,000 in C's hands under § 732(b) ($20,000 predistribution basis in C's partnership interest, less $15,000 cash distributed).

If the basis adjustment provisions of § 734(b) are inapplicable because no § 754 election is in effect, the partnership incurs no tax consequences as a result of the distribution. If the partnership has a § 754 election in effect, it is entitled to increase the bases of assets Y and Z by a total of $2,000 under

§ 734(b)(1)(B) (the excess of the partnership's $7,000 predistribution basis in asset X, over the $5,000 basis of asset X in C's hands).

[b] Property Distributions as Section 736(a)(2) Payments

Matters become a bit complicated if the total value of cash and property distributed exceeds the value of the distributee's interest in § 736(b) property. In these circumstances, the excess value must be treated as a § 736(a) payment. It is unclear, however, how the distributed assets should be allocated between §§ 736(a) and 736(b).

Assume that instead of $15,000 cash and asset X, C receives $15,000 cash and asset Z (fair market value $15,000) in liquidation of his interest. Because the amount of the distribution, $30,000, exceeds the value of C's interest in the partnership's § 736(b) property by $5,000, C is in receipt of a $5,000 guaranteed payment under § 736(a)(2).

Does the § 736(a) portion of the distribution consist entirely of cash or entirely of property, or is it a mixture of both? In the absence of an agreement among the partners, it could be argued that all items distributed should be apportioned ratably between §§ 736(a) and 736(b) payments, in which case one sixth of the cash ($2,500) and one sixth of the value of asset Z ($2,500) would be viewed as guaranteed payments pursuant to §§ 736(a)(2) and 707(c). However, there is no reason to think that an allocation agreement between the partnership and the retiring partner would not be respected. Thus, for example, if the parties agree that all of asset Z should be treated as distributed under § 736(b) and the cash should be divided $5,000 to § 736(a)(2) and $10,000 to § 736(b), the agreement should be respected.

Ratable approach analysis. In the absence of an agreement, assuming the ratable approach is the default rule, C would be viewed as receiving cash of $12,500 and five sixths of asset Z (value $12,500, basis to the partnership of $2,500) as a § 736(b) distribution, and cash of $2,500 and one sixth of asset Z (value $2,500, partnership basis $500) as a § 736(a)(1) guaranteed payment. Thus, C's taxable income consists of $5,000 of ordinary income under § 707(c). The cash distribution pursuant to § 736(b) reduces the basis of C's partnership interest from $20,000 to $7,500, which becomes the basis of five sixths of asset Z. This represents a $5,000 increase over its predistribution basis in the hands of the partnership, so the partnership will be required to reduce the basis of its other assets by $5,000 if it has a § 754 election in effect or the basis reduction is substantial under § 734(d). The other one sixth of Z takes a fair market value basis of $2,500 under § 707(c),[133] giving C a total basis of $10,000 ($7,500 plus $2,500) and a built-in gain of $5,000 for Z.

---

[133] As discussed in ¶ 14.03[5], a transfer of property to a partner as part of a guaranteed payment should be treated as a taxable disposition of the property by the partnership

The partnership's side of the transaction looks like this: (1) The partnership recognizes gain of $2,000 on the transfer of one sixth of Z to C as part of the guaranteed payment; (2) the partnership is entitled to reduce its taxable income by $5,000 to reflect the guaranteed payment to C; and (3) the partnership's basis in its remaining assets is unaffected unless a § 754 election is in effect or the potential basis reduction under § 754 is "substantial" under § 734(d), either of which will result in the partnership reducing the basis of its remaining assets by $5,000 (the amount of the basis increase in the five sixths of Z distributed to C).

Allocation by agreement. If the proposed allocation agreement is respected, the entire § 736(a)(2) payment consists of cash so the partnership had no imputed gain on the payment, just a $5,000 reduction of its ordinary income. Under § 736(b), the partnership is viewed as distributing cash of $10,000, reducing C's partnership basis from $20,000 to $10,000, which becomes the basis of Z in the hands of C. This is an increase of $7,000 from the partnership's predistribution basis, so the partnership may have a basis reduction of $7,000 instead of $5,000 in its other assets. This is very likely to be a better result for the continuing partners, who effectively have traded an immediate $2,000 recognized gain for a possible $2,000 increase in their built-in gain in other partnership assets.

C has the same $5,000 of income from the guaranteed payment as he had under the ratable allocation approach and the same $10,000 basis in Z as under the ratable approach, so he is largely indifferent to such an agreement.[134]

The relative indifference of the retiring partner to the allocation method in this example is common, although not universal. There are a number of possible exceptions. For example, the retiring partner may be affected by the choice of allocation method if his predistribution basis in his partnership interest is less than the amount of cash distributed because an allocation of too much cash to the § 736(b) portion of the payment may trigger gain under § 731(a)(1). Another example is the differences that may arise if the property distribution consists of multiple properties. The basis allocation rules of § 732(c), which apply to § 736(b) distributions, look to the predistribution bases of property in the hands of the partnership, while property distributed under § 736(a)(2) takes on a cost basis, so the allocation of basis among properties in the hands of the retiring partner may be affected by the choice of formulas.

---

for its fair market value, generating gain or loss to the partnership equal to the difference between the value of the property and the partnership's basis; the recipient of the property should be required to include the fair market value of the property in income and take a fair market value basis for the property.

[134] A minor advantage to C under the proposed agreement is the avoidance of a possible short-term holding period problem for the one sixth of Z received as part of the guaranteed payment under the ratable approach.

[2] Distributions That Result in Section 736(a)(2) Guaranteed Payments to Retiring General Partners From Service Partnerships That Own Unrealized Receivables

If a distribution of property in liquidation of a retiring general partner's interest is made by a service partnership that owns unrealized receivables, the analysis is complicated considerably by the application of § 751(b) and the limited exclusion of unrealized receivables from the definition of "§ 736(b) property." As discussed above,[135] this exclusion only applies to retiring or deceased general partners of partnerships in which capital is not a material income-producing factor. Again, the problems that arise in this context can be examined best through an example, which will be referred to in the subsections below.

EXAMPLE 22-10: Equal general partner F retires from the DEF accounting firm partnership at a time when its balance sheet is as follows:

	Adjusted Basis	Fair Market Value
Assets:		
Cash	$30,000	$ 30,000
Unrealized receivables	0	45,000
Capital assets:		
P	7,000	10,000
Q	4,000	5,000
R	4,000	15,000
Total	$45,000	$105,000
Capital:		
D	$15,000	$ 35,000
E	15,000	35,000
F	15,000	35,000
Total	$45,000	$105,000

[a] Distributions of Cash and Property Other Than Unrealized Receivables

Assume that $15,000 in cash and assets Q and R are distributed to F in liquidation of his interest. F has received a distribution of § 736(b) assets for his interest in both § 736(b) property and unrealized receivables. The $15,000 portion of the distribution that he receives for his interest in unrealized receivables must be treated as a § 736(a)(1) "payment," and the question is what

---

[135] See ¶ 22.02[1].

portion of each distributed asset is allocable to this payment. This allocation question is similar to that discussed in the previous section.[136]

There is no reason to think that an allocation agreement between the partnership and the retiring partner would not be respected in this context as well. Thus, for example, if the parties agree that all of the $15,000 cash is distributed pursuant to § 736(a)(2) and assets Q and R are distributed pursuant to § 736(b), the agreement should be respected.

Ratable approach analysis. In the absence of an agreement, assuming the ratable allocation approach is the default rule, F would be viewed as receiving (1) cash of $8,570 (four sevenths of $15,000), a four-sevenths interest in asset Q (partnership basis $2,290, value $2,860), and a four-sevenths interest in asset R (partnership basis $2,290, value $8,570) as a § 736(b) distribution; and (2) cash of $6,430 (three sevenths of $15,000), a three-sevenths interest in asset Q (partnership basis $1,710, value $2,140), and a three-sevenths interest in asset R (partnership basis $1,710, value $6,430) as a guaranteed payment under § 736(a)(2). Thus, F's taxable income consists of $15,000 of ordinary income under § 707(c). The $8,570 cash distribution pursuant to § 736(b) reduces the basis of F's partnership interest from $15,000 to $6,430, which becomes the basis of the four sevenths of assets Q and R distributed pursuant to § 736(b). Four sevenths of these assets had a predistribution basis of $4,580 (four sevenths of $8,000), so their basis to F represents a $1,850 basis increase, which means the partnership will be required to reduce the basis of asset P by $1,850 if it has a § 754 election in effect or the basis reduction is substantial under § 734(d). The other three sevenths of Q and R take a total fair market value basis of $8,570 under § 707(c), giving F a total basis of $15,000 ($8,570 plus $6,430) and a built-in gain of $5,000 for them.

The partnership's side of the transaction looks like this: (1) the partnership recognizes gain of $5,150 ($430 plus $4,720) on the transfer of three sevenths of Q and R to F as part of the guaranteed payment; (2) the partnership is entitled to reduce its taxable income by $15,000 to reflect the guaranteed payment to C; and (3) the partnership's basis in its remaining assets is unaffected unless a § 754 election is in effect or the potential basis reduction under § 754 is "substantial" under § 734(d), either of which will result in the partnership reducing the basis of asset P by $1,850 (the amount of the basis increase in the assets distributed to F).

It is worth noting that in this scenario (involving a general partner, a service partnership, and only traditional unrealized receivables), the operating rules of § 736 effectively insulate the transaction from § 751(b). However, this is not a free ride for any of the participants. The creation of a guaranteed payment equal to the retiring partner's share of unrealized receivables is a surrogate for the ordinary income that would have been taxed to the retiree under §

---

[136] See ¶ 22.06[1][b].

751(b). The continuing partners will eventually be taxed on the retiree's share of the receivables, but this seeming injustice should be effectively offset by their guaranteed payment deduction.

Allocation by agreement. If the proposed allocation agreement is respected, the arithmetic is a lot easier. The entire § 736(a)(2) payment consists of cash so the partnership had no imputed gain on the payment, just a $15,000 reduction of its ordinary income. Under § 736(b), the basis of Q and R to F is $15,000, an increase of $7,000 from the partnership's predistribution basis, so the partnership may have a basis reduction of $7,000 (instead of $1,850) in asset P. This is very likely to be a better result for the continuing partners, who effectively have traded an immediate $5,150 recognized gain under the ratable allocation for a possible additional $5,150 ($7,000 less $1,850) increase in their built-in gain in asset R.

F has the same $15,000 of income from the guaranteed payment as he had under the ratable allocation approach and the same total $15,000 basis in Q and R as under the ratable approach, so he is largely indifferent to such an agreement.

[b] Distributions of Unrealized Receivables as Section 736(a)(2) Guaranteed Payments

Assume next that F receives $35,000 of unrealized receivables in liquidation of his interest. Of this distribution, $20,000 is payment for F's $20,000 interest in § 736(b) property and is taxed as a regular partnership distribution. Under § 751(b)(1), F is considered to have received a preliminary distribution of his one-third interest in partnership assets other than § 751 property (with a value of $20,000 and a basis of $15,000), and to have sold this property to the partnership for $20,000 of receivables. Thus, F recognizes $5,000 of capital gain and receives a $20,000 basis in the portion of the receivables distributed in exchange for his interest in § 736(b) property. The partnership recognizes $20,000 of ordinary income as a result of its § 751(b) exchange of $20,000 of zero-basis receivables for F's interest in other assets. The partnership also receives a $20,000 basis in the assets "purchased" from F, thereby increasing its basis in these assets by $10,000.

In addition to $20,000 of receivables received for his interest in § 736(b) property, F receives $15,000 of receivables, which represents his proportionate share of the partnership's receivables. Under the statutory language, it seems the distribution of these receivables constitutes a § 736(a)(2) guaranteed payment to F. Under this analysis, both F and apparently the partnership[137] recognize immediate ordinary income of $15,000. The partnership's income is offset

---

137 See ¶ 14.03[5].

by a § 707(c) deduction of $15,000 and F obtains a $15,000 basis in the distributed receivables.

Alternatively, it can be argued that the distribution to F of his $15,000 proportionate share of partnership receivables should not be treated as a "payment" for purposes of § 736, so that the normal distribution provisions apply.[138] Applying these provisions, neither F nor the partnership would recognize any income at the time of the distribution under § 731(a). Instead, under § 732(c), the receivables would continue to have a zero basis in F's hands and, under § 735(a)(1), F would recognize ordinary income upon their collection. There would be no § 707(c) deduction for the partnership under this approach.

If a retiring partner receives liquidating distributions of both unrealized receivables and other property, the analysis is further complicated. Assume that F receives $15,000 of the unrealized receivables and assets Q and R in liquidation of his interest. Because this distribution results in F receiving his proportionate share of unrealized receivables and § 736(b) assets equal to his proportionate interest in such property, it may be argued that the distribution does not constitute a § 736 payment in any respect, and thus the normal distribution provisions apply.[139] On its face, however, § 736 seems to clearly apply, and thus the only real issues are how to allocate the distributed assets between §§ 736(b) and 736(a)(2) in the absence of an allocation agreement and whether an allocation agreement among the partners, if one exists, should be given effect.

Finally, assume that F receives assets Q and R and $20,000 of receivables. The $5,000 excess of the $40,000 value of this distribution over the $35,000 value of F's interest in all listed partnership assets is a § 736(a) payment, presumably for F's interest in goodwill. Applying § 736 by its terms, F receives a § 736(b) payment of $20,000 and a § 736(a)(2) payment of $20,000 ($15,000 for his interest in unrealized receivables and $5,000 for his interest in goodwill). The distributed assets (unrealized receivables with a value of $20,000 and assets Q and R) must be allocated between these payments. Possible methods of allocation are discussed above.[140]

---

[138] Oblique support for normal distribution treatment may be gleaned from Example (6) in Regulations § 1.751-1(g). The liquidating distribution in this example consists in part of an unrealized receivable. The example treats the portion of the distributed receivable equal to the distributee's share of partnership unrealized receivables as received under the normal distribution provisions. See Reg. § 1.751-1(g) Example (6)(d)(2). On the face of § 736, it seems this portion of the distribution should constitute a guaranteed payment under § 736(a)(2). The example, however, contains absolutely no mention of § 736, and seems premised on the assumption that § 736 is wholly inapplicable to the transaction. It is unclear whether the failure of this example to take § 736 into account was deliberate or inadvertent.

[139] See note 138.

[140] See ¶ 22.06[1][b].

[3] Property Distributions in Satisfaction of Section 736(a)(1) Distributive Shares

If a retiring partner is entitled to a § 736(a)(1) distributive share that is satisfied by a property distribution, the tax consequences should be analyzed in two steps:

1. The retiring partner's § 736(a)(1) distributive share is computed under the general rules of § 704, without regard to the type of property distributed, and the retiring partner is taxed under § 702(a).
2. The distribution itself is taxed under the normal distribution rules of §§ 731 through 735.

These steps may be illustrated using the facts of Example 22-10. Assume that F retires, receiving $30,000 in cash and asset Q. In addition, F is entitled to a § 736(a)(1) distributive share of 10 percent of the partnership's net profit for the year following his retirement. During the next year, the partnership's net income is $100,000 so that F is entitled to a $10,000 distribution, which the partnership satisfies by distributing asset P to F.

The initial distribution of cash and asset Q is taxed in the manner previously described[141] and is not of present interest. The present inquiry relates to the taxation of the distribution of asset P in satisfaction of F's § 736(a)(1) distributive share of $10,000. Under the two-step analysis suggested above, F is taxed on a $10,000 distributive share of partnership income under § 702(a)(8). As a result, his basis in his partnership interest is increased from zero to $10,000. The distribution of asset P is then taxed under the normal distribution rules. Thus, under § 731(a), F realizes no income upon the distribution of P, and, under § 732(b), his basis in P equals the $10,000 predistribution basis of his partnership interest. These results are entirely rational: F is taxed on $10,000 of partnership income and receives property with a basis of $10,000.

Rational results may also be obtained if the partnership distributes $10,000 of unrealized receivables to F, but the analysis is more complicated: Section 751(b) applies to the extent F receives unrealized receivables, which are § 751 property, in exchange for his interest in "other property." Arguably, F has no interest in the partnership's unrealized receivables, because he will not share in the proceeds of the future collection of such receivables. Moreover, since F will not share in the proceeds of gain realized on future sales of the partnership's other property, his interest in other property may be viewed as an interest only in the basis of such property. Therefore, F may be treated as relinquishing a $10,000 interest in other property with a basis of $10,000 for $10,000 of unrealized receivables in a § 751(b) exchange. As a result of this exchange, F realizes no income and obtains a basis of $10,000 in the dis-

---

[141] See ¶ 22.06[2][a].

tributed receivables. The partnership, on the other hand, recognizes $10,000 of ordinary income. Under this analysis, *F* is taxed on a $10,000 distributive share of partnership income and receives unrealized receivables with a basis of $10,000—again, an entirely rational result.

¶ 22.07 APPLICATION OF SECTION 409A TO SECTION 736(a) PAYMENTS

When Section 736 was enacted in 1954, Congress anticipated that § 736(a) would, in part, serve a retirement payout function,[142] in effect permitting the partnership to make continuing compensatory payments to retired partners for past services. In 2004, Congress enacted § 409A, providing detailed rules for the taxation of nonqualified deferred compensation plans.[143] Section 409A generally provides that if a nonqualified deferred compensation plan does not meet specified requirements regarding (1) the timing of deferred compensation distributions, (2) restrictions on the ability to accelerate deferred compensation, and (3) elections to defer compensation, then all compensation deferred under the plan is immediately includible in gross income where it is not subject to a substantial risk of forfeiture. The legislative history of § 409A does not consider whether or how § 409A might apply to payments under § 736(a). In Notice 2005-1, the Service stated that it would not apply the requirements of § 409A to payments made under § 736(a) unless otherwise provided in applicable Regulations.[144] Regulations issued under § 409A reserve comment on the application of the statute to arrangements between partnerships and partners[145] and the preamble to the final regulations indicates that taxpayers can continue to rely on Notice 2005-1 and the preamble to the proposed regulations until new guidance is issued.[146]

---

[142] S. Rep. No. 1622, 83d Cong., 2d Sess. 296 (1954).

[143] For purposes of applying § 409A, a nonqualified deferred compensation plan is any plan that provides for a deferral of compensation other than a "qualified employer plan" under § 219(g)(5), § 457(b), or § 415(m) and any bona fide vacation leave, sick leave, compensatory time, disability pay, or death benefit plan. § 409A(d).

[144] Notice 2005-1, 2005-2 IRB 1. The uncertainty regarding the application of § 409A to § 736(a) payments has been the focus of some commentary. See Postlewaite & Rosenzweig, "Anachronisms in Subchapter K of the Internal Revenue Code: Is It Time to Part With Section 736?" 100 Nw. U.L. Rev. 379, 396 (2006); ABA Tax Section Members Comment on Application of Section 409A to Partnership Transactions, Tax Notes Today, May 24, 2005, 2005 TNT 99-28 (LEXIS).

[145] Reg. § 1.409A-1(b)(7).

[146] REG-158080-04 (Dec. 16, 2005).

CHAPTER **23**

Special Problems Relating to the Death of a Partner

¶ 23.01 ALLOCATING YEAR-OF-DEATH PARTNERSHIP INCOME

Section 706(c)(2)(A) provides that the taxable year of a partnership closes "with respect to a partner whose entire interest ... terminates (whether by reason of death, liquidation or otherwise)." By automatically closing the partnership year with respect to deceased partners, this rule assures that the deceased partner's distributive share of partnership income or loss for the short partnership year that ends at death is included on the partner's final income tax return.

However, the taxable year of the partnership does not close upon the death of a partner under the general rule in § 706(c)(1). Thus, the decedent's share of year-of-death income or loss must be apportioned between the decedent and his estate or successor under § 706(d).[1]

Generally, individual partners and most partnerships are on the calendar year so the mandatory closing of the partnership year with respect to a decedent cannot cause more than twelve months of partnership income or loss to be "bunched" on the decedent's final income tax return.[2]

---

[1] See ¶ 12.03.

[2] Prior to enactment of the Taxpayer Relief Act of 1997, the partnership year of a partner who died prior to 1998 did not close automatically, no apportionment was required, and the decedent's entire share of partnership income or loss for the year of death was taxed to the decedent's estate or successor. This eliminated any possible bunching.

¶ 23.02 PARTNERSHIP ITEMS OF INCOME IN RESPECT OF A DECEDENT

[1] The General Rules: Sections 691 and 1014(c)

Section 691 prescribes rules for the income taxation of items of "income in respect of a decedent" (IRD). While IRD is not defined in the statute (or its legislative history), it has come to mean, in general, items of income that are substantially "earned" (in a very loose sense) but not properly includible in taxable income prior to death under the decedent's accounting method.[3] Items of IRD are subject to estate tax[4] and, under § 691, are also subject to income tax upon accrual or collection by the decedent's estate or beneficiary. Section 691(c) grants partial relief from this double taxation by allowing an income tax deduction to the recipient of the income in an amount equal to the estate, inheritance, legacy, and succession taxes paid by the estate with respect to IRD items.

An essential part of the pattern of taxing IRD is § 1014(c), which denies an estate or beneficiary a § 1014(a) fair-market-value-at-death basis for items of IRD. Were it not for § 1014(c), IRD items would obtain a basis equal to their value at the decedent's death under § 1014(a), thereby eliminating the inherent income that § 691 is intended to tax to estates and beneficiaries.

[2] Items of Income in Respect of a Decedent Attributable to Partnership Interests

Two classes of IRD may arise in connection with the ownership of partnership interests by decedents.[5] The first is statutorily defined as the amount of any § 736(a) payments made to a decedent-partner's successor in liquidation of his partnership interest.[6] The second class, which is a creature of case law, includes that portion of a decedent's partnership interest that is attributable to the

---

While bunching is possible under current law, it is rare because of the prevalence of the calendar tax year for individuals and partnerships.

[3] See Reg. § 1.691-1(b).

[4] § 2033; cf. Reg. § 1.691(c)-1(a).

[5] For taxable years beginning before 1998, there was a third class of IRD that could arise in connection with partnership interests owned by decedents. That class, as defined by Regulations §§ 1.706-1(c)(3)(v) and 1.753-1(b), was the distributive share attributable to the decedent's partnership interest for the period ending with the date of his death that was includible in the income of his estate or other successor. As discussed supra ¶ 23.01, a decedent-partner's final tax return now includes his share of partnership income or loss for the short partnership year that ends at death, thus eliminating this class of IRD.

[6] § 753. See generally ¶ 22.03 for a discussion of § 736(a).

decedent's interest in certain partnership items, such as zero-basis accounts receivable, that would be IRD if held directly by the decedent.

[a] Section 736(a) Payments

Section 753 provides that "[t]he amount includible in the gross income of a successor in interest of a deceased partner under section 736(a) shall be considered income in respect of a decedent under section 691." Under Regulations § 1.753-1(a), if a retired partner dies before his partnership interest has been completely liquidated, any § 736(a) payments made to his successor also constitute IRD. Thus, § 753 ensures that § 736(a) payments to a decedent's successor are taxable in their entirety by preventing the basis of the decedent's partnership interest from being increased under § 1014(a) to the extent of the value of the § 736(a) payments, and accords the decedent's successor the right to a § 691(c) deduction for the estate tax attributable to the § 736(a) payments.

Section 736(a) may embrace items not considered IRD outside Subchapter K. For example, goodwill is not an IRD item if held directly by a decedent. However, § 736(b)(2) provides that a distribution to a retired or deceased general partner for her interest in partnership goodwill is a § 736(a) payment if capital is not a material income-producing factor in the partnership business.[7] Consequently, this type of distribution is IRD.

Although § 753 literally requires *all* § 736(a) payments to successors of deceased partners to be treated as IRD, it should be limited to payments pursuant to binding contractual or statutory obligations in force at the decedent's death. If § 736(a) payments are subsequently negotiated by the decedent's successor on his or her own behalf, the payments are not included as such in the decedent's estate and thus IRD treatment under § 753 is inappropriate. However, to the extent such payments reflect the decedent's share of cash-method accounts receivable and other income rights held by the partnership at the decedent's death, IRD treatment may result under the case law discussed below.[8]

If a decedent's successor disposes of his right to receive future § 736(a) payments by sale to a third party, Regulations § 1.753-1(a) permits the successor to treat gain realized from the sale as IRD, thereby entitling the successor to a § 691(c) deduction for the estate tax attributable to the value of the § 736(a) rights.

[b] Court-Established Items of Income in Respect of a Decedent

The Tax Court and two circuit courts of appeal have recognized the existence of a second class of partnership IRD items by treating a decedent's inter-

---

[7] See ¶ 22.04.
[8] See ¶ 23.02[2][b].

est in zero-basis accounts receivable of a service partnership as IRD.[9] The legitimacy of this second class of IRD has been the subject of disagreement among commentators.[10] However, these decisions have remained unchallenged for many decades.

The statutory argument against treating partnership-held income rights (such as zero-basis accounts receivable) as IRD is based on § 691(e), which provides that "[f]or application of this section [691] to income in respect of a deceased partner, see section 753," and § 753, which provides only that § 736(a) payments are IRD. Because "for application" of § 691 with respect to a deceased partner, the Code cross-references § 753 exclusively, and since § 753 applies only to § 736(a) payments, no other partnership item should qualify as IRD.

In *George Edward Quick Trust*,[11] however, the Tax Court (in a decision subsequently affirmed by the Eighth Circuit) rejected the notion that §§ 691(e) and 753 preclude any partnership item other than a § 736(a) payment from being IRD.[12] Instead, based on its reading of §§ 691, 742, and 1014 in light of the legislative history, the court determined that a partnership interest is not "a unitary res, incapable of further analysis," but may "be appropriately viewed as a bundle of rights."[13] Having concluded that a partnership interest is not a single property, but rather a bundle of property rights, the court had no difficulty in concluding that "a major constituent element [of the decedent's] interest was the right to share in the proceeds of the accounts receivable as they were collected,"[14] and that, therefore, the zero-basis accounts receivable were IRD items. Similarly, in *Chrissie H. Woodhall*,[15] the Tax Court (in a memorandum decision affirmed by the Ninth Circuit) held that a decedent's share of a partnership's zero-basis accounts receivable is an IRD item.

The rationale of *Quick Trust* and *Woodhall* strongly suggests that partnership items other than zero-basis accounts receivable may qualify as IRD.

---

[9] George Edward Quick Trust, 54 TC 1336 (1970) (acq.), aff'd per curiam, 444 F2d 90 (8th Cir. 1971); Chrissie H. Woodhall, 28 TCM 1438 (1969), aff'd, 454 F2d 226 (9th Cir. 1972); cf. Rev. Rul. 66-325, 1966-2 CB 249.

[10] See, e.g., Ferguson, "Income and Deductions in Respect of Decedents and Related Problems," 25 Tax L. Rev. 5, 102–103 (1969); Tenen, "Tax Problems of Service Partnerships," 16 NYU Inst. on Fed. Tax'n 137, 162–164 (1958); Willis, Little & McDonald, "Problems on Death, Retirement, or Withdrawal of a Partner," 16 NYU Inst. on Fed. Tax'n 1033, 1042 (1959).

[11] George Edward Quick Trust, 54 TC 1336 (1970) (acq.), aff'd per curiam, 444 F2d 90 (8th Cir. 1971).

[12] George Edward Quick Trust, 54 TC 1336, 1344 n.13 (1970). Section 691(f) was redesignated § 691(e) by the Tax Reform Act of 1976.

[13] George Edward Quick Trust, 54 TC 1336, 1345 (1970).

[14] George Edward Quick Trust, 54 TC 1336 (1970).

[15] Chrissie H. Woodhall, 28 TCM 1438 (1969), aff'd, 454 F2d 226 (9th Cir. 1972); cf. Rev. Rul. 66-325, 1966-2 CB 249.

Under this analysis, IRD includes any partnership item that would be IRD if held by the decedent in his individual capacity. Whether this analysis will be extended beyond general partners in service partnerships is uncertain.

If, contrary to *Quick Trust* and *Woodhall*, partnership income rights are not treated as IRD, a § 754 election would entitle a deceased partner's successor to a fair-market-value-at-death basis for his share of such rights in the hands of the partnership, and thus the successor would never be subject to income tax on his share of such income rights. On the other hand, in the absence of a § 754 election, a successor-partner is generally better off if the income rights are treated as IRD, because IRD treatment entitles him to a § 691(c) deduction for estate taxes. Under these circumstances, treatment of the rights as IRD requires the successor to accept a lower basis in his partnership interest under § 1014(a), but does not affect the basis of partnership assets or his share of subsequent taxable income with respect to such rights.

¶ 23.03 BASIS OF A PARTNERSHIP INTEREST IN THE HANDS OF A DECEDENT'S SUCCESSOR

[1] General

Under Regulations § 1.742-1, the basis of a partnership interest acquired from a decedent is the fair market value of the interest as of the date of death, or the alternative valuation date, with the following two adjustments:

1. The value of the interest for estate tax purposes is increased by the successor's share of partnership liabilities and
2. The value is decreased by items of IRD under § 691.[16]

[a] Inclusion of Partnership Liabilities

Consistent with the theory of § 752(a), Regulations § 1.742-1 provides that the basis of a partnership interest in the hands of a decedent's successor is increased over its estate tax value by the successor's proportionate share of partnership liabilities. The addition of partnership liabilities is necessary to

---

[16] See Priv. Ltr. Rul. 9102018 (Oct. 12, 1990) (basis excludes partner's distributive share of partnership income for period ending with date of his death). See also Reg. § 1.742-1(a), as amended by TD 9811, 2017-7 IRB 869 (Jan. 19, 2017) (basis of a partnership interest acquired from a decedent is determined under § 1022 if the decedent died in 2010 and the decedent's executor elected to have § 1022 apply to the decedent's estate; conforming language).

maintain the integrity of the overall basis scheme of Subchapter K. Because the § 1014(a) basis of a partnership interest in the hands of a decedent's successor is its date-of-death value, net of the decedent's share of partnership liabilities, failure to add back liabilities in computing the successor's basis would result in the exclusion of partnership liabilities from basis and create an unwarranted discrepancy between the outside basis of the partners' partnership interests and the inside basis of the partnership's assets.

[b] Exclusion of Value Attributable to Income in Respect of a Decedent

Regulations § 1.742-1 provides that the basis of a partnership interest acquired from a decedent includes the fair market value of the interest at death (or the alternative valuation date), "reduced to the extent that such value is attributable to items constituting income in respect of a decedent."[17] Excluding the value of partnership IRD items from a successor's basis protects the § 691 scheme of IRD taxation by ensuring that the successor is taxed on all partnership items that constitute IRD.

[2] Basis Adjustments Under Sections 754 and 743(b)

If a § 754 election is in effect with respect to the transfer of a decedent's partnership interest to his successor or if the partnership has a substantial built-in loss, the bases of the partnership's assets are increased or decreased, with respect to the successor, by the difference between the adjusted basis of the interest in the successor's hands and his proportionate share of the basis of partnership assets. The § 743(b) increase or decrease is apportioned among the partnership's assets pursuant to § 755. These basis adjustment provisions are discussed in detail in Chapter 24.[18]

---

[17] See Rev. Rul. 66-325, 1966-2 CB 249.

[18] See ¶ 24.08 for discussion of the application of basis adjustment provisions upon the death of a partner.

¶ 23.04 SELECTING THE DECEASED PARTNER'S SUCCESSOR IN INTEREST

[1] Selecting the Immediate Successor in Interest

Upon the death of a partner, his interest passes to his estate, unless, pursuant to Regulations § 1.706-1(c)(3)(iii), he has previously designated another successor under the partnership agreement. In determining whether the estate or some other taxpayer should be selected as the immediate successor to his interest, a partner should consider whether by designating an individual, rather than his estate or a trust, as immediate successor, he can avoid the complexity, discussed below, of having both Subchapter K and Subchapter J (relating to the taxation of trust and estate income) apply to the partnership interest.

[2] Selecting the Ultimate Successor

While certain tax benefits may be gained from the judicious selection of the immediate successor to a partner's interest, these benefits are temporary. Proper selection of the ultimate successor is more important. In selecting his ultimate successor, a partner should be cognizant that the partnership interest will continue to generate income or loss to the successor subsequent to his death. This projected income or loss should be taken into account in determining who will succeed to the interest. For example, a partnership interest that is expected to generate significant continuing losses may be best utilized by an heir who materially participates in the partnership's business because the utility of such losses to such an heir will not be affected by the passive loss rules.[19] If, on the other hand, a partnership interest is likely to generate substantial passive income, it may be more valuable to heirs who have accumulated passive losses or who expect to have ongoing passive losses. As discussed elsewhere,[20] special problems may arise where a partnership interest is held by a tax-exempt entity. Therefore, a partner should carefully consider the effects of bequeathing a partnership interest to charity.

[3] Determining Who Is the Decedent's Successor in Interest

The decedent's successor in interest is his estate unless, pursuant to the partnership agreement, he designates another as his successor. If, in accordance with the terms of the partnership agreement, he designates a successor other

---

[19] § 469. See generally ¶ 11.08.
[20] See ¶¶ 9.03[3], 16.05[2][b] .

than his estate, the Regulations indicate that the designation is effective for tax purposes, apparently on the theory that the interest passes by contract rather than by will or intestacy.[21] The Service has ruled that a deceased partner may have more than one successor in interest, provided each successor receives an undivided share of all of the decedent's rights with respect to the partnership.[22]

Similar successor-in-interest rules apply if a retired partner dies prior to the complete liquidation of his interest under § 736, in which case any person designated by the retired partner as his successor in interest is taxable on all § 736 payments made subsequent to the retired partner's death.[23]

¶ 23.05 SPECIAL PROBLEMS RELATING TO THE INCOME TAXATION OF PARTNERSHIP INTERESTS HELD BY ESTATES AND TRUSTS

[1] Allocation of Partnership Income and Loss Between the Trust or Estate and Beneficiaries

If a partnership interest passes to an estate or trust, the post-mortem share of partnership income or loss associated with the interest is allocated, in accordance with the rules of Subchapter J, among the estate or trust and its beneficiaries.[24] Generally, an estate or trust (other than a grantor trust) is a taxable

---

[21] Reg. § 1.706-1(c)(3)(iii).

[22] Rev. Rul. 71-271, 1971-1 CB 206. Some of the complications that may arise in connection with specific bequests of rights with respect to partnership interests are illustrated by Revenue Ruling 68-215, 1968-1 CB 312, in which a deceased partner made specific bequests to several beneficiaries of certain rights with respect to his partnership interest, including the right to undistributed profits for the partnership year during which death occurred. Prior to the end of the partnership year during which the decedent died, the estate assigned these rights to the designated beneficiaries, but retained the right to receive undistributed partnership income from prior years. Under these circumstances, the Service concluded that the estate, rather than the beneficiaries, was the decedent's successor at the end of the year and was taxable on the entire distributive share of partnership income for the year of death. The ruling indicates, however, that if the estate had assigned undivided interests in its entire partnership interest to the designated beneficiaries prior to the end of the partnership's taxable year, the beneficiaries would have been the decedent's successors and would have been taxable on partnership income for the year of death.

[23] Rev. Rul. 71-507, 1971-2 CB 331; cf. Reg. § 1.753-1(a) (last sentence) (payments made to successor for § 736(a) liquidation right constitute IRD).

[24] See generally H. Zaritsky, N. Lane & R. Danforth, Federal Income Taxation of Estates and Trusts (Thomson Reuters/Tax & Accounting, 3d ed. 2001); M. Ferguson & M. Ascher, Federal Income Taxation of Estates and Beneficiaries (Wolters Kluwer, 4th ed. 2018).

entity.[25] However, under §§ 661 and 662, an estate or trust may shift the incidence of tax on its income to its beneficiaries by making distributions of cash or property to them. Section 661 accords the estate or trust a deduction, up to the amount of its distributable net income (DNI),[26] for cash distributions or the value of property distributions to beneficiaries. Concomitantly, § 662 requires that a beneficiary include as income any DNI distributed to him under § 661.

If an estate or trust holds depreciable, depletable, or amortizable property, the depreciation, depletion, or amortization must be apportioned between the entity and its beneficiaries.[27] In general, if the entity is an estate, its depreciation and depletion deductions are allocated, under §§ 167(d) and 611(b)(4), among the estate and the beneficiaries "on the basis of the income of the estate [computed without regard to depreciation or depletion] allocable to each."[28] If a trust owns depreciable or depletable property, its cost recovery deductions are allocated "in accordance with the pertinent provisions of the instrument creating the trust," or, if the instrument contains no such provisions, on the basis of income allocable to the trust and each of its beneficiaries.[29]

While depreciation or depletion deductions allocable to an estate or trust and an estate's or trust's share of any other partnership deductions and losses decrease its income as well as its DNI,[30] any portion of such items allocated to the beneficiaries does not. Therefore, if an estate or trust is a partner, the partnership must separately state its depreciation and depletion items under § 702(a)(7) so that the estate or trust can compute its income properly.[31]

If an estate or trust has a net operating loss, the loss is not deductible by the beneficiaries; instead, it must be carried over by the entity.[32] If an estate or trust has an unused net operating loss at the time it is finally liquidated, the loss becomes available to the beneficiaries who succeed to the residuary property of the estate.[33]

The passive loss rules of § 469 apply to estates,[34] as do, apparently, the at-risk rules of § 465.[35] The application of these rules to investments (including

---

[25] § 641.

[26] See § 643(a) (definition of "DNI").

[27] §§ 642(e), 642(f), 167(d), 611(b)(4).

[28] See Rev. Rul. 74-71, 1974-1 CB 158; cf. Reg. §§ 1.167(h)-1(c), 1.611-1(c)(5). The allocation is based on "income" in the fiduciary accounting sense. See also §§ 642(e), 642(f).

[29] §§ 167(d), 611(b)(4); cf. Reg. § 1.48-6(b) (allocation of investment credit between estate or trust and beneficiaries).

[30] § 642(e).

[31] See ¶ 9.01[3][b].

[32] § 642(d).

[33] § 642(h).

[34] § 469(a)(2)(A).

[35] See Prop. Reg. § 1.465-1(d) (1979).

partnership interests) held by estates is relatively straightforward, at least with respect to the application of the passive activity loss rules to distributions of partnership interests by estates.

When a passive activity interest is transferred upon the death of the owner, the decedent's unused passive activity losses are deductible on her final return to the extent they do not exceed the amount by which the basis of the interest is stepped up under § 1014; any excess loss is lost forever.[36] With regard to post-mortem passive losses, § 469(j)(12)[37] provides that upon the distribution of an interest in any passive activity by an estate or trust, the basis of the distributed interest immediately before the distribution is stepped up in the hands of the estate or trust by the amount of any passive activity losses allocable to the interest. Such losses are not allowable as a deduction for any year. While the § 469 regulations do not comprehensively address the treatment of estates and trusts and their beneficiaries,[38] they generally take an almost pure look-through approach to passive activities conducted through partnerships and other pass-through entities.[39] Thus, under § 469(j)(12) it is reasonable to assume that the distribution of a partnership interest by an estate or trust will be treated as a distribution of its interest in any passive activities in which it is engaged. On this basis, any unused passive losses of the estate or trust related to the activity are lost on the distribution and the basis of the partnership interest is stepped up by the amount of such losses.[40]

The statutory at-risk rules in § 465 are devoid of any guidance with regard to the details of their application to partnerships in general, as well as the consequences following the death of a partner.[41] The following is based largely

---

[36] § 469(g)(2); see ¶ 11.08[g][3][a].

[37] Added by PL 100-647 (Technical and Miscellaneous Revenue Act of 1988). HR Rep. No. 100-795, 100th Cong., 2d Sess. [*] (July 26, 1988) states:

The bill provides that if a trust or estate distributes its entire interest in a passive activity to the beneficiary of the trust or estate, the basis of the property immediately before the distribution shall be increased by the amount of the passive activity losses allocable to the activity. Gain or loss to the trust or estate and the basis of the property in the hands of the beneficiary will then be determined under the usual rules applicable under the Code.

While the legislative history does not elucidate the meaning of "passive activity losses allocable to the activity," presumably the intent is to include all losses prior to the distribution date that have not been previously deducted by the trust or estate under the passive activity rules.

[38] Reg. § 1.469-8 ("Application ... to trusts, estates and their beneficiaries" is "Reserved").

[39] See, e.g., Temp. Reg. §§ 1.469-2T(c)(2)(i)(B), 1.469-2T(d)(5), 1.469-2T(e)(3).

[40] While the mechanical rules relating to the treatment of passive activity losses associated with partnership interests distributed by trusts are clear, the determination of whether the activities of trust-owned partnership interests are passive or active is not. See generally ¶ 11.08[3].

[41] See generally ¶ 11.06[2].

on the legislative history of this provision (from 1976 and 1978) and Regulations proposed in 1979 but never finalized.

If a partnership is engaged in an activity subject to the at-risk rules, the rules are applied at the partner level. Each partner who is an individual taxpayer (or a closely held C corporation) must compute and take into account her individual at-risk amount for each of the partnership's at-risk activities. The full amount of any losses from the activity reduces the basis of each such partner, regardless of whether the deductibility of the loss is deferred under § 465. Upon the death of a partner, the Proposed Regulations provide the following:

1. If the decedent's at-risk amount, after being (a) reduced by losses previously suspended, and (b) adjusted for any changes in the at-risk amount occasioned by the decedent's death, is greater than zero, it is added to her successor's at risk amount; and

2. Her successor's at-risk amount is also increased by any step-up in the basis of the activity under § 1014.[42]

EXAMPLE 23-1: Individual partner *P* dies owning an interest in Partnership. Partnership is engaged in a single activity that is subject to the at-risk rules. At the time of her death, *P*'s basis in Partnership is $6,000, her at-risk amount (net of losses previously suspended) is $2,500, and the estate tax value of her interest is $12,500. The amount at risk is not affected by her death. *P*'s sole heir is individual *P2*. *P2* takes a basis of $12,500 in Partnership. *P2*'s initial at-risk amount with respect to Partnership is $2,500 plus the entire $6,500 basis step-up in Partnership, all of which relates to the at-risk activity, for a total of $9,000.[43]

[2] Distributions of Partnership Interests by Estates and Trusts

[a] General

The rules governing the tax consequences of property distributions by trusts and estates are complex and are beyond the scope of this treatise.[44] Nevertheless, a brief overview is necessary in order to understand the even more

---

[42] Prop. Reg. § 1.465-69 (1979).

[43] Cf. Prop. Reg. § 1.465-69(b) (1979).

[44] See generally Freeland, Maxfield & Sawyer, "Estate and Trust Distribution of Property in Kind After the Tax Reform Act of 1984," 40 Tax L. Rev. 449 (1985), hereinafter "Freeland, Maxfield & Sawyer."

complex interaction of the rules of Subchapter K with the rules of Subchapter J relating to property distributions by trusts and estates.

In general, if property, including a partnership interest, is specifically bequeathed to a legatee, its formal transfer from the estate to the legatee is not given independent effect for tax purposes.[45] Instead, the transfer is viewed as if the property had been transferred directly from the decedent to the legatee. . Consequently, the transfer is tax-free to the legatee under § 102(a) and the legatee's basis in the property is determined as if he received it directly from the decedent under § 1014. The estate recognizes no gain or loss,[46] and is not entitled to a deduction for the transfer under § 661. Moreover, the distributee includes no amount under § 662, even if the estate has DNI.

By contrast, an estate's transfer of property in satisfaction of a specific pecuniary bequest is generally treated as a sale or exchange in which the estate satisfies a monetary obligation with appreciated or depreciated property. Such transfers are generally regarded as taxable sales and exchanges for all purposes.[47]

Additionally, it appears that any distribution by an estate or trust of property subject to liabilities (except for transfers of specific property in satisfaction of a specific bequest of such property) constitutes a sale or exchange in part, even if the distribution of the net value of the property is not treated as a sale or exchange under the rules described below.[48] In this regard, it seems that an otherwise tax-free distribution by an estate or trust of a partnership interest constitutes a sale or exchange to the extent that the estate is required by § 752(d) to include its share of partnership liabilities in its amount realized in such sale or exchange.[49]

Most distributions of property by estates and trusts are subject to the rules of § 643(e). Under § 643(e)(2), a distribution of property is deductible by the estate or trust under § 661 and includible by the distributee under § 662, up to the estate's or trust's DNI. Under the general rule, the amount deducted and included under §§ 661 and 662 is the lesser of the estate's or trust's basis in the property or the fair market value of the property.[50] The estate or trust may elect, however, to recognize gain or loss "in the same manner as if such property had been sold to the distributee at its fair market value."[51] If this election

---

[45] § 663(a)(1); Reg. § 1.663(a)-1. A bequest of the residuary of an estate is not a specific bequest for this purpose. Reg. § 1.663(a)-1(b)(2).

[46] Reg. § 1.661(a)-2(f)(1).

[47] Reg. §§ 1.661(a)-2(f)(1), 1.1014-4(a)(3). See Kenan v. Commissioner, 114 F2d 217 (2d Cir. 1940).

[48] See Freeland, Maxfield & Sawyer, at 454 n.20.

[49] See ¶ 7.02[6].

[50] § 643(e)(2).

[51] § 643(e)(3)(A). A trust, but not an estate, is precluded from recognizing a loss by § 267.

is made, the amount taken into account under §§ 661 and 662 is the fair market value of the property.[52]

The basis of the property in the hands of the distributee is the same as the basis of the property in the hands of the estate or trust, increased or decreased by any gain or loss recognized by the estate or trust as a result of the distribution.[53] Thus, if the estate or trust elects to recognize gain or loss under § 643(e)(3), the distributee takes the distributed property at a basis equal to its fair market value.

The general rules discussed above do not apply to distributions by estates of rights to IRD under § 691.[54] Instead, the right to an item of IRD is treated as transferred directly from the decedent to the distributee, who includes the income on his tax return when realized under the normal rules of § 691. As discussed previously,[55] IRD items include a deceased partner's right to receive liquidating payments under § 736(a) as well as the decedent's share of certain partnership receivables that existed on the date of death. Thus, a distribution by an estate of a deceased partner's right to unpaid § 736(a) payments is not treated as a sale or exchange of the right or a distribution subject to §§ 661, 662, and 643(e); instead, the distributee simply includes the payments in his or her income when received.

Several cases have held that a general partner's interest in the receivables of a service partnership is IRD and the estate's basis in the interest is not increased to reflect their value.[56] This analysis effectively divides the partnership interest into two components: The indirect interest in partnership receivables is a separate zero basis tax asset; the remainder of the partnership interest is a separate tax asset that takes a fair market value basis under § 1014. Upon a distribution of the partnership interest by the estate, the distribution should be bifurcated into a distribution of the remaining partnership interest with a fair market value basis and a distribution of an interest in the receivables with a zero basis.

Conventional receivables and a variety of recapture items under §§ 1245, 1250, and a host of other sections are all treated as "unrealized receivables" for purposes of § 751. The basic purpose of § 751 is to reduce the opportunities for taxpayers to convert ordinary income into capital gains.[57] The aggregation of these diverse sources of ordinary income under § 751 does not mean they should all be treated the same for purposes of the IRD rules. They are

---

[52] § 643(e)(3)(A)(iii).

[53] § 643(e)(1). The basis consequences are not affected by whether the distribution is fully "covered" by DNI.

[54] See § 691(a). A distribution of IRD in satisfaction of a pecuniary bequest, however, is a taxable disposition of the IRD item.

[55] See ¶ 23.02.

[56] § 1014(c). See ¶ 23.02[2][b].

[57] See ¶ 17.03.

fundamentally different. Unrealized receivables represent contractual rights to payments that are not sufficiently mature to justify current income taxation, whereas potential recapture items represent mere expectations (not "rights") to future payments.[58] The treatment of conventional receivables as IRD fosters uniform tax treatment regardless of whether the receivables are held directly or through a partnership. Treatment of potential partnership recapture items as IRD would do just the opposite: It would create numerous unexplored disparities between directly owned and partnership owned recapture property. For directly owned property, potential recapture generally ceases to exist upon the death of the owner.[59] Encapsulation of potential recapture at death for partnership owned property in separate IRD items would produce quite different results and require the creation of an entire lattice of currently unknown rules.

The most commonly applicable recapture provisions explicitly exempt decedents and their heirs from the recapture of pre-death recapture items in connection with "transfers at death."[60] There is some possible uncertainty as to the scope of this phrase. Specifically, how should it be applied with respect to (1) indirect transfers of partnership owned recapture property upon the death of a partner; and (2) at a more granular level, transfers from a decedent to her estate or trusts, and transfers from her estate and trusts to beneficiaries in connection with her death. For the reason discussed in the preceding paragraph, it seems clear that these transfer at death exemptions should be fully applicable to partnership-owned recapture properties, either because there has not been an actual transfer of the property or because, under the aggregate theory, the application of the exemptions should apply directly to the partnership-owned properties.[61] In this context, it seems clear that fragmentation should be rejected in light of the statutory and regulatory scheme dealing with basis adjustments on the death of a partner. Absent a § 754 election, § 743(a) states that no adjustment to the basis of partnership assets is permitted, and the transferee inherits the decedent's recapture position. Conversely, if a § 754 election is in effect, the basis of partnership property is adjusted and the recapture amount is zero.[62] These rules are simply inconsistent with a fragmentation approach to partnership-owned recapture properties.

---

[58] See ¶ 17.03[3].

[59] See, e.g., §§ 1245(b)(2), 1250(d)(2) (transfers at death do not trigger recapture); Reg. §§ 1.1245-2(c)(1)(iv), 1.1250-3(b)(2)(i)(a) (complete elimination of pre-death potential recapture on death).

[60] See, e.g., §§ 1245(b)(2), 1250(d)(2).

[61] The aggregate approach has been adopted in Holiday Village Shopping Ctr. v. United States, 5 Cl. Ct. 566 (1984), aff'd, 773 F2d 276 (Fed. Cir. 1985) (distribution by corporation) but rejected by the Fifth Circuit in Petroleum Corp. of Tex. v. United States, 939 F2d 1165 (5th Cir. 1991) (same; joint stipulation that all transactions had valid business purposes used to justify different conclusion). See generally ¶ 16.03[1].

[62] Reg. §§ 1.1245-1(e)(3)(ii), 1.1250-1(f). See ¶ 24.07.

[b] Distributions as Sales or Exchanges for Subchapter K Purposes

A sale or exchange of a partnership interest may trigger the application of several provisions of Subchapter K. Under § 706(c)(2)(A), the taxable year of a partnership closes with respect to a partner when he sells or exchanges his entire interest in the partnership.[63] Under § 743(b), if a § 754 election is in effect or if the partnership has a substantial built-in loss, a person who acquires a partnership interest in a sale or exchange or on the death of a partner is entitled to a special adjustment in the basis of the partnership's assets in an amount equal to the difference between such person's initial basis in the interest and his proportionate share of the partnership's common basis in its assets.[64] Section 761(e) provides as follows:

> Except as otherwise provided in regulations, for purposes of—
>
> (1) section 708 (relating to continuation of partnership),
> (2) section 743 (relating to optional adjustment to basis of partnership property), and
> (3) any other provision of this subchapter specified in regulations prescribed by the Secretary,
>
> any distribution of an interest in a partnership (not otherwise treated as an exchange) shall be treated as an exchange.

Although § 761(e) was added to the Code in 1984, the only Regulation that has been issued under § 761(e) is Regulations § 1.761-1(e), relating to the technical termination rule in former § 708(b)(1)(B).[65] Following the repeal of the technical termination rule in 2017, this Regulation and § 761(e)(1) of the statute are effectively deadwood. In the absence of future Regulations, § 761(e) can be condensed to read as follows: *for purposes of § 743, any distribution of a partnership interest is treated as an exchange of the interest.*

However, not every transfer of a partnership interest to or from an estate or trust is a distribution. As discussed in ¶ 21.05[2][a], property specifically bequeathed to a legatee is treated as passing directly from the decedent to the legatee, and, therefore, no "distribution" should be deemed to occur when the estate formally transfers it to the legatee. Similarly, transfers of items of IRD, subject to § 691, generally are not treated as distributed by the estate to the transferee.

Although § 761(e) requires that a distribution of a partnership interest be treated as a sale or exchange for purposes of § 743, it does not mandate sale

---

[63] See ¶ 12.02.
[64] See Chapter 24.
[65] See ¶ 13.03.

or exchange treatment for § 706 purposes.[66] Regulations § 1.706-1(c)(2)(i) provides that a sale or exchange does not include "any transfer of a partnership interest which occurs at death as a result of inheritance or any testamentary disposition." The accompanying example makes clear that a distribution of a decedent's partnership interest (as well as all other estate assets) to his widow upon liquidation and termination of the estate "is not a sale or exchange," and that the spouse is taxable on the entire share of partnership income for the partnership year in which the distribution occurs. These Regulations are absolute on their face: Even if an estate makes a § 643(e)(3) election to recognize gain or loss on the distribution, no sale or exchange apparently occurs for purposes of § 706.

¶ 23.06 INSURANCE FUNDING OF PARTNERSHIP BUY-SELL AND REDEMPTION AGREEMENTS

It is common for partnership buy-sell and redemption agreements to be funded in whole or in part through insurance on the lives of the partners. This section focuses on the estate tax consequences of the ownership of insurance for this purpose.

[1] Buy-Sell Agreements

The simplest method for providing insurance funding of a buy-sell agreement among a small number of partners in a relatively stable partnership is for each partner to purchase an insurance policy on the life of each of the other partners, with each purchasing partner naming himself as beneficiary. Upon the death of a partner, each surviving partner applies the insurance proceeds he receives to purchase a portion of the decedent's interest. Under this sort of arrangement, the insurance proceeds are not includible in the decedent's estate under § 2042.[67] Instead, only the value of the partnership interest (which is sold in exchange for the proceeds) is included in the deceased partner's estate.

---

[66] The Treasury has the authority to treat partnership interest distributions as sales or exchanges for purposes of Code provisions other than §§ 708 and 743, but this authority has not been exercised. § 761(e)(3).

[67] See Rev. Rul. 56-397, 1956-2 CB 599, involving the reciprocal life insurance funding of a buy-sell agreement between corporate shareholders. The ruling concludes that the decedent-shareholder had no incidents of ownership in the policy held by the surviving shareholder on the decedent's life. The ruling specifically rejects the applicability of the reciprocal trust doctrine established by Lehman v. Commissioner, 109 F2d 99 (2d Cir. 1940)IRD items (cert. denied) in this context. See also Estate of C.C. Ealy, 10 TCM 431 (1951).

At least three practical problems are inherent in this simple arrangement:

1. If a large number of partners is involved, a multiplicity of policies must be issued on the life of each partner.
2. Whenever a new partner is admitted, he must acquire a policy on the life of each of the other partners, with premiums based on the other partners' ages and physical conditions at the time of the new partner's admission. The expense of acquiring insurance on older or physically unstable partners may be prohibitive, or such insurance may not be available at any price.
3. The successor of a deceased partner has no assurance that the insurance proceeds will be used for their intended purpose—namely, the purchase of the decedent's interest. For example, the proceeds may be squandered by the surviving partners or attached by their creditors.

The first two problems can be avoided if a single policy is acquired on each partner's life, with each of the other partners owning a portion of the policy and being responsible for payment of a portion of the premiums.[68] Any partner admitted to the partnership after the policies have been acquired may be assigned an undivided interest in each policy[69] and thereafter be responsible for his share of the premiums.

A more dangerous partial solution for the first two problems involves the acquisition by each partner of a policy on his *own* life, subject to an agreement with his partners that they will be responsible for premiums and will be named as beneficiaries. The difficulty with this arrangement is that the insured may be deemed to possess "incidents of ownership" with respect to the policy under § 2042(2), in which case the proceeds will be included in his estate even

---

[68] For ease of administration, there seems to be no reason why the policy could not be acquired by a nominee or trustee on behalf of the partners other than the insured partner. See Priv. Ltr. Ruls. 9328010, 9328012 (Apr. 16, 1993) (approving ownership of policies by trusts, shifting of "unmatured" trust interests upon deaths of partners).

[69] Notwithstanding the general rule regarding the taxation of the proceeds from insurance policies that have been acquired for value, a partner who pays value for the assignment of an insurance policy on the life of his partner is not taxable on the receipt of the proceeds upon the death of the insured. § 101(a)(2)(B). The enactment of the commercial transaction limitation relating to "reportable policy sales" in 2017 should not adversely affect this conclusion. See § 101(a)(3); HR Rep. No. 466, 115th Cong., 1st Sess. 485 (2017) (Conference Report). See Priv. Ltr. Rul. 9410039 (Dec. 14, 1993) (law partnership owns life insurance policy on nonpartner "Managing Director"; admissions/withdrawals of partners not § 101(a)(2) transfers for value); Priv. Ltr. Rul. 9309021 (Dec. 3, 1992) (policies owned by two corporations; shareholders form partnership to purchase corporate-owned policies to facilitate shareholder buy-sell agreement; § 101(a)(2)(B) applicable); Priv. Ltr. Rul. 9012063 (Dec. 28, 1989) (same, preexisting partnership); Priv. Ltr. Rul. 9347016 (Aug. 24, 1993) (transfers of life insurance policies on shareholders from corporation to shareholders within § 101(a)(2)(B) exception, since all shareholders also were partners in preexisting partnership engaged in unrelated passive investments).

though they are collected by the surviving partners as beneficiaries and used by them to purchase the decedent's partnership interest. Under this analysis, both the value of the decedent's partnership interest and the amount of the insurance proceeds used to acquire that interest would be included in the decedent's gross estate. In at least two cases, however, the courts have refused to sanction such double inclusion on the ground that the decedent, by collateral contract, had surrendered all of the incidents of ownership conferred upon him by the policy.[70] Nevertheless, it is generally advisable to avoid this type of arrangement because the incidents of ownership of the policy are conferred upon the owner-partner by the policy itself and are effectively negated only if the collateral contract is both comprehensive and enforceable.[71]

Attempts to solve the third problem, ensuring that insurance proceeds are actually applied to purchase the interest of a deceased partner, may create more difficult tax problems. A common approach is to name the estate of the insured partner as the beneficiary of policies acquired by the other partners to fund the purchase of his partnership interest. The buy-sell agreement between the partners then provides that the purchase price of the insured's interest is reduced by the insurance proceeds payable to his estate. Two questions arise with regard to these arrangements: (1) whether the value of the decedent's gross estate should include *both* the insurance proceeds under § 2042(1) and the value of the partnership interest to be purchased with such proceeds and (2) whether the basis of the surviving partners in the partnership interest acquired from the decedent includes the insurance proceeds payable to the decedent's estate.

The courts generally have avoided double inclusion in the decedent's gross estate by holding that the insurance proceeds are includible in the decedent's estate under § 2042(1), but that the estate tax value of the decedent's partnership interest is reduced by the insurance proceeds to the extent that they reduce the purchase price of the decedent's interest as fixed in a binding buy-sell agreement.[72] A better rationale, adopted by the Tax Court in *Victor G. Mushro*,[73] is to recognize that the arrangement is nothing more than a security

---

[70] See First Nat'l Bank v. United States, 358 F2d 625 (5th Cir. 1966); Estate of Bert L. Fuchs, 47 TC 199 (1966) (acq.).

[71] In Estate of Howard F. Infante, 29 TCM 903 (1970), the Service argued that a decedent-partner possessed incidents of ownership within the meaning of § 2042(2) because he had the right by contract to veto the exercise by his partner of incidents of ownership conferred on the partner by the insurance policy. The court held that the right to veto the exercise of incidents of ownership was not, in itself, a sufficient incident of ownership to bring § 2042(2) into effect.

[72] See, e.g., Estate of Ray E. Tompkins, 13 TC 1054 (1949) (acq.); Estate of John T.H. Mitchell, 37 BTA 1 (1938) (acq.); M.W. Dobrzensky, 34 BTA 305 (1936) (nonacq.).

[73] Victor G. Mushro, 50 TC 43 (1968) (nonacq.). The Service's nonacquiescence in *Mushro* reflects its position that the transaction should have been treated as a liquidation rather than a sale of the decedent's interest and some computational issues arise from the

device to ensure that the surviving partners, who are the true beneficiaries of the policies in an economic sense, will apply the proceeds to the purchase of the decedent's interest. Under this rationale, the proceeds are treated as received by the surviving partners and applied by them to the purchase of the decedent's partnership interest.

In determining the basis of the surviving partners in the partnership interest acquired from a deceased partner pursuant to this sort of arrangement, a vintage decision by the Board of Tax Appeals, *Paul Legallet*,[74] held that the basis of the surviving partners did not include insurance proceeds paid directly to the decedent's estate even though the surviving partners paid the premiums on the insurance and the proceeds reduced the buy-sell price for the decedent's interest. The theory of *Legallet* is that, by agreeing to a reduction in the purchase price of his interest in exchange for the insurance proceeds, the decedent effectively paid the premiums for the policy of which his estate was the beneficiary. In *Mushro*, on the other hand, the Tax Court, recognizing the arrangement as a security device, held that the surviving partners' bases in the interest acquired from the decedent included the amount of the insurance proceeds, just as if the proceeds had been received by the surviving partners and paid over to the decedent's estate. The Tax Court in *Mushro* distinguished *Legallet* on the ground that the arrangement in *Legallet* was not intended as a security device, but rather as an arrangement to allow the wife of the deceased partner to receive an annuity for life. Regardless of the validity of this distinction, it seems clear that *Mushro* goes a long way toward ensuring that the surviving partners' bases include the amount of insurance proceeds applied to reduce the purchase price of a deceased partner's interest.

[2] Redemption Agreements

Questions as to the possible double inclusion of insurance proceeds in the estate of a deceased partner are also raised by arrangements under which the partnership itself owns insurance on the lives of partners, with a view to using the proceeds to fund an obligation to liquidate the interests of deceased partners. The key question here is whether, for purposes of applying § 2042(2), the partnership is treated as an entity or as an aggregate. Under the aggregate theory, each partner would be treated as possessing incidents of ownership

---

Tax Court's failure to take into account the surviving partners' disproportionate interests. AOD, 1970-2 CB xxii (Aug. 21, 1970). In different contexts, at least two Tax Court memorandum opinions have followed the *Mushro* approach of examining the intent of the parties and the substance of the transaction in determining whether a transaction is a sale or a security arrangement. Dorothy Vickers, 36 TCM 391 (1977); Commercial Capital Corp., 27 TCM 897, 939 (1968).

[74] Paul Legallet, 41 BTA 294 (1940).

with respect to a policy on his life "in conjunction with" his partners, and the proceeds would be includible in his estate under § 2042(2). Additionally, the value of a decedent-partner's interest in other partnership assets would be includible in his estate, even though his interest in these assets would be acquired by the partnership using the insurance proceeds.

Under an entity theory, on the other hand, no incidents of ownership of partnership-owned life insurance should be attributable to any partner if the proceeds are payable to the partnership,[75] even though the partnership applies the proceeds to the redemption price of a deceased partner's interest. However, the portion of the proceeds attributable to the decedent's partnership interest may increase the estate tax value of the interest,[76] unless a redemption agreement that is binding during the decedent's life fixes the value of the interest without regard to the proceeds.[77]

In Revenue Ruling 83-147,[78] the Service applied an aggregate approach, holding that the decedent-partner possessed incidents of ownership under § 2042(2) where the partnership owned a life insurance policy and the decedent's child was the beneficiary. However, at the same time the Service indicated, in Revenue Ruling 83-148,[79] that it will not treat a deceased partner as having incidents of ownership of a partnership-owned policy if the proceeds are paid to or for the benefit of the partnership.[80]

Even under an entity theory, a number of old cases indicate that the proceeds of partnership-owned insurance are includible in the decedent's estate under § 2042(1) if they are payable directly to the estate.[81] The full value of the decedent's partnership interest may also be included in his estate. Double inclusion can be avoided, however, if (1) the liquidation price of the interest is fixed by agreement at its date-of-death value, less the amount of insurance

---

[75] Under Regulations § 20.2042-1(c)(6), incidents of ownership of insurance policies on the life of a corporate shareholder are not attributable to the shareholder unless the shareholder is in control of the corporation and the proceeds are not payable to or for the benefit of the corporation. Cf. Prunier v. Commissioner, 248 F2d 818 (1st Cir. 1957).

[76] See Reg. § 20.2031-2(f).

[77] See Reg. § 20.2031-2(h).

[78] Rev. Rul. 83-147, 1983-2 CB 158. See Priv. Ltr. Rul. 9623024 (Mar. 6, 1996) (partners had no incidents of ownership in insurance policies; partnership was owner and beneficiary; policies not pledged to or for benefit of partners or their estates; proportionate share of policy proceeds includible in deceased partner's estate); Priv. Ltr. Rul. 200111038 (Dec. 15, 2000) (limited partners have no incidents of ownership over partnership-owned policies on their lives; no rights to vote or control partnership activities).

[79] Rev. Rul. 83-148, 1983-2 CB 157.

[80] See Estate of Frank H. Knipp, 25 TC 153 (1955) (acq. in result), aff'd on other issues, 244 F2d 436 (4th Cir. 1957) (cert. denied).

[81] See cases cited in note 72; cf. Reg. § 20.2042-1(c)(6).

proceeds payable directly to the estate, and (2) the price so fixed is binding for estate tax valuation purposes.[82]

A better approach, analogous to that adopted by the Tax Court in *Mushro*, is to recognize that if the proceeds of partnership-owned insurance are payable directly to the decedent's estate in reduction of the redemption price of his interest, the designation of the estate as beneficiary is merely a security device to ensure that the partnership (which is the economic owner and beneficiary) will apply the proceeds to the purchase of the decedent's interest. Under the *Mushro* approach, the proceeds are not includible in the decedent's estate under § 2042(1); instead, the decedent's partnership interest is includible in his estate at its full value, as determined by the redemption agreement, and is not reduced by the insurance proceeds. The *Mushro* approach is better for three reasons. First, it reflects business reality. Second, it permits the surviving partners to increase the bases of their partnership interests under § 705(a)(1)(B) by a proportionate amount of the insurance proceeds applied to redeem the decedent's interest.[83] (If the proceeds were directly includible in the decedent's estate under § 2042(1), the surviving partners would obtain no basis increase.[84]) Third, applying the § 2042(1) approach of the older cases may lead to unwarranted avoidance of both estate and income tax.

> **EXAMPLE 23-2:** Assume the proceeds of partnership-owned insurance are payable to someone other than the decedent's estate (e.g., the decedent's children). The proceeds would not be includible in the value of the decedent's gross estate under § 2042(1). Furthermore, if the decedent is held not to possess any incidents of ownership with respect to the insurance, the proceeds cannot be included in his gross estate under § 2042(2). Accordingly, the proceeds are not includible in the decedent's gross estate. Moreover, if the redemption price of the decedent's interest is fixed by a binding redemption agreement at its value, net of the proceeds, the interest would apparently be includible in the gross estate based on the reduced redemption price.[85] The estate, therefore, could completely escape tax on the proceeds.

The § 2042(1) approach of the pre-*Mushro* cases may also lead to the avoidance of tax on § 736(a) payments.

> **EXAMPLE 23-3:** A general partnership engaged in a service business has zero-basis accounts receivable at the time of a decedent-partner's death,

---

[82] Reg. § 20.2042-1(c)(6).

[83] Even under *Mushro*, a portion of the proceeds may be allocable to the decedent's interest unless the partnership agreement specifically provides that the proceeds are allocable entirely to the surviving partners. The survivors do not receive any basis increase with respect to proceeds allocable to the decedent's interest.

[84] See Paul Legallet, 41 BTA 294 (1940).

[85] See cases cited in note 72.

and the redemption price of the decedent-partner's interest includes an amount attributable to the value of his share of the receivables. Under § 736(a), partnership distributions for the deceased partner's interest in such receivables are taxed as ordinary income to his successor in interest. If, however, the partnership's responsibility to make such distributions is fulfilled by the direct payment of insurance proceeds to the successor, the application of the § 2042(1) approach would require that the successor's receipt of the proceeds be treated as a tax-free receipt of insurance proceeds under § 101, rather than as a taxable § 736(a) payment.

By contrast, the *Mushro* approach precludes both the estate and income tax avoidance possibilities that seem to be inherent in the § 2042(1) approach of the older cases.

¶ 23.07 VALUATION OF PARTNERSHIP INTERESTS FOR ESTATE AND GIFT TAX PURPOSES

[1] General Valuation Concepts; Discounts and Premiums

For estate and gift tax purposes, partnership interests are generally valued in the same manner as interests in other business enterprises. Accordingly, under Regulations § 20.2031-3, the fair market value of a partnership interest is the "net amount which a willing purchaser ... would pay for the interest to a willing seller, neither being under any compulsion to buy or to sell and both having reasonable knowledge of relevant facts." The factors to be taken into account in valuing partnership interests generally include the fair market value of the tangible and intangible assets (including goodwill) of the partnership business, the earning capacity of the business, and the effect of any agreements restricting the disposition of interests in the partnership.[86] Other relevant factors include the partnership's position in the industry in which it is engaged, the outlook in such industry, the competence of its continuing management, the value of nonoperating assets, including the proceeds from any insurance policies payable to or for the benefit of the partnership, the degree of control of the business represented by the interest to be valued, and the effect of any options or contracts relating to the interest.[87]

Because the asset to be valued is an interest in the partnership business and not the business itself, factors related to the interest must also be taken into account. The value of a 5 percent interest in a business is seldom the same as 5 percent of the value of the business. This fundamental difference

---

[86] Reg. § 20.2031-3.

[87] Reg. §§ 20.2031-2(f), 20.2031-2(h).

has given rise to a wide variety of recognized premiums and discounts that may be taken into account in placing a fair market value on a partnership interest: Control premiums (or lack of control discounts), minority discounts, discounts for lack of liquidity, and blockage are the most common.

Other important estate planning techniques involve the use of so-called "estate freezes" and "family limited partnerships" (FLPs) to shift future increases in the value of family-owned assets from senior family members to more junior family members while preserving the senior members' operational control over the assets. Widespread use of these techniques has generated both statutory and regulatory changes as well as extensive litigation.

Application of these discounts and premiums, the "anti-freeze" legislation and regulations, and the concurrent rise in the popularity of FLPs has generated a large and constantly growing body of case law that is factually intensive, frequently ambiguous, and sometimes difficult to reconcile. The volume of reported cases bears witness to both the hostility of the Service toward the allegedly improper use of these techniques and the aggressiveness of practitioners in exploring and stretching their limits.

This flood of litigation, which shows no sign of abating as long as estate and gift taxes are part of the system, is beyond the scope of this work and is covered in great detail in a number of excellent treatises devoted to these matters.[88]

[2] Includibility of Goodwill

While the value of a decedent-partner's interest in partnership goodwill is included in his gross estate,[89] the courts have generally been reluctant to ascribe independent estate tax value to goodwill in service partnerships and have valued interests in such partnerships with reference to the value of other partnership assets.[90]

---

[88] See, e.g., J. Bogdanski, Federal Tax Valuation (Thomson Reuters/Tax & Accounting 1996); R. Stephens, G. Maxfield, S. Lind & D. Calfee, Federal Estate and Gift Taxation (Thomson Reuters/Tax & Accounting, 9th ed. 2013); H. Zaritsky, N. Lane & R. Danforth, Federal Income Taxation of Estates and Trusts (Thomson Reuters/Tax & Accounting, 3d ed. 2001); H. Zaritsky & R. Aucutt, Structuring Estate Freezes: Analysis With Forms (Thomson Reuters/Tax & Accounting, 2d ed. 1997).

[89] See, e.g., Estate of George Marshall Trammell, 18 TC 662 (1952) (acq.); Estate of Robert A. Goddall, 24 TCM 807 (1965), aff'd in part and rev'd in part, 391 F2d 775 (8th Cir. 1968); Estate of Gertrude G. Rubenstein, 10 BTA 864 (1928).

[90] See, e.g., Wilmot Eng'g Co., 65 TC 847, 861 (1976) ("ability, experience, acquaintanceship, or other personal attributes" of partners held not to constitute part of partnership goodwill); Estate of Robert R. Cannon, 21 TC 1073 (1954); Estate of Henry A. Maddock, 16 TC 324 (1951) (acq.); Estate of Leopold Kaffie, 44 BTA 843 (1941)

[3] Includibility of the Decedent's Final Profit Share

The portion of a decedent-partner's final distributive share of income that has not been withdrawn prior to his death is generally included in the estate tax value of his interest unless the decedent's right to his unwithdrawn share is conditioned upon his survival to the end of the year.[91] Predeath income withdrawn by the deceased partner prior to his death is not included in the estate tax value of the deceased partner's partnership interest.

[4] Includibility of the Value of a Future Profits Interest

Although the U.S. Supreme Court, in *Bull v. United States*,[92] held that the value of the right of a deceased partner's estate to share in future partnership income was not includible in the decedent's gross estate, it is fairly clear that the rule in *Bull* is no longer valid. The decedent, in *Bull*, had been a partner of a service partnership in which no significant capital had been invested. Subsequent to his death, the decedent's estate had a choice of either withdrawing from the partnership or continuing to share in postmortem partnership profits. The estate elected to take the post-mortem profits. The Court found the post-mortem profits to be taxable as income to the estate, but held that the value of the right to share in post-mortem profits was not includible in the decedent's gross estate.

Bull was decided prior to the enactment of the predecessor to § 691(c), which accords the recipient of IRD a deduction for estate tax attributable to the IRD income right, and was apparently motivated by the Supreme Court's unwillingness to subject the income to both estate and income taxes. With the enactment of the predecessor to § 691(c), Congress provided a method of mitigating double taxation on IRD, and subsequent decisions have distinguished *Bull* virtually out of existence.[93]

While it is now well settled that the estate tax value of a partnership interest is determined by reference to its claim on future profits, as well as its claim on the liquidating value of partnership assets and other factors,[94] there

---

(nonacq.); Estate of Arthur J. Brandt, 8 TCM 820 (1949). But cf. Bateman v. United States, 490 F2d 549 (9th Cir. 1973).

[91] See Estate of Frank H. Knipp, 25 TC 153 (1955) (nonacq.), aff'd, 244 F2d 436 (4th Cir. 1957).

[92] Bull v. United States, 295 US 247 (1935).

[93] See Estate of Riegelman v. Commissioner, 253 F2d 315 (2d Cir. 1958); McClennen v. Commissioner, 131 F2d 165 (1st Cir. 1942); Estate of Arthur H. Hull, 38 TC 512 (1962) (acq.), rev'd on other grounds, 325 F2d 367 (3d Cir. 1963); Winkle v. United States, 160 F. Supp. 348 (WD Pa. 1958); cf. Rev. Rul. 66-20, 1966-1 CB 214.

[94] See, e.g., Henry J. Knott, 55 TCM 424 (1988).

are a few peculiarities about valuing a deceased partner's interest in future profits that should be borne in mind. First, as discussed in the following section, a variety of special rules applicable to the basis of partnership assets and allocations of partnership income may cause the apparent value of an interest in partnership profits to be overstated or understated. Second, most partners do not receive salaries or § 707(c) guaranteed payments for their services, while most shareholders who perform services for their corporations receive separately stated and paid compensation for their services. Thus, when the net profits of a closely held corporation are computed for purposes of determining value, they are reduced by salaries that must be paid if the corporation is to continue in business. Similarly, in determining the value of future partnership profits, it seems appropriate to reduce projected future profits by that portion of such profits that are likely to be needed to compensate the partners or others for future services. Otherwise, future partnership profits will be overstated when compared to the profits of a similar enterprise conducted in corporate form, and partnership interests will be similarly overvalued.

[5] Effect of Income Tax Factors

Peculiarities relating to the computation of the basis of partnership assets may affect the value of a partnership interest.[95] If the value of partnership assets exceeds the partnership's basis therein, one of the key income tax factors in valuing an interest in the partnership may be whether there is in effect a § 754 election to adjust the basis of partnership assets under § 743(b). If such an election is in effect, the bases of partnership assets are adjusted upon the death of a partner to reflect the estate tax value of the decedent's interest and on any subsequent sale of the interest, thereby giving heirs and purchasers a basis in their shares of partnership assets that approximates a "cost" basis. Failure to adjust the basis of partnership assets under these circumstances is likely to increase the distributive share of taxable income allocated to the interest *without* increasing the distributive share of economic income (for example, by decreasing the share of depreciation deductions), and hence *decrease* the amount a "willing purchaser" would pay for the interest.[96] Similar consideration should be given to other provisions of the partnership agreement that affect the tax

---

[95] For a discussion of the valuation of tax shelter limited partnerships, see Paley, "Post-Mortem Planning for Tax Shelter Interest Aided by Use of Revocable Trust," 44 J. Tax'n 278, 278–279 (1976).

[96] See Reg. § 20.2031-3; cf. Obermer v. United States, 238 F. Supp. 29 (D. Haw. 1964); Mary A.B. DuPont Laird, 38 BTA 926 (1938) (nonacq.). But cf. G.R. Robinson, 69 TC 222 (1977) (value of installment obligation held by estate *not* discounted by potential income tax liability on sale or collection); Estate of Frank A. Cruikshank, 9 TC 162 (1947).

benefits or burdens of a potential transferee, including special allocations of losses or deduction items as well as allocations with respect to contributed property under § 704(c).

[6] Special Valuation of Partnership Farm Property and Closely Held Business Property: Section 2032A

Normally, property held by a decedent is valued for estate tax purposes at its fair market value, that is, the price a willing buyer would pay to a willing seller, neither being under any compulsion to buy or sell and both having reasonable knowledge of relevant facts.[97] In determining fair market value, it is presumed that the property would be sold for a price based on the "highest and best use" to which the property could be put, regardless of the actual use of the property by the seller at the time of the sale.

Real property used as a family farm or in a family business is often not put to its highest and best use. For example, the highest and best use of farm property may be for commercial development. When a decedent dies owning an interest in such property, highest-and-best-use valuation may impose such a substantial estate tax burden that the heirs are compelled to sell the land in order to pay estate taxes. To mitigate this problem, Congress adopted § 2032A, which permits certain real property to be valued with regard to its current use, rather than its highest and best use, where it is used *both before and after* a decedent's death in a family farming or business operation. However, the aggregate decrease in the estate tax value of such real property under § 2032A cannot exceed $750,000 for decedents dying after 1983.[98]

Section 2032A is a complex provision, even by Code standards. In general, under § 2032A(b)(1), real property qualifies for special-use valuation if the following requirements are satisfied:

1. Fifty percent or more of the "adjusted value of the gross estate"[99] consists of real or personal property that, on the date of the decedent's death, was being used for a "qualified use"[100] by the decedent

---

[97] See Reg. § 20.2031-1(b).

[98] § 2032A(a)(2). The $750,000 figure is adjusted for post-1997 inflation. § 2032A(a)(3). See Estate of Hoover v. Commissioner, 69 F3d 1044 (10th Cir. 1995).

[99] "Adjusted value of the gross estate" means the value of the gross estate less deductions under § 2053(a)(4) (mortgages and indebtedness on property included in gross estate). § 2032A(b)(3)(A).

[100] "Qualified use" means the devotion of property to use "(A) as a farm for farming purposes, or (B) use in a trade or business other than the trade or business of farming." § 2032A(b)(2).

or a member of the decedent's "family,"[101] and was acquired or passed from the decedent to a "qualified heir";[102]

2. At least 25 percent of the adjusted value of the gross estate consists of the "adjusted value of real property"[103] that satisfies requirement 1 above and requirement 3 below;

3. During the eight-year period ending on the date of the decedent's death, there have been periods aggregating five years or more during which such real property was owned by the decedent or family member and used for a qualified use[104] by the decedent or family member, and there was "material participation"[105] by the decedent or family member in the operation of the farm or other business; and

4. The real property is designated in an agreement described by § 2032A(d)(2).

The complexity of this provision with respect to real property held by partnerships is aggravated by the fact that the statute contains no guidelines for valuing decedents' interests in partnerships that own real property for family farming or business purposes, providing only that "[t]he Secretary shall prescribe regulations setting forth the application of this section ... in the case of an interest in a partnership ... which, with respect to the decedent, is an interest in a closely held business (within the meaning of paragraph (1) of section 6166(b))."[106] The Regulations provide as follows:

> The real property may be owned directly or may be owned indirectly through ownership of an interest in a corporation, a partnership, or a trust. Where the ownership is indirect, however, the decedent's interest in the business must, in addition to meeting the tests for qualification under section 2032A, qualify under the tests of section 6166(b)(1) as an interest in a closely-held business on the date of the decedent's death and for sufficient other time (combined with periods of direct ownership) to equal at least 5 years of the 8 year period preceding the death.[107]

---

[101] The term "member of the family" includes an individual's ancestors, spouse, lineal descendants (and their spouses), and spouse's lineal descendants (and their spouses). § 2032A(e)(2).

[102] "Qualified heir" is a member of the decedent's family who acquires property from the decedent. § 2032A(e)(1).

[103] § 2032A(b)(3)(B).

[104] "Qualified use" is not a very stringent standard. It means use as a farm for farming purposes or use in any other trade or business.

[105] "Material participation" is generally defined by cross-reference to § 1402(a)(1). § 2032A(e)(6). See Reg. § 20.2032A-3. Regulations § 20.2032A-3(f) provides special rules for defining material participation where the real property is owned by partnerships, corporations, or trusts.

[106] § 2032A(g).

[107] Reg. § 20.2032A-3(b)(1).

Thus, for a partnership interest to qualify for special-use valuation, both the requirements of § 2032A (applied on an aggregate basis) and the requirements of § 6166(b)(1) must be satisfied.

Under § 6166(b)(1)(B), a decedent's partnership interest qualifies as an "interest in a closely held business," if the partnership is carrying on a trade or business, and either

1. Twenty percent or more of the total capital interest in the partnership is included in determining the decedent's gross estate; or
2. The partnership had partners at the time of the decedent's death.[108]

The special-use valuation benefits of § 2032A may be elected if (1) the decedent-partner's interest in partnership real property would satisfy the § 2032A requirements if his interest in the property were held directly and (2) the partnership interest qualifies as an interest in a closely held business under § 6166(b)(1). The election must be made no later than the time for filing the estate tax return, with extensions.[109]

If a valid election is made, the qualifying real property is valued with respect to its current use rather than its highest and best use. If the real property is a farm, it must generally be valued under the rules set forth in § 2032A(e)(7)(A). If the property is closely held business property or farm property that is not valued under § 2032A(e)(7)(A), it is valued under rules prescribed in § 2032A(e)(8).

The tax benefit conferred by § 2032A is subject to recapture if, within ten years of the decedent's death and before the death of the qualified heir, the qualified heir (1) disposes of any interest in the qualified real property to anyone other than a member of his family or (2) ceases to use the qualified real property for a qualified use.[110] If recapture occurs, the amount recaptured is the lesser of (1) the estate tax benefit of the special-use valuation or (2) the excess of the amount realized with respect to the property over the value of the interest determined under the special-use valuation.[111] Qualified heirs are personally liable for recapture,[112] and, in addition, the property is subject to a special tax lien under § 6324B.

---

[108] See generally ¶ 23.07[7].

[109] § 2032A(d)(1).

[110] § 2032A(c)(1). "Cessation of qualified use" is defined by § 2032A(c)(6). See Priv. Ltr. Rul. 200840018 (May 13, 2008) (sale of qualified conservation easement not within § 2032A(c)(8) exception).

[111] § 2032A(c)(2).

[112] § 2032A(c)(5).

[7] Extension of Time to Pay Estate Tax: Section 6166

The Code contains the following two provisions that can extend the time for the payment of estate tax:

1. Under § 6161(a)(2), the Commissioner has the discretion, upon a showing of "reasonable cause," to extend the time for the payment of estate tax for a reasonable period, not in excess of ten years from the date that the estate tax return is due. Section 6161(a)(2) presents no unusual problems in the partnership context.

2. Section 6166 provides an elective procedure for the payment of estate tax attributable to a decedent's "interest in a closely held business" in installments, with the entire tax deferred for up to five years and thereafter payable in up to ten consecutive equal annual installments. Although no tax is due for up to five years if a valid § 6166 election is made, interest accrued on the unpaid tax liability is payable annually.[113] Under § 6601(j), interest on a portion of the tax deferred under § 6166 accrues at the rate of 4 percent per year. Interest on the balance accrues at the rates established from time to time with respect to other underpayments under § 6621.

The benefits of § 6166 may be elected with respect to an "interest in a closely held business" that is included in the gross estate of the decedent if the estate tax value of the interest exceeds 35 percent of the decedent's adjusted gross estate. The value of a closely held business to which § 6166 applies is the "closely held business amount."[114] Such value does not include the value of certain passive assets.[115]

A decedent's partnership interest qualifies as an "interest in a closely held business" under § 6166 if (1) the partnership carries on a trade or business[116] and (2) either (a) 20 percent or more of the total capital interest in the partner-

---

[113] § 6166(f)(1).

[114] § 6166(b)(5).

[115] § 6166(b)(9).

[116] § 6166(b)(1)(B); see Rev. Rul. 61-55, 1961-1 CB 713 (for purposes of § 6166A, now repealed, ownership, development, and operation of oil and gas properties is trade or business, but mere ownership of royalty interests in oil properties is not). The Service maintains that management of rental property is not a § 6166 trade or business and that § 6166 was intended to apply only to manufacturing, mercantile, or service enterprises. See Rev. Rul. 75-365, 1975-2 CB 471; Rev. Rul. 75-367, 1975-2 CB 472. However, in Private Letter Ruling 9223028 (Mar. 4, 1992), interests in two partnerships that owned and managed rental apartments were treated as interests in closely held businesses for purposes of § 6166. Because of the number of apartment units involved, the scale of management activities in these partnerships was much greater than in Revenue Ruling 75-365.

ship[117] is included in determining the decedent's gross estate[118] or (b) the partnership at the time of the decedent's death had forty-five or fewer partners.[119]

For purposes of these tests, a partnership interest that is held by a husband and wife as community property or as joint tenants, tenants by the entirety, or tenants in common is treated as owned by one partner;[120] property owned directly or indirectly by a corporation, partnership, or trust is treated as owned proportionately by or for its shareholders, partners, or beneficiaries;[121] and all stock and partnership interests held by the decedent or any member of his family (as defined by § 267(c)(4)) are treated as owned by the decedent.[122] Also, for purposes of § 6166, interests in two or more partnerships may be treated as an interest in a single closely held business if 20 percent or more of the total value of each partnership is included in the decedent's gross estate.[123]

The maximum amount of estate tax that can be deferred under § 6166 is that portion of the estate tax (less credits) that bears the same ratio to the total estate tax (less credits) as the value of the partnership interest bears to the adjusted gross estate.[124]

Section 6166(g)(1) provides that the unpaid portion of the estate tax deferred under § 6166 becomes immediately due and payable if 50 percent or more of the value of the interest in the closely held business is sold, exchanged, disposed of, or withdrawn.[125] Failure to pay an installment when due also results in acceleration.[126] Partial acceleration may occur, in certain cases, if the estate has undistributed net income.[127] Finally, § 6324A provides for a lien to secure tax deferred under § 6166. If the conditions of this lien are violated, the § 6166 deferral is terminated.[128]

---

[117] Although "capital interest" is not defined, the term probably refers to the value of partnership assets distributable to the partners upon liquidation of the partnership. See Reg. § 1.704-1(e)(1)(v). If so, a mere interest in future partnership profits does not qualify under § 6166.

[118] § 6166(b)(1)(B)(i).

[119] § 6166(b)(1)(B)(ii).

[120] § 6166(b)(2)(B).

[121] § 6166(b)(2)(C).

[122] § 6166(b)(2)(D).

[123] § 6166(c).

[124] § 6166(a)(2).

[125] In Private Letter Ruling 9222040 (Feb. 28, 1992), the distribution of a partnership's assets to its partners in liquidation, followed by the contribution of the distributed assets to separately owned S corporations, was treated as a mere change in form. Consequently, there was no acceleration of estate taxes deferred with respect to an interest in the partnership under § 6166.

[126] § 6166(g)(3).

[127] § 6166(g)(2).

[128] § 6324A(d)(5).

If a deceased partner's successor in interest receives a series of payments in liquidation of the decedent's interest under § 736, the successor is treated as a continuing partner until the interest is completely liquidated.[129] It is unclear whether the estate tax with respect to an interest that is liquidated in installments under § 736 may be deferred under § 6166. The difficulty is that § 6166(g)(1)(A) requires the acceleration of deferred estate tax where the interest with respect to which tax is deferred is withdrawn or "distributed, sold, exchanged, or otherwise disposed of." The Service may argue that the surrender of a partnership interest in exchange for the partnership's obligation to make a series of liquidating distributions constitutes an immediate "disposition" of the interest under § 6166(g)(1)(A), even though the successor in interest is considered a continuing partner for income tax purposes. Even if the execution of an agreement surrendering a partnership interest in exchange for an installment liquidation-obligation of the partnership is not an immediate disposition, deferred estate tax is nevertheless accelerated under § 6166 when one half of the liquidation payments have been received.

---

[129] Reg. § 1.736-1(a)(6).

CHAPTER **24**

Adjustments to the Bases of Partnership Assets in Connection With Transfers of Partnership Interests

¶ 24.01 OVERVIEW OF SECTION 743 RULES

[1] The General No-Adjustment Rule of Section 743(a)

Under the aggregate theory of partnership taxation, the purchaser of a partnership interest would be entitled to a cost basis for his undivided interest in partnership assets, while under the entity approach, the acquirer's basis would attach solely to his partnership interest and would not affect the basis of partnership assets. Prior to 1954, the effect of the purchase of a partnership interest on the basis of partnership assets was not covered clearly by the statute. However, a substantial body of case law had adopted the entity approach and had rejected efforts of transferee-partners to claim basis increases for partnership assets. In these cases, the courts denied relief primarily on the theory that the transferee had acquired an interest in the partnership, rather than a direct interest in partnership assets, and hence the cost-basis provisions applied to the partnership interest itself rather than to the underlying assets.[1] These cases were consistent with, and occasionally relied on,[2] the developing case law under the 1939 Code, and generally adopted an entity approach to sales of partnership interests.[3] Section 743(a) codifies the general entity approach of the pre-1954 case law as follows: "The basis of partnership property shall not be adjusted as the result of a transfer of an interest in a partnership by sale or exchange or on the death of a partner...."[4]

[2] The Basis Adjustment Rule of Section 743(b)

If the partnership makes a valid election under § 754,[5] or if the partnership has a substantial built-in loss,[6] the general entity rule of § 743(a) gives way to the aggregate approach under § 743(b). Under § 743(b), the basis of partnership

---

[1] See, e.g., Wasson v. United States, 56-2 USTC ¶ 9886 (ND Tex. 1956), aff'd on another issue, 250 F2d 826 (5th Cir. 1958) (cert. denied); Robert E. Ford, 6 TC 499 (1946) (acq.); Henry W. Healy, 18 BTA 27 (1929) (nonacq.), modified without opinion (2d Cir. 1931).

[2] See, e.g., Estate of Aaron Lowenstein, 12 TC 694 (1949), aff'd sub nom. First Nat'l Bank v. Commissioner, 183 F2d 172 (5th Cir. 1950) (cert. denied).

[3] See ¶ 17.01[1].

[4] Under the 1954 Code, the Service initially took the position that a purchaser of a partnership interest was entitled to a cost basis for his share of partnership § 751 property, even if the partnership had not made a § 754 election. See GCM 36329 (July 3, 1975). This position was reversed in GCM 38186 (Nov. 30, 1979).

[5] See infra ¶ 24.10 for a discussion of the § 754 election.

[6] See infra ¶ 24.01[4] for a discussion of the mandatory application of § 743(b) where a partnership has a substantial built-in loss.

assets is adjusted with respect to the transferee-partner only upon the transfer of a partnership interest "by sale or exchange or upon the death of a partner." The amount of the § 743(b) adjustment is equal to the difference between the transferee's initial basis for his partnership interest and his "proportionate share of the adjusted basis of the partnership property." If the transferee's basis in his partnership interest is greater than his share of the basis of partnership property, the adjustment increases the basis of partnership property with respect to the transferee. If it is less, the basis of partnership property is decreased with respect to the transferee.

After application of § 743(b), a transferee-partner's share of the basis of all partnership assets generally equals the initial basis of his partnership interest. In this respect, § 743(b) reflects the aggregate approach to partnership taxation. Overall, the transferee's basis in partnership assets is the same as it would have been had the transferee acquired a direct interest in the assets. However, the allocation of the transferee's total basis among these assets is controlled by § 755, which does not adopt a pure aggregate approach to this allocation—although it is reasonably close.[7] Accordingly, a transferee's adjusted § 743(b) basis for a specific partnership asset may not equal the basis such asset would have been accorded if the transferee had acquired a direct interest in it. Notwithstanding the possible distortions introduced by § 755 with respect to the bases of individual partnership assets, equating the overall basis adjustment to the adjustment that would arise upon the acquisition of a direct interest in partnership assets is helpful in comprehending the intricacies of § 743(b).

[3] The Impact of Section 743(b) on the Timing, Character, and Amount of Income Realized

Both the timing and character of income realized by a transferee-partner may be affected by whether he is entitled to adjust the basis of partnership assets under § 743(b). These changes generally occur if partnership assets, the bases of which would be affected by § 743(b), are subject to depreciation, amortization, or depletion, or are disposed of by the partnership in a taxable transaction during the period the transferee holds his partnership interest. If a transferee's initial basis in his partnership interest exceeds his proportionate share of the basis of partnership assets, the absence of a § 743(b) basis adjustment is apt to increase the transferee's share of partnership income. Conversely, if a transferee's initial basis in his partnership interest is less than his share of the part-

---

[7] The application of § 755 to transfers of partnership interests is discussed infra ¶ 24.04. For transfers on or after December 15, 1999, the § 755 Regulations are closer to the aggregate approach with respect to § 743(b) adjustments than the Regulations applicable to pre−December 15, 1999 transfers. Reg. § 1.755-1; see infra ¶ 24.04.

nership's basis for its assets, the absence of a § 743(b) adjustment is likely to result in a decrease in the transferee's share of partnership income.

In either case, the increase or decrease in the transferee's share of income is generally offset by an equal change in either (1) the amount of gain or loss recognized by the transferee when he ultimately disposes of his partnership interest or (2) the built-in gain or loss in partnership assets distributed to him in-kind.[8] Thus, the applicability of § 743(b) may either defer or accelerate a portion of the transferee's income from his partnership interest. The overall character of the transferee's income may also be affected if the character of the gain or loss realized upon disposition of the interest or of assets distributed in-kind differs from the character of the increase or decrease in the transferee's share of partnership income.[9]

It is less common, but nonetheless possible, for the overall amount of income realized with respect to a transferred partnership interest to be affected by a § 743(b) adjustment. Generally, distortions in the amount of income realized are a consequence of the death of a transferee (either while a partner or while holding assets distributed in-kind by the partnership), and the application of the fair-market-value-at-death basis rule of § 1014.

Estate of Dupree v. United States[10] can be used to illustrate the effect of § 743(b) on the timing, character, and amount of income with respect to a transferred partnership interest. Upon the death of his wife, Mr. Dupree inherited an interest in a limited partnership. His basis in the interest was increased to its date-of-death value under § 1014(a), but the basis of partnership assets was not increased under § 743(b) to reflect this increase, because the court found the partnership had not made a timely election under § 754. Three years later, the partnership's principal asset, a motel, was sold, and Mr. Dupree was taxed on his full share of the partnership's gain from the sale, without reduction by reason of the increase in the basis of his partnership interest upon the death of his wife. His basis in his partnership interest was increased by his share of the gain, giving him a basis in the interest that was substantially in excess of the market value of the assets subsequently distributed to him in liquidation of the partnership. Unfortunately, because a portion of these assets (the motel purchaser's promissory notes) was distributed in-kind, no loss was

---

[8] This offset occurs because the increase or decrease in the transferee's share of partnership income causes an equal increase or decrease in the basis of his partnership interest, which subsequently affects the gain or loss realized upon disposition of the interest or carries over to the basis of the distributed assets.

[9] For example, upon the transfer of an interest in a partnership that holds property subject to depreciation recapture, the transferor of the interest may be subject to ordinary income tax on his share of such recapture income under § 751, and, if § 743(b) does not apply to the transfer, the transferee may also be required to treat all or a portion of the same amount as recapture upon a subsequent disposition of his interest or the recapture property. See infra ¶ 24.07.

[10] Estate of Dupree v. United States, 391 F2d 753 (5th Cir. 1968).

allowable on the liquidating distribution under § 731(a)(2).[11] Under § 732(b), the notes were assigned a basis considerably in excess of their face amount.

If Mr. Dupree had lived to collect these notes in full, he would have realized a loss on their collection, which would have exactly offset the artificial gain he previously realized on the partnership's sale of the motel, and, therefore, his overall gain would have been equal to his economic income from the partnership. Of course, the timing of this income would have been distorted (as a consequence of the deferred realization of the artificial loss on the notes), and the character of the gains and losses realized might also have been affected. However, Mr. Dupree died shortly after the partnership was liquidated and before the notes were collected in full. Presumably, the basis of the notes was reduced to the notes' market value upon his death pursuant to the basis-at-death rules of § 1014(a), and hence the offsetting loss was never realized.

If a § 754 election had been in effect upon the death of Mrs. Dupree, Mr. Dupree's share of the partnership's basis in the motel would have been increased under § 743(b) to reflect the § 1014(a) increase in the basis of the partnership interest he inherited from Mrs. Dupree, and, therefore, his share of the gain on sale of the motel would have been reduced. As a consequence, the basis of the notes he received upon liquidation of the partnership would not have exceeded their face amount, no artificial gain or loss would have been created, and the distortion caused by Mr. Dupree's subsequent death would not have occurred.[12]

The salutary consequences of a § 754 election under facts similar to the *Dupree* case should not obscure the fact that § 754 is a double-edged sword. If the transferee's share of the basis of partnership assets exceeds his initial basis in his partnership interest, the immediate effect of a § 754 election is an overall decrease in the basis of partnership assets with respect to the transferee under § 743(b), a consequence more likely to favor the fisc than the transferee. As discussed immediately below, in ¶ 24.01[4], however, negative adjustments often must be made regardless of whether a § 754 election is in effect.

[4] Mandatory Section 743(b) Basis Adjustments

Section 743(d) provides that § 743(b) basis adjustments are mandatory if the partnership has a "substantial built-in loss" immediately after the transfer of a

---

[11] See ¶ 19.05.

[12] Another unfortunate example of a failure to make a timely § 754 election is Estate of Ernest D. Skaggs, 75 TC 191 (1980), aff'd per curiam, 672 F2d 756 (9th Cir. 1982) (cert. denied), in which the failure of a husband-wife partnership to make the election prevented a basis step-up for all of the partnership's assets upon the death of the husband under the rules applicable to community property (see infra ¶ 24.03[3]).

partnership interest. A substantial built-in loss exists if (1) the adjusted basis of partnership property exceeds its value by $250,000 (§ 743(d)(1)(A)), or (2) the transferee partner would be allocated a loss of more than $250,000 if partnership assets were sold for cash equal to their fair market value immediately after the transfer (§ 743(d)(1)(B)). Because § 743(d)(1)(A) focuses on the partnership as a whole, it can trigger mandatory application of § 743(b) even if the built-in loss associated with the transferred interest is miniscule. The addition of § 743(d)(1)(B) in 2017 creates a second, relatively narrow category of transfers that are encompassed by § 743(d), but does nothing to reduce the unfortunate breadth of § 743(d)(1)(A).[13] Despite the breadth of § 743(d)(1)(A), a partnership can have significant built-in losses and yet escape its grasp as long as the losses are offset (within $250,000) by built-in gains.[14]

Regulations proposed § 743 in 2014 would explicate the application of the $250,000 threshold in § 704(d)(1)(A) as follows: (1) in determining basis, any basis adjustments under § 743 or § 704(c)(1)(C) with regard to partners other than the transferee are disregarded[15] and (2) the fair market value of an upper-tier partnership's (UTP) interest in a lower-tier partnership (LTP) is the sum of: (a) the amount of cash the UTP would receive upon a liquidation of its interest in the LTP following an arm's-length sale of the LTP's assets to an unrelated party, satisfaction of the LTP's liabilities (other than § 1.752-7 liabilities), and payment to an unrelated person to assume the LTP's § 1.752-7 liabilities in an arm's-length, taxable transaction[16] and (b) the UTP's share of the LTP's liabilities as determined under § 752.[17]

Reporting by partnerships and transferees required to adjust the basis of property following a transfer as the result of a partnership having a substantial built-in loss would be controlled by the reporting rules in Regulations § 1.743-1(k) just as if a § 754 election were in effect.[18]

The temptation for taxpayers to avoid these rules by manipulating the makeup of partnership assets in advance of a transfer led to a broad grant of regulatory authority to carry out the purposes of the section by "aggregating

---

[13] Section 743(d)(1)(B) was added by the 2017 Tax Cuts and Jobs Act (Pub. L. No. 115-97, § 13502) (Dec. 22, 2017)), effective for transfers after 2017. The expansion created by this addition is not likely to be very significant: transactions that are picked up by § 743(d)(1)(B) that would not otherwise be picked up by § 743(d)(1)(A) will be rare and unlikely to involve inadvertent blunders by unsophisticated taxpayers. This point is brought home by an example in the legislative history suggesting the primary impact of § 743(d)(1)(B) is likely to be on transfers of interests that represent disproportionately large shares of loss assets. See HR Rep No. 466, 115th Cong., 1st Sess., "Conference Report to Accompany HR 1," at 513 (2017).

[14] See Notice 2005-32, 2005-16 IRB 895.

[15] Prop. Reg. § 1.743-1(a)(2)(ii) (2014).

[16] Prop. Reg. § 1.743-1(a)(2)(iii)(A) (2014).

[17] Prop. Reg. § 1.743-1(a)(2)(iii)(B) (2014).

[18] Prop. Reg. §§ 1.743-1(k)(1)(iii)(B), 1.743-1(k)(2)(iv) (2014).

related partnerships and disregarding property acquired by the partnership in an attempt to avoid such purposes."[19] Even though the built-in gain is allocable to the contributor under § 704(c), it nevertheless would offset the partnership's overall loss position and mechanically take § 743(d)(1)(A) (first clause) out of play.[20] The enactment of § 743(d)(1)(B) in 2017 relieves some of the pressure on the anti-abuse rules: If a transferee's potential loss is more the $250,000, § 743(d) applies. Game over.

Carveouts from the mandatory application of § 743(b) (but not § 734(b)) are provided for "electing investment partnerships" and "securitization partnerships." These are very narrow provisions.[21] Electing investment partnerships are essentially limited to securities investing and trading vehicles formed by cash contributions with a life of fifteen or fewer years.[22] The ability of transferees of interests in such partnerships to take losses is highly restricted.[23] A securitization partnership is one whose sole business activity is to issue debt-like securities serviced by a pool of financial assets that will convert to cash over a finite period.[24]

Extensive Proposed Regulations dealing with the carve out for electing investment partnerships were issued in 2014.[25] Considerably less extensive Regulations relating to securitization partnerships were part of the same package.[26]

[5] Interaction of Section 743(b) and the Consolidated Return Rules

Intercompany transactions between members of the same consolidated group are governed by Regulations § 1.1502-13, which provides that the amount and location of the members' intercompany items are determined on a separate entity basis, but that the timing, character, source, and other attributes of these

---

[19] § 743(d)(2).

[20] Proposed Regulations issued in 2014 would create a specific anti-abuse rule for built-in loss transactions, giving the Commissioner authority to recast the transaction "as appropriate." This provision would apply if, based on all the facts and circumstances, a principal purpose of a transaction is to achieve a tax result inconsistent with the purpose of the Regulations. For example, under this provision, the Commissioner could (1) aggregate property held by related partnerships to undo transfers undertaken with a principal purpose of avoiding the substantial built-in loss provision or (2) disregard contributions of appreciated property made with the same purpose. Prop. Reg. § 1.743-1(m) (2014).

[21] See Notice 2005-32, 2005-16 IRB 895.

[22] § 743(e)(6).

[23] § 743(e)(2).

[24] § 743(f).

[25] Prop. Reg. § 1.743-1(n) (2014).

[26] Prop. Reg. § 1.743-1(o) (2014).

items are determined as though the members were divisions of a single corporation.[27] The touchstone of single entity treatment in the context of the transfer
of a partnership interest giving rise to a § 743(b) adjustment is the "matching"
rule of Regulations § 1.1502-13(c), which dictates that the members' intercompany items are to be redetermined so as to produce the same effect on consolidated taxable income as if the members were divisions of a single corporation.
Under this rule, any gain or loss on the sale of a partnership interest is recognized only as the corresponding benefit or burden of the § 743(b) adjustment
is recognized.

The § 1502 Regulations illustrate the operation of this rule by positing an
intercompany sale at a gain of an interest in a partnership that owns appreciated depreciable property, all of the gain from which would be subject to recapture if sold by the partnership.[28] If the partnership has a § 754 election in
effect, the selling member takes the gain into account each year in an amount
equal to the buying member's increased depreciation deduction attributable to
the § 743(b) basis adjustment, and the character of the gain is ordinary (both
timing and character are "matched"). If the partnership sells the property subject to the § 743(b) adjustment, the selling member takes into account additional gain equal to the amount of the remaining § 743(b) adjustment enjoyed
by the buying member on the sale, and the character of the gain is determined
as if the selling and buying members were divisions of a single corporation
and the sale had been made to a third party (e.g., ordinary gain under the recapture rules and/or § 1231 gain).[29]

Chief Counsel Advice 201726012 (Mar. 28, 2017) considers the consequences of a tax-free reorganization transaction in which one member of a
consolidated group acquired partnership interests from another member. The
partnership had a § 754 election in effect, and due to historic differences between the basis of the transferred partnership interests and the share of inside
basis allocable to the transferred interests, the transferee member was entitled
to a positive § 743(b) adjustment even though the transferor member recognized no income. This Advice applies Regulations § 1.1502-13 to deny the
group the benefit of the basis step-up.

---

[27] Reg. § 1.1502-13(a)(2).

[28] Reg. § 1.1502-13(c)(7)(ii) Example (9).

[29] Chief Counsel Advice 201726012 (Mar. 28, 2017) considers the consequences of a
tax-free reorganization in which one member of a consolidated group acquires partnership
interests from another member. The partnership had a § 754 election in effect, and due to
historic differences between the basis of the transferred partnership interests and the share
of inside basis allocable to the transferred interests, the transferee member was entitled to
a positive § 743(b) adjustment even though the transferor member recognized no income.
This Chief Counsel Advice applies Regulations § 1.1502-13 to deny the group the benefit
of the basis step-up.

¶ 24.02 THE MECHANICS OF SECTION 743(b): THE "PROPORTIONATE SHARE" RULE

[1] Determining a Transferee-Partner's Proportionate Share of the Basis of Partnership Assets

In order to equalize the transferee-partner's initial basis in his partnership interest and his "proportionate share" of the basis of partnership assets,[30] the transferee's basis adjustment under § 743(b) is equal to the difference between (1) the initial basis of his partnership interest[31] and (2) his share of the adjusted basis to the partnership of the partnership's property.[32] The transferee's initial basis in his interest is determined under the generally applicable basis rules.[33] The determination of the second factor in this formula, the transferee's proportionate share of the basis of partnership assets, is a problem that is unique to the optional basis adjustment provisions.

The Regulations rely on § 704(b) capital account concepts for the computation of a partner's proportionate share of the basis of partnership assets. A transferee's share of basis equals the sum of (1) the transferee's interest in a partnership's "previously taxed capital" and (2) the transferee's share of liabilities.[34] A partner's interest in previously taxed capital is equal to the amount of cash the partner would receive if the partnership sold all of its assets for cash equal to their fair market value in a fully taxable transaction (the "hypothetical transaction") and then distributed all of its cash to its partners in complete liq-

---

[30] The stated purpose of § 743(b) is to ensure that a transferee's distributive share of income, gain, loss, deduction, or credit is the same "as though the partnership had dissolved and been reformed, with the transferee of the interest a member of the partnership." See HR Rep. No. 1337, 83d Cong., 2d Sess. 70 (1954); S. Rep. No. 1622, 83d Cong., 2d Sess. 97 (1954). The House version of § 743(b) did not limit the effect of the adjustment to the transferee-partner. This aspect of the section was changed by the Senate. Under the final section, which adopts the Senate approach, it is more accurate to view the transferee as acquiring a direct undivided interest in partnership assets.

[31] The Regulations contain references to the provisions governing the computation of a partner's initial basis for a partnership interest. See Reg. § 1.743-1(c) (referring to §§ 742 and 752, and Reg. §§ 1.752-1, 1.752-5).

[32] Reg. §§ 1.743-1(b)(1), 1.743-1(b)(2).

[33] See ¶ 16.01[2].

[34] Reg. § 1.743-1(d)(1).

uidation,[35] increased by the partner's share of any unrealized tax loss[36] and decreased by the partner's share of any unrealized tax gain.[37]

The Regulations require the partnership to take any § 743(b) adjustments into account in preparing the Schedule K-1s of transferee-partners.[38] They make clear, however, that a § 743(b) basis adjustment has no effect on the partnership's computation of any item under § 703,[39] nor does it impact the transferee's capital account.[40] The transferee's gain or loss from the sale or exchange of a partnership asset is thus equal to the transferee's share of partnership gain or loss (including remedial allocations), minus the amount of any positive adjustment (which can convert a partnership gain to a partner loss) or plus the amount of any negative adjustment (which can convert a partnership loss to a partner gain).[41] Depreciation and depletion computations are more complex, as discussed at ¶ 24.07.

The operation of these rules in a relatively simple factual context is illustrated in Example 24-1.

EXAMPLE 24-1: *A* has a one-third interest in the equal *ABC* partnership. *A* sells its interest to *T* for a $22,000 cash payment. *ABC* has a § 754 election in effect. *ABC*'s balance sheet is as follows:

Assets		
	Adjusted Basis	*Fair Market Value*
Cash	$ 5,000	$ 5,000
Accounts Receivable	10,000	10,000
Inventory	20,000	21,000
Depreciable Assets	20,000	40,000
Total	$55,000	$76,000

Liabilities and Capital		
	Adjusted Basis	*Fair Market Value*

---

[35] Reg. §§ 1.743-1(d)(1)(i), 1.743-1(d)(2). If the partnership maintains capital accounts in compliance with the § 704(b) Regulations, this amount is equal to the partner's capital account adjusted for the hypothetical transaction.

[36] This is the amount of any tax loss (including any Reg. § 1.704-3(d) remedial allocations) that would be allocated to the partner as a result of the hypothetical transaction. Reg. § 1.743-1(d)(1)(ii).

[37] This is the amount of any tax gain (including any Reg. § 1.704-3(d) remedial allocations) that would be allocated to the partner as a result of the hypothetical transaction. Reg. § 1.743-1(d)(1)(iii).

[38] See Reg. § 1.743-1(j)(2).

[39] Reg. § 1.743-1(j)(1).

[40] Reg. § 1.743-1(j)(2).

[41] Reg. § 1.743-1(j)(3).

Liabilities	$10,000	$10,000
Capital:		
A	15,000	22,000
B	15,000	22,000
C	15,000	22,000
Total	$55,000	$76,000

T's basis in its partnership interest is $25,333 (cash paid plus one third of *ABC*'s liabilities). *T*'s interest in previously taxed capital is $15,000 ($22,000 cash *T* would receive if the partnership liquidated after the hypothetical sale of its assets less the $7,000 gain allocated to *T* from the hypothetical transaction). *T*'s share of the adjusted basis to the partnership of the partnership's property is thus $18,333 ($15,000 of previously taxed capital, plus $3,333 share of partnership liabilities). *T*'s § 743(b) adjustment is thus $7,000 (*T*'s $25,333 basis in its interest, less $18,333 share of adjusted basis to partnership of partnership property).

Mechanically, the § 743 Regulations provide that the transferee's § 743(b) adjustment with respect to each partnership asset is segregated from the partnership's "common basis" in the asset.[42] Accordingly, separate records must be maintained that reflect both the common basis and each transferee's § 743(b) basis adjustment for each partnership asset. Separate accounting is necessary for a variety of purposes, including computation of depreciation and determination of adjustments in connection with subsequent transfers or distributions.

Regulations § 1.743-1(k)(1)(i) requires the partnership to attach a statement to its tax return for the year of the transfer, setting forth the name and taxpayer identification number of the transferee, as well as the computation of the adjustment and the partnership properties to which the adjustment has been allocated. If the partnership holds oil and gas property that is depleted at the partner level under § 613A(c)(7)(D), the transferee must attach a statement to its return with the computation and allocation information.[43]

[2] Consequences of Section 704(c) Allocations and Special Allocations Under Section 704(b)

Section 704(c) requires that income, gain, loss, and deduction with respect to the property contributed in-kind to a partnership must be allocated among the partners in a manner that takes into account the difference between the basis of the property and its fair market value at the time it is contributed to the part-

---

[42] See Reg. § 1.743-1(j)(1).
[43] Reg. § 1.743-1(k)(1)(ii).

nership.[44] Section 704(c) must be taken into account in making the special basis adjustment under § 743(b).[45]

A partner's § 743(b) adjustment is computed with reference to his share of the partnership's "previously taxed capital." Any unresolved book-tax differences (including any Regulations § 1.704-3(d) remedial allocations) under § 704(c) are taken into account in making this computation.

> **EXAMPLE 24-2:** *A* contributes property with a basis of $400 and a value of $1,000 to equal partnership *ABC*. *B* and *C* each contribute $1,000 cash. The property appreciates in value to $1,300. *A* sells his interest to *D* for $1,100. *D*'s share of partnership previously taxed capital is $400, computed as his $1,100 share of hypothetical liquidation proceeds, less $600 of § 704(c) gain, less $100 share of appreciation in the property. *D*'s § 743(b) adjustment is $700.[46]

The "hypothetical transaction" approach of Regulations § 1.743-1(d) makes it clear that special allocations valid under § 704(b) are taken into account just as fully as § 704(c) allocations. For example, income or gain "chargebacks" (special allocations of income or gain designed to offset prior allocations of loss or deduction) are treated just like the § 704(c) allocation in Example 24-2;[47] if, in Example 24-2, *A* had received a special allocation of depreciation of $600 subject to an offsetting chargeback of $600, *D*'s § 743(b) adjustment would still be $700.

---

[44] See ¶ 11.08.

[45] Section 704(c)(1), as in effect before 1984, provided as a general rule that no special allocations need be made with respect to contributed property. If a partnership is subject to the pre-1984 rule in § 704(c)(1), it may be impossible to maintain equality between the bases of partnership assets and the bases of the partners in their interests, even if an election to adjust the basis of partnership assets is in effect. For example, assume *A*, *B*, and *C* contribute three properties to *ABC*, each worth $1,000, with bases of $600, $800, and $1,000 respectively. If *A* subsequently sells his interest to *D* for $1,000, *D*'s § 743(b) adjustment is $200 ($1,000, less $800, or one third of the partnership's $2,400 common basis for its assets), so that the sum of the partnership's common basis and *D*'s § 743(b) adjustment is $2,600. On the other hand, the aggregate basis of *B*, *C*, and *D* in their partnership interests is $2,800. In contrast, if § 704(c) of current law is applicable, *D*'s § 743(b) adjustment is $400 ($1,000, less $600 share of partnership previously taxed capital) and equality of basis is preserved.

[46] Reg. § 1.743-1(d)(3) Example (2). See HR Rep. No. 2543, 83d Cong., 2d Sess. 63–64 (1954). The examples in Regulations § 1.743-1(d)(3) deal with three-partner examples, rather than the two-partner examples in the report, presumably because the two-partner examples failed to take into account the termination rules in the 1954 version of § 708(b)(1)(B) (repealed by the 2017 Tax Cuts and Jobs Act. Pub, L. No. 115-97, § 13504(a) (Dec. 22, 2017).Pub. L. No. 115-97, § 13504(a) (Dec. 22, 2017).

[47] See R. Whitmire, W. Nelson, W. McKee, M. Kuller, S. Hallmark & J. Garcia, Jr., Structuring and Drafting Partnership Agreements: Including LLC Agreements ¶ 5.02[1] (Thomson Reuters/Tax & Accounting, 3d ed. 2003, 2016-2018) for a discussion of chargebacks.

Although *D*, in Example 24-2, is indifferent as to whose partnership interest he purchases if the partnership's property is not depreciable or if it is immediately sold, *D* must carefully analyze the partnership's assets and § 704(c) elections in all other cases. If the partnership is using the "traditional method" of Regulations § 1.704-3(b) to deal with the book-tax difference inherent in *A*'s contributed property, *D* generally will be better off purchasing *A*'s interest, as a consequence of the operation of the "ceiling rule" of Regulations § 1.704-3(b)(1).[48] This rule grants to *D* one third of the depreciation attributable to the property purchased with the $2,000 contributed by *B* and *C*. *D* is also entitled to all of the depreciation attributable to his $700 special basis adjustment, so he receives depreciation on $1,367 of basis even though he only paid $1,100 for *A*'s interest.[49] Conversely, a purchase of *B*'s interest carries with it one third of the depreciation on $2,000, one half of the depreciation on $400 (because of the "ceiling rule") and all of the depreciation on *D*'s $100 special basis adjustment. Thus, *D* receives depreciation on a total basis of $967, despite the fact that he paid $1,100 for *B*'s interest.[50] As discussed at ¶ 24.07, *D*'s special basis adjustment may not be depreciable under the same rules as his share of the common partnership basis.

If, in Example 24-2, the partnership uses the "traditional method with curative allocations,"[51] *D* is likely to be disadvantaged by purchasing *A*'s interest. *D*'s § 743(b) adjustment must be recovered as if it were newly purchased property.[52] The burden of the curative allocations inherent in the interest purchased from *A* is amortized over the remaining § 704(b) book life of the contributed property.[53] If this remaining book life is shorter than the recovery period for newly purchased property of the same type, *D* will suffer a timing detriment by purchasing *A*'s interest. For example, assume the property contributed by *A* in Example 24-2 is ten-year recovery property that has a remaining five-year § 704(b) book life at the time of *A*'s contribution. *B* and *C* are each allocated $67 per year of § 704(b) book depreciation ($1,000/5 years/3), but only $40 of tax depreciation ($400/5 years/2). *ABC* makes a curative allocation of $54 of gross income per year to *A* to make up the shortfall to *B* and *C* ($27 each times 2). If *D* buys *A*'s interest immediately before the property

---

[48] See generally ¶ 11.04[2].

[49] *D* inherits *A*'s § 704(c) account of $600. Reg. § 1.704-3(a)(7). Thus, while the partnership has a total of $2,400 of common basis, § 704(c) continues to operate to cause the consequences of this common basis to be shared disproportionately by the partners despite the transfer of partnership interests.

[50] This phenomenon is explored in some detail in Marich & McKee, "Sections 704(c) and 743(b): The Shortcomings of Existing Regulations and the Problems of Publicly Traded Partnerships," 41 Tax L. Rev. 627, 655–668 (1986).

[51] See Reg. § 1.704-3(c); ¶ 11.04[3][c].

[52] Reg. § 1.743-1(j)(4)(i)(B)(1).

[53] See Reg. § 1.704-3(c)(1); ¶ 11.04[3][c].

appreciates, he recovers his $600 § 743(b) adjustment over ten years, at the rate of $60 per year. For five years, he has $67 per year of book depreciation ($1,000/5 years/3) not matched by tax depreciation ($333 shortfall), plus $54 per year ($267 total) of curative income (a detriment of $120 per year, or $600 total). The $600 of gain in A's contributed property is thus taxed to D over five years, while D recovers his $600 § 743(b) adjustment over ten years.

This distortion is not present if ABC, in Example 24-2, uses remedial allocations.[54] In this circumstance, D recovers his § 743(b) adjustment over the period he is burdened with remedial income allocations.[55] D should therefore be indifferent as to which interest he purchases.

If, in Example 24-2, the partnership owns property that would be subject to § 197 but for the fact that the property fails § 197's effective date provisions,[56] A's interest is more attractive, unless the partnership uses the remedial method with respect to the § 197 property. Section 197(f)(9)(E) provides that a post-effective date purchaser of a partnership interest is generally entitled to amortize any § 743(b) adjustment allocable to the otherwise nonamortizable intangibles. If A's contributed property is a § 197 intangible that fails to qualify under the effective date provisions, A's purchaser will qualify for amortization of his § 743(b) adjustment under § 197(f)(9)(E). Because the partnership's common basis does not qualify for § 197 treatment, however, it is not amortizable. The § 197 Regulations provide that a partnership may make remedial allocations of amortization deductions with respect to a contributed intangible as long as the partners enjoying the remedial allocations are not related to the contributor.[57] Absent the benefit of remedial allocations, B, C, and their purchasers are disadvantaged.

---

[54] See Reg. § 1.704-3(d); ¶ 11.04[3][d].

[55] Reg. § 1.743-1(j)(4)(i)(B)(2). ABC's election to use remedial allocations at the outset came at a price to B and C, however, because it lengthened the period over which they received depreciation deductions with respect to A's contributed property (which, of course, yielded an equal benefit to A).

[56] See Reg. § 1.197-2(d)(1); Temp. Reg. § 1.197-1T.

[57] Reg. §§ 1.197-1(g)(4)(ii), 1.197-2(h)(12)(vii)(B). Remedials are also precluded if, as a part of a series of transactions including the contribution, the contributing partner or a related person (other than the partnership) becomes (or remains) a direct user of the intangible. Id.

¶ 24.03 TRANSFERS COVERED BY SECTION 743(b)

[1] Statutory Limitations on Types of Transfers

Section 743(b) is applicable only to transfers of partnership interests between partners. It does not apply to the acquisition of a partnership interest upon a contribution of money or property to the partnership.[58] Moreover, § 743(b) does not apply to all transfers of partnership interests: It is limited to transfers "by sale or exchange or on the death of a partner."[59] Although the legislative history of the provision does not make clear the purpose of this limitation, the major effect seems to be the exclusion of transfers by inter vivos gift.[60] Most other transfers, including any distribution of a partnership interest by a corporation or partnership,[61] will come within the broad ambit of the phrase "sale or exchange."[62]

---

[58] See Reg. § 1.743-1(a). Similarly, it does not apply when a partnership interest is "transferred' upon its redemption by the partnership. That is the province of § 734(b), discussed in Chapter 25.

[59] See Rev. Rul. 79-84, 1979-1 CB 223 (death of grantor triggers § 743(b) with respect to partnership interest held by grantor trust).

[60] Final revision of § 743(b) by the Conference Committee in 1954 resulted in computation of the adjustment with respect to the differences between the transferee's initial basis in his partnership interest and his share of the partnership's asset basis. As originally proposed, the adjustment under § 743(b) would have been the difference between the transferee's and transferor's bases in the partnership interest itself. This change in computing the amount of the adjustment puts additional (and apparently unintended) pressure on the definition of the types of transfers subject to the section. For example, if the adjustment were computed with reference to the difference between the transferor's and transferee's basis for the interest, it would be immaterial whether exchanges under § 351 or similar carryover basis sections are within § 743(b), since the transferee's basis in the partnership interest is generally the same as the transferor's under these sections. However, under the adjustment formula in the final version of § 743(b), where this type of exchange triggers a § 743(b) adjustment, the exchange may serve as a vehicle for a partner who acquired his interest in a transaction with respect to which a valid § 754 election was not in effect to rectify discrepancies between his basis for his interest and his share of the basis of partnership assets. This might be accomplished, for example, by a conveyance of the interest from an individual partner to his wholly owned corporation in exchange for stock in a § 351 transaction. See ¶ 16.07.

[61] See § 761(e); HR Rep. No. 801, 98th Cong., 2d Sess. 863–865 (1984). The legislative history of § 761(e) does not mention distributions by estates and trusts. Hence, the treatment of such distributions remains unclear. Part gift/part sale transfers of partnership interests should result in a pro rata adjustment with respect to the sale portion of the transaction. See also CCA 201726012 (Mar. 28, 2017). See generally ¶¶ 16.05, 16.07.

[62] Compare § 1001.

[2] Status of the Transferee as a Partner

The statutory language of § 743(b) is arguably inconsistent in the use of the phrases "transfer of an interest in a partnership" and "transferee partner." The former suggests that the status of the transferor and transferee as partners is not significant, while the latter can be construed to require that the transferee must be a "partner" in order for § 743(b) to be applicable. Thus, there is a technical argument that a mere assignee of a partnership interest, who is not a "member" of the partnership for state law purposes, is not a "partner" and hence not entitled to the benefits (or detriments) of § 743(b).[63] The Service has ruled, however, that an unadmitted assignee of a limited partner is a partner for tax purposes.[64] Moreover, the failure of § 743 in particular, and Subchapter K in general, to distinguish partners from mere assignees, or expressly to provide separate treatment for assignees, argues strongly against making this technical distinction between a mere assignee and a partner.[65]

[3] Community Property Considerations

If a partnership interest is held as community property, the death of either spouse may affect the basis of the entire interest. The deceased spouse's community property share of the interest is accorded a basis equal to its date-of-death (or alternate valuation date) value under § 1014(a) upon its transfer to his successor. The same basis consequences follow with respect to the surviving spouse's share of the interest (even though no actual transfer of this part of the interest took place) under § 1014(b)(6), which provides that, under most circumstances, the surviving spouse's community property share of the interest "shall be considered to have been acquired from or to have passed from the decedent" for purposes of § 1014(a).[66]

---

[63] See ¶ 3.02[4][c].

[64] Rev. Rul. 77-137, 1977-1 CB 178; see ¶ 3.01[2].

[65] Cf. Evans v. Commissioner, 447 F2d 547 (7th Cir. 1971); Rev. Rul. 77-332, 1977-2 CB 484. See generally ¶ 3.02[4][c].

[66] See ¶ 23.04[1]. If the date of death is after December 31, 1976, and before November 7, 1978, the carryover basis rules of former § 1023 may be applicable on an elective basis. See § 401(d) of the Crude Oil Windfall Profit Act of 1980. Section 1023 accorded a new basis to both halves of community property held by decedents with respect to whom the election was made. Section 1023 provided that "carryover basis property" acquired from a decedent takes a carryover basis equal to its adjusted basis in the hands of the decedent, as further adjusted under § 1023. As defined in § 1023(b)(1), "carryover basis property" included "any property which is acquired from or passed from a decedent (within the meaning of section 1014(b))." The parenthetical reference to § 1014(b)) makes it clear that the surviving spouse's share of any community property is carryover basis property, the basis of which is subject to adjustment under § 1023.

The Service has ruled that § 743(b) applies to the entire partnership interest held as community property, regardless of which spouse dies first.[67] Although this result promotes the Subchapter K policy of maintaining equality between a partner's basis in his partnership interest and his share of the partnership's basis in its assets, it masks two significant technical problems. First, § 743(b) is limited to "a transfer ... upon the death of a partner." Literally, there is no state law transfer of the surviving spouse's community property share, nor does the taxing statute create an artificial transfer for this purpose.[68] Second, the statutory language limits § 743(b) to transfers upon the death of a "partner." It is not entirely clear that a spouse of a partner is also a partner under Subchapter K solely by reason of his ownership of community property rights with respect to a partnership interest.[69]

Provided that the deceased partner's partnership interest is worth more than his or her share of the tax basis of partnership assets, the Service's ruling is favorable to taxpayers, and therefore not likely to be challenged. However, if the interest is worth less,[70] this ruling may be subject to attack by aggrieved taxpayers on the technical grounds outlined previously, particularly if the decedent is the nonpartner spouse. In this situation, the stakes are a full basis step-down under the ruling, as opposed to a *no* basis step-down if the decedent is not a partner for purposes of Subchapter K.

---

[67] Rev. Rul. 79-124, 1979-1 CB 224.

[68] This aspect of § 743(b) contrasts with the artificial transfer of the surviving spouse's interest created by § 1014(b)(6) for purposes of determining the basis of community property under § 1014(a). No comparable artificial transfer is created for purposes of § 743(b).

[69] Cf. Reg. § 1.702-1(d) (husband and wife who hold partnership interest as community property and file separate returns must each report one half of their distributive share of partnership income).

[70] The likelihood that the decedent's interest may be valued at less, rather than more, than his or her share of the basis of partnership assets is increased by the availability of significant discounts for minority interests and liquidity in determining the estate tax values of partnership interests. See ¶ 23.02. Thus, a decedent's partnership interest may be valued at less than his share of the basis of partnership assets even if the partnership assets are worth more than their tax basis!

If the value of the partnership's assets is less than the aggregate basis of such assets by more than $250,000, § 743(b) adjustments are mandatory for transfers after October 22, 2004. The § 743(b) adjustments are also mandatory for transfers after 2017 where the decedent's interest would be allocated a loss of more than $250,000 if partnership assets are sold at fair market value. Accordingly, the Service's position in Revenue Ruling 79-124, 1979-1 CB 224, is potentially significant even if the partnership does not have a § 754 election in effect.

[4] Section 367 Transfers

If a partnership (whether foreign or domestic) transfers property to a foreign corporation in an exchange described in § 367(a)(1), each U.S. person that is a partner is treated as transferring his proportionate share of the transferred property.[71] If the partnership has a § 754 election in effect, the Temporary § 367 Regulations state that "solely for purposes of determining the basis of the partnership in the stock of the transferee foreign corporation," each partner who is required to recognize gain is treated as acquiring a new interest in the partnership for an amount equal to the gain recognized, thereby allowing the basis of partnership assets to be adjusted under § 743(b).[72] The apparent intent of the Temporary § 367 Regulations is to give each partner a special basis adjustment with respect to the stock of the foreign corporation in an amount equal to the gain recognized by that partner under § 367. The complex mechanics of the basis adjustment rules of §§ 743(b) and 755, however, will almost never produce this result; for example, if the partnership has other appreciated capital or § 1231 assets, a portion of the adjustment must be allocated to these other assets. It is unclear whether taxpayers are free to ignore these niceties in order to achieve the result apparently intended by the Temporary Regulations.

A similar construct applies to the transfer of a partnership interest by a U.S. person to a foreign corporation in a § 367(a)(1) exchange: The transferor partner is treated as transferring to the foreign corporation its proportionate share of the partnership's assets.[73] The transferee foreign corporation's basis in the transferred interest is increased by the gain recognized, and the partnership's basis in the property held by it is determined as though "the U.S. person ... acquired an interest in the partnership (for an amount equal to the gain recognized), permitting the partnership to make an optional adjustment to basis pursuant to sections 743 and 754."[74] The goal of the Temporary Regulations appears to be to grant the partnership a basis increase to its assets equal to the gain recognized on the transfer. It is unclear whether this increase is solely for the account of the transferee foreign corporation (as is typically the case with § 743(b) adjustments) or is intended to create partnership common basis (as the quoted language suggests). Again, it is difficult to square the mechanical rules of §§ 743(b) and 755 with the apparent goal of the Temporary Regulations. Transfers of limited partnership interests regularly traded on an established securities market are not subject to these special rules, but are treated as transfers of stock or securities.[75]

---

[71] Temp. Reg. § 1.367(a)-1T(c)(3)(i)(A) (1990).
[72] Temp. Reg. § 1.367(a)-1T(c)(3)(i)(B) (1990).
[73] Temp. Reg. § 1.367(a)-1T(c)(3)(ii)(A) (1990).
[74] Temp. Reg. § 1.367(a)-1T(c)(3)(ii)(B)(3) (1990).
[75] Temp. Reg. § 1.367(a)-1T(c)(3)(ii)(C) (1990).

¶ 24.04 ALLOCATIONS OF SECTION 743(b) ADJUSTMENTS TO PARTNERSHIP ASSETS: SECTION 755

[1] The Allocation Rules

The overall scheme for allocating basis adjustments under § 743(b) is set forth in Regulations § 1.755-1(a)(1). First, the partnership must determine the value of each of its assets under subparagraphs (a)(2) through (5) of Regulations § 1.755-1(a)(1). Second, the basis adjustment is allocated between the two classes of property described in § 755(b). Those classes consist of capital assets and § 1231(b) property (together referred to as capital gain property), and any other property of the partnership (referred to as ordinary income property). For purposes of categorizing partnership property, the § 755 Regulations specifically provide that "properties and potential gain treated as unrealized receivables under section 751(c) and the regulations thereunder shall be treated as separate assets that are ordinary income property." Finally, the portion of the basis adjustment allocated to each class is allocated among the items of property within the class.

The current § 755 allocation scheme is close to a pure aggregate approach.[76] The bases of properties (or a class of properties) that have declined in value can be decreased, even if the overall § 743(b) adjustment is an increase (or zero). Conversely, the bases of properties (or a class of properties) that have appreciated can be increased, even if the overall § 743(b) adjustment is a decrease (or zero).[77] Special rules are provided for substituted basis exchanges.

[a] General Rules of Regulations §§ 1.755-1(b)(2) Through 1.755-1(b)(4).

Under the general rules of Regulations §§ 1.755-1(b)(2) through 1.755-1(b)(4),[78] allocations are based on the amounts of income, gain, or loss (including remedial allocations under Regulations § 1.704-3(d)) that would be

---

[76] The § 755 Regulations apply to transfers of partnership interests on or after December 15, 1999.

[77] Reg. § 1.755-1(b)(1); see Reg. §§ 1.755-1(b)(2)(ii) Example (1) (decrease basis of ordinary income property, increase basis of capital gain property, and give effect to § 704(c) allocations), 1.755-1(b)(2)(ii) Example (2) (even though § 743(b) adjustment is zero, decrease basis of ordinary income property to reflect market value, and increase basis of capital gain property by a like amount).

[78] As proposed, the general rules applied in all cases. See REG-209682-94, 1998-1 CB 944. When finalized, a special rule was carved out for transferred basis exchanges (Reg. § 1.755-1(b)(5)(i), see ¶ 24.04[1][b]), with an admonition that attempts to avoid the general rules by structuring into the special rule would be closely scrutinized. TD 8847,

allocated to the transferee-partner with respect to each partnership property if all of the properties were sold for their fair market values in a fully taxable transaction (the "hypothetical transaction").[79] The portion of the basis adjustment allocated to ordinary income property is equal to the total income, gain, and loss (including remedial allocations) that would be allocated to the transferee with respect to the sale of ordinary income property in the hypothetical transaction.[80] The basis adjustment to capital gain property is equal to the total § 743(b) basis adjustment reduced by the amount allocated to ordinary income property.[81] If the basis adjustment to capital gain property turns out to be a decrease under this formula, it may not exceed "the partnership's basis (or in the case of property subject to the remedial allocation method, the transferee's share of any remedial loss under § 1.704-3(d) from the hypothetical transaction) in capital gain property."[82] The balance of any decrease is applied "to reduce the basis of ordinary income property."[83]

This approach effectively allocates any overpayment or underpayment to the basis of capital gain property, so that a transferee who overpays for a partnership interest generally will find the basis of his share of partnership capital gain property inflated by the entire amount of the overpayment, whereas a transferee who underpays generally will have the entire underpayment applied against the basis of partnership capital gain property.

Within the class of ordinary income property, the basis of each property is generally adjusted by an amount equal to the income, gain, or loss (including remedial allocations) that would be allocated to the transferee upon a sale of the property in the hypothetical transaction.[84] Within the class of capital gain property, the basis of each property is generally adjusted by (1) an amount equal to the income, gain, or loss (including remedial allocations) that would be allocated to the transferee upon a sale of the property in the hypothetical transaction, minus (2) a portion (based on the market value of a particular property compared to the aggregate market value of all capital gain properties) of the following amount:

1999-2 CB 701, 704. The reach of the special rule was subsequently extended to substituted basis exchanges on or after June 9, 2003. Reg. § 1.755-1(b)(5) (second sentence).

[79] Reg. § 1.755-1(b)(1)(ii).

[80] Reg. § 1.755-1(b)(2)(i).

[81] Reg. § 1.755-1(b)(2)(i).

[82] Reg. § 1.755-1(b)(2)(i)(B).

[83] Reg. § 1.755-1(b)(2)(i)(B).

[84] Reg. § 1.755-1(b)(3)(i)(A). The adjustment is reduced by a portion (based on the relative fair market value of a particular ordinary income property to the aggregate value of all ordinary income properties) of any basis decrease allocated to ordinary income property under Regulations § 1.755-1(b)(2)(i)(B).

The total amount of gain or loss (including any remedial allocations under § 1.704-3(d)) that would be allocated to the transferee (to the extent attributable to the acquired partnership interest) from the hypothetical sale of all items of capital gain property, minus the amount of the positive basis adjustment to all items of capital gain property or plus the amount of the negative basis adjustment to capital gain property.[85]

While the drafting of this provision is opaque to say the least, it is apparently intended to allocate overpayments and underpayments among capital gain assets in proportion to their relative fair market values.

EXAMPLE 24-3:[86] Transferee-partner T is entitled to a $35,000 basis increase under § 743(b) upon the purchase of a 50 percent partnership interest. The basis of ordinary income property is reduced by $1,250, producing a positive basis adjustment of $36,250 to be allocated between the following assets: Asset 1 (basis $25,000, value $75,000; the first $25,000 of gain is allocated to partner T under § 704(c)), and Asset 2 (basis $100,000, value $117,500; no special allocations). In the hypothetical transaction, T would be allocated $37,500 of gain with respect to Asset 1 and $8,750 with respect to Asset 2, a total of $46,250. T's basis in these assets is first increased by these amounts. The basis of T in these assets must then be reduced by the excess of $46,250 (total gain allocable to T) over $36,250 ($T$'s basis adjustment), or $10,000. This reduction is allocated in proportion to the relative fair market values of the two assets: 38.96 percent to Asset 1 ($75,000 divided by $192,500, the sum of $75,000 and $117,500) and 61.04 percent to Asset 2 ($117,500 divided by $192,500), or $3,896 to Asset 1 and $6,104 to Asset 2. The net adjustment to the basis of Asset 1 is $33,604 ($37,500 minus $3,896) and the net adjustment to the basis of Asset 2 is $2,646 ($8,750 minus $6,104).

Example 24-3 illustrates the operation of the allocation rules when the purchaser of a partnership interest underpays for the interest. While the results may appear somewhat capricious, at least the intended operation of the rule is relatively clear. If the purchaser overpays for the interest, the rules are more complex, as discussed at ¶ 24.04[3][d].

---

[85] Reg. § 1.755-1(b)(3)(ii). For transfers on or after June 9, 2003, an asset for which the transferee-partner has no interest in income, gain, losses, or deductions is not taken into account in applying this rule. Reg. §§ 1.755-1(b)(3)(iii)(A), 1.755-1(e)(2). Similarly, no basis decrease to an item of capital gain property can exceed the partnership's adjusted basis in that item (or the transferee's share of any remedial loss from a hypothetical sale of the item); any remaining decrease is allocated to other capital gain assets pro rata in proportion to their adjusted basis (as adjusted for the transfer). Reg. §§ 1.755-1(b)(3)(iii)(B), 1.755-1(e)(2).

[86] Reg. § 1.755-1(b)(3)(iv) Example (2).

As has long been the case, no part of a § 743(b) basis adjustment is allocable to items constituting income in respect of a decedent.[87]

[b] Special Rules for Substituted Basis Exchanges.

An entirely different set of rules is applicable to "substituted basis exchanges"—that is, exchanges in which the transferee's basis is determined (1) in whole or in part by reference to the transferor's basis or (2) for exchanges on or after June 9, 2003, by reference to other property held at any time by the transferee.[88]

Application of the general rules to common nonrecognition transactions, such as §§ 721 and 351 contributions, would lead to all sorts of mischief because taxpayers could take advantage of these rules to shift basis among assets at no tax cost. The § 755 Regulations appropriately provide a separate set of rules, which are similar to those applicable to § 734(b) adjustments, in order to deal with these issues.

If the amount of the § 743(b) basis adjustment triggered by a substituted basis exchange is zero (as is usually the case), no basis adjustments are made. Beyond this simple baseline case, little is totally clear. While the Treasury has issued detailed Regulations for allocations triggered by substituted basis transactions (Reg. § 1.755-1(b)(5)), it has also acknowledged that these Regulations "can result in unintended consequences," and in 2014, issued Proposed Regulations to correct the perceived shortcomings in the existing Regulations.[89] The effective date of the Proposed Regulations is January 16, 2014.[90] The authors believe it is highly likely the Proposed Regulations will eventually be finalized in substantially the form proposed. Accordingly, the balance of this discussion reflects a composite of the existing Regulations § 1.755-1(b)(5)and the retroac-

---

[87] See Reg. § 1.755-1(b)(4); infra ¶ 24.08[1].

[88] Reg. § 1.755-1(b)(5)(i). For transfers on or after December 15, 1999 and before June 9, 2003, Regulations § 1.755-1(b)(5) only applied to "transferred basis exchanges" in which the transferee's basis is determined, in whole or in part, by reference to the transferor's basis, such as under § 721 or § 351 contributions. One inappropriate consequence of this limitation was the exclusion of certain § 731(a) partnership distributions of interests in other partnerships. This was corrected by TD 9059, 68 Fed. Reg. 34,293 (June 9, 2003). See Reg. § 1.755-1(b)(5)(i) (last sentence, final clause). Prior to this correction, a distribution of an interest in a lower-tier partnership could result in a fair market value reset of the basis of the distributee's share of the lower-tier partnership's ordinary assets, while any gain or loss inherent in the distributed interest was reflected in the basis of the distributee's interest in the lower-tier partnership's capital assets.

Regulations proposed in 2014 would delete the reference to "June 9, 2003" in Regulations § 1.755-1(b)(5)(i), presumably as "dead wood."

[89] Preamble to REG-1444468-05 (Jan. 16, 2014).

[90] Prop. Reg. § 1.755-1(f)(2) (2014). Taxpayers considering gaming the existing Regulations do so at their own risk.

tive changes proposed in 2014. Major differences related to the Proposed Regulations are noted in footnotes.

The first step in the allocation process is to allocate any basis increase or decrease between the two classes of property. If there is a basis increase, it must be allocated between capital gain property and ordinary income property in proportion to, and to the extent of, the gross gain or gross income (including any remedial allocations) that would be allocated to the transferee upon the hypothetical sale of all partnership property. The balance, if any, of an increase must be allocated between the classes in proportion to the fair market value of all property in each class.

If there is a basis decrease, it must be allocated between capital gain property and ordinary income property in proportion to, and to the extent of, the gross loss (including remedial allocations) that would be allocated to the transferee upon the hypothetical sale of all partnership property. The balance, if any, of a decrease must be allocated between the classes in proportion to the transferee's shares of the bases (as adjusted pursuant to the prior sentence) of all property in each class.[91]

Within each class, increases are first allocated to properties with unrealized appreciation in proportion to the transferee's share of such unrealized appreciation until the transferee's share of the appreciation is eliminated; any remaining amount is allocated among assets in the class in proportion to their fair market values.[92]

Decreases are allocated to properties in the class with unrealized depreciation in proportion to the transferee's shares of such unrealized depreciation until they are eliminated; remaining decreases are allocated to all assets in the class (regardless of whether there is any unrealized depreciation) in proportion to the transferee's share of their remaining bases until the transferee's share of the basis of all assets in the class is reduced to zero.[93] Any remaining decrease

---

[91] Prop. Reg. § 1.755-1(b)(5)(ii) (2014). Thus, the Proposed Regulations effectively remove the requirements (built into the existing Regulations) that (1) there be an overall net gain or net income in partnership property for an increase in basis to be allocated to a particular class of property, and (2) there be an overall net loss in partnership property for a decrease in basis to be allocated to a particular class of property. See Reg. § 1.755-1(b)(5)(ii).

[92] See Prop. Reg. § 1.755-1(b)(5)(iii)(A) (2014); Regulations § 1.755-1(b)(5)(iii)(A) is similar except the allocation of any remaining amount is in proportion to the transferee's share of the "amount realized" from the hypothetical sale of each asset in the class. Technically, a partner has no share of the "amount realized" from a sale; the gross income or loss item is the gain or loss measured by first subtracting basis. See Reg. § 1.61-6(a). The Proposed Regulations correct this technical flaw and also clarify that all references to a "transferee's share" of an item is limited to the portion that is attributable to the transferred interest.

[93] See Prop. Reg. §§ 1.755-1(b)(5)(iii)(A), 1.755-1(b)(5)(iii)(B), 1.755-1(b)(5)(iii)(C) (2014); Reg. §§ 1.755-1(b)(5)(iii)(B), 1.755-1(b)(5)(iii)(C), 1.755-1(b)(5)(iii)(D).

is carried forward by the partnership and applied when the partnership subsequently acquires property of a like character to which an adjustment can be made.[94]

The general rule under § 743(b) is that a transferee's basis adjustment is determined without regard to any prior transferee's basis adjustments.[95] The Proposed Regulations will create an exception to this rule for subsequent substituted basis transfers: in these transfers, the transferee succeeds to that portion of the transferor's basis adjustment attributable to the transferred partnership interest and this adjustment is taken into account in determining the transferee's share of the adjusted basis to the partnership for purposes of Regulations §§ 1.743-1(b) and 1.755-1(b)(5).[96]

[c] Section 755 and Partnership Terminations.

Prior to 2018, the sale or exchange during a twelve-month period of 50 percent or more of the interests in partnership capital and profits triggered a partnership termination under former § 708(b)(1)(B). The terminated partnership was treated as contributing its assets to a new partnership in exchange for interests in the new partnership, and distributing those interests in liquidation of the terminated partnership. If the terminated partnership had a § 754 election in effect but the new partnership did not, Regulations § 1.743-1(h)(1) provides that a partner with a basis adjustment in the terminated partnership continues to have the same basis adjustment in the new partnership with respect to property deemed contributed by the terminated partnership, "regardless of whether the new partnership makes a 754 election."

If both the terminated partnership and the new partnership made a § 754 election, it is unclear whether the basis adjustments with respect to the new partnership arising from the § 708(b)(1)(B) termination override those carried over from the terminated partnership. In order to eliminate this conflict, the application of Regulations § 1.743-1(h)(1) should probably be limited to cases in which the new partnership does not make a § 754 election.

Basis adjustments resulting from the terminated partnership's distribution of interests in the new partnership (with a § 754 election in effect) are governed by the "(b)(5) rules." Because a taxable transfer of an interest in the terminated partnership is governed by the "(b)(2)–(b)(4) rules," purchasing

---

[94] Prop. Reg. § 1.755-1(b)(5)(iii)(D) (2014); Reg. § 1.755-1(b)(5)(iii)(B).

[95] Reg. § 1.743-1(f)(1).

[96] Prop. Reg. § 1.743-1(f)(2) (2014). This aspect of the Proposed Regulations does not have a 2014 effective date. It is effective only upon finalization of the Proposed Regulations. Prop. Reg. § 1.743-1(p) (2014). This is a "one-time" exception. If the transferee subsequently re-transfers the interest in a transfer that is not a substituted basis transfer, the general rule applies and the new transferee ignores all prior adjustments. See Prop. Reg. § 1.743-1(f)(2) Example (iii) (2014).

taxpayers could choose which set of rules they preferred: If they liked the "(b)(2)–(b)(4) rules" treatment, the terminated partnership made a § 754 election and the new one did not; if they preferred the outcome of the "(b)(5) rules," the terminated partnership did not make the election, but the new one did.

> **EXAMPLE 24-4:** *A* and *B* formed the equal *AB* partnership. *A* contributed § 1245 recapture property with a basis of $0 and a value of $50, and B contributed land with a basis of $100 and a value of $50, and a depreciable § 1231 asset with a basis of $0 and a value of $50.

[d] Transfers Before December 15, 1999

Regulations finalized in 1999 substantially revised the manner in which § 743(b) basis adjustments are allocated among partnership assets.[97] The discussion in this subsection applies to transfers occurring before December 15, 1999.

The procedure for allocating § 743(b) basis adjustments among partnership assets under § 755 is as follows:

1. Partnership assets are divided into two classes;[98] those that are either capital assets or § 1231(b) property[99] ("capital gain assets"[100]), and those that are not ("ordinary income assets").
2. The portion of the transferee's basis in his partnership interest allocable to the value of the assets in each class and the transferee's pro-

---

[97] See supra ¶ 24.04[1][a].

[98] See § 755(b); Reg. §§ 1.755-1(a)(1)(i), 1.755-1(b) (as in effect for transfers before December 14, 1999).

[99] Section 1231(b) property is depreciable or real property that is used in a trade or business and held for more than the long-term holding period, other than (1) inventory; (2) property held primarily for sale to customers in the ordinary course of business; (3) copyrights, compositions, letters, memoranda, and similar property; and (4) certain publications of the U.S. government. The term specifically includes timber, coal, and iron ore (with respect to which § 631 applies); livestock used for draft, breeding, dairy, or sporting purposes (if held for at least twelve months or, in the case of cattle or horses, at least twenty-four months); and certain unharvested crops, but excludes poultry.

[100] This nomenclature, which is not found in the statute or the Regulations, is used because gains from sales or exchanges of both types of "capital gain assets" are ordinarily treated as capital gain. The dichotomy between capital gain assets and ordinary income assets is not perfect (e.g., a portion of the gain from a "capital gain asset" may be treated as ordinary income under § 1245 or § 1250), but this defect in the terminology mirrors a defect inherent in the statute. The current Regulations under § 755 remedy this imperfection by treating potential gain treated as an unrealized receivable under § 751(c) as a separate asset that is ordinary income property. See Reg. § 1.755-1(a) (as in effect for transfers after December 19, 1999).

portionate share of the partnership's common basis for assets in each class are determined.

3. The portion of the § 743(b) adjustment allocable to each class of assets is equal to the difference between the portion of the transferee's basis for his partnership interest that is attributable to the value of assets in the class, and his share of the partnership's common basis for the assets in the class.[101] However, if one class of partnership assets has appreciated while the other has declined in value, any net positive adjustment is allocated entirely to the appreciated class, while any net negative adjustment is allocated entirely to the class that has declined in value.[102]

4. The portion of the § 743(b) adjustment allocable to a class of assets is allocated among assets in the class so as to reduce proportionately the difference between the fair market value and the adjusted basis to the partnership of each asset in the class.[103] If the § 743(b) adjustment is positive, assets in the class that have bases equal to or in excess of their market values (i.e., assets with respect to which the partnership has unrealized losses) are ignored in this allocation; this is because allocation of a portion of the basis increase to these assets would *increase* the difference between market value and basis, the opposite of the required result.[104] Conversely, if the § 743(b) adjustment is negative, assets that have bases less than their market values (i.e., assets with respect to which the partnership has unrealized gains) are excluded.[105]

The refusal of the § 755 Regulations to (1) allow downward basis adjustments with respect to assets that have declined in value if the class of which they are a part has increased in value, or (2) permit basis increases for appreciated assets in a class that has, in the aggregate, declined in value, would often lead to consequences in which a transferee-partner's total basis in each partnership asset was significantly different than the basis such partner would have had if an undivided interest in the assets of the partnership had been purchased. As discussed at ¶ 24.04[1][a], such distortions are largely eliminated by the § 755 Regulations applicable to transfers of partnership interests occurring on or after December 15, 1999.

---

[101] Reg. § 1.755-1(b)(2) (as in effect for transfers before December 14, 1999).

[102] See Reg. §§ 1.755-1(a)(1)(i), 1.755-1(b)(2), 1.755-1(c) Examples (1), (2) (as in effect for transfers before December 14, 1999).

[103] See § 755(a); Reg. § 1.755-1(a)(1) (as in effect for transfers before December 14, 1999).

[104] See Reg. § 1.755-1(a)(1)(ii) (as in effect for transfers before December 14, 1999).

[105] See Reg. § 1.755-1(a)(1)(iii) (as in effect for transfers before December 14, 1999).

[2] Types of Assets to Which Section 743(b) Adjustments Are Allocable

Section 743(b) adjustments are allocated to all types of assets that have value, regardless of whether the assets are tangible or intangible, appear on the books and records of the partnership, or have a basis for tax purposes.[106] While the most common (and troublesome) intangible asset that is taken into account under § 743(b) is partnership "goodwill" or "going concern value,"[107] other types of intangible assets are also taken into account. For example, in *G. Ralph Bartolme*,[108] the Tax Court permitted allocation of a portion of a § 743(b) increase to a partnership asset described as "unamortized prepaid interest," thereby allowing a transferee-partner to amortize the portion of the cost of his partnership interest allocable to partnership's prepaid interest. The court found that the interest prepayment was a partnership asset, the value of which had been taken into account by the transferor when he purchased his interest in the partnership.[109]

The § 755 Regulations specifically provide that the optional basis adjustment provisions are fully applicable to transfers of interests in partnerships holding "unrealized receivables"[110] and "inventory."[111] This is clearly correct. Failure to make the adjustment, and to coordinate the amount of the adjustment with the amount of ordinary income realized by the transferor under § 751(a),[112] may result in double taxation of the ordinary income attributable to § 751 assets: once to the transferor upon the sale of his interest, and a second time to the transferee upon realization of the income by the partnership (or on a subsequent resale of the transferee's interest).[113]

---

[106] See G. Ralph Bartolme, 62 TC 821, 829–831 (1974).

[107] See infra ¶ 24.04[4].

[108] G. Ralph Bartolme, 62 TC 821 (1974).

[109] G. Ralph Bartolme, 62 TC 821, 829 (1974). Bartolme's transferor apparently also deducted his share of the partnership's interest, but was allowed to escape ordinary income treatment under § 751(a) on the sale of the interest to Bartolme. Id. at 825, 826. Whether the Service might have been successful in pursuing the transferor under § 751(a) is unclear. See ¶ 17.03[2]. Prepaid interest is generally no longer deductible. § 461(g).

[110] See Reg. § 1.755-1(a).

[111] See Reg. § 1.755-1(b)(5)(iv) Example (2).

[112] See ¶ 17.02.

[113] But see Barnes v. United States, 253 F. Supp. 116 (SD Ill. 1966), in which the transferee of an interest in a medical partnership was, in effect, allowed to apply the cost of his interest to partnership assets, including unrealized receivables, for purposes of applying § 751(a) to a subsequent resale of his interest. *Barnes* should not be relied on. See generally Rudolph, "Collapsible Partnerships and Optional Basis Adjustments," 28 Tax L. Rev. 211 (1973).

[3] Valuation Problems: Partnership Goodwill

[a] Section 1060(d): Background

Section 1060(a) generally requires the value of "goodwill" or "going concern value" to be determined under the "residual method" in connection with "applicable asset acquisitions." Under the residual method, any portion of the transferee's initial basis that is in excess of the fair market value of identifiable tangible and intangible assets (other than goodwill and going concern value) must be allocated to goodwill and going concern value.[114]

Section 1060(c) defines "applicable asset acquisition" as any direct or indirect transfer of assets comprising a "trade or business" if the transferee's basis is determined wholly by reference to the consideration paid for the assets. For this purpose, a group of assets constitutes a "trade or business" if the assets comprise an active trade or business within the meaning of § 355 or are of a character such that "goodwill or going concern value could under any circumstances" attach to them.[115]

The interrelationship between § 1060 and the § 755 allocation rules is controlled by § 1060(d), which provides as follows:

> In the case of a distribution of partnership property or a transfer of an interest in a partnership—
>
> (1) the rules of [§ 1060(a)] shall apply but only for purposes of determining the value of section 197 intangibles for purposes of applying section 755, and
> (2) if section 755 applies, such distribution or transfer (as the case may be) shall be treated as an applicable asset acquisition for purposes of [§ 1060(b), relating to certain information reporting requirements].

The legislative history of this provision suggests that Congress intended § 1060 to be broadly applicable to partnership distributions and transfers for purposes of making § 755 allocations.[116] Unfortunately, there is a curious lack of parallelism between § 1060(d)(1) and § 1060(d)(2), which is not mentioned

---

[114] See Reg. §§ 1.338-6, 1.338-7, 1.1060-1(a)(1).

[115] Temp. Reg. § 1.1060-1T(b)(2). The assets of most partnerships, including partnerships engaged in the active ownership of rental real estate, constitute an active trade or business for purposes of § 355. See Reg. §§ 1.355-3(b)(2)(iv)(B), 1.355-3(c) Example (12). However, the passive ownership of stock, securities, land, or other property is not an active trade or business for this purpose (see Reg. § 1.355-3(b)(2)(iv)), and generally does not involve any "attached" goodwill or going concern value that would bring such assets within the expansive trade or business definition in Regulations § 1.1060-1(b)(2).

[116] See HR Rep. No. 795, 100th Cong., 2d Sess. 7071 (1988); S. Rep. No. 313, 99th Cong., 2d Sess. 254 (1986).

in the legislative history and which creates an element of uncertainty as to the scope of § 1060(d). Section 1060(d)(1), unlike § 1060(d)(2), does not state directly that the transfer or distribution "shall be treated as an applicable asset acquisition"; it merely states that the rules of § 1060(a) shall apply. These rules, on their face, only apply to "applicable asset acquisitions," so apparently § 1060(a) (unlike § 1060(b)) does not apply unless (1) the transferred assets constitute a trade or business and (2) the transferee's basis is determined wholly by reference to the consideration paid for the assets.[117]

With regard to transfers, the Regulations take the position that the residual method of valuing § 197 intangibles for purposes of § 755 applies to basis adjustments under §§ 743(b) and 732(d) if "the assets of the partnership constitute a trade or business (as described in § 1.1060-1(b)(2))."[118] The primary effect of this rule is to exclude from the ambit of § 1060 all transfers of interests in partnerships engaged in purely passive investment activities, which is welcome news indeed for partners in such partnerships. Curiously, however, these Regulations do not acknowledge the second requirement of the "applicable asset acquisition" definition in § 1060(c), namely, that the transferee's basis be determined by reference to the consideration paid for the assets. The Service apparently believes that transfers of partnership interests are subject to § 1060(a) regardless of whether this part of the § 1060(c) definition is satisfied; this is a seemingly inconsistent and untenable position given the concession that the trade or business requirement in § 1060(c) must be satisfied. If, contrary to these Regulations, both requirements of § 1060(c) must be satisfied in connection with transfers, then transfers at death as well as various other types of transfers (e.g., contributions to corporations under § 351, as well as distributions by corporations and partnerships) would not be subject to § 1060.

The Regulations' position is also rather tenuous with regard to § 755 allocations of § 734(b) basis adjustments. Most distributions that trigger § 734(b) adjustments would fail the "trade or business" requirement in § 1060(c) if such requirement applies to the transferee. Further, although it is difficult to define exactly how to apply the requirement that basis be determined wholly by reference to "consideration paid" in this context, it would seem highly unlikely that this requirement will ever be satisfied. Nevertheless, the Regulations on their face apply to § 734(b) basis adjustments.

The following subsection discusses Regulations § 1.755-1(a), which provides the interface between § 1060 and § 755. This Regulation provision represents a reasonable approach to the issue; despite the technical niceties discussed above, there is little doubt that it will be upheld.

---

[117] The impact of this difference seems limited to requiring § 1060(b) reporting for transfers and distributions that are not subject to § 1060(a) because the partnership is not engaged in a trade or business.

[118] Reg. § 1.755-1(a)(2).

[b] Valuing Partnership Property for Section 755 Purposes: Regulations § 1.755-1(a)

Regulations § 1.755-1(a) provides rules for allocating basis adjustments under §§ 743(b), 734(b), and 732(d) with respect to transfers of partnership interests and distributions of property from partnerships.[119] These rules require that the "residual method" be applied to value partnership intangibles only where the assets of the partnership constitute a trade or business as described by Regulations § 1.1060-1(b)(2),[120] and apply the residual method to value all of the partnership's § 197 intangibles,[121] not just goodwill and going concern value.

[i] Value of partnership property other than Section 197 intangibles.
Regulations § 1.755-1(a) provides that "the fair market value of each item of partnership property other than § 197 intangibles shall be determined on the basis of all the facts and circumstances, taking into account section 7701(g)." Under § 7701(g), the fair market value of property is treated as being "less than the amount of any nonrecourse indebtedness to which it is subject."

[ii] Value of partnership Section 197 trade-or-business intangibles.

[A] *General.* For purposes of § 755, if the assets of the partnership constitute a trade or business (as described in Regulations § 1.1060-1(b)(2)), the partnership must use the residual method to assign values to the partnership's § 197 intangibles.[122] Applying the residual method involves the following steps. First, the partnership must determine the value of its assets other than § 197 intangibles using a facts and circumstances methodology. Second, the partnership must determine "partnership gross value" under Regulations § 1.755-1(a)(4). Third, partnership gross value is then compared to the aggregate value of all partnership property other than § 197 intangibles. If partnership gross value exceeds the value of all assets other than § 197 intangibles, the excess is the "residual" value of partnership assets that must be allocated to all § 197 intangibles in order to assign a value to them under the rules of Regulations § 1.755-1(a)(5). If the gross value of partnership assets is less than

---

[119] Reg. § 1.755-1(e).

[120] Reg. § 1.755-1(a)(2).

[121] The term § 197 intangibles includes all § 197 intangibles (as defined in § 197), as well as any goodwill or going concern value that would not qualify as a § 197 intangible under § 197. Reg. § 1.755-1(a)(2).

[122] Reg. § 1.755-1(a)(2).

the aggregate individual values of non−§ 197 assets, then the value of all § 197 intangibles is deemed to be zero.[123]

[B] *Partnership gross value.* The § 755 Regulations and § 1060(d) are based generally on the assumption that differences between the aggregate value of the individual trade or business assets other than intangibles and the value of the trade or business as a going concern are attributable to the positive value of intangibles, including goodwill and going concern value.

As a conceptual matter, partnership gross value is determined by the value of the partnership as a going concern, generally without regard to the values of specific partnership assets. It is the comparison of such gross going concern value to the (supposedly) known values of specific partnership assets (other than § 197 intangibles) that determines a residual value to be allocated to such intangibles so that the sum of the parts (i.e., the aggregate value of all partnership assets, including intangibles) equals its value as a going concern. When a § 743(b) adjustment results from a taxable sale of a partnership interest, the Regulations adopt the view that partnership gross value can be inferred from the price paid for the interest. Thus, Regulations § 1.755-1(a)(4)(i)(A) provides that, for purposes of allocating a basis adjustment under § 743(b), "partnership gross value generally is equal to the amount that, if assigned to all partnership property, would result in a liquidating distribution to the partner equal to the transferee's basis in the transferred partnership interest immediately following the relevant transfer (reduced by the amount, if any, of such basis that is attributable to partnership liabilities)."

For example, suppose a partner pays $100 to purchase an interest representing a pro rata 25 percent interest in a partnership that has $150 of liabilities and none of such liabilities are allocated to the purchasing partner under § 752. Thus, the purchasing partner's initial basis is $100. If the partnership sold its assets and liquidated, the purchaser would receive a liquidating distribution of $100 only if the partnership sold assets for $550 (gross proceeds of $550, less $150 to pay liabilities, times 25 percent interest in liquidating distributions). Gross asset value, therefore, is $550.[124]

Regulations § 1.755-1(a)(4)(i)(C) provides a special rule for determining partnership gross value where § 743(b) applies as a result of the transfer of a partnership interest at death. Generally, the amount of the § 743(b) adjustment is based on the post-death basis of the interest under § 1014. While § 1014 provides for the adjustment of the basis of a decedent's property to its

_____

[123] Reg. § 1.755-1(a)(5).

[124] Note that $550 is not necessarily the "real" gross partnership value. For example, the purchaser may have paid less than 25 percent of the real gross value of the interest to account for the facts that the interest is illiquid and does not control the partnership. Thus, gross partnership value is really the gross value of the partnership to the holder of the interest at issue.

date-of-death value, § 1014 does not, however, apply to items of "income in respect of a decedent" (IRD) under § 691. As discussed at ¶ 24.08, the basis of a decedent's partnership interest is not increased under § 1014 for the decedent's share of partnership property that would be IRD if held directly by the decedent at death. To assure that gross partnership value is determined without regard to these limitations relating to IRD, Regulations § 1.755-1(a)(4)(i)(C) provides that, solely for the purpose of determining partnership gross value, the basis of a partnership interest is determined without regard to § 1014(c), and is deemed to be adjusted for that portion of the interest, if any, that is attributable to items of IRD.[125]

The relatively simple algorithm that applies to determine gross partnership value when a simple pro rata interest is acquired in a taxable transaction (or transfer at death) is problematic where "partnership gross value may vary depending on the values of particular section 197 intangibles held by the partnership" (such as where income or loss with respect to particular § 197 intangibles are allocated differently among partners). In these "special situations," Regulations § 1.755-1(a)(4)(i)(B) requires that the partnership assign value, first, among § 197 intangibles (other than goodwill and going concern value) in a reasonable manner that is consistent with the ordering rule in Regulations § 1.755-1(a)(5) and will cause the appropriate liquidating distribution to the transferee-partner. If the actual fair market value of all § 197 intangibles (other than goodwill and going concern value) is not sufficient to cause the appropriate liquidating distribution, then the fair market value of goodwill and going concern value is presumed equal to an amount that, if assigned to goodwill and going concern value, would cause the appropriate liquidating distribution.

Unlike the general rule that determines gross partnership value without regard to the value of any partnership asset, the special rule requires that all partnership assets (including § 197 intangibles other than goodwill and going concern value) be valued separately and allocated separately in order to determine gross partnership value. Nevertheless, while there is a certain dissonance between the theory of the residual method and the determination of gross partnership value by summing the separate values of individual intangible assets, the special rule does assure that the transferee-partner's share of the aggregate value of the partnership's assets is equal to an amount that correlates to the purchase price paid by the transfer for that interest.

---

[125] The interface of the IRD rules and the § 755 allocation rules is demonstrated by the example contained in Regulations § 1.755-1(b)(4)(ii). As that example shows, in order to ensure that an appropriate § 743(b) adjustment is made to partnership intangibles, it is necessary to determine the basis of a partnership interest (which in turn is used to determine partnership gross value) without regard to § 1014(c). The same rules apply if the transferee's basis was determined under former § 1022 (decedents dying in 2010). TD 9811, 82 Fed. Reg. 6235 (Jan. 19, 2017).

Regulations §§ 1.755-1(a)(4)(ii) and 1.755-1(a)(4)(iii) provide rules to determine gross partnership value where the transaction giving rise to the § 755 adjustment does not provide a reliable indicator of the value of the partnership as a going concern. Regulations § 1.755-1(a)(4)(ii) applies if a § 743(b) adjustment results from an "exchange in which the transferee's basis in the partnership interest is determined in whole or in part by reference to the transferor's basis in the interest or to the basis of other property held at any time by the transferee (substituted basis transactions)." In the case of a substituted basis transaction, partnership gross value equals the value of the entire partnership as a going concern, increased by the amount of partnership liabilities at the time of the exchange that triggered the basis adjustment. Examples of substituted basis exchanges include a contribution of a partnership interest to a corporation in a nonrecognition exchange under § 351 and a § 731 distribution of an interest in a lower-tier partnership by an upper-tier partnership.

The difference between the rule for determining partnership gross value in connection with a taxable exchange (or transfer at death) and the rule for determining partnership gross value in connection with a substituted basis exchange is that the former correlates partnership gross value to the actual value of the transferred interest at the time it is transferred, while, in the latter case, partnership gross value does not correlate to the value of the transferred interest, but simply requires that the value of the partnership as a going concern be determined. The value determined under each rule may be substantially different because the price that a willing buyer will pay for a partnership interest may be affected by external factors that are not directly related to, or dependent on, the value of the partnership as a going concern. For example, the purchase price of a partnership interest that is a minority interest or is not marketable may be discounted below its indirect claim on the partnership's value as a going concern. Such external factors are not taken into account in determining partnership gross value in a substituted basis exchange. Thus, partnership gross value with respect to a transfer of a partnership interest may vary significantly depending on how the interest is transferred.

Regulations § 1.755-1(a)(4)(iii) provides rules for determining partnership gross value in connection with § 734(b) basis adjustments resulting from partnership distributions. As is the case with § 743(b) adjustments resulting from substituted basis exchanges, the starting point for the § 743(b) distribution rules is a determination of the value of the entire partnership as a going concern immediately following the distribution causing the adjustment, increased by the amount of partnership liabilities immediately following the distribution.

[C] *Allocating residual value to assign values to specific intangibles.* Under Regulations § 1.755-1(a)(5)(i), if the aggregate value of partnership property other than § 197 intangibles is equal to or greater than partnership gross value, then all § 197 intangibles are deemed to have a value of zero for purposes of § 755. This does not mean that such intangibles have no value; rather, it means that they are treated as having no value for purposes of § 755, and, hence, their bases after application of § 755 are deemed to be zero.

If gross partnership value exceeds the aggregate value of partnership property other than § 197 intangibles, the aggregate value of the partnership's § 197 intangibles is deemed to equal such excess or residual value. If there is a residual value and multiple § 197 intangibles, Regulations § 1.755-1(a)(5)(i) requires that the residual value be allocated first among § 197 intangibles other than goodwill and going concern value. The value assigned to each § 197 intangible (other than goodwill and going concern value) is limited to its actual fair market value (determined on the basis of all the facts and circumstances) on the date of the transfer. Any remaining residual value is then allocated to goodwill and going concern value.

If the residual value is less than the sum of the actual fair market values of all of the partnership's § 197 intangibles (other than goodwill and going concern value), then the residual § 197 intangibles value is allocated among the individual § 197 intangibles (other than goodwill and going concern value) in the following order. First, the residual value is assigned to any § 197 intangibles (other than goodwill and going concern value) with built-in gain that would be treated as unrealized receivables under the flush language of § 751(c) ("flush language receivables") to the extent of their basis plus the amount of income the partnership would recognize if they were sold for their actual fair market values (determined based on all the facts and circumstances) (collectively, the "flush language receivables value"). If the value assigned to § 197 intangibles (other than goodwill and going concern value) is less than the flush language receivables value, then the assigned value is allocated among the properties giving rise to the flush language receivables in proportion to their values.

Second, any remaining residual value is allocated among the remaining portions of the § 197 intangibles (other than goodwill and going concern value) in proportion to the actual fair market values of such portions (determined based on all the facts and circumstances).

Finally, the fair market value of goodwill and going concern value is the amount, if any, by which the residual § 197 intangibles value exceeds the aggregate value of the partnership's § 197 intangibles (other than goodwill and going concern value).

[D] Examples. Regulations § 1.755-1(a)(6) contains several examples of the application of the residual approach to valuing partnership § 197 intangibles. These examples assume that the partnerships have § 754 elections in effect at the time of the transfers, and that the assets of each partnership constitute a trade or business. Except as otherwise stated, no partnership asset (other than inventory) is property described in § 751(a), and partnership liabilities are secured by all partnership assets.

Regulations § 1.755-1(a)(6) Example (1). A is the sole general partner of PRS, a limited partnership with three equal partners. If no value is attached to goodwill and going concern value, the fair market value balance sheet of *PRS* is as follows:

Inventory	$1,000,000
Building (capital asset)	2,000,000
Intangible 1	50,000
Intangible 2	50,000
Goodwill and going concern value	—
Total Assets	$3,100,000
Liability (allocated to *A*: § 752)	$1,000,000
Equity:	
A	700,000
B	700,000
C	700,000
Total Liabilities & Equity	$3,100,000

A sells his interest to *D* for $650,000, with *D* becoming solely liable for the $1,000,000 liability. *D*'s basis (excluding liabilities) is $650,000. The partnership gross value is $2,950,000 ($650,000 times 3, plus $1,000,000). This is less than the value of the tangibles, so all of the intangibles, including goodwill and going concern value, are assigned values of zero for purposes of allocating any § 743(b) adjustment. This Example concludes that the values assigned to the two intangibles are "inventory, $1,000,000; Building $2,000,000."[126]

Regulations § 1.755-1(a)(6) Example (2). Same facts as Example (1), except each of the intangibles has a $300,000 fair market value and *A* sells his interest to *D* for $1 million, with *D* becoming solely liable for the $1 million liability. *D*'s basis (excluding liabilities) is $1 million. The partnership gross value is $4 million ($1,000,000 times 3, plus $1,000,000). This is $1 million more than the value of the tangibles, so $1 million of value must be allocated among the intangibles. A portion of this amount equal to the fair market value of the intangibles other than goodwill and going concern value is assigned to Intangibles *1* and *2* ($300,000 each), and the $400,000 residual is assigned to goodwill and going concern value. The tangibles are assigned their true values. These assigned values are used to allocate any § 743(b) adjustment.

---

[126] Unfortunately, there is only $2,950,000 of gross value available for this allocation. *A* sold his interest to *D* for $50,000 less than its fair market value, indicating the partnership as a whole has value that is $150,000 less than the stated asset values on the fair market value balance sheet. By coincidence, $100,000 of this difference is resolved by treated the identified intangibles as having zero values, leaving a $50,000 difference between the computed partnership gross value of $2,950,000 and the $3,000,000 stated fair market value of the tangible assets on the balance sheet. Under Regulations § 1.755-2, the § 742(b) basis adjustment is first allocated to the inventory equal to the ordinary income that would be allocated to D on its hypothetical sale, and any remaining adjustment is allocated to the building.

Regulations § 1.755-1(a)(6) Example (3). Same facts as Example 1, except Intangible 1 is a § 751(c) unrealized receivable to the extent of $250,000 of unrealized gain, each of the intangibles has a $300,000 fair market value, and *A* sells his interest to *D* for $750,000, with *D* becoming solely liable for the $1 million liability. *D*'s basis (excluding liabilities) is $750,000. The partnership gross value is $3,250,000 ($750,000 times 3, plus $1,000,000). This is $250,000 more than the value of the tangibles, so $250,000 of value must be allocated among the intangibles. Because Intangible *1* is a § 751(c) unrealized receivable with a total value of $300,000, the entire $250,000 is allocated to Intangible *1*. Intangible *2* and the *PRS*'s goodwill and going concern are assigned values of zero. The tangibles are assigned their true values. These assigned values are used to allocate any § 743(b) adjustment.

Regulations § 1.755-1(a)(6) Example (4). Same facts as Example 1, except each of the intangibles has a $300,000 fair market value and *A* transfers his interest to *E*, his wholly owned corporation, in a § 351 transaction, with *E* becoming solely liable for the $1 million liability. This transaction generates a § 743(b) adjustment other than zero. At the time, *PRS* has a going concern value of $3 million, so partnership gross value is $4 million. This is $1 million more than the value of the tangibles, so $1 million of value must be allocated among the intangibles. A portion of this amount equal to the fair market values of the intangibles other than goodwill and going concern value is assigned to Intangibles *1* and *2* ($300,000 each), and the $400,000 residual is assigned to *PRS*'s goodwill and going concern value. The tangibles are assigned their true values. These assigned values are used to allocate the § 743(b) adjustment.

[c] The *Cornish* and *Muserlian* Decisions

Prior to the enactment of § 1060, the courts had the opportunity to consider the application of § 755 to partnerships owning intangible assets. These cases continue to be relevant because Regulations § 1.755-1(a) deals directly only with § 197 intangibles involved in a partnership trade or business.

The leading case is *United States v. Cornish*,[127] in which the price paid for a partnership interest exceeded the buyer's share of the market value of the partnership's tangible and intangible assets (other than going concern value or goodwill) by a considerable amount. The Service argued that the excess was allocable entirely to the goodwill or the going concern value of the partnership business. The Ninth Circuit rejected this approach and remanded the case with

---

[127] United States v. Cornish, 348 F2d 175 (9th Cir. 1965), rev'g and remanding 221 F. Supp. 658 (D. Or. 1963). See also Arthur G. Rudd, 79 TC 225 (1982) (acq.); James T. McKay, 27 TCM 1478 (1968).

instructions to divide the price paid by the transferee-partner into the following three categories:

1. The fair market value of tangible assets and certain identifiable intangible assets other than going concern value;
2. Going concern value; and
3. "[T]he balance, representing partnership overvaluation, which should be pro rated between the tangibles and nondepreciable intangibles."[128]

Having concluded that the buyer simply paid too much,[129] the Ninth Circuit was confronted with a much narrower technical problem in applying the § 755(a)(1) directive that the transferee's basis adjustment be allocated so as to reduce the differences between the market values and the bases of partnership assets. Specifically, as a consequence of the court's conclusion that the transferee had overpaid for his partnership interest, the basis adjustment under § 743(b) substantially exceeded the difference between the value and the basis of partnership assets. The Service argued that in no event should the adjustment cause the basis of tangible assets to exceed their value. The Ninth Circuit, however, rejected this argument, characterizing § 755(a) as "intended to establish a formula for allocating all of the increase in adjusted bases on a proportional basis, not to withhold from allocation such part of the increase which might exceed the fair market value of the class of property to which it attaches."[130] The court concluded that the adjustment should be allocated so as to preserve "the percentage of difference between the fair market value and the adjusted basis of each [class of depreciable properties]."[131]

Another pre−§ 1060 "buyer-overpayment" case is *Muserlian v. Commissioner*,[132] in which a partnership composed of the wife and children of a partner purchased a portion of his partnership interest. The entire purchase price was represented by a twelve-year note, payable interest only (at the rate of 6 percent per year) until the end of the twelfth year. The purchasers used the face amount of the note as the cost basis of their interest—a position that was not challenged by the Service under § 483. This approach produced a basis to

---

[128] United States v. Cornish, 348 F2d 175, 185−186 (9th Cir. 1965).

[129] United States v. Cornish, 348 F2d 175, 182−184 (9th Cir. 1965). The buyer's willingness to "overpay" is explainable in part by the lack of interest charged on deferred payments (the transaction occurred prior to the enactment of § 483), and in part by the apparent expectation (without contractual support) that the seller would continue to manage the business.

[130] United States v. Cornish, 348 F2d 175, 186 n.17 (9th Cir. 1965). Contra Tech. Adv. Mem. 8348001 (undated) (issue 2) (no basis increase for partnership's sole asset on death of a partner where partnership basis exceeded fair market value; basis attributable to partnership liabilities in excess of asset's value).

[131] United States v. Cornish, 348 F2d 175, 186 (9th Cir. 1965).

[132] Muserlian v. Commissioner, 932 F2d 109 (2d Cir. 1991), aff'g 58 TCM 100 (1989).

be allocated under § 743(b) that was nearly double the fair market value of the purchaser's share of the partnership's tangible assets. Refusing to adopt or reject the *Cornish* partnership overvaluation analysis, the Tax Court, in *Muserlian,* found that, as a factual matter, there were only two classes of assets reflected in the purchase price: tangible assets and nondepreciable intangibles.[133] For purposes of § 743(b), the court allocated a portion of the purchase price to the tangible assets equal to their fair market value and the balance to a "nondepreciable intangible asset in the nature of goodwill or going concern value."[134] The Second Circuit, in affirming the Tax Court, found *Cornish* inapposite because (1) the *Cornish* transaction occurred prior to the effective date of § 483 and (2) the seller in *Muserlian* did not intend to exact an overvaluation premium from his family, as evidenced by the negligible difference between the appraised value of the partnership interest and the present value of the note.[135]

These attempts to distinguish *Cornish* miss the mark, however. Manifestly, the present value of the buyer's note was significantly less than its face amount in both cases, so there was no substantial economic overpayment in either case—merely apparent overpayments created by the no-interest note in *Cornish* and the low-interest note in *Muserlian*. Although it is true that the Service could not assert § 483 in *Cornish*, because it was not yet in effect, it is also true that the Service failed to assert § 483 in *Muserlian*, so that effectively § 483 is not relevant in either case. In reality, both cases involve illusory overpayments that, in an economic sense, were offset by favorable financing terms that the tax law did not deal with effectively by creating additional interest expense. Both cases should have been decided in a consistent manner and, because they were not, the law remains unsettled for cases not covered by Regulations § 1.755-1(a).

---

[133] Muserlian v. Commissioner, 58 TCM 100, 110 (1989). The Tax Court made a factual determination that the discounted present value of the note was approximately equal to the fair market value of the partnership's tangible assets, a determination that was consistent with its conclusion that the father-seller would not deliberately inflate the value of a partnership interest that he was selling to "members of his family whom he intended to benefit." Id. at 109–110.

[134] Muserlian v. Commissioner, 58 TCM 100, 110 (1989).

[135] Muserlian v. Commissioner, 932 F2d 109, 113 (2d Cir. 1991).

¶ 24.05 DISTRIBUTIONS OF PARTNERSHIP PROPERTY SUBSEQUENT TO SECTION 743(b) BASIS ADJUSTMENTS

A distribution of partnership property with respect to which a transferee-partner has a special basis adjustment under § 743(b) may necessitate a reallocation of the special basis adjustment. The principles governing reallocations in connection with distributions are set forth in Regulations § 1.743-1(g).[136] In applying these reallocation rules, § 755 divides property into two classes: (1) capital gain property and (2) ordinary income property.[137]

If property with respect to which a partner has a special basis adjustment is distributed to other partners, the distributees do not take the adjustment into account in determining their basis in distributed property under § 732.[138] The partner entitled to the special basis adjustment with respect to the distributed property reallocates it under § 755 to remaining partnership property of the same class.[139] If the partnership owns no property in the right class or if the adjustment would reduce the basis of such property below zero, the adjustment is deferred (in whole or in part) until the partnership acquires the right kind of property.[140]

If a distribution is solely to a partner entitled to a special basis adjustment with respect to the distributed property, the distributee is entitled to add (or subtract) his special basis adjustment to (or from) the partnership's adjusted basis in the property for purposes of determining his post-distribution basis in the property under § 732.[141]

If property is distributed to partners entitled to a special basis adjustment and to other partners in the same transaction, the reallocation rules are more complex:

1. A distributee who is not entitled to a special basis adjustment does not take another's adjustment into account in determining the basis of property distributed to such distributee.

2. A distributee entitled to a special basis adjustment with respect to both property distributed to him and property distributed to other partners takes into account his entire basis adjustment with respect to the property he receives.[142] Additionally, the distributee's special basis

---

[136] Regulations § 1.743-1(g) is based on the 1954 Senate Report. See S. Rep. No. 1622, 83d Cong., 2d Sess. 400 (1954).

[137] Reg. §§ 1.755-1(a), 1.755-1(c)(1); see Reg. § 1.743-1(g).

[138] Reg. § 1.743-1(g)(2)(i).

[139] Reg. § 1.743-1(g)(2)(ii).

[140] Reg. §§ 1.743-1(g)(2)(ii), 1.755-1(c)(4).

[141] Reg. § 1.743-1(g)(1)(i).

[142] Reg. § 1.743-1(g)(1)(i).

adjustment with respect to the property distributed to other partners is reallocated among the "remaining items" of partnership property.[143] A good argument can be made that the term "remaining items" should be read to include property distributed as part of the same distribution, but the § 743 Regulations are not as clear as one might like on this point.[144]

If the distribution is in complete liquidation of the distributee's interest, he is required to reallocate any special basis adjustments in property retained by the partnership to any property of the same class distributed to him.[145] This special rule for liquidating distributions does not affect the distributee's aggregate basis in property distributed in liquidation; under § 732(b), that amount is equal to the distributee's basis in his partnership interest (less any cash distributed).

¶ 24.06 TRANSFERS OF PARTNERSHIP INTERESTS SUBSEQUENT TO SECTION 743(b) BASIS ADJUSTMENTS

If several transfers of partnership interests occur, the general rule is that each transferee's § 743(b) adjustment is determined solely with respect to his share of the partnership's common basis in its assets, without regard to any § 743(b) adjustments of the transferor or any other transferees.[146]

EXAMPLE 24-5: Equal partnership ABC has a single asset with a basis of $3,000. If C sells his partnership interest to D for $1,100 at a time when the partnership's asset has a value of $3,300, D is entitled to a $100 adjustment under § 743(b). If the asset appreciates to $3,600 and D sells his partnership interest to E for $1,200, E's § 743(b) adjustment is $200 ($1,200 less $1,000, his one-third share of the partnership's $3,000 common basis). D's special basis adjustment is ignored in computing E's adjustment. If E purchases his interest from B rather than D, E's adjustment remains $200.

---

[143] Reg. § 1.743-1(g)(2)(ii).

[144] The suggested reading is consistent with the operation of the "liquidation" rule in Regulations § 1.743-1(g)(3). Example (1) in Regulations § 1.743-1(b)(2)(ii), which disappeared when such Regulations were revised in 1999, allowed the distributee, in this type of situation, to include his entire special basis adjustment for property distributed to other partners as part of the same distribution. Although this rule was arguably overly simplistic and overly pro-taxpayer, it had the virtues of clarity and relative ease of application.

[145] Reg. § 1.743-1(g)(3).

[146] See Reg. § 1.743-1(f).

While the § 743 Regulations do not specifically provide for a pro tanto reduction of a partner's § 743(b) adjustment upon a subsequent transfer of a portion of his partnership interest, such a reduction is consistent with the purpose of § 743(b). If, in Example 24-5, *D* sold one half of his partnership interest to *E*, one half of *D*'s § 743(b) adjustment should be eliminated by the sale, and *D*'s remaining § 743(b) adjustment should be $50 (one half of the original $100). The same type of analysis should apply in computing the additional § 743(b) adjustment, if a transferee-partner subsequently acquires an additional interest in the partnership: The new adjustment should first be determined and allocated solely with respect to the new interest acquired, and then be merged with the transferee's existing § 743(b) adjustment.

For gifts of partnership interests made on or after December 15, 1999, the portion of a donor's § 743(b) adjustment that relates to a transferred interest is treated as transferred by the donor and received by the donee.[147] For donative transfers before this date, matters are less certain. The language of the statute and the then-applicable Regulations may cause a permanent loss of the purchaser's § 743(b) adjustment: The donee is clearly not entitled to an adjustment as a consequence of the gift, because he did not acquire his interest by sale, exchange, or inheritance; and, under the Regulations then in effect, the donee apparently is not entitled to inherit his donor's adjustment.[148]

Regulations proposed in 2014 would create a special rule under which transferees would succeed to their transferor's pre-existing § 743(b) basis adjustments when a subsequent transfer is a substituted basis transaction within the meaning of Regulations § 1.755-1(b)(5).[149] To the extent a transferee would be required to reduce the basis of a property pursuant to Regulations §§ 1.743-1(b)(2) and 1.755-1(b)(5), the decrease first reduces any positive § 743(b) adjustments that the transferee succeeds to.[150]

> **EXAMPLE 24-6:**[151] *A* and *B* are 60/40 partners in *LTP*. *B*'s basis in its interest is $50 and its value is $70. *LTP* has two capital assets, Asset 1 with a basis of $25 and a value of $100 and Asset 2 with a basis of $100 and a value of $75. *B* sells its *LTP* interest to *UTP* for $70. Both partnerships have § 754 elections in effect. *UTP*'s § 743(b) basis adjustments are $30 for Asset 1 and ($10) for Asset 2.

---

[147] Reg. § 1.743-1(f); Prop. Reg. § 1.743-1(f)(1) (2014).

[148] This result might be avoided, and the donee allowed to succeed to his donor's § 743(b) basis adjustment if the word "transfer" in the first sentence of Regulations § 1.743-1(b)(2)(iv) (as in effect for transfers prior to December 15, 1999) were construed as encompassing only transactions that trigger § 743(b). However, this interpretation of the Regulations seems strained.

[149] Prop. Reg. § 1.743-1(f)(2) (2014).

[150] Prop. Reg. § 1.743-1(f)(2) Example (2014).

[151] See Prop. Reg. § 1.743-1(f)(2) Example (ii) (2014).

In an unrelated transaction, *UTP* subsequently distributes its *LTP* interest to one of the *UTP* partners, *C*, who has a $40 basis in its *UTP* interest. The *LTP* values have not changed. *C*'s substituted basis in the distributed *LTP* interest is $40. *C* succeeds to *UTP*'s § 743(b) adjustment, which is taken into account in computing *C*'s share of the adjusted basis of *LTP* property. *C* would receive $70 cash on a liquidation of *LTP* and be allocated no gain or loss on the hypothetical sale (since *C* succeeded to *UTP*'s $30 and ($10) basis adjustments). Thus *C*'s $70 previously taxed capital exceeds its $40 basis, requiring a $30 negative § 743(b) adjustment. *LTP*'s only asset class is capital gain property. Taking into account the § 743(b) adjustments, *C* has no share of *LTP* unrealized depreciation, so the downward adjustment is allocated in proportion to *C*'s share of adjusted basis. Taking into account *UTP*'s § 743(b) adjustments, these are $40 for Asset 1 (40% x $25 common basis + $30 § 743(b) adjustment) and $30 for Asset 2 (40% x $100 common basis - $10 negative § 743(b) adjustment). Thus the $30 downward adjustment goes 40/70 to Asset 1 ($17.14) and 30/70 to Asset 2 ($12.86). The downward adjustment to Asset 1 first reduces *UTP*'s § 743(b) adjustment to which *C* succeeded, leaving *C* with a $10 share of common basis and a net § 743(b) adjustment of $12.86 for Asset 1 ($30 - $17.14). *C* has a $40 share of common basis and a total negative § 743(b) adjustment of $22.86 for Asset 2 ($10 plus $12.86).

The recovery periods for these adjustments is not entirely clear. Presumably, basis adjustments to which the transferee succeeds continue to be amortized according to their original schedule, and new adjustments start afresh.[152] Under the 2014 Proposed Regulations, whenever there has been a prior § 743(b) adjustment, subsequent negative adjustments generated in a substituted basis transaction would first reduce positive § 743(b) adjustments to which the transferee had previously succeeded. This can deprive the new owner of depreciation benefits if a shorter remaining life was associated with the prior positive adjustment.[153]

¶ 24.07 EFFECT OF THE SECTION 743(b) ADJUSTMENT ON DEPRECIATION, DEPLETION, AND INVESTMENT CREDIT

If the cost of partnership property to which the § 743(b) adjustment relates is being recovered under ACRS, then the adjustment is treated as if it were

---

[152] See Reg. § 1.743-1(j)(4)(i)(B).
[153] Prop. Reg. § 1.743-1(f)(2) (2014). See ¶ 24.07.

newly purchased recovery property placed in service at the time of transfer.[154] Any applicable recovery period and method may be used for a deemed newly purchased item of property.

Section 168(i) provides for 100-percent bonus depreciation for property acquired after September 27, 2017.[155] The bonus percentage phases down over a number of years and is scheduled to fully expire after 2027. Prior to the 2017 changes, only new property was eligible for § 168(k) treatment; however, used property is now eligible for the first time.[156] To reduce opportunities for taxpayers to churn used property to generate accelerated depreciation deductions, § 168(k)(2)(E)(ii) limits bonus depreciation to property that "was not used by the taxpayer at any time prior to such acquisition."

> **EXAMPLE 24-7:** Partner A contributes property X with a basis of $100 and a value of $500, and partner B contributes $500 to a 50-50 partnership.[160] At the time the partnership is formed, the remaining recovery period for property X is five years, so the $100 of tax basis is recovered over five years. The partnership elects to use the remedial allocation method for property X. If the partnership had purchased X at the time of the contribution, it would have used a ten-year recovery period; accordingly, the $400 of built-in gain at the time of contribution is amortized over a ten-year period for purposes of computing remedial allocations. The partnership's § 704(b) book depreciation for each of years one and two is $60 [($400 ÷ 10) plus ($100 ÷ 5)]. Each year, B is entitled to all of the partnership's $20 of tax depreciation and, in addition, receives a remedial expense allocation of $10. A receives a remedial income allocation each year of $10. Except for depreciation deductions, the partnership breaks even during its first two years, so that, at the end of two years, A's share of the adjusted basis of partnership property is $120 ($100, plus two $10 remedial income allocations), while B's share is $440 ($500, less two $20 depreciation deductions and less two $10 remedial expense allocations).
>
> At the end of two years, A sells his interest to C for $440. A § 754 election is in effect, so C is entitled to increase the basis of his share of partnership assets by $320 ($440 purchase price, less $120 share of "previously taxed capital"[161]). Under § 755, the entire increase is allocated to

---

[154] See W. McKee, W. Nelson & R. Whitmire, Federal Taxation of Partnerships and Partners ¶ 24.07 (Thomson Reuters/Tax & Accounting, 3d ed. 1997) if the partnership owns property that is being depreciated under the pre-1981 depreciation rules in § 167.

[155] § 168(k), as amended by the 2017 Tax Cuts and Jobs Act, Pub. L. No. 115-97, § 13021(a) (Dec. 22, 2017).

[156] § 168(k)(2)(E)(ii), as amended.

[160] This example is based on Regulations § 1.743-1(j)(4)(i)(C) Example (2).

[161] See supra ¶ 24.02.

property X. At the time of the sale, $320[162] of the original $400 of built-in gain from property X is still reflected on the partnership's books, so C's entire $320 § 754 basis increase is attributable to built-in gain and must be recovered over the remaining recovery period for the § 704(c) built-in gain (i.e., eight years).

Any § 743(b) basis decrease allocable to an item of partnership cost recovery property is "recovered" over the remaining useful life of the property by (1) reducing the transferee's share of depreciation with respect to such property, (2) then, if necessary, decreasing the transferee's share with respect to other partnership property, and (3) finally, if necessary, creating ordinary income for the transferee.[163] The amount recovered during any year is equal to the amount of the initial basis decrease allocable to an item of property multiplied by a fraction, the numerator of which is the portion of the adjusted basis of the property recovered by the partnership during such year and the denominator of which is the adjusted basis of the property on the date of transfer.[164]

EXAMPLE 24-8: Partner A contributes property Y with a basis of $100 and a value of $100, and partner B contributes $100 cash to the equal AB partnership. Y has a remaining recovery period of five years at the time of its contribution, and therefore the partnership's initial basis of $100 is recovered at the rate of $20 per year for five years. Except for depreciation, the partnership's income and expenses are equal in each of its first two years of operation. After two years, A's share of the basis of partnership property is $80 ($100, less two $10 depreciation allocations).

After two years, when the value of Y has declined to $30, A sells his interest to C for $65, its market value.[165] A § 754 election is in effect. The amount of the negative § 743(b) adjustment is $15 ($65 basis of the interest to C, less $80 of "previously taxed capital" allocable to C's interest). Assume the entire basis reduction is allocated to property Y. At the time of this sale, the remaining recovery period for property Y is three years, so $5 of the negative adjustment must be recovered annually. Accordingly, C's net share of depreciation for each of the next three years is $5 ($10 share of partnership depreciation, less $5 negative basis recovery).[166]

---

[162] Annual book depreciation is $60; thus, the book value of property X at this time is $380 ($500, less two $60 book depreciation deductions), compared to tax basis of $60 ($100, less two $20 depreciation deductions), producing a remaining book-tax difference (built-in gain) of $320. Note that these computations differ from the depreciation computations required for § 704(b) capital account purposes. See Reg. § 1.704-1(b)(2)(iv)(g)(3).

[163] Reg. § 1.743-1(j)(4)(ii).

[164] Reg. § 1.743-1(j)(4)(ii)(B).

[165] Assume the transaction occurs after the effective date of the repeal of § 708(b)(1)(B) in 2017.

[166] See Reg. § 1.743-1(j)(4)(ii)(C) Example (2).

Any § 743(b) adjustments to the basis of depletable partnership property are taken into account by the transferee-partner in separately computing its share of depletion. The other partners' depletion calculations are unaffected.[167] This may result in the partners finding that it is inefficient for all to use the same depletion method.[168]

Upon a subsequent disposition of depreciation recapture property by the partnership, a transferee-partner will not be subject to the recapture rules with respect to his predecessor's share of partnership depreciation if a § 754 election was in effect with respect to the transfer of his interest.[169] However, in the absence of a § 754 election, a transferee may effectively be subject to recapture with respect to his predecessor's share of partnership depreciation deductions. Although arguably unwarranted in view of the provisions of § 751, this result seems mandated by the Regulations.

If an adjustment is made to the basis of partnership property subject to depletion, § 743(b) provides that any depletion allowable will be determined separately for the transferee-partner with respect to his interest in such property. The apparent purpose of this rule is to prevent a transferee-partner from effectively claiming both cost depletion and percentage depletion with respect to the same production. The § 743(b) Regulations contain the following example, which is drawn from the legislative history.

> EXAMPLE 24-9: *A*, *B*, and *C* contribute $5,000 cash each to form partnership *PRS*, which purchases a coal property for $15,000. *A*, *B*, and *C* have equal interests in capital and profits. *C* subsequently sells its partnership interest to *T* for $100,000 when *PRS* has a § 754 election in effect. *T* has a basis adjustment under § 743(b) for the coal property of $95,000 (the difference between *T*'s basis, $100,000, and *T*'s share of the basis of partnership property, $5,000). Assume that the depletion allowance computed under the percentage method would be $21,000 for the taxable year, so that each partner would be entitled to $7,000 as its share of the deduction for depletion. Under the cost depletion method, at an assumed rate of 10 percent, the allowance with respect to *T*'s one-third interest, which has a basis to him of $100,000 ($5,000 plus its basis adjustment of $95,000), is $10,000, although the cost depletion allowance with respect to the one-third interests of *A* and *B* in the coal property, each of which has a basis of $5,000, is only $500. For partners *A* and *B*, percentage depletion is greater than cost depletion, and each will deduct $7,000 based on the percentage depletion method. However, as to *T*, the transferee-partner, the

---

[167] Reg. § 1.743-1(j)(5).

[168] See Reg. § 1.743-1(j)(6) Example.

[169] See Reg. §§ 1.1245-1(e)(3)(ii), 1.1250-1(f); but see REG-151416-06, 79 Fed. Reg. 65,151 (Nov. 3, 2014) (noting in the preamble to Proposed § 751(b) Regulations that the § 1245 Regulations (Reg. § 1.1245-1(e)) are "out of date" and can cause issues and uncertainties).

cost depletion method results in a greater allowance, and *T* will, therefore, deduct $10,000 based on cost depletion under § 613(a).[170]

Example 24-9 appears to require that the partnership separately track for each partner a share of the common partnership basis in the property. Thus, although the normal rules under §§ 611 through 613 would require the partnership to reduce the basis of the coal property to zero, under the approach of the example (which is supported by the legislative history), partners *A* and *B* will each have a share of common basis of zero ($5,000 − $7,000, but not less than zero) and *C* will have a share of common basis of $4,500 ($5,000 − $500). Presumably, a transferee of *C*'s interest would succeed to *C*'s separate share of remaining common basis, much like the rule for partnership oil and gas properties under § 613A(c)(7)(D).[171]

The transferor of a partnership interest may be subject to the recapture of a portion of his share of any investment credit previously claimed with respect to partnership assets.[172] However, his transferee is apparently not entitled to an investment credit with respect to partnership assets, regardless of whether he is entitled to adjust the basis of partnership assets under § 743(b).[173]

---

[170] Reg. § 1.743-1(j)(6) Example. See also S. Rep. No. 1622, 83d Cong., 2d Sess. 400 (1954).

Under regulations proposed in 2014:

1. Upon any transfer of an interest in an upper-tier partnership (UTP), there would be a deemed transfer of any lower-tier partnership (LTP) interest "attributable" to the transferred UTP interest. See Prop. Reg. § 1.743-1(l)(1) (2014).
2. Upon a transfer of a UTP interest by sale, exchange, or death, if the UTP has a substantial built-in loss "with respect to the transfer," each LTP would be deemed to have made a § 754 election under the Proposed Regulations. See Prop. Reg. § 1.743-1(l)(1) (2014) (referencing Rev. Rul. 87-115).

An illustration of this proposed rule tests for the $250,000 threshold by computing the amount of the UTP's built-in loss in the LTP at the time of the transfer (possibly indicating that if there are multiple LTPs each will be examined separately for this purpose). Because the UTP in this example is determined to have more than $250,000 of built-in loss with respect to an LTP, the UTP must adjust the basis of its interest in the LTP and the LTP must adjust the basis of its assets. See Prop. Reg. § 1.743-1(l)(2) Example (2014).

[171] In the case of oil or gas property, the basis of which has been allocated to the partners pursuant to § 613A(c)(7)(D), the basis adjustment is made with reference to the transferor-partner's adjusted basis in the oil and gas property. See Reg. § 1.613A-3(e)(6)(iv).

[172] See Reg. § 1.47-6(a)(2).

[173] See Reg. § 1.48-3(a)(2)(i); Rev. Rul. 82-213, 1982-2 CB 31 (Situation 2). Since the property continues to be used by the same person (i.e., the partnership) following the transfer of a partnership interest, a § 743(b) basis adjustment should not qualify for the credit.

If application of § 743(b) increases the basis of partnership intangibles that are subject to § 197,[174] the increase is usually treated as a new § 197 intangible with a fresh fifteen-year amortization period under § 197(f)(2).[175] The transferee is not subject to the § 197(f)(9) anti-churning rules with respect to this new intangible, unless he is "related," within the meaning of § 197(f)(9)(C)(i), to the partner who transferred the interest to him; any relationships between the transferee and the other partners or the partnership are irrelevant.[176]

¶ 24.08 SPECIAL PROBLEMS UPON THE DEATH OF PARTNER

Upon the death of a partner, § 743(b) provides for the adjustment of the basis of partnership assets to reflect the initial basis of the decedent's partnership interest in the hands of his successor. Generally, interests acquired from decedents take an initial basis equal to their date-of-death (or alternate valuation date) value under §§ 1014(a) and 742.[177]

[1] Partnership Items of Income in Respect of Decedent

If property acquired from a decedent constitutes income in respect of a decedent (IRD) under § 691, its basis in the hands of the decedent carries over to his successor and is not adjusted under § 1014. If a portion of a decedent's partnership interest is treated as IRD, the interest is fragmented for basis purposes:[178] The IRD portion takes a carryover basis from the decedent, while the basis of the non-IRD portion is adjusted as provided in § 1014.

The statute and Regulations set forth only two grounds for characterizing a portion of a partnership interest as IRD. Section 753 provides that "any

---

[174] See generally ¶ 9.02[3][t].

[175] Regulations § 1.197-2(g)(3) provides that for purposes of determining the amortization period under § 197 with respect to the basis increase, the intangible is treated as having been acquired at the time of the transaction that causes the basis increase, except as provided in Regulations § 1.743-1(j)(4)(i)(B)(2) (relating to the remedial allocation method).

[176] See § 197(f)(9)(E); Reg. § 1.197-2(h)(12)(v); HR Rep. No. 213, 103d Cong., 1st Sess. 235 (1993).

[177] See ¶ 23.04[1]. The basis of a partnership interest acquired from a decedent is determined under § 1022 if the decedent died in 2010 and the decedent's executor elected to have § 1022 apply to the decedent's estate. Reg. § 1.742-1(a), as amended by TD 9811, 2017-7 IRB 869 (Jan. 19, 2017).

[178] See ¶ 23.03. See also Reg. § 1.755-1(b)(4).

amount includible in the gross income of a successor in interest of a deceased partner under Section 736(a)" is IRD, and Regulations § 1.753-1(b) treats as IRD the decedent's share of partnership income earned during the portion of the partnership's taxable year ending on the date of his death to the extent it is taxable to his estate or other successor. Section 706(c) was amended by the Taxpayer Relief Act of 1997 to provide that the taxable year of a partnership closes with respect to a partner upon the death of the partner. This means that income attributable to the period prior to the partner's death will be included in the deceased partner's final tax return, and thus is not taxable to his estate or other successor. Accordingly, this change to § 706(c) appears to eliminate this category of IRD.

Except to the extent § 736(a) applies, zero-basis accounts receivable and other partnership assets that would constitute IRD if inherited directly are not classified as IRD under these rules. Thus, it might seem that these rules would permit a decedent's successor to take into account the value of such assets in computing the initial basis of his partnership interest under § 1014(a). The inclusion of the value of these assets in the basis of the successor's partnership interest might then entitle the successor to a basis increase under § 743(b) with respect to the assets themselves, and thereby reduce or eliminate his share of partnership income subsequently realized with respect to the assets. The Tax Court, with the approval of two circuit courts, has, however, refused to permit the bases of inherited partnership interests to be increased to reflect the value of partnership assets that would be IRD if inherited directly.[179] As a consequence of this holding, the § 743(b) adjustments available to the successor partners were reduced. The truncated § 743(b) adjustment remaining after this exclusion was allocable entirely to partnership assets other than those treated as IRD.[180]

[2] Selection of Alternate Valuation Date

Section 1014(a) generally provides that the basis of property in the hands of a person acquiring it from a decedent is the fair market value of the property as of the date of the decedent's death or the alternate valuation date (as limited by § 1014(f) to the value used for estate tax purposes).[181] The alternate valua-

---

[179] See George Edward Quick Trust, 54 TC 1336 (1970) (acq.), aff'd per curiam, 444 F2d 90 (8th Cir. 1971); Chrissie H. Woodhall, 28 TCM 1438 (1969), aff'd, 454 F2d 226 (9th Cir. 1972); cf. Rev. Rul. 66-325, 1966-2 CB 249; ¶ 23.03[2][c].

[180] Reg. § 1.755-1(b)(4)(ii) Example (ii) (effective for transfers on or after December 15, 1999). See generally Kalish & Scheider, "Is There Partnership Basis After Death?" 35 Tax Law. 143, 154–158 (1981) (prior law).

[181] See §§ 2032, 2032A. Under § 1014(f), the basis must be "consistent with" (i.e., may not exceed) the value used for estate tax purposes.

tion date is generally six months after the date of the decedent's death. If the alternate valuation date is applicable to a partnership interest with respect to which a § 743(b) adjustment is to be made, it seems that the amount of the adjustment should be determined with reference to the value of the interest on the alternate valuation date[182] but there is no clear authority for handling intervening taxable events or for dealing with changes in the values or composition of partnership assets during the interim period between the date of death and the alternate valuation date.

A relatively simple approach would be to make the adjustment as of the alternate valuation date with respect to assets still held by the partnership on that date, but make the adjustment with respect to assets sold by the partnership before the alternate valuation date as of the date of the sale.

Alternatively, the statutory language furnishes at least some support for application of the adjustment as of the date of the decedent's death. Problems created by the lapse of time between death and the alternate valuation date could be solved through the filing of amended returns, if necessary. However, the potential problems inherent in this approach with respect to (1) the treatment of partnership distributions, (2) the consequences of purchases or sales of assets by the partnership, and (3) the computation of partnership income during the period between the date of death and the alternate valuation date are substantial. This suggests that the simplest solution may well be the best in this case.

¶ 24.09 APPLICATION OF SECTION 743(b) TO TIER PARTNERSHIPS

If a transferee acquires an interest in a partnership that holds an interest in another partnership, the basis of the upper-tier partnership (UTP) in its interest in the lower-tier partnership (LTP) is adjusted under § 743(b) if the UTP has a § 754 election in effect. The Service has ruled that a corresponding adjustment to the basis of the assets held by the LTP is made if the LTP also has a § 754

---

[182] The Regulations provide that the valuation date is the same for both § 743(b) and § 1014 purposes. See Reg. §§ 1.743-1(k)(2)(ii) (transferee's statement must include valuation of partnership interest as of the "applicable date of valuation set forth in section 1014"), 1.755-1(b)(4)(ii) Example (ii)(same). See also Prop. Reg. § 1.742-1 (2015) (for decedents dying in 2010, executors may make § 1022 election to pay no estate tax and forgo § 1014 basis step up; conforming language).

election in effect,[183] and has proposed regulations addressing multi-tier partnership structures.[184]

The fragmentary evidence currently available indicates that the Service's general approach to multi-tier partnership structures is based on a look-through approach while simultaneously (1) respecting (as appropriate) the separate existence of each partnership in the structure, (2) applying § 743 on a partnership-by-partnership basis,[185] and (3) creating special rules as deemed appropriate to deal with potential abuse situations.[186] Accordingly, it seems prudent for practitioners to assume the following:

1. Any transfer of a UTP interest will be treated as a transfer of all LTP interests "attributable" to the transferred UTP interest;[187]
2. Except in connection with substantial built-in losses, each UTP and LTP will be required and permitted to make its own § 754 election;[188] and
3. If there is a substantial built-in loss "with respect' to a transfer of a UTP interest by sale, exchange, or death, the UTP and some or all of the LTPs will be subject to the mandatory § 743 adjustments for substantial built-in losses.[189]

There is some ambiguity, exacerbated by the enactment of § 743(d)(1)(B) in 2017, as to the treatment of LTPs in connection with the mandatory application of § 743 to a UTP. The single illustration in the Proposed Regulations involves a UTP that has only one asset, a 25 percent interest in an LTP that owns a single asset, Land, that has a very large built-in loss, so that both the

---

[183] Rev. Rul. 87-115, 1987-2 CB 163; Rev. Rul. 78-2, 1978-1 CB 202. Regulations § 1.705-2(c), dealing with the interaction of §§ 705 and 1032 in the tiered partnership context, adopts a similar approach. See ¶ 6.02[3][d]. See also Priv. Ltr. Ruls. 9338004, 9338005, 9338006 (June 10, 1993) (extensions granted for § 754 election by second-, third-, and fourth-tier partnerships following death of partner in top-tier partnership; timely § 754 election by top-tier partnership, but not by any other partnerships); Priv. Ltr. Rul. 9327068 (Apr. 12, 1993) (extension granted for § 754 election by lower-tier partnership following death of partner in upper-tier partnership holding 50 percent interest in lower-tier partnership; timely § 754 election by upper-tier partnership).

[184] Prop. Reg. § 1.743-1(l) (2014) (focused on the mandatory application of § 743 in connection with built-in losses).

[185] Similar concepts seem to be guiding the Service's approach under § 734. See Rev. Rul. 92-15, 1992-1CB 215, discussed at ¶ 25.07.

[186] See Reg. § 1.705-2(c); Prop. Reg. § 1.743-1(l) (2014): Rev. Rul. 87-115. 1987-2 CB 163; Rev. Rul. 78-2 1978-1 CB 202; cf. Rev. Rul. 92-15, 1992-1 CB 215.

[187] See Prop. Reg. § 1.743-1(l)(1) (2014).

[188] The willingness of the Service to allow each separate entity to elect in or out of § 754 is explicit in Rev. Rul. 87-115 and the private letter rulings cited in note 195, and is implicit in the 2014 Proposed Regulations under § 743.

[189] See Prop. Reg. § 1.743-1(l)(1) (2014); Rev. Rul. 87-115, 1987-2 CB 163.

UTP (with regard to its 25 percent share) and the LTP are clearly subject to the mandatory application of § 743 under any analysis, leaving open a number of questions, few of which are clearly answered by the text of the Proposed Regulation:

1. What are the consequences if the built-in loss in the Land owned by 25 percent owned LTP is more than $250,000 but less than $1,000,000? Likely answer: LTP is subject to mandatory application of § 743 (even though the interest transfer is indirect) but UTP is not;

2. If UTP has assets other than LTP with built-in losses in excess of $250,000, but LTP does not, is LTP subject to mandatory application of § 743? Likely answer: No.

3. If UTP has multiple LTPs with built-in losses that collectively cause UTP to be subject to mandatory application of § 743, are the LTP's subject to mandatory application? Likely answer: an LTP is subject to mandatory application only if its built-in loss is greater than $250,000.

The publication of the Proposed Regulation predates the addition of § 743(d)(1)(B) in 2017, creating a host of new issues to be addressed by the next iteration of the Proposed Regulations.

There are also mechanical problems inherent in the application of § 743(b) to tiered partnership structures, particularly inside-outside basis differences in LTPs. Some of these are illustrated in Revenue Ruling 87-115,[190] which provides the basis for the following examples:

EXAMPLE 24-10: *A, B, C,* and *D* are equal partners in *UTP.* Each partner contributed 30x cash on formation of *UTP* and has a 30x interest in *UTP*'s capital and surplus. Neither *UTP* nor *LTP* have any liabilities. *UTP* is an equal one-third partner, with *X* and *Y*, in *LTP. LTP* was formed by *X, Y*, and *Z*, who each contributed 110x cash to *LTP* on its formation. *UTP* purchased its interest in *LTP* from *Z* for 80x dollars at a time when *LTP* did not have a § 754 election in effect. *UTP, X,* and *Y* each have a 110x dollar interest in partnership capital and surplus of LTP.

UTP has an adjusted basis of 120x in its property: 80x in its *LTP* partnership interest and 40x in its inventory. The fair market value of the *LTP* interest is 120x and the value of the inventory is 80x. *LTP* has only one asset, a capital asset that is not a § 751 asset.[191] *LTP's* asset has an adjusted basis of 330x and a value of 360x.

---

[190] Rev. Rul. 87-115, 1987-2 CB 163.

[191] If *LTP* holds inventory or unrealized receivables, the interest in *LTP* should be bifurcated into a capital asset portion and an ordinary portion for purposes of applying § 755. The principal support for such an approach is § 751(f), which provides that in determining whether property of a partnership is an unrealized receivable or an inventory item, the partnership is treated as owning its proportionate share of the property of any other

A sells its entire interest in *UTP* to *E* for 50x dollars at a time when both *UTP* and *LTP* have § 754 elections in effect.

UTP increases the adjusted basis of its property by 20x, the excess of *E*'s 50x cost basis in its *UTP* interest over its 30x share of the adjusted basis of *UTP*'s property. *E*'s 20x § 743(b) basis adjustment raises *UTP*'s adjusted basis in the property to 140x, and the additional 20x must be segregated and allocated solely to *E*. Under § 755, the 20x is allocated 10x to *UTP*'s interest in *LTP* and 10x to *UTP*'s inventory.

The sale of *A*'s partnership interest in *UTP* is treated as a deemed sale of an interest in *LTP*. The selling price of *E*'s share of *UTP*'s interest in *LTP* is deemed to equal *E*'s share of *UTP*'s adjusted basis in *LTP*, 30x (1/4 of 80x plus 10x, the portion of *E*'s § 743(b) basis adjustment allocated to *UTP*'s interest in *LTP*). Under § 743(b), *LTP* must increase the adjusted basis of its partnership property by 2.5x, the excess of *E*'s share of *UTP*'s adjusted basis in *LTP* (30x) over *E*'s share of the adjusted basis of *LTP*'s property (the capital asset) of 1/4 of 110x, or 27.5x. The 2.5x adjustment must be segregated and allocated solely to *UTP* and *E*, the transferee partner of *UTP*.

The result is that transferee *E* only gets the benefit of 12.5x for its 20x basis increase due to *UTP*'s pre-existing difference between the basis of its *LTP* interest and its share of the basis of *LTP*'s assets, which effectively absorbs 75 percent of the basis increase that would otherwise have been allocated to *LTP*'s capital asset.

If *UTP* has a § 754 election in effect but *LTP* does not, there is no § 743(b) increase in the basis of *LTP*'s assets. If only *LTP* has a § 754 election in effect, there are no basis increase for the assets of either partnership.

The Service has adopted a similar approach to the application of § 734(b) to distributions by an upper-tier partnership, giving full recognition to the separateness of partnerships in different tiers and independent effect to each partnership's § 754 election (or lack thereof).[192]

---

partnership in which it is a partner. Section 751(f) appears to be made applicable by Regulations § 1.755-1(a)(1), which requires that properties and potential gain treated as unrealized receivables under § 751(c) be treated as separate assets that are ordinary income property. Although the § 755 Regulations refer explicitly only to unrealized receivables, treating partnership interests differently based on whether the partnership holds unrealized receivables or inventory items would seem to be inconsistent with the purposes of §§ 751(f) and 755.

[192] See Rev. Rul. 92-15, 1992-1 CB 215, discussed at ¶ 25.07.

¶ 24.10 CONTRIBUTIONS OF PROPERTY SUBJECT TO SECTION 743(b) ADJUSTMENTS

The § 743 Regulations provide that § 743(b) adjustments are preserved upon a contribution of partnership property to a lower-tier partnership.[193] They also provide that, upon a contribution of partnership property to a corporation in a § 351 transaction, the corporation's basis for the contributed property generally includes the full amount of any § 743(b) basis adjustments with respect to the property.[194] Special rules provide for situations in which the contributing partner recognizes gain on a § 351 transfer: Partnership gain is computed without regard to any § 743(b) adjustments, but each partner's share of the gain is adjusted (up or down, as the case may be) to reflect any § 743(b) adjustments with respect to contributed property.[195] Any such basis adjustment that reduces a partner's gain is ignored in computing the corporation's initial basis for the contributed property.[196] The partnership's initial basis for the stock received in the § 351 transaction is equal to its basis in the contributed property, exclusive of any § 743(b) adjustments; however, each partner is entitled to a § 743(b) basis adjustment with respect to the stock, to the extent the partner's § 743(b) adjustment was not used to offset gain that would otherwise have been recognized in the transaction.[197]

In the context of a contribution of partnership property to a lower-tier partnership, it is unclear whether the contributed basis adjustment retains its status as a § 743(b) basis adjustment or becomes common basis to the lower tier partnership (and thus, survives a subsequent transfer of the interest subject to the adjustment). The language of Regulations § 1.743-1(h)(1), which applies generally to contributions from upper-tier partnerships to lower-tier partnerships, leans strongly towards the common basis approach. It provides that the "lower tier's basis in the contributed assets and the upper tier's basis in the partnership interest received ... are determined with reference to the basis adjustment." This Regulation goes on to provide that the relevant portions of each basis must be segregated and allocated to the transferee. If the adjustment retained its status as a § 743(b) basis adjustment, it would be allocated automatically to the transferee. Moreover, the "determined with reference" language is also used in Regulations § 1.743-1(h)(2)(i) to describe a corporation's basis in contributed assets subject to § 743(b) basis adjustments, which be-

---

[193] See Reg. § 1.743-1(h)(1) (applicable to transfers on or after December 15, 1999).

[194] Reg. § 1.743-1(h)(2)(i).

[195] Reg. § 1.743-1(h)(2)(ii).

[196] A corporation's initial basis for contributed property is increased to reflect any gain recognized by contributing shareholders under § 362(a). Accordingly, the corporation should not be entitled to a basis increase to the extent that a § 743(b) basis adjustment reduces the gain recognized by partners in a contributing partnership.

[197] Reg. § 1.743-1(h)(2)(iii).

comes the common basis to the corporation. However, the transferee-partnership's common basis in the corporate stock received is specifically not determined with reference to the § 743(b) basis adjustment.[198] This common basis adjustment approach makes some sense in a multi-tiered partnership setting, if for no other reason than to advance the cause of administrative simplicity. It is hard to justify in the context of an "assets over" partnership merger, however, because the tiered partnership structure created by Regulations § 1.708-1(c)(3)(i) is transitory.[199] Nevertheless, the alternative § 743(b) status approach is difficult to square with the final sentence of Regulations § 1.743-1(h)(1), which specifically provides that, in the case of a § 708(b)(1)(B) termination, a partner with a § 743(b) basis adjustment in the terminated partnership retains the adjustment in the new partnership. The contrast in the language and the approach taken in this final sentence with the rest of Regulations § 1.743-1(h)(1) is hard to ignore. While the repeal of § 708(b)(1)(B) in 2017[200] nullifies the direct impact of this sentence, it is not yet clear whether it will also resolve the apparent confusion.

¶ 24.11 THE SECTION 754 ELECTION TO ADJUST THE BASIS OF PARTNERSHIP ASSETS

[1] Application of the Election to Transfers of Partnership Interests and Partnership Distributions

Although there are substantial differences between adjustments to the basis of partnership assets under § 743(b) in connection with transfers of partnership interests and adjustments under § 734(b) in connection with partnership distributions,[201] the application of both provisions on a nonselective basis is activated by the filing of a single election under § 754. A § 754 election applies to all distributions and transfers during the taxable year "with respect to which such election was filed" and during all subsequent years, until the election is revoked in accordance with the Regulations. Both the statute and the Regulations make it clear that a § 754 election applies to both transfers and distribu-

---

[198] See Reg. § 1.743-1(h)(2)(iii).
[199] See ¶ 13.06[1].
[200] 2017 Tax Cuts and Jobs Act, Pub. L. No. 115-97, § 13504(a) (Dec. 22, 2017).
[201] See Chapter 25.

tions. A partnership is not permitted to limit the election to transfers or distributions alone.[202]

[2] Form of the Election

No particular form is required for a § 754 election. The § 754 Regulations merely require that the election include the name and address of the electing partnership, a declaration that the partnership elects, under § 754, to apply the provisions of §§ 734(b) and 743(b), and the signature of any partner.[203]

In Field Service Advice 200025017, issued March 23, 2000, the Service considered the efficacy of a U.S. parent's filing of a partnership return (Form 1065) with a § 754 election (as part of its consolidated U.S. tax return) on behalf of a foreign partnership not required to file a U.S. return. While the U.S. parent had no direct interest in the foreign partnership, the election would be advantageous because, in the following year, a lower-tier foreign subsidiary increased its interest and other subsidiaries acquired interests in the foreign partnership. The Service ruled that a § 754 election made in this manner is not effective. The Service noted that

> [w]here a United States citizen is a partner in a partnership which is not required to file a United States return because it does no business in the United States, and the citizen desires an election in accordance with the provisions of section 703 to be made by or for the partnership, a return must be filed by the partnership. Treas. Reg. section 1.6031-1(d)(2). The filing of a return for a taxable year of the partnership by a citizen or resident partner constitutes a filing for the partnership of such partnership return. Treas. Reg. section 1.6031-1(d)(2).

---

[202] Reg. § 1.754-1(a). This aspect of a § 754 election would have been changed by HR 9662, 86th Cong., 2d Sess. § 780 (1960) (separate elections with respect to transfers and distributions).

[203] Reg. § 1.754-1(b). Presumably, the signature of "any partner" must be authorized under state law to constitute an effective election. Otherwise, disagreements among partners as to whether to elect could easily be "resolved" in favor of those desiring to make the election. See Atlantic Veneer Corp., 85 TC 1075 (1985), aff'd, 812 F2d 158 (4th Cir. 1987) (foreign partnership with U.S. partner; domestic partner must file partnership return and attach statement making § 754 election; copy of foreign partnership's tax return and supporting statements, not in English but reflecting stepped-up basis, is not sufficient); Tech. Adv. Mem. 8142017 (June 18, 1981) (same). Even if no return is otherwise required of a foreign partnership, Regulations § 1.6031-1(d)(2) requires a return to be filed (presumably by the domestic partner) in order to make partnership elections, including the § 754 election. Proposed Regulations published in 2017 would resolve all issues relating to the signature requirement by altogether eliminating this requirement. Prop. Reg. § 1.754-1(b)(1) (2017), REG-116256-17 (Oct. 12, 2017).

Under the facts, a Form 1065 was never filed by, or on behalf of, the partnership. The partnership return was merely included as an exhibit in the U.S. parent's consolidated return. Because this type of inclusion is not the same as the filing of a return, the § 754 election was never properly made.[204]

[3] Timing of the Election

The statute provides that a § 754 election applies to all transfers and distributions during the taxable year "with respect to which" the election is filed and all subsequent years, thus leaving open the question of whether a retroactive election can be filed "with respect to" prior taxable years. The original Regulations promulgated under § 754 attempted to resolve this uncertainty by requiring that the election be filed "with the partnership return for the first taxable year to which the election applies."[205] The phrase "to which the election applies" introduced a further ambiguity in situations where the partners did not claim any benefit from the election until a year subsequent to the year in which the transfer or distribution occurred.[206] The § 754 Regulations were amended in 1972, and presently require that the election be filed with a timely return for the taxable year "during which the distribution or transfer occurs"; although, if a valid election has been made for a preceding year and not revoked, a new election is not required to be made.[207]

While the validity of the original version of the § 754 Regulations was successfully challenged on two occasions,[208] the 1972 version has been consistently upheld.[209] Accordingly, the issue now seems settled in favor of the validity of the Regulations.[210]

---

[204] See Atlantic Veneer Corp., 85 TC 1075 (1985), aff'd, 812 F2d 158 (4th Cir. 1987).

[205] Reg. § 1.754-1(b) (TD 6175, 1956-1 CB 211, 302).

[206] The ambiguity in this Regulation was accentuated by Revenue Ruling 57-347, 1957-2 CB 365, which stated that the election must accompany the return for the first year "for which the partners wish the election to become effective."

[207] Reg. § 1.754-1(b)(1).

[208] Neel v. United States, 266 F. Supp. 7 (ND Ga. 1966); Allison v. United States, 379 F. Supp. 490 (MD Pa. 1974) (opinion vacated because taxpayer's refund claim barred by statute of limitations). But cf. Estate of Dupree v. United States, 391 F2d 753 (5th Cir. 1968) (effect given to Regulation under different factual circumstances).

[209] Jones v. United States, 553 F2d 667 (Ct. Cl. 1977); Estate of Ernest D. Skaggs, 75 TC 191 (1980), aff'd per curiam, 672 F2d 756 (9th Cir. 1982) (cert. denied). See Gindes v. United States, 661 F2d 194 (Ct. Cl. 1981).

[210] An additional year within which to make the election would have been allowed under HR 9662, 86th Cong., 2d Sess. § 780 (1960). See Anderson & Coffee, "Proposed Revision of Partner and Partnership Taxation: Analysis of the Report of the Advisory Group on Subchapter K (Second Installment)," 15 Tax L. Rev. 497, 523–524 (1960).

Under Regulations § 301.9100-2, an automatic twelve-month extension from the due date for making a § 754 election is available provided that the taxpayer takes "corrective action." This automatic extension is available regardless of whether the partnership filed a timely return for the year the election should have been made.

"Corrective action," for this purpose, means—

taking the steps required to file the election in accordance with the statute or the regulation published in the Federal Register, or the revenue ruling, revenue procedure, notice, or announcement published in the Internal Revenue Bulletin (see §601.601(d)(2) of this chapter). For those elections required to be filed with a return, corrective action includes filing an original or an amended return for the year the regulatory or statutory election should have been made and attaching the appropriate form or statement for making the election. Taxpayers who make an election under an automatic extension (and all taxpayers whose tax liability would be affected by the election) must file their return in a manner that is consistent with the election and comply with all other requirements for making the election for the year the election should have been made and for all affected years; otherwise, the IRS may invalidate the election.[211]

To qualify for the automatic extension, certain procedural requirements must be followed. First, the return or election must provide the following statement at its top: "FILED PURSUANT TO § 301.9100-2." Next, any filing made to obtain an automatic extension "must be sent to the same address that the filing to make the election would have been sent had the filing been timely made."

Under circumstances where the automatic twelve-month extension is not available, a discretionary extension of time to file the § 754 election may still be requested from the Service, and will generally be granted if the requirements of Regulations § 301.9100-3 are met.[212] To obtain an extension under this provision, the taxpayer must provide evidence that establishes to the "satisfaction of the Commissioner" that the taxpayer acted reasonably and in good faith, and that the grant of the extension will not "prejudice the interests of the Government."[213]

---

[211] Reg. § 301.9100-2(c). The Service routinely grants relief pursuant to this section.

[212] See, e.g., FSA 200202022 (Sept. 24, 2001) (six partnerships eligible to request relief under Reg. § 301.9100-1).

[213] Regulations § 301.9100-3(c) states that

1. The interests of the Government are prejudiced if granting relief would result in a taxpayer having a lower tax liability in the aggregate for all taxable years affected by the election than the taxpayer would have had if the election had been timely made (taking into account the time value of money). Similarly, if the tax consequences of more than one taxpayer are affected by the election, the Gov-

Regulations § 301.9100-3 indicates that a taxpayer will be deemed to have acted reasonably and in good faith with regard to the requested extension if the taxpayer

1. Requests relief before the failure to make the election is discovered by the Service;
2. Failed to make the election because of intervening events beyond the taxpayer's control;
3. Failed to make the election because, after exercising reasonable diligence (taking into account the taxpayer's experience and the complexity of the return or issue), the taxpayer was unaware of the necessity for the election;
4. Reasonably relied on the written advice of the Service; or
5. Reasonably relied on a qualified tax professional (including an employee), and the tax professional failed to make, or advise the taxpayer to make, the election.[214]

Reasonable reliance on a qualified tax professional will not exist if the taxpayer knew or should have known that (1) the professional was not "competent to render advice on the regulatory election" or (2) the professional was not aware of all relevant facts.[215]

Further, a taxpayer will not be viewed as having acted "reasonably and in good faith" with regard to a requested extension if the taxpayer

1. Seeks to alter a return position for which an accuracy-related penalty has been or could be imposed at the time the taxpayer requests relief (taking into account any qualified amended return filed), and the new position requires or permits a regulatory election for which relief is requested;
2. Was informed in all material respects of the required election and related tax consequences, but chose not to file the election; or

---

ernment's interests are prejudiced if extending the time for making the election may result in the affected taxpayers, in the aggregate, having a lower tax liability than if the election had been timely made.

2. The interests of the Government are ordinarily prejudiced if the taxable year in which the regulatory election should have been made or any taxable years that would have been affected by the election had it been timely made are closed by the period of limitations on assessment under section 6501(a) before the taxpayer's receipt of a ruling granting relief under this section. The IRS may condition a grant of relief on the taxpayer providing the IRS with a statement from an independent auditor (other than an auditor providing an affidavit pursuant to paragraph (e)(3) of this section) certifying that the interests of the Government are not prejudiced under the standards set forth in paragraph (c)(1)(i) of this section.

[214] Reg. § 301.9100-3(b).
[215] Reg. § 301.9100-3(b)(2).

3. Uses hindsight in requesting relief.[216]

Further, to obtain this discretionary extension, the taxpayer must submit a detailed sworn affidavit (1) describing the events that led to the failure to make a valid election and to the discovery of the failure; (2) indicating the existence of the grounds for the extension, along with sworn affidavits by others that support these grounds; and (3) stating whether the taxpayer's return or returns for the taxable year(s) in which the election should have been made (or any taxable years that would have been affected by the election had it been timely made) are either being examined by the Service or being considered by an appeals office or a federal court.[217] Additionally, the taxpayer must submit a copy of any documents that refer to the election, and, when requested, the taxpayer must submit a copy of the taxpayer's return for any taxable year for which the taxpayer requests an extension of time to make the election and any return affected by the election, along with a copy of the returns of other taxpayers affected by the election.

[4] Revocation of the Election

Once made, a § 754 election is revocable only with the approval of the District Director for the district in which the partnership's returns are filed.[218] Regulations § 1.754-1(c) provides several examples of the types of situations that may be grounds for approval of a revocation application:

1. A change in the nature of the partnership business;
2. A substantial increase in the assets of the partnership;
3. A change in the character of partnership assets; and
4. An increased frequency of retirements or shifts of partnership interests, thereby increasing the administrative burden of the election.

---

[216] Reg. § 301-9100-3(b)(3). If specific facts have changed since the due date for making the election and that change results in the election being advantageous to a taxpayer, the Service will not ordinarily grant relief. In such a case, the Service will grant relief only when the taxpayer provides strong proof that the taxpayer's decision to seek relief did not involve hindsight. Reg. § 301.9100-3(b)(3)(iii). See Priv. Ltr. Rul. 200626003 (Feb. 28, 2006).

[217] Reg. § 301.9100-3(e).

[218] Reg. § 1.754-1(c). The application must be filed within thirty days of the end of the partnership year with respect to which the revocation is intended to take effect and may be signed by any partner. Presumably, this filing deadline may be extended by the Service pursuant to Regulations § 1.9100-1(a) under appropriate circumstances.

This Regulations provision specifically provides that avoidance of potential decreases in the basis of partnership assets is not an acceptable purpose for revoking a § 754 election.[219]

[5] Determining Whether to Elect Under Section 754

The decision to make an election to adjust basis under § 754 should take into account a number of considerations. Of prime importance are the essentially irrevocable character[220] of the election and its mandatory application to both transfers of partnership interests and distributions of partnership assets. Thus, any initial benefits that may flow from the election in the form of increases in the bases of partnership assets during the first year of the election must be weighed against the detriment of possible basis *decreases* in subsequent years. Because basis decreases are mandatory if the partnership has a substantial built-in loss at the time of the transfer, however, this detriment is not too severe.[221] Downwards basis adjustments are also mandatory in the case of distributions that would trigger downwards basis adjustments to partnership property in excess of $250,000 if a § 754 election were in effect. As discussed at ¶ 25.01[7], the failure to have a § 754 election in effect upon a transfer of an interest can have unpleasant consequences if the transferee subsequently receives a liquidating distribution that triggers this mandatory downwards basis adjustment.[222] Accordingly, having a § 754 election in place is more likely to be helpful than harmful.

---

[219] The Regulations finalized in 1999 substantially modified the way basis adjustments are made under §§ 734(b), 743(b), and 755. As a consequence, the Service granted every partnership having a § 754 election in effect a one-time opportunity to revoke the election by filing a statement revoking the election with the partnership's timely filed return (including extensions) for the year including December 14, 1999. Reg. § 1.754-1(c)(2).

[220] It would be extremely hazardous to assume that the partnership will be successful in obtaining permission to revoke the election (see supra ¶ 24.11[4]), and hence it is probably best to view the election as irrevocable for planning purposes.

[221] See supra ¶ 24.01[4]. A partnership has a substantial built-in loss with respect to a transfer of an interest if (1) the partnership's adjusted basis for its assets exceeds their value by more than $250,000 (§ 743(d)(1)(A)), or (2) after 2017 (see Pub. L. No. 115-97, § 13502 (Dec. 22, 2017)), the transferee partner would be allocated a loss of more than $250,000 if the partnership assets were sold for cash equal to their fair market value immediately after such transfer. § 743(d)(1)(B).

[222] After 2017, the basis decrease is also mandatory if the transferee partner would be allocated a loss of more than $250,000 upon a hypothetical sale of partnership assets for cash equal to their fair market value immediately after the transfer. § 743(d)(1)(B), as amended by the 2017 Tax Cuts and Jobs Act, Pub. L. No. 115-97, § 13502 (Dec. 22, 2017).

A significant drawback of the election is the consequent increase in the records that must be maintained by the partnership. The extent of this clerical burden is a function of the number of assets held by the partnership, as well as the frequency with which transfers of partnership interests and certain types of distributions occur. These problems may not be important in a closely held partnership, but they can be substantial in a widely held partnership that owns many assets, particularly if those assets are depreciable. Clerical burdens and other administrative considerations were the apparent reason for exempting certain investment partnerships and securitization partnerships from the mandatory application of § 743(b) as discussed above.[223]

The decision whether to make a § 754 election is further complicated by the fact that the benefits of the election do not fall evenly on the partners in the case of transfers of partnership interests, where § 743(b) adjustments benefit only transferee-partners.[224] The continuing partners may well decide that the benefits of the election to their new partners are more than outweighed by the potential long-term detriments to themselves, in the form of record-keeping headaches and possible future basis decreases as to their partnership interests. By contrast, § 734(b) adjustments triggered by distributions of partnership property generally inure to the benefit or detriment of all partners;[225] therefore, conflict among the interests of the partners does not usually arise in connection with the decision to make a § 754 election on the occasion of such a distribution.

One obvious lesson from this analysis is that a prospective purchaser of an interest in a partnership holding appreciated assets should either assure himself that a § 754 election is in effect or obtain contractual assurances that one will be made. The latter will, in most cases, require three-way negotiations between the buyer, the seller, and the continuing partners. The buyer and seller may find it necessary to make some concessions to the continuing partners to induce them to make the election. Conversely, the purchaser of an interest in a partnership holding a mix of assets that do not have an overall loss in excess of $250,000, or a loss of more than $250,000 allocable to the purchased interest (thus avoiding mandatory application of § 743(b)), but nevertheless having favorable basis-value relationships (i.e., high basis depreciable assets, low basis capital assets), might be dissuaded from purchasing an interest in the partnership by the existence of an election and may wish to obtain assurances that none is in effect.

The possible reluctance of continuing partners to make an election for the primary benefit of an incoming partner suggests that the inclusion of provisions in the original partnership agreement concerning the election is desirable.

---

[223] See supra ¶ 24.01[4].
[224] See supra ¶ 24.01[3].
[225] See ¶ 25.01[2].

For example, the partnership agreement might give any transferor-partner or his transferee the contractual right to require that the election be made. If such a provision were included in the partnership agreement, the first transferee who is in a position to benefit from the § 754 election will be able to require that one be made. A more sophisticated version of this approach would be to limit the right of a transferor or his transferee to require the election to transfers in which the transferee will be entitled to a specified minimum basis increase as a result of the election. The idea here, familiar to experienced drafters, is to obtain an agreement between the partners before it becomes clear whose ox is apt to be gored.

[6] Application of the Election to Partnerships Terminated Prior to 2018

Former § 708(b)(1)(B) provided for the termination of a partnership upon the sale or exchange of 50 percent or more of the interests in partnership capital and profits within a twelve-month period. For tax years beginning before 2018, Regulations § 1.708-1(b)(4) provides that if a partnership terminates under § 708(b)(1)(B), the following is deemed to occur: The partnership contributes all of its assets and liabilities to a new partnership in exchange for an interest in the new partnership; and, immediately thereafter, the terminated partnership distributes, in liquidation of the terminated partnership, interests in the new partnership to the purchasing partner and the other remaining partners (in proportion to their respective interests in the terminated partnership), either for the continuation of the business by the new partnership or for its dissolution and winding up.

Regulations § 1.708-1(b)(5) provides:

> If a partnership is terminated by a sale or exchange of an interest in the partnership, a section 754 election (including a section 754 election made by the terminated partnership on its final return) that is in effect for the taxable year of the terminated partnership in which the sale occurs, applies with respect to the incoming partner. Therefore, the bases of partnership assets are adjusted pursuant to sections 743 and 755 prior to their deemed contribution to the new partnership.

Under Regulations § 1.761-1(e), for purposes of § 708(b)(1)(B), the deemed distribution of an interest in a new partnership by a partnership that terminates under § 708(b)(1)(B) is treated as an exchange of the interest in the new partnership for purposes of § 743. Thus, a § 754 election may be made by the new partnership, as a result of which the bases of the new partnership in its assets will be adjusted under § 743(b) with respect to the partners of the new partnership.[226]

[7] Reporting Requirements

A transferee who acquires a partnership interest by sale or exchange or upon the death of a partner is required to notify the partnership of the transfer. The notice must (1) be written; (2) include the names, addresses, and taxpayer identification numbers of the transferor (if known) and transferee, the date of the transfer, the relationship (if any) between the transferee and the transferor; and (3) (a) in the case of a sale or exchange, include the amount of money and the fair market value of any other consideration given or to be given for the interest, or (b) in the case of a transfer upon the death of a partner, include the fair market value of the interest on the applicable valuation date under § 1014, the date of death, and the manner in which market value was determined.[227] The notice must be given within thirty days of a sale or exchange (but no later than January 15 of the next calendar year) or within one year of the death of a deceased partner.[228]

The partnership is not required to take any action, unless it receives a notice (as described above) or the partner who has responsibility for federal income tax reporting has "knowledge" (apparently, actual knowledge) that a transfer has occurred.[229] If a partnership has notice or knowledge of a transfer, it must attach a statement to its return for the year of the transfer setting forth the name and taxpayer identification number of the transferee, as well as the computation of the § 743(b) adjustment and the properties to which it has been

---

[226] These rules are generally applicable to terminations of partnerships under § 708(b)(1)(B) occurring on or after May 9, 1997, or, by election of the partners, to terminations occurring on or after May 9, 1996, and before 2018. See generally supra ¶ 24.04[1][b][iv]. Prior to the effective date of Regulations § 1.708-1(b)(5), the Service ruled that a § 754 election by a terminated partnership is applicable to the transferee of the partnership interest that causes the § 708(b)(1)(B) termination, reasoning that the transferee is properly viewed as a partner in the terminated partnership for the instant prior to its termination. Rev. Rul. 86-73, 1986-1 CB 282. The Service apparently believes that, under the duty of consistency, a taxpayer is bound in future years by the factual representations inherent in these computations. FSA 200234006 (Feb. 22, 2002).

[227] Reg. §§ 1.743-1(k)(2), 1.743-1(k)(3). The partnership is entitled to rely on the written notice, unless the partner who is responsible for federal income tax reporting has knowledge of facts indicating that the notice is clearly erroneous. See Reg. § 1.743-1(k)(3). If the partnership interest is transferred to a nominee that is required to furnish a § 6031(c) statement to the partnership, the nominee may satisfy both notice requirements with a single statement containing all required information. See Reg. § 1.743-1(k)(2)(iii).

[228] Reg. § 1.743-1(k)(2).

[229] Reg. § 1.743-1(k)(4).

allocated.[230] If the transferee fails to provide notice, the partnership must attach a statement to its return in the year it is notified of the transfer. The statement must set forth the name and identification number (if known) of the transferee, and must "prominently display" the following statement in capital letters on the first page of the return and on the first page of any schedule relating to the transferee's allocations for the year: "RETURN FILED PURSUANT TO § 1.743-1(k)(5)."[231]

¶ 24.12 SPECIAL POST-ADJUSTMENT PROBLEMS

Following a § 743(b) adjustment, the partners will have different bases with respect to various partnership assets. As a result, certain types of partnership accounting elections under § 703(b) may have disparate consequences for the partners, or may affect certain partners but not others. For example, a replacement of involuntarily converted partnership property under § 1033 should allow some partners to defer gain on the conversion without precluding the deductibility of losses by other partners.

More difficult problems may arise if the partnership has a loss on the transaction (measured with respect to common basis), but certain partners have gains. In this situation, it is not clear that the partnership is eligible to make special Code-provided elections that only apply to gains (e.g., § 1033 elections). Nevertheless, it would appear both advisable and appropriate for such partners to attempt to make any elections that may be necessary to protect partners who realize gains on the transaction.[232]

---

[230] Reg. § 1.743-1(k)(1).

[231] Reg. § 1.743-1(k)(5). Provision is also made for belated notices by transferees. Id.

[232] See Tax Clinic, 9 Tax Adviser 335, 337 (1978).

CHAPTER **26**

Special Basis Adjustments in Connection With Distributions to Transferee-Partners: Section 732(d)

¶ 26.01 TRANSFEREES' SPECIAL BASIS ADJUSTMENTS IN CONNECTION WITH SUBSEQUENT DISTRIBUTIONS

If a partnership interest is acquired by sale or exchange or upon the death of a partner[1] and § 743(b) is inapplicable to the acquisition of such interest,[2] § 732(d) provides special rules for determining the partnership's basis in property (other than money) when subsequently distributed to the transferee-partner.[3] For purposes of computing the distributee's basis in distributed assets under subsections (a) through (c) of § 732, the assets are treated as having adjusted partnership bases equal to the bases they would have had if § 743(b) had been applicable to the distributee's acquisition of his interest. Application of § 732(d) may be either

1. *Elective*, at the option of the distributee, with respect to any property distributions within two years of the acquisition of the distributee's partnership interest,[4] or
2. *Mandatory*, regardless of when the distribution occurs, if the market value of partnership property (other than money) exceeds 110 percent of its basis at the time the acquisition occurs and certain other conditions are met.[5]

Section 732 became part of the Code when Subchapter K was enacted in 1954. As originally enacted, § 732(c) required that the basis of a liquidated partnership interest (or the basis of a partnership interest in a distribution to which § 732(a)(2) applied) be allocated first to any unrealized receivables and inventory items in an amount equal to the adjusted basis of each such property

---

[1] See Reg. § 1.732-1(d)(l)(i).

[2] By its terms, § 732(d) potentially applies to all cases where "the election provided in section 754 is not in effect." Prior to amendment in 2004, § 743(b) applied only if an election under § 754 was in effect. Section 743(b) was amended, by the American Jobs Creation Act, Pub. L. No. 108-357 (Oct. 22, 2004), and subsequently by the 2017 Tax Cuts and Jobs Act, Pub. L. No. 115-97 (Dec. 22, 2017), to apply to transfers of partnership interests if the partnership has a "substantial built-in loss" immediately after such transfer, regardless of whether an election under § 754 is in effect. See ¶ 24.01[4]. Section 732(d) should not apply in a case where application of § 743(b) is mandatory, because of the existence of a substantial built-in loss.

[3] General Counsel Memorandum 39502 (May 7, 1986) indicates that § 732(d) applies in connection with the constructive distribution of partnership assets to a transferee-partner who has acquired his interest in a transaction that causes a termination of the partnership under § 708(b)(1)(B) before May 9, 1997. See ¶ 13.05[2] n. 93; Priv. Ltr. Rul. 9232022 (May 5, 1992); infra ¶ 26.03. Cf. Rev. Rul. 86-73, 1986-1 CB 282 (§ 754 election applies to transferee in same situation); see ¶ 24.10[4]. Section 708(b)(1)(B) was repealed by the 2017 Tax Cuts and Jobs Act for partnership tax years beginning after 2017. Pub. L. No. 115-97, § 13504(a) (Dec. 22, 2017).

[4] See infra ¶ 26.02.

[5] See infra ¶ 26.03.

to the partnership and then to all other distributed assets in proportion to their
predistribution basis to the partnership. Congress recognized that this relatively
simple method of allocating basis could result in unwarranted shifts of basis in
the case of transferee-partners, and, in response, adopted § 732(d) to reduce
the likelihood of such unwarranted shifts occurring.[6]

The basis allocation scheme of § 732(c) was substantially amended by the
Taxpayer Relief Act of 1997. As amended, § 732(c) continues to require that
the basis of a liquidated partnership interest be reduced by any money received
in liquidation, and then allocated (1) first to distributed unrealized receivables
and inventory in an amount equal to their predistribution bases to the partnership[7] and (2) thereafter to other distributed assets in an amount equal to their
predistribution bases to the partnership.[8] However, the methodology for allocating basis shortfalls and excess basis among distributed assets was modified
significantly. If the partnership interest basis available to be allocated to a particular class of assets is less than the partnership's basis for such assets, the
shortfall is first allocated among all depreciated assets (assets whose values are
less than their bases) to reduce proportionately the differences between the bases and values of these assets, and then the remaining shortfall, if any, is allocated among all distributed assets in proportion to their bases, as so reduced.[9]
On the other hand, if the partnership interest basis available to be allocated to
assets other than unrealized receivables and inventory items (which are prohibited from having their bases increased) exceeds the partnership's basis for such
assets, the excess is first allocated among all appreciated assets (assets whose
values are greater than their bases) to reduce proportionately the differences
between the values and the bases of these assets, and then the remaining excess, if any, is allocated among all distributed assets in proportion to their respective fair market values.[10]

These rules reduce the opportunity to shift basis from non-depreciable to
depreciable assets, since both the § 732(c) rules and the § 743(b) rules try to
adjust the bases of assets towards fair market value and then apply any excess
to assets other than inventory and unrealized receivables in proportion to
value. As the basic schemes are quite similar, a partner whose interest is liqui-

---

[6] The 1954 legislative history to § 732(d) contains two examples. In the first example, the normal application of § 732(c) operates to shift a transferee partner's basis from
inventory to capital and depreciable assets. In the second example, a shift from nondepreciable to depreciable assets occurs. In each case, the application of § 732(d), whether elective or mandatory, prevented such basis shifts from occurring. See S. Rep. No. 1622, 83d
Cong., 2d Sess. 392 (1954).

[7] § 732(c)(1)(A)(i). See generally ¶ 19.06[2].

[8] § 732(c)(1)(B)(i).

[9] § 732(c)(3). See generally ¶ 19.06[2].

[10] § 732(c)(2)(B). See generally ¶ 19.06[2].

dated will often be indifferent as to whether a § 754 election was in effect at the time she acquired her interest.

One major difference in the basis allocation schemes remains, however, giving continuing vitality to § 732(d). Basis determinations for distributed property start with a carryover basis (which for inventory and unrealized receivables cannot be increased), while the fair market value purchase of a partnership interest to which § 743(b) applies will cause the bases of partnership assets to be set at fair market value.[11] Accordingly, in this respect, a distributee-partner can have a significantly different outcome depending on whether a § 754 election was in effect when she acquired her interest, because the basis of distributed property for purposes of § 732 includes the distributee's § 743(b) adjustment, if any, made upon the acquisition of her partnership interest.[12] If, assuming a § 754 election was in effect, the § 743(b) adjustment to inventory and unrealized receivables is positive, distributees of such property will generally want to invoke § 732(d), since to do so will increase the basis of ordinary income assets upon distribution to them. Similarly, under such circumstances, if the partnership holds appreciated depreciable assets and depreciated nondepreciable capital assets, invoking § 732(d) will shift basis to the depreciable property. It is questionable whether the tax stakes in these cases are high enough to warrant the mandatory application of § 732(d). Nevertheless, the Treasury decided to retain the mandatory aspect of § 732(d) when it looked at the issue in 1999.[13]

[1] Computation of the Adjustment

The aggregate amount of the § 732(d) adjustment is computed under § 743(b) as if a § 754 election had been in effect with respect to the distributee's acquisition of his partnership interest. A major modification to the rules governing computation of this adjustment[14] is engrafted on the statute by Regulations § 1.732-1(d)(1)(iv), which provides that the amount of the adjustment is not diminished by any interim depletion or depreciation that would have been al-

---

[11] See generally ¶ 24.04.

[12] Reg. §§ 1.732-2(b), 1.732-2(c).

[13] On January 29, 1998, the Treasury Department released proposed amendments to the § 732(d) Regulations to conform those Regulations to the changes made to § 732(c) by the Taxpayer Relief Act of 1997. The preamble to the Proposed Regulations noted that the amendments to § 732(c) made the basis distortions that were the target of the existing Regulations less likely to occur, and requested comments regarding under what circumstances, if any, the Treasury Department should exercise its authority to mandate the application of § 732(d) to a transferee. In TD 8847, 1999-2 CB 701, which adopted final § 732(d) Regulations, the preamble stated that the mandatory application of § 732(d) was still necessary because distortions caused by § 732(c) could still occur.

[14] See discussion at ¶ 24.02.

lowable with respect to the portion of the basis arising from the adjustment itself. As this provision of the Regulations notes, such depletion or depreciation is not allowable for the period prior to the distribution. Consequently, it makes little sense to reduce the basis adjustment by taking it into account.

[2] Allocation of the Adjustment to Specific Partnership Assets

Like § 743(b), § 732(d) relies on § 755 for the allocation of the aggregate § 732(d) adjustment to specific partnership properties.[15] In connection with this allocation, Regulations § 1.732-1(d)(1)(v) deals with problems that may arise if the property distributed is not property with respect to which the distributee would have been entitled to a special basis adjustment under § 743(b). This situation may arise with respect to (1) property acquired by the partnership subsequent to the distributee's acquisition of his partnership interest,[16] or (2) property that, although held by the partnership at the time, would not have been subject to adjustment for a variety of reasons.[17] In these cases, the § 732 Regulations seem to apply the same concepts to the shifting of hypothetical adjustments as are applicable to the shifting of actual adjustments under Regulations § 1.743-1(g), as well as to provide (for the application to distributed property) adjustments with respect to "like property," in which the transferee has relinquished an interest in exchange for the distributed property.[18]

[3] The Impact of Section 732(d) Adjustments

Section 732(d) does not directly adjust the basis of distributed property in the hands of the distributee. Instead, it provides for adjustment of the partnership's basis in distributed property immediately prior to its distribution. The distributee's basis in the property is then determined under the usual rules set forth in subsections (a) through (c) of § 732.

---

[15] TD 8847 states that in calculating basis adjustments, a "partnership should apply the final regulations under section 743 and 755 if the distribution to which section 732(d) applies occurs on or after December 15, 1999." The Regulations under §§ 743 and 755 were significantly modified by TD 8847, effective for transfers of partnership interests on or after December 15, 1999. Thus, it appears that those revised Regulations will apply to a distribution triggering § 732(d) that occurs on or after December 15, 1999, even though the prior Regulations under §§ 743 and 755 would have applied to the transfer of the partnership interest had a § 754 election been in effect at the time of such transfer.

[16] See Regulations § 1.732-1(d)(1)(vi) Example, stating that it is "immaterial" to the application of § 732(d) whether distributed inventory was on hand when the distributee acquired his interest.

[17] See ¶ 24.04.

[18] These rules are described at ¶ 24.05.

If the distributee takes a carryover basis in distributed property under the general rule applicable to current distributions pursuant to § 732(a)(1), the § 732(d) adjustment with respect to the distributed property is included in his carryover basis from the partnership, and, consequently, has a dollar-for-dollar effect on the distributee's basis. However, if the distributee's basis in distributed property is limited to his predistribution basis in his partnership interest under (1) § 732(a)(2) with respect to current distributions or (2) § 732(b) with respect to liquidating distributions, the § 732(d) adjustment generally does not affect the distributee's aggregate basis in distributed property,[19] but may affect the manner in which his basis in his partnership interest is allocated among the distributed assets under § 732(c).[20]

[4] Application to Section 751(b) Distributions and Section 751(a) Transfers

If a distribution changes the distributee's interest in the partnership's § 751 property, § 751(b) creates a hypothetical current distribution of the class of property with respect to which the distributee's interest is reduced, followed by a taxable exchange of such property for partnership property in the class with respect to which the distributee's interest is increased upon the distribution.[21] In determining the distributee's basis in property received in a hypothetical § 751(b) distribution, § 732(d) basis adjustments are taken into account even though no actual distribution occurs.[22]

Conversely, § 732(d) has no application upon the sale or exchange of a partnership interest. For transferees of interests before December 15, 1999, the regulatory scheme computed the seller's ordinary income by postulating a current distribution of his share of the partnership's ordinary income assets, followed by a sale of those assets; § 732(d) was fully applicable to the constructive current distribution.[23] The 1999 amendments of the § 751 Regula-

---

[19] An exception to this generalization occurs in connection with current distributions if the distributee's basis in his partnership interest is greater than the partnership's basis in the distributed property, computed without reference to § 732(d), but less than the partnership's basis as increased under § 732(d). In this situation, the aggregate basis of distributed property in the hands of the distributee is increased by the application of § 732(d), and the allocation of this basis among the distributed assets under § 732(c) may also be affected.

[20] See Arthur G. Rudd, 79 TC 225 (1982) (acq.) (mandatory application of § 732(d) shifts transferee-distributee's basis from furniture and fixtures to goodwill upon liquidation of partnership; portion of purchase price paid for partnership interest by distributee attributable to goodwill); see generally ¶¶ 19.04, 19.06.

[21] See ¶ 21.01.

[22] Reg. §§ 1.732-1(e), 1.751-1(b)(2)(iii), 1.751-1(b)(3)(iii).

[23] Reg. § 1.751-1(a)(2) (1956).

tions to a partnership-level hypothetical sale approach deprived taxpayers of the potential benefits of § 732(d), thereby increasing the chances that the fisc could tax partnership ordinary income twice (once to the first seller, and again to the purchaser/seller who failed to cause the partnership to make a § 754 election at the time of his acquisition of his interest).

¶ 26.02 ELECTIVE ADJUSTMENTS

If partnership property is distributed to a transferee within two years of the date he acquires his interest, the transferee may elect to compute the basis of the distributed property under § 732(d). The election to compute basis under § 732(d) must accompany the distributee's return for (1) the year of the distribution, if the distribution includes depreciable, depletable, or amortizable property, or (2) any taxable year not later than the first year in which the basis of distributed property is pertinent to the distributee's income tax liability, if the distribution does not include such property.[24] No particular form of election is required by the § 732 Regulations. However, the election must include a statement that the distributee elects to adjust the basis of distributed property under § 732(d), and a computation of the amount of the adjustment and the properties to which it is allocated under § 755.[25] If a transferee-partner notifies a partnership that it plans to make the election under § 732(d), the partnership is required to provide the transferee with the information necessary for the transferee to properly compute basis adjustments under § 732(d). The partnership is also required to supply information to the transferee-partner if the mandatory adjustment rule of Regulations § 1.732-1(d)(4) is applicable.[26]

[1] Elective Application of Section 732(d) Following the Purchase of a Partnership Interest

The application of § 732(d) following the purchase of a partnership interest may be illustrated as follows.

> **EXAMPLE 26-1:** *ABC* is an equal partnership that has two assets: cash of $600 and inventory with a basis of $2,100 and a market value of $2,400. *C* sells his interest to *D* for $1,000, its market value. *A* and *B* refuse to permit an election to be filed under § 754, pointing out (correctly) that the election will be of no immediate benefit to them and may ultimately

---

[24] Reg. § 1.732-1(d)(2).
[25] Reg. § 1.732-1(d)(3).
[26] Reg. § 1.732-1(d)(5).

operate to their detriment.[27] Consequently, D is not entitled to an increase in basis with respect to his share of the inventory. If the inventory is sold by the partnership, D's share of the partnership's ordinary income will be $100 even though he has no economic profit.

This unfortunate result can be avoided, with some cooperation on the part of A and B, if D's share of the inventory is distributed to him in kind, so that by electing to take advantage of § 732(d), he can obtain a basis (the "would have been" basis under § 743(b)) of $800 in the inventory. On a subsequent sale of the inventory by D for $800, no gain is realized because his basis is equal to the market value of the property.

The advantage of § 732(d) in this context is that, unlike §§ 754 and 743(b), its use by D does not commit the partnership to continue to make basis adjustments in connection with subsequent transfers and distributions.

Although the elective adjustments under § 732(d) may be helpful in certain cases in curing basis inequities confronting an acquiring partner who is not entitled to adjustments under § 743(b), its powers in this regard should not be overestimated. Its limitations are apparent from an examination of the two types of assets the bases of which are likely to be of concern to a new partner. The first is appreciated property that is slated for sale by the partnership, such as the inventory in the preceding example. The second is appreciated property with respect to which the partners are entitled to continuing deductions (amortization, depreciation, or depletion) computed with reference to the property's basis.

If distributions of property in the first category are followed closely by sales of the distributed property, the transaction may be vulnerable to attack on the theory that, in substance, the distribution was of the sale proceeds, rather than the property. Although there is a dearth of case law under the partnership provisions,[28] analogous cases dealing with corporate distributions are likely to provide compelling authority in analyzing transactions of this sort.[29] A subsequent recontribution of the sales proceeds is particularly likely to prove fatal to the hoped-for application of § 732(d).[30] Finally, the Service may assert the au-

---

[27] For discussion of the considerations involved in a § 754 election, see ¶ 24.11[5].

[28] Cf. Rev. Rul. 75-113, 1975-1 CB 19; see ¶ 16.02[3][d].

[29] Under Subchapter C, the courts have analyzed corporate distributions in terms of the identity of the "real" seller of the distributed property. If the distributing corporation is found to be the seller, the transaction is taxed as a sale by the corporation followed by a distribution of the proceeds. Compare Commissioner v. Court Holding Co., 324 US 331 (1945) (sale by corporation) with United States v. Cumberland Pub. Serv. Co., 338 US 451 (1950) (sale by shareholders).

[30] This fact pattern raises questions not only as to what was distributed but also as to whether anything was distributed.

thority to recast the transaction as a sale by the partnership under the anti-abuse rule contained in the § 701 Regulations.[31]

Economic considerations may create problems with respect to distributions of the second type of property, particularly if the property's use is integral to the operation of the partnership business. If the new partner is the only recipient of the distribution, the remaining partners will presumably insist on a rearrangement of interests in partnership capital and profits. If all partners receive distributions of undivided interests in property, there may be a question as to whether a distribution has in fact occurred. These problems are accentuated if the partnership needs to continue to use the property, although there is some evidence that a carefully structured leaseback may achieve the desired results, at least with respect to disproportionate distributions.[32] The anti-abuse rule in the § 701 Regulations can come into play in this context as well.

[2] Elective Application of Section 732(d) Following the Death of a Partner

Although not particularly effective as a planning tool following the purchase of a partnership interest, a § 732(d) election may reduce the amount of ordinary income realized under § 751(b) upon the liquidation of a partnership interest within two years of the death of a partner.

¶ 26.03 MANDATORY ADJUSTMENTS

The mandatory aspect of § 732(d) is one of the least-known provisions of Subchapter K. Because of its obscurity and its potential applicability many years after the occurrence of the transfer that triggers its application, it constitutes a particularly insidious trap for the unwary. Fortunately, perhaps, the virtual absence of reported litigation involving this aspect of § 732 seems to indicate a lack of awareness, not only on the part of taxpayers and their representatives, but among Service personnel as well.[33] Furthermore, as discussed at ¶ 26.01, amendments made to § 732(c) by the Taxpayer Relief Act of 1997 substantially change and limit, but do not eliminate, the mandatory effect of § 732(d).

---

[31] Reg. § 1.701-2, discussed at ¶ 1.05.

[32] Cf. Leon A. Harris, Jr., 61 TC 770 (1974).

[33] But see Arthur G. Rudd, 79 TC 225 (1982) (acq.) (mandatory application of § 732(d) at behest of taxpayer to generate post-dissolution abandonment loss with respect to partnership name); PBD Sports, Ltd., 109 TC 423 (1997) (taxpayer invoked mandatory application of § 732(d) to achieve increased basis allocation to short-lived assets).

The statute delegates to the § 732 Regulations most of the responsibility for defining the conditions under which mandatory application of § 732(d) is called for, requiring only that the fair market value of partnership assets (other than money) must exceed 110 percent of the adjusted basis of the assets at the time of the transfer. The § 732 Regulations[34] add two additional requirements:

1. An allocation of basis under § 732(c), upon a hypothetical liquidation of the transferred interest immediately after the transfer, would have resulted in a "shift" of basis to depreciable, depletable, or amortizable property from other property; and
2. Application of § 743(b) would change the basis of property actually distributed to the transferee.

The apparent purpose of the mandatory application of § 732(d) was to avoid potential distortions that could arise under the pre−1997 Act version of § 732(c) whenever such distortions would favor the taxpayer by inflating the basis of depreciable, depletable, or amortizable property above its market value.[35] This type of distortion could occur because under certain circumstances, including liquidation of a partner's interest, old § 732(c)(2) provided for allocation of a portion of a partner's basis to distributed property (other than unrealized receivables and inventory) in proportion to the partnership's adjusted bases in the assets without reference to their market values.[36]

As discussed earlier in ¶ 26.01, the 1997 amendments to § 732(c) reduce substantially the circumstances in which these distortions can arise. These

---

[34] Reg. § 1.732-1(d)(4).

[35] But see Arthur G. Rudd, 79 TC 225 (1982) (acq.) (mandatory application of § 732(d) benefits taxpayer).

[36] See ¶¶ 19.04, 19.06. In Private Letter Ruling 9232022 (May 5, 1992), the purchase by C and D of the equal partnership interests of A and B in the X partnership caused X to be treated as terminated under § 708(b)(1)(B). Under the Regulations then in effect, the terminated partnership was treated as distributing its assets to C and D in liquidation. The Service ruled that § 732(d) applied to the "deemed" liquidating distributions on a mandatory basis, provided only that the usual conditions to its application were satisfied: (1) the value of partnership assets was greater than 110 percent of their basis to X; (2) an allocation of basis under § 732(c) would shift basis from nondepreciable property to depreciable property; and (3) application of § 743(b) would change the basis of property "actually distributed." The Service's position that § 732(d) was applicable when a purchase of partnership interests causes a termination of the partnership under § 708(b)(1)(B) is consistent with its analysis that the terminating partnership may make a § 754 election in the same circumstances, although the absence of an actual distribution of assets under § 708(b)(1)(B) is an apparent technical flaw in this application of § 732(d). See Rev. Rul. 88-42, 1988-2 CB 265; GCM 39502 (May 7, 1986); ¶ 24.10[6]. Section 708(b)(1)(B) terminations, occurring in partnership taxable years beginning before 2018 and triggered by transfers of interests on or after May 9, 1997, did not result in deemed liquidating distributions of partnership assets. See ¶ 13.05[2]. However, for partnership tax years beginning after 2017, this is no longer a concern since § 708(b)(1)(B) was repealed by the 2017 Tax Cuts and Jobs Act, Pub. L. No. 115-97, § 13504(a) (Dec. 22, 2017).

amendments also highlight the issue of when a prohibited "shift" of basis occurs, since both § 732(c) and § 743(b) work towards getting basis equal to value. The § 732 Regulations do not set forth a standard for determining whether a "shift" of basis from nondepreciable to depreciable property would occur in connection with a hypothetical liquidation immediately after the transfer of an interest. Under one view, a comparison is made between the tax basis that would be attributed to depreciable property under § 732(c) in a pro rata liquidation assuming no § 754 election and the tax basis that would be attributed to depreciable property assuming a § 754 election had been in effect with regard to the transfer. If the tax basis of depreciable property is higher in the hypothetical liquidation without a § 754 election than with an election, then a "shift" has occurred.

Under an alternative and more supportable view, a "shift" occurs only if a hypothetical pro rata liquidation would result in an allocation of basis to depreciable property under § 732(c) that both (1) causes the basis of the depreciable property to exceed its fair market value and (2) causes the basis of such property to exceed its basis in the hands of the partnership. This approach is more consistent with the apparent policy goal of § 732(d), which is to prevent the use of the basis allocation regime of § 732(c) to produce a better result for the taxpayer than the result the taxpayer would get if no distribution of assets triggering application of § 732(c) had occurred. Although there is no authority directly confirming this view, it is consistent with the example contained in the legislative history to § 732(d) and with examples previously contained in the § 732 Regulations.[37] Additionally, this reading respects the independent vitality of the requirements that both a "shift" of basis occur and a § 743(b) adjustment would have changed the basis of the property in fact distributed.

Although the 1997 amendments to § 732(c) largely eliminate the possibility of any type of basis "shift," as discussed earlier in ¶ 26.01, at least two types of potential shifts remain. First, if appreciated inventory is distributed along with depreciable property, § 732(c) limits the basis of the inventory to its basis in the hands of the partnership and allocates all remaining basis to the depreciable property. While this is a "shift" of basis from nondepreciable to depreciable property, the cost to the fisc depends on when the inventory is sold versus how rapidly the depreciable basis is recovered. Ironically, the mandatory application of § 732(d) in this context is likely to favor the taxpayer. Second, if nondepreciable property is distributed along with depreciable property, § 732(c) may allocate more basis to the depreciable property in some cases; such allocation of basis, however, may not constitute a prohibited "shift" under the alternative view expressed above.

---

[37] See S. Rep. No. 1622, 83d Cong., 2d Sess. 392 (1954); Reg. § 1.732-1(d)(4) Examples 1, 2 (1956).

EXAMPLE 26-2: *ABC* is an equal partnership that has four assets: inventory with a basis of $2,100 and a market value of $2,400, and three depreciable assets each with a basis and value of $200. *C* sells his interest to *D* for $1,000 when no § 754 election is in effect. The partnership subsequently retires *D*'s interest, distributing $800 of inventory with a basis of $700 and one of the three depreciable assets. In this case, the fair market value of all partnership property exceeds 110 percent of its adjusted basis to the partnership at the time of the transfer of the partnership interest. In a hypothetical pro rata liquidation immediately following the transfer of the partnership interest, *D* would receive one third of the inventory, taking a basis of $700, and one third of each depreciable asset, with each asset receiving a basis of $100. Since, under § 732(c), the total basis of the depreciable assets (1) is in excess of the fair market value of such property ($300 of tax basis and $200 fair market value) and (2) exceeds the basis of such property in the hands of the partnership ($200), a "shift" of basis has occurred. Finally, a basis adjustment under § 743(b) would have changed the basis of the property actually distributed, since the basis of the inventory would have been $800 (including *D*'s $100 § 743(b) adjustment). On these facts, the application of § 732(d) is mandatory, even though the fisc is likely to be harmed by such application.

EXAMPLE 26-3: *ABC* is an equal partnership that has four assets: a nondepreciable capital asset with a basis of $900 and a market value of $1,500, and three depreciable assets, each with a basis of $300 and a market value of $200 (total value of $2,100). *C* sells his interest to *D* for $700 when no § 754 election is in effect. The partnership subsequently retires *D*'s interest, distributing one third of the nondepreciable capital asset and one of the depreciable assets. The fair market value of partnership property at the time of the transfer ($2,100) is more than 110 percent of the basis of the property ($1,800). A hypothetical liquidation immediately after the transfer of the partnership interest would result in *D* receiving one third of the nondepreciable capital asset with a basis under § 732(c) of $400, and depreciable assets with a basis of $300. In this case, even though the basis of hypothetically distributed depreciable property exceeds its fair market value, it does not exceed the basis of that property in the hands of the partnership. Thus, no "shift" arguably occurs even though a § 743(b) adjustment would have resulted in the distributed nondepreciable assets having a basis of $500 and the depreciable asset having a basis of $200.[38] The mandatory application of § 732(d) should not be required.

---

[38] Under the first view of when a "shift" occurs, there would have been a shift on these facts, since a hypothetical liquidation without a § 743(b) adjustment leads to a higher basis for distributed depreciable property than a hypothetical liquidation with § 743(b) adjustments.

All basis shifts that favor taxpayers are not the subject of mandatory pro-government adjustments under § 732(d). Although shifts of basis from nondepreciable to depreciable property may trigger mandatory application of § 732(d), shifts from long-lived depreciable property to short-lived depreciable property do not.[39] As discussed earlier in ¶ 26.01, the amendment of § 732(c) has greatly reduced the likelihood of such shifts.

---

[39] In Technical Advice Memorandum 9734003 (Apr. 14, 1997), one of the assets of a corporation acquired in a § 338(g) transaction was an 80 percent interest in a mining partnership, triggering a § 708(b)(1)(B) termination of the partnership under the pre-1997 termination rules. There was no § 754 election in effect for the terminated partnership, and *T* did not elect to apply § 732(d) on an elective basis. As a result, there was a substantial increase in the basis of relatively short-lived depreciable assets of the partnership and no increase in the basis of relatively long-lived depreciable assets of the partnership. As a consequence, *T* claimed substantially larger depreciation deductions than it would have been entitled to if it had acquired an interest in the partnership assets directly. The National Office concluded that application of § 732(d) is not mandatory if there is a substantial business purpose for the transaction and the effect of the § 732(c) basis allocation rules is merely to shift basis from longer-lived to shorter-lived property. See Reg. § 1.732-1(d)(4)(ii). Section 708(b)(1)(B) was repealed by the 2017 Tax Cuts and Jobs Act, for partnership tax years beginning after 2017. Pub. L. No. 115-97, § 13504(a) (Dec. 22, 2017).

WG&L Tax Series

FEDERAL TAXATION OF PARTNERSHIPS AND PARTNERS

FOURTH EDITION

2021 Cumulative Supplement
to Abridged Student Edition

WILLIAM S. McKEE
Member of the Virginia
and District of Columbia
Bars

WILLIAM F. NELSON
Member of the Georgia
and District of Columbia
Bars

ROBERT L. WHITMIRE
Member of the California
Bar

GARY R. HUFFMAN
Member of the Texas and
District of Columbia Bars

JAMES P. WHITMIRE
Member of the Colorado
and Virginia Bars

THOMSON REUTERS™

This publication is designed to provide accurate and authoritative information in regard to the subject matter covered. It is sold with the understanding that the publisher is not engaged in rendering legal, accounting, or other professional service. If legal advice or other expert assistance is required, the services of a competent professional person should be sought.—From a Declaration of Principles jointly adopted by a Committee of the American Bar Association and a Committee of Publishers and Associations.

PRINTED IN THE UNITED STATES OF AMERICA

 THOMSON REUTERS™

How to Use This Supplement

THIS SUPPLEMENT brings the abridged student edition of *Federal Taxation of Partnerships and Partners, Fourth Edition*, up to date with coverage of significant developments that were not covered in the student edition but that occurred prior to January 1, 2021.

This supplement includes references to and appropriate discussions of important cases, published rulings, proposed regulations, final regulations, and legislation. It also includes references to private letter rulings that were made available for public inspection prior to January 1, 2021. Private letter rulings may not be cited as precedent in tax controversies, but they may provide valuable insight regarding the position of the Service on legal questions and may aid practitioners in preparing ruling requests on similar issues.

For economy, the publisher has included all material from the professional edition supplement. Therefore, this supplement contains references to some paragraphs that are not included in the student edition. Except for this, each entry in this supplement is keyed to a chapter, paragraph, and specific page number in the student edition. An italicized instruction line located under the reference in the student edition indicates exactly where the new material belongs in relation to the original text and/or footnotes of the student edition. Entries labeled "[New]" indicate sections introduced in the supplement. When using the student edition, you can quickly find whether there have been post-publication developments by locating the corresponding place in the supplement. The sequences of both the student edition and this supplement are identical. As a further aid to locating material in the supplement, the top of each page carries a reference to the paragraph number of the student edition to which it is related. The supplement also contains a series of cumulative tables and a cumulative index to both the student edition and the supplement.

Summary of Contents

VOLUME 1

VOLUME 2

Table of Contents

VOLUME 1

3 Defining "Partnerships" and "Partners" for Tax Purposes

PART II ACQUISITIONS OF PARTNERSHIP INTERESTS

4

Receipt of a Partnership Interest in Exchange for a Contribution of Property

TABLE OF CONTENTS

10   TEFRA Partnership Audit and Litigation Rules

10A   Centralized Partnership Audit Regime

11   Determining the Partners' Distributive Shares

12 Distributive Share Allocations in Connection With Shifts in the Partners' Interests

VOLUME 2

PART V TERMINATIONS; PARTNERSHIP-PARTNER TRANSACTIONS; AND FAMILY PARTNERSHIP RULES

13 Termination of a Partnership

14   Transactions Between Partnerships and Partners

15   Family Partnership Rules

PART VI   TRANSFERS OF PARTNERSHIP INTERESTS

17   Transfers of Interests in Collapsible Partnerships

18   Incorporation of a Partnership

PART VII   PARTNERSHIP DISTRIBUTIONS

19   Distributions That Do Not Alter the Partners' Interests in Section 751 Property

21   Distributions That Alter the Partners' Interests in Section 751(b) Property

PART VIII   DEATH OR RETIREMENT OF A PARTNER

22   Payments in Liquidation of the Interest of a Retired or Deceased Partner

23   Special Problems Relating to the Death of a Partner

PART IX   ADJUSTMENTS TO THE BASES OF PARTNERSHIP ASSETS

24   Adjustments to the Bases of Partnership Assets in Connection With Transfers of Partnership Interests

25   Adjustments to the Bases of Partnership Assets in Connection With Distributions of Partnership Assets

26   Special Basis Adjustments in Connection With Distributions to Transferee-Partners: Section 732(d)

General Concepts

CHAPTER 1

An Overview of Subchapter K

¶ 1.01 THE OPERATING RULES OF SUBCHAPTER K

[1] Partnership Operations

Page 1-3:

Replace note 9 with the following.

⁹ § 704(e)(1) (former § 704(e)(2) renumbered on 2016 repeal of § 704(e)(1), which is discussed at ¶ 3.00).

¶ 1.02 THE AGGREGATE AND ENTITY CONCEPTS

[3] Blending of the Entity and Aggregate Concepts

Page 1-9:

Add new note 41.1 at end of list item 2.

41.1 See Grecian Magnesite Mining, Industrial & Shipping Co, SA. v. Commissioner, 149 TC No 3 (2017), aff'd, 926 F3d 819 (DC Cir. 2019), citing and quoting this text.

¶ 1.04 CAPITAL GAINS AND SUBCHAPTER K

Replace last paragraph of subsection with the following.

The American Taxpayer Relief Act of 2012[52.1] increased the maximum capital gains rate (to 20%). The 2017 Tax Cuts and Jobs Act set the maximum marginal rate on ordinary income at 37 percent. Thus, the spread between the maximum ordinary income and long-term capital gains rates has been reduced only slightly (from 20% to 17%).

52.1 Pub. L. No. 112-240, § 101(b)(2)(A).

¶ 1.05 SUBCHAPTER K ANTI-ABUSE RULE

[1] Overview

[c] Neutral Principles and Tax Avoidance Motives

Page 1-20:

Add to note 68.

The IRS National Office has granted "blanket approval" for agents to apply the anti-abuse rule in seven specific areas: (1) transactions described in CCA 200704030 (Oct. 6, 2006) (dealing with the use of a partnership to facilitate the sale of state tax credits); (2) transactions described in Notice 2000-44, 2000-2 CB 255 (assumption by a partnership of obligation to deliver property under a sold call option); (3) partnership straddle shelters described in Notice 2002-50, 2002-2 CB 690; (4) straddle transactions described in Notice 2002-65, 2002-2 CB 690; (5) transactions involving compensatory options sold to related persons as described in Coordinated Issue Papers based on Notice 2003-47, 2004-2 CB 48; (6) transactions described in Notice 2004-31, 2004-1 CB 830, that avoid limitations on interest deductibility under former § 163(j); and (7) transactions described in a Coordinated Issue Paper entitled "Redemption Bogus Optional Basis Tax Shelter" (Jan. 31, 2006), where the transaction involves a special purpose partnership. See "IRS Gives Blanket Authority to Apply Partnership Anti-abuse Reg.," 2007 TNT 51-5 (Mar. 15, 2007). Any hope that the IRS National Office would seriously monitor assertions of the anti-abuse rule were somewhat dimmed by the Service's issuance of an FPAA asserting that the anti-abuse rule supported the disregarding of a partnership whose sole tax benefit was the reduction of *state* taxes; this assertion was, however, dropped on the eve of trial. See Virginia Historic Tax Credit Fund 2001 LP, 98 TCM 630 (2009), rev'd, 2011-1 USTC ¶ 50,308 (4th Cir. 2011).

Replace note 69 with the following.

[69] Jade Trading v. United States, 60 Fed. Cl. 558 (2004) (denying taxpayer's motions for partial summary judgment, one of which was based on the asserted invalidity of Regulations § 1.701-2; issue held not ripe for decision because of alternate theories asserted by government; unclear which theories government would actually rely on). As discussed below (see text at note 72), the government ultimately did not assert the anti-abuse Regulations in this case, which it won on economic substance grounds.

Page 1-21:

Replace first and second full paragraphs with the following.

The government's reluctance to assert the anti-abuse rule has faded with time, and the courts seem receptive to its assertion. At least two district courts have relied on the anti-abuse rule to strike down aggressive tax shelters, albeit as alternative holdings.[71.1]

Eventually, the Court of Federal Claims decided *Jade Trading* in favor of the government, without mention of the anti-abuse rules,[72] relying instead on the economic substance doctrine as interpreted by the Federal Circuit in *Coltec Industries, Inc. v. United States*.[73] While the government's failure to assert the abuse-of-Subchapter-K rule in *Jade Trading* might be viewed as a concession that the transaction should be respected according to its form and that its tax consequences are consistent with the intent of Subchapter K, the Court of Federal Claims simply ignored this possible inference in deciding in favor of the government. The court held that despite compliance with the literal terms of Subchapter K, the taxpayer's "Son-of-BOSS" transaction lacked economic sub-

---

[71.1] Kearney Partners Fund, LLC v. United States, 2013-1 USTC ¶ 50,303 (MD Fla. 2013), aff'd per curiam, 803 F3d 1280 (11th Cir. 2015); Nevada Partners Fund, LLC v. United States, 2010-1 USTC ¶ 50,379 (SD Miss. 2010), aff'd, 2013-2 USTC ¶ 50,398 (5th Cir. 2013) (no discussion by Fifth Circuit of anti-abuse issue).

[72] Jade Trading, LLC v. United States, 80 Fed. Cl. 11 (2007).

[73] Coltec Indus., Inc. v. United States, 454 F3d 1340 (Fed. Cir. 2007).

stance. Following *Coltec* and *Jade Trading*, the common law sub-stance-over-form doctrine may have swallowed the abuse-of-Subchapter-K rule, at least in the Federal Circuit.

[2] Abuse-Of-Subchapter-K Rule

Page 1-26:

Add new note 84.1 at the end of fourth sentence (beginning with "The second negative factor...") of carryover paragraph.

[84.1] In CCA 200650014 (Sept. 7, 2006), the Service cites the second factor in support of its application of the abuse-of-Subchapter-K rule to a distribution of property acquired by a partnership apparently for the sole purpose of immediately distributing the property to a partner and circumventing any gain recognition under § 731(a). The Service's recast of this transaction (presumably as a distribution of cash, followed by the acquisition of the property in exchange for cash) contains precisely the same number of steps as the actual transaction. As a general rule, the Service's ability to reorder steps of a transaction under the step-transaction doctrine is limited. See Esmark v. Commissioner, 90 TC 171 (1988), aff'd without published opinion, 886 F2d 1318 (7th Cir. 1989). But see Long Term Capital Holdings v. United States, 330 F. Supp. 2d 122 (D. Conn. 2004), aff'd, 150 Fed. Appx. 40 (2d Cir. 2005). Application of the abuse-of-Subchapter-K rule in this context is consistent with the Service's aggressive view of the step-transaction doctrine.

Add the following after the carryover paragraph and before the first full paragraph.

Regulations proposed in 2008 would provide that an additional factor indicating a possible violation of the abuse-of-Subchapter K rule is the use of the remedial allocation method by related partners to make remedial allocations of items of income, gain, loss, or deduction to one partner and allocations of offsetting remedial items to a related partner.[84.2]

[84.2] Prop. Reg. § 1.704-3(a)(1) (2008). See ¶ 11.04[3][d] for a discussion of the remedial allocation method.

Page 1-27:

Add to note 87.

For the Service's application of the abuse-of-subchapter-K rule to purported equity that the Service believes is more appropriately taxable as debt, see Tech. Adv. Mem. 200807015 (Nov. 7, 2007).

[3] The Regulations § 1.701-2(d) Examples Used to Illustrate Application of the Anti-Abuse Rule

Page 1-31:

Replace note 93 with the following.

[93] The discussion notes, immediately following its explanation of what is permitted by § 704(b), that § 704(e)(1) (formerly § 704(e)(2) renumbered on 2016 repeal of former § 704(e)(1)), relating to partnership interests created by gift, is not applicable. It is unclear whether this reference is supposed to cast some light on the consistency of the allocations with the purposes of § 704(b), or is meant only to dismiss as irrelevant the rules of current § 704(e)(1) (2016 repeal discussed at ¶ 3.00).

Page 1-32:

Add new note 97.1 at the end of title of paragraph heading numbered 3.

[97.1] See CCA 200704030 (Oct. 6, 2006) and CCA 200704028 (Oct. 6, 2006) (each applying the anti-abuse rule to a partnership created for the purpose of purchasing and transferring state tax credits to its partners).

[4] Relationship to Existing Judicial Doctrines

[a] Bona Fide Partnership

Page 1-41:

Replace first full paragraph (ending with note callout 114).

In response to the confusion created by the *Culbertson* intent test, in 1951 Congress enacted the predecessor to now former § 704(e)(1), following its 2016 repeal, which provides that "[a] person shall be recognized as a partner for purposes of this subtitle if he owns a capital interest in a partnership in which capital is a material income producing factor, whether or not such interest was derived by purchase or gift from any other person." Former § 704(e)(1) was repealed by the Bipartisan Budget Act of 2015, effective for partnership taxable years beginning after December 31, 2015, while § 704(e)'s remaining provisions, "Distributive share of donee includible in gross income" and "Purchase of interest by member of family" were renumbered §§ 704(e)(1) and 704(e)(2), respectively.[114] For a complete discussion of the rationale for, as well as the ramifications of, this repeal, see ¶ 3.00.

---

[114] Bipartisan Budget Act of 2015, § 1102(c), Pub. L. No. 114-74 (Nov. 2, 2015).

Page 1-42:

Replace note 119 with the following.

[119] ASA Investerings Partnership v. Commissioner, 201 F3d 505, 512 (DC Cir. 2000). See also Boca Investerings v. United States, 314 F3d 625 (DC Cir. 2003) (cert. denied) (partnership entity not respected in absence of nontax business need for its existence; relying on *Culbertson* and *ASA Investerings*); Chemtech Royalty Assocs., LP v. United States, 2013-1 USTC ¶ 50,204 (MD La. 2013), aff'd, 766 F3d 453 (5th Cir. 2014) (cert. denied) (partnership not respected despite asserted nontax business purposes of off-balance

sheet financing because "[t]here were cheaper and less complex alternatives to [the effec-tuated transaction] that could achieve the goal of obtaining [off-balance sheet financing]"); New Millennium Trading, LLC, 113 TCM 1033 (2017) (partnership entity not respected; all partnership activity undertaken in furtherance of tax avoidance purpose). But see TIFD III-E, Inc. v. United States, 342 F. Supp. 2d 94 (DC Conn. 2004), rev'd on other grounds and remanded, 459 F3d 220 (2d Cir. 2006), on remand, 660 F. Supp. 2d 367 (D. Conn. 2009), rev'd, 666 F3d 836 (2d Cir. 2012) (*ASA* and *Boca* do not enunciate new standard; use of partnership must have business purpose, which is satisfied if partners share an in-vestment in a specific business; creation of a partnership need not be only way to achieve purpose of financing assets). See ¶ 3.03[2]. See also Fidelity International Currency Advi-sor A Fund, LLC v. United States, 2010-1 USTC ¶ 50,418 (D. Mass. 2010) (partnership anti-abuse Regulations benignly described as "a complement to the common-law doctrines addressed above [*ASA, Culbertson, TIFD III-E,* etc.]"), aff'd, 661 F3d 667 (1st Cir. 2011).

Page 1-43:

Replace last sentence of subsection with the following.

There is no doubt that the partnership in Example (8) meets the tests of *Cul-bertson*, and even *ASA Investerings*, and thus is a valid partnership for federal tax purposes. The assertion to the contrary is an attempt to simultaneously reo-pen and preempt a debate that the Service lost in the courts and in Congress more than forty years ago.

[b] Substantial Business Purpose

[i] Introduction to the sham transaction doctrine.

Page 1-43:

Add new note 122.1 at end of first paragraph of subsection.

[122.1] Two courts have relied on the abuse-of-Subchapter-K rule to invalidate transac-tions that were also found to lack economic substance. See Nevada Partners Fund, LLC, 714 F. Supp. 2d 598 (SD Miss. 2010), aff'd, 720 F3d 594 (5th Cir. 2013) (partnership straddle transactions found to lack economic substance; claimed losses held invalid be-cause inconsistent with the intent of Subchapter K); Kearney Partners Fund, LLC v. United States, 2013-1 USTC ¶ 50,303 (MD Fla. 2013) (same), aff'd per curiam, 803 F3d 1280 (11th Cir. 2015).

[vi] Comparison of judicial decisions to abuse-of-Subchapter-K rule.

Page 1-51:

Add the following before last paragraph of subsection.

The only court to have considered the application of the substan-tial-business-purpose component of the abuse-of-subchapter-K rule ignored the impact of the super factor. In *Countryside Limited Partnership*,[149.1] the Tax Court held that a partner's business purpose of converting his partnership interest into distributed promissory notes constituted a substantial business purpose under the abuse-of-Subchapter-K rule without weighing the tax benefits to the partners (i.e., avoidance of § 731 gain if cash had been distributed) against such business purpose. That court validated an upper-tier partnership's distribution of an interest in a partnership that held non-marketable securities to a partner in complete liquidation of the distributee partner's upper-tier partnership interest because the transaction was "imbued with economic substance," and, in fact, resulted in the taxpayer's receipt of non-marketable securities. Because the court's review addressed only the recognition of gain on the distribution of the partnership interests—and not the formation of the lower-tier partnership (which occurred three months prior to the distribution and appeared to have little purpose other than protecting the inside basis of the non-marketable securities)—the court was prevented from examining the application of the abuse-of-Subchapter-K rule to the transaction as a whole.[149.2]

[149.1] Countryside Ltd. Partnership, 95 TCM 1006 (2008). But see Pritired I, LLC v. United States, 816 F. Supp. 2d 693 (SD Iowa 2011) (favorable view of "substantial business purpose" aspect of rule).

[149.2] Countryside Ltd. Partnership, 95 TCM 1006 (2008).

[5] Validity of Abuse-Of-Subchapter-K Rule

Page 1-63:

Replace note 170 with the following.

[170] While *Chevron* was not a tax case, the Supreme Court has held that *Chevron* applies fully to tax cases. Mayo Foundation for Medical Research v. United States, 562 US 44 (2011). *Mayo Foundation* rejected the analysis contained in the Court's prior decision in National Muffler Dealers Ass'n v. United States, 440 US 472 (1979). *National Muffler Dealers* considered such factors as whether an agency's interpretation of a statute had been consistent over time, whether it was promulgated years after the statute was enacted, and whether it was issued in response to an adverse judicial decision. Such factors are irrelevant under *Mayo Foundation*.

[b] Intent-Of-Subchapter-K Element of the Rule

Pages 1-69–1-70:

Replace second paragraph of subsection (after numbered list) with the following.

If the Service can successfully argue that implicit gaps exist in the statutory scheme, the U.S. Supreme Court's decision in *Mayo Foundation for Med-*

ical Research v. United States,[192] strongly supports the validity of the regulations, at least to the extent of the gap.

---

[192] Mayo Foundation for Medical Research v. United States, 562 US 44 (2011).

[i] Bona fides of partnership.

Replace last two sentences of first paragraph of subsection (following block quote) with the following.

While this definition includes a number of words (e.g., business, financial operation, or venture) that might be viewed as "so general ... as to render an interpretive regulation appropriate,"[194] none of the words used in the statute even remotely suggests that the potential for obtaining tax benefits through an organization has any bearing on whether the organization qualifies as a partnership. Lastly, though case law and the legislative history of former § 704(e)(1) are sharply to the contrary, as discussed above, it should be noted that § 704(e)(1) was repealed by the Bipartisan Budget Act of 2015, effective for partnership taxable years beginning after December 31, 2015; see discussion of this repeal, its purposes, and its ramifications at ¶ 3.00.

---

[194] National Muffler Dealers Ass'n v. United States, 440 US 472, 476 (1979), quoting Helvering v. Reynolds Co., 306 US 110, 114 (1939). This aspect of *National Muffler Dealers* appears unaffected by Mayo Foundation for Medical Research v. United States, 562 US 44 (2011).

Pages 1-70–1-71:

Delete last paragraph of subsection.

[6] Abuse-Of-Entity-Treatment Rule

Page 1-76:

Add to note 206.

; CCA 201917007 (Apr. 26, 2019) (Service asserts ability to apply Regulations § 1.701-2(e) to disregard special allocations of § 367(d)(2) income and treat partnership as aggregate of partners).

Selection of the Form of Business Organization

¶ 2.02 PARTNERSHIPS, C CORPORATIONS, AND S CORPORATIONS: GENERAL SCHEMES OF TAXATION

[2] Taxation of C Corporations

Page 2-4:

In first paragraph of subsection, replace fourth sentence with the following.

Thus, "dividends" (i.e., distributions out of the corporation's current or accumulated earnings and profits) are included in shareholders' gross income (though they are generally taxed at a maximum rate of 20 percent[18.1]) and do not affect shareholders' bases in their shares.[19]

[18.1] American Taxpayer Relief Act of 2012, Pub. L. No. 112-240, § 102(b). For taxable years beginning on or before December 31, 2012, dividends were generally subject to a maximum rate of 15 percent.

[19] Corporate shareholders are generally entitled to a dividends-received deduction (DRD) for all or a portion of the dividends that they receive. § 243. The effect of the DRD is to prevent corporate earnings from being taxed more than once at full corporate rates. When a parent and subsidiary join in the filing of a consolidated return, the parent's basis in the subsidiary's stock is increased by the subsidiary's income and decreased by the subsidiary's losses in much the same way that a partner's basis in a partnership interest is increased and decreased under § 705 by the partner's share of partnership income and loss. Reg. § 1.1502-32. Dividends paid by the subsidiary are generally tax-free to the parent (Reg. § 1.1502-13(f)(2)(ii)) and reduce its basis in the subsidiary stock (Reg. § 1.1502-32).

Page 2-5:

Replace note 23 with the following.

 [23] § 1014(a).

Replace note 24 with the following.

 [24] §§ 531–537. The tax rate is 20%.

Page 2-6:

Replace note 25 with the following.

 [25] §§ 541–547. The tax rate is 20%.

Add at end of subsection.

 The 2017 Tax Cuts and Jobs Act significantly altered the tax calculus relating to the use of corporate entities after 2017. It reduced the corporate tax from a graduated tax with a maximum rate of 35 percent to a flat rate tax of 21 percent,[27.1] reduced the maximum individual rate from 39.6 percent to 37 percent,[27.2] and introduced a new deduction of as much as 20 percent for the qualified business income of pass-through entities.[27.3] The overall impact of these changes is to significantly lower the effective tax rates on corporations and owners of qualified businesses. However, the impact on the differential between double-taxed corporate income and directly taxed income from qualified businesses has not changed very much, suggesting that pass-through treatment

---

 [27.1] § 11, amended by Pub. L. No. 115-97, § 13001 (Dec. 22, 2017).

 [27.2] § 1, amended by Pub. L. No. 115-97, § 11001 (Dec. 22, 2017).

 [27.3] § 199A, added by Pub. L. No. 115-97, §§ 11011 (Dec. 22, 2017); see ¶ 9.02[3][z].

will continue to be the optimum tax choice for many businesses. Consider the following (somewhat oversimplified) examples:

EXAMPLE 2-1: In 2017, corporation X, a C corporation, has income on which it pays a 35 percent tax. X distributes a portion of this income to its shareholders, all of whom are individuals, in the form of qualified dividends subject to tax at the maximum 20 percent rate. The total federal tax on $100 of corporate income that is distributed as dividends can be computed as 35 percent of $100 plus 23.8 percent (20 percent plus the 3.8 percent Medicare contribution tax) of the $65 after-tax distribution, a total of $50.47 representing a combined federal tax rate of 50.47 percent on this income, compared to the maximum federal income tax of $43.40 that would have been payable if X had been a pass-through entity and its owners had been in the highest income tax bracket, representing a reduction of 7.07 percent in the effective federal tax rate on the income.[27.4]

EXAMPLE 2-2: In 2018, the same corporation X has income on which it pays a 21 percent federal tax. X distributes a portion of this income to its shareholders, all of whom are individuals, in the form of qualified dividends subject to federal tax at the maximum total 23.8 percent rate. The total federal tax on $100 of corporate income that is distributed as dividends can be computed as 21 percent of $100 plus 23.8 percent of the $79 after-tax distribution, a total of $39.80, representing a combined federal tax rate of 39.8 percent on this income. This is a significant reduction in the overall federal tax burden versus the 2017 results. However, if X had been a pass-through entity and all of the income had qualified for the new 20-percent deduction, the maximum federal income tax would have been $33.40,[27.5] representing a reduction of 6.40 percent in the effective federal tax rate on the income.[27.6] While this represents a slight (0.67 percent) reduction of the corporate double-tax burden, the additional burden remains a meaningful tax planning consideration.

[27.4] This analysis disregards the impact of state taxes, which can be punitive in the corporate setting for shareholders that reside in states that tax individual income. Further, if the owners of a partnership are not subject to the 3.8 percent Medicare contribution tax under § 1411 (see ¶ 9.01(3)(b)) or the self-employment tax of § 1401(b) on partnership income, the combined tax rates would be 50.47 percent (35 percent plus 23.8 percent of 65 percent) versus 39.6 percent, a reduction of 10.87 percent in the effective tax rate.

[27.5] The 3.8 percent Medicare contribution tax is not reduced by the new 20-percent "pass-thru deduction," so the total tax is 3.8 percent of $100 ($3.80) plus 37 percent of $80 ($29.60), or $33.40.

[27.6] This analysis disregards the impact of state taxes, which can be punitive in the corporate setting for shareholders that reside in states that tax individual income. If the owners are not subject to the 3.8 percent Medicare contribution tax or the self-employment tax of § 1401(b) on their share of partnership income, the combined tax rates would be 39.8 percent (21 percent plus 23.8 percent of 79 percent) versus 29.60 percent (37 percent of $80), a reduction of 10.2 percent in the effective tax rate.

For businesses that generate and regularly distribute a significant portion of their taxable income to equity owners who are individuals, the use of a C corporation will continue to come at a very high annual tax cost.

[3] Subchapter S Taxation

Page 2-8:

Add to note 46.

Although nonresident aliens generally cannot be shareholders of S corporations, after January 1, 2018, a nonresident alien can be a potential current beneficiary of an electing small business trust that owns stock of an S corporation. See § 1361(c)(2)(B)(v), last sentence, added by § 13541 of the 2017 Tax Cuts and Jobs Act. The taxation of electing small business trusts is so onerous that this apparent largess is unlikely to become a popular tax strategy.

¶ 2.04 QUALIFIED PLANS AND OTHER FRINGE BENEFITS

[2] Other Fringe Benefits

[a] Employee Benefits That Exclude Partners

Page 2-17:

Add the following as first paragraph of subsection and before ¶ 2.04[2][a].

As explained below, while some fringe benefits available to employees are also available to partners, others are not.

Under Regulations § 301.7701-2(c)(2), a business entity that has a single owner and is not a corporation under Regulations § 301.7701-2(b) is disregarded as an entity separate from its owner. However, Regulations § 301.7701-2(c)(2)(iv)(B) provides that a disregarded entity is nevertheless treated as a corporation for purposes of employment taxes imposed under subtitle C of the Code. Therefore, the disregarded entity, rather than its owner, is considered to be the employer of the entity's employees for purposes of employment taxes imposed by subtitle C.

Temporary Regulations § 301.7701-2T adds a sentence to clarify that partners in a partnership that owns a disregarded entity cannot be treated as employees of the disregarded entity. Therefore, they are subject to self-employment tax and are treated as partners, and not employees, for fringe benefit purposes.

[c] Statutory Fringe Benefits and the Rules of Section 132

Page 2-19:

Add to note 96.

Section 132(f) is suspended for tax years beginning after December 31, 2017, and before January 1, 2026. Pub. L. No. 115-97, § 11047 (Dec. 22, 2017).

Add to note 97.

Except for certain active duty military members, § 132(g) is suspended for tax years beginning after December 31, 2017, and before January 1, 2026. Pub. L. No. 115-97, § 11048 (Dec. 22, 2017).

Defining "Partnerships" and "Partners" for Tax Purposes

Page 3-3:

Add new ¶ 3.00 at beginning of Chapter 3 (and before ¶ 3.01).

¶ 3.00 REPEAL OF FORMER SECTION 704(E)(1) CREATES UNCERTAINTY REGARDING THE DEFINITION OF PARTNERSHIPS AND PARTNERS [NEW]

[NOTE: In this Chapter 3, there are several instances in which former § 704(e)(1) is discussed and its impact analyzed. Section 704(e)(1) was repealed, as discussed below, effective for partnership taxable years beginning in 2016. For partnership taxable years beginning before then, the existing discussion of former § 704(e)(1) in this chapter remains relevant to the extent the repeal can be interpreted as a change to, rather than a clarification of, pre-2016 law; the following discussion addresses, among other things, this concern.]

The Bipartisan Budget Act of 2015 (BBA 2015)[0.1] repealed former § 704(e)(1), and renumbered former §§ 704(e)(2) and 704(e)(3) as §§ 704(e)(1) and 704(e)(2), respectively. These changes are effective for partnership taxable years beginning in 2016. Prior to its repeal, former § 704(e)(1) read as follows:

> A person shall be recognized as a partner for purposes of this subtitle if he owns a capital interest in a partnership in which capital is a material income producing factor, whether or not such interest was derived by purchase or gift from any other person.

The predecessor to former § 704(e)(1) was enacted in 1951 to assure that owners of partnership capital were taxed as partners even though they acquired the capital interest for no reason other than tax minimization. For reasons explained in the following discussion, the most immediate impact of the repeal of former § 704(e)(1) is likely to be creation of a zone of uncertainty about when preferred equity investments in partnerships (the equivalent of nonparticipating preferred stock in the corporate context) will be recognized as partnership interests. The implications, however, are broader and can only be understood in the context of the history of the development of the definition of the terms "partnership" and "partner." This history is chronicled in detail throughout Chapter 3, as well as Chapter 15.

[0.1] Bipartisan Budget Act of 2015, § 1102(c), Pub. L. No. 114-74 (Nov. 2, 2015) (hereinafter "BBA 2015").

Because the effect of the repeal of former § 704(e)(1) can only be understood in its historical context, the history of this provision is summarized below in ¶ 3.00[1].

[1] Brief History of Former Section 704(e)(1)

The metes and bounds of the interrelated definitions of the terms "partnership"
and "partner" have expanded and contracted over the years. Initially, the Code
included no definition of the term "partnership." Instead, the original drafters
simply provided for the tax treatment of "partnerships" and "partners" as those
terms were defined for non-tax purposes.

The definitions of these terms for non-tax purposes are found in the common law of partnership and the early versions of the Uniform Partnership Act,
which were grounded in the law of agency. Partners were mutual general
agents of each other, and so each had the power to bind the others. Agency relationships depend on the intent of the parties. That is, under agency law, a
person could not be an agent of another unless that other person intended an
agency relationship to exist. Once established, an agency relationship could be
dissolved at will. Thus, intent became key to the definition of the term "partnership" in the commercial law context.

Under certain circumstances, this intent was inferred from the fact that the
participants in a commercial enterprise shared profits and losses. This factor
was especially important, but not conclusive, when the participants themselves
disputed whether they were partners. Other factors could, however, establish a
partnership, including, for example, holding one's self out as a partner, which
was virtually conclusive if non-participants were seeking to establish that such
person was jointly and severally liable as a partner.

Early on, participants in unincorporated economic ventures that were not
partnerships under commercial law took the view that they were not partners
for tax purposes, and so were not taxable on profits produced by the venture—
at least until they received actual possession of those profits. This led Congress, in 1932, to add a definition of "partnership" to the Code, one that still
appears as both the first sentence of § 761(a) and as § 7701(a)(2):

> [T]he term "partnership" includes a syndicate, group, pool, joint venture,
> or other unincorporated organization through or by means of which any
> business, financial operation, or venture is carried on, and which is not,
> within the meaning of this title, a corporation or a trust or estate.

The clear purpose of this definition was to apply the partnership classification to every sort of economic relationship in which the participants pooled
capital and services, unless the relationship took on another label for tax purposes.[0.2] An arrangement might be a corporation, trust, or estate, or it might be

---

[0.2] HR Rep. No. 708, 72d Cong., 1st Sess. 53 (1932); S. Rep. No. 665, 72d Cong.,
1st Sess. 59 (1932).

an employee/employer relationship, a lender/borrower relationship, or lessee/ lessor relationship, etc., but if the arrangement (1) involved the use of capital and performance of services by multiple parties and (2) did not fit any other Code defined category, the new "partnership" definition was intended to classify it as such for federal income tax purposes, even if the participants had absolutely no intention to be partners in the commercial law sense.

At the same time that Congress added the broad statutory definition of "partnership" to the Code, it statutorily defined the term "partner" as simply a "member" of a partnership.[0.3] By comparison, § 7701(a)(8) defines the term "shareholder" as including " a member in an association, ..." (i.e., an arrangement that is classified as a corporation).

In the 1940s, a structure—the family partnership—was widely adopted as a tax avoidance strategy, and its use put considerable stress on the definition of "partner." At the time, much business activity was conducted by sole proprietorships or traditional general partnerships, and the marginal tax rates that applied to individuals were quite high. High earning sole proprietors and partners sought to mitigate their tax bills by transferring partnership interests in their businesses to their non-working spouses (joint returns had not been invented) or minor children, and thereby divert partnership income to them. As chronicled in ¶ 3.02[2], the family partnership wars led ultimately to two inconclusive Supreme Court decisions: *Commissioner v. Tower*,[0.4] and *Commissioner v. Culbertson*,[0.5] both of which resurrected the concept of intent as an important component of the "partner" and "partnership" definitions. *Culbertson*, in particular, drew on commercial law concepts and interpretations[0.6] in formulating its oft-repeated statement of the partnership test:

[0.3] The "member" reference appears in the current Code as the first sentence of § 761(b) and the second independent clause of § 7701(a)(2).

[0.4] Commissioner v. Tower, 327 US 280 (1946).

[0.5] Commissioner v. Culbertson, 337 US 733 (1949).

[0.6] The Court's reliance, in *Culbertson*, on commercial law and not the Code definition of "partnership" and "partner" is stated most clearly by Justice Frankfurter in his concurring opinion:

[I]n defining the relevant considerations for determining the existence of a partnership, the Court in the *Tower* case relied on familiar decisions formulating the concept of partnership for purposes of various commercial situations in which the nature of that concept was decisive. It is significant that among the cases cited was the leading case of *Cox v. Hickman*, 8 H. L. Cas. 268. The Court today reaffirms this reliance by its quotation from the *Tower* case. The final sentence of the portion quoted underlines the fact that the Court did not purport to announce a special concept of "partnership" for tax purposes differing from the concept that rules in ordinary commercial-law cases. The sentence is:

"We see no reason why this general rule should not apply in tax cases where the Government challenges the existence of a partnership for tax purposes." (citations omitted)

Commissioner v. Culbertson, 337 US 733, 750 (1949).

The question is not whether the services or capital contributed by a partner are of sufficient importance to meet some objective standard supposedly established by the *Tower* case, but whether, considering all the facts—the agreement, the conduct of the parties in execution of its provisions, their statements, the testimony of disinterested persons, the relationship of the parties, their respective abilities and capital contributions, the actual control of income and the purposes for which it is used, and any other facts throwing light on their true intent—the parties in good faith and acting with a business purpose intended to join together in the present conduct of the enterprise.[0.7]

There were three problems with the Court's *Tower* and *Culbertson* decisions. First, they largely ignored the Code definitions of "partnership" and "partner" in favor of the intent-based commercial definitions.

Second, while *Culbertson*, in particular, saluted and indeed purported to apply the assignment of income principle, subsequent courts were drawn to the language that focused on subjective intent, and not on the aspects of the opinion that emphasized the assignment of income principle. To the extent that application of the *Culbertson* intent standard is read to exclude owners of capital from partner status, it creates a direct conflict with the assignment of income principle, which *Culbertson* itself described as the "first principle of income taxation."[0.8]

A third problem with *Tower* and *Culbertson* was latent. These cases made references to the notion that partners share profits,[0.9] but no issue about profit participation was before the Court in either case. Rather, the issue in each case was whether the family members participated in producing the partnership's income by providing services or owning an interest in income-producing capital. This point is explicit in *Culbertson*:

The cause must therefore be remanded to the Tax Court for a decision as to which, if any, of respondent's sons were partners with him in the operation of the ranch during 1940 and 1941. As to which of them, in other words, was there a bona fide intent that they be partners in the conduct of the cattle business, *either because of services to be performed during those years, or because of contributions of capital of which they were the true owners,* as we have defined that term in the *Clifford, Horst,* and *Tower* cases? *No question as to the allocation of income between capital*

[0.7] Commissioner v. Culbertson, 337 US 733,742 (1949).

[0.8] Commissioner v. Culbertson, 337 US 733, 740 (1949).

[0.9] "Furthermore, our decision in *Commissioner* v. *Tower,* clearly indicates the importance of participation in the business by the partners during the tax year. We there said that a partnership is created 'when persons join together their money, goods, labor, or skill for the purpose of carrying on a trade, profession, or business and when there is community of interest in the profits and losses.... This is, after all, but the application of an often iterated definition of income—the gain derived from capital, from labor, or from both combined—to a particular form of business organization.'" Commissioner v. Culbertson, 337 US 733, 741 (1949).

and services is presented in this case, and we intimate no opinion on that subject.[0.10]

Thus, *Culbertson* declared that the intent requirement would be satisfied by the fact that a person either provides services or owns capital that contributes to the earning of partnership income, and, importantly, the decision also expressly disavowed offering any view about how such income should be allocated or shared. This view is entirely consistent with the assignment of income principle, under which income is taxed to the person whose services and capital produce the income and not to the persons who receive it.

Nevertheless, after *Culbertson*, confusion continued in the courts. In the family partnership context, the income-from-services branch of the assignment of income principle and the courts' intuitive notions about whether a service provider should be treated as an earner of the income at issue generally jibed. If a family member actually worked in the business, he or she was likely to be accepted as a partner.

However, the income-from-capital branch of the assignment of income principle ran directly contrary to some courts' intuitive notions about who should be a partner. Under the assignment of income principle, a minor child can own capital and so the income produced by the capital is taxed to the child. Intuitively accepting a minor, non-working child as a partner did not square with traditional notions of who is a real partner, especially when recognizing that child as partner facilitated significant tax reduction.

In 1951, expressly to assure that owners of partnership capital are recognized as partners, Congress added § 3797(a)(2) to the 1939 Code. This provision appeared in the 1954 and 1986 Codes as § 704(e)(1), and, as noted, § 704(e)(1) was later repealed by the BBA 2015 without explanation (except for a post-repeal explanatory statement by the Staff of the Joint Committee on Taxation).

In the years after the enactment of the 1939 Code predecessor to former § 704(e)(1), the provision was seldom cited. This is largely attributable to the fact that the Service and the Treasury pursued expansive definitions "partnership" and "partner" with the intent that all equity (i.e., non-debt) investments be classified either as stock, if the issuer is classified as a corporation, or as partnership interests, if the issuer is classified as a partnership. During this period, the Service resisted taxpayer entreaties to allow passive investment vehicles that issued "tranched" interests in asset pools to be taxed as trusts, because partnership taxation simplified reporting requirements. Thus, as explained in ¶ 3.02[4], the Treasury, in 1986, promulgated Regulations § 301.7701-4(c), which mandated that multi-class investment trusts be classified as either corporations or partnerships, and not classified as trusts. These trusts were designed to hold a single income-producing asset or group of assets and disaggregate the income and losses produced by the investments into tranches

---

[0.10] Commissioner v. Culbertson, 337 US 733, 748 (1949) (emphasis added).

or classes whose economics did not mimic or track the total performance of the underlying assets. Trusts subject to these rules included trusts that issued "senior" tranches that were insulated from risk by the capital investments attributable to junior tranches in exchange for limited upside potential, while the junior tranches were entitled to residual upside profits in exchange for taking first risk. There is no hint in Regulations § 301.7701-4(c), or the explanations that accompanied it, that a tranche would not be treated as a partnership interest if it did not sufficiently share both upside and downside. Indeed, the Service issued a number of revenue procedures *mandating* that non-sharing equity investments in trusts that invest in tax exempt bonds be treated as partnership interests.[0.11]

Further, in 1996, the Treasury promulgated the so-called check-a-box Regulations, explained in detail in ¶¶ 3.02[5] and 3.03. These regulations eliminated any substantive distinctions between arrangements that are classified as partnerships and those that are classified as corporations, and instead created a new tax classification—a "business entity"—and declared that, with certain *per se* exceptions, any business entity could elect to be treated as a partnership or corporation. Logically, this change might have been expected to render *Tower* and *Culbertson* archaic. After all, the portions of these decisions that focus on intent and even their glancing references to profit sharing are all derived from the commercial law of partnership and had no logical application to corporations. Nevertheless, the Service and courts continue to apply *Culbertson* to decide whether a business entity that elects partnership status is a partnership for tax purposes, and whether a "member" of such an entity is a partner, even though, if the entity elected corporate status, *Culbertson* would be entirely irrelevant in answering similar questions.

With the advent of the check-a-box Regulations, taxpayers began to use the elective freedom provided by those regulations to create investment and finance entities that elected to be treated as partnerships for federal income tax purposes, but which did not fit the traditional mold of partnerships. Usually, such vehicles were formed as limited liability companies. They were capitalized with assets or pools of assets, and raised funds by issuing multiple tranches of interests, ranging from very debt-like tranches to risky junior or residual tranches. The debt-like tranches, however, were not legal debts of the issuer entity or its "sponsors," who would hold all or most of the residual upside in the entity's assets and whose equity interests bore all or most of the practical risk of loss that the assets might produce. In view of the check-a-box Regulations and the fact that the Service had long since ruled that preferred stock, though the equivalent of short-term debt or commercial paper, is never-

---

[0.11] See, e.g., Revenue Procedure 2003-84, 2003-2 CB 1159, which even describes the non-sharing tranches as the economic equivalent of a "bond." These authorities were not intended to be taxpayer favorable. To the contrary, these authorities represented advertent rejections of requests by taxpayer groups that these passive, multi-class investment vehicles not be treated as partnerships.

theless stock (and not debt) for tax purposes,[0.12] the notion that a partnership interest could be quite debt like seemed reasonable—indeed, mandatory.

What had not been contemplated in the development of all this authority was that applying the rules of Subchapter K to certain fixed-return equity investments, especially if the investments were held by non-U.S. persons, could produce some rather spectacular tax benefits, which the Service felt compelled to attack aggressively. In three cases, *TIFD III-E* (also known, and referred to herein, as the *Castle Harbour* case), *Southgate*, and *Chemtech*, the courts declared that a putative foreign partner was not a partner for tax purposes, because the foreign investor did not participate adequately in partnership profits and losses to be recognized as partner for tax purposes.[0.13] In *Castle Harbour* and *Chemtech*, the foreign investors contributed millions of dollars, which the partnerships held and deployed for years, in exchange for interests whose profit share resembled a cumulative fixed rate dividend plus a small share of upside profit, and whose loss exposure was protected by the other partner's subordinated capital. In *Chemtech*, the Fifth Circuit clearly did *not* hold that the foreign investors were not partners because their preferred interests were debt. Instead, the Fifth Circuit held that the foreign investors' interests did not participate adequately in partnership profits, even if the interests were equity investments in the partnership, for them to be treated as partners for federal income tax purposes. There was no discussion of the assignment of income principle, nor any discussion of former § 704(e)(1).

The Second Circuit rendered two opinions in *Castle Harbour*. In the first,[0.14] the Second Circuit appeared not to hold that the foreign investors were not partners because they were lenders, but held that their interests did not participate sufficiently in profit and loss to be partners under *Culbertson*. It remanded the case to the U.S. district court to determine whether foreign investors were nevertheless partners under former § 704(e)(1). On remand, the district court held that the foreign investors were partners under former § 704(e)(1) because their interests were equity capital and therefore were capital interests within the meaning of former § 704(e)(1).[0.15] On appeal, the § 704(e)(1) issue was squarely before the Second Circuit, but it dodged the question whether a partnership equity interest can be disregarded as a valid partnership interest because the interest lacks sufficient participation in partnership profits and losses. Instead, the court held that former § 704(e)(1) could not apply because the foreign investors were lenders after all. That a partnership debt obligation is not a partnership interest was never at issue.

[0.12] See Rev. Rul. 90-27, 1990-1 CB 50.

[0.13] TIFD III-E v. United States, 666 F3d 836 (2d Cir. 2012), on remand, 8 F. Supp. 3d 142 (D. Conn. 2014), rev'd, 604 Fed. Appx. 69 (2d Cir. 2015), cert. denied, 136 S. Ct. 796 (2016) (also known as the *Castle Harbour* case, discussed in detail in ¶ 3.02[A]); Southgate Master Fund, LLC v United States, 659 F3d 466 (5th Cir. 2011); Chemtech Royalty Assocs. v. United States, 766 F3d 453 (5th Cir. 2014) (cert. denied).

[0.14] TIFD III-E v. United States, 459 F3d 220 (2d Cir. 2006).

[0.15] TIFD III-E v. United States, 660 F. Supp. 2d 367 (D. Conn. 2009).

In sum, *Chemtech* clearly holds that an equity investor in a partnership will not be recognized as a partner under *Culbertson* if it does not participate in the varying profits and losses of the partnership, but does not discuss former § 704(e)(1). The first *Castle Harbour* opinion also holds that a debt-like equity investment in partnership cannot be a partnership interest under *Culbertson*, and remanded the case to the district court to decide whether former § 704(e)(1) applied. The Second Circuit's second opinion in *Castle Harbour* holds that former § 704(e)(1) was inapplicable because the investors were lenders. Thus, neither court directly addressed the question whether under former § 704(e)(1) a person who holds a nonparticipating interest in partnership equity capital is a partner.

We turn now, finally, to the repeal of former § 704(e)(1), effective for partnership taxable years beginning on or after January 1, 2016.

[2] Repeal of Former Section 704(e)(1)

Former § 704(e)(1) was, as stated, repealed by BBA 2015, effective for partnership tax years beginning in 2016. At the same time, Congress added the following sentence to § 761(b):

> In the case of a capital interest in a partnership in which capital is a material income-producing factor, whether a person is a partner with respect to such interest shall be determined without regard to whether such interest was derived by gift from any other person.

It is far from clear what Congress intended to accomplish with the enactment of this sentence and with the repeal of former § 704(e)(1), but it seems to have thought that it was enacting a substantive change in the law because it attached a revenue estimate of about $1.9 billion. There are no committee reports, however, to explain Congress's thinking and analysis.

Furthermore, since the government had won both the *Castle Harbour* and *Chemtech* cases despite the existence of former § 704(e)(1), it is not clear why repealing § 704(e)(1) attracted a material revenue estimate, unless Congress was under the impression that former § 704(e)(1) mandated that nonparticipating capital interests be recognized as partnership interests and wanted to change that result.

Following enactment, the Staff of the Joint Committee on Taxation provided an explanation (in the "Blue Book") that raises as many questions as it purports to answer.[0.16]

The Blue Book refers to the district court's opinion on remand from the first appeal of *Castle Harbour*, in which the district court held that former § 704(e)(1) provided an alternative test to the *Culbertson* intent test. The Blue Book says that Congress sought to affirm that there is only one test for deter-

---

[0.16] Joint Committee on Taxation, General Explanation of Tax Legislation Enacted in 2015 (JCS-1-16), p 83 (Mar. 2016).

mining partner status. The Blue Book, however, does not say that the Second Circuit correctly stated that sole test for partner status in its first *Castle Harbour* opinion, and it does not even cite *Chemtech* or *Southgate*. Therefore, the Blue Book is agnostic on the specific question whether material upside and downside profit and loss participation is necessary for partner status or determining whether an interest is a partnership interest.

Ironically, the only guidance that Blue Book offers regarding the intended unitary test for partner status is the following sentence that describes what Congress did *not* intend:

> The provision is not intended to change the principle that the real owner of a capital interest is to be taxed on the income from the interest, regardless of the motivation behind or the means of the transfer of the interest.[0.17]

This is a virtual restatement of former § 704(e)(1), which required that the real owner of a capital interest in a partnership be recognized as a partner. If Congress did not intend to allow courts to disregard some capital investments as valid partnership interests, then the repeal of former § 704(e)(1) changed little or nothing.

Accordingly, the implications of former § 704(e)(1)'s repeal seem to be:

1. Repeal increases the likelihood that non-participating partnership equity interests will be disregarded as partnership interests, at least in those cases where the government wants to press the point.
2. Repeal leaves unanswered the question how much entrepreneurial profit and loss a preferred interest must carry in order to clear the participation bar (if there is a participation bar).
3. Repeal provides no guidance as to how a capital interest that is not a partnership interest *and* not debt should be taxed.

In repealing former § 704(e)(1), Congress failed to reconcile the apparent conflict between the check-a-box Regulations, which clearly adopt a single test for a business entity that can elect to be treated as a partnership or corporation for income tax purposes, and the test for partnership status that the courts derived from the commercial law of partnership and which has no plausible application to corporations. (In fact, if the Service and the courts view the repeal of former § 704(e)(1) as affirming the use of a partnership-only test based on *Culbertson* and commercial partnership law, the repeal will exacerbate the already irreconcilable gap between the business entity regulations and cases such as *Castle Harbour* and *Chemtech*.)

Ironically, the fact that former § 704(e)(1) has been repealed without any statement of approval of the specific tests applied by the courts could lead to the sensible conclusion that, under the check-a-box Regulations, there is a sin-

---

[0.17] Joint Committee on Taxation, General Explanation of Tax Legislation Enacted in 2015 (JCS-1-16), p. 84 (Mar. 2016).

gle test for a partnership that is the same test as the test for a corporation. That conclusion, however, would not square with a $2 billion revenue estimate.

The authors of the repeal of former § 704(e)(1) were apparently oblivious to the fact that the check-a-box Regulations adopt a unitary definition of the term business entity that applies equally to partnerships and corporations. The courts in *Castle Harbour* and *Chemtech* were unconcerned that the unitary test they derived in *Culbertson*, sourced from then-existing commercial law, cannot be reconciled with tax regulations applying a single unitary test (the business entity test) to determine arrangements that can be taxed as either partnerships or corporations.

¶ 3.01 THE DEFINITIONAL PATTERN

Page 3-4:

Add to note 3.

; Priv. Ltr. Rul. 201305006 (Oct. 15, 2012) (contractual "Profit Participation Agreement" between taxpayer and wholly owned affiliate, though not creating a separate juridical legal entity, and under which taxpayer will retain legal ownership of all assets and liabilities, created a separate business entity for tax purposes that may elect corporate treatment).

[1] Statutory Provisions

Page 3-8:

Replace last two paragraphs of subsection.

In addition to the general definitions, the Code had included another provision that was intended to substantially simplify and focus the definition of a "partner," and hence the definition of a "partnership." That now repealed provision was former § 704(e)(1);[15] see repeal discussion at ¶ 3.00. Former § 704(e)(1) provided:

> A person shall be recognized as a partner for income tax purposes if he owns a capital interest in a partnership in which capital is a material income- producing factor, whether or not such interest was derived by purchase or gift from any other person.

(In § 704(e)(1)'s repeal, a version of this provision was relocated to § 761(b).)

---

[15] Former § 704(e)(1) was, however, repealed by the Bipartisan Budget Act of 2015, effective for partnership taxable years beginning after December 31, 2015, while § 704(e)'s remaining provisions, "Distributive share of donee includible in gross income" and "Purchase of interest by member of family" were renumbered §§ 704(e)(1) and 704(e)(2), respectively. See Bipartisan Budget Act of 2015, § 1102(c), Pub. L. No. 114-74 (Nov. 2, 2015).

Although located in § 704(e), which was captioned "Family Partnerships" (but post-repeal is captioned "Partnership Interests Created by Gift), former § 704(e)(1) applies to all owners of capital interests in partnerships in which capital is a material income-producing factor, regardless of whether there is any family involvement.[16] Former § 704(e)(1) is discussed in greater detail in ¶¶ 3.02[3] and 3.04[2] of this chapter.

If a putative partner does not own a capital interest or if capital is not a material income-producing factor, the meaning of "partner" and "member" are more ambiguous. A vast body of pre–check-a-box case law that addresses the meaning of the term "partner" may continue to provide Delphic guidance where former § 704(e)(1) does not apply. However, the check-a-box Regulations may have significantly influenced the meaning of "member" and hence the definition of "partner" as well. These matters are discussed in detail in both ¶¶ 3.00 (concerning the repeal of former § 704(e)(1)) and 3.04 of this chapter.

---

[16] See ¶ 3.02[3].

[2] The Check-A-Box Regulations

Page 3-10:

Add to note 24.

See CCA 201323015 (June 7, 2013) (collaboration agreement to develop and commercialize a product found to be a partnership; factors listed in Hubert M. Luna, 42 TC 1067 (1964) analyzed). In Sun Capital Partners III, LP v. New England Teamsters & Trucking Industry Pension Fund, 943 F3d 49 (2019), rev'g 172 F. Supp. 3d 447 (D. Mass. 2016), two investment funds formed an LLC taxed as a corporation to acquire a target corporation. The target subsequently went bankrupt. If the arrangement between the funds created a "partnership in fact," the funds would be liable for the target's pension liabilities. The First Circuit analyzed the *Luna* factors and found that no tax partnership existed. The opinion makes no mention of the check-a-box regulations.

Add to note 26.

See Tech. Adv. Mem. 200701032 (Sept. 20, 2006) (mere co-ownership is limited to circumstances equivalent to a tenants-in-common ownership "in which each owner has a right to, and the responsibility for, an undivided fractional interest in each asset that is owned").

[3] Members and Non-Members

Page 3-12:

Add new note 35.1 at end of third to last sentence of subsection.

[35.1] Rev. Proc. 2007-65, 2007-2 CB 967, as revised by Ann. 2007-112, 2007-2 CB 1175, and Ann. 2009-69, 2009-2 CB 475, creates a safe harbor for certain allocations of income, deduction, and § 45 credits in wind energy partnerships. This safe harbor encompasses a specific allocation arrangement involving "flips" and other shifts in which both partners have an interest of at least 1.0% in all allocations at all times. However, the Service also sets forth a second example involving a similar allocation scheme in which one partner's interest is 0.5%, instead of 1.0%, during a certain period, and states that "[u]nder these facts, the wind energy LLC's classification as a valid partnership would not be governed by the safe harbor in this revenue procedure." Id. at § 5.02. This statement suggests the Service may believe that a participant in a partnership arrangement cannot be a partner for tax purposes unless it owns a certain minimum interest (apparently 0.5% may be too little, but 1.0% is enough) in profits and losses at all times. There is no apparent basis for this distinction.

[4] The Time a Partnership Comes Into Existence

Page 3-12:

Add to note 36.

See 436, Ltd., TC Memo. 2015-28 (partnership does not come into existence until it begins activities; activities furthering purpose to avoid tax are not business activities).

¶ 3.02 DEFINING "PARTNERSHIPS" AND "PARTNERS": A NECESSARY HISTORY

Page 3-13:

Add before first paragraph of subsection.

[NOTE: In this section, there are several instances in which former § 704(e)(1) is discussed and its impact analyzed. Former § 704(e)(1) was repealed, as discussed in ¶ 3.00, effective for partnership taxable years beginning in 2016. For partnership taxable years beginning before then, the existing discussion of former § 704(e)(1) in this section remains relevant to the extent the repeal can be interpreted as a change to, rather than a clarification of, pre-2016 law; the discussion in ¶ 3.00 addresses, among other things, this concern. Also, in the repeal of former § 704(e)(1), former §§ 704(e)(2) and 704(e)(3) were renumbered as §§ 704(e)(1) and 704(e)(2), respectively, without any other change, aside from clarifying that they are applicable for purposes of applying § 704(e).]

Page 3-21:

Add new ¶ 3.02[2A].

[2A] The Questionable Requirement of Participation under *Culbertson* [New]

[NOTE: In this section, there are several instances in which former § 704(e)(1) is discussed and its impact analyzed. Former § 704(e)(1) was repealed, as discussed in ¶ 3.00, effective for partnership taxable years beginning in 2016. For partnership taxable years beginning before then, the existing discussion of for-

mer § 704(e)(1) in this section remains relevant to the extent the repeal can be interpreted as a change to, rather than a clarification of, pre-2016 law; the discussion in ¶ 3.00 addresses, among other things, this concern. Also, in the repeal of former § 704(e)(1), former §§ 704(e)(2) and 704(e)(3) were renumbered as §§ 704(e)(1) and 704(e)(2), respectively, without any other change, aside from clarifying that they are applicable for purposes of applying § 704(e).]

Since 2006, at least two circuit courts have adduced the view that implicit in the *Culbertson* standard is a requirement that a person must "participate" to some material extent in the partnership's profits and losses to be recognized as a partner. Both circuit court cases denied partner status to investors who made investments determined to have economic substance (to a partnership whose activities were determined to have economic substance) because the investors did not participate sufficiently in profits and losses to satisfy a "participation" requirement the courts inferred from *Culbertson*. Neither circuit court resolved the question of whether an equity investor who does not participate sufficiently to be a partner under *Culbertson* can nevertheless be a partner under § 704(e)(1).[68.1]

The source of this participation requirement is the Second Circuit's first opinion in *TIFD III-E v. United States* (commonly referred to as *Castle Harbour*, the name of the partnership involved). The case actually involves four different opinions—two by the district court and two by the Second Circuit. For convenience, these cases are referred to as *Castle Harbour I*,[68.2] *Castle Harbour II*,[68.3] *Castle Harbour III*,[68.4] and *Castle Harbour IV*.[68.5]

Castle Harbour series involved a partnership that owned and operated a large fleet of leased commercial aircraft and also indirectly owned a large portfolio of liquid investment assets. Two Dutch banks invested about $117 million in the partnership. The investors were entitled to a return of their investment plus a preferred return, computed like a variable cumulative preferred stock dividend. In addition, the investors had an upside participation right, which the district court thought was real but the Second Circuit dismissed as de minimis. Further, the banks were generally protected against loss because the vast majority of their investment would not bear losses until the other partners' very substantial capital had been lost. If the banks were partners, the operation of § 704(c) would have allocated a substantial amount of partnership taxable income in excess of their § 704(b) income to the banks, which, being foreign, would not have been liable for any U.S. income tax on such taxable income.

[68.1] See infra ¶ 3.02[3].

[68.2] TIFD III-E v. United States, 342 F. Supp. 2d 94 (D. Conn. 2004).

[68.3] TIFD III-E v. United States, 459 F3d 220 (2d Cir. 2006).

[68.4] TIFD III-E v. United States, 660 F. Supp. 2d 367 (D. Conn. 2009).

[68.5] TIFD III-E v. United States, 666 F3d 836 (2d Cir. 2012).

Structurally, the banks' interests resembled debt in the same sense that modern preferred stock can resemble debt, though such stock is generally respected as equity. In *Castle Harbour I*, the district court held that, despite the similarity of the banks' interests to debt, such interests were equity. The district court also held that the partnership and the banks' interests had economic effect and that the overall arrangement was motivated by a substantial non-tax business purpose. In its analysis, the district court applied the *Culbertson* intent test, which included an analysis of the banks' limited rights to variable partnership profits and limited exposure to downside risk. It held that the banks' interests were partnership interests under *Culbertson*, but did not address the taxpayer's separate argument that, regardless of *Culbertson*, the banks were partners under the alternative test of § 704(e)(1).

Though it appealed, the government did not challenge either the district court's determinations relating to business purpose or economic substance, nor did it not directly challenge the district court's holding that the banks' interests were not debt. Instead, the government argued that even if the banks' interests had economic substance and were not debt, the banks did not participate sufficiently in the entrepreneurial results of partnership operations to be considered partners under *Culbertson*. In *Castle Harbour II*, the Second Circuit appeared to adopt the government's interpretation of *Culbertson*, namely, that the banks' interests were so overwhelmingly debt-like that they failed to qualify as "bona fide partnership equity participations" under *Culbertson*.

In *Castle Harbour II*, the Second Circuit did not address the taxpayer's alternative theory that, regardless of their lack of participation and similarity to debt, the banks' interests were equity, and as equity, were "capital interests" under § 704(e)(1). As explained in ¶ 3.02[3], § 704(e)(1) requires that the owner of capital interest in a partnership be treated as a partner if capital is a material factor in the partnership's business. Instead, *Castle Harbour II* remanded the § 704(e)(1) issue to the district court. In *Castle Harbour III*, the district court determined that the banks' interests were indeed partnership capital interests under § 704(e)(1) because (despite their similarity to debt) they were equity. The district court did not think participation was a criterion of a § 704(e)(1) capital interest.

On appeal, in *Castle Harbour IV*, the Second Circuit did not resolve the § 704(e)(1) issue and, perhaps unwittingly, relegated its disquisition in *Castle Harbour II* on the necessity of participation under *Culbertson* to the status of dictum. In *Castle Habour IV*, the Second Circuit adopted a revisionist interpretation of its prior opinion. According to *Castle Harbour IV*, *Castle Harbour II* had determined that the banks' interests were in fact debt, not merely an interest "in the nature of" debt. Partnership debt (including "participating" partnership debt) cannot qualify as a partnership interest for the simple reason that debt *of* a partnership cannot be an interest *in* the partnership, any more than the debt of a corporation can be stock.

Thus, while the Second Circuit's opinions in *Castle Harbour* make much of participation, the participation analysis ultimately informed the court's determination that the banks' interests were debt for tax purposes, and not whether the banks' interests would have been denied partner status if they were highly secure, non-participating preferred equity for tax purposes. Further, because the relevance of *Culbertson* to a debt-equity analysis is tertiary at best, the Second Circuit's reliance on *Culbertson* seems entirely misplaced in view of its ultimate determination that the banks' interests were debt.

Nevertheless, in *Historic Boardwalk Hall, LLC v. Commissioner*,[68.6] the Third Circuit picked up the participation theme from *Castle Harbour II*, and applied it in a case in which the government conceded that the interest at issue was not debt. *Historic Boardwalk* involved a partnership formed between a tax exempt governmental entity and a taxable investor to rehabilitate historic property, with the expectation of earning historic rehabilitation tax credits under § 47 and then to own and operate the property. The investor contributed funds and, under the partnership agreement, was allocated the tax credits. The Service determined that the investor was not a partner and that the transaction was merely an attempted sale of tax credits by a governmental entity that could not use them to a taxable entity that could. The investor negotiated for and received various protections against loss and also entered into collateral agreements which, in the Third Circuit's view, virtually eliminated profit over and above a 3 percent preferred return. While the investor's interest had some similarity to debt, the government conceded that the interest was not debt.

The Tax Court, in *Historic Boardwalk*, had determined that the arrangement had economic substance and that the investor was a partner entitled to the credits. The Third Circuit did not overturn those determinations. Instead, the Third Circuit reversed, relying heavily on the Second Circuit's participation analysis in *Castle Harbour II* (which, as explained above, was effectively mooted when *Castle Harbour IV* held that the interests in question could not be partnership interests because they were debt).

Several aspects of a participation requirement are noteworthy. First, if participation is the issue, the question must be participation in what? If a partnership is formed by equal partners to invest in short-term Treasury bills, there may be little upside or downside in the partnership's activity. Nevertheless, the partners participate fully in the benefits and burdens (however limited) that are inherent in the underlying enterprise, and so must be recognized as partners under any participation standard. Similarly, some tax-recognized partnerships are not formed to earn a profit at all. For example, *Madison Gas & Electric*

[68.6] Historic Boardwalk Hall, LLC v. Commissioner, 694 F3d 425 (3d Cir. 2012) (cert. denied), rev'g and remanding 136 TC 1 (2011). See also Chief Counsel Memo. 20124002F (Aug. 30, 2012) (applying participation analysis to treat tax equity investor's interest in partnership as debt). The Tax Court refused to apply *Historic Boardwalk* to evaluate the bona fides of a partnership interest to determine whether refined coal production by the partnership entitled a partner to production tax credits under § 45. See Cross Refined Coal LLC, TC No. 19502-17 (Aug. 29, 2019) (bench opinion).

Co.[68.7] involved a venture among electric power companies to own and operate a generating facility that would not sell its output, but would permit its owners to access and sell their shares of electricity produced by the facility. The owners participated fully in the joint enterprise and were deemed partners.

Second, the participation requirement simply does not square with modern tax law that accords equity status to very debt-like instruments issued by partnerships and corporations.[68.8]

Third, the absence of participation in entrepreneurial profit and loss fairly informs the question of whether an investment is debt or equity. But if, despite the absence of participation, an investment is equity, and not debt, for tax purposes, then the investment should be recognized as a valid partnership interest. Otherwise, the investment falls into a category to which no established tax regime applies. The tax law makes elaborate provision to determine the tax consequences of debt, on the one hand, and equity, on the other. No existing rules, however, apply to an equity investment in a partnership that is not recognized as a bona fide partnership interest.

Prodded in part by persistent pleas for guidance from a variety of tax-credit stakeholders, the Service in 2014 created a safe harbor to address the *Historic Boardwalk* participation requirement.[68.9] To the disappointment of some members of the tax credit community, this safe harbor is explicitly limited to § 47 rehabilitation credits, leaving purveyors and consumers of other nonrefundable credits as well as their advisors to their own devices.[68.10] The safe harbor provides that the Service will not challenge allocations of § 47 rehabilitation credits if a partnership and its partners satisfy all of the following requirements:

1. Each partner authorized to act for the partnership (each a "Principal") must have a minimum one percent interest in all material items of income, gain, loss, deduction, and credit at all times.
2. Each non-Principal partner (each an "Investor") must have a minimum interest in each such material item at all times equal to at least 5 percent of the Investor's interest during the year in which it is the largest (subject to adjustment for sales, redemptions, and dilutions).
3. Each Investor's partnership interest must be a "bona fide equity investment" with a reasonably anticipated value "commensurate" with

---

[68.7] Madison Gas & Electric Co. 72 TC 521 (1979), aff'd, 633 F2d 512 (7th Cir. 1980).

[68.8] See, e.g., Rev. Rul. 90-27, 1990-1 CB 50; Rev. Proc. 2003-84, 2003-2 CB 1159.

[68.9] See Rev. Proc. 2014-12, 2014-3 IRB 415.

[68.10] See CCA 20161101F (Mar. 11, 2016) (refined coal; investor not bona fide partner under *Historic Boardwalk*). Tech. Adv. Mem. 201729020 (July 21, 2017) (same); AM 2018-002 (Feb. 28, 2018) (refined coal structures; factors to consider). The § 47 safe harbor resembles the § 45 wind energy production tax credit safe harbor. See Rev. Proc. 2007-65, 2007-2 CB 967, as revised by Ann. 2007-112, 2007-2 CB 1175, and Ann. 2009-69, 2009-2 CB 475, discussed supra Chapter 3, n. 35.1.

the Investor's overall percentage interest in the partnership *without regard to any deductions, allowances, credits, or other tax attributes* allocated to the Investor.[68.11] An interest is a bona fide equity interest only if its value is dependent on the partnership's net income, gain, and loss, and is not substantially fixed in amount. The Investors must not be substantially protected from loss and must participate in profits in a manner that is not limited to a "preferred return." The value of the Investors' partnership interests cannot be reduced through fees, leases, distributions, or other arrangements that do not reflect fair market values.

4. At least 20 percent of the Investors' total expected capital contributions (a) must be made before the building is placed in service, excluding any Investor notes and other obligations, (b) must be maintained throughout the duration of the Investor's ownership of its partnership interest, and (c) must not be protected against loss. Furthermore, at least 75 percent of the Investor's expected capital contributions must be fixed in amount before the building is placed in service.

5. Only certain types of unfunded guarantees can be provided to the Investors.

6. Loans from related parties to Investors are generally prohibited.

7. Calls and puts with related parties relating to an Investor's interest are generally prohibited.

8. Investors may not acquire interests with the intent to abandon them after the rehabilitation is completed.

[68.11] This language implies that an Investor must reasonably expect a pre-tax (cash-on-cash) profit on its investment "commensurate" with the partnership as a whole in order to come within the safe harbor. Such a requirement, however, would be at odds with both commercial reality and congressional intent (as well as case law) relating to most incentive tax credit regimes. It would also make the safe harbor essentially useless. Fortunately, Example 1 in section 5.01 of Revenue Procedure 2014-12, 2014-3 IRB 415 implies no pre-tax profit expectation is required provided that (1) the Investor has at least a 5 percent post-flip interest and (2) the value of that interest is not eroded by unreasonable fees, lease terms, or similar devices. The language in Revenue Procedure 2014-12 could, however, use some clarification on this point.

[3] Congress's Response to *Culbertson:* Section 704(e)(1) and the Assignment-of-Income Principle

Page 3-25:

Add to last paragraph of subsection.

The district court thereupon found that the banks held capital interests in a partnership in which capital was a material income-producing factor, and thus owned partnership interests for tax purposes.[78.1] This conclusion was similarly reversed, on appeal, by the Second Circuit,[78.2] which reasoned that a person will be treated as holding a partnership "capital interest" (i.e., an "interest in the assets of the partnership") only if the return on such interest is subject to meaningful risk based upon the value of the partnership assets or connected to the partnership's success or failure. The court was quite careful throughout the opinion to reiterate that its holding applied equally to both debt and "an interest overwhelmingly in the nature of debt," thus continuing the delicate tiptoe between debt and equity that characterized its earlier decision. In footnote 8, however, the Second Circuit abruptly made an about face, rebuking the taxpayer for failing to understand that, despite its repeated and careful dance around the issue, the banks' interests were required to "be treated as debt for tax purposes."[78.3] This simple statement, while wreaking havoc on taxpayers who have previously relied upon authorities such as Revenue Ruling 90-27 and Revenue Procedure 2003-84,[78.4] nonetheless obviated the need for any further discussion of § 704(e)(1) in that circumstance; if the banks' interests are properly treated as debt, they clearly cannot be partnership interests under § 704(e)(1).

To summarize, regarding the scope of § 704(e)(1), *TIFD III-E* changed virtually nothing. The district court held that the banks' interests were not debt. Therefore, since those interests represented economically substantial investments in a partnership, they must be equity, albeit preferred and non-participating equity. Finding no reason why the term capital interest as used in § 704(e)(1) could or should be limited to participating equity, the district court held that the banks' interests were § 704(e)(1) capital interests. Rather than address the question whether preferred, non-participating equity is a capital interest, in its second opinion in *TIFD III-E*, the Second Circuit declared that it had decided in its first opinion that the banks' interests were debt after all, and not merely an interest in the nature of debt. Debt, of course, is not equity, and the debt of a partnership is not a partnership interest under any definition. Therefore, the district court's opinion, namely, that preferred, non-participating equity of a partnership was neither, was neither affirmed nor reversed.

[78.1] TIFD III-E, Inc. v. United States, 660 F. Supp. 2d 367 (D. Conn. 2009); cf. Devonian Program, 100 TCM 37 (2010), aff'd unpub. opinion, 2011-2 USTC ¶ 50,564 (3d Cir. 2011) (no reference to § 704(e)(1) test in evaluating whether purported tax matters partner was truly a partner). In Crescent Holdings, LLC, 141 TC No. 15 (2013), relying on Revenue Procedure 93-27, 1993-2 CB 343, the Tax Court defined a partnership capital interest as "an interest that would give the holder a share of the proceeds if the partnership's assets were sold at fair market value and then the proceeds were distributed in a complete liquidation of the partnership."

[78.2] TIFD III-E, Inc. v. United States, 666 F3d 836 (2d Cir. 2012).

[78.3] TIFD III-E, Inc. v. United States, 666 F3d 836, 847 n.8 (2d Cir. 2012).

[78.4] See infra ¶ 3.05[3] (discussing Rev. Rul. 90-27, 1990-1 CB 50; Rev. Proc. 2003-84, 2003-2 CB 1159).

[4] The "Investment Trust" Regulations: The Inclusive Approach Affirmed

Page 3-27:

Add to note 86.

See also Notice 2008-80, 2008-40 IRB 820, proposing technical modifications and clarifications to Rev. Proc. 2003-84.

Replace last paragraph of subsection with the following.

The Second Circuit rendered two opinions in *TIFD III-E*.[87] The first opinion held that an economically substantial investment in non-participating preferred partnership equity cannot be a partnership interest under the subjective intent test of *Culbertson*.[88] This holding was very difficult to square with the "investment trust" regulations, as well as other authorities, such as Revenue Procedure 2003-84,[88.1] which contemplate and intend that all equity interests in a non-corporate business entity be treated as partnership interests. In its second opinion,[88.2] the Second Circuit adopted a revisionist interpretation of its first opinion, asseverating that its initial opinion had determined that the non-participating interests at issue were debt, and not merely "in the nature of" or like debt. Debt, of course, is not a partnership interest under any circumstances.

---

[87] TIFD III-E v. United States, 459 F3d 220 (2d Cir. 2006); TIFD III-E v. United States, 666 F3d 836 (2d Cir. 2012).

[88] Commissioner v. Culbertson, 337 US 733 (1946).

[88.1] Rev. Proc. 2003-84, 2003-2 CB 1159.

[88.2] TIFD III-E v. United States, 666 F3d 836 (2d Cir. 2012). See discussion infra ¶ 3.05[3].

¶ 3.03 DEFINING "BUSINESS ENTITIES": THE SUBSTANCE TESTS

Page 3-28:

Add before first paragraph of subsection.

[NOTE: In this section, there are several instances in which former § 704(e)(1) is discussed and its impact analyzed. Former § 704(e)(1) was repealed, as discussed in ¶ 3.00, effective for partnership taxable years beginning in 2016. For partnership taxable years beginning before then, the existing discussion of former § 704(e)(1) in this section remains relevant to the extent the repeal can be interpreted as a change to, rather than a clarification of, pre-2016 law; the discussion in ¶ 3.00 addresses, among other things, this concern. Also, in the repeal of former § 704(e)(1), former §§ 704(e)(2) and 704(e)(3) were *renumbered as §§ 704(e)(1) and 704(e)(2), respectively, without any other change, aside from clarifying that they are applicable for purposes of applying § 704(e).]*

Page 3-29:

Add to note 99.

See Priv. Ltr. Rul. 201305006 (Feb. 1, 2013) (profit participation agreement between corporation and wholly owned affiliate created a separate business entity; no separate juridical entity created).

Add at end of third paragraph of subsection.

The Treasury Department, in 2010, ventured into the "entity" thicket by issuing Proposed Regulations § 301.7701-1(a)(5) (2010), dealing with the classification of "series" LLCs. A number of states have enacted statutes providing that an LLC can establish one or more series of members, managers, LLC interests, or assets. Each series generally has a number of rights typically associated with separate entity status. The proposed regulations take a very broad view of entity status. They provide that each series will be treated as a separate entity if it represents a segregated group of assets and liabilities established pursuant to a "series statute," regardless of whether the series is a judicial person under local law. The key feature of the enabling series statute is that it must provide for the segregation of the assets and liabilities of each series. The proposed regulations are not effective until finalization, but would grandfather the treatment of series organizations as a single entity if such organizations were established on or before September 14, 2010. They are generally inapplicable to foreign entities.

Meanwhile, courts and taxpayers continue to apply pre–check-a-box law in deciding whether a partnership exists, leading to soft analysis and ambiguity, if not always to wrong answers. *Long v. Commissioner*,[101.1] is a case in point. On its face, *Long* is unremarkable. Over a period of time, a company called Steelervest and its owner invested in Mr. Long's real estate activities. Usually, these investments were denominated as loans. In return, Mr. Long agreed to repay the advanced amounts with various commitments to share the proceeds from his real estate projects. The contracts and commitments were renegotiated and extended numerous times. Evidence indicated that the parties did not treat any of these arrangements as a partnership. Ultimately, Mr. Long, through a wholly owned entity called LOT (formed as a corporation, but operated by Mr. Long as a sole proprietorship), brought a lawsuit related to his real estate business, and agreed to pay Steelervest 50% of the proceeds from the lawsuit up to $875,000. When Mr. Long realized a substantial sum from the lawsuit, he paid $600,000 to Steelervest, in accordance with this agreement.

[101.1] Long, TC Memo. 2013-233.

As with their prior arrangements, the parties did not treat their deal regarding the lawsuit as a partnership nor did they file partnership returns. At trial in the Tax Court, Mr. Long argued that Steelervest received the $600,000 as its share of the income from their joint venture. The year at issue was 2006, a decade after the check-a-box regulations adopted a unitary test for a business entity that could be classified as either a partnership or a corporation.

Nevertheless, the Tax Court addressed the question of whether there was joint venture under traditional state partnership law without so much as a mention of the check-a-box regulations or considering whether the arrangement at issue was a business entity at all. The court determined that Steelervest "did contribute money" and concluded that it undeniably had a real right to share in Mr. Long's profits from LOT, especially with regard to the success of the lawsuit. However, the court held that the arrangement was not a partnership, because (1) Steelervest had no right to control LOT, (2) it had no liability for LOT's losses, (3) its interest in the lawsuit proceeds was capped at $875,000, (4) "[n]either Long's ownership of LOT nor LOT's operations were conducted in Steelervest's name," (5) no separate books were maintained, and (6) no partnership returns were filed.

To be clear, on the same facts, the court might well have determined there was no business entity under the check-a-box regulations that could be classified as a partnership. But, in such event, its analysis almost certainly would have been different. Moreover, as is typical when the government challenges a partnership in court and the court decides that no partnership exists, the *Long* court neglected to say how the arrangement should be classified after concluding that it was not a joint venture.

Add new note 101.2 to last sentence of subsection.

[101.2] While this seemed inevitable as of the initial writing of the Fourth Edition of this treatise, the infallible logic of this approach may have fallen prey to the inartful drafting of a transaction's promoter. In Superior Trading, LLC, TC Memo. 2012-110, the petitioners, who were represented by the lawyer that had designed and marketed the partnership transactions at issue, appeared to contend (by motion) that the check-a-box regulations overruled the traditional partnership test for entity recognition. We say "appeared" because the motion (which was derided by the Tax Court as "beyond the pale of zealous advocacy" and quoted with notations of "[o]missions, insertions, and awkward grammar") was not a model of coherency. In response, the court noted that "[t]he import of these *Luna* factors has not dissipated any after the promulgation of sec. 301.7701-3(a)." The Seventh Circuit concurred with this analysis, observing that the purpose of the check-a-box regulations is "merely to determine whether the default tax treatment of the entity shall be under the corporate or the partnership provisions of federal tax law, not whether it shall be entitled to the benefits ... created by those provisions should they be found inapplicable for other reasons." Superior Trading, LLC v. Commissioner, 728 F3d 676, 681 (7th Cir. 2013), aff'g 137 TC 70 and TC Memo. 2012-110. Accord Jimastowlo Oil, LLC, TC Memo. 2013-195; Markell Co., Inc., TC Memo 2014-86. While this observation is true, the Seventh Circuit misses the inference of the check-a-box regulations detailed herein: Separate entity recognition tests for corporations and partnerships are inconsistent with the optionality of the check-a-box regulations, which require that the existence of an entity be established before the classification of such entity is chosen. See also Kenna Trading

LLC, 143 TC 181 (2014) ("check-the-box regulations do not supersede *Culbertson* insofar as the putative members must still come together to form an entity"). In *Ad Inv. 2000 Fund LLC*, 110 TCM 471 (2015), vacated and reentered, 112 TCM 660 (2016), however, Judge Halpern noted that "important cases dealing with the nature of entities recognized as separate from their owners for Federal tax purposes ... predate the check-a-box regulations ... which may place the question of whether there is a tax-recognized entity ahead of the classification of the entity as a partnership or corporation for tax purposes" (citing this text). See also Order (filed Feb. 13, 2018) (citing *AD Inv. 2000 Fund*), denying Commissioner's motion for partial summary judgement, Peking Inv. Fund LLC v. Commissioner, TC Memo. 2013-288.

[2] Pre−Check-A-Box Partnership Entity Recognition Tests: The Conflation of *Moline Properties* and *Culbertson*

Page 3-35:

Add new note 129.1 at end of first full paragraph.

129.1 See Fidelity International Currency Advisor A Fund, LLC v. United States, 2010-1 USTC ¶ 50,418 (D. Mass. 2010), aff'd, 661 F3d 667 (1st Cir. 2011) (an entity is a sham and will not be recognized for tax purposes if it has no business purpose other than the creation of tax deductions; the absence of a nontax business purpose is "fatal," quoting from *ASA*).

Page 3-37:

Replace note 134 with the following.

134 Boca Investerings v. United States, 314 F3d 625, 632 (DC Cir. 2003) (cert. denied). The "elaborate partnership" reference may be read as establishing a separate recognition test for those transactions that are designed with significant tax reduction purposes. See also TIFD III-E, Inc. v. United States, 459 F3d 220 (2d Cir. 2006), rev'g and remanding 342 F. Supp. 2d 94 (D. Conn. 2004), on remand, 660 F. Supp. 2d 367 (D. Conn. 2009), rev'd, 666 F3d 836 (2d Cir. 2012).

Replace note 135 with the following.

135 TIFD III-E, Inc. v. United States, 342 F. Supp. 2d 94, 114 n.39 (D. Conn. 2004)(rev'd on other grounds and remanded, 459 F3d 220 (2d Cir. 2006), on remand, 660 F. Supp. 2d 367 (D. Conn. 2009), rev'd, 666 F3d 836 (2d Cir. 2012)):

> [s]ome language in the Boca Investerings decision supports a reading that merely demonstrating a business *purpose* for forming a partnership is insufficient, and instead, a taxpayer must demonstrate a business *necessity*....I think that other language, see, e.g. ("We do not of course suggest that in every transaction using a partnership a taxpayer must justify that to form"), as well as a reading of the case as a whole, shows that the D.C. Circuit meant nothing more than that, when there appears to be no non-tax reason for creating a separate entity to effect a given transaction, the creation of the entity is likely a sham.

Page 3-38:

Add to carryover paragraph.

Unfortunately, the Fifth Circuit may have done just this, and possibly more, in *Southgate Master Fund, LLC v. United States.*[139.1] *Southgate* involved a pre-2004 built-in loss transaction in which China Cinda, an institution owned by the Chinese government, contributed nonperforming loans, with a high tax basis but little value, to a partnership as a prelude to further transactions designed to shift the built-in loss in these loans to a United States taxpayer (Beal).

The holding of the Fifth Circuit's decision is unremarkable: "Southgate's acquisition of the [distressed debt] should be recharacterized as a direct sale from Cinda to Beal."[139.2] This holding follows that of other courts which have addressed similar transactions.[139.3] The essence of these decisions is that the seller of the high basis assets never became a partner in the partnership to which it transferred the assets;[139.4] rather, the seller intended to sell the assets, and the partnership was merely the vehicle through which the sale was effectuated. The Fifth Circuit's opinion repeatedly emphasizes that Cinda had no continuing economic stake in Southgate's business.[139.5] Thus, the Fifth Circuit's decision is best read as a fairly straightforward "substance over form" holding.

[139.1] Southgate Master Fund, LLC v. United States, 659 F3d 466 (5th Cir. 2011).

[139.2] Southgate Master Fund, LLC v. United States, 659 F3d 466, 492 (5th Cir. 2011). See also Chemtech Royalty Assocs., LP v. United States, 2013-1 USTC ¶ 50,204 (MD La. 2013), aff'd, 766 F3d 453 (5th Cir. 2014) (cert. denied) (suggesting that not only is a non-tax business purpose required, but that such non-tax business purpose must be accomplished in the cheapest and simplest manner possible without considering tax consequences).

[139.3] Long-Term Capital Holdings v. United States, 330 F. Supp. 2d 122 (D. Conn. 2004), aff'd by summary order, 150 Fed. Appx. 40 (2d. Cir. 2005); Superior Trading, LLC, 137 TC 70 (2011), motion for reh'g denied, 103 TCM 1604 (2012), aff'd, 728 F3d 676 (7th Cir. 2013); Rovakat, LLC, 102 TCM 264 (2011), aff'd unpub. opinion, 2013-1 USTC ¶ 50,386 (3d Cir. 2013); Kenna Trading LLC, 143 TC 181 (2014); Santa Monica Pictures, LLC, 89 TCM 1157 (2005); Derringer Trading LLC, TC Memo. 2018-59 (2018). But see Order (filed Feb. 13, 2018), Peking Inv. Fund LLC v. Commissioner, TC Memo. 2013-288 (DAD transaction, government's motion for summary judgement denied; showing profit objectives satisfies *Culbertson* even if outweighed by tax motive).

[139.4] The Fifth Circuit focused on the Chinese member's lack of economic participation in the Southgate business in looking for "a legitimate, profit-motivated reason to operate as a partnership." The Chinese company had none. Southgate Master Fund, LLC v. United States, 659 F3d 466, 492 n.80 (5th Cir. 2011). While the court concluded that there was no partnership between Cinda and Beal, it left open the question of whether there was a partnership between Beal and the manager of the entity, who held a 1% interest in the partnership.

[139.5] In concluding that the Chinese company had no economic interest in the partnership's success or failure, the court emphasized that the Chinese partner held its purported partnership interest, in its own words, only "symbolically." The Chinese partner did not abide by the partnership agreement and took affirmative steps that hindered the profitability of the venture. The partners entered into an identical second partnership despite the

What is disturbing about the *Southgate* decision, however, is not its holding, but the language used by the Fifth Circuit to get there. Despite finding the partnership's underlying acquisition of nonperforming loans had both economic substance and a realistic possibility of producing a profit, the Fifth Circuit nonetheless disregarded the partnership vehicle involved in the transaction, stating:

> The fact that a partnership's underlying business activities had economic substance does not, standing alone, immunize the partnership from judicial scrutiny. *The parties' selection of the partnership form must have been driven by a genuine business purpose.* This is not to say that tax considerations cannot play any role in the decision to operate as a partnership. It is only to say that tax considerations cannot be the only reason for a partnership's formation. If there was not a legitimate, profit-motivated reason to operate as a partnership, then the partnership will be disregarded for tax purposes even if it engaged in transactions that had economic substance.[139.6] (footnotes omitted and emphasis added)

The court went on to test the viability of the partnership under *Culberston* and found it lacking, concluding that the partnership was a sham "under our analysis, which trains exclusively on the question whether there was a nontax business purpose that necessitated the partnership's existence."[139.7]

A broad reading of these statements would bring *Southgate* into direct conflict with applicable Treasury Regulations as well as the cases cited above. The statement that "[t]he parties' selection of the partnership form must have been driven by a genuine business purpose"[139.8] should not be read as mandating either that a taxpayer's choice of entity requires a business purpose or that, in order for a partnership to be respected for tax purposes, its partners must have a business need for the formation of an underlying state law entity. The first interpretation would be inapposite to Regulations § 301.7701-3, which explicitly allows a tax-recognized entity to elect, solely for tax reasons, to be taxable as either a partnership or a corporation. The second reading would be inconsistent with Regulations § 301.7701-1(a), which mandates that an entity can exist for tax purposes even if there is no juridical entity under local law.[139.9] Thus a co-ownership or other contractual arrangement may create a separate entity for federal tax purposes despite the complete lack of any entity

---

foundering of the first. The court also emphasizes Beal's near-total control over the income of the partnership. Southgate Master Fund, LLC v. United States, 659 F3d 466, 485–488 (5th Cir. 2011).

[139.6] Southgate Master Fund, LLC v. United States, 659 F3d 466, 484 (5th Cir. 2011).

[139.7] Southgate Master Fund, LLC v. United States, 659 F3d 466, 491 (5th Cir. 2011) (emphasis added).

[139.8] Southgate Master Fund, LLC v. United States, 659 F3d 466, 484 (5th Cir. 2011).

[139.9] Reg. § 301.7701-1(a)(1) (whether an entity is recognized for federal tax purposes "is a matter of federal tax law and does not depend on whether the organization is recognized as an entity under local law").

recognized under state law.[139.10] Because the existence of a separate legal entity is not a prerequisite to the creation of a taxable entity, whether a business need exists for the formation of an entity cannot be a prerequisite to the recognition of the arrangement as a taxable entity. Indeed, there are numerous situations in which the Treasury Department forces entity status on taxpayers without regard to business purpose or necessity.[139.11] Finally, as discussed immediately below, the Treasury Department's own "partnership anti-abuse" regulations confirm that no business purpose is required to operate as a partnership.

Similarly, the court's statement that "our scrutiny of a taxpayer's choice to use the partnership form is especially stringent" should not be interpreted as requiring a different legal analysis of partnerships than of corporations. The entity classification regulations first ask whether an organization is a separate entity that must be classified; any business entity that is not a *per se* corporation can *choose* its classification. There cannot be a more stringent test for partnerships than for corporations if the choice between the two is made after business entity status has been determined. And since this election cannot have a non-tax effect, there can be no more stringent requirement for choosing to be taxed as a partnership rather than a corporation, or vice versa. Again, a better reading of *Southgate* would be to call for careful scrutiny of the bona fides of the underlying business activity (or the participation of a purported member in that activity) whenever the claimed tax consequences of the transaction are unusual or extraordinary—hardly a surprising statement.

Hard cases (*Boca* and *Southgate* clearly are hard cases) often make bad law. These cases can be read to say that partnerships, unlike all other types of tax-recognized entities, will only be recognized if there is a need (*Boca*) and a profit-motivated reason (*Southgate*) for their existence. That has not been the law prior to these cases. It turns traditional business purpose doctrine on its head and ignores the check-the-box regulations, *Moline Properties* and the like. They are better read for what they are—overbroad statements in reaction to perceived tax abuses.

Nevertheless, these cases render the tax landscape uncertain. Transactions that generate "unusual" or "extraordinary" tax advantages are at risk (as they always have been), perhaps especially so if a partnership is involved.

[139.10] Reg. § 301.7701-1(a)(2); see Madison Gas & Elec. Co. v. Commissioner, 633 F2d 512 (7th Cir. 1980) (taxpayer's characterization as mere co-ownership rejected; partnership status imposed); Bentex Oil Corp., 20 TC 565 (1953); see infra ¶ 3.05[5].

[139.11] Reg. § 301.7701-4(c) (requiring that passive investment trusts with non-pro rata interests be classified as corporations or partnerships); Rev. Proc. 2003-84, 2003-2 CB 1159 (refusing to let owners avoid partnership tax status because of the non-pro rata allocation of income and gain from a bond); see supra ¶ 3.02[4].

Page 3-39:

Add new note 140.1 at end of carryover paragraph.

[140.1] Notice 2009-7, 2009-1 CB 312, identifies as "transactions of interest" structures in which a domestic partnership is interposed between a U.S. parent and its controlled foreign corporations to act as a "blocker" facilitating deferral of the taxation of subpart F income to the parent. The interposition of the domestic partnership has no apparent purpose other than the avoidance of subpart F income. Notice 2009-7 suggests this deferral "is contrary to the purpose and intent of subpart F of the Code," and therefore warrants further scrutiny by the Service. Any such scrutiny may implicate the issues involved in this discussion of the so-called "business need" requirement for entity recognition. See ¶ 9.01[4][c][iv][C].

Subsequently, in Notice 2010-41, 2010-22 IRB 1, the Service announced that it would issue Regulations classifying domestic partnerships as foreign solely for the limited purpose of identifying the United States shareholders of a controlled foreign corporation if the following conditions are satisfied: (1) the partnership is a United States shareholder of a foreign corporation that is a CFC (within the meaning of § 957(a) or § 953(c)) (the "Subsidiary CFC") and (2) if the partnership were treated as foreign, (a) the Subsidiary CFC would continue to be a CFC and (b) at least one United States shareholder of the Subsidiary CFC would be (i) treated under § 958(a) as indirectly owning stock of the Subsidiary CFC and (ii) required to include an amount in gross income under § 951(a) with respect to the Subsidiary CFC. The Notice is implemented by Proposed Regulations § 1.951-1(h) (2018), which is to be retroactively applied to taxable years of domestic partnerships ending on or after May 14, 2010.

¶ 3.04 DEFINING "MEMBER" UNDER THE CHECK-A-BOX REGULATIONS

Page 3-40:

Add before first paragraph of subsection.

[NOTE: In this section, there are several instances in which former § 704(e)(1) is discussed and its impact analyzed. Former § 704(e)(1) was repealed, as discussed in ¶ 3.00, effective for partnership taxable years beginning in 2016. For partnership taxable years beginning before then, the existing discussion of former § 704(e)(1) in this section remains relevant to the extent the repeal can be interpreted as a change to, rather than a clarification of, pre-2016 law; the discussion in ¶ 3.00 addresses, among other things, this concern. Also, in the repeal of former § 704(e)(1), former §§ 704(e)(2) and 704(e)(3) were renumbered as §§ 704(e)(1) and 704(e)(2), respectively, without any other change, aside from clarifying that they are applicable for purposes of applying § 704(e).]

[1] Shareholders as Members Prior to the Check-A-Box Regulations

Page 3-41:

Add to note 146.

Cf. Terry Nathan Norman, TC Summ. Op 2006-102 (taxpayer entered into limited partnership agreement and received 10 percent preferred return plus 4 percent of partnership profits, but argues that interest is debt, not equity; court refuses to let him disavow form of transaction and treats entity as partnership).

[2] Partners as Members: Section 704(e)(1)

Page 3-41:

Replace first two sentences of subsection with the following.

Section 704(e)(1) provides, in part, that "[a] person shall be recognized as a partner ... if he owns a capital interest in a partnership in which capital is an income-producing factor...." The Regulations, in turn, define a "capital interest in a partnership" as "an interest in the assets of the partnership, which is distributable to the owner of the capital interest upon his withdrawal from the partnership or upon liquidation of the partnership."[146.1]

[146.1] See Crescent Holdings, LLC, 141 TC No. 15 (2013) (relying on Rev. Proc. 93-27, 1993-2 CB 343, to define a "capital interest" as an interest that would give the holder a "share of the proceeds if the partnership's assets were sold at fair market value and then the proceeds were distributed in a complete liquidation of the partnership").

[3] Partners as Members: Other Considerations

[a] Dividing Profits

Page 3-42:

Add to note 153.

See Virginia Historic Tax Credit Fund 2001 LP, 98 TCM 630 (2009) (investors respected as partners through sole benefit was state historic rehabilitation tax credits; nominal one percent profits interest shared by more than 100 partners), rev'd, 2011-1 USTC ¶ 50,308 (4th Cir. 2011).

Page 3-43:

In second paragraph of subsection, add new note 153.1 at end of last sentence.

[153.1] See Priv. Ltr. Rul. 200832024 (Aug. 8, 2008) (partnership between United States subsidiary (US1), foreign subsidiary (F2), and third party; US1 allocated profits solely from U.S. business, F2 allocated profits solely from foreign business, and third party's share apparently minimal; partnership exists despite lack of sharing between US1 and F2).

Add to fourth paragraph of subsection (ending with note callout 155).

In Notice 2008-80, however, the Service proposed to modify Revenue Procedure 2003-84, quoted above, by requiring that the variable-rate interests have at least a 5% share of any gains from the underlying bonds.[155.1]

[155.1] Notice 2008-80, 2008-40 IRB 820.

Page 3-44:

Add at end of first full paragraph.

On remand, the district court found the investment to be a partnership interest under § 704(e)(1).[156.1] On appeal of the remand, the Second Circuit reiterated its earlier conclusion that the interest was too debt-like to be considered equity, but clarified that its earlier opinion intended to treat the banks' interests as debt. As a result, not surprisingly, § 704(e)(1) did not apply to the banks' interests. The Second Circuit stopped short, however, of addressing any conflict between *Culbertson*, upon which it relied for its initial holding, and § 704(e)(1).[156.2]

[156.1] TIFD III-E, Inc. v. United States, 660 F. Supp. 2d 367 (D. Conn. 2009), rev'd, 666 F3d 836 (2d Cir. 2012). In 2015, the Second Circuit reversed the U.S. district court for the third time in *TIFD III-E*. In an unpublished summary order, it held there was no reasonable basis for the taxpayer's reporting position, reversed the district court's finding to the contrary, and imposed the 20 percent negligence penalty on the taxpayer. TIFD III-E v. United States, 2015-1 USTC ¶ 50,308 (2d Cir. 2015) (summary order). See also Pritired I, LLC v. United States, 816 F. Supp. 2d 693 (SD Iowa 2011) (purported equity investment in substance a loan; holder not a partner).

[156.2] TIFD III-E, Inc. v. United States, 666 F3d 836, 847 n.8 (2d Cir. 2012). ("Even assuming, however, that there may be circumstances in which the application of *Culbertson* and § 704(e)(1) yields different results as to whether the purported holder of a partnership interest qualifies as a partner, we see no reason why the results should differ in this case."). The Second Circuit reversed the U.S. district court for a third time in 2015. See TIFD III-E v. United States, 2015-1 USTC ¶ 50,308 (2d Cir. 2015) (summary order) (no reasonable basis for taxpayer's position, reversing district court's finding to the contrary; 20 percent negligence penalty imposed).

In note 160, add the following after citation to Cokes.

; David H. Methvin, TCM 2015-81 (same);

[b] Other Factors

[i] Loss sharing.

Page 3-47:

Add to note 168.

; WB Acquisition, Inc., 101 TCM 1157 (2011) (no loss sharing), aff'd per curiam, 803 F3d 1014 (9th Cir. 2015).

[iii] Participation in management.

Page 3-48:

In note 175, replace last sentence with the following.

Compare Craig v. United States, 451 F. Supp. 378 (D. SD 1978) and Claire A. Ryza, 36 TCM 269, 273 (1977) (joint control evidence of partner-partnership relationship), with WB Acquisition, Inc., 101 TCM 1157 (2011), aff'd per curiam, 803 F3d 1014 (9th Cir. 2015); Fred P. Fiore, 39 TCM 64 (1979); and Ian T. Allison, 35 TCM 1069 (1976) (absence of joint control evidence of no partner-partnership relationship).

[iv] Performance of substantial services.

Add new note 178.1 at end of first sentence of subsection.

178.1 See WB Acquisition, Inc., 101 TCM 1157 (2011) (contributions of little value weigh against partnership status), aff'd per curiam, 803 F3d 1014 (9th Cir. 2015).

[v] Partnership agreements and tax returns.

Page 3-49:

Add to note 179.

In WB Acquisition, Inc., 101 TCM 1157 (2011), aff'd per curiam, 803 F3d 1014 (9th Cir. 2015), a formal agreement existed but was not followed, which cut against partnership status.

Add to last paragraph of subsection.

On the other hand, the absence of partnership tax return filings does not preclude the Service from finding that an entity classified as a partnership exists.180

---

180 See CCA 201323015 (June 7, 2013), (collaboration agreement to develop and commercialize a product found to be a partnership; documents provided no partnership intended; no tax return filed; *Luna* factors analyzed).

Add new ¶ 3.04[4].

[4] Optionholders as Members [New]

Regulations proposed in 2003 and finalized ten years later recharacterize holders of noncompensatory options (NCOs) as partners of a partnership where a two-pronged conjunctive test is satisfied as of the date of any measurement event (a "Measurement Date").[180.1] An NCO is any option other than an option issued in connection with the performance of services.[180.2] The term "option," for this purpose, means a call option, warrant, other similar arrangement, or the conversion feature of convertible debt or equity. It also means other types of contractual agreements, including forward contracts or notional principal contracts, if the Commissioner determines that such treatment is necessary to achieve the purposes of Regulations § 1.761-3.[180.3]

A Measurement Date is any date on which any of the following events occurs:

1. The issuance of the NCO;
2. A modification of the NCO or the underlying partnership interest; or
3. A transfer of the NCO if the option may be exercised more than 12 months after its issuance or the transfer is pursuant to a plan on a Measurement Date with a principal purpose of substantially reducing the present value of the NCO holder's and the partners' aggregate federal tax liabilities. (a "Tax Reduction").[180.4]

The two-pronged conjunctive test treats the holder of an NCO as a partner where the NCO both (1) provides the option holder with rights that are "substantially similar to the rights afforded a partner"[180.5] and (2) there is a strong likelihood that not treating the option holder as a partner would result in a Tax Reduction.[180.6] This test is meant to be additive to the current common law treatment of option holders as partners, and is not intended to override such

---

[180.1] Reg. § 1.761-3.

[180.2] Reg. § 1.761-3(b)(2).

[180.3] Reg. § 1.761-3(b)(3).

[180.4] Reg. § 1.761-3(c). Proposed Regulations issued under Regulations § 1.761-3 would add additional Measurement Dates, but only if a principal purpose of Tax Reduction existed on that date. The additional Measurement Dates include those upon which any of the following events occur: (1) issuance, transfer, or modification of an interest in, or liquidation of, the issuing partnership; (2) issuance, transfer, or modification of an interest in any look-through entity that directly, or indirectly through one or more look-through entities, owns the NCO; and (3) issuance, transfer, or modification of an interest in any look-through entity that directly, or indirectly through one or more look-through entities, owns an interest in the issuing partnership. Prop. Reg. § 1.761-3(c)(1)(iv) (2013). Adding such Measurement Dates would increase significantly the frequency with which partnerships would be obligated to review the status of an NCO holder (and thus, the costs of compliance with the Regulations).

[180.5] Reg. § 1.761-3(a)(1)(i).

[180.6] Reg. § 1.761-3(a)(1)(ii). If this language seems familiar, that's because it is similar to the language of the substantiality rule contained in Regulations § 1.704-1(b)(2)(iii)(a), and, in fact, the final regulations modified the test to address some of the issues that arose in the substantiality context. See TD 9612, Summary of Comments and Explanation of Provisions, § 3.B (Feb. 5. 2013). Unlike the substantiality rule, however, the NCO test provides a solid baseline for comparison between the option holder being treated as an option holder and the option holder being treated as a partner.

law.[180.7] The term "additive" apparently means that the Regulations are intended to override the common law treatment of option holders as option holders and not the common law treatment of option holders as partners.[180.8]

[a] The "Substantially Similar" Test

The "substantially similar" test is also a two-prong test, but here, the test is disjunctive, rather than conjunctive. An option holder has rights that are "substantially similar to the rights afforded a partner" if the option is either (1) reasonably certain to be exercised or (2) the option holder possesses partner attributes.

[i] Reasonable certainty of exercise. Whether an option is reasonably certain to be exercised is based on all of the facts and circumstances as of a Measurement Date. The final Regulations spell out a series of potential facts and circumstances for consideration, but assign no weight, or even merit, to such factors. The facts and circumstances are all economically driven and read like the factors considered in a Black-Scholes Model:

1. The fair market value of the partnership interest that is the subject of the NCO;
2. The strike price of the NCO;
3. The term of the NCO;
4. The volatility of the value or income of the issuing partnership or the underlying partnership interest;
5. Anticipated distributions by the partnership during the term of the NCO;
6. Any other special option features, such as a strike price that fluctuates; and
7. Any other arrangements affecting or undertaken with a principal purpose of affecting the likelihood that the NCO will be exercised.

One thing that is clear from the list is that some of the identified facts and circumstances cannot be considered in isolation. The fact that a partner-

---

[180.7] Reg. § 1.761-3(a)(2).

[180.8] Prior to Regulations § 1.761-3, existing authority applied the substance-over-form doctrine to treat option holders as owning the underlying property only where the economic likelihood of exercise was near certain. See, e.g., Rev. Rul. 85-87, 1985-1 CB 268 (based on economic factors, "no substantial likelihood" that the put would not be exercised); Rev. Rul. 82-150, 1982-2 CB 110 (option to acquire 100% of stock of a foreign corporation is treated as ownership of $100,000 worth of underlying stock where strike price was $30,000). Regulations § 1.761-3 expands the Service's recharacterization authority to situations where the option is not economically certain to be exercised but the option holder obtains "partner attributes," as well as situations where the option is only "reasonably certain" to be exercised. Additionally, Regulations § 1.761-3 authorizes recharacterization at dates other than issuance; no authority previously existed for such recharacterizations.

ship interest is worth $1 or $1,000,000 is irrelevant to the issue of certainty of exercise standing on its own, but becomes highly significant when coupled with a strike price of $100,000. In other words, it is the "spread" between the strike price and value that is relevant to likelihood of exercise, not the strike price or value individually.[180.9] Conversely, regardless of any other facts or circumstances, the longer the term of an option, generally the more likely it is to be exercised at some point.

The relevance of the volatility factor is unclear. Generally speaking, the higher the volatility of an underlying partnership interest, the higher the value of the NCO. However, the Regulations do not look to the value of the NCO, but to likelihood of exercise. With a highly volatile asset, the upside can be greater, but the downside can be greater as well. Because the option holder participates only in the upside, increased volatility decreases the similarities between a partner and an option holder and so may make exercise less likely in certain circumstances (particularly for a holder of an in-the-money option).

The addition of safe harbors would generally clarify the facts and circumstances test, but the two safe harbors proffered by the final Regulations are significantly limited in their application.[180.10] Under the first of these safe harbors, an NCO will not be considered reasonably certain to be exercised if the term of the option is limited to 24 months and the strike price is no lower than 110 percent of the fair market value of the underlying partnership interest as of the exercise date.[180.11] The second safe harbor exempts any NCO that allows the holder to acquire the partnership interest only at fair market value or higher as of the exercise date.[180.12]

An example in the Regulations approves an option similar to the first safe harbor, but with a 36-month term and an unpredictable business.

> **EXAMPLE 3-5:** PRS is a partnership engaged in an active real estate business. At a time when a 10% interest in PRS is worth $100, PRS sells a noncompensatory option to A to acquire a 10% interest in PRS at any time during the next three years for $110. The premium for the NCO is $100. Despite the high premium, the unpredictable nature of the real estate business means that the NCO is not reasonably certain to be exer-

---

[180.9] See, e.g., Rev. Rul. 85-87, 1985-1 CB 268 (taking into account spread, term, premium, historic volatility of the underlying asset, and "other objective factors" in concluding there was "no substantial likelihood that the put would not be exercised").

[180.10] Additionally, even NCOs that satisfy one of the safe harbors will not be safe if the partnership and option holder had a principal purpose of substantially reducing the present value of the aggregate federal tax liabilities of the partners and NCO holder. Reg. § 1.761-3(d)(2)(ii)(C).

[180.11] Reg. § 1.761-3(d)(2)(ii)(A)(1).

[180.12] Reg. § 1.761-3(d)(2)(ii)(A)(2). An option will be considered to have an exercise price equal to or greater than fair market value as of the date of exercise if the parties agree upon a formula at the time the option is issued that constitutes a bona fide attempt to arrive at a fair market value as of the time of exercise and is to be applied based on the facts and circumstances in existence on the exercise date. Reg. § 1.761-3(d)(2)(ii)(B).

cised. As long as *A* does not possess partner attributes, the NCO will not be treated as a partnership interest under Regulations § 1.761-3.

By erring so closely to the side of safety, the example in the Regulations and the safe harbors provide almost no guidance in interpreting the "reasonable certainty of exercise" test. Although the final Regulations explicitly remove any presumption that an NCO that fails to satisfy one of the safe harbors will be treated as reasonably certain to be exercised,[180.13] taxpayers wishing to issue what were once considered plain vanilla options will need to carefully weigh the risk of the option holder being treated as a partner under the final Regulations where there is any significant possibility of the option reducing the parties' tax liabilities.

[ii] Partner attributes. Even if an NCO is not reasonably certain to be exercised, it can still be considered to provide its holders with rights substantially similar to the rights afforded to a partner if the option holder possesses "partner attributes," the evaluation of which depends on the facts and circumstances. However, the Regulations provide us with certainty as to some factors which conclusively constitute partner attributes and some factors which are not partner attributes. Factors that conclusively constitute partner attributes include (1) the right of an NCO holder to participate in current operating or liquidating distributions with respect to the underlying partnership interests prior to exercise of the NCO and (2) an obligation on the part of an NCO holder to bear obligations that are similar to those of a partner who bears partnership losses.[180.14] Thus, the holder of an NCO that guarantees partnership debt would generally be treated as possessing partner attributes.

By contrast, an NCO holder will not be treated as having partner attributes simply because the holder has the ability to impose reasonable restrictions on partnership distributions or dilutive issuances of partnership equity or options during the term of the NCO, or because the holder has the ability to choose the partnership's § 704(c) methodology.[180.15] Exceptions to the "partner attributes" rules apply where such attributes arise as a result of the NCO holder's separate position as a partner in the partnership.[180.16]

[b] Substantial Tax Reduction

In addition to satisfying the "substantially similar" test, in order for the holder of an NCO to be treated as a partner, there must be a strong likelihood that the treatment of the NCO as an NCO would result in a substantial reduction in the present value of the partners' and NCO holders' aggregate federal tax liability. The substantial tax reduction test takes into account the interac-

---

[180.13] Reg. § 1.761-3(d)(2)(ii)(D).

[180.14] Reg. § 1.761-3(d)(3)(ii).

[180.15] Reg. § 1.761-3(d)(3)(iii)(C).

[180.16] See Reg. § 1.761-3(d)(3)(iii).

tion between partnership items and the partners' and NCO holder's federal tax attributes (including the federal tax attributes of the members of the partner or NCO holder if it is a look-through entity or the rest of the group if a member of a consolidated group),[180.17] as well as (1) the timing of income and deductions and (2) both the absolute and relative amount of the reduction (in comparison to the overall federal tax liability).[180.18] Caution is advised, as it may be difficult after the fact to demonstrate that substantial tax savings were attributable to unexpected events.

[c] Consequences of Partner Treatment

Regulations § 1.761-3 provides for the treatment of an option holder as a partner in certain situations, but does little to clarify the consequences of such treatment. We know that upon exercise of an NCO, the newly minted partner acquires the partnership interest with a basis equal to the sum of the premium paid and the basis of any property transferred in exercise of the NCO.[180.19] When no property has yet been transferred in exercise of the NCO, however, presumably the new partner's basis is limited to the premium paid to exercise the option until such time as the new partner legally exercises the option by delivering the exercise price to the partnership.[180.20] Similarly, the new partner's capital account should not include the exercise price prior to the date of exercise. This treatment is comparable to a partner with a deferred capital contribution.

[180.17] Reg. § 1.761-3(e)(2).

[180.18] Reg. § 1.761-3(e)(1).

[180.19] Reg. § 1.721-2(a). Discussed infra ¶ 4.01[1][d].

[180.20] Giving the holder of the NCO basis for the exercise price appears to be a recipe for abuse.

¶ 3.05 DISTINGUISHING PARTNERSHIPS FROM OTHER ECONOMIC RELATIONSHIPS

Page 3-49:

Add before first paragraph of subsection.

[NOTE: In this section, there are several instances in which former § 704(e)(1) is discussed and its impact analyzed. Former § 704(e)(1) was repealed, as discussed in ¶ 3.00, effective for partnership taxable years beginning in 2016. For partnership taxable years beginning before then, the existing discussion of former § 704(e)(1) in this section remains relevant to the extent the repeal can be interpreted as a change to, rather than a clarification of, pre-2016 law; the discussion in ¶ 3.00 addresses, among other things, this concern. Also, in the repeal of former § 704(e)(1), former §§ 704(e)(2) and 704(e)(3) were

renumbered as §§ 704(e)(1) and 704(e)(2), respectively, without any other change, aside from clarifying that they are applicable for purposes of applying § 704(e).]

[1] Partnerships Distinguished From Employment or Independent Contractor Relationships

Page 3-52:

Add after carryover paragraph.

In *Rigas v. United States*,[188.1] the district court applied a "facts and circumstances" test to determine that a business relationship was not a partnership, but was instead a service arrangement. The contract forming the relationship was styled as a Loan Management and Services Agreement, pursuant to which the taxpayers obligated themselves to manage a portfolio of energy properties. The contract expressly negated any intent to form a partnership, and, in fact, no partnership tax return was filed that included the taxpayers. While the court noted that the taxpayers' were compensated based on business profits and were indirectly exposed to business losses, this alone was insufficient to support a conclusion that a partnership existed. As a result, the plaintiff taxpayers' shares of the proceeds of asset sales were ordinary income rather than capital gain.

By contrast, in *United States v. Stewart*,[188.2] the U.S. district court concluded that a partnership was established between a capital providing investor with no experience in the oil and gas industry and an experienced management team (which received a 20 percent profits interest in sale proceeds from acquired property). Of importance to the court was the contribution of experience by the management team and financing by the investor, which when combined created a tax partnership despite the parties' failure to file a joint tax return or operate under a joint name.

[188.1] Rigas v, United States, 2011-1 USTC ¶ 50,372 (SD Tex. 2011).

[188.2] United States v. Stewart, 2015-2 USTC ¶ 50,443 (SD Tex. 2015), appeal filed by government (Oct. 16, 2015).

[2] Partnerships Distinguished From Purchaser-Seller Relationships

Page 3-53:

Add to note 192.

An entity will be treated as having only one member where 100% of the interests are attributed to the same taxpayer through one or more disregarded entities. See 6611, Ltd. Ricardo Garcia, Tax Matters Partner, 105 TCM 1309 (2013).

[3] Partnerships Distinguished From Lender-Borrower Relationships

Page 3-56:

Delete note 204.

Add to note 205.

See also Notice 2008-80, 2008-40 IRB 820, proposing technical modifications and clarifications to Rev. Proc. 2003-84.

Page 3-57:

Add at the end of subsection.

After a long and winding road involving four opinions, rendered over a span of eight years, in *TIFD III-E* (commonly referred to as the *Castle Harbour* case), the Second Circuit finally determined that the preferred interests of two Dutch banks in a partnership called Castle Harbour were so debt-like that they were debt for tax purposes, and therefore were not partnership interests,[210.1] and sent the case back to the U.S. district court to determine whether the taxpayer was subject to the 20 percent accuracy-related negligence penalty under § 6662. Somewhat predictably, U.S. district court Judge Underhill (who had consistently supported the taxpayer in two prior decisions) held that the taxpayer's position had a reasonable basis and therefore the taxpayer was not negligent. The Second Circuit found this factual finding to be erroneous and reversed, imposing a 20 percent penalty on the taxpayer.[210.2] In a previous opinion the Second Circuit had appeared to accept the district court's determination that the banks' interests were not debt (a determination that the government did not appeal), but nevertheless the Second Circuit appeared to hold that, due to the debt-like nature of the banks' interests, the banks did not "participate" sufficiently in profits and losses for their interests to be treated as partnership interests under *Culbertson v. Commissioner.*[210.3]

[210.1] TIFD III-E v. United States, 666 F3d 836 (2d Cir. 2012).

[210.2] TIFD III-E v. United States, 2015-1 USTC ¶ 50,308 (2d Cir. 2015) (summary order).

[210.3] TIFD III-E v. United States, 459 F3d 220 (2d Cir. 2006).

[4] Partnerships Distinguished From Lessor-Lessee Relationships

[b] Ostensible Partnerships Treated as Leases: Section 7701(e)

Page 3-59:

In note 216, replace § 50(d)(1) with former § 46(e)(3).

[5] Partnerships Distinguished From Co-Ownership of Property

Page 3-63:

In note 228, add the following at end of first sentence (following citation of Bentex Oil).

; Jimastowlo Oil, LLC, 106 TCM 161 (2013).

Page 3-65:

In second full paragraph, replace fourth sentence (containing note 236) with the following.

Nevertheless, given the pervasive uncertainty in this area[236] and the critical nature of this distinction, particularly in the context of § 1031 exchanges,[236.1] it is predictable that practitioners as well as revenue agents will give great deference to these guidelines in planning and auditing transactions.

---

[236] But see Priv. Ltr. Rul. 200327003 (July 3, 2003).

[236.1] Interests in partnerships are treated as direct interests in partnership assets for purposes of § 1031 (§ 1031(e), as amended by the Pub. L. No. 115-97, § 13303(b) (Dec. 22, 2017), if a partnership has a valid § 761(a) election in effect (see ¶ 3.08[3]). Thus, a § 761(a) election may provide greater comfort under § 1031 than even a carefully crafted co-ownership arrangement. After 2017, § 1031 exchanges are limited to exchanges of real property under the 2017 Tax Cuts and Jobs Act, Pub. L. No. 115-97, § 13303(a) (Dec. 22, 2017).

Page 3-67:

Add to note 246.

Some grace from the Service may be available in the application of this requirement. See PMTA 2010-005 (Mar. 15, 2010) (temporary non-pro rata pooling of funds not "sufficiently extensive" to cause co-owners to be treated as partners; note extenuating circumstances).

Page 3-69:

Add to note 258.

In Priv. Ltr. Rul. 201622008 (Feb. 23, 2016), the Service applied Revenue Procedure 2002-22, 2002-1 CB 733, to rule that co-ownership of property arrangement will not be a partnership even though one of the co-owners is the lessee of the property under a triple net lease. Further, the arrangement envisioned the possibility of a creeping acquisition of the property by the lessee-co-owner from the lessor−co-owner through a series of puts and calls.

[7] Tax Consequences of Improperly Classifying an Economic Relationship

Page 3-72:

Add to penultimate paragraph of subsection (ending with note callout 264).

The consequences in the international arena can be especially harsh, including subjecting foreign partners to United States taxation because the deemed partnership is engaged in a U.S. trade or business.[264.1]

[264.1] See Kadet & Koontz, "Profit Shifting Structures and Unexpected Partnership Status," 151 Tax Notes 335 (2016).

¶ 3.06 ELECTIVE CLASSIFICATION FOR ELIGIBLE ENTITIES UNDER THE CHECK-A-BOX REGULATIONS

[1] The Historical Perspective

Page 3-76:

Replace note 274 with the following.

[274] Littriello v. United States, 2005-1 USTC ¶ 50,385 (WD Ky. 2005), aff'd, 484 F3d 372 (6th Cir. 2007), cert. denied, 128 S. Ct. 1290 (2008). Accord McNamee v. Department of Treasury, 488 F3d 372 (6th Cir. 2007); Kandi v. United States, 295 Fed. Appx. 873 (9th Cir. 2008); Medical Practice Solutions LLC, 132 TC 125 (2009), supplemented by 99 TCM 1392 (2010).

[3] Single-Owner Business Entities

Page 3-78:

Add to note 292.

See Notice 2012-52, 2012-35 IRB 317 (contributions to U.S. charity's wholly-owned disregarded entity generally treated as made to charity).

Replace last sentence of subsection with the following.

If an entity is disregarded, its activities are treated in the same manner as a sole proprietorship, branch, or division of the owner.[292.1]

[292.1] Prior to 2009 (see Reg. § 301.7701-2(c)(2)(iv)(B), supra ¶ 2.04[2]), disregarded entities were entirely disregarded as separate entities for employment tax purposes. See Heber E. Costello LLC, 112 TCM 396 (2016) (single-member LLC and its sole member "are a single taxpayer or person who is personally liable for" employment taxes of the entity).

[4] *Per Se* **Corporations**

[b] *Per Se* **Foreign Corporations**

[i] General.

Page 3-80:

Add the following country to "per se" list after Brazil.

Bulgaria, Aktsionerno Druzhestvo[302.1]

[302.1] Temp. Reg. § 301.7701-2T(b)(8)(vi) (effective for any Aktsionerno Druzhestvo formed after January 1, 2007, pursuant to Notice 2007-10, 2007-1 CB 354).

[5] Elective Classification by Eligible Entities

[a] Default Classification of Eligible Entities

[i] General.

Page 3-85:

In second paragraph of subsection, replace second sentence with the following.

Foreign business entities that do not fall under the grandfather rule are separated into two categories to determine their default classification: those that possess the characteristic of limited liability and those that do not.[321.1]

[321.1] See George C. Huff, 138 TC 258 (2012) (U.S. Virgin Islands LLC).

[b] Election to Adopt or Change a Classification

Page 3-88:

Add to note 335.

See Rev. Proc. 2009-41, 2009-39 IRB 439 (Sept. 3, 2009) (extension of relief for late classification election to within 3 years and 75 days of requested effective date).

Replace note 338 with the following.

[338] Reg. § 301.7701-3(c)(1)(ii).

Replace note 339 with the following.

[339] Reg. § 301.7701-3(c)(1)(ii).

Replace note 340 with the following.

340 Reg. § 301.7701-3(c)(1)(ii).

Page 3-89:

Add at end of subsection.

The IRS allows taxpayers to correct otherwise valid elections for foreign eligible entities where the election misstates the actual number of owners of the entity. Thus, where a qualified entity files a Form 8832, electing to be treated as a disregarded entity (or a partnership), but is determined to have two members rather than one (or one, rather than two), the entity's election will remain valid, but will be treated as making an election to be taxable as a partnership (or disregarded entity) for federal income tax purposes, provided that the entity files a corrected Form 8832 and attaches the corrected Form 8832 to the owners' (or owner's) amended return for the taxable year in which the original election was filed.343.1

343.1 Rev. Proc. 2010-32, 2010-36 IRB 320. An entity is a "qualified entity" for these purposes if (1) it is an eligible entity under Regulations § 301.7701-3(a); (2) it is foreign under Regulations § 301.7701-5(a); (3) it would be treated as an association taxable as a corporation if no election were made under Regulations § 301.7701-3; (4) it elected, pursuant to Regulations § 301.7701-3(c), to be taxable as either a disregarded entity or a partnership; (5) either (a) no information or tax returns have been required to be filed since the effective date of the election or (b) the business entity and its owners have treated the entity consistently with the election on the otherwise valid Form 8832 on all filed information and tax returns; and (6) the period of limitations under § 6501(a) has not ended for any taxable year of the business entity or its owners affected by the election made on the otherwise valid Form 8832.

[d] Limited Partnerships as S Corporations

Page 3-90:

Replace note 349 with the following.

349 The Service is currently "addressing" this problem by refusing to issue one-class-of-stock rulings related to state law limited partnerships under 1361(b)(1)(D). Rev. Proc. 2019-3, 3.01(100), 2019-1 IRB 130 .

¶ 3.07 PARTNERSHIPS INVOLVING SHAREHOLDERS AND CORPORATIONS

[2] Partnerships Between Shareholders and Controlled Corporations

Page 3-94:

Add to note 368.

But see DJB Holding Corp v. Commissioner, 2016-2 USTC ¶ 50,509 (9th Cir. 2015) (alleged partnership involving tax-exempt retirement plans not respected; *Maxwell* distinguished).

Page 3-95:

In note 373, replace § 704(e)(1) *with* former § 704(e)(1) (2016 repeal discussed at ¶ 3.00).

¶ 3.08 ELECTION TO BE EXCLUDED FROM SUBCHAPTER K: SECTION 761(a)

[3] Uses and Tax Costs of the Election

Page 3-102:

In second to last paragraph of subsection, replace last sentence with the following.

Section 1031(a)(2) was amended by the Revenue Reconciliation Act of 1990 to provide that, for purposes of § 1031, an interest in a partnership that has made a valid § 761(a) election is treated as an interest in each of the assets of the partnership.[403.1]

[403.1] This aspect of former § 1031(a)(2) has been moved to § 1031(e) by the 2017 Tax Cuts and Jobs Act, Pub. L. No. 115-97, § 13303(b) (Dec. 22, 2017).

[4] Applicability of the Election Outside of Subchapter K

Page 3-103:

Add to note 406.

In 2015, *David H. Methvin*, TCM 2015-81, the Tax Court reaffirmed its position in *Cokes*, namely, that a § 761(a) election has no effect on the applicability of the § 1402(a) rule that an individual's self-employment income includes his distributive share of trade or business income from partnerships of which he is a member.

¶ 3.09 PUBLICLY TRADED LIMITED PARTNERSHIPS: SECTION 7704

[1] General

Page 3-105:

Add to note 414.

Publicly traded foreign partnerships that otherwise qualify for pass-through treatment are treated as foreign corporations for purposes of the foreign inversion rules of § 7874 if the partnership would, but for § 7704(c), be treated as a corporation under § 7704(a) at the time (or following that time if pursuant to a plan that existed at the time) of the partnership's acquisition of (1) substantially all of the properties held by a domestic corporation or (2) substantially all of the properties constituting a trade or business held by a domestic partnership. See Reg. § 1.7874-2(g). These Regulations are designed to prevent the avoidance of the corporate inversion rules through the use of partnerships.

[3] Readily Tradable on Secondary Market or Substantial Equivalent Thereof

Page 3-106:

Add to note 420.

See also Priv. Ltr. Rul. 201527039 (Mar. 19, 2015) (partnerships holding investment portfolios ruled not "publicly traded"; interests therein were held by domestic life insurance companies, directly or through separate accounts, with benefits and burdens of ownership of such portfolios allocated among holders of variable annuity contracts and variable life insurance contracts based on investment direction of contract holders).

[4] Certain Transfers Disregarded

[b] "Private Transfers" Disregarded

[ii] Redemptions treated as private transfers.

Page 3-108:

Add to note 427.

Priv. Ltr. Rul. 200852005 (Sept. 24, 2008) (repurchase/redemption program is closed end redemption plan, as described in Reg. § 1.7704-1(e)).

[d] Transfers Through Qualified Matching Service Disregarded

Page 3-110:

Add to note 432.

See also Priv. Ltr. Rul. 201213004 (Nov. 10, 2011) (website operated by broker-dealer offers both qualifying and non-qualifying matching services; qualifying service satisfies requirements); Priv. Ltr. Rul. 201710019 (Mar. 3, 2017) (same); Priv. Ltr. Rul. 202017008 (Apr. 24, 2020) (qualified matching service requirements satisfied).

[6] Effective Date and Transition Rules Under the Regulations

Page 3-113:

Add to note 445.

See Priv. Ltr. Rul. 201314025 (Apr. 5, 2013) (activities closely related to pre-existing business will not constitute a new line of business under § 7704(g)(2)).

Pages 3-113–3-117:

Replace ¶ 3.09[7] with revised ¶ 3.09[7], and add new ¶ 3.10.

[7] Limited Exception for Partnerships With Passive-Type Income [Revised]

Publicly traded partnerships, 90 percent or more of whose gross income is passive-type income, are not treated as corporations under § 7704.[447] To qualify for this exception, a partnership must meet the 90-percent test for its first taxable year after 1987 in which it is a publicly traded partnership and every year thereafter.

Even if a publicly traded partnership avoids being treated as a corporation under the 90-percent passive income test, its partners may incur certain tax disadvantages under the passive loss rules of § 469, which are applied to such partnerships in a particularly harsh fashion.[448]

Passive-type income generally consists of interest, dividends, real property rents, gains from the sale or other disposition of real property, income and gains from certain natural resource activities, and any gain from the sale or disposition of a capital or § 1231 asset held for the production of any of the foregoing types of income.[449] Interest that is derived from the conduct of a fi-

---

[447] See § 7704(c).

[448] See § 469(k).

[449] § 7704(d). See Reg. § 1.7704-3(a) (certain investment income); Priv. Ltr. Rul. 9743006 (July 18, 1997) (rental income qualifies); Priv. Ltr. Rul. 200411018 (Nov. 26, 2004) (interest income from obligations of directly and indirectly owned companies qualifies).

Regulations § 1.7704-3(a)(1) provides that "qualifying income includes…income from notional principal contracts (as defined in [Reg.] § 1.446-3) and other substantially similar income from ordinary and routine investments to the extent determined by the Commissioner. Income from a notional principal contract is included in qualifying income only if the property, income, or cash flow that measures the amounts to which the partnership is entitled under the contract would give rise to qualifying income if held or received directly by the partnership." Private Letter Ruling 200841017 (June 16, 2008) treats a "Treasury lock" as generating qualifying income under § 7704(d)(1) and Regulations § 1.7704-3(a)(1). The Treasury locks were used to fix the interest on planned debt offerings between the times the borrowing decisions were made and the closings of the debt transactions (the exposure period). Each consisted of a counterparty agreement under which an unrelated party agreed to purchase Treasury bonds from the putative borrower based on prevailing rates at the start of the exposure period and sell them back at the end

nancial or insurance business[450] and rent that is contingent upon profits[451] do not qualify as passive-type income. "Inventory costs" are excluded in determining gross income from real property held for sale in the ordinary course of business under § 1221(1),[452] thus making it easier to satisfy the 90-percent threshold. Finally, the definition of passive-type income from natural resources is quite broad, including income and gain from processing, transporting, or marketing any natural resource, including fertilizer and timber.[453]

---

of the exposure period. The transaction was settled on a net basis at the end of the exposure period without any Treasury bonds actually being bought or sold. Neither a Treasury lock or an interest rate swap involves the payment of interest (there is no borrowing between the counterparties and hence no compensation for the use or forbearance of money), but both involve payments measured by reference to an underlying interest rate or interest rate index and hence are not excluded from qualifying income under § 856(f). The ruling concludes that Treasury locks "will be common and routine transactions, entered into for the same purpose as interest rate swaps" (to manage the risk of interest rate movement), and therefore the income from Treasury locks and interest rate swaps is qualifying income under § 7704(d). See also Priv. Ltr. Rul. 200919019 (Jan. 23, 2009); Priv. Ltr. Rul. 201208021 (Nov. 1, 2011); Priv. Ltr. Rul. 201315008 (Apr. 12, 2013) (same analysis and conclusion).

Similarly, the Service has announced that cancellation of indebtedness income is qualifying income if it is attributable to debt incurred in direct connection with activities that generate qualifying income. "Direct connection" can be established using "any reasonable method." Rev. Proc. 2012-28, 2012-27 IRB 4.

[450] § 7704(d)(2)(A). In general, partnerships that do not originate or actively place loans or leases should not be treated as engaging in a "financial" business merely because they purchase and hold for investment multiple tranches of such instruments.

[451] § 7704(d)(3). "Qualifying rents" are amounts that would qualify as rent from real property under § 856(d) (dealing with REITs) without regard to the independent contractor rules of § 856(d)(2)(C). See Reg. § 1.856-4. A 5-percent de minimis rule applies for purposes of the attribution of holdings to partnerships in the application of the related-party rule of § 856(d)(2)(B). § 7704(d)(3)(B). See HR Rep. No. 795, 100th Cong., 2d Sess. 401 (1988); Priv. Ltr. Rul. 201549013 (Aug. 19, 2015) (income derived from ground leases for billboards, cellular towers, rooftop internet installations, wind turbines, and solar panel sites constitutes qualifying income under § 7704(d)(1)(C)).

[452] § 7704(d)(5).

[453] § 7704(d)(1)(E). According to the Conference Report, passive-type income includes income of partnerships "whose exclusive activity is transporting refined petroleum products by pipeline ... but the income of a partnership whose exclusive activities are transporting refined petroleum products by truck, or retail marketing with respect to refined petroleum products (e.g., gas station operators) is not intended to be treated as passive-type income." HR Rep. No. 495, 100th Cong., 1st Sess. 947 (1987); HR Rep. No. 1104, 100th Cong., 2d Sess. 17 (1988). Apparently, Congress intended for income from wholesale activities to be treated as passive-type income, but was unwilling to treat retail income from marketing as passive. See HR Rep. No. 795, 100th Cong., 2d Sess. 401 (1988); HR Rep. No. 1104, 100th Cong., 2d Sess. 18 (1988) (sales of fertilizers to farmers in amounts of one ton or more are not considered retail sales; income qualifies as passive). See Priv. Ltr. Rul. 9105015 (Nov. 1, 1990) (income from sawmilling processes is passive-type income); Priv. Ltr. Rul. 9338028 (June 25, 1993) (plywood and medium-density fiberboard operations of timber partnership generate passive-type income); Priv. Ltr. Rul. 9339014 (June 28, 1993) (income from sale of chemical by-products pro-

duced during conversion of natural gas into plant fertilizers is passive-type income, as are gains from disposition of natural gas futures contracts); Priv. Ltr. Rul. 200740010 (June 27, 2007) (income derived from operating pipeline systems and terminals for petroleum products is passive-type income); CCA 200749012 (Aug. 15, 2007) (income derived from distribution and marketing of propane to end users at retail level is passive-type income); Priv. Ltr. Rul. 200821021 (Feb. 19, 2008) (income from power production is not passive-type income); Priv. Ltr. Rul. 200845035 (Nov. 7, 2008) (income from pipeline transportation customers as reimbursement for pipeline extensions is qualifying income under § 7704(d)(1)(E) up to, but not exceeding, construction costs); Priv. Ltr. Rul. 200848018 (Nov. 28, 2008) (Section 7701(d)(1)(E) includes income from refining and blending, as well as income from packaging, marketing, and distributing refined and processed products); Priv. Ltr. Rul. 200921010 (Feb. 10, 2009) (fees derived from short and long term storage of petroleum, as well as ancillary services, are qualifying income); Priv. Ltr. Rul. 200939016 (June 25, 2009) (income from transportation of § 7704(d)(1)(E) products is qualifying income); Priv. Ltr. Rul. 200927002 (Mar. 23, 2009) (income from production, marketing, and distribution of straight-run and modified asphalt (other than marketing to end users at the retail level) is qualifying income; Priv. Ltr. Rul. 201005018 (Oct. 8, 2009) (rent from lease of a facility qualifies; the facility included a system of physically connected and functionally interdependent assets designed to receive, store, and distribute a product at elevated temperatures); Priv. Ltr. Rul. 201027003 (July 9, 2010) (income from marine transportation services provided under both spot and term contracts is qualifying income where products transported are described in § 7704(d)(1)(E)); Priv.Ltr. Rul. 201043024 (July 12, 2010) (gross income from selling, removing, treating, and disposing of fracturing fluid and acid mine discharge constitutes qualifying income); Priv. Ltr. Rul. 201129028 (Apr. 7, 2011) (income derived from processing refined petroleum distillates and lube oil base stocks into specialty lubricating oils constitutes qualifying income); Priv. Ltr. Rul. 201206004 (Oct. 31, 2011) (income derived from additization and ethanol blending activities at refined products terminals constitutes qualifying income); Priv. Ltr. Rul. 201241004 (July 2, 2012) (income from sale, storage, and transportation of olefins (derived from cracking ethane and propane), used in the manufacture of chemical derivatives, is qualifying income); Priv. Ltr. Rul. 201314038 (Apr. 5, 2013) (income derived from processing natural gas into premium diesel fuel and marketing same is qualifying income); Priv. Ltr. Rul. 201314029 (Apr. 5, 2013) (income derived from customer construction of terminalling, storage, and pipeline assets is qualifying income); Priv. Ltr. Rul. 201315015 (Apr. 12, 2013) (income from processing natural gas into gasoline and liquefied petroleum gas constitutes qualifying income); Priv. Ltr. Rul. 201322024 (May 31, 2013) (income derived from providing hydraulic fracturing services constitutes qualifying income); Priv. Ltr. Rul. 201324002 (June 14, 2013) (income derived from processing and marketing gasoline, liquefied petroleum gas, methanol, and synthesis gas produced from natural gas constitutes qualifying income); Priv. Ltr. Rul. 201414004 (Sept. 11, 2013) (income derived from mining, marketing, and transportation of frac sand constitutes qualifying income under § 7704(d)(1)(E)); Priv. Ltr. Rul. 201417005 (Oct. 21, 2013) (income derived from transporting crude oil, refined crude oil, refined petroleum products, and certain other products constitutes qualifying income under § 7704(d)(1)(E)); Priv. Ltr. Rul. 201414002 (Dec. 16, 2013) (income derived from supplying fresh water, transporting fracturing fluid, and transporting fracturing and flowback water to disposal facilities constitutes qualifying income under § 7704(d)(1)(E)); Priv. Ltr. Rul. 201416003 (Dec. 27, 2013) (income derived from supplying fresh water, transporting fracturing fluid, and transporting flowback water and other wastes to disposal facilities constitutes qualifying income under § 7704(d)(1)(E)); Priv. Ltr. Rul. 201541008 (June 29, 2015) (income derived from transportation, storage and marketing of fuel constitutes qualifying income under § 7704(d)(1)(E)); Priv. Ltr. Rul. 201545002 (Aug. 5, 2015) (income derived from delivery

In an attempt to reduce the increasing volume of requests for private rulings relating to the scope of the natural resource exception, the Treasury issued Regulations in 2017 intended to clarify the exception.[454] Under the Regulations, "qualifying income" from natural resource activities is defined as income and gains from a "qualifying activity." There are two types of qualifying activities: (1) those described in § 7704(d)(1)(E), consisting of the exploration, development, mining or production, processing, refining, transportation, or marketing of minerals or natural resources ("§ 7704(d)(1)(E) activities"),[455] and (2) those limited support activities that are intrinsic to § 7704(d)(1)(E) activities ("intrinsic activities"). A support activity would not be an intrinsic activity unless it satisfied three requirements: (1) it must be "specialized" to support a § 7704(d)(1)(E) activity; (2) it must be "essential" to the completion of the § 7704(d)(1)(E) activity; and (3) it must require the provision of significant services to support the § 7704(d)(1)(E) activity.[456]

The Regulations generally apply to income earned by a partnership in a taxable year beginning on or after January 19, 2017. However, during a "transition period" that ends on the last day of a partnership's taxable year that includes January 19, 2017, a partnership may treat income from an activity as qualifying income if

1. The partnership received a private letter ruling holding that income from the activity is qualifying income;
2. Prior to May 6, 2015, the partnership was publicly traded, engaged in the activity, treated the activity as giving rise to qualifying income under § 7704(d)(1)(E), and the income was qualifying income under the statute as reasonably interpreted prior to May 6, 2015;
3. Prior to May 6, 2015, the partnership was publicly traded and had entered into a binding agreement for construction of assets to be used in the activity that would give rise to income that was qualifying income under the statute as reasonably interpreted prior to May 6, 2015; or
4. The partnership is publicly traded and engages in the activity after May 6, 2015 but before January 19, 2017, and the income from the activity is qualifying income under the proposed version of the Regulations issued May, 6, 2015.[457]

Publicly traded partnerships that are registered under the Investment Company Act of 1940 (e.g., entities that would be regulated investment companies

---

of water and collection treatment as well as transportation of flowback, produced water, and other fluids constitutes qualifying income under § 7704(d)(1)(E)); Priv. Ltr. Rul. 201548013 (Aug. 5, 2015) (income derived from fluid handling, treatment, processing, and disposal services constitutes qualifying income under § 7704(d)(1)(E)).

[454] Reg. § 1.7704-4; TD 9817 (Jan. 24, 2017).

[455] Reg. § 1.7704-4(c).

[456] Reg. § 1.7704-4(d).

[457] Reg. § 1.7704-4(g). See REG-132634-14 for May 6, 2015 proposed regulations.

under § 851(a) if they were domestic corporations) generally do not qualify for the passive income exception, and thus are treated as corporations.[458] To the extent provided in the regulations, however, the exception from corporate treatment may be made available to such partnerships whose principal activity is buying and selling commodities, options, or futures or forward contracts with respect to commodities.[459]

Relief, in the form of continued partnership treatment, from a failure to meet the 90-percent passive income requirement is available if

1. The Secretary determines that the failure was inadvertent;
2. The partnership takes steps within a reasonable time (one year unless otherwise provided in regulations) to meet the 90-percent requirement; and
3. The partnership and each of its partners (during the failure period) agree to make such adjustments or pay such amounts as required by the Secretary.[460]

The passive loss rules of § 469 are applied separately to the income and loss of each publicly traded partnership.[461] Losses may only be deducted against income from the same partnership, and unused losses are suspended and carried forward until they are either used against future income from the same partnership or freed from the restrictions of § 469 upon the disposition of the taxpayer's entire interest in the partnership.

---

[458] § 7704(c)(3).

[459] § 7704(c)(3).

[460] § 7704(e); see HR Rep. No. 495, 100th Cong., 1st Sess. 950 (1987). The amount paid should be the corporate tax that the partnership would have paid if it had been taxed as a corporation during the disqualification period. HR Rep. No. 795, 100th Cong., 2d Sess. 399 (1988). See Priv. Ltr. Rul. 201818001 (Feb. 1, 2018) (§ 965 inclusion triggered by the 2017 Tax Cuts and Jobs Act satisfies inadvertent requirement).

[461] § 469(k). See HR Rep. No. 495, 100th Cong., 1st Sess. 951–953 (1987). The low-income housing credit of § 42 and the rehabilitation credit of § 47 are not subject to the special rules applicable to publicly traded partnerships to the extent these credits exceed the regular tax liability attributable to the income from the partnership. § 469(k)(1).

¶ 3.10 QUALIFIED JOINT VENTURES AMONG SPOUSES [NEW]

Section 761(f), added to the Code in 2007, provides an exclusion from partnership status for a "qualified joint venture" conducted by a husband and wife who file a joint return. Congress enacted § 761(f) to alleviate what it viewed as the unnecessary complexity of filing a partnership return in cases where the only members of a business joint venture are a husband and wife who file a joint return.[462] There was also concern that if the spouses were not filing a partnership return, but instead reporting all of the trade or business income on a single Schedule C, only the spouse treated as having net earnings from self-employment from the venture would receive credit for purposes of determining Social Security benefits.[463]

Under § 761(f), if both spouses elect § 761(f) treatment, their qualified joint venture is not treated as a partnership for federal income tax purposes.[464] All of the qualified joint venture's items of income, gain, loss, deduction, and credit are then divided between the spouses in accordance with their respective interests in the venture,[465] and each spouse must take into account his or her respective shares of such items as if they were attributable to a trade or business conducted by such spouse as a sole proprietor.[466] Where a § 761(f) election is made for a joint venture previously treated as a partnership for tax purposes, the venture is treated as having terminated, presumably under § 708(b)(1)(A), at the end of the taxable year immediately preceding the taxable year for which the election takes effect.[467]

"Qualified joint venture" is defined as any joint venture involving the conduct of a trade or business if (1) the only members of the joint venture are a husband and wife, (2) both spouses materially participate (within the meaning of § 469(h) without regard to paragraph (5) thereof) in such trade or business, and (3) both spouses elect the application of § 761(f).[468]

The election is not available for a business conducted by a state law entity, such as a general partnership, limited partnership, or limited liability company.[469] Once made, the election remains in effect for as long as the joint venture continues to meet the requirements for filing the election.[470] Thus, for example, if separate returns are later filed by the spouses or if a non-spouse becomes a member of the venture, the election ceases to be effective for the

---

[462] See HR Rep. No. 14, 110th Cong., 1st Sess. 15 (2007).

[463] See HR Rep. No. 14, 110th Cong., 1st Sess. 15 (2007).

[464] § 761(f)(1)(A). This differs from the treatment afforded by an election under § 761(a), which only excludes a partnership from the application of Subchapter K.

[465] § 761(f)(1)(B).

[466] § 761(f)(1)(C). As a result of this rule, each spouse should file a separate Schedule C reporting his or her respective share of the items of the venture. The Service provides specific guidance for the § 761 election on its website, at: http://www.irs.gov (search "qualified joint venture"; then follow hyperlink entitled "Election for Husband and Wife Unincorporated Businesses").

[467] See http://www.irs.gov (search "qualified joint venture"; then follow hyperlink entitled "Election for Husband and Wife Unincorporated Businesses").

[468] § 761(f)(2).

[469] See http://www.irs.gov (search "qualified joint venture"; then follow hyperlink entitled "Election for Husband and Wife Unincorporated Businesses"). Trades or businesses co-owned by spouses are eligible, but co-owned property that is not a trade or business is not.

[470] See http://www.irs.gov (search "qualified joint venture"; then follow hyperlink entitled "Election for Husband and Wife Unincorporated Businesses").

taxable year with respect to which the separate returns are filed or during which the new non-spouse member joins the venture.[471] Spouses make the § 761(f) election on a jointly filed Form 1040 by dividing all items of income, gain, loss, deduction, and credit between them in accordance with each spouse's respective interest in the joint venture, with each spouse filing with the joint return a separate Schedule C or Schedule F, and, if otherwise required, a separate Schedule SE reporting self-employment tax.[472]

---

[471] See http://www.irs.gov (search "qualified joint venture"; then follow hyperlink entitled "Election for Husband and Wife Unincorporated Businesses").

[472] See http://www.irs.gov (search "qualified joint venture"; then follow hyperlink entitled "Election for Husband and Wife Unincorporated Businesses").

PART II

Acquisitions of
Partnership Interests

Receipt of a Partnership Interest in Exchange for a Contribution of Property

¶ 4.01 PROPERTY CONTRIBUTIONS: AN OVERVIEW

[1] The General Rule of Nonrecognition and Substituted Basis

[a] Nonrecognition Treatment

Pages 4-3–4-4:

Replace second paragraph of subsection (ending with note callout 7)

There are five principal exceptions to the nonrecognition rule of § 721(a). First, §§ 721 through 723 are applicable only if "property" is contributed to a partnership. (A major consequence of this limitation is that transactions in which partnership interests are issued in exchange for services are not eligible for nonrecognition treatment under § 721.[4]) Second, § 721(a) does not apply to contributions to a "partnership investment company."[5] Third, transfers of ap-

---

[4] The tax consequences of transfers of interests in exchange for services are discussed in Chapter 5.

[5] See discussion infra ¶ 4.07.

preciated property to partnerships with foreign partners related to the transferor may be taxable under § 721(c) if certain conditions are not met.[5.1] Fourth, a contribution is taxable if it is part of a "disguised sale" under § 707(a).[6] Finally, the interaction of §§ 721, 731, and 752 may result in gain (but not loss) recognition when a partner contributes property and the partnership takes the property subject to or assumes the contributing partner's liabilities.[7]

[5.1] See discussion infra ¶ 4.01[5][b].

[6] See discussion infra ¶¶ 4.01[4], 14.02[3][b].

[7] See discussion infra ¶ 4.03.

Pages 4-6–4-8:

Replace ¶ 4.01[1][d] with the following.

[d] Noncompensatory Options [Revised]

Final Regulations under Regulations § 1.721-2 clarify that, unless the option holder is treated as a partner upon issuance of a noncompensatory option (NCO), the issuance of an NCO is governed by generally applicable open transaction principles: There is no income to either the partnership or the option holder on issuance of the NCO or on payment of an option premium in cash.[16]

If an NCO lapses, (1) § 721 is inapplicable, (2) the option premium is taxable to the partnership as ordinary income, and (3) the option holder has a loss equal to his basis in the option in the lapse year under § 1234.[17] If an NCO is exercised, the option holder is viewed as making a contribution, under § 721, of the option premium and the exercise price, which contribution will generally have no taxable consequences for either the option holder or the partnership.[18] Where an NCO is issued by a disregarded entity that would de-

---

[16] If the option premium is paid with property (instead of cash) or the option is issued in satisfaction of a partnership obligation, the general nonrecognition rule of § 721 will not apply, and the transaction will be taxed in accordance with general tax principles. Reg. § 1.721-2(b)(1). The exception to this rule occurs where a conversion feature is granted in connection with convertible equity to which § 721 otherwise applies. Reg. § 1.721-2(b)(2).

[17] Proposed Regulations issued under § 1234 would confirm that the term "securities" under § 1234 includes partnership interests, thus subjecting the lapse of a partnership NCO to § 1234. Prop. Reg. § 1.1234-3(b)(2) (2013).

[18] Reg. § 1.721-2(a)(1). Where the exercise price is satisfied with the cancellation of a partnership obligation for unpaid rents, royalties, or interest, any of which accrued during the option holder's holding period in the option, § 721 will not apply to such cancellation with respect to the option holder. The partnership in such a scenario, however, will not recognize gain or loss on the issuance of a partnership interest. Reg. § 1.721-2(a)(2). Another exception to the general nonrecognition rule occurs where the option holder receives a capital account that is less than the exercise price, in which case general tax prin-

fault to partnership status if the NCO were to be exercised, the general nonrecognition rule of § 721 does not apply upon exercise of the NCO.[19]

"NCO" defined. An NCO is any option issued by a partnership to acquire a partnership interest "other than an option issued in connection with the performance of services."[20] The term "option," for this purpose, means a call option, warrant, other similar arrangement, or the conversion feature of convertible debt or equity.[21]

> **EXAMPLE 4-2:** *N* buys an NCO on a one-third interest in the *LM* partnership. *N* is not treated as a partner under Regulations § 1.761-3. *N* pays the option premium by transferring Property *E* (adjusted basis $600, market value $1,000) to *LM*. The exercise price is $5,000, payable in either cash or property. *N* eventually exercises the option by transferring Property *F* (adjusted basis $3,000, market value $5,000) to the partnership.
>
> Section 721(a) does not apply to the transfer of Property *E* to the partnership in exchange for the option, so *N* recognizes gain of $400 and the partnership takes a $1,000 basis in Property *E* upon issuance of the option. Under general open transaction principles, the partnership recognizes no income or gain on issuance of the option. On exercise of the option, § 721 applies, and thus neither the partnership nor *N* recognizes gain on the contribution of appreciated Property *F* to the partnership and the issuance of a one-third partnership interest to *N*. *N*'s initial basis for his partnership interest is $4,000 ($1,000 basis in option, plus $3,000 basis of contributed Property *F*). Under § 723, the partnership has a carryover basis of $3,000 for Property *F*.[22]

---

ciples will apply, presumably to potentially create a compensatory capital shift under Regulations § 1.721-1(b)(1).

[19] See TD 9612, Summary of Comments and Explanation of Provisions, § 1.B.iii (Feb. 5. 2013).

[20] Reg. § 1.721-2(f).

[21] Reg. § 1.721-2(g)(1).

[22] Reg. § 1.721-2(h) Example. Special capital account maintenance rules apply under § 704(b) upon exercise of an NCO; certain corrective allocations may be required and reverse § 704(c) principles may come into play. See Reg. §§ 1.704-1(b)(2)(iv)(*s*), 1.704-1(b)(4)(*x*). See ¶ 11.02[3][e][ii].

[3] Disguised Capital Contributions

Page 4-12:

In note 41, delete second sentence with cross reference to ¶ 3.05[4]

Pages 4-13—4-14:

Replace ¶ 4.01[5] with revised ¶ 4.01[5].

[5] Transfers to Foreign Partnerships and Certain Partnerships with Related Foreign Partners [Revised]

[a] Transfers to Foreign Partnerships

Prior to its repeal by the Taxpayer Relief Act of 1997, § 1491 was one of the most insidious traps in the Code, imposing an excise tax on the transfer of property to a foreign partnership by a U.S. citizen or resident, a domestic partnership, or a U.S. corporation.[44] Congress believed that the imposition of enhanced information reporting obligations with respect to foreign partnerships (including §§ 6038, 6038B, and 6046A) would eliminate the need for § 1491.[45] In particular, §§ 6038B(a)(1)(B) and 6038B(b)(1) impose reporting requirements on any "United States person" who contributes property to a foreign partnership if (1) such person, immediately after the transfer, holds (directly, indirectly, or by attribution) at least a 10 percent interest in the partnership, as defined in § 6038(e)(3)(C), or (2) the value of the property transferred (when added to the value of all property transferred by such person and any related person to such partnership or a related partnership during the twelve-month period ending on the date of transfer) exceeds $100,000.[46] Property is valued at its fair market value as of the date transferred.[47] Reporting requirements that might be triggered by a § 482 adjustment are excused if the adjustment was initiated by the Service, but not if it was initiated by the taxpayer.[48]

Additionally, the Regulations impose ongoing filing requirements on any United States person who is subject to the § 6038B filing requirements in connection with a contribution of property to a foreign partnership, but only if the contributed property had built-in gain at the time of contribution. For so long as the United States person remains a direct or indirect partner, she must re-

---

[44] The repeal of § 1491 was effective on August 5, 1997. See Pub. L. No. 105-34, § 1131(a). The tax imposed was equal to 35 percent of the excess of the fair-market value of the transferred property over the sum of its basis and any gain recognized at the time of the transfer.

[45] See Staff of the Joint Comm. on Taxation, General Explanation of Tax Legislation Enacted in 1997, Part Two: Taxpayer Relief Act of 1997, 314–315 (Dec. 17, 1997).

[46] See Reg. § 1.6038B-2(a). The Regulations provide special rules for "indirect transfers" through domestic partnerships:

1. If the domestic partnership complies with the § 6038B reporting requirements, its direct and indirect partners are excused. Reg. § 1.6038B-2(a)(2)..
2. Reporting is also excused if the transferee-partnership validly elects out of Subchapter K under § 761(a). Reg. § 1.6038B-2(f).
3. Transfers must be reported on Form 8865. Reg. § 1.6038B-2(a)(5).

Effective date provisions are set forth in Regulations § 1.6038B-2(j).

[47] § 6038B(a)(1) (flush language at end).

[48] § 6038B(b)(2); Reg. § 1.6038B-2(g) (for taxpayer-initiated adjustments, information is timely furnished if filed by due date (including extensions) of return for taxable year during which adjustment is made).

port any disposition of the property by the partnership, unless the disposition qualifies as a nonrecognition transaction in which the partnership receives substituted basis property that has built-in gain under Regulations § 1.704-3(a)(8).[49]

If a United States person fails to timely comply with these reporting requirements, the entire gain inherent in the appreciated property as of the contribution date becomes taxable. To add further insult, a penalty is levied in an amount equal to 10 percent of the fair market value of the property as of the same date.[50] The penalty (but not the amount of gain that may be recognized under this draconian rule) is limited to $100,000 unless the failure to report was due to intentional disregard.[51] Fortunately, there is a reasonable cause exception that applies to both the penalty and the gain recognition provisions.[51.1]

[b] Transfers to Certain Partnerships with Related Foreign Partners

In addition to the enhanced information reporting requirements that accompanied the repeal of the § 1491 excise tax, the Taxpayer Relief Act of 1997 included two provisions granting the Secretary regulatory authority to override nonrecognition treatment under § 721(a). Section 721(c) gives the Secretary authority to write regulations overriding § 721(a) if gain realized on a transfer of property to a partnership, when recognized, would be includible in the gross income of a non-U.S. person. Section 367(d)(3), which is somewhat narrower in scope, provides the Secretary with regulatory authority to apply the rules of § 367(d)(2) to transfers of intangible property to partnerships in circumstances consistent with the purposes of § 367(d).

After a hiatus of almost two decades, the Service got around to exercising part of this authority by publishing temporary regulations under § 721(c) on January 19, 2017.[51.2] Publication of the Temporary Regulations was prompted by concerns on the part of the Treasury and the Service regarding transactions "in which certain taxpayers purport to be able to contribute, consistently with sections 704(b), 704(c), and 482, property to a partnership that allocates the income or gain from the contributed property to related foreign partners that are

---

[49] See Reg. § 1.6038B-2(a)(4). This Regulations provision has not been updated to reflect the 2005 amendments to Regulations § 1.704-3(a)(8). These amendments extend the treatment of substituted basis property in what is now Regulations § 1.704-3(a)(1)(i) to installment sales of § 704(c) property and property acquired pursuant to contracts that are § 704(c) property. See Reg. §§ 1.704-3(a)(8)(ii), 1.704-3(a)(i)(iii) ; ¶ 11.04[3][a].

[50] § 6038B(c)(1); Reg. § 1.6038B-2(h)(1).

[51] § 6038B(c)(3); Reg. § 1.6038B-2(h)(1)(i).

[51.1] § 6038B(c)(2); Reg. § 1.6038B-2T(h)(3) (reasonable cause to be determined by District Director based on "all the facts and circumstances").

[51.2] TD 9814, 82 Fed. Reg. 7582–7611 (Jan. 19, 2017). The Treasury and the Service had previously announced their intent to issue regulations under § 721(c) in Notice 2015-54, 2015-2 CB 210.

not subject to U.S. tax."[51.3] The Treasury and the Service determined that exercising regulatory authority under § 721(c), rather than § 367(d)(3), was more appropriate "because the transactions at issue are not limited to transfers of intangible property."[51.4]

In 2020, the Temporary Regulations were finalized with some modifications.[51.4a]

[i] Overview of the Regulations. The target of the Regulations is narrow, and their general thrust fairly easy to articulate: § 721(a) will not apply to a contribution of appreciated property by a U.S. person to a partnership (foreign or domestic) if (1) a related foreign person is a direct or indirect partner and (2) the U.S. person and related persons own, directly or indirectly, 80 percent or more of the interests in partnership capital, profits, deductions, or losses. However, § 721(a) is reactivated if the partnership elects to apply the remedial allocation method under Regulations § 1.704-3(d) to the contributed property and complies with certain other administrative requirements. While the general rule is relatively straightforward, the Regulations are fearsomely detailed and complex, requiring numerous subsections, defined terms, special rules for tiered partnerships and "acceleration events" (and exceptions to acceleration events), and corresponding changes or temporary additions to regulations under §§ 197, 704(b), 704(c), and 6038B.

[ii] General rule of gain recognition: contribution of Section 721(c) property to a Section 721(c) partnership. As a general rule, nonrecognition treatment under § 721(a) does not apply to gain realized by a contributing partner upon a contribution of "§ 721(c) property" to a "§ 721(c) partnership."[51.5]

    [A] *Section 721(c) property.* Section 721(c) property is property with built-in gain that is contributed to a partnership by a "U.S. transferor," determined on a property-by-property basis.[51.6] A "U.S. transferor" is a United

---

[51.3] See Preamble to TD 9814, 82 Fed. Reg. 7582, 7583.

[51.4] See Preamble to TD 9814, 82 Fed. Reg. 7582, 7583.

[51.4a] TD 9891, 85 FR 3833 (Jan. 24, 2020).

[51.5] Reg. § 1.721(c)-2(b). The Regulations apply to all contributions, actual or deemed, of property to a partnership, including, for example, a contribution of property that occurs as a result of (1) a partnership merger, consolidation, or division in the Assets-Over form, (2) a change in entity classification that occurs pursuant to Regulations § 301.7701-3, or (3) a transaction described in Revenue Ruling 99-5, 1999-1 CB 434. However, the termination of a partnership under now-repealed § 708(b)(1)(B) generally will not cause a partnership to become a § 721(c) partnership. Reg. § 1.721(c)-2(d)(2). In addition, a de minimis exception applies if the sum of the built-in gain with respect to all § 721(c) property contributed to a § 721(c) partnership during a taxable year does not exceed $1 million.

[51.6] Reg. § 1.721(c)-1(b)(15). Section 721(c) property does not include "excluded property" consisting of (1) a cash equivalent; (2) a security within the meaning of §

States person within the meaning of § 7701(a)(30), other than a domestic partnership.[51.7] If a U.S. transferor is a direct or indirect partner in a partnership (which is or will be an upper-tier partnership) and the upper-tier partnership contributes all or a portion of its property to a lower-tier partnership, the U.S. transferor is treated as contributing to the lower-tier partnership its share of the property actually contributed by the upper-tier partnership to the lower-tier partnership (under the "partnership look-through rule").[51.8] When a U.S. transferor is treated as transferring its share of upper-tier partnership property to a lower-tier partnership, the entire property is treated as § 721(c) property.[51.9]

[B] *Section 721(c) partnership.* A domestic or foreign partnership is a § 721(c) partnership if there is a transfer of § 721(c) property to the partnership and, after the contribution, (1) a "related foreign person" with respect to the U.S. transferor is a direct or indirect partner in the partnership, and (2) the U.S. transferor and "related persons" own 80 percent or more of the interests in partnership capital, profits, deductions, or losses.[51.10] A related person with respect to a U.S. transferor is a person that is related within the meaning of § 267(b) or § 707(b)(1) to the U.S. transferor.[51.11] A related foreign person is a related person that is not a U.S. person.[51.12] These definitions, while seemingly straightforward, are somewhat of a trap for the unwary: A partnership may be a § 721(c) partnership if a related foreign person owns any interest, direct or

---

475(c)(2), without regard to § 475(c)(4); (3) tangible property with a book value exceeding adjusted tax basis by no more than $20,000 or with an adjusted tax basis in excess of book value; or (4) an interest in a partnership if 90 percent or more of the property (as measured by value) held by the partnership (directly or indirectly through interests in one or more partnerships that are not excluded property) consists of excluded property. Reg. § 1.721(c)-1(b)(6).

[51.7] Reg. § 1.721(c)-1(b)(18).

[51.8] Reg. § 1.721(c)-2(d)(1). For purposes of the Regulations, a "direct or indirect partner" is a person (other than a partnership) that owns an interest in a partnership directly or through one or more partnerships. Reg. § 1.721(c)-1(b)(5). The Regulations provide no guidance regarding how to determine a partner's "share" of a particular partnership property.

[51.9] Reg. § 1.721(c)-1(b)(15)(i). As a result of this rule, if the lower-tier partnership is a § 721(c) partnership, absent use of the gain deferral method (discussed infra at ¶ 4.01[5][b][iii]) by the lower-tier partnership to the entire property and by the upper-tier partnership to its interest in the lower-tier partnership, the upper-tier partnership will recognize the entire built-in gain in the § 721(c) property. See Preamble to TD 9814, 82 Fed. Reg. 7582, 7586–7587.

[51.10] Reg. § 1.721(c)-1(b)(14). The Regulations provide no guidance regarding how to determine a partner's interest in partnership capital, profits, deductions, or losses.

[51.11] Reg. § 1.721(c)-1(b)(12). However, for this purpose, § 267(b) is applied without regard to § 267(c)(3), which provides that "an individual owning (otherwise than by the application of paragraph (2)) any stock in a corporation shall be considered as owning the stock owned, directly or indirectly, by or for his partner." Reg. § 1.721(c)-1(b)(12)(ii).

[51.12] Reg. § 1.721(c)-1(b)(11).

indirect, in the partnership so long as a U.S. transferor and all related persons together meet the 80-percent requirement.[51.13]

[iii] The gain deferral method. Section 721(a) may be reactivated, and so gain otherwise required to be recognized on a contribution of § 721(c) property to a § 721(c) partnership can therefore be avoided (or at least deferred), if all five requirements of the "gain deferral method" are satisfied. In general, § 721(a) applies under the gain deferral method only to the extent that a contribution of § 721(c) property to a § 721 partnership does not give rise to an opportunity to shift the incidence of the tax on built-in gain to a related foreign person.

[A] *Remedial allocations or effectively connected income.* The gain deferral method applies only if one of the following two requirements is satisfied:

1. Both (a) the § 721(c) partnership adopts the remedial allocation method with respect to the § 721(c) property,[51.14] and (b) the § 721(c) partnership applies the "consistent allocation method" with respect to the § 721(c) property, or
2. For the period beginning on the date of the contribution of the § 721(c) property and ending on the date when there is no remaining built-in gain with respect to the property, (a) all distributive shares of income and gain with respect to the § 721(c) property for all direct and indirect partners that are related foreign persons with respect to the U.S. transferor will be subject to taxation as income effectively connected with a trade or business within the U.S. (under either § 871 or § 882), and (b) neither the § 721(c) partnership nor a related foreign person claims benefits under an income tax convention that would exempt the income or gain from tax or reduce the rate of tax to which the income or gain is subject.[51.15]

[B] *Consistent allocation method.* The gain deferral method applies only if a § 721(c) partnership employs the "consistent allocation method" with respect to § 721(c) property. Under the consistent allocation method, for each taxable year of a § 721(c) partnership with respect to which there is "remaining built-in-gain" in a § 721(c) property, the § 721(c) partnership must allocate each item of book income, gain, deduction, and loss with respect to the §

[51.13] See Preamble to TD 9814, 82 Fed. Reg. 7582, 7585 ("[t]he Treasury Department and the IRS are concerned that even a small ownership interest held by a related foreign person may be used for a meaningful shift of gain or income outside of the United States").

[51.14] For a discussion of the remedial allocation method, see ¶ 11.04[3][d].

[51.15] Reg. § 1.721(c)-3(b)(1).

721(c) property to the U.S. transferor in the same percentage.[51.16] Section 721(c) property has remaining built-in gain if there is a book-tax disparity with respect to the property, disregarding increases or decreases arising from revaluation events.[51.17]

For purposes of applying the consistent allocation method, a § 721(c) partnership must attribute book income and gain to each item of § 721(c) property in a consistent manner using a reasonable method that takes into account all facts and circumstances.[51.18] The partnership is required to apply the principles of Regulations §§ 1.861-8 and 1.861-8T to allocate and apportion its items of deduction and loss (other than interest expense and research and experimental expenditures) to the income and gain attributed to a § 721 property.[51.19]

[C] Acceleration events.

General rules. For the gain deferral method to apply, a U.S. transferor is required to recognize gain in connection with any "acceleration event," which is generally defined to include any event that either (1) would reduce the amount of built-in gain that a U.S. transferor would recognize with respect to § 721(c) property under the gain deferral method if the event had not occurred or (2) could defer the recognition of the built-in gain.[51.20] An acceleration event expressly includes a failure by any party to comply with any condition of the gain deferral method with respect to a § 721(c) property.[51.21] A reduction in built-in gain with respect to a partnership interest that occurs as a result of allocations from a lower-tier partnership is excepted from status as an acceleration event. jxj[51.22]

If an acceleration event occurs, the gain deferral method requires the U.S. transferor to recognize gain in an amount equal to the remaining built-in gain that would have been allocated to the U.S. transferor if the § 721(c) partnership had sold the § 721(c) property immediately before the acceleration event for fair market value.[51.23] The U.S. transferor increases its basis in its partnership interest by the amount of gain recognized in an acceleration event, and the § 721(c) partnership increases its basis in the § 721(c) property by the

---

[51.16] Reg. § 1.721(c)-3(c)(1). An exception is provided for certain regulatory allocations and creditable foreign tax expenditures. See Reg. § 1.721(c)-3(c)(4).

[51.17] Reg. § 1.721(c)-1(b)(13)(i). A special rule applies to tiered partnerships. Reg. § 1.721(c)-1(b)(13)(ii).

[51.18] Reg. § 1.721(c)-3(c)(2).

[51.19] Reg. § 1.721(c)-3(c)(3). Interest expense and research and experimental expenses may be allocated under any reasonable method. Id.

[51.20] Reg. § 1.721(c)-4(b).

[51.21] A failure to comply with certain reporting requirements is not an acceleration event unless the failure is willful. Reg. § 1.721(c)-4(b)(2)(ii).

[51.22] Reg. § 1.721(c)-4(b)(3).

[51.23] Reg. § 1.721(c)-4(c)(1).

same amount.[51.24] The ancillary tax consequences of an acceleration event are then determined taking into account the partnership's increased basis in § 721(c) property.[51.25] If the § 721(c) property remains in the partnership following an acceleration event, the increased basis may be recovered using any applicable recovery period and depreciation (or other cost recovery) method, and the § 721(c) property is no longer subject to the gain deferral method.[51.26]

Exceptions and special rules. There are a number of exceptions and special rules, which are discussed in the following paragraphs.

Termination events. No acceleration event occurs, and § 721(c) property is released from the gain deferral method, in the following circumstances where built-in gain in § 721(c) property can no longer be shifted to a related foreign person (i.e., "termination events"): (1) § 721(c) property is contributed to a domestic corporation in a § 351(a) transaction; (2) a § 721(c) partnership is incorporated into a domestic corporation (other than via a method involving an actual distribution of partnership property to the partners); (3) § 721(c) property is distributed to the U.S. transferor; (4) a § 721(c) partnership ceases to have any direct or indirect partners that are related foreign persons with respect to the U.S. transferor; (5) a § 721(c) partnership disposes of § 721(c) property in a fully taxable transaction; or (6) a U.S. transferor (or a partnership in which a U.S. transferor is a direct or indirect partner) disposes of its entire interest in a § 721(c) partnership in a fully taxable transaction.[51.27]

Successor events. The following events (i.e., "successor events") are not acceleration events, but require continued application of the gain deferral method: (1) a U.S. transferor or an upper-tier partnership transfers an interest in a § 721(c) partnership to a domestic corporation in a transaction to which § 351 or § 381 applies if the gain deferral method is continued by treating the transferee domestic corporation as the U.S. transferor;[51.28] (2) a U.S. transferor that is a member of a consolidated group transfers (directly or indirectly through one or more partnerships) an interest in a § 721(c) partnership to another member if the gain deferral method is continued by treating the transferee member as the U.S. transferor;[51.29] (3) a § 708(b)(1)(B) termination of a § 721(c) partnership if the gain deferral method is continued by treating the new partnership as the prior § 721(c) partnership;[51.30] or (4) a contribution of §

[51.24] Reg. §§ 1.721(c)-4(c)(1), 1.721(c)-4(c)(2). If the U.S. transferor is an indirect partner in a § 721(c) partnership through one or more tiered partnerships, appropriate basis adjustments must be made to the interests in the tiered partnerships. Reg. §§ 1.721(c)-4(c)(1), 1.721(c)-4(c)(2). Presumably, any such basis increases inure solely to the benefit of the indirect U.S. transferor.

[51.25] Reg. § 1.721(c)-4(c)(2).

[51.26] Reg. § 1.721(c)-4(c)(2).

[51.27] Reg. §§ 1.721(c)-5(b)(2) through 1.721(c)-5(b)(7).

[51.28] Reg. § 1.721(c)-5(c)(2).

[51.29] Reg. § 1.721(c)-5(c)(3).

[51.30] Reg. § 1.721(c)-5(c)(4). Section 708(b)(1)(B) is repealed for years beginning after December 31, 2017.

721(c) property to a lower-tier partnership or a contribution of an interest in a § 721(c) partnership to an upper-tier partnership provided that, in either case, certain specified requirements with respect to continued application of the gain-deferral method are met.[51.31]

Partial acceleration events. Certain transactions or events (i.e., "partial acceleration events") trigger gain in part, but not in whole, under the acceleration rule.[51.32] If a partial acceleration event occurs, the rules of Regulations § 1.721(c)-4(c) regarding the consequences of an acceleration event apply to the extent a U.S. transferor is required to recognize gain.[51.33] The gain deferral method continues to be applicable to any remaining built-in gain with respect to § 721(c) property following a partial acceleration event.[51.34] A partial acceleration event occurs if (1) a "regulatory allocation" is made that does not satisfy the consistent allocation method to the extent the allocation is not an allocation of income or gain to the U.S. transferor (or a member of its consolidated group), or is an allocation of deduction or loss to a partner other than the U.S. transferor (or a member of its consolidated group),[51.35] or (2) there is a distribution of property that results in a basis increase to § 721(c) property under § 734.[51.36]

In the case of a regulatory allocation, a U.S. transferor must recognize gain (but not in excess of the remaining built-in gain) equal to the amount of the allocation that would have been made if the consistent allocation method had applied. In the case of a § 734 basis increase, the U.S. transferor generally must recognize an amount of gain (but not in excess of remaining built-in gain) equal to the amount of the basis increase.

Section 367 transfers of § 721(c) property. If (1) a § 721(c) partnership transfers § 721(c) property or (2) a U.S. transferor or a partnership in which a U.S. transferor is a direct or indirect partner transfers (directly or indirectly through one or more partnerships) all or a portion of an interest in a § 721(c) partnership that owns § 721(c) property, to a foreign corporation in a transaction described in § 367, then the property is no longer subject to the gain

---

[51.31] Reg. § 1.721(c)-5(c)(5).

[51.32] Reg. § 1.721(c)-5(d).

[51.33] Reg. § 1.721(c)-5(d).

[51.34] Reg. § 1.721(c)-5(d).

[51.35] Reg. § 1.721(c)-5(d)(2). A "regulatory allocation" is (1) an allocation pursuant to a minimum gain chargeback, as defined in Regulations § 1.704-2(b)(2); (2) a partner nonrecourse deduction, as determined in Regulations § 1.704-2(i)(2); (3) an allocation pursuant to a partner minimum gain chargeback, as described in Regulations § 1.704-2(i)(4); (4) an allocation pursuant to a qualified income offset, as defined in Regulations § 1.704-1(b)(2)(ii)(*d*); (5) an allocation with respect to the exercise of a noncompensatory option described in Regulations 1.704-1(b)(2)(iv)(*s*); and (6) an allocation of partnership level ordinary income or loss described in Regulations § 1.751-1(a)(3). Reg. § 1.721(c)-1(b)(10).

[51.36] Reg. § 1.721(c)-5(d)(3).

deferral method. The tax consequences of the transaction are determined under § 367.[51.37]

Taxable dispositions of part of a partnership interest. If a U.S. transferor or a partnership in which a U.S. transferor is a direct or indirect partner disposes (directly or indirectly through one or more partnerships) of a portion of an interest in a § 721(c) partnership in a transaction in which all gain or loss, if any, is recognized, no acceleration event occurs with respect to the portion of the interest transferred. The gain deferral method continues to apply to the § 721(c) property of the § 721(c) partnership.[51.38]

[D] *Tiered-partnership rules.* The Regulations are unusually explicit in describing how the requirements of the gain deferral method are applied in circumstances involving tiered partnerships.

Where § 721(c) property is a partnership interest. If the § 721(c) property contributed to a § 721(c) partnership is an interest in a lower-tier partnership that is a "controlled partnership"[51.39] with respect to the U.S. transferor, the lower-tier partnership (and any subsidiary partnerships that are also controlled partnerships with respect to the U.S. transferor) must satisfy the following three requirements under the gain deferral method:

1. The partnership must revalue all of its property under Regulations § 1.704-1(b)(2)(iv)(*f*)(*6*) if the revaluation would result in a separate positive difference between book value and adjusted tax basis in at least one property that is not excluded property;[51.40]
2. The partnership must apply the gain deferral method for each property (other than excluded property) for which there is a separate positive difference between book value and adjusted tax basis resulting from the revaluation (i.e., a "new positive reverse § 704(c) layer"), and the partnership must apply the remedial allocation method to any new positive reverse § 704(c) layer;[51.41] and
3. The partnership must treat a partner that is a partnership in which the U.S. transferor is a direct or indirect partner as if it were the U.S. transferor solely for purposes of applying the consistent allocation method.[51.42]

[51.37] Reg. § 1.721(c)-5(e). See Reg. §§ 1.367(a)-1(c)(3)(i), 1.367(a)-1(c)(3)(ii), 1.367(d)-1(d)(1), and 1.367(c)-2(b)(1)(iii) (generally providing an aggregate treatment of partnerships for purposes of applying the outbound transfer rules of § 367).

[51.38] Reg. § 1.721(c)-5(f).

[51.39] A partnership is a controlled partnership with respect to a U.S. transferor if, taking all facts and circumstances into account, the U.S. transferor and related persons control the partnership. Control is deemed to exist if a U.S. transferor and related persons own, in the aggregate (directly or indirectly through one or more partnerships), more than 50 percent of the interests in partnership capital or profits. Reg. § 1.721(c)-1(b)(4).

[51.40] Reg. § 1.721(c)-3(d)(1)(i).

[51.41] Reg. § 1.721(c)-3(d)(1)(ii).

[51.42] Reg. § 1.721(c)-3(d)(1)(iii).

If a lower-tier partnership is required to apply these rules, it is deemed to be a § 721(c) partnership for purposes of the gain deferral method.[51.43]

For purposes of applying the gain deferral method to tiered partnerships, Regulations § 1.704-1(b)(2)(iv)(f)(6) provides that if an interest in a partnership is contributed to a § 721(c) partnership, the partnership whose interest is contributed may revalue its property immediately before the contribution. If the partnership whose interest is contributed owns an interest in another partnership, the partnership in which it owns an interest may also revalue its property. When multiple partnerships revalue their property under this rule, the revaluation occurs in order from the lowest-tier partnership to the highest-tier partnership. When a revaluation pursuant to Regulations § 1.704-(b)(2)(iv)(f)(6) occurs, the principles of Treasury Regulations § 1.704-3(a)(9) apply, and an upper-tier partnership must treat its distributive share of lower-tier partnership items of gain, loss, amortization, depreciation, or other cost recovery with respect to the lower-tier partnership's § 721(c) property as though they were items of gain, loss, amortization, depreciation, or other cost recovery with respect to the upper-tier partnership's interest in the lower-tier partnership.[51.44]

Where § 721(c) property is indirectly contributed by a U.S. transferor under the partnership look-through rule. If a U.S. transferor is treated as contributing § 721(c) property (including an interest in a controlled partnership) to a § 721(c) partnership under the partnership look-through rule, the following requirements must be satisfied under the gain deferral method:

1. The § 721(c) partnership must treat the upper-tier partnership as the U.S. transferor of the § 721(c) property solely for purposes of applying the consistent allocation method;[51.45]
2. The upper-tier partnership, if it is a controlled partnership with respect to the U.S. transferor, must apply the gain deferral method with respect to its interest in the § 721(c) partnership;[51.46] and
3. If the U.S. transferor is an indirect partner in the upper-tier partnership through one or more partnerships, rules (1) and (2) above must be applied with respect to those partnerships that are controlled partnerships with respect to the U.S. transferor.[51.47]

[E] *Special rules with respect to Section 197(f)(9) intangibles.* The Regulations contain a complex set of rules that alter the application of the § 704(c) remedial allocation method and the § 197(f)(9) anti-churning rules where the § 721(c) property contributed to a § 721(c) partnership consists of a

---

[51.43] Reg. § 1.721(c)-1(b)(14)(ii). This rule is intended to reach the same result as if an aggregate approach governed the application of Regulations § 1.704-3(a)(9) in the context of the gain deferral method. See Preamble to TD 9814, 82 Fed. Reg. 7582, 7594.

[51.44] Reg. §§ 1.704-3(a)(13)(i), 1.704-3(a)(13)(ii).

[51.45] Reg. § 1.721(c)-3(d)(2)(i).

[51.46] Reg. § 1.721(c)-3(d)(2)(ii).

[51.47] Reg. § 1.721(c)-3(d)(2)(iii).

§ 197(f)(9) intangible.[51.48] If the gain deferral method applies to the contribution of a § 197(f)(9) intangible that was not an amortizable § 197 intangible in the hands of the contributor, the § 721(c) partnership must amortize excess book basis over the 15-year period provided by § 197.[51.49] If allocations of book amortization deductions are made to a related person with respect to the U.S. transferor, the partnership does not create a remedial item of deduction to allocate to the related person. Instead, the partnership increases the adjusted tax basis of the § 197(f)(9) intangible by the amount of the book amortization deduction allocated to the related person, and creates an offsetting remedial income allocation to the U.S. transferor.[51.50]

The basis adjustment inures only to the benefit of the related person; it does not constitute common basis.[51.51] The basis adjustment is not amortizable, but reduces the related partner's distributive share of gain (or increases its distributive share of loss) if the partnership disposes of the § 197(f)(9) intangible.[51.52] In general, if the related person transfers all or part of its partnership interest, the portion of the basis adjustment attributable to the interest transferred is eliminated.[51.53] If the interest is transferred in a transaction in which the transferee's basis in the partnership is determined in whole or in part by reference to the transferor's basis, the transferee succeeds to that portion of the transferor's basis adjustment for the § 197(f)(9) intangible attributable to the interest transferred, including for purposes of applying § 743(b).[51.54]

[F] *Procedural and reporting requirements.* Regulations § 1.721(c)-6 provides an elaborate and detailed set of procedural and reporting requirements that must be complied with under the gain deferral method. Separate requirements exist for (1) a U.S. transferor, both with respect to the initial transfer of § 721(c) property to a § 721 partnership as well as on an annual basis thereafter;[51.55] (2) contributions where the gain deferral method is applied to § 721(c) property that produces effectively connected income;[51.56] (3) tiered partnerships;[51.57] and (4) partnerships with an obligation to file a partnership tax return under § 6031.[51.58]

[51.48] For a general discussion of the application of the anti-churning rules to contributions of § 197(f)(9) intangibles, see ¶ 9.02[3][k].

[51.49] Reg. § 1.704-3(d)(5)(iii)(B).

[51.50] Reg. § 1.704-3(d)(5)(iii)(C).

[51.51] Reg. § 1.704-3(d)(5)(iii)(D)(1).

[51.52] Reg. § 1.704-3(d)(5)(iii)(D)(2).

[51.53] Reg. § 1.704-3(d)(5)(iii)(E)(1).

[51.54] Reg. § 1.704-3(d)(5)(iii)(E)(2).

[51.55] Reg. §§ 1.721(c)-6(b)(2), 1.721(c)-6(b)(3).

[51.56] Reg. § 1.721(c)-6(c)(1).

[51.57] Reg. § 1.721(c)-6(c)(2).

[51.58] Reg. § 1.721(c)-6(d).

[iv] Effective/applicability dates. In general, the Regulations apply to contributions occurring on or after January 18, 2017, and to contributions occurring before January 18, 2017, that result from an entity classification election under Regulations § 301.7701-3 that is filed on or after August 6, 2015.

[6] Transfers to Foreign Corporations

Page 4-15:

Add to note 52.

See AM (CCA) 2008-006, Doc. 2008-11938 (May 21, 2008) (partners, rather than partnership, required to file Form 926).

Replace note 53 with the following.

[53] Temp. Reg. § 1.367(a)-1T(c)(3)(ii); Reg. § 1.367(a)-1(c)(3)(ii).

[8] Formation of Limited Liability Company

Page 4-16:

Add to note 59.

; CCA 201326014 (Mar. 4, 2013) (illustrating application of Revenue Ruling 99-5).

In first paragraph, replace last sentence with the following.

On the other hand, a type two transaction closely followed by a distribution of partnership funds to the original owner does not appear to be subject to recharacterization; rather, the original owner is subject to § 707(a)(2)(B)'s disguised-sale-of-assets rules.[62]

---

[62] See generally ¶ 14.02[3][b].

¶ 4.02 QUALIFYING FOR NONRECOGNITION TREATMENT

[1] Defining "Property" Contributed for a Partnership Interest

Page 4-17:

Replace note 66 with the following.

[66] See Reg. § 1.453-9(c)(2), providing that the transfer of an installment obligation to a partnership under § 721 is not a "disposition" under § 453(d) (redesignated as § 453B by the Installment Sales Revision Act of 1980). The Service has ruled privately that Regulations § 1.453-9(c)(2) survived the enactment of § 453B in 1980. Priv. Ltr. Rul. 8824044 (Mar. 22, 1988). See Prop. Reg. § 1.453B-1(c)(1)(i)(B) (2014). See also Irving J. Hayutin, 31 TCM 509 (1972), aff'd on other issues, 508 F2d 462 (10th Cir. 1975); J.C. Wynne, 47 BTA 731 (1942) (nonacq.). If the partnership is the obligor of contributed installment ob-

ligations, the transaction is treated as a "satisfaction" of the obligations, resulting in income to the contributing partners. § 453B(f). If installment obligations acquired from a decedent are subsequently transferred to a partnership, gain may be triggered under § 691(a)(2) notwithstanding the general nonrecognition rule of § 721(a). See M. Ferguson, J. Freeland & M. Ascher, Federal Income Taxation of Estates and Beneficiaries ¶ 3:24 (Aspen Law & Business 1995). In Gladys G. Wilkinson, 49 TC 4 (1967), the taxpayer-shareholders held corporate installment obligations. Immediately prior to the liquidation of the corporation, the taxpayers contributed the obligations to a partnership in hopes of preventing the merger of the obligations upon the liquidation of the corporation. The Tax Court simply disregarded the transfer of the obligations to the partnership and held that a taxable merger of the estate of the corporate obligor and shareholder-obligees resulted from the liquidation—that is, a portion of the corporate liquidation proceeds was distributed in payment of the obligations. See Prop. Reg. § 1.453B-1(c)(1)(ii) (2014).

Page 4-22:

In note 88, add the following at end of first sentence (following citation of Rev. Rul. 68-629).

; VisionMonitor Software, LLC, 108 TCM 256 (2014).

Page 4-24:

In last paragraph of subsection, add new note 95.1 at end of first sentence.

95.1 But see AM 2011-003 (Aug. 8, 2011) (in a check-a-box conversion of insolvent foreign corporation to a partnership, assets distributed were treated as worthless for purposes of § 165(g), yet subsequent contribution of such distributed assets to partnership was treated as valid § 721 contribution).

[3] Cancellation of Partnership Indebtedness as a Contribution of "Property"

Page 4-28:

Add at end of subsection.

The "debt-for-equity" scheme has been fleshed out in final regulations, effective for exchanges occurring on or after November 17, 2011.[110.1]

In general, provided that certain requirements are satisfied, the Regulations allow the partnership and the creditor to value the partnership interest transferred to the creditor in a debt-for-equity exchange (i.e., the "debt-for-equity interest") based on liquidation value.[110.2] For this purpose, liquidation value equals the amount of cash that the creditor would receive with respect to the debt-for-equity interest if, immediately after the transfer, the partnership sold all of its assets (including goodwill, going concern value, and any other intangibles associated with the partnership's operations) for cash equal to the fair market value of those assets, and then liquidated.

[110.1] Reg. § 1.108-8.
[110.2] Reg. § 1.108-8(b).

Valuing the debt-for-equity interest at its liquidation value requires that the following conditions are met:

1. The creditor, the partnership, and its partners treat the fair market value of the indebtedness as being equal to the liquidation value of the debt-for-equity interest for purposes of determining the tax consequences of the debt-for-equity exchange;
2. All debt-for-equity interests transferred as part of the same overall transaction are valued at liquidation value;
3. The debt-for-equity exchange is an arm's-length transaction; and
4. Subsequent to the debt-for-equity exchange, neither the partnership redeems nor any person related (under § 267(b) or § 707(b)) to the partnership or its partners purchases the debt-for-equity interest as part of a plan at the time of the debt-for-equity exchange that has as a principal purpose the avoidance of cancellation of indebtedness income by the partnership.

If any of the above requirements are not satisfied, all of the facts and circumstances are considered in determining the fair market value of the debt-for-equity interest for purposes of applying § 108(e)(8).[110.3] In the case of tiered partnerships, the liquidation value of an upper-tier partnership is determined by taking into account the liquidation value of a lower-tier partnership.[110.4]

Even though a transfer of a partnership's debt to the partnership for a debt-for-equity interest results in the partnership's recognition of cancellation of indebtedness income equal to the excess of the transferred debt over the value of the interest, Regulations § 1.721-1(d)(1) provides that § 721(a) applies to the creditor. Thus, a creditor who receives the debt-for equity interest does not recognize a bad debt loss that corresponds to the partnership's § 108 income as a result of the transaction. Instead, under § 722, the creditor's basis is the entire basis of the transferred debt and, under § 1223(1), the creditor's holding period for the debt-for-equity interest includes the holding period of the transferred debt. These rules result in a difference between the aggregate tax basis of the partnership's assets and the aggregate tax basis of the partners in their partnership interests equal in amount to any cancellation of indebtedness income recognized by the partnership in the debt-for-equity exchange.

Section 721 does not apply, however, to the extent the partnership interest is exchanged for the partnership's obligation for unpaid rent, royalties, or interest that accrued on or after the beginning of the creditor's holding period for the indebtedness.[110.5] If the partnership owns appreciated assets, one might think that the partnership would recognize gain by transferring an interest in appreciated property in satisfaction of a liability. Regulations § 1.721-1(d)(2)

[110.3] Reg. § 1.108-8(b)(1).

[110.4] Reg. § 1.108-8(b)(2)(ii).

[110.5] Reg. § 1.721-1(d)(2).

specifically disavows this approach, which is consistent with the no-gain position taken by the Treasury in the compensatory context.[110.6]

Any minimum gain triggered by the debt-for-equity exchange includes the resultant cancellation of indebtedness income as a first-tier item under the chargeback rules; these rules are discussed at ¶ 11.02[4][f][v]. Finally, if the creditor transfers an installment obligation of the partnership back to the partnership, proposed regulations provide that gain or loss must be recognized under § 453B; the general nonrecognition rule of Regulations § 1.453-9(c)(2) is turned off.[110.7]

Under § 108(i), added by the American Recovery and Reinvestment Act of 2009 (ARRA), partnerships and other debtors may elect to defer the taxation of discharge of indebtedness income arising in 2009 or 2010.[110.8] This debt discharge income is deferred for five years if the discharge occurs in 2009 or four years if the discharge occurs in 2010, and the deferred income is then included in income at the rate of 20% per year over a five-year period generally starting in 2014.[110.9]

If the election is made, all four of the income exclusions in §§ 108(a)(1)(A)–(D) are inapplicable to the debt discharge income—namely, the exclusions for debt discharges (1) in bankruptcy, (2) when the taxpayer is insolvent, (3) of qualified farm indebtedness, or (4) of qualified real property business indebtedness (available to noncorporate taxpayers only).[110.10] The § 108(i) election is made at the partnership level and binds all of the partners,[110.11] whereas these exclusions are applied on a partner-by-partner basis at the partner level under § 108(d)(6).

Under Regulations § 1.108(i)-2, a partnership may elect to defer all or a portion of the COD income realized from the reacquisition of an applicable debt instrument. A partnership that elects to defer less than all of its COD income must first allocate the realized COD income among the persons who were partners in the partnership immediately before the reacquisition and do so in the manner in which such income would have been allocated under § 704(b) if the COD income had been recognized at that time.[110.12] Amounts so allocated to a partner increase that partner's capital account at the time of the reacquisition.[110.13] This rule effectively freezes each partner's share of deferred COD in-

---

[110.6] See ¶ 5.02[8][d].

[110.7] TD 9557 (Nov. 17, 2011).

[110.8] § 108(i) (applicable to discharges after 2008, see ARRA § 1231(b)). This election is limited to discharges in connection with "reacquisitions" of "applicable debt instruments," as defined in §§ 108(i)(3) and 108(i)(4). Significant modifications of a debt instrument, complete forgiveness, and acquisitions by "related persons" (as defined in § 108(e)(4)) are treated as "reacquisitions."

[110.9] § 108(i)(1).

[110.10] § 108(i)(5)(B)(iii).

[110.11] §§ 108(e)(4), 108(i)(5)(C).

[110.12] Reg. § 1.108(i)-2(b)(1).

[110.13] Reg. § 1.108(i)-2(b)(2)(ii).

come as of the date of the reacquisition of a debt, so that subsequent changes in distributive shares (e.g., upon the admission of additional partners), which apparently do not accelerate deferred discharge income (see § 108(i)(5)(D)(ii)), are ignored in eventually allocating the deferred income among the partners. This may come as a bit of an unpleasant surprise to the original partners, but would be a welcome relief to subsequently admitted partners and, possibly, their professional advisors.

A deferring partnership must then determine, in any manner, the portion (if any) of each partner's allocable COD income amount that is the partner's "deferred amount" and the portion (if any) of each partner's COD income amount that is the partner's "included amount."[110.14] Under this rule, one partner's deferred amount could conceivably be zero, while another partner's deferred amount could equal the partner's entire COD income allocation, subject to the limits imposed by the initial § 704(b) allocation of COD income. A partner may exclude from income the partner's included amount under §§ 108(a)(1)(A), 108(a)(1)(B), 108(a)(1)(C), or 108(a)(1)(D), if applicable.

A partner's outside basis in its partnership interest is not increased at the time of the cancellation of indebtedness realization for the component of the COD income treated as the partner's "deferred amount," although it is increased for the "included amount." Instead, the partner's outside basis is increased in the year in which the partnership takes the deferred income into account.[110.15]

Any decrease in a partner's share of partnership debt "as a result" of a debt discharge covered by § 108(i) is not taken into account at the time of the discharge for purposes of § 752 "to the extent it would cause the partner to recognize gain under section 731."[110.16] The obvious thrust of these rules is to avoid creating situations in which the deferral objective of § 108(i) is undone by the taxable distribution rules in § 731(a). Instead, the Regulations require the maintenance of a "deferred § 752 amount" equal to the portion of the partner's § 752(b) distribution arising from the reacquisition that would be treated as gain under § 731 absent the application of § 108(i)(6). A partner's deferred § 752 amount is then treated as a distribution at the same time and, to the extent remaining, in the same amount as the partner recognizes the deferred amount with respect to the reacquired debt instrument.[110.17] In determining the amount of gain the partner would otherwise recognize, the amount of any deemed distribution under § 752(b) that is to be treated as an advance or draw under Regulations § 1.731-1(a)(1)(ii) is determined as if no COD income resulting from the reacquisition of the applicable debt instrument is deferred under § 108(i).[110.18] The Regulations require each direct partner of an electing

---

[110.14] Reg. § 1.108(i)-2(b)(1).

[110.15] Reg. § 1.108(i)-2(b)(2)(i).

[110.16] § 108(i)(6).

[110.17] Reg. § 1.108(i)-2(b)(3)(i).

[110.18] Reg. § 1.108(i)-2(b)(3)(ii).

partnership under § 108(i) to provide to the partnership, within 30 days of the partnership's request, a written statement, made under penalty of perjury, containing such information as is necessary for the partnership to determine the partner's deferred § 752 amount.[110.19]

Similar relief is provided to deal with the at-risk recapture rule of § 465(e). If the reacquisition of the applicable debt instrument would cause a partner to have income under § 465(e) because the partner's at-risk amount is reduced, the reduction is not taken into account until the partner recognizes the deferred amount.[110.20]

If a partnership issues (or is treated as issuing) new debt in connection with a debt discharge and makes a § 108(i) election with respect to the discharge, all or a portion of any deductions for original issue discount with respect to the new debt may be deferred and amortized over the same five-year period as the previously deferred debt discharge income is included in gross income.[110.21]

As with deferred COD income, no outside basis adjustment occurs for the partner to whom the deferred deduction is allocated until the item accrues, but a capital account adjustment is made.[110.22]

An upper-tier partnership that receives an allocation of COD income, some of which is deferred under § 108(i), allocates all of that COD income in the same manner as the lower-tier partnership allocated the income—as directed under § 704(b) among the partners that were partners immediately prior to the acquisition. The upper-tier partnership then determines the portion of each partner's COD income that is deferred and the portion that is included. The aggregate amount of COD income deferred and included by the partners must equal the upper-tier partnership's share of such deferred and included amounts from the electing lower-tier partnership.[110.23] Each upper-tier partnership's partner's deferred § 752 amount with respect to a debt instrument is simply equal to such partner's share of the upper-tier partnership's deferred § 752 amount with respect to that debt instrument, determined with regard to such partner's relative share of deferred COD income from that instrument.[110.24]

Deferred debt discharge income (and deferred OID deduction) is accelerated upon the death of a taxpayer, the liquidation or sale of substantially all the taxpayer's assets, the cessation of business by the taxpayer, or any similar event.[110.25] In the partnership context, acceleration can occur as a result of either (1) a partnership-level event (e.g., liquidation of the partnership, sale, exchange, transfer, or gift of substantially all of the partnership's assets,

[110.19] Reg. § 1.108(i)-2(b)(3)(iv).

[110.20] Reg. § 1.108(i)-2(d)(3).

[110.21] Reg. §§ 1.108(i)-2(a), 1.108(i)-2(d)(2).

[110.22] Reg. § 1.108(i)-2(b)(2).

[110.23] Reg. § 1.108(i)-2(b)(4)(i).

[110.24] Reg. § 1.108(i)-2(b)(4)(ii).

[110.25] § 108(i)(5)(D).

cessation of the partnership's business, or filing of a bankruptcy petition in a Title 11 or similar case) or (2) a partner-level event (e.g., death or liquidation of the partner, or sale, exchange, redemption, abandonment, transfer, or gift of all or a portion of the partner's separate interest in the partnership).[110.26] Certain nonrecognition transfers, including § 721 contributions, of the electing partnership's assets or the partner's separate interest are exempted from triggering an acceleration under § 108(i).[110.27]

Partnerships making § 108(i) elections may rely upon the procedures established in Revenue Procedure 2009-37[110.28] as to:

1. General procedures for making the election,
2. Required contents of an election statement,
3. Procedures for elections by foreign partnerships, and
4. Election year reporting by tiered pass-through entities.

[110.26] Reg. § 1.108(i)-2(b)(6).
[110.27] Reg. § 1.108(i)-2(b)(6)(iii).
[110.28] Rev. Proc. 2009-37, 2009-36 IRB 309.

[6] Nonpartner Contributions to Capital

Page 4-29:

Add to note 121.

See also Uniquest Delaware LLC v. United States, 2018-1 USTC ¶ 50,199 (WDNY 2018) (*Cuba Railroad* not applicable to partnership; § 118 not available even though partners are corporations).

¶ 4.03 TREATMENT OF LIABILITIES AND CONTINGENT OBLIGATIONS IN CONNECTION WITH PROPERTY CONTRIBUTIONS

[5] Contingent Liabilities and Cash-Method Payables

Page 4-39:

In note 156, replace Rev. Rul. 80-189, 1980-2 CB 113, *with* Rev. Rul. 80-198, 1980-2 CB 113.

¶ 4.05 CONTRIBUTIONS OF RECAPTURE PROPERTY AND OTHER SPECIAL TYPES OF PROPERTY

[3] Investment Credit Recapture Property

Page 4-44:

In first paragraph of subsection, replace second sentence with the following.

Section 48C added the qualifying advanced energy project credit to this list in 2009. All or a portion of the investment credit is recaptured if investment credit property is disposed of or ceases to qualify as investment credit property within five years of the date it is placed in service.[175]

---

[175] § 50(a)(1).

Page 4-46:

In third to last paragraph of subsection, replace last sentence with the following.

Section 50(a) requires recapture of all or a portion of the credit if the property with respect to which the credit was allowed is disposed of or ceases to be § 38 property within five years of being place in service.[183]

---

[183] Reg. § 1.47-3(f)(5)(i). Cf. Jerry L. Moudy, 59 TCM 280 (1990) (incorporation of partnership followed by repossession of property by creditors; recapture triggered to former partners).

Replace note 186 with the following.

[186] The reduction is 50% in the case of the energy credit. § 50(c)(3) .

Replace note 187 with the following.

[187] § 50(c)(2). The increase is 50% of the recapture amount in the case of the energy credit. § 50(c)(3)(B).

[5] Computation of Depreciation for the Year of Contribution and Subsequent Years

Page 4-48:

In note 194, replace last two sentences and citations (after reference to Reg. § 1.168(d)-1(b)(6)) with the following.

If the contributing partner placed the contributed property in service in a short taxable year, then for purposes of applying the applicable convention and allocating the depreciation deduction between the partner and the partnership, the contributing partner is treated as having a full twelve-month taxable year commencing on the first day of the short year. Reg. § 1.168(d)-1(b)(7)(ii).

[6] Unrealized Receivables and Inventory Items

Page 4-49:

In second paragraph of subsection, replace first sentence with the following.

Section 724 provides that, where a partner contributes unrealized receivables (as defined in § 751(c)) the partnership will recognize ordinary income upon any subsequent disposition (or collection) of such receivables, regardless of how long they are held.[199.1]

[199.1] The term "unrealized receivables" does not include recapture property. These items are brought within the definition only pursuant to the second sentence of § 751(c), which is limited to §§ 731, 732, 741, and 751. Section 735 is similar in operation. See ¶ 20.02, n. 7.

Page 4-51:

Replace ¶ 4.05[8] with revised ¶ 4.05[8].

[8] Contributions of Businesses Subject to Unamortized Section 481 Adjustments [Revised]

The Service's view is that a contribution of assets of a trade or business as to which a § 481 adjustment relates, to a partnership, results in an acceleration of any outstanding § 481 adjustments.[205]

---

[205] Rev. Proc. 2011-14, 2011-4 IRB 330, § 5.04(3)(c)(ii)(E). The Services' original position was to the contrary. See Rev. Rul. 66-206, 1966-2 CB 206; Priv. Ltr. Rul. 8946071 (Aug. 24, 1989).

[12] Importation of Built-In Losses

Page 4-54:

Add at end of subsection.

Regulations finalized in 2016 flesh out the rules applicable to transactions involving partnerships.

In the case of a transfer of a partnership interest, the value of the transferred interest includes the § 752 liabilities allocated to the transferee.[211.1] The partnership's property is tentatively divided into separate portions in proportion to the amount of gain or loss that would be allocated to each partner for purposes of determining whether it is "importation property."[211.2] Each portion that is importation property is aggregated to determine if the transaction is a loss importation transaction.[211.3] The entire property is then re-aggregated to make

---

[211.1] Reg. § 1.362-3(c)(4).
[211.2] Reg. § 1.362-3(e).
[211.3] Reg. § 1.362-3(e)(2).

the required basis adjustments. The following two examples illustrate the operation of these rules.[211.4]

> **EXAMPLE 4-11 (asset transfer):** U.S. person A and foreign person F are equal partners in a foreign partnership (FP). FP owns property X, with a basis of $100 and a value of $70. FP transfers property X to a domestic corporation (DC) in a § 351 transaction.
>
> Upon a hypothetical sale of property X, F's share of the gain or loss would not have been taken into account for U.S. tax purposes, so F's portion of property X is importation property, with a basis of $50 and a value of $35, and the transaction is a loss importation transaction. DC's basis in F's portion of property X is thus $35. DC's carryover basis of $85 in the aggregated property exceeds its $70 value, such that under the usual anti-loss duplication rule of § 362(e)(2), DC must reduce its basis in property X to $70. FP's basis in its DC stock is $100 under § 358.
>
> If a § 362(e)(2)(C) election is made to have the § 362(e)(2) basis reduction applied to the stock of DC (instead of the asset), the basis of property X is $85 and FP's basis in its DC stock is reduced to $85. The $15 reduction in FP's basis in its DC stock reduces A's basis in its partnership interest by $15 under § 705(a)(2)(B).[211.5]

> **EXAMPLE 4-12 (transfer of interest):** Foreign person F and two other individuals are equal partners in a foreign partnership (FP). F's basis in FP is $247, $150 of which is attributable to FP's liabilities. F transfers its interest to a domestic corporation (DC) in a § 351 transaction. If DC were to sell the FP interest immediately after the transfer, DC would receive $100. DC's share of FP's liabilities is $145.
>
> DC's basis in the FP interest is $242 ($F$'s $247 basis, reduced by F's $150 share of FP's liabilities and increased by DC's $145 share). Since the value of the interest to DC is deemed to be $245 ($100 cash value plus $145 liability share), the transfer is not a loss importation transaction.

For purposes of § 755, a basis determination under the loss importation rules is not treated as a substituted basis transaction and thus not governed by Regulations § 1.755-1(b)(5), but rather is subject to the general rules of Regulations § 1.755-1(b)(2)-(4).[211.6]

Of note, the determination of whether partnership gain or loss would be subject to federal income tax is made by reference to the treatment of the partners, taking into account all partnership items for the year of the § 362 transaction.[211.7] The partnership is not permitted to use the closing-of-the-books method in making this determination.[211.8]

[211.4] Reg. § 1.362-3(f).

[211.5] Reg. § 1.362-4(e)(1).

[211.6] Reg. §§ 1.362-3(b)(4)(i); 1.755-1(b)(1)(i).

[211.7] Reg. § 1.362-3(e)(1).

[211.8] TD 9759, 2016-15 IRB 545 (Apr. 11, 2016).

Page 4-54:

Add new ¶ 4.05[13].

[13] Contributions of LIFO Inventory [New]

The contribution to a partnership of LIFO inventory property is a contribution of built-in gain property subject to § 704(c). The Service has ruled privately that the partnership may elect to aggregate each item of inventory for purposes of making allocations under § 704(c), and that if the partnership elects to use the LIFO method, § 704(c) will not apply to the separate items of contributed inventory. Rather, the partnership will treat the aggregate basis of the contributed inventory as its opening inventory acquired at the time of contribution. Any LIFO "layers" of the contributor are lost.[211.9]

[211.9] Priv. Ltr. Rul. 200123035 (June 8, 2001); see Priv. Ltr. Rul. 9644027 (July 25, 1996).

¶ 4.06 PARTNERSHIP ORGANIZATION AND SYNDICATION EXPENSES

Page 4-56:

Add to note 218.

Regulations issued in 2011 provide that a taxpayer is deemed to have elected to deduct/amortize organizational expenses for the tax year in which the partnership begins business unless it affirmatively elects to capitalize organizational expenses on a timely filed (including extensions) return for the year. Once made, this election is irrevocable. Any change in the characterization of an item as an organizational expense (if the partnership reports the item consistently for two or more years) or the year in which the trade or business begins (if the partnership amortizes organizational expenses for two or more years) is a change in accounting method. Reg. § 1.709-1(b)(2).

Although effective for organizational expenses paid on or after August 16, 2011, taxpayers may apply the 2011 Regulations to expenses paid or incurred after October 22, 2004, provided the statute of limitations for the year of the election has not run. Alternatively, taxpayers may apply Regulations § 1.709-1 (as in effect at that time) to pre-September 8, 2008 organizational expenses. Reg. § 1.709-1(b)(5).

Add to note 220.

See Reg. § 1.709-1(b)(3) (§ 165 loss for unamortized organizational expenses; no partnership deduction with respect to capitalized syndication expenses.)

Pages 4-56–4-57:

Replace third paragraph of subsection (ending with note callout 221) with the following.

An election to amortize organizational costs is deemed made by a partnership unless it chooses to forgo the election by electing to capitalize its organizational expenses on its timely filed return (including extensions) for the tax year in which it begins business.[221]

---

[221] Reg. § 1.709-1(b)(2). Under prior law, an affirmative election was required. See Frank M. Lieber, 66 TCM 529, 538–540 (1993) (minor flaws in election filed prior to publication of any Proposed or Temporary Regulations do not invalidate election); Priv. Ltr. Rul. 9501007 (Sept. 29, 1994) (return not timely filed; extension to make election granted under Reg. § 301.9100-1).

Page 4-58:

Replace last paragraph of subsection with the following.

The amortization election applies to all organization expenses.[229]

Regulations applicable to terminations occurring after December 9, 2013, preclude a technical termination of a partnership under § 708(b)(1)(B) (by sale or exchange of more than 50% of the partnership interests) from being treated as a disposition of a business for purposes of applying §§ 195 and 709. Instead, the new partnership resulting from such a technical termination is required to amortize the terminated partnership's §§ 195 and 709 expenses using the same amortization period used by the terminated partnership.[230]

---

[229] Reg. § 1.709-1(b)(1).
[230] Reg. §§ 1.195-2(a), 1.708-1(b)(6), 1.709-1(b)(3)(ii).

¶ 4.07 CONTRIBUTIONS TO PARTNERSHIP INVESTMENT COMPANIES

[1] Definition of "Investment Company"

Page 4-60:

Add to note 240.

See also Priv. Ltr. Rul. 202016013 (Jan. 8, 2020) (contribution of assets to publicly traded partnership (PTP) coupled with transfer of contributed assets from PTP to master limited partnership (MLP) more than 50 percent owned by PTP not subject to § 721(b); look-through rule applied to PTP's interest in MLP; 80 percent test applied to the value of PTP's assets (including its ratable share of MLP's assets) immediately after the transaction).

Add to note 241.

For purposes of determining whether a partnership is an investment company, interests the partnership owns in a publicly traded partnership can be ignored if those interests represent more than 50 percent of the value of all interests in the publicly traded partnership. Instead, the partnership may look through to its ratable share of the assets of the publicly traded partnership in determining its status as an investment company. Priv. Ltr. Rul. 201547003 (May 19, 2015). While this private letter ruling does not cite Treasury Regulations § 1.351-1(c)(4) (providing a look-through rule for 50-percent owned corporate subsidiaries), it appears to be an effort to provide parallel treatment for 50-percent owned publicly traded partnerships. See Priv. Ltr. Rul. 201633028 (Aug. 12, 2016) (same).

[2] The Diversification Requirement

Page 4-62:

Add to note 249.

; Priv. Ltr. Rul. 200931042 (Apr. 28, 2009) (§ 721(b) not applicable where all transferors contribute cash, diversified portfolios of stocks and securities, or a combination thereof).

¶ 4.08 ACQUISITIONS OF INTERESTS IN SPECIALIZED SMALL BUSINESS INVESTMENT COMPANIES FOLLOWING DISPOSITIONS OF PUBLICLY TRADED SECURITIES: SECTION 1044

Page 4-63:

Add the following before the first paragraph of subsections

NOTE: Section 1044 was repealed for sales occurring after December 31, 2017, by the 2017 Tax Cuts and Jobs Act.[251.1] The following discussion remains applicable for sales occurring prior to January 1, 2018.

[251.1] Pub. L. No. 115-97, § 13313 (Dec. 22, 2017).

Transfer of a Partnership Interest in Exchange for Services

Chapter 5 was revised effective September 2020. The revised chapter can be found in the front of this student edition.

PART

Basis of a Partner's Partnership Interest and the Impact of Partnership Liabilities

Determining the Basis of a Partner's Partnership Interest

¶ 6.02 THE GENERAL RULE FOR DETERMINING BASIS: SECTION 705(a)

[1] Basis as a History of Partnership Transactions

Page 6-5:

Add to note 15.

See also VisionMonitor Software, LLC, 108 TCM 256 (2014).

Page 6-6:

Add to note 18.

Section 1044 was repealed, effective as of December 31, 2017, by the 2017 Tax Cuts and Jobs Act, Pub. L. No. 115-97, § 13313 (Dec. 22, 2017).

Replace note 19 with the following.

   [19] § 1014(a).

[2] Adjustments to the Basis of a Partner's Interest: The Purpose of Section 705(a)

Page 6-7:

Replace note 24 with the following.

   [24] § 705(a)(2)(B). Section 199A (see ¶ 9.02[3][z]) creates a deduction for individual taxpayers that may be based in whole or in part on trades or businesses operated by partnerships. Each individual partner must take into account his or her share of income generated by a partnership business as well as a share of W-2 wages related to the business and the basis of certain property used in the business. The deduction, however, is not computed at the partnership level; it is computed by the partners individually based on information provided by the partnership. The § 199A Regulations provide clearly that the § 199A deduction has no effect on the basis of a partner's interest in a partnership. Reg. § 1.199A-1(e)(1). This rule is clearly correct and consistent with the scheme of § 705(a), since the deduction is not treated as a partnership expense and does not decrease the basis of any partnership asset.

[3] The Less Common Basis Adjustments

[a] Tax-Exempt Income

Page 6-11:

Add the following after carryover paragraph.

A less obvious kind of tax-exempt income can arise in connection with energy credit property under § 48. Under §§ 48(a)(2) and 48(a)(5)(A), the energy credit is 10% or 30% of the basis of energy property placed in service, depending on the type of property. Generally, § 50(c)(3) provides that the basis of energy property is reduced by 50% of the energy credit. In lieu of claiming the credit, however, taxpayers may elect to apply for a "grant" under § 1603 of the American Recovery and Reinvestment Act of 2009 (ARRA). The amount of the grant is the same as the amount of the credit. Grants are available for certain types of energy property (see ARRA § 1603(d)) placed in service during 2009, 2010, and 2011 (or thereafter, under certain circumstances). Section 48(d)(3)(A) provides that grant payments "shall not be included in the gross income of the taxpayer."

If energy property is disposed of or ceases to be qualifying property within the five-year period starting with the date it is placed in service, the credit (or grant) is subject to recapture under § 50(a)(1)(A) and ARRA § 1603(f). The initial recapture percentage is 100%, and decreases by 20% for every full year the facility has been in service.[32.1]

If energy property is placed in service by a partnership that claims a § 1603 grant, half of the amount of the grant should be viewed as tax-exempt income under § 705(a)(1)(B), as demonstrated by the following example:

> **EXAMPLE 6-2.1:** Equal partners *C* and *D* each contribute $300 to the *CD* partnership. The *CD* partnership borrows $1,400 and constructs and places in service a qualified solar facility with a cost of $2,000 during 2009. The *CD* partnership files for and receives a $600 grant under ARRA § 1603 during 2009. The grant proceeds are distributed equally to each partner during 2009. At the end of 2009, assuming the partnership has no other income, loss, etc., the adjusted basis of each partner's partnership interest should be calculated as follows:

[32.1] These recapture percentages are set forth in § 50(a)(1)(B) for credits. Although § 1603(f) refers to § 50, it also states that the Secretary "shall provide for the recapture of the appropriate percentages of the grant amount in such manner as the Secretary...deems appropriate." Given the clear congressional intent that the grant "mimic" the credit (see HR Rep. 111-16, 111th Cong., 1st Sess. 444 (Feb. 12, 2009)), it seems unlikely that this language was intended to give the Treasury authority to vary the recapture percentages. Rather, it should be interpreted to provide authority as to the mechanics for repaying a portion of the grant.

Capital contribution	$ 300	Cash
Share of partnership debt	700	50% of $1,400
Less: distribution of ½ of grant	(300)	50% of $600
Plus: tax-exempt portion of grant	150	§ 705(a)(1)(B)
Year-end partner's adjusted basis	$ 850	

Each partner's year-end basis includes a liability share of $700, which is equivalent to a tax-basis capital account of $150 ($850 less $700).

At the end of 2009, the tax basis balance sheet of the *CD* partnership is as follows:

Asset	Tax Basis	Liabilities	Amount
Solar Facility	$1,700	Debt	$1,400
		Capital	
		C	150
		D	150
Total Assets	$1,700	Total Liabilities and Capital	$1,700

Although the entire grant payment is tax exempt under § 48(d)(3)(A), half of the grant payment reduces the tax basis of the solar facility and thus represents a payment that is merely tax-deferred, rather than tax exempt, for purposes of § 705. Effectively, this portion of the grant payment will be taxed on the disposition of the facility.

If the partnership receives an energy credit, rather than a grant, a different type of basis adjustment is required. As discussed in ¶ 6.02[3][c], § 50(c)(5) provides that the bases of the partners' partnership interests must be "appropriately adjusted" to take into account the § 50(c)(3) reduction in the basis of energy property.

Add to note 39.

See also Principal Life Ins. Co. v. United States, 2015-1 USTC ¶ 50,184 (Ct. Cl. 2015) (discussing application of § 705(a)(1)(B) to a distribution of previously taxed income from a controlled foreign corporation).

Page 6-12:

Add at end of subsection.

Under § 108(i), added by ARRA, partnerships and other debtors may elect to defer the taxation of discharge of indebtedness income realized during 2009 and 2010. This election and its consequences for partners and partnerships are explored in ¶ 4.02[3].

Partnerships that own stock of controlled foreign corporations (CFCs) are treated as foreign partnerships for purposes of the Subpart F and GILTI (global intangible low-taxed income) regimes.[40.1] Foreign partnerships are not United States shareholders of CFCs, and thus cannot have Subpart F or GILTI inclusions. Instead, these inclusions occur at the partner level, and the basis increase arising from the inclusion is made to the partnership interest in the partnership that actually owns the stock.[40.2] Presumably, the partnership is entitled to a corresponding increase to its basis in the CFC stock, but this conclusion is uncertain.[40.3]

Section 250 allows a deduction for domestic corporations equal to 50 percent of their GILTI. This deduction is a partner-level deduction and has no impact on the corporate partner's basis in its partnership interest.[40.4]

Section 245(b) provides for a 100 percent deduction for dividends received by a domestic corporation from a foreign corporation. This deduction is available to domestic corporate partners.[40.5] The deduction is at the partner level and has no impact on partnership accounts (such as the partner's basis

---

[40.1] Prop. Reg. § 1.958-1(d) (2019). Taxpayers may rely on the Proposed Regulations for taxable years of foreign corporations beginning after December 31, 2017.

[40.2] Reg. § 1.961-1(b)(1)(ii).

[40.3] See Jackel & Crnkovich, "CFC Stock Held by Foreign Partnerships: Confusion Galore," Tax Notes 709 (Aug. 17, 2009).

[40.4] Preamble, REG-104464-18 (2019) III.A.3.

[40.5] See Joint Committee on Taxation, General Explanation of Public Law No. 115-97 (JCS-1-18), p. 349 (Dec. 2018).

for its partnership interest). This treatment is comparable to the treatment accorded to dividends eligible for the § 243 dividends received deduction.

[c] Nondeductible Expenditures

Page 6-13:

Replace note 44 with following.

⁴⁴ The partners' bases are reduced by the basis, not the fair market value, of contributed capital gain property. Rev. Rul. 96-11, 199-1 CB 138. Consistent with this ruling, new § 704(d)(3)(B) (added by the 2017 Tax Cuts and Jobs Act, Pub. L. No. 115-97, § 13503 (Dec. 22, 2017), which is effective for partnership taxable years beginning after December 31, 2017, confirms that a partner's share of the excess of the fair market value of contributed partnership property over its fair market value is not taken into account in applying the § 704(d) loss limitation. See infra ¶ 11.05[1][b].

Page 6-14:

Add at end of numbered list.

   8. Reductions in basis of partnership-owned corporate stock under Sections 362(e)(2)[46.1] and 1059.[46.2]

[46.1] Reg. § 1.362-4(e)(1).

[46.2] Reg. § 1.701-2(e)(2) Example 2.

Replace last paragraph of subsection with the following.

   Conversely, expenditures "chargeable to capital account" in the sense that they increase the bases of partnership assets should not reduce the partners' bases under § 705(a)(2)(B). Capital expenditures generally do not deplete partnership assets or the aggregate bases thereof, and merely represent a change in the type of assets held by the partnership. Consequently, no basis adjustment at the partner level is appropriate. Section 709 organization and syndication costs should be treated as chargeable to capital account for purposes of § 705(a)(2)(B), and hence should not reduce the bases of the partners in their partnership interests.[47]

   As discussed in ¶ 6.02[3][a], taxpayers who place qualified energy property in service during certain time periods are entitled to an energy credit under §§ 48(a)(2) and 48(a)(5)(A) equal to either 10% or 30% of the basis of the qualifying property, depending on the type of property. Generally, § 50(c)(3) provides that the basis of energy property is reduced by 50% of the

---

[47] But cf. Reg. § 1.704-1(b)(2)(iv)(*i*)(*2*) (partnership organization and syndication costs, other than organization costs with respect to which a § 709(b) amortization election has been made, are treated as § 705(a)(2)(B) expenses "solely" for purposes of computing capital accounts). See generally ¶ 4.06.

energy credit, and § 50(c)(5) provides that the bases of the partners' partnership interests must be "appropriately adjusted" to take into account the § 50(c)(3) reduction in the basis of energy property placed in service by the partnership. In the event all or a portion of the credit is recaptured, an appropriate portion of the adjustment to the basis of the energy property is reversed. An identical process should occur with respect to the partners' bases for their partnership interests.

To maintain parity between the bases of partnership assets and the aggregate bases of the partners' in their partnership interests at the time energy property is placed in service, the "appropriate" adjustment is a reduction in the partners' bases equal to the reduction in the basis of the partnership's energy property. While this adjustment may not technically be a § 705(a)(2)(B) adjustment,[48] it mimics one very closely, as illustrated below.

> **EXAMPLE 6-3.1:** As in Example 6-2.1, equal partners C and D each contribute $300 to the CD partnership. The CD partnership borrows $1,400 and constructs and places in service a qualified solar facility with a cost of $2,000 during 2009. The CD partnership does not apply for a grant under ARRA § 1603, and, consequently, the partners are entitled to a $600 credit (30% of $2,000) for 2009. At the end of 2009, assuming the partnership has no other income, loss, etc., the basis of each partner's partnership interest should be calculated as follows:

---

[48] Cf. Reg. § 1.704-1(b)(2)(iv)(*j*) (capital account adjustments corresponding to § 48(q)(1) and § 48(q)(3) basis adjustments; § 48(q)(6) provides for the bases of the partners to be "appropriately adjusted," and is virtually identical to current § 50(c)(5)). This Regulation explicitly provides that the basis reduction at the partner level is pursuant to § 48(q)(6) and that no additional adjustment is to be made under § 705(a)(2)(B). Presumably, this concept will reappear if any Regulations are ever adopted under § 50(c). The clear statement that there is not to be a duplicate reduction is obviously welcome. Whether it makes any difference whether the adjustment is made under § 48(q)(6) (now § 50(c)(5)) or § 705(a)(2)(B) is unclear. Certainly, the amounts are identical. The only § 50 Regulations issued to date do not directly address partnerships that own (rather than lease) credit property, but clearly reject any notion that a duplicate adjustment is appropriate by treating the required 50 percent income inclusion as a partner-level income item, thereby avoiding a § 705 basis increase for the partner and maintaining inside/outside basis parity. See Reg. § 1.50-1(b), relating to the income inclusion rules applicable to lessees following an election pursuant to Reg. § 1.48-4 to treat the lessee as having purchased the credit property).

Capital contribution	$ 300	Cash
Share of partnership debt	700	50% of $1,400
Less: share of basis reduction	(150)	§ 50(c)(5)
Year-end partner's adjusted basis	$ 850	

Each partner's year-end basis includes a liability share of $700, which is equivalent to a tax basis capital account of $150 ($850 less $700).

At the end of 2009, the tax basis balance sheet of the CD partnership is as follows:

Asset	Tax Basis	Liabilities	Amount
Solar Facility	$1,700	Debt	$1,400
		Capital	
		C	150
		D	150
Total Assets	$1,700	Total Liabilities and Capital	$1,700

The tax and economic results to the partners are identical in Examples 6-3.1 and 6-2.1. In both cases, the partners have recovered their entire capital contributions (as a result of the distribution of the grant funds in Example 6-2.1 or the claiming of the credit in Example 6-3.1). In both cases, their capital accounts and outside bases are aligned. This is consistent with the congressional intent in enacting the grant system as part of ARRA.[48.1]

[48.1] The operation of the grant rules was intended to "mimic" the operation of the energy credit rules. See HR Rep. No. 16, 111th Cong., 1st Sess. 444 (Feb. 12, 2009).

¶ 6.04 THE RELATIONSHIP BETWEEN A PARTNER'S BASIS AND CAPITAL ACCOUNT

Page 6-27:

In note 91, replace second sentence with the following.

However, any liability of a partnership that is assumed by a partner is credited to his capital account.

Basis Consequences of Partnership Liabilities

¶ 7.03 WHAT IS A "LIABILITY"?

[2] The Shift to a Policy-Driven Definition of "Liability"

Page 7-17:

Add to note 60.

At least one internal memorandum prepared by the Service acknowledges that the Service's position in Revenue Ruling 95-26 is contrary to *Helmer*. A portion of this memorandum was inadvertently produced by the Service during discovery. See Jade Trading, LLC v. United States, 80 Fed. Cl. 11, 44 n. 65 (2007), referring to the "Helmer/Cram memo" produced in Marriott Int'l Resorts, LP v. United States, 63 Fed. Cl. 144, 145–146 (2004).

Page 7-18:

Add to note 62.

In COLM Producer, Inc. v. United States, 460 F. Supp. 2d 713 (ND Tex. 2006), aff'd sub nom. Kornman & Assoc. v. United States, 527 F3d 443 (5th Cir. 2008), the district court was confronted with a taxpayer who similarly argued that an obligation to deliver securities pursuant to a short sale transaction was not a liability for § 752 purposes, and, therefore, should not be considered an amount realized in the context of a transfer of an interest in the partnership. In agreement with *Salina Partnership*, the court held that the obligation constituted a liability under the plain meaning of the word, and ruled that the liability was not contingent, because the obligation itself was legally enforceable and the amount of the obligation (the basis of the securities to be delivered) was fixed at the time that the partnership interest was transferred. Accord Marriott Intl. Resorts, L.P., 83 Fed. Cl. 291 (2008), aff'd, 2009-2 USTC ¶ 50,719 (Fed. Cir. 2009) (Treasury bills). In Cemco Investors, LLC v. United States, 2007-1 USTC ¶ 50,385 (ND Ill. 2007), aff'd, 515 F3d 749 (7th Cir. 2008), a U.S. district court faced the similar issue of whether an obligation to deliver foreign currency pursuant to a sold option created a liability for § 752 purposes. The court did not reach the issue of whether *Salina Partnership* was controlling, because all parties to the motion for summary judgment before the court apparently agreed that Regulations § 1.752-6 results in a retroactive change to the definition of "liability" for purposes of § 752. The conclusion that Regulations § 1.752-6 retroactively alters the definition of liability for purposes of § 752 is erroneous. Regulations § 1.752-1(a)(4)(iv) provides that the revised definition of "liability" applies only to liabilities incurred or assumed by a partnership on or after June 24, 2003. Regulations § 1.752-6, if valid, merely provides that the basis of a partner's interest is reduced for § 358(h)(3) liabilities assumed by the partnership during the period from October 18, 1999, through June 23, 2003. While the ultimate conclusion in *Cemco* would have been the same if the transactions had been properly analyzed (and if Regulations § 1.752-6 can validly be applied retroactively), the misguided analysis caused the court to avoid confronting the issue addressed in *Salina Partnership*. See also Stobie Creek Inv., LLC v. United States, 82 Fed. Cl. 636 (2008) (retroactive application of Reg. § 1.752-6 invalid; *Helmer* followed; transaction disregarded under economic substance doctrine), aff'd, 2010-1 USTC ¶ 50,455 (Fed. Cir. 2010) (no economic substance). But see Markell Co., TC Memo. 2014-86 (Temp. Reg. § 1.752-6T valid based on specific congressional grant of authority).

Page 7-19:

Add to note 66.

See also COLM Producer, Inc. v. United States, 460 F. Supp. 2d 713 (ND Tex. 2006), aff'd sub nom. Kornman & Assoc. v. United States, 527 F3d 443 (5th Cir. 2008) (district court cited Black's Law Dictionary for definition of "liability" in the context of a short sale obligation; Fifth Circuit rejected this approach).

Add at end of subsection.

In *Cemco Investors, LLC v. United States*,[67.1] the Seventh Circuit avoided the issue of whether an option created a liability in contravention to *Helmer* by validating the basis reduction approach set forth in Regulations § 1.752-6 (see

---

[67.1] Cemco Investors, LLC v. United States, 515 F3d 749 (7th Cir. 2008).

discussion at ¶ 7.04[2]). The Claims Court, in *Stobie Creek Investments, LLC v. United States*, declined to follow *Cemco*.[67.2]

[67.2] Stobie Creek Inv., LLC v. United States, 82 Fed. Cl. 636 (2008), aff'd, 2010-1 USTC ¶ 50,455 (Fed. Cir. 2010) (*Cemco* court failed to offer thorough analysis of retroactive application of Reg. § 1.752-6).

[3] Leveling the Playing Field

Page 7-19:

Add to note 68.

See also Jade Trading, LLC v. United States, 80 Fed. Cl. 11 (2007) (option not a liability for purposes of § 752, following *Helmer*; transaction disregarded due to lack of economic substance); Stobie Creek Inv., LLC v. United States, 82 Fed. Cl. 636 (2008), aff'd, 2010-1 USTC ¶ 50,455 (Fed. Cir. 2010) (same); Maguire Partners—Master Investments, LLC v. United States, 2009-1 USTC ¶ 50,215 (CD Cal. 2009) (no economic substance; alternatively, step-transaction and substance-over-form doctrines apply to disallow claimed losses; further, short option part of contractually interlocked long and short options is a § 752 liability under *Kornman*; finally, even if short option is not a § 752 liability, Temp. Reg. § 1.752-6 applies retroactively under *Cemco* to reduce outside basis), aff'd unpub. opinion, 2011-2 USTC ¶ 50,517 (9th Cir. 2011); New Phoenix Sunrise Corp. 132 TC 161 (2009) (option transaction is a sham under Sixth Circuit precedent; transaction lacked economic substance), aff'd unpub. opinion, 2010-2 USTC ¶ 50,740 (6th Cir. 2010); Candyce Martin 1999 Irrevocable Trust v. United States, 2011-2 USTC 50,670 (ND CA 2011) (option was a liability for § 752 purposes; transaction disregarded as lacking economic substance).

¶ 7.04 "NON-LIABILITY OBLIGATIONS"

[2] Regulations § 1.752-6 (October 18, 1999 to June 23, 2003)

Page 7-22:

In third paragraph of subsection, replace second sentence with the following.

First, a basis reduction generally is not required if the trade or business with which the liability is associated is transferred to the partnership assuming the liability.[77.1]

[77.1] An offsetting option transaction described in Notice 2000-44, 2000-2 CB 255, does not create, by itself, a trade or business under this exception. Clearmeadow Investments, LLC v. United States, 87 Fed. Cl. 509 (Fed. Cl. 2009).

Page 7-23:

Add to note 79.

In Cemco Investors, LLC v. United States, 515 F3d 749 (7th Cir. 2008), the Seventh Circuit took a broad view of the congressional authorization granted to the Service in Public Law No. 106-554, § 309(c), finding that it included "basis reduction rules for many transactions." The court therefore found Regulations § 1.752-6 valid as applied to a transaction described in Notice 2000-44. Accord Maguire Partners—Master Investments v. United States, 2009-1 USTC ¶ 50,215 (CD Cal. 2009), aff'd unpub. opinion, 2011-2 USTC ¶ 50,517 (9th Cir. 2011). Contra Stobie Creek Inv., LLC v. United States, 82 Fed. Cl. 636 (2008), aff'd, 2010-1 USTC ¶ 50,455 (Fed. Cir. 2010) (*Cemco* court failed to offer thorough analysis of retroactive application of Reg. § 1.752-6); Sala v. United States, 552 F. Supp. 2d 1167 (DC Colo. 2008), motion for a new trial denied, 251 FRD 614 (d. Colo. 2008), rev'd on other grounds, 106 AFTR2d 2010-5406 (10th Cir. 2010) (transaction had no economic substance).

In note 81.1, add the following after citation to Klamath Strategic Inv. Fund, LLC v. United States.

In a subsequent opinion, the district court held that the underlying transactions at issue in *Klamath* lacked economic substance, thus effectively rendering moot the issues of whether the transactions created liabilities for purposes of § 752 and whether Regulations § 1.752-6 can validly be applied on a retroactive basis. See Klamath Strategic Inv. Fund, LLC v. United States, 472 F. Supp. 2d 885 (ED Tex. 2007), aff'd, 568 F3d 537 (5th Cir. 2009). A Colorado district court judge came to the opposite conclusion in Sala v. United States, 552 F. Supp. 2d 1167 (D. Colo. 2008), motion for new trial denied, 251 FRD 614 (D. Colo. 2008), rev'd on other grounds, 106 AFTR2d 2010-5406 (10th Cir. 2010) (transaction had no economic substance), holding the retroactive application of Regulations § 1.752-6 invalid because it does not provide partnership rules comparable to the § 358(h) corporate rules, does not address the acceleration or duplication of losses, and does not apply to the types of liabilities described in § 358(h)(3) (liabilities assumed by corporations). Accord Stobie Creek Inv., LLC v. United States, 82 Fed. Cl. 636 (2008), aff'd, 2010-1 USTC ¶ 50,455 (Fed. Cir. 2010) (retroactive application of Reg. § 1.752-6 invalid; *Helmer* followed); MURFAM Farms, LLC v. United States, 88 Fed. Cl. 516 (2009) (retroactive application of Reg. § 1.752-6 invalid).

In note 81.2, add the following case history to citation of Klamath Strategic Inv. Fund.

, aff'd, 568 F3d 537 (5th Cir. 2009).

Page 7-24:

Add to note 81.3.

Accord Sala v. United States, 552 F. Supp. 2d 1167 (D. Colo. 2008), rev'd on other grounds, 106 AFTR2d 2010-5406 (10th Cir. 2010) (transaction had no economic substance).

In note 81.4, add the following case history to citation of Klamath Strategic Inv. Fund.

, aff'd, 568 F3d 537 (5th Cir. 2009).

¶ 7.05 RECHARACTERIZATION OF LOANS

[1] Partner Loans as Partnership Liabilities: The Thin Partnership Doctrine

Page 7-43:

Replace note 165 with the following.

[165] TIFD III-E, Inc. v. United States, 459 F3d 220, 241 (2d Cir. 2006), rev'g and remanding 342 F. Supp. 2d 94 (D. Conn. 2004) (banks' interest not a bona fide equity participation; also not debt, according to district court; query what it is?), on remand, 660 F. Supp. 2d 367 (D. Conn. 2009) (interest a partnership interest under § 704(e)(1)), rev'd, 666 F3d 836 (2d Cir. 2012) (§ 704(e)(1) inapplicable to interests that are debt). See also Andantech, LLC v. Commissioner, 331 F3d 972 (DC Cir. 2003); Boca Investerings v. United States, 314 F3d 625 (DC Cir. 2003), rev'g 167 F. Supp. 2d 298 (DDC 2001) (cert. denied); Saba Partnership v. Commissioner, 273 F3d 1135 (DC Cir. 2001); ASA Investerings v. Commissioner, 201 F3d 505 (DC Cir 2000) (cert. denied); Chemtech Royalty Assocs., LP v. United States, 2013-1 USTC ¶ 50,204 (MD La. 2013), aff'd, 766 F3d 453 (5th Cir. 2014) (cert. denied). See generally ¶ 3.04[4]. Section 704(e)(1) was repealed by the Bipartisan Budget Act of 2015, effective for partnership taxable years beginning after December 31, 2015. See discussion at ¶ 3.00.

Determining a Partner's Share of Partnership Liabilities for Basis Purposes

Chapter 8 was revised effective June 2020. The revised chapter can be found in the front of this student edition.

PART IV

Tax Aspects of Partnership Operations; Audit and Litigation; and Distributive Share Rules

CHAPTER **9**

Tax Accounting for Partnership Operations

¶ 9.01 TAXATION OF PARTNERSHIP OPERATIONS: GENERAL CONCEPTS

[1] Blending Aggregate and Entity Concepts

Page 9-7:

Add to note 1.

; Burke v. Commissioner, 485 F3d 171 (1st Cir. 2007) (partner's current year gross income includes share of partnership income earned during year even though partnership earnings were held in escrow pending resolution of dispute among partners regarding their shares of such earnings; no deferral of partner income recognition due to escrow restriction where partnership itself received income "free and clear"); Les Hicks, TC Summ. Op. 2009-68 (partner must include distributive share of partnership income even though no distributions made). But see Solomon Windheim, TC Memo. 2009-136 (partner not beneficial owner of partnership interest, and thus not taxable on allocable share of partnership income).

[2] Computation of Partnership Taxable Income

Page 9-10:

Replace note 14 with the following.

[14] See Frederick S. Klein, 25 TC 1045 (1956); Peter A. McLauchlan, TC Memo. 2011-289; Tech. Adv. Mem. 9316003 (Dec. 23, 1992) (if partnership agreement or partnership practice requires partner to bear certain types of partnership business expenses out of partner's funds, partner is entitled to § 162 deductions for such expenses; not subject to § 67(a) floor; however, partner cannot deduct expenses for which he was entitled to, but failed to seek, reimbursement); Tech. Adv. Mem. 9330004 (Apr. 14, 1993) (same). See also Tech. Adv. Mem. 9330001 (Apr. 13, 1993), discussed infra note 128.

For individual partners, the distinction between § 162 and § 212 treatment is accentuated by the 2017 Tax Cuts and Jobs Act. This Act replaces the 2-percent floor in § 67 with a flat denial of all "miscellaneous itemized deductions" (a phrase that includes § 212 deductions) by individuals for tax years beginning after December 31, 2017, and before January 1, 2026. Pub. L. No. 115-97, § 11045 (Dec. 22, 2017).

Page 9-11:

Add to note 16.

The 2017 Tax Cuts and Jobs Act eliminates the deductibility of foreign real property taxes and severely limits the deductibility of other foreign taxes (other than those related to a trade or business or a § 212 activity) during 2018 through 2025. See § 164(b)(6), as amended by Pub. L. No. 115-97, § 11042 (Dec. 22, 2017), effective for tax years beginning after December 31, 2017.

Page 9-12:

Add to end of section.

For taxable years beginning after December 31, 2017, and before January 1, 2026, § 164(b)(6) limits an individual's deduction under § 164(a) for certain state and local taxes (so-called SALT deductions) to $10,000 ($5,000 for married persons filing separately). In connection with the enactment of this limitation, Congress indicated that "taxes imposed at the entity level, such as a business tax imposed on pass-through entities, that are reflected in a partner's or S corporation shareholder's distributive or pro-rata share of income or loss on a Schedule K-1 (or similar form), will continue to reduce such partner's or shareholder's distributive or pro-rata share of income as under present law."[18.1] In other words, business taxes imposed on such entities are not subject to the SALT limitation.

Following enactment of this limitation, some high-SALT states have enacted (or are considering the enactment) of legislation that would impose either a mandatory or elective entity-level income tax on partnerships and S corporations. In some instances, the legislation would provide a corresponding or offsetting owner-level tax benefit, such as a full or partial credit, deduction, or exclusion. The Service is aware of this legislative activity and has announced that it will issue Proposed Regulations to "clarify" that certain state and local income taxes imposed on and paid by a partnership or an S corporation on its income are allowed as a deduction by the partnership or S corporation in computing its non-separately stated income or loss.[18.2] Consequently, such taxes would not be subject to limitation under § 164(b)(6) at the partner level.

_____

[18.1] HR Rep. No. 115-466, 115th Cong., 1st Sess. 260 n. 172 (2017).

[18.2] Notice 2020-75, 2020-49 IRB 1453. "Specified Income Tax Payments" are (1) deductible by partnerships and S corporations in computing their non-separately stated income or loss; (2) not separately taken into account by partners or S corporation shareholders; and (3) not separately taken into account by individuals who are partners or shareholders in applying the SALT deduction limit. The Regulations to be proposed will apply to payments made on or after November 9, 2020, but taxpayers may generally rely on them prior to issuance with respect to all payments, including those prior to November 9, 2020.

[3] Specifically Segregated Partnership Items

[a] Items Listed in the Statute

[iv] Dividends.

Page 9-16:

Delete last paragraph of subsection.

[v] Foreign taxes.

Add to note 30.

The 2017 Tax Cuts and Jobs Act eliminates the deductibility of foreign real property taxes as well as severely limits the deductibility of other foreign taxes and all state and local income, property, and sales taxes (other than those related to a trade or business or a § 212 activity) during 2018 through 2025. See § 164(b)(6), as amended by Pub. L. No. 115-97, § 11042 (Dec. 22, 2017), effective for tax years beginning after December 31, 2017.

Page 9-16:

Add the following at end of subsection.

Proposed Regulations issued under § 901 provide that an amount paid to a foreign country is not a compulsory payment, and thus is not a tax described in § 901, where the foreign payment is attributable to certain kinds of transactions intentionally structured to generate foreign tax liability.[30.1] Presumably, although these Proposed Regulations do not address the issue, taxes paid by a partnership to a foreign country that fall subject to this proposed rule would not require a separate statement under § 702(a)(6), since such taxes are not described in § 901. However, a partner's distributive share of any such taxes paid by the partnership should reduce the basis of its partnership interest under § 705(a)(2)(B).[30.2] As a result, a partner's taxable income from such an arrangement may exceed the partner's economic income, with no tax credits available to neutralize the difference.

[30.1] REG-156779-06 (Mar. 30, 2007).

[30.2] See ¶ 6.02[3][c].

[b] Additional Items

Page 9-17:

Replace list item 7 with the following.

7 Alimony payments (§ 215);[35.1]

[35.1] The § 215 alimony deduction (as well as the related income inclusion provision in former § 61(8) and other related provisions) was repealed by the 2017 Tax Cuts and Jobs Act, effective for agreements executed after December 31, 2018, as well as prior agreements that provide for application of the new rules. See Pub. L. No. 115-97, § 11051 (Dec. 22, 2017).

Page 9-21:

Replace note 63 with the following.

[63] The § 68 limitation was suspended for tax years beginning during 2010, 2011, and 2012. Pub. L. No. 111-312, § 101(a) (Dec. 17, 2010). See also Temp. Reg. § 1.67-2T(b)(1). Section 68 was resurrected and revised by the American Taxpayer Relief Act of 2012, Pub. L. No. 112-240, § 101(b)(2)(A), effective for tax years beginning after December 31, 2012. The revisions increase the adjusted gross income floors for 2013 (to $300,000 for joint returns) and indexes them for inflation after 2013. The § 68 limitation was again suspended (for tax years beginning after December 31, 2017, and before January 1, 2026, by the 2017 Tax Cuts and Jobs Act, Pub. L. No. 115-97, § 11046 (Dec. 22, 2017).

Add at end of subsection.

For tax years beginning after 2012, individuals (other than nonresident aliens) are subject to the new 3.8% Medicare contribution tax, which is imposed on the lesser of (1) "net investment income" or (2) the excess of adjusted gross income (increased by net amounts excluded under § 911(a)(1)) over a threshold amount (i.e., $250,000 for joint return filers and $200,000 for single filers).[63.1] The term "net investment income" targets all sources of passive income, and is equal to the excess of:

1. The sum of (a) gross income from interest, dividends, annuities, royalties, and rents, other than such income derived in the ordinary course of a qualified trade or business, (b) all other gross income from a disqualified trade or business, and (c) taxable net gain attributable to the disposition of property that is not held in a qualified trade or business, over

2. The allowable deductions allocable to such gross income or net gain.[63.2]

A partnership interest is generally not considered "property held in a qualified trade or business" unless the partnership is engaged in a "qualified trade or business."[63.3] Self-employment income taxed under § 1401(b) is exempt from the Medicare contribution tax.[63.4]

"Qualified trades or businesses" generally include trades or businesses that are nonpassive in nature. A qualified trade or business is any trade or business defined as such for § 162 purposes, other than (1) any trade or business with respect to which the taxpayer is passive (within the meaning of § 469) and (2) any trade or business of trading in financial instruments or commodities (as defined in § 475(e)(2)), regardless of whether it is active or passive with respect to the taxpayer.[63.5]

[63.1] § 1411; REG-130507-11, 77 Fed. Reg. 72,612 (Dec. 5, 2012). Dispositions of partnership interests are addressed in Prop. Reg. § 1.1411-7 (2012). See ¶ 16.08[7].

[63.2] § 1411(c)(1); see Prop. Reg. § 1.1411-4(a) (2012). The statutory listing of portfolio income items would be expanded by the proposed regulations to include "substitute interest payments, and substitute dividend payments." Prop. Reg. § 1.1411-4(a)(1)(ii) (2012). Special rules are provided for (1) the timing of the inclusion in net investment income of income from any controlled foreign corporation (CFC) and any passive foreign investment company that a domestic partnership has elected to treat as a qualifying electing fund (QEF), (2) the determination of a partner's outside basis in his interest in a partnership that owns an interest in a CFC or QEF, (3) the computation of a partnership's adjusted basis in its CFC or QEF stock, and (4) conforming adjustments to the partners' modified adjusted gross income. Prop. Reg. § 1.1411-10 (2012).

[63.3] See Prop. Reg. § 1.1411-4(d)(3)(ii)(B)(1) (2012). Gain from the sale of a partnership interest is therefore generally included in net investment income except to the extent excluded under the look-through rule in § 1411(c)(4). See Prop. Reg. § 1.1411-7 (2012). See generally ¶ 16.08[7].

[63.4] § 1411(c)(6).

[63.5] § 1411(c)(2); see Prop. Reg. § 1.1411-5 (2012).

For partnership activities, the determination of whether an activity is "trading in financial instruments or commodities" is made at the entity level. For all other activities, passivity is tested, partner-by-partner, at the partner level.[63.6]

Application of the Medicare contribution tax to partners will require a variety of items to be separately stated by partnerships. Most of these (such as interest, dividends, annuities, royalties, and rents) are already required to be separately stated. However, a few items will need to be added to this list, including substitute interest payments and substitute dividend payments.[63.7] Multi-activity partnerships will need to allocate and separately state income and expense items relating to different activities if the activities may be subject to different rules at the partner level under § 1411.

The application of the self-employment tax to partners is discussed in ¶ 9.02[5][b]. Guaranteed payments to partners are subject to an entirely different set of rules, discussed in ¶ 14.03[6][b].

[63.6] Prop. Reg. § 1.1411-4(b)(2) (2012).

[63.7] Prop. Reg. § 1.1411-4(a)(1)(ii) (2012).

[4] Impact of Entity Concept on Characterization Issues

[a] Partnership-Level Characterization

Page 9-22:

Add to note 68.

The Service's partnership-level characterization view was strongly reaffirmed in Rev. Rul. 2008-39, 2008-31 IRB 252, in which it ruled that management fees paid by an upper-tier partnership (UTP) are § 212 expenses where UTP's activity consists of investing in lower-tier partnerships (LTPs) engaged in the business of trading securities. Management fees paid by the LTPs, however, are § 162 expenses, which retain their character as they flow up through UTP to its partners.

Page 9-23:

Add at end of subsection.

While the tax character and attributes partnership items must be determined at the partnership level, a partnership is not a sentient being capable forming intent. Therefore, when intent, motive, and purpose inform the tax character of an item, reference must be made to thoughts and intent of the human participants. In *Klamath Strategic Investment Fund v. United States*,[72.1] the Fifth Circuit generally disallowed the tax benefits of a partnership's operations because they lacked economic substance. However, the partnership had incurred certain expenses that would nevertheless be allowed as deductions if

---

[72.1] Klamath Strategic Investment Fund v. United States, 568 F3d 537 (5th Cir. 2009).

they had been incurred with legitimate investment intent. The court remanded the case to the district court to resolve the question of intent, declaring that the relevant intent is the intent of the individuals who control the partnership's activities.

On remand, the district court determined that the investors in the partnership were motivated by legitimate investment purposes, while the promoter who controlled day-to-day operations participated solely to produce a tax benefit.[72.2] The district court declared, "Anatomically speaking, control is the head and management is the hands." Since the investors were the "head," their motive controlled. Accordingly, the deductions for the expenses were allowed.

[72.2] Klamath Strategic Investment Fund, LLC v. United States, 110 AFTR2d 13627 (ED Tex. 2012), aff'd, 2014-1 USTC ¶ 50,199 (5th Cir. 2014).

[c] Entity and Aggregate Concepts in International Transactions

Page 9-26:

Add after first (and sole) paragraph of subsection.

The 2017 Tax Cuts and Jobs Act (2017 Act) added §§ 250 and 951A to the CFC regime.[88.1] These provisions provide domestic corporations with reduced rates of U.S. tax on their foreign-derived intangible income (FDII)[88.1a] and global intangible-low-taxed income (GILTI). Application of these provisions is dependent, in part, on the computation of qualified business asset investment (QBAI). In computing QBAI, a CFC that holds an interest in a partnership includes its distributive share of the aggregate of the partnership's adjusted bases in tangible property to the extent (1) the property is used in the trade or business of the partnership, (2) is of a type with respect to which a deduction is allowable under § 167, and (3) is used in the production of "tested income" (based on the CFC's distributive share of income with respect to the property). The CFC's distributive share of the adjusted basis of property is the CFC's distributive share of income with respect to the property.[88.2]

[88.1] 2017 Tax Cuts and Jobs Act, Pub. L. No. 115-97, §§ 14201, 14202 (Dec. 22, 2017), effective for tax years beginning after December 31, 2017.

[88.1a] Reg. § 1.250(b)-3(e)(1) provides that a partnership is a "person" for purposes of determining whether a sale of property or the provision of services to or by a partnership comes within the FDII rules. Thus, a sale of property to a foreign partnership for foreign use comes within the rules, whereas the same sale to a domestic partnership does not. This dichotomy is stark, since the status of a partnership as foreign or domestic is of little commercial significance.

[88.2] § 951A(d)(3), as amended. Note the apparent numbering error: there are two (d)(3)s. "Tested income" is defined in § 951A(c)(2)(A). Under Reg. § 1.951A-3(g)(4)(ii), a CFC's distributive share of a partnership's adjusted basis in partnership "specified tangible property" is based on its "proportionate share ratio." This ratio reflects the partner's share of depreciation. The preamble to the final Regulations asserts "that a partner's share of a depreciation deduction ... is a plausible proxy for determining a CFC's distributive

Domestic partnerships that own stock of CFCs present difficult computational problems. The GILTI inclusion amount is an aggregation of the U.S. shareholder's pro rata share of tested income, tested loss, QBAI, tested interest expense, and tested interest income of each of its CFCs. A partner is deemed to own its proportionate share of CFC stock owned by the partnership.[88.3] Thus, a partner can be a U.S. shareholder with respect to stock owned by a partnership and should therefore be entitled to aggregate its pro rata share of GILTI attributes from the partnership CFC with its other GILTI attributes from its other CFCs. On the other hand, a domestic partnership can itself be a U.S. shareholder even if one or more of its partners is not (an equal 50 percent partnership may own 10 percent of a CFC's stock even though neither of its partners does), in which case the partnership has a GILTI inclusion.

After considering a hybrid approach in proposed regulations (where the partnership is treated as an entity for shareholders that are not U.S. Shareholders of any CFC owned by the partnership, but is treated as an aggregate for all other shareholders), the Treasury Department opted instead for a full aggregate approach that looks through a domestic partnership and treats the partners as owning proportionately the stock of CFCs owned by the partnership. Throwing years of viewing domestic partnerships as entities under subpart F out the window, the Treasury declared that in the GILTI context, the 2017 Tax Act "fundamentally changed the policies relating to the taxation of CFC earnings relative to those in 1962."[88.4]

Rather than creating a whole new approach to aggregate taxation, Regulations § 1.951A-1(e)(1), like Proposed Regulations § 1.951-1(h) (2018), treats a domestic partnership in the same manner as a foreign partnership, thereby adopting "relatively well-developed" rules relating to aggregation. This treatment is intended to apply solely for purposes of § 951A and the § 951A regulations (as well as any other provision that applies by reference to a GILTI inclusion amount).

Thus, whether a partner is a U.S. shareholder with respect to a foreign corporation owned by a partnership is determined under an entity analysis, while that partner's share of GILTI income will be computed on an aggregate basis.[88.5] This principle is best illustrated by Example 2 of the regulations:

> USP, a domestic corporation, and Individual A, a United States citizen, own 90% and 10%, respectively, of PRS1, a domestic partnership. PRS1

---

share of income" and that this rule is necessary to "avoid uncertainty and controversy." TD 9866, Preamble at V.E. (June 19, 2019). This blatant departure from the statutory mandate is unlikely to withstand a well-articulated challenge, as seasoned subchapter K practitioners have little difficulty distinguishing a distributive share of income from depreciation.

[88.3] §§ 951(b) (United States shareholder defined), 958(b) (applying constructive ownership rules of § 318).

[88.4] TD 9866 (June 21, 2019).

[88.5] Regulations § 1.951A-1(e)(2).

and Individual B, a nonresident alien individual, own 90% and 10%, respectively, of PRS2, a domestic partnership. PRS2 owns 100% of the single class of stock of FC, a foreign corporation. USP, Individual A, and Individual B are unrelated to each other.[88.6]

Because PRS1 owns, indirectly, more than 50 percent of the total combined voting power of FC, it is considered to own 100 percent of the stock of FC entitled to vote under § 958(b)(2). Rather than looking through PRS1 and PRS2 and treating Individual A as indirectly owning 9 percent of FC (and thus avoiding status as a U.S. shareholder), A is treated as owning an indirect 10 percent interest in FC and is thus a U.S. shareholder for purposes of applying GILTI. However, for purposes of calculating A's share of GILTI items from FC, A is entitled to look through both partnerships and reflect her 9 percent share of tested items of FC.

This aggregate approach would be extended to subpart F in general by Proposed Regulations § 1.958-1(d) (2019) ("for purposes of section 951 and section 951A ... a domestic partnership is treated in the same manner as a foreign partnership ...."). Taxpayers may apply this rule retroactively to taxable years of a foreign corporation beginning after December 31, 2017.[88.7]

[88.6] Regulations § 1.951A-1(e)(3)(ii) (Example 2).

[88.7] Prop. Reg. § 1.958-1(d)(4) (2019).

[iii] The *Brown Group* Regulations.

[A] *Foreign personal holding company exception.*

Page 9-30:

Replace note 105 with the following.

[105] Reg. §§ 1.954-2(a)(5)(ii)(C), 1.954-2(a)(5)(iii) Example (2).

Page 9-32:

Replace ¶ 9.01[4][c][iii][D] with revised ¶ 9.01[4][c][iii][D].

[D] *Section 956 exception [revised].* The Regulations provide that, for purposes of § 956, where a CFC is a partner in a partnership that owns property that would be treated as "United States property" if owned directly by the CFC, the CFC is treated as holding an ownership interest in "United States property" equal to its ownership interest in the partnership.[111]

The amount of the investment is computed by reference to the partnership's inside basis in the relevant property, rather than to the CFC partner's

---

[111] Reg. § 1.956-2(a)(3).

outside basis in its partnership interest.[112] Ownership interest (for taxable years of a CFC ending on or after November 3, 2016, and for taxable years of United States shareholders in which or with which such taxable years end, with respect to property acquired on or after November 3, 2016) for a CFC partner in a partnership is generally treated as the portion of partnership property equal to the portion of the aggregate proceeds such partner would receive from the partnership in a partnership liquidation at fair market value (i.e., its "liquidation value percentage").[113] A CFC partner is required to recompute this portion (and hence, such partner's share of United States property) on each determination date. Determination dates include the formation of the partnership, the occurrence of any revaluation event described in Regulations § 1.704-1(b)(2)(iv)(f)(5) or § 1.704-1(b)(2)(iv)(s)(1) (regardless of whether the partnership's capital accounts are actually adjusted), or the first day of each taxable year (if any partner's portion would change by more than 10 percentage points from the last determination date).[113.1] Partnerships with special allocations relating to United States property are allowed to deviate from the general rule and utilize the partner's special allocation to determine such partner's share of the United States property, as long as the special allocation has substantial economic effect under § 704(b) and does not have a principal purpose of avoiding the purposes of § 956.[113.2]

The Regulations provide that the amount of United States property held indirectly by a CFC can be increased to include all property acquired by a partnership that is controlled by the CFC.[113.3] United States property will be treated as held indirectly by the CFC only if a principal purpose of creating, organizing, or funding (including through capital contributions or debt) the partnership is to avoid the application of § 956 with respect to the CFC.[113.4] This anti-avoidance rule applies only to the extent it would increase the amount of United States property that is treated as held by the CFC under Regulations § 1.956-4; however, a CFC does not have to include duplicative amounts of United States property as a result of a partnership obligation.[113.5]

> **EXAMPLE 9-0.1:** *P* is a domestic corporation that owns all of the stock of a foreign corporation, *FS1*. *FS1* has substantial earnings and profits. *P* and

---

[112] Reg. § 1.956-4(b)(1). Temporary and Proposed Regulations were issued in 2015, which were finalized on November 3, 2016.

[113] Reg. §§ 1.956-4(b)(1), 1.956-4 (f)(1).

[113.1] Reg. § 1.956-4(b)(2)(i)(B).

[113.2] Reg. § 1.956-4(b)(2)(ii). Under Proposed Regulations § 1.956-4(b)(2)(iii) (2016), the exception for special allocations would be turned off in the case of a partnership controlled by the partner. A partner is treated as controlling a partnership if they are related under § 267(b) or § 707(b), substituting "at least 80 percent" for "more than 50 percent."

[113.3] Reg. § 1.956-1(b)(1)(iii). For these purposes, control exists if the CFC and the partnership are related under § 267(b) or § 707(b). Reg. § 1.956-1(b)(2).

[113.4] Reg. § 1.956-1(b)(1)(iii).

[113.5] Reg. § 1.956-1(b)(3).

FS1 are the only partners in foreign partnership FPRS. *FS1* contributes $600 cash to FPRS for a 60 percent interest, and *P* contributes $400 of foreign real estate for a 40 percent interest. FPRS loans $100 to *P*. Under Regulations § 1.956-4(b), *FS1* is treated as holding United States property of $60. Under Regulations § 1.956-1(b), if a principal purpose of creating, organizing or funding FPRS is to avoid the application of § 956, *FS1* is considered to hold an additional $40 of United States property.

This rule applies to taxable years of a CFC ending on or after September 1, 2015, and to taxable years of United States shareholders in which or with which such taxable year ends, but only with respect to property acquired on or after September 1, 2015.[113.6]

The Regulations dramatically expand the application of § 956 to obligations of foreign partnerships. They adopt a strong aggregate approach by treating each partner as owning its share (measured by its liquidation value percentage) of an obligation of a foreign partnership.[113.7] This rule is called off if neither the CFC, nor any related person (under § 954(d)(3)), is a partner in the partnership. The scope of the application of § 956 to obligations of foreign partnerships is significantly expanded by a special "but for" rule (assuming the rule has not been called off). An obligation of a foreign partnership that is held[113.8] by a CFC is treated as a separate obligation of a partner when the foreign partnership distributes money or property to the partner and the foreign partnership would not have made the distribution but for a funding of the foreign partnership through the obligation. The amount treated as an obligation of the distributee partner is the lesser of the "but for" distribution or the amount of the obligation.[113.9]

EXAMPLE 9-0.2: *P*, a domestic corporation, owns *FS*, a CFC. *P* owns 70 percent of FPRS, a foreign partnership. An unrelated domestic corporation owns 30 percent of FPRS. FPRS borrows $100 from *FS* and distributes $80 to *P*. If FPRS would not have made the distribution "but for" the funding by *FS*, *FS* is considered to hold $80 of United States property.

The "but for" standard represents a significant hurdle for a taxpayer. In order to escape § 956 treatment with respect to an amount distributed by the foreign partnership to a partner, the partnership must have liquid assets sufficient to make the distribution determined immediately prior to the distribution.[113.10] Few affected partnerships are likely to pass this test.

[113.6] Reg. § 1.956-1(g)(2).

[113.7] Reg. § 1.956-4(c).

[113.8] Or, would be treated as "held" under Regulations § 1.956-2(c) (dealing with pledges and guarantees) if the obligation were an obligation of a United States person.

[113.9] Reg. § 1.956-4(c)(3)(i). An upper-tier partnership's share of an obligation of a lower-tier partnership is treated as an obligation of the upper-tier partnership in applying these rules. Reg. § 1.956-4(c)(1). The effective date provisions are in Reg. § 1.956-4(f).

[113.10] Reg. § 1.956-4(c)(3)(ii)(A).

This rule is applied in reverse chronological order to the extent that multiple obligations of the foreign partnership are incurred.[113.11]

Notably, a pure entity approach is applied to the obligations of a domestic partnership, which are treated as obligations of a United States person regardless of the status of its partners.[113.12]

[113.11] Reg. § 1.956-4(c)(3)(ii)(B).

[113.12] Reg. § 1.956-4(e).

[iv] Open issues relating to the *Brown Group* Regulations.

[C] *Aggregate versus entity.*

Page 9-34:

Add at end of subsection.

Notice 2009-7 describes a transaction involving the interposition of a U.S. partnership between first and second tier CFCs as a "transaction of interest."[117.1] Notice 2009-7 provides the following example.

> In a typical transaction, a U.S. taxpayer (Taxpayer) wholly owns two CFCs (*CFC1* and *CFC2*). *CFC1* and *CFC2* are partners in a domestic partnership (USPartnership). USPartnership owns 100% of the stock of another CFC (*CFC3*). Some or all of the income of *CFC3* is subpart F income (as defined in § 952). As part of the transaction, Taxpayer takes the position that the subpart F income of *CFC3* is currently included in the income of USPartnership (which is not subject to U.S. tax) and is not included in the income of Taxpayer. The result of the claimed tax treatment is that income that would otherwise be taxable currently to Taxpayer under subpart F of the Code is not taxable to Taxpayer because of the interposition of a domestic partnership in the CFC structure. Without the interposition of USPartnership, the § 951 (a) inclusion resulting from the subpart F income of *CFC3* would be taxable currently to Taxpayer. In some variations of the transaction, there may be more than one person that owns the stock of *CFC1* and/or *CFC2*, USPartnership may own less than all of the stock of *CFC3*, a domestic trust may be used instead of a domestic partnership, or the § 951 (a) inclusion amount may result from an amount determined under § 956.

Notice 2009-7 states that the Service is concerned that "taxpayers are taking the position that structures described in this notice result in no income inclusion to Taxpayer under section 951," and that "the IRS and Treasury Department believe that the position there is no income inclusion to Taxpayer under section 951 is contrary to the purpose and intent of the provisions of subpart F of the Code." The Notice, however, does not explain why the posi-

---

[117.1] Notice 2009-7, 2009-3 IRB 312.

tion is technically wrong, nor does it add the examined structure to the list of "listed" tax avoidance transactions within the meaning of Regulations § 1.6011-4(b)(3). Rather, the Notice simply treats the structure as a "transaction of interest."

While the position taken by taxpayers who adopt the structure may be viewed fairly as inconsistent with the intent and purpose of subpart F, this position is not so clearly contrary to the plain meaning of the Code. In the structure described by Notice 2009-7, USPartnership is a "United States shareholder," within the meaning of § 951(b), of *CFC3*, and is required by § 951(a) to include *CFC3*'s subpart F income in its gross income. However, USPartnership is not a taxpayer and, while *CFC1* and *CFC2* are partners of USPartnership, they are not "United States shareholders" of *CFC3* or subject to U.S. tax. The question then is whether the distributive shares of USPartnership's gross income inclusion under § 951(a) constitute subpart F income to its partners, *CFC1* and *CFC 2*, so that Taxpayer, as the owner of *CFC1* and *CFC2*, would itself have to include such amounts under § 951(a). *CFC1*'s and *CFC2*'s distributive shares of § 951(a) gross income do not fit well into the § 952 definition of "subpart F income," because § 951(a) does not preserve the § 952 character of *CFC3*'s items of subpart F income.

Of course, applying a pure aggregate approach—ignoring the partnership—would resolve subpart F policy concerns identified in Notice 2009-7, but would be hard to square with the fact that subpart F clearly adopts an entity approach, which treats USPartnership as a "United States person." For example, suppose *FC* (a foreign corporation) and *DC* (a domestic corporation unrelated to *FC*) form a U.S. partnership (*USPS*), with *FC* owning a 60% interest and *DC* owning a 40% interest. *USPS* owns all of the stock of a foreign corporation (*FS*). Section 7701(a)(30), which is incorporated into subpart F, by § 957(c), defines the term "United States person" to include a "domestic partnership." Therefore, *USPS* is a "United States shareholder," as defined by § 951(b), and, because *USPS* owns all of the stock of *FS*, *FS* is a CFC. (Under an aggregate approach, *USPS* would be ignored and *FS* would not be a CFC, because it would be owned only 40% by a "United States shareholder.") Accordingly, under § 951(a), *USPS* must include *FS*'s subpart F income in its gross income and *DC* must include its 40% distributive share of *USPS*'s § 951(a) income.

The point of this example is that subpart F expressly adopts an entity approach that treats a domestic partnership as a "United States person" and, as a result, *DC* must include its distributive share of *USPS*'s subpart F income even though, under an aggregate approach, *FS* would not be a CFC. (If *USPS* could be ignored, *DC* and *FC* would be treated as directly owning *FS*, and, therefore, *FS* would not be a *CFC* because "United States shareholders" would own less than 50% of *FS*.) It is difficult to rationalize an argument under the existing statutory scheme that simultaneously recognizes and ignores a partnership for subpart F purposes.

In Notice 2010-41, 2010-22 IRB 1, the Service announced that it would issue Regulations classifying domestic partnerships used in these structures as foreign solely for the limited purpose of identifying the United States shareholders of a controlled foreign corporation. Foreign classification will occur under these Regulations if (1) the partnership is a United States shareholder of a foreign corporation that is a CFC (within the meaning of § 957(a) or §953(c)) (the "Subsidiary CFC") and (2) if the partnership were treated as foreign, (a) the Subsidiary CFC would continue to be a CFC and (b) at least one United States shareholder of the Subsidiary CFC would be (i) treated under § 958(a) as indirectly owning stock of the Subsidiary CFC and (ii) required to include an amount in gross income under § 951(a) with respect to the Subsidiary CFC. The Regulations will provide similar results in the case of tiered-partnership structures.

While treating a domestic partnership as a foreign partnership may correct the concern noted in Notice 2009-7, the Service's authority to so treat the partnership appears to be limited, under § 7701(a)(4), to situations where regulations have actually been issued. Notice 2010-41, however, purports to be effective for taxable years of domestic partnerships ending on or after May 14, 2010.[117.2]

[117.2] See Jackel, "IRS Notice Wrongly Treats Domestic Partnership as Foreign," 2010 TNT 105-5 (June 2, 2010).

Page 9-34:

Add new ¶¶ 9.01[4][c][v]– 9.01[4][c][ix].

[v] Section 954(c)(6) [new]. Section 954(c)(6) provides that dividends, interest, rents, and royalties received by one CFC from a related CFC will not be subpart F income to the extent properly allocable to the related CFC's non-subpart F income. The application of these rules to CFCs that are partners in partnerships is governed by Regulations §§ 1.954-2(b)(4)(i)(B) and 1.954-2(b)(5)(i)(B).[117.3] These Regulations apply § 704(b) principles to determine the amount which a corporate partner will be treated as paying or receiving with respect to the item in question.

[vi] Partnership blocker structures [new]. Proposed Regulations § 1.951-1(h) (2018) treats a controlled domestic partnership as a foreign partnership for purposes of determining the ownership of the stock of a CFC in certain cases when necessary to prevent avoidance of Subpart F. The classic case, illustrated in the proposed regulations, is a U.S. parent corporation (USP) which owns two CFCs (CFC1 and CFC2), which in turn are 60/40 partners in DPS, a domestic partnership. DPS owns all the stock of CFC3. Absent the proposed regulation (authorized by § 7701(a)(4)), DPS would have a § 951(a)

[117.3] Notice 2007-9, 2007-5 IRB 401.

inclusion, but USP would not (CFC1 and CFC2 have a distributive share of DPS's § 951(a) inclusion, but this does not create Subpart F income at the CFC1 and CFC2 level). Treating DPS as a foreign partnership makes USP a U.S. shareholder of CFC3 under the attribution rules of § 958. Blocker structures were considered sufficiently abusive such that the 2018 proposed regulations are retroactively applied to taxable years of domestic partnership ending on or after May 14, 2010. Proposed Regulations issued in 2019 clarify that the treatment of a domestic partnership as a foreign partnership applies with respect to all partners (not just a specific U.S. shareholder). Prop. Reg. § 1.951-1(h)(2) (2019).

[vii] **Aggregate approach to the base erosion and anti-abuse tax (BEAT) [new].** To reduce erosion of the U.S. tax base, Congress enacted a tax on certain deductible payments made by corporations to foreign related parties. Section 59A, titled "Tax on base erosion payments of taxpayers with substantial gross receipts," imposes this base erosion and anti-abuse tax (BEAT). In general, BEAT is a tax on certain corporate taxpayers, and is paid in addition to any other federal income tax liabilities imposed on the corporations to which BEAT applies. While BEAT does not apply to partnerships as such, Regulations § 1.59A-7 generally adopts an aggregate approach for purposes of BEAT. This aggregate approach is limited to BEAT computations; Subchapter K continues to operate as usual outside of § 59A.

A corporation to which BEAT applies is referred to as an "applicable taxpayer."[117.4] An applicable taxpayer is a corporation other than an S corporation, a REIT, or a RIC, with average annual gross receipts of $500 million over the preceding three taxable years, and whose "base erosion percentage" is at or above a specified percentage (either 3 percent or, in the case of certain affiliated group members, 2 percent).[117.5]

In general, the additional tax is the excess of 10 percent of the applicable taxpayer's "modified taxable income," over the taxpayer's regular tax liability with some adjustments.[117.6] In general, modified taxable income is an applicable taxpayer's regular taxable income increased by "base erosion tax benefits" taken into account in computing regular taxable income.[117.7] Base erosion tax benefits are deductions attributable to payments made to foreign persons who are related to the applicable taxpayer.[117.8]

As noted above, BEAT does not apply to partnerships. Instead, partnerships are treated as aggregates for purposes of applying BEAT to applicable taxpayers.[117.9] In general, this means that a partner who is an applicable tax-

---

[117.4] § 59A(e).
[117.5] § 59A(e).
[117.6] § 59A(b).
[117.7] § 59A(c).
[117.8] § 59A(c)(2).
[117.9] Reg. § 1.59A-7.

payer is treated as directly receiving its distributive share of partnership gross income and as directly paying or incurring its distributive share of partnership expenses, depreciation, and amortization. Aggregate principles also apply to determine those persons who are related parties to an applicable person.

A series of examples illustrates the application of the BEAT rules to partnership transactions. It is helpful to keep in mind the conceptual underpinnings of these rules:

1. No netting is permitted. The measurement of a base erosion payment is made on a gross basis.[117.9a]
2. The aggregate approach is applied strictly and literally. Thus, base erosion payments can arise from property transfers.
3. The measurement of the base erosion tax benefit is based on a partner's distributive share of any deduction or reduction in gross receipts attributable to a base erosion payment.[117.9b]

In Example 1,[117.9c] a domestic corporation (DC) and a related foreign corporation (FC) each contribute depreciable property with a basis and value of $100 to the equal PRS partnership. DC is treated as making a base erosion payment to FC of 50 percent of the property DC contributed to PRS and the base erosion tax benefit is the depreciation allocable to DC on the property contributed by FC. The fact that DC gives up half of the depreciation on the property it contributed to PRS is ignored. If FC's contributed property has a basis of only $40 and PRS adopts the remedial method under Reg. § 1.704-3(d), the base erosion tax benefit includes the remedial deduction.[117.9d] If DC purchases a partnership interest from FC, DC is treated as purchasing FC's share of the depreciable property of PRS. The base erosion tax benefit is any depreciation from the deemed purchased property, which drives off of FC's share of PRS's basis in the property, increased by any § 743(b) basis adjustment available to DC.[117.9e] Tiered partnerships are treated on a look-through basis.[117.9f] A distribution from PRS to FC that reduces FC's partnership interest and increases DC's interest creates a base erosion payment from DC to FC (again, pure aggregate treatment), such that the depreciation attributable to DC's increased share of PRS property, plus DC's share of any concomitant § 734(b) basis adjustment, constitute base erosion tax benefits.[117.9g] Similar principles apply to distributions of PRS property to DC. Any reduction in DC's share of PRS property is treated as a base erosion payment, and the base erosion tax benefit is the sum of DC's share of any depreciation on FC's historic

---

[117.9a] Reg. § 1.59A-3(b)(2)(iii).

[117.9b] Reg. §§ 1.59A-7(d)(1), 1.59A-7(e)(1).

[117.9c] Reg. § 1.59A-7(g)(2)(i).

[117.9d] Reg. § 1.59A-7(g)(2)(ii) Example 2.

[117.9e] Reg. §§ 1.59A-7(g)(2)(iii), 1.59A-7(g)(2)(iv) Examples 3, 4.

[117.9f] Reg. § 1.59A-7(g)(2)(vi) Example 6.

[117.9g] Reg. § 1.59A-7(g)(2)(vii) Example 7.

basis in the distributed property, plus any § 732(b) basis increase to FC's historic share of such property.[117.9h]

The Regulations make clear that curative allocations under Regulations § 1.704-3(c) can give rise to base erosion tax benefits,[117.9i] and add the seemingly mandatory anti-abuse rules to deal with transactions involving derivatives and abusive allocations.[117.9j]

The decision to apply a pure aggregate approach with no netting in applying the BEAT rules can produce strange results in transactions governed by Revenue Ruling 99-5, 1999-1 CB 434. Assume a U.S. corporation (DC) sells to a related foreign corporation (FC) a 50 percent interest in a disregarded entity whose sole asset is depreciable property. Under Revenue Ruling 99-5, FC is treated as purchasing a 50 percent interest in the depreciable property and then FC and DC contribute the property to an equal partnership. The contribution by DC is a base erosion payment, and the depreciation on the property deemed contributed by FC is a base erosion tax benefit. The deemed transaction falls squarely within Example 1. That a sale of property can give rise to a "payment" resulting in a base erosion tax benefit suggests something is awry.

A corporate taxpayer may elect to forgo allowable deductions that would otherwise constitute base erosion tax benefits (BEAT waiver election).[117.9k] Any deduction waived pursuant to a BEAT waiver election is waived for all U.S. federal income tax purposes.[117.9l] A corporate partner (not the partnership) may make a BEAT waiver election with respect to its distributive share of partnership deductions.[117.9m] Waived deductions are treated as non-deductible expenditures for purposes of § 705(a)(2)(B) and thus reduce the tax basis of the corporate partner's interest in the partnership.[117.9n] Waived deductions may also increase the corporate partner's § 163(j) limitation computation.[117.9o]

[viii] Determining passive foreign investment company status and ownership of stock [new]. Sections 1291 through 1298 set forth special tax regimes for U.S. persons that are shareholders of a passive foreign investment company (PFIC). In general, a foreign corporation is classified as a PFIC if either (a) 75 percent or more of its gross income for a taxable year is passive, or (b) the average percentage of assets held by the foreign corporation during a taxable year that produce (or are held for production of) passive income is at least 50 percent.[117.10] For purposes of applying the asset test, a foreign corpora-

---

[117.9h] Reg. § 1.59A-7(g)(2)(viii) Example 8.

[117.9i] Reg. §§ 1.59A-7(c)(5)(v), 1.59A-7(g)(2)(x) Example 10.

[117.9j] Reg. §§ 1.59A-9(b)(5), 1.59A-9(b)(6).

[117.9k] Reg. § 1.59A-3(c)(6).

[117.9l] Reg. § 1.59A-3(c)(6)(iii).

[117.9m] Reg. § 1.59A-3(c)(6)(iv)(A).

[117.9n] Reg. § 1.59A-3(c)(6)(iv)(B).

[117.9o] Reg. § 1.59A-3(c)(6)(iv)(C).

[117.10] § 1297(a).

tion that owns at least 25 percent of the value of all interests in a partnership is treated as owning its proportionate share of the assets of the partnership.[117.11] In general, a corporation's proportionate share of a partnership asset is treated as producing passive income, or being held to produce passive income, to the extent the asset produced, or was held to produce, passive income in the partnership's hands, taking into account only the partnership's activities.[117.12] If a foreign corporation owns less than 25 percent of the value of all interests in a partnership, the partnership interest is treated as a passive asset.[117.13]

Section 1298(a)(3) provides that stock owned directly or indirectly by a partnership is treated as owned proportionately by the partners if the effect of such attribution is to treat stock of a PFIC as owned by a U.S. person. Under § 1298(a)(2)(A), if 50 percent or more of the stock of a corporation is owned, directly or indirectly by or for any person, that person is considered to own the stock owned directly or indirectly by the corporation in proportion to the person's ownership of the corporation. Stock considered to be owned by attribution is treated as directly owned by a person to whom ownership is attributed, and the attribution rules are applied by successively treating a person as actually owning its proportionate share of stock directly held by an entity directly owned by the person.[117.14]

> **EXAMPLE 9-4.1:** *A*, a U.S. citizen, owns 50 percent of the interests in Foreign Partnership, the remainder of which is owned by an unrelated foreign person. Foreign Partnership owns 100 percent of the stock of FC1 and 50 percent of the stock of FC2, the remainder of which is owned by an unrelated foreign person. Both FC1 and FC2 are foreign corporations that are not PFICs. FC1 and FC2 each own 50 percent of the stock of FC3, a foreign corporation that is a PFIC.
>
> Under Regulations § 1.1291-1(b)(8), for purposes of determining whether *B* is a shareholder of FC3, *B* is considered to actually own 50 percent of the stock of FC1 and 25 percent of the stock of FC2. *B* is then considered to own 25 percent of the stock of FC3 indirectly through FC1, and thus is a shareholder of FC3 for purposes of the PFIC provision. Because *B* is considered to own less than 50 percent of FC2, *B* is not considered to own any stock of FC3 indirectly through FC2.

[ix] Passive character for foreign tax credit purposes [new]. Generally, a partner's distributive share of partnership income is characterized as passive income to the extent it is passive at the partnership level.[117.15] However, a limited partner that owns less than 10 percent of the value of a partnership

---

[117.11] Reg. §§ 1.1297-2(g)(4), 1.1297-2(b)(3).

[117.12] Reg. § 1.1297-2(b)(3).

[117.13] Reg. § 1.1297-1(d)(4).

[117.14] Reg. § 1.1291-1(b)(8).

[117.15] Reg. § 1.904-4(n)(1)(i).

treats the entire distributive share as passive.[117.16] Value is measured as "10 percent of the capital and profits interest of the partnership," and is determined at the end of the partnership's taxable year.[117.17]

[117.16] Reg. § 1.904-4(n)(1)(ii).
[117.17] Reg. § 1.904-4(n)(3).

[5] Distinguishing Partnership Items from Partner Items

Page 9-37:

Add to note 128.

For individual partners, the distinction between § 162 as opposed to § 212 treatment is accentuated by the 2017 Tax Cuts and Jobs Act, which replaces the 2-percent floor in § 67 with a flat denial of all "miscellaneous itemized deductions" (a phrase that includes § 212 deductions) by individuals for tax years beginning after December 31, 2017, and before January 1, 2026. Pub. L. No. 115-97, § 11045 (Dec. 22, 2017).

In note 129, add the following after first sentence (ending with the citation of Theodore G. Arens).

See Rev. Rul. 2008-39, 2008-31 IRB 252 (strict partnership level analysis, characterizing *Butler* as involving unreimbursed payment by partner on behalf of partnership).

[6] Accounting Methods

Page 9-39:

In second paragraph of subsection, replace second sentence with the following.

The limitation does not apply to any farming business (within the meaning of § 263A(e)(4))[139] or to any entity that had no more than $25 million (adjusted for post−2018 inflation) in average annual gross receipts (excluding returns and allowances) for the three-year period ending with each such prior taxable year.[140]

---

[139] §§ 448(b)(1), 448(d)(1).

[140] §§ 448(b)(3), 448(c)(1). For purposes of applying the three-year rule, an entity not in existence for the entire three-year period applies this rule with reference to its term of existence (§ 448(c)(3)(A)), and gross receipts for any short taxable year are annualized (§ 446(c)(3)(B)). Gross receipts of certain related entities are aggregated for purposes of the "$25-million rule." § 448(c)(2).

Page 9-40:

Add to note 142.

The performance of services in these fields has been broadly defined without regard to local licensure requirements. See, e.g., Kraatz & Craig Surveying Inc., 134 TC 167 (2010) (surveyor performs engineering services even though not a licensed engineer); Rainbow

Tax Service Inc., 128 TC 42 (2007) (tax return preparation and bookkeeping services performed by non-CPAs are accounting services).

In note 144, replace Rev. Proc. 84-74, 1984-2 CB 736, *with* Rev. Proc. 2011-14, 2011-4 IRB 330.

[7] Elections

Add to note 163.

See also Robert W. Parker, 104 TCM 823 (2012) (§ 453 election out ineffective, despite the partnership's intent, where election not actually made).

Page 9-43:

Replace list item 11 with the following.

    11. The election to capitalize organizational expenses under § 709(b);[166]

---

   [166] Reg. § 1.709-1(c).

Page 9-44:

Add list item 18 (following note callout 172).

    18. The election by a domestic partnership to treat a passive foreign investment company as a qualified electing fund.[172.1]

   [172.1] Reg. § 1.1295-1(d)(2).

Page 9-45:

Add new list item 5 (following note callout 178).

    5. The election under § 59(e) to write off certain tax preferences over ten years.[178.1]

   [178.1] § 59(e)(4)(C).

[8] Effects of Partnership Ownership: Entity Versus Aggregate Treatment

[d] Foreign Corporations

Page 9-48:

Add to note 201.

Temporary Regulations, issued in late 2007, conform the rules of § 904 to this principle. These Temporary Regulations treat gain from the sale of a partnership interest by a partner who owns 25% or more of the partnership as general category, as opposed to passive, income for purposes of § 904. Temp. Reg. § 1.904-5T(o)(3)(ii) (2007).

[e] Private Activity Bonds

Page 9-49:

Add the following at end of subsection.

This ruling is consistent with Proposed Regulations under § 141 that would treat a partnership comprised wholly of "governmental persons" as "disregarded" for purposes of determining whether a partnership's bond is a private activity bond under § 141. If any of the partners is nongovernmental, however, the partnership would be treated as a separate entity that is a nongovernmental person for these purposes.[207.1]

[207.1] Prop. Reg. § 1.141-1 (2006).

Page 9-49:

Add new ¶¶ 9.01[8][f], 9.01[8][g], and 9.01[8][h].

[f] Section 311(e) Election [New]

Prior law provided individuals with a special 18 percent capital gains rate for certain property held for more than five years. Section 311(e) of the Taxpayer Relief Act of 1997 was a transition rule that allowed noncorporate taxpayers an election to treat an asset as sold and reacquired on the same date in order to restart the asset's holding period so as to come within the effective date of the special 18 percent rate provision. The Service has ruled privately that a partnership is not eligible to make this election if all of its partners are corporations.[207.2] Since a partnership is a noncorporate taxpayer, the Service's position, while technically deficient, is entirely consistent with the purpose of the election.

[207.2] Priv. Ltr. Rul. 200701030 (Sept. 29, 2006).

[g] Trust Classification [New]

An "investment" trust is not classified as a trust for tax purposes if there is a power under the trust agreement to vary the investments of the beneficiaries.[207.3] The Service has taken the position that a trust that holds an interest in a partnership is not a trust for tax purposes where the partnership has the power to vary the partnership's investments.[207.4] This position was taken under

---

[207.3] Reg. § 301.7701-4(c); Commissioner v. North Am. Bond Trust, 122 F2d 545 (2d Cir. 1941).

[207.4] AM 2007-005 (Feb. 5, 2007).

facts indicating that the trust had no investment power at all, but the partnership was apparently controlled by a subset of the trust's beneficiaries. If the partnership was managed by unrelated third parties, one would think that the trust would be classified as a trust for tax purposes, although the Service's position on this point is unclear.

[h] Cooperatives [New]

The Service has taken the position that a cooperative that is a partner in an LLC treated as a partnership for federal income tax purposes cannot treat the partnership as an aggregate for purposes of applying the special rules applicable to cooperatives.[207.5]

[207.5] LAFA 20150801F (Apr. 22, 2014).

[10] Partnership as a "Person" or "Taxpayer"

Page 9-50:

Replace note 212 with the following.

[212] United States v. Galletti, 541 US 114 (2004) (unpaid employment tax properly assessed against partnership need not also be assessed against general partners liable under state law; "it is the tax that is assessed, not the taxpayer"; Service has ten years from date of assessment against partnership to collect tax from partners under § 6502). See CCN 2005-003 (Jan. 19, 2005) (*Galletti* does not affect Service's long-standing practice of collecting unpaid partnership employment taxes from general partners based on their state law liability). See also Priv. Ltr. Rul. 8443084 (July 25, 1984).

¶ 9.02 TREATMENT OF SPECIFIC ITEMS OF INCOME, GAIN, LOSS, DEDUCTION, AND CREDIT

[1] Gains and Losses

[a] Capital Asset Status: The Dealer Issue

Page 9-52:

Add to note 224.

See also CCA 201423019 (Jan. 22, 2014) (partnership's status as dealer in securities not attributable to partner).

[c] Like-Kind Exchanges: Section 1031

[i] In general.

Page 9-55:

Add to note 235.

The need for the § 1031(a)(2)(D) exclusion of partnership interests (as well as several of the other exclusions in former § 1031(a)(2)) has been obviated by the requirement, effective for exchanges after 2017, that qualifying property must be "real property." 2017 Tax Cuts and Jobs Act, Pub. L. No. 115-97, § 13303 (Dec. 22, 2017). See § 1031(a)(1); Prop. Reg. § 1.1031(a)-3(a) (2020) (definition of real property).

Add the following after first paragraph of subsection.

For exchanges after 2017, the scope of § 1031 was narrowed by the 2017 Tax Cuts and Jobs Act: "qualifying property" is now limited to *real property* held for productive use in a trade or business or for investment that is not held primarily for sale.[235.1]

[235.1] §§ 1031(a)(1), 1031(a)(2). See Prop. Reg. § 1.1031(a)-3(a) (2020) (definition of real property). For this purpose, an interest in a partnership that has a § 761(a) election in effect is treated as direct interests in the assets (including real estate) owned by the partnership. § 1031(e), as amended by the 2017 Jobs and Tax Cut Act, Pub. L. No. 115-97, § 13303 (Dec. 22, 2017). In connection with deferred exchanges of real property, Proposed Regulations would allow the tax-free receipt of "incidental personal property" of the type typically transferred with the real property with a value not to exceed 15 percent of the replacement real property. Prop. Reg. § 1.1031(k)-1(g)(7)(iii) (2020).

[v] Exchanges involving partnership interests.

Page 9-61:

Replace first (and sole) paragraph of subsection with the following.

Section 1031(a)(2)(D) provides that § 1031(a) does not apply to any exchange of "interests in a partnership."[254.1] There are two exceptions to this exclusion, however. One exception is statutory: Where a partnership has made a valid § 761(a) election to be excluded from all of the provisions of Subchapter K, the last sentence of § 1031(a)(2) provides that interests in the partnership are treated as direct interests in partnership assets, rather than as partnership interests, for purposes of § 1031(a). The other exception is based on case law and supported by the Service in a 1984 revenue ruling: Where the acquisition of a partnership interest results in the acquirer owning all of the outstanding partnership interests, the acquirer is treated as acquiring an interest in partnership assets directly.[254.2] Additionally, although interests in the same partnership can-

---

[254.1] While § 1031(a)(2)(D) was removed from the Code by the 2017 Jobs and Tax Cuts Act, the exclusion of partnership interests remains as a consequence of the new limitation, created by this Act, and so limiting the scope of § 1031 to exchanges of "real property." Pub. L. No. 115-97, § 13303 (Dec. 22, 2017).

[254.2] See Priv. Ltr. Rul. 200807005 (Nov. 9, 2007).

not be exchanged tax-free under § 1031(a), the Service has ruled that similar results can be obtained under §§ 721 and 731.[255]

---

[255] Rev. Rul. 84-52, 1984-1 CB 157.

[B] Interests in partnerships that cease to exist.

Page 9-62:

Delete last paragraph of subsection (including notes 259 and 260).

[vi] Section 1031 planning.

Page 9-62:

Replace heading of ¶ 9.02[1][c][vi][A] with the following revised heading.

[A] Planning to avoid the real property requirement [revised heading].

Replace first paragraph of subsection with the following.

It is not uncommon for a partner to be interested in exchanging his partnership interest for either an interest in a different partnership or a direct ownership interest in other property. Conversely, a person who owns a direct interest in property may be interested in exchanging it for a partnership interest. If undertaken directly, all of these exchanges would run afoul of the real property requirement, and thus would be fully taxable. What can be done to turn these transactions into exchanges that will qualify for nonrecognition under § 1031 or some other nonrecognition provision? Many different approaches to nonrecognition treatment are possible. Two of the more promising are as follows:

[C] The "held for" doctrine.

Page 9-65:

Replace last sentence of subsection with the following.

Despite rejection of the doctrine by the Ninth Circuit and the Tax Court,[269] the Service does not appear to have entirely backed off its position,[270] although it has ruled privately that neither a contribution to a disregarded entity, nor a distribution from a trust, violates the "held for" requirement.[271]

---

[269] Magneson v. Commissioner, 753 F2d 1490 (9th Cir. 1985), aff'g 81 TC 767 (1983) (post-exchange contribution of replacement property to a partnership does not violate "held for" requirement). Taxpayers should not rely too heavily upon *Magneson.* The Ninth Circuit rejected the application of the step-transaction doctrine to the facts, noting that, even if the transaction was collapsed into an exchange of a fee interest for a partnership interest, the exchange would still satisfy § 1031. Now that the real property limitation in § 1031(a) precludes the like-kind exchange of partnership interests, it is unclear whether the taxpayer would have prevailed in *Magneson.* See also Bolker v. Commissioner, 760 F2d 1039 (9th Cir. 1985), aff'g 81 TC 782 (1983) (exchange of property by shareholder after receiving it in distribution from corporation did not violate "held for" requirement); Bonny B. Maloney, 93 TC 89 (1989) (exchange by closely held corporation, followed by liquidating distribution of replacement property; no violation of "held for" requirement).

[270] See Priv. Ltr. Rul. 200521002 (Feb. 24 2005) (§ 1031 exchange by testamentary trust valid, despite trust's required termination at a later date, distributing the replacement property; trust not acquiring property "in order to dispose of the property pursuant to a prearranged plan").

[271] Priv. Ltr. Rul. 200651030 (Sept. 19, 2006) (contribution of § 1031 exchange rights to wholly owned LLC by trust followed by distribution of LLC interests to beneficiaries in termination of trust interests; § 1031 applies because LLC is "functionally a continuation of the Trust."); Priv. Ltr. Rul. 200131014 (May 2, 2001) (contribution of replacement property to disregarded entity does not violate "held for" requirement). See also Priv. Ltr. Rul. 200812012 (§ 708(b)(1)(B) termination (prior law) of partnership in the midst of a § 1031 exchange will not preclude identified replacement property from being held for investment or for the productive use in a trade or business).

Add new ¶ 9.02[1][d].

[d] Carried Interests: Conversion of Long-Term Capital Gain to Short-Term Capital Gain—Section 1061 [New]

[i] Statutory enactment and interpretation. Service providers who receive partnership profits interests ("carried interests") generally are not taxed upon the receipt of their interests.[271.1] To the extent the partnership subsequently generates long-term capital gains that are allocated to a service provider holding a carried interest, the overall fortuitous tax effect for the service provider is to convert what is arguably service income into long-term capital gains. The apparent unfairness of this result relative to the manner in which

---

[271.1] Rev. Proc. 93-27, 1993-2 CB 343; Rev. Proc. 2001-43, 2001-2 CB 191, discussed in ¶ 5.02[7].

most service income is taxed has been highlighted in recent years by the increasing aggregation of large pools of capital in investment vehicles (taxable
as partnerships) managed by groups of individuals whose compensation may
be measured as a percentage of the gains realized by the vehicles. Thus, for
example, the manager of a venture capital fund may receive 20 percent of the
fund's gains as compensation for managing the fund as well as selecting, managing, and arranging for the liquidation of its investments. While the compensation is entirely dependent upon appreciation of the fund's investments—the
hallmark of capital gains taxation—the connection between services provided
and low tax rates resulted in an optically displeasing result for many tax ob-
servers.

After many years of debate, Congress took a tenuous baby-step toward
addressing this disparity by enacting § 1061 as part of the 2017 Tax Cuts and
Jobs Act.[271.2] Section 1061 extends the long-term holding period for certain
capital gains from one year to three years, thereby creating at least the possibility of a reduced rate disparity with regard to the income of fund managers if
the holding period of the fund's investments is less than three years.[271.3] Unfortunately, it seems likely the three-year period will become both an obvious target for managers seeking to optimize their after-tax income and a source of
conflict between managers and investors.

While the purpose and consequence of § 1061 are relatively simple to articulate, the drafters had considerable difficulty with the details of separating
the lambs' (investors') gains (subject to the usual one-year holding period)
from the wolves' (service providers') gains (subject to the extended holding
period requirement). The result is a series of intricately intertwined, and surprisingly ambiguous rules and definitions, that start with an admission of de-
feat: to wit, § 1061(b) grants regulatory authority to the Treasury to make sure
that the three-year rule does not apply to income or gain that is not related to
portfolio investments made on behalf of third-party investors.[271.4]

The ambiguity of § 1061 begins with its "general rule":

[271.2] 2017 Tax Cuts and Jobs Act, Pub. L. No. 115-97, § 13309(a)(2) (Dec. 22, 2017),
effective for tax years beginning after December 31, 2017.

[271.3] There are many types of investment vehicles in place today, and new types are
being developed at a rapid pace. Section 1061 does not create a level playing field for different types of funds. At the risk of oversimplification: (1) hedge funds, which generally
hold investments for less than 12 months, are not likely to be affected by § 1061; (2) private equity funds typically hold investments for more than three years are also not likely
to be affected; and (3) only other types of funds, including activist funds, are likely to be
impacted.

[271.4] "Third-party investor" is defined in § 1061(c)(5) as a holder of an interest in the
partnership that is not held in connection with an applicable trade or business, and who is
not (and has not been) an active service provider or related (within the meaning of §
318(a)(1)) to an active service provider. See also § 1061(d)(2). Also note that § 1061(b) is
limited to "subsection (a)" rather than the entirety of § 1061, leaving open the question of
how it might affect the application of § 1061(d).

IN GENERAL.—If one or more applicable partnership interests are held by a taxpayer at any time during the taxable year, the excess (if any) of—

> (1) the taxpayer's net long-term capital gain with respect to such interests for such taxable year, over
>
> (2) the taxpayer's net long-term capital gain with respect to such interests for such taxable year computed by applying paragraphs (3) and (4) of sections 1222 by substituting "3 years" for "1 year", shall be treated as short-term capital gain, notwithstanding section 83 or any election in effect under section 83(b).

The most basic question relates to the scope of § 1061(a): What is the intent of the phrase "net long-term capital gain with respect to such interests"? On its face, the answer is straightforward: substitute "3 years" for "1 year" whenever an asset's holding period is relevant. Thus if a taxpayer has a distributive share of capital gain with respect to an applicable partnership interest, its status as long or short term is determined using a three-year period for the partnership, regardless of the partner's holding period for its interest.[271.4a] Similarly, capital gain or loss with respect to the disposition of the interest (including § 731(a) gain from partnership distributions) is long or short term based on the partner's holding period for the interest. Holding periods are determined under the usual rules.

The first conclusion (that the partnership's holding period governs) is consistent with the House Ways and Means Committee Report: If the holder of an applicable partnership interest is allocated gain from the sale of property held for less than three years, that gain is treated as short-term capital gain and is subject to tax at the rates applicable to ordinary income."[271.5]

The second conclusion (that the long/short-term character of gain from the disposition of a partnership interest is determined by the holding period of the interest) is less certain. Section 1061(d) provides special rules for transfers of applicable interests to related persons. Section 1061(d)(1) states that:

> [T]he taxpayer shall include in gross income (as short term capital gain) the excess (if any) of (A) so much of the taxpayer's long-term capital gains with respect to such interest for such taxable year attributable to the sale or exchange of any asset held for not more than 3 years as is allocable to such interest, over (B) any amount treated as short term capital gain under subsection (a) with respect to the transfer of such interest.

Clause (B) (aka the rule against double-counting[271.6]), provides that there can be an amount treated as short-term gain under § 1061(a) "with respect to

---

[271.4a] Rev. Rul. 68-79, 1968-1 CB 310.

[271.5] HR Rep No 409, 115th Cong., 1st Sess., "Report of House Ways & Means Comm. on HR 1," at 277 (2017).

[271.6] HR Rep No. 466, 115th Cong., 1st Sess., "Conference Report to Accompany HR 1," at 422 (2017).

the transfer of such interest." Therefore § 1061(a) must encompass gains from transfers.

The computation required by § 1061(d)(1) appears to require a look-through approach akin to that of § 751(a). The long-term gain from the transfer of the interest is apparently reduced by the portion of the gain attributable to partnership assets held by the partnerships for less than three years.[271.6a] Since the partial look-through approach of § 1061(d) is limited to related-party transfers, it suggests that an entity approach should prevail in all other cases.

Regulations proposed in 2020 would adopt a look-through approach to the transfer of partnership interests subject to § 1061(d). These regulations are addressed in more depth below.

An "applicable partnership interest"[271.7] is a partnership interest that is, directly or indirectly, transferred to (or held by) the taxpayer in connection with the performance of services in any "applicable trade or business." The services that taint the interest may be performed by the taxpayer or by anyone related to the taxpayer in any applicable trade or business.[271.8] An applicable partnership interest does not include any interest that (1) is directly or indirectly held by a corporation or (2) is a capital interest.[271.9]

An "applicable trade or business" is "any activity conducted on a regular, substantial and continuous basis" that consists, in whole or in part, of raising or returning capital, and either (1) investing in (or disposing of) specified assets (or identifying specified assets for investing or disposition), or (2) devel-

---

[271.6a] Subparagraph (A) starts with the taxpayers' long-term gain "attributable to the sale or exchange of any asset held for not more than three years." Presumably this is gain from a hypothetical sale, since any actual sale would produce short-term gain.

[271.7] § 1061(c).

[271.8] An interest held by a person who is employed by another entity that is conducting a trade or business (which is not an applicable trade or business) and who provides services only to the other entity is not an applicable partnership interest. § 1061(c)(1). If the service provider also makes capital contributions to the partnership, the Treasury is directed to provide guidance to prevent the contribution from insulating the entire interest from the services taint. HR Rep No. 466, 115th Cong., 1st Sess., "Conference Report to Accompany HR 1," at 420 (2017).

[271.9] § 1061(c)(4). The exclusion of partnership interests held by "corporations" from § 1061 has tempted some practitioners to consider having C corporations that hold carried interests otherwise subject to § 1061 elect to become S corporations. Notice 2018-18, 2018-12 IRB, announced Treasury's intent to promulgate regulations interpreting the term "corporations" to refer solely to corporations taxable under Subchapter C. Whether the Treasury is authorized to promulgate such regulations under § 1061 remains to be seen. While § 1061(f) authorizes the Secretary to "issue such regulations or other guidance as is necessary or appropriate to carry out the purposes of this section," it is far from clear that Congress intended the language to only apply to C corporations. Treasury's intent was fulfilled in Proposed Regulations § 1.1061-3(b)(2) (2020), which is more authoritative than the Notice, but bears the same caveats stated above with respect to Treasury's authority.

oping specified assets.[271.10] "Specified assets" include "securities" (generally as defined under rules for mark-to-market accounting for securities dealers); "commodities" (as defined under rules for mark-to-market accounting for commodities dealers); real estate held for rental or investment; cash or cash equivalents; and options or derivative contracts with respect to any of the foregoing, as well as an interest in a partnership to the extent of the partnership's proportionate interest in any of the foregoing.[271.11]

Searching for the purpose and effect of the special conversion rule in § 1061(d) is difficult. It seems to be intended to disfavor certain transfers involving related parties,[271.12] but the legislative history is entirely silent as to its purpose. The use of the word "transfer" rather than "sale or exchange" seems to suggest the scope of this rule may not be limited to taxable sales.[271.13] Again, there is nothing helpful beyond the bare language of the Code.

As noted above, § 1061(d)(1)(A) was apparently intended to identify and call out for short-term capital gain treatment that portion of the unrealized appreciation in a transferor partner's partnership interest attributable to assets held for three years or less. This interpretation would effectively require creation of a look-through rule for related-party transfers of applicable partnership interests while the general rule of § 1061(a) would not. The words of the existing statute are unclear on this point. Clarification is appropriate.

Sections 1061(e) and 1061(f) authorize the Treasury to issue both reporting requirements and regulations or other guidance. This forthcoming guidance is to "address prevention of the abuse of the purposes of the provision, including through the allocation of income to tax-indifferent parties. Guidance is also to provide for the application of the provision in the case of tiered structures of entities."[271.14]

[271.10] § 1061(c)(2). "Developing specified assets takes place, for example, if it is represented to investors, lenders, regulators, or others that the value, price, or yield of a portfolio business may be enhanced or increased in connection with choices or actions of a service provider or of others acting in concert with or at the direction of a service provider." HR Rep No. 466, 115th Cong., 1st Sess., "Conference Report to Accompany HR 1," at 421 (2017).

[271.11] § 1061(c)(3).

[271.12] Including any person "who performed a service within the current calendar year or the preceding three calendar years in any applicable trade or business in which or for which the taxpayer performed a service," referred to in the legislative history as a "colleague." HR Rep No. 466, 115th Cong., 1st Sess., "Conference Report to Accompany HR 1," at 422 (2017). (Perhaps the first appearance of an "anti-colleague" rule in the Code?)

[271.13] The same issue is inherent in § 1061(a) if it encompasses changes in the ownership of applicable partnership interests, although the word "transfer" is never mentioned.

[271.14] HR Rep No. 466, 115th Cong., 1st Sess., "Conference Report to Accompany HR 1," at 422 (2017).

[ii] Proposed Regulations Sections 1.1061-1 through 1.1061-6 (2020).
Proposed Regulations Sections 1.1061-1 through 1.1061-6 were issued in Au-

gust 2020. Like many other things in 2020, the Proposed Regulations reflect an attempt to deal with a hopelessly flawed situation.

The framework of the Proposed Regulations begins in Proposed Regulations § 1.1061-1 with a laundry list of definitional references and then continues in Proposed Regulations § 1.1061-2 with the initial classification of a partnership interest as an applicable partnership interest ("API"). For those partners that hold both APIs ("API Holders") and capital interests, Proposed Regulations § 1.1061-3 provides the means to isolate an API Holder's capital investment from the recharacterization potential of § 1061(a). Proposed Regulations § 1.1061-4 identifies the formulas and calculations necessary to determine an API Holder's "Recharacterization Amount" (the capital gain recognized with respect to an API that is recharacterized from long term to short term), while Proposed Regulations § 1.1061-5 attempts to wrangle the related-party dictate of § 1061(d) into a coherent set of rules.

Proposed Regulations § 1.1061-6 would require partnerships to provide API Holders with certain information necessary to complete the calculations required under § 1061. In the event the partnership fails to provide such information and the API Holder is not otherwise able to substantiate the information, many of the exceptions that might otherwise be available to the API Holder to avoid recharacterization of gain would be denied.[271.15]

[271.15] Prop. Reg. § 1.1061-6(a)(2) (2020).

[A] *Wolves in sheep's clothing.* Many fund managers, at the behest of their investors (after all, who trusts a bartender that doesn't drink?), will contribute significant capital to the fund alongside their investors. If the investors are lambs and the service providers are wolves, and § 1061 attempts to bifurcate the treatment of the two while adhering to Subchapter K's principles, Proposed Regulations § 1.1061-3 would attempt to skin the sheep's clothing from the wolves in order to tax it at a lower rate (insert joke about the value of sheepskin here). What seems at first to be a simple process quickly devolves into massive complexity as multiple tiers are considered, necessitating a dizzying variety of terms that will quickly become standard nomenclature for tax lawyers advising funds and their general partners.

Under the Proposed Regulations, the sheepskin is named Capital Interest Gains and Losses and these amounts would be excluded from the recharacterization rule of § 1061(a). Long-term capital gains and losses with respect to an API are called API Gains and Losses and are subject to recharacterization. Capital Interest Gains and Losses would include Capital Interest Allocations, Passthrough Interest Capital Allocations, and Capital Interest Disposition Amounts. Capital Interest Allocations would be just what they sound like—direct allocations to an interest in a partnership in which an API Holder has an API (a "Passthrough Interest"), but that are attributable to a capital interest, rather than the API. Passthrough Interest Capital Allocations would be indirect allocations from a partnership that holds a Passthrough Interest and can consist of either Passthrough Capital Allocations (Capital Interest Allocations from the partnership's Passthrough Interest) or Passthrough Interest Direct Investment Allocations (allocations from an investment other than a Passthrough Investment).[271.16] Finally, Capital Interest Disposition Amounts would be gains attributable to the disposition of a Passthrough Interest that is a capital interest. We warned you things would get complex fast.

Key to all of these definitions is parsing allocations to capital interests from allocations to APIs, and the Proposed Regulations would do that by providing an effective safe harbor whereby an allocation will be attributable to a capital interest where it is "based on the relative capital accounts of the partners ... receiving the allocation...." (hereinafter referred to as the "pro-rata rule").[271.17] Taxpayers would be allowed to use capital accounts as determined under the relevant partnership agreements if they either maintain capital accounts in accordance with Regulations § 1.704-1(b)(2)(iv) or they use principles similar to those provided in Regulations § 1.704-1(b)(2)(iv).[271.18] The Proposed Regulations are silent as to the consequences for a partnership that does not maintain capital accounts under those principles, but presumably any partnership that fails to do so would not be able to treat any allocations as Capital Interest Allocations.

Note that the pro-rata rule does not require that all partners of a partnership be allocated amounts proportionate to their capital accounts, but only that partners receiving the allocation be allocated pro-rata amounts, thus preserving the possibility of long-term capital gain treatment for managers of funds that allow investors to participate in different aspects of fund investments. In order to prevent abuse of this rule, the Proposed Regulations would require that Capital Interest Allocations at least be made to Unrelated Non-Service Partners (which means exactly what it sounds like) that hold at least 5 percent of the aggregate partnership capital account balance.[271.19]

The Proposed Regulations would apply the pro-rata rule at each level in order to preserve the capital interest component of an allocation. Thus, Passthrough Capital Allocations must satisfy the pro-rata rule when allocated at the parent passthrough level, as must Passthrough Interest Direct Investment Allocations.[271.20]

Upon the disposition of a Passthrough Interest, all long-term capital gain from such event would be deemed to be API Gain, except to the extent com-

---

[271.16] Prop. Reg. § 1.1061-3(c)(5)(i) (2020).

[271.17] Prop. Reg. § 1.1061-3(c)(3)(i) (2020). The Preamble to the Proposed Regulations, Fed. Reg. Vol. 85, No. 158 p. 49753, at 49762 (Aug. 14, 2020) provides that, at least with respect to Passthrough Interest Direct Investment Allocations, the pro-rata rule will be satisfied as long as the terms of the allocations to the API Holders are no more beneficial than the terms of the allocations to the Unrelated Non-Service Providers.

[271.18] Prop. Reg. § 1.1061-3(c)(3)(iii)(A) (2020).

[271.19] Prop. Reg. § 1.1061-3(c)(4)(ii) (2020).

[271.20] Prop. Reg. §§ 1.1061-3(c)(5)(ii), 1.1061-3(c)(5)(iii) (2020).

prised of Capital Interest Disposition Amounts.[271.21] The Proposed Regulations would require taxpayers to engage in a three-step calculation of this amount:

1. Calculate the long-term capital gain that would be allocated to the Passthrough Interest from a hypothetical sale of all of the Passthrough Entity's assets (and all subsidiary passthrough entities);[271.22]
2. Calculate the Capital Interest Allocations and Passthrough Interest Capital Allocations that would be allocated to the Passthrough Interest upon such hypothetical liquidation;[271.23] and
3. Multiply the long-term capital gain recognized in the actual disposition by a fraction equal to (2), divided by (1).[271.24]

The statutory scheme of § 1061 does not fit well within the structure of Subchapter K, in that the former presumes that a portion of a partnership interest (an API) can be segregated from the interest as a whole, while the latter does not. This inconsistency shows up most clearly in the interplay between the unitary basis rules and the fragmented carried interest approach of the Proposed Regulations.

> **EXAMPLE 9-13.1:** Partnership PRS, which conducts an active trade or business, provides that all limited partner capital providers receive their capital back first, and then residual profits are shared 80 percent to the limited partners and 20 percent to the general partner, A. In addition to its general partnership (GP) interest, A contributes $10,000 to PRS as a limited partner, in exchange for a 2 percent limited partnership interest. Two years later, at a time when no gain or loss has been recognized by PRS, but A's limited partnership interest is worth $15,000 and its general partnership interest (which is an API) is worth $85,000, A sells its limited partnership interest for $15,000. All allocations of long-term capital gain with respect to A's limited partnership interest are Capital Interest Allocations. PRS holds no hot assets under § 751(a).
>
> Because Subchapter K regards a partner as having a unitary basis in its partnership interest, A's sale of its limited partnership interest will be treated as a sale of 15 percent of its PRS interest. A will thus recognize $13,500 of long-term capital gain on the disposition as a result of a recovery of 15 percent of its $10,000 basis against the $15,000 amount realized.
>
> To determine the percentage of the long-term capital gain that is treated as a Capital Interest Disposition Amount, A determines the amount of long-term capital gain that would be allocated to the portion of A's interest sold if PRS sold all of its assets for fair market value and liquidated immediately before the disposition. Because the limited partner-

---

[271.21] These rules would apply to both long-term capital gains and long-term capital losses under the Proposed Regulations.

[271.22] Prop. Reg. § 1.1061-3(c)(6)(ii)(A) (2020).

[271.23] Prop. Reg. § 1.1061-3(c)(6)(ii)(B) (2020).

[271.24] Prop. Reg. § 1.1061-3(c)(6)(ii)(D) (2020).

ship interests are only entitled to allocations that are Capital Interest Allocations and are not entitled to allocations of API Gain or Loss, all of the $13,500 long-term capital gain is Capital Interest Disposition Gain.[271.25]

The result is odd for two reasons. First, because Section 1061 takes a separate asset approach to the capital interest and the API, we would expect that the sale of the limited partnership interest would result in gain limited to the actual built-in gain in the asset itself. However, the Proposed Regulations would rightfully acknowledge the primacy of the unitary basis approach in which Subchapter K is grounded, and the transaction results in gain in excess of that which we might expect under a separate asset approach. The Proposed Regulations then overlay a bifurcated asset approach to recharacterization, resulting in the avoidance of Section 1061 recharacterization for appreciation with respect to the API.

In addition to these consequences being odd, applying the unitary basis approach to this situation opens the door to what tax advisors like to call "opportunities" (others, perhaps, use the term "shenanigans").

EXAMPLE 9-13.2: Assume the same facts as in Example 9-13.1, but after two years of the investment, a third-party approaches PRS and offers to purchase 100 percent of the interests in PRS for $1 million. *A*'s GP interest has a value of $100,000 (20 percent of the excess of $1 million over the initial limited partnership (LP) investment of $500,000), while *A*'s LP interest has a value of $18,000 (2 percent of the aggregate LP value of $900,000). Immediately prior to the sale, PRS borrows $100,000 and redeems out *A*'s GP interest in PRS for its fair market value of $100,000.

Because *A* has a unitary basis in its PRS interest, the distribution triggers no gain to A under § 731.[271.26]

When a third party then purchases *A*'s LP interest in PRS for $18,000 (and the remaining interests for $882,000, resulting in total proceeds, including the loan, of $1 million), the Proposed Regulations would simply not apply—no API would exist at the time of the sale.

[271.25] Prop. Reg. § 1.1061-3(c)(7)(v) Example 5 (2020).

[271.26] Prop. Reg. §§ 1.1061-4(a)(4)(i)(B), 1.1061-4(a)(4)(ii)(C) (2020) (API calculations with reference to § 731(a) gains).

[B] *Determination of the recharacterization amount.* Once gain attributable to its capital interest has been shorn from an API Holder's gain, any remaining long-term capital gain recognized with respect to such API needs to be broken down into the One-Year Gain Amount and the Three-Year Gain Amount. An API Holder's Three-Year Gain Amount would be a subset of its One-Year Gain Amount, and would be subtracted from its One-Year Gain Amount in order to determine the API Holder's Recharacterization Amount (i.e., the gain treated as short-term capital gain pursuant to § 1061).[271.27] Each Gain Amount would be comprised of both a Disposition Amount, generally reflecting long-term capital gain recognized upon the sale or other disposition of an API, and a Distributive Share Amount, generally reflecting long-term capital gain allocated to the API Holder with respect to its API.[271.28]

An API Holder's Disposition Amount would include long-term capital gain recognized upon (a) the disposition of all or a portion of an API; (b) a distribution of cash in excess of basis under § 731; (c) the disposition of property distributed with respect to the API in a nonrecognition transaction; and (d) the application of § 751(b) with respect to the API.[271.29] All such long-term capital gain would be included in the taxpayer owner's One-Year Disposition Amount, while any such long-term capital gain generally would be included in the taxpayer owner's Three-Year Disposition Amount to the extent that the underlying API was held for more than three years.[271.30]

An API Holder's Distributive Share Amount would include its distributive share of net long-term capital gain from the partnership for the taxable year, subject to certain exceptions, discussed below.[271.31] All such net long-term capital gain would be included in an API Holder's One-Year Distributive Share Amount, while it would only be included in Three-Year Distributive Share Amount to the extent it arose with respect to an asset with a holding period in excess of three years.[271.32]

For purposes of determining the applicable holding period, the Proposed Regulations would confirm the longstanding rule under Subchapter K that the holding period of the seller of assets controls for purposes of § 1061 and not the holding period of the API Holder in its partnership interest.[271.33] Further in keeping with applicable law, the holding period with respect to gain recog-

---

[271.27] Prop. Reg. § 1.1061-4(a)(1) (2020).

[271.28] Prop. Reg. § 1.1061-4(a)(2) (2020).

[271.29] Prop. Reg. § 1.1061-4(a)(4) (2020).

[271.30] Prop. Reg. § 1.1061-4(a)(4) (2020). Note, however, that with respect to gain recognized as a result of the disposition of property distributed with respect to an API, if the property has a holding period in excess of three years as of the date of disposition, any gain is excluded from both the One-Year Disposition Amount and the Three-Year Disposition Amount. Prop. Reg. § 1.1061-4(a)(4)(i)(C) (2020).

[271.31] Prop. Reg. § 1.1061-4(a)(3) (2020). Certain regulated investment company (RIC) and real estate investment trust (REIT) dividend income would be excluded from One-Year Amounts or included in Three-Year Amounts, if appropriate disclosures are made by the applicable payor of the dividend. Prop. Reg. § 1.1061-4(b)(4) (2020). Special rules would also apply to a partnership's pro-rata share of passive foreign investment companies (PFICs) that have made qualifying electing fund (QEF) elections. Prop. Reg. § 1.1061-4(b)(5) (2020).

[271.32] Prop. Reg. § 1.1061-4(a)(3)(ii) (2020).

[271.33] Notice of Proposed Rulemaking, Fed. Reg. Vol. 85, No. 158 p. 49753, at 49767 (Aug. 14, 2020).

nized under an installment sale would be determined as of the date of the installment sale and not as of the date of any installment payment.[271.34]

There are a number of exceptions to the calculation of both the Distribution Amount and the Distributive Share Amount, as outlined below.

1. *Excluded Items*

Proposed Regulations § 1.1061-4(b)(6) would exclude the following items from consideration for purposes of determining an API Holder's Distributive Share Amount: (a) § 1231 gain or loss; (b) § 1256 gain or loss; (c) qualified dividends under § 1(h)(11)(B); and (d) certain gains or losses that are characterized as long or short term regardless of holding period (such items referred to as "Excluded Items").[271.35] While Excluded Items are not specifically excluded from the calculation of an API Holder's Disposition Amount, property that generates Excluded Items factor into such determination under the Lookthrough Rule (discussed below).

Section 1231 generally provides for long-term capital gain or loss on the disposition of property used in the taxpayer's business, eligible for depreciation, and held for more than one year. Section 1231 property thus includes depreciable equipment (although not depreciation recapture, which is excluded from § 1061 recharacterization as a result of being treated as a hot asset under § 751(c)), as well as goodwill and other intangible assets of an ongoing business. Additionally, § 1231 property includes certain livestock, unharvested crops, timber, coal, and iron ore.[271.36]

The Section 1231 exclusion creates another reason for private equity investors to favor pass-through investment for operating businesses, rather than C corporation investment. The majority of appreciation in many privately held businesses accrues with respect to goodwill, the disposition of which, if held for more than one year, generates long-term capital gain pursuant to § 1231. As a result, API Holders who invest in private businesses through partnerships and are looking to exit within three years can avoid the impact of § 1061 by exiting through asset dispositions (or transactions taxable as asset dispositions) where the majority of gain will be attributable to goodwill appreciation.

> **EXAMPLE 9-13.3:** Assume GP holds an API in Fund, an investment vehicle that holds, among other investments, 90 percent of the partnership interests in PRS, a partnership that conducts Business *X.* Fund invested $100 in PRS in Year 1 in exchange for its 90 percent interest and has been allocated $10 of loss over the past two years. Now, in Year 3, less than three years after its initial investment, Buyer is offering $300 for either 100 percent of the PRS interests or Business *X.*

[271.34] Prop. Reg. § 1.1061-4(b)(3) (2020).

[271.35] Prop. Reg. §§ 1.1061-4(b)(6)(i)−1.1061-4(b)(6)(iv) (2020). Gains and losses characterized without regard to holding period specifically include mixed straddles under § 1092(b).

[271.36] § 1231(b).

If Fund sells its 90 percent partnership interest in PRS, it will recognize $180 of gain (90 percent of the $300 purchase price, less its $90 basis in PRS). Assume that 20 percent of this gain ($36) would be allocated to GP. As Fund held the PRS interest for less than three years, all $36 of the gain would be included in GP's One-Year Distributive Share Amount, while none of the gain would be included in GP's Three-Year Distributive Share Amount, resulting in all $36 being recharacterized as short-term capital gain under § 1061.

Alternatively, if PRS sells Business X for $300, PRS will recognize $200 of gain. To the extent that this gain is attributable to § 1231 property, including goodwill, it will be excluded in computing both GP's One-Year Distributive Share Amount and its Three-Year Distributive Share Amount, significantly reducing the gain being recharacterized as short-term capital gain under § 1061.

2. *The Lookthrough Rule.*

The "Lookthrough Rule" of Proposed Regulations § 1.1061-4(b)(9) would apply to override the general rule that gain recognized by an API Holder upon its disposition of an API is a Three- Year Amount if the interest has been held by the API Holder for more than three years. Under the Lookthrough Rule, if "substantially all" (i.e., 80 percent) of a partnership's capital assets have a holding period of three years or less, a portion of any gain with respect to an API in such partnership would be excluded from treatment as a Three-Year Amount (but still included as a One-Year Amount, thus increasing the amount recharacterized as short-term capital gain).[271.37] The portion treated as excluded would be equal to a fraction where the numerator is the built-in capital gain with respect to the partnership's capital assets with a holding period of three years or less and the denominator is the partnership's built-in capital gain with respect to all of its assets.[271.38] This exclusion is a one-way street—the Lookthrough Rule cannot be applied to treat as a Three-Year Amount any gain recognized on the disposition of an API held less than three years based on the underlying makeup of the partnership's assets. Further, in the event that an asset of the partnership being looked through is a partnership interest, that interest would also be looked through, but only if it has been held for more than three years.[271.39]

3. *Transition Amounts.*

The Proposed Regulations would authorize a partnership to make a one-time, irrevocable election to exclude any gains or losses with respect to assets held for more than three years as of December 31, 2017 ("Transition

---

[271.37] Prop. Reg. § 1.1061-4(b)(9) (2020).

[271.38] Prop. Reg. § 1.1061-4(b)(9)(ii)(C) (2020). In applying the "substantially all" test and in determining the exclusion percentage, assets that produce Excluded Items are not considered.

[271.39] Compare Reg. §§ 1.1061-4(c)(2)(i) and 1.1061-4(c)(2)(ii) (2020).

Amounts"), from consideration under the § 1061 rules. But wait, you might be asking, aren't such assets already excluded from consideration under the § 1061 rules? While it is easiest to think of such assets in that fashion, in fact they are just included on both sides of the § 1061 ledger as both One-Year Amounts and Three-Year Amounts. As a result, Transition Amounts can impact § 1061, but the direction of that impact depends on whether the partnership is expecting a gain or loss with respect to such asset.

> **EXAMPLE 9-13.4:** Assume PRS has a greater-than-three-year holding period in stock as of December 31, 2017. Two years later, in the same year that PRS has a $75 gain from two-year property subject to § 1061 and a $50 loss from three-year property subject to § 1061, PRS sells the stock at a $25 loss. If PRS has made or makes the Transition Amount election, the $25 loss is excluded from the § 1061 calculation and PRS' recharacterization amount is equal to its One-Year Gain Amount of $25 ($75 gain, less $50 loss), less its Three-Year Gain Amount of $0, or $25.[271.40] Conversely, if PRS does not make a Transition Amount election, the $25 loss is included in both the One-Year Gain Amount and the Three-Year Gain Amount. Because the One-Year Gain Amount is zero ($25 loss, $75 gain, $50 loss), PRS' recharacterization amount is zero.[271.41]

> **EXAMPLE 9-13.5:** Assume the same facts as Example 9-13.4, except the Transition Amount property is sold at a $100 gain and the three-year property that is not Transition Amount Property is sold at a $100 loss. In that situation, if the Transition Amount election is not made, PRS' One-Year Gain Amount is $75 ($100 gain, plus $75 gain, less $100 loss) and its Three-Year Gain Amount is $0 ($100 gain, less $100 loss), resulting in a recharacterization amount of $75. If the Transition Amount election is made, PRS' One-Year Gain Amount is reduced to $0 ($75 gain, less $100 loss) and PRS' recharacterization amount is zero.

The above examples illustrate the Transition Amount rules at the partnership level, while § 1061 applies its rules at the partner level. The Proposed Regulations would translate a partnership's Transition Amount, to the extent that it would have been allocated to an API Holder under the partnership's allocation scheme for the 2017 taxable year, into an API Holder Transition Amount and apply the API Holder Transition Amount in a manner that correlates to the partnership examples above.[271.42] How exactly this translation would work under the targeted allocation method favored by most investment partnerships is a mystery, however.

While potentially beneficial in limited situations, a Transition Amount election is irrevocable and needs to be made with a timely filed tax return filed

---

[271.40] See Prop. Reg. § 1.1061-4(b)(2) (2020) (Three-Year Gain Amount cannot be negative).

[271.41] Prop. Reg. § 1.1061-4(b)(1) (2020).

[271.42] Prop. Reg. § 1.1061-4(b)(7)(ii) (2020).

for the first year in which a Transition Amount is to be excluded from the §
1061 calculations.[271.43] Partnerships willing to make such an election should be
prepared for the reporting requirements, the unpredictable and potentially inju-
rious allocations of Transition Amounts to API Holders, and the potential to be
whipsawed by the election in the future.[271.44]

[271.43] Prop. Reg. § 1.1061-4(b)(7)(iii)(A) (2020).

[271.44] Prop. Reg. § 1.1061-4(b)(7)(iii)(C) (2020). The partnership is generally required
to maintain books and records sufficient to demonstrate the appropriateness of the Transition Amount exclusion.

[C] *Section 1061(d).* The statutory language of § 1061(d) requires API
Holders who transfer APIs to related persons to recognize, potentially, some
amount as short-term capital gain. As noted in our discussion of the statutory
language, what that amount is and how it is calculated is anyone's guess. The
Proposed Regulations would clarify § 1061(d) to serve as an acceleration device for transfers—whether taxable or otherwise tax-free—to related persons.
Whether the statutory language supports this conclusion is less than clear.

The Proposed Regulations would expand upon the statutory language in
two meaningful ways: first, by including amounts into the API Holder's gross
income as short-term capital gain in the year of transfer regardless of whether
such gain is recognized under other provisions of the Code; and second, by applying an aggregate approach to look through an API Holder's transfer of an
API in order to recharacterize gain based on the assets held by the underlying
partnership.

The acceleration and recharacterization provisions of Proposed Regulations § 1.1061-5 apply where an API Holder transfers[271.45] either an API or
property distributed with respect to an API, to a related person.[271.46] Related
persons for these purposes include family and co-workers, as well as any pass-
through entities in which family or co-workers hold an interest.[271.47] The gain
recognized in the context of such a transfer is equal to the amount of gain the
API Holder would recognize if the partnership sold all of its assets held for
three years or less as of the date of the transfer for their fair market value at
that time,[271.48] but only to the extent in excess of gain actually recognized and
recharacterized under the general rule of Proposed Regulations § 1.1061-4.[271.49]

[271.45] The term "transfer" for these purposes includes contributions, distributions, sales
and exchanges, and gifts, although Proposed Regulations § 1.1061-5(e)(2) (2020) at least
helpfully excepts § 721 contributions to a partnership from the definition.

[271.46] Prop. Reg. § 1.1061-5(a) (2020).

[271.47] Prop. Reg. § 1.1061-5(e) (2020).

[271.48] Prop. Reg. § 1.1061-5(c)(1) (2020).

[271.49] Prop. Reg. § 1.1061-5(a)(2) (2020).

[2] Income

[a] Cancellations of Partnership Debt

[i] Reduction of tax attributes of debtor: general principles.

Page 9-68:

Add to note 287.

Revenue Procedure 2014-20, 2014-9 IRB 1, creates a QRPBI safe harbor for indebtedness secured by a 100 percent interest in a disregarded entity (DRE) holding real property. This safe harbor applies if (1) the indebtedness is incurred by the taxpayer or a DRE wholly owned by the taxpayer (the "borrower"); (2) the borrower owns (directly or indirectly) 100 percent of the ownership interest in a separate DRE owning real property; (3) the borrower pledges to the lender a first priority security interest in the ownership interest and any further encumbrance is subordinate to the lender's security interest; (4) at least 90 percent of the fair market value of the total assets of the DRE consists of real property used in a trade or business and any other assets held by the DRE are incidental to the acquisition, ownership, and operation of the real property; and (5) upon default and foreclosure, the lender will replace the borrower as the sole owner of the DRE. This safe harbor is not intended to preclude debt that is not within the safe harbor from being QRPBI.

[ii] Application of the general principles to partnerships.

[A] *Aggregate/entity.*

Page 9-68:

Add after first sentence of subsection (ending with note callout 288).

Regulation § 1.108-9(b) provides: "[I]n the case of a partnership, section 108(a)(1)(A) and (B) applies at the partner level. If a partnership holds an interest in a grantor trust or a disregarded entity, the applicability of section 108(a)(1)(A) and (B) to the discharge of indebtedness income is tested by looking to each partner to whom the income is allocable."

[C] *Basis reductions.*

Page 9-72:

Add to note 311.

The Service will not follow these decisions. See AOD 2015-1, 2015-6 IRB 579. Further, in the preamble to Regulations § 1.108-9 (TD 9771), the Service reiterated its objection to these cases.

Page 9-74:

Add to note 317.

In 2008, the Service issued Proposed Regulations under §§ 108(e)(8) and 721, providing a safe harbor that allows a partnership interest issued in exchange for partnership debt to be valued based upon the liquidation value of the partnership interest, and confirming that the contributor is generally entitled to nonrecognition treatment upon the contribution of partnership debt in exchange for a partnership interest. REG-164370-05, 73 Fed. Reg. 64,903 (Oct. 31, 2008), discussed in ¶ 4.02[3].

Add at end of subsection.

Under § 108(i), added by the American Recovery and Reinvestment Act of 2009 (ARRA), partnerships and other debtors may elect to defer the taxation of discharge of indebtedness income from certain discharges occurring during 2009 and 2010. This election and its consequences for partners and partnerships are explored in ¶ 4.02[3].

[b] Tax-Benefit Rule

Page 9-75:

Add to note 322.

; CCA 200909032 (Jan. 15, 2009) (State of New York QRZE Credit for Real Property Taxes; credit claim not inconsistent with prior § 164 deduction under tax benefit rule; however, receipt of credit payment is inconsistent, and must be separately stated; no opinion if intervening change in partners).

[d] Gross Income

Page 9-79:

In note 336, add the following after first sentence.

See United States v. G-1 Holdings, Inc., 2009 US Dist. Lexis 115850 (D. NJ 2009) (share of gross receipts determined with reference to distributive share of partnership income in complex sharing arrangement; three-year limitations period applies).

Page 9-80:

Add to note 347.

; Priv. Ltr. Rul. 201314005 (Apr. 5, 2013) (corporation must include its distributive share of partnership gross receipts for purposes of applying § 165(g)(3)(B)).

[f] Long-Term Contracts

Page 9-82:

Add to end of section.

Section 460(e) exempts from the ambit of § 460 certain contracts entered into by a taxpayer (other than a taxpayer classified as a tax shelter) that meets the gross receipts test of § 448(c). Section 448(c) generally authorizes the cash method of accounting for taxpayers that average less than $25 million a year in gross receipts (indexed for post-2018 inflation). Proposed Regulations under § 460(e) would generally require a partner to include its distributive share of a partnership's gross receipts in applying this test.[352.1]

[352.1] Prop. Reg. § 1.460-3(b)(3)(ii)(C) (2020).

[g] Source of Income From Sales of Inventory and Natural Resources

Page 9-82:

Replace note 353 with the following.

[353] Reg. § 1.863-3(f). Partnership transactions involving possessions of the United States are governed by the rules of Regulations § 1.863-3(f). Reg. § 1.863-3(e)(5).

Replace note 354 with the following.

[354] Reg. § 1.863-3(f)(2)(i).

Replace note 355 with the following.

[355] Reg. § 1.863-3(f)(2)(ii). The partner apparently takes on a proportionate share of the partnership's basis in its assets, including any § 743(b) special basis adjustment allocable to the partner. Reg. §1.863-3(f)(2)(iii). No specific guidance is furnished if a partner's basis in his partnership interest differs from his proportionate share of the partnership's basis in its assets. One possible approach would be to calculate a partner's basis in the partnership's assets under a constructive liquidation assumption, although the Regulations arguably ignore these differences and apply a pure look-through approach.

Page 9-83:

Replace note 356 with the following.

[356] Reg. § 1.863-3(f)(2)(ii).

Replace note 357 with the following.

[357] See Reg. § 1.863-3(f)(3) Example 1.

Replace note 358 with the following.

[358] See Reg. § 1.863-3(f)(3) Example 2.

[h] Source of Interest Income

Page 9-84:

Add to end of section.

Interest paid by a domestic partnership is U.S. source if it is engaged in a trade or business in the United States at any time during its taxable year.[360.1] Otherwise, it is foreign source.[360.2]

Loans made to a partnership by a United States person that is a partner (directly or indirectly) in the partnership could potentially cause a sourcing mismatch (and therefore inappropriately impact the computation of the foreign tax credit limitation under § 904), since the rules governing the source of the interest expense and the partner's distributive share of the partnership's interest expense are different. Regulations § 1.861-9(e)(8)(ii) remedies this mismatch by assigning the interest income to the same statutory and residual groupings as those from which the interest expense is deducted. Regulations § 1.861-9(e)(8)(v) extends these rules to transactions that are not loans but give rise to deductions that are allocated and apportioned in the same manner as interest expense. Regulations § 1.861-9(e)(9) (2019) extends these rules to loans from partnerships to its partners ("upstream partnership loans"). Guaranteed payments are treated as giving rise to income and deductions equivalent to interest.[360.3]

[360.1] Reg. § 1.861-2(a)(2)(iii).

[360.2] Reg. § 1.861-2(a)(i).

[360.3] Reg. § 1.861-9(b)(8).

[3] Deductions

[a] Excessive Employee Remuneration

Page 9-84:

Add to note 361.

; Priv. Ltr. Rul. 200727008 (Apr. 2, 2007).

Add to end of section.

However, for taxable years beginning on or after December 30, 2020, a corporate partner's distributive share of a partnership's deduction for compensation paid to a covered employee of the corporation must be taken into account by the corporation when it applies § 162(m).[361.1]

[361.1] Reg. § 1.162-33(c)(3)(ii). Application of this rule is illustrated by Regulations § 1.162-33(c)(3)(iv)(C) Example 3.

[b] Investment Interest Expense: Section 163(d)

Page 9-84:

Replace note 363 with the following.

³⁶³ Rev. Rul. 2008-12, 2008-1 CB 520. See Rev. Rul. 2008-38, 2008-2 CB 249 (interest incurred in partnership trade or business, though characterized as "investment interest" under § 163(d)(3)(A) by reason of § 163(d)(5)(A)(ii), retains its character as a business deduction under § 62(a)(1), and thus is not subject to limitation as an itemized deduction); Ann. 2008-65, 2008-31 IRB 279 (explaining need for Rev. Rul. 2008-38). Interest incurred to purchase a partnership interest, however, is determined at the partner level, generally depending upon whether the partner materially participates in the activity of the partnership. See S. Rep. No. 313, 99th Cong., 2d Sess. 805 (1986); Tech. Adv. Mem. 8235004 (May 21, 1982). Interest incurred to purchase a limited partnership interest in a limited partnership carrying on a trade or business will generally give rise to a passive deduction subject to § 469. Temp. Reg. §§ 1.163-8T, 1.469-2T(d)(3). See Notice 88-37, 1988-1 CB 522; Notice 88-20, 1988-1 CB 487. See William C. Lipnick, 153 TC 1 (2019) (partnership interests acquired by gift and bequest treated as debt-financed acquisitions; interest expense on partnership debt allocated among partnership assets for purposes of § 163(d)).

Proposed Regulations promulgated in 2020 would provide guidance as to the allocation of interest expense attributable to debt-financed distributions. Under these rules, partnerships (and S corporations) would need to allocate debt traceable to distributions made to equity holders first to any "available expenditures" of the entity during the taxable year and then to the distribution itself. Prop. Reg. § 1.163-14(d)(1) (2020). Any such treatment would be debt-financed distribution interest expense, which would generally be further allocated under the rules of Temporary Regulations § 1.163-8T to the distributee's use of the proceeds of the distribution. Prop. Reg. § 1.163-14(d)(1)(ii) (2020). Any amounts not treated under these two categories (for example, debt-financed distribution interest expense allocated to a partner who acquired its interest from an unrelated distributee of a debt-financed distribution) would be treated as "excess interest expense" and allocated among the assets of the entity based on their relative adjusted tax bases. Prop. Reg. § 1.163-14(d)(3)(iii) (2020).

Pages 9-85 – 9-86:

Replace ¶ 9.02[3][c] with the following revised ¶ 9.02[3][c].

[c] Limits on Interest Deductions: Section 163(j) [Revised]

Prior to 2018, the so-called "interest-stripping" rules in § 163(j) applied only to limit deductions for interest on loans from U.S. corporations to related parties not subject to U.S. taxation. These rules are discussed in ¶ 9.02[3][c][ii]. For tax years beginning after December 31, 2017,³⁶⁴ the scope of § 163(j) has been greatly expanded to limit the deductibility of business interest paid by all types of taxpayers to all creditors. The post-2017 rules are discussed in ¶ 9.02[3][c][i].

---

³⁶⁴ 2017 Tax Cuts and Jobs Act, Pub. L. No. 115-97, § 13301(c) (Dec. 22, 2017).

[i] Limited deductibility for business interest: Section 163(j) post-2017. For tax years beginning after December 31, 2017, the deductibility of all types of taxpayers' business interest expense (BIE) is limited to the sum of (a) the business interest income (BII) of the taxpayer, plus (b) 30 percent (subject to exception in 2019 and 2020 discussed below) of the taxpayer's adjusted taxable income (ATI), plus (c) the "floor plan financing interest" of the taxpayer.[365] Small businesses (generally, those with less-than-average annual gross receipts of not more than $25 million) are not subject to the limitation.[366]

Business interest is interest paid or accrued on indebtedness properly allocable to a trade or business and does not include investment interest.[367] Similarly, BII is limited to interest properly allocable to a trade or business and does not include investment income.[368] ATI means the taxable income of the taxpayer exclusive of (1) items not properly allocable to a trade or business, (2) business interest or business interest income, (3) any net operating loss (NOL), (4) any § 199A deduction, and (5) for taxable years beginning before January 1, 2022, any deduction for depreciation, amortization, or depletion.[369]

This limitation applies at the partnership level and the deduction for business interest must be taken into account in determining partnership § 702(a)(8) "bottom-line" income or loss.[370] If any partnership business interest is not deductible at the partnership level as a result of the § 163(j) limitation, it becomes excess business interest expense (EBIE), which is allocated to the partners based on a methodology discussed below. At the partner level, any EBIE is carried forward and potentially deductible by a partner to the extent of such partner's excess taxable income (ETI) from the same partnership in a subsequent taxable year.[371] Additionally, a partner's share of any ETI of the partnership (but not the partner's share of any item of partnership income, gain, loss, or deduction that has already been applied in computing the partnership's BIE in determining the partnership-level limitation) is included in the partner's ATI in order to determine whether the § 163(j) limitation is applied

---

[365] § 163(j)(1). Any interest disallowed under this rule is carried forward and treated as paid or accrued in the next tax year. § 163(j)(2). The effect of including floor plan financing interest in the formula is to allow this type of interest expense to be fully deductible. HR Rep. No. 466, 115th Cong., 1st Sess., "Conference Report to Accompany HR 1," at 387 (2017).

[366] See ¶ 9.02[3][c][i][E]. Certain public utilities and electing real estate and farming businesses are not subject to § 163(j), nor is the business of performing services as an employee. § 163(j)(7). See ¶ 9.02[3][c][i][F].

[367] § 163(j)(5). The determination of "properly allocable" is surprisingly complex and is subject to an elaborate scheme set forth in Proposed Regulations issued in 2020, discussed at ¶ 9.02[3][b].

[368] § 163(j)(6).

[369] § 163(j)(8).

[370] § 163(j)(4)(A)(i). If partnership BIE is deductible at the partnership level, it is not retested at the partner level. Reg. § 1.163(j)-6(c)(3). Since floor plan financing interest is deductible at the partnership level, it is not again deductible by the partners. Reg. § 1.163(j)-6(e)(4)(ii).

[371] § 163(j)(4)(B)(ii).

with respect to any business interest incurred directly by the partner,[372] as well as any BIE "freed up" from the carryforward limitation.

Excess taxable income is generally equal to the amount by which 30 percent of the partnership's ATI exceeds its business interest.[373]

> **EXAMPLE 9-18:** X and Y are equal partners in partnership PRS. In Year 1, PRS has $100 of ATI and $40 of BIE. PRS's § 163(j) limitation is $30, allowing it to deduct $30 of BIE. The remaining $10 is EBIE and is allocated to X and Y, $5 each. X and Y are not required to retest under § 163(j) their distributive shares of the $30 of interest expense that is deductible at the PRS level. In Year 2, PRS has $10 of ATI, and no other items. That $10 passes through to X and Y as ETI and "frees up" the $10 of Year 1 EBIE, which now becomes $10 of BIE. Assuming no other income or loss for X and Y, each would have Year 2 ATI of $5 and be able to deduct $1.50 of the previously suspended EBIE after running the 30 percent § 163(j) gauntlet at the partner level. Each partner would have $3.50 of EBIE that would carry forward to Year 3. However, if X has a $5 loss from another source, that loss would offset the $5 of ETI from PRS and its ATI would be zero, eliminating X's ability to deduct any interest in Year 2.

Conversely, if X has no losses, X will prefer the timing in Example 9-18, since the $3.50 carryforward is BIE (versus EBIE in Example 9-18.1).

The Regulations' approach to partner- and partnership-level limitations puts a premium on timing—a partnership's ATI in the year of an interest expense can be more valuable than ATI in the year following the interest expense because the second year's ATI can be offset by losses at the partner level.

> **EXAMPLE 9-18.1:** Assume the same facts as in Example 9-18, except PRS has $110 of ATI in Year 1 and no ATI in Year 2. In Year 1, PRS's § 163(j) limitation is $33, all of which is included in PRS's non-separately stated income or loss during Year 1. Even if X has a $5 loss from another source, under this fact pattern, it will not limit X's otherwise-deductible business expense of $16.50. X has $3.50 of EBIE in Year 2. Contrast this result with the final sentence of Example 9-18, where X's $5 loss in Year 2 limits its ability to deduct the $1.50 EBIE in Year 2, limiting its total benefit from the same net ATI to $15.

The different results highlighted in Example 9-18.1 stem from the complete segregation of partnership activities from a partner's directly conducted activities. If a taxpayer directly engages in an activity that generates a loss, that loss must be subtracted from the income of the taxpayer's other directly owned business activities in measuring ATI, potentially reducing an otherwise allowable business interest deduction by 30 percent. If the loss-generating ac-

---

[372] § 163(j)(4)(A)(ii).
[373] Reg. § 1.163(j)-1(b)(17).

tivity is conducted through a partnership, however, the loss is ignored in computing partner-level ATI, thereby effectively increasing each partner's allowable interest deduction by 30 percent of its share of the loss.

The planning opportunities offered by the segregation of partnership activity in applying the § 163(j) limitation were not lost on the Regulations' drafters—the Regulations contain a general anti-avoidance rule, one example of which specifically targets separating a partnership's loss-generating business in a lower-tier partnership to improve the upper tier's § 163(j) position.[374] All arrangements with a principal purpose of avoiding the rules of § 163(j) or its Regulations run afoul of the rule's scope.

A less significant consequence of the Regulations' segregation of partnership activity is that it may facilitate the allocation of interest expense to investment activity by placing the interest expense in a partnership carrying on an investment activity, thus avoiding the uncertainty inherent in the "properly allocable" rule generally applicable to characterizing interest as business interest versus investment interest.

---

[374] Reg. §§ 1.163(j)-2(j)(1), 1.163(j)-2(j)(2)(ii) Example 2.

[A] Interest on indebtedness. Section 163(j) applies by its terms solely to "business interest," but the Regulations expand upon items commonly understood to be interest, and under the guise of an anti-avoidance rule, include within the ambit of business interest payments that are clearly not business interest, such as guaranteed payments for the use of capital.[375] The example illustrating the application of the anti-avoidance rule to a guaranteed payment asserts that a generic guaranteed payment on capital that otherwise would be funded by a loan generates interest expense for the partnership and interest income to the partner for § 163(j) purposes.[375.1] Few guaranteed payments for contributions of money are likely to escape this rule.

The validity of this position is questionable. Regulations § 1.707-1(c) provides that guaranteed payments are considered as made to one who is not a member of a partnership only for purposes of Sections 61(a) and 162(a), meaning that for purposes of applying Section 163(j), a guaranteed payment should be treated as a partner's distributive share of ordinary income. Further, the difference between a guaranteed payment and a preferred return is not always clear, especially when the preferred return is calculated with respect to gross income. In Revenue Ruling 81-300,[375.2] the Service ruled that a 5 percent gross income allocation is a "guaranteed payment," despite the fact that it is calculated with respect to partnership (gross) income. This is contrary to Pratt,[375.3] in which the Tax Court held that a gross income allocation was a dis-

---

[375] Reg. § 1.163(j)-1(b)(22)(iv).

[375.1] Reg. § 1.163(j)-1(b)(22)(v)(E) Example 5.

[375.2] Rev. Rul. 81-300, 1981-2 CB 143.

[375.3] Edward T. Pratt, 64 TC 203 (1975), aff'd, 550 F2d 1023 (5th Cir. 1977).

tributive share. The anti-avoidance rule will shine a spotlight on this narrow distinction.

[B] *Calculating partnership ATI.* A partnership takes § 734(b) basis adjustments into account in calculating its ATI, but excludes § 743(b) adjustments and remedial items.[375.4] These items are instead taken into account at the partner level in calculating the partner's ATI for purposes of calculating the § 163(j) limitation on non-partnership income (or the deductibility of carried-forward EBIE).[375.5] This treatment, which is consistent with the statute, creates a significant difference between the treatment of depreciation and amortization attributable to partnership assets and depreciation and amortization attributable to § 743(b) special basis adjustments. While of less importance for years prior to 2022, beginning in 2022, when ATI is reduced for a partnership's depreciation and amortization deductions, this rule will play a critical role in determining the § 163(j) limitation and practitioners should be planning ahead for its application.

> **EXAMPLE 9-18.2:** *X* wholly owns PRS, which conducts an operating business. At a time when PRS's sole asset is Asset *A*, a § 197 amortizable intangible with a zero basis and a value of $300, *Y* purchases 50 percent of *X*'s interest in PRS for $150. Pursuant to Revenue Ruling 99-5, *Y* is treated as purchasing an undivided 50 percent interest in *A* for $150 and contributing the assets to PRS in exchange for a partnership interest therein. PRS applies the traditional method to amortization of Asset *A*.
>
> Assume that the tax year following *Y*'s acquisition of the PRS interest is a year that begins after December 31, 2021, and that PRS has $30 of ATI (excluding items of depreciation and amortization) and $9 of BIE. PRS is entitled to $10 of amortization deductions attributable to the intangible asset deemed contributed by *Y*, reducing its ATI to $20 and its § 163(j) limitation to $6. $6 of BIE is included in PRS's non-separately stated income or loss, while the remaining $3 is EBIE and is allocated to *X* and *Y* for use in future years to the extent of PRS's future ETI.

> **EXAMPLE 9-18.3:** Assume the same facts as in Example 9-18.2, but immediately prior to *Y*'s purchase, *X* contributes 1 percent of its PRS interest to its wholly owned corporation, *Z*, and makes a § 754 election for the newly formed partnership PRS. As a result, *Y*'s purchase of a 50 percent interest in PRS from *X* is treated as an acquisition of a partnership interest for federal income tax purposes. PRS does not adjust its tax basis in its assets as a result of this purchase, but because of PRS's § 754 election, *Y* receives a partner-level special basis adjustment of $150.
>
> In the year when PRS has $30 of ATI (it has no items of depreciation or amortization) and $9 of BIE, *Y* is entitled to $10 of amortization deductions attributable to its $150 § 743(b) adjustment, but these deductions do not reduce PRS's ATI. As a result, PRS's ATI is $30 and its §

[375.4] Reg. § 1.163 (j)-6(d)(2).
[375.5] Reg. § 1.163(j)-6(e)(2).

163(j) limitation is $9. $9 of BIE is included in PRS's non-separately stated income or loss and no BIE is subject to limitation. Y's ATI is reduced by the $10 of amortization of its § 743(b) asset, but PRS's § 163(j) limitation is not impacted.[375.6]

Given the potential impact of this differential on the deductibility of interest expense starting in 2022, transaction planners should consider structuring any acquisition of an interest in a disregarded entity as an acquisition of a partnership interest for federal tax purposes. Additionally, consideration should be given to maintaining the ongoing existence of a partnership in an acquisition of 100 percent of an entity taxable as a partnership.

[375.6] See Reg. § 1.163(j)-6(o)(6) Example 6(ii).

[C] *Partner basis and capital account adjustments, § 704(d), and dispositions.* A partner's basis in its interest is reduced (but not below zero) by EBIE allocated to it in the allocation year (even though it produces no deduction). If the partner disposes of the interest before all of the carried-forward excess business interest has been deducted, its basis in the transferred interest is increased by any remaining carry-forward amount, and the carry forward disappears.[375.7] Proposed Regulations would require that immediately before the disposition, the partnership increase its basis in its capital gain property by a like amount in the same manner as a positive § 734(b) adjustment. This basis adjustment is not depreciable or amortizable.[375.8] If the disposition is because the partnership interest is liquidated, any § 734(b) adjustment is made first[375.9] and is not subject to the no-amortization rule. Upon the disposition of a portion of a partnership interest, a proportionate share of any EBIE remains with the transferor partner.[375.10]

The interaction of these rules with § 704(d), which limits a partner's ability to deduct losses to its outside basis, is complex. Where multiple classes of losses are suspended under Section 704(d), Regulations § 1.704-1(d)(2) apportions such suspended losses among the classes proportionately based on the character of such losses.[375.11] Deductible BIE and EBIE embedded in a suspended loss becomes a "negative § 163(j) expense." Since the partner's basis must be zero in order to bring § 704(d) into play, these negative § 163(j) expenses have no impact on the partner's basis and a disposition of the interest does not "free up" these items.[375.12] To the extent the suspended losses are no

---

[375.7] § 163(j)(4)(B)(iii); Reg. § 1.163(j)-6(h)(3). The liquidation of a partner's interest is a "disposition." Id.

[375.8] Prop. Reg. § 1.163(j)-6(h)(5) (2020).

[375.9] Prop. Reg. § 1.163(j)-6(h)(5) (2020).

[375.10] Reg. § 1.163(j)-6(h)(3).

[375.11] See ¶ 11.05[1].

[375.12] Upon a partial disposition of an interest, all of the negative § 163(j) expense remains with the transferor partner, not just a proportionate amount. Reg. § 1.163(j)-6(h)(3).

longer subject to § 704(d) (say, because income is allocated to the partner), the negative § 163(j) items spring to life and become subject to the general § 163(j) rules.[375.13]

Since the entire suspended loss remains with the transferor, this is the correct result. See ¶ 11.05[2].

[375.13] Reg. §§ 1.163(j)-6(h)(3), 1.163(j)-6(o)(7) Example 7.

[D] *Partner's share of deductible business interest and Section 163(j) excess items.* The partnership-level application of § 163(j) implicates the application of § 163(j) at the partner level. Business interest deductible at the partnership level becomes part of the partnership's income or loss, and is not again tested at the partner level.[375.14] But the § 163(j) analysis does not end there because components of the partnership's activities can affect the partner's ability to deduct both current-year and future interest expense deductions ("§ 163(j) excess items"). These § 163(j) excess items include (1) business interest not deductible by the partnership (EBIE), which is passed through to the partners and carried forward by them to be tested in future years for deductibility; (2) a partnership's excess capacity to deduct business interest (ETI); and (3) BII in excess of its BIE (excess business interest income, or EBII).[375.15] Which partners are entitled to (or burdened by) these attributes? These § 163(j) excess items are not tax items themselves; they are subsets of a partners' distributive share of other items governed by § 704(b). Accordingly, they cannot be specially allocated among the partners. The statute provides that a partner's share of EBIE and ETI are to be determined in the same manner as the non-separately stated taxable income or loss of the partnership. Rather than simply allocating these items according to bottom-line income or loss, however, the Regulations provide an extraordinarily complex formula for allocating all § 163(j) excess items, as well as the partnership's deductible BIE. While mathematically elegant, few practitioners will be able to apply it. For all but the largest taxpayers, these rules are likely to be ignored. Fortunately, small taxpayers are exempted from the rules (discussed later at ¶ 9.02[3][c][i][E]), and an exemption is provided for "straight up" allocation schemes.

The allocation formula is an eleven-step process:[375.16] The first two steps are easy:

Step 1: Determine the partnership's § 163(j) limitation. This calculation will produce the partnership's EBII, ETI, EBIE (not including, floor plan financing interest) (such items referred to herein as the "§ 163(j) excess items"), and the partnership's deductible BIE for the year.

[375.14] Reg. § 1.163(j)-6(c)(3).
[375.15] Reg. § 1.163(j)-6(b)(6).
[375.16] Reg. § 1.163(j)-6(f)(2).

> Step 2: Determine each partner's allocable share of each § 163(j) item[375.17] under §§ 704(b) and 704(c). Section 743(b) adjustments, remedial items, and investment income and expense are not taken into account. If each partner has a pro-rata share of each allocable § 163 excess item (or, if such items do not exist), each such item is allocated in the same proportion *and the allocation process is complete.* Many, if not most, partnerships should satisfy this standard, and thus avoid the mind-numbing complexity of Steps 3 through 11.

Steps 3 through 11 address the tension between the partnership-level application of § 163(j) and the need to reflect the deductible BIE and the § 163(j) excess items at the partner level. Obtaining the deduction for business interest is obviously desirable. The excess items can be very valuable, since EBII increases a partner's interest deduction capacity dollar-for-dollar, ETI increases it by 30 percent, and EBIE can be carried forward. When the partners' distributive shares of ATI, BII, and BIE vary, deciding who should get these items is critical. Allowing partners to decide for themselves would lead to severe gamesmanship and a significant revenue loss to the Fisc. Accordingly, the Treasury determined that the § 163(j) excess item allocation scheme must be airtight.

As noted earlier, many partnerships will not need to deal with these rules because they either meet the small partnership exception or satisfy the pro-rata rule. Most of the rest will find that the intuitively correct answer is indeed the actual answer. Aggressive allocation structures, on the other hand, such as those that fragment ATI into both positive and negative amounts, are in for a long day at the office.

A pared down version of example 17 of Regulations § 1.163(j)-6(o)(17) illustrates a fairly common fact pattern.

EXAMPLE 9-18.4: *A* and *B* are the only partners of PRS. PRS has $100 of ATI, $20 of BII, and $60 of BIE. PRS allocates all $100 of ATI to *A* and its BII and BIE equally to *A* and *B*. PRS's § 163(j) limitation is $50 ($100 × 30% + $20). PRS has no EBIE nor any ETI (PRS used all its capacity). *A* and *B* are each allocated $30 of BIE ($60 total), but only $50 is deductible. Intuitively, *A* provided $40 of deduction capacity (ATI of $100 × 30% plus $10 share of business income) and *B* only $10 ($10 share of business income). Thus, all of *A*'s $30 share of BIE should be deductible. *B* gets a free ride in that *B* gets to deduct $20 of business interest even though contributing only $10 of capacity. But *A* cannot deduct more business interest than *A*'s allocable share ($30), so *B* is the beneficiary of the entity application of § 163(j): *B* can deduct $20 even though providing just $10 of capacity. *B*'s nondeductible $10 of EBIE carries over to the next year. Example 17 confirms that these intuitively correct results are identical to those yielded by the eleven-step formula.

[375.17] Reg. § 1.163(j)-6(b)(1).

Intuiting the correct result is also possible when BII exceeds BIE, but they are disproportionately allocated such that even though the partnership has EBII, a partner has a net BIE. Here, the commonsense answer is to allocate the EBII in proportion to each partner's positive contribution to the partnership's capacity, and the "free ride" (the ability to deduct some interest despite providing no capacity) is shared among the free riders in proportion to their distributive shares of interest expense. For example, assume the ABC partnership has $60 of BII, allocated 100 percent to *A*, and $30 of BIE, allocated equally to *B* and *C*. ABC is entitled to deduct $30 of BIE. *A* contributes $60 of capacity, *B* and *C* none. Nevertheless, each of *B* and *C* deducts $15 of BIE as a free rider. *A* is entitled to $30 of EBII; although *A* provided $60 of capacity, the entity-level application of § 163(j) limits his benefit to $30. These results are consistent with Steps 3 through 5 of the eleven-step formula.

One partner's ability to use excess capacity of a partner can yield a planning opportunity where one partner has material BII, as illustrated by the following example.

EXAMPLE 9-18.5: Assume the same facts as in Example 9-18.4, but in a transaction that does not have a principal purpose of avoiding the rules of § 163(j), *C*, a financial institution, contributes an asset that generates $10 of BII to PRS. The $10 of BII (and no other PRS item) is allocated to *C*. PRS's § 163(j) limitation is increased to $60 and, due to the entity-level application of § 163(j), PRS's $60 of BIE is fully deductible.

Steps 6 through 11 provide the rules for dealing with complex situations, specifically cases where a partnership fragments its ATI into both positive and negative numbers. Since a partner with negative ATI contributes no capacity to the partnership but may still receive an allocation of deductible BIE, apportioning this "free rider" penalty among the other partner is exceedingly complex.[375.18] Example 18-21 of Regulations § 1.163(j)-6(o) lays out the mechanics of this process in great detail. We encourage the reader facing such a problem to consult these examples and we pass along our condolences.

[375.18] See Reg. § 1.163(j)-6(f)(2)(vii) (skipping Step 8 if ATI of no partner is negative).

[E] *Small business exception.* Section 163(j)(3) exempts taxpayers (other than tax shelters) that meet the gross receipts test of § 448(c) for the taxable year ($25 million, indexed for post-2018 inflation) from the deduction limitation rules (such a taxpayer is referred to as an exempt entity). The gross receipts test is applied at the partnership level. A partner's distributive share of business interest from an exempt entity is not subject to § 163(j).[375.19] A partner's share of an exempt entity's trade or business income is included in its ATI computation, but its share of a loss is not. If a partner has an excess BIE

[375.19] Reg. § 1.163(j)-6(m)(1).

carry forward from a partnership and the partnership becomes an exempt entity, the carry forward becomes BIE of the partner for such year, subject to the usual § 163(j) rules at the partner level.[375.20]

[F] *Excepted trades or businesses.* Section 163(j)(7) excepts certain trades or businesses from the limitation rules of § 163(j). Specifically, the business of performing services as an employee, an electing real estate business, an electing farming business, and regulated utilities are excepted.[375.21] Elections with respect to a partnership trade or business must be made by the partnership.[375.22] If a partnership owns both excepted and non-excepted trades or businesses, its overall interest income and interest expense is allocated between the businesses based on the partnership's relative adjusted bases in the assets of each business.[375.23] A partner's interest in a partnership is treated as an asset of the partner, and its basis is allocated between excepted or non-excepted trades or business by looking through the partnership to the partner's share of the partnership's basis to its assets, using any reasonable method. The partners' interest basis subject to allocation is determined without including its share of partnership liabilities under § 752. Various de minimis rules and the like can come into play.[375.24] Gain or loss from the disposition of a partnership interest is allocated among excepted, non-excepted, and investment assets using the same basis rules (and enters the partner's ATI calculation accordingly), except that if 90 percent or more of the basis is allocable to either excepted or non-excepted trades or businesses, all of the gain or loss is allocated to the dominant category.[375.25]

[G] *Corporate partners.* All interest income and expense of a C corporation is treated as properly allocable to a trade or business.[375.26] Thus any investment interest, income, or expense of a partnership that is allocated to a corporate partner is treated as properly allocable to a non-excepted trade or business of that corporate partner.[375.27] A corporate partner that disposes of a partnership interest previously subject to suspended excess business interest (and thus whose basis, and earnings and profits, was reduced by the suspended

---

[375.20] Reg. §§ 1.163(j)-6(m)(3), 1.163(j)-6(o)(13) Example 13, 1.163(j)-6(o)(14) Example 14, 1.163(j)-6(o)(15) Example 15.

[375.21] Reg. § 1.163(j)-1(b)(44)(ii).

[375.22] Reg. § 1.163(j)-9(d)(4). Special rules are provided for real estate investment trusts (REITs) owning partnership interests. Reg. § 1.163(j)-9(h).

[375.23] Reg. § 1.163(j)-10(c)(1)(i).

[375.24] Reg. § 1.163(j)-10(c)(5)(ii).

[375.25] Reg. § 1.163(j)-10(b)(4)(ii).

[375.26] Reg. § 1.163(j)-4(b)(1).

[375.27] Reg. §§ 1.163(j)-4(b)(1), 1.163(j)-4(b)(3), 1.163(j)-4(b)(7)(ii) Example 2, 1.163(j)-10(b)(6), 1.163(j)-10(b)(7)(ii) Example 2.

interest) must increase its earnings and profits by the upwards basis adjustment triggered by the disposition.[375.28]

[H] *Traders.* Partnerships engaged in trading activities present unique problems, since they are per-se non-passive activities under § 469. Proposed Regulations issued in 2020 would bifurcate such a partnership's activities into the portion in which partners materially participate and the portion in which they do not. Section 163(j) applies to the active portion at the partnership level, while the non-active portion is passed through to the partners and potentially subject to the investment interest limitation of § 163(d).[375.29]

[I] *Self-charged interest.* Absent a self-charged rule, the partnership-level application of § 163(j) to loans to partnerships from partners could create harsh results. For example, assume *A* in the equal *AB* partnership loans $10,000 at 10 percent interest to *AB*, which has ATI of zero. *A* has $1,000 of interest income from the loan, while *AB*'s entire deduction from accrued interest is limited (its § 163(j) limit is $0 × 30%, or $0). Since *A* effectively loaned half of the funds to itself and half to *B*, economically *A* only has $500 of income.

Proposed Regulations issued in 2020 would remedy this unfairness by deeming an allocation of excess business income to the lending partner equal to the lesser of the lender's EBIE from the partnership or the interest income attributable to the self-charged lending transaction.[375.30] In the example above, *A*'s $500 allocation of EBIE gives rise to a deemed allocation to *A* of $500 of excess business income, thus allowing *A* to deduct the $500 EBIE. Note that if *AB* had an additional $1,500 of EBIE from another unrelated loan, of which $750 was allocable to *A*, the deemed allocation of excess business income would increase to $1,000 (the lesser of *A*'s EBIE of $1,500 or the interest income attributable to the self-charged lending transaction of $1,000). This result stands in sharp contrast to the self-charged rules in the § 469 passive loss regulations, which limit the offset to the "applicable percentage" of the lending partner's interest income (essentially, an aggregate outcome).[375.31] The entity-level application of § 163(j) and the complexity of the eleven-step approach to determining a partner's share of EBIE makes the aggregate approach of the § 469 scheme impossible to apply.

[375.28] Reg. § 1.163(j)-4(c)(3).

[375.29] Prop. Reg. §§ 1.163(j)-6(c)(1), 1.163(j)-6(c)(2), 1.163(j)-6(c)(4) (2020). Proposed Regulations § 1.469-4(d)(6) (2020) would prevent the groupings rules from converting a partner's investment interest expense to BIE.

[375.30] Prop. Reg. §§ 1.163(j)-6(n), 1.163(j)-6(o)(26) Example 26 (2020).

[375.31] See ¶ 11.08[5][a].

[J] *Tiered partnerships.* EBIE is suspended at the partner level, awaiting an allocation of ETI from the partnership that generated the EBIE. In the tiered partnership context, an upper-tier partnership (UTP) that has suspended EBIE from a lower-tier partnership (LTP) has a valuable tax attribute that must eventually be allocated to the UTP partners, some (or all) of whom may not have been around when the EBIE was generated. The 2020 Proposed Regulations[375.32] provide an elaborate scheme to deal with the tiered-partnership problem.

At its heart, EBIE is treated as a § 705(a)(2)(B) expenditure for capital account purposes throughout the tiered structure, but results in a basis reduction only with respect to UTP's interest in LTP. The partners of UTP do not adjust downwards their bases in their UTP interests. UTP creates a non-depreciable capital asset (UTP EBIE) with a fair market value of zero and a tax basis equal to the basis reduction UTP made with respect to its LTP interest. This UTP EBIE carries the carry forward component with it (it is "freed up" by allocations of ETI from LTP). When the "free up" occurs, the resulting BIE is allocated to its "specified partner," which is the UTP partner that suffered the § 705(a)(2)(B) capital account reduction from the original EBIE allocation. The rules are designed to prevent "trafficking" in EBIE deductions. Thus, while §§ 734(b) and 743(b) basis adjustments of transferee partners do not affect carry-forward amounts, once the EBIE is freed up, these adjustments generally eliminate the amount of EBIE that becomes available to a transferee.[375.33] While the conceptual structure of the tiered partnership rules is fairly easily summarized—a UTP's EBIE from a LTP creates a fictional loss asset whose book/tax difference is subject to § 704(c)-type principles, and a transfer of a UTP interest is subject to § 743(b) adjustment with respect to the UTP EBIE regardless of whether a § 754 election is in effect—its mechanics are horrifically complex. A significant portion of the complexity deals with cases in which a partner withdraws from the partnership, stranding the UTP EBIE (the "specified partner" is gone).[375.34] This stranded UTP EBIE does not create any associated BIE that is allocable to UTP's partners. In order to make the books balance, a "§ 1.163(j)-6(j)(8)(ii) account" is created.[375.35] On the other hand, a distribution of an interest can carry UTP EBIE with it to the extent the distributee had a pre-distribution interest in the UTP EBIE,[375.36] and a contribution of a UTB EBIE interest makes the contributor a specified partner with respect to the contributed UTP EBIE.[375.37]

[375.32] Prop. Reg. § 1.163(j)-6(j) (2020).

[375.33] Although the UTP EBIE is generally treated as a capital asset, it is treated as ordinary for the purpose of Regulations § 1.755-1(b), thus generally matching the negative adjustment equal to the difference between the zero value and the tax basis of the fictional UTP EBIE asset. Prop. Reg. §§ 1.163(j)-6(j)(7)(i), 1.163(j)-6(o)(28)(ii) (2020). If no § 754 election is in effect at the time of the transfer, the computations are made as though it were. Prop. Reg. §§ 1.163(j)-6(j)(8)(i), 1.163(j)-6(o)(28)(v) (2020).

[375.34] Prop. Reg. § 1.163(j)-6(j)(6)(ii)(A) (2020).

[375.35] See Prop. Reg. § 1.163(j)-6(o)(29) Example 29 (2020).

[375.36] Prop. Reg. § 1.163(j)-6(j)(6)(ii)(A) (2020).

[375.37] Prop. Reg. § 1.163(j)-6(j)(6)(ii)(B) (2020).

[K] *Controlled foreign corporations.* Regulations § 1.163(j)-7(b) provides that in computing a "relevant" foreign corporation's deductible BIE for the purpose of determining its taxable income, § 163(j) generally applies in the same manner to a controlled foreign corporation (CFC) as it would to a domestic corporation. Domestic corporations generally must treat all interest income and expense as properly allocable to a trade or business (i.e., they do not have investment interest). While § 163(j) is generally applicable to CFCs on an entity-by-entity approach, under Proposed Regulations issued in 2020, a group of commonly owned CFCs would be able to elect to be treated like a consolidated group of domestic corporations.[375.38] If an applicable CFC is a partner in a partnership, the rules generally apply to the partnership in the same manner as if the CFC were a domestic corporation.[375.39] Under the normal rules, a U.S. shareholder of a CFC does not include GILTI or subpart F inclusions in determining ATI due to double-counting concerns, as such amounts were otherwise used in applying § 163(j) at the CFC level. A domestic partnership that is a U.S. shareholder also does not include GILTI or subpart F inclusions in ATI if attributable to a trade or business.

[L] *Special rules in 2019 and 2020.* Section 163(j)(10) increases the limit on deductions for BIE from 30 percent to 50 percent of ATI for taxable years beginning in 2019 and 2020. For partnerships, however, the 30 percent limitation remains in effect for 2019 but 50 percent of any excess BIE is treated as fully deductible business interest in 2020. The remaining 50 percent is treated as EBIE subject to the usual carry-forward rules. Partnerships may elect out of this regime.[375.40] In addition, a partnership may elect to substitute its 2019 ATI for its 2020 ATI.[375.41]

[375.38] If a "CFC group election" is made, § 163(j) is applied on a group basis. Prop. Reg. §§ 1.163(j)-7(c)(2), 1.163(j)-7(e) (2020).

[375.39] Reg. § 1.163(j)-7(b).

[375.40] § 163(j)(10)(A)(ii); Prop. Reg. § 1.163(j)-6(g)(4) (2020).

[375.41] § 163(j)(10)(B)(i); Prop. Reg. § 1.163(j)-6(d)(5) (2020).

[ii] Earnings Stripping: Section 163(j) Pre−2018. The earnings-stripping rules limit the deductibility for U.S. tax purposes of interest paid by a corporation to a related party where the related party is not subject to U.S. tax on such interest and the payor has a debt-to-equity ratio in excess of 1.5 to 1.[375.42] Interest paid to a related party that is subject to a reduced rate of tax on interest under a treaty is subject to a reduced earnings-stripping limitation.[375.43] Interest subject to the earnings-stripping limitation is deductible only to the extent of 50 percent of the corporation's adjusted taxable income.[375.44]

[375.42] §§ 163(j)(1)(A), 163(j)(2)(A).

[375.43] § 163(j)(5)(B).

[375.44] § 163(j)(2)(B)(i). Additionally, failure to utilize the corporation's yearly allotment of adjusted taxable income entitles the corporation to roll such income over into a

Adjusted taxable income is taxable income computed without deductions for net interest expense, net operating losses, depreciation, amortization, or depletion.[375.45] Net interest expense is the excess of interest expense over interest income for the year.[375.46] Interest not deductible by reason of § 163(j) is carried forward for up to three years.[375.47]

> **EXAMPLE 9-18:** A foreign corporation, *FCo*, which pays no tax on U.S. interest under the applicable treaty, has a U.S. subsidiary, *USCo*, which it has financed in part with debt. *USCo* has a debt-to-equity ratio in excess of 1.5 to 1, no interest income, $100 of taxable income each year (before deducting interest), and no net operating losses, depreciation, amortization, depletion, or interest payments other than $60 of interest paid each year to *FCo*. The earnings-stripping limitation allows a deduction for $50 of interest paid to *FCo* and denies a deduction for $10 of such interest— that is, the amount by which *USCo*'s $60 total of interest payments exceeds $50 (one half of its taxable income before interest deductions).
>
> Assume that *USCo* wants to borrow additional funds from an unrelated third party to invest in a project that will not produce any taxable income (without regard to deductions for interest, depreciation, amortization, or depletion) for several years. If *USCo* pays $20 of interest each year on its new borrowing, *USCo*'s total interest payments would be $80 ($30 greater than one half of its adjusted taxable income). As a result, the earnings-stripping limitation would deny a deduction for $30 of the interest paid to *FCo*. The $20 of added interest payments to the unrelated party effectively causes an additional $20 of interest payments to *FCo* to be nondeductible. *USCo*'s taxable income after interest deductions would be $50.

Proposed Regulations issued in 1991 apply these rules to partnerships with corporate partners in a quite logical manner. For purposes of determining the debt-equity ratio of a corporate partner, a partnership's debt is allocated among its partners pursuant to the rules of § 752.[375.48] The determination of a corporate partner's interest income and interest expense is made by treating the partner's § 704 distributive share of interest income and expense as incurred directly by the partner.[375.49]

Whether interest paid or accrued to a partnership is subject to tax is determined at the partner level.[375.50] If a foreign entity is treated as a partnership for U.S. tax purposes but is recognized as an entity under the applicable income

---

subsequent year, thereby increasing the amount of net interest expense allowable under § 163(j). §§ 163(j)(2)(B)(ii), 163(j)(2)(B)(iii).

[375.45] § 163(j)(6).

[375.46] § 163(j)(6)(B).

[375.47] § 163(j)(2)(B)(ii).

[375.48] Prop. Reg. § 1.163(j)-3(b)(3) (1991).

[375.49] Prop. Reg. §§ 1.163(j)-2(e)(4), 1.163(j)-2(e)(5) (1991).

[375.50] Prop. Reg. § 1.163(j)-4(a) (1991).

tax treaty (e.g., a *Belgian société en nom collectif*), this rule produces inaccurate results because it measures the effective tax rate at the wrong level. One hopes that this problem will be rectified in the event the Proposed § 163 Regulations are ever finalized.

An exception to the earnings-stripping rules is provided for interest payments by a corporation to a partnership if persons who are not subject to U.S. tax hold less than 10 percent of the capital and profits interests in the partnership. This exception is inapplicable to interest includible in the gross income of a partner that is itself related to the payor of the interest.[375.51]

The Proposed § 163 Regulations reserve the definition of "interest equivalents."[375.52] Accordingly, the treatment of guaranteed payments as interest for purposes of § 163(j) is uncertain, although the Service's general position is that they are to be treated as interest payments to the recipient but not for the payor.[375.53]

[375.51] Prop. Reg. §§ 1.163(j)-2(g)(4)(i), 1.163(j)-2(g)(5) Example (4) (1991).

[375.52] Prop. Reg. § 1.163(j)-2(e)(3) (1991).

[375.53] GCM 38133 (Oct. 10, 1979); GCM 36702 (Apr. 12, 1976). The Service has announced that it will attack related-party transactions that use guaranteed payments to avoid § 163(j). Notice 2004-31, 2004-17 IRB 830, discussed at ¶ 14.03[6][i].

[g] Additional First-Year Depreciation: Section 179

Pages 9-88 – 9-89:

Replace first two paragraphs of subsection with the following.

Section 179 allows taxpayers to elect to expense the cost of up to $1 million ($500,000 in the case of taxable years beginning before 2018) of certain property. The dollar limitation is subject to reduction for each dollar in excess of $2.5 million ($2 million in the case of taxable years beginning before 2018) of § 179 property placed in service during the year, and is further limited to the taxpayer's trade or business income for the year.[386] All of these dollar amounts are subject to inflation adjustments for years after 2018.[386.1]

The definition of § 179 property was expanded after 2017 to include tangible § 168 property or computer software described in § 197(e)(3)(A)(i), which is (1) § 1245 property or, at the election of the taxpayer, "qualified real

---

[386] For enterprise zone businesses, the $500,000 limit is increased by the lesser of $35,000 or the cost of the § 179 property that is qualified zone property and is put in service during the year. Furthermore, only 50 percent of the cost of qualified zone property is taken into account in applying the $2 million limit. § 1397A.

[386.1] § 179(b)(6), as amended by the 2017 Tax Cuts and Jobs Act, Pub. L. No. 115-97, § 13101(a)(3)(A) (Dec. 22, 2017).

property," and (2) acquired by purchase for use in the active conduct of a trade or business.[386.2]

These limits apply at both the partnership and partner levels,[387] but the election to expense the cost of § 179 property, as well as the determination of whether property is § 179 property, is made at the partnership level.[388] The dollar limitations are applicable (and the § 179 expenses are deductible) in the partner's year in which the partnership's year ends.[389]

For purposes of assessing the trade or business income limitation, a partnership must aggregate its net income (or loss) from all trades or businesses actively conducted by the partnership during the year, determined under § 702(a) (excluding credits, tax-exempt income, and § 707(c) guaranteed payments). Once the § 179 expenditure is limited by this amount, each partner again applies the limitation with respect to his trade or business income. At the partner level, a partner may include his distributive share of partnership active trade or business income as long as he is engaged in the active conduct of at least one of the partnership's trades or businesses.[390] However, partners are not required to take into account the cost of partnership § 179 property in applying the $2.5 million limit at the partner level.[391] A partner's share of partnership § 179 expenses is determined under § 704 and the Regulations thereunder.[392]

[386.2] § 179(d)(1), as amended by the 2017 Tax Cuts and Jobs Act, Pub. L. No. 115-97, § 13101(a)(3)(A) (Dec. 22, 2017). Property described in § 50(b) (other than paragraph (2) thereof) is not eligible. "Qualified real property" means qualified improvement property described in § 168(e)(6) as well as the following improvements to nonresidential real property placed in service after such property was placed in service: roofs, heating, ventilation and air-conditioning property, fire protection and alarm property, and security systems. § 179(f), as amended.

[387] § 179(d)(8); Reg. § 1.179-2(c)(2). The validity of this provision of the Regulations, which is based squarely on the statute, was upheld in Dennis L. Hayden, 112 TC 115 (1999), aff'd, 204 F3d 772 (7th Cir. 2000).

[388] Reg. § 1.179-1(h); see Rev. Rul. 89-7, 1989-1 CB 178.

[389] Reg. §§ 1.179-2(b)(3)(iv), 1.179-2(c)(2)(ii).

[390] Reg. § 1.179-2(c)(2)(v).

[391] Reg. § 1.179-2(b)(3).

[392] Reg. § 1.179-2(b)(3)(iii). See generally ¶ 11.03[2][b].

[j] Start-Up Expenses: Section 195

Page 9-92:

Replace note 416 with the following.

[416] § 195(a). Section 195(b) allows the taxpayer to elect to deduct the lesser of the amount of the start-up expenditures or $5,000, in the latter case reduced by the amount by which the start-up expenditures exceed $50,000. The remainder is amortized over the 180-month period beginning with the month in which the active trade or business begins. A taxpayer is deemed to have elected § 195(b) treatment for the tax year in which the active trade or business begins unless he affirmatively elects to capitalize start-up expenditures on a timely filed (including extensions) return for the year. Once made, an election

is irrevocable for the trade or business. Any change in the characterization of an item as a start-up expenditure (if the taxpayer reports the item consistently for two or more years) or the year in which the trade or business begins (if the taxpayer amortizes start-up expenditures for two or more years) is a change in accounting method. Reg. § 1.195-1(b). See Rev. Rul. 81-150, 1981-1 CB 119 (partnership organized to construct and own offshore drilling rig; payments to general partner for supervision of construction required to be capitalized as part of cost of rig; payments to general partner for general management services during construction period may be amortized under § 195).

[k] Intangibles

[i] Section 197 generally.

Page 9-95:

Add to note 428.

Special rules apply if there is a contribution of a § 197(f)(9) intangible to a § 721(c) partnership. See ¶ 4.01[5][b][iii][E].

In first full paragraph, replace third sentence with the following.

The exchange is tax-free under § 1031(a), and *A* takes a $400 basis in *I-2* under § 1031(d).[429.1]

[429.1] Tax-free exchanges of intangibles are no longer possible following the 2017 changes to § 1031(a), limiting qualifying exchanges to exchanges of real property, made by the 2017 Tax Cuts and Jobs Act, Pub. L. No. 115-97, § 13303 (Dec. 22, 2017).

[l] Expenses for the Production of Income: Section 212

Page 9-103:

Add to note 463.

The 2017 Tax Cuts and Jobs Act replaces the 2-percent floor in § 67 with a flat denial of all "miscellaneous itemized deductions" (a phrase that includes § 212 deductions) by individuals for tax years beginning after December 31, 2017, and before January 1, 2026. Pub. L. No. 115-97, § 11045 (Dec. 22, 2017).

[m] Uniform Capitalization Rules: Section 263A

[i] Overview.

Page 9-104:

Replace note 467 with the following.

[467] § 263A(b). Exceptions are provided for personal-use property and certain timber property. §§ 263A(c)(1), 263A(c)(5). Small businesses (i.e., taxpayers (other than tax shelters) meeting the gross receipts test of § 448(c)) are also exempt under § 263A(i). A part-

ner would include its distributive share of partnership gross receipts in applying this test. Prop. Reg. § 1.263A-1(j)(2)(iii) (2020).

Page 9-105:

Add to note 468.

For tax years beginning after December 31, 2021, the 2017 Tax Cuts and Jobs Act is scheduled to amend § 174 and convert research and experimental expenditure deductions into intangibles generally amortizable over five years. Pub. L. No. 115-97, § 13206 (Dec. 22, 2017).

[t] Interest Subject to Allocation Under Section 864(e)

Page 9-113:

Replace last sentence, including footnote 508, with the following.

A special entity rule is provided for all less-than-10-percent limited partners.[508]

---

[508] Reg. § 1.861-9(e)(4). Prior to tax years that both begin after December 31, 2017, and end on or after December 4, 2018, the entity rule also applied to corporate general partners. Reg. § 1.861-9(k).

Pages 9-113–9-115:

Replace ¶ 9.02[3][u] with revised ¶ 9.02[3][u].

[u] Fifty Percent Exclusion of Gain From Certain Small Business Stock; Rollover of Gain From Qualified Small Business Stock to Another Qualified Small Business Stock [Revised]

Section 1202 permits noncorporate taxpayers to exclude from income 50 percent of the gains from certain small business stocks that were issued after August 10, 1993, and held for five or more years. The exclusion percentage is 100% for qualified small business stock acquired between September 27, 2010, and January 1, 2014,[509] and the exclusion percentage was 75% for qualified small business stock acquired between February 17, 2009, and September 28, 2010.[509.1] Where such gains are recognized by a partnership, a noncorporate partner's share of the gain can qualify for the exclusion provided that: (1) the stock was held by the partnership for more than five years; (2) the gain would have been eligible for the exclusion if the stock had been held by an individual; and (3) the partner held his interest in the partnership from the time the partnership acquired the stock to the time it disposed of the stock.[509.2] A part-

---

[509] § 1202(a)(4).

[509.1] § 1202(a)(3).

[509.2] See § 1202(g). If the partner's interest in the partnership increases while the small business stock is held by the partnership, the portion of the gain attributable to the increased interest is not eligible for the exclusion. See § 1202(g)(3).

ner who acquires small business stock from a partnership and who has held his interest in the partnership for the entire period that the partnership held the stock generally is entitled to tack on the partnership's holding period (for purposes of meeting the five-year holding requirement) and is treated as having acquired the stock in the same manner as the partnership.[510]

Section 1045(a) generally provides for deferral of gain that would otherwise be currently taxable on the sale of qualified small business (QSB) stock (1) held by a taxpayer (other than a corporation) for more than six months and (2) with respect to which such taxpayer elects to defer gain recognition. If § 1045 applies, gain is recognized only to the extent of the greater of (1) the amount by which the amount realized on the sale exceeds the cost of any QSB stock acquired by the taxpayer within the sixty-day period beginning on the date of the sale or (2) the ordinary income realized on the sale of such stock. Section 1045(a) apparently operates before § 1202, because gain not recognized under § 1045(a) is not available to be partially excluded from gross income under § 1202.

Regulations under § 1045 govern the manner in which gain may be deferred upon a partnership's sale of QSB stock.[511] In general, these Regulations allow partners considerable flexibility in their use of § 1045,[512] and provide as follows:

1. A partnership that holds QSB stock for more than six months, sells such QSB stock, and purchases replacement QSB stock may elect to apply § 1045;
2. An eligible partner of a partnership that sells QSB stock may elect to apply § 1045 if the eligible partner purchases replacement QSB stock directly or through a purchasing partnership;
3. A taxpayer (other than a C corporation) that holds QSB stock for more than six months, sells such QSB stock, and purchases replacement QSB stock through a purchasing partnership may elect to apply § 1045;
4. A partnership that holds QSB stock for more than six months, sells such QSB stock, and purchases replacement QSB stock may elect to apply § 1045 in accordance with Regulations § 1.1045-1(h).[513]

If a partnership elects to apply § 1045, then generally eligible partners will not recognize their distributive share of any partnership § 1045 gain.[514] A

---

[510] See § 1202(h).

[511] Rev. Proc. 98-48, 1998-2 CB 367, provides procedures for making an election under § 1045 to defer recognition of gain on the sale of QSB stock.

[512] Reg. § 1.1045-1(a).

[513] Reg. § 1.1045-1(b)(1).

[514] For this purpose, partnership § 1045 gain equals the partnership's gain from the sale of the QSB stock reduced by the greater of —

partner's distributive share of partnership § 1045 gain is proportionate to his distributive share of the partnership's gain from the sale of the QSB stock.[515]

Under Regulations § 1.1045-1(b)(3)(i), the adjusted basis of an eligible partner's interest in a partnership is not increased under § 705(a)(1) by gain from a partnership's sale of QSB stock that is not recognized by the partner as the result of a partnership election under Regulations § 1.1045-1(b)(1).

Under Regulations § 1.1045-1(b)(3)(ii)(A), the basis of a partnership's re-placement QSB stock is reduced (in the order acquired) by the amount of gain from the partnership's sale of QSB stock that is not recognized by an eligible partner as a result of the partnership's election under § 1045. Such a basis ad-justment constitutes an adjustment to the basis of the partnership's replacement QSB stock with respect to that partner only.[516] If a partnership (1) sells QSB stock with respect to which such a basis adjustment has been made and (2) makes an election with respect to the sale and purchases replacement QSB stock, the basis adjustment generally carries over to the replacement QSB stock.

Under Regulations § 1.1045-1(b)(4), an eligible partner may opt out of the partnership's § 1045 election with respect to QSB stock either by recogniz-ing the partner's distributive share of the partnership § 1045 gain or by making a partner-level § 1045 election with respect to the partner's distributive share of the partnership § 1045 gain. Opting out of a partnership's § 1045 election, as provided in Regulations § 1.1045-1(b)(4) , does not constitute a revocation of the partnership's election, which continues to apply to the partnership's other partners.

Under Regulations § 1.1045-1(c)(1)(i), an eligible partner of a partnership that sells QSB stock (i.e., the selling partnership) may elect, in accordance with Regulations § 1.1045-1(h), to apply § 1045 if replacement QSB stock is purchased by an eligible partner. An eligible partner of a selling partnership may elect to apply § 1045 if replacement QSB stock is purchased by a partner-ship in which the taxpayer is a partner (directly or through an upper-tier part-nership) on the date on which the partnership acquires the replacement QSB stock (i.e., the purchasing partnership). A taxpayer (other than a C corporation) that sells QSB stock held for more than six months at the time of the sale may

---

1. The amount of the gain from the sale of the QSB stock that is treated as ordinary income; or
2. The excess of the amount realized by the partnership on the sale over the total cost of all replacement QSB stock purchased by the partnership (excluding the cost of any replacement QSB stock purchased by the partnership that is other-wise taken into account under § 1045).

[515] Reg. § 1.1045-1(b)(2). For this purpose, the partnership's gain from the sale of QSB stock and the partner's distributive share of that gain are determined without regard to basis adjustments under § 743(b) and Regulations § 1.1045-1(b)(3)(ii).

[516] Except as modified by Regulations § 1.1045-1(b)(3)(ii)(A), the effect of such a basis adjustment is determined under the principles set forth in Reg. §§ 1.743-1(g), 1.743-1(h), and 1.743-1(j).

elect to apply § 1045 if replacement QSB stock is purchased by a purchasing partnership (including a selling partnership).

Under Regulations § 1.1045-1(c)(1)(ii), an eligible partner of a selling partnership that elects to apply § 1045 with respect to his/her purchase of replacement QSB stock must recognize his/her distributive share of gain from the sale of QSB stock by the selling partnership only to the extent of the greater of (1) the amount of the eligible partner's distributive share of the selling partnership's gain from the sale of the QSB stock that is treated as ordinary income or (2) the excess of (a) the eligible partner's share of the selling partnership's amount realized on the sale of the QSB stock (excluding the cost of any replacement QSB stock purchased by the selling partnership) over (b) the cost of any replacement QSB stock purchased by the eligible partner (excluding the cost of any replacement QSB stock that is otherwise taken into account under § 1045).

Under Regulations § 1.1045-1(c)(1)(iii)(A), an eligible partner that (1) treats his/her interest in QSB stock purchased by a purchasing partnership as a purchase of replacement QSB stock by the eligible partner and (2) elects to apply § 1045 with respect to such purchase must recognize his/her total gain (i.e., the eligible partner's distributive share of gain from the selling partnership's sale of QSB stock and any gain taken into account under Regulations § 1.1045-(1)(c)(5) from the sale of replacement QSB stock), but only to the extent of the greater of (1) the amount of the eligible partner's distributive share of the selling partnership's gain from the sale of the QSB stock that is treated as ordinary income or (2) the excess of (a) the eligible partner's share of the selling partnership's amount realized on the sale of the QSB stock (excluding the cost of any replacement QSB stock purchased by the selling partnership) over (b) the eligible partner's share of the purchasing partnership's cost of the replacement QSB stock (excluding the cost of any QSB stock that is otherwise taken into account under § 1045).

Under Regulations § 1.1045-1(c)(1)(iii)(B), if a partner (other than a C corporation) treats his/her interest in QSB stock purchased by a purchasing partnership (with respect to which he/she is a partner) as a purchase of replacement QSB stock by the partner, such partner must recognize his/her gain from the sale of the QSB stock, but only to the extent of the greater of (1) the amount of gain from the sale of the QSB stock that is treated as ordinary income or (2) the excess of (a) the amount realized by the partner on the sale of the QSB stock over (b) the partner's share of the purchasing partnership's cost of the replacement QSB stock (excluding the cost of any QSB stock that is otherwise taken into account under § 1045).

Under § 705(a)(1), the adjusted basis of an eligible partner's interest in a selling partnership that sells QSB stock generally is increased by the partner's distributive share of gain. However, if the selling partnership is also the purchasing partnership, the adjusted basis of an eligible partner's interest in a partnership that sells QSB stock may be reduced as well.

A partner that treats his interest in QSB stock purchased by the purchasing partnership as the partner's replacement QSB stock must reduce (in the order replacement QSB stock is acquired) the adjusted basis of the partner's interest in the purchasing partnership by the partner's distributive share of the gain on the sale of the selling partnership's QSB stock that is not recognized by the partner or by the gain on a sale of QSB stock by the partner that is not recognized by the partner under § 1045, as applicable.

Pages 9-116–9-121:

Replace ¶ 9.02[3][w] with revised ¶ 9.02[3][w], and add new ¶¶ 9.02[3][x], 9.02[3][y], 9.02[3][z], and 9.02[3][aa].

[w] Domestic Production Deduction: Section 199 [Revised]

The ongoing efforts by Congress to provide an export-related tax benefit that will not be seen as a "prohibited export subsidy" by the World Trade Organization (WTO) may have ended with the repeal of § 199 by the 2017 Tax Cuts and Jobs Act in conjunction with the overall revision of both individual and corporate tax rates and the creation of a new 20-percent deduction for qualified business income of individuals and pass-through entities. Prior to its repeal, § 199 provided a deduction equal to a percentage (9 percent as of its repeal) of the lesser of (1) "qualified production activities income" (QPAI) or (2) taxable income. The deduction was limited to 50 percent of the W-2 wages paid during the tax year.[524]

NOTE: The following discussion, in this ¶ 9.02[3][w], does not apply to tax years beginning after December 31, 2017:

QPAI is the excess of domestic production gross receipts (DPGR) over the sum of (1) the cost of goods sold that are allocable to those receipts (CGS); (2) other deductions, expenses, or losses directly allocable to those receipts; and (3) a ratable portion of all other deductions, expenses, or losses not directly allocable to any specific class of income. Final § 199 Regulations require taxpayers to use a reasonable method to allocate CGS between DPGR and non-DPGR.[527] Deductions attributable to DPGR (as well as deductions that are not directly allocable to DPGR or to another class of income) are allocated under one of the three following explicitly "reasonable" methods: (1) the § 861 method (which is available to all taxpayers); (2) the simplified deduction method (which is only available to taxpayers which meet maximum gross receipt and asset requirements); and (3) the small business simplified overall method (which is only available to qualifying small taxpayers).[528]

With respect to partnerships and other pass-through entities, § 199(d)(1) provides that § 199 will be applied at the partner or similar level, and gives

---

[524] § 199(b).

[527] Reg. § 1.199-4(b).

[528] Reg. § 1.199-4(c).

the Treasury the authority to promulgate rules relating to the allocation of the deduction among partners and additional reporting requirements. Section 199(d)(1) also provides that each partner shall be treated as having W-2 wages for the taxable year equal to such partner's allocable share of the W-2 wages of the partnership for the taxable year.[529]

Initial guidance with respect to the application of § 199 was provided by Notice 2005-14.[530] Subsequently, Proposed Regulations provided that a taxpayer could rely either upon the Proposed Regulations or upon Notice 2005-14.[531] Final Regulations were issued on May 24, 2006, applicable to taxable years beginning on or after June 1, 2006. Taxpayers may generally apply these Regulations to prior periods.[532] Legislation enacted on May 17, 2006, however, changed the wage allocation rules applicable to partnerships, such that the final Regulations (as drafted) were obsolete in this regard. Accordingly, the partnership provisions of these Regulations (contained in Regulations § 1.199-9) were inapplicable to taxable years beginning after May 17, 2006.[533] On October 19, 2006, the Treasury Department promulgated Proposed and Temporary Regulations reflecting the May 17, 2006 legislation.[534] The final Regulations, which replaced those Proposed Regulations, apply to taxable years beginning after May 17, 2006. The following rules outline the general rules applicable to partnerships with respect to § 199, noting differences between the various regimes where relevant:

---

[529] Regulations provide that a partnership must generally allocate W-2 wages among its partners in the same manner it allocates wage expense. The partner must then aggregate its allocable share of W-2 wages from the partnership with its W-2 wages from non-partnership sources in order to determine the amount of the partner's W-2 wages properly allocable to domestic production gross receipts. See Reg. § 1.199-5(b)(3). The Regulations are applicable to taxable years beginning after October 19, 2006. However, a taxpayer may apply the provisions of the Regulations to taxable years beginning after May 17, 2006, and before October 19, 2006. Where a partner's taxable year differs from a partnership's taxable year, these effective dates are based upon the partnership's taxable year. For taxable years beginning on or before May 17, 2006, § 199(d)(1)(B) provided that W-2 wages paid by partnerships must be allocated to each partner in an amount equal to the lesser of: (1) the wages the partner would have been allocated without regard to § 199(d)(1); or (2) two times the applicable percentage for the year (3 percent, 6 percent, or 9 percent) of the QPAI allocated to the partner.

The wage allocation provisions of Regulations § 1.199-5(b) apply to all partnerships, regardless of whether the partnership has elected, under § 761(a), to be excluded from the application of Subchapter K.

[530] Notice 2005-14, 2005-1 CB 498.

[531] Prop. Reg. § 1.199-8(g) (2005). A taxpayer could not interpret the absence of a rule in Notice 2005-14, 2005-1 CB 498, that was contained in the Proposed Regulations as creating a contrary rule.

[532] See Reg. § 1.199-8(i).

[533] See Reg. § 1.199-9(k).

[534] TD 9293, 2006-48 IRB 957.

1. A partner's share of any item relevant to the computations under § 199 (i.e., income, gain, loss, and deduction; CGS allocated to those items of income; and gross receipts included in those items of income) is equal to the partner's distributive share of the item under §§ 702 and 704. Special allocations are respected provided they have substantial economic effect and are otherwise valid under the § 704(b) Regulations.[535]

2. In applying § 199 at the partner level, each partner must aggregate its share of partnership § 199 items (to the extent such items are not otherwise disallowed under the Code) with (a) expenses incurred directly by the partner that are attributable to the partnership's qualified production activities and (b) the partner's § 199 items from all sources other than the partnership.[536]

3. Partnership § 199 expenses are taken into account by each partner only if the partner's distributive share of partnership losses and deductions is not limited under §§ 704(d), 465, 469, or any other Code provision. A proportionate share of partnership § 199 expenses is taken into account if a portion of a partner's share of losses is limited under any of these provisions, with deferred expenses potentially taken into account in future years.[537]

4. For taxable years beginning after May 17, 2006,[538] a partner's share of W-2 wages is equal to his allocable share of partnership W-2 wages (which generally must be allocated in the same manner as partnership wage expenses are allocated among the partners). The partner must then add its share of W-2 wages to its W-2 wages from non-partnership sources, and apportion such wages between DPGR and non-DPGR pursuant to Regulations § 1.199-2(e)(2).[539]

   For taxable years beginning before May 18, 2006, a partner's share of W-2 wages is equal to the lesser of the partner's distributive share of partnership W-2 wages (giving effect to any allocations that are valid under § 704(b)) or two times the applicable percentage of the partner's QPAI, computed by taking into account only the items of the partnership allocable to the partner for the taxable year. This

---

[535] See Reg. § 1.199-5(b)(1) and Reg. § 1.199-9(b)(1)(i) (for taxable years beginning before May 18, 2006); Notice 2005-14, § 4.06(1)(a)(i), 2005-1 CB 498.

[536] See Reg. § 1.199-5(b)(1) and Reg. § 1.199-9(b)(1)(i) (for taxable years beginning before May 18, 2006); Notice 2005-14, § 4.06(1)(a)(i), 2005-1 CB 498 (omitting requirement that items be otherwise allowable under the Code).

[537] See Reg. § 1.199-5(b)(2) and Reg. § 1.199-9(b)(2) (for taxable years beginning before May 18, 2006) Notice 2005-14, § 4.06(1)(a)(ii), 2005-1 CB 498.

[538] If a partner's taxable year differs from the partnership's taxable year, the partnership's taxable year must begin after May 17, 2006.

[539] Reg. § 1.199-5(b)(3). Partnerships that elect out of Subchapter K pursuant to § 761(a) are still treated as partnerships for purposes of Regulations §§ 1.199-1 through 1.199-8.

share is aggregated with the partner's W-2 wages paid from all other qualified production activity sources for purposes of § 199. However, if a partner does not have positive QPAI from a partnership for the year, no partnership W-2 wages may be taken into account in computing the partner's § 199 deduction.[540] In the case of tiered partnerships, the W-2 wage limitation of § 199(d)(1) in effect prior to May 18, 2006, is applied separately for each partnership entity. Further, the W-2 wages of a partner in a partnership that owns an interest in one or more pass-through entities are equal to the sum of the partner's allocable share of W-2 wages of the upper-tier partnership (determined by including its own W-2 wages, plus its allocable share of lower-tier W-2 wages, subject to the limitation of § 199(d)(1)) and the partner's other W-2 wages.[541]

5. DPGR generally does not include gain or loss from dispositions of partnership interests or partnership distributions. However, if § 751(a) or § 751(b) applies to a partner, the partner must take into account gain or loss allocable to partnership assets that would give rise to DPGR if disposed of by the partnership.[542]

6. Section 199 is generally applicable to all tax years beginning after December 31, 2004. Despite the general pass-through approach of § 199, partners are not entitled to any share of partnership § 199 items for partnership years that begin in 2004 and end in 2005.[543]

While the above rules evidence an aggregate flavor to the application of § 199 to partnerships, the determination of whether an item of partnership gross receipts is DPGR is generally made by treating the partnership as a separate entity.[544] There are two exceptions to this entity rule in the cases of "qualifying in-kind partnerships" and expanded affiliated group (EAG) partnerships.

If a partnership (1) is engaged solely in (a) the extraction, refining, or processing of oil, natural gas, petrochemicals, or products derived therefrom, in whole or significant part in the United States, (b) the production or generation of electricity in the United States, or (c) an activity or industry designated by the Secretary; and (2) distributes a share of the property to a partner, the partnership is a "qualifying in-kind partnership" and its activities are attributed

---

[540] See Reg. § 1.199-5(a)(3) and Reg. § 1.199-9(b)(3) (for taxable years beginning before May 18, 2006); Notice 2005-14, § 4.06(1)(a)(iii), 2005-1 CB 498.

[541] See Reg. § 1.199-9(g) (for taxable years beginning before May 18, 2006); Prop. Reg. § 1.199-5(f) (2005).

[542] See Reg. § 1.199-5(f) and Reg. § 1.199-9(f) (for taxable years beginning before May 18, 2006); Notice 2005-14, § 4.06(2), 2005-1 CB 498.

[543] See Reg. § 1.199-8(i)(2); Notice 2005-14, § 4.06(3), 2005-1 CB 498.

[544] See Reg. § 1.199-5(g) and Reg. § 1.199-9(b) (for taxable years beginning before May 18, 2006). See Jackel and Huffman, "Partnerships Under the Proposed Domestic Production Activities Deduction Regulations," 110 Tax Notes 251 (2006).

to the partner to the extent of the distribution.[545] In Revenue Ruling 2007-30,[545.1] the Service expanded the definition of "qualifying in-kind partnership" to include partnerships engaged solely in the extraction and processing of minerals within the United States.

Similarly, if all of the interests of a partnership are owned by members of a single EAG[546] (which, for purposes of § 199, is treated as a single taxpayer), the partnership is treated as part of the EAG.[547] The activity of an EAG partnership is attributed to the members of the EAG (or the activity of a member of an EAG is attributed to an EAG partnership) for purposes of determining DPGR if the partnership produces property and distributes, leases, rents, licenses, sells, exchanges, or otherwise disposes of the property to a member of the EAG (or the EAG member produces property and disposes of that property to an EAG partnership).

---

[545] See Reg. § 1.199-9(i); Reg. § 1.199-3(i)(7).

[545.1] Rev. Rul. 2007-30, 2007-21 IRB 1277.

[546] An EAG is an affiliated group as defined in § 1504(a), determined by substituting "more than 50 percent" for "at least 80 percent" everywhere it appears and without regard to §§ 1504(b)(2) and 1504(b)(4). § 199(d)(4)(B).

[547] § 199(c)(4).

[x] Branch Currency Transaction Rules [New]

Section 987 requires that in the case of a qualified business unit (QBU) that has a functional currency other than that of the taxpayer-owner, the taxable income of the taxpayer with respect to the QBU is computed by determining the taxable income or loss of the QBU and then translating that income into U.S. currency at the appropriate exchange rate. Regulations proposed in 2006 and finalized in 2016 are designed to prevent the deduction of non-economic losses available under prior Proposed Regulations. Partnerships are generally treated as entities under the new Regulations, with the result that where a partnership has a functional currency different from that of its partners it will be treated as a § 987 QBU. However, where all of the capital and profits interests of a partnership are owned, directly and indirectly, by persons that are related within the meaning of § 267(b) or § 707(b), the partnership is treated as a § 987 aggregate partnership and each partner is treated as owning its share of assets and liabilities of any § 987 QBU owned indirectly through the partnership.[548]

Final Regulations issued in 2019 are intended to limit the ability of a taxpayer to selectively recognize foreign currency losses by terminating a § 987 QBU. These Regulations effect this outcome by ignoring certain transactions

---

[548] Reg. § 1.987-1(b)(5). A partner's share is determined using any reasonable method. TD 9857 (May 10, 2019), withdrawing liquidation value approach of Temp. Reg. § 1.987.7T(b).

between existing § 987 QBUs and deferring the recognition of § 987 gain or loss in the context of other transactions.[548.1]

[548.1] See Reg. §§ 1.987-2(c)(9), 1.987-12.

[y] Determining Who Is the Insured: Section 831 [New]

Where a partnership or other entity was the named insured under an insurance policy, the Service took the position that the entity should be treated as the insured for purposes of measuring the transfer and distribution of an insurance risk of economic loss unless some or all of the members are exposed to liability in excess of the assets of the entity, in which case the exposed members would be the insured.[549] Thus, general partners, rather than the general or limited partnership in which they have interests, are treated as the insured, but limited liability company mangers and corporate shareholders are ordinarily not viewed as the insured. The existence of limited deficit restoration obligations presumably will require a more nuanced analysis under this approach.

---

[549] Tech. Adv. Mem. 200816029 (Dec. 3, 2007).

[z] Qualified Business Income Deduction: Section 199A [New]

A temporary qualified business income (QBI) deduction for individual taxpayers was added to the Code as § 199A by the 2017 Tax Cuts and Jobs Act (the 2017 Act).[550] It was intended to leaven, to some extent, the differences between the 2017 Act's prodigious reduction in the corporate tax rates (from a maximum of 35 percent to 21 percent) and the more miserly concurrent reduction in the individual tax rates (from a maximum of 39.6 percent to 37 percent).[550.1] Computationally, § 199A(a) provides that the QBI deduction is the lesser of (1) the "combined qualified business income amount" of an individual taxpayer, as determined under § 199A(b)(1); or (2) an amount equal to 20 percent of the excess, if any, of the taxpayer's taxable income over the taxpayer's net capital gain for the year. Section 199A(b)(1) defines "combined qualified business income" as the sum of (1) the amounts determined under § 199A(b)(2) for each of the taxpayer's "qualified trades and businesses"

---

[550] § 199A, added by Pub. L. No. 115-97, § 11011 (Dec. 22, 2017). This new deduction can be claimed by taxpayers regardless of whether they itemize their deductions (§ 63(d)(3), as amended by the 2017 Act), does not reduce adjusted gross income (§ 62(a), as amended by the 2017 Act), and is not taken into account in applying the limitation on itemized deductions (§ 63(d), as amended by the 2017 Act).

[550.1] See discussion and Examples 2-1 and 2-2 in ¶ 2.02[2].

(QBs);[550.2] (2) 20 percent of qualified REIT dividends;[550.3] and (3) 20 percent of qualified publicly-traded partnership (PTP) income.[550.4]

Generally, the amount determined under § 199A(b)(2) for each QB is the lesser of (1) 20 percent of the QBI from the QB; or (2) the greater of (a) 50 percent of the W-2 wages with respect to the QB or (b) 25 percent of the W-2 wages plus 2.5 percent of the unadjusted basis immediately after acquisition (UBIA) of the QB's qualified property.[550.5] However, if the taxpayer's taxable income does not exceed certain threshold amounts ($315,000 for 2018 joint returns, $157,500 for all other 2018 returns, adjusted for cost-of-living increases), the impact of any reductions pursuant to clause (2) of this formula is reduced or eliminated.[550.6] Conversely, if the taxpayer's taxable income exceeds these threshold amounts and the QB is a "specified services trade or business" (SSTB), all or a portion of the SSTB may be disqualified as a QB under § 199A(d), thereby effectively reducing the available QBI deduction, as discussed in ¶ 9.02[3][z][ii] below.

If these computational gyrations seem confusing, it's because they are. The Regulations attempt to articulate the computations in a more cohesive and logical order, with mixed success, by propounding a relatively straight-forward set of rules for taxpayers whose taxable income is less than the applicable threshold amounts and a much more complex set of rules for those with excessive income.[551] For those (like the authors) requiring further assistance, an extensive and helpful set of examples is provided in Regulations § 1.199A-1(d)(4).

The use of taxable income as the measuring rod for these limitations seems only distantly related to the policies underlying the creation of the 20-percent deduction, and can produce very odd results that will force individual taxpayers and relevant pass-through entities (RPEs) into extraordinarily meticulous tax planning to efficiently utilize this new deduction.

This temporary deduction is effective for tax years beginning after December 31, 2017, and before January 1, 2026.[551.1]

[550.2] §§ 199A(b)(1), 199A(b)(2)(A); Reg. §§ 1.199A-1(b)(5), 1.199A-3(b).

[550.3] Reg. §§ 1.199A-1(b)(8), 1.199A-3(c)(2).

[550.4] Reg. §§ 1.199A-1(b)(7), 1.199A-3(c)(3).

[550.5] § 199A(b)(2).

[550.6] § 199A(b)(3). If taxable income exceeds the threshold amount by less than a phase-in amount ($100,000 for a joint return, $50,00 for all others, with no cost-of-living adjustment), the reduction is "phased-in."

[551] Reg. §§ 1.199A-1(c), 1.199A-1(d).

[551.1] 2017 Tax Cuts and Jobs Act, Pub. L. No. 115-97, § 11011 (Dec. 22, 2017); § 199A(i).

---

[i] In general. Section 199A(c) provides that QBI generally includes the net amount of income, gain, deduction, and loss with respect to each QB carried on by the taxpayer, excluding portfolio income, capital gains and losses, employment income, § 707(c) guaranteed payments to partners for services rendered to the partnership, and certain other payments to partners under § 707(a) as prescribed by Regulations.[551.2]

Only items that are effectively connected with the conduct of a trade or business in the United States and included in the calculation of taxable income may be taken into account in computing QBI.[551.3] Performing services as an employee is not a qualified trade or business for purposes of § 199A.[551.4]

The Regulations include detailed rules addressing several specific items: §§ 751(a) and 751(b) gains and losses are included in QBI; guaranteed payments for the use of capital are excluded unless within the scope of a trade or business of the recipient; § 481 adjustments are included but only if the adjustment arises in a year ending after 2017; previously deferred losses under §§ 465, 469, 704(d), and 1366(d) are allowed and taken into account on a FIFO basis if they are from years after 2017; § 172 NOLs are excluded but excess business losses deferred under § 461(l) are taken into account in the subsequent year in which they are deducted; the deductible portions of the self-employment tax, the deduction for the cost of self-employed health insurance, and § 404 deductions for contributions to qualified plans are taken into account.[551.5]

[551.2] §§ 199A(c)(3)(B), 199A(c)(4), 199A(d)(1)(B). The Regulations illustrate and clarify these QBI exclusions. See Reg. § 1.199A-3(b)(2)(ii). Long- and short-term capital gains and losses as well as any items treated as long- or short-term capital gains and losses are excluded. § 199A(c)(3)(B)(ii); Reg. § 1.199A-3(b)(2)(ii). Presumably, § 1231 gains generally will be excluded under this provision, although the Regulations are purposefully vague as to the treatment of § 1231 gains and losses because of a number of complexities noted in the Preamble to the final Regulations. See TD 9847, Preamble III.B.10 (Feb. 8, 2019). Guaranteed payments for services or for the use of capital are excluded from QBI, but a partnership's deduction for such guaranteed payments will reduce QBI if properly allocable to a partnership business and deductible by the partnership. Reg. §§ 1.199A-3(b)(1)(ii), 1.199A-3(b)(2)(ii)(l). Payments received under § 707(a) are excluded from QBI, but a partnership's deduction for such payments will reduce QBI if properly allocable to a partnership business and deductible by the partnership. Reg. § 1.199A-3(b)(2)(ii)(J).

[551.3] § 199A(d)(1)(B); Reg. § 1.199A-1(b)(14).

[551.4] Reg. § 1.199A-3(b)(1). In determining whether a person is an employee, the worker's status for Federal employment tax purposes is not relevant. Reg. § 1.199A-5(d)(2). Instead, the term seems to encompass both workers who are subject to federal employment taxes and those who are common-law employees. See TD 9847, Preamble to the Final Regulations III.A (Feb. 8, 2019); Reg. §§ 1.199A-5(d)(3)(i), 1.199A-5(d)(3)(iii)(A) Example 1, 1.199A-5(d)(3)(iii)(B) Example 2, 1.199A-5(d)(3)(iii)(C) Example 3, 1.199A-5(d)(3)(iii)(D) Example 4 (all referencing "common-law employee" classification rules). There is a strong but rebuttable presumption that anyone who has been classified as an employee for federal employment tax purposes and who continues to perform substantially the same services must remain an employee for § 199A purposes for at least three years. Reg. § 1.199A-5(d)(3). See Reg. § 1.199A-5(d)(3)(iii) for examples of possible valid rebuttal approaches.

[551.5] Reg. §§ 1.199A-3(b)(1)(i)–1.199A-3(b)(1)(vi).

The rental or licensing of tangible or intangible property is always treated as a trade or business under § 199A if the activity rises to the level of a § 162 trade or business.[551.6] Even if this standard is not met, the rental activity may be a QB if it involves related or commonly controlled entities, without regard to whether they are aggregated.[551.7]

QBI with respect to a QB can be negative, resulting in the netting of such losses against positive QBI of other QBs carried on by the taxpayer.[551.8]

An individual can conduct a QB directly[551.9] or indirectly as an owner of an interest in a partnership or S corporation.[551.10] A pass-through approach is generally adopted for partnerships, S corporations, and other types of relevant pass-through entities, and § 199A is applied only at the individual partner, shareholder, or owner level based on the individual's allocable or pro rata share of QBI and all other relevant items.[551.11] Special rules are provided for the application of the separate share rule to beneficiaries of estates and trusts, and the computations necessary for recipients of unitrust and annuity amounts from charitable remainder trusts.[551.11a] Special rules are also provided to integrate the § 199A deduction with the general mirror system of taxation for Puerto Rico.[551.12]

[551.6] Reg. § 1.199A-1(b)(14).

[551.7] Reg. § 1.199A-1(b)(14); see ¶ 9.02[3][z][iv].

[551.8] §§ 199A(c)(1) (QBI is a net amount), 199A(c)(2) (a net QBI loss for a year carries forward).

[551.9] The activities of all types of single-owner disregarded entities are attributed to their owner. Disregarded entities are fully disregarded under § 199A. Reg. § 1.199A-1(e)(2).

[551.10] § 199A(f)(1). The Regulations create a definition of "relevant pass-through entity" (RPE) that includes partnerships (other than publicly traded partnerships), S corporations, common trust funds (Reg. § 1.6032-1T), religious and apostolic organizations (§ 501(d)), and trusts and estates that pass through QBI and related items to their owners or beneficiaries. Reg. § 1.199A-1(b)(10). Regulated investment companies (RICs) are RPEs. Detailed rules relating to the computation and treatment of § 199A dividends from RICs are included in Regulations § 1.199A-3(d).

[551.11] § 199A(f)(1); Reg. § 1.199A-1(e)(1).

[551.11a] See Reg. §§ 1.199A-6(d)(3)(iii), 1.199A-6(d)(3)(v).

[551.12] § 199A(f)(1)(C); Reg. § 1.199A-1(e)(4).

[ii] Computational rules.

[A] *In general.* The § 199A(b)(2) amount for a specific QB generally is equal to the *lesser* of (1) 20 percent of QBI, or (2) the greater of (a) 50 percent of W-2 wages or (b) 25 percent of W-2 wages plus 2.5 percent of UBIA. However, the statute modifies this formula in two significant ways. Each modification involves thresholds and phase-in provisions. The threshold amounts for tax years beginning in 2018 are taxable income[551.13] of $315,000 for joint returns and $157,500 for all others. These amounts are inflation adjusted for subsequent years to reflect increases in the cost-of-living as determined under § 1(f)(3).[551.14] The phase-ins are based on a "phase-in range" between (1) the threshold amount and (2) the threshold amount plus $100,000 for joint returns and $50,000 for all others.[551.15] The phase-in ranges are not inflation adjusted.

One of the modifications is general (it applies to all QBs); the other is a limitation that is specific to certain types of QBs known as specified service trades or businesses (SSTBs).[551.16] The SSTB limitation is applied before the general modification.

The SSTB limitation is as follows:

1. If the taxpayer's taxable income is in excess of the sum of the threshold amount and the phase-in range ($415,000 for 2018 joint returns, $207,500 for all others), *none of the taxpayer's SSTBs are treated as QBs*;

2. If the taxpayer's taxable income is more than the threshold amount and less than the sum of the threshold amount and the phase-in range, then *a percentage of each SSTB is disqualified,* based on the amount by which taxable income exceeds the threshold amount (e.g., if the amount of the taxable income in excess of the relevant threshold amount is 60 percent of the phase-in range, then 60 percent of the SSTB is disqualified, so only 40 percent of the SSTB's QBI, W-2 wages, and UBIA are taken into account under § 199A); and

3. If the taxpayer's taxable income is less than the threshold amount, *each of the taxpayer's SSTBs is treated 100 percent as a QB.*[551.17]

The general modification is also based on the taxpayer's taxable income and affects all QBs, not just SSTBs. This modification allows taxpayers to compute their § 199A(b)(2) amounts without giving full effect to potential reductions as a consequence of the application of § 199A(b)(2) (relating to W-2 wages and UBIA) if their taxable income is less than the sum of their threshold amount and phase-in range:

1. If taxable income is more than the threshold amount and less than the sum of the threshold amount and the phase-in range, then the § 199A(b)(2) amount is 20 percent of QBI less the "reduction amount"; and

---

[551.13] Solely for purposes of applying § 199A, § 199A(e)(1) provides that taxable income is determined without regard to the § 199A deduction.

[551.14] § 199A(e)(2); Reg. § 1.199A-1(b)(12).

[551.15] Reg. § 1.199A-1(b)(4). Thus, the phase-in range for 2018 is $315,000 to $415,000 for joint returns and $157,500 to $207,500 for all other returns.

[551.16] § 199A(d)(2); Reg. § 1.199A-5; see ¶ 9.02[3][z][v] below.

[551.17] § 199A(d)(3); Reg. § 1.199A-1(d)(2)(ii).

2. If taxable income does not exceed the threshold amount, the § 199A(b)(2) amount is simply 20 percent of QBI (W-2 wages and UBIA are irrelevant).

The "reduction amount" is the amount by which 20 percent of QBI exceeds the greater of (1) 50 percent of W-2 wages or (2) the sum of 25 percent of W-2 wages and 2.5 percent of the QB's UBIA (the "excess amount") multiplied by the ratio that the taxpayer's taxable income in excess of the threshold amount bears to the taxpayer's phase-in range.[551.18]

Taxpayers must measure QBI from each of their directly or indirectly held QBs against their allocable share of W-2 wages and UBIA of qualified property from that specific QB to determine the § 199A(b)(2) amount with respect to that QB. If a QB has negative QBI, its negative QBI is apportioned to (and reduces the QBI of) the QBs that have positive QBI in proportion to their positive QBI amounts, but the W-2 wages and UBIA from the negative QB are not taken into account in computing the § 199A(b)(2) amounts from the positive QBs.[551.19] If the combined QBI from all QBs is negative, it is carried forward as a loss from a separate trade or business for purposes of § 199A, but the related W-2 wages and UBIA are not taken into account currently and are not carried forward under § 199A.[551.20]

For partnerships operating QBs, § 199A is not applied at the partnership level. It is applied only at the partner level on a QB-by-QB basis.[551.21] A partner's allocable share of partnership W-2 wages for each QB is based on the partner's allocable share of the wage expense for that QB.[551.22] A partner's share of UBIA for each QB is based on the partner's share of depreciation related to that QB.[551.23] QBI does not include any compensation paid to the taxpayer by any QB of the taxpayer, any § 707(c) guaranteed payments to the

---

[551.18] Reg. §§ 1.199A-1(b)(9), 1.199A-1(d)(2)(iv). While the articulation of this formula in the Regulations might be read to suggest otherwise, it is clear from the overall scheme of the statute that the "reduction amount" should never exceed the "excess amount."

[551.19] Reg. § 1.199A-1(d)(2)(iii)(A); see Reg. § 1.199A-1(d)(4)(ix) Example 9 (negative QBI from loss QB is apportioned to and reduces QBI, of positive QBs; W-2 wages (and, presumably, UBIA) of loss QB do not transfer or carry forward). If only a portion of QBI is taken into account after application of one of the limitations, only a corresponding portion of W-2 wages and UBIA is taken into account. Reg. § 1.199A-1(d)(2)(i).

[551.20] Reg. §§ 1.199A-1(d)(2)(iii)(B), 1.199A-1(d)(4)(xi)(A) Example 11(A); see Reg. § 1.199A-1(d)(4)(xi)(B) Example 11(B) (in subsequent year, negative QBI carryforward is combined with any negative QBI from loss QBs and the total reduces QBI of positive QBs in proportion to their positive QBIs).

[551.21] § 199A(f)(1)(A)(i). Each partner's allocable share of partnership qualified income, gain, deduction, and loss is included in QBI.

[551.22] § 199A(f)(1)(A).

[551.23] § 199A(f)(1)(A). Presumably, it is the partner's share of depreciation with respect to tangible property in question. See § 199A(b)(6)(A).

partner for services, or any § 707(a) payments to the partner for services.[551.24] To assure that partners have the partnership information needed to comply with these rules, the Regulations provide detailed computational and reporting requirement for partnerships and other RPEs, PTPs, trusts, and estates.[551.25]

[551.24] § 199A(c)(4); Reg. §§ 1.199A-3(b)(2)(ii)(I), 1.199A-3(b)(2)(ii)(J).

[551.25] Reg. § 1.199A-6; see ¶ 9.02[3][z][vi][A] below.

[B] *Regulatory methodology.* The Regulations attempt to simplify matters somewhat for lower-income taxpayers. They provide two sets of detailed computational rules for § 199A deductions, depending on whether an individual's taxable income is over or under the relevant threshold amount.

If a taxpayer's income is not over the threshold amount, the base case deduction rules are relatively simple:

1. Add 20 percent of net QBI from all directly and indirectly held QBs to 20 percent of the combined amount of qualified REIT dividends and qualified PTP income;

2. Compare that sum to 20 percent of the individual's taxable income (before giving effect to the § 199A deduction) in excess of his or her capital gain (§ 1(h)); and

3. The lesser of these two amounts is the § 199A deduction.[551.26]

The carryover rules for taxpayers under the threshold are also relatively simple:

1. If total QBI is negative, the current deduction related to QBI is zero and the negative QBI is carried forward to the next year as negative QBI from a separate trade or business; and

2. If the combined amount of qualified REIT dividends and qualified PTP income is less than zero, the current deduction related to these sources is zero and the negative amount is carried forward and reduces the combined REIT and PTP amount in the next year.[551.27]

If a taxpayer's taxable income is over the threshold amount, the deduction rules are as follows:

1. Add the "QBI component" to the "qualified REIT dividend/qualified PTP income component";

[551.26] Reg. § 1.199A-1(c)(1); see Reg. §§ 1.199A-1(c)(3)(i) Example 1 (deduction limited by individual's taxable income), 1.199A-1(c)(3)(ii) Example 2 (exclusion of net capital gain from taxable income limitation), 1.199A-1(c)(3)(iii) Example 3 (wages paid by S corporation to owner are not QBI to recipient but are deductible in determining QBI of S corporation pass through to owner), 1.199A-1(c)(3)(iv) Example 4 (inclusion of qualified REIT dividends and qualified PTP income in determining § 199A deduction).

[551.27] Reg. § 1.199A-1(c)(2). With regard to the negative QBI carryforward, related W-2 wages and UBIA disappear in the process.

    2. Compare that sum to 20 percent of the individual's taxable income (before giving effect to the § 199A deduction) in excess of his or her capital gain (§ 1(h)); and

    3. The lesser of these two amounts is the § 199A deduction.[551.28]

The carryover rules are only slightly more complicated than in the base case:

    1. If the QBI component is negative, the current deduction related to QBI is zero and the negative QBI is carried forward to the next year as negative QBI from a separate trade or business; the W-2 wages and UBIA related to QBs with negative QBI are not carried forward;[551.29] and

    2. If the qualified REIT dividend/qualified PTP income component is less than zero, the rule is the same as in the base case: The current deduction related to these sources is zero and the negative amount is carried forward and reduces the combined REIT and PTP amount in the next year.[551.30]

The devil, of course, is in the details, specifically the details of computing the QBI component and, to a much lesser extent, the qualified REIT dividend/qualified PTP income component. For taxpayers whose taxable income is in excess of the relevant threshold amount, the preliminary steps in computing the QBI component are to apply the following rules in the following order:

    1. First, for each SSTB, if taxable income is within the phase-in range, compute the "applicable percentage" and apply it to the QBI, W-2 wages, and UBIA of the SSTB to determine the amounts to be taken into account for each SSTB. (If taxable income exceeds the phase-in range, no QBI, W-2 wages, or UBIA from any SSTB is taken into account.);[551.31]

[551.28] Reg. § 1.199A-1(d)(1).

[551.29] Reg. §§ 1.199A-1(d)(2)(iii)(B), 1.199A-1(d)(4)(xi)(A) Example 11(A); see Reg. § 1.199A-1(d)(4)(xi)(B) Example 11(B) (in subsequent year, negative QBI carryforward combined with negative QBIs from loss QBs; total reduces QBI of positive QBs in proportion to positive QBIs).

[551.30] Reg. § 1.199A-1(d)(3)(iii).

[551.31] Reg. § 1.199A-1(d)(2)(i). Similar rules apply if an SSTB has qualified PTP income. See Reg. § 1.199A-1(d)(3)(ii) (apply "applicable percentage" if taxable income is within phase-in range, disallow entirely if taxable income in excess of phase-in range). There is no comparable rule for qualified REIT dividends. This omission does not appear to be inadvertent. Compare Reg. § 1.199A-5(a)(2) (second sentence; limited to SSTB's interests in PTPs), with Reg. § 1.199A-6(b)(2)(iv) (RPEs must separately report qualified REIT dividends and qualified PTP income).

2. Second, if the taxpayer elects to "aggregate" trades or businesses,[551.32] determine the aggregated QBI, W-2 wages, and UBIA of each aggregated trade or business;[551.33]

3. Third, if any trade or business or aggregated trade or business has negative QBI, the QBI of each trade or business or aggregated trade or business that has positive QBI must be reduced proportionately by the total negative QBI. (The W-2 wages and UBIA of the trade or businesses and aggregate trade or businesses that have negative QBI are not taken into account currently and cannot be carried forward.);[551.34] and

4. Fourth, if the taxpayer's combined QBI from all trades and businesses is negative, the QBI component for the year is zero and the negative amount is carried forward to the next year as a negative QBI from a separate trade or business.[551.35]

After making these adjustments in the prescribed order, the taxpayer's QBI component for the year can now be computed based on the QBI, W-2 wages, and UBIA, as so adjusted, for each trade or business and aggregated trade or business. For each trade or business or aggregated trade or business, the taxpayer computes the lesser of (1) 20 percent of QBI or (2) the greater of 50 percent of W-2 wages or 25 percent of W-2 wages plus 2.5 percent of UBIA, and the QBI component is the sum of such amounts for all trades or businesses and aggregated trades or businesses.[551.36]

However, if the taxpayer's taxable income is in the phase-in range, and (1) 20 percent of QBI for any trade or business or aggregated trade or business is less than (2) the greater of 50 percent of W-2 wages or 25 percent of W-2 wages plus 2.5 percent of UBIA, then the QBI component for that trade or business or aggregated trade or business is equal to 20 percent of QBI reduced by the reduction amount.[551.37] The reduction amount is the excess, if any, of 20 percent of the QBI amount over the W-2 wages and UBIA amount, multiplied by the ratio that the taxable income in excess of the threshold amount bears to $50,000 ($100,000 for joint returns).[551.38]

[551.32] The aggregation rules are discussed in ¶ 9.02[3][z][iv] below. SSTBs cannot be aggregated.

[551.33] Reg. § 1.199A-1(d)(2)(ii).

[551.34] Reg. § 1.199A-1(d)(2)(iii)(A); see Reg. § 1.199A-1(d)(4)(ix) Example 9.

[551.35] Reg. § 1.199A-1(d)(2)(iii)(B); see Reg. § 1.199A-1(d)(4)(xi) Example 11 (in subsequent year, negative QBI carryforward combined with negative QBIs from loss QBs; total reduces QBI of positive QBs in proportion to positive QBIs).

[551.36] Reg. § 1.199A-1(d)(2)(iv)(A).

[551.37] Reg. § 1.199A-1(d)(2)(iv)(B). See Reg. § 1.199A-1(d)(4)(v) Example 5 (reduction calculations for QB that is not an SSTB).

[551.38] Reg. § 1.199A-1(b)(9).

[C] *Examples and analysis.*

EXAMPLE 9-24.1: *D* is unmarried and operates a sole proprietor business that is not an SSTB. In 2018, the business has no employees and uses qualified property owned by *D* with a UBIA of $10 million. The business generates $4 million of QBI. *D*'s total taxable income (exclusive of the § 199A deduction) is $3,980,000. The 20 percent of QBI amount is $2 million. The W-2 wages and UBIA amount (consisting entirely of UBIA) is $250,000 (2.5 percent of $10 million). The reduction amount (using a ratio of 1.00) is $1,750,000, so the QBI component is $250,000, which is less than 20 percent of *D*'s taxable income ($796,000, or 20 percent of $3,980,000), so the § 199A deduction is $250,000.[551.39]

If a taxpayer with taxable income in the phase-in range has interests in SSTBs, the first step is to determine the portion of each SSTB that is treated as a QB. Then, the generally applicable rules are applied to the down-sized QB.

EXAMPLE 9-24.2: *B* and *C* are married and file a joint return for 2018 showing taxable income of $375,000, none of which is net capital gain, prior to the application of § 199A. *B* is a shareholder in an S corporation that operates a QB that is not an SSTB. For 2018, *B*'s share of the S corporation's QBI is $300,000; her share of W-2 wages is $40,000 and the S corporation has no UBIA; 20 percent of *B*'s share of QBI is $60,000 and 50 percent of her share of the S corporations W-2 wages is $20,000. *B* and *C*'s joint taxable income of $375,000 exceeds their $315,000 threshold amount by $60,000, which is 60 percent of their $100,000 phase-in range. Their excess amount is $40,000 (20 percent of QBI, or $60,000, less 50 percent of W-2 wages, or $20,000). Their reduction amount is 60 percent of $40,000, or $24,000, which reduces their QBI component from $60,000 (20 percent of $300,000 QBI) to $36,000. This is less than 20 percent of their taxable income, so their § 199A deduction is $36,000 for 2018.[551.40]

EXAMPLE 9-24.3: Same facts as Example 9-24.2 except the QB is an SSTB. Because *B* and *C* are in the phase-in range, the first step is to reduce their QBI, W-2 wages, and UBIA to the "applicable percentage" of these items. Their applicable percentage is 100 percent less the percentage equal to the ratio that $60,000 (the amount of their taxable income in excess of their threshold amount) bears to their $100,000 phase-in range, or 40 percent (100 percent less 60 percent). Their reduced amounts are thus QBI of $120,000 (40 percent of $300,000) and W-2 wages of $16,000 (40

[551.39] See Reg. § 1.199A-1(d)(4)(ii) Example 2. The methodology in this Example suggests a computational shortcut in some cases: if taxable income is in excess of the threshold amount plus the phase-in range, there is no need to compute the "reduction amount." The § 199A deduction is simply the lesser of the wages and UBIA amount or 20 percent of taxable income.

[551.40] See Reg. § 1.199A-1(d)(4)(v) Example 5.

percent of $40,000), and therefore their excess amount is now $16,000 (20 percent of QBI = $24,000, less 50 percent of W-2 wages = $8,000). As in the previous example, their reduction amount is based on applying 60 percent to their now reduced excess amount of $16,000, so their reduction amount is $9,600, which reduces 20 percent of QBI from $24,000 to $14,400. This is less than 20 percent of their taxable income, so their § 199A deduction is $14,400 for 2018.[551.41]

EXAMPLE 9-24.4: Same facts as Example 9-24.2 except combined taxable income is less than the threshold amount. Regardless of whether the QB is an SSTB, the § 199A deduction is simply $60,000 (20 percent of QBI).[551.42]

If the taxable income limitation is not in play, the available § 199A deduction for individuals depends on only three factors: (1) the amount of taxable income relative to the threshold taxable income amount and the applicable phase-in range; (2) the "excess amount" (20 percent of QBI less the greater of 50 percent of W-2 wages or the sum of 25 percent of W-2 wages and 2.5 percent of UBIA); and (3) whether a QB is or is not an SSTB. Based on the $300,000 QBI and the excess amount of $40,000 assumed in each of the preceding examples, the § 199A deduction may be generalized as follows:

[551.41] See Reg. § 1.199A-1(d)(4)(vi) Example 6.
[551.42] §§ 199A(b)(3)(A), 199A(d)(3).

	Non-SSTB	SSTB
Deduction if taxable income < threshold	$60,000	$60,000
Deduction if taxable income > threshold + phase-in	$20,000	zero
Taxable income within phase-in range (60% of phase-in)	$36,000	$14,400

Mathematically, for joint return filers, § 199A deductions in the phase-in range are reduced by $400 (reflecting 1 percent of the excess amount) for each $1,000 by which taxable income exceeds the threshold amount. If the QB is an SSTB, the reduction is $600 (reflecting 1 percent of 20 percent the QBI without regard to W-2 wages or UBIA).

[D] *Qualified REIT dividends/qualified PTP income component.* The qualified REIT dividends/qualified PTP income component is generally equal to 20 percent of the sum of the taxpayer's direct and indirect (through RPEs) qualified REIT dividends and qualified PTP income. However, if the taxpayer's taxable income is within the phase-in range, the "applicable percentage" must be computed and applied to reduce the qualified PTP income from any SSTBs. If taxable income exceeds the phase-in range, no qualified PTP income from any SSTB is taken into account.[551.43]

[551.43] See Reg. § 1.199A-1(d)(3)(ii). There is no comparable rule for qualified REIT dividends—an omission that does not appear to be inadvertent. Compare Reg. § 1.199A-5(a)(2) (second sentence; limited to SSTB's interests in PTPs), with Reg. §

If, after making this adjustment, the taxpayer's combined qualified REIT dividends and qualified PTP income for a year is negative, the qualified REIT dividends/qualified PTP income component is treated as zero and does not reduce the § 199A deduction for the year. Instead, solely for purposes of § 199A, it is carried over and reduces combined qualified REIT dividends and qualified PTP income in subsequent years.[551.44]

1.199A-6(b)(2)(iv) (RPEs must separately report qualified REIT dividends *and* qualified PTP income).

[551.44] Reg. § 1.199A-1(d)(3)(iii).

[E] *W-2 wages and UBIA.* The computation of W-2 wages and UBIA is addressed by §§ 199A(b)(4), 199A(b)(5), and 199A(b)(6), as well as Regulations § 1.199A-3. W-2 wages for each trade or business (or aggregated trade or business) must be computed by the individual or RPE that directly conducts the business.[551.45] The Regulations provide a three-step process for each responsible individual or RPE to determine the W-2 wages paid with respect to a trade or business that are properly allocable to QBI: First, determine the total W-2 wages paid for the year; second, allocate the wages among the trades and businesses if the individual or RPE operates several trades or businesses; and, third, determine the amount of such wages with respect to each trade or business that is properly allocated to the QBI of the trade or business.[551.46]

Generally, the Forms W-2 "Wage and Tax Statement" issued by the operator of the business are sufficient, but there are many modifications, refinements, and exceptions to this rule, as detailed in Regulations §§ 1.199A-3(b)(2), 1.199A-3(b)(3), and 1.199A-3(b)(4). If there are multiple trades or businesses, the individual or RPE that conducts them must allocate the calculated W-2 wages among the trades and businesses that generated the wages in the same manner as the expenses associated with the wages are allocated pursuant to Regulations § 1.199A-3(b)(5).[551.47]

The wages allocated to a given trade or business are "properly allocable" to the QBI for the trade or business if the associated wage expense is taken into account in computing QBI under Regulations § 1.199A-3(b)(5).[551.48] Thus, if the trade or business is conducted by a partnership or other RPE, the wage expense must be allocated among, and reported to, the owners of the RPE.

Regulations § 1.199A-2(c)(3)(i) generally provides that UBIA means the § 1012 basis of qualified property on the date it is placed in service. However, UBIA is not adjusted to reflect § 1016(a)(2) or § 1016(a)(3) adjustments or any adjustments for tax credits claimed by the owner or any portion of the ba-

---

[551.45] Reg. § 1.199A-2(a)(2). If wages are not determined and reported they are presumed to be zero.

[551.46] Reg. § 1.199A-2(b)(1).

[551.47] Reg. § 1.199A-2(b)(3). See ¶ 9.02[3][z][iii][A] below.

[551.48] Reg. § 1.199A-2(b)(4). See ¶ 9.02[3][z][iii][A] below.

sis that is expensed (for example, under § 179). A variety of special rules are provided to determine or adjust the basis of qualified property involved in transactions subject to §§ 1031, 1033, and 168(i)(7)(B).[551.49] The UBIA of qualified property acquired from a decedent that is immediately placed in service in the business is its fair market value at the date of death under § 1014.[551.50]

UBIA is based on tangible property that is depreciable under § 167, held by (or available for use in) the trade or business at the end of the tax year, used at some point during the year in the trade or business, and within the depreciable period for the property.[551.51] Solely for purposes of § 199A, "depreciable period" means the period beginning when the property is placed in service and ending on the later of (1) ten years thereafter or (2) the last day of the last year of the § 168(c) recovery period (without regard to § 168(g)).[551.52] Basis adjustments to qualified property under § 734(b) are ignored, but excess § 743(b) basis adjustments are taken into account as qualified property and treated as placed in service as of the date of the transfer of the partnership interest.[551.53] The Regulations also provide a variety of special rules relating to additional first year depreciation (not taken into account), and property acquired in §§ 1031, 1033, and 168(i)(7)(B) transactions.[551.54]

While these UBIA rules are extensive and detailed, their impact is limited by their purposes, which are two-fold: (1) establish the amount of basis included in UBIA upon the acquisition of property and (2) determine the recovery period of each item of property included in UBIA that has a § 168(c) recovery period of less than ten years so the basis of the item can be eliminated from UBIA at the end of the recovery period. *The actual depreciation deductions for qualified property are wholly irrelevant under § 199A.*

[551.49] Reg. §§ 1.199A-2(c)(3)(ii), 1.199A-2(c)(3)(iii), 1.199A-2(c)(3)(iv). A special anti-stuffing rule applies to all of these types of transactions. Reg. § 1.199A-2(c)(3)(vi).

[551.50] Reg. § 1.199A-2(c)(3)(v).

[551.51] Reg. § 1.199A-2(c)(1)(i). However, to discourage "stuffing," property acquired within 60 days of the end of the year and held for less than 120 days generally is excluded unless it has been used in the trade or business for at least 45 days. Reg. § 1.199A-2(c)(1)(iv).

[551.52] Reg. § 1.199A-2(c)(2)(i).

[551.53] Reg. § 1.199A-2(c)(2)(v). If the § 743(b) adjustment is positive, a fresh recovery period is created for it. If it is negative, it is recovered over the remaining useful life of the qualified property. See Reg. §§ 1.743-1(j)(4)(i)(B) (positive), 1.743-1(j)(4)(ii)(B) (negative).

[551.54] Reg. §§ 1.199A-2(c)(2)(ii), 1.199A-2(c)(2)(iii), 1.199A-2(c)(2)(iv).

[iii] Qualified business income, qualified REIT dividends, and qualified PTP income: details.

[A] *QBI.* QBI is the net amount of any qualified items of income, gain, deduction, and loss from a trade or business of the taxpayer. QBI excludes any income not effectively connected with a United States trade or business.[551.55] Also (1) with respect to partnerships, QBI includes any ordinary income under the collapsible partnership rules (§§ 751(a) and 751(b)) attributable to partnership assets in a trade or business;[551.56] (2) with respect to partnerships, QBI excludes any guaranteed payments for the use of capital except to the extent allocable to a trade or business of the recipient;[551.57] (3) QBI includes positive and negative § 481 adjustments arising in tax years ending after 2017;[551.58] (4) QBI includes previously disallowed losses (§§ 461(l), 465, 469, 704(d), and 1366(d)) from tax years ending after 2017;[551.59] (5) while net operating loss deductions are generally not taken into account in computing QBI, excess business losses under § 461(l) are included in QBI in the subsequent tax years in which they are deducted;[551.60] and (6) QBI takes into account all other deductions commonly taken into account, including the deductible portion of the tax on self-employment income under § 164(f), the self-employed health insurance deduction under § 162(l), and deductions for contributions to qualified § 404 retirement plans to the extent the individual's gross income for the trade or business is taken into account in calculating the allowable deduction.[551.61]

The following items are not taken into account as qualified items: (1) capital gains and losses and all items treated as capital gains and losses unless treated as anything other than capital gains or losses;[551.62] (2) dividends and the like;[551.63] (3) interest income not properly allocable to a trade or business;[551.64] (4) items described in §§ 954(c)(1)(C), 954(c)(1)(D), and 954(c)(1)(F);[551.65] (5) amounts from annuities not received in connection with a trade or business;[551.66] (6) qualified REIT dividends and qualified PTP income;[551.67] (7) "reasonable" compensation received by a shareholder from an S corporation;[551.68]

[551.55] Reg. § 1.199A-3(b)(2)(i).

[551.56] Reg. § 1.199A-3(b)(1)(i).

[551.57] Reg. § 1.199A-3(b)(1)(ii).

[551.58] Reg. § 1.199A-3(b)(1)(iii).

[551.59] Reg. § 1.199A-3(b)(1)(iv). The reference to § 461(l) in the parenthetical list was added in 2020 "to clarify" this point. See TD 9899, 85 Fed. Reg. 38060, 38061 (June 25, 2020).

[551.60] Reg. § 1.199A-3(b)(1)(v).

[551.61] Reg. § 1.199A-3(b)(1)(vi).

[551.62] Reg. § 1.199A-3(b)(2)(ii)(A).

[551.63] Reg. § 1.199A-3(b)(2)(ii)(B).

[551.64] Reg. § 1.199A-3(b)(2)(ii)(C).

[551.65] Reg. §§ 1.199A-3(b)(2)(ii)(D), 1.199A-3(b)(2)(ii)(E).

[551.66] Reg. § 1.199A-3(b)(2)(ii)(F).

[551.67] Reg. § 1.199A-3(b)(2)(ii)(G).

[551.68] Reg. § 1.199A-3(b)(2)(ii)(H). However, the S corporation's deduction for the payment generally will reduce the QBI of the trades or businesses to which the payment is allocable.

and (8) § 707(c) guaranteed payments and § 707(a) payments to partners for services rendered.[551.69]

Pursuant to § 199A(f)(1(C), the term "United States" includes the Commonwealth of Puerto Rico for purposes of determining QBI for any taxable year in the case of any taxpayer with QBI from sources within the Commonwealth of Puerto Rico if all such receipts are taxable under § 1 for such year.[551.70]

Expenses for all wages must be taken into account in computing QBI regardless of the application of the W-2 wage limitation in Regulations § 1.199A-1(d)(2)(iv).[551.71] Items of QBI must be reasonably allocated among multiple trades or businesses conducted by the individual or RPE directly conducting the trades or businesses.[551.72]

[551.69] Reg. §§ 1.199A-3(b)(2)(ii)(I), 1.199A-3(b)(2)(ii)(J). However, the partnership's deduction for the payment generally will reduce the QBI of the trades or businesses to which the payment is allocable.

[551.70] Reg. § 1.199A-3(b)(3).

[551.71] Reg. § 1.199A-3(b)(4). The referenced limitation relates to the reduction of QBI items for taxpayers in the phase-in range. This "clarification" seems largely unnecessary.

[551.72] Reg. § 1.199A-3(b)(5). Different reasonable methods can be chosen for different items of income, gain, loss, deduction, and credit. The methods chosen must be consistent from year to year, must clearly reflect income and expenses of each trade or business, and must be consistent with the books and records maintained for each trade or business.

[B] *Qualified REIT dividends and qualified PTP income.* Qualified REIT dividends and the net qualified PTP income earned directly or through an RPE are combined for each tax year. If the annual total is positive, it is multiplied by 20 percent and becomes the "qualified REIT dividends/qualified PTP income component" that is added to the "QBI component," and then compared to 20 percent of the individual's taxable income (excluding net capital gain) in determining the § 199A deduction. If the annual total is negative, it is treated as zero in computing the current § 199A deduction and carried forward to subsequent years as a loss in the calculation of future qualified REIT dividends/qualified PTP income components.[551.73]

Qualified REIT dividends exclude capital gains dividends (§ 857(b)(3)), qualified dividend income (§ 1(h)(11)), dividends on stock held for short periods (§§ 246(c)(3) and 246(c)(4)), and dividends to the extent the recipient is obligated to make offsetting payments with respect to substantially similar or related property.[551.74] Qualified PTP income means the sum of the taxpayer's allocable share of income, gain, deduction, and loss from a PTP (as defined in § 7704(b)) that is not taxed as a corporation under § 7704(a) and any ordinary

---

[551.73] Reg. §§ 1.199A-1(c)(2), 1.199A-1(d)(3)(iii), 1.199A-1(c)(3)(iv) Example 4 (inclusion of qualified REIT dividends and qualified PTP income in determining § 199A deduction), discussed in ¶ 9.02[3][z][ii] above.

[551.74] Reg. § 1.199A-3(b)(2).

income under §§ 751(a) and 751(b) that is attributable to trades or businesses conducted by the PTP.[551.75] In general, the rules applicable to the determination of QBI also apply to the determination of PTP income.[551.76]

[551.75] Reg. § 1.199A-3(b)(3)(i).

[551.76] Reg. § 1.199A-3(b)(3)(ii).

[iv] Aggregation rules. The Regulations allow taxpayers to elect to aggregate trades or businesses that are not SSTBs. Aggregation, if available, is unlikely to have any adverse effects for electing taxpayers and may have significant benefits by allowing the aggregation of QBI, W-2 wages, and UBIA for purposes of applying the limitations in § 199A(b) and Regulations § 1.199A-1(d)(2)(iv).

> **EXAMPLE 9-24.5:** *F*, an unmarried individual, owns three businesses. Business *X* generates $1,000,000 of QBI and pays $500,000 of W-2 wages for 2018. Business *Y* generates $1,000,000 of QBI and pays no W-2 wages. Business *Z* generates $2,000 of QBI and pays $500,000 of W-2 wages. *F*'s taxable income for 2018 is over $2 million. If the businesses are not aggregated, the § 199A(b) limit for Business *X* is $200,000 (the lesser of 20 percent of $1,000,000 of QBI and 50 percent of $500,000 of W-2 wages). The limit for Business *Y* is zero (the lesser of 20 percent of $1,000,000 of QBI and 50 percent of zero in W-2 wages). The limit for Business *Z* is $400 (the lesser of 20 percent of $2,000 of QBI and 50 percent of $500,000 of W-2 wages). *F*'s total QBI component is $200,400 ($200,000 plus zero plus $400).[551.77]

> **EXAMPLE 9-24.6:** The facts are the same as Example 9-24.5, except *F* makes a valid aggregation election. The aggregate QBI for the three businesses is $2,002,000 and the aggregate W-2 wages is $1,000,000. The limit for the aggregated businesses is $400,400, that is, the lesser of $400,400 (20 percent of QBI of $2,002,000) and $500,000 (50 percent of W-2 wages of $1,000,000).[551.78] In this situation, the aggregation election allows *F* to approximately double her § 199A deduction.

Understandably, the potential benefits of aggregation have led the Treasury to severely restrict its availability as follows:

1. SSTBs cannot be aggregated.
2. All the aggregated trades or businesses must file returns using the same taxable year.
3. During a majority of the tax year, including the last day, the same person or group of persons must own (directly or by § 267(c) or §

[551.77] Reg. § 1.199A-1(d)(4)(vii) Example 7.

[551.78] Reg. § 1.199A-1(d)(4)(viii) Example 8. See also Reg. § 1.199A-1(d)(4)(ix) Example 9, and Reg. § 1.199A-1(d)(4)(x) Example 10, in which aggregation increases *F*'s § 199A deduction from $140,000 to $280,000.

707(b) attribution) 50 percent or more of each aggregated trade or business.

4. Two or more of the following three factors must be satisfied by the aggregated trades or businesses: (a) they provide products, property, or services that are the same or customarily offered together; (b) they share facilities or significant centralized business elements (personnel, accounting, legal, manufacturing, purchasing, HR, IT); and (c) each is operated in coordination with, or reliance upon, other trades or businesses in the aggregated group.[551.79]

If an aggregation election is made, the owner must consistently report the aggregated trades or businesses and file annual disclosure statements in subsequent years.[551.80] The disclosure statements must include (1) a description of each aggregated trade or business, (2) the name and EIN of each entity in which an aggregated trade or business is operated, (3) information identifying each aggregated trade or business that was formed, ceased operations, was acquired or disposed of during the year, (4) information identifying any aggregated trade or business of an RPE in which the owner has an ownership interest, and (5) any other information that may be required on forms, instructions, or other published guidance.

[551.79] Reg. § 1.199A-4(b)(1); see Reg. § 1.199A-4(d) Examples.

[551.80] Reg. § 1.199A-4(c). If the owner is an individual, the annual statement must be attached to the return for the year. If the owner is an RPE, it must be attached to each K-1 for the year. Failure to attach a required statement allows the Commissioner to disaggregate the trades or businesses for the year, in which case the taxpayer cannot re-aggregate for three tax years. Reg. §§ 1.199A-4(c)(2), 1.199A-4(c)(3).

[v] Specified service trades or businesses (SSTBs). Regulations § 1.199A-5(b)(1) defines an "SSTB" as any trade or business involving the performance of services in the following fields: health, law, accounting, actuarial science, performing arts, consulting, athletics, financial services, brokerages services, investing and investment management, trading, dealing securities, partnership interests or securities, or any other trade or business where the principal asset of the trade or business is reputation or skill of one or more of its employees or owners.[551.81]

The Regulations provide several special rules, including a de minimis exception for trades or businesses if less than 10 percent of the gross receipts of the business are attributable to the performance of services in one of these

---

[551.81] The scope of each of these fields is explored in some detail in Regulations §§ 1.199A-5(b)(2) and 1.199A-5(b)(3) Examples. Architecture and engineering services are not on the list; and services provided by architects and engineers are explicitly excluded from treatment as "consulting." The trade or business of performing services as an employee cannot be a trade or business for this or any other purpose under § 199A. Reg. § 1.199A-5(d).

fields.[551.82] If this exception does not apply, the entire trade or business is an SSTB even though a very large portion of its receipts is unrelated to the performance of services.

> **EXAMPLE 9-24.7:** Landscape LLC sells lawncare and landscaping equipment and also provides advice and counsel ("consulting") for large office parks and residential buildings. Although it invoices separately for its consulting services, Landscape maintains one set of books and records and treats the equipment sales and the design services as a single business for purposes of §§ 162 and 199A. It has gross receipts of $2 million, of which $250,000 is attributable to the design services, an SSTB. Since $250,000 is more than 10 percent of $2 million, the entirety of Landscape's trade or business is an SSTB.[551.83]

Fortunately, Example 2 in Regulations § 1.199A-5(c)(1)(iii)(B) provides a road map for avoiding this potentially ugly result: maintain separate books and records, separate employees providing design services from employees selling equipment, and treat the two activities as separate trades or businesses for purposes of §§ 162 and 199A.

Another special rule provides that any trade or business that provides goods or services to an SSTB will be treated as an SSTB (in whole or in part) if they share 50 percent or more common ownership, taking into account both direct ownership and attributed ownership under §§ 267(b) and 707(b).[551.84] The portion of the trade or business converted to SSTB status is based on the ratio of goods and services provided to the commonly controlled SSTB versus other customers.[551.85]

[551.82] Reg. § 1.199A-5(c)(1). The 10 percent figure is reduced to 5 percent if the trade or business has annual gross receipts in excess of $25 million.

[551.83] Reg. § 1.199A-5(c)(1)(iii)(A) Example 1.

[551.84] Reg. § 1.199A-5(c)(2).

[551.85] Reg. § 1.199A-5(c)(2)(iii)(B) Example 2.

[vi] Reporting requirements. Entities that operate trades or businesses and pass some or all of the tax incidents of the trade or business to its owners or beneficiaries are required to make certain determinations and computations as well as file certain reports annually so their owners and beneficiaries can determine their § 199A deductions. The Regulations create three categories of reporting entities and three sets of reporting rules: (1) partnerships, S corporations, and other RPEs; (2) PTPs; and (3) trusts (other than grantor trusts) and estates.[551.86]

[A] *Partnerships, S corporations and other RPEs.* Every RPE[551.87] is required to apply the following rules:

1. Determine whether it is engaged in a trade or business. If it is, then it must determine whether any of its trades or businesses is an SSTB, and if it operates multiple trades or businesses, decide whether to aggregate them;

2. Determine the QBI for each trade or business (or aggregated trade or business) engaged in directly;

3. Determine the W-2 wages and UBIA of qualified property for each trade or business (or aggregated trade or business) engaged in directly; and

4. Determine whether it has any qualified REIT dividends earned directly or through another RPE, and also whether it has any qualified PTP income earned directly or through another RPE.[551.88]

It must then separately identify and report on the Schedule K-1 issued to each owner the following information for each trade or business (or aggregated trade or business) it is directly engaged in: (1) the owner's allocable share of QBI, W-2 wages, and UBIA of qualified property for each such trade or business; and (2) whether any of the identified trades or businesses are SSTBs.[551.89] It must also report, on an attachment to the K-1, any QBI, W-2 wages, and UBIA of qualified property, or SSTB determinations reported to it by any RPE in which it has an interest[551.90] together with the owner's allocable share of any qualified REIT dividends and any qualified PTP income or loss received (directly or indirectly) through interest it holds in other RPEs.[551.91]Any reporting failure by an RPE results in the QBI, W-2 wages, and UBIA shares of the affected direct (or indirect) owners being presumed to be zero.[551.92]

[551.86] Reg. § 1.199A-6(a). Single-owner disregarded entities are not included in any of these categories because their activities are attributed to their owners. Reg. § 1.199A-1(e)(2).

[551.87] RPE includes partnerships (other than publicly traded partnerships), S corporations, common trust funds (Reg. § 1.6032-1T), religious and apostolic organizations (§ 501(d)), and trusts and estates that pass through QBI and related items to their owners. Reg. § 1.199A-1(b)(10).

[551.88] Reg. § 1.199A-6(b)(2).

[551.89] Reg. § 1.199A-6(b)(3)(i).

[551.90] Reg. § 1.199A-6(b)(3)(i). Presumably, the reporting should reflect the owner's allocable share of these items, but that is not what the Regulation says.

[551.91] Reg. § 1.199A-6(b)(3)(ii). Evidencing awareness of one of the obvious issues with these tiered reporting requirements, the last sentence of this Regulation provides: "Such information can be reported on an amended or late filed return to the extent that the period of limitations remains open."

[551.92] Reg. § 1.199A-6(b)(3)(iii).

For some partnerships and LLCs, the decisions relating to aggregation of trades or businesses and the categorization of a particular trade or business as an SSTB may affect different owners differently. In these situations, it may help to protect the decision maker if the owners agree in advance as to how these decisions will be made.

[B] *PTPs.* A PTP must determine the QBI (but not the W-2 wages or the UBIA) and the SSTB status of each directly operated trade or business and report this information on its partners' Schedules K-1 together with any qualified REIT dividends and qualified PTP income or loss received through an RPE, REIT, or another PTP.[551.93]

[C] *Trusts, estates, and beneficiaries.* A trust or estate computes its § 199A deduction based on the QBI, W-2 wages, UBIA of qualified property, qualified REIT dividends, and qualified PTP income that are allocated to the trust or estate. An individual beneficiary of a trust or estate takes into account his or her shares of any QBI, W-2 wages, UBIA of qualified property, qualified REIT dividends, and qualified PTP income allocated from a trust or estate in calculating the beneficiary's § 199A deduction, just as he or she would if the items had been allocated from an RPE.[551.94] Thus, trusts and estates are effectively treated as RPEs to the extent they allocate QBI and other items to their beneficiaries, and are treated as individuals with their own § 199A deductions to the extent they retain QBI and other items.

To the extent a trust is treated as owned by a grantor or other person under §§ 671 through 679, such owner computes its § 199A deduction as if it directly conducted its share of the trust's activities.[551.95]

Non-grantor trusts and estates calculate their QBI, W-2 wages, UBIA, qualified REIT dividends, and qualified PTP income at the trust or estate level.[551.96] After adjusting for allocations to beneficiaries, remaining QBI, W-2 wages, UBIA, qualified REIT dividends, and qualified PTP income are allocated to the trust or estate, and a § 199A deduction for the trust or estate is computed using a 2018 threshold amount of $157,500.

Attempts to use multiple trusts to reduce taxes have been a staple of the tax system for many decades. To discourage the formation of multiple trusts created for the purpose of multiplying the available threshold amount, an anti-abuse rule is included in the Regulations.[551.97]

[551.93] Reg. § 1.199A-6(c).

[551.94] Reg. § 1.199A-6(d)(1).

[551.95] Reg. § 1.199A-6(d)(2).

[551.96] Reg. § 1.199A-6(d)(3)(i). Special rules apply in computing and allocating QBI among the trust or estate and its beneficiaries that take into account how trust distributable net income is distributed (or required to be distributed). See Reg. §§ 1.199A-6(d)(3)(i), 1.199A-6(d)(3)(ii), 1.199A-6(d)(3)(viii) Example.

[551.97] Reg. §§ 1.643(f)-1, 1.199A-6(d)(3)(vii) (trust aggregation rule if principal purpose is avoidance).

Electing small business trusts are entitled to deductions under § 199A as computed pursuant to Regulations § 1.199A-6(d)(3)(vi).

[aa] Loss Limitation for Noncorporate Taxpayers: Section 461(l)

Noncorporate taxpayers are not permitted to deduct "excess business losses" under § 461(l), added by the 2017 Tax Cuts and Jobs Act. This temporary limitation is effective for tax years beginning after December 31, 2017, and before January 1, 2026.[551.98] "Excess business losses" are trade or business losses in excess of $250,000 ($500,000 for joint returns, inflation adjusted after 2018 in both cases).[551.99] This limitation is applied at the partner level.[551.100]

[551.98] Pub. L. No. 115-97, § 11012 (Dec. 22, 2017). During this period, the limitation on excess farm losses is suspended. § 461(l)(1)(A).

[551.99] § 461(l)(3). Losses under this limitation are computed after application of the passive activity loss rules. § 461(l)(6). Presumably, other loss limitations (such as § 704(d)) should also be applied first. Disallowed losses are carried forward indefinitely. § 461(l)(2). The Regulations relating to the treatment of previously disallowed losses were amended in 2020 to provide more detail for the following: (a) "previously disallowed losses" include, but are not limited to, losses disallowed under §§ 461(l), 465, 469, 704(d), and 1366(d) (§ 461(l) was not included in this list prior to 2020; however, the preamble to the 2020 amendment makes clear that this addition was not intended as a substantive change but only "to clarify" the regulation); (b) "previously disallowed losses" are taken into account on a first-in, first-out (FIFO) basis; (c) rules for partial disallowances are provided; and (d) the attributes of the losses (including application of the SSTB rules) are determined in the years the losses were incurred and are preserved for purposes of § 199A. Reg. § 1.199A-3(b)(1)(iv).

[551.100] § 461(l)(4).

[4] Credits

[a] Credit for Fuels From Nonconventional Sources

Page 9-121:

Replace second sentence of subsection with the following.

The Service has ruled privately that four corporate partners, none of whom have a 50% or more interest in the partnership, are "unrelated persons" to their partnership for purposes of applying the predecessor to § 45K(a)(2)(A).[552]

---

[552] Priv. Ltr. Rul. 8443084 (July 25, 1984).

Replace ¶ 9.02[4][b] with revised ¶ 9.02[4][b].

[b] Alcohol Fuels Credit [Revised]

Section 40(b)(4) grants a credit to any eligible small ethanol producer for each gallon of qualified ethanol fuel produced, up to a maximum of 15 million gallons per taxable year.[553] An eligible small ethanol producer is a person who cannot produce more than 60 million gallons of alcohol per year. These limitations are applicable at both the partnership and the partner levels.[554] Moreover, persons under common control within the meaning of § 52(b) (determined by treating an interest of more than 50% as a controlling interest) are treated as one person for purposes of applying the limitation.[555]

---

[553] § 40(b)(4)(C).

[554] § 40(g)(3).

[555] § 40(g)(2). For the application of § 52(b) in the partnership context, see supra ¶ 9.02[4][c]. In ruling on the 60 million gallon limitation on the definition of "eligible small ethanol producer," the Service has taken a representation that the partners and the partnership collectively produce fewer than 60 million gallons of alcohol per year. Priv. Ltr. Ruls. 200046023 (Aug. 18, 2000), 200021034 (Feb. 23, 2000).

[c] Credit for Increasing Research Activities

Page 9-122:

Replace first sentence of subsection with the following.

The § 41 research credit is 20% of the sum of (1) any excess of the qualified research expenses for the year over the "base amount," (2) the basic research payments for the year, and (3) the amounts paid or incurred (including as contributions), in carrying on any trade or business of the taxpayer, to an energy consortium for energy research.[556]

---

[556] § 41(a). The credit is not available for any amount paid or incurred after December 31, 2011. § 41(h)(1). For tax years beginning after December 31, 2021, the 2017 Tax Cuts and Jobs Act will convert § 174 research and experimental expenditure deductions into intangibles generally amortizable over five years. Pub. L. No. 115-97, § 13206 (Dec. 22, 2017).

In second paragraph of subsection, add the following after second sentence.

Computation of the excess of qualified research expenses over the base amount on an aggregate basis may result in no excess or a minimal excess even though a substantial excess may exist in a specific partnership.

Replace note 560 with the following.

[560] See Reg. §§ 1.41-2(a)(4)(ii)(C), 1.41-2(a)(4)(ii)(D), 1.41-2(a)(4)(ii)(E), 1.41-2(a)(4)(iii) Examples.

[d] Low-Income Housing Credit

Page 9-126:

Add at end of subsection.

Section 1602 of the American Recovery and Reinvestment Act of 2009 (ARRA) authorizes state housing credit agencies to make subawards to finance the acquisition or rehabilitation of qualified low-income projects. Subawards are made in the same manner, and are subject to the same limitations, as § 42 credits (ARRA § 1602(c)(2)). Recapture is also required during the compliance period (ARRA § 1602(c)(2)). Subawards must be made prior to 2011 (ARRA § 1602(d)). Like § 42 credits, ARRA § 1602 grants are not taxable to the recipient and do not affect the basis of qualified low-income buildings.[580.1]

[580.1] § 42(i)(9)(B).

[e] Disabled Access Credit

Page 9-127:

Replace note 582 with the following.

[582] § 44(d)(2)(A).

[g] New Markets Tax Credit

Page 9-128:

Add to note 589.

See Prop. Reg. §§ 1.45D-1(e)(3)(iii) (2008) (expanding pro rata safe harbor), 1.45D-1(e)(4) (2008) (§ 708(b)(1)(B) termination not a recapture event).

Page 9-128:

Replace ¶ 9.02[4][h] with revised ¶ 9.02[4][h].

[h] Investment Tax Credit [Revised]

The § 46 investment credit currently has five components: (1) the § 47 rehabilitation credit, (2) the § 48 energy credit, (3) the § 48A qualifying advanced coal project credit, (4) the § 48B qualifying gasification project credit, and (5) the § 48C qualifying advanced energy project credit. The investment credit is part of the § 38 general business credit.

Each of the credits included in the investment credit is subject to several special rules collected in § 50. These include (1) the recapture rules in § 50(a) (recapture if property is disposed of or ceases to be investment credit property within five years of being placed in service—full recapture if disposition within one year, and reduced by 20% per year thereafter), (2) the ineligible property rules in § 50(b) (disqualifying property used outside the United

States, certain property used for lodging, and property used by certain tax-exempt organizations, governmental units, or foreign persons or entities), and (3) the basis adjustment rules (and the reversal thereof in the case of recapture of the credit) in § 50(c). There are a number of points at which the investment credit rules and the special rules in § 50 intersect the rules of Subchapter K. The major points of intersection are as follows:

1. The investment credit for property owned by a partnership flows through to the partners. The manner in which the credit is allocated among the partners is discussed in ¶ 11.03[2][a].

2. The credit pass-through does not directly affect either the partners' adjusted bases for their partnership interests or their § 704(b) capital accounts. However, the reduction of the partnership's basis for its investment credit property under § 50(c) triggers corresponding changes in the partners' capital accounts and the adjusted bases of their partnership interests under Regulations § 1.704-1(b)(2)(iv)(j) and § 50(c)(5). Special issues are presented with respect to energy property because the basis reduction is only 50% of the credit (see § 50(c)(3)) and, in some cases, an election may be made to receive a grant in lieu of the credit.[590] These matters are discussed in ¶¶ 6.02[3][a] and 6.02[3][c].

3. Recapture triggers the reversal of all or a portion of the partners' prior basis or capital account adjustments.[591]

4. In addition to the recapture rules set forth in § 50(a)(1) that are triggered by the investment credit property's early disposition or premature failure to qualify, additional rules are provided for recapture at the partner level upon a premature transfer of a partner's partnership interest in profits or other events that reduce a partner's interest in profits to less than two thirds of the partner's original interest in the credit.[591.1]

5. Generally, elections with respect to partnership investment credit property are made by the partnership.[591.2] However, there is at least one exception to this rule.[591.3]

6. Limitations in § 50(b) related to the identity of the owner of the investment credit property are applied partner-by-partner at the partner-

---

[590] See American Recovery and Reinvestment Act of 2009 (ARRA) § 1603.

[591] § 50(c)(5); Reg. § 1.704-1(b)(2)(iv)(j).

[591.1] Reg. § 1.47-6(a)(2). See ¶ 16.08[2].

[591.2] § 703(b). See ARRA § 1603(a) ("application" for grant filed by person who places property in service); cf. Reg. 1.43-6(b) (enhanced oil recovery credit; election out made by partnership).

[591.3] See Chapter 9, note 180.

ship level.[591.4] Similar look-through rules are applied if the user of the property is a partnership that includes disqualified partners.[591.5]

The investment tax credit is generally not available to states and their political subdivisions, nor to tax-exempt organizations.[591.6] The Service has adopted an aggregate approach to these provisions, holding that the credit is not available to partners who would not qualify for the credit if they held the property directly, but is available to other partners (e.g., investor-owned utilities) with respect to their shares of a partnership credit.[591.7]

[591.4] See ¶ 9.02[5][h].

[591.5] See §§ 168(h)(5), 168(h)(6); ¶ 9.03[b].

[591.6] See §§ 50(b)(3), 50(b)(4) (formerly §§ 48(a)(4), 48(a)(5)).

[591.7] See Rev. Rul. 78-268, 1978-2 CB 10; see also Rev. Rul. 80-219, 1980-2 CB 18; Priv. Ltr. Ruls. 8011040 (Dec. 19, 1979), 7846031 (Aug. 16, 1978).

[i] New Employee Jobs Credit

Page 9-128:

Replace first sentence of subsection with the following.

Sections 51 and 52 provide a "work opportunity credit" for "qualified" wages paid to certain individuals hired on or before December 31, 2013.[592]

---

[592] §§ 51(b), 51(c)(4).

Page 9-128:

Replace heading of ¶ 9.02[4][j] with the following revised heading.

[j] Pre−2018 Foreign Tax Credit [Revised Heading]

Add the following before first paragraph of ¶ 9.02[4][j].

The indirect foreign tax credit provisions of former § 902 were repealed by the 2017 Tax Cuts and Jobs Act for taxable years of foreign corporations beginning after 2017. The following discussion remains relevant to prior years.

[5] Other Matters

[b] Self-Employment Tax

[i] General rules.

Page 9-130:

Add to note 598.

Passive income from non-farm rental real estate generally is not subject to self-employment tax under § 1402(a)(1). See, e.g., CCA 200816030 (Mar. 18, 2008) (under § 761(f), income from rental real estate business conducted by husband and wife through a "qualified joint venture" is not self-employment income) (tax years beginning after 2006). Presumably, the result was the same for husband-wife ventures treated as partnerships prior to the enactment of § 761(f); the purpose of § 761(f) was merely to eliminate a reporting burden (i.e., the filing of an unnecessary partnership return by husbands and wives who file joint returns).

Under Regulations § 301.7701-2(c)(2), a business entity that has a single owner and is not a corporation under Regulations § 301.7701-2(b) is disregarded as an entity separate from its owner. However, Regulations § 301.7701-2(c)(2)(iv)(B) provides that a disregarded entity is nevertheless treated as a corporation for purposes of employment taxes imposed under subtitle C. Therefore, the disregarded entity, rather than the owner, is considered to be the employer of the entity's employees for purposes of employment taxes imposed by subtitle C. Regulations § 301.7701-2(c)(2)(iv)(C)(2) provides that partners in a partnership that owns a disregarded entity cannot be treated as employees of the disregarded entity. Therefore, they are subject to self-employment tax and are treated as partners, and not employees, for fringe benefit purposes.

Add to note 600.

In Lauren A. Howell, 104 TCM 519 (2012), the court held that, in the absence of strong proof that the originally reported position was incorrect, taxpayers were bound by their LLC's reported position that payments made to its members in accordance with their respective ownership interests should be taxed as § 707(c) guaranteed payments, rather than distributive share allocations of income. Further, because taxpayers provided some services to the LLC and failed to submit evidence as to the portion of the guaranteed payments not related to those services, the whole of each payment was determined to be subject to employment tax pursuant to § 1402(a)(13).

Page 9-131:

Add to note 604.

; David H. Methvin, TCM 2015-81 (same).

[ii] Distinguishing limited partners from general partners.

Page 9-132:

In note 614, add the following after first sentence.

This provision was accompanied by a "Sense of the Senate" resolution that called for withdrawal of the Proposed Regulations and explicitly reserved to Congress the authority to determine the self-employment status of limited partners. 143 Cong. Rec. 13297 (1997).

Page 9-135:

Add at end of subsection.

With these now-ancient Proposed Regulations still in limbo, the Tax Court was faced with the self-employment tax issue in the context of a Kansas limited liability partnership engaged in the practice of law.[624.1] After recounting the history of the controversy and the status of the Proposed Regulations, as well as noting the lack of any congressional action, Judge Jacob looked first to the statute and found the term "limited partner" had become "obscured over time because of the increasing complexity of partnership and other flow-through entities as well as the history of section 1402(a)(13)."

This ambiguity opened the door for the court to consult the legislative history. The 1977 House Report states that the purpose of § 1402(a)(13) is to exclude from social security coverage "certain earnings which are basically of an investment nature. However, the exclusion from coverage would not extend to guaranteed payments (as described in 707(c) of the Internal Revenue Code), such as salary and professional fees, received for services actually performed by the limited partner for the partnership."[624.2] The insight provided by this language led to the court's conclusion that the intent of this section

> was to ensure that individuals who merely invested in a partnership and who were not actively participating in the partnership's business operations (which was the archetype of limited partners at the time) would not receive credits toward Social Security coverage. The legislative history of section 1402(a)(13) does not support a holding that Congress contemplated excluding partners who performed services for a partnership in their capacity as partners (i.e., acting in the manner of self-employed persons), from liability for self-employment taxes.[624.3]

Consequently, limited liability partners in a law partnership are not limited partners with respect to their distributive shares of income arising from the provision of legal services.

[624.1] Renkemeyer, Campbell & Weaver, LLP, 136 TC 137 (2011). See also CCA 201436049 (2014) (applying *Renkemeyer* to a state law limited liability company operating as an investment manager).

[624.2] HR Rep. No. 702 (Part 1), 95th Cong., 1st Sess. 11 (1977).

[624.3] Renkemeyer, Campbell & Weaver, LLP, 136 TC 137, 150 (2011). See also CCA 201436049 (2014) (applying *Renkemeyer* to a state law limited liability company operating as an investment manager); Riether v. United States, 919 F. Supp. 2d 1140 (DNM 2012) (summary judgment); ILM 201640014 (2016) (limited partner is "operating manager" of limited partnership's franchised restaurants; both distributive share (arguably reflecting capital investment) and guaranteed payments are self-employment income; relying in part on requirements of franchise agreements). See also Vincent J. Castigliola, 113 TCM 1296 (2017) (lawyers in professional LLC; no negligence penalty).

[c] Section 481 Adjustments

Page 9-135:

Replace note 625 with the following.

[625] See generally Rev. Proc. 2011-14, 2011-4 IRB 330, § 5.04.

Pages 9-135–9-136:

Replace last paragraph of subsection with the following.

Upon the incorporation of a partnership, any outstanding § 481 adjustment to the partners is accelerated.[629] Similarly, the Service's view is that the contribution of assets of a trade or business to which a § 481 adjustment relates, to a partnership, results in an acceleration of any outstanding § 481 adjustment.[630] In neither case does the unamortized § 481 adjustment carry over to the transferee of the business, which is consistent with the proposition that these unamortized adjustments belong with the tax returns of those that actually pay the tax (i.e., the partners), and not the partnership.[631]

---

[629] Rev. Rul. 85-134, 1985-2 CB 160; Rev. Rul. 77-264, 1977-2 CB 187; Rev. Proc. 2011-14, 2011-4 IRB 330, § 5.04(3)(c)(ii)(A).

[630] Rev. Proc. 2011-14, 2011-4 IRB 330, § 5.04(3)(c)(ii)(E). The Service has changed its original position to the contrary. See Rev. Rul. 66-206, 1966-2 CB 206.

[631] But cf. Grogan v. Commissioner, 475 F2d 15 (5th Cir. 1973). The taxpayer, in *Grogan*, changed from sole proprietor to a 91.6 percent partner in a partnership, after which the Service placed the partnership on the accrual method of accounting. In response to the partnership's claim that it was entitled to the benefits of § 481(a) with respect to pre-1954 inventories, the Service argued that the partnership, as an entity, had no pre-1954 inventory, since the taxpayer formed the partnership after 1954. The court held that the purposes of § 481(a) were better served by treating the partnership as the "taxpayer" that had pre-1954 inventory.

Page 9-136:

Add new ¶ 9.02[5][e].

[e] Qualified Opportunity Funds Organized as Partnerships [New]

The 2017 Tax Cuts and Jobs Act provides two new incentives to encourage investment in qualified opportunity zones.[633.1] A "qualified opportunity fund" is an investment vehicle organized as a corporation or a partnership for the purpose of investing in qualified opportunity zone property and that holds at least 90 percent of its assets in qualified opportunity zone property.[633.2] First, it allows taxpayers to elect to defer capital gains that are reinvested in a quali-

---

[633.1] "Qualified opportunity zones" are low-income areas designated under this provision.

[633.2] § 1400Z-1.

fied opportunity fund.[633.3] The deferral is preserved through a reduced basis in the investment. In the case of a partnership investment, the taxpayer's outside basis in its partnership interest is reduced, but the partnership takes a carryover basis under § 723 in the contributed property.[633.3a] For example, if *A* elects to defer $100 of capital gain under § 1400Z-2(a)(i) and contributes $100 of cash to a partnership that is a qualified opportunity zone partnership, *A*'s basis in her partnership interest is zero but the partnership's basis in its cash is $100. Acknowledging the potential for mischief created by this inside-outside basis disparity, the Treasury and the Service requested comments on this point.[633.3b]

This disparity also creates a serious trap for taxpayers: Although a partnership merger does not trigger the deferred amount,[633.3c] Step 2 in an assets-over merger (distribution of interest in resulting partnership from terminating partnership)[633.3d] could cause a downward basis adjustment to the resulting partnership's assets. Thus, if the partnership above invested its $100 in property and then merged into a larger partnership, the resulting partnership would take on the $100 basis in the property and the terminating partnership would take a $100 basis in its transitory interest in the resulting partnership after Step 1 of the assets-over construct. But the distribution of the interest to *A* (Step 2) would reduce the basis of the distributed interest to zero. If a § 754 election is in effect with respect to the resulting partnership (or there is a substantial built-in loss),[633.3e] a downwards basis adjustment of $100 with respect to *A* may arise.[633.3f]

The deferral obtained through an investment in a qualified opportunity zone fund lasts until the earlier of the date the investment is sold or December 31, 2026. In addition, the taxpayer's basis in the investment is increased by 10 percent of the gain deferred if the investment is held for at least five years (15 percent if held for at least seven years). This basis increase results in a reduction in the amount of gain recognized when the deferred period ends.[633.3g] The basis increase produces a corresponding increase to the basis of the partnership interest, which is then increased by the recognized deferred gain when recog-

---

[633.3] § 1400Z-2(b)(1). The gain being deferred may be from any sale or exchange of property to an unrelated party.

[633.3a] Preamble to Proposed Regulations, REG-120186-18, Explanation of Provisions, VII, D 1. See Reg. § 1.1400Z2(a)-1(b)(10)(iv)(A) Example 1 (carryover basis under § 362).

[633.3b] Preamble to Proposed Regulations, REG-120186-18, Explanation of Provisions, VII, D 1. This disparity will be resolved when the deferred gain is recognized on the earlier of when the investment is sold or December 31, 2026.

[633.3c] Reg. § 1.400Z2(b)-1(c)(6)(ii)(C)(1).

[633.3d] See generally ¶ 13.06[1].

[633.3e] See generally ¶ 24.01[2].

[633.3f] See TAM 201929019 (Apr. 30, 2019) (Step 2 in assets over merger an exchange under § 761(e) triggering application of § 743(b)).

[633.3g] Reg. § 1.1400Z2(b)-1(e)(5).

nized.[633.3h] These adjustments tier up to upper-tier partnerships and their partners.[633.3i]

A partnership may make the deferral election[633.3j] or, if it does not, each partner may separately elect to defer her distributive share .[633.3k]

Second, it allows exclusion of any post-acquisition capital gains on investments in opportunity zone funds for which an election is made that are held for at least ten years.[633.4] The exclusion is effectuated by an adjustment to fair value of a taxpayer's basis in the disposed of qualified investment. If the basis of a partnership interest is so adjusted, a corresponding adjustment is made to the basis of partnership assets using § 743(b) principles.[633.4a] If the partnership disposes of qualified property, the taxpayer can elect to exclude the gain from gross income, and the excluded amount is treated as an income item under § 705(a)(1), producing an increase to outside basis.[633.4b] Taxpayers can continue to recognize losses associated with investments in qualified opportunity zone funds as under current law.[633.5]

Partnership interests issued for services do not qualify for the benefits of opportunity zone treatment.[633.5a] If a partner contributes both non-qualifying property and property for which the deferral election is made (in either case, including cash), she is treated for § 1400Z purposes as holding two separate interests, and the allocations between the two are based on relative capital contributions.[633.5b] If a profits interest is received for services, the allocation between the two interests is based on the highest share of residual profits allocable to the profits interest.[633.5c] Since this scheme can inappropriately deny opportunity zone benefits to partners who contribute both capital and services (the upside on the "carry" will drag with it a portion of the economics on the capital), these arrangements should be structured so that the profits interest stands separate and apart from the capital interest (for example, by placing it in a separate entity).

[633.3h] See Reg. § 1.1400Z2(b)-1(f)(3) Example 3.

[633.3i] Reg. § 1.1400Z2(b)-1(g).

[633.3j] Reg. § 1.1400Z2(a)-1(c)(1)(i).

[633.3k] Reg. § 1.1400Z2(a)-1(c)(2)(ii)(B).

[633.4] § 1400Z-2(c).

[633.4a] Reg. § 1.1400Z2(c)-1(b)(2). There is apparently some flexibility in applying these rules. The regulation uses the phrase "similar" to the § 743(b) adjustments that would have been made in a cash purchase, and the preamble to the final regulations dictates that the adjustments be made to the extent necessary to eliminate gain or loss. TD 9889 at IV.E.3, 85 Fed. Reg. 1866, 1894 (Jan. 13, 2020).

[633.4b] Reg. § 1.1400Z2(c)-1(b)(2)(ii)(C).

[633.5] HR Rep. No. 466, 115th Cong., 1st Sess., "Conference Report to Accompany HR 1," at 539 (2017).

[633.5a] Reg. § 1.1400Z2(a)-1(b)(9).

[633.5b] Reg. § 1.1400Z2(b)-1(c)(6)(D).

[633.5c] Reg. § 1.1400Z2(b)-1(c)(6)(D).

If a qualified opportunity fund fails to meet the 90-percent requirement without reasonable cause, the fund is required to pay a monthly penalty on the shortfall multiplied by the underpayment rate.[633.6] If the fund is a partnership, the penalty is taken into account "proportionately" as part of each partner's distributive share.[633.7]

[633.6] § 1400Z-2(f)(1).

[633.7] § 1400Z-2(f)(2). The correct application of the "proportionately" standard is not clear for partnership arrangements based on disproportionate allocations.

¶ 9.03 SPECIAL TYPES OF PARTNERS

[1] Corporations

[a] Interaction With Subchapter C

Pages 9-137—9-142:

Replace ¶ 9.03[1][a][ii] with revised ¶ 9.03[1][a][ii].

[ii] Deemed redemptions of corporate stock [revised]. Following the repeal of the *General Utilities* doctrine in 1986, corporations are required to recognize gain on the distribution of appreciated assets to their shareholders. The possibility of avoiding this undesirable result led some taxpayers to utilize partnership "mixing bowl" structures, in which corporate partners contributed appreciated property to partnerships that held or acquired stock of the contributing corporation.[638] Subsequently, the partnership might redeem the corporate partner's interest in exchange for the corporate partner's own stock without triggering the recognition of any gain to the corporate partner.

The Service rather promptly announced, in Notice 89-37, its disapproval of this and all similar efforts to end-run the repeal of *General Utilities*.[639] Proposed Regulations to the same effect under § 337(d) were published in 1992.[640] The 1992 Proposed Regulations were greeted with some criticism by the tax bar, generally along the lines that they created an extremely complex (and technically flawed) elephant gun to repel a minor flea invasion.[641]

---

[638] See B. Bittker & J. Eustice, Federal Taxation of Corporations and Shareholders ¶ 9.23[2][a] (Thomson Reuters/Tax & Accounting, 7th ed. 2000).

[639] Notice 89-37, 1989-1 CB 679.

[640] Prop. Reg. § 1.337(d)-3 (1992); PS91-90, 1993-1 CB 919. Section 337(d) authorizes the Secretary to prescribe "necessary or appropriate" Regulations to carry out the purposes of the 1986 repeal of the *General Utilities* doctrine.

[641] The Service recanted a bit in Notice 93-2, 1993-1 CB 292, but otherwise ignored this criticism.

These events were followed by over two decades of silence: the Proposed Regulations (which had a stated effective date of March 9, 1989) lay fallow and largely ignored. In the meantime, a number of other Subchapter K developments, capped by the 1999 enactment of § 732(f), seemed to lessen the need for any additional regulations.[642] Nevertheless, the Treasury ultimately refocused its attention on this area and, in 2015, issued a fulsome set of final, Temporary, and Proposed Regulations, as well as some related Proposed Regulations, generally applicable to transactions occurring on or after June 12, 2015.[643] Those Regulations, which retain the June 12, 2015 applicability date, were finalized, with minor clarifications, on June 8, 2018.[643.1]

[A] *The fundamental concept.* The basic thrust of these Regulations is to trigger gain to a corporate partner whenever a transaction has the economic effect of an exchange by the partner of appreciated property for an interest in its stock (or stock of an affiliate) owned, acquired, or distributed by the partnership.[644] These Regulations effectively treat a corporation's interest in stock held by a partnership as if it were owned directly by the issuing corporation.

The breadth of the Regulations may not be obvious from this simple articulation of its guiding principle. Under the Regulations, it is not necessary for stock to be distributed to a corporate partner to trigger gain. Instead, any acquisition of stock by a partnership or any partnership distribution or other transaction that creates or increases a corporate partner's direct or indirect interest in its own stock can trigger gain to the corporate partner.[645]

While perhaps appropriate to minimize the opportunities to use partnerships to avoid the repeal of *General Utilities,* the quasi look-through aspect of the Regulations does not fit easily within the general framework (the plumbing, if you will) of Subchapter K. It is difficult enough to deal with corporate partner stock that is owned by a partnership and which is subject to the usual rules of Subchapter K applicable to partnership assets. Layering in the § 337(d) Regulations, which effectively treat such stock as distributed to the issuing corporation (or an affiliate) in whole or in part, from time to time, for

---

[642] In between the issuance of the Proposed Regulations in 1992 and the addition of § 732(f) in 1999, the "mixing bowl" example was included in the final disguised-sale Regulations (see Reg. § 1.707-3(f) Example 8), §§ 731(c) and 737 were added to the Code, and the partnership anti-abuse rules were added in Regulations § 1.701-2.

[643] See TD 9722, 2015-26 IRB 1094 (June 12, 2015), as corrected at 80 Fed. Reg. 38,940 (July 8, 2015) and 80 Fed. Reg. 38,941 (July 8, 2015); REG 149518-03, 80 Fed. Reg. 33,451 (June 12, 2015). The Temporary Regulations had a sunset date of June 11, 2018. See also Prop. Reg. § 1.732-3 (2015), discussed in ¶ 19.10, this supplement.

[643.1] See TD 9833, 83 Fed. Reg. 26,580 (June 8, 2018).

[644] Reg. § 1.337(d)-3(a).

[645] See, e.g., Reg. § 1.337(d)-3(h) Example 1 (formation of partnership triggers gain recognition). For the treatment of distributions, see Reg. § 1.337(d)-3(h) Examples 3 and 4, discussed at ¶ 9.03[1][a][ii][D].

gain recognition purposes, creates complexity that only the most hardened Subchapter K practitioners will be able to process.

Some of the resultant difficulties are addressed by a series of special mechanical rules built into the Regulations, contributing mightily to their complexity.

Other difficulties will come to light as practitioners explore the nuances of the Regulations and the interaction of Subchapter K with these special rules.[646] Compliance with these Regulations, as well as their application on audit, is likely to require feats of mental gymnastics not commonly present in the ranks of tax practitioners or the Service's audit staff. Compliance and enforcement will suffer accordingly.

[B] *An overview of the mechanics; definitions.* The § 337(d) Regulations require a *"Corporate Partner"* to recognize gain (but not loss) under either (1) the *"Deemed Redemption"* rule in Regulations § 1.337(d)-3(d), or (2) the *"Distribution of Stock"* rule in Regulations § 1.337(d)-3(e) "when a transaction has the effect of the Corporate Partner acquiring or increasing an interest in its own stock in exchange for appreciated property in a manner that contravenes the purpose of this section...."[647]

Several defined terms are involved in the application of this recognition rule:

1. *"Corporate Partner"* means any entity that is classified as a corporation for federal income tax purposes and holds or acquires an interest in a partnership.[648]
2. *"Stock of the Corporate Partner"* includes the *Corporate Partner's* stock or other equity interests (including options, warrants, and similar interests) in the *Corporate Partner* or a corporation that controls the *Corporate Partner* within the meaning of § 304(c), except that §§ 318(a)(1) and 318(a)(3) do not apply.[649] *Stock of the Corporate Part-*

---

[646] For example, the Regulations ignore the collateral consequences if depreciable property is contributed by a corporate partner in exchange for stock.

[647] Reg. § 1.337(d)-3(b).

[648] Reg. § 1.337(d)-3(c)(1).

[649] Reg. § 1.337(d)-3(c)(2). Application of the § 304(c) control rules means the controlling corporation generally must hold at least 50 percent of either the combined voting power of all classes of stock of the *Corporate Partner* or the value of all shares of all classes of stock of the *Corporate Partner*. The impact of this relatively low threshold is offset somewhat by the exclusions of attribution pursuant to §§ 318(a)(1) (family members) and 318(a)(3) (corporations and other entities). Because of these exclusions, upward entity attribution under § 318(a)(2)(C) will apply, but downward entity attribution under § 318(a)(3)(C) will not apply. While this would effectively limit "control" to upper-tier corporations, which seems consistent with the overall scheme of the Regulations, the Service and the Treasury Department have indicated that they may remove or revise the § 318(a)(3) exclusions in future amendments to the § 337(d) Regulations. See TD 9833, 83 Fed. Reg. 26,580 (June 8, 2018). Proposed Regulations issued in 2019 would substantially modify the application of the § 304(c) control rules. Prop. Reg. § 1.337(d)-3(c)(2) (2019).

ner also includes interests in any entity to the extent the value of the interest is attributable to *Stock of the Corporate Partner*.[650]

3. A "*Section 337(d) Transaction*" is a "transaction (or series of transactions) that has the effect of an exchange by a *Corporate Partner*of its interest in appreciated property for an interest in *Stock of the Corporate Partner* owned, acquired, or distributed by a partnership."[651] Examples include (but apparently are not limited to):

    a. A contribution by a *Corporate Partner* of appreciated property to a partnership that owns *Stock of the Corporate Partner*;

    b. An acquisition of *Stock of the Corporate Partner* by a partnership;[651.1]

Stock of a Corporate Partner would be limited to entities that own a direct or indirect interest in the Corporate Partner. For purposes of testing direct or indirect ownership of an interest in the Corporate Partner, ownership of the stock of the Corporate Partner would be attributed under § 318(a)(2) (without regard to the 50 percent limitation) and § 318(a)(4), but otherwise without regard to § 318 (§§ 318(a)(1) and 318(a)(3) would not apply). But once an entity is found to own an interest in stock of the Corporate Partner, all of the § 304(c) rules would be applied to determine whether the tested entity is a Controlling Corporation. For purposes of applying these rules, stock of a corporation that controls a *Corporate Partner* is treated as *Stock of the Corporate Partner* without regard to the ratio of the controlling corporation's interest in the *Corporate Partner* to the controlling corporation's total assets. See Example 3 of Reg. § 1.337(d)-3(h).

[650] Reg. § 1.337(d)-3(c)(2)(i). The scope of the "Value Rule" is breathtaking. For example, assume *X*, a publicly traded corporation, has a portfolio investment in *P*, another publicly traded corporation. *P* controls *CP*, a Corporate Partner, so *P*'s stock is Stock of a Corporate Partner. Thus *X* stock is stock of a Corporate Partner to the extent of the value of *X*'s interest in *P*. If *CP*'s partnership acquires *X* stock, the rules of § 337(d)(3) could come into play. See Preamble, REG-135671-17 (2019), at 3. The Proposed Regulations would limit the Value Rule to cases where the entity (*X* in the example) owns, directly or indirectly, 5 percent or more of the vote or value of the stock of the Corporate Partner. Prop. Reg. § 1.337(d)-3(c)(2)(ii) (2019). There is a single, very narrow exception to this definition: "Stock of the Corporate Partner does not include any stock or other equity interests held or acquired by a partnership if all interests in the partnership's capital and profits are held by members of an affiliated group as defined in section 1504(a) that includes the Corporate Partner." Reg. § 1.337(d)-3(c)(2)(ii). Proposed Regulations issued in 2019 would eliminate this exception. Prop. Reg. § 1.337(d)-3(c)(2) (2019).

[651] Reg. § 1.337(d)-3(c)(3).

[651.1] The Service and the Treasury Department acknowledge that, in certain circumstances, a partnership's acquisition of *Stock of the Corporate Partner* does not have the effect of an exchange of appreciated property for that stock. For example, if a partnership with an operating business uses the cash generated in that business to purchase *Stock of the Corporate Partner*, the *Deemed Redemption* rule does not apply because the *Corporate Partner's* share in appreciated property has not been reduced. Taxpayers hoping to show that a transaction does not have the effect of an exchange of appreciated property for *Stock of the Corporate Partner* are cautioned, however, to carefully document the source of funds for a purchase of stock by the partnership. See TD 9833, 83 Fed. Reg. 26580 (June 8, 2018).

    c. A distribution of appreciated property to a partner other than a *Corporate Partner* by a partnership that owns *Stock of the Corporate Partner;*

    d. A distribution by a partnership of *Stock of the Corporate Partner* to the *Corporate Partner;* and

    e. An amendment of a partnership agreement that increases a *Corporate Partner*'s interest in *Stock of the Corporate Partner*, which amendment may be in connection with a contribution to, or distribution from, the partnership.

  4. A *"Corporate Partner's Gain Percentage"* is a fraction, the numerator of which is the value of the *Corporate Partner*'s interest in the appreciated property effectively exchanged for *Stock of the Corporate Partner* under the *Deemed Redemption* rule, and the denominator of which is the value of the *Corporate Partner*'s interest in the appreciated property immediately before the *Section 337(d) Transaction*. Under the *Deemed Redemption* rule, the *Corporate Partner*'s aggregate gain in appreciated property is multiplied by the *Corporate Partner's Gain Percentage* to determine the amount of gain recognized.[652]

[C] *The Deemed Redemption rule.* The timing, amount, and character of the gain recognized by a *Corporate Partner* under these rules is generally controlled by the *Deemed Redemption* rule.[653] Upon the occurrence of a *Section 337(d) Transaction*, the *Corporate Partner* recognizes gain to the extent its interest in other appreciated partnership property is reduced in exchange for an increased interest in *Stock of the Corporate Partner*.[654] Generally, the *Corporate Partner*'s interest in any partnership property (stock or otherwise) is based on all the facts and circumstances, including the allocation and distribution rights set forth in the partnership agreement.[655] However, to avoid possible duplica-

---

[652] Reg. § 1.337(d)-3(c)(4). "Gain Percentage" is a bit of a misnomer in this context and may be confusing. "Recognition Percentage" or "Transfer Percentage" might be more appropriate.

[653] The primary function of the *Distribution of Stock* rule is to assure that distributions of *Stock of the Corporate Partner* do not create basis distortions. Gain is recognized under this rule only if distributed stock is treated as having excess basis. See ¶ 9.03[1][a][ii][D].

[654] Reg. § 1.337(d)-3(d)(1). If a distribution of *Stock of the Corporate Partner* has the effect of an exchange by the *Corporate Partner* of an interest in appreciated property for an interest in *Stock of the Corporate Partner*, the distribution is treated as if it were immediately preceded by a *Section 337(d) Transaction* in the form of an amendment to the partnership agreement to allocate 100 percent of the distributed *Stock of the Corporate Partner* to the distributee *Corporate Partner*. See Reg. § 1.337(d)-3(h) Example 4.

[655] The examples in the Regulations all involve simple partnerships in which each partner has the same economic interest in every distribution and every allocation. More complex partnership allocation or distribution schemes may present greater challenges in ascertaining the partners' interests in partnership assets.

tive gain recognition, the Regulations provide a special rule under which a *Corporate Partner's* interest in an identified share of *Stock of the Corporate Partner* is never less than the largest interest (by value) in such share that was taken into account in determining whether there had been a prior *Section 337(d) Transaction* (regardless of whether the *Corporate Partner* recognized gain in such prior transaction).[656]

The amount of recognized gain under the *Deemed Redemption* rule is determined by multiplying the *Corporate Partner's Gain Percentage* by the *Corporate Partner's* share of the gain from the appreciated property involved in the exchange.[657] The *Corporate Partner's* share of the gain is determined "by applying the principles of section 704(c), including any remedial allocations under § 1.704-3(d)" and basis adjustments under § 743(b).[658] The character of gain recognized by a *Corporate Partner* is the same as the character of gain that would be recognized if the *Corporate Partner* had sold the relevant appreciated property immediately prior to the *§ 337(d) transaction*.[658.1]

The recognition of gain under these rules triggers two (or more[659]) basis increases, one relating to the appreciated property involved in the exchange and the other relating to the *Corporate Partner's* interest in the partnership—each equal to the amount of gain recognized.[659.1]

[D] *The Distribution of Stock rule.* The *Distribution of Stock* rule applies to distributions of *Stock of the Corporate Partner* to the *Corporate Partner* if two conditions are met:

1. Section 732(f) does not apply to the distribution; and
2. The stock has previously been the subject of a *Section 337(d) Transaction* or becomes the subject of a *Section 337(d) Transaction* as a result of the distribution.

---

[656] Reg. § 1.337(d)-3(d)(2); see Reg. § 1.337(d)-3(h) Example 7. However, this special rule does not apply if there is a plan or arrangement to circumvent the purpose of the Regulations. Reg. § 1.337(d)-3(h) Example 8 (special rule not applicable; tainted plan to circumvent).

[657] Reg. § 1.337(d)-3(d)(3). The amount of gain is based on a hypothetical taxable sale at fair market value (taking into account § 7701(g)) of all partnership assets, reduced by any gain the *Corporate Partner* recognizes under any other provision of the Code.

[658] Reg. § 1.337(d)-3(d)(3)(i) (last sentence). See ¶ 9.03[1][a][ii][D], discussing Reg. § 1.337(d)-3(h) Examples 3 and 4.

[658.1] Reg. § 1.337(d)-3(d)(3)(ii).

[659] If gain is recognized at any level other than the upper level in a tiered partnership structure, the basis of the upper tier's direct or indirect interest in each lower-tier partnership is also adjusted. See Reg. §§ 1.337(d)-3(g), 1.337(d)-3(h) Example 9.

[659.1] Reg. § 1.337(d)-3(d)(4). The increase in the basis of the appreciated property is mandated regardless of whether a § 754 election is in effect and is treated as property that is placed in service by the partnership in the taxable year of the § 337(d) transaction. While the body of the Regulations is silent on this point, Example 4 in Regulations § 1.337(d)-3(h) makes it clear that this basis increase, like a § 743(b) basis adjustment, is allocated entirely to the *Corporate Partner*.

Once these two conditions are met, the *Distribution of Stock* rule provides that the *Deemed Redemption* rule applies as though the partners had amended the partnership agreement to allocate a 100 percent interest in the distributed stock to the *Corporate Partner* immediately prior to the distribution; concurrently, an appropriately reduced interest in other partnership property is allocated away from the *Corporate Partner*.[659.2]

In addition, the *Corporate Partner* is required to recognize gain on the distribution in the event the partnership's basis in the distributed stock is in excess of the *Corporate Partner*'s basis in its partnership interest immediately before the distribution (reduced by any cash distributed in the transaction).[659.3]

The *Distribution of Stock* rule recognizes that the basis of distributed stock in the hands of the *Corporate Partner* is of little or no significance, and therefore focuses on making sure the amount of basis allocated to the distributed stock does not create basis distortions elsewhere in the structure. As a consequence,

1. If the partnership distributes other non-cash property along with the *Stock of the Corporate Partner*, the *Corporate Partner*'s basis in its partnership interest is allocated first to the distributed stock, with any balance is allocated in accordance with the usual § 732(c) rules;[659.4] and

2. The partnership's basis for the distributed stock is the greater of (a) the partnership's basis for the distributed stock immediately prior to the distribution; and (b) the fair market value of the distributed stock immediately prior to the distribution reduced by the *Corporate Partner*'s allocable share of gain from all of the *Stock of the Corporate Partner* if the partnership sold all of its assets for cash equal to their fair market value (taking into account § 7701(g)) in a fully taxable transaction immediately before the distribution.

The application of these rules is illustrated by three examples in the Regulations.[659.5]

EXAMPLE 9-27: In Year 1, *X*, a corporation, and *A*, an individual, form partnership *AX* as equal partners in all respects. *X* contributes Asset 1 with a fair market value of $100 and a basis of $20. *A* contributes *X* stock, which is *Stock of the Corporate Partner*, with a fair market value and a tax basis of $100. Upon the formation of the *AX* partnership, there is an exchange by *X* of a 50 percent interest in appreciated property, Asset 1, for a 50 percent interest in the *X* stock. This is a *Section 337(d)*

[659.2] Reg. § 1.337(d)-3(e)(1).

[659.3] Reg. § 1.337(d)-3(e)(3).

[659.4] Reg. § 1.337(d)-3(e)(2)(i). See Reg. § 1.732-1(c)(1)(iii), adopted at the same time (and with the same effective and sunset dates) as the § 337(d) Regulations, discussed in ¶¶ 19.04[1] and 19.06.

[659.5] Reg. § 1.337(d)-3(h) Examples 1, 3 and 4.

Transaction, and X recognizes gain of $40 (Gain Recognition Percentage of 50 percent times total gain of $80 in Asset 1), which results in a $40 increase in the basis of X's partnership interest and a $40 increase in the basis of the appreciated property, Asset 1.

EXAMPLE 9-28: Assume the same facts as in Example 9-27. In Year 9, when Asset 1 and the X stock have each appreciated to $200, the partnership liquidates. Each partner receives a 50 percent interest in each asset. X's interests in the assets do not change as a result of the liquidation, so the liquidation is not a *Section 337(d) Transaction*. However, because there was a prior *Section 337(d) Transaction* and § 732(f) is not applicable, the *Distribution of Stock* rules must be applied. The distribution of 50 percent of X stock is deemed to immediately precede the distribution of 50 percent of Asset 1 to X for basis purposes. The basis of the distributed X stock is treated as $50—the greater of (a) $50, which is 50 percent of the pre-liquidation $100 basis of the stock to the partnership, and (b) $50, which is the $100 value of the stock distributed to X reduced by the $50 gain that would have been allocated to X on a hypothetical sale of the stock (50 percent of $200 value less $100 basis). Thus, X must reduce its basis in the partnership by $50, from $60 to $10, and that amount becomes its basis for the distributed 50 percent interest in Asset 1. No gain is recognized by X under the *Distribution of Stock* rule, since the basis of its partnership interest was greater than the partnership's basis for the distributed stock.

EXAMPLE 9-29: Assume the same facts as in Example 9-28, except X receives 75 percent of X stock and 25 percent of Asset 1 in liquidation of the partnership in Year 9. As a result of the disproportionate distributions, there is a deemed amendment of the partnership agreement immediately before the liquidation in which X is treated as exchanging an additional 25 percent of Asset 1 for an additional 25 percent of the stock. This is a *Section 337(d) Transaction*. X must recognize gain equal to the product of X's *Gain Percentage* and the gain from Asset 1 that X would have recognized if the partnership had sold all of its assets for cash equal to their fair market values in a fully taxable transaction for cash.

If Asset 1 were sold for its value, X's allocable share of the gain would have been $90 (the sum of X's $40 remaining § 704(c) gain and $50 of the $100 post-contribution appreciation). X's *Gain Percentage* is 50 percent (the $50 value of X's 25 percent interest in Asset 1 exchanged for X stock, divided by the $100 value of X's 50 percent interest in Asset 1 immediately before the liquidation). Thus, X recognizes $45 of gain ($90 multiplied by 50 percent) under the *Deemed Redemption* rule. X's basis in its partnership interest increases from $60 to $105 and the partnership basis in Asset 1 increases from $60 to $105.

Because there was a prior *Section 337(d) Transaction* and § 732(f) is not applicable, the *Distribution of Stock* rules must be applied. The distribution of 75 percent of X stock is deemed to immediately precede the distribution of 25 percent of Asset 1 to X for basis purposes. The basis to the partnership of the 75 percent of the X stock distributed to X is treated as $100—the greater of (a) $75, equal to 75 percent of the pre-liquidation $100 basis of the stock to the partnership, and (b) $100, equal to X's 75 percent share of the value of the distributed stock ($150, or 75 percent of $200) less the $50 gain that would have been allocated to X (50 percent of the $100 gain on a hypothetical sale of the stock for $200 less its $100 basis). Thus, X must reduce its basis in the partnership by $100, from $105 to $5, and that becomes X's basis for the distributed 25 percent interest in Asset 1. No further gain is recognized by X, since the basis of its partnership interest was greater than the partnership's basis for the distributed stock.

These results should be tested against the stated objective of the Regulations to trigger gain to a *Corporate Partner* in an appropriate amount to the extent a transaction has the economic effect of an exchange by the *Corporate Partner* of appreciated property for an interest in its stock.[659.6] To achieve this objective, the gain from the *Corporate Partner*'s share of the portion of the appreciated property that is disposed of in an economic sense should be recognized, and the built-in gain in the portion of the property retained should be preserved.

Scrutinizing Example 9-27 on this basis, 50 percent of Asset 1 (value $100, basis $20, and unrealized gain of $80) is disposed of in Year 1. Corporation X recognizes gain of $40 and the basis of Asset 1 is increased to $60, decreasing X's remaining built-in gain in its remaining 50 percent interest in Asset 1 (which is potential § 704(c) gain) to $40. This is consistent with what would happen on a sale of 50 percent of Asset 1.

The computations are more complicated in Example 9-29 when another 25 percent interest in Asset 1 is disposed of by X in Year 9 after the value of Asset 1 has increased to $200. Prior to this disposition, Asset 1 has a value of $200, a basis of $20 (ignoring the basis adjustment that occurred in Year 1 under the § 337(d) Regulations), and a book value of $100 to the partnership. This results in the following thoughts and concerns:

1. If the partnership disposed of 100 percent of Asset 1 for $200, its value, in a taxable transaction in Year 9, there would be book gain of $100 and tax gain of $180. The book gain would be allocated equally (i.e., $50 to each partner). Under § 704(c), the tax gain would be allocated $50 to partner A, the noncontributing partner, to match his tax gain, and the balance of $130 of tax gain would be allocated to X, the contributing partner. However, X has already been taxed on $40 of this gain in Year 1, so X's net recognized tax gain in Year 9 should be $90.

2. Of course, X is only disposing of 50 percent of its remaining interest in Asset 1 in Year 9, so X should recognize gain of only $45, that is, 50 percent of the tax gain it would recognize upon a transfer of its

---

[659.6] See Reg. § 1.337(d)-3(a), discussed in ¶ 9.03[1][a][ii][A].

entire interest in Asset 1. As illustrated in Example 9-29, this is exactly the result reached under the Regulations.

3. The next question is: What should X's basis be in the 25 percent interest in Asset 1 X receives in liquidation of the partnership? Simplistically, one might assume it should be 25 percent of X's original $20 basis in Asset 1, and that is exactly the result reached Example 9-29.

4. Is this the right result? Economically, X has disposed of a 50 percent interest in a $100 asset in Year 1, a 25 percent interest in a $200 asset in Year 9, and still owns a 25 percent interest in a $200 asset. That totals $150 of total value to X versus $20 of tax basis. One would expect X to have a combined total of $130 of recognized gain and built-in gain. In fact, X recognizes a total of $85 of tax gain in Years 1 and 9, and holds a $50 interest in Asset 1 with built-in gain of $45 (i.e., $50 value less $5 basis), a total of $130, which is the correct total of recognized and built-in gain, at least in this situation.

[E] *Exceptions.* Section 1.337(d)-3(f) of the Regulations creates two general exceptions to these rules:[659.7] the "de minimis exception" and the "inadvertence exception." The de minimis exception provides that these gain recognition rules do not apply if three requirements are met: (1) the *Corporate Partner* (and related persons under § 267(b) or § 707(b)) owns less than five percent of the partnership; (2) the value of the *Stock of the Corporate Partner* held by the partnership is less than two percent of the partnership's total gross asset value; and (3) the partnership never holds stock of the *Corporate Partner* with a value of more than $1 million or more than two percent of any class of *Stock of the Corporate Partner.*[659.8] A special rule is provided if a partnership satisfies this rule at the time it acquires the *Stock of the Corporate Partner* but subsequently ceases to satisfy this rule.[659.9]

The inadvertence exception gives partnerships that run afoul of these rules a short-lived opportunity to reverse the transaction that would otherwise trigger application of the gain recognition rule. Any acquisition of *Stock of the Corporate Partner* that is unwound before the due date (including extensions) of the partnership return for the year during which the stock is acquired is ignored so long as the acquisition is not part of a plan to circumvent the Regulations and the unwinding does not result in a transfer of an interest in the stock to the *Corporate Partner* or its parent.[659.10]

[659.7] While not acknowledged as such, the affiliated group rule in Regulations § 1.337(d)-3(c)(2)(ii), discussed in note 650 of this chapter, is effectively a third general exception to these rules.

[659.8] Reg. § 1.337(d)-3(f)(1)(i).

[659.9] Reg. § 1.337(d)-3(f)(1)(ii).

[659.10] Reg. § 1.337(d)-3(f)(2). See Prop. Reg. § 1.337(d)-3(F)(2)(ii) (2019).

[iii] Dividends-received deduction, including debt-financed portfolio stock.

Page 9-142:

In first paragraph of subsection, replace last two sentences (including footnotes 662 and 663) with the following.

Finally, if a partnership owns stock of any member of a corporate partner's consolidated return group, the corporate partner's distributive share of dividends on such stock should not be eliminated under the consolidated return regulations. Under Regulations § 1.1502-13(f)(2)(ii), the exclusion of an intercompany distribution from the gross income of a member is available only to the extent there is a corresponding negative adjustment reflected in the stock of the distributing member under Regulations § 1.1502-32. Because the basis adjustments under Regulations § 1.1502-32 can only be made to stock held by a member of the consolidated group, no corresponding negative adjustment can be made by the partnership.

Page 9-143:

Add to note 664.

The indirect foreign tax credit provisions of former § 902 were repealed by the 2017 Tax Cuts and Jobs Act for taxable years of foreign corporations beginning after 2017.

[iv] Consolidated returns.

Page 9-145:

Add to note 678.

Proposed Regulations § 1.706-1(c)(2)(iii) (2009) would confirm this result.

Page 9-148:

Add to note 689.

Prop. Reg. § 1.1502-13(h)(2) Example 4 (2014) (updated to reflect subsequent change from five to seven years).

[v] Reorganizations.

Page 9-149:

In note 694, replace last sentence with the following.

See Reg. § 1.368-1(d)(5) Example (8) (active management and 20% partnership interest sufficient), Example (9) (active management and one percent partnership interest not sufficient), Example (10) (no management; 33¹/₃% interest sufficient), Example (11) (similar), Example (12) (similar; aggregation of interests of members of group), Example (13) (tiered partnerships). If the stock of the target is transferred to a partnership, the partnership must be part of the acquiring group determined under § 362(c) principles (a § 362(c) controlled partnership) in order to maintain continuity. Reg. § 1.368-1(d)(4)(iii)(D); see Reg. § 1.368-1(d)(5) Example (14) (corporate group members own all of the interests in partnership; target stock treated as owned by qualified group), Example (15) (target stock transferred to partnership 50% owned by unrelated party; continuity of business enterprise requirement not satisfied). See also Reg. § 1.368-2(k)(1)(ii); Reg. § 1.368-2(k)(2) Example (5) (transfer of target stock to 50% owned partnership; partnership outside controlled group; control requirement not satisfied), Example (8) (transfer of target assets to 33⅓% owned partnership does not disqualify reorganization).

Add to note 696.

See also Reg. § 1.368-2(k)(1)(ii) (transfer of target stock permitted as long as target remains part of controlled group; transfer presumably includes distribution from partnerships).

   [vi] Corporate divisions.

Page 9-150:

Add to second to last paragraph of subsection.

The Service subsequently expanded its look-through approach by holding that a corporation with a "significant interest" in a partnership will be treated as engaged in the active conduct of the partnership's (otherwise qualifying) business.[697.1] A one-third interest is significant, a one-fifth interest is not.[697.2]

[697.1] Rev. Rul. 2007-42, 2007-28 IRB 44; see Prop. Reg. § 1.355-3(d)(2), Examples (8), (22), (23), and (24) (2007); cf. Reg. § 1.368-1(d)(5) Example (9).

[697.2] Rev. Rul. 2007-42, 2007-28 IRB 44.

Add to note 699.

Proposed Regulations would further narrow the ability to utilize partnership nonrecognition transactions to ameliorate the impact of the five-year rule. Proposed Regulations § 1.355-3 (2007) treats partnership contributions and distributions as transactions in which gain or loss is recognized for purposes of the five-year rule if they are, in substance, exchanges of the corporate partner's assets. Thus, a corporation's contribution of assets to an existing partnership whose active business would be attributed to the corporation under the "significant interest" rule is treated as a taxable transaction that blocks the tacking of the partnership's period of operations for purposes of the five-year rule. Distributions are similarly treated. Exceptions are provided, however, to deal with cases in which the partnership's business was already attributed to the corporate partner before the contribution or distribution occurred. While the Service's concerns with efforts to circumvent the five-year rule are justifiable, providing that statutorily mandated nonrecognition transactions are to be treated as transactions in which gain or loss is recognized is indeed a bold move. Given the horrendous consequences of failing to meet the requirements of § 355, it will take an equally bold taxpayer to challenge the validity of this position. See Prop. Reg. § 1.355-9 (2016) (so-called "hot dog stand" Proposed Regulations applied to partnership interests).

Page 9-152:

Add new ¶ 9.03[1][a][x].

[x] **Section 385 [new].** Section 385 authorizes regulations to determine whether an interest in a corporation should be treated as stock or debt. As part of its attack on inversions that escape the § 7874 net, Treasury has issued a massive set of regulations applicable to instruments issued by domestic corporations that have the potential to erode the U.S. tax base by creating interest deductions. The perceived abuse involves closely related parties—for example, a U.S. subsidiary of a foreign parent distributes a note as a dividend, and subsequently deducts the interest on the note. Accordingly, the Regulations only apply to corporate groups—so-called "expanded groups," which are generally 80 percent or more controlled groups. Partnerships among expanded group members are "controlled partnerships." The usual hornet's nest of attribution rules and the like can render problematic a determination of whether one is in the grasp of these rules.

In order to minimize the technical issues raised by the interaction of those Regulations with the mechanical rules of Subchapter K, a pure aggregate approach is adopted.[709.1] Thus, if a controlled partnership acquires an interest in a member of an expanded group, each partner is treated as acquiring its share of that instrument in a distribution from the partnership, and the § 385 Regulations operate at the partner level.[709.2] A partner's share of the interest is determined using the increasingly familiar liquidation value percentage.[709.3]

Issuances of interests by a controlled partnership are a bit more complex. The Regulations adopt the same conduit approach to address these issues. Upon the occurrence of an event that would otherwise cause the partnership's obligation to be treated as equity, the expanded group member that holds the debt instrument is deemed to contribute its receivable to the expanded group partner in exchange for equity. The interest paid by the partnership on its debt instrument is deemed paid to the partner, which then distributes the amount to the expanded group member as an equity distribution.[709.4] By adopting this approach, there appear to be no significant problems with the interaction of these § 385 rules with Subchapter K. The specifics of the conduit approach are discussed in the Preamble to Treasury Decision 9790, at H.4.b.

[709.1] Preamble to TD 9790, at H.3 (Oct. 13, 2016).

[709.2] See Reg. §§ 1.385-3(f)(2)(i)(A), 1.385-3(h)(3)(xii) Example 12.

[709.3] See Reg. §§ 1.385-3(f)(2)(i)(B), 1.385-3(g)(7).

[709.4] See Preamble to TD 9790, at H.4.a.; Reg. §§ 1.385-3(f)(2)(i)(A), 1.385-3(h)(3)(xiii) Example 13.

[3] Tax-Exempt Entities

[a] Impact on Partnership ACRS Deductions

[ii] Reduction in available ACRS benefits to partnership having tax-exempt entity partners: Section 168(h)(6).

Page 9-161:

In third paragraph of subsection, add new note 743.1 at end of last sentence.

743.1 While the statute admits of no other exceptions, the legislative history suggests another possibility that has been used to good effect in a 2007 private letter ruling. The relevant legislative history is from 1984 and relates to former § 168(j), the predecessor of current § 168(h). It sets forth an example of an allocation in which a particular item is excluded or segregated without violating the "qualified allocation" rules. In this example, a U.S. corporation and a foreign country are equal partners in a partnership created under the laws of that foreign country. Under those laws, the U.S. corporation's share of the partnership's profits are taxed, but not the foreign government's share. However, the tax is imposed on and paid by the partnership rather than the U.S. corporation partner directly. The partnership agreement allocates all partnership items equally between the partners except for the tax expense, which is allocated entirely to the U.S. corporation. The cash distributions to the partners reflect this expense allocation. Assuming those allocations possess substantial economic effect, the 1984 Conference Report indicates that the conferees did not intend the partnership agreement to be treated as containing an unqualified allocation. See HR Rep. No. 861, 98th Cong., 2d Sess. 792 (1984). In Priv. Ltr. Rul. 200752002 (Sept. 20, 2007), based on this example, the Service ruled favorably under § 168(h)(6) with respect to a special allocation of "tax expense recovery income" to the taxable members of a limited liability company subject to regulation (including rate-setting) by the Federal Energy Regulatory Commission (FERC). Although this particular special allocation apparently was required under a FERC policy statement, it appears the allocation would have fallen within the spirit of the 1984 example even in the absence of an administrative compulsion.

[iii] Section 470.

Pages 9-163–9-164:

Replace last sentence of subsection with the following.

As originally enacted, § 470 did not provide any exception to its application in situations where partnerships are considered to hold tax-exempt use property solely by reason of § 168(h)(6) (i.e., because a partnership has both taxable and tax-exempt partners and makes nonqualified allocations to tax-exempt partners).[761] This failure was recognized fairly quickly by both Congress and the Service,[762] but it was not until the end of 2007 that an appropriate amend-

---

[761] See supra ¶ 9.03[3][a][iii].

[762] Notice 2007-4, 2007-2 IRB 1, superseding and modifying Notice 2006-2, 2006-2 IRB 278, and Notice 2005-29, 2005-13 IRB 796. Notice 2007-4 notes the introduction of

ment (effective as if included in the original 2004 legislation) was enacted as part of the Technical Corrections Act of 2007.[762.1]

---

the Tax Technical Corrections Act of 2006, introduced in Congress on September 29, 2006, which addresses the application of § 470 to partnerships and other pass-through entities with tax-exempt use property as a result of § 168(h)(6). The legislation, as of the time of the Notice, had not been enacted, but bore with it a retroactive effective date so as to apply to property acquired after March 12, 2004. The Notice observes that the Description of the Tax Technical Corrections Act of 2006, prepared by the Joint Committee on Taxation (Oct. 2, 2006), states that the retroactive effective date of the proposed legislation is not intended to supersede the rules of Notice 2006-2 and Notice 2005-29. Accordingly, for taxable years beginning before January 1, 2007, the Service will not apply § 470 to disallow losses associated with property that is treated as tax-exempt use property solely as a result of the application of § 168(h)(6).

[762.1] Section 470(c)(2)(B), as amended by § 7(c) of Pub. L. No. 110-172, provides that the term "tax-exempt use property" does "not include any property which would (but for this subparagraph) be tax-exempt use property solely by reason of section 168(h)(6)."

[b] Investment Tax Credit

Page 9-164:

Replace note 763 with the following.

[763] The § 46 investment credit currently consists of the § 47 rehabilitation credit, the § 48 energy credit, the § 48A qualifying advanced coal project credit, the § 48B qualifying gasification project credit, and the § 48C qualifying advanced energy project credit.

Add at end of subsection.

Additionally, generally no investment tax credit is available under Section 48 with respect to property used predominantly outside the United States. An exception exists under Section 50(b)(1)(B) for property described in Section 168(g)(4), which includes property predominantly used outside of the United States that is (1) owned by a domestic corporation (other than a corporation which has an election in effect under former Section 936) or by a U.S. citizen (other than a citizen entitled to the benefits of Section 931 or Section 933) and (2) used predominantly in a U.S. possession by such persons. The Service has adopted an aggregate approach to the application of Section 50(b)(1)(B), ruling that a domestic partnership owned solely by approved corporations and individuals under Section 168(g)(4)(G) will be entitled to claim the investment tax credit with respect to property used predominantly in a U.S. possession.[765.1]

[765.1] Priv. Ltr. Rul. 201426013 (Mar. 19, 2014).

[c] Unrelated Business Taxable Income

Page 9-164:

Replace note 768 with the following.

768 Whether a business engaged in by a partnership generates unrelated business taxable income is determined at the partner level. § 512(c)(1). Section 512(a)(6) provides that an organization with more than one unrelated trade or business must calculate its UBTI separately with respect to each trade or business, and losses from one cannot be netted with profits from another. Exempt organizations that invest in partnerships that carry on multiple trades or business, often in tiered structures, would have great difficulty complying with this rule. Regulations issued in 2020 provide some relief, permitting the aggregation of such trades or businesses in de minimis situations (no more than a 2 percent partnership interest) or lack of control situations (no more than 20 percent interest, no control or influence over the partnership). This latter rule appears to be the most useful. See Reg. §§ 1.512(a)-6(c)(3), 1.512(a)-6(c)(4) (consistent with Notice 2018-67, 2018-36 IRB 409).

[ii] Preferred returns and guaranteed payments.

Page 9-167:

Add to first paragraph of subsection (ending with note callout 780).

Proposed Regulations would expand the exclusion for items of income and gain allocated to a partner with respect to a preferred return (currently subject to a matching rule, discussed below) if the partnership agreement requires priority distributions (other than reasonable tax distributions) with respect to such preferred return.780.1

780.1 Prop. Reg. §§ 1.514(c)-2(d)(2)(ii) (2016), 1.514(c)-2(d)(2)(iii) (2016).

Page 9-168:

In last paragraph of subsection, add the following after note callout 788.

The Treasury Department has proposed regulations in 2016 that would eliminate this matching requirement with respect to preferred returns, having concluded that the potential for abuse is limited so long as the preferred return is given priority over other returns.788.1

788.1 REG-136978-12 (Nov. 23, 2016). See Prop. Reg. §§ 1.514(c)-2(d)(ii) (2016), 1.514(c)-2(d)(iii) (2016).

[iii] Chargebacks and offsets.

Page 9-169:

Add the following after next to last paragraph of subsection (ending with note callout 798).

For taxable years ending on or after November 23, 2016, Proposed Regulations would allow a partnership to disregard two additional chargeback items,

both of which offset items that originally were not taken into account in computing overall partnership income or loss under the fractions rule: First,
chargebacks against partner-specific expenditures that were disregarded originally may be disregarded (and must be disregarded for taxable years ending after the date any final Regulations are adopted). Second, chargebacks against
prior allocations of unlikely losses and deductions that were disregarded originally may (and must, at a later date) also be disregarded.[798.1]

[798.1] Prop. Reg. §§ 1.514(c)-2(e)(1)(vi) (2016), 1.514(c)-2(e)(1)(vii) (2016). The Proposed Regulations would also add an example explicating a chargeback of prior allocations of unlikely losses and deductions. Prop. Reg. § 1.514(c)-2(e)(5) Example 5 (2016).

[iv] Allocations relating to certain administrative costs, unlikely losses and deductions, and certain partner nonrecourse loans.

Page 9-170:

Add to note 800.

For taxable years ending on or after November 23, 2016, Proposed Regulations would allow (and mandate, for taxable years ending on or after the date
final Regulations are published) a partnership to disregard expenditures for
management and similar fees, so long as such fees do not exceed for a taxable
year, in the aggregate, 2 percent of a partner's capital commitment. Prop. Reg.
§ 1.514(c)-2(f)(4) (2016).

Page 9-171:

Replace last paragraph of subsection with the following.

Allocations of partner nonrecourse deductions, as well as compensating
allocations of other items of loss or deduction to other partners, are not taken
into account for purposes of the fractions rule until the taxable years in which
the allocations are made. Moreover, a violation of the fractions rule will be
disregarded if a nontax-motivated allocation of partner nonrecourse deductions
to one qualified organization causes another qualified organization's violation.[803]

---

[803] Reg. § 1.514(c)-2(j).

[v] Special rules.

Page 9-171:

Add the following after second paragraph of subsection.

Proposed Regulations would disregard changes in allocations for purposes
of applying the fractions rule in the context of staged closings (i.e., when investors come into an investment in timed stages), so long as four conditions
are met: First, each new investor invests in the partnership no later than 18

months following the formation of the partnership. Second, the partnership agreement provides for such delayed investment. Third, the partnership agreement specifies a method for allocations and determining any interest factor paid in accordance with the delayed investment. Fourth, the interest factor is less than or equal to 150 percent of the highest applicable federal rate in effect when the partnership was formed.[806.1]

[806.1] Prop. Reg. § 1.514(c)-2(k)(1)(ii) (2016).

[vi] Tiered partnerships.

Page 9-173:

Add to last paragraph of subsection (ending with note callout 812).

Proposed Regulations would clarify that a violation of the fractions rule in a lower-tier entity would cause a violation of the fractions rule only with respect to an upper-tier partnership's investment in the lower-tier entity and not with respect to all other investments of the upper-tier partnership.[812.1]

[812.1] Prop. Reg. § 1.514(c)-2(m)(2) Example 3(ii) (2016).

[4] Nonresident Aliens and Foreign Corporations

[a] General

Page 9-175:

Add to note 822.

The 10-percent shareholder test is applied at the partner level. Reg. § 1.871-14. This aggregate approach considerably broadens the scope of the portfolio interest exception because partnership-level application coupled with the attribution rules would treat many foreign partnerships as 10-percent shareholders (since the partnership is treated as owning stock held by its partners). Partner-level treatment is also far more administrable.

Page 9-176:

Add to note 825.

In Technical Advice Memorandum 200811019 (Nov. 29, 2007), the Service expressed its view that the aggregate approach is applied in determining whether a foreign partner's distributive share of partnership fixed or determinable annual or periodical income or capital gains is effectively connected under Regulations § 1.864-4(c) . This technical advice memorandum relies heavily on Revenue Ruling 91-32, 1991-1 CB 107, which applies an aggregate approach to determine whether gain from the sale of a partnership interest by a foreign person is effectively connected with the conduct of a U.S. trade or business of the partnership. (The Service reaffirmed the position taken in Revenue Ruling 91-32 in Chief Counsel Memorandum 20123903F (July 17, 2012).) In *Grecian Magnesite Mining, Industrial & Shipping Co., SA v. Commissioner*, 149 TC No. 3 (2017), aff'd, 926 F3d 819 (DC Cir. 2019), the Tax Court rejected use of the aggregate approach as applied in Revenue Ruling 91-32. That rejection undercuts the analysis in Technical Advice Memorandum 200811019, though the issues addressed in the technical advice and *Grecian Magnesite* differ. The issue in Technical Advice Memorandum 200811019 is whether a partner's share of the fixed or determinable annual or periodical income (FDAP) of a partnership that has no U.S. office may be effectively connected to the U.S. office of a foreign partner. In *Grecian Magnesite*, a foreign partner that directly conducted no U.S. business sold an interest in a partnership that conducted a U.S. business through a U.S. office. Accordingly, the Tax Court did not address the issue considered by Technical Advice Memorandum 200811019.

In second paragraph of subsection, replace last sentence with the following.

Accordingly, such foreign partners are generally not exempt from tax by treaty.[828]

---

[828] Rev. Rul. 85-60, 1985-1 CB 187; but see Priv. Ltr. Rul. 201027041 (July 9, 2010) (Russian resident partner not taxable on distributive share of partnership's ECI; U.S.-Russian treaty provision requires Russian resident to be present in the United States for more than 183 days in a calendar year in order to be taxable in the United States on income from independent personal services).

Pages 9-176—9-177:

Replace third paragraph of subsection (containing notes 829 through 831) with the following.

The Service and the Tax Court disagree about the sourcing of gain or loss realized by a foreign partner on the sale or redemption of an interest in a partnership. Revenue Ruling 91-32,[829] involves the sale by a foreign partner who does not directly operate a U.S. business of an interest in a partnership that does conduct a U.S. business. On the other hand, *Grecian Magnesite Mining, Industrial & Shipping Co., SA v. Commissioner*,[830] considers the sourcing of gain or loss realized on the liquidation of an interest in a U.S. partnership held by a foreign partner who directly conducts no U.S. business. In *Grecian Magnesite*, the Tax Court treated sales, subject to § 741, and redemptions, subject to §§ 736(b) and 731(a), as equivalent transactions.[831]

The analysis in Revenue Ruling 91-32 is grounded on the view that, in the applying the rules of Subchapter N (relating to the sourcing of income of foreign persons), partnerships should be viewed as aggregations of partners, and not as entities. Under an aggregate approach, the sourcing rules would be

---

[829] Rev. Rul. 91-32, 1991-1 CB 107.

[830] Grecian Magnesite Mining, Industrial & Shipping Co., SA v. Commissioner, 149 TC No. 3 (2017), aff'd, 926 F3d 819 (DC Cir. 2019).

[831] Under § 736(b)(1) liquidation payments in exchange for a partner's interest in partnership property are treated as distributions, subject to § 731, and § 731(a) provides that gain or loss recognized from distributions "shall be considered as gain or loss from the sale or exchange of the partnership interest of the distributee partner."

applied by treating the selling partner as selling interests in the partnership's assets.

By contrast, in *Grecian Magnesite*, the Tax Court rejected the aggregate approach in favor of an entity approach. Under an entity approach, a partnership interest is treated as an item of personal property that is separate from the partnership's assets, and, under § 865(a)(1), gain or loss from the sale of a partnership interest by a nonresident of the U.S. is generally sourced outside the United States. On appeal to the D.C. Circuit, the Service declined to pursue the aggregate theory, instead chasing an interpretation of § 865(e)(2)(A) that would treat gain from the sale of an interest in a partnership that conducted a U.S. trade or business as "attributable to [the U.S. office] or other fixed place of business." In affirming the Tax Court, the D.C. Circuit dismissed the Service's position in Revenue Ruling 91-32 as "a single unreasoned sentence in a Ruling that spans four pages of the Cumulative Bulletin."[831.0] Instead, the court agreed with the taxpayer (and the Tax Court) and declined to apply § 865(e)(2)(A) to a sale of a partnership interest.

Congress attempted to resolve this disagreement in 2017 by adding new § 864(c)(8) to the definition of "effectively connected income."[831.1] Under § 864(c)(8), gain or loss from the sale or exchange of a partnership interest is effectively connected with a U.S. trade or business to the extent that the transferor would have had effectively connected gain or loss upon a hypothetical sale by the partnership of all of its assets at fair market value on the date of the sale or exchange. Such gain or loss must be allocated among the partners in the same manner as residual income and loss.[831.2]

Regulations elucidating § 864(c)(8) were finalized in late 2020.[831.2a] The regulations require a foreign transferor to first determine its gain or loss on the transfer of a partnership interest ("outside gain" and "outside loss") under all relevant provisions of the Code and the regulations thereunder. Under §§ 741 and 751, the seller of a partnership interest can have both capital gain (or loss) and ordinary income (or loss). The hypothetical sale of each partnership asset would generate deemed sale effectively connected income (ECI). The foreign transferor must determine its distributive share of the aggregate deemed sale EC ordinary gain (if the aggregate results in a gain) or aggregate deemed sale EC ordinary loss (if the aggregate results in a loss). Parallel computations are

---

[831.0] *Grecian Magnesite Mining, Industrial & Shipping Co., S.A. v. Commissioner*, 926 F3d. 819 (DC Cir. 2019), aff'g, 149 TC 63 (2017).

[831.1] 2017 Tax Cuts and Jobs Act, Pub. L. No. 115-97, § 13501(a) (Dec. 22, 2017); HR Rep No. 466, 115th Cong., 1st Sess., "Conference Report to Accompany HR 1," at 509 (2017). The definitional change applies to sales and exchanges.

[831.2] It is not clear why Congress decided to use residual sharing interests as opposed to the actual sharing interests that would have applied the gain or loss from the hypothetical sale under the terms of the partnership agreement. Use of residual interests, which may not be reflective of real economic interests, would seem to be an invitation to manipulation.

[831.2a] Reg. § 1.864(c)(8)-1.

made with respect to capital items. The gain/loss computed under the usual §§ 741 and 751 rules is effectively connected to the extent it does not exceed the foreign transferor's distributive share of aggregate deemed sale EC ordinary/ capital gain/loss, as the case may be. Examples are provided illustrating that EC capital gain cannot exceed outside capital gain and that an outside ordinary loss precludes taxing a distributive share of EC ordinary gain.

> **EXAMPLE 9-31A:** Foreign Corp. sells its entire 50 percent interest to Buyer Corp. for $110, at a time when its outside basis is $100 and the Partnership's balance sheet is as follows:

> U.S. Asset: $100 Adjusted Basis /$150 FMV ($50 gain)
> Foreign Asset: $100 Adjusted Basis / $70 FMV ($30 loss)

> Foreign Corp. recognizes $10 of capital gain under § 741. The deemed sale would result in a $50 capital gain, all of which is EC gain attributable to the U.S. business. There would be no deemed EC gain or loss on the foreign asset (despite the $30 loss on the asset) as it has never generated any ECI. Foreign Corp.'s aggregate deemed sale EC capital gain is $25. Since the outside capital gain of $10 is lower than the aggregate deemed sale EC capital gain, Foreign Corp. only recognizes the $10 of gain as EC capital gain.

> **EXAMPLE 9-31B:** Foreign Corp. sells its entire 50 percent interest to Buyer Corp. for $95, at a time when its outside basis is $100 and the Partnership's balance sheet is as follows:

> | | |
> |---|---|
> | U.S. Business Capital Asset: | $20 Adjusted Basis / $50 FMV ($30 gain) |
> | U.S. Business Inventory: | $30 Adjusted Basis / $50 FMV ($20 gain) |
> | Foreign Business Capital Asset: | $100 Adjusted Basis / $80 FMV ($20 loss) |
> | Foreign Business Inventory: | $50 Adjusted Basis / $10 FMV ($40 loss) |
> | Total | $200 Adjusted Basis / $190 FMV ($10 loss) |

> Foreign Corp. recognizes a $5 capital gain and $10 ordinary loss under §§ 741 and 751. The total deemed EC gain is $30 for the capital asset, and $20 for the inventory. Foreign Corp.'s aggregate deemed sale EC capital gain is $15 (50 percent of $30) and its aggregate deemed sale EC ordinary loss is $0 (because there is no ordinary loss property that is EC loss property). The $5 capital gain is treated as EC gain because its aggregate deemed sale EC capital gain ($15) is greater than $5. The $10 outside ordinary loss is treated as effectively connected loss *to the extent that it does not exceed Foreign Corp.'s aggregate deemed sale EC loss*, which is

$0. Thus, Foreign Corp. has no effectively connected loss. From an ECI perspective, this makes sense, as the reason that Foreign Corp. generated an overall loss on the sale of its partnership interest is due to the fact that its 50 percent share of the loss in the Partnership non-ECI assets exceeded its 50 percent share of gain in the Partnership ECI assets by $5.

EXAMPLE 9-31C: Foreign Corp. sells its 50 percent interest in Partnership for $100. Foreign Corp. had a $100 outside basis in its Partnership interest. Partnership has only ECI assets, which consist of

$160 Basis / $180 FMV ordinary asset ($20 gain)
$40 Basis / $20 FMV capital asset ($20 loss)

Despite the fact that Foreign Corp. sold its interest for an amount equal to its outside basis, it nevertheless recognizes the $10 of ECI ordinary income and has a $10 EC capital loss. If Foreign Corp. has no ECI capital gain, it will owe U.S. tax on more income that it has economically generated.

It is noteworthy that the regulations do not deal with non-taxable distributions to foreign persons of non-ECI assets. The Preamble notes that this may result in abuses and that the Treasury and Service are considering rules to address this issue.[831.2b]

To enforce new § 864(c)(8), Congress modified the withholding rules, adding § 1446(f), which requires that if any portion of the gain on the disposition of a partnership would be effectively connected with a U.S. trade or business, the transferee of a partnership interest must withhold 10 percent of the amount realized on the sale or exchange of a partnership interest unless the transferor certifies that the transferor is not a nonresident alien individual or foreign corporation.[831.3] If the transferee fails to withhold any portion of amount, the partnership is required to deduct and withhold the shortfall from distributions to the transferee partner.

In 2020 the Treasury finalized Regulations under § 1446(f) that would implement the § 1446(f) withholding regime.

The Regulations generally authorize a transferee to rely upon certification from a transferor of the various exceptions to withholding (described below), where such certification contains the transferor's name, address, tax identification number (TIN) (if the person providing the certification has a TIN), and is

---

[831.2b] TD 9919, Preamble II.D., Section 731 Distributions, 85 Fed. Reg. 70958, 70963 (Nov. 6, 2020).

[831.3] Notice 2018-8, 2018-7 IRB 352 suspended withholding obligations for dispositions of interests in publicly traded partnerships (within the meaning of § 7704(b)). Withholding on dispositions of interests in publicly traded partnerships is currently governed by Regulations § 1.1446(f)-4.

signed under penalties of perjury.[831.4] The transferee is allowed to rely on any such certification issued no earlier than thirty days prior to the transfer.[831.5]

The Regulations authorize multiple exceptions to a transferee's obligation to withhold, expanding some and narrowing others. The exceptions are as follows:

1. Where the transferor certifies its non-foreign status (generally through a certification or a valid Form W-9);[831.6]
2. Where the transferor certifies it has not realized gain in connection with the transaction;[831.7]
3. Where the underlying partnership certifies that if it sold all of its assets at their fair market value, the percentage of the total gain that would have been effectively connected with the conduct of a trade or business within the United States would have been less than 10 percent;[831.8]
4. Where the transferor certifies that the ECI allocated to it by the partnership was, during each of the transferor's three prior full taxable years: (a) less than $1 million; (b) less than 10 percent of the total taxable income allocated to it by the partnership; and (c) reported on a federal income tax return by the transferor (or its foreign partners) and all tax due thereon has been paid;[831.9]
5. Where the transferor certifies that no gain or loss is required to be recognized by the transferor by reason of a nonrecognition provision of the Code;[831.10] or
6. The transferor certifies that it is not subject to tax pursuant to a treaty benefit and provides a valid Form W-8BEN to the transferee.[831.11]

In situations 2 through 4 described above, where a partnership is the transferee to the partner by reason of a distribution, it would be able to rely upon its books and records in applying the relevant exception.[831.12]

The required withholding is generally equal to 10 percent of the transferor partner's amount realized in the transfer, including the partner's share of liability relief under § 752(d).[831.13] A transferor may generally rely upon a certifica-

---

[831.4] Reg. § 1.1446(f)-1(c)(2)(i).

[831.5] Reg. § 1.1446(f)-1(c)(2)(i).

[831.6] Reg. § 1.1446(f)-2(b)(2).

[831.7] Reg. § 1.1446(f)-2(b)(3).

[831.8] Reg. § 1.1446(f)-2(b)(4).

[831.9] Reg. § 1.1446(f)-2(b)(5).

[831.10] Reg. § 1.1446(f)-2(b)(6). Note that the certification must be for full nonrecognition—the exception generally does not apply in the case of partial nonrecognition.

[831.11] Reg. § 1.1446(f)-2(b)(7).

[831.12] Reg. §§ 1.1446(f)-2(b)(3)(iii), 1.1446(f)-2(b)(4)(ii), 1.1446(f)-2(b)(5)(iv).

[831.13] Reg. § 1.1446(f)-2(c)(2). A partnership is allowed to rely on its books and records to determine the amount of liability relief for a transferor partner in a distribution.

tion from the underlying partnership as to the transferor's share of partnership liabilities.[831.14] Recognizing, however, that some transferees may be challenged in obtaining liability relief calculations from partnerships, the Regulations generally authorize a transferee (other than the underlying partnership) to rely on a certification from the transferor partner that provides the partner's identified share of partnership liabilities on its most recent Schedule K-1.[831.15]

The Regulations also provide for reduced withholding obligations on the part of a transferee under the following situations:

1. Where the transferor is a foreign partnership and can certify that some of its partners are not foreign;[831.16]

2. Where the transferor certifies its "maximum tax liability" in connection with the transfer (which generally requires certification as to the transferor's tax basis and effective tax rates on applicable gain);[831.17]

3. Where the amount required to be withheld (based on the transferor's decreased share of partnership liabilities) exceeds the cash paid by the transferee; or

4. Where the transferee is unable to determine the transferor partner's share of liabilities.[831.18]

The Regulations make clear that the withholding of tax by the transferee does not relieve the transferor partner from its obligation to file a U.S. income tax return with respect to the transfer; nor does it eliminate such partner's obligation to pay any additional tax due with respect to the transfer.[831.19]

Section 1446(f)(4) serves as a backstop to § 1446(f)(1) by imposing upon the underlying partnership the obligation to withhold any amounts with respect to the transferee partner if the transferee does not satisfy its obligations to withhold. Regulations § 1.1446(f)-3 provides limited exceptions to this obligation where the transferee certifies that it has complied with the withholding requirements of § 1446(f)(1).[831.20] The partnership's obligation to withhold includes both the initial withholding obligation and any interest on such obligation, computed at the underpayment rate.[831.21]

Different rules apply to transfers of interests in publicly traded partnerships. Because the transferee generally has no idea of the identity of the transferor partner, the obligation to withhold is passed along to any broker (where a

---

[831.14] Reg. § 1.1446(f)-2(c)(2)(ii)(C).

[831.15] Reg. § 1.1446(f)-2(c)(2)(ii)(B).

[831.16] Reg. § 1.1446(f)-2(c)(2)(iv).

[831.17] Reg. § 1.1446(f)-2(c)(4).

[831.18] Reg. § 1.1446(f)-2(c)(3).

[831.19] Reg. § 1.1446(f)-2(e).

[831.20] Reg. § 1.1446(f)-3(b)(1) (see Reg. § 1.1446(f)-2(d)(2) for transferee's certification requirement).

[831.21] Reg. § 1.1446(f)-3(c)(2).

broker is involved in the transfer).[831.22] The broker is then entitled to rely on a series of exceptions, including non-foreign status certification, designation of a distribution as a qualified current income distribution, certification of the application of an income tax treaty, and certification that less than 10 percent of the gain recognized by a publicly traded partnership in connection with a sale of all of its assets would be classified as ECI.[831.23]

[831.22] Reg. § 1.1446(f)-4(a).
[831.23] Reg. § 1.1446(f)-4(b).

[b] Foreign Investment in Real Property Tax Act of 1980

Page 9-178:

Add to note 836.

Priv. Ltr. Rul. 200851023 (Dec. 19, 2008) describes an elaborate reorganization of U.S. real property interests in which several "United States real property holding companies," within the meaning of § 897(c)(2), were transferred to a foreign partnership. The letter ruling concludes that the transaction is a nonrecognition transfer under § 721 and not a taxable event under § 897.

[c] Withholding

[ii] Fixed or determinable, annual or periodical income.

Page 9-179:

Add to note 839.

Section 1441 technically applies only to nonresident alien individuals and foreign partnerships. Section 1442(a) provides for withholding for foreign corporations "in the same manner and on the same items of income as provided in Section 1441...."

Page 9-180:

Replace note 847 with the following.

[847] See Rev. Proc. 2017-21, 2017-6 IRB 791 (agreement for withholding foreign partnership agreements; revising and updating agreements set forth in Rev. Proc. 2014-47, 2014-35 IRB 393, which updated and revised Rev. Proc. 2003-64, 2003-2 CB 306, to coordinate with FATCA).

[iii] Gain from the disposition of U.S. real property interests.

Page 9-180:

Replace third sentence of subsection with the following.

Section 1445(e)(1) imposes a 35 percent (or, where provided in the Regulations, a 20 percent[848.1]) withholding tax on the amount of gain realized from the disposition of U.S. real property interests by domestic partnerships to the extent such gain is allocable to a foreign person.[849]

[848.1] American Taxpayer Relief Act of 2012, Pub. L. No. 112-240, § 102(c)(1)(C). For taxable years beginning on or before December 31, 2012, the withholding tax rate was a minimum of 15 percent.

[849] Reg. § 1.1445-5(c)(1)(ii). See supra ¶ 9.03[4][b].

[iv] Effectively connected income.

Page 9-182:

Add to note 861.

See Ann. 2013-30 (2012 rates for withholding for taxable years beginning in 2012; foreign partners in fiscal year partnership with taxable year ending in 2013 must nevertheless pay tax at 2013 rates).

Page 9-183:

Add to note 872.

For partnership taxable years beginning after December 31, 2007, Regulations § 1.1446-6 restates the elaborate system under which foreign partners may "certify" certain losses and deductions to partnerships that may be subject to § 1446 withholding, thereby potentially reducing the required withholding.

Page 9-185:

Add to note 885.

For partnership taxable years beginning after December 31, 2007, the rules regarding submission of certificates are set forth in Regulations § 1.1446-6. A partner providing a certificate must use Form 8804-C "Certificate of Partner-Level Items to Reduce Section 1446 Withholding." See Reg. § 1.1446-6(c)(2)(i).

Add to note 886.

For partnership taxable years beginning after December 31, 2007, this rule, which applies only to nonresident alien individual partners, is found in Regulations § 1.1446-6(c)(1)(ii). This provision of the Regulations includes a de minimis rule under which no withholding is required for individuals if the properly estimated amount of withholding is less than $1,000.

Add to note 887.

For partnership taxable years beginning after December 31, 2007, a foreign partner must have filed federal income tax returns and paid the tax liability shown on such returns for the current year and the preceding three years. See Reg. § 1.1446-6(b).

Add to note 888.

For partnership taxable years beginning after December 31, 2007, the rules governing a partnership's reliance on certificates are found in Regulations § 1.1446-6(a)(2).

[e] Eligibility of Partnership Income for Reduced Treaty Withholding Rates Applicable to Foreign Partners: Section 894(c)

Page 9-188:

Add to note 899.

On the flip side, there is no corollary to § 894(c)(1) in the Canadian tax law. The Tax Court of Canada has held that a Delaware LLC is a U.S. resident because the United States taxes its world-wide income (including its Canadian branch income), albeit at the U.S resident member level. Accordingly, the LLC was entitled to the reduced 5% withholding rate under the Canada-U.S. treaty (prior to the Fifth Protocol). See TD Securities (USA) LLC v. The Queen, 2010 TCC 186 (Apr. 8, 2010). This decision apparently will not be appealed by the Canada Revenue Agency, which has announced it will accept refund claims from certain U.S. LLCs for periods prior to the effective date of the Fifth Protocol. See 2010 TNT 132-6 (July 9, 2010).

[f] Partnerships as Controlled Commercial Entities of Foreign Governments: Section 892

Page 9-190:

Add at end of subsection.

Where the foreign government conducts its activities through a controlled entity (generally a separate juridical entity in which the foreign government has actual or effective control), the exemption does not apply if the controlled entity carries on a commercial activity.[909.1] Except for partners of publicly traded partnerships, commercial activities of a partnership are attributable to both its general and limited partners.[909.2] The Treasury has proposed regulations to mitigate the harshness of this "all or nothing" rule by cutting off attribution to limited partners.[909.3] A limited partner is defined by the proposed regulations as a member in an entity classified as a partnership who has no right to participate in the management and conduct of the partnership's business at any time during the partnership's year.[909.4] An exception from the "all or nothing" rule is also provided, in the proposed regulations, for partners in partnerships engaged in securities trading activities.[909.5]

[909.1] Temp. Reg. § 1.892-5T(a).

[909.2] Temp. Reg. § 1.892-5T(d)(3).

[909.3] Prop. Reg. § 1.892-5(d)(5) (2011).

[909.4] Prop. Reg. § 1.892-5(d)(5)(iii) (2011).

[909.5] Prop. Reg. § 1.892-5(d)(5)(ii) (2011).

¶ 9.04 TAXABLE YEAR CONSIDERATIONS; TIME OF INCLUSION OF PARTNER'S DISTRIBUTIVE SHARE

[1] Partnership's Taxable Year

[a] Least Aggregate Deferral

Page 9-197:

Add to note 939.

Reg. § 1.706-1(b)(6)(ii) (applicable on or after October 1, 2019) removed the exclusion for foreign personal holding companies, and excludes only CFCs with respect to which a U.S. shareholder owns stock within the meaning of § 958(a). The narrowing of the CFC exclusion was triggered by the repeal of § 958(b)(4) (blocking downward attribution for determining CFC status), which vastly expanded the universe of CFCs to include corporations with no U.S. shareholders. Since such entities do not impact the U.S. tax system, they should not be relevant to determine a partnership's tax year.

In first full paragraph, fourth sentence, clause (2), replace the word or *with the word* and.

[4] Monthly Reporting for Partners in Tax-Exempt Bond Partnerships

Page 9-210:

Add after second paragraph of subsection.

The Service has proposed a new revenue procedure to modify and supersede Revenue Procedure 2003-84. While prospective for bond partnerships formed 30 days after the new revenue procedure is finalized,[1005.1] tax-exempt bond partnerships may rely on the proposed revenue procedure with respect to monthly closing elections made on or after September 17, 2008.[1005.2]

The proposed revenue procedure would add three new eligibility requirements for a partnership to make a monthly closing election.[1005.3] The first deals with "tender option termination events." Investors in these partnerships are generally protected against loss because they can put their partnership interest to the sponsor or related person on short notice. The proposed revenue procedure requires that this put right must terminate upon at least one significant event (such as bankruptcy of the issuer), thus exposing the investor to at least

---

[1005.1] Notice 2008-80, 2008-40 IRB 820, Form of Proposed Revenue Procedure, § 9.01.

[1005.2] Notice 2008-80, 2008-40 IRB 820, Form of Proposed Revenue Procedure, § 3.

[1005.3] Notice 2008-80, 2008-40 IRB 820, Form of Proposed Revenue Procedure, § 3.02.

some risk of loss from the partnership's activities. The second requires that the investor have at least a 5% share of any gain recognized by the partnership, and the third requires that the partnership in fact recognize such gain on or before the date on which 80% of the bond's maturity date has elapsed.

What is striking about the proposed revenue procedure is the fine line that it draws between a tax-recognized partnership and a financing transaction. In all but the rarest of cases, the investor is looking to the put option, not the partnership, as the source of its return. Nevertheless, the presence of one rather remote "tender option termination event," together with a 5% share of a relatively small amount of potential gain, is enough to confer partner status on the investor.

The markets in which these instruments are traded require certainty. Thus, while tax purists may raise an eyebrow at the precise line drawn by the proposed revenue procedure, the Service is to be commended for providing clear guidance in this area.

Replace last sentence of subsection with the following.

An exempt-interest dividend is any dividend paid by a RIC and designated by the RIC as an exempt-interest dividend in a written notice mailed to its shareholders.[1007]

[1007] § 852(b)(5)(A).

¶ 9.05 ALTERNATIVE MINIMUM TAX COMPUTATIONS

Page 9-211:

Replace first paragraph of subsection with the following

Following enactment of the 2017 Tax Cuts and Jobs Act, corporations are spared from the alternative minimum tax (AMT), although individuals remain subject to its invidious application.[1008] The base for the AMT is alternative minimum taxable income (AMTI), which is generally equal to taxable income, increased by certain tax preferences, and adjusted to reflect the recomputation of a number of items taken into account in computing regular taxable income.[1009] The AMT is equal to the "tentative minimum tax" less the "regular tax" for the year.[1010] The tentative minimum tax is equal to 26 percent of the "taxable excess" up to $175,000, plus 28 percent of the taxable excess in excess of $175,000, reduced by any "alternative minimum tax foreign tax credit"

[1008] The elimination of the corporate AMT is effective for tax years beginning after December 31, 2017. Pub. L. No. 115-97, § 12001(c) (Dec. 22, 2017).

[1009] See § 55(b)(2).

[1010] § 55(a)

for the year.[1011] The "taxable excess" is the excess, if any, of AMTI over the exemption amount.[1012] Under certain circumstances, a credit for AMT payments may be allowed against subsequent years' tax liabilities.[1012.1]

[1011] § 55(b)(1)(A).

[1012] § 55(b)(1)(B). The exemption amounts for 2018 through 2026 are $109,400 for joint returns and surviving spouses, $70,300 for unmarried individuals who are not surviving spouses, $54,700 for married persons filing separately, and $22,500 for estates and trusts. § 55(d)(4)(A)(i). These exemption amounts are reduced by 25 percent of the AMTI in excess of certain amounts (§§ 55(d)(2), 55(d)(4)((A)(ii)), and most of these amounts are adjusted for inflation after 2018. § 55(d)(4)(B).

[1012.1] See § 53.

¶ 9.06 PROCEDURAL AND REPORTING MATTERS

[1] Returns

[a] General Returns

Page 9-219:

Add to note 1047.

If a foreign partnership that is not required to file a return makes a payment or accrual that is treated as a base erosion payment of a partner under Regulations § 1.59A-7(c), a corporate partner required to file Form 8991 (computing base erosion and anti-abuse tax (BEAT)) must include the information necessary to report those base erosion payments. Reg. § 1.6031(a)-1(b)(7).

Page 9-220:

Replace first full paragraph (ending with note callout 1055) with the following.

Under § 6072(b), the partnership return must be filed on or before the fifteenth day of the third month following the end of the partnership's taxable year.[1053.1] An automatic five-month extension is allowed upon filing an application.[1054] Regulations § 1.6031(a)-1(e)(1) requires the return to be filed in the district in which the partnership has its principal office or place of business within the United States. The return must be signed by a partner, and any part-

---

[1053.1] Notice 2017-71, 2017-51 IRB 561, provides penalty relief for returns filed after March 15, 2017, but before April 18, 2017 (i.e., returns that would have been timely under prior law).

[1054] Reg. § 1.6081-2.

ner's signature is prima facie evidence of his authority to sign the return on behalf of the partnership.[1055]

For partnership tax years beginning after 2017, § 6031(b) generally prohibits partnerships subject to the centralized partnership audit procedures enacted as part of the Bipartisan Budget Act of 2015 ("BBA partnerships") from amending the information required to be furnished to their partners (including Forms 1065 and K-1) after the due date of the return without filing an administrative adjustment request pursuant to § 6227. The Treasury is authorized to provide relief from this requirement, which it exercised in Revenue Procedure 2020-23.[1055.1] Section 3 of this Revenue Procedure gives BBA partnerships that filed returns prior to the issuance of the Revenue Procedure an option to file amended returns and issue amended Schedules K-1 for tax years beginning in 2018 and 2019 prior to September 30, 2020.

[1055] § 6063. The Service takes the position that the signature by a person that is a general partner when the return is signed is effective even if such person was not a partner during the taxable period covered by the return. FSA 563 (Nov. 4, 1992). See CCA 201945027 (July 12, 2019) (minor errors in e-file Signature Authorization do not render return invalid); CCA 201425011 (Feb. 21, 2014) (return signed in name of foreign entity holding interest in LLC; LLC not an individual acting for entity; invalid return).

[1055.1] Rev. Proc. 2020-23, 2020-18 IRB 749.

Add to note 1058.

In *Battle Flat, LLC*, the U.S. district court granted deference to, and enforced, Revenue Procedure 84-35. Battle Flat, LLC v. United States, 2015-2 USTC ¶ 50,490 (DSD 2015).

Page 9-221:

Add after carryover paragraph.

The adoption of the original version of the § 1.704-1(b) Regulations on December 24, 1984, ushered in a brave new world for determining, reporting, and testing the ways in which partnership tax items are allocated among partners.[1062.1] Central to this new regime are the interwoven relationships among the allocations of these tax items, the partners' capital accounts, and the sharing of the economic benefits and burdens of partnership activities among partners. The new regime recognizes and respects the enormous freedom afforded to partners and limited liability company members under state law to share these economics in virtually any way imaginable. Within this freedom, it attempts to ensure, to the extent possible, that the tax allocations correlate with the economics.

At the center of this correlation is the key question of the partners' capital accounts: Exactly how should these capital accounts be determined? The answer to this question must bridge the gap between tax and economic consider-

---

[1062.1] TD 8065, 86-1 CB 254, 50 Fed. Reg. 53420 (Dec. 24, 1985). See ¶ 11.02.

ations if the tax allocations are to reflect the sharing of the economics. To accomplish this goal, the drafters of these Regulations developed a previously unknown methodology and birthed a new vocabulary in the process.[1062.2] The governing capital accounts, which have come to be known as "§ 704(b) book capital accounts" must comply with some very precise rules.

Critically, the § 704(b) book capital accounts must be part of a partnership balance sheet that is "balanced" in the sense that the sum of the partners' capital accounts is equal to the difference between the aggregate book value of the partnership's assets and liabilities. This means that the construction of the capital accounts must take into account a host of differences between the tax basis and the book value of assets, including the taxability (or not) of receipts, the deductibility (or not) of expenditures, differences in tax versus nontax rules for capitalization, depreciation and amortization of capital items, and differences in the treatment of various liabilities.

Historically, the return forms for partnerships (principally Form 1065 "U.S. Return of Partnership Income" and Form Schedule K-1 (Form 1065) "Partner's Share of Income, Deductions, Credits, etc.") have addressed the blending of tax and economic concepts as follows:

- The basic reporting of income, deductions, loss, credits, etc. in the first section of Form 1065 and Schedule K necessarily reflects taxable amounts except for a few specific items (e.g., tax-exempt income and nondeductible expenses on Line 18);
- The Balance Sheets in Schedule L explicitly reflect "book" (typically GAAP book, not § 704(b) "book");
- Schedules M-1, M-2, and M-3 (if required) blend and reconcile taxable amounts and book amounts;
- On Schedule K-1 (Form 1065) Part II, Box L "Partner's capital account analysis" gives the partnership several choices: tax basis, GAAP, Section 704(b) book, Other (explain);
- Part II, Box M of Schedule K-1 (Form 1065) asks whether the partner has contributed property with built-in gain or loss, thereby addressing one of the common sources of book-tax differences; and
- Part III, "Partner's Share of Current Year Income, Deductions, Credits, and Other Items" mirrors Form 1065 Schedule K and hence generally reflects tax amounts except as otherwise indicated (e.g., Line 18).

Over the years, it has become apparent that the latitude afforded taxpayers under Boxes L and M of Schedule K-1 significantly reduces the usefulness of this information as an audit tool for the Service.[1062.3] For audit purposes, the

---

[1062.2] See ¶ 11.02[2][c].

[1062.3] It can also be a great source of confusion for partners and their advisors: Depending on the method selected for these boxes, there may be no correlation whatsoever between the adjustment amounts in these boxes and the income and deduction amounts reflected in Part III of a K-1.

single most important piece of information regarding a partner is probably the tax basis (or, for some types of partners, the at-risk basis) of the partner's partnership interest. The historical version of Schedule K-1 does not give the Service a clue as to either of these amounts. The reason for this is relatively simple: There are many situations in which a partnership cannot determine, from its own records, the amount of a partner's basis for his partnership interest. The majority of these situations involve transfers of partnership interests or partnership distributions that do not trigger internal partnership basis adjustments due to the lack of a § 754 basis adjustment election by the partnership. The Treasury is well aware of this: The newly minted Regulations under the Bipartisan Budget Act of 2015 (BBA) audit regime explicitly provide that the basis of a partner's interest is not a "partnership-related item" within the scope of the BBA rules.[1062.4] Why not? Because a partnership cannot compute a partner's basis without taking "into account the facts and circumstances specific to that partner."

However, the inability of the Service to require partnerships to provide definitive basis information for partners' interests does not mean they cannot come a lot closer to getting meaningful information than the historical forms provide. Almost three and a half decades after the advent of the 1984 Regulations, the Service began to focus on the usefulness of better basis information. Schedule K-1 of the 2019 Form 1065 includes the following changes that relate, directly or indirectly, to the bases of partners in their interests:[1062.5]

- Item N—A new item was added for reporting a partner's share of net unrecognized § 704(c) gain or (loss), at the beginning and the end of the tax year. 2019 Instructions p. 31.[1062.6]
- Box/Line 11—Code F was repurposed to reflect any net positive income effect from § 743(b) adjustments. 2019 Instructions p. 34.
- Box/Line 13—New code V was added for any net negative income effect from § 743(b) adjustments. 2019 Instructions p. 37.
- Box/Line 20—Code AA is now used for the net income/loss effect for all § 704(c) adjustments. 2019 Instructions p. 51.
- Box/Line 20—Code AH, Other, now includes net § 743(b) adjustments for partners with basis adjustments. 2019 Instructions p. 52.

All of these changes will ease the audit process for the Service and may red-flag some possible basis issues for auditors.

In addition, the original Instructions for the 2019 version of Form 1065 proposed to add a requirement that Schedules K-1 must include "tax basis cap-

---

[1062.4] Reg. § 301.6241-1(a)(6)(iii), discussed in ¶ 10A.02[3].

[1062.5] 2019 Instructions for Form 1065, pp. 1–2, Internal Revenue Service (Feb. 13, 2020) (2019 Instructions).

[1062.6] Item N is an expansion of Item M, which simply asks whether the partner contributed property with a built-in gain or loss. Item M was added to Schedule K-1 in 2009.

ital account" information for all partners.[1062.7] While this amount is not a completely accurate indicator of the tax basis of a partner's partnership interest in the absence of a § 754 election, it is certainly useful: In many situations, the basis of a partner's interest can be approximated as the sum of the partner's tax basis capital account and the partner's share of partnership liabilities, an amount that is also included on Schedule K-1 (Box K). While the Service has relented on this requirement for 2019, it has also announced it is considering a slightly different approach going forward. In Notice 2020-43,[1062.8] it proposed two (and only two) ways for partnerships to comply with the new "tax capital reporting requirement" for 2020 and subsequent tax years. The two proposed methods are as follows:

1. Modified Outside Basis Method. The partnership computes, or obtains from its partners, each partner's adjusted basis in its partnership interest, determined under the principles and provisions of Subchapter K (including those contained in §§ 705, 722, 733, and 742), and subtracts from that basis the partner's share of partnership liabilities under § 752; or

2. Modified Previously Taxed Capital Method. This method is based on Regulations § 1.743-1(d)(1) and generally provides that a partnership interest transferee's share of the adjusted basis of partnership property is equal to the sum of the transferee's interest as a partner in the partnership's previously taxed capital, plus the transferee's share of partnership liabilities. This Regulation also provides that the transferee's previously taxed capital is the sum of (i) the amount of cash the partner would receive on a liquidation of the partnership following a hypothetical liquidation transaction, plus (ii) the tax loss (including any remedial allocations under Regulations § 1.704-3(d)) that would be allocated to the partner from the hypothetical transaction; less (iii) the amount of tax gain (including any remedial allocations under Regulations § 1.704-3(d)) that would be allocated to the partner from the hypothetical transaction. The hypothetical transaction is a disposition by the partnership of all of its assets in a fully taxable transaction for cash equal to the fair market value of the assets. See Regulations § 1.743-1(d)(2).

Modified outside basis is, of course, exactly the information the Service would like to have but, as implicitly acknowledged by the "or obtains from its partners" clause, the partnership may not be able to deliver it without the voluntary (in most cases) assistance of its partners.

The Service has requested comments on this proposal. They are likely to be critical and voluminous.

[1062.7] See Notice 2019-20, 2019-1 CB 927, Notice 2019-66, 2019-2 CB 1509.
[1062.8] See Notice 2020-43, 2020-27 IRB 1.

[c] Returns for Controlling U.S. Partners of Foreign Partnerships

Page 9-224:

Add to note 1077.

See also Prop. Reg. § 1.6038-3(g)(4) (2019) (reporting requirements in connection with claiming deduction under § 250, relating to foreign derived intangible income and GILTI).

Page 9-225:

Add at end of numbered list.

> 7. A § 362(e)(2)(C) election to reduce the basis of corporate stock re-
> ceived by a controlled foreign partnership in exchange for loss prop-
> erty in a § 351 transaction.[1077.1]

[1077.1] Reg. § 1.362-4(d)(3)(ii)(B).

Add to last sentence of subsection.

In addition, for tax years beginning after June 30, 2016, any U.S. person that is the "ultimate parent" of a U.S. multinational enterprise group is required to file annual country-by-country returns on Form 8975.[1078.1]

[1078.1] Reg. § 1.6038-4; see TD 9773 (June 29, 2016).

[2] Reportable Transaction Disclosure Requirements

[a] Reportable Transactions

Page 9-228:

Add to note 1089.

The deductibility by individuals of most personal casualty losses was eliminated by the 2017 Tax Cuts and Jobs Act during the period from 2018 through 2025. § 165(h)(5) (as amended by Pub. L. No. 115-97, § 11044(a) (Dec. 22, 2017)).

[6] Liens

Page 9-237:

Add to note 1151.

; Pitts v. United States, 2016-2 USTC ¶ 50,399 (9th Cir. 2016) (not for publication) (fed-eral tax lien valid; liability of general partner for unpaid employment taxes arises under federal law (§ 6231) as well as state law; state statute of limitations not controlling).

CHAPTER **10**

TEFRA Partnership Audit and Litigation Rules

¶ 10.01 OVERVIEW

Page 10-2:

Add the following before first paragraph of subsection.

The procedures for examining partnership returns and collecting resulting deficiencies were completely overhauled on November 2, 2015, for taxable years beginning after December 31, 2017.[0.1]

The legislation creates a single, streamlined set of partnership audit rules, and repeals the 1982 Tax Equity and Fiscal Responsibility Act (TEFRA) unified partnership audit rules as well as the electing large partnership rules.

Broadly, the legislation eliminates the ability of partners to participate in partnership examinations, and empowers a sole partnership representative (who need not be a partner) to control partnership examinations and bind all partners. While the legislation also makes the partnership directly liable for any deficiencies, it provides two mechanisms whereby the partnership can shift part or all of any deficiency obligation to the persons who were partners in the partnership during the tax year under examination.

These rules will apply to all partnerships that have more than 100 partners or who have a direct partner that is classified as a partnership for federal tax purposes. Partnerships that have 100 or fewer partners, none of which are partnerships, can elect out of the new regime.

These rules are discussed in ¶ 10.08.

[0.1] Partnerships may elect to apply these new rules for taxable years beginning after November 2, 2015. Bipartisan Budget Act of 2014, § 1101(g)(4).

Page 10-3:

Add to note 9.

All trusts are pass-thru partners. Colin P. Murphy, 129 TC 82, 88 (2007); Block Developers, LLC, 2014 TNT 39-16 (Feb. 26, 2014) (Tax Court CLC order dated Feb. 25, 2014, denying partial summary judgment; Roth IRA is a trust and therefore a pass-thru partner, relying on *Murphy.*

¶ 10.02 STRUCTURAL ASPECTS

[1] Small Partnership Exception

Page 10-4:

In second paragraph of subsection, replace second sentence with the following.

Specifically, the small partnership exception will not apply where a partnership has any partners who are nonresident aliens, partnerships, disregarded entities,[17.1] S corporations, or trusts.[17.2]

[17.1] Rev. Rul. 2004-88, 2004-32 IRB 165. See Seaview Trading, LLC v. Commissioner, 2017-1 USTC ¶ 50,243 (9th Cir. 2017) (Rev. Rul. 2004-88 followed); Mellow Partners v. Commissioner, 890 F3d 1070 (DC Cir. 2018) (same).

[17.2] The presence of a prohibited type of partner prevents a partnership from qualifying as a small partnership even if the partner holds only a small interest. See Charles Brumbaugh, TCM 2015-65 (partnership holds a 0.02 percent interest in second partnership; second partnership is not a "small partnership").

Page 10-5:

Add to note 23.

Merely identifying a tax matters partner on a Form 1065 does not constitute a TEFRA election. Larry J. Wadsworth, 93 TCM 940 (2007).

Add to note 24.

But see Gardner, TC Memo. 2018-42 (TEFRA procedures inapplicable to taxpayer who invested in Son-of-BOSS transaction through legal partnership that failed to file a federal tax return where partnership was disregarded under *Culbertson*).

Add to note 25.

The issuance of an FPAA may be treated as a determination by the Service that TEFRA applies even if the Service also issues a notice of deficiency relating to the same partnership items. See John C. Bedrosian, 143 TC 83 (2014).

Add to note 26.

DeWayne Bridges, TC Memo. 2020-51 (2020) (Service's determination that TEFRA does not apply was reasonable, rejecting taxpayer's argument that because the returns were "internally inconsistent and irreconcilable" it was impossible for the Service to make a reasonable determination): "Petitioner cannot litter his returns with misleading and inaccurate information, selectively rely upon the information, and then expect to bamboozle his way to a procedural victory." In John C. Bedrosian, 143 TC 83 (2014), the Tax Court held that it would not be reasonable for the Service to conclude that TEFRA does not apply if the partnership return, including Schedules K-1, contains sufficient information identifying one or more pass-through partners.

Add to note 27.

See CCA 201016079 (Mar. 31. 2010) (reliance is not reasonable if Service is aware of "contradicting facts").

[2] Tax Matters Partners

Page 10-6:

In second paragraph of subsection, add new note 31.1 at end of first sentence.

[31.1] In Devonian Program, 100 TCM 37 (2010), aff'd unpub. opinion, 2011-2 USTC ¶ 50,564 (3d Cir. 2011), a partner challenged the status of the purported tax matters partner of a tax partnership as a partner for tax purposes, arguing that the purported tax matters partner had no interest in capital or profits (the purported tax matters partner contributed $3,000 to the partnership in exchange for a 17% net revenue interest, which the petitioner characterized as a "contingent interest" received in exchange for services). The Tax Court rejected the petitioner's claim, relying on Commissioner v. Culbertson, 337 US 733 (1949) to conclude that the purported tax matters partner had an intent to join together in the conduct of a business enterprise and thus was a partner.

Add to second paragraph of subsection.

It is not necessary for a partner to bear liability in a partnership proceeding in order to serve as tax matters partner.[33.1]

[33.1] Gateway Hotel Partners LLC, TC Memo. 2009-128.

Page 10-7:

Add to note 35.

Cambridge Partners, LP, 114 TCM 392 (2017) (individual who filed petition was not the tax matters partners; case dismissed for lack jurisdiction).

Page 10-11:

Add to note 61.

Since state law determines who can bind the entity, a tax matters partner of an LLC may not have the authority to sign for the LLC. See CCA 201312042 (Feb. 5, 2013); CCA 201312043 (Feb. 6, 2013).

[3] Partnership Items

Page 10-12:

Add to note 65.

Neither the issuance of an unnecessary "affected items" deficiency notice, following a partner-level proceeding, to a partner nor any computational error reflected therein provides the Tax Court with jurisdiction to review the partner's petition appealing the notice or tolls the period of assessment relating to such notice. Randall J. Thompson, 137 TC 220 (2011), rev'd, 729 F3d 869 (8th Cir. 2013).

Add to note 67.

Similarly, in Alpha I, L.P. v. United States, 84 Fed. Cl. 209 (2008), withdrawn in part, 2009-1 USTC ¶ 50,267 (Ct. Fed. Cl. 2009), the court held that the question of whether a contribution of a partnership interest to a charitable remainder unitrust is a sham is not a partnership item. *Alpha I* was reversed on appeal. 2012-1 USTC ¶ 50,401 (Fed. Cir. 2012). Although the IRS argued that the charitable remainder unitrust's distributive share would be allocated back to the contributor, thus apparently bringing the case within the purview of *Grigoraci*, the Federal Circuit noted that the taxpayers had not agreed to this reallocation and so the issue remained open. Accordingly, partner identity is a partnership item because partner identity *could* affect the distributive shares of the other partners (even though such would not be true if the IRS's argument prevails).

Add to note 68.

See RJT Investments, 491 F3d 732 (8th Cir. 2007) (partnership's sham status treated as a partnership item determinable in a partnership-level proceeding); Petaluma FX Partners, LLC. v. Commissioner, 591 F3d 649 (DC Cir. 2010), aff'g in part and rev'g in part 131 TC 84 (2008); see also CCN 2009-027 (Aug. 21, 2009) (defining "partnership items").

Pages 10-12−10-13:

In third paragraph of subsection, replace second sentence with the following.

The Regulations contain an extensive list of matters that are within the definition of "partnership items," including (1) all items of partnership income, gain, loss, deduction, or credit, and each partner's share thereof;[69] (2) partnership liabilities and each partner's share thereof;[70] (3) guaranteed payments;[71] (4) optional adjustments to the basis of partnership property pursuant to a § 754 election;[72] and (5) partnership contributions and distributions,[73] payments to a partner under § 707(a), and the application of §§ 751(a) and 751(b).[73.1] Partnership items also include partnership liabilities.[73.2]

---

[69] Reg. § 301.6231(a)(3)-1(a)(1)(i).

[70] Reg. § 301.6231(a)(3)-1(a)(1)(v). This includes the release of a partner from a liability. See Bassing v. United States, 80 Fed. Cl. 710 (2008).

[71] Reg. § 301.6231(a)(3)-1(a)(2).

[72] Reg. § 301.6231(a)(3)-1(a)(3).

[73] Reg. §§ 301.6231(a)(3)-1(a)(4), 301.6231(a)(3)-1(c)(2). See Dakotah Hills Offices Ltd. Partnership, 71 TCM 1942 (1996) (amount of § 752(b) distribution is a partnership item); FSA 200049023 (Sept. 6, 2000) (disputed recharacterization of contributions and distributions as disguised sales; contributions and distributions are partnership items).

[73.1] Reg. § 301.6231(a)(3)-1(a)(1)(vi)(E).

[73.2] Reg. § 301.6231(a)(3)-1(a)(1)(v). Likewise, the cancellation of partnership liabilities is a partnership item.

Add to note 74.

; CCA 201139009 (Sept. 19, 2011) (application of § 183 is a partnership item).

Add the following after note callout 75.

The Federal Circuit Court of Appeals has held that a partner's release from a deficit restoration obligation is a partnership item.[75.1] In *Michael E,*

[75.1] Charles W. Bassing III v. United States, 563 F3d 1280 (Fed. Cir. 2009).

Napoliello,[75.2] the Tax Court held that the basis of securities distributed from a disregarded sham partnership is an "affected item" that may be determined in a partner-level proceeding following a related TEFRA (partnership-level) proceeding.

In *Petaluma FX Partners, LLC v. Commissioner*,[75.3] the D.C. Circuit reviewed the Tax Court's decision concerning certain "partnership item" determinations in *Petaluma FX Partners, LLC*.[75.4] In doing so, the appellate court affirmed the Tax Court's holding that whether a partnership is a sham or lacks economic substance is a partnership item to be resolved in a TEFRA proceeding.[75.4a] However, the appellate court held that a partner's basis in his partnership interest is not a partnership item that can be determined in a TEFRA proceeding even though the determination of a partnership item in that proceeding (here, that the partnership was a sham) directly affects the partner's basis, reversing the Tax Court's decision to the contrary. Accordingly, the appellate court affirmed the Tax Court's determination that the partnership was a sham, but ruled that the Tax Court lacked jurisdiction to determine that the basis of the partner's interest was zero (as a result of the partnership being a sham). The appellate court also concluded that the Tax Court lacked jurisdiction to consider penalties that might be applicable if the partner's basis is determined to be zero.

The scope and consequences of the "partnership item" definition created so much confusion and conflict among the lower courts that the Supreme Court, in *United States v. Woods,* finally entered the fray to attempt to address the chaos.[75.5] The impact of *Woods* is far reaching and pervasive, and was still

---

[75.2] Michael E. Napoliello, 97 TCM 1536 (2009), aff'd, 655 F3d 1060 (9th Cir. 2011).

[75.3] Petaluma FX Partners, LLC v. Commissioner, 591 F3d 649 (DC Cir. 2010). Accord AD Global FX Fund v. United States, 113 AFTR2d 2014-1582 (SDNY 2014) (outside basis is not a partnership item, although sham nature of partnership and inside basis of assets are partnership items).

[75.4] Petaluma FX Partners, LLC, 131 TC 84 (2008).

[75.4a] See 436, Ltd., TC Memo. 2015-28 (determination of whether partnership exists is a partnership item); John C. Bedrosian, 144 TC 152 (2015); LAFA 20162901F (Mar. 21, 2016) (whether partnership exists or is valid is a partnership item; statute of limitations determined under § 6229(a) based on filing date of return for sham partnership).

[75.5] United States v. Woods, 571 US 31 (2013). See Robert C. Gunther, TC Memo 2019-6 (2019). In *Gunther*, the Tax Court had determined in a partnership-level proceeding that the partnership was a sham and the partners were subject to both deficiencies and penalties. Gunther's subsequent action challenging his personal deficiencies and penalties as a partner was dismissed by the Tax Court with respect to the penalties for lack of jurisdiction, pointing out that *Woods* only noted that an aggrieved "partner remains free to raise, in subsequent partner-level proceedings, any reasons why the penalty may not be imposed on him specifically." United States v. Woods, 571 US 31, 42 (2013). Under § 6230, the only available venue for partners to raise subsequent challenges to penalties is in a "post-payment" refund action. *Woods* does not modify § 6230, contrary to the unfounded hopes of Mr. Gunther (and, no doubt, many others hoping to avoid payment up front).

being worked out even as Congress replaced TEFRA itself in 2018.[75.5a] In *Woods*, the Supreme Court determined that TEFRA courts do indeed have the jurisdiction to provisionally determine the applicability of certain tax penalties on partners. In *Woods*, the substantive result of the lower courts' decisions was to ignore partnerships that had no business purpose or economic substance, and so were "shams." Any deficiency resulting from these determinations, however, depended on a determination that the taxpayer-partners had no basis in their sham partnership interests. The taxpayer, in *Woods*, argued that, because a partner's basis in his partnership interest is not a partnership item, a court sitting in a TEFRA case has no jurisdiction to determine penalties that might result from overstatement of a partner's basis. The Supreme Court disagreed:

> Under TEFRA's two-stage structure, penalties for tax underpayment must be *imposed* at the partner level, because partnerships themselves pay no taxes. And imposing a penalty always requires some determinations that can be made only at the partner level. Even where a partnership's return contains significant errors, a partner may not have carried over those errors to his own return; or if he did, the errors may not have caused him to underpay his taxes by a large enough amount to trigger the penalty; or if they did, the partner may nonetheless have acted in good faith with reasonable cause, which is a bar to the imposition of many penalties, see § 6664(c)(1). None of those issues can be conclusively determined at the partnership level. Yet notwithstanding that every penalty must be imposed in partner-level proceedings after partner-level determinations, TEFRA provides that the *applicability* of some penalties must be determined at the partnership level. The applicability determination is therefore inherently provisional; it is always contingent upon determinations that the court in a partnership-level proceeding does not have jurisdiction to make. Barring partnership-level courts from considering the applicability of penalties that cannot be imposed without partner-level inquiries would render TEFRA's authorization to consider some penalties at the partnership level meaningless.[75.6]

In *Randall J. Thompson*,[75.7] the Tax Court held that it had no jurisdiction in a partner-level proceeding to examine the partner's ability to deduct losses realized upon the liquidation of his partnership interest where the partnership's

---

[75.5a] See Chapter 10A (Centralized Partnership Audit Regime); this regime was enacted as part of the Bipartisan Budget Act of 2015, Pub. L. No. 114-74).

[75.6] United States v. Woods, 571 US 31, 38, 564 (2013). Applying *Woods*, the Tax Court, in an unpublished order affirmed by the Court of Appeals for the 11th Circuit, held, in a partner-level deficiency proceeding, that it did not have jurisdiction over a gross-valuation misstatement penalty previously determined to be applicable at the partnership level where the partnership was determined to be a sham lacking economic substance. Highpoint Tower Technology Inc. v. Commissioner, 931 F3d 1050 (11th Cir. 2019) (affirming an unpublished order of the Tax Court).

[75.7] Randall J. Thompson, 137 TC 220 (2011), rev'd, 729 F3d 869 (8th Cir. 2013).

losses had been disallowed pursuant to a partnership-level proceeding in which the court found absence of business purpose, absence of economic substance, and absence of any profit motive for the underlying transactions or the acquisition of the partnership interest. The Eighth Circuit, in *Thompson*, reversed on the ground that outside basis is an affected item that must be determined in a partner level proceeding.[75.8]

In *United States v. Steinbrenner*,[75.9] an adjustment to partnership income resulted in a trust that was a partner having a net operating loss. The trust elected to carry back the net operating loss to a prior year, thereby permitting a trust beneficiary to claim a refund of taxes for the prior year. The IRS asserted that the refund claim was time-barred by § 6230(c)(2)(B)(i) because the refund claim was "attributable to a partnership item" for purposes of § 6511(g). The district court summarily dismissed the notion that a partnership item could include the decision of a trustee to carry back a loss to a preceding year. The court then rejected the IRS's proffered "but for" standard for determining whether the refund claim was "attributable to" a partnership item, ruling that the carryback determination related only to the individual circumstances of the trust, and so had no connection to the tax attributes of the partnership.

[75.8] Randall J. Thompson v. Commissioner, 729 F3d 869 (8th Cir. 2013). See Erwin v. United States, 118 AFTR2d 2016-5343 (WD Ky. 2016) (denying cross motions for summary judgment; relying on *United States v. Woods*, 134 S. Ct. 557 (2013)).

[75.9] United States v. Steinbrenner, 2013-1 USTC ¶ 50,371 (MD Fla. 2013).

Add to note 76.

; CCN 2009-027 (Aug 21, 2009) (the extent to which a partner is at risk includes both partnership-level and partner-level determinations).

Page 10-13:

Replace note 77 with the following.

[77] Gemini Twin Fund III, 62 TCM 104 (1991). Cf. University Heights at Hamilton Corp., 97 TC 278 (1991); Dial USA, Inc., 95 TC 1 (1990); LB&M Assocs., Inc., 75 TCM 1595 (1998); Israel Greenwald, 142 TC 308 (2014) (outside basis in bona fide partnership is an affected item requiring partner-level determination). But see Countryside Ltd. Partnership, 95 TCM 1006 (2008) (partner's outside basis can be a partnership item if all basis components are partnership items); CCA 201534010 (Aug. 21, 2015) (outside basis partnership item when partnership makes § 754 election); see also CCN 2009-027 (Aug 21, 2009) (determination that partnership is a sham includes determination that putative partners' outside bases are zero).

Replace note 78 with the following.

[78] NCF Energy Partners, 89 TC 741 (1987); Span Hansa Mgmt. Co. v. United States, 91-1 USTC ¶ 50,213 (WD Wash. 1991); Weiner v. United States, 255 F. Supp. 2d 673 (SD Tex. 2003), aff'd, 2005-1 USTC ¶ 50,137 (5th Cir. 2004) (doctor in tax shelter avoids § 6621(c)); Irvine v. United States, 2012-1 USTC ¶ 50,330 (SD Tex. 2012) (*Weiner* followed; no § 6621(c) interest imposed); Robert C. Olson, 72 TCM 433 (1996); Rowland v. United States, 2011-2 USTC ¶ 50,490 (ND Tex. 2011). Penalties cannot be

partnership items because they are not set forth in Subtitle A of the Code; however, the application of penalties must be determined in a TEFRA proceeding. See, e.g., §§ 6221, 6226(f).

Add to note 80.

These authorities all deal with the pre-1999 version of the § 751 Regulations, which used a hypothetical distribution construct to measure a seller's ordinary income or loss. The current Regulations hypothesize a sale by the partnership of all of its § 751 property, and measure the seller's ordinary income or loss by the amount that would be allocated to it on the hypothetical sale by the partnership. Whether this distinction makes a difference is uncertain.

Page 10-14:

Add to note 82.

; Prati v. United States, 81 Fed. Cl. 422, 433 (2008), aff'd, 603 F3d 1301 (Fed. Cir. 2010); Rowland v. United States, 2011-2 USTC ¶ 50,490 (ND Tex. 2011); Varela v. United States, 2011-1 USTC ¶ 50,432 (SD Tex. 2011); Acute Care Specialists II, Ltd. v. United States, 2012-1 USTC ¶ 50,106 (ND Ill. 2011), aff'd, 727 F3d 802 (7th Cir. 2013); Kettle v. United States, 104 Fed. Cl. 699, 2012-2 USTC ¶ 50,692 (Fed. Cl. 2012) (thorough discussion; syndicated tax shelter, statute of limitations, and tax-motivated penalty interest are partnership items). In companion cases, Kerchner v. United States, 2013-2 USTC ¶ 50,507 (5th Cir. 2013), and Irvine v. United States, 2013-2 USTC ¶ 50,508 (5th Cir. 2013), the Fifth Circuit reached the unsurprising conclusion that § 6229(a) extends the § 6501 statute of limitations, and thus whether a partner's statute is open or closed is a partnership item that cannot be raised in a partner-level proceeding. With respect to penalty interest, however, the Fifth Circuit held it had jurisdiction to decide whether the partnership-level proceeding had determined that a tax motivated transaction occurred. In *Kerchner*, it found that the Tax Court made the requisite findings such that jurisdiction was lacking in the partner-level refund suit. In *Irvine*, however, the individual partners had settled before the district court made its findings. Thus, the district court had jurisdiction to determine whether the tax motivated determination had been made. The lynchpin for jurisdiction at the partner level is that penalty interest requires the underpayment be "attributable to" a tax motivated transaction. Whether or not the tax motivated determination has been made at the partnership level can apparently be contested in a partner-level proceeding. See Bush v. United States, 717 F3d 920 (Fed. Cir. 2013). In Isler v. United States, 118 AFTR2d 2016-6377 (Cl. Ct. 2016), the Court of Federal Claims concluded that it lacked jurisdiction over an untimely assessment claim by a partner relating to partnership items that had been resolved in a partnership-level settlement. The application of the statute of limitations to the partner's assessed tax liability was a partnership level item (despite loose language in the settlement agreement intimating that it was not) and so the court lacked jurisdiction under § 7422(h).

Replace note 84 with the following.

[84] FSA 1998-314 (May 7, 1993). Section 1446 withholding tax is found in Subtitle A of the Code, a prerequisite to an item being a partnership item. § 6231(a)(3). The Tax Court agrees with the Service. YA Global Investments, LP, 151 TC No. 2 (2018).

Add to note 87.

A putative innocent spouse cannot invoke these procedures until the partnership proceedings are completed and a notice of computational adjustment is mailed. See Peter D. Adkison, 129 TC 97 (2007) (result not changed by issuance of premature (and invalid) notice of deficiency to partner), aff'd, 2010-1 USTC ¶ 50,181 (9th Cir. 2010).

Add the following before last paragraph of subsection.

Partnership items include not only items of income, gain, loss, deduction, or credit (i.e., items that have an immediate tax effect), but also any factual determinations that underlie these items.[87.1] Partnership items may also include contributions and distributions, including the basis to the partnership of contributed property.[87.2] Because these types of determinations may affect multiple years, the Service may adjust the item in any year to which the adjustment relates. For example, in *Wilmington Partners L.P.*,[87.3] the Tax Court held that it could determine the partnership's basis in a note that was contributed in 1993 even though the TEFRA proceeding related the 1999 year because the basis in the note affected items reported in 1999.

The tax treatment of a payment made by the parent of an affiliated group to a partnership in which a member of the affiliated group is a partner is not a partnership item.[87.4]

The references to the partnership's "taxable year" in § 6231(a)(3) and Regulations § 301.6231(a)(3)-1(a) seem to suggest that partnership items for one taxable year are different "items" than similar items for a different taxable year. Thus, for example, it seems that partnership depreciation for 2008 is a different "item" than partnership depreciation for 2009. However, in *Mueth v. United States*,[87.5] the parties expended considerable energy and ink arguing whether a settlement relating to partnership losses for 1981 and 1982 was a valid closing agreement under § 7121 that converted 1983 losses into a nonpartnership item under § 6231(b)(1)(C). The court held that the settlement relating to the earlier years was not a validly executed closing agreement, so that the 1983 losses were not converted to nonpartnership items and the § 6629(a) statute of limitations for the 1983 partnership items remained applicable. The parties (and the opinion) ignored the underlying question of whether a settlement for one partnership taxable year, even if a valid closing agreement, can convert items in a different year into nonpartnership items.

In addition to the issue of whether something is a partnership item, questions sometimes occur as to the year in which the partnership item arises or, in

---

[87.1] Reg. § 301.6231(a)(3)-1(b).

[87.2] Reg. § 301.6231(a)(3)-1(c)(2)(iv).

[87.3] Wilmington Partners L.P., 98 TCM 138 (2009), aff'd in part and remanded in part, 2012 WL 3892637, 110 AFTR2d 2012-5860 (2d Cir. 2012).

[87.4] Rev. Rul. 2006-11, 2006-1 CB 635. The Service's position is, in some respects, internally inconsistent. The ruling states that the consolidated parent's "status as a partner for purposes of section 6231(a)(2)(B) does not make [the parent] a partner in [the partnership] for purposes of Subchapter K." Yet, the question of whether a partner is bound by a TEFRA proceeding turns on the definition of "partnership" for TEFRA purposes, and not the Subchapter K definition in § 761.

[87.5] Mueth v. United States, 2008-2 USTC ¶ 50,427 (SD Ill. 2008).

the case of tiered structures, the entity in which the partnership item arises. For example, in *Cemco Investors, LLC*, the Service adjusted the basis of property sold by Cemco, thus disallowing a loss reported on the sale.[87.6] Cemco had received the property in a carryover basis transaction from another pass-through entity, CIP. The taxpayer argued that the Service should have made the adjustment with respect to CIP because Cemco was required to take CIP's basis in the property under § 723. Judge Easterbrook, writing for the Seventh Circuit, roundly rejected this contention, noting that "no statute requires the IRS to treat identically two or more entities just because they have some partners in common."[87.7] Similarly, in *Bausch & Lomb*,[87.8] the Tax Court invalidated a notice of deficiency that reflected the Service's adjustment to the basis of contributed property in the year of contribution when such basis was already being contested in a partnership proceeding concerning a later year.

[87.6] Cemco Investors, LLC v. United States, 515 F3d 749 (7th Cir. 2008), aff'g 2007-1 USTC ¶ 50,385 (ND Ill. 2007).

[87.7] Cemco Investors, LLC v. United States, 515 F3d 749 (7th Cir. 2008), aff'g 2007-1 USTC ¶ 50,385 (ND Ill. 2007). See Sugarloaf Fund LLC, 141 TC No. 4 (2013) (trust was a transferee of partnership property; trust held a carryover basis in such property; neither trust nor beneficiary of trust was a direct or indirect partner for TEFRA purposes under § 6231(a)(2)).

[87.8] Bausch & Lomb Inc., 97 TCM 1577 (2009). See also Bausch & Lomb Inc., 103 TCM 1095 (2011).

Add to note 88.

; Bush v. United States, 2011-2 USTC ¶ 50,721 (Fed. Cl. 2011) (penalty interest assessment was partnership item not challengeable in a partner-level proceeding). Nevertheless, the Tax Court has held that the Service does not bear the burden of production under § 7491(c) with respect to penalties asserted in a partnership level proceeding because a partnership is not an "individual." Dynamo Holdings Ltd., 150 TC No. 10 (2018).

Add at the end of subsection.

When penalty-related items are determined in a partnership-level proceeding, the correct application of "partner-level defenses" is less than clear. For example, in *Santa Monica Pictures*, the Tax Court acknowledged that partner-level defenses must be raised in a partner-level refund proceeding.[89.1] However, the court then went on to devote twenty-eight pages of its slip opinion in the partnership-level proceeding to analyze the reasonable cause defense of a partner. Similarly, the court, in *Klamath Strategic Investment Fund*, analyzed

---

[89.1] Santa Monica Pictures, LLC, 89 TCM 1157, n.187 (2005). In Ackerman v. United States, 643 F. Supp. 2d 140 (DDC 2009), a partner in Santa Monica Pictures attempted to raise partner-level defenses in a subsequent refund proceeding. That case was dismissed, however, because the taxpayer did not follow the procedures for paying the tax and filing a claim for refund. See §§ 6230(c)(1)(C) and 6230(c)(2)(A). Accord Clearmeadow Investments, LLC v. United States, 87 Fed. Cl. 509 (Fed. Cl. 2009).

the reasonable cause defense in a partnership-level proceeding.[89.2] The court held that the reasonable cause defense is properly considered in the partnership-level proceeding "if it involves actions by the managing member partner."[89.3] In *Klamath*, "the Service delved into these taxpayers' defenses during the administrative process." "[N]o administrative benefit would be gained" by addressing the partner-level defenses in a separate proceeding. To the contrary, however, is *Stobie Creek Investments LLC v. United States*,[89.4] where the Court of Federal Claims held fast to its refusal to consider a non-manager member's reasonable cause defense in a partnership-level proceeding, despite the "eminently reasonable argument" that to do so would promote judicial economy. In *Michael V. Domulewicz*,[89.5] the Tax Court concluded that it lacked jurisdiction to determine penalty issues in an affected item deficiency notice.

In *New Millennium Trading, L.L.C.*,[89.6] the Tax Court held that neither it (nor any court considering a petition from an FPAA) has the jurisdiction to

---

[89.2] Klamath Strategic Inv. Fund v. United States, 472 F. Supp. 2d 885 (ED Tex. 2007), aff'd, Klamath Strategic Inv. Fund v. United States, 568 F3d 537 (5th Cir. 2009).

[89.3] Klamath Strategic Inv. Fund v. United States, 472 F. Supp. 2d 885, 904 (ED Tex. 2007), aff'd, Klamath Strategic Inv. Fund v. United States, 568 F3d 537 (5th Cir. 2009). Accord American Boat Co., LLC v. United States, 2009-2 USTC ¶ 50,665 (7th Cir. 2009). In Kearney Partners Fund, LLC v. United States, 2013-1 USTC ¶ 50,345 (MD Fla. 2013), aff'd per curiam, 803 F3d 1280 (11th Cir. 2015), the parties filed cross-motions for summary judgment relating to accuracy-related penalties asserted in an FPAA despite an apparent attempt by the "controlling member" of a chain of partnerships to make a disclosure statement complying with the "penalty-protection" disclosure rules in Announcement 2002-2, 2002-1 CB 304. The district court denied the government's motion for summary judgment because the court could not resolve material factual issues relating to the authority of the controlling member to submit the required disclosure on behalf of the partnership, and, as a consequence, could not determine whether it had subject matter jurisdiction in a partnership-level proceeding to determine the validity of the asserted penalty defense.

[89.4] Stobie Creek Investments, LLC v. Unites States, 82 Fed. Cl. 636 (2008), aff'd, 2010-1 USTC ¶ 50,455 (Fed. Cir. 2010).

[89.5] Michael V. Domulewicz, 129 TC 11 (2007), aff'd in part and remanded sub nom. Desmet v. Commissioner, 581 F3d 297 (6th Cir. 2009) (Tax Court affirmed on jurisdictional issue, but case remanded for further consideration on statute of limitations issue).

[89.6] New Millennium Trading, L.L.C., 131 TC 275 (2008); J. Winston Krause v. United States, 105 AFTR 2d 2010-1899 (WD Tex. 2010) (40% gross valuation overstatement penalty cannot be challenged at partner level), aff'd per curiam, 2010-2 USTC ¶ 50,668 (5th Cir. 2010); Randall J. Thompson, 108 TCM 104 (2014) (citing Regulations § 301.6221-1(c) for the rule that partner-level defenses may be raised only in a post-payment refund suit); Shasta Strategic Investment Fund, LLC v. United States, 2014-2 USTC ¶ 50,383 (ND Cal. 2014) (citing United States v. Woods, 571 US 31 (2013) for the proposition that determination of applicability of penalties at the partnership level is merely provisional because each partner remains free to raise defenses in subsequent partner-level proceedings, 551 Fed. Appx. 203, 2014-2 USTC ¶ 50,438 (5th Cir. 2014)), 2015-1 USTC ¶ 50,122 (ND Cal. 2015) (further proceedings in *Shasta Strategic Investment Fund, LLC*); New Millennium Trading, LLC, 113 TCM 1033 (2017) (following *Woods*).

consider partner-level defenses, including a partner's defense of reasonable cause under § 6664(c)(1). In its opinion, the court rejected the taxpayer's challenge to the validity of Regulations §§ 301.6221-1T(c) and 301.6221-1T(d), which prevent partner-level defenses from being asserted in a partnership-level proceeding. In *Tigers Eye Trading LLC*,[89.7] the Tax Court confirmed the validity of the Temporary Regulations, but asserted jurisdiction over the reasonable cause defense in a partnership-level proceeding. Under the Tax Court's rationale, the reasonable cause defense is only a partner-level defense where each partner has a unique defense. The Tax Court had jurisdiction to review whether the law firm, whose opinion the partners relied upon, was a promoter of the transaction whose opinion was "inherently unreliable," because this issue was not personal to any partner. In *McNeill v. United States*[89.71] a divided Tenth Circuit panel reversed a district court decision that refused to allow a managing (also referred to as the "tax matters" and "controlling") partner to pursue the reasonable cause and good faith penalty defense. Parsing § 6230(c)(4) sentence by sentence, the Tenth Circuit held that the general provision in the third sentence of this Code section, allowing a partner to assert "any partner-level defenses that may apply," creates an exception to the specific language in the second sentence, providing that any decision in a partnership-level proceeding relating to the applicability of penalties is "conclusive," and noted that the third sentence is applicable "notwithstanding the preceding [second] sentence."

It is not uncommon for the Service to assert multiple theories in connection with the issuance of an FPAA.[89.8] Some of these theories, if sustained in litigation, might support valuation misstatement penalties under § 6662(b)(3) at either the 20% rate in § 6662(a) or the 40% rate in § 6662(h) (i.e., gross valuation misstatements). Other theories propounded by the Service might not. If a taxpayer gets weak knees in the middle of litigation, a 2008 decision by the Court of Federal Claims suggests that the Service's usual shotgun approach may give the taxpayer an opportunity to elect to concede the case on the basis of one of the Service's theories that would not support a valuation misstate-

---

[89.7] Tigers Eye Trading LLC, 97 TCM 1622 (2009). In Rawls Trading LP, 104 TCM 732 (2012), another partnership-level proceeding, Judge Vasquez found the Tax Court had jurisdiction over the penalty aspect of the proceedings, and then concluded that the reasonable cause defense under § 6664(c) was applicable, quoting and relying upon Superior Trading, LLC, 137 TC 70, 91 (2011), aff'd, 728 F3d 676 (7th Cir. 2013), for the proposition that the determination of reasonable cause and good faith is made "at the partnership level, taking into account the state of mind of the general partner."

[89.71] McNeill v. United States, 836 F3d 1282 (10th Cir. 2016).

[89.8] In Kearney Partners Fund, LLC v. United States, 2013-1 USTC ¶ 50,303 (MD Fla. 2013), aff'd per curiam, 803 F3d 1280 (11th Cir. 2015), the court held that the Service is not limited to litigating partnership items on the theories set forth in an FPAA.

ment penalty and thereby permit the taxpayer to escape the penalty while conceding the tax.[89.9]

[89.9] Alpha I, L.P. v. United States, 2009-1 USTC ¶ 50,125 (Ct. Fed. Cl. 2008). On appeal, *Alpha I* was reversed. 2012-1 USTC ¶ 50,401 (Fed. Cir. 2012). The Federal Circuit focused on whether the valuation misstatement was central to the tax avoidance scheme, and, while remanding to the trial court for a factual analysis, threw cold water on the taxpayers' attempt to avoid the 40 percent penalty.

[4] Conversion of Partnership Items

Page 10-15:

Add to note 94.

See CCA 201319024 (May 10, 2013) (husband and wife, in community property state, treated as separate partners; conversion of one spouse does not automatically convert partnership items of other spouse; but, if non-settling spouse not listed on partnership return, all partnership items converted).

Page 10-16:

Add to note 101.

In Central Valley AG Enterprises v. United States, 531 F3d 750 (9th Cir. 2008), the court held that the Bankruptcy Code permitted the review of the debtor's tax liability stemming from a TEFRA partnership despite the fact that an FPAA had been issued, the 150-day period for contesting the FPAA had lapsed, and the debtor did not file for bankruptcy until after the 150-day period had expired.

Add after first paragraph of subsection.

Regulations proposed in 2009, and withdrawn in 2017, would expand this concept by giving the Service authority to convert partnership items related to "listed transactions" into nonpartnership items.[102.1] The transaction must be a listed transaction under Regulations § 1.6011-4 on the date the Service notifies the partner that the partner's partnership items will be treated as nonpartnership items.[102.2] The fact that a transaction becomes a listed transaction after the date on which the taxpayer engages in the transaction would not preclude the conversion of items under the proposed regulations. The proposed regulations would give the Service complete authority to make conversion determinations on a partnership-by-partnership and partner-by-partner basis.[102.3] Partnership

---

[102.1] REG-138326-07, 74 Fed. Reg. 7205 (Feb. 13, 2009), withdrawn, REG-136118-15, 82 Fed. Reg. 27,334 (June 14, 2017).

[102.2] Prop. Reg. § 301.6231(c)-9(a) (2009), withdrawn, REG-136118-15, 82 Fed. Reg. 27,334 (June 14, 2017).

[102.3] However, any such determination affects all tax years of the identified partnership ending on or before the date of the notice. Prop. Reg. § 301.6231(c)-9(a) (2009) (sixth sentence), withdrawn, REG-136118-15, 82 Fed. Reg. 27,334 (June 14, 2017).

items related to listed transactions would remain subject to the TEFRA partnership procedures until the Service notifies the partner in writing that the items will be treated as nonpartnership items. Such notices to indirect partners could identify only the lower-tier partnership and not the pass-through partner.[102.4]

[102.4] Prop. Reg. § 301.6231(c)-9(a) (2009) (last sentence), withdrawn, REG-136118-15, 82 Fed. Reg. 27,334 (June 14, 2017). See also Prop. Reg. § 301.6231(c)-9(b) Examples (2009).

Add to note 103.

See also McNaughton v. United States, 118 Fed. Cl. 274 (2014), in which the Court of Federal Claims held that the taxpayer was barred by § 7422(h) from filing a partner-level refund suit because he had not made a timely administrative adjustment request, and the claim did not relate to computational errors.

[5] Affected Items

Page 10-17:

In note 110, insert the following before reference to Estate of Quick.

Michael V. Domulewicz, TC Memo 2010-177 (deductibility of fees by partner is an affected item where fees paid for establishment of partnership and partnership was later disregarded as sham); John C. Bedrosian, 144 TC No. 10 (2015) (same);

Page 10-18:

Add to note 113.

; LeBlanc, Jr. v. United States, 2011-1 USTC ¶ 50,209 (Fed. Cir. 2011) (same). See also CCN 2009-011 (Mar. 11, 2009) (if the outcome of partnership-level proceedings affects the amounts of losses claimed by partners with respect to dispositions of their partnership interests or assets distributed from the partnership, deficiency notices to the partners with respect to these affected items and any penalties should be issued within eight months of the conclusion of the partnership proceedings to assure coming within the one-year period for assessment under § 6229(d)); ECC 201017045 (Mar. 24, 2010) (excise tax of direct and indirect partners is affected item).

Add to note 116.

; David Soward, 92 TCM 475 (2006) (notice of deficiency issued to partner invalid because issued with respect to partnership items that were potentially the subject of stayed Tax Court proceeding).

Add to note 119.

; Russian Recovery Fund Ltd. v. United States, 81 Fed. Cl. 793 (2008) (FPAA that adjusted only one partner's amount at risk—an affected item but not a partnership item—was held valid and tantamount to a "no change"); Alex Meruelo, 132 TC 131 (2009) (Service entitled to challenge deductibility of partner's allocated loss under §§ 465 and 704(d), as well as application of accuracy-related penalty under § 6662, provided it accepted partnership's return as filed).

Page 10-19:

Add before first full paragraph (after indented quote).

Meruelo v. Commissioner,[119.1] involves a further strengthening of the Services's ability to proceed against partners with respect to affected items when no FPAA has been issued. In *Meruelo*, at a time when no partnership level proceeding had been commenced, the Service issued a statutory notice to partners (relating to affected items) shortly before the normal three-year partnership item adjustment period of § 6229(a) expired. The three-year § 6229(a) period then expired without any partnership proceeding being commenced. The Service, however, thereafter commenced a partnership-level proceeding to investigate the possibility of fraud at the partnership level (based on § 6229(c), which provides an extended period for adjusting partnership items due to fraud), that was later closed without adjustment. The Ninth Circuit affirmed the Tax Court's determination that the statutory notice of deficiency was valid despite the subsequent initiation of a partnership-level proceeding because no partnership proceeding was commenced prior to the normal § 6229(a) period and ultimately the partnership return was accepted as filed.

[119.1] Meruelo v. Commissioner, 691 F3d 1108 (9th Cir. 2012), aff'g 132 TC 355 (2009).

Page 10-20:

Add new note 127.1 at end of second full paragraph.

[127.1] See Michael V. Domulewicz, 129 TC 11 (2007) (Tax Court has jurisdiction over affected item deficiency notice relating to the determination of capital gain on partner-level sale of distributed property; deficiency not a computational adjustment, because partner-level determinations required), aff'd in part and remanded sub. nom Desmet v. Commissioner, 581 F3d 297 (6th Cir. 2009) (Tax Court affirmed on jurisdictional issue, but case remanded for further consideration on statute of limitations issue).

Page 10-21:

Add new note 129.1 at end of first sentence of third full paragraph.

[129.1] See Countryside Ltd. Partnership, 95 TCM 1006 (2008) (partner's outside basis can be a partnership item if all basis components are partnership items).

[6] Consistency Requirement

Page 10-23:

Add to note 137.

A failure to file consistently may expose the partner to a negligence penalty, which may be collected through a deficiency procedure against the partner. Bernard P. Malone, 148 TC No. 18 (2017).

¶ 10.03 ADMINISTRATIVE PROCEEDING

[1] Notice Requirements

Page 10-25:

Add to note 146.

Notwithstanding the statutory notice requirement concerning the beginning of a partnership proceeding, in General Legal Advice Memorandum 2015-003 (Mar. 3, 2015), the IRS National Office advised revenue agents that they do not have to link notice partners to the examination at its beginning and need not even give notice of the beginning of a partnership proceeding if it does not culminate in an FPAA.

Add to note 148.

; Austin Inv. Fund, LLC v. United States, 2009-1 USTC ¶ 50,173 (Fed. Cl. 2009) (FPAA need not contain reasoning underlying adjustments).

Page 10-26:

Add to note 152.

The Service may, but is not required to, use other information available to it to determine the identity of partners for purposes of satisfying the § 6223(a) notice requirement. Kearney Partners Fund, LLC v. United States, 2013-1 USTC ¶ 50,249 (MD Fla. 2013).

Add to note 153.

See also Stone Canyon Partners, 94 TCM 618 (2007) (taxpayer failed to comply with TEFRA change of address requirements; notices sent to partners' addresses as shown on partnership return and schedules K-1 sufficient for notice purposes).

Add to note 154.

In addition, the Service may use, but is not obligated to use, other information in its possession. Reg. § 301.6223(c)-1(f). Thus, the Service is permitted to send notice to an indirect partner. Colin P. Murphy, 129 TC 82 (2007).

Add the following to second paragraph of subsection (ending with note callout 160).

If the IRS receives actual notice of information, it may, but is not required to, use such information.[160.1]

[160.1] See Taurus Partners FX Partners LLC v Commissioner, TC Memo. 2013-168; Block Developers, LLC v. Commissioner, TC Memo. 2017-142.

Page 10-27:

Add to note 162.

Notwithstanding the statutory notice requirement concerning the beginning of a partnership proceeding, in General Legal Advice Memorandum 2015-003 (Mar. 3, 2025), the IRS National Office advised revenue agents that they do not have to link notice partners to the examination at its beginning and need not even give notice of the beginning of a partnership proceeding if it does not culminate in an FPAA. As a consequence, notice partners will receive notice of the actual commencement of an examination only if the tax matters partner provides such notice. This advice to revenue agents merely confirms what had become standard practice. In theory, the Service will try to send a Notice of the Beginning of the Administrative Proceeding (NBAP) to all notice partners 150 days before it expects to send an FPAA; however, the delay in sending NBAPs will likely continue to protract TEFRA examinations that are already overly protracted.

Add to note 164.

In JT USA LP, 131 TC 59 (2008), rev'd, 2014-2 USTC ¶ 50,504 (9th Cir. 2014), the Service failed to give notice as required by § 6223(a). As a result, partners who did not receive notice had the right to elect under § 6223(e)(3) to have their partnership items treated as nonpartnership items. During the year to which the FPAA related, the taxpayers were both direct and indirect partners. The taxpayers made a timely § 6223(e)(3) election, in their capacity as indirect partners, to have their partnership items treated as nonpartnership items. They did not elect, in their capacity as direct partners, to have their partnership items treated as nonpartnership items. The Service argued that a § 6223(e)(3) election should apply or not to the taxpayers' entire interests, that is, the Service argued that for § 6223(e)(3) purposes, a partner's direct and indirect interests should be treated a unitary interest. The Tax Court rejected this argument, holding that for TEFRA purposes a partner's direct and indirect interests must be treated separately. The election was thus valid only as to the taxpayers' indirect interests. The dissenting opinion in the Ninth Circuit's reversal of *JT USA* characterizes the Service as having "struck out" and seeking a "do-over" by disallowing the taxpayers' election to opt out of the TEFRA proceedings. The majority appeared troubled by the fact that the Tax Court decision allowed the taxpayer to avoid $10 million in tax from a "bogus tax shelter."

Page 10-28:

Add to note 166.

The filing of a petition in response to an erroneously issued partner-level notice of deficiency does not constitute substantial compliance with Section 6223(e)(3) if the petition is not filed in strict accordance with the requirements of Regulations § 301.6223(e)-2(d). See John C. Bedrosian, 143 TC 83 (2014).

Add to note 167.

See American Milling, LP, TC Memo. 2015-192 (partnership proceeding for lower-tier partnership did not preclude partnership proceeding with respect to upper-tier partnership's items, regardless of similarities of issues). In NPR Invs. v. United States, 732 F. Supp. 2d 676 (ED Tex. 2010), aff'd on this issue, 740 F3d 998 (5th Cir. 2014), the taxpayer's inaccurate statement on its Form 1165 that it was not a partnership subject to the TEFRA provisions was held to be "materially misleading" under § 6223(f).

[2] Settlement Agreements

Page 10-34:

Add to note 212.

But cf. LeBlanc, Jr. v. United States, 2010-1 USTC ¶ 50,104 (Fed. Cl. 2009) (conversion only with respect to partnership items specifically settled), rev'd on other grounds, 2011-1 USTC ¶ 50,209 (Fed. Cir. 2011).

Page 10-35:

Add new note 216.1 at the end of third to last paragraph of subsection.

[216.1] In addition to resolving the taxable year before the court, the decision can have a collateral effect on other taxable years. For example, in *Nault*, a taxpayer claimed that the disallowance of partnership expenses resulting from a Tax Court decision had the correlative effect of restoring the partner's basis in his partnership interest, thus entitling him to a loss when the partnership terminated. Nault v. United States, 2007-1 USTC ¶ 50,326 (DNH 2007). The prior Tax Court decision stated that the underlying transactions "lacked economic substance" under the tax-motivated interest provision of former § 6621(c). The district court with jurisdiction over the refund proceeding held the determination that the transactions lacking economic substance was sufficient to disallow the loss on the partnership's termination for § 165 purposes.

Add to note 218.

; Jean Mathia, 97 TCM 1611 (2009), aff'd, 2012-1 USTC ¶ 50,134 (10th Cir. 2012) (settlement between tax matters partner and Service does not necessitate a partner-level proceeding, and therefore cannot cause partnership items to become nonpartnership items under § 6231(b)(1)(C)).

[3] Assessments

Page 10-36:

In note 220, add the following after cite to Olson v. United States

; Gosnell v. United States, 2011-2 USTC ¶ 50,488 (D. Ariz. 2011), aff'd in unpub. opinion, 525 Fed. Appx. 598, 2013-1 USTC ¶ 50,347 (9th Cir. 2013).

Page 10-37:

Add to note 223.

The Service is similarly bound by the four corners of the FPAA. For example, if the FPAA fails to make determinations to support the assessment of interest under former § 6621(c), the Service would not be permitted to make such assessment based on a defaulted FPAA. McGann v. United States, 81 Fed. Cl. 642 (2008).

Add at end of subsection.

In *David Soward*,[223.1] the taxpayer-partner was able to take advantage of a jurisdictional issue in the district court case filed by the Tax Matters Partner to file a protective petition with respect to an FPAA in the Tax Court. The Tax Court held that the filing of the protective Tax Court petition was sufficient to prevent the assessment of tax by the Service on the taxpayer for all partnership and affected items.

[223.1] David Soward, 92 TCM 475 (2006).

[4] Computational Adjustments

Page 10-37:

In first paragraph of subsection, replace last two sentences with the following.

The U.S. district court, in *Gosnell v. United States*,[225.1] has provided this example of a computational adjustment with respect to an affected item:

> An example of an affected item that requires no further factual determination at the partner level would be a partner's medical expense deduction, pursuant to, I.R.C. §213(a). The allowable deduction is a function of the partner's adjusted gross income, which in turn depends on the partner's distributive share of the partnership income or loss. Determining the allowed deduction is a mathematical calculation and requires no further factual finding. Callaway v. Comm'r, 231 F.3d 106, 110 n.4 (2d Cir. 2000) (citation omitted).

It does not matter that the IRS had need to ask the taxpayer certain questions as long as no 'individualized factual determination takes place as to the correctness of the originally declared figures or any other factual matter....'[225.2] However, changes in tax liability attributable to "affected items which require a partner level determination (other than penalties, additions to tax, and additional amounts that relate to adjustments to partnership items)"[225.3] cannot be

---

[225.1] Gosnell v. United States, 2011-2 USTC ¶ 50,488 (D. Ariz. 2011), aff'd in unpub. opinion, 525 Fed. Appx. 598, 2013-1 USTC ¶ 50,347 (9th Cir. 2013).

[225.2] Gosnell v. United States, 2011-2 USTC ¶ 50,488 (D. Ariz. 2011), aff'd in unpub. opinion, 525 Fed. Appx. 598, 2013-1 USTC ¶ 50,347 (9th Cir. 2013) (quoting Olson v. United States, 172 F3d 1311, 1317 (Fed. Cir. 1999).

[225.3] § 6230(a)(2)(A)(i). The parenthetical clause was added in 1997 to clarify that penalties are to be determined in partnership-level proceeding, subject to the rights of partners to raise partner-level defenses in refund forums. See note 224 supra. Thus, the Tax Court does not have jurisdiction over a deficiency notice asserting an accuracy-related penalty attributable to partnership items. The notice is unnecessary and invalid insofar as it relates to the penalties. Michael V. Domulewicz, 129 TC 11 (2007); see also John C. Bedrosian, 94 TCM 614 (2007), aff'd memo., 2009-2 USTC ¶ 50,783 (9th Cir. 2009); John C. Bedrosian, 143 TC 83 (2014), aff'd 940 F3d 467 (9th Cir. 2019). This rule can

assessed immediately following a partnership-level proceeding. Instead, they are subject to the normal deficiency procedures that allow administrative and judicial review of all partner-level determinations.[226] Adjustments that rely on determinations made in a partnership-level proceeding necessarily occur after the partnership-level proceeding. Consequently, the Tax Court has held that an affected item notice of deficiency issued while a TEFRA proceeding is ongoing is premature, and thus invalid.[226.1] Likewise, in a tiered partnership structure, a notice of final partnership administrative adjustment addressed to the middle-tier entity may be predicated on adjustments to the lower-tier partnership. Such a notice, issued prior to the conclusion of the lower-tier partnership-level proceeding, would likewise be premature and invalid.[226.2]

In *Bedrosian v. Commissioner*,[226.3] the Tax Court drew a relatively bright line difference between an affected item that may be taken into account as a computational adjustment and an affected item that requires partner-level proceedings. In an FPAA, the Service determined that a partnership in which the taxpayers had invested was a sham. Because no petition was filed to challenge the FPAA, the Service's partnership-level determination became final. At issue in this partner-level proceeding was the question whether the court had jurisdiction to consider if the taxpayers could deduct legal fees that they incurred in connection with their investment in the disregarded partnership.

The court held:

A partner-level determination must be made as to whether those fees related to the Bedrosians' participation in the partnership that has been held to be a sham. The answer to this question may be known to the parties; it

---

create situations, apparently not anticipated by Congress when it amended § 6230(a)(2)(A)(i), in which a partner is not entitled to a deficiency notice with regard to a penalty even though the affected item on which it is based is subject to the usual deficiency procedures and has not yet been adjudicated. See Michael V. Domulewicz, 129 TC 11, 23–24 (2007) (plain reading of statute must be followed unless it results in an "absurd or futile result," citing Arlington Cent. Sch. Dist. Bd. of Educ. v. Murphy, 548 US 291 (2006)).

[226] § 6230(a)(2)(A)(i). See also Reg. §§ 301.6231(a)(5)-1 (definition of "affected item"), 301.6231(a)(6)-1 (computational adjustments may only include certain affected items); see also George Wayne Bradley, 100 TC 367 (1993) (notice of computational adjustment not required prior to issuance of deficiency notice with respect to affected items); Michael V. Domulewicz, 129 TC 11 (2007) (same), aff'd in part and remanded sub. nom Desmet v. Commissioner, 581 F3d 297 (6th Cir. 2009); Bush v. United States, 78 Fed. Cl. 76, aff'd, 655 F3d 1323 (Fed. Cir. 2011) (application of at-risk limitation is a computational adjustment if no partner-level facts are alleged to place partner at-risk).

[226.1] See GAF Corp., 114 TC 519 (2000); Bausch & Lomb, Inc., 103 TCM 1095 (2012).

[226.2] Rawls Trading, LP, 138 TC 271 (2012). Judge Vasquez subsequently determined that the taxpayers in *Rawls* were entitled to rely on the reasonable cause defense under § 6664(c) to avoid imposition of the § 6662(a) accuracy-related penalty. Rawls Trading LP, 104 TCM 732 (2012).

[226.3] John C. Bedrosian, 144 TC No. 10 (2015).

may be a fact to which the parties are willing to stipulate. But a factual determination at the partner level over which there is no dispute nonetheless remains a factual determination at the partner level. Accordingly, the deductibility of the professional fees is a factual affected item subject to deficiency procedures and over which we have jurisdiction [in a partner-level proceeding].

In *Bedrosian*, the Service had included disallowance of the legal fees in a post-partnership proceeding deficiency notice issued pursuant to § 6230(a)(2), rather than in the form of a computational adjustment. Nevertheless, the court's analysis should apply equally where the Service includes a factual affected item in a computational adjustment and then tries to avoid deficiency proceedings by arguing that the resolution of the partner-level issue is self-evident.

Page 10-38:

Add to note 230.

This proceeding must await the outcome of the partnership-level proceeding. Peter D. Adkison, 129 TC 97 (2007).

Add to note 233.

Similarly, limitations applicable to deficiency procedures do not apply to computational adjustments. Bush v. United States, 2012-2 USTC ¶ 50,558 (Fed. Cl. 2012) (no need to review partners' individual returns). Interest charged under § 6621(c) on a large corporate underpayment is a computational adjustment that is directly assessed. A claim that the Service used an improper starting date to compute interest due under § 6621(c) is treated as a claim that the Service erroneously computed a computational adjustment, and therefore is subject to the six-month statute of limitations. General Mills, Inc. v. United States, 123 Fed. Cl. 576 (2015).

¶ 10.04 ADJUDICATION OF DISPUTES CONCERNING PARTNERSHIP ITEMS

Add to note 235.

The 90-day period in § 6226(a), and hence the following 60-day period in § 6226(b)(1), begins on the date of mailing without regard to when, or even whether, the FPAA is actually received. See Gary J. Yusko, 89 TC 806 (1987); Donald V. Crowell, 102 TC 683 (1994); Biomage, LLC, 106 TCM 196 (2013); Han Kook LLC I-I, 102 TCM 256 (2011).

Page 10-39:

Add to note 238.

; Berkshire 2006-5, LLP v. Commissioner, 111 TCM 1103 (2016) (same). In Wise Guys Holdings, LLC, 140 TC 193 (2013), the Tax Court held that if the IRS issues two FPAAs with respect to the same partnership taxable year, the mailing of the first FPAA starts the period for filing a petition because the subsequent FPAA is invalid under § 6223(f). An

FPAA issued to an upper-tier partnership following the conclusion of a partnership proceeding at a lower-tier partnership, however, is not invalid; each partnership is treated separately for purposes of applying § 6223(f). American Milling, LP, 110 TCM 326 (2015).

Add to note 239.

In PCMG Trading Partners XX, L.P., 131 TC 206 (2008), the Tax Court confirmed that indirect partners can join together to constitute a 5-percent group, which can file a valid petition to an FPAA. See also A.I.M. Controls, LLC v. Commissioner, 2012-1 USTC ¶ 50,211 (5th Cir. 2012) (150-day period jurisdictional; no "equitable tolling" of statute of limitations).

Page 10-40:

Add to note 245.

The IRS takes the position that the deposit must include amounts due in all years affected by the FPAA, not just the year in question. The courts, however, are split on this. *Compare* Kislev Partners, L.P. v. United States, 84 Fed. Cl. 378 (2008) (NOLs generated in FPAA year; deposit must include tax increases in carryforward years), motion for reconsideration denied, 84 Fed. Cl. 385 (2008) and Russian Recovery Fund, Ltd. v. United States, 90 Fed. Cl. 698 (2008), *with* Prestop Holdings LLC v. United States, No. 05-576T, 106 AFTR 2d 2010-7246 (Fed. Cl. Dec. 7, 2010) (FPAA adjustments, if correct, would not have resulted in any underpayment of tax for the FPAA year, but would have resulted in underpayments in carryforward years; no deposit was required because the deposit requirement is limited to the underpayment for the FPAA year).

Page 10-41:

In fourth paragraph of subsection, add the following after first sentence (ending with note callout 246).

The Service's position has been that the amount required to be deposited must take into account the tax effect of all partnership items that have been adjusted, even if those tax effects occur in years not before the court. The Court of Federal Claims split on this issue.[246.1]

[246.1] *Compare* Kislev Partners, L.P. v. United States, 84 Fed. Cl. 378 (2008) *with* Prestop Holdings LLC v. United States, No. 05-576T, 106 AFTR 2d 2010-7246 (Fed. Cl. Dec. 7, 2010).

Add to note 248.

; Kislev Partners, L.P. v. United States, 84 Fed. Cl. 378 (2008) (same); Gail Vento, LLC v. United States, 2015-1 USTC ¶ 50,109 (3d Cir. 2014) (cert. denied) (same).

¶ 10.05 AMENDED RETURNS: ADMINISTRATIVE ADJUSTMENT REQUESTS

Page 10-43:

Replace note 261 with the following.

[261] An explanation of the changes is also required (see Reg. § 301.6227(c)-1(a)), as well as any other information required by the appropriate form. An administrative adjustment request is filed electronically on Form 8082 or on Form 1065X if a hard copy is filed.

Page 10-44:

Replace note 267 with the following.

[267] Rothstein v. United States, 98-1 USTC ¶ 50,435 (Fed. Cl. 1998); Hamilton v. United States, 120 AFTR2d 2017-5701 (D. Ind. 2017); § 6227(a). Currently, all administrative adjustment requests are made on Form 8082. But see Wall v. United States, 89 F3d 848 (9th Cir. 1996) (failure to file Form 8082 not a bar to refund action; *Wall* "substantially complied" with § 6227(b)).

[2] Partner Requests

Page 10-45:

Add to note 278.

The administrative adjustment request must be made on the prescribed form or on a statement providing substantially the same information. See Henry F. Samueli, 132 TC 336 (2009) (amended return not an AAR because it failed to substantially comply with requirements for a partner AAR); United States v. Stewart, 2016-2 USTC ¶ 50,451 (5th Cir. 2016) (same). Currently, the proper form depends on whether the request is being made electronically or in hard copy. Electronic requests are made through Form 8082; hard copy requests are made on Form 1065X.

Page 10-46:

Add at end of subsection.

In *Rigas v. United States*,[283.1] the court considered several issues relating to administrative adjustment requests filed by partners. Pursuant to Regulations § 301.6227(d)-(1)(a), the Service requires administrative adjustment requests be filed on Form 8082. In *Rigas*, the taxpayer partners filed an amended return on a Form 1040X and later filed a Form 8082. The court first considered the Form 8082, which was filed about one month before the taxpayers filed suit in the district court. Because § 6228(b) requires a partner to wait at least six months after filing an administrative adjustment request to file suit, the court disregarded the Form 8082 and focused on the earlier filed amended return. Applying the doctrine of substantial compliance, the court determined that the amended return satisfied the requirements for an administrative adjustment request and permitted the action to continue.

[283.1] Rigas v, United States, 2011-1 USTC ¶ 50,372 (SD Tex. 2011).

¶ 10.06 STATUTES OF LIMITATIONS

[1] General

Page 10-46:

Replace first sentence of subsection with the following.

Under § 6229(a), the period for assessing tax "attributable to any partnership item (or affected item)" for a partnership taxable year does not expire before three years after the later of (1) the filing of the partnership return[283.1] or (2) the last day for the filing of the partnership return (determined without regard to extensions).[284]

[283.1] Unless a valid partnership return is filed (properly executed, etc.), the statute of limitations does not begin to run. See CCA 200907029 (Aug. 18, 2009). A return is not considered properly filed unless it is filed with the service center prescribed in the relevant IRS revenue procedure, publication, form, or instructions to a form. See Seaview Trading, LLC, TC Memo 2019-122.

[284] Returns, payments, and all other filings are generally treated as filed on the date received by the Service, not the date mailed. See United States v. Lombardo, 241 US 73, 76 (1916); Phinney v. Bank of Southwest NA, 335 F2d 266, 268 (5th Cir. 1964); Poynor v. Commissioner, 81 F2d 521, 522 (5th Cir. 1936); Chasar v. IRS, 733 F. Supp. 48, 49 (ND Tex. 1990). The "mail box" rule (mailing treated as filing) in § 7502(a) only comes into play when a return, payment, or the like, that is required to be filed or paid on or before a certain date, is mailed on or before the critical date but delivered thereafter. Thus, a partnership return both mailed to and received by the Service before the extended due date is deemed filed on the date received. See Natalie Holdings, Ltd. v. United States, 2003-1 USTC ¶ 50,233 (WD Tex. 2003).

Page 10-47:

Replace note 286 with the following.

[286] § 6229(b)(1); see Reg. § 301.6229(b)-1 (procedural requirements). See also Cambridge Research & Dev. Group, 97 TC 287 (1991) (extension signed by general partner other than tax matters partner valid despite lack of separate writing specifically authorizing extension; authority flows from state law and written partnership agreement; elaborate procedural requirements in Temporary Regulations not mandatory); Summit Vineyard Holdings, LLC, 110 TCM 113 (2015) (apparent authority; extension valid); Iowa Investors Baker, 64 TCM 611 (1992) (grant of authority to general partner to "manage all partnership affairs" sufficient to validate execution of extension of the period of limitations by general partner; same result under provisions of applicable limited partnership act (California) in absence of specific provision in agreement); CCA 200245002 (July 18, 2002) (extension executed by tax matters partner's successor-in-interest by merger is valid); Peking Inv. Fund, LLC, 106 TCM 688 (2013)(Service not estopped from arguing that an extension was valid).

Courts have been willing to declare statute extensions invalid under limited circumstances where a tax matters partner is under formal criminal investigation. In Transpac Drilling Venture, 1982-12 v. Commissioner, 147 F3d 221 (2d Cir. 1998), the Second Circuit declared an extension invalid because a criminal tax investigation of the tax matters partner resulted in a conflict of interest between the tax matters partner and other partners. However, whether the conflict of interest between the partners and the tax matters partner is significant is a highly factual inquiry. In Leatherstocking 1983 Partnership, 92 TCM 106 (2006), rev'd unpub. opinion, 2008-2 USTC ¶ 50,597 (2d Cir. 2008), the Tax Court rejected an argument against the validity of a statute extension signed by a tax matters partner under a criminal investigation because it was not convinced that the tax matters partner was under a "disabling conflict when he signed the consents." In fact, none of the limited partners called to testify at trial were able to testify that they would have objected to the consents had they known of them. The Second Circuit, in an unpublished opinion, reversed the Tax Court in *Leatherstocking*, finding that "the existing record demonstrates the existence of a disabling conflict of interest." In River City Ranches #1 LTD, 94 TCM 1 (2007), aff'd, 2009-1 USTC ¶ 50,257 (9th Cir. 2009), the Tax Court invalidated an extension of the statute of limitations signed by a TMP whose interests conflicted with those of the investor-partners, because the tax matters partner was concealing his theft. Unfortunately for the investor-partners, the court went on to find that the six-year statute applied because the tax matters partner signed fraudulent returns with the intent to evade taxes. See also Madison Recycling Assocs. v. Commissioner, 295 F3d 280 (2d Cir. 2002), aff'g Madison Recycling Assocs., 64 TCM 1063 (1992) ("We did not hold that the existence of a criminal investigation by the IRS automatically disqualifies a TMP or his representative from negotiating or entering into agreements with the IRS."). But see Sixty-Three Strategic Investment Funds v. United States, 2017-1 USTC ¶ 50,254 (9th Cir. 2017) (*Transpac* distinguished); Twenty-Two Strategic Investment Funds v. United States, 2017-1 USTC ¶ 50,245 (9th Cir. 2017) (same); BCP Trading and Investments, LLC, 114 TCM 151 (2017) (same).

Add to end of carryover paragraph.

In a tiered partnership structure, a partner in an upper-tier partnership that is exempt from TEFRA under the small partnership exception is nevertheless subject to § 6229's statute extension with respect to items from a lower-tier partnership; these items are "affected items."[287.1]

[287.1] Raghunathan Sarma, 116 TCM 540 (2018).

Replace note 288 with the following.

[288] § 6229(b)(3). Rhone-Poulenc Surfactants & Specialties, LP, 114 TC 533, 549–550 (2000); WHO515 Inv. Ptnrs., 104 TCM 567 (2012), aff'd, 2019-2 USTC ¶ 50,269 (DC Cir. 2019) (taxpayers' purported intent to extend statute only with respect to certain items does not override explicit language of the Form 872-I). See also Foam Recycling Assocs., 64 TCM 1243 (1992), aff'd, 159 F3d 1346 (2d Cir. 1998) (Form 872-A executed by partner referred to "return(s) of the aforementioned entity(ies) which also affect your return"; partnership one of listed entities; partner consented to extension with respect to partnership even though phrase "partnership items" not used); Alan H. Ginsburg, 127 TC 75 (2006) (statute extension silent as to partnerships; § 6229(b)(3) applies to affected items; Service precluded from challenging distributive share of partnership loss flowing up through S corporation partner on grounds that (1) partnership interest had insufficient basis, (2) at-risk limitation of § 465 applied, (3) § 469 passive loss rules applied, or (4) S corporation loss limitation rules of § 1366 applied); Candyce Martin 1999 Irrevocable Trust v. United States, 2014-1 USTC ¶ 50,134 (9th Cir. 2014) (extension for adjustment "attributable to" upper-tier partnership items includes loss on liquidation of lower-tier partnership; FPAA issued to lower-tier partnership). The *Martin* court distinguished the decision of the Court of Federal Claims in Russian Recovery Fund Ltd. v. United States,

2011-2 USTC ¶ 50,727 (Fed. Cl. 2011) (Form 872-P signed by upper-tier partnership extends statute only for partnership items "qua [upper tier] partnership items"), on the grounds that the loss in *Martin* actually occurred at the upper-tier level. The *Martin* decision agrees with *Russian Recovery* in that it holds that losses that originated at the lower-tier level were time barred.

Add to note 290.

In BASR Partnership v. United States, 113 Fed. Cl. 181, (Fed. Cl. 2013), aff'd, 2015-2 USTC ¶ 50,412 (Fed. Cir. 2015), no partner had the prohibited intent to evade tax; the fraud was committed by the promoter. The court held the statute was not extended, since § 6229(c) requires partner participation and §§ 6229(c) and 6501 must be read in harmony. In subsequent proceedings involving the same controversy, the aggrieved taxpayers recovered an award of more than $300,000 for litigation costs under § 7430. BASR Partnership v. United States, 130 Fed. Cl. 286 (2017), aff'd, 915 F3d (Fed. Cir. 2019).

Pages 10-47–10-48:

In third paragraph of subsection, replace third sentence and note 292 with the following.

If the partnership omits gross income from the partnership return in an amount in excess of 25% of the gross income shown on the partnership return, the period of limitations with respect to partnership items for the taxable year is extended to six years under § 6229(c)(2).[292] The 25-percent-omission rule in § 6229(c)(2) is framed in the same terms as the generally applicable substantial omission rule in § 6501(e)(1),[292.1] but does not explicitly include either of the clarifying rules set forth in § 6501(e)(1)(A)(i) (based on gross receipts

---

[292] See, e.g., Highwood Partners, 133 TC 1 (Aug. 13, 2009).

[292.1] This similarity has led the courts to consider precedent under § 6501(e)(1) in interpreting § 6229(c)(2). See, e.g., UTAM, Ltd. v. Commissioner, 645 F3d 415 (DC Cir. 2011); Salman Ranch Ltd v. United States, 79 Fed. Cl. 189 (2007), rev'd and remanded on other grounds, 2009-2 USTC ¶ 50,528 (Fed. Cir. 2009); Bakersfield Energy Partners, 128 TC 207, 212 (2007), aff'd, 568 F3d 767 (9th Cir. 2009); M.I.T.A. Partners, Tax Court No. 17832-07 (2010).

from sales of goods or services)[292.2] or § 6501(e)(1)(A)(ii) (no omission if adequate disclosure).[292.3]

[292.2] The 1939 Code version of § 6501(e)(1) did not include a special directive to take into account gross income from sales of goods or services. In the absence of a special rule, the Supreme Court concluded that a substantial overstatement of the costs of residential lots did not constitute an omission of gross income, relying in part on the legislative history and in part on the Webster's Dictionary definition of "omit." Colony, Inc. v. Commissioner, 357 US 28 (1958). In connection with recent "Son-of-BOSS" litigation, the courts divided over the correct interpretation of *Colony* in the context of § 6229(c)(2). The Supreme Court resolved this conflict in United States v. Home Concrete & Supply, LLC, 132 S.Ct. 1836 (2012), holding that *Colony* establishes that a basis overstatement does not constitute an omission from gross income. See Beverly Clark Collection, LLC, 118 TCM 405 (2019) (reporting some of transaction's gain rather than all, not omission of entire item, no six-year statute). Since *Colony* interpreted the statute, there was no room to issue regulations interpreting the statute in this regard. Accordingly, Reg. § 301.6229(c)(2)-1 and its twin, Reg. § 301.6501(e)-1(a)(1)(iii), promulgated in 2010 in an effort to overturn *Colony*, are invalid. The battle that led to *Home Concrete* was fierce. These cases typically involved capital assets, as opposed to inventory property, leading one court to conclude that both *Colony* and the "sale of goods" rule in § 6501(e)(1)(A)(i) are inapplicable on the facts. Because the omission being tested is of "gross income," which generally includes only gains (as opposed to the gross receipts) from property dealings, this court concluded that the existence and amount of an omission should be based on the amount of gain, rather than the gross amount realized, from sales of capital assets. Thus, a basis overstatement should be taken into account in measuring an omission since basis is taken into account in measuring gross income. See Brandon Ridge Partners v. United States, 2007-2 USTC ¶ 50,573 (MD Fla. 2007). However, other courts interpreted *Colony* more broadly, and ignored basis overstatements in testing for a 25% omission. See, e.g., Salman Ranch Ltd v. United States, 573 F3d 1362 (Fed. Cir. 2009), rev'g 79 Fed. Cl. 189 (2007); Bakersfield Energy Partners, 128 TC 207 (2007), aff'd, 568 F3d 767 (9th Cir. 2009); Grapevine Imports, Ltd. v. United States, 77 Fed. Cl. 505 (2007). Several courts held the § 6501 regulations to be invalid. See Intermountain Ins. Serv., 134 TC 211 (2010), rev'd, 650 F3d 691 (DC Cir. 2011); Home Concrete & Supply LLC v. United States, 634 F3d 249 (4th Cir. 2011); Burks v. United States, 633 F3d 347 (5th Cir. 2011). Both *Home Concrete* and *Burks* were decided after the Supreme Court's decision in Mayo Foundation for Medical Research v. United States, 562 US 44, 131 S. Ct. 704 (2011), which emphasizes *Chevron* deference to agency interpretations of taxing statutes. Post-*Mayo Foundation*, the Tax Court stayed with its position set forth in *Intermountain*. Carpenter Family Investments, LLC, 136 TC 373 (2011). Several circuit courts of appeals, on the other hand, found these regulations valid. Grapevine Imports, Ltd. v. United States, 636 F3d 1368 (Fed. Cir. 2011); Intermountain Insurance Service of Vail LLC v. Commissioner, 650 F3d 691 (DC Cir. 2011); UTAM, Ltd. v. Commissioner, 645 F3d 415 (DC Cir. 2011); Salman Ranch, Ltd. v. Commissioner, 647 F3d 929 (10th Cir. 2011).

[292.3] Notwithstanding the absence of an explicit adequate disclosure rule in § 6229(c)(2), the courts have generally recognized that one applies. See CC&F W. Operations Ltd. Partnership, 80 TCM 345 (2000), aff'd, 273 F3d 402 (1st Cir. 2001) (gains treated as omitted from return because no adequate disclosure on return).

Page 10-48:

Add to note 296.

See also Michael O. Williams, 97 TCM 1870 (2009) (IRS computer system transcripts do not memorialize any assessments made within one-year extension period; court accepted IRS testimony that assessments were made manually within required period).

Add to note 297.

In *Gaughf v. Commissioner*, 139 TC 219 (2012), the Tax Court determined that the § 6229(e) extended period for assessing unidentified indirect partners applied because the notice of the partners' identities had not been provided according to the prescribed procedure, even though the Service had actual knowledge of their identities and had acted on that information. The District of Columbia Circuit Court of Appeals affirmed *Gaughf*, 738 F3d 415 (DC Cir. 2013).

Page 10-49:

Add to note 298.

; Michael J. McElroy, 108 TCM 174 (2014) (under § 6229(f), period open for one year after partner files bankruptcy, and partner's partnership items become non-partnership items even though named TMP was under criminal investigation, and thus disqualified from serving as TMP, when FPAAs were mailed).

Page 10-50:

Add at end of subsection.

If a partner wants to assert a statute of limitations defense, she must do so in the partnership proceeding. Section 6226(d) provides that a partner "shall be permitted to participate ... solely for the purpose of asserting that the period of limitations for assessing any tax attributable to partnership items has expired with respect to such person, and the court having jurisdiction of such action shall have jurisdiction to consider such assertion." In *MK Hillside Partners v. United States*,[307.1] the Ninth Circuit rejected a partner's argument that, while the Tax Court has the jurisdiction to "consider" a partner's assertion that the statute of limitations has expired with respect to him or her, its jurisdiction to consider the assertion does not give it jurisdiction to determine that the partner's limitations period has in fact expired. In *MK Hillside Partners*, the Tax Court had considered and rejected the partner's statute of limitations assertion. The partner then sought to renew the assertion outside the TEFRA proceeding on the grounds that the Tax Court lacked jurisdiction to determine that the limitations period had indeed expired. The Ninth Circuit made short shrift of the argument.

[307.1] MK Hillside Partners v. United States, 826 F3d 1200 (9th Cir. 2016).

[2] Section 6229: A Statute of Extension or Limitation?—The *Rhône-Poulenc* Case

Pages 10-50–10-51:

Replace first paragraph of subsection with the following.

During the first decade of this century, there was intense disagreement between taxpayers and the Service regarding the interaction between the partnership-level statute of limitations and the general statute of limitations.[308]. From its enactment, taxpayers and the Service viewed § 6229 as providing a unified period of limitations during which the partnership's tax treatment of partnership items must be challenged—if at all. During the 1990s, the Service began to assert that § 6229 does not supplant the normal assessment limitation period of § 6501, which applies to nonpartnership items, but rather that § 6229 merely extends the individual § 6501 assessment periods of the partners.[309] Under this view, there is no uniform period of limitations applicable to partnership items. In *Rhône-Poulenc Surfactants & Specialties, LP*[310] (hereinafter *R-P*), the Tax Court subscribed to the Service's view, and all other courts that have considered the issue have followed *R-P*.[311]

---

[308] See, e.g., AD Global Fund, LLC v. United States, 481 F3d 1351 (Fed. Cir. 2007); Schumacher Trading Ptnrs. II v. United States, 72 Fed. Cl. 95 (2006); Grapevine Imports, Ltd. v. United States, 71 Fed. Cl. 324 (2005).

[309] See, e.g., LGM 199905040 (Sept. 25, 1998). However, in some situations, the Service is not willing to assert this theory. See FSA 1999-829 (undated) (partnership return timely filed and not audited; partner filed own return late, after § 6229(a) period had expired, reporting all partnership items consistently with partnership return; Service concludes it must accept partner's return as filed with regard to partnership items; "not an appropriate test case"). Because courts have held that the expiration of the period of limitations is an affirmative defense that must be raised in the partnership proceeding, one of the drawbacks to the Service's position is that the partners must separately assert their own statute of limitations defense in the partnership-level proceeding. See, e.g., Thomas v. United States, 97-1 USTC ¶ 50,368 (ND Ga. 1997); Vann v. United States, 97-1 USTC ¶ 50,415 (DNJ 1997).

[310] Rhône-Poulenc Surfactants & Specialties, LP, 114 TC 533 (2000).

[311] Andantech LLC v. Commissioner, 331 F3d 972 (DC Cir. 2003); AD Global Fund, LLC v. United States, 481 F3d 1351 (Fed. Cir. 2007); Curr-Spec Ptnrs., L.P. v. Commissioner, 579 F2d 391 (5th Cir. 2009) (cert. denied); Schumacher Trading Ptnrs. II v. United States, 72 Fed. Cl. 95 (2006); Grapevine Imports, Ltd. v. United States, 71 Fed. Cl. 324 (2005); see Gail Vento, LLC v United States, 2015-1 USTC ¶ 50,109 (3d Cir. 2014)(cert. denied) (treating issue as settled law).

Page 10-54:

Add to note 318.

The U.S. Court of Claims has held that "the reference in section 6229(d) to 'the period specified in subsection (a)' is a reference to the limitations period in section 6501(a), as extended by section 6229," citing *Grapevine*, *AD Global* and *Rhone-Poulenc*. Epsolon Ltd. v. United States, 78 Fed. Cl. 738, 762 (2007).

Page 10-55:

Add new note 318.1 at end of last sentence of subsection.

[318.1] In Epsolon Ltd. v. United States, 78 Fed. Cl. 738, 760 (2007), the U.S. Court of Claims held that an FPAA issued after the § 6229 period had expired was timely because the § 6501(a) statute of limitations for at least one of the partners had been suspended under § 7609(e), relating to delays in the final resolution of the production of information sought pursuant to third-party summonses. The § 7609(e) suspension rule specifically refers to § 6501 but does not mention § 6229.

¶ 10.07 OVERSHELTERED RETURNS

Page 10-56:

Add the following at end of subsection.

The Second Circuit has held that the Tax Court has jurisdiction under the normal deficiency procedures of §§ 6211 through 6216 in a case where neither *Munro* nor § 6234 was applicable.[323.1] In *Chai*, the Service asserted a deficiency in self-employment taxes resulting from the taxpayer's failure to report approximately $2 million of income. While the case was pending in the Tax Court, losses the taxpayer had reported for the same taxable year were denied in a TEFRA partnership proceeding. The Service filed an amended answer in the Tax Court proceeding, seeking to collect additional income taxes with respect to the $2 million of unreported income. The Tax Court held that because income tax attributable to the disallowed loss was not an affected item, § 6230(a)(1) precluded the Service from using any mechanism other than a computational adjustment to assess and collect the additional income tax due. The Second Circuit acknowledged the "odd posture" of the case, noting that § 6234 was not available, because of the asserted self-employment tax deficiency, and that *Munro* was "inconsequential" because the TEFRA proceeding had concluded before the personal deficiency proceeding. Relying on *Harris*,[323.2] the Second Circuit reversed the Tax Court, holding that once the TEFRA proceeding concluded, the Tax Court had jurisdiction over the income tax deficiency by reason of its usual deficiency jurisdiction under § 6212.

[323.1] Chai v. Commissioner, 851 F3d 190 (2d Cir. 2017).
[323.2] Joseph R. Harris, 99 TC 121 (1992).

Page 10-56:

Add new ¶ 10.08.

¶ 10.08 CENTRALIZED AUDIT REGIME [NEW]

For taxable years beginning after December 31, 2017, the general rule is that partnership examinations are managed at the partnership level by a sole partnership representative (who need not be a partner), who has the power to bind the partnership and all its partners.[324] Discussion and analysis of this centralized partnership audit regime is the subject of Chapter 10A.

---

[324] The Treasury and the Service have requested comments on a detailed list of issues. Notice 2016-23, 2016-1 CB 490.

CHAPTER **10A**

Centralized Partnership Audit Regime

Chapter 10A was revised effective March 2021. The revised chapter can be found in the front of this student edition.

104

CHAPTER **11**

Determining the Partners' Distributive Shares

¶ 11.01 THE PARTNERS' DISTRIBUTIVE SHARES: THE STATUTORY SCHEME

[1] Distributive Shares: The Interface Between the Partnership and Its Partners

Page 11-6:

Add to note 4.

; Stephan F. Brennan, 104 TCM 100 (2012), aff'd, 619 Fed. Appx. 564 (9th Cir. 2015).

[2] Determining the Partners' Distributive Shares: An Overview

Page 11-7:

Add to note 11.

An amount received by a non-partner who performs services for a partnership cannot be a distribution with respect to an interest in the partnership. The amount is simply Schedule C income to the non-partner. These concepts are equally applicable even if the non-partner exercises near total control over the partnership, through family members and other related persons, and receives the payments through another partnership that is arguably a sham. See Martin G. Plotkin, 102 TCM 450 (2011), aff'd in an unpublished opinion, 2012-2 USTC ¶ 50,688 (4th Cir. 2012) (taxpayer who orchestrated transactions may not benefit from "sham" argument; absence of provision for the payments in partnership agreement prevents their characterization as distributions).

Replace list item 2 with the following.

2. Section 704(e)(1) (former § 704(e)(2) renumbered on 2016 repeal of § 704(e)(1), which is discussed at ¶ 3.00) provides special rules for allocating partnership income between a donor and a donee of a partnership interest. The allocation rules of § 704(e)(1)[12] supersede the allocation provisions of the partnership agreement, even if these provisions would otherwise pass muster under § 704(b)(2)'s "substantial economic effect" test.

___

[12] The allocation rules of § 704(e)(1) (formerly § 704(e)(2)) are discussed at ¶ 15.05. Former § 704(e)(1) was repealed by the Bipartisan Budget Act of 2015, effective for partnership taxable years beginning after December 31, 2015, while § 704(e)'s remaining provisions, "Distributive share of donee includible in gross income" and "Purchase of interest by member of family" were renumbered §§ 704(e)(1) and 704(e)(2), respectively. See Bipartisan Budget Act of 2015, § 1102(c), Pub. L. No. 114-74 (Nov. 2, 2015).

¶ 11.02 TESTING ALLOCATIONS UNDER SECTION 704(b)

[1] Overview

Page 11-13:

Replace note 30 with the following.

[30] See TIFD III-E, Inc. v. United States, 342 F. Supp. 2d 94 (DC Conn. 2004) (partner's interest in the partnership will generally differ from allocations in the agreement when allocations are based on the taxable characteristics of specific items; allocation under examination the same under both the agreement and the partner's interest test; tax-advantaged transaction), rev'd on other grounds and remanded, 459 F3d 220 (2d Cir. 2006), on remand, 2009-2 USTC ¶ 50,711 (D. Conn. 2009).

Page 11-14:

Replace note 33 with the following.

[33] Reg. § 1.704-1(b)(3). See TIFD III-E, Inc. v. United States, 342 F. Supp. 2d 94 (DC Conn. 2004) (partner's interest analysis concerning allocation of 98% of operating income to tax-indifferent partners focuses on economic consequences of operating income allocation; partner's interest in operating income found to be same as 98% allocation because tax-indifferent partners enjoyed economic benefit of 98% allocation), rev'd on other grounds and remanded, 459 F3d 220 (2d Cir. 2006), on remand, 2009-2 USTC ¶ 50,711 (D. Conn. 2009).

Page 11-16:

In last paragraph of subsection, second sentence, replace § 704(e)(2) with § 704(e)(1) (former § 704(e)(2) renumbered on 2016 repeal of § 704(e)(1), which is discussed at ¶ 3.00).

[2] Substantial Economic Effect

[a] Economic Effect

[ii] Limited deficit makeup provisions; the alternate test for economic effect.

[C] *Special adjustments under the alternate test.*

Page 11-25:

In third paragraph of subsection, named "Reasonably expected future loss and deduction allocations," replace § 704(e)(2) with § 704(e)(1) (former § 704(e)(2) renumbered on 2016 repeal of § 704(e)(1), which is discussed at ¶ 3.00).

Page 11-32:

Add new ¶ 11.02[2][a][iv].

    [iv] Anti-abuse rules [new]. A deficit capital account restoration obligation is ignored if it is not legally enforceable or the facts and circumstances otherwise indicate a plan to circumvent or avoid the obligation.[85.1] Four non-exclusive factors are listed:

1. The partner is not subject to commercially reasonable provisions for enforcement and collection of the obligation.
2. The partner is not required to provide (either at the time the obligation is made or periodically) commercially reasonable documentation regarding the partner's financial condition to the partnership.
3. The obligation ends or could, by its terms, be terminated before the liquidation of the partner's interest in the partnership or when the partner's capital account as provided in § 1.704-1(b)(2)(iv) is negative other than when a transferee partner assumes the obligation.
4. The terms of the obligation are not provided to all the partners in the partnership in a timely manner.

It is especially noteworthy that these factors do *not* require that a partner have sufficient assets to satisfy the deficit. Although factor 2 draws an adverse inference if the partner is not required to provide reasonable documentation regarding their financial condition, the factor does not require that the partner's financial condition be sufficient to satisfy the deficit. These factors stand in sharp contrast to the requirement in the § 752 Regulations that a payment obligation must satisfy a "reasonable expectation of payment" standard in order to be recognized.[85.2] The thrust of these rules seems to be a requirement that the parties take the obligation seriously, not that it necessarily will be satisfied.

    The anti-abuse regulation also disregards a deficit restoration obligation to the extent it is a bottom dollar payment obligation that is not recognized under Regulations § 1.752-2(b)(3). A close inspection of this requirement reveals it as more of a trap for the unwary than a substantive hurdle for well-advised taxpayers. In order to avoid "bottom dollar" status, the obligation must require the partner "to restore the full amount of the partner's deficit capital account." A well-drafted partnership agreement will invariably satisfy this requirement, since it will not allocate losses to partners that cannot validly use them, and will allocate gross income to partners who receive distributions that would otherwise leave them with a negative capital account in excess of their restoration obligation.[85.3] With one possible exception, discussed below, partners should

---

[85.1] Reg. § 1.704-1(b)(2)(ii)(c)(4)(A).

[85.2] Reg. § 1.752-2(k).

[85.3] R. Whitmire, W. Nelson, W. McKee & S. Brodie, Structuring and Drafting Partnership and LLC Agreements ¶ 4.03[2][a] (Thomson Reuters/Tax & Accounting, 4th ed. 2021).

always be fully liable for any capital account deficit, thus taking the "bottom dollar" rule off the table.

The one exception to this otherwise benign state of affairs lies in the interaction with the nonrecourse deduction regime. As discussed later at ¶ 11.02[4][f], nonrecourse deductions are matched with "minimum gain." Although nonrecourse deductions reduce a partner's capital account,[85.4] the capital account is generally restored via a "minimum gain chargeback." If there are not enough partnership items to satisfy the chargeback requirement, it carries forward to subsequent years. If a partner's interest is liquidated before the chargeback is fully implemented, the "bottom dollar" anti-abuse rule would apparently require that the partner contribute money to the partnership to satisfy the resulting deficit capital account balance. Partners who face this dilemma may wish to retain partner status long enough to allow the chargeback to fully operate.

The four factors and the "bottom dollar" rule are applicable to partnership taxable years ending on or after October 9, 2019. Although the four factors flesh out the "plan to circumvent or avoid" rule, they are not a material change to the rule. And the "bottom dollar" requirement is of little practical significance. Thus, the effective date aspect of these rules is not particularly material.

[85.4] Reg. § 1.704-2(f)(7) Example 1.

[b] Substantiality

[i] Overview.

Page 11-35:

Add the following at the end of the subsection.

For partnership taxable years beginning on or after May 19, 2008, and before December 28, 2012, the tax attributes of "de minimis" partners do not have to be considered. A de minimis partner is any partner (including a look-through entity) that (1) owns, directly or indirectly, less than 10% of the capital and profits of a partnership and (2) is allocated less than 10% of each partnership item of income gain, loss, deduction, and credit.[94.1] If this de minimis rule was relied on, the partnership's allocations were required to be retested without regard to the de minimis rule on the first day of the first partnership taxable year beginning on or after December 28, 2012.[94.2] In short, the de minimis rule had a short and relatively useless existence.

[94.1] Reg. § 1.704-1(b)(2)(iii)(e)(*1*).
[94.2] Reg. § 1.704-1(b)(2)(iii)(e)(*2*)(*ii*).

[iv] Overall-tax-effect rule.

Page 11-46:

Replace note 115 with the following.

[115] TIFD III-E, Inc. v. United States, 342 F. Supp. 2d 94 (DC Conn. 2004), rev'd on other grounds and remanded, 459 F3d 220 (2d Cir. 2006), on remand, 660 F. Supp. 2d 367 (D. Conn. 2009), rev'd, 666 F3d 836 (2d Cir. 2012).

Pages 11-49 – 11-54:

Replace ¶¶ 11.02[2][b][v] and 11.02[2][b][vi] with revised ¶ 11.02[2][b][v], new ¶ 11.02[2][b][vi], revised ¶ 11.02[2][b][vii] (previously ¶ 11.02[2][b][vi]) and new ¶ 11.02[2][b][viii].

[v] Determining the baseline [revised]. Each of the rules described above requires a comparison of the consequences expected to result from the allocation scheme contained in the partnership agreement with the consequences that would be expected if such allocations were not contained in the partnership agreement.[119] In order to make this comparison, these rules require the construction of a "baseline" allocation scheme that omits the allocations suspected of lacking substantiality.

For partnership tax years beginning after May 18, 2008, the Regulations explicitly provide that the baseline is the allocations that would be determined under the partners'-interests-in-the-partnership rule, disregarding the allocations being tested.[120] This rule seems to require the baseline to be drawn by hypothetically allocating the items at issue to the partners in the same proportions as they share other partnership items.

If the partners' economic deal consists of a few items that are specially allocated among the partners and a fixed residual sharing ratio that governs the sharing of all other items, the delineation of the baseline is relatively straightforward. Example (5) of Regulations § 1.704-1(b)(5), discussed above in ¶ 11.02[2][b][iv], illustrates this process. In Example (5), the partnership agreement specially allocates most of an investment partnership's tax-exempt income to high-bracket partner *I* and all of the taxable interest and dividends

---

[119] While not explicitly stated, even the general substantiality rule of Regulations § 1.704-1(b)(2)(iii)(*a*) implies that a comparison is required, since one must ask "compared with what?" when faced with the question of whether one or more allocations hold out a reasonable possibility of affecting substantially the amounts that the partners will receive from the partnership on a pre-tax basis.

[120] Reg. § 1.704-1(b)(2)(iii)(*a*) (last sentence, added in 2008). Under the Proposed Regulations, this rule was limited to drawing a baseline solely for purposes of the overall-tax-effect rule. See Prop. Reg. § 1.704-(1)(b)(iii)(*a*) (2005). Under the final Regulations, it applies generally for all comparisons under the substantiality rules in Regulations § 1.704-1(b)(2)(iii). This rule was arguably inherent in the Regulations in place prior to 2008, most notably in Example (5) of Regulations § 1.704-1(b)(5), and was foreshadowed by the district court decision in TIFD III-E, Inc. v. United States, 342 F. Supp. 2d 94 (DC Conn. 2004), rev'd on other grounds and remanded, 459 F3d 220 (2d Cir. 2006), on remand, 660 F. Supp. 2d 367 (D. Conn. 2009), rev'd, 666 F3d 836 (2d Cir. 2012).

to low bracket partner *J.* All other partnership items are allocated equally to the partners.[121] Part (i) of Example (5) tests the two special allocations against a 50/50 baseline, and finds them lacking substantial economic effect under the overall-tax-effect rule. Since the only allocation set forth in the agreement other than the allocations being tested is 50/50, the use of a 50/50 baseline is reasonably obvious.

However, not all partnership agreements are quite so simple. Depending on the circumstances and the complexity of the economic deal among the partners, serious difficulties may emerge in the determination of the baseline required by the Regulations. Resolution of these difficulties should be accomplished in a way that creates at least a strong likelihood that the capital accounts of the partners under the baseline will not differ substantially from the capital accounts that would result if full effect were given to the allocations being tested.[122] Otherwise, the baseline will not reflect the partners' economic deal. The following two scenarios illustrate the types of difficulties that may emerge in constructing the baseline:

Scenario (1). If the partners' residual interests may change from time to time, should the baseline for the current year reflect their interests for the current year or a reasonable projection, as of the time the allocations are agreed to, of their residual interests over the life of the partnership? The use of projections seems appropriate, but the language of the Regulations provides little guidance.[123]

> **EXAMPLE 11-0:** Under the *XY* partnership agreement, which complies with the mechanical economic effect rules, residual profits and losses are allocated 90% to *X* and 10% to *Y* until *X* has received a 12% return on invested capital, and 30% to *X* and 70% to *Y* thereafter. What are the baseline partners' interests for purposes of evaluating a contested item allocation?

---

[121] Example (5) actually provides that "gains and losses from the sale of the partnership's investment securities" are shared equally by the partners. Since the partnership is stated to be an "investment partnership," perhaps this agreement relating to gains and losses is substantially equivalent to an allocation of all other partnership items, although it ignores unexpected items as well as miscellaneous expenses (accounting fees, annual filing and other fees, § 709 deductions, etc.) that many partnerships incur. The preamble to the 2008 amendment to the Regulations supports the gloss suggested in the text on this aspect of Example (5): "the partners shared all other items equally." TD 9398, Summary, Part B, 2008-14 IRB 1143. It might have been easier to have simply amended Example (5) in connection with the 2008 changes.

[122] See Reg. § 1.704-1(b)(5) Examples (1)(xi), (2), (3), (6), (7), (8)(ii), (10)(ii), and (17). If the baseline is being constructed for use in connection with the overall-tax-effect test, some leniency may be necessary and appropriate in complying with this rule.

[123] Cf. Reg. § 1.704-1(b)(5) Example (5)(i), which is based on a "strong likelihood" of income projections over "several years," but which is concerned with the amounts of the items being allocated rather than constructing the baseline itself.

Scenario (2). The Regulations generally provide that a partner does not have a single overall "interest in the partnership." Rather, a partner's interest is determined on an item-by-item basis.[124] If the partnership agreement contains item allocations other than the allocations being tested, it is unclear which "partners' interests" control the hypothetical allocation of the contested items. Again, projections over the life of the partnership taking into account all specially allocated items (other than those being tested) and residual items seems appropriate, but there is scant guidance.

> **EXAMPLE 11-0.1:** Under the *AB* partnership agreement, which complies with the mechanical economic effect rules, depreciation is allocated 90% to *A* and 10% to *B*, interest expense is allocated 25% to *A* and 75% to *B*, and residual profits and losses are allocated 45% to *A* and 55% to *B*. If the substantiality of the depreciation allocation is being tested, are the partners' interests in the partnership 25% and 75%, 45% and 55%, or some blending of these ratios?

[vi] Consequences of baseline violations [new]. If the allocations being tested lack substantiality relative to the baseline, they are invalid and the items involved are reallocated in accordance with the partners' interests in the partnership. For this purpose, however, part (ii) of Example (5) of Regulations § 1.704-1(b)(5) makes it very clear that the determination of the partners' interests must be accomplished in a much different way. Unlike the baseline determination, there are no projections involved, the partners' interests are determined annually after the fact and may change from year-to-year, and the interests to be determined are the partners' interests in the combined invalidly allocated items. Each invalidly allocated item is allocated annually based on the economic sharing ratios of the combined invalidly allocated items for the year.

> **EXAMPLE 11-0.2:**[125] After it has been determined that the agreed-upon allocations of tax-exempt interest, taxable interest, and dividends lack substantiality and are invalid, the *IJ* partnership has $450 of tax-exempt interest (allocated $360 to *I* and $90 to *J* under the agreement) and $550 of taxable interest and dividends (allocated entirely to *J* under the agreement). Thus, economic income of $360 has been allocated to *I* (36% of the total) and $640 to *J* (64% of the total). Thus, the partners' actual economic interests in the combined items for the year are 36% and 64%. Consequently, *I* is allocated 36% of each item and *J* is allocated 64% of each item under the partners'-interests-in-the-partnership rule. These ratios preserve and reflect the partners' real economic deal[126] while undoing

---

[124] See infra ¶ 11.02[3].

[125] Based on Example (5)(ii) of Regulations § 1.704-1(b)(5).

[126] Use of the baseline partners' interests (50/50) would not reflect the economics agreed upon by the partners.

their tax-driven allocation provisions. This is precisely the objective of the substantiality rules.

[vii] Flow-through partners: determining tax consequences of allocations [revised]. In testing the substantiality of allocations, the Regulations long required an examination of the impact of the allocations on the tax liability of the *partners*.[127] Because the Regulations were specific in their reference to "partners," a strong case could be made that the substantiality requirement was automatically met in cases where the partners did not pay U.S. federal income taxes.[128] Regulations issued on May 19, 2008, effective for partnership taxable years beginning on or after that date, eliminate this technical fault in the rules.[129] The Regulations provide that the interaction of a partnership allocation with the tax attributes of owners of look-through entities must be taken into account when testing the substantiality of the allocation to a partner that is a "look-through" entity. For purposes of this rule, look-through entities include partnerships, S corporations, trusts, estates, certain controlled foreign corporations, and entities that are disregarded for federal tax purposes.[130] Real estate investment trusts and regulated investment companies are not treated as look-through entities for this purpose. Additionally, in determining the after-tax economic benefit or detriment of an allocation to any partner that is a member of a consolidated group (within the meaning of Regulations § 1.1502-1(b)), the tax consequences that result from the interaction of the allocation with the tax attributes of the consolidated group and with the tax at-

---

[127] Reg. § 1.704-1(b)(2)(iii)(*a*) (overall-tax-effect test looks to after-tax economic consequences to a "partner"); Reg. § 1.704-1(b)(2)(iii)(*b*) (shifting allocation test looks to total tax liability of the "partners"); Reg. § 1.704-1(b)(2)(iii)(*c*) (transitory allocation test looks to total tax liability of the "partners").

[128] A similar issue was addressed by the Tax Court in its second consideration of the *Brown Group* case. Brown Group, Inc., 104 TC 105 (1995). At the time of that case, the § 702 Regulations required a partner to take into account separately its distributive share of any partnership item which, if separately taken into account by any partner, would result in an income tax liability for that *partner* different from the liability that would result if that *partner* did not take the item into account separately. On the facts of the case, none of the partners of the partnership were U.S. taxpayers, and thus, under a literal reading of the Regulations, the partnership was not required to separately state certain commission income that it earned. A majority of the Tax Court, over strenuous objections by the minority, concluded that separate statement was required under § 702 if the item would affect the U.S. tax liability of a partner or an owner of the partner. The Tax Court was reversed by the Eighth Circuit, which, on its analysis, did not need to address the § 702 issue. The Regulations under § 702 were subsequently amended to require separate statement of any item where separate statement would result in a different income tax liability for a partner "or for any other person."

[129] See Reg. § 1.704-1(b)(2)(iii)(*d*).

[130] Reg. § 1.704-1(b)(2)(iii)(*d*)(*2*).

tributes of another member with respect to a separate return year must be taken into account.[131]

In applying the Regulations to partners that are controlled foreign corporations, only allocations of items of income, gain, loss, or deduction that enter into the corporation's computation of subpart F income, or would enter into that computation if such items were allocated to the corporation, are taken into account.[132]

---

[131] Reg. § 1.704-1(b)(2)(iii)(d)(1).

[132] Reg. § 1.704-1(b)(2)(iii)(d)(2)(v). This limitation appears to prevent the substantiality rules from policing special allocations of foreign tax expense among partners that are controlled foreign corporations (CFCs), even though special allocations of foreign tax expense may allow for improved after-tax results to the U.S. shareholder of a CFC upon a repatriation of CFC earnings. Perhaps, this reflects a view that Regulations § 1.704-1(b)(4)(iii), dealing with allocations of creditable foreign taxes, provides adequate protection for the fisc.

[viii] The De Minimis Rule (2008–2012) [new]. In 2008, the Treasury carved a "de minimis rule" out of the substantiality provisions. The de minimis rule provides that the tax attributes of any partner holding less than 10 percent of the interests in partnership capital and profits need not be taken into account in applying the entity look-through rule.[133] The de minimis rule was short-lived due to concerns about possible abuses. It was withdrawn in 2012 with respect to allocations that become part of a partnership agreement on or after December 28, 2012; pre-existing allocations must be retested for the first partnership taxable year beginning on or after December 28, 2012, without giving effect to the de minimis rule.[134]

---

[133] Reg. § 1.704-1(b)(2)(iii)(e) (2008).

[134] Reg. § 1.704-1(b)(2)(ii)(e)(2). TD 9607, 77 Fed. Reg. 76,380 (Dec. 28, 2012).

[c] The Importance of Capital Accounts

Pages 11-58–11-66:

Replace ¶ 11.02[2][c][ii] with the following.

[ii] Contributions, distributions, and revaluations of property [revised]. Section 704(c) requires that contributed property be "booked" at fair market value in order to prevent the shifting of built-in gain or loss away from the contributing partner. The § 704(b) Regulations follow the policy expressed by § 704(c),[151] and provide an elaborate set of rules to deal with the resulting book-tax disparities.

Although the Regulations mandate that a contributing partner's capital account be credited with the value, rather than the basis, of contributed property,

---

[151] Reg. § 1.704-1(b)(2)(iv)(d)(1).

and provide other instances in which the partnership must, or may, adjust the book value of its property to a value different from basis, they do not sanction the use of generally accepted accounting principles or other accounting conventions for purposes of computing the partners' capital accounts. Once a book value is established for an item of partnership cost recovery property, tax principles are applied to determine the rate and manner by which that book value is recovered and charged to the partners' capital accounts. In dealing with the Regulations, therefore, it is important to remember that references to "book value" do not refer to the value of an asset for financial accounting purposes, and references to "book income" or "book loss" do not refer to income or loss as determined for financial accounting purposes.

Promissory notes. The principal amount of a promissory note contributed to partnership capital by the maker of the note (or by a partner who is related to such maker)[152] is not immediately credited to the contributor's capital account, except in those rare situations where the contributed note is readily tradable on an established securities market. Rather, the contributor's capital account is generally increased when there is a taxable disposition of the note by the partnership or when the partner makes principal payments on the note.[153] Similarly, the distribution of a partnership's promissory note generally causes a reduction in the distributee's capital account only if the note is readily tradable on an established securities market, when there is a taxable disposition of the note by the partner, or when the partnership makes principal payments on the note. However, upon liquidation of a partner's partnership interest, the following special rules apply on account of such notes:

1. The partner whose interest is liquidated is treated as satisfying his deficit capital account restoration obligation to the extent of (a) the fair market value, at the time of contribution, of any negotiable notes, of which he is the maker, that he contributes to the partnership on or after the date of liquidation and within the time permitted by the deficit capital account restoration rules,[154] and (b) the fair market value, at the time of liquidation, of the unsatisfied portion of any such notes he previously contributed to the partnership;[155]

---

[152] Reg. § 1.704-1(b)(2)(ii)(c) (last sentence, added in 1988). Although the reference in this sentence has not been updated, the relevant "related party" definition is currently located in Regulations § 1.752-4(b) (disregarding Regulations § 1.752-4(b)(2)(iii), which provides that persons owning interests in the same partnership are not treated as related persons for purposes of determining who bears the economic risk of loss for partnership liabilities).

[153] Reg. § 1.704-1(b)(2)(iv)(d)(2). See Gemini Twin Fund III, 62 TCM 104 (1991), aff'd unpub. opinion (9th Cir. 1993). In effect, a partner's note is generally treated as the equivalent of a partnership agreement provision requiring the partner to make additional capital contributions.

[154] See Reg. § 1.704-1(b)(2)(ii)(b)(3).

[155] Reg. § 1.704-1(b)(2)(iv)(d)(2).

2. The liquidated partner's capital account is reduced by (a) the fair market value, at the time of distribution, of any negotiable notes, of which the partnership is the maker, that the partnership distributes to him on or after the date of liquidation and within the period required under the capital account distribution rules,[156] and (b) the fair market value, at the time of liquidation, of the unsatisfied portion of any such notes previously distributed to him by the partnership;[157] and

3. For purposes of these special rules, the fair market value of a note is no less than its outstanding principal balance on the valuation date, provided it bears interest at no less than the applicable federal rate at that time.[158]

Contributions and distributions of property. A partner's capital account must be increased or decreased by the fair market value (not the tax basis) of property contributed by or distributed to him, as the case may be.[159] In the case of a distribution, however, the capital accounts of all partners must first be adjusted to reflect the manner in which the unrealized income, gain, loss, and deduction inherent in such property (which had not previously been reflected in the partners' capital accounts) would be allocated among the partners if there were a taxable disposition of the property for its fair market value (taking § 7701(g) into account) on the date of distribution. After this readjustment, the fair market value of the distributed property will also be its book value, and the distribution will not cause the balance sheet not to balance. Moreover, in most cases, it will be desirable for the partners to restate the value of all partnership assets before a non–pro rata distribution of an item of partnership property in order to prevent economic distortions.[160]

In the case of either a contribution or distribution of property, the Regulations, citing § 752(c) as authority, state that § 7701(g) (which provides generally that property encumbered by nonrecourse debt has a value at least equal to the amount of the debt) does not apply to the fair market value determination.[161]

Noncompensatory options. Special capital account adjustments and allocations are necessary in connection with the issuance and exercise of noncom-

---

[156] See Reg. § 1.704-1(b)(2)(ii)(*b*)(*2*).

[157] Reg. § 1.704-1(b)(2)(iv)(*e*)(*2*).

[158] Reg. §§ 1.704-1(b)(2)(iv)(*d*)(*2*), 1.704-1(b)(2)(iv)(*e*)(*2*).

[159] Reg. §§ 1.704-1(b)(2)(iv)(*d*)(*1*), 1.704-1(b)(2)(iv)(*e*)(*1*).

[160] See infra Example 11-3 and accompanying text.

[161] See HR Rep. No. 861, 98th Cong., 2d Sess. 846 (1984); Staff of Joint Comm. on Taxation, 98th Cong., 2d Sess., General Explanation of Revenue Provisions of Deficit Reduction Act of 1984, at 239 n.15 (Comm. Print 1984).

pensatory options (NCOs) by partnerships.[162] An NCO is any option[163] issued by a partnership to acquire an interest in the issuing partnership "other than an option issued in connection with the performance of services."[164] The term "option" means a call option, warrant, or the conversion feature of convertible debt or equity.[165]

Upon the issuance of an NCO, the holder is not treated as a partner (unless Regulations § 1.761-3 comes into play to make the option holder a partner upon issuance of the option or some other "measurement date"[166]), and so has no capital account. Further, the existing partners' capital accounts are apparently undisturbed by the partnership's receipt of the option premium, which is not taken into income by the partnership, under general principles, pending the exercise or lapse of the NCO. However, the partnership may elect, pursuant to Regulations § 1.704-1(b)(2)(iv)(f), to adjust capital accounts to reflect a revaluation of partnership property upon the issuance of an NCO (so long as the underlying interest is not of de minimis value).[167] In making this adjustment (or any adjustment while NCOs are outstanding), the value of partnership property must be adjusted to account for outstanding NCOs.[168]

Upon exercise of an NCO, the fair market value of the exercising partner's capital contribution is the sum of the fair market value of the consideration paid to the partnership to acquire the option (the "option premium") and the fair market value of any property contributed to the partnership on exercise of the NCO.[169] If the option is embedded in convertible partnership equity, this amount is increased by the partner's capital account immediately before the conversion.[170] If the option is embedded in convertible debt, this amount is in-

---

[162] Reg. §§ 1.704-1(b)(2)(iv)(d)(4), 1.704-1(b)(2)(iv)(f)(1), 1.704-1(b)(2)(iv)(h)(2), 1.704-1(b)(2)(iv)(s). These Regulations are effective for NCOs issued on or after February 5, 2013. Reg. § 1.704-1(b)(2)(iv)(s)(1).

[163] Options under which the holder is treated as a partner upon issuance (see Regulations § 1.761-3, discussed at ¶ 3.04[4]) result in immediate § 721 contributions subject to the normal capital account adjustments for contributions, rather than the NCO capital account adjustment rules discussed in this subsection.

[164] Reg. § 1.721-2(f).

[165] Reg. § 1.721-2(g)(1).

[166] Reg. § 1.761-3. Discussed at ¶ 3.04[4].

[167] Reg. § 1.704-1(b)(2)(iv)(f)(5)(iv).

[168] Reg. § 1.704-1(b)(2)(iv)(h)(2). If the value of the NCO on the date of the adjustment exceeds the NCO premium paid, the value of partnership property must be reduced by such excess, but only to the extent of unrealized income or gain inherent in such partnership property. Conversely, if the value of the NCO is less than the NCO premium paid, the value of partnership property must be increased by such deficit. In each case, any adjustment will be allocated only to property with unrealized gain (for reductions) or loss (for increases), in proportion to their respective amounts of such gain or loss.

[169] Reg. § 1.704-1(b)(2)(iv)(d)(4).

[170] Prop. Reg. § 1.704-1(b)(2)(iv)(d)(4) (2003). While this provision was removed when the Regulations were finalized in 2013, "no substantive change [was] intended by

creased by the adjusted issue price of the debt and the accrued but unpaid qualified stated interest on the debt immediately before its conversion.[171]

Revaluations of partnership property. The Regulations permit the partners' capital accounts to be increased or decreased to reflect the revaluation of partnership property[172] on the partnership's books if the adjustments are made principally for a substantial nontax business purpose either (1) in connection with a contribution or distribution of money or other property (other than a de minimis amount) as consideration for the acquisition or relinquishment of an interest in the partnership; (2) under generally accepted industry accounting practices, provided substantially all of the partnership's property (excluding money) consists of stock, securities, commodities, options, warrants, futures, or similar instruments that are readily tradable on an established securities market;[173] (3) in connection with a liquidation of the partnership;[174] (4) in connection with a grant of a non de minimis interest in the partnership as consideration for the performance of services to or for the benefit of the partnership;[175] or (5) in connection with the issuance of an NCO (other than an NCO to acquire a de minimis partnership interest).[176] In certain circumstances, the Regulations also permit a partnership to revalue its assets if an interest in the partnership is contributed to another partnership.[176.1]

Proposed regulations issued in 2014 would expand the scope of permitted revaluation events to include (1) if a partnership that revalues its property owns an interest in another partnership, the other partnership may revalue its assets, (2) if an interest in a partnership that revalues its property is owned by

---

this revision." TD 9612 (Feb. 5. 2013), Summary of Comments and Explanation of Provisions, § 2.C.

[171] Reg. § 1.704-1(b)(2)(iv)(*d*)(*4*).

[172] This includes intangible property such as goodwill.

[173] The Service has issued a large number of identical private letter rulings dealing with the mark-to-market rules. See, e.g., Priv. Ltr. Rul. 9327011 (Apr. 6, 1993) (issue 4) (agreement has "economic effect").

[174] This third category of permitted book-up events is somewhat puzzling. To the extent that assets are sold in connection with the liquidation of the partnership, a revaluation is superfluous; to the extent assets are distributed to the partners in kind, the Regulations mandate (as opposed to permit) the revaluation of the distributed assets. The only apparent explanation for the inclusion of this third category relates to the rule permitting installment notes to continue to be held by the partnership upon its liquidation (see supra note 50). If installment notes are retained by the partnership beyond the normal liquidation period, the Regulations require that a revaluation take place. In the absence of an actual distribution of the notes, a revaluation might not be required or permitted. However, if the installment note situation is the sole reason for this category of the revaluation rules, the category should have been specifically limited thereto to prevent confusion as to whether a revaluation is required, or only optional, upon liquidation of the partnership.

[175] Reg. § 1.704-1(b)(2)(iv)(*f*)(*5*)(*iii*).

[176] Reg. § 1.704-1(b)(2)(iv)(*f*)(*5*)(*iv*).

[176.1] Reg. § 1.704-1(b)(2)(iv)(f)(6), discussed in ¶ 4.01[5][b][iii][D] (§ 721(c) partnerships).

another partnership, such other partnership may revalue its property, and (3) if the partners agree to change (other than a de minimis change) the manner in which they share any item or class of items of partnership income, gain, loss, deduction, or credit.[176.2] This expansion is entirely appropriate, and taxpayers are likely to be tempted to make these revaluations even prior to the finalization of these regulations.[176.3]

Indeed, the Regulations warn taxpayers that a failure to restate capital accounts or to achieve a similar result through special allocations of gain or loss[177] upon the acquisition or relinquishment of an interest could have substantial adverse tax consequences.[178] In any case, where the partnership agreement provides for liquidation in accordance with capital accounts, it is generally advisable to book up the partners' capital accounts upon the acquisition or relinquishment of an interest in the partnership in order to avoid the significant economic distortions that may otherwise result.

> **EXAMPLE 11-1:** The equal *DE* partnership has cash of $300, and owns property *Z* with a basis of $200 and a value of $300. *Z* is not § 751 property. Each partner has a basis of $250 in his partnership interest. Capital accounts are properly maintained, and the partners are liable for deficit capital account balances. The partnership distributes cash of $150 to *D*, reducing his interest to one third. The basis of *D*'s interest is reduced to $100. *E*'s capital account remains $250. The assets of the partnership now consist of *Z*, with a basis of $200, and cash of $150. If *Z* is sold for $300, the partnership gain of $100 will be allocated $33 to *D* (one third) and $67 to *E* (two thirds). *D*'s capital account is increased to $133 and *E*'s to $317.
>
> The "one-third/two-thirds" agreement between *D* and *E* means that their capital accounts should be $150 and $300, not $133 and $317. The failure to book up capital accounts prior to the distribution deprived *D* of his full $50 share of the $100 of unrealized appreciation in property *Z*. He received credit for only $33 when *Z* was sold; the $17 shortfall arises because of the failure to book up capital accounts upon the reduction of *D*'s interest.

The mechanics of dealing with restated capital accounts (if they are to comply with the Regulations) include the following steps:

[176.2] Prop. Reg. § 1.704-1(b)(2)(iv)(f) (2014).

[176.3] See Reg. § 1.704-1(b)(2)(iv)(q) (adjustments where guidance is lacking).

[177] See infra ¶ 11.02[2][c][v] (discussion of Example (14)(iv) of Regulations § 1.704-1(b)(5)).

[178] Reg. § 1.704-1(b)(2)(iv)(f). Presumably, the Regulations refer to (1) the capital shift that may accompany a failure to adjust capital accounts when a partner is admitted or when he retires and (2) the concomitant tax effect if the capital shift is a disguised payment for the performance of services or the transfer of property, or related parties are involved.

1. The adjustments must be based on the fair market value of partner-ship property (taking § 7701(g) into account) and must reflect the manner in which the unrealized income, gain, loss, or deduction in-herent in the property (which has not been previously reflected in the capital accounts) would be allocated among the partners if there had been a taxable disposition of the property at its fair market value on that date. The fair market value assigned to contributed, distributed, or revalued property (which value is determined on a prop-erty-by-property basis, except to the extent otherwise permitted by the § 704(c) Regulations) will be regarded as correct if it is reasonably agreed to among the partners in arm's-length negotiations and if the partners have sufficiently adverse interests.[179]

2. The partners' capital accounts must be subsequently adjusted for *book* depreciation, depletion, amortization, and gain or loss with respect to the booked-up value of the property.[179.1]

3. The partners' distributive shares of *tax* depreciation, depletion, amor-tization, and gain or loss with respect to the property must be deter-mined so as to take account of the resulting book/tax disparity according to the rules of § 704(c).[179.2]

Revaluations: effect of outstanding noncompensatory options. The eco-nomic effect of any outstanding NCOs must be taken into account whenever partnership properties are revalued.[179.3] If the fair market value, as of any reval-uation date, of outstanding NCOs exceeds the consideration paid for the op-tions, the values of partnership properties must be reduced by the excess to the extent of the unrealized income or gain in the properties (not previously re-flected in capital accounts). This reduction is applied to properties with unreal-ized appreciation in proportion to their respective amounts of unrealized appreciation. Conversely, if the consideration paid for outstanding NCOs ex-ceeds their fair market value as of the revaluation date, the values of partner-ship properties must be increased by the excess to the extent of the unrealized deduction or loss in the properties (not previously reflected in capital ac-counts). This increase is applied to properties with unrealized depreciation in proportion to their respective amounts of unrealized depreciation. All adjust-

---

[179] Otherwise, if the value assigned to this property is overstated or understated (by more than an insignificant amount), the partnership's capital accounts will be deemed not to be maintained according to the Regulations, and its allocation scheme will not have ec-onomic effect.

[179.1] See infra ¶ 11.02[2][c][iii].

[179.2] Reg. § 1.704-1(b)(2)(iv)(*f*). This includes the "ceiling rule" of Regulations § 1.704-3(b)(1). See Rev. Rul. 75-458, 1975-2 CB 258; see infra ¶ 11.04[2]

[179.3] Reg. § 1.704-1(b)(2)(iv)(*h*)(*2*). These Regulations are effective for options issued on or after February 5, 2013. Reg. § 1.704-1(b)(2)(iv)(*s*)(*1*).

ments must take into account the economic arrangement of the partners with respect to the property.[179.4]

The examples used in the Regulations suggest that the fair market value of an outstanding NCO may be determined by comparing the exercise price of the NCO with the share of the then fair market value of partnership properties to which the option holder would be entitled upon exercise based upon a liquidation analysis, rather than a valuation that takes into account the inherent option value, such as a Black-Scholes model valuation. Specifically, in Example (33) of Regulations § 1.704-1(b)(5), the holder of an outstanding NCO has the right to become a one-fourth partner upon payment of an exercise price of $15,000. Following exercise, the partnership would own property with a value of $37,000 and cash of $35,000, or a total of $72,000, one fourth of which is $18,000, or $3,000 more than the exercise price. The example states, without explication, that the fair market value of the NCO is $3,000. This approach to option valuation seems sound and was confirmed by the Treasury Decisionin finalizing the Regulations.[179.5]

Revaluations: special rules upon exercise of noncompensatory options. Upon exercise of an NCO, Regulations § 1.704-1(b)(2)(iv)(*s*) provides that capital accounts will not be treated as determined and maintained in accordance with the § 704(b) Regulations unless all of the following requirements are met:

1. The partnership must *not* revalue its property immediately *before* the exercise and must revalue its property immediately *after* the exercise;[179.6]

2. In revaluing and restating the partners' § 704(b) capital accounts, items of unrealized income, gain, loss, or deduction must first be allocated to the exercising partner to the extent necessary to reflect such partner's right to share in capital under the partnership agreement, with any remaining allocations going to the historical partners to reflect the way such items would be allocated upon a taxable disposition of the partnership property for its fair market value;[179.7]

3. If the allocations to the exercising partner mandated by the preceding requirement are not sufficient to give it a § 704(b) capital account equal to the share of partnership capital it is entitled to under the partnership agreement, the partnership must reallocate sufficient capi-

---

[179.4] This provision is intended to address partnerships with special allocations. See TD 9612, Summary of Comments and Explanation of Provisions, § 2.B (Feb. 5, 2013).

[179.5] See TD 9612, Summary of Comments and Explanation of Provisions, § 2.B (Feb. 5, 2013) ("The Treasury Department and the IRS believe that ... the examples sufficiently illustrate that the fair market value of an outstanding option may be based on the liquidation value of the option assuming exercise.").

[179.6] Reg. § 1.704-1(b)(2)(iv)(*s*)(*1*).

[179.7] Reg. § 1.704-1(b)(2)(iv)(*s*)(*2*).

tal from (or, less likely, to) the historical partners to (or from) the exercising partner to accomplish this result;[179.8] and

4. The partnership agreement must require "corrective allocations" to be made pursuant to Regulations § 1.704-1(b)(4)(x) to reflect any such capital account reallocations; corrective allocations are "tax only" allocations (consisting of a pro rata share of each item) of any and all items of gross income and gain, or gross loss and deduction, that differ from the partnership's allocation of the corresponding book items.

These rules are explicated in the following two scenarios:

Scenario #1: the base case. In Example (31) of Regulations § 1.704-1(b)(5), an equal two-person partnership that owns property, with basis of $18,000 and book value of $20,000, and has no debt sells (for $1,000) an NCO to acquire a one-third interest for an exercise price of $15,000. The holder of the NCO is not treated as a partner under Regulations § 1.761-3. At the time the option is exercised, the value of the property has increased to $35,000, and the partnership still holds $1,000 cash and has no debt. Exercise of the NCO for $15,000 requires the value of the partnership assets to be restated as $51,000 ($35,000 plus $1,000 plus $15,000). The exercising partner's capital account is credited with both the option premium and the exercise price, for a total of $16,000, whereas his agreed share of the value of partnership capital is one third of $51,000, or $17,000. The $1,000 discrepancy triggers Regulations § 1.704-1(b)(2)(iv)(s). The unrealized appreciation in partnership property is $15,000 ($35,000 market value less $20,000 book value). The first $1,000 of this unrealized gain must be booked into the exercising partner's capital account, with the $14,000 remainder booked into the capital accounts of the original two partners. Subsequent tax gain must be allocated in accordance with § 704(c) principles.

Scenario #2: corrective allocation required. Example (32) of Regulations § 1.704-1(b)(5) shares the same basic facts as Example (31) but squeezes the unrealized gain out of the partnership property prior to the exercise of the outstanding NCO, so that, upon exercise, there is insufficient unrealized appreciation to fully book-up the exercising partner's capital account. This triggers the capital account reallocation and corrective allocation provisions of the Regulations. The need for these reallocation and corrective provisions arises because the option holder is not a partner when the gain is realized but is economically entitled to share a portion of the gain that is, by necessity, initially allocated to the historical partners. The net effect of these provisions is to undo, in part, the initial gain allocation to the extent it did not reflect the actual economics.

In this scenario, the partnership property is sold for $40,000 prior to the exercise of the NCO, and gain of $22,000 is allocated to the original partners. New nondepreciable property is acquired for $40,000, and has increased in value by $1,000 at the time the NCO is exercised. The partnership still holds

---

[179.8] Reg. § 1.704-1(b)(2)(iv)(s)(3).

$1,000 cash and has no debt. Exercise of the NCO for $15,000 increases the value of the partnership assets to $57,000 ($41,000 property plus $16,000 total cash). The exercising partner's capital account is credited with both the option premium and the exercise price, for a total of $16,000, whereas his agreed share of the value of partnership capital is one third of $57,000, or $19,000. The $3,000 discrepancy triggers Regulations § 1.704-1(b)(2)(iv)(s). However, the unrealized appreciation in partnership property is only $1,000, all of which must be booked into the exercising partner's capital account. Under Regulations § 1.704-1(b)(2)(iv)(s)(3), the remaining discrepancy must be eliminated immediately by transferring $2,000 of capital from the § 704(b) capital accounts of the original partners to the exercising partner, thus giving him a § 704(b) capital account of $19,000, which is consistent with the partners' economic agreement. After this capital shift, it is apparent that the original partners have been taxed on an excessive share of the realized gain—a problem that the Regulations address by requiring a "corrective allocation" of $2,000 of gross income or gain to the new partner.[179.9] This is a "tax only" allocation; the book gross income is shared equally among the three partners. Finally, the example goes on to state that "the tax items from [the property] must be allocated in accordance with section 704(c) principles." In this context, § 704(c) will require the next $1,000 of tax gain from the partnership property to be allocated to the exercising partner to bring his tax and book capital accounts into balance.

[179.9] Technically, the exercising partner will be allocated $3,000 (his pro rata share of the $3,000 of income ($1,000) plus a corrective allocation of $2,000).

[v] Optional basis adjustments.

Page 11-68:

Replace note 189 with the following.

[189] See CCA 201726012 (Mar. 28, 2017). However, to the extent the distribution gives rise to a common basis adjustment under Regulations § 1.734-2(b)(1) (see ¶ 25.04), the adjustment is allocated to all partners' capital accounts in proportion to their interests in the partnership (under Regulations § 1.704-1(b)(3)) to the extent it complies with the requirements of Regulations § 1.704-1(b)(2)(iv)(m)(5) applicable to § 734(b) adjustments.

Page 11-69:

In EXAMPLE 11-2, second paragraph, fourth sentence (ending with note callout 193, replace § 743(b) basis with § 734(b) basis.

[viii] Basis adjustments to Section 38 property.

Page 11-78:

Replace note 211 with the following.

[211] Although the § 46 Regulations deal explicitly with basis adjustments to property where the owner of the property claims a tax credit, they are silent on the consequences where the owner elects to pass the credit to a lessee under former § 48(d)(5) (current § 50(d)(5) provides that rules similar to former § 48(d) apply). In lieu of mandating a basis reduction for the lessor in this situation, former § 48(d) required the lessee to include ratably in gross income an amount equal to 50 percent of the credit allowable to the lessee. This income inclusion is the rough economic equivalent of the basis reduction that would have impacted the lessor if it had retained the credit.

The Regulations under § 50(d)(5), which apply to property placed in service after September 19, 2016, are consistent with the Regulations under former § 48(d). They provide that lessors who have elected to pass credits to lessees are unaffected by subsequent recapture events and the lessee is generally required to include an additional amount in income. See Reg. § 1.50-1(b). In this type of situation, lessees that are partnerships (or S corporations) are subject to special recapture rules in Reg. § 1.50-1(b)(3). Because the lessee is treated as having acquired the property only for purposes of the credit rules, these rules treat both the income inclusion and the credit itself as occurring outside the partnership-lessee at the level of the "ultimate credit recipient" (each partner who files a Form 3468 to claim the credit). This treatment means that the income does not increase the basis of the partners in their partnership interests—a result clearly intended and defended by the Treasury both in connection with the adoption of these Regulations (TD 9872, Supplementary Information, Summary of Comments and Explanation of Provisions, part I (July 17, 2019)) and their prior issuance as temporary and proposed regulations (TD 9776, Supplementary Information, Explanation of Provisions, part C (July 21, 2016)). The income inclusion is the amount of the credit (or 50 percent of the § 38(c) credit for energy property) amortized over the shortest recovery period that could apply under § 168, commencing on the date the property is placed in service. See Reg. § 1.50-1(b)(2). Detailed recapture rules and a related election are set forth in Regulations §§ 1.50-1(c) and 1.50-1(d).

[3] Partners' Interests in the Partnership

Page 11-80:

Add to note 215.

Renkemeyer, Campbell & Weaver, LLP, 136 TC 137 (2011) ("bald assertion" of a "special allocation" in missing partnership agreement not sufficient).

Pages 11-83:

Replace note 224 with the following.

[224] See TIFD III-E, Inc. v. United States, 342 F. Supp. 2d 94 (DC Conn. 2004) (partner's interest analysis concerning allocation of 98% of operating income to tax-indifferent partners focuses on economic consequences of operating income allocation; partner's interest in operating income found to be same as 98% allocation because tax-indifferent partners enjoyed economic benefit of 98% allocation), rev'd on other grounds and remanded, 459 F3d 220 (2d Cir. 2006), on remand, 660 F. Supp. 2d 367 (D. Conn. 2009), rev'd, 666 F3d 836 (2d Cir. 2012).

Replace note 227 with the following.

227 Under certain circumstances, this same methodology is useful in drafting partnership allocation provisions. See R. Whitmire, W. Nelson, W. McKee & S. Brodie, Structuring and Drafting Partnership and LLC Agreements ¶ 5.05[2] (Thomson Reuters/Tax & Accounting, 4th ed. 2021) ("forced allocation" method). In the preamble to the disguised-payment-for-services regulations, the Treasury noted that this drafting technique can have surprising consequences: If the partnership agreement provides that a partner has an increased right to share in partnership property on liquidation and the partnership has no net income, that partner must be allocated gross income or receive a guaranteed payment to properly reflect the increased right. Notice of Proposed Rulemaking, 80 Fed. Reg. 43,652 (July 23, 2015). But see PNRC Ltd. Partnership, 66 TCM 265, 270 n.18 (1993) (neither party raised Regulations § 1.704-1(b)(3)(iii) approach); Interhotel Co., 74 TCM 819 (1997), vacated and remanded, 2000-1 USTC ¶ 50,501 (9th Cir. 2000) (not for publication) (Tax Court; application of comparative liquidation test in context of two-tiered partnership; effect of nonrecourse deductions and minimum gain chargebacks from lower-tier partnerships ignored). The Tax Court's analysis in *Interhotel* is flawed. Analyzing the economics of the upper-tier partnership using a capital account analysis requires an elimination of the effect of nonrecourse deductions from those capital accounts regardless of whether they arise at the upper tier or at some lower tier. Nonrecourse deductions cannot affect the amount of money that a partner actually receives from a partnership, which is the focus of the comparative liquidation analysis. The Service acknowledged its error in the Ninth Circuit. See Lipton, "Nonrecourse Deductions of Lower-Tier Partnerships: No Room at the *Interhotel*?" 88 J. Tax'n 42 (1998).

Page 11-84:

Replace second full paragraph with the following.

Prior to May 19, 2008, there existed a rebuttable presumption that each partner had an equal interest in the partnership at all times.**230** The Treasury Department eliminated this presumption, feeling that it "failed to consider factors relevant to a determination of the manner in which the partners agreed to share the economic benefits or burdens corresponding to the allocation of partnership items."**230.1**

---

230 Former Reg. § 1.704-1(b)(3)(i). Compare Randal and W. Holdner, 100 TCM 108 (2010), aff'd in an unpublished opinion, 2012-2 USTC ¶ 50,626 (9th Cir. 2012) (taxpayers unable to rebut presumption of equal sharing where no agreement exists and all cash distributions have been made equally); with Bill McDonald, 68 TCM 1400, 1408 (1994) (partners provide sufficient evidence of oral agreement to support unequal sharing arrangement).

230.1 TD 9398 (May 19, 2008).

[4] Special Rules

[b] Allocations of Credits

Page 11-88:

In first paragraph of subsection, add new note 240.1 at end of third sentence.

240.1 See CCA 200812023 (Nov. 9, 2007) (special allocation of losses to avoid deficit capital account for non-managing member causes § 42 credits to be allocated in ratio in which losses actually shared, and not in accordance with general allocation provisions (as desired by taxpayer)).

In first paragraph of subsection, add new note 240.2 at end of fourth sentence.

240.2 See Rev. Proc. 2007-65, 2007-2 CB 967, as revised by Ann. 2009-69, 2009-40 IRB 475 (safe harbor for certain partnership allocations of § 45 energy credit (1.5 cents per kilowatt hour of electricity produced and sold); allocations must be made in accordance with Reg. § 1.704-1(b)(4)(ii); among other requirements, investors must (1) maintain minimum percentages of all material items of partnership income, gain, loss, deduction, and credit, (2) make minimum unconditional investments, and (3) limit contingent consideration to 25% of all contributions).

[f] Nonrecourse Debt: Post-1991 Agreements

[iii] Computing partnership minimum gain.

Page 11-124:

In second to last paragraph of subsection, replace last sentence with the following.

The recourse portion of the liability is superior to the nonrecourse portion and absorbs the first $100,000 of adjusted basis attributable to property, leaving only $630,000 of basis to be allocated to the $700,000 nonrecourse liability.306.1

306.1 This analysis of "top" and "bottom" guarantees is based on Regulations § 1.704-2(m) Example 1(vii). This Example 1(vii) would be excised by Regulations proposed in 2014. See REG 119305-11, 79 Fed. Reg. 4826 (Jan. 29, 2014). These Proposed Regulations create a new set of requirements that top and bottom partner guarantees must satisfy in order to be recognized for purposes of allocating partnership liabilities, as discussed in ¶ 8.02[4][b][i].

[v] Minimum gain chargeback provisions.

Page 11-130:

Add to note 321.

Any cancellation of indebtedness income attributable to nonrecourse debt encumbering partnership property is included in the first tier of chargeback items. Reg. § 1.704-2(f)(6).

Pages 11-144–11-145:

Replace ¶ 11.02[4][g] with the following.

[g] Noncompensatory Partnership Options [Revised]

Regulations § 1.704-1(b)(4)(ix) provides that partnership allocations cannot have economic effect while certain NCOs are outstanding. Specifically, the requirement applies to NCOs issued by the partnership to acquire partnership interests where the partnership interests would have capital accounts that differ from the sum of the premium and exercise price of the NCO.[357] While such NCOs are outstanding, partnership allocations cannot have economic effect because it is impossible to determine who will receive the economic benefit (or bear the economic detriment) of partnership income, gain, loss, or deduction pending the exercise or lapse of outstanding NCOs. However, allocations during this period will be deemed to be in accordance with the partners' interests in the partnership if three conditions are met:

1. The holder of the NCO is not treated as a partner under Regulations § 1.761-3;
2. The partnership agreement requires the partnership to comply with Regulations §§ 1.704-1(b)(2)(iv)(f) and 1.704-1(b)(2)(iv)(s);[358] and
3. All material allocations and capital account adjustments unrelated to NCOs are recognized under § 704(b).

Upon exercise of an NCO, a mandatory "corrective allocation" of tax items of gross income and gain, or gross deduction or loss may be necessary if there is a "capital account reallocation" under Regulations § 1.704-1(b)(2)(iv)(s)(3).[359]

---

[357] Regulations § 1.704-1(b)(4)(ix) is effective for NCOs issued on or after February 5, 2013. Reg. § 1.704-1(b)(2)(iv)(s)(1).

[358] Discussed supra ¶ 11.02[2][c][ii].

[359] Reg. § 1.704-1(b)(4)(x).

¶ 11.03 OTHER CONSIDERATIONS AFFECTING ALLOCATIONS OF PARTICULAR ITEMS

[2] Allocations of Particular Items

[a] Investment Tax Credit

Page 11-147:

Replace note 370 with the following.

[370] Reg. § 1.46-3(f)(2)(i). The investment credit currently consists of the § 47 rehabilitation credit, the § 48 energy credit, the § 48A qualifying advanced coal project credit, the § 48B qualifying gasification project credit, and the § 48C qualifying advanced energy project credit. § 46.

In note 371, second paragraph, first sentence, replace Regulations § 1.47-3(f) *with* Regulations § 1.46-3(f).

[b] Expensing of Certain Depreciable Business Assets

Page 11-148:

Replace note 376 with the following.

[376] See ¶ 9.02[3][g] (limitation on § 179 depreciation available to partners).

Pages 11-160–11-165:

Replace ¶ 11.03[2][i] with revised ¶ 11.03[2][i].

[i] Foreign Taxes [Revised]

Section 164(a)(3) generally allows a deduction for foreign income taxes.[421.1] Under certain circumstances, § 901 allows taxpayers to claim a credit in lieu of this deduction. Entities treated as partnerships for U.S. tax purposes may be subject to entity-level taxes by foreign jurisdictions.[421.1a] When such taxation occurs, § 702(a)(6) requires that each partner's distributive share of "taxes, described in section 901, paid or accrued to foreign countries and to possessions of the United States" be separately stated and passed through to the partners, rather than deducted by the partnership in computing the partnership's residual taxable income under § 702(a)(8).

Section 703(b)(3) provides that the election whether to claim a § 164 deduction or a § 901 credit for a partner's share of foreign taxes must be made

---

[421.1] The 2017 Tax Cuts and Jobs Act limits the deductibility of foreign income taxes (other than those related to a trade or business or a § 212 activity) during 2018 through 2025. § 164(b)(6) (as amended by Pub. L. No. 115-97, § 11042(a) (Dec. 22, 2017)). Most foreign income taxes paid by partnerships are likely to come within the trade or business or § 212 activity exclusion, and hence not be impacted by this limitation.

[421.1a] Regulations dealing with the "technical taxpayer" rule under § 901 confirm that if foreign law imposes an entity-level tax on the income of an entity treated as a partnership for U.S. income tax purposes, the hybrid partnership is considered to be legally liable for such tax under foreign law, and thus is considered to pay the tax for U.S. income tax purposes. See Reg. § 1.901-2(f)(4). Under the Regulations, if a hybrid partnership's U.S. taxable year closes for all partners as the result of a termination under § 708(b)(1)(B) while the partnership's foreign taxable year does not close, then the foreign tax paid or accrued by the hybrid partnership with respect to the foreign taxable year that ends with or within the new partnership's first U.S. taxable year must be allocated between the terminating partnership and the new partnership. The allocation must be made under the principles of Regulations § 1.1502-76(b) based on the respective portions of the partnership's taxable income (as determined under foreign law) for the foreign taxable year that are attributable to the period ending on and the period ending after the last day of the terminating partnership's U.S. taxable year. Similar principles are to be applied if the hybrid partnership's U.S. taxable year closes under § 706 with respect to some but not all of the partners. Reg. § 1.901-2(f)(4).

at the partner level on a partner-by-partner basis. Section 901(b)(5) provides that a person who is a partner will, subject to certain limitations, qualify for the foreign tax credit for his proportionate share of the partnership's taxes paid or accrued during the taxable year to a foreign country or to any possession of the United States.

From an economic perspective, foreign income taxes that are imposed on a partnership have real economic effect that is substantial. They are noncapital partnership expenses in the same manner as rent, interest, or state income taxes. As such, they should reduce the partners' bases in their partnership interests under § 705 and should be charged against the partners' capital accounts.

Nevertheless, in 2006, the Treasury issued Regulations based on the premise that foreign income taxes imposed on a partnership "do not have substantial economic effect."[422] These Regulations provide that "such expenditures must be allocated in accordance with the partners' interests in the partnership."[423] The general effect of these Regulations is to prevent the special allocation of creditable foreign taxes and to force the allocation of such taxes in the same manner that the partnership's foreign income is allocated.

Any doubt about the appropriateness of the approach of the 2006 Regulations[424] was put to rest by the 2010 enactment of § 909, which is designed to prohibit "Foreign Tax Credit splitting events." Any partnership allocation scheme that has the effect of separating foreign tax credits from their related income would run afoul of the policy underlying these rules.[425]

The Treasury has implemented this policy through the § 704(b) Regulations, and sharply narrowed the application of § 909 so as to apply only to partnership inter-branch payment splitter arrangements, which are a creature of an earlier version of the 2006 Regulations.[426] Nevertheless, the legislative intent is clear—foreign taxes and their related income are to be reported by the same taxpayer.

Regulations § 1.704-1(b)(4)(viii)(a) provides a safe harbor under which an allocation of a creditable foreign tax expenditure will be deemed in accord with the partners' interests in the partnership. Specifically, this safe harbor applies if (1) "[t]he [creditable foreign tax expenditure (CFTE)] is allocated (whether or not pursuant to an express provision in the partnership agreement) to each partner and reported on the partnership return in proportion to the partners' CFTE category shares of income to which the CFTE relates," and (2) al-

---

[422] Reg. § 1.704-1(b)(4)(viii)(a).

[423] Reg. § 1.704-1(b)(4)(viii)(a).

[424] The legislative history to the 1954 Code clearly contemplated that foreign tax expenditures were subject to the general allocation rules. S. Rep. No. 1622, 83d Cong., 2d Sess. 5021 (1954).

[425] See Reg. § 1.909-1(b) (split taxes determined at partner level).

[426] See Reg. § 1.909-2(b)(4).

locations of all other partnership items that materially affect the CFTEs allocated to a partner are valid.[427]

A CFTE is a foreign tax that is (1) paid or accrued by a partnership and (2) eligible for a credit under § 901(a) or an applicable U.S income tax treaty.[428] A foreign tax is a creditable foreign tax for these purposes without regard to whether a partner receiving an allocation of such foreign tax elects to claim a credit for such amount.[429]

While the idea of tying foreign tax credits to their related foreign income is simple, the actual mechanics are quite complex, given the differences between U.S. and foreign tax rules. The first step in applying the safe harbor is for the partnership to compute its net income in each CFTE category, which is itself a three-step process:[430]

1. First, the partnership determines all of its partnership items as computed for U.S. federal income tax purposes (*not* § 704(b) book purposes). The partners' § 743(b) adjustments are ignored (since they are personal to the partners), but the partnership's § 743(b) adjustments with respect to lower-tier partnerships are taken into account (since they fairly impact the partnership's income).

2. Second, the partnership items are assigned to its activities.

3. Third, the items assigned to each activity are aggregated within the relevant CFTE category.

Whether a partnership has one or more activities, and the scope of each activity, is a facts-and-circumstances determination to be conducted in a reasonable manner.[431]

The principal consideration is to tie the CFTEs to their related foreign income. Critically, income from a divisible part of a single activity is treated as income from a separate activity if necessary to prevent separating CFTEs from their related foreign income, such as when income from divisible parts of a single activity is subject to different allocations. Conversely, allocations (or

---

[427] Under the Temporary Regulations, an allocation of CFTE had to comply with the substantial economic effect safe harbor. The language of the 2006 Regulations was expanded to include allocations that satisfy the economic effect equivalence standard of Reg. § 1.704-1(b)(2)(ii)(*i*).

[428] Regulations issued under § 901 provide that an amount paid to a foreign country is not a compulsory payment, and thus is not a tax described in § 901, if the foreign payment is attributable to certain forms of transactions intentionally structured to generate foreign tax liability. Reg. § 1.901-2(e)(5)(iv). Taxes paid by a partnership that fall subject to these § 901 Regulations would not be subject to these Regulations under § 704(b), because such taxes would not be CFTEs.

[429] Reg. § 1.704-1(b)(4)(viii)(*b*)

[430] Reg. § 1.704-1(b)(4)(viii)(c)(3)(i).

[431] Reg. § 1.704-1(b)(4)(viii)(c)(2)(iii).

guaranteed payments) determined with reference to all the income from a single activity generally will not cause the activity to be divided.[432]

The assignment of partnership gross income items to activities (the second step) is made under "any reasonable method."[433] Expenses, losses, and other deductions are allocated under the rules of Regulations § 1.861-8 and Temporary Regulations § 1.861-8T, as well as Regulations §§ 1.861-9 through 1.861-13T (interest) and 1.861-17 (research and experimental expenditures).

The third step is to aggregate the items assigned to each activity within the relevant CFTE category. The partnership's activities are included in a single CFTE category unless the allocations from the activities differ, in which case the income from each activity or group of activities that is subject to a different allocation is treated as a separate CFTE category.[434]

The partnership's net income in each CFTE category is then allocated among the partners.[435] Three adjustments are made to the net income in a CFTE category for purposes of determining the partners' CFTE category shares of income. First, the net income in the CFTE category is increased by the amount of any guaranteed payment that is not deductible (in any year) under foreign law. This nondeductible (for foreign law purposes) guaranteed payment is treated as an allocation for purposes of determining the partners' CFTE category shares of income.[436]

Second, if foreign law allows a deduction for an allocation (or distribution of an allocated amount), the net income from the CFTE category is reduced by the allocated amount.[436.1] Finally, if foreign law excludes an item from its tax base because of the status of a partner, the net income in the relevant CFTE category is reduced by the excluded amount.

CFTEs are then allocated and apportioned among the CFTE categories in accordance with the principles of Regulations § 1.861-20.[436.2]

The operation of the Regulations is demonstrated by Regulations § 1.704-1(b)(5) Example 24.

EXAMPLE 11-22: *A* and *B* form *AB*, an eligible entity treated as a partnership for U.S. tax purposes. *AB* conducts business *M* in country *X* through *DE1* and business *N* in country *Y* through *DE2. DE1* and *DE2* are corporations for country *X* and *Y* tax purposes, but are disregarded entities for U.S. tax purposes. The tax rates in *X* and *Y* are 40 percent and 20 percent, respectively. In 2012, *DE1* has $100,000 of income and *DE2* has $50,000 of income, each as determined under the principles of Regulations § 1.904-6. *DE1* makes payments of $75,000 to *DE2* that are

---

[432] Reg. § 1.704-1(b)(4)(viii)(c)(2)(iii).
[433] Reg. § 1.704-1(b)(4)(viii)(c)(2)(iii).
[434] Reg. § 1.704-1(b)(4)(viii)(c)(2)(i).
[435] Reg. § 1.704-1(b)(4)(viii)(c)(4)(i).
[436] Reg. § 1.704-1(b)(4)(viii)(c)(4)(ii).
[436.1] Reg. § 1.704-1(b)(4)(viii)(c)(4)(iii).
[436.2] Reg. § 1.704-1(b)(4)(viii)(d)(1).

deductible by *DE1* for country *X* tax purposes and includible in income by *DE2* for country *Y* tax purposes. As a result of the payments, *DE1* has taxable income of $25,000 for country *X* tax purposes, on which $10,000 of taxes are imposed, and *DE2* has $125,000 of taxable income for country *Y* purposes, on which $25,000 of taxes are imposed. The *AB* partnership agreement generally allocates income from business *M* 75 percent to *A* and 25 percent to *B*; income from business *N* is allocated equally among the partners.

Part (ii) of Example 24 indicates the partners may satisfy the partners'-interests-in-the-partnership rules if they allocate $100,000 of business *M* income 75 percent to *A* and 25 percent to *B*, and allocate $25,000 of CFTEs (composed of $10,000 of tax imposed by country *X* plus $15,000 of tax imposed by country *Y* on the $75,000 payment) in the same ratios. The business *N* income of $50,000 and the remaining $10,000 of country *Y* taxes may be allocated equally.

Part (iii) of Example 24 addresses the consequences if the parties modify the terms of their economic deal so that "in order to reflect the $75,000 payment ...[,] the partnership agreement allocates $75,000 of the income attributable to business *M* equally between *A* and *B*," and treats the payment as a "divisible part" of the business *M* activity. The apparent economic consequence of this modification is to shift $18,750 (25 percent of $75,000) of economic income from *A* to *B*. Because $75,000 of the income from business *M* and all of the income from business *N* are now being allocated in the same proportions (i.e., equally to *A* and *B*), both are treated as being in the same CFTE category. *AB* allocates $25,000 of business *M* income and the $10,000 of country *X* taxes 75 percent to *A* and 25 percent to *B*. The remaining $125,000 of income (i.e., the $75,000 payment plus $50,000 of business *N* income) and the $25,000 of country *Y* taxes are allocated equally. All CFTE allocations are deemed to be in accordance with the partners' interests in the partnership.

In both Part (ii) and Part (iii) of revised Example 24, no foreign tax credit splitting event should exist.

The preamble to the 2006 Regulations states that "the IRS and the Treasury Department believe that only in unusual circumstances (such as where the CFTEs are deducted and not credited) will allocations that fail to satisfy the safe harbor be in accordance with the partners' interests in the partnership."[436.3] The Regulations contain a number of examples that illustrate how the safe harbor applies,[436.4] as well as one example that describes a situation in which the safe harbor does not apply.[436.5]

[436.3] TD 9292, 2006-2 CB 914.

[436.4] Reg. § 1.704-1(b)(5) Examples 20 through 27; Reg. § 1.704-1(b)(6) Examples 2, 3.

[436.5] Reg. § 1.704-1(b)(5) Example 24 (iii).

The following example is based on Example 1(b) of Regulations § 1.704-1(b)(6).[436.5a]

EXAMPLE 11-22.1: U.S. Parent (a corporation) owns two U.S. subsidiaries, *US 1* and *US 2*. Each of *US 1* and *US 2* owns a controlled foreign corporation, *CFC A* and *CFC B*. *CFC A* and *CFC B* are members of a partnership that conducts a business in Country *X*. *CFC A* contributes $6,000 to the partnership, while *CFC B* contributes $4,000. To compensate *CFC A* for its extra $2,000 of capital, the partnership agreement allocates the first $100 of its gross income to *CFC A*. All remaining gross income and all expenses, including creditable foreign taxes, are shared equally by *CFC A* and *CFC B*. Thus, *CFC A* and *CFC B* will each bear half the foreign tax expenditures.

For its first taxable year, the partnership has $300 of gross income from Country *X* business; it also has $100 of expenses other than foreign taxes, and it pays Country *X* taxes of $40.

Thus, the partnership has net economic income of $160 ($300 gross income, minus $100 of non-tax expenses, minus $40 of tax expenditures). Of this amount, *CFC A* has a $130 (81.25 percent) economic share ($100 gross income allocation, plus $100 share of remaining gross income, minus $50 of non-tax expenses and $20 of tax expenditures). *CFC B* has an economic share of $30 (18.75 percent) ($100 share of remaining gross income, minus $50 of non-tax expenses and $20 of tax expenditures). If the partnership was liquidated, each would receive a distribution equal to its original investment, plus its share of net economic income.

The safe harbor provided by Regulations § 1.704-1(b)(4)(viii)(*a*) does not apply on these facts, because the agreement does not allocate CFTEs in the same proportion that it allocates the related creditable foreign income. The creditable foreign income is $200 ($300 gross income, minus $100 of non-tax expenses), of which $150 (75 percent) is allocated to *CFC A* and $50 (25 percent) is allocated to *CFC B*, while the agreement allocates the $40 of foreign tax expenditures equally between *CFC A* and *CFC B*. Example (1)(b) confirms that the safe harbor does not apply on these facts, and assuming the partners do not reasonably expect to claim a deduction for the CFTEs, reallocates the CFTEs under the partners'-interests-in-the-partnership rules, 75 percent to *CFC A* and 25 percent to *CFC B* based upon their proportionate shares of net income.

[436.5a] Oddly, the text of this Example may be found both in Reg. § 1.704-1(b)(6) Example 1 and in Temp. Reg. § 1.704-1T(b)(5) Example 25. Similarly, Reg. § 1.704-1(b)(6) Examples 2 and 3 are duplicated in Reg. § 1.704-1(b)(5) Examples 36 and 37. These oddities are explained in the Explanation section of the Preamble in TD 9871 (Aug. 12, 2019), 2019-33 IRB 624 as follows: "In order to comply with new Federal Register formatting requirements, *Examples 25, 36 and 37* in § 1.704-1T(b)(5) in the 2016 temporary regulations appear without further changes in § 1.704-1(b)(6)(i) through (iii) of these final regulations, *Examples 1, 2, and 3,* respectively."

This example illustrates two problems with the regulatory approach. First, allocating the $40 of foreign tax expenditures in accordance with the partners' shares of creditable foreign income (i.e., $30 to *CFC A* and $10 to *CFC B*) is inconsistent with their economic arrangement because *CFC A*'s economic entitlement is $130, not $120. The example notes that the reallocation may cause the partners' capital accounts to not reflect their contemplated economic arrangement, such that the partners may need to reallocate other partnership items to ensure that tax follows economics over the life of the partnership. This reallocation may in turn impact the partners' shares of creditable foreign income.

The second problem is related to the first. Namely, the partner's interest in the partnership rule allocates items according to how the partners share the economic benefit or burden of the item in question. The approach of the 2006 Regulations gives effect to all of the partnership's allocations other than that of the foreign tax expenditure. The capital accounts prior to consideration of the foreign tax expenditure are $150 for CFC *A* and $50 for *CFC B*; the only way to reflect the partners' economic deal—$130 for *CFC A* and $30 for *CFC B*—is to allocate $20 of the foreign tax expenditure to each partner. This result is obviously not what the drafters of the 2006 Regulations had in mind.

Presumably, the reallocations necessary to have capital accounts reflect economics would be to allocate 81.25 percent of all items (including CFTEs) to *CFC A* and 18.75 percent to *CFC B*. It is uncertain why Example 1(b) does not mention this result.

The Temporary and Proposed § 901(m) Regulations[436.5b] concerning that section's covered asset acquisition rules would add to the complexity of the CFTE allocation. The general concept of § 901(m) is that, where a taxpayer engages in a transaction in which it receives a basis adjustment for U.S. tax purposes but no basis adjustment for foreign tax purposes, its future foreign taxable income should be adjusted to reflect that basis adjustment. The provision therefore requires that a portion of a taxpayer's foreign income tax attributable to basis adjustments in connection with "covered asset acquisitions" be disregarded in determining its foreign tax credit. In the partnership context, the adjustment needs to happen at the partnership level in order to appropriately reflect the economics of the partners' arrangement. Thus, Proposed Regulations under § 704(b) would require that items attributable to such basis adjustments be factored back into the computations for the relevant CFTE category.[436.5c]

[436.5b] TD 9800, 81 Fed. Reg. 88, 102 (Dec. 7, 2016); REG-129128-14, 81 Fed. Reg. 88,562 (Dec. 7, 2016).

[436.5c] Specifically, a partner's CFTE category share of income would be increased for cost recovery and disposition amounts attributable to a positive basis adjustment, and decreased for cost recovery and disposition amounts attributable to a negative basis adjustment. Prop. Reg. §§ 1.704-1(b)(4)(viii)(*c*)(4)(*v*) (2016), 1.704-1(b)(4)(viii)(*c*)(4)(*vi*) (2016), 1.704-1(b)(4)(viii)(*c*)(4)(*vii*) (2016). The current Regulations already disregard § 743(b) adjustments partners may have in determining net income in a CFTE category.

Special transition rules are available for partnership agreements entered into prior to April 21, 2004, which have not been materially modified and which cannot be amended without the consent of an unrelated party.[436.6] Relief is also provided for partnership agreements entered into before February 14, 2012, that complied with certain inter-branch payment rules contained in an earlier version of the CFTE regulations.[436.7]

Complexities arise in the case of serial disregarded payments subject to withholding tax, as illustrated by two examples in the regulations.[436.8] The ABC partnership operates through three disregarded entities (*DEX, DEY*, and *DEZ*) treated as corporations in three separate countries (countries *X, Y*, and *Z*). *DEZ* owns intellectual property that is licensed and sublicensed from *DEZ* to *DEY*, then to *DEX*, and then on to third parties. Country *X* imposes both an income tax on the third party royalties earned by *DEX* and a withholding tax on royalties paid from *DEX* to *DEY*. The partners share the results of each disregarded entity in different proportions. (*DEX* operates business *X* in country *X, DEY* operates business *Y* in country *Y*, and *DEZ* operates business *Z* in country *Z*; all of which business relates to the licensing and sublicensing of *DEZ*'s intellectual property).

For U.S. income tax purposes, the only item recognized is the third party royalty income earned by *DEX*. The inter-branch payments to *DEY* and then to *DEZ* are ignored. Accordingly, all of the income is attributable to the business activity conducted by *DEX*. The partnership agreement allocates this income according to the *DEX* sharing ratios. All of the foreign taxes are allocable to the business *X* CFTE category, and the foreign taxes are allocable among the partners in accordance with the sharing ratios for *DEX*.

As an economic matter, the partners likely intended that the sharing ratios for *DEY* and *DEZ* control the allocation of the respective profits of each. If the partnership agreement specially allocates portions of the third party income earned by *DEX* to the business activities conducted by *DEY* and *DEZ* to reflect the inter-branch payments (and thus according to the different applicable sharing ratios), these portions become divisible parts of the business *X* activity and therefore separate activities. The income tax imposed by country *X* is allocated to the business *X* CFTE category. The withholding tax imposed by country *X* is apportioned between business *Y* and business *Z* CFTE categories based on the relative amounts of net royalty income earned by each. To satisfy the safe harbor, each partner has CFTEs based on its share of the foreign income generated by each activity.

Reg. § 1.704-1(b)(4)(viii)(*c*)(*3*)(*i*). The interaction between this rule and the specifics of the Temporary § 901(m) Regulations require these additional adjustments in certain circumstances, particularly where a partnership (which cannot be a "§ 901(m) payor") acquires the relevant foreign asset. See REG-129128-14, at X, 81 Fed. Reg. 88,562 (Dec. 7, 2016).

[436.6] Reg. § 1.704-1(b)(1)(ii)(b)(2).

[436.7] Reg. § 1.704-1(b)(1)(ii)(b)(3).

[436.8] Reg. § 1.704-1(b)(6) Examples 2, 3.

[3] Partnership Allocations and Section 482

Page 11-166:

In note 440, replace § 704(e)(2) *with* § 704(e)(1) (former § 704(e)(2) renumbered on 2016 repeal of § 704(e)(1), which is discussed at ¶ 3.00).

¶ 11.04 ALLOCATIONS AND DISTRIBUTIONS WITH RESPECT TO CONTRIBUTED PROPERTY: SECTION 704(c)

[1] Traditional Method

[b] Contribution of Loss Property

Page 11-179:

Add at end of subsection.

The Treasury took a major step toward redemption from its interim guidance failure under the 2004 Jobs Act with the publication of a massive and thoughtful set of Proposed § 704(c)(1)(C) Regulations on January 15, 2014.[481.1]

[i] **Basic concepts and definitions [new].** If a partner ("§ 704(c)(1)(C) partner") contributes property with a built-in loss ("§ 704(c)(1)(C) property") to a partnership, the excess of the adjusted basis of the property over its fair market value at the time of contribution (the "§ 704(c)(1)(C) basis adjustment") is effectively stripped away from the common basis of the contributed property in the partnership's hands and allocated entirely to the contributing partner under § 704(c)(1)(C).[481.2]

Effectively, the § 704(c)(1)(C) basis adjustment becomes a separate, high-basis, tax-only item of intangible property in the partnership's hands, the tax incidents of which must be allocated entirely to the § 704(c)(1)(C) partner. These tax allocations have no economic consequences and so are not taken into account in determining the partners' § 704(b) capital accounts.

Each § 704(c)(1)(C) basis adjustment has the same tax characteristics as the underlying tangible property to which it relates. If the underlying property

---

[481.1] REG-144468-05, 79 Fed. Reg. 3041 (Jan. 15, 2014), 2014-6 IRB 474. In addition to providing much needed guidance as to the application of § 704(c)(1)(C), these Proposed Regulations would address a number of collateral issues created by § 704(c)(1)(C), modify the basis allocation rules relating to substituted basis transactions, provide additional guidance for allocations following revaluations of partnership properties, and update the regulations for the Tax Reform Act of 1997.

[481.2] Prop. Reg. § 1.704-3(f) (2014).

is depreciable, amortizable, or subject to some other cost recovery method, so is the related § 704(c)(1)(C) basis adjustment. The entire amount of these deductions with respect to the § 704(c)(1)(C) basis adjustment must be allocated to the § 704(c)(1)(C) partner. For tax return purposes, these deductions augment the § 704(c)(1)(C) partner's share of the comparable items generated by the underlying § 704(c)(1)(C) property. Over time, the amount of the § 704(c)(1)(C) basis adjustment asset will be reduced (eventually to zero if the basis of the underlying property is fully recoverable). Upon disposition of the underlying property, the gain or loss realized or recognized by the § 704(c)(1)(C) partner will reflect the sum of the remaining § 704(c)(1)(C) basis adjustment and the § 704(c)(1)(C) partner's share of the partnership's common adjusted basis for the underlying asset.[481.3]

[ii] Transfers of partnership interests by § 704(c)(1)(C) partners [new]. If a § 704(c)(1)(C) partner transfers all (or a portion) of its partnership interest in a recognition transaction, an amount equivalent to all (or a portion) of its § 704(c)(1)(C) basis adjustment will be included in the adjusted basis of the transferred interest and hence reduce the gain (or increase the loss) recognized on the transfer. Having been taken into account, this portion of the § 704(c)(1)(C) basis adjustment is eliminated.[481.4] However, if the transfer is a nonrecognition transfer or a gift of the interest, the following special rules apply:

1. The transferee in a nonrecognition transfer of all (or a portion) of the partnership interest becomes a § 704(c)(1)(C) partner and succeeds to all or a portion of the § 704(c)(1)(C) partner's § 704(c)(1)(C) basis adjustment. However, (a) regardless of whether there is a substantial built-in loss or there is a § 754 election in effect, the amount of the transferee's § 704(c)(1)(C) basis adjustment is reduced by the amount of any negative § 743(b) adjustment that would be allocated to the § 704(c)(1)(C) property if the partnership had a § 754 election in effect, and (b) if gain or loss is recognized on the transfer, appropriate adjustment is made to the amount of the transferee's § 704(c)(1)(C) basis adjustment.[481.5]

2. If a § 704(c)(1)(C) partner makes a gift of a partnership interest, the donee does not succeed to any part of the donor's § 704(c)(1)(C) basis adjustment. The portion of the donor's § 704(c)(1)(C) basis adjustment that relates to the gifted interest is eliminated.[481.6]

[481.3] Prop. Reg. § 1.704-3(f)(3)(ii) (2014).

[481.4] See Prop. Reg. §§ 1.704-3(f)(3)(iii)(A), 1.704-3(f)(3)(iii)(C) Examples 1 and 2 (2014).

[481.5] Prop. Reg. §§ 1.704-3(f)(3)(iii)(B)(1), 1.704-3(f)(3)(iii)(C) Examples 3 and 4 (2014).

[481.6] Prop. Reg. §§ 1.704-3(f)(3)(iii)(B)(2), 1.704-3(f)(3)(iii)(C) Example 5 (2014).

[iii] Transfers of Section 704(c)(1)(C) properties by partnerships [new]. A taxable disposition of § 704(c)(1)(C) property allows the § 704(c)(1)(C) partner to take the full remaining amount of the § 704(c)(1)(C) basis adjustment into account in determining his share of the gain or loss from the disposition.[481.7] Accordingly, the § 704(c)(1)(C) basis adjustment evaporates at the same instant. Matters can be a bit more complex if the disposition is a nonrecognition transaction, as detailed below.

Like-kind § 1031 exchanges. If § 704(c)(1)(C) property is exchanged for like-kind property in an exchange that is wholly or partially tax-free pursuant to § 1031, the new property is treated as § 704(c)(1)(C) property with respect to the § 704(c)(1)(C) partner and the § 704(c)(1)(C) basis adjustment (net of any amount taken into account in computing the § 704(c)(1)(C) partner's gain or loss from the exchange) reattaches to the new property.[481.8]

Section 721 contributions. If § 704(c)(1)(C) property is contributed to a lower-tier partnership (LTP) pursuant to § 721, the interest in the LTP is treated by the upper-tier partnership (UTP) as § 704(c)(1)(C) property with the same § 704(c)(1)(C) basis adjustment as the original § 704(c)(1)(C) property. The basis of the LTP in the § 704(c)(1)(C) property is computed without regard to the § 704(c)(1)(C) basis adjustment, but the LTP succeeds to the UTP's § 704(c)(1)(C) basis adjustment. Thus, there are now (1) two "high basis" assets (namely, the § 704(c)(1)(C) partner's interest in the UTP, as before, and the UTP's interest in the LTP) and (2) two § 704(c)(1)(C) basis adjustments (namely, the UTP's adjustment with regard to its LTP interest and the LTP's adjustment with regard to the actual property). The portion of the UTP's basis for its LTP interest that is attributable to the § 704(c)(1)(C) basis adjustment must be segregated and allocated entirely to the original contributor of the § 704(c)(1)(C) property to UTP. Similarly, the portion of LTP's interest in the actual property attributable to the § 704(c)(1)(C) basis adjustment must be allocated entirely to the UTP and the original contributor of the § 704(c)(1)(C) property. The amount of the § 704(c)(1)(C) basis adjustment must be appropriately adjusted if gain or loss is recognized on the contribution.[481.9]

To the extent a § 704(c)(1)(C) basis adjustment is recovered or reduced at any level in a tiered partnership structure, it must be recovered or reduced at all levels "to prevent duplication of loss."[481.10] In the event the value of § 704(c)(1)(C) property is less than its basis at the time of its contribution to an LTP, a second layer of § 704(c)(1)(C) basis adjustment is created for the §

[481.7] Prop. Reg. § 1.704-3(f)(3)(ii)(C) (2014).

[481.8] Prop. Reg. § 1.704-3(f)(3)(iv)(A)(*1*) (2014).

[481.9] Prop. Reg. §§ 1.704-3(f)(3)(iv)(B)(*1*), 1.704-3(f)(3)(iv)(B)(*3*) Examples 1 and 2 (2014).

[481.10] Prop. Reg. § 1.704-3(f)(3)(iv)(B)(*2*)(*a*) (2014).

704(c)(1)(C) property and must be allocated to the partners in the UTP so as to reflect their shares of the new loss layer.[481.11]

Section 351 transactions. If a partnership contributes § 704(c)(1)(C) property to a corporation in a § 351 transaction, the § 704(c)(1)(C) basis adjustment transfers to the § 704(c)(1)(C) partner's interest in the corporate stock. The corporation determines its basis in the contributed § 704(c)(1)(C) property under § 362, taking into account the § 704(c)(1)(C) basis adjustment for the property. If any gain is recognized by the partnership, the share of the partnership gain allocated to the § 704(c)(1)(C) partner is offset by the partner's § 704(c)(1)(C) basis adjustment and is reduced accordingly.[481.12]

Section 708(b)(1)(B) terminations. A § 704(c)(1)(C) partner in a partnership that terminates under § 708(b)(1)(B) has the same basis adjustment for § 704(c)(1)(C) property deemed contributed by the terminated partnership to the new partnership. The deemed contribution is not subject to § 704(c)(1)(C) and does not create any new § 704(c)(1)(C) basis adjustments.[481.13]

Installment sales. If a partnership disposes of § 704(c)(1)(C) property in an installment sale, the installment obligation received by the partnership is treated as § 704(c)(1)(C) property with the same § 704(c)(1)(C) basis adjustment as the original § 704(c)(1)(C) property, adjusted for any gain recognized on the sale.[481.14]

Contributed contracts. If a partner contributes a contract (including, but not limited to, an option, forward contract, or futures contract) that is § 704(c)(1)(C) property, and the partnership subsequently acquires property pursuant to the contract without recognizing all the built-in loss in the contract, the acquired property is treated as § 704(c)(1)(C) property with the same § 704(c)(1)(C) basis adjustment as the contract, adjusted by any gain or loss recognized on the acquisition.

[iv] Distributions of Section 704(c)(1)(C) property [new]. If § 704(c)(1)(C) property is distributed to the § 704(c)(1)(C) partner who contributed it in a current distribution, the § 704(c)(1)(C) basis adjustment is taken into account under § 732.[481.15] If the current distribution is to another partner, the § 704(c)(1)(C) basis adjustment is not taken into account under § 732 unless the distribution triggers loss recognition under § 704(c)(1)(B), in which case the § 704(c)(1)(C) basis adjustment is taken into account in determining the amount of the loss. To the extent a § 704(c)(1)(C) basis adjustment is not

---

[481.11] Prop. Reg. §§ 1.704-3(f)(3)(iv)(B)(2)(*b*), 1.704-3(f)(3)(iv)(B)(*3*) Example 3 (2014) (two basis adjustment layers).

[481.12] Prop. Reg. § 1.704-3(f)(3)(iv)(C)(2)(*b*) (2014).

[481.13] Prop. Reg. § 1.704-3(f)(3)(iv)(D) (2014).

[481.14] Prop. Reg. § 1.704-3(f)(3)(iv)(E) (2014).

[481.15] Prop. Reg. § 1.704-3(f)(3)(v)(A) (2014).

taken into account under these rules, it is reallocated among the remaining items of partnership property under Regulations § 1.755-1(c).[481.16]

A different set of rules applies if a § 704(c)(1)(C) partner receives distributions in complete liquidation of its interest. For purposes of determining the § 704(c)(1)(C) partner's basis in distributed property under § 732, the adjusted basis of the distributed property to the partnership immediately before the distribution includes the § 704(c)(1)(C) partner's § 704(c)(1)(C) basis adjustment for the § 704(c)(1)(C) property in which the liquidating partner is relinquishing an interest. The basis adjustment in relinquished property must be reallocated to distributed property of a like character; if no like character property is distributed, the basis adjustment is not reallocated, and under Proposed Regulations § 1.734-2(c)(2) (2014) is treated as a positive § 734(b) adjustment.

The operation of these rules is illustrated in Example 3 of Proposed Regulations § 1.704-3(f)(3)(v)(D) (2014). In this example, Partner *A* contributes built-in loss Property *1* (with a basis of $15,000 and market value of $10,000) and built-in gain Property *2* (with a basis of $5,000 and market value of $20,000) in exchange for a one-third partnership interest. Both properties are capital assets. In a later year, *A* receives Property *2* (value unchanged) and $10,000 cash in complete liquidation of his interest. The § 704(c)(1)(C) property stays in the partnership. Consequently, the $5,000 § 704(c)(1)(C) basis adjustment shifts to Property *2* immediately before the distribution, increasing the basis of this property to $10,000. Partner *A* takes a $10,000 basis in this property on liquidation (that is, a $20,000 basis in its partnership interest less the $10,000 cash distributed), so no partnership basis adjustment is required under § 734.

[481.16] Prop. Reg. § 1.704-3(f)(3)(v)(B) (2014).

[2] Limitation on Section 704(c) Allocations Under the Traditional Method: The "Ceiling Rule"

Page 11-180:

Replace note 482 with the following.

[482] See Reg. § 1.704-3(b)(1). The Service apparently believes that it can override the effects of the ceiling rule by invoking § 482 to allocate the "excess" income back to the contributing partner. FSA 199936007 (May 25, 1999). If this is indeed the case, one wonders why the § 704(c) Regulations contain such a carefully crafted anti-abuse rule. See Reg. § 1.704-3(a)(10), discussed infra ¶ 11.04[3][a]; TIFD III-E, Inc. v. United States, 342 F. Supp. 2d 94 (DC Conn. 2004) (ceiling rule applied), rev'd on other grounds and remanded, 459 F3d 220 (2d Cir. 2006), on remand, 660 F. Supp. 2d 367 (D. Conn. 2009), rev'd, 666 F3d 836 (2d Cir. 2012).

[3] Section 704(c) Regulations: "Other Reasonable Methods"

[a] General

Page 11-182:

In note 487, second paragraph, replace first two sentences (including citation) with the following.

It is unclear whether, once adopted, a § 704(c) method can be changed by filing an amended return. The better view is that it cannot. Under the doctrine of election, once one of several methods is chosen, (such as a § 704(c) method), the election cannot be changed. See Pacific Nat'l Co. v. Welch, 304 US 191 (1938); Grynberg v. Comm'r, 83 TC 255 (1984); Tech. Adv. Mem. 200041005 (June 14, 2000). In addition, if the use of a § 704(c) method constitutes the adoption of a method of accounting, then the filing of two or more tax returns using the method apparently constitutes adoption, and so the § 704(c) method adopted on the original return(s) cannot be changed by filing an amended return. Rev. Rul. 90-38, 1990-1 CB 57; see Reg. § 1.446-1(e)(2)(i) (generally, the Service must consent to a change in method of accounting).

In note 487, third paragraph, replace Rev. Proc. 2003-3, § 6.06, 2003-1 CB 113 *with* Rev. Proc. 2019-3, § 6.05, 2019-1 IRB 130

Page 11-184:

Add to note 493.

Revaluations would create separate § 704(c) layers, and so "netting" reverse § 704(c) adjustments against prior adjustments might not be permitted under Regulations proposed in 2014. See Prop. Reg. § 1.704-3(a)(6)(i) (2014). But see Prop. Reg. § 1.704-4(c)(4)(ii)(F) Example 3 (2007) (netting required). The 2014 Proposed Regulations apparently reflect a change of heart by the Treasury.

Page 11-185:

Replace note 494 with the following.

[494] Reg. § 1.704-3(a)(7). But see Long-Term Capital Holdings v. United States, 330 F. Supp. 2d 122 (D. Conn. 2004) (step-transaction doctrine used to treat contribution followed fifteen months later by sale of interest as sale of contributed property followed by contribution; purchase price of property includes share of partnership profits for fifteen-month period), aff'd by summary order, 150 Fed. Appx. 40 (2d Cir. 2005); Russian Recovery Fund Ltd. v. United States, 2015-2 USTC ¶ 50,433 (Ct. Fed. Cl. 2015), aff'd, 851 F3d 1253 (Fed. Cir. 2017) (similar transaction; contributor not a partner under *Culbertson*); Southgate Master Fund, LLC v. United States, 659 F3d 466 (5th Cir. 2011) (similar transaction treated as sale from alleged contributor to tax-benefitted "partner"); Kenna Trading LLC, 143 TC 181 (2014); Superior Trading, LLC, 137 TC 70 (2011), motion for reh'g denied, 103 TCM 1604 (2012), aff'd, 728 F3d 676 (7th Cir. 2013); Rovokat, LLC, 102 TCM 264 (2011), aff'd unpub. opinion, 2013-1 USTC ¶ 50,386 (3d Cir. 2013); Santa Monica Pictures, LLC, 89 TCM 1157 (2005); Derringer Trading LLC, TC Memo. 2018-59 (2018). But see Order (filed Feb. 13, 2018), Peking Inv. Fund LLC v. Commissioner, TC Memo. 2013-288 (DAD transaction, government's motion for summary judgement denied; showing profit objectives satisfies *Culbertson* even if outweighed by tax motive). This rule does not apply to any person who acquires a partnership interest from a "§1.752-7 liability partner" in a transaction to which Regulations § 1.752-7(e) applies. A "§ 1.752-7 liability partner" is a partner from whom a partnership assumes a § 1.752-7 liability on or after June 24, 2003. TD 9207, 2005-26 IRB 1344. See also Temp. Reg. §§ 1.704-3T(a)(13)(i), 1.704-3T(a)(13)(ii) (generally treating tiered partnerships on a look-through basis for purposes of applying the "gain deferral method" under § 721(c)), discussed in ¶ 4.01[5][b][iii][D].

Page 11-186:

Add at end of subsection.

The anti-abuse rule was amended in 2010[501.1] to provide that "[a]n allocation method (or combination of methods) is not reasonable if the contribution of property (or event that results in reverse section 704(c) allocations) and the corresponding allocation of tax items with respect to the property are made with a view to shifting the tax consequences of built-in gain or loss among the partners in a manner that substantially reduces the present value of the partners' aggregate tax liability."[501.2] For purposes of the anti-abuse rule, all references to the partners includes both direct and indirect partners. For this purpose, an indirect partner is (1) any direct or indirect owner of a partnership, S corporation, or controlled foreign corporation (as defined in § 957(a) or § 953(c)), or direct or indirect beneficiary of a trust or estate, that is a partner in the partnership, and (2) any consolidated group of which the partner in the partnership is a member (within the meaning of Regulations § 1.1502-1(h)). However, an owner (whether directly or through tiers of entities) of a controlled foreign corporation is treated as an indirect partner only with respect to allocations of items of income, gain, loss, or deduction that enter into the computation of a United States shareholder's inclusion under § 951(a) with respect to the foreign corporation, or would enter into those computations if such items were allocated to the controlled foreign corporation.[501.3]

The amended Regulations apply to taxable years beginning after June 9, 2010.[501.4]

[501.1] TD 9485, 2010-26 IRB 771 (June 9, 2010).

[501.2] Reg. § 1.704-3(a)(10)(i).

[501.3] Prop. Reg. § 1.704-3(a)(10)(ii) (2008).

[501.4] Reg. § 1.704-3(f).

[b] Unavailability of Traditional Method

Page 11-186:

Add to note 502.

But see Reg. § 1.704(b)(5) Example 26 (contribution of appreciated property by U.S. partner to partnership with foreign partner; traditional method sanctioned).

Page 11-187:

Replace last sentence in carryover paragraph with the following.

If the advantage is substantial, the government will likely assert that the anti-abuse rule should apply. Given the rather explicit language to the contrary in the legislative history of § 704(c), such an assertion seems problematic.[504.1]

[504.1] HR Rep. No. 861, 98th Cong., 2nd Sess. 856 (1984) ("The conferees do not intend for the Treasury to require such variation to be eliminated by allocations of operating income and loss attributable to the contributed property."). See Reg. § 1.704-3(b)(2) Example 2(i) (anti-abuse rule inapplicable to traditional method with curative gain allocation). The Service has nonetheless asserted the application of the anti-abuse rule on similar facts, without citing either of these authorities. Chief Counsel Memorandum 20204201F (Apr. 22, 2020).

[d] Remedial Allocation Method

Page 11-190:

In note 519, add after first full sentence.

However, excess book basis may not be recovered under the bonus depreciation rules of § 168(k). See Reg. § 1.168(k)-2(a)(3)(iv)(A).

[e] Exceptions and Special Rules; Securities Partnerships

Page 11-193:

Add to note 529.

See also Priv. Ltr. Ruls. 201028016, 201028017 (July 16, 2010) (limited partnership entitled to use the full netting approach of Regulations § 1.704-3(e)(3)(v) for making forward and reverse § 704(c) allocations where potential for abuse is minimal), 201032003 (same for statutory trust taxable as partnership).

Page 11-194:

Add to note 530.

See generally Priv. Ltr. Rul. 200633019 (Apr. 19, 2006) (formation of securities partnership).

Add to note 531.

The rules with respect to the treatment of partnership interests as qualified financial assets are relaxed in the case of certain qualified partnerships. Rev. Proc. 2007-59, 2007-40 IRB 745.

[4] Partnership Distributions of Contributed Property

[a] In General

Page 11-198:

Add to note 541.

A trust and a remainder beneficiary of the trust who were treated as contributing corporate shares to a new partnership as set forth in Situation 1 of Revenue Ruling 99-5, 1999-1 CB 434, and who subsequently receive distributions of the contributed shares are treated as contributors under § 704(c)(1)(B). Priv. Ltr. Rul. 200824005 (Mar. 6, 2008); Priv. Ltr. Rul. 200824009 (Mar. 6, 2008).

[b] Exceptions

[vii] Complete transfer to another partnership.

Page 11-200:

Replace note 557 with the following.

[557] Rev. Rul. 2005-10, 2005-1 CB 492.

Page 11-203:

Add at end of subsection.

The Service has issued Proposed Regulations that would confirm and supplement Revenue Ruling 2004-43.[561.1]

Proposed Regulations § 1.704-4(c)(4)(i) (2007) provides that § 704(c)(1)(B) would not apply to the transfer in an Assets-Over merger by a partnership (the "transferor-partnership," which is considered to be the terminated partnership as a result of the merger) of all of its assets and liabilities to another partnership (the "transferee-partnership," which is considered to be the resulting partnership after the merger), that is followed by a distribution of the interest in the transferee-partnership in liquidation of the transferor-partnership as part of the same plan or arrangement. However, Proposed Regulations § 1.704-4(c)(4)(ii) (2007) provides that § 704(c)(1)(B) would apply to the transferee-partnership's subsequent distribution of § 704(c) property contributed by the transferor-partnership to the transferee-partnership in an Assets-Over merger. Proposed Regulations §§ 1.704-4(c)(4)(ii)(A) (2007) through 1.704-4(c)(4)(ii)(D) (2007) describe how § 704(c)(1)(B) would apply to such subsequent distributions.[561.2]

Under Proposed Regulations § 1.704-4(c)(4)(ii)(A) (2007), the seven-year period in § 704(c)(1)(B) would not restart with respect to original § 704(c) gain or loss as a result of the transfer of the § 704(c) property to the transferee-partnership. For this purpose, the amount of original § 704(c) gain or loss would be the difference between the property's fair market value and the

---

[561.1] REG-143397-05, 72 Fed. Reg. 46,932–46,939.

[561.2] Proposed Regulations § 1.737-2(b) (2007) would provide similar rules for applying § 737 in Assets-Over mergers.

contributing partner's adjusted tax basis at the time of contribution, to the extent such difference has not been eliminated by § 704(c) allocations, prior revaluations,[561.3] or in connection with the merger. A subsequent distribution by the transferee-partnership of property with original § 704(c) gain or loss to a partner other than the partner that contributed such property to the transferor-partnership would be subject to § 704(c)(1)(B) if the distribution occurs within seven years of the contribution of the property to the transferor-partnership.[561.4]

Under Proposed Regulations § 1.704-4(c)(4)(ii)(B) (2007), a subsequent distribution of property with new § 704(c) gain or loss by the transferee-partnership to a partner other than the contributing partner would be subject to § 704(c)(1)(B) if the distribution occurs within seven years of the transferor-partnership's contribution of the property to the transferee-partnership. For these purposes, a partner of the transferor-partnership would be deemed to have contributed to the transferee-partnership an undivided interest in the property of the transferor-partnership. The determination of the partner's undivided interest for this purpose would be made by the transferor-partnership using any reasonable method. New § 704(c) gain or loss would be allocated among the transferor-partnership's partners in a manner consistent with the principles of Regulations §§ 1.704-3(a)(7) and 1.704-3(a)(10).[561.5]

Under Proposed Regulations § 1.704-4(c)(4)(ii)(C)(1) (2007), revaluations after a merger that reflect a reduction in the amount of built-in gain or loss inherent in property would reduce new § 704(c) gain or loss prior to reducing original § 704(c) gain or loss. Revaluations would create separate § 704(c) layers, and "netting" reverse § 704(c) adjustments against prior adjustments might not be permitted under Regulations proposed in 2014.[561.6]

Under Proposed Regulations § 1.704-4(c)(4)(ii)(C)(2) (2007), if less than all of a § 704(c) property is distributed, then a proportionate amount of original and new § 704(c) gain or loss would be recognized.

Under Proposed Regulations § 1.704-4(c)(4)(ii)(D) (2007), if the transferee-partnership (the first transferee-partnership) is subsequently merged into another partnership (a new transferee-partnership), the new § 704(c) gain or loss that resulted from the merger of the transferor-partnership into the first transferee-partnership would be subject to § 704(c)(1)(B) for seven years from

---

[561.3] See Prop. Reg. § 1.704-4(c)(4)(ii)(F) Example (3) (2007) (original § 704(c) gain reduced by revaluation loss). But see Prop. Reg. § 1.704-3(a)(6)(i) (2014) (separate layers required; no netting).

[561.4] Proposed Regulations § 1.737-2(b)(1)(ii)(A) (2007) would provide a similar rule for in the context of § 737.

[561.5] See Proposed Regulations § 1.737-2(b)(1)(ii)(B) (2007) for a similar rule in the context of § 737.

[561.6] See Prop. Reg. § 1.704-3(a)(6)(i) (2014). But see Prop. Reg. § 1.704-4(c)(4)(ii)(F) Example 3 (2007) (netting required). The 2014 Proposed Regulations apparently reflect a change of heart by the Treasury on the netting issue.

the time of the transferor-partnership's contribution to the first trans-feree-partnership (in the original merger) and new § 704(c) gain or loss that resulted from the merger of the first transferee-partnership into the new trans-feree-partnership (in the subsequent merger) would be subject to § 704(c)(1)(B) for seven years from the time of the subsequent merger.[561.7]

Proposed Regulations § 1.704-4(c)(7) (2007) confirms that these rules would not apply to reverse § 704(c) gain or loss, as described in Regulations § 1.704-3(a)(6)(i).

In addition, Proposed Regulations § 1.704-4(c)(4)(ii)(E) (2007) would provide limited exceptions to the application of these rules where both the transferor-partnership and the transferee-partnership are owned by the same owners in the same proportions or the difference in ownership is de minimis. The transferor-partnership and the transferee-partnership would be considered owned by the same owners in the same proportions if (1) each partner owns identical interests in book capital and in each item of income, gain, loss, de-duction, and credit in both the transferor-partnership and transferee-partnership and (2) each partner has identical shares of distributions and liabilities in both the transferor-partnership and transferee-partnership. A difference in ownership would be de minimis if 97 percent of the interests in book capital and in each item of income, gain, loss, deduction, credit, shares of distributions, and liabil-ities of the transferor partnership and transferee partnership are owned by the same owners in the same proportions.[561.8]

Proposed Regulations § 1.704-3(a)(9) (2007) would provide rules for se-lecting an allocation method for applying these rules.

Proposed Regulations § 1.737-2(b)(2) (2007) would provide that § 737 does not apply in divisive transactions involving a transfer by a partnership (the transferor-partnership) of all of the § 704(c) property contributed by a partner to a second partnership (the transferee-partnership) in an exchange de-scribed in § 721, followed by a distribution as part of the same plan or ar-rangement of an interest in the transferee-partnership (and no other property) in complete liquidation of the interest of the partner that originally contributed the § 704(c) property to the transferor-partnership (i.e., divisive transactions). However, after such a divisive transaction, a subsequent distribution of prop-erty by the transferee-partnership to a partner of the transferee-partnership that was formerly a partner of the transferor-partnership would be subject to § 737 to the same extent that a distribution from the transferor-partnership would have been subject to § 737.

If promulgated, these Proposed Regulations will apply to distributions of property after January 19, 2005, with respect to property contributed in an As-sets-Over merger after May 3, 2004.

[561.7] See Proposed Regulations § 1.737-2(b)(1)(ii)(D) (2007) for a similar rule in the context of § 737.

[561.8] See Proposed Regulations § 1.737-2(b)(1)(ii)(E) (2007) for a similar rule in the context of § 737.

The Service received a number of comments on the proposed regulations' treatment of § 704(c) layers in connection with partnership mergers, especially with regard to Example 3 (which called for netting § 704(c) layers when a book-up is followed by a book-down). In Notice 2009-70,[561.9] the Service requested comments on the appropriate treatment of § 704(c) layers. The finalization of the proposed regulations will undoubtedly await the resolution of this issue.

[561.9] Notice 2009-70, 2009-34 IRB 255 (Aug. 12, 2009).

¶ 11.05 THE BASIS LIMITATION ON THE DEDUCTIBILITY OF A PARTNER'S SHARE OF PARTNERSHIP LOSSES: SECTION 704(d)

Page 11-211:

Add to note 593 after F.A. Falconer *citation.*

Rock Bordelon, 119 TCM 1157 (2020) (guarantee of LLC loan increases partner's basis; § 704(d) does not limit losses);

[1] Application of the Limitation

Page 11-212:

Add the following after first paragraph of subsection (ending with note callout 596).

These Regulations do not yet reflect the 2017 amendment of § 704(d).[596.1] For tax years beginning after 2017, § 704(d)(1) reflects prior § 704(d) and limits the deductibility of a partner's share of partnership loss (including capital loss) to the adjusted basis of its interest. New § 704(d)(3)(A) provides that each partner's share of separately stated charitable contribution deductions (§ 702(a)(4)) and foreign taxes described in § 901 (§ 702(a)(6)) will be taken into account in determining loss for purposes of the § 704(d)(1) limitation. Finally, new § 704(d)(4) confirms (consistent with Revenue Ruling 96-11[596.2]) that a partner's share of the excess of the fair market value over the adjusted basis of contributed partnership property is not taken into account for purposes of § 704(d).[596.3]

[596.1] 2017 Tax Cuts and Jobs Act, Pub. L. No. 115-97, § 13503 (Dec. 22, 2017), discussed in ¶ 11.05[1][b].

[596.2] Rev. Rul. 96-11, 1996-1 CB 140.

[596.3] See ¶ 6.02[3][c].

Pages 11-214–11-215:

Replace ¶ 11.05[1][b] with revised ¶ 11.05[1][b].

[b] Exclusion of Charitable Contributions From the Limitation: Repeal by the 2017 Tax Cuts and Jobs Act [Revised]

Prior to 2017, partnership charitable contributions were excluded from the computation of partnership income or loss, and hence were not subject to the § 704(d) limitation on the deductibility of partnership losses.[601] This was a technical flaw finally corrected by Treasury as part of the 2017 Tax Cuts and Jobs Act.[602]

For pre–2018 tax years, this potential flaw allowed zero-basis partners to reap the benefits of a partnership charitable contribution without offsetting decreases in the bases of their interests, whereas fellow partners who happened to have a positive bases could do so only at the cost of bases decreases.[603] Under certain circumstances, these rules could produce counterintuitive results in pre–2018 taxable years, as indicated by the following examples.

> **EXAMPLE 11-34:** *A* and *B* form the equal *AB* partnership, with *A* contributing $500 cash and *B* contributing land that has a basis of zero and a value of $500. Some time thereafter, with the partnership holding the same assets and not having realized any income or loss or made any distributions in the interim, the partnership makes a charitable contribution of the land. Each partner is entitled to a $250 charitable contribution deduction, but neither partner's outside basis in his partnership interest is affected (*A* continues to have a $500 basis, while *B* continues to have a zero basis). On a subsequent liquidation of the partnership, each partner receives $250 cash. *A* thus has a $250 capital loss and *B* has a $250 capital gain on the liquidation. Over the term of the partnership, each partner has an economic "loss" (actually a charitable contribution) of $250, but *A*

---

[601] See §§ 703(a)(2)(C) (excluding charitable contribution deductions from the computation of partnership income), 704(d) (prior to amendment by the 2017 Tax Cuts and Jobs Act).

[602] Pub. L. No. 115-97, § 13503 (Dec. 22, 2017). See HR Rep No. 466, 115th Cong., 1st Sess., "Conference Report to Accompany HR 1," at 513, n.1120 (2017) (citing and quoting the Fourth Edition of this Treatise).

[603] Prior to 2018, foreign taxes were subject to the same treatment as charitable contributions. They are separately stated under § 702(a)(4), and not listed in Regulations § 1.704-1(d)(2). Since foreign taxes cannot be specially allocated, but must be allocated along with the income that generates the foreign taxes (see supra ¶ 11.03[2][i]), this treatment seems to have been of little practical consequence, but was nonetheless corrected by the 2017 amendment to § 704(d)(3)(A) for post–2017 tax years.

Post–1974 oil and gas depletion deductions are also excluded from the computation of partnership taxable income or loss (see § 703(a)(2)(F)), and hence are not subject to § 704(d). The significance of this exclusion from § 704(d) is limited, however, because post–1975 deductions of this kind will generally be subject to the "at-risk" provisions of § 465. See infra ¶ 11.06.

deducts a total of $500 ($250 charitable contribution deduction plus $250 capital loss), while B has a net tax loss of zero (ignoring character differences) because his $250 charitable deduction is offset by a capital gain of $250.

EXAMPLE 11-35: The facts are the same as Example 11-34, except that after the charitable contribution of the land, partner B contributes his partnership interest to charity, claiming a $250 charitable contribution deduction. Thereafter, the partnership liquidates, distributing $250 cash to partner A and $250 to the charity. The results to A are the same as in the previous example ($250 economic outlay, with a $500 of tax deduction and capital loss), but now partner B has an economic outlay and tax deductions of $500.

[c] Carryover of Disallowed Losses

Page 11-215:

Add to note 607.

See LeBlanc, Jr. v. United States, 2010-1 USTC ¶ 50,104 (Fed. Cl. 2009) (illustration of § 704(d) and basis computation), rev'd on other grounds, 2011-1 USTC ¶ 50,209 (Fed. Cir. 2011).

[3] Year-End Planning Under Section 704(d)

Page 11-220:

Add to note 622.

; see Southgate Master Fund, LLC v. United States, 2009-2 USTC ¶ 50,593 (ND Tex. 2009) (contribution of assets subject to recourse debt in attempt to increase basis disregarded for lack of economic substance).

¶ 11.06 THE AT-RISK LIMITATION ON THE DEDUCTIBILITY OF PARTNERSHIP LOSSES: SECTION 465

[1] General Concepts

Page 11-223:

Replace note 631 with the following.

[631] Films and videotapes, farming, leasing personal property, oil and gas ventures, and geothermal ventures. § 465(c)(3)(D). The requisite regulations have been issued extending this rule to all activities covered by the at-risk rules. See Reg. § 1.465-8(a), effective for amounts borrowed after May 3, 2004.

Add to note 634.

A partner's right of subrogation and reimbursement from a partnership does not cause such partner's guarantee of partnership debt to be treated as not at risk. However, a partner's co-guarantee of partnership debt will be ineffective to create at-risk basis where the guarantor has a right of contribution or reimbursement against the other guarantors under local law. CCA 201308028 (Nov. 14, 2012).

[2] Application to Partnerships

[b] Computation of a Partner's At-Risk Amount

Page 11-227:

Replace note 647 with the following.

[647] Movies and videotapes, farming, leasing § 1245 property, oil and gas ventures, and geothermal ventures. § 465(c)(3)(D). The requisite regulations have been issued extending this rule to all activities covered by the at-risk rules. See Reg. § 1.465-8(a), effective for amounts borrowed after May 3, 2004.

Replace note 648 with the following.

[648] See § 465(b)(3). Thus, amounts borrowed from a partner or a person related to a partner are not at risk. See James Peters, 77 TC 1158 (1981) (partnership borrowed funds from persons related to partners under § 267(b); borrowing not at risk). Similarly, borrowings from a creditor who has the right to convert his loan into a partnership interest may be excluded from the partners' at-risk amounts.

Page 11-230:

Add at end of subsection.

However, the Tax Court, on remand from a Sixth Circuit decision mandating that the debt of an LLC (treated as a partnership for tax purposes) could be included in a member's at-risk amount only where the member was a "payor of last resort," concluded that a deficit restoration obligation under Wyoming law did not render the member-obligors the "payors of last resort."[661.1] The deficit restoration obligation created an obligation on the part of the members to contribute capital only upon liquidation of the LLC. Because a default under the relevant recourse debt was not an event that caused a liquidation of the LLC under Wyoming law, the Tax Court held that the members were not entitled to include the recourse debt in their amounts at-risk.

[661.1] Hubert Enterprises, 95 TCM 1194 (2008).

¶ 11.07 THE AT-RISK LIMITATION ON INVESTMENT TAX CREDIT

Page 11-233:

Add to note 683.

The concept of energy property has been expanded to include not only property eligible for the § 48 energy credit, but also property covered by the § 48A qualifying advanced coal project credit, the § 48B qualifying gasification project credit, and the § 48C qualifying advanced energy project credit. See § 46.

¶ 11.08 PASSIVE LOSS RULES

[2] Definition of "Passive Activities"

Page 11-237:

Add to note 707.

For tax years beginning after December 31, 2021, the 2017 Tax Cuts and Jobs Act is scheduled to convert § 174 research and experimental expenditure deductions into intangibles generally amortizable over five years. Pub. L. No. 115-97, § 13206 (Dec. 22, 2017).

Page 11-240:

Add to beginning of note 730.

Compliance with the 750-hour requirement is, as one might expect, based on the evidentiary requirements in Temporary Regulations § 1.469-5T(f)(4), relating to the general 500-hour requirement in Temporary Regulations § 1.469-5T(a)(1). See Zaid Hakkak, TC Memo. 2020-46 (2020) (evidence presented by taxpayer fails to prove compliance with 750-hour requirement); ¶ 11.08[2].

[6] Material Participation

Page 11-256:

Add to note 816.

While no specific record keeping requirements are imposed by the Regulations, the gold standard that has developed under the case law is contemporaneous daily logs or appointment books including descriptions of activities and time spent. In the absence of this type of comprehensive written evidence, taxpayers frequently seek to satisfy this requirement based on narrative summaries of their activities but have rarely prevailed in the absence of significant and credible third-party testimony or other corroborating evidence (flight logs, phone records, credit card invoices, etc.). Compare, e.g., Jose A. Lamas, 109 TCM 1299 (2015) (taxpayer prevails); Stefan A. Tolin, 107 TCM 1339 (2014) (same), with Scott Wesley Williams, 108 TCM 128 (2014), aff'd, 771 Fed Appx 365 (9th Cir. 2019) (memorandum) (taxpayer loses; lack of corroboration); Randy G. Sellers, TC Memo. 2020-84 (2020) (same).

Replace last sentence of subsection with the following.

Members of limited liability partnerships and LLCs are not treated as limited partners for these purposes where state law does not preclude the member from participating in the business of the entity;[818] however, Proposed Regulations § 1.469-5(e) would treat an interest in an entity as an interest in a limited partnership for purposes of Section 469(h)(2) only if the entity is both classified as a partnership for federal tax purposes and the holder of the interest does not have rights to manage the entity at all times during the relevant taxable year of the entity.[818.1] If finalized, these regulations would apply to taxable years beginning on or after the date of publication of any final regulations.[818.2]

---

[818] Paul D. Garnett, 132 TC 368 (2009) (Iowa LLP and LLC); Gregg v. United States, 186 F. Supp. 2d 1123 (D. Or. 2000) (Oregon LLC); Thompson v. United States, 87 Fed. Cl. 728 (2009) (Texas LLC); Lee E. Newell, 99 TCM 1107 (2010) (California LLC). The IRS has recommended formal acquiescence in the results of *Garnett, Gregg* and *Thompson.* See AOD 2010-02.

[818.1] Prop. Reg. § 1.469-5(e)(3)(i) (2011). The taxpayer may also avoid limited partner status by holding another interest in the entity that is not a limited partner interest (such as a general partnership interest). Prop. Reg. § 1.469-5(e)(3)(ii) (2011).

[818.2] Prop. Reg. § 1.469-5(e)(4) (2011).

[7] Definition of "Activity"

Page 11-257:

Add to note 820.

For tax years beginning after December 31, 2021, the 2017 Tax Cuts and Jobs Act is scheduled to convert § 174 research and experimental expenditure deductions into intangibles generally amortizable over five years. Pub. L. No. 115-97, § 13206 (Dec. 22, 2017).

Page 11-258:

Add to note 831.

In Stephen P. Hardy, 113 TCM 1070 (2017), the Tax Court rejected an attempt by the Service to regroup the taxpayer's activities because the taxpayer's groupings reflected appropriate economic units and did not have a purpose to circumvent § 469.

Distributive Share Allocations in Connection With Shifts in the Partners' Interests

Chapter 12 was revised effective December 2020. The revised chapter can be found in the front of this student edition.

Terminations; Partnership-Partner Transactions; and Family Partnership Rules

CHAPTER **13**

Termination of a Partnership

¶ 13.01 THE GENERAL RULE OF NONTERMINATION

Page 13-2:

Replace first paragraph of subsection with the following:

Section 708(a) sets forth the general rule that a partnership continues to exist for purposes of Subchapter K until it is "terminated." As amended by the 2017 Tax Cuts and Jobs Act, § 708(b) provides that a partnership is terminated "only if no part of any business, financial operation, or venture of the partnership continues to be carried on by any of its partners in a partnership."[0.1] Prior to the 2017 Tax Cuts and Jobs Act, partnerships could also be terminated (by a so-called "technical termination") if 50 percent of more of the interests in partnership capital and profits were sold or exchanged during a 12-month period. Paragraph 13.03 addresses issues related to technical terminations prior to 2018.

[0.1] Pub. L. No. 115-97, § 13504(a) (Dec. 22, 2017).

Page 13-4:

Replace heading of ¶ 13.02 with the following revised heading.

¶ 13.02 TERMINATION UPON DISCONTINUATION OF THE PARTNERSHIP BUSINESS: SECTION 708(B)(1)(A)— SECTION 708(B)(1) AFTER 2017 [REVISED HEADING]

Add the following before first paragraph of subsection.

NOTE: Due to the elimination of "technical terminations" following the repeal of § 708(b)(1)(B) by the 2017 Tax Cuts and Jobs Act (Pub. Law. No 115-97, § 13504(a)), references to § 708(b)(1)(A) in ¶ 13.02 refer to § 708(b)(1) for partnership tax years beginning after December 31, 2017.

Page 13-5:

Add to note 13.

7050, LTD, 95 TCM 1413 (2008) (no termination; partnership continued to hold foreign currency in an inactive account); Priv. Ltr. Rul. 201244004 (Nov. 2, 2012) (sale of partnership business, with portion of sale proceeds distributed to partners and balance placed in a liquidating trust to satisfy known and unknown partnership liabilities; trust interests distributed to partners; on date state law status as a limited partnership terminated, partnership terminated for tax purposes under § 708(b)(1)(A) [now § 708(b)(1)]).

Pages 13-5–13-6:

Replace fifth paragraph of subsection (including note 15) with the following.

Cases holding that a partnership continues under § 708(b)(1)(A) [now § 708(b)(1)] subsequent to the sale of its primary business have not, however, considered the effect of the "sale-of-a-going-business" doctrine on the partnership's existence. Under this doctrine, which is of uncertain scope under current law, a partnership's sale of the assets representing its entire going business may be treated as a sale by the partners of their partnership interests for purposes of determining the character of the partners' gains or losses.[15]

---

[15] See Barran v. Commissioner, 334 F2d 58 (5th Cir. 1964). But cf. Estate of Aaron Levine, 72 TC 780 (1979), aff'd, 634 F2d 12 (2d Cir. 1980) (exchange by partnership of principal asset; no sale of partnership interests and no termination). See generally ¶ 16.03[3].

Page 13-6:

Add to note 16.

; FAA 20132101F (May 24, 2013); CCA 201315026 (Apr. 12, 2013) (original partnership merges into a disregarded entity (DRE) owned by New Partnership; partners of Original Partnership contribute interests to New Partnership for interests therein; Rev. Rul. 66-264 applies).

Add to note 17.

Less problematic is the Service's more recent analysis in ILM 201315026 (Apr. 12, 2013) (triangular merger of existing state law partnership with a disregarded entity held by a new state law partnership, with partners in existing partnership acquiring same interests in new partnership, does not cause a termination; use of different taxpayer identification number by new partnership irrelevant).

Pages 13-6–13-7:

Replace second to last paragraph of subsection (including notes 18–20) with the following.

The facts of the ruling did not raise the question of whether this type of transaction may have caused a termination under § 708(b)(1)(B) (prior to its repeal for post–2017 taxable years), since the continuing partners held more than 50 percent of the capital and profits interests in the original partnership. However, the ruling notes the possibility that the withdrawal of the other partners might be treated as a retirement of their interests under appropriate factual circumstances.[18] The retirement of a partner's interest could not have resulted in a termination under § 708(b)(1)(B) (prior to its repeal), because it is not a

---

[18] See ¶ 16.02[3].

"sale or exchange" of an interest.[19] Accordingly, it might have been possible to avoid a § 708(b)(1)(B) termination under the logic of the ruling even where the continuing partners owned less than 50 percent of the capital and profits interests in the original partnership. It might also have been possible, under appropriate circumstances, to have brought outsiders into the new partnership without causing a § 708(b)(1)(B) termination of the old partnership. However, if the new partners' interests had exceeded 50 percent, their admission, in conjunction with the retirement of the interests of some of the original partners, could have caused the transaction to be wholly or partially recast as a sale or exchange under § 707(a)(2)(B), and thereby result in a termination under § 708(b)(1)(B).[20]

---

[19] See Reg. § 1.708-1(b)(2).

[20] See ¶ 14.02[3][b]. See also Reg. §§ 1.708-1(b)(2), 1.731-1(c)(3); Mahoney v. United States, 81-2 USTC ¶ 9761 (Ct. Cl. 1981), aff'd, 229 Ct. Cl. 794 (Cl. Ct. 1982); Walter K. Oehlschlager, 55 TCM 839 (1988).

Page 13-8:

Replace heading of ¶ 13.03 with the following revised heading.

¶ 13.03 SALE OR EXCHANGE OF 50 PERCENT OR MORE OF INTERESTS IN PARTNERSHIP CAPITAL AND PROFITS: SECTION 708(B)(1)(B)—PRE–2018 LAW [REVISED HEADING]

Replace first paragraph of subsection with the following:

Former Section 708(b)(1)(B) came into the Code in 1954 and left it in 2017. It was apparently designed to prevent trafficking in partnerships with advantageous taxable years and thereby to inhibit avoidance of the § 706(b) limitations on a partnership's ability to elect a taxable year other than that of its principal partners,[23] but that concern faded through the years as subsequent changes in the Code have greatly reduced the ability of partnerships to adopt or retain favorable taxable years, leading Congress to revoke the rule as part of the 2017 Tax Cuts and Jobs Act.[24]

NOTE: *The remainder of this ¶ 13.03 addresses the law applicable to taxable years beginning before January 1, 2018.*

---

[23] See Jackson et al., "The Internal Revenue Code of 1954: Partnerships," 54 Colum. L. Rev. 1183, 1198 (1954).

[24] Pub. L. No. 115-97, § 13504(a) (Dec. 22, 2017).

¶ 13.04 EFFECT OF PARTNER'S DEATH OR WITHDRAWAL ON PARTNERSHIP'S EXISTENCE

Pages 13-21–13-14:

Replace ¶ 13.04[1] with revised ¶ 13.04[1].

¶ 13.05 TAX CONSEQUENCES OF A PARTNERSHIP'S TERMINATION

[1] The Effects of Termination by Cessation of Business Activity

Page 13-23:

Add the following before first paragraph of subsection.

NOTE: Due to the elimination of "technical terminations" following the repeal of § 708(b)(1)(B) by the 2017 Tax Cuts and Jobs Act (Pub. Law. No 115-97, § 13504(a)), references to § 708(b)(1)(A) in ¶ 13.05 refer to § 708(b)(1) for partnership tax years beginning after December 31, 2017.

Page 13-25:

Replace heading of ¶ 13.05[2] with the following revised heading.

[2] The Effects of Termination by Sale or Exchange of Capital and Profits Interests—Prior to 2018 [Revised Heading]

Add the following before first paragraph of subsection.

NOTE: For taxable years beginning prior to January 1, 2018, former § 708(b)(1)(B) provided for a "technical termination" of a partnership upon the sale or exchange within a twelve-month period of more than 50 percent of the interests in partnership profits and capital. The technical termination rule of former § 708(b)(1)(B) were eliminated as part of the 2017 Tax Cuts and Jobs Act,[92.1] but the consequences of such a termination are outlined below to provide readers with an understanding of the historic consequences of certain partnership transactions.

[92.1] Pub. L. No. 115-97, § 13504(a) (Dec. 22, 2017).

Page 13-25:

Add to note 93.

The Service has ruled privately that the termination of a partnership pursuant to § 708(b)(1)(B) in the midst of a § 1031 exchange will not preclude identified replacement property from being held for investment or for the productive use in a trade or business. Priv. Ltr. Rul. 200812012 (Dec. 19, 2007).

[b] Effect on Partnership Elections

Page 13-26:

Add to note 98.

However, the Service is willing to rule that the new partnership is entitled to rely on a ruling received by the terminated partnership provided that the new partnership is willing to pay its $10,000 fee. See Priv. Ltr. Ruls. 200806002 (Oct. 30, 2007), 200806003 (Oct. 30, 2007), 200806004 (Oct. 30, 2007), 200808013 (Oct. 30, 2007), 200808014 (Oct. 30, 2007).

[c] Effects of Hypothetical Contribution and Distribution Under Sections 704(b), 704(c), and 737

Page 13-27:

Add to note 100.

See also Prop. Reg. § 1.737-1(c)(3)(ii) (2014): "A termination of the partnership under section 708(b)(1)(B) does not begin a new seven-year period for each partner with respect to built-in gain and built-in loss property that the terminated partnership is deemed to contribute to the new partnership under § 1.708-1(b)(4)."

[d] Recognition of Gain or Loss on the Hypothetical Distribution

Page 13-28:

Replace note 103 with the following.

[103] Reg. § 1.453-9(c)(2). The statutory language under which this provision of the Regulations was promulgated is now found in § 453B; presumably, this provision continues to be applicable. See Prop. Reg. § 1.453B-1(c)(1)(i)(B) (2014). See also Letter, 31 Tax Law. 449 (1978).

[f] Holding Period and Character of Old Assets and Interests in the New Partnership

Page 13-29:

Replace last two sentences of sole paragraph of subsection (after note callout 108) with the following.

The holding periods of interests in the new partnership, however, are determined under § 735(b), which includes the partnership's holding period in the distributed asset in the partner's holding period. If the terminated partnership's holding period in the new partnership interests is bifurcated under Regulations § 1.1223-3 (e.g., where the contributed assets consisted of both capital and non-capital assets in the hands of the terminated partnership), it appears that the new partners' holding periods in the new partnership interests will be similarly bifurcated.

[g] Recapture of Investment Credit

Page 13-29:

Replace note 109 with the following.

[109] Currently, the investment credit of § 38 is equal to the sum of the rehabilitation credit (§ 47), the energy credit (§ 48), the qualifying advanced coal project credit (§ 48A), the qualifying gasification project credit (§ 48B), and, as of 2009, the § 48C qualifying advanced energy project credit. § 46.

Page 13-30:

Add to note 112.

See also Prop. Reg. § 1.45D-1(e)(4) (2008) (no recapture of § 45D new markets tax credit on § 708(b)(1)(B) termination).

[m] Organization and Syndication Fees; Start-Up Expenditures

Page 13-37:

Replace note 143 with the following.

[143] § 709(b)(2); Reg. § 1.709-1(b)(3).

Replace note 144 with the following.

[144] Reg. § 1.709-1(b)(3); Rev. Rul. 85-32, 1985-1 CB 186.

Page 13-38:

Replace second and third paragraphs of subsection with the following.

For § 708(b)(1)(B) terminations occurring on or after December 9, 2013, no disposition of the partnership's trade or business is deemed to occur for purposes of § 195(b)(2).[147] Similarly, no liquidation of the partnership occurs under § 709(b)(2).[148] Rather, the partnership continues to amortize any start up or organizational expenditures over the remaining portion of the amortization period adopted by the terminated partnership.[149]

It appears that a § 708(b)(1)(B) termination after May 9, 1997, and before December 9, 2013, should be treated as a liquidation for purposes of § 709.[149.1]

---

[147] Reg. § 1.195-2.

[148] Reg. § 1.709-1(b)(3)(ii).

[149] Reg. § 1.708-1(b)(6).

[149.1] Under the prior § 708 construct, the § 708(b) Regulations did not use the term "liquidate," but they did provide that a partnership was deemed to "distribute its properties to the purchaser and the other remaining partners" upon a § 708(b)(1)(B) termination.

Accordingly, the terminated partnership should be entitled to a § 165 deduction on its final return for the unamortized balance of any organization costs that are subject to a § 709(b) election. However, no partnership-level deduction should be permitted with respect to syndication costs or any organization costs that are not being amortized under § 709(b).[149.2] Further, partners should not be able to claim losses under § 731(a)(2) upon a § 708(b)(1)(B) termination.[149.3]

With respect to a termination before December 9, 2013, it is unclear whether the balance of any start-up expenses that are being amortized over a period of 180 months under § 195 can be deducted on a § 708(b)(1)(B) termination. Section 195(b)(2) provides for the deduction of such unamortized expenses as a § 165 loss when the "trade or business is completely disposed of by the taxpayer" before the end of the amortization period. Because the partnership is the taxpayer owning the business and the partnership ceases to exist (thereby apparently disposing of the business upon its constructive contribution to the new partnership), the statutory requirements appear to be satisfied. However, it is unclear to what extent the fiction of the § 708(b)(1)(B) Regulations will be given effect outside Subchapter K—an uncertainty that is highlighted by the limiting language in the general rule of § 708(a), which only applies "for purposes of this subchapter...." Accordingly, significant uncertainty exists as to the deductibility of unamortized start-up expenses upon a § 708 partnership termination.

Reg. § 1.708-1(b)(1)(iv) (prior to amendment by TD 8717). As amended by TD 8717, 1997-1 CB 125, Regulations § 1.708-1(b)(4) refers to distributions "in liquidation of the terminated partnership," thus eliminating any possible confusion on this point.

[149.2] Analytically, it seems that syndication costs and organization costs which are not being amortized under § 709(b) should be treated as a capitalized "asset" contributed by the terminating partnership to the new partnership. This analysis, however, seems inconsistent with the suggestion in Revenue Ruling 87-111, 1987-1 CB 160, that such costs may contribute to a § 731(a)(2) loss upon liquidation, since a liquidating distribution that includes this type of asset (whatever it is, it is not money, inventory, or an unrealized receivable) could not possibly generate a loss under § 731(a)(2). The only way to make sense out of Revenue Ruling 87-111 is to apply the highest form of Subchapter K sorcery to make these costs "disappear" for purposes of the distribution rules. Under that view, the question would become whether such costs are an asset of the terminated partnership that can be contributed to the new partnership or, if they cannot be transferred, simply become worthless and deductible at the time the old partnership terminates.

[149.3] A liquidating distribution must consist solely of money, unrealized receivables, and inventory in order for a loss to be allowable to the distributee-partner.

[3] The Effects of Termination of a Two-Person Partnership

Page 13-39:

Add the following before first paragraph of subsection.

NOTE: Due to the elimination of "technical terminations" following the repeal of § 708(b)(1)(B) by the 2017 Tax Cuts and Jobs Act (Pub. Law. No

115-97, § 13504(a)), references to § 708(b)(1)(A) in ¶ 13.05[3] refer to § 708(b)(1) for partnership tax years beginning after December 31, 2017.

¶ 13.06 PARTNERSHIP TERMINATIONS AND CONTINUATIONS RESULTING FROM MERGERS AND DIVISIONS

[1] Mergers

Page 13-42:

Add to note 165.

Following the repeal of § 708(b)(1)(B) in 2017 (see Pub. L. No. 115-97, § 13504(a) (Dec. 22, 2017)), it is now entirely clear that the distribution of resulting partnership interests by terminating partnerships cannot trigger a termination.

Add to note 167.

Following the repeal of § 708(b)(1)(B) in 2017 (see Pub. L. No. 115-97, § 13504(a) (Dec. 22, 2017)), there is no longer any possibility that these sales may trigger a partnership termination.

Page 13-44:

In note 175, replace first sentence with the following.

Generally, § 50(a)(1) requires recapture of all or a portion of the investment credit if investment credit property is disposed of or ceases to be qualifying property within five years of the date the property is placed in service.

Add to note 178.

The merger of two partnerships with identical ownership does not create built-in gain regardless of the date of the distribution. Notice 2005-15, 2005-1 CB 527; Priv. Ltr. Rul. 200631014, (May 1, 2006). The Service subsequently issued proposed regulations largely following Revenue Ruling 2004-43, 2004-18 IRB 842 (Apr. 12, 2004), revoked by Rev. Rul. 2005-10, 2005-1 CB 492. Prop. Reg. §§ 1.704-4(c)(4), 1.737-2(b)(2007). In Notice 2009-70, 2009-34 IRB 255 (Aug. 12, 2009), the Service asked for comments on certain § 704(c) issues raised by the proposed regulations. This issue may someday be put to rest upon the finalization of Proposed Regulations § 1.737-1(c)(3)(ii) (2014): "A termination of the partnership under section 708(b)(1)(B) does not begin a new seven-year period for each partner with respect to built-in gain and built-in loss property that the terminated partnership is deemed to contribute to the new partnership under § 1.708-1(b)(4)." If there is no new seven-year period, presumably there is no new layer of § 704(c) gain or loss. The repeal of § 708(b)(1)(B) in 2017 (see Pub. L. No. 115-97, § 13504(a) (Dec. 22, 2017)), should put this issue to rest by making it clear that there is no new seven-year clock and no new gain or loss layer.

Page 13-45:

Add to note 183.

See Priv. Ltr. Rul. 201643016 (Oct. 21, 2016) (Reg. § 1.708-1(c)(4) invoked).

Add after Example 13-5.

Special rules are provided for dealing with mergers involving partnerships with liabilities in excess of basis. The "netting rule" of Regulations § 1.752-1(f) (§ 752 increases and decreases from same transaction netted) applies to partnership mergers, which makes the application of § 743(b) to the second step of the assets-over construct problematic.

> **EXAMPLE 13-5.1:** *B* is a partner in both *S* and *T*. *T*'s sole asset is property *X*, with a basis of $600 and a value of $1,000, encumbered by $900 of debt. *T* merges into *S* (property value of $1,000 encumbered by $100 debt), taking back a 10 percent *S* interest with a $100 share of liabilities in *S* (the merged partnership). Absent the netting rule, *T* would have a $200 § 731(a) gain ($800 § 752 distribution versus $600 basis). All of the liabilities are netted against *B*'s final outside basis in *S*, however, such that the net § 752(b) distribution is from *S* to *B*.[183.1]

While the result in Example 13-5.1 is favorable to taxpayers, it makes the § 743(b) computation on the step 2 distribution on the liquidation of *T* problematic to say the least. *T*'s basis in its *S* interest after step 1 of the assets-over merger is *negative* $200. Absent indulging in the fiction of negative basis, the inside-outside basis mechanics of § 743(b) simply cease to function. The better view may well be that § 743(b) doesn't apply in the merger context.

A Technical Advice Memorandum,[183.2] however, concluded that in an assets-over merger, the deemed distribution of interests in the resulting partnership is a deemed distribution under § 761(e)(2), which is treated as an exchange for the purposes of § 743(b). The memorandum concludes further that (1) the deferred income under § 108(i)[183.3] is not tax gain under Regulations § 1.743-1(d), and (2) the "netting rule" of Regulations § 1.752-1(f) does not apply (at least in the manner provided by the Regulation) in determining the appropriate § 743(b) adjustment for the merger as a whole. Although the facts of the memorandum are completely redacted, it is apparent[183.4] that the resulting partnership's assets had a "substantial built-in loss" under § 743(d)(1),

---

[183.1] Reg. § 1.752-1(g) Example 2.

[183.2] TAM 201929019 (July 19, 2019).

[183.3] Under § 108(i), taxpayers (including partnerships) are permitted to elect to defer the inclusion of cancellation of indebtedness income for debt discharged in 2009 and 2010.

[183.4] See Jackel, Assets-Over Merger Blunders on Negative Adjustments, 164 Tax Notes 859 (Aug. 5, 2019) (hereinafter, Jackel).

which IRS Chief Counsel argued triggered the mandatory application of §
743(b). The memorandum has been criticized by a prominent commentator,[183.5]
and its analysis appears to be fatally flawed. This commentator opined that the
memorandum is contrary to the clear indication in four Regulation packages
(the 2000 and 2001 merger and division Regulations, as well as the 2014 and
2016 disguised sale Regulations) that an assets-over merger should not produce substantive tax consequences.[183.6] Finally, in calculating the § 743(b) adjustment, Chief Counsel invented a liability-sharing rule not contained in the
applicable § 752 Regulations to deal with a perceived anomaly caused by the
netting rule.

[183.5] See Jackel (arguing that TAM 201929019 should have concluded that either the
deferred cancellation of indebtedness income under § 108(i) is be treated as tax gain, or
that there is no mandatory application of § 743(b) in an assets-over merger).

[183.6] See Jackel at 864.

[2] Divisions

Page 13-47:

Add to note 190.

; Priv. Ltr. Rul. 200921009 (Feb. 13, 2009) (same).

Page 13-50:

Add to note 203.

Regulations § 1.761-1(e) has not yet been amended to reflect the repeal of § 708(b)(1)(B)
in 2017 by the 2017 Tax Cuts and Jobs Act, Pub. L. No. 115-97, § 13504(a) (Dec. 22,
2017).

Page 13-53:

Add to note 214.

See Priv. Ltr. Rul. 201643016 (Oct. 21, 2016) (division followed by merger of larger
value resulting partnership into newly formed partnership; form respected; structure appears to utilize the "no form" rule for treating the divided partnership as the more valuable partnership, such that the subsequent merger involves the "old and cold" divided
partnership).

Transactions Between Partnerships and Partners

¶ 14.01   THE STATUTORY FRAMEWORK: SECTION 707

[2] Distinguishing Among Payments Subject to Sections 707(a), 707(c), and 704

Page 14-5:

Add new note 8.1 at end of first sentence of subsection.

    8.1 Payments to a non-partner are not subject to the provisions of § 707 or § 704. Instead, payments to non-partners for services are simply Schedule C income to the non-partner. These concepts are equally applicable even if the non-partner exercises near total control over the partnership, through family members and other related persons, and receives the payments through another partnership that is arguably a sham. See Martin G. Plotkin, 102 TCM 450 (2011), aff'd in an unpublished opinion, 2012-2 USTC ¶ 50,688 (4th Cir. 2012) (taxpayer who orchestrated transactions may not benefit from "sham" argument).

¶ 14.02   PARTNERS ACTING IN NONPARTNER CAPACITIES: SECTION 707(a) TRANSACTIONS

[1] Loan Transactions

Page 14-10:

Replace note 31 with the following.

[31] See Todd A. Dagres, 136 TC 263 (2011) (member-manager is deemed to carry on trade or business of his LLC; loan to third party gives rise to business bad debt); Theodore G. Arens, 59 TCM 589, 591 (1990) ("cases too numerous to cite have held that the business of a partnership is the business of its partners"; business of general partnership attributed to partner for purposes of avoiding short-year accelerated cost recovery system rules); Tech. Adv. Mem. 7907001 (July 29, 1977) (espousing principle that partners are viewed as engaged in partnership's business). The taxpayer in *Butler* was a limited partner. There may be more justification for treating debts owed to general partners as business debts because limited partners may not participate actively in the partnership's business. In this respect, it has been suggested that the taxpayer in *Butler* was in fact more than a passive investor. See Young, "Income Tax Consequences of Investment Losses of Individuals," 27 Tax L. Rev. 1, 26–28 (1971). See also GCM 38201 (Dec. 14, 1979) (trust holds 10 percent interest in limited partnership engaged in business enterprise; business of partnership not attributed to trust for purposes of entity classification Regulations; broad application of *Butler* rejected); ¶ 9.02[3][e] . The Service expressed a narrow view of *Butler* in Rev. Rul. 2008-39, 2008-31 IRB 252, stating that it stands for the proposition that a partner may deduct unreimbursed amounts paid by the partner on behalf of the partnership (itself engaged in a trade or business). The Service's effort to reconcile *Butler* with its general entity-level characterization view (see ¶ 9.01[4][a]) seems strained and perhaps driven by its acquiescence in *Butler.*

[3] Sales

[b] Disguised Sales

[i] In general.

Page 14-16:

Add new note 56.1 at end of second sentence of subsection.

[56.1] See Virginia Historic Tax Credit Fund 2001 LP, 98 TCM 630 (2009) (no disguised sale on contribution of cash for allocation of state income tax credits; government's claim that gain was triggered by partnership's sale of zero basis credits rejected), rev'd, 639 F3d 129 (4th Cir. 2011). Footnote 8 of the Fourth Circuit's opinion, in *Virginia Historic Tax Credit Fund,* tells the story: the Service sought to tax the difference between what the promoters paid to the property developers to get the credits, plus expenses, and what the investors paid for the credits. Since the promoters owned 99% of the partnership, the Service concluded that they should be taxed on the profit. Not an unreasonable assertion, which the Fourth Circuit wholeheartedly embraced.

See Route 231, LLC, 107 TCM 1155 (2014) (following the Fourth Circuit's decision in *Virginia Historic Tax Credit Fund* under *Golsen* rule), aff'd, 2016-1 USTC ¶ 50,143 (4th Cir. 2016); SWF Real Estate LLC, 109 TCM 1327 (2015) (same); Bosque Canyon Ranch, L.P., 110 TCM 48 (2015) (contribution of cash followed by real property distribution five months later treated as disguised sale); vacated and remanded, 2017-2 USTC ¶ 50,306 (5th Cir. 2017) (portion of transaction treated as sale sharply reduced; distributive share of charitable deduction cannot be included as consideration).

By comparison, in Gateway Hotel Partners, 107 TCM 1023 (2014), the Tax Court found, after a detailed factual analysis, that only a portion of one of three transfers of

Missouri historic preservation tax credits from a partnership to a partner constituted a taxable sale by the partnership. One of the two non-sale transfers occurred eighteen months after the transferee's capital contribution, within the two-year presumption period; the other was more than 24 months after the capital contribution, outside the presumption period. The Tax Court examined each of these transfers in the context of the "nonexhaustive" ten-factor list in Regulations § 1.707-3(b)(2), and found that only two of the factors supported disguised sale treatment: (1) factor nine, relating to disproportionately large distributions relative to a partner's profits interest, and (2) factor ten, relating to the lack of an obligation to return or repay distributed property. After weighing these two factors against the other eight, the Tax Court concluded that the transfers were not disguised sales. The transferee partner bore substantial entrepreneurial risk.

A single transaction may be, in part, a contribution or distribution subject to the nonrecognition rules of Subchapter K and, in part, a disguised sale. In that case, it is necessary to decide what part of the transaction is a disguised sale. *Bosque Canyon Ranch LP v. Commissioner*, 867 F3d 547 (5th Cir. 2017), rev'g TC Memo. 2015-130, is an example. In *Bosque Canyon*, a partnership acquired a tract of property. Under a plan, it developed a part of the property into lots and contributed a conservation easement on the remainder of the property, claiming a large charitable contribution. Under the plan, investors would contribute money for partnership interests and the right to receive a distribution of a lot at a later time, along with "appurtenant rights" to use common areas. In addition, the investors would receive allocations of the charitable contribution deduction. Both the Tax Court and the Fifth Circuit agreed that the transaction involved a disguised sale of lots by the partnership to the investor partners, but disagreed about the metes and bounds of the disguised sale. The Tax Court held that all of the investor partners' cash contributions was consideration paid to the partnership in disguised sales, even though the lots, valued separately, were worth much less than the allocable consideration. In the Tax Court's view, the contributions were disguised-sale payments for the appurtenant rights and tax deductions, as well as lots. The Fifth Circuit reversed, holding that only a small portion of the contributions were disguised-sale payments.

Page 14-17:

Add at end of subsection.

The proposed disguised-sale-of-partnership-interests Regulations have been withdrawn.[63.1] Thus, where two parties contribute property to a partnership and one of the partners receives a related distribution from the partnership, the transaction should be evaluated under the disguised-sale-of-property rules of Regulations § 1.707-3.

These rules, coupled with the Service's position in Revenue Ruling 99-5[63.2]—treating the sale of an interest in a disregarded entity as a sale of the underlying assets, followed by proportionate asset contributions to a partnership or, alternatively, as a contribution of assets and cash to a disregarded entity as multiple § 721 contributions—give taxpayers a choice as to how a partnership formation transaction is to be taxed. If sale treatment is desired, the seller may transfer the assets to a disregarded entity and sell an interest in the entity to the buyer for the agreed consideration.[63.3] If treatment under the dis-

---

[63.1] REG-149519-03 (Jan. 16, 2009); Ann. 2009-4, 2009-8 IRB 597.

[63.2] Rev. Rul. 99-5, 1995-1 CB 434.

[63.3] See Rev. Rul. 99-5, 1995-1 CB 434 (Situation 1).

guised-sale-of-property Regulations is preferred (potentially due to the favorable treatment of reimbursements of preformation expenditures, discussed at ¶ 14.02[3][b][iii][C] below), the seller may again transfer the assets to a disregarded entity, but the buyer would then transfer the consideration to the disregarded entity, which would, in turn, transfer the consideration to the seller.[63.4]

[63.4] See Rev. Rul. 99-5, 1995-1 CB 434 (Situation 2).

[ii] Unencumbered property contributions.

Add to note 66.

Section 708(b)(1)(B) has been repealed, effective as of December 31, 2017. 2017 Tax Cuts and Jobs Act, Pub. L. No. 115-97, § 13504(a) (Dec. 22, 2017).

Page 14-18:

Replace note 68 with the following.

[68] Reg. § 1.707-3(c)(1). See Superior Trading, LLC, 137 TC 70 (2011), motion for reh'g denied, 103 TCM 1604 (2012), aff'd, 728 F3d 676 (7th Cir. 2013), involving a pre-2004 distressed asset transaction. There was a partnership distribution of cash to the contributor of the distressed (i.e., built-in loss) assets within 10 months of the contribution of the assets to the partnership. Based on the evidence presented, Judge Wherry states that the court "may conclude from petitioner's failure to rebut this [2-year] presumption" that there was a disguised sale of the assets. However, he then discussed the step-transaction doctrine at great length, and concluded there was a sale of the assets under this doctrine. Query whether the judicial step-transaction doctrine continues (or should continue) to have independent vitality in this context after Congress has enacted detailed statutory rules and the Treasury has promulgated extensive Regulations to address the perceived abuse. See also Kenna Trading LLC, 143 TC 181 (2014) and Derringer Trading LLC, TC Memo. 2018-59 (2018) (each *Superior Trading*); Rovakat, LLC, 102 TCM 264 (2011) (losses from built-in loss transaction denied for lack of economic substance; structure of transaction relating to foreign currency loss "leads us to conclude that" there was either an actual or disguised sale), aff'd unpub. opinion, 2013-1 USTC ¶ 50,386 (3d Cir. 2013). Taxpayers who take the position that no sale has occurred notwithstanding this presumption are required to provide notice of their position to the Service unless the transfers from the partnership fall within one of the safe harbors relating to guaranteed payments, preferred returns, or operating cash flow distributions. Reg. § 1.707-3(c)(2). See generally infra ¶ 14.02[3][b][iii]. Buyuk, LLC, TC Memo. 2013-253, is another case in which the Tax Court determined that a disguised sale occurred in a distressed debt transaction. In *Buyuk*, the contribution and distribution were not simultaneous, but occurred within the two-year presumption period. The distribution was expected and highly likely to occur, however, there was no right to receive the distribution.

Page 14-19:

Add after carryover paragraph (ending with note callout 71).

The first case to fully analyze these factors is *United States v. G-1 Holdings, Inc.*[71.1] The court found that a contribution of assets followed by a nonrecourse borrowing against the partnership interest received constituted a disguised sale. The court found that, "in substance," the borrowing was incurred by the partnership and the borrowed funds were distributed by the partnership to the asset-contributing partner. The opinion focuses on the terms of the partnership agreement, which prevented the capital account of G-1 Holdings from falling below a specific amount and allocated partnership losses entirely to the credit-worthy counterparty, who was liable for any resulting deficit in its capital account. This minimum capital account enabled G-1 Holdings to secure nonrecourse financing in an amount nearly equal to the minimum balance. Absent this fact, a nonrecourse borrowing against a partnership interest should generally not trigger the disguised sale rules, although there is language in the court's opinion that may encourage the government to attack such transactions.

[71.1] United States v. G-1 Holdings, Inc., 2009 US Dist. Lexis 115850 (D. NJ 2009).

[iii] Special rules for guaranteed payments for capital, preferred returns, operating cash flow distributions, and reimbursements of preformation expenditures.

[C] *Reimbursements of preformation expenditures.*

Page 14-27:

Add to note 93.

Both private letter rulings and *Park Realty* deal with newly formed partnerships.

In first paragraph of subsection, add the following after note 93 callout.

The term "capital expenditure" generally has the same meaning for purposes of Regulations § 1.707-4(d) as it does for other purposes of the Code, except that it includes capital expenditures that the partner elects to deduct, but excludes deductible expenditures that the partner elects to capitalize.[93.1] Additionally, if expenditures are funded by a qualified liability assumed or taken subject to by the partnership in connection with a contribution of property, a transfer of money or other consideration to the contributing partner is not treated as reimbursement for such capital expenditure to the extent it exceeds the partner's

---

[93.1] Reg. § 1.707-4(d)(5).

share of the qualified liability allocable to the property under Regulations § 1.163-8T.[93.2]

[93.2] Reg. § 1.707-4(d)(4).

Add to note 94.

For transactions where all transfers occur after October 5, 2016, this rule is generally applied on a property-by-property basis. Reg. § 1.707-4(d)(1)(ii)(B). Apparently, after the aggregate amount of eligible preformation capital expenditure is computed on a property-by-property basis, all amounts received from the partnership may be exempted from disguised sale treatment up to the aggregate amount; the consideration is not first apportioned among the transferred assets. The example used to illustrate the rule computes the amount of eligible preformation capital expenditure and concludes that the eligible reimbursement is limited to this amount. Reg. § 1.707-4(d)(6) Example. There is no suggestion that the amount received from the partnership must first be allocated between the transferred assets. Indeed, the example strongly suggests that the contributing partner could receive an amount equal to the entire qualifying preformation capital expenditure free of disguised sale treatment, even though all of the capital expenditure was incurred with regard to only one of the transferred assets.

A partner may aggregate transferred property for purposes of applying the limitation to the extent that the total fair market value of the property is not greater than the lesser of (1) 10 percent of the total fair market value of all property transferred by the partner to the partnership, or (2) $1,000,000; provided that no single property may be aggregated if its fair market value exceeds one percent of the total fair market value of the aggregated property. Reg. § 1.707-4(d)(1)(ii)(B). This limited grant of aggregation permission is limited by the requirement that the partner consistently apply a reasonable aggregation method as well as an anti-abuse rule. Reg. §§ 1.707-4(d)(1)(ii)(B)(2), 1.707-4(d)(1)(ii)(B)(3).

[iv] Encumbered property contributions: qualified liabilities.

Page 14-28:

Add after first paragraph of subsection ending with note callout 98.

Prior to the issuance of Temporary Regulations in 2016, the disguised sale Regulations adopted the definitions and allocation framework of the § 752 Regulations, with certain modifications. Thus, "recourse liability" and "nonrecourse liability" generally had the same meanings as set forth in Regulations §§ 1.752-1(a)(1) and 1.752-1(a)(2), but also included any obligation that would be treated as a recourse or nonrecourse liability if it were treated as a liability for purposes of those provisions.[98.1] Recourse liabilities were allocated among the partners in accordance with the § 752 Regulations.[98.2] All nonrecourse lia-

---

[98.1] See Reg. §§ 1.707-5(a)(2)(i), 1.707-5(a)(2)(ii), prior to amendment by Temp. Reg. § 1.707-5T(a)(2).

[98.2] See Reg. § 1.707-5(a)(2)(i), prior to amendment by Temp. Reg. § 1.707-5T(a)(2).

bilities were (and are) treated as "excess nonrecourse liabilities" and allocated in accordance with Regulations § 1.752-3(a)(3).[98.3]

Proposed regulations issued in 2014 would have removed contingent liabilities from the scope of the definition of liability for purposes of the disguised sale rules.[98.4] In 2018, the 2014 Proposed Regulations were withdrawn, and replaced with new proposed regulations that would reinstate the prior rules with respect to contingent liabilities.[98.5]

In addition, Temporary Regulations § 1.707-5T(a)(2), issued on October 5, 2016, provides that, for the transactions in which all transfers occur on or after January 3, 2017, a partner's share of recourse liabilities is determined as if the liabilities were nonrecourse liabilities, except that such share may not exceed the partner's actual share of such liabilities under § 752. In response to Executive Order 13789,[98.6] the Treasury and the Service issued proposed regulations on June 19, 2018, that would withdraw the 2016 Temporary Regulations and reinstate the prior final Regulations. These 2018 Proposed Regulations would be effective 30 days following their publication as final Regulations; however, partnerships and their partners are permitted to apply these 2018 Proposed Regulations, rather than the 2016 Temporary Regulations, to any transaction with respect to which all transfers occur on or after January 3, 2017.[98.7]

[98.3] See Reg. § 1.707-5(a)(2)(ii), prior to amendment by Temp. Reg. § 1.707-5T(a)(2); Temp. Reg. § 1.707-5T(a)(2).

[98.4] See REG 119305-11, 79 Fed. Reg. 2826 (Jan. 29, 2014) (Preamble, "Explanation of Provisions," ¶¶ 5.1, 5.b).

[98.5] See REG 131186-17, 83 Fed. Reg. 28,397 (June 19, 2018).

[98.6] EO 13789, 82 Fed. Reg. 19,317 (Apr. 26, 2017).

[98.7] See Prop. Reg. § 1.707-9(a)(4) (2018).

[B] *Definitional matters.*

Add to note 104.

For transactions where all transfers occur on or after October 5, 2016, Regulations add a fifth category of qualified liability: Any liability incurred in connection with a trade or business in which property transferred to the partnership was used or held, but only if (1) it was not incurred in anticipation of the transfer and (2) all assets material to the continuation of that trade or business were included in the transfer. Reg. § 1.707-5(a)(6)(i)(E). The intent of this new category is to clarify that a liability is not required to encumber transferred property to be "qualified" if the property transferred is an entire trade or business. REG 119305-11, 79 Fed. Reg. 4826 (Jan. 29, 2014) (Preamble, "Explanation of Provisions," ¶ 3).

Any Category 2 or Category 5 liability incurred within two years of the transfer (or, if earlier, the date the partner agrees in writing to make the transfer) is presumed to have been incurred in anticipation of the transfer and must be disclosed in accordance with Regulations § 1.707-8 if reported as a qualified liability. Reg. § 1.707-5(a)(7)(ii).

The treatment of Regulations § 1.752-7 contingent liabilities is uncertain; the Temporary Regulations reserve on this issue. Temp. Reg. § 1.707-5T(a)(2)(ii). The Preamble to Treasury Decision 9788 (Oct. 5, 2016) notes that, in many cases, contingent liabilities will be qualified liabilities. See also Preamble to Proposed Regulations § 1.707-5, REG-13186-17, 83 Fed. Reg. 28,397 (June 19, 2018) (to similar effect).

Page 14-30:

Add to note 105.

In a situation in which an assumed recourse liability, which exceeded the fair market value of contributed encumbered property, was immediately extinguished when the creditor simultaneously contributed its position to the partnership, the Service concluded that the disguised sale rules did not apply to the extent that the partnership recognized discharge of indebtedness income under § 108(e)(8) and allocated the income to the property-contributing partner. See Priv. Ltr. Rul. 201103018 (Sept. 23, 2010).

Add to note 106.

For purposes of determining whether a liability is qualified, the Regulations (1) clarify that liabilities of a lower-tier partnership (LTP) that are treated as liabilities of an upper-tier partnership (UTP) are treated as incurred by the UTP on the same day they are incurred by the LTP (see Reg. § 1.707-5(b)(1)), and (2) provide that liabilities transferred from an LTP to a UTP that become liabilities of the UTP under Regulations § 1.752-4(a) would become qualified liabilities of the UTP to the extent they would have been qualified if they had been assumed or taken subject to by the UTP as part of a transfer of all of the LTP's property. Reg. § 1.707-5(e)(2); see REG 119305-11, 79 Fed. Reg. 4826 (Jan. 29, 2014) (Preamble, "Explanation of Provisions," ¶ 5) (appropriate to treat LTP as an aggregate for this purpose).

Add at end of subsection.

Similarly, qualified liabilities incurred by a person other than the contributing partner are treated as incurred by the contributing partner to the extent such partner assumed or took property subject to the liability from the person who incurred the liability in a nonrecognition transaction described in § 351, § 381(a), § 721, or § 731.[106.1]

[106.1] Reg. § 1.707-5(a)(8).

[v] Encumbered property contributions: nonqualified liabilities.

Page 14-30:

In first paragraph of subsection, replace sentence ending with note callout 108 with the following.

For transactions where any transfer occurs prior to January 3, 2017, a partner's share of a recourse liability is determined in accordance with the § 752 Regulations.[108] For transactions where all transfers occur on or after January 3,

---

[108] Reg. § 1.707-5(a)(2)(i) (2016). For such time period, the § 752 Regulations also are used to determine whether a particular liability is recourse or nonrecourse. Id. See CCA 200246014 (Aug. 8, 2002) (corporate partner's guarantee of nonqualified debt disre-

2017, a partner's share of recourse liabilities is determined in the same manner as such partner's share of nonrecourse liabilities, except that such share is limited to the partner's share of such liabilities under § 752 (thus effectively allocating to the partner the lesser of its recourse or nonrecourse shares of the liability).[108.1]

---

garded under anti-abuse rule in Regulations § 1.752-2(j) because partner "severely undercapitalized," transforming recourse debt into nonqualified debt; partners' agreement to allocate "tier three" (excess) nonrecourse debt disregarded because not consistent with any significant allocation of profit or loss; allocation of debt based on general partnership profit-sharing ratios triggers disguised sale upon distribution to guarantor partner funded in large part with borrowing proceeds).

[108.1] Temp. Reg. § 1.707-5T(a)(2). The Treasury has announced that it is considering revoking these Temporary Regulations and reinstating the prior regulations. See EO 13789 (Oct. 2, 2017). A literal reading of the limitation of the Temporary Regulations (to the "partner's share of the partnership liability under § 752 and applicable regulations") would apply tiers one and two of Regulations § 1.752-3(a)(3) to a transferor partner, but only adversely. For example, where 100 percent of a nonrecourse liability was allocated to a partner other than the transferor partner under tiers one and two of Regulations § 1.752-3(a)(3), the transferor partner's share of a partnership liability for disguised sale purposes would also be zero. This interpretation is inappropriate as these two rules have nothing to do with disguised sales. While the Treasury has indicated informally that the language of Temporary Regulations § 1.707-5T(a)(2) is not intended to make tiers one and two relevant, a formal correction would be advisable. See Madara, Matthew, "Official Gives Details on Corrections to Disguised Sale Rules," 2017 TNT 16-2 (Jan. 26, 2017).

Page 14-31:

Add at end of second paragraph of subsection (ending with note callout 112).

For liabilities incurred, taken subject to, or assumed by a partnership on or after October 5, 2016, Regulations § 1.752-3(a)(3) requires the partnership utilize only the general method of allocating excess nonrecourse liabilities (i.e., allocation in proportion to the partners' interests in partnership profits, taking into account all facts and circumstances) in allocating nonrecourse (and recourse) liabilities for purposes of the disguised sale rules.[112.1]

[112.1] Reg. § 1.752-3(a)(3) (third to last sentence).

Page 14-32:

In third paragraph of subsection, replace first and second sentences (ending with note callout 113) with the following.

The Regulations include an anti-abuse rule pursuant to which a partner's post-contribution share of any qualified or nonqualified liability is decreased to the extent it is anticipated that (1) the partner's share of the liability will be reduced after the partnership assumes or takes subject to the liability and (2) the anticipated reduction is not subject to the entrepreneurial risks of partnership operations. This rule applies only where the reduction is part of a plan that has as one of its principal purposes the minimization of the amount of the liability that would otherwise be treated as sale proceeds.[113]

---

[113] Reg. § 1.707-5(a)(3).

[vi] Liability assumptions in connection with partnership mergers.

Page 14-34:

Add new note 119.1 at end of last sentence of subsection.

[119.1] Regulations proposed in 2014 would have provided for liability netting in Assets-Over mergers and consolidations. Prop. Reg. § 1.707-5(f) (2014). However, the Treasury did not include the provision in the final Regulations issued in 2016, determining that such a rule was unnecessary given the adoption of the "step-in-the-shoes" rule of Regulations § 1.707-5(a)(8) in the context of transactions governed by §§ 721 and 731. See TD 9787 (Oct. 14, 2016).

[vii] Debt-financed distributions.

Page 14-34:

Add to note 120.

For transactions where all transfers occur on or after October 5, 2016, liabilities of a lower-tier partnership (LTP) that are treated as liabilities of an upper-tier partnership (UTP) are treated as incurred by the UTP on the same day they are incurred by the LTP. Reg. § 1.707-5(b)(1). The debt-financed distribution rules are applied before application of the rules in Regulations § 1.707-4. See Reg. § 1.707-5(b)(3). The application of these ordering rules as well as the general application of the Regulations are illustrated by a series of Examples in Regulations § 1.707-5(f). (New Example 11 illustrates the operation of the ordering rule.)

Add to note 122.

For transactions where all transfers occur on or after October 5, 2016, a subsequent reduction of a partner's share of a liability is taken into account immediately after the partnership incurs the liability if (1) at the time the partnership incurs the liability it is anticipated that the partner's share of the liability that is allocable to a transfer of money or other consideration to the partner will be reduced; (2) the anticipated reduction is not subject to the entrepreneurial risks of partnership operations; and (3) the reduction is part of a plan one of the principal purposes of which is minimizing the extent to which the distribution to the partner is treated as part of a disguised sale. If the reduction occurs within two years of the time the liability is incurred, the reduction is presumed to be anticipated and must be disclosed pursuant to Regulations § 1.707-8. See Prop. Reg. § 1.707-7(b)(2)(iii) (2014).

Page 14-35:

Add at end of subsection.

The potential for deferral through this technique, as well as one of the pit-falls in utilizing the technique, is illustrated in *Canal Corporation*,[122.1] where the taxpayer attempted to defer $524 million of capital gain through a lever-aged distribution transaction with the purchaser of its assets. The deferral was lost when the allocation of debt to the distributee-partner was denied under the anti-abuse rule of Regulations § 1.752-2(j).

[122.1] Canal Corp., 135 TC 199 (2010). See also ILM 201324013 (June 14, 2013) (cit-ing *Canal*, and applying a similar analysis to invoke Regulations § 1.752-2(j) to disregard an indemnity in a debt-financed distribution).

[ix] Disclosure rules.

Page 14-36:

Add new note 128.1 at end of list item 1.

[128.1] Notably absent from the list of exempted distributions are those that are reim-bursements for pre-formation capital expenditures. It seems illogical to require disclosure of amounts that are not treated as part of a disguised sale while not requiring disclosure for preferred returns and operating cash flow distributions that are only presumed to not be part of a disguised sale, but it is difficult to conclude otherwise.

Page 14-37:

In last paragraph of subsection, replace first sentence with the following.

The Service issued, and then withdrew, proposed regulations that would extend the disclosure period from two to seven years.[132] The extended disclosure pe-riod rules were part of the ill-fated disguised-sale-of-a-partnership-interest reg-ulation package, discussed at ¶ 14.02[3][b][xi]. The package was withdrawn because the disguised sale portion was severely criticized. The extended dis-closure period rules are worthy of discussion, as they may reappear as part of another project.

---

[132] Notice of Proposed Rulemaking, 69 Fed. Reg. 68,838 (Nov. 26, 2004), 2004-2 CB 1009. The proposed regulations were issued in response to a report of the Joint Committee on Taxation. See Staff of Joint Comm. on Taxation, 108th Cong., 1st Sess., Report of In-vestigation of Enron Corporation and Related Entities Regarding Federal Tax and Com-pensation Issues, and Policy Recommendations 29 (Feb. 2003). The proposed regulations were withdrawn by REG-149519-03 (Jan. 16, 2009); Ann. 2009-4, 2009-8 IRB 597.

[xi] Disguised sales of partnership interests.

Pages 14-40–14-47:

After first three paragraphs of ¶ 14.02[3][b][xi], replace the remaining discussion in this subsection with the following.

This feeling was confirmed in 2009 when the Treasury Department withdrew the regulations proposed in 2004, stating that:

> The Treasury Department and the IRS will continue to study this area and may issue guidance in the future. Until new guidance is issued, any determination of whether transfers between a partner or partners and a partnership is a transfer of a partnership interest will be based on the statutory language, guidance provided in legislative history, and case law.[147]

Despite the promise to continuing studying this area and the attempt to restore the law to the status quo ante, it seems unlikely that there will be any significant regulatory activity in this area in the near future. Making lemonade (or even sense) out of this lemon of a statute is obviously a daunting and labor-intensive task that may better be left undone. Nevertheless, the project is on the Priority Guidance Plan.[147.1]

---

[147] REG-149519-03 (Jan. 16, 2009); Ann. 2009-4, 2009-8 IRB 597.

[147.1] https://www.irs.gov/pub/irs-utl/2019-2020_pgp_4th_quarter_update.pdf.

[4] Services by Partners

[a] Scope of Section 707(a)

Page 14-47:

Add to note 184.

In Herman v. United States, 2017-1 USTC ¶ 50,260 (Ct. Cl. 2017), the taxpayer became a partner in a U.K. partnership for U.K. tax purposes, but was indirectly compensated by its U.S. sponsor, Paulson & Co., an S corporation. She received her bonus in 2009, the year in which she paid her U.K. taxes. The Service claimed the bonus year was part of her 2008 distributive share, creating a mismatch between the income and the foreign tax credits. The court found that the bonus was for services outside her capacity as a partner in the U.K. partnership.

Page 14-51:

Add to note 189.

Nevertheless, the U.S. district court, in United States v. G-1 Holdings, Inc., 2009 US Dist. Lexis 115850 (D. NJ 2009), carefully considered four of the six factors in a disguised sale case under § 707(a)(2)(B). The court found that the contributed property had been properly valued, which should have moved the analysis out of the allocation-distribution scheme of § 707(a)(2)(A). It did not, leading the court to dismiss the taxpayer's nontax business motives for entering into the transactions (factor four above). This aspect of the G-1 Holdings decision seems misguided.

[b] Collateral Consequences of Section 707(a) Treatment

Page 14-55:

Add at end of subsection.

The Service has reaffirmed its position that "bone fide members of a partnership are not employees of the partnership" for purposes of FICA, FUTA, and wage withholding, and if a partner provides services to the partnership as an independent contractor, the partner is viewed as a self-employed individual, and not as an employee.[201.1]

[201.1] Preamble to TD 9766 (May 4, 2016). Comments were requested as to whether exceptions should be made for partnership employees who obtain small ownership interests as employee compensation awards, and how to deal with tiered partnership structures.

[c] Nonqualified Deferred Compensation Plans: Section 409A

Page 14-56:

In note 202, replace last sentence and Proposed Regulations cite with the following.

TD 9321, 2007-19 IRB 1123, 72 Fed. Reg. 19,234, 19,243–19,244 (Apr. 17, 2007). The Regulations are silent on the application of § 409A to partnerships. Reg. § 1.409A-1(b)(7) ("Arrangements between partnerships and partners. [Reserved]").

Add to note 206.

Limited transition relief has been granted. See TD 9321, 2007-1 CB 1123, 72 Fed. Reg. 19,234, 19,272 (Apr. 17, 2007); Notice 2007-78, 2007-2 CB 780, as revoked and superseded by Notice 2007-86, 2007-2 CB 990.

Add new ¶ 14.02[4][d].

[d] Proposed Regulations § 1.707-2 [New]

On July 23, 2015, in an effort to crack down on what some perceived as abusive fee waiver provisions for private equity firms and other investment funds, the Treasury issued Proposed Regulations under § 707(a)(2)(A), which seek to draw lines between payments received by partners in exchange for services performed in their partner capacity and those made in exchange for services performed in their non-partner capacity.

The transaction that drew the concern of the Treasury generally worked as follows. In many investment funds, the management team is generally entitled to two types of payments: (1) a management fee designed to fund operations of the investment manager equal to 2 percent of committed capital, and (2) a "carried interest" consisting of 20 percent of the profits earned with respect to the investment. Many funds structure these payments for receipt by separate but related entities: that is, (1) a general partner that invests into the fund and holds the carried interest, and (2) a related management company that is not a partner in the fund, but is entitled to receive the 2 percent management fee.

Prior to the enactment of the Proposed Regulations, many fund agreements provided the management company with the option of "waiving" its right to its management fee in exchange for an increased share of partnership profits, issued either to it or to the related general partner. The service provider would take the position that the increased interest in partnership profits was a tax-free issuance of a profits interest pursuant to Revenue Procedure 93-27,[206.1] and so the ultimate receipt of proceeds from such interest was long-term capital gain (to the extent its allocable share of fund profits was so characterized). The Proposed Regulations seek to identify when these transactions are effective to create the above-described results sought by the investment funds and when they constitute disguised payments for services under § 707(a)(2)(A).

The Proposed Regulations would generally rely upon the five factors identified by Congress in the legislative history to § 707(a)(2)(A) and would also add a sixth. Neither the existence nor absence of any of these factors would be determinative, however, of whether an arrangement is treated as a disguised payment for services.

The following factors identified within the Proposed Regulations would not be exclusive, leaving considerable concern for the expansive reading of provisions that seem intended to effect a narrow result.

"Significant entrepreneurial risk" factor. As reflected in the legislative history, the presence or absence of significant entrepreneurial risk with respect to an allocation of income would be the most significant factor in determining whether a disguised payment has occurred. In fact, the Notice of Proposed Rulemaking underlying the Proposed Regulations requests comments as to whether there are any circumstances under which an allocation that lacks significant entrepreneurial risk should nevertheless be characterized as a distributive share under § 704(b).[206.2] The Proposed Regulations' description of this factor diverges significantly from the legislative history, however, focusing not on whether the payment itself lacks significant entrepreneurial risk in a vacuum, but on whether the payment lacks significant entrepreneurial risk relative to the overall entrepreneurial risk of the partnership.[206.3]

Presumably, the Proposed Regulations' revision to this factor is intended to distinguish interests in partnerships with low-risk investments from those arrangements designed to limit a service partner's risk in order to increase the certainty of such partner's return. But, it is not clear that this change is appropriate. Relative certainty may be just as risky to the provider of services as empirical uncertainty, and a partner who provides services in exchange for the first 10 percent of gross income from a speculative oil play is exposed to significant empirical uncertainty with respect to its payment, despite the certainty

---

[206.1] Rev Proc 93-27, 1993-2 CB 343.

[206.2] Notice of Proposed Rulemaking, 80 Fed. Reg. 43,652 (July 23, 2015).

[206.3] Prop. Reg. § 1.707-2(c)(1) (2015).

of payment relative to the other partners. Conversely, a partner who renders services in exchange for a 10 percent profits interest in a partnership holding high-quality debt instruments may have certainty of payment, but relative entrepreneurial risk.

The significant entrepreneurial risk factor is, itself, determined by a multi-sub-factor test, the presence of any one sub-factor of which would create a presumption that an arrangement lacks significant entrepreneurial risk. Such presumption would then be rebuttable by facts and circumstances establishing the presence of significant entrepreneurial risk by clear and convincing evidence.[206.4] A presumption is established by the presence of any one of the following sub-factors:

1. A capped allocation of partnership income if the cap is reasonably expected to apply in most years;
2. An allocation for one or more years under which the service provider's share of income is reasonably certain;
3. An allocation of gross income;
4. An allocation that is predominately fixed in amount, is reasonably determinable under all the facts and circumstances, or is designed to assure that sufficient net profits are highly likely to be available to make the allocation to the service provider;[206.5] or
5. An arrangement in which a service provider waives its right to receive payment for the future performance of services in a manner that is non-binding or fails to timely notify the partnership and its partners of the waiver and its terms.

While the first four of these sub-factors generally track the legislative history of § 707(a)(2)(A),[206.6] the final, fifth sub-factor does not and was clearly included to target the practice of fund managers who waive their rights to management fees in exchange for increased interests in their funds.

Remaining factors identified by legislative history. The Proposed Regulations would identify as relevant to whether an arrangement constitutes a payment for services the remaining four factors identified in the legislative history:

1. Whether a partner's interest is transitory or continuing;

[206.4] Prop. Reg. § 1.707-2(c)(1) (2015).

[206.5] For example, where a service provider receives a priority allocation of partnership net gain and controls the partnership's ability to revalue assets as well as the valuation of those assets, such allocation would be "designed to assure that sufficient net profits are highly likely to be available to make the allocation to the service provider." Prop. Reg. § 1.707-2(d) Example 3(iii) (2015).

[206.6] Senate Comm. on Finance, 98th Cong., 2d Sess., Deficit Reduction Act of 1984, S. Prt. No. 169, 223 (Comm. Print 1984). Note, however, that the legislative history allows that gross income allocations may "in very limited instances represent an entrepreneurial return." Presumably, such an instance would rebut the presumption created by Proposed Regulations § 1.707-2(c)(1)(iii) (2015).

2. Whether the time frame of receipt of payment under an allocation and distribution scheme mimics that which would be expected in a payment scenario;

3. Whether a service provider became a partner primarily to obtain tax benefits unavailable outside of the partner context; and

4. Whether the service provider's interest in general partnership profits is small in comparison to the allocation and distribution in question.[206.7]

The new, sixth factor. The Proposed Regulations would add a sixth factor to those identified in the legislative history—specifically, whether the "arrangement provides for different allocations or distributions with respect to different services received, the services are provided either by one person or by persons that are related under sections 707(b) or 267(b), and the terms of the differing allocations or distributions are subject to levels of entrepreneurial risk that vary significantly."[206.8] This factor is clearly aimed at identifying payments made in lieu of fees historically earned and paid to fund managers as disguised payments for services,[206.9] but it is not clear why these facts are necessarily indicative of a payment rather than a partnership interest. For example, if a father and daughter form a law partnership, and the father, as the principal generator of business, receives an interest in all partnership revenue, while the daughter receives an interest only in the partnership revenue from services rendered to those clients that she originates or bills, is the daughter's interest a disguised payment for services? If an entity manages funds with differing levels of risk—one fund providing mezzanine-type financing through preferred equity investments and the other providing true equity investment—and both funds invest into an operating partnership in exchange for preferred and common equity, respectively, are payments to the mezzanine-type fund disguised payments for services? Neither of these fact patterns is particularly indicative of a disguised payment for services. The Proposed Regulations appear to have ample ammunition to fire at the management fee-waiver situation—the new, proposed sixth factor may well be unnecessary.

The Proposed Regulations' Examples. While the rules of the Proposed Regulations generally mimic the legislative history's guidance, practitioners will look to the examples contained in Proposed Regulations § 1.707-2(d) for guidance as to the application of these rules in real life contexts. Examples 1 and 2 replicate examples provided by Congress in the legislative history to § 707(a)(2)(B), while Examples 3 through 6 provide new guidance on the operation of the Proposed Regulations in the context of management fee waivers.

[206.7] Prop. Reg. §§ 1.707-2(c)(2) through 1.707-2(c)(5) (2015).

[206.8] Prop. Reg. § 1.707-2(c)(6).

[206.9] The Notice of Proposed Rulemaking underlying the Proposed Regulations illustrates the factor with a standard general partner/management company structure outlined in the text above. See Notice of Proposed Rulemaking, 80 Fed. Reg. 43,652 (July 23, 2015).

The following four principles can be gleaned from these six examples:

1. The presence or absence of significant entrepreneurial risk would be the primary driver of whether an agreement constitutes a disguised payment for services.

2. An interest in partnership net profits would generally not be viewed as lacking significant entrepreneurial risk;[206.10] however, where the allocation of net gain is not measured over the life of the partnership, but is instead measured over a shorter period *and* the partner (or a related party) controls the timing of any gain recognition, the allocation may constitute a disguised payment for services.[206.11]

3. The waiver of a right to receive a payment would not necessarily turn the arrangement into a disguised payment as long as the partnership interest received in exchange satisfies the "significant entrepreneurial risk" test.[206.12]

4. While not stated, the Regulations' examples imply that the absence of a "clawback obligation" (which generally requires a distributee to return funds to the partnership to the extent necessary return thresholds are not met over the life of the partnership) may cause the arrangement to lack significant entrepreneurial risk.[206.13]

Effective date. The Proposed Regulations would be effective for arrangements entered into or modified on or after the date the final Regulations are published. The preamble to the Proposed Regulations cautions, however, that for arrangements entered into prior to that time, the Proposed Regulations "generally reflect Congressional intent as to which arrangements are appropriately treated as disguised payments for services."[206.14]

[206.10] See Prop. Reg. § 1.707-2(d) Examples (3)(ii), (4)(ii), (5)(iii), (6)(iii) (2015).

[206.11] See Prop. Reg. § 1.707-2(d) Examples (3)(iii), (3)(iv) (2015).

[206.12] See Prop. Reg. § 1.707-2(d) Example (6) (2015).

[206.13] See Prop. Reg. § 1.707-2(d) Examples (3)(ii), (5), (6) (2015).

[206.14] Notice of Proposed Rulemaking, 80 Fed. Reg. 43,652 (July 23, 2015).

¶ 14.03 PARTNERS ACTING IN THEIR CAPACITIES AS PARTNERS: SECTION 707(c) GUARANTEED PAYMENTS

[3] Computation of Partnership Income and Partners' Distributive Shares

Page 14-66:

Add at end of subsection (following note callout 234).

Proposed Regulations, issued in 2015, would change the results described in Examples 14-9 through 14-11.[234.1] These Proposed Regulations would change Example 2 of Regulations § 1.707-1(c) to indicate that any minimum payment required to be made to a partner should be treated as a guaranteed payment regardless of the net income of the partnership. Thus, in Example 14-9, if the *CD* partnership had $60,000 of net income for a taxable year, partner *C* would be entitled to $18,000, $10,000 of which would be treated as a guaranteed payment and $8,000 of which would be *C*'s distributive share. If *CD* had $20,000 of net income for a taxable year, the $10,000 received by *C* would similarly be treated as a guaranteed payment. The issues raised in Examples 14-10 and 14-11 would thus no longer exist.

The change that would be effected by finalization of Proposed Regulations § 1.707-1(c), Example 2 (2015) was necessary, in the eyes of the Treasury, to ensure consistency between Proposed Regulations § 1.707-2 (2015), which mandates the existence of significant entrepreneurial risk in order for an allocation to be treated as a partner's distributive share, and the guaranteed payment rules of § 707(c).[234.2] A minimum distribution like that described in Example 2 of Regulations § 1.707-1(c) would, in the eyes of the Treasury, minimize a partner's entrepreneurial risk.[234.3] It is unclear whether the Treasury intended that the modification apply to partners contributing capital, but this appears to be the result.

[234.1] Prop. Reg. § 1.707-1(c) Example (2) (2015).

[234.2] Notice of Proposed Rulemaking, 80 Fed. Reg. 43,652 (July 23, 2015).

[234.3] While it is conceivable that a partnership would be economically distressed enough to subject even a minimum payment to significant entrepreneurial risk, the Proposed Regulations, which assume significant net operating income for the partnership, do not provide such an example.

[4] Guaranteed Payments for Capital and Other Nondeductible Expenditures

Page 14-68:

Add to note 243.

One taxpayer attempted to recharacterize obvious guaranteed payments for services as guaranteed payments for capital in order to avoid self-employment tax with respect to such payments. The Tax Court rejected this approach where the recipient provided services, but no capital to the partnership. Seismic Support Servs., LLC, TC Memo. 2014-78.

[5] Transfers of Property as Guaranteed Payments: Gain or Loss Recognition by the Partnership

Page 14-69:

Add to second paragraph of subsection.

The Servive agrees with this view.[247.1]

[247.1] Rev. Rul. 2007-1 CB 1426.

Add to second paragraph of subsection..

The Service agrees with this view.247.1[247.1]

[247.1] Rev. Rul. 2007-40, 2007-1 CB 1426.

Page 14-71:

Replace list item 2 with the following.

2. For all other purposes, the payment is viewed as a distributive share of partnership income. Accordingly, (a) the basis of the distribu-tee-partner's partnership interest is increased by the amount of his distributive share (i.e., the market value of the property);[249.1] (b) the distributed property itself takes a carryover basis in his hands under § 732; and (c) under § 733(2), the basis of the distributee-partner's partnership interest is decreased by the amount of the § 732 carryover basis. The partnership realizes neither gain nor loss on the distribution of the property under § 731(b).

[249.1] But see CCA 201741018 (Oct. 13, 2017), which states "guaranteed payment does not affect the recipient's basis in its partnership interest." This assertion is more than questionable, as it leads to the conclusion that a right to a guaranteed payment is a separate asset with its own tax basis. Consider the sale of a partnership interest with the right to an accrued but unpaid guaranteed payment—since the selling partner has included the guaranteed payment in income, it must have the associated basis. There is nothing in the scheme of Subchapter K that creates this basis other than through increasing the basis of the sold partnership interest. Also, consider the case of a retiring partner receiving a § 736(a)(2) guaranteed payment—presumably, she treats the payment right as part of her partnership interest.

[6] Interaction of Section 707(c) and Other Code Provisions

[b] Employment Tax and Withholding Provisions

Add to note 258.

The Service and Treasury have reaffirmed their position in Revenue Ruling 69-184, 1969-1 CB 256. Preamble to TD 9766 (May 4, 2016). See also Reg. § 301.7701-2(c)(2)(iv)(C)(2) (partner in partnership that owns a disregarded entity subject to same self-employment tax rules as partner in partnership that does not own a disregarded entity).

Page 14-73:

Add to note 259.

See Lauren A. Howell, 104 TCM 519 (2012) (partners bound by partnership return's characterization of payments to partner as § 707(c) guaranteed payments; payments subject to employment tax under § 1402(a)(13)).

Page 14-74:

Add at end of subsection.

Proposed Regulations § 1.1411-4(g)(10) confirms generally that a § 707(c) guaranteed payment for services is not included in "net investment income," subject to the 3.8% Medicare contribution tax, whether or not such guaranteed payment qualifies as self-employment income.[261.1] These proposed regulations would also confirm that guaranteed payments for the use of capital are included in net investment income under § 1411.

[261.1] REG-130843-13, 78 Fed. Reg. 72,451 (Dec. 2, 2013). The tax is 3.8% of the lesser of (1) "net investment income" or (2) the excess of "modified adjusted gross income" over the applicable "threshold amount" (i.e., $250,000 for joint returns and $200,000 for single filers). See § 1411; REG-130507-11, 77 Fed. Reg. 72,612 (Dec. 5, 2012).

[h] Uniform Capitalization Rules

Page 14-78:

Add after first, and only, sentence of subsection (ending with note callout 281).

Conversely, a guaranteed payment for services is treated as employee compensation for purposes of the general capitalization rules of § 263, and therefore not subject to capitalization, at least in the context of the acquisition of an intangible.[281.1]

[281.1] Reg. § 1.263(a)-4.

[i] Guaranteed Payments as Substitutes for Interest Payments

Page 14-78:

Replace note 282 with the following:

[282] See Reg. § 1.163(j)-6(e)(2) (guaranteed payment not interest per se, but often treated as interest under anti-avoidance rule); Reg. § 1.267A-5(b)(5)(ii)(B) (similar approach taken under § 267A hybrid transaction/hybrid entity rules).

¶ 14.04 SPECIAL RULES FOR TRANSACTIONS BETWEEN PARTNERSHIPS AND PARTNERS OR RELATED PERSONS

[3] Loss Transactions With Related Nonpartners: Section 267(a)(1)

Page 14-87:

Add to note 312.

See Kahn, "Sales Between a Partnership and Non-Partners," 136 Tax Notes 827 (2012) (arguing for invalidity of regulation requiring proportionate loss disallowance).

Family Partnership Rules

Page 15-2:

Add new ¶ 15.00 at beginning of Chapter 15 (and before ¶ 15.01).

¶ 15.00 REPEAL OF SECTION 704(E)(1) CREATES UNCERTAINTY REGARDING THE DEFINITION OF PARTNERSHIPS AND PARTNERS [NEW]

[NOTE: In this Chapter 15, there are several instances in which former §
704(e)(1) is discussed and its impact analyzed. Former § 704(e)(1) was re-
pealed, as discussed below, effective for partnership taxable years beginning in
2016. For partnership taxable years beginning before then, the existing discus-
sion of former § 704(e)(1) in this chapter remains relevant to the extent the re-

peal can be interpreted as a change to, rather than a clarification of, pre-2016 law; the following discussion addresses, among other things, this concern.]

The Bipartisan Budget Act of 2015 (BBA 2015)[0.1] repealed former § 704(e)(1), and renumbered former §§ 704(e)(2) and 704(e)(3) as §§ 704(e)(1) and 704(e)(2), respectively. These changes are effective for partnership taxable years beginning in 2016. Prior to its repeal, former § 704(e)(1) read as follows:

> A person shall be recognized as a partner for purposes of this subtitle if he owns a capital interest in a partnership in which capital is a material income producing factor, whether or not such interest was derived by purchase or gift from any other person.

For reasons explained below, the most immediate impact of the repeal of former § 704(e)(1) is likely to be creation of a zone of uncertainty about when preferred equity investments in partnerships (the equivalent of nonparticipating preferred stock in the corporate context) will be recognized as partnership interests. The implications are, however, broader and can only be understood in the context of the history of the development of the definition of the terms "partnership" and "partner." This history is chronicled in detail throughout Chapter 15, as well as Chapter 3.

At the same time, former § 704(e)(1) was repealed by BBA 2015, Congress added the following sentence to § 761(b):

> In the case of a capital interest in a partnership in which capital is a material income-producing factor, whether a person is a partner with respect to such interest shall be determined without regard to whether such interest was derived by gift from any other person.

It is far from clear what Congress intended to accomplish with the enactment of this sentence matched with the repeal of former § 704(e)(1), but it seems to have thought that it was enacting a substantive change in the law because it attached a revenue estimate of about $1.9 billion. There are no committee reports, however, to explain its thinking and analysis.

Furthermore, since the government had won both the *Castle Harbour* and *Chemtech* cases (discussed in this chapter, as well as at ¶ 3.00), despite the existence of former § 704(e)(1), it is not clear why repealing § 704(e)(1) attracted a material revenue estimate, unless Congress was under the impression that former § 704(e)(1) mandated that nonparticipating capital interests be recognized as partnership interests and wanted to change that result.

[0.1] Bipartisan Budget Act of 2015, § 1102(c), Pub. L. No. 114-74 (Nov. 2, 2015) (hereinafter "BBA 2015").

Following enactment, the Staff of the Joint Committee on Taxation provided an explanation (in the "Blue Book") that raises as many questions as it purports to answer.[0.2]

The Blue Book refers to the district court's opinion on remand from the first appeal of *Castle Harbour*, in which the district court held that former § 704(e)(1) provided an alternative test to the *Culbertson* intent test. The Blue Book says that Congress sought to affirm that there is only one test for determining partner status. The Blue Book, however, does not state that the Second Circuit correctly expressed that unitary test in its first *Castle Harbour* opinion, and it does not even cite *Chemtech* or *Southgate*. Therefore, the Blue Book is agnostic on the specific question whether material upside and downside profit and loss participation is necessary for partner status or determining whether an interest is a partnership interest.

Ironically, the only guidance that Blue Book offers regarding the intended unitary test for partner status or whether an interest is a partnership interest is the following sentence that describes what Congress did *not* intend:

> The provision is not intended to change the principle that the real owner of a capital interest is to be taxed on the income from the interest, regardless of the motivation behind or the means of the transfer of the interest.[0.3]

This is a virtual restatement of former § 704(e)(1), which required that the real owner of a capital interest in a partnership be recognized as a partner. If Congress did not intend to allow courts to disregard some capital investments as valid partnership interests, then the repeal of former § 704(e)(1) changed little or nothing.

Accordingly, the implications of former § 704(e)(1)'s repeal seem to be:

1. Repeal increases the likelihood that non-participating partnership equity interests will be disregarded as partnership interests, at least in those cases where the government wants to press the point.
2. Repeal leaves unanswered the question how much entrepreneurial profit and loss a preferred interest must carry in order to clear the participation bar (if there is a participation bar).
3. Repeal provides no guidance as to how a capital interest that is not a partnership interest *and* not debt should be taxed.

It seems clear that, in repealing former § 704(e)(1), Congress failed to reconcile the apparent conflict between the check-a-box Regulations, which clearly adopt a single test for a business entity that can elect to be treated as a partnership or corporation for income tax purposes, and the test for partnership status that the courts derived from the commercial law of partnership and

---

[0.2] Joint Committee on Taxation, General Explanation of Tax Legislation Enacted in 2015 (JCS-1-16), p 83 (Mar. 2016).

[0.3] Joint Committee on Taxation, General Explanation of Tax Legislation Enacted in 2015 (JCS-1-16), p. 84 (Mar. 2016).

which has no plausible application to corporations. (In fact, if the Service and the courts view the repeal of former § 704(e)(1) as affirming the use of a partnership-only test based on *Culbertson* and commercial partnership law, the repeal will exacerbate the already irreconcilable gap between the business entity regulations and cases such as *Castle Harbour* and *Chemtech.*)

Ironically, the fact that former § 704(e)(1) has been repealed without any statement of approval of the specific tests applied by the courts could lead to the sensible conclusion that, under the check-a-box Regulations, there is a single test for a partnership that is the same test as the test for a corporation. That conclusion, however, would not square with a $2 billion revenue estimate.

The authors of the repeal of former § 704(e)(1) were apparently oblivious to the fact that the check-a-box Regulations adopt a unitary definition of the term business entity that applies equally to partnerships and corporations. The courts in *Castle Harbour* and *Chemtech* were unconcerned that the unitary test they derived in *Culbertson*, sourced from then-existing commercial law, cannot be reconciled with tax regulations applying a single unitary test (the business entity test) to determine arrangements that can be taxed as either partnerships or corporations.

¶ 15.01 DEVELOPMENT OF THE FAMILY PARTNERSHIP RULES

Page 15-2:

Add before first paragraph of subsection.

[NOTE: In this section, there are several instances in which former § 704(e)(1) is discussed and its impact analyzed. Former § 704(e)(1) was repealed, as discussed principally in ¶ 3.00 as well as ¶ 15.00, effective for partnership taxable years beginning in 2016. For partnership taxable years beginning before then, the existing discussion of former § 704(e)(1) in this section remains relevant to the extent the repeal can be interpreted as a change to, rather than a clarification of, pre-2016 law; the discussions at ¶¶ 3.00 and 15.00 address, among other things, this concern. Also, in the repeal of former § 704(e)(1), former §§ 704(e)(2) and 704(e)(3) were renumbered as §§ 704(e)(1) and 704(e)(2), respectively, without any other change, aside from clarifying that they are applicable for purposes of applying § 704(e).]

[2] The Enactment of Section 704(e): Capital Ownership Supersedes Intent and Business Purpose as the Test for Partner Status

Page 15-4:

Add at end of subsection.

The relationship between *Culbertson* and § 704(e)(1) (as discussed at ¶ 3.00, former § 704(e)(1) was repealed by the Bipartisan Budget Act of 2015, effective for partnership taxable years beginning after December 31, 2015) was vigorously tested in *TIFD III-E, Inc. v. United States*.[8.1] The Second Circuit held that an investment by a group of banks in an aircraft leasing partnership, though equity and not a sham, failed to meet the *Culbertson* intent test. On remand, the district court held that the banks were partners under § 704(e)(1). This holding was reversed on appeal by the Second Circuit, which ruled that § 704(e)(1) is inapplicable to an interest that is debt. *TIFD III-E, Inc.* is discussed at ¶ 3.02[3].

[8.1] TIFD III-E, Inc. v. United States, 342 F. Supp. 2d 94 (D. Conn. 2004), rev'd on other grounds and remanded, 459 F3d 220 (2d Cir. 2006), on remand, 660 F. Supp. 2d 367 (D. Conn. 2009), rev'd, 666 F3d 836 (2d Cir. 2012). The Second Circuit reversed the U.S. district court for a third time in 2015. See TIFD III-E v. United States, 2015-1 USTC ¶ 50,308 (2d Cir. 2015) (summary order) (no reasonable basis for taxpayer's position, reversing district court's finding to the contrary; 20 percent negligence penalty imposed).

[5] Application of Section 704(e) to Nonfamily Partnerships

Page 15-5:

Replace note 12 with the following.

[12] See Evans v. Commissioner, 447 F2d 547 (7th Cir. 1971); TIFD III-E, Inc. v. United States, 660 F. Supp. 2d 367 (D. Conn. 2009), rev'd, 666 F3d 836 (2d Cir. 2012). See also ¶ 3.04[2][a].

¶ 15.02 EFFECT OF CAPITAL OWNERSHIP ON PARTNER STATUS

Page 15-6:

Add before first paragraph of subsection.

[NOTE: In this section, there are several instances in which former § 704(e)(1) is discussed and its impact analyzed. Former § 704(e)(1) was repealed, as discussed principally in ¶ 3.00 as well as ¶ 15.00, effective for partnership taxable years beginning in 2016. For partnership taxable years beginning before then, the existing discussion of former § 704(e)(1) in this section remains relevant to the extent the repeal can be interpreted as a change to, rather than a clarification of, pre-2016 law; the discussions at ¶¶ 3.00 and 15.00 address, among other things, this concern. Also, in the repeal of former § 704(e)(1), former §§ 704(e)(2) and 704(e)(3) were renumbered as §§ 704(e)(1) and

704(e)(2), respectively, without any other change, aside from clarifying that they are applicable for purposes of applying § 704(e).]

[1] Determining Whether Capital Is a Material Income-Producing Factor

Page 15-6:

*Replace note 14 with the following.*Reg. § 1.704-1(e)(1)(iv).

Replace note 15 with the following.

[15] Reg. § 1.704-1(e)(1)(iv). See TIFD III-E Inc. v. United States, 660 F. Supp. 2d 367 (D. Conn. 2009) (capital material income-producing factor in partnership aircraft leasing business; does not matter whether particular partner's capital contribution produced income), rev'd on other grounds, 666 F3d 836 (2d Cir. 2012); Estate of Emerson Winkler, 73 TCM 1657 (1977) (capital is material income-producing factor for family partnership that purchased lottery tickets). See also § 911(d)(2)(B); Reg. § 1.911-3(b)(2).

[2] Establishing Ownership of a Capital Interest

Page 15-8:

Add to note 21.

But see TIFD III-E, Inc. v United States, 666 F3d 836 (2d Cir. 2012) (putative partner did not have interest in partnership assets where interest was debt for tax purposes).

¶ 15.03 RECOGNITION OF DONEES AS PARTNERS: THE GENERAL RULES

Page 15-10:

Add before first paragraph of subsection.

[NOTE: In this section, there are several instances in which former § 704(e)(1) is discussed and its impact analyzed. Former § 704(e)(1) was repealed, as discussed principally in ¶ 3.00 as well as ¶ 15.00, effective for partnership taxable years beginning in 2016. For partnership taxable years beginning before then, the existing discussion of former § 704(e)(1) in this section remains relevant to the extent the repeal can be interpreted as a change to, rather than a clarification of, pre-2016 law; the discussions at ¶¶ 3.00 and 15.00 address, among other things, this concern. Also, in the repeal of former § 704(e)(1), former §§ 704(e)(2) and 704(e)(3) were renumbered as §§ 704(e)(1) and 704(e)(2), respectively, without any other change, aside from clarifying that they are applicable for purposes of applying § 704(e).]

¶ 15.04 RECOGNITION OF FAMILY PARTNERS: SPECIAL SITUATIONS

Page 15-19:

Add as first paragraph of subsection (and before ¶ 15.04[1]).

[NOTE: In this section, there are several instances in which former § 704(e)(1) is discussed and its impact analyzed. Former § 704(e)(1) was repealed, as discussed principally in ¶ 3.00 as well as ¶ 15.00, effective for partnership taxable years beginning in 2016. For partnership taxable years beginning before then, the existing discussion of former § 704(e)(1) in this section remains relevant to the extent the repeal can be interpreted as a change to, rather than a clarification of, pre-2016 law; the discussions at ¶¶ 3.00 and 15.00 address, among other things, this concern. Also, in the repeal of former § 704(e)(1), former §§ 704(e)(2) and 704(e)(3) were renumbered as §§ 704(e)(1) and 704(e)(2), respectively, without any other change, aside from clarifying that they are applicable for purposes of applying § 704(e).]

¶ 15.05 ALLOCATIONS OF PARTNERSHIP INCOME AND LOSS AMONG RELATED PARTNERS

Page 15-23:

Add before first paragraph of subsection.

[NOTE: As previously discussed, former § 704(e)(1) was repealed (see discussion at ¶¶ 3.00 and 15.00), effective for partnership taxable years beginning in 2016. In the repeal of § 704(e)(1), former §§ 704(e)(2) and 704(e)(3), discussed throughout this section, were renumbered as §§ 704(e)(1) and 704(e)(2), respectively, without any other change, aside from clarifying that they are applicable for purposes of applying § 704(e).]

PART **VI**

Transfers of Partnership
Interests

CHAPTER **16**

Sales, Exchanges, and Other Transfers of Partnership Interests

¶ 16.01 TRANSFERS OF PARTNERSHIP INTERESTS: TAX CONSEQUENCES GENERALLY

[1] Treatment of Transferor-Partners

Page 16-6:

Add the following before last paragraph of subsection.

For tax years beginning after 2012, a look-through approach is also embedded in the 3.8% Medicare contribution tax on "net investment income."[13.1] Net investment income includes any taxable net gain attributable to dispositions of property, except property held in a nonpassive trade or business (other than a trade or business of trading in financial instruments or commodities within the scope of § 475(e)(2)).[13.2] Gains and losses from dispositions of partnership interests are included in net gain to the extent of the net gain that would have been taken into account by the transferor if the partnership had sold all of its assets for fair market value immediately before the disposition.[13.3]

[13.1] The tax is 3.8% of the lesser of "net investment income" or the excess of "modified adjusted gross income" over the applicable "threshold amount" (i.e., $250,000 for joint returns and $200,000 for single filers). See § 1411; REG-130507-11, 77 Fed. Reg. 72,612 (Dec. 5, 2012).

[13.2] § 1411(c)(1)(A)(iii).

[13.3] §§ 1411(c)(4)(A), 1411(c)(4)(B). See infra ¶ 16.08[7].

[2] Treatment of Transferee-Partners

Page 16-7:

In second paragraph of subsection, replace last sentence (and note 17) with the following.

Further, with respect to gain from the pre−2018 sale of publicly traded securities that was deferred under § 1044,[17] as a consequence of the purchase of an interest in a partnership that is a specialized small business investment corporation, the basis of the purchased interest is its cost, less the amount of gain deferred.[17.1]

---

[17] Section 1044 was repealed for sales occurring after December 31, 2017, by the 2017 Tax Cuts and Jobs Act, Pub. L. No. 115-97, § 13313 (Dec. 22, 2017).

[17.1] See § 1044(d). See generally ¶ 4.08.

Replace note 18 with the following.

[18] A partnership has a substantial built-in loss with respect to a transfer of an interest if (1) the partnership's adjusted basis for its assets exceeds their value by more than $250,000, or (2) after 2017 (see Pub. L. No. 115-97, § 13502 (Dec. 22, 2017)), the transferee partner would be allocated a loss of more than $250,000 if the partnership assets were sold for cash equal to their fair market value immediately after such transfer. § 743(d)(1). Certain investment partnerships are entitled to elect out of the mandatory basis adjustment rules. See § 743(e). See generally ¶ 24.01[4].

[4] Allocation of Partnership Profit or Loss Between Transferor and Transferee

Page 16-9:

Add to note 26.

; Prop. Reg. § 1.706-4 (2009).

¶ 16.02 TRANSFERS OF PARTNERSHIP INTERESTS BY SALE OR EXCHANGE: TAX CONSEQUENCES OF LIQUIDATIONS COMPARED

[2] Comparison of the Consequences of Liquidations and Transfers

[d] Termination of the Partnership

Page 16-14:

Replace first sentence of subsection with the following:

For taxable years beginning prior to January 1, 2018, the sale of a withdrawing partner's interest to his co-partners terminated the partnership under § 708(b)(1)(B) if 50 percent or more of the total interest in partnership capital and profits was sold within a twelve-month period.[44.1]

[44.1] Section 708(b)(1)(B) has been repealed, effective for taxable years beginning after December 31, 2017. 2017 Tax Cuts and Jobs Act, Pub. L. No. 115-97, § 13504(a) (Dec. 22, 2017).

Page 16-15:

Add the following at end of subsection.

Following the 2017 repeal of § 708(b)(1)(B),[45.1] the so-called technical termination rule, neither a liquidation nor a transfer of a partnership interest can cause a termination provided at least two partners remain after the transfer or liquidation is completed.[45.2]

[45.1] Pub. L. No. 115-97, § 13504(a) (Dec. 22, 2017).

[45.2] Terminations and their consequences are discussed in Chapter 13.

[3] Categorization Problems: Sales vs. Liquidations

[b] Two-Person Partnerships

Page 16-22:

Add to note 79.

The inconsistent treatment of the seller (*S*) and buyer (*B*) create a unique issue under the consolidated return regulations: How do the matching rules of Reg. § 1.1502-13(b) apply when *B* is not buying what *S* is selling? The Service has ruled privately that *S* should be treated as though it had received assets in a liquidating distribution, which it then sells to *B*. The deferred gain or loss, however, is computed with reference to the sold partnership interest, leaving unanswered how the matching computation is done if the partnership's assets have both gains and losses (or different characters) which aggregate to a single number at the partnership interest level. See Priv. Ltr. Ruls. 201528007 (Apr. 7, 2015), 200737013 (June 21, 2007), 200737006 (Sept. 27, 2006), 200334037 (May 13, 2003). See, generally, Dubroff, Blanchard, Broadbent & Duvall, Federal Income Taxation of Corporations Filing Consolidated Returns § 31.05[2][b] (Matthew Bender, 2d ed. 2003); Hennessey, Yates, Banks & Pellervo, The Consolidated Tax Return ¶ 6.02 (Thomson Reuters/WG&L, 6th ed. 2002).

Add to note 83.

Section 708(b)(1)(B) has been repealed, effective for taxable years beginning after December 31, 2017. 2017 Tax Cuts and Jobs Act, Pub. L. No. 115-97, § 13504(a) (Dec. 22, 2017).

Page 16-23:

Add to note 86.

See Priv. Ltr. Rul. 200807005 (Nov. 9, 2007) (acquisition of 100% of partnership interests; § 1031 applied relying on Rev. Rul. 99-6). See also Priv. Ltr. Rul. 201505001(Jan. 30, 2015) (LLC agreement amended to provide that in event of deemed or actual liquidation, each partner will receive its § 704(c) property (or derivative substituted basis property); agreement respected to avoid potential § 732(f) issues on deemed distribution to seller). Giving effect to the otherwise meaningless amendment protects the fisc from basis distortions that might otherwise arise from the Rev. Rul. 99-6 construct. Interpreting the Rev. Rul. 99-6 construct to trigger tax to the buyer (for example, by applying § 704(c)(1)(B) to the deemed distribution to the seller) seems a stretch, but cautious practitioners may decide to include the protective language described in the private letter ruling in their agreements.

¶ 16.03 TRANSFERS OF PARTNERSHIP INTERESTS: TRANSFERS OF PARTNERSHIP ASSETS COMPARED

Page 16-37:

Add new note 126.1 at end of first sentence of subsection.

[126.1] For tax years beginning after 2012, Congress has embedded the aggregate approach in the new 3.8% Medicare contribution tax on "net investment income" in § 1411. The tax is 3.8% of the lesser of (1) "net investment income" or (2) the excess of "modified adjusted gross income" over the applicable "threshold amount" (i.e., $250,000 for joint returns and $200,000 for single filers). Net investment income includes any taxable net gain attributable to dispositions of property, except property held in a trade or business with respect to which the taxpayer is nonpassive (other than a trade or business of trading in financial instruments or commodities within the scope of § 475(e)(2)). § 1411(c)(1)(A)(iii). For this purpose, gains and losses from dispositions of partnership interests are included in net gain to the extent of the net gain that would have been taken into account by the transferor if the partnership had sold all of its assets for fair market value immediately before the disposition. §§ 1411(c)(4)(A), 1411(c)(4)(B). See infra ¶ 16.08[7].

[1] Aggregate-Entity Theory

Page 16-38:

Add to note 128.

For taxable years beginning after December 31, 2012, the capital gains rate for high-income taxpayers has been increased to 20 percent. American Taxpayer Relief Act of 2012, Pub. L. No. 112-240, § 102(b).

Page 16-39:

Add at beginning of note 136.

The Service's aggregate view of § 1239 is apparently limited to cases in which the partnership goes out of existence, such that the buyer ends up with depreciable property. See Priv. Ltr. Rul. 8052086 (Oct. 1, 1980) (sale of partnership interest not subject to § 1239 since interest not depreciable property).

Add at end of fifth paragraph of subsection (following note callout 138).

In *Grecian Magnesite Mining, Industrial & Shipping Co, SA. v. Commissioner*, the Tax Court refused to apply the aggregate approach to vindicate policies under non-Subchapter K provisions of the Code, when the policies and text of Subchapter K provisions mandate the entity approach.[138.1]

[138.1] Grecian Magnesite Mining, Industrial & Shipping Co, SA. v. Commissioner, 149 TC No. 3 (2017).

Page 16-40:

Add to note 144.

Cf. Pope & Talbot Inc. v. Commissioner, 162 F3d 1236 (9th Cir. 1999) (contribution of timber to newly formed partnership followed by distribution of partnership units to corporation's shareholders; corporate gain measured by value of timber, not lesser value of partnership units).

¶ 16.04 DEFERRED PAYMENT SALES AND EXCHANGES OF PARTNERSHIP INTERESTS

[1] Deferred Payment Sales of Partnership Interests

[b] Installment Sales of Partnership Interests

Page 16-50:

Add to note 199.

See Lori M. Mingo, 105 TCM 1857 (2013), aff'd, 2014-2 USTC ¶ 50,538 (5th Cir. 2014) (§ 751(a) applies to deny installment sale treatment to payments for a partnership interest to the extent attributable to the partnership's cash-method accounts receivable). See also CCA 200722027 (Apr. 27, 2007) (installment reporting denied for portion of gain from sale of partnership interest attributable to unrealized receivables); CCA 200728001 (July 5, 2007) (same).

[2] Exchanges of Partnership Interests

Page 16-51:

Replace ¶ 16.04[2][a] with revised ¶ 16.04[2][a].

[a] Exchanges of Partnership Interests for Interests in Other Partnerships [Revised]

Following the restriction, in 2017, of qualifying exchanges to exchanges of interests in real property, § 1031(a) no longer applies to exchanges of partnership interests.[201] Accordingly, exchanges of partnership interests for interests in other partnerships are fully taxable under the general rules of § 1001. The possibility of distributing assets from a partnership and subsequently engaging in a like-kind exchange of the distributed assets is discussed above.[202] Section 1031(e) also provides that an interest in a co-ownership arrangement that would otherwise be taxable as a partnership but that has made a valid election under § 761(a) to be excluded from all of Subchapter K is treated as an interest in each of the co-owned assets, thus laying the groundwork for possible § 1031 exchanges.[203]

---

[201] 2017 Tax Cuts and Jobs Act, Pub. L. No. 115-97, § 13303(a) (Dec. 22, 2017).

[202] See ¶ 9.02[1][c][vi][C].

[203] See ¶ 3.08. The utility of § 761(a) elections in facilitating § 1031 exchanges is severely circumscribed by the Service's position that this election is only available with respect to jointly-owned properties, and has no application to properties owned by state-law partnerships or other types of state-law entities. See Reg. §§ 1.761-2(a)(2)(i), 1.761-2(a)(3)(i).

[b] Exchanges of Interests in the Same Partnership

Page 16-51:

Add to note 204.

The alteration of a partner's economic rights through an amendment to the partnership agreement does not involve an exchange. See CCA 201517006 (Apr. 24, 2015) (conversion of incentive distribution rights in publicly traded partnership to common units not an exchange, but a readjustment of partnership items among existing partners).

Page 16-52:

Add to note 206.

The exchange construct adopted by Revenue Ruling 84-52, 1984-1 CB 157, could prove troublesome if the partnership has foreign trade or business assets that produce income in the same basket as a taxpayer-partner's overall foreign loss (OFL) account. The disposition of a partnership interest is treated as the disposition of a proportionate share of each asset of the partnership. Reg. § 1.904(f)-2(d)(5)(ii). A disposition includes a contribution to a partnership, Reg. § 1.904(f)-2(d)(5)(i), and includes a disposition in which no gain is recognized. Reg. § 1.904(f)-2(d)(4). The notion that a conversion of a partnership to an LLC could trigger OFL recapture seems bizarre, but the applicable technical provisions are not comforting.

¶ 16.05 GRATUITOUS TRANSFERS OF PARTNERSHIP INTERESTS

Page 16-53:

Add to note 209.

Section 708(b)(1)(B) has been repealed, effective for taxable years beginning after December 31, 2017. 2017 Tax Cuts and Jobs Act, Pub. L. No. 115-97, § 13504(a) (Dec. 22, 2017).

Add to note 211.

Section 708(b)(1)(B) has been repealed, effective for taxable years beginning after December 31, 2017. 2017 Tax Cuts and Jobs Act, Pub. L. No. 115-97, § 13504(a) (Dec. 22, 2017).

[1] Treatment of Partnership Liabilities Under Section 752

[a] Broad Interpretation of Section 752(d)

Page 16-55:

Add to note 215.

See Kornman & Assoc. v. United States, 527 F3d 443, 459, n. 15 (5th Cir. 2008) (§ 752(d) controls transfer for consideration).

[4] Summary of Related Problems

Page 16-63:

In list item 3, replace first sentence with the following.

> The termination rule of § 708(b)(1)(B), repealed for taxable years beginning after December 31, 2017, were applicable only to sales and exchanges of partnership interests.[240.1]

[240.1] The technical termination rule in § 708(b)(1)(B) has been repealed, effective for taxable years beginning after December 31, 2017. 2017 Tax Cuts and Jobs Act, Pub. L. No. 115-97, § 13504(a) (Dec. 22, 2017).

¶ 16.06 ABANDONMENTS, FORFEITURES, AND WORTHLESSNESS OF PARTNERSHIP INTERESTS

[2] Consequences in the Absence of Liabilities

Page 16-65:

Add the following at the end of sole paragraph of subsection.

The Service has also ruled that a partner is entitled to an ordinary loss on the worthlessness of a partnership interest.[256.1]

Notwithstanding decades of near consensus that the mere abandonment of property is not a sale or exchange, in *Pilgrim's Pride Corp. v. Commissioner*,[256.2] the Tax Court adopted an analysis of § 1234A under which an abandonment of any partnership interest will be treated as a sale or exchange. In so doing, the court rejected Revenue Ruling 93-80,[256.3] in which the Service had ruled to the contrary. On appeal, however, the Fifth Circuit made short work of the Tax Court's reasoning, holding that the "plain terms" of § 1234A(1) do not apply to the termination of ownership of the capital asset itself.[256.4] It remains to be seen whether the Tax Court sticks with its position.

Pilgrim's Pride involved an abandonment of stock, but the court's analysis applies to the abandonment of any personal property, including a partnership interest. The value of the stock at issue in this case had declined very substantially below the taxpayer-shareholder's adjusted basis. While the issuer offered to redeem the stock for a fraction of the taxpayer's basis, a redemption would have produced a large capital loss for which the taxpayer had little use. As a consequence, the taxpayer decided to abandon the stock to the issuer for no consideration in order to secure an ordinary loss under § 165 equal to its entire basis in the stock. The expected tax benefit of this ordinary loss was worth more than the combined value of the meager redemption proceeds and the tax savings generated by the capital loss that would have been recognized on a redemption.

The Service's challenge to the taxpayer's ordinary abandonment loss apparently did not include reliance on § 1234A or disavowal of its position in Revenue Ruling 93-80, under which an abandonment of a property produces an ordinary loss unless the abandoning taxpayer receives some consideration (e.g., a § 752(b) distribution). Nevertheless, the court, on its own motion, raised the question of whether § 1234A requires the abandonment of any item of personal property be treated as a sale or exchange, and so result in capital gain or loss.

Prior to its amendment in 1997, § 1234A mandated capital gain or loss treatment for certain non−sale-or-exchange dispositions of rights with respect to actively-traded personal property. In 1997, the "actively traded" limitation was removed, so that (as applicable to the year at issue in *Pilgrim's Pride*) § 1234A provides as follows:

[256.1] Rev. Rul. 93-80, 1993-2 CB 239.

[256.2] Pilgrim's Pride Corp., 141 TC 533 (2013), rev'd, Pilgrim's Pride Corp. v. Commissioner, 779 F3d 311 (5th Cir. 2015).

[256.3] Rev. Rul. 93-80, 1993-2 CB 239.

[256.4] Pilgrim's Pride Corp. v. Commissioner, 779 F3d 311 (5th Cir. 2015).

Gain or loss attributable to the cancellation, lapse, expiration, or other termination of-(1) a right or obligation (other than a securities futures contract, as defined in § 1234B with respect to property which is (or on acquisition would be) a capital asset in the hands of the taxpayer, ... shall be treated as gain or loss from the sale of a capital asset.

The court rejected the taxpayer's argument (based on examples in the legislative history to the 1997 amendment) that Congress intended § 1234A to apply only to "contractual and other derivative rights with respect to property and not to the inherent property rights and obligations arising from the ownership of property."[256.5] Instead, the court engaged in a plain meaning analysis of the phrase "with respect to," and determined that the inherent property rights of property owners are rights with respect to the property. "[W]e do not think that the examples in the legislative history do more than show that § 1234A applies broadly to derivative contractual rights and obligations as well as inherent property rights."[256.6]

Because Revenue Ruling 93-80 predated the 1997 amendment to § 1234A, the court did not consider it dispositive, even though the Service had not withdrawn Revenue Ruling 93-80 during the 15-year period between the 1997 amendment of § 1234A and the publication of the court's opinion in *Pilgrim's Pride*. Instead, the court said, "the Commissioner is not required to assert a particular position as soon as the statute authorizes such an interpretation, whether that position is taken in a regulation or in a revenue ruling."[256.7]

[256.5] Pilgrim's Pride Corp., 141 TC 533 (2013), rev'd, Pilgrim's Pride Corp. v. Commissioner, 779 F3d 311 (5th Cir. 2015).

[256.6] Pilgrim's Pride Corp., 141 TC 533 (2013), rev'd, Pilgrim's Pride Corp. v. Commissioner, 779 F3d 311 (5th Cir. 2015).

[256.7] Pilgrim's Pride Corp., 141 TC 533 (2013), rev'd, Pilgrim's Pride Corp. v. Commissioner, 779 F3d 311 (5th Cir. 2015).

[3] The Effect of Liabilities

Page 16-66:

Add to note 259.

Cf. Thomas E. Watts, TC Memo. 2017-114, 113 TC 1507 (2017) (failure to prove absence of liabilities).

Replace the last paragraph of subsection with the following.

The Eleventh Circuit has held that a partner forfeiting his entire interest does not realize his share of partnership liabilities if he remains liable as a guarantor thereof.[260] Similarly, the Fifth Circuit and the Tax Court have both held that a partner may claim a loss on the worthlessness of a partnership interest, apparently without requiring the recognition of the partner's share of partnership liabilities.[261] Thus, a partner who abandons a partnership interest but remains liable for a partnership liability, or who claims a loss based on the worthlessness of a partnership interest but remains a partner, has received neither an actual nor a deemed distribution and should be entitled to an ordinary loss.[261.1] Subject to these limitations, the *Stillwell* analysis is correct, and taxpayers should assume that Revenue Ruling 93-80 accurately describes the law.

---

[260] Weiss v. Commissioner, 956 F2d 242 (11th Cir. 1992), criticized supra ¶ 16.05[1][c]. See In re Kreidle, 91-1 USTC ¶ 50,371 (D. Colo. 1991).

[261] Echols v. United States, 935 F2d 703, reh'g denied per curiam, 950 F2d 209 (5th Cir. 1991), rev'g 93 TC 553 (1989) (taxpayer-partners entitled to loss deductions under § 165(a) with respect to partnership interests in partnership that had liabilities; § 752 not discussed); MCM Investment Management, LLC, 118 TCM 437 (2019) (ordinary loss equal to basis of partnership interest, apparently attributable to partnership liabilities); Tejon Ranch Co., 49 TCM 1357 (1985) (corporate partner allowed ordinary loss under § 165 on worthlessness of investment in partnership; fact that partnership had unsatisfied liabilities not considered by court); cf. Larry E. Webb, 23 TC 1035 (1955) (acq.).

[261.1] A subsequent reduction in the partner's share of partnership liabilities would be taxable to the partner under §§ 752 and 731(a).

Pages 16-66—16-67:

Delete ¶ 16.06[4].

¶ 16.07 TRANSFERS OF PARTNERSHIP INTERESTS TO AND FROM CORPORATIONS AND OTHER PARTNERSHIPS

[1] Transfers to Corporations

Add to note 269.

Reg. § 1.367(a)-1(c)(3)(ii)(A). The foreign corporation is apparently intended to be the beneficiary of a § 743(b) basis adjustment in the amount of the gain recognized, although the wording of the Regulations is difficult to square with the mechanics of the basis adjustment rules. See ¶ 24.03[4].

Page 16-68:

Add after second paragraph of subsection (ending with note callout 269).

If the § 351 exchange would result in the transfer of a loss to the transferee corporation, the rules of § 362(e)(2) come into play to prevent loss duplication.

In general, these rules require the corporation to reduce the carryover basis of the contributed assets by the amount of the loss. An election can be made to instead reduce the basis of the stock received in the exchange. If the transferred property is a partnership interest, the computations are made by taking into account the transferee's § 752 share of partnership liabilities immediately after the transfer.[269.1]

[269.1] Reg. §§ 1.362-4(g)(12)(ii), 1.362-4(h) Example 8.

Replace list item 2 with the following.

    2. A termination of the partnership occurring in a taxable year beginning before January 1, 2018, could result under the provisions of § 708(b)(1)(B);[271]

---

[271] See Rev. Rul. 81-38, 1981-1 CB 386; Priv. Ltr. Rul. 8851004 (Aug. 21, 1988); Priv. Ltr. Rul. 8047105 (Aug. 29, 1980); Priv. Ltr. Rul. 7902086 (Oct. 16, 1978). Section 708(b)(1)(B) has been repealed, effective for taxable years beginning after December 31, 2017. 2017 Tax Cuts and Jobs Act, Pub. L. No. 115-97, § 13504(a) (Dec. 22, 2017).

[2] Distributions by Corporations

Page 16-70:

In second paragraph of subsection, replace list item 3 with the following.

    3. *Other distributions and redemptions.* All other distributions with respect to shares, as well as distributions in connection with redemptions not within one of the five categories of § 302(b), are taxed to the distributee under § 301(c) as follows: first, as an item of gross income to the extent the distribution is a dividend out of current or accumulated earnings and profits; second, as a reduction of the distributee's basis in his shares; and third, as a gain from the sale or exchange of property. With respect to property distributions, the amount of the distribution and the basis of the distributed property in the hands of the distributee is the fair market value of the property.[277]

---

[277] §§ 301(b)(1), 301(d).

Page 16-71:

In third paragraph of subsection, replace penultimate sentence (ending with note 279) with the following.

Corporate distributions of partnership interests, occurring in taxable years beginning before January 1, 2018, could be treated as exchanges for purposes of the now repealed technical termination rule of § 708(b)(1)(B).[279]

---

[279] The technical termination rule in § 708(b)(1)(B) has been repealed, effective for taxable years beginning after December 31, 2017. 2017 Tax Cuts and Jobs Act, Pub. L. No. 115-97, § 13504(a) (Dec. 22, 2017).

[4] Distributions by Other Partnerships

Page 16-72:

Replace first sentence of subsection with the following.

Section 761(e) provides that a distribution by a partnership of an interest in another partnership is a sale or exchange for both § 708 and § 743 purposes. Presumably, Regulations will eventually be issued to also treat such a distribution as a sale or exchange for § 706(c) purposes., although the reference to § 708 is of diminished significance following the repeal of § 708(b)(1)(B) (the technical termination rule) in 2017.[286.1]

[286.1] 2017 Tax Cuts and Jobs Act, Pub. L. No. 115-97, § 13504(a) (Dec. 22, 2017).

¶ 16.08 COLLATERAL CONSEQUENCES OF TRANSFERS OF PARTNERSHIP INTERESTS

[5] Transfers of Interests in Partnerships Holding a Sports Franchise Subject to Section 1056

Page 16-81:

In second paragraph of subsection, add new note 323.1 at end of first sentence.

[323.1] Section 708(b)(1)(B) was repealed in 2017. 2017 Tax Cuts and Jobs Act, Pub. L. No. 115-97, § 13504(a) (Dec. 22, 2017).

[6] Transfers of Interests in Partnerships Holding Collectibles, Small Business Stock, or Real Estate Subject to Section 1250

Page 16-82:

Replace first paragraph of subsection with the following.

For individual taxpayers, the Code currently imposes multiple maximum capital gains rates for different types of capital assets. The maximum rate is presently set at 28 percent for gains and losses from sales or exchanges of collectibles held for more than one year ("collectibles gain"),[324] as well as a portion of the gain from the sale of § 1202 "small business" stock, reduced by any net short-term capital loss for the year and any long-term capital loss carryover to the year under § 1212(b)(1)(B) ("28 percent rate gain").[325] The maximum rate is 25 percent for unrecaptured § 1250 gain.[326] This is the amount of long-term gain (but not in excess of the taxpayer's net § 1231 gain for the year) from § 1250 property that would be subject to recapture if all § 1250 depreciation were subject to recapture. Finally, the maximum rate is 20 percent for net long-term capital, excluding 28 percent rate gain and unrecaptured § 1250 gain ("20 percent rate gain").[327]

---

[324] The term "collectibles" is defined in § 408(m) as any work of art, rug or antique, metal or gem, stamp or coin, alcoholic beverage, or other tangible personal property identified by Regulations. The definition of "collectibles" contained in § 1(h)(6) expressly includes certain types of coin or bullion excluded by § 408(m)(3).

[325] § 1(h)(5).

[326] § 1(h)(1)(D).

[327] § 1(h)(1)(C). For tax years beginning before January 1, 2013, the maximum rate was 15 percent for net long-term capital gains excluding 28 percent rate gain and unrecaptured § 1250 gain. For tax years ending beginning after December 31, 2012, the maximum rate was increased to 20 percent. However, certain lower income taxpayers may continue to enjoy the 15 percent rate for some or all of their net long-term capital gains. American Taxpayer Relief Act of 2012, Pub. L. No. 112-240, § 102(b).

Page 16-83:

In last sentence of last full paragraph, insert (now 20) *before percent rate gain.*

Page 16-85:

Replace next to last paragraph of subsection with the following.

   The Regulations' refusal to treat look-through § 1250 gain as § 1231 gain works to the taxpayer's detriment since she is taxed at the 25% rate on look-through § 1250 gain even if she has net § 1231 losses in excess of this gain from other sources. If the partnership had actually sold the § 1250 property, of course, the § 1231 character would have passed through, been netted against her § 1231 losses, and then eliminated her tax entirely. Although at first blush it may appear that the rule can work in the taxpayer's favor when the § 1250 look-through gain is her only § 1231 gain for the year, such is not the case. While the taxpayer's net § 1231 gain in this case is zero, and thus the § 1(h)(6)(B) limit is zero, the limit is inapplicable to gain from sales of partnership interests since such sales are not themselves § 1231 transactions.[339.1]

[339.1] See TD 8902, 2000-2 CB 232.

Page 16-85:

Add new ¶ 16.08[7].

[7] Medicare Contribution Tax: Dispositions of Partnership Interests [New]

For tax years beginning after 2012, a look-through approach to dispositions of partnership interests is embedded in the new 3.8% Medicare contribution tax on "net investment income."[342] Net investment income includes any taxable net gain from dispositions of property, except property held in a nonpassive trade or business (other than the trade or business of trading in financial instruments or commodities within the scope of § 475(e)(2)).[343] Any gain or loss from the disposition of a partnership interest is included in net gain only to the extent of the net gain or net loss that would have been included in the computation of net gains under § 1411(c)(1)(A)(iii) by the disposing partner if the partnership had sold all of its assets for fair market value immediately before the disposition.[344]

On December 5, 2012, the Treasury issued a massive set of proposed regulations dealing with a host of computational issues under § 1411, including the look-through computations on dispositions of partnership interests.[345] While the conceptual rules underlying these proposed regulations may be stated fairly simply, the detailed computations they require are on the same level of complexity as the collapsible partnership rules under § 751 and the optional basis adjustment rules under § 754.[346]

---

[342] The tax is 3.8% of the lesser of (1) "net investment income" or (2) the excess of "modified adjusted gross income" over the applicable "threshold amount" (i.e., $250,000 for joint returns, $200,000 for single filers). § 1411.

[343] § 1411(c)(1)(A)(iii).

[344] §§ 1411(c)(4)(A), 1411(c)(4)(B). A partnership interest generally is not property held in a trade or business (see Prop. Reg. § 1.1411-4(d)(3)(ii)(B)(1) (2012)), and therefore the gain from the sale of a partnership interest is generally included in net investment income except to the extent excluded under the look-through rule in § 1411(c)(4).

[345] REG-130507-11, 77 Fed. Reg. 72,612 (Dec. 5, 2012). Dispositions of partnership interests are addressed in Proposed Regulations § 1.1411-7 (2012). The general effective date for the proposed regulations is taxable years beginning after December 31, 2013. However, taxpayers may rely on the proposed regulations until the effective date of final regulations. See REG-130507-11, 77 Fed. Reg. 72,612 (Dec. 5, 2012), Preamble to Proposed Regulations, Explanation of Provisions, part 12, *Taxpayer Reliance on Proposed Regulations.*

[346] This extraordinary complexity is achieved without even addressing the truly complicated issues—most notably, the interaction between the look-through rules of § 1411

The basic concepts are as follows:

1. Generally, gains and losses from property dispositions are excluded from the computation of net gain for § 1411 purposes if the property is held in a trade or business (§ 1411(c)(1)(A)(iii));

2. However, gains and losses from dispositions of property held in a trade or business that is (a) a passive § 469 activity or (b) a trade or business of trading financial instruments or commodities (a "trading business") are not excluded from the computation of § 1411 net gain (§ 1411(c)(2)); and

3. Upon the disposition[347] of a partnership interest, any recognized gain or loss is adjusted (subject to certain limitations) by the amount of gain or loss allocable to the transferor partner that would have been excluded under rules 1 and 2 above upon a "deemed sale" of the entity's assets, taking into account the application of §§ 704(b), 704(c), and 743 (§ 1411(c)(4)).[348]

---

and the similar, but critically different, look-through rules of § 751. The § 1411 proposed regulations would allow taxpayers to offset capital losses against ordinary income only to the extent provided in § 1211(b). See Prop. Reg. §§ 1.1411-4(d)(2) (2012), 1.1411-4(d)(2)(h), Example 1(ii) (2012). Upon the sale of a partnership interest, § 751 may operate to characterize a portion of the gain as ordinary and a portion as capital. The proposed regulations appear to contemplate a single gain or loss on the sale of a partnership interest and limitations based on that single gain or loss. See Prop. Reg. § 1.1411-7(c) (2012). Where a partner has both ordinary income and capital gain, or ordinary income and capital loss, on the sale of a partnership interest, it is unclear how the proposed regulations are intended to operate. Is the "deemed sale" structure of Proposed Regulations § 1.1411-7(c) (2012) applied separately to hot assets and cold assets? Is § 751 ignored for these purposes and the partnership interest treated as an entity interest, subject to adjustment solely as provided in Proposed Regulations § 1.1411-7(c) (2012)? These questions will get even more interesting if and when regulations are proposed to address distributions in excess of basis under § 731 and the interaction of § 1411 with § 751(b) is explored. See REG-130507-11, 77 Fed. Reg. 72,612 (Dec. 5, 2012), Preamble to Proposed Regulations, Explanation of Provisions, part 8.A.i, *Dispositions of Interests in Partnerships and S Corporations, Mechanics of section 1411(c)(4), In general.*

[347] The Treasury, recognizing that a partner may have taxable gain as a result of a distribution in excess of basis and that the deemed sale model may not work well in this type of situation, has requested "comments on how to determine a partner's interest in section 1411 assets upon a distribution in which gain is recognized pursuant to section 731." See REG-130507-11, 77 Fed. Reg. 72,612 (Dec. 5, 2012), Preamble to Proposed Regulations, Explanation of Provisions, part 8.A.i, *Dispositions of Interests in Partnerships and S Corporations, Mechanics of section 1411(c)(4), In general.*

[348] Special rules would affect (1) the timing of the inclusion in net investment income of income from any controlled foreign corporations (CFCs) and any passive foreign investment company that a domestic partnership has elected to treat as a qualifying electing fund (QEF), (2) the determination of a partner's outside basis in his interest in a partnership that owns an interest in a CFC or QEF, (3) the computation of a partnership's adjusted basis in its CFC or QEF stock, and (4) conforming adjustments to the partners' modified adjusted gross income. Prop. Reg. § 1.1411-10 (2012).

In many situations, the deemed sale rules do not come into play. In these situations, the § 1411 rules are easy to apply, and produce simple, straightforward results:

1. If a partnership is not engaged in a trade or business, all gain or loss from disposition of a partnership interest is *included* in the computation of § 1411 net gain;
2. If a partnership is only engaged in trading businesses described in § 1411(c)(2)(B), all gain or loss from disposition of a partnership interest is *included* in the computation of § 1411 net gain;
3. If a partnership is only engaged in non-trading businesses, gain or loss from disposition of a partnership interest is *included* in the computation of § 1411 net gain if all of the partnership's businesses are passive with respect to the partner disposing of the interest;[349] and
4. If a partnership is only engaged in non-trading businesses, gain or loss from disposition of a partnership interest is *excluded* from the computation of § 1411 net gain if the partner disposing of the interest is active in each of the partnership's businesses.

However, if (1) a partnership is engaged in multiple trades or businesses or non-§ 162 activities and (2) some (but not all) are trading businesses or all are non-trading businesses and the disposing partner is nonpassive with respect to any of the businesses, the deemed sale rules kick in. The objective of these rules is to separate the disposing partner's share of the gain (or loss) from disposition of his interest into (1) gain or loss from nonpassive, non-trading businesses (excluded from the computation of § 1411 net gain) and (2) all other gain or loss (included in the computation of § 1411 net gain).

The mechanics adopted in the proposed regulations are as follows:

1. *Deemed sale of partnership properties.* The partnership is deemed to dispose of all of its properties (including goodwill) in a fully taxable transaction for cash equal to the fair market value of the properties immediately before the disposition of the interest in the entity.[350]

---

[349] The determination of whether an activity is passive is made on a partner-by-partner basis at the partner level; however, the existence of a trade or business and the categorization of a trade or business as a trading business are done at the partnership level at which the activity occurs and apply equally to all partners. Prop. Reg. §§ 1.1411-4(b)(2) (2012), 1.1411-4(b)(3), Example 1 (2012) (dividends received by lower-tier partnership not engaged in trade or business; not derived in trade or business with respect to partner in upper tier partnership engaged in a trade or business even though included in income allocated to partner through upper-tier partnership).

[350] This deemed sale is "similar to § 1.743-1(d)(2)" (see Prop. Reg. § 1.1411-7(c)(2) (2012)); however, the Treasury and the IRS "recognize that the Deemed Sale may impose an administrative burden on owners of partnerships and S corporations in certain circumstances [and therefore] request comments on other methods that would implement the provisions of section 1411(c)(4) without imposing an undue burden on taxpayers." 77 Fed. Reg. 72,612 (Dec. 5, 2012).

2. *Gain or loss is determined on a property-by-property basis.* The hypothetical gain or loss from the deemed sale is computed on a property-by-property basis.

3. *Gain or loss is allocated to the partners on a property-by-property basis.* The disposing partner's share of the gain or loss from each property is determined, taking into account §§ 704(b) and 704(c), as well as any § 743 basis adjustments.

4. *Determination of disposing partner's share of the net gain (or loss) from properties held in nonpassive, non-trading businesses.* The disposing partner's shares of the net gains and losses from properties held in non-trading businesses in which the partner is nonpassive are aggregated; a net gain is treated as a negative adjustment, while a net loss is treated as a positive adjustment, to the disposing partner's total gain or loss from the disposition of the partnership interest.[351]

A negative adjustment reduces (but not below zero) the disposing partner's total gain (if any) from disposition of the interest includible in net gain under § 1411; if the disposing partner has a total loss from disposition of the interest, the negative adjustment is ignored. A positive adjustment reduces the disposing partner's total loss (if any) from the disposition of the interest taken into account in determining net gain for purposes of § 1411, but any excess does not create a gain; if the disposing partner has a total gain from disposition of the interest, the positive adjustment is ignored.[352]

The 2012 proposed regulations were finalized by Treasury Decision 9644 on November 26, 2013. In addition, the Treasury has issued proposed regulations that deal, among other things, with the application of § 1411 to § 707(c) guaranteed payments, § 736 distributions made to a retiring partners, and sales or exchanges of partnership interests.[353]

Proposed Regulations § 1.1411-7 provides rules for applying § 1411 to sales and exchanges of interests in partnerships and S corporations. In general, under Proposed Regulations § 1.1411-7(b)(1)(i), if a partner recognizes a gain from the sale of a partnership interest, the amount taken into account as investment income for § 1411 purposes is the lesser of (1) the gain the selling partner recognizes from the sale or (2) the net gain that the selling partner would recognize from a sale by the partnership of its assets other than assets that are held in connection with a trade or business of the partnership in which the selling partner does not materially participate. For this purpose, the passive

---

[351] Prop. Reg. § 1.1411-7(c) (2012). Property used in more than one trade or business must be allocated among such businesses in a way that reasonably reflects the use of the property during the 12-month period ending on the date of the deemed sale. Goodwill is allocated among an entity's trades or businesses based on the relative fair market values of the noncash properties held in each trade or business. Prop. Reg. § 1.1411-7(c)(5)(ii) (2012).

[352] Prop. Reg. §§ 1.1411-7(c)(5)(iii) (2012), 1.1411-7(c)(5)(iv) (2012).

[353] Reg-130843-13 (Dec. 2, 2013).

loss rules of Regulations § 1.469-2T(e)(3) are incorporated. However, the amount cannot be less than zero.

Under Proposed Regulations § 1.1411-7(b)(1)(ii), if the selling partner recognizes a loss from a sale of a partnership interest, the amount of the net loss that is taken into account for § 1411 purposes is the lesser of (1) the loss (expressed as a positive number) that the selling partner recognizes from the sale of the interest or (2) the net loss that the seller would recognize from a sale by the partnership of its assets other than assets that are held in connection with a trade or business of the partnership in which the seller does not materially participate. For this purpose, the passive loss rules of Regulations § 1.469-2T(e)(3) are also incorporated.

Proposed Regulations § 1.1411-7(b)(2) illustrates these rules with the following examples.

Example 1: A owns a one-half interest in P, a calendar year partnership. In Year 1, A sells its interest for $200,000. A's adjusted basis for the interest sold is $120,000. Thus, A recognizes $80,000 of gain from the sale. P is engaged in three trade or business activities, X, Y, and Z. P also owns marketable securities. For Year 1, A materially participates in activity Z; however, A does not materially participate in activities X and Y. Because P is engaged in at least one trade or business and A materially participates in at least one of those trades or businesses, A determines its amount of gain or loss on net investment income under Proposed Regulations § 1.1411-7. The fair market value and adjusted basis of the gross assets used in P's activities are as follows:

Activity gain/loss	Adjusted basis	Fair market value	Gain/loss	A's Share
X (Passive as to A)	$136,000	$ 96,000	($ 40,000)	($20,000)
Y (Passive as to A)	60,000	124,000	64,000	32,000
Z (Non-passive as to A)	40,000	160,000	120,000	60,000
Marketable securities	4,000	20,000	16,000	8,000
Total	240,000	400,000	160,000	80,000

A's allocable share of gain on a deemed sale of P's assets and business (other than the assets and business related to activity Z in which A materially participates) is $20,000 (($20,000) from X + $32,000 from Y + $8,000 from the marketable securities). Because the $20,000 allocable to A from a deemed sale is less than A's $80,000 gain, A includes $20,000 as investment income under § 1.1411.

Example 2: Assume the same facts as *Example 1,* but A materially participates in activities Y and Z and does not materially participate in activity X. Under Proposed Regulations§ 1.1411-7(b)(1)(i), A's allocable share of P's of loss from the deemed sale is ($12,000) (($20,000) from X + $8,000 from the marketable securities). Because A sold its interest for a gain, the amount allocable to A from a deemed sale cannot be less than zero. Accordingly, A includes no gain or loss under § 1411.

Transfers of Interests in Collapsible Partnerships

Chapter 17 was revised effective June 2021. The revised chapter can be found in the front of this student edition.

CHAPTER **18**

Incorporation of a Partnership

¶ 18.01 NONRECOGNITION TRANSFERS OF PROPERTY TO A CORPORATION UNDER SECTION 351: THE GENERAL RULES

[3] The Effect of Boot Received and Liabilities Assumed in the Exchange

Page 18-4:

Delete note 9.

[4] Determining Basis

Page 18-5:

Add the following after second paragraph of subsection.

If the aggregate basis of the contributed property exceeds its fair market value, § 362(e)(2) limits the corporation's basis in the contributed property to such fair market value. Section 362(e)(2)(C) provides that the parties may instead elect to reduce the basis of the contributor's stock to fair market value. In the partnership context, Regulations § 1.362-4(e)(1) provides that any reduction to stock basis is treated as a § 705(a)(2)(B) expenditure, reducing the partners' bases in their partnership interests. There are apparently no consequences if the requisite basis reduction exceeds the partners' bases in their interests, which stands in sharp contrast to the rule applicable to § 358(h) contingent liabilities. Regulations § 1.358-7(b) provides that any excess of the required basis reduction in this latter context triggers gain equal to the excess.

Additional rules come into play if (1) the transferor is not subject to tax but the transferee corporation is, and (2) the transferred property has a net built-in loss (i.e., a loss importation transaction). Since a basis reduction to the transferor's stock is meaningless if the transferor is not subject to tax, the stock basis reduction election is unavailable, and so the transferee's basis in the contributed property (both gain and loss assets) is the property's fair market value. If the transferor is a partnership, § 362(e)(1)(B) provides that each partner is treated as owning its proportionate share of the partnership's property. Proposed Regulations § 1.362-3(e) (2013) flesh out this rule by tentatively dividing each asset among the partners in proportion to the amount of gain or loss allocable to each on a hypothetical sale at fair market value. After application of the loss importation rules, the acquiring corporation has a single asset whose basis is the sum of fair value for the loss importation portion and carryover for the rest. If the carryover portion is itself loss property, a separate basis reduction must be made (either to the asset or, electively, to the stock).[10.1]

[10.1] See Prop. Reg. § 1.362-3(f) Example 5.

¶ 18.02 APPLYING THE SECTION 351 NONRECOGNITION RULES TO THE INCORPORATION OF A GOING PARTNERSHIP BUSINESS

[6] Investment Credit Recapture Upon Contributions to Corporations

Page 18-14:

Replace note 43 with the following.

[43] The investment credit currently consists of the § 47 rehabilitation credit, the § 48 energy credit, the § 48A qualifying advanced coal project credit, the § 48B qualifying gasification project credit, and the § 48C qualifying advanced energy project credit. See § 46.

¶ 18.03 METHODS OF INCORPORATING A PARTNERSHIP BUSINESS

[6] Subchapter S Status of the Transferee-Corporation

Page 18-21:

Add the following at end of sole subparagraph of subsection.

The Service has ruled that Alternative I incorporations are consistent with S corporation status where the S election is effective on January 1 with respect to calendar year taxpayers.[71.1] The Service reasoned that the deemed asset transfer to the corporation occurs immediately before the close of the day before the election is effective. Accordingly, the partnership's taxable year closes on December 31, and the corporation's first year begins on January 1; the partnership is thus not deemed to own any of the corporation's stock during any portion of the corporation's first taxable year beginning January 1. Since the S election need only be made during the first two and one-half months of the taxable year and the classification election may be made retroactively for a 75-day period, calendar year taxpayers may elect to incorporate a partnership and make an S election during the first two and one-half months of the year as long as the effective date of the incorporation and S election is January 1 of that year.

[71.1] Rev. Rul. 2009-15, 2009-21 IRB 1035.

Partnership Distributions

Distributions That Do Not Alter the Partners' Interests in Section 751 Property

¶ 19.02 DEFINING THE DISTRIBUTION

[5] Distributions of a Partner's Debt to the Debtor-Partner

[a] Direct Partnership Loans to Partners: Regulations § 1.731-1(c)(2)

Page 19-15:

Add to note 53.

See Priv. Ltr. Rul. 201314004 (Oct. 22, 2012).

¶ 19.03 CURRENT DISTRIBUTIONS

Page 19-24:

Add new note 74.1 at the end of the first sentence of subsection.

[74.1] Additionally, the Service has taken the position that a distribution of property, where the property was "selected by the distributee, acquired by the partnership immediately before the distribution solely for the purpose of the distribution, and was unrelated to the partnership's business activity," should be treated as a distribution of money by the partnership under § 731(a). CCA 200650014 (Sept. 7, 2006).

Add to note 75.

Further complexity may result from the enactment, effective for tax years beginning after 2012, of the 3.8% Medicare contribution tax on "net investment income" in § 1411. Net investment income includes any taxable net gain from dispositions of property, except property held in a nonpassive trade or business (other than the trade or business of trading in financial instruments or commodities within the scope of § 475(e)(2)). § 1411(c)(1)(A)(iii). For this purpose, gains and losses from "dispositions" of partnership interests are included in net gain to the extent of the net gain that would have been taken into account by the transferor if the partnership had sold all of its assets for fair market value immediately before the disposition. §§ 1411(c)(4)(A), 1411(c)(4)(B). Despite the somewhat inelegant use of the word "disposition," it appears this tax is intended to apply to taxable distributions under § 731, although the Treasury seems somewhat unsure as to exactly how to do the computations. See REG-130507-11, 77 Fed. Reg. 72,612 (Dec. 5, 2012), Preamble to Proposed Regulations, Explanation of Provisions, part 8.A.i, *Dispositions of Interests in Partnerships and S Corporations, Mechanics of section 1411(c)(4), In general,* as discussed in ¶ 16.08[7].

[2] Advances or Draws Distinguished From Distributions

Page 19-26:

Replace note 85 with the following.

    [85] Willis & Postelwaite, Partnership Taxation ¶ 13.02[4][a] n. 151 (Thomson Reuters/ WG&L, 6th ed. 1997).

¶ 19.04 BASIS CONSEQUENCES OF CURRENT DISTRIBUTIONS

[1] Allocations of Basis Under Section 732

Page 19-30:

Add at end of subsection (following EXAMPLE 19-7).

    If the distribution includes "Stock of a Corporate Partner" subject to the special rules in Regulations § 1.337(d)-3(e)(1), the basis to be allocated to properties distributed to the "Corporate Partner" under § 732(a)(2) must be allocated first to such stock before it can be allocated to any other distributed property.[92.1] For this purpose, the amount to be allocated to the stock is determined under Regulations § 1.337(d)-3(e)(2).[92.2]

    [92.1] Reg. § 1.732-1(c)(1)(ii) (effective date June 12, 2015).
    [92.2] See ¶ 9.03[1][a][ii][D].

¶ 19.05 DISTRIBUTIONS IN COMPLETE LIQUIDATION OF A PARTNERSHIP INTEREST

Page 19-31:

Replace second sentence of subsection with the following.

Provided neither of these sections applies, the recognition of gain or loss by the distributee-partner is governed by § 731(a), which provides for (1) nonrecognition of gain except to the extent an amount of money is distributed in excess of the distributee-partner's basis in his partnership interest[94.1] and (2)

    [94.1] For tax years beginning after 2012, all or a portion of any gain recognized by a partner in this context may be subject to the 3.8% Medicare contribution tax on "net investment income" in § 1411. Net investment income includes any taxable net gain from dispositions of property, except property held in a nonpassive trade or business (other than the trade or business of trading in financial instruments or commodities within the scope of § 475(e)(2)). § 1411(c)(1)(A)(iii). For this purpose, gains and losses from "disposi-

nonrecognition of loss unless a distribution in complete liquidation consists solely of money, unrealized receivables (as defined in § 751(c)), and inventory (as defined in § 751(d)).[95]

---

tions" of partnership interests are included in net gain to the extent of the net gain that would have been taken into account by the transferor if the partnership had sold all of its assets for fair market value immediately before the disposition. §§ 1411(c)(4)(A), 1411(c)(4)(B). Despite the somewhat inelegant use of the word "disposition," it appears this tax is intended to apply to taxable distributions under § 731, although the Treasury seems somewhat unsure as to exactly how to do the computations. See REG-130507-11, 77 Fed. Reg. 72,612 (Dec. 5, 2012), Preamble to Proposed Regulations, Explanation of Provisions, part 8.A.i, *Dispositions of Interests in Partnerships and S Corporations, Mechanics of section 1411(c)(4), In general,* as discussed in ¶ 16.08[7].

[95] See ¶¶ 17.03, 17.04. The statute makes it clear that the inventory need not be "substantially appreciated" within the meaning of § 751(b)(3) to permit the recognition of loss.

¶ 19.06 BASIS OF PROPERTY RECEIVED IN COMPLETE LIQUIDATION OF A PARTNERSHIP INTEREST

Page 19-37:

Add the following after first paragraph of subsection.

If the distribution includes "Stock of a Corporate Partner" subject to Temporary Regulations § 1.337(d)-3T(e)(1), a special rule must be applied prior to the application of this two-step algorithm. The basis to be allocated to properties distributed to the "Corporate Partner" under § 732(c) must be allocated first to such stock before it can be allocated to any other distributed property.[117.1] For this purpose, the amount to be allocated to the stock is determined under Temporary Regulations § 1.337(d)-3T(e)(2).[117.2]

[117.1] Temp. Reg. § 1.732-1T(c)(1)(ii) (effective date June 12, 2015; sunset date June 11, 2018).

[117.2] See ¶ 9.03[1][a][ii][D].

¶ 19.07 COLLATERAL CONSEQUENCES OF PARTNERSHIP DISTRIBUTIONS

[1] General Rules

Replace note 134 with the following.

[134] See Chapter 13. Section 708(b)(1)(B) was repealed in 2017by the 2017 Tax Cuts and Jobs Act, Pub. L. No. 115-97, § 13504(a) (Dec. 22, 2017). However, a liquidating distribution may terminate the partnership under § 708(b)(1)(A) [§ 708(b)(1), after 2017].

If the distribution is reclassified as a sale or exchange of the distributee's interest, a termination may result. See § 707(a)(2)(B); ¶¶ 14.02[3], 14.02[3][b].

Page 19-43:

In third paragraph of subsection, replace first sentence with the following.

The distribution of property with respect to which the partnership has taken investment credit, within five years after the date the property is placed in service, will generally trigger a recapture of the credit with respect to the non-distributee-partners, and, potentially, also with respect to the distributee-partner.[138]

---

[138] See § 50(a)(1), Reg. § 1.47-6(a)(1). Recapture apparently occurs even if the other partners receive distributions of an equivalent amount of investment credit recapture property, since the recapture rule operates on a property-by-property basis. Reg. § 1.47-6(a)(1).

Add at end of subsection.

For tax years beginning after 2012, all or a portion of any gain recognized by a partner under § 731 upon the receipt of partnership distributions may be subject to the 3.8% Medicare contribution tax on "net investment income" in § 1411. Net investment income includes any taxable net gain from dispositions of property, except property held in a nonpassive trade or business (other than the trade or business of trading in financial instruments or commodities within the scope of § 475(e)(2)).[142.1] For this purpose, gains and losses from "dispositions" of partnership interests are included in net gain to the extent of the net gain that would have been taken into account by the transferor if the partnership had sold all of its assets for fair market value immediately before the disposition.[142.2] Despite the somewhat inelegant use of the word "disposition," it appears this tax is intended to apply to taxable distributions under § 731, although the Treasury seems somewhat unsure as to exactly how to do the computations.[142.3]

[142.1] § 1411(c)(1)(A)(iii).

[142.2] §§ 1411(c)(4)(A), 1411(c)(4)(B).

[142.3] See REG-130507-11, 77 Fed. Reg. 72,612 (Dec. 5, 2012), Preamble to Proposed Regulations, Explanation of Provisions, part 8.A.i, *Dispositions of Interests in Partnerships and S Corporations, Mechanics of section 1411(c)(4), In general*, as discussed in ¶ 16.08[7].

[2] Distributions of Contracts Accounted for Under a Long-Term Contract Method of Accounting

Page 19-44:

In second paragraph of subsection, replace first sentence with the following.

The constructive completion rules do not, however, apply to distributions and contributions pursuant to either technical terminations under § 708(b)(1)(B) or Assets-Over mergers under Regulations § 1.708-1(c)(3)(i). (The technical termination rule in § 708(b)(1)(B) was repealed by the 2017 Tax Cuts and Jobs Act, effective for partnership taxable years beginning after December 31, 2017.[146.1])

[146.1] 2017 Tax Cuts and Jobs Act, Pub. L. No. 115-97, § 13504(a) (Dec. 22, 2017).

¶ 19.08 DISTRIBUTIONS OF PROPERTY TO PARTNERS WHO CONTRIBUTED OTHER PROPERTY: SECTION 737

Page 19-45:

Add to note 150.

Proposed Regulations § 1.737-1(c)(3)(i) (2014) would provide that the seven-year period begins on (and includes) the date of the contribution and ends on (and includes) the last date within the seven-year period (e.g., May 15, 2016, to May 14, 2023).

[2] Computation and Character of Gain

[f] Character of Gain

Page 19-51:

Replace first sentence of subsection with the following.

The character of any gain recognized under § 737 is determined by the "proportionate character of the net precontribution gain."[171]

---

[171] § 737(a).

[3] Exceptions and Special Rules Under Section 737(a)

[a] Previously Contributed Property

Page 19-52:

Add new note 173.1 at end of first sentence of subsection.

[173.1] For this purpose, a trust and a remainder beneficiary of the trust who were treated as contributing corporate shares to a new partnership as set forth in Situation 1 of Revenue Ruling 99-5, 1999-1 CB 434, and subsequently receive distributions of the contributed shares are treated as contributing partners. Priv. Ltr. Rul. 200824005 (Mar. 6, 2008); Priv. Ltr. Rul. 200824009 (Mar. 6, 2008).

Page 19-54:

Add to note 180.

 See also Priv. Ltr. Rul. 201537002 (May 13, 2015) (distributed stock treated as previously contributed where adequately identified by certificate).

Page 19-54:

Replace heading of ¶ 19.08[3][b] with the following revised heading.

[b] Application Following Section 708(b)(1)(B) Termination—Prior to 2018 [Revised Heading]

Add the following before first paragraph of subsection.

   For taxable years beginning prior to January 1, 2018, the sale of a withdrawing partner's interest to his co-partners terminated the partnership under § 708(b)(1)(B) (the "technical termination" rule) if 50 percent or more of the total interest in partnership capital and profits was sold within a twelve-month period. Following the 2017 repeal of this rule, neither a liquidation nor a transfer of a partnership interest will cause a termination provided at least two partners remain after the transfer or liquidation is completed.[181.1]
   NOTE: The remainder of this ¶ 19.08[3][b] addresses the law in effect with respect to taxable years beginning prior to January 1, 2018.

 [181.1] Terminations and their consequences are discussed in Chapter 13.

Page 19-55:

Add to note 183.

Prop. Reg. § 1.737-1(c)(3)(ii) (2014) (termination does not start new seven-year period with respect to partnership properties).

¶ 19.09 DISTRIBUTIONS OF MARKETABLE SECURITIES

[1] General Rule

Page 19-64:

 Add to note 217.

The technical termination rule in § 708(b)(1)(B) has been repealed, effective for taxable years beginning after December 31, 2017. 2017 Tax Cuts and Jobs Act, Pub. L. No. 115-97, § 13504(a) (Dec. 22, 2017).

[2] Marketable Securities

Page 19-66:

Add to note 227.

The Service has ruled privately that the distribution of a group flexible premium variable life insurance policy is not a distribution of a marketable security under § 731(c). Priv. Ltr. Rul. 200651023 (Sept. 21, 2006).

In Countryside Ltd. Partnership, 95 TCM 1006 (2008), the Service contended that the willingness of an issuer to consider a modification or repurchase of notes rendered the notes "marketable securities." There, an upper-tier partnership distributed an interest in a lower-tier partnership that held four privately issued notes issued by AIG Matched Funding Corp. The notes had a ten-year term and were redeemable at the holder's option less than three years from issuance. Additionally, each note provided the holder with the option of changing the due date of the note upon the affirmative vote of holders of 100% of the outstanding notes. The court ruled that this "right to renegotiate" did not indicate the presence of an arrangement to readily exchange the AIG notes for cash under § 731(c)(2)(B)(ii).

[3] Exceptions

Page 19-67:

Add to note 234.

A trust and a remainder beneficiary of the trust who were treated as contributing corporate shares to a new partnership as set forth in Situation 1 of Revenue Ruling 99-5, 1999-1 CB 434, and subsequently receive distributions of the contributed shares are treated as contributing the securities and fall within this exception. Priv. Ltr. Rul. 200824005 (Mar. 6, 2008); Priv. Ltr. Rul. 200824009 (Mar. 6, 2008).

Page 19-68:

Add to note 239.

; Priv. Ltr. Rul. 200627013 (Mar. 31, 2006) (distributee not eligible partner, because assets contributed to partnership not listed in § 731(c)(3)(C)(i)).

[5] Anti-Abuse Rule

Page 19-70:

Add the following to last paragraph of subsection.

These examples, in the words of the Tax Court, "presumably illustrate the universe of circumstances considered abusive for purposes of section 731(c)."[250.1]

[250.1] Countryside Ltd. Partnership, 95 TCM 1006 (2008), noting the Commissioner's comment in the preamble to the final § 731(c) Regulations, that "the text of the regulations adequately described several situations that would be considered abusive...and...additional examples are unnecessary." TD 8707.

¶ 19.10 DISTRIBUTIONS OF CORPORATE STOCK TO A CORPORATE PARTNER

Page 19-71:

Add to note 253.

See also Reg. § 1.732-3(a), which requires application of the aggregation rules under Reg. § 1.1502-34 to determine control, and Reg. § 1.732-3(b), which limits the amount of the § 732(f) basis reduction to the excess, if any, of the partnership's adjusted basis in the distributed stock immediately before the distribution over the aggregate basis of the distributed stock in the hands of corporate partners that are members of the same consolidated group (within the meaning of Reg. § 1.1502-1(h)) immediately after the distribution if the following two conditions are met: (1) two or more of the corporate partners receive a distribution of stock in another corporation, and (2) the corporation whose stock is distributed is (or becomes) a member of the same consolidated group following the distribution.

Page 19-72:

Add following to second full paragraph (ending with note callout 259).

Anticipating an apparent weakness in the "control" test, the Treasury issued regulations that treat a corporate partner as having control of the corporation whose stock is distributed if the corporate partner engages in a "Gain Elimination Transaction" (GET) following the distribution. A GET is any transaction in which the distributed stock is disposed of and less than all of the gain is recognized unless the nonrecognition occurs as part of an exchanged basis transaction or a transaction in which the distributed stock is transferred basis property in the hands of the transferee.[259.1]

[259.1] Reg. § 1.732-3(c). A GET may include a corporate reorganization or division.

Add to note 260.

See Reg. § 1.732-3(d).

Page 19-73:

Add new note 263 at end of last sentence of subsection.

[263] See generally ¶ 25.02[1][a] with regard to § 755(c). Proposed Regulations were issued under § 755(c) during 2014, effective for distributions on or after December 15, 1999. Prop. Reg. §§ 1.755-1(e), 1.755-1(f)(1) (2014).

CHAPTER **21**

Distributions That Alter the Partners' Interests in Section 751(b) Property

¶ 21.01 RECOGNITION OF GAIN INHERENT IN PARTNERSHIP ORDINARY INCOME PROPERTY: SECTION 751(b)

[3] Collateral Effects of Section 751(b)

Page 21-8:

Add at end of subsection.

Some or all of any income recognized by partners under § 751(b) during tax years beginning after 2012 may be subject to the 3.8% Medicare contribution tax on "net investment income" in § 1411, although the interaction between the two provisions is far from clear and creates complications that are unresolved by proposed regulations under § 1411. Net investment income includes any taxable net gain from dispositions of property, except property held in a nonpassive trade or business (other than the trade or business of trading in financial instruments or commodities within the scope of § 475(e)(2)).[23.1] For this purpose, gains and losses from "dispositions" of partnership interests are included in net gain to the extent of the net gain that would have been taken into account by the transferor if the partnership had sold all of its assets for fair market value immediately before the disposition.[23.2] Despite the somewhat inelegant use of the word "disposition," it appears this tax applies to taxable distributions under § 731, although the Treasury seems somewhat unsure as to exactly how to do the computations.[23.3] While neither the preamble nor the proposed regulations mention gains recognized on distributions under § 751(b), the Medicare contribution tax may also apply to these gains.

[23.1] § 1411(c)(1)(A)(iii).

[23.2] §§ 1411(c)(4)(A), 1411(c)(4)(B).

[23.3] See REG-130507-11, 77 Fed. Reg. 72,612 (Dec. 5, 2012), Preamble to Proposed Regulations, Explanation of Provisions, part 8.A.i, *Dispositions of Interests in Partnerships and S Corporations, Mechanics of section 1411(c)(4), In general*, as discussed in ¶ 16.08[7].

Page 21-11:

Add new ¶ 21.01[6].

[6] 2014 Proposed Regulations [New]

[a] Overview and Effective Date

Proposed § 751(b) regulations were issued on November 3, 2014. They completely revamp the existing regulatory scheme. While generally prospective from the date of finalization, they are partially applicable as of November 3,

2014, on an elective basis, which greatly increases their significance. A result of the request for comments on suggested approaches to dealing with § 751(b) contained in Notice 2006-14,[35.1] the Proposed Regulations are a thoughtful and technically profound effort.

In the Proposed Regulations, the gross value approach of the existing regulations is abandoned in favor of a system that is driven by a partner's share of the unrealized gain or loss in partnership § 751 property: Section 751(b) is triggered only if a distribution reduces a partner's net § 751 unrealized gain or loss. Grossly simplified, ordinary income is recognized by the partner whose share is reduced, and the basis of the corresponding § 751 property is increased by a like amount. Net § 751 unrealized gain or loss is measured using a hypothetical sale approach, which coordinates § 751(b) with § 704(c).

The devil, of course, is in the details. The allocations resulting from a hypothetical sale are impacted by § 704(c) and the reverse § 704(c) allocations attributable to revaluations of partnership assets (namely, "book-ups"). If a partnership does not maintain capital accounts in accordance with Regulations § 1.704-1(b)(2)(iv), it must make the hypothetical sale determination as if it did. Special rules are provided for tiered partnerships, which include mandatory book-ups for controlled lower-tier partnerships.

A reduction in a partner's § 751 unrealized gain or loss is a "section 751(b) amount" (hereinafter § 751(b) amount) giving rise to a "section 751(b) distribution" (hereinafter § 751(b) distribution). The partnership must choose a "reasonable approach" consistent with the purposes of § 751(b) under which each partner recognizes ordinary income (or sacrifices a basis adjustment) equal to its § 751(b) amount. Two approaches are generally sanctioned: (1) the "deemed gain" approach and (2) the "hot asset sale" approach. The deemed gain approach is straightforward: The partnership is deemed to recognize ordinary income equal to each partner's § 751(b) amount, allocates that amount to each partner, and makes appropriate adjustments for the partnership's basis in its assets. The hot asset sale approach creates a deemed taxable exchange of § 751 property for cash. Neither approach produces the correct result in all cases—hence, the flexibility (and complexity).

A distributee partner is required to recognize capital gain to the extent necessary to prevent a § 734(b) adjustment that would reduce unrealized § 751 gain or loss. The hypothetical sale approach measures a partner's net § 751 unrealized gain or loss after the distribution without regard to basis adjustments arising from distributions under the "reasonable approach" chosen by the partnership. Thus, any adjustment which could impact § 751 unrealized gain or loss must be prevented. The capital gain (or ordinary income, if the partnership has elected out of the special recapture/§ 1231 rules summarized in the next paragraph) recognized by the distributee increases outside basis, thus eliminating the offending inside basis adjustment. Partners can elect to recognize capital gain to the extent a distribution would otherwise cause an increase

---

[35.1] Notice 2006-14, 2006-1 CB 498.

in their net unrealized § 751 gain or loss (e.g., upon the distribution of § 751 property with a greater than zero basis to a zero basis partner).

The Proposed Regulations also make a significant change to the current basis adjustment rules. A distribution of capital gain property can yield a basis adjustment to capital gain property under either § 732(c) or § 734(b), which can have the effect of reducing ordinary income by increasing a property's basis (for example, recapture under § 1245). In order to negate this result, the Proposed Regulations provide that the basis adjustment is not taken into account for purposes of determining both (1) the partnership's basis for purposes of §§ 617(d)(1), 1245(a)(1), 1250(a)(1), 1252(a)(1), and 1254(a)(1) (i.e., the recapture provisions), and (2) the partner's or the partnership's gain or loss under §§ 995(c), 1231(a), and 1248(a). Thus, a positive § 734(b) basis adjustment to § 1231 property, for example, will not reduce the recapture on disposition, nor will it reduce the § 1231 gain; rather, it can produce a capital loss on a disposition as to which gain is otherwise recognized. Taxpayers offended by these rules can opt out of them, although potentially at the cost of recognizing ordinary income instead of capital gain in certain cases. While the election may be beneficial in many cases, once made, it cannot be revoked without the consent of the Commissioner, which makes the election problematic.

[b] Distributions to Which Section 751(b) Applies

A distribution is a § 751(b) distribution if it gives rise to a § 751(b) amount for any partner.[35.2] A § 751(b) amount measures the reduction in a partner's share of partnership ordinary income or loss, and equals the reduction in ordinary income (or increase in ordinary loss) caused by the distribution. More precisely, it equals the greater of

1. The excess of the partner's net § 751 unrealized gain immediately before the distribution over net § 751 unrealized gain immediately after the distribution;
2. The excess of the partner's net § 751 unrealized loss immediately after the distribution over net § 751 unrealized loss immediately before the distribution; or
3. The partner's net § 751 unrealized gain immediately before the distribution plus the partner's net § 751 unrealized loss immediately after the distribution (where neither number equals zero).[35.3]

A partner's net § 751 unrealized gain or loss is determined by hypothesizing a sale at fair market value (taking into account § 7701(g), which deems property encumbered by nonrecourse debt to have a value at least equal to the debt), including remedial allocations under Regulations § 1.704-3(d) and tak-

---

[35.2] Prop. Reg. § 1.751-1(b)(2)(i) (2014).

[35.3] Prop. Reg. § 1.751-1(b)(2) (2014). The parenthetical in the third alternative is necessary to prevent it from negating the first two.

ing into account § 743(b) basis adjustments. Basis adjustments arising from the distribution itself are taken into account, but those arising from the transaction deemed to occur under the "reasonable approach" selected by the partnership are not. Basis adjustments that cannot be made because the partnership does not own § 751 property to which the adjustment can attach (termed "carryover basis adjustments")[35.4] are treated as though made to new partnership § 751 property with a value of zero. The post-distribution computation is made by summing the distributee's remaining partnership share (if any) with the ordinary income or loss the distributee would recognize if she immediately disposed of the distributed assets at fair market value (taking into account § 7701(g)). All partnership computations are made assuming a revaluation (i.e., a "book-up") is made immediately prior to the distribution.[35.5]

The basic mechanics of determining whether a distribution is a § 751(b) distribution are illustrated by Examples 2 and 3 of Proposed Regulations § 1.751-1(g). A, B, and C each contribute $120 to partnership ABC for a one-third interest. ABC buys land for $100 in Year 1. At the end of Year 3, when ABC holds $260 in cash, the land is still worth $100, and ABC has generated $90 of zero basis unrealized receivables, ABC distributes $50 cash to C, reducing C's interest from one third to one fourth. C's share of ABC's § 751 income immediately before the distribution is $30 ($C$'s net § 751 unrealized gain). Since the revaluation locks in the $30 of ordinary income to C under § 704(c) principles, C's post-distribution share of § 751 unrealized gain remains $30, and no § 751(b) distribution occurs. But, if ABC distributes $150 cash to C in retirement of C's interest, C's post-distribution net § 751 unrealized gain is zero, C has a § 751(b) amount of $30, a § 751(b) distribution has occurred, and C must recognize $30 of ordinary income.

The complexities of dealing with carryover basis adjustments are illustrated by Proposed Regulations § 1.751-1(g) Example 4.[35.6] A and B are equal partners in AB, which owns a $50 value unrealized receivable (with a zero basis) and non-depreciable real property (with a basis of $50 and a value of $100). A's outside basis is $25, B's is $50, and B has a $25 § 743(b) basis adjustment allocable to the unrealized receivable. AB distributes the unrealized receivable to A. Immediately before the distribution, a sale of the unrealized

---

[35.4] See ¶ 24.05 (distributed § 751 property, basis adjustment of non-distributee partner, partnership holds no other § 751 property); Reg. §§ 1.755-1(b)(5)(iii)(D), 1.755-1(c)(4).

[35.5] Prop. Reg. § 1.751-1(b)(2)(iv) (2014). If the partnership does not maintain capital accounts, it must make the computations as if it did. In the tiered partnership context, the lower-tier partnership must revalue its assets if (1) it owns § 751 property and (2) the upper-tier partnership controls the lower-tier partnership (i.e., the same persons own, directly or indirectly (through one or more entities) more than 50 percent of the capital and profits interests in both partnerships). Absent control, the upper-tier partnership must allocate its distributive share of lower-tier partnership items as though the revaluation had taken place.

[35.6] Prop. Reg. § 1.751-1(g) Example 4 (2014).

receivable for $50 would produce $50 of ordinary income, shared equally, and *B* would offset its $25 share with its $25 § 743(b) adjustment. Thus, *A*'s net § 751 unrealized gain is $25, and *B*'s is zero. After the distribution, a hypothetical sale by the partnership would produce no net income or loss from § 751 property. But, *B* must take into account its $25 carryover adjustment created by the distribution to *A* of property in which *B* had a § 743(b) adjustment.[35.7] This deemed $25 adjustment to deemed zero-value property creates, for *B*, a $25 net § 751 unrealized loss. *A* has a $50 net § 751 unrealized gain since *A* owns a zero basis $50 value unrealized receivable. Since *B*'s $25 net § 751 unrealized loss immediately after the distribution exceeds its zero net § 751 unrealized loss immediately before the distribution, the distribution is a § 751(b) distribution.

[c] Tax Consequences of a Section 751(b) Distribution

The Proposed Regulations sanction any reasonable approach to determining the tax consequences of the § 751(b) distribution as long as each partner with a § 751(b) amount either (1) recognizes an equal amount of ordinary income or (2) takes it into account by eliminating a basis adjustment. Once adopted, the reasonable approach must be consistently applied, even after a § 708(b)(1)(B) termination, unless it produces results inconsistent with the purpose of § 751, in which case another "reasonable approach" must be adopted.[35.8]

Proposed Regulations § 1.751-1(g) Example 4 illustrates the flexibility accorded by the rule.[35.9] Again, the equal AB partnership owns a zero-basis $50 value unrealized receivable and land with a basis of $50 and value of $100. *A* and *B* have outside bases of $25 and $50, respectively, and *B* has a $25 § 743(b) basis adjustment. AB distributes the unrealized receivable to *A*. *B*'s § 751 amount is $25, attributable to its carryover § 743(b) adjustment. The "deemed gain" approach would presumably require that *B* recognize $25 of ordinary income, and would also apparently leave AB with a $25 basis in a nonexistent asset, *A* with $50 of potential ordinary income, and *B* with a $25 loss in its interest—a most unsatisfactory result, since *A* should have only $25 of ordinary income and *B*'s original $50 outside basis equaled the $50 value of its interest. Fortunately, the hot asset sale approach eliminates these problems. *B* is deemed to receive its $25 share of the unrealized receivable in a current distribution, sell it back to AB, and then contribute the cash to AB. Since the current distribution of the unrealized receivable carries with it *B*'s § 743(b) adjustment, *B* takes a $25 basis and has no gain on the deemed sale back to AB. The receivable now has a $25 basis that goes to *A* in the actual distribution, and all distortions are eliminated.

[35.7] See Reg. § 1.743-1(g)(2)(ii).

[35.8] Prop. Reg. § 1.751-1(b)(3)(i) (2014).

[35.9] Prop. Reg. § 1.751-1(g) Example 4 (2014).

The requirement that the AB partnership must continue to use the hot asset sale approach for future § 751(b) distributions, or cannot use it if AB previously used the deemed gain approach, seems unreasonable, however. Since only approaches that satisfy the purposes of § 751(b) are ever permitted, partnerships should be entitled to choose any approach that yields reasonable results. The deemed gain approach produces patently unreasonable results under the facts of Example 4. Perhaps, an adversely affected taxpayer can point to the last sentence of Proposed Regulations § 1.751-1(b)(3)(i) (2014), which mandates a change in approach on a one-time basis if the adopted approach produces results inconsistent with the purpose of § 751.

If the chosen approach produces a § 734(b) adjustment that would reduce unrealized § 751 gain or loss, the distributee must recognize capital gain, which increases outside basis to the extent necessary to eliminate the offending § 734(b) adjustment.[35.10] This principle is illustrated by Proposed Regulations § 1.751-1(g) Examples 5 and 6.[35.11] These two examples also address two significant open issues under current law: (1) whether § 734(b) adjustments triggered by actual distributions are taken into account in computing the § 751(b) exchange and (2) whether some § 734(b) adjustments reduce the § 704(c) account of the distributee and some do not; the difference is unclear.

Example 5 postulates the equal ABC partnership that owns Unrealized Receivable *1* (with a basis of zero and value of $90), Unrealized Receivable *2* (with a basis of zero and value of $30), and nondepreciable real property (with a basis of zero and value of $180). Each of *A*, *B*, and *C* has a zero outside basis, and ABC has a § 754 election in effect.[35.12] ABC revalues its assets ("books up") and makes a current distribution of Unrealized Receivable *1* to *A*.

Before the distribution, each partner has $40 of net § 751 unrealized gain (one third of $120 total unrealized receivables gain). After the distribution (but before taking § 751(b) into account), each partner has $10 of net income from Unrealized Receivable *2* and *A* has $90 of net income from Unrealized Receivable *1*. Since each of *B* and *C* have more net § 751 unrealized gain before the distribution than after, the distribution is a § 751(b) distribution, and the § 751(b) amount of each equals the difference, that is, $30. Accordingly, *B* and *C* must each recognize $30 of ordinary income. Example 5 sets forth three approaches, two reasonable (i.e., the deemed gain and hot asset sale approaches),

---

[35.10] Prop. Reg. § 1.751-1(b)(3)(ii)(A) (2014). If the partnership makes an election under Proposed Regulations § 1.755-1(c)(2)(vi) (2014) to negate the special basis adjustment rules applicable to recapture, § 1231, and similar property, the gain may be ordinary income or a dividend, as appropriate.

[35.11] Prop. Reg. § 1.751-1(g) (2014).

[35.12] Example 5 stipulates that no partner has a capital loss carryforward. The suggestion is that if the capital gain generated by the § 751(b) distribution were offset by a capital loss carryforward (but not a current year capital loss), the result would somehow be different. Since no other result makes sense, this caveat seems gratuitous.

as well as one unreasonable (i.e., the violation of no basis adjustment rule approach).

Under the deemed gain approach, B and C each recognize $30 of ordinary income and ABC increases its basis in Unrealized Receivable 1 to $60. Upon the distribution of Unrealized Receivable 1 to A, its basis would be reduced to zero (A's outside basis), and since ABC has a § 754 election in effect, a $60 basis adjustment would be made to Unrealized Receivable 2. Since this adjustment would alter the computation of net § 751 unrealized gain or loss, $60 of capital gain must be recognized by A in order to increase A's outside basis and eliminate the § 734(b) adjustment. Unrealized Receivable 1 thus takes a $60 basis in A's hands. The correlative basis adjustment to reflect the capital gain is to the real property, and it eliminates A's reverse § 704(c) account therein. The deemed gain approach is thus reasonable.

Under the hot asset sale approach, B and C are each deemed to receive a $30 portion of Unrealized Receivable 1, sell it back to ABC for $30, and then contribute the $30 cash back to ABC. In order to avoid a prohibited § 734(b) basis adjustment on the distribution of Unrealized Receivable 1, A must recognize $60 of capital gain. To accomplish this, A is deemed to receive a $60 interest in the zero-basis real property, sell it back to ABC for $60 cash, and then contribute the cash back to ABC. The $60 capital gain reduces A's reverse § 704(c) account in the real property. The hot asset sale approach is thus reasonable.

A hot asset sale approach that fails to recognize the $60 of capital gain to A and thus produces a $60 § 734(b) adjustment to Unrealized Receivable 2 is not reasonable, however, because it generates a prohibited basis adjustment.

Proposed Regulations § 1.751-1(g) Example 6 varies the facts of Example 5 by assuming that Unrealized Receivable 1 has a basis of $9 and that each partner has an outside basis of $3. Thus, the distribution of Unrealized Receivable 1 to A produces a $6 § 734(b) adjustment to Unrealized Receivable 2 (resulting in the $9 basis in Unrealized Receivable 1 being reduced to $3), which is taken into account in measuring the § 751(b) transaction. Each partner's pre-distribution net § 751 unrealized gain is $37 (1/3 x [$120 unrealized receivables value - $ 9 basis]). Each partner's share of ABC's post-distribution ordinary income is $8 (1/3 x [$30 unrealized receivables value - $6 basis]). B and C thus each have a § 751(b) amount of $29 (i.e., $37 pre-distribution net § 751 unrealized gain - $8 post-distribution ordinary income).

Under the deemed gain approach, B and C each recognize $29 of ordinary income, the basis of Unrealized Receivable 2 is increased by $58 (from $9) to $67, and the distribution to A (who has a $3 outside basis) would produce a $64 § 734(b) basis adjustment, instead of the $6 adjustment from the actual distribution. Accordingly, A recognizes $58 of capital gain to avoid a prohibited basis adjustment, all of which reduces A's reverse § 704(c) account with respect to the real property. A takes a $61 basis in Unrealized Receivable 1, thus preserving his $37 total ordinary income position (namely, $29 in Unrealized Receivable *1* and $8 in Unrealized Receivable *2*). The deemed gain approach is thus reasonable.

The hot asset sale approach produces the same results. The deemed distribution of a portion of Unrealized Receivable *1* with a basis of zero and a value of $29 to each of *B* and *C*, followed by a deemed sale for cash and a re-contribution of the cash, produces $29 of ordinary income to each. The resulting $58 basis increase to Unrealized Receivable *1* requires *C* to recognize $58 of capital gain to avoid using this basis to generate a prohibited § 734(b) basis increase to Unrealized Receivable *2*—ergo, a correlative distribution and re-sale of a $58 portion of the real property with *A*. The distribution of Unrealized Receivable *1* with a basis of $67 ($58 + $9) to *A*, whose outside basis is $61 ($3 + $58), produces the same $6 § 734(b) adjustment to the basis of Unrealized Receivable *2*.

Critically, the $6 § 734(b) adjustment reduced each partner's reverse § 704(c) account in Unrealized Receivable *2* by $2, while in both Examples 5 and 6, the capital gain reduces only the distributee's reverse § 704(c) account in the real property. There are two differences in the adjustments. First, the $6 adjustment is with respect to an actual distribution, as opposed to a transaction invented by the § 751(b) construct. Second, the adjustment is with respect to ordinary income versus capital gain property. Neither difference seems compelling. On the other hand, treating the $6 § 734(b) adjustment as reducing only *A*'s § 704(c) account produces a perfectly sensible outcome. By leaving *B* and *C* with $2 more ordinary income in Unrealized Receivable *2*, it reduces the § 751(b) amount of each by $2, such that each has only $27 of ordinary income. Since the basis increase to Unrealized Receivable *1* is $4 less, the prohibited § 734(b) basis increase potentially caused by the distribution of Unrealized Receivable *1* is $4 less, and *A*'s required capital gain is $4 less. The incremental $4 reduction to *A*'s § 704(c) account in Unrealized Receivable *2* is matched by *A*'s basis in Unrealized Receivable *1* being less by $4 (and thus having $4 more potential gain). The position taken by Example 6 has the effect of accelerating the recognition of ordinary income to *B* and *C*, with a matching acceleration of capital gain to A. The justification for this outcome is difficult to ascertain.

The elective capital gain recognition option is illustrated by Proposed Regulations § 1.751-1(g) Example 7, which assumes the same facts as Example 6 except that ABC does not have a § 754 election in effect. Thus, the distribution of Unrealized Receivable *1* to *A* does not produce a prohibited § 734(b) adjustment and *A* is not required to recognize capital gain. *A* may nevertheless elect to recognize capital gain in an amount necessary to eliminate the downwards § 732 adjustment to Unrealized Receivable *1* in order to prevent *A*'s net § 751 unrealized gain from increasing as a result of the distribution.

Proposed Regulations § 1.751-1(g) Examples 8 and 9 provide guidance on the interaction of § 751(b) with § 1248, which recharacterizes as a dividend certain gain from the sale of stock in a controlled foreign corporation. These examples make clear that a § 751(b) distribution creates a sale or exchange for purposes of § 1248, thus characterizing the recognized ordinary income as a dividend. The dividend reduces § 704(c) (as well as reverse § 704(c)) accounts. Section 1248(g)(2)(B), which provides that § 1248 is inapplicable if any other provision of the Code mandates ordinary income on disposition of the stock, is ignored, and so a subsequent disposition by the distributee partner of the distributed stock, the gain on which is ordinary under § 735(a), triggers § 1248(a). Mechanically, these examples fragment the stock into its ordinary income and capital gain components, and treat them as separate assets for purposes of determining the consequences of a § 751(b) distribution.

[d] Basis Adjustments to Recapture and § 1231 Property

The application of § 734(b) basis adjustments to recapture property has always been troublesome. Since the § 734(b) adjustment increases common basis, it can have the effect of reducing the recapture amount on the disposition of the property. The same phenomenon can occur upon a distribution in liquidation of a partner's interest.

Regulations proposed in 2014 seek to remedy this apparent defect in the regulatory scheme.[35.13] An increase to the basis of capital gain property is not taken into account in computing "recomputed basis" under § 1245(a)(1) (and thus the ordinary income recapture is not reduced by the basis increase). Similar rules apply for purposes of §§ 617(d)(1), 1250(a)(1), 1251(a)(1), and 1254(a)(1). Somewhat surprisingly, the adjustment is also not taken into account for purposes of §§ 1231, 1248, and 995. A companion set of rules applies in determining a partner's basis in property received in a distribution in liquidation of its interest.[35.14] Whether the fisc has enough at stake under these provisions to warrant this level of complexity is a fair question.

The following detailed example illustrates the rule.[35.15] The equal ABC partnership owns depreciable property X (with a basis of $30, value of $150, and subject to $120 of recapture) and depreciable property Y (basis and value of $30). Each partner has an outside basis of $20. ABC distributes property Y to A in a current distribution, and makes a § 754 election. Property X is revalued such that its $120 of appreciation is booked into the capital accounts, $40 to each partner. The current distribution does not create a § 751(b) amount for any partner.

Since A's basis is only $20, ABC has a $10 § 734(b) upwards basis adjustment. Property X is fragmented into two assets: (1) a zero-basis, $120-value unrealized receivable and (2) capital gain property with a basis and value of $30. The $10 basis increase is allocated to the capital gain property, increasing its basis to $40. If ABC then sells X for its $150 value, it has $120

[35.13] Prop. Reg. §§ 1.755-1(c)(2)(iii) (2014) through 1.755-1(c)(2)(vi) (2014).

[35.14] Prop. Reg. §§ 1.732-1(c)(2)(iii) (2014) through 1.732-1(c)(2)(vi) (2014).

[35.15] Prop. Reg. § 1.755-1(c)(6) Example 2 (2014).

of ordinary income and a capital loss of $10; the § 734(b) adjustment is not taken into account for purposes of computing ABC's recapture amount.

Complexity increases if ABC holds Property X, takes $15 of depreciation on the $30 of original basis and $1 of depreciation on the $10 § 734(b) step up adjustment, and then sells X for $170. The recapture amount is $136, that is, the original $120 of recapture plus the $16 of additional depreciation taken. For purposes of § 1231, the § 734(b) adjustment is not taken into account, so that § 1231(a)(1) applies to the $19 portion of the gain not recaptured as ordinary income (that is, $170 sales proceeds - $15 adjusted basis = $155 gain; $155 gain - $136 recapture amount = $19 non-recapture gain). The remaining § 734(b) adjustment of $9 is recovered as a capital loss.

A partnership may elect to have these special basis adjustment rules not apply.[35.16] This election also makes inapplicable the companion set of rules under the Proposed § 732 Regulations designed to prevent basis increases to distributed capital gain property from reducing recapture as well as similar amounts.[35.17] The election applies to all distributions for the taxable year for which the election is made and all subsequent partnership taxable years (including all taxable years after a § 708(b)(1)(B) termination). The election must be in writing and timely filed (including extensions) with the partnership return for the year, and is a method of accounting which can be changed only with the consent of the Commissioner.

In the base case, the election is highly favorable. For instance, in the example above, applying the $10 § 734(b) basis adjustment directly to Property X increases its basis from $30 to $40. On a disposition for $150, the resulting $110 of gain is ordinary (versus the consequence in the above example, namely, $120 of ordinary income and a $10 capital loss if the election is not made).

The actual cost of the election arises, however, if a § 751(b) distribution occurs. Basis adjustments that are created by the transactions deemed to occur under the partnership's "reasonable approach" must be made, but if making them alters the net § 751 unrealized gain or loss of any partner, gain must be recognized by the putative distributee in order to increase its outside basis and thereby avoid the prohibited basis adjustment. If an election has been made under Proposed Regulations § 1.755-1(c)(2)(vi) (2014), this gain is ordinary.

Proposed Regulations § 1.751-1(g) Example 9 illustrates the election provided by Proposed Regulation § 1.755-1(c)(2)(vi) (2014) to ignore the newly proposed rules that prevent § 734(b) adjustments from reducing recapture and § 1231-type amounts. Under the facts of Example 9, a current distribution of stock subject to § 1248 is a § 751(b) distribution that would produce a prohibited § 734(b) basis adjustment. Because of the election, the distributee recognizes § 1248 dividend income equal to the forgone basis adjustment, and the

---

[35.16] Prop. Reg. § 1.755-1(c)(2)(vi) (2014) (election to not apply the rules of Prop. Reg. §§ 1.755-1(c)(2)(iii) (2014) through 1.755-1(c)(2)(v) (2014)).

[35.17] Prop. Reg. §§ 1.732-1(c)(2)(iii) (2014) through 1.732-1(c)(2)(vi) (2014).

partnership then increases the basis of the ordinary asset to which the prohibited basis adjustment would have applied.

[e] Anti-Abuse Rule

The breadth of the requisite anti-abuse rule will likely test the limits on the guidance set forth in decisions such as *RLC Industries*.[35.18] "[I]f a principal purpose of a transaction is to achieve a tax result that is inconsistent with the purpose of section 751, the Commissioner may recast the transaction for federal tax purposes as appropriate to achieve tax results that are consistent with the purpose of section 751."[35.19] Two categories of situations are presumed to establish that a transaction is inconsistent with the purpose of § 751. The first category exists if a transaction would be subject to § 751(b) but for the application of the principles of § 704(c) and any one of the five following conditions is also present:

1. The distributee's net § 751 unrealized gain is at least four times greater than its booked up post-distribution capital account; presumably, it is the net unrealized gain remaining in the partnership that counts, although the language could be read (nonsensically) to include the ordinary income imbedded in distributed property;
2. The distributee is substantially protected from loss and has little or no participation in profits other than a preferred return;
3. The distributee engages in a transaction that causes its net worth to be less than its tax liability inherent in partnership § 751 property;
4. The distributee transfers within five years a portion of its interest in a nonrecognition transaction to a nontaxable transferee; or
5. The partnership transfers to a corporation in a nonrecognition transaction § 751 property other than a transfer of all property used in a trade or business.

The second category of transaction that is presumed inconsistent with the purposes of § 751 is an amendment to the partnership allocation provisions that reduces a partner's net § 751 unrealized gain.

If a partner participates in either category of transaction and does not report its share of ordinary income from § 751 property for the taxable year of the transaction, it must file a Form 8275-R for that year.[35.20]

The anti-abuse rule is problematic in that the remedy for its application is uncertain. It is difficult to see how a distribution would be recast to achieve the deemed (by the Commissioner) result other than to characterize it as a recognition transaction. There is no obvious authority for just triggering the of-

---

[35.18] RLC Indus. Co. v. Commissioner, 58 F3d 413 (9th Cir. 1995) (Service's attempt to vest in itself overriding power to decide reasonableness of particular taxpayer's timber depletion allowance ruled invalid).

[35.19] Prop. Reg. § 1.751-1(b)(4)(i) (2014).

[35.20] Prop. Reg. § 1.751-1(b)(4)(ii) (2014).

fending partner's remaining share of partnership ordinary income (or, in the case of the four-to-one rule, the amount of ordinary income in excess of the permitted amount). Nor is there any authority, obvious or not, for converting a statutory nonrecognition transaction into a fully taxable transaction. Perhaps, the gross value asset exchange approach of the current regulations could be invoked, although this approach is likely irreconcilable with § 704(c). The lack of any example in the Proposed Regulations illustrating the rule suggests that the drafters shared this uncertainty. Nevertheless, the situations that bring the anti-abuse rule into play validate the Treasury's concerns. Whether it is appropriate to address those concerns in the final or Proposed § 751(b) Regulations is another question.

[f] Successor Rules

Section 751(b)(2)(A) provides that § 751(b) does not apply to a distribution of property previously contributed by the distributee. The Proposed Regulations provide a detailed set of successor rules.[35.21] The transferee of a partnership interest in a nonrecognition transaction is treated as the contributing partner. If the partnership disposes of § 751 property in a nonrecognition transaction, the substituted basis property received in the exchange is treated as contributed § 751 property. An interest in an entity is not treated as previously contributed property to the extent it is "stuffed" with non-contributed property.

[g] Statements Required

For each § 751(b) distribution made during the year, the partnership must include, with its return for the year of the distribution, a statement with a caption identifying the statement as the disclosure for the § 751(b) distribution with the date of the distribution, and a brief description of the "reasonable approach" adopted by the partnership for recognizing ordinary income and, if applicable, capital gain. If relevant, the statement must say whether the approach varies from an approach previously adopted for any of the three prior years.

In addition, the partnership must include a statement for each partner attached to its K-1 that includes the date of the § 751(b) distribution and the amount of ordinary income and capital gain recognized.

[h] Effective Date

The Proposed § 751(b) Regulations are prospective only, and thus will apply to distributions on or after they are finalized. However, a partnership and its partners may apply, on or after November 3, 2014, the rules for determining a partner's interest in partnership § 751 property contained in Proposed Regulations § 1.751-1(b)(2) (2014), provided they comply with the anti-abuse rule and they consistently apply these rules. The "reasonable approach" rules

---

[35.21] Prop. Reg. § 1.751-1(b)(5) (2014).

of Proposed Regulations § 1.751-1(b)(3) (2014) may not be used, however, so the full exchange approach of the existing regulations remains applicable until the Proposed § 751(b) Regulations are finalized.

¶ 21.03 DETERMINING THE TAX CONSEQUENCES OF A SECTION 751(b) DISTRIBUTION: THE SEVEN-STEP ANALYSIS

[4] Step 4: Determine Which Assets Are Involved in the Section 751(b) Exchange

[c] The Effect of Express Agreements Among the Parties as to the Assets Exchanged

Page 21-23:

Replace note 61 with the following.

⁶¹ See Reg. § 1.751-1(g)(3)(c) Examples (3)(c), (3)(d)(1), 4(c), (5)(c), 6(c). The agreement is recognized even though it has no economic effect.

Page 21-25:

Add to second to last paragraph of Example 21-7.

To the extent that the agreement does not facilitate ordinary income shifting, however, it should be respected. Thus, if the distributee receives multiple items of other property, an agreement as to which of these properties is acquired by the distributee in the exchange should be given effect. The amount of ordinary income triggered in the exchange is not impacted by the agreement.

Death or Retirement of a Partner

Payments in Liquidation of the Interest of a Retired or Deceased Partner

Chapter 22 was revised effective December 2019. The revised chapter can be found in the front of this student edition.

Special Problems Relating to the Death of a Partner

Chapter 23 was revised effective March 2020. The revised chapter can be found in the front of this student edition.

Adjustments to the Bases of Partnership Assets

PART IX

Adjustments to the Bases of Partnership Assets in Connection With Transfers of Partnership Interests

¶ 24.07   Effect of the Section 743(b) Adjustment on Depreciation,
             Depletion, and Investment Credit S24-1

Chapter 24 was revised effective August 2019. The revised chapter can be found in the front of this student edition. Updates occurring after that date appear below.

¶ 24.07 EFFECT OF THE SECTION 743(b) ADJUSTMENT ON DEPRECIATION, DEPLETION, AND INVESTMENT CREDIT

Page 24-44:

In first full paragraph, first sentence, replace Section 168(i) *with* Section 168(k).

Replace second and third full paragraphs with the following.

Regulation § 1.168(k)-2(b)(iv)(D) takes an aggregate approach to applying the bonus depreciation rules to § 743(b) adjustments: Each partner is treated as having a depreciable interest in the its share of partnership property. Consequently, a § 743(b) basis increase is not eligible for bonus depreciation unless all of the following requirements are satisfied: (1) Neither the transferee partner or a predecessor had any depreciable interest in the deemed transferred property;[157] (2) the acquisition of the partnership interest meets the requirements of §§ 179(d)(2)(A) (acquisition not from a related person under §§ 267 and 707, with minor modifications, tested at partner level),[157.1] 179(d)(2)(B) (controlled group prohibition), and 179(d)(2)(C) (carryover basis and § 1014 prohibition); and (3) the acquisition of the partnership interest meets the requirements of § 179(d)(3) (cost of property does not include basis attributable to other property held at any time by transferee partner).[157.2] However, a § 743(b) adjustment is not eligible for bonus depreciation if the purchaser disposes of the partnership interest in a taxable transaction in the same taxable year in which the interest was acquired.[157.3]

Computation of the recovery allowance for the balance of the property is unaffected.[158] As a general rule, if the partnership is using the remedial allocation method with respect to an item of partnership property, then any § 743(b) increase with respect to such item that is attributable to § 704(c) built-in gain would be recovered over the remaining recovery period for the partnership's excess book basis.[159] However, if a partnership (other than a publicly traded partnership) elects to claim bonus depreciation with respect to a partner's § 743(b) adjustment, the portion of the adjustment attributable to § 704(c) built-in gain may be deducted under the applicable bonus depreciation rule.[159.1]

---

[157] The definition of "predecessor" for purposes of this rule is supplied by Reg. § 1.168(k)-2(a)(2)(iv).

[157.1] For purposes of applying this rule, a partner is not treated as having a depreciable interest in partnership property solely by virtue of being a partner in the partnership. See TD 9916, Preamble I.B.2, Application to Partnerships, 85 Fed. Reg. 71734, 71737 (Nov. 10, 2020). For taxable years ending before January 1, 2021, taxpayers may elect to apply Proposed Regulations § 1.168(k)-2(b)(3)(iii)(B)(5) (2019) (partner's prior depreciable interest in partnership property based on percentage of depreciation deductions allocable to such partner; five-year lookback period). The intricacies of this look-through rule and related issues (such as the interface with Rev. Rul. 99-6) is explained by the New York State Bar Association in Report No. 1428 (Nov. 25, 2019). Guidance with respect to an election to apply Proposed Regulations § 1.168(k)-2(b)(3)(iii)(B)(5) is provided in Revenue Procedure 2020-50, 2020-48 IRB 1122.

[157.2] Reg. § 1.168(k)-2 is generally applicable to qualified property placed in service by a taxpayer during or after the taxpayer's taxable year that includes September 24, 2019. Reg. § 1.168(k)-2(h)(1)(i). A taxpayer may generally choose to apply the regulation, in its entirety, to qualified property acquired and placed in service after September 27, 2017. Reg. §§ 1.168(k)-2(h)(2)(i), 1.168(k)-2(h)(3)(i) (relying on proposed regulation).

[157.3] Reg. § 1.168(k)-2(g)(1)(i).

[158] Reg. § 1.743-1(j)(4)(i)(B)(1) (applicable to transfers of interests on or after December 14, 1999).

[159] Reg. § 1.743-1(j)(4)(i)(B)(2); see Reg. § 1.704-3(d)(2). But see Reg. § 1.704-1(b)(2)(iv)(g)(3) (entire book basis must be recovered at same rate as tax basis for purposes of § 704(b) capital account maintenance rules; failure to amend to reflect contrary rule in remedial allocation Regulations is apparent technical oversight).

[159.1] Reg. § 1.743-1(j)(4)(i)(B)(2) (last sentence).

CHAPTER **25**

Adjustments to the Bases of Partnership Assets in Connection With Distributions of Partnership Assets

¶ 25.01 OVERVIEW OF THE SECTION 734 RULES

[3] Basis Relationships Under Section 734(b)

Page 25-9:

Add to note 18.

Following the repeal of § 708(b)(1)(B) for taxable years beginning after December 31, 2017, this gambit is no longer available. 2017 Tax Cuts and Jobs Act, Pub. L. No. 115-97, § 13504(a) (Dec. 22, 2017).

[5] Effect of Section 734(b) on Property Subject to Depreciation or Depletion

Page 25-11:

In note 27, add after first full sentence.

However, § 168(k) bonus depreciation may not be claimed with respect to a § 734(b) basis increase. Reg. § 1.168(k)-2(b)(3)(iv)(C).

Page 25-12:

Replace note 28 with the following.

²⁸ Reg. § 1.734-1(e)(2).

[7] Mandatory Section 734(b) Basis Adjustments

Page 25-17:

Add at end of subsection.

Proposed Regulations relating to mandatory application of § 734(b) in connection with distributions that produce substantial basis reductions were issued during 2014. Pending finalization of these proposals, the highlights of these Proposed Regulations are as follows:

1. Although the statute and the Proposed Regulations refer to a "substantial basis reduction" (in excess of $250,000) as the trigger for mandatory application of § 734(b), the basis reduction in question reflects the total of (a) any losses recognized upon liquidation of a partner's interest (see § 734(b)(2)(A)), and (b) decreases in the basis of remaining partnership property to reflect increases in the basis of distributed property in the hands of a distributee (see § 734(b)(2)(B)).[43.1]

2. The mandatory adjustment triggered by a substantial basis reduction is a one-time event; unlike the elective application of § 734(b), a mandatory adjustment only affects the distribution that triggers the substantial basis reduction.[43.2]

3. Special rules are provided for tiered partnerships.[43.3]

[43.1] Prop. Reg. § 1.734-1(a)(2) (2014).

[43.2] Prop. Reg. § 1.734-1(d) (2014).

[43.3] Prop. Reg. § 1.734-1(f) (2014). See infra ¶ 25.07[1].

4. Securitization partnerships (as defined in Regulations § 1.743-1(o)(2)) are excluded from the mandatory application of § 734(b).[43.4]

[43.4] Prop. Reg. § 1.734-1(d) (2014).

[8] Relationship of Section 734(b) and Section 704(c)(1)(C)

Add to note 48.

Section 708(b)(1)(B) was repealed for partnership tax years beginning after 2017 by 2017 Tax Cuts and Jobs Act, Pub. L. No. 115-97, § 13504(a) (Dec. 22, 2017).

Page 25-18:

Add at end of subsection.

Proposed Regulations § 1.734-2(c)(1) (2014) provides: "Section 704 (c)(1)(C) basis adjustments will be taken into account in determining the basis adjustment under section 734(b). However, section 704(c)(1)(C) basis adjustments, other than a section 704(c)(1)(C) basis adjustment applied as an adjustment to the basis of partnership property pursuant to paragraph (c)(2) of this section, will not be taken into account in making allocations under § 1.755-1(c)."

The reference to "paragraph (c) (2)" is to a complex set of rules relating to § 704(c)(1)(C) partners who receive liquidating distributions, as discussed supra ¶ 11.04[1][b][iv]. If a § 704(c)(1)(C) partner receives distributions in complete liquidation of its interest, § 704(c)(1)(C) basis adjustments that are treated as basis in distributed property under § 732 are "taken into account" in determining the basis adjustment under § 734(b), regardless of whether the distributed property is § 704(c)(1)(C) property. Such § 704(c)(1)(C) basis adjustments are taken into account as follows:

1. If the adjustment "cannot be reallocated to distributed property in connection with the distribution," it is treated as a positive § 734(b) adjustment;

2. If the distribution also gives rise to a negative § 734(b) adjustment without regard to the § 704(c)(1)(C) basis adjustment reallocation, then the negative § 734(b) adjustment and the § 704(c)(1)(C) basis adjustment reallocation are netted and the net amount is allocated under Regulations § 1.755-1(c); and

3. If the partnership does not have a § 754 election in effect at the time of the liquidating distribution, it is treated as having made a § 754 election solely for purposes of computing any negative § 734(b) adjustment that would arise from the distribution.[49.1]

[49.1] Prop. Reg. § 1.734-2(c)(2) (2014).

The application of item 1 above is illustrated in Example 3 of Proposed Regulations § 1.734-2(c)(3) (2014), in which A contributes capital gain Property 1 (with a basis of $35x$ and value of $30x$), B contributes inventory Property 2 (with a basis and value of $30x$), and C contributes $30x$ cash. A has a $5x$ § 704(c)(1)(C) basis adjustment with respect to Property 1. Subsequently, at a time when none of the values have changed, A's interest is completely liquidated for $30x$ cash. A recognizes a ($5x$) loss on the distribution under § 732(a)(2). The partnership has a § 754 election in effect. The distribution results in a negative § 734(b) adjustment to capital gain property of ($5x$) (that is, the amount of loss A recognizes under § 731(a)(2)). Because A is a § 704(c)(1)(C) partner who is unable to take into account his § 704(c)(1)(C) basis adjustment in Property 1 upon the distribution of the cash, the unused basis adjustment is treated as a positive § 734(b) adjustment. This positive $5x$ adjustment and the negative ($5x$) adjustment under the usual § 734(b) rules are netted, resulting in no adjustment under § 734(b). Therefore, the partnership's basis in Property 1 and Property 2 remains $30x$.

Example 4 of Proposed Regulations § 1.734-2(c)(3) (2014) is based on the same facts as Example 3, except that more than seven years after formation of the partnership, partner A's interest is completely liquidated in exchange for inventory Property 2 (with a $30x$ value and basis to the partnership). A cannot include his § 704(c)(1)(C) adjustment in the basis of the distributed property, because the § 704(c)(1)(C) property and the distributed property are of different characters.[49.2] Therefore, the basis of Property 2 to A is $30x$, and A has a capital loss of $5x$ under § 731(a)(2), reflecting his original built-in loss on Property 1. This capital loss triggers a negative ($5x$) basis adjustment under § 734(b), which is netted against A's unused § 704(c)(1)(C) adjustment of positive $5x$ to produce a net § 734(b) adjustment of zero.

Under the Proposed Regulations, the analysis of the allocations in Example 25-10 would be as follows:

1. The "common" basis of property X to the partnership is limited to its $500,000 value at the contribution date;[49.3]
2. Because properties X and Y are both capital assets, and a liquidating distribution is being made to partner A, who is a § 704(c)(1)(C) partner, the partnership's adjusted basis in the property distributed to partner A is increased, immediately before the distribution, by the adjustment related to the § 704(c)(1)(C) property in which he is relinquishing an interest (that is, property X, which has a $500,000 § 704(c)(1)(C) adjustment);[49.4]
3. Therefore, the adjusted basis of property Y immediately before the distribution and in A's hands is $1,000,000; and

[49.2] See Prop. Reg. § 1.704-3(f)(3)(v)(C) (2014), discussed supra ¶ 11.04[1][b][iv].
[49.3] Prop. Reg. § 1.704-3(f)(1) (2014).
[49.4] Prop. Reg. § 1.704-3(f)(3)(v)(C) (2014).

4. As a result there is no basis reduction and no adjustment to be made under § 734(b), regardless of whether a § 754 election is in effect.

¶ 25.02 ALLOCATIONS OF SECTION 734(b) ADJUSTMENTS TO PARTNERSHIP ASSETS: SECTION 755

[1] The Allocation Rules

[a] Distributions on or After December 15, 1999

Page 25-23:

Replace sole sentence of last paragraph of subsection with the following.

Section 755(c) is applicable to partnership distributions made after October 22, 2004.[68.1]

[68.1] Proposed Regulations were issued under § 755(c) during 2014. Prop. Reg. §§ 1.755-1(e), 1.755-1(f)(1) (2014) (effective for transactions on or after December 15, 1999). These Proposed Regulations cast little light on the questions raised in the text.

¶ 25.07 APPLICATION OF SECTION 734(b) TO TIER PARTNERSHIPS

[1] Distributions of Assets Other Than Lower-Tier Partnership Interests

Page 25-42:

Add to note 119.

Section 708(b)(1)(B) was repealed by the 2017 Tax Cuts and Jobs Act for partnership tax years beginning after 2017. Pub. L. No. 115-97, § 13504(a) (Dec. 22, 2017).

Page 25-43:

Add to note 121.

See Prop. Reg. § 1.734-1(f)(1) (2014) (would apply § 743(b) approach whether § 754 election or substantial basis reduction triggers adjustments).

Replace last sentence of subsection with the following.

It is not clear, however, whether the holding of Revenue Ruling 92-15 should apply to require UTP's adjustment to filter down to the assets of LTP in circumstances where LTP does not have a § 754 election in place.[122.1]

[122.1] See Prop. Reg. § 1.734-1(f)(1) (2014) (if UTP is subject to a mandatory § 734(b) adjustment, basis adjustments filter down to LTP properties regardless of whether LTP has a § 754 election in effect; Rev. Rul. 92-15, 1992-1 CB 215, followed). The Treasury seems to believe the reach of a mandatory adjustment is greater than that of an elective adjustment.

[2] Distributions by Upper-Tier Partnerships of Lower-Tier Partnership Interests

Page 25-43:

Add new note 123.1 at end of first paragraph of subsection.

[123.1] The significance of the reference to § 708 in § 761(e) has been greatly diminished by the repeal of § 708(b)(1)(B) as part of the 2017 Tax Cuts and Jobs Act, Pub. L. No. 115-97, § 13504(a) (Dec. 22, 2017).

Page 25-44:

In second to last paragraph of subsection (following note callout 126), replace first two sentences with the following.

Under § 761(e), the distribution of an LTP interest is treated as an exchange for purposes of § 743(b).

Special Basis Adjustments in Connection With Distributions to Transferee-Partners: Section 732(d)

Chapter 26 was revised effective December 2018. The revised chapter can be found in the front of this student edition.

Cumulative Table of IRC Sections

[Text references are to paragraphs; note references are to chapters (boldface numbers) and notes ("n."). References to the supplement are preceded by "S."]

[Text references are to paragraphs; note references are to chapters (boldface numbers) and notes ("n."). References to the supplement are preceded by "S."]

[Text references are to paragraphs; note references are to chapters (boldface numbers) and notes ("n."). References to the supplement are preceded by "S."]

[Text references are to paragraphs; note references are to chapters (boldface numbers) and notes ("n."). References to the supplement are preceded by "S."]

[Text references are to paragraphs; note references are to chapters (boldface numbers) and notes ("n."). References to the supplement are preceded by "S."]

*[Text references are to paragraphs; note references are to chapters (boldface numbers)
and notes ("n."). References to the supplement are preceded by "S."]*

IRC §

173 . . . . 9.05[1][e]; 9.05[2]
174 . . . . **1** n.133; 9.02[3][j]; 9.02[4][c]; 9.05[2];
    9 n.468; **S9** ns. 468, 556; 11.08[2];
    11.08[7]; **S11** ns. 707, 820
174(a) . . . . 9.05[1][e]; 9.05[2]
175 . . . . . . 9.01[3][b]; 17.03[3][d]; 20.03[3]
175(b) . . . . 9.02[2][d]
179 . . . . 9.01[3][b]; 9.01[7]; 9.02[3][d];
    9.02[3][g]; S9.02[3][g];
    S9.02[3][z][ii][E]; **9** ns. 45, 386;
    11.03[2][b]; 11.05[2][c]; **11** n.376; **17**
    n.93
179(b) **9** n.376; **12** n.40
179(b)(3)(B) . . . . 9.02[3][g]
179(b)(6) **S9** n.386.1
179(d)(1) **S9** n.386.2
179(d)(2)(A) 24.07; S24.07
179(d)(2)(B) 24.07; S24.07
179(d)(2)(C) 24.07; S24.07
179(d)(3) 24.07; S24.07
179(d)(8) . . . . **9** ns. 376, 387
179(f) **S9** n.386.2
179A **17** n.93
183 . . . . 1.05[4][b][iii]; 1.05[4][b][iv];
    1.05[4][b][v]; **1** ns. 133, 135, 136;
    9.01[3][b]; 9.01[7]; 9.02[3][h]; **9** ns. 76,
    403, 404, 413, 634, 1142; **S10** n.74
183(a) . . . . 9.02[3][h]
183(b) . . . . 9.02[3][h]
183(c) **1** n.134
183(d) . . . . 9.01[7]; 9.02[3][h]; **9** ns. 399, 402,
    403
183(e) . . . . 9.01[7]; 9.02[3][h]; **9** ns. 399, 402,
    403
185 . . . . **17** n.93
188 . . . . **17** n.93
190 . . . . **17** n.93
191 (1939 Code) . . . . . **1** n.186; **3** ns. 15, 70
191(a) (1939 Code) . . . . **3** ns. 15, 70
191(b) (1939 Code) . . . . **3** ns. 15, 70
193 . . . . **17** n.93
194 . . . . 9.02[3][d]; 9.02[3][i]; **9** n.414; **17** n.93
194(b)(1) **9** n.378
194(b)(2)(B) . . . . **9** ns. 378, 414
195 . . . . . . 4.06; S4.06; 9.02[3][j]; S9.02[3][j]; **9**
    n.416; **S9** n.416; 13.05[2][m];
    S13.05[2][m]
195(a) . . . . . . **9** n.416; **S9** n.416; 13.05[2][m]
195(b) **9** n.416; **S9** n.416
195(b)(2) . . . . 13.05[2][m]; S13.05[2][m]

IRC §

197 . . . . . . S4.01[5][b][i]; S4.01[5][b][iii][E];
    4.05[9]; 7.04[3][d]; 9.02[3][k][i];
    S9.02[3][k][i]; 9.02[3][k][ii];
    9.02[3][k][ii][D]; **9** ns. 425, 437, 462;
    11.04[3][f]; 13.05[2][n]; 14.04[8]; **14**
    n.58; 16.02[2][a]; 16.02[3][b]; **17** ns. 49,
    170; 20.05; **20** n.68; 22.04[1]; **22** ns.
    118, 121; 24.02[2]; 24.04[3][a];
    24.04[3][b]; 24.04[3][b][i];
    24.04[3][b][ii]; 24.04[3][b][ii][A];
    24.04[3][b][ii][B]; 24.04[3][b][ii][C];
    24.04[3][b][ii][D]; 24.04[3][c]; 24.07; **24**
    ns. 121, 175; 25.01[6]; 25.02[6]
197(a) . . . . . . 4.05[9]; 11.04[3][f]; **16** n.314;
    25.01[6]
197(c) **9** n.423
197(c)(1) . . . . 11.04[3][f]
197(d)(1) **11** n.533
197(d)(1)(A) – 197(d)(1)(F) . . . . . 9.02[3][k][i]
197(d)(1)(A) – 197(d)(1)(C) . . . . 9.02[3][k][i]; **9**
    n.424
197(d)(1)(E) **16** n.314; **22** n.121
197(d)(2) **9** n.424
197(d)(3) **9** n.424
197(e) **9** n.425
197(e)(3)(A)(i) . . . . S9.02[3][g]
197(f)(2) . . . 4.05[9]; 9.02[3][k][i]; 13.05[2][n];
    13 n.151; 20.05; 24.07
197(f)(9) . . . . . S4.01[5][b][iii][E]; 4.05[9]; **S4**
    n.51.48; 9.02[3][k][ii]; **9** n.423; **S9**
    n.428; 11.04[3][f]; 14.04[8]; 16.02[3][b];
    20.05; 24.07; 25.01[6]; **25** n.8
197(f)(9)(A) . . . . 9.02[3][k][ii]; 20.05
197(f)(9)(B) **9** n.438; **20** n.69
197(f)(9)(C)(i) **9** n.439; **20** n.70; 24.07
197(f)(9)(C)(ii) **9** n.439; **20** n.70
197(f)(9)(E) . . . . . . 9.02[3][k][ii][C]; **9** ns. 437,
    440; 14.04[8]; 16.02[3][b]; 20.05;
    24.02[2]; **24** n.176; **25** n.33
197(f)(9)(F) **20** n.68
199 . . . 9.02[3][w]; S9.02[3][w]; **9** ns. 524, 532;
    S9 n.524
199(b) . . . . **9** n.526; **S9** ns. 524, 526
199(c)(4) **9** n.543; **S9** n.547
199(d)(1) . . . 9.02[3][w]; S9.02[3][w]; **9** n.528;
    S9 n.529
199(d)(1)(B) **9** n.528; **S9** n.529
199(d)(4)(B) **9** n.542; **S9** n.546
199A . . . . . **S2** n.27.3; **S6** n.24; S9.02[3][c][i];
    S9.02[3][z]; S9.02[3][z][i];
    S9.02[3][z][ii][A]; S9.02[3][z][ii][B];
    S9.02[3][z][ii][C]; S9.02[3][z][ii][D];
    S9.02[3][z][ii][E]; S9.02[3][z][iii][B];
    S9.02[3][z][iv]; S9.02[3][z][v];
    S9.02[3][z][vi]; S9.02[3][z][vi][C]; **S9** ns.
    550, 551.4, 551.9, 551.10, 551.13,
    551.39, 551.59, 551.73, 551.78, 551.81
199A(b) . . . . . S9.02[3][z]; S9.02[3][z][iv]; **S9**
    n.551.7
199A(b)(1) . . . . S9.02[3][z]; **S9** n.550.2

[Text references are to paragraphs; note references are to chapters (boldface numbers) and notes ("n."). References to the supplement are preceded by "S."]

[Text references are to paragraphs; note references are to chapters (boldface numbers) and notes ("n."). References to the supplement are preceded by "S."]

IRC §

267(c)(3) . . . **S4** n.55.11; 14.04[2][b]; 14.04[4]; 14.04[5]; **14** ns. 34, 43; **16** n.311; 18.02[4]

267(c)(4) . . . . . 3.09[4][b]; **14** ns. 34, 303; **16** n.304; 23.07[7]

267(c)(5) . . . . 9.06[1][c]; **14** ns. 304, 305, 317

267(d) . . . **1** n.206; **6** ns. 3, 30; 14.04[9]; **14** ns. 288, 313; 16.08[3][a]; **16** n.310

267(d)(2) . . . . 16.08[3][a]

267(e)(1)   8.04; **8** n.107; **11** ns. 80, 277, 334; 14.04[5]

267(e)(1)(A) **14** n.323

267(e)(1)(B) **14** n.323

267(e)(1)(C) . . . . 14.04[5]

267(e)(1)(D) . . . . . . 14.04[5]; **14** n.324

267(e)(3) . . . . 14.04[5]

267(e)(4) . . . . 14.04[5]

267(e)(5) . . . . 14.04[5]

267(f) . . . . 14.04[9]; 16.08[3][a]

267(f)(1) . . . . 14.04[9]

267(f)(1)(A) . . . . 8.04; **11** ns. 277, 334

267A **S14** n.282

269 . . . . 1.05[5][a][i]; **1** n.175

274 . . . . **2** n.104; 9.02[3][d]

274(b)(1) . . . . **9** ns. 377, 494

274(b)(2)(A) . . . . . . 9.02[3][o]; **9** ns. 377, 495

280A . . . . 9.02[3][p]

280A(d)(3) . . . . 9.02[3][p]

280C 9.05

280C(a) 9.05; **9** n.1022

291 . . . . 9.03[1][d]; 9.03[1][d][ii]; **9** n.714; 17.03[3][b]; 21.05[3]; **21** n.136

291(a) . . . . 9.03[1][d][ii]

291(a)(1) . . . 9.03[1][d][i]; **9** n.714; 17.03[3][b]

291(a)(2) . . . . 9.03[1][d][ii]

291(a)(3) **9** n.713

291(a)(4) **9** n.713

291(b) . . . . 9.03[1][d][iii]; **11** n.417

291(b)(1)(A) . . . . 9.03[1][d][iii]

291(b)(1)(B) . . . . 9.03[1][d][iii]

291(b)(2) . . . 9.03[1][d][iii]; **9** n.468; **11** n.417

291(b)(3) . . . . 9.03[1][d][iii]

301(c) . . . . 16.07[2]

301(b)(1) **16** n.277

301(c)(2) **2** n.20

301(c)(3) **2** n.20

301(d) **16** n.277

302 . . . . 16.02[3][e]

302(a) . . . . 16.07[2]

302(b) . . . . 16.07[2]

304 . . . . 9.03[1][a][iv]

304(c) . . . . . . S9.03[1][a][ii][B]; **S9** n.649

306 . . . . **17** n.157

306(a) . . . . **16** ns. 174, 200; 17.04[2]

311 . . . . 2.02[3]; 2.02[5]; **2** ns. 22, 38; 9.03[1][a][ii][B]; 16.07[2]

311(b) . . . . 9.03[1][a][ii][D]; **9** n.656; 19.02[1]

311(b)(1) . . . . 16.07[2]

311(b)(3) . . . . . **1** n.186; 16.07[2]; **16** n.281

312(k) . . . . 9.03[1][a][i]

318 . . . . **9** n.905; **S9** ns. 88.3, 649; 13.02

318(a) . . . . 14.04[6]

318(a)(1) . . . S9.02[1][d]; S9.03[1][a][ii][B]; **S9** ns. 271.4, 649

318(a)(2) **S9** n.649

318(a)(2)(C) **S9** n.649

318(a)(3) . . . . S9.03[1][a][ii][B]; **S9** n.649

318(a)(3)(C) **S9** n.649

318(a)(4) . . . . **S9** n.649; 14.04[6]

331(a) . . . . 16.07[2]

332 . . . . . . **2** n.22; **3** ns. 355, 356; **7** n.181; **9** n.653; **11** n.450; **13** n.49; **14** n.95; 16.07[2]; **19** n.251

333 . . . . **19** n.46

333 (former) . . . . . . 16.03[1]; 19.02[5][b]

333(e) (former) . . . . 16.03[1]

333(e)(2) . . . . **16** n.144; 19.02[5][b]

333(f)(1) . . . . 19.02[5][b]

334(a) . . . . 16.07[2]

334(b) . . . . 16.07[2]

334(b)(1) **19** n.251

334(b)(2) (1954 Code) . . . . . 17.01[2]; **18** n.66

336 . . . . . . 2.02[3]; **2** n.22; 16.07[2]; **16** n.132

336(a) . . . . 16.07[2]

337 . . . . 17.04[2]

337(a) . . . . **2** n.22; 16.07[2]

337(d) . . . . . S9.03[1][a][ii]; S9.03[1][a][ii][A]; S9.03[1][a][ii][B]; S9.03[1][a][ii][C]; S9.03[1][a][ii][D]; **9** n.640; **S9** ns. 640, 649, 650, 654, 659.1, 659.4

337(d)(3) **S9** n.650

338 . . . . . . 13.03[1][d]; **13** ns. 47, 49; **18** n.66

338(g) **26** n.39

338(h)(10) **10** n.51

341(e) (former) **17** n.154

351 . . . . **1** n.37; 2.02[5]; 4.01[1][a]; 4.01[2][a]; S4.01[5][b][iii][C]; 4.01[6]; 4.02[1]; 4.02[4]; 4.02[5]; 4.05[6]; S4.05[12]; 4.07; 4.07[1]; 4.07[2]; **4** ns. 3, 28, 65, 77, 78, 80, 84, 87, 102, 103, 108, 177; 9.03[1][a][viii]; 9.03[1][a][ix]; S9.06[1][c]; **9** n.692; 11.03[3]; 11.04[1][b]; S11.04[1][b][iii]; 11.04[3][d]; 11.08[3][a]; **11** n.496; 12.02[2]; **12** ns. 8, 30; **13** n.46; S14.02[3][b][iv][B]; 16.07[1]; S16.07[1]; 16.07[3]; **16** ns. 264, 268, 270, 274; 18.01; S18.01; S18.01[1]; 18.01[2]; 18.01[3]; 18.01[4]; 18.02; 18.02[1]; 18.02[2]; 18.02[3]; 18.02[4]; 18.03[1]; 18.03[3]; 18.03[4]; 18.03[9]; **18** ns. 4, 21, 29; 19.08[3][a]; 19.08[3][d]; **19** ns. 45, 262; 24.04[1][b]; 24.04[3][a]; 24.04[3][b][ii][B]; **24** ns. 60, 88

351(a) . . . . . S4.01[5][b][iii][C]; 4.07; 18.01[4]; 18.02[4]

351(b) . . . 18.01[3]; 18.02[4]; 18.03[2]; 18.03[3]

351(c) **18** n.6

351(e) . . . . . . 1.05[3]; 1.05[4][b][vi]; 3.03[2]

351(e)(1) **4** n.241

351(e)(1)(B) . . . . 4.07[1]

351(g) . . . . 3.05[3]

[Text references are to paragraphs; note references are to chapters (boldface numbers) and notes ("n."). References to the supplement are preceded by "S."]

[Text references are to paragraphs; note references are to chapters (boldface numbers) and notes ("n."). References to the supplement are preceded by "S."]

[Text references are to paragraphs; note references are to chapters (boldface numbers) and notes ("n."). References to the supplement are preceded by "S."]

*[Text references are to paragraphs; note references are to chapters (boldface numbers)
and notes ("n."). References to the supplement are preceded by "S."]*

[Text references are to paragraphs; note references are to chapters (boldface numbers) and notes ("n."). References to the supplement are preceded by "S."]

IRC §

702(a) . . . . . **1** n.4; 9.01[1]; 9.01[2]; 9.01[3][a];
9.01[3][a][ii]; 9.01[4][a]; 9.01[4][b];
9.02[2][a][ii][A]; 9.02[3][g]; 9.02[3][l];
9.02[3][q]; 9.03[4][c][iv]; 9.04[3][f][i]; **9**
ns. 24, 985; 10A.06; 10A.06[1][c];
10A.06[1][d]; 10A.06[2][b]; **10A** ns.
109, 116, 122, 123, 131, 242; 11.01[1];
11 n.598; **17** n.73; 22.06[3]
702(a)(1)−702(a)(8) . . . . 9.02[2][d]
702(a)(1)−702(a)(7) . . . . 9.01[3][a]; 9.02[3][q];
9.02[5][b][i]; **9** n.15; 11.03[1]; **11** n.371
702(a)(1)−702(a)(6) **10A** n.161
702(a)(1) . . . . 9.01[3][a][i]; 11.05[1]
702(a)(2) . . . . . 9.01[2]; 9.01[3][a][i]; 11.05[1];
14.03[3]; 22.03[2][b]
702(a)(3) . . . . 9.01[3][a][ii]; 11.05[1]; 17.03[2]
702(a)(4) . . . **6** n.44; 9.01[3][a][iii]; 9.01[4][b];
S11.05[1]; 11.05[1][b]; **11** n.602; **S11**
n.603
702(a)(5) . . . . 9.01[3][a][iv]; 9.03[1][a][iii]
702(a)(6) . . . 9.01[3][a][v]; S9.01[3][a][v]; **S10**
n.373; 11.03[2][i]; S11.03[2][i];
S11.05[1]
702(a)(7) . . . 9.01[3][b]; 9.02[2][c]; 9.02[3][d];
9.02[3][l]; 9.02[3][n]; 9.02[3][q];
9.02[5][b][i]; 9.03[1][d][i]; 9.03[4][a]; **9**
ns. 31, 51; **10A** n.161; 11.05[1];
21.03[6][a]; **21** n.74; 23.05[1]
702(a)(8) . . . . 9.01[3][a]; 9.01[3][a][ii];
9.01[3][b]; 9.02[2][d]; S9.02[3][c][i];
9.02[3][q]; 9.02[5][b][i]; 9.03[4][e]; **9** ns.
15, 31, 51, 601; **10A** n.161;
11.02[4][e][i]; 11.02[4][f][i]; 11.03[1];
11.03[2][a]; 11.03[2][i]; S11.03[2][i];
11.05[1]; **11** ns. 371, 413; 13.03[2][b];
14.03[3]; **14** ns. 232, 241; **21** n.74;
22.06[3]
702(a)(9) **11** n.371
702(b) . . . . 3.02[4]; 3.04[3][a]; 9.01[1]; 9.01[4];
9.02[3][l]; **9** ns. 17, 64−66; 22.03[2][b]
702(c) . . . . . 9.01[1]; 9.02[2][d]; **9** ns. 347, 348
703 . . . . . . **1** n.38; 3.08[4]; 9.01[1]; 9.01[4][a];
9.02[3][l]; 9.06[1][a]; **9** n.51; **11** n.520;
14.01[1][c]; 24.02[1]; 24.11[2]
703(a) . . . . **1** ns. 2, 3; 6.02[2]; 9.01[1]; 9.01[2];
9.01[3][a]; 9.02[3][l]; 9.03[1][a];
9.03[1][d][ii]; 9.04[3][f][ii]; **9** ns. 15, 399;
11 ns. 397, 487, 598; 14.03[6][e]
703(a)(1) . . . 9.01[2]; 9.03[4][c][iv]; **9** n.16; **11**
n.598
703(a)(2) . . . . 9.01[2]
703(a)(2)(C) **6** n.44; **S11** n.601
703(a)(2)(D) **11** n.601
703(a)(2)(F)   6.02[3][b]; **11** n.605; **S11** n.603
703(b) . . . . . **1** n.2; 9.01[1]; 9.01[7]; **9** ns. 135,
156, 179; **S9** n.591.2; **17** n.108; 24.12
703(b)(1) . . . . **9** ns. 177, 291
703(b)(2) **9** n.176; **11** n.150

IRC §

703(b)(3) . . . . **9** n.175; 11.03[2][i]; S11.03[2][i]
704 . . . . 1.05[3]; 8.03[4]; **8** n.72; 9.01[1];
9.01[4][a]; 9.02[3][c]; 9.02[3][w];
S9.02[3][w]; 9.03[4][c][iv]; 9.03[5];
11.01[1]; 11.04[3][d]; 11.05[1][a]; **11** ns.
15, 37; 12.04[1]; 14.01[1][c]; 14.01[2];
S14.01[2]; 14.02[4][a]; 14.03[1][a]; **S14**
n.8.1; 22.01[3]; 22.03[2][b]; 22.06[3]; **22**
n.66
704(a) . . . . **1** n.5; 11.01[2]; 12.04[1]
704(b)−704(e) . . . . 12.04[1]
704(b) . . . . 1.05[1][a]; 1.05[2]; 1.05[3];
1.05[4][d]; **1** ns. 6, 89, 93, 94, 96, 97,
186, 202; **S1** n.93; S3.02[2A]; 3.02[4];
3.04[3][a]; S4.01[5][b]; S4.01[5][b][i];
4.02[1]; S4.02[3]; **4** ns. 24, 136; **S4**
n.22; 5.01[2]; 5.02[3][g][i]; 5.02[3][h];
5.03[5]; 6.04; **6** ns. 6, 88, 89; 7.04[3][b];
7.04[3][d]; 7.04[3][e]; **7** ns. 111, 197,
199; 8.02[2]; 8.02[3]; 8.02[4][b][v][D];
8.03[2]; 8.03[3][a]; 8.03[4]; 8.03[5];
8.04; **8** n.144; S9.01[4][c][iii][D];
S9.01[4][c][v]; 9.02[1][c][iii];
S9.02[3][c][i][D]; 9.02[3][q]; 9.02[3][w];
S9.02[3][w]; 9.02[4][d]; S9.02[4][h];
9.03[1][a][i]; 9.03[2]; 9.03[3][a][ii];
9.03[5]; 9.05; S9.06[1][a]; **9** ns. 448,
927; **S9** n.551.11; 10A.01; 10A.06[1][b];
10A.06[3]; 10A.06[3][b][i];
10A.06[3][b][ii]; 10A.06[3][c]; 10A.08;
10A.10[3]; **10A** ns. 108, 330; 11.01[2];
11.02; 11.02[1]; 11.02[2][a][ii][C];
11.02[2][b][v]; 11.02[2][c];
11.02[2][c][i]; 11.02[2][c][ii];
S11.02[2][c][ii]; 11.02[2][c][iii];
11.02[2][c][x]; 11.02[4][a]; 11.02[4][e];
11.02[4][e][i]; 11.02[4][e][vi];
11.02[4][e][vii]; 11.02[4][f][i];
11.02[4][g]; S11.02[4][g]; 11.03[1];
11.03[2][a]; 11.03[2][b]; 11.03[2][f];
11.03[2][i]; S11.03[2][i]; 11.03[3];
11.03[4][c]; 11.04[1]; S11.04[1][b][i];
11.04[2]; 11.04[3][a]; 11.04[3][b];
11.04[3][c]; 11.04[3][d]; 11.04[3][f];
11.04[4][b][vii]; **11** ns. 35, 43, 52, 65,
98, 111, 204, 211, 259, 292, 371, 405,
440, 489, 519; **S11** n.428; 12.04[1];
12.04[2]; **12** n.84; 13.05[2][c]; 13.06[1];
13 n.146; S14.02[4][d]; 14.03[3];
14.03[6][a]; 14.04[1][a]; **14** ns. 187, 189,
218, 222, 276.1; 15.01[4]; 15.05[1][c];
S16.08[7]; **16** n.302; 18.01[4]; 21.03[8];
24.02[1]; 24.02[2]; 24.07; **24** ns. 35,
159, 162; **S24** n.159; 25.01[6]
704(b)(2) . . . . **1** n.176; 6.04; 9.03[3][c]; 11.01[2];
S11.01[2]; 11.02[2][c]; 11.03[1]; **11**
n.2833

[Text references are to paragraphs; note references are to chapters (boldface numbers) and notes ("n."). References to the supplement are preceded by "S."]

[Text references are to paragraphs; note references are to chapters (boldface numbers) and notes ("n."). References to the supplement are preceded by "S."]

IRC §

704(e)(1) (repealed effective 2016 by BBA 2015)
. . . . S1.05[4][a]; 1.05[5][b][i]; S1.05[5][b][i]; S3.00; S3.00[1]; S3.00[2]; 3.01[1]; S3.01[1]; 3.02; S3.02; 3.02[2]; S3.02[2A]; 3.02[3]; S3.02[3]; 3.02[4]; S3.03; 3.03[2]; S3.04; 3.04[2]; S3.04[2]; 3.04[2A]; 3.04[3][a]; S3.04[3][a]; 3.04[3][b]; S3.05; 3.05[1]; 3.05[5]; 3.09[7][a]; **3** ns. 15, 50, 70, 71, 73, 75, 132, 151, 174, 186, 373; **S3** ns. 15, 78.1, 156.2, 373; **5** n.125; **S7** n.165; S11.01[2]; **S11** n.12; S15.00; S15.01; 15.01[2]; S15.01[2]; 15.01[3]; 15.01[4]; 15.01[5]; 15.02; 15.02[2]; 15.02[3]; 15.02[4]; 15.03; S15.03; 15.03[1]; 15.03[2]; 15.03[4]; S15.04; 15.04[1]; S15.05; 15.05[2]; **15** ns. 18, 22, 27

704(e)(1) (current) . . . . . **S1** ns. 9, 93; **S3** n.15; S11.01[2]; S11.02[1]; S11.02[2][a][ii][C]; **S11** ns. 12, 440; **12** ns. 10, 15, 17

704(e)(2) (renumbered as 704(e)(1) by BBA 2015)
. . . . **S1** n.93; S3.00; S3.02; S3.02[2A]; S3.03; S3.04; 3.04[3][a]; S3.05; **3** ns. 15, 70; 11.01[2]; S11.01[2]; 11.02[1]; S11.02[1]; 11.02[2][a][ii][C]; **11** ns. 12, 440; **S11** ns. 12, 440; **12** ns. 10, 15, 17; S15.00; 15.01[4]; 15.01[5]; 15.03[4]; 15.05[1]; 15.05[1][a]; 15.05[1][b]; 15.05[1][c]; 15.05[2]; **15** ns. 11, 79, 90, 94, 95

704(e)(2) (current) **S3** n.15

704(e)(3) (renumbered as 704(e)(2) by BBA 2015)
. . . . . . S3.00; S3.02; S3.02[2A]; S3.03; S3.04; 3.04[3][a]; S3.05; **3** ns. 15, 70; **S3** n.15; S15.00; 15.01[4]; 15.05[1][a]; **15** n.11

705 . . . . 2 n.19; **S2** n.19; 6.01; S6.02[3][a]; 6.02[3][d][ii]; 7.02; 7.02[6]; 9.02[2][a][ii][B]; S9.06[1][a]; 10.02[5]; 10A.06[3]; 11.03[2][i]; S11.03[2][i]; 11.05[1]; 11.05[2][b]; **11** n.211; 14.01[1][c]; 16.01[1]; 16.01[4]; **24** n.183

705(a) . . . . . 1.01[1]; 1.02[3]; **1** n.42; 6.01; 6.02; 6.02[1]; 6.02[2]; 6.02[3][a]; 6.02[3][b]; 6.02[5]; 6.03; 6.04; **6** ns. 22, 82; 7.02; **S6** n.24; 7.02[3]; 7.02[4]; 7.06[3]; **9** n.15; **14** n.248; 22.03[2][b]; 25.01[1][b]

705(a)(1) . . . . 6.02[2]; 6.02[5]; 9.02[3][u]; S9.02[3][u]; S9.02[5][e]; 19.03[2]; **19** n.88

705(a)(1)(A) . . . . 6.02[3][a]; 6.02[3][b]; 6.02[3][d][ii]; 9.02[1][c][ii]; **9** n.15; 11.05[1]; **11** n.598

705(a)(1)(B) . . . . 6.02[3][a]; S6.02[3][a]; 6.02[3][d][i]; **6** n.30; **S6** n.39; **11** n.461; **14** n.289; 19.05; 23.06[2]

705(a)(1)(C) . . . . . 6.02[3][b]; 9.03[1][d][ii]; **11** n.397; **14** n.276.1

705(a)(2) . . . 6.02[2]; 6.02[4]; 6.02[5]; 7.02[3]; 7.02[4]

705(a)(2)(A) . . . . . . 6.02[3][b]; 11.05[2][a]; **16** n.307

705(a)(2)(B) . . . 1.05[6]; S4.05[12]; 4.06; **4** ns. 215, 216; 6.02[3][c]; S6.02[3][c]; **6** ns. 24, 43, 48; **S6** ns. 24, 47, 48; S9.01[3][a][v]; S9.01[4][c][vii]; S9.02[3][c][i][J]; 9.02[4][f]; 9.03[3][c][iii]; **9** n.778; 10A.06[3][b][ii]; 10A.06[3][c]; 11.02[2][c][i]; 11.02[2][c][vii]; 11.02[2][c][viii]; 11.02[4][b]; 11.02[4][e][ii]; 11.02[4][f][ii]; 11.05[1][b]; **11** n.298; **13** n.146; **14** n.290; 18.01[4]; S18.01[4]

705(a)(3) . . . . 6.02[2]; 6.02[3][b]; 6.02[4]

705(b) . . . . 6.01; 6.02[1]; 6.03; **6** n.76

705(b)(1)(B) . . . . 10A.06[3][b][ii]

705(b)(2)(B) . . . . 10A.06[3]

706 . . . . . 9.01[1]; 9.03[1][a][iv]; 11.02[1]; **S11** n.421.1a; 12.02[2][c]; 12.04[1]; **14** n.298; 16.01[4]; 16.07[2]; 21.01[5]; 23.05[2][b]

706(a) . . . 1.01[1]; 9.01[1]; **9** n.925; 14.03[6][a]

706(a)(2)(A) **12** n.9

706(b) . . . . 1.01[1]; **1** n.39; **3** ns. 401, 403; 9.04[1]; 9.04[1][a]; 9.04[1][b]; 9.04[3]; 9.04[3][a]; 9.04[3][b]; 9.04[3][e]; 9.04[3][f][i]; **9** ns. 2, 927; 12.02[3]; 13.03; S13.03; **13** n.60; **14** n.256

706(b)(1) 9.04; **9** n.957

706(b)(1)(B)(i) **9** n.926

706(b)(1)(B)(ii) **9** n.931

706(b)(1)(B)(iii) **9** n.933

706(b)(1)(C) . . . . 9.04[1]; 9.04[1][b]

706(b)(2) . . . . .9.04[2]

706(b)(3) . . . . . **9** n.932; 14.03[6][a]; **14** n.256

706(b)(4)(A) **9** n.928

706(b)(4)(A)(i) **14** n.256

706(b)(4)(B) **9** n.929

706(b)(5) **9** n.930

706(c) . . . . **1** n.186; 12.01; 12.02[2][b]; 12.02[2][d]; 12.02[2][e]; **12** n.84; 13.01; 13.06[1]; **15** n.94; 16.07[1]; 16.07[4]; S16.07[4]; 24.08[1]

706(c)(1) . . . . 12.01; 12.02[1]; **12** ns. 2, 4; 13.06[1]; **13** ns. 87, 94; 23.01

706(c)(2) . . . . 12.03[1][c]; **17** n.10; **22** n.15

706(c)(2)(A) . . . . **11** ns. 47, 611; 12.01; 12.02[2]; 12.02[2][a]; 12.02[2][c]; 12.02[3]; 12.02[4][a]; 12.02[4][b]; 12.02[4][c]; **12** ns. 7, 9, 14, 30, 67; **15** n.94; 16.01[4]; 23.01; 23.05[2][b]

706(c)(2)(B) . . . 11.05[2][a]; 12.01; 12.02[4][b]; **12** ns. 12, 75; **15** ns. 94, 95; 16.01[4]; **16** n.209

706(d) . . . . . 1.01[1]; **1** n.186; 4.02[3]; 11.01[2]; 11.02[2][a][ii][C]; 11.02[2][c][vii]; **11** ns. 43, 65, 373; 12.01; 12.03[1]; 12.03[2]; 12.04[1]; 12.04[2]; 15.05[3]; **15** ns. 94, 95; 23.01

[Text references are to paragraphs; note references are to chapters (boldface numbers) and notes ("n."). References to the supplement are preceded by "S."]

IRC §

708(b) . . . . 1.01[1]; 12.02[1]; 12.02[2]; **12** n.4; S13.01; 13.03[1]; **13** n.147; **S13** n.149.1; 14.02[3][a]; 14.03[6][a]; 16.01[3]; 16.02[3][b]; **22** n.14

708(b)(1) . . . . 8.02[6]; 12.02[1]; 13.01; S13.02; 13.04[1]; S13.05[1]; S13.05[3]; **S19** n.134; 22.03[3]

708(b)(1)(A) . . . . . . 3.03[2]; 3.06[6][a]; S3.10; 9.02[1][c][v][B]; **9** n.259; 10.02[3]; 13.02; S13.02; 13.05[1]; S13.05[1]; 13.05[2]; 13.05[3]; S13.05[3]; **13** ns. 13, 112, 135, 142; **S13** n.13; **14** n.298; **16** ns. 19, 83; 19.07[2]; **19** n.134; **S19** n.134

708(b)(1)(B) . . . . **1** n.67; 3.06[4][b][ii]; 3.06[5][a][ii]; 3.09[6]; S4.01[5][b][iii][C]; S4.06; **4** ns. 104, 200; **S4** n.55.30; 7.03[2]; 7.04[3][b]; 9.02[1][c][v][B]; 9.02[3][k][i]; 9.02[4][d]; **9** ns. 259, 578, 972; **S9** ns. 271, 589; 11.02[2][a][i]; 11.02[2][c][iv]; 11.02[4][f][v]; S11.04[1][b][iii]; 11.04[4][b][v]; 11.04[4][f]; 11.04[4][f][i]; 11.04[4][f][ii]; **11** ns. 49, 316; **S11** n.421.1a; 12.01; 13.02; 13.03; 13.03[1]; 13.03[1][b]; 13.03[1][d]; 13.03[1][e]; 13.03[2]; 13.03[2][a]; 13.03[2][b]; 13.03[3]; 13.05[2]; 13.05[2][a]; 13.05[2][c]; 13.05[2][d]; 13.05[2][e]; 13.05[2][g]; 13.05[2][i]; 13.05[2][j]; 13.05[2][k]; 13.05[2][m]; S13.05[2][m]; 13.05[2][n]; 13.06[2]; **13** ns. 31, 33, 34, 39, 48, 49, 52, 60, 63, 79, 80, 93, 100–102, 108, 110, 112, 114, 136, 139, 147, 165, 167, 203; **S13** ns. 93, 100, 112, 149.1, 178; 14.02[3][b][xi]; **14** n.66; 16.02[2][d]; 16.05[4]; 16.07[1]; 16.07[2]; 16.08[5]; **16** ns. 83, 209, 211; 19.07[1]; 19.07[2]; 19.08[3][b]; **19** n.217; S21.01[6][c]; S21.01[6][d]; 25.07[1]; 25.07[2]; **25** ns. 18, 48; **26** ns. 3, 36, 39

708(b)(1)(B) (repealed as of 2018) . . . . **S4** n.51.5; 12.01; 12.02[1]; 12.02[2][b]; **12** ns. 3, 7, 8; S13.02; S13.03; S13.04[1]; S13.05[1]; S13.05[2]; S13.05[3]; S13 ns. 79, 80, 165, 167, 178, 203; **S14** n.66; S16.02[2][d]; S16.05[4]; S16.07; S16.07[4]; S16 ns. 18, 44.1, 83, 209, 211, 240.1, 271, 279, 323.1; S19.07[2]; S19.08[3][b]; S19 ns. 134, 217; 23.05[2][b]; 24.04[1][c]; 24.10; 24.11[6]; **24** ns. 46, 165, 226; 26 ns. 3, 36, 39

708(b)(2)(A) . . . . 11.04[4][b][vii]; 13.01; 13.06[1]; **13** n.165

708(b)(2)(B) . . . . . 3.06[4][b][ii]; 3.06[5][a][ii]; 13.01; **13** ns. 17, 187, 193; 14.02[3][a]; **19** ns. 185, 217

IRC §

709 . . . . . . **4** ns. 212, 214–217, 220; S4.06; **5** n.157; 6.02[3][c]; S6.02[3][c]; 9.01[7]; 11.02[2][c][vii]; **S11** n.121; 13.05[2][m]; S13.05[2][m]; 14.02[3][b][iii][C]; 14.02[4][a]

709(a) . . . . . 4.06; **4** ns. 214, 216; 13.05[2][m]

709(b) . . . 4.06; **4** ns. 216, 218, 224; **6** n.48; **S6** n.47; S9.01[7]; 11.02[2][c][vii]; 13.05[2][m]; S13.05[2][m]; **13** n.148; **S13** n.149.2

709(b)(1) . . . . **4** ns. 218, 220

709(b)(2) . . . . **4** n.220; S13.05[2][m]; **13** n.143; **S13** n.143

709(b)(3) **4** n.222

721–724 . . . . 1.01

721–723 . . . . 4.01[1][a]; 4.03[1][a]; **11** n.517; 16.07[3]

721 . . . . . . 1.02[4]; **1** ns. 14, 167; 4.01[1][a]; S4.01[1][a]; 4.01[1][b]; 4.01[1][d]; S4.01[1][d]; S4.01[5][b][iii]; S4.01[5][b][iii][B]; S4.01[5][b][iii][F]; 4.01[7]; 4.02[1]; 4.02[2]; S4.02[3]; 4.02[4]; 4.03[1][a]; 4.03[3]; 4.05[1]; 4.05[3]; 4.05[4]; 4.05[9]; 4.05[10]; **4** ns. 1, 3, 20, 43, 64–67, 77, 79, 80, 84, 85, 249; **S4** ns. 16, 18, 66, 95,1; 5.02[1]; 5.02[3][f]; 5.02[4][a]; 5.02[4][b]; 5.02[4][c]; 5.02[4][d]; **5** ns. 2, 16, 52, 74; 7.04[3][g]; **7** n.174; 9.02[1][c][v]; S9.02[1][c][v]; 9.02[3][k][i]; 9.03[1][a][vi]; 9.03[1][a][viii]; 9.03[1][a][ix]; **9** ns. 462, 692, 836; **S9** ns. 271.45, 317, 551.11, 836; 11.03[3]; S11.04[1][b][iii]; S11.04[4][b][vii]; 11.08[3][a]; **11** ns. 163, 451, 459; **S11** n.163; 12.02[2]; **12** n.9; 13.03[1][b]; 13.05[2][d]; 13.05[2][k]; 13.05[2][n]; **13** ns. 34, 136, 193; 14.02[3][b]; S14.02[3][b][i]; S14.02[3][b][iv][B]; 14.04[9]; **14** ns. 22, 54; **S14** n.119.1; 16.04[2][b]; **16** n.284; 18.01; 19.08[3][c]; **20** n.35; 24.04[1][b]; **24** n.88

721(a) . . . . 3.03[2]; 4.01[1][a]; S4.01[1][a]; 4.01[1][c]; 4.01[1][d]; S4.01[1][d]; 4.01[5]; S4.01[5][b]; S4.01[5][b][i]; S4.01[5][b][ii]; S4.01[5][b][iii]; 4.02[3]; 4.02[7]; 4.05[11]; 4.07; **4** ns. 66, 85, 103, 104, 231, 236, 249; **S4** n.66; 5.02[1]; 5.02[4][c]; 7.04[2]; 7.04[3][d]; **7** n.174; 9.02[3][u]; 13.05[2][d]; 13.05[2][k]; 14.02[3][a]; 20.02

721(b) . . . . **1** n.17; **3** n.140; 4.01[1][b]; 4.01[1][c]; 4.07; 4.07[1]; 4.07[2]; 4.07[3]; **4** ns. 127, 128, 149, 231, 232, 236, 243, 244, 247, 249, 250; **S4** ns. 240, 249

[Text references are to paragraphs; note references are to chapters (boldface numbers) and notes ("n."). References to the supplement are preceded by "S."]

IRC §

721(c) . . . . . . S4.01[1][a]; 4.01[5]; S4.01[5][b];
S4.01[5][b][ii]; S4.01[5][b][ii][A];
S4.01[5][b][ii][B]; S4.01[5][b][iii];
S4.01[5][b][iii][A]; S4.01[5][b][iii][B];
S4.01[5][b][iii][C]; S4.01[5][b][iii][D];
S4.01[5][b][iii][E]; S4.01[5][b][iii][F]; **S4**
ns. 51.2, 51.5, 51.6, 51.9; **S9** n.428; **S11**
ns. 176.1, 494

722 . . . . . . **1** ns. 15, 42; 4.01[1][b]; 4.01[1][c];
S4.02[3]; 4.03[1][a]; 4.03[1][b]; 4.07[3];
4 ns. 25, 127, 128; 6.01; 6.02[1]; **6** ns.
22, 94; 7.02; 7.02[3]; 7.02[4]; 7.04[3][f];
7.06[3]; S9.06[1][a]; 10.02[5]; 11.04[1];
11.04[2]; 11.05[2][c]; **19** n.77

723 . . . 1.02[4]; **1** n.16; S4.01[1][a]; 4.01[1][c];
4.01[1][d]; S4.01[1][d]; 4.03[1][a];
4.05[1]; 4.07[3]; **4** ns. 20, 43, 128, 149,
171; 5.03[5]; 6.01; **6** n.1; **7** n.182;
S9.02[5][e]; S9.06[1][a]; **S9** n.551.11;
S10.02[3]; 11.04[1]; 11.04[2];
13.05[2][e]; 13.06[1]; 25.01[4]

724 . . . . 1.04; **1** ns. 19, 186; 4.05[6];
S4.05[5][b]; **4** n.201; **11** n.466; **13** n.108;
17.04[2]; **17** n.85

724(a) . . . . 17.03; 17.03[3]

724(c) . . . . 4.05[6]; **11** n.451

724(d)(3) . . . . 4.05[6]

731–737 . . . . 1.01

731–736 . . . . 11.01[1]; 21.01[1]

731–735 . . . . 16.02[1][a]; 19.01[1];
19.01[2][b][i]; 19.02[1]; 19.02[4];
21.01[2]; 21.02[2]; 22.06[3]

731–733 . . . . . . 6.02[5]; 7.02; **14** n.241; 25.03

731 . . . . S1.05[4][b][vi]; **1** ns. 48, 167;
2.04[2][a]; 3.07[3]; **3** n.367; 4.01[1][a];
S4.01[1][a]; 4.01[2][a]; S4.02[3]; **S4**
n.199.1; 5.02[3][h]; 6.01; 9.02[1][c][v];
S9.02[1][c][v]; S9.02[1][d][ii][A];
S9.02[1][d][ii][B]; 9.02[2][a][ii][B];
9.02[3][k][i]; 9.03[1][a][ii][B];
9.03[1][a][ii][D]; **9** ns. 462, 653, 656; **S9**
n.831; **S10** n.349.7; 10A.06[2][b]; **10A**
n.210; 11.03[4][b]; 11.04[4][d]; **11**
n.526; 13.05[2][d]; 13.05[2][n]; **13** ns.
102, 193; 14.01[1][c]; 14.02[3][b];
S14.02[3][b][iv][B]; 14.03[1];
14.03[1][b]; **14** ns. 17, 22, 40; **S14**
n.119.1; 16.02[1]; 16.02[3]; 16.02[3][d];
S16 ns. 346, 347; 17.03; 17.03[3];
17.03[3][j]; **17** ns. 26, 83; 19.01[2][b][i];
19.01[2][c][vi]; 19.02[1]; 19.02[4];
19.02[5][b]; 19.02[5][d]; 19.03; 19.05;
S19.07[1]; 19.08[2][f]; 19.09[4]; **19** ns.
1, 31, 46; **S19** ns. 75, 94.1; 20.03;
20.05; **20** ns. 7, 35; 21.01[1]; S21.01[3];
21.02[3][c]; 21.05[3]; 22.01; 22.01[4];
22.01[6]; 22.02[4][a]; 22.02[4][a];
22.02[4][d][i]; 22.02[5][b];
24.04[3][b][ii][B]; 25.01[4]; 25.03; **25**
n.21

731(a) . . . . **1** n.21; **S1** n.84.1; S4.02[3];
4.03[1][c]; 4.03[4]; **4** ns. 29, 43, 130;
6.02[2]; 6.02[5]; **7** n.9; S9.02[1][d][i];
9.02[2][a][ii][B]; S9.03[4][a]; **9** n.295;
S9 ns. 271.26, 831; 11.03[4][a];
11.03[4][c]; **11** ns. 460, 757; 13.05[2][d];
S13.06[1]; 14.03[1][b]; **14** n.223;
16.02[1][a]; 16.03[4]; 16.05[1][b];
16.05[1][c]; 16.05[2][b]; **S16** n.261.1;
18.03[5]; 19.01[2][a][i]; 19.02[1]; 19.03;
19.03[2]; 19.05; S19.05; 19.08[4][a]; **19**
ns. 88, 101; **S19** n.74.1; 21.04[1];
21.04[4]; 22.01[4][a]; 22.02[4][b];
22.02[5][a]; 22.02[5][b]; 22.03[2][b];
22.06[1][a]; 22.06[2][b]; 22.06[3]; **24**
n.88; 25.01[1][a]; 25.01[2]; 25.01[4];
25.03; **25** n.99

731(a)(1) . . . . **1** n.22; 4.03[1][a]; 4.05[1];
6.02[2]; 6.02[4]; 6.04; 7.02; 7.06[3];
9.02[1][c][iv]; 11.04[2]; 11.05[2][b]; **14**
n.223; 16.04[2][b]; **16** n.39; 19.02[5][a];
19.02[5][b]; 19.02[5][c]; 19.03[1];
19.03[2]; 19.08[1]; **19** ns. 24, 107, 214;
21.03[5]; **21** n.70; 22.06[1][b]; 25.01[2];
25.01[3]; 25.01[6]; 25.02[4]; 25.02[8];
25.03; 25.04; **25** n.101

731(a)(2) . . . . . . **1** n.24; 9.02[1][c][iii]; 11.04[2];
13.05[2][m]; S13.05[2][m]; **13** ns. 146,
148; **S13** n.149.2; 6.05[1][b]; **16** n.223;
17.03; **17** n.83; 19.02[5][a]; 19.02[5][b];
19.05; **19** ns. 4, 115, 214; **22** n.55;
24.01[3]; 25.01[1][b]; 25.01[2];
25.01[2][a]; 25.01[3]; 25.01[8];
S25.01[8]; 25.02[5]

731(a)(2)(B) . . . . 17.04[2]; 25.02[5]

731(b) . . . . 14.03[5]; S14.03[5]; 16.06[3];
19.01[2][b][iii]; 19.02[5][a]; 19.02[5][b];
19.03; 19.05; **19** n.130

731(c) . . . . **1** ns. 23, 186; **S9** n.642; 19.03;
19.08[6]; 19.09[1]; 19.09[3]; 19.09[4];
19.09[5]; S19.09[5]; **19** ns. 16, 153,
216–218, 232, 234, 246; **S19** ns. 227,
250.1

731(c)(1) . . . . . 14.02[3][b][xi]; **16** n.55; **19** ns.
214, 247; **21** n.69; **25** ns. 4, 5, 79

731(c)(1)(B) **19** n.215

731(c)(2) . . . . 4.07[1]; 19.09[1]

731(c)(2)(A) **19** n.223

731(c)(2)(B)(i)(II) **19** n.226

731(c)(2)(B)(ii) **19** n.227; **S19** n.227

731(c)(2)(B)(iii) **19** n.228

731(c)(2)(B)(iv) **19** n.230

731(c)(2)(B)(v) . . . . **19** ns. 217, 231

731(c)(2)(B)(vi) **19** n.232

731(c)(2)(C) **19** n.224

731(c)(2)(C)(i)(VII) **19** n.241

731(c)(3)(A)(i) **19** n.234

731(c)(3)(A)(iii) **19** n.239

731(c)(3)(B) . . . . 19.08[6]; **19** ns. 216, 217

731(c)(3)(C)(i) . . . **19** ns. 240, 241; **S19** n.239

731(c)(3)(C)(iii) **19** n.239

[Text references are to paragraphs; note references are to chapters (boldface numbers) and notes ("n."). References to the supplement are preceded by "S."]

IRC §

731(c)(3)(C)(iv) **19** n.243
731(c)(4) **1** n.25; **19** n.221; **25** n.79
731(c)(5) . . . . **25** ns. 4, 79
731(c)(6) **19** n.221
731(d) **19** n.130; 25.03
732 . . . . . . .1.05[4][d]; **1** n.100; 3.09[4][b]; **S4** n.199.1; 6.01; 7.02[4]; 9.02[3][k][ii]; **9** n.653; S11.04[1][b][iv]; 11.04[4][d]; 14.03[5]; S14.03[5]; 14.04[8]; 16.01[2]; 16.02[1]; **16** n.217; 17.03; 17.03[3]; 17.03[3][j]; **17** ns. 31, 33, 82; 18.03[4]; 19.02[4]; 19.02[5][b]; 19.03; 19.04[1]; 19.05; 19.07[2]; 19.09[1]; 19.10; **19** ns. 126, 214; 20.03; 20.05; **20** n.7; 21.01[1]; S21.01[6][c]; S21.01[6][d]; 21.03[5]; 24.05; 25.01[4]; S25.01[8]; 25.03; 25.04; 25.06; **25** ns. 21, 106; 26.01; 26.01[2]; 26.02; 26.03
732 (former) . . . . 1.05[3]; 1.05[4][d]; **1** n.100 26.01; 26.01[3]
732(a)−732(c) . . . . 26.01; 26.01[3]
732(a) . . . . . 1.05[4][d]; **1** ns. 21, 25; **9** n.1024; 19.03; 19.08[4][a]; 21.03[4][c]
732(a)(1) . . . 6.02[4]; **13** n.136; 19.01[2][a][ii]; 19.02[5][b]; 19.04[1]; 19.04[2]; 19.05; 19.08[3][a]; **19** n.2; 20.03[1]; **20** n.39; 21.03[5]; 21.04[1]; 21.04[2]; 21.04[3]; **22** n.85; 25.01[2]; 25.01[2][b]; 26.01[3]
732(a)(2) . . . **1** n.103; 6.02[2]; 6.02[4]; **6** ns. 64, 65, 67, 69; 11.05[2][b]; 16.08[3][a]; 19.01[2][a][ii]; 19.02[5][b]; 19.04[1]; S19.04[1]; 19.10; **19** n.68; 20.01; **20** n.18; 21.03[5]; 21.06[2][a]; 25.01[2]; 25.01[2][b]; 25.03; S25.01[8]; **25** n.102; 26.01; 26.01[3]
732(b) . . . 1.05[3]; **1** ns. 21, 25, 103; 6.02[2]; **6** n.10; 7.02[5]; 9.01[4][c][vii]; 9.02[3][k][ii]; 9.02[3][k][ii][C]; 9.02[3][k][ii][D]; 9.03[1][a][vi]; **9** n.1024; 13.06[1]; **13** ns. 104, 112, 136; 16.02[3][e]; 16.08[3][a]; **18** n.61; 19.01[2][b][ii]; 19.02[5][b]; 19.06; 19.07[1]; 19.10; **19** ns. 3, 68; 20.01; 20.03[2][c]; 20.03[2][d]; 20.05; **20** n.18; 21.06[2][a]; 21.06[2][c]; 22.01; 22.06[1][a]; 22.06[3]; 24.01[3]; 24.05; 25.01[2]; 25.01[2][b]; 25.01[3]; 25.01[4]; 25.01[7]; 25.02[1][a]; 25.02[1][b]; 25.03; 25.04; **25** n.20; 26.01[3]
732(c) . . . . 1.05[3]; **1** ns. 45, 91, 196; S9.03[1][a][ii][D]; 11.04[4][f][ii]; 13.06[1]; **13** n.112; 17.03; **17** n.82; 18.03[4]; **18** n.63; 19.01[2][b][ii]; 19.02[5][b]; 19.06; S19.06; 19.06[2]; 19.08[1]; 19.08[4][a]; 19.10; 20.03[2][d]; 20.05; **20** ns. 46, 71; S21.01[6][a]; 21.03[5]; **21** n.3; 22.06[1][b]; 22.06[2][b]; 25.02[1][a]; 25.02[1][b]; **25** n.77; 26.01; 26.01[3]; 26.03; **26** ns. 6, 13, 19, 36, 39
732(c) (former) . . . 1.05[1][a]; 1.05[4][d]; **1** ns. 105

732(c)(1) . . . . 17.04[2]; 19.05; 21.01[1]; **21** ns. 14, 18; 22.02[5][b]; 25.02[1][b]; 25.02[2]; 25.02[5]; **25** n.80.
732(c)(1)(A) . . . . 19.06[2]; **19** n.90
732(c)(1)(A)(i) . . . 19.06[2]; **19** n.118; **25** n.77; **26** n.7
732(c)(1)(A)(ii) . . . . 21.04[4]; **21** n.122
732(c)(1)(B) . . . . **9** n.1024; 19.06[2]; **19** n.112; **25** n.77
732(c)(1)(B)(i) **19** n.121; **26** n.8
732(c)(2) . . . . . . 19.06[2]; 25.02[1][b]; 26.03
732(c)(2)(A) **19** n.124
732(c)(2)(B) **19** n.125; **26** n.10
732(c)(3) **25** n.68; **26** n.9
732(c)(3)(A) . . . . **19** ns. 91, 119, 122
732(c)(3)(B) . . . . **19** ns. 92, 120, 123; **21** n.121
732(d) . . . 1.05[4][d]; **1** n.186; 9.02[3][k][ii][B]; 9.02[3][k][ii][D]; **9** n.432; **11** n.188; 12.03[1]; 16.01[2]; 17.02[3][d]; 18.03[4]; 19.01[2][c][iii]; 21.03[5]; **21** n.25; 22.02[5][b]; 22.02[5][c]; 22.02[6]; **22** n.94; 24.04[3][a]; 24.04[3][b]; 25.02[6]; 25.05; **25** n.15; 26.01; 26.01[1]; 26.01[2]; 26.01[3]; 26.01[4]; 26.02; 26.02[1]; 26.02[2]; 26.03; **26** ns. 2, 3, 6, 13, 15, 16, 19, 20, 33, 35, 36, 39
732(e) 25.03
732(f) . . . . 9.03[1][a][ii]; S9.03[1][a][ii]; S9.03[1][a][ii][D]; **9** ns. 641, 653; 19.10; **S9** n.642; **S16** n.86; **19** ns. 252, 253; **S19** n.253; 25.02[1][a]
732(f)(1) . . . . **19** ns. 254, 258
732(f)(2) **19** n.259
732(f)(3)(A) **19** n.255
732(f)(3)(B) **19** n.256
732(f)(4) **19** n.257
732(f)(6) . . . . **19** ns. 261, 262
732(f)(7) 19.10
732(f)(8) **19** n.260
733 . . . . . . **1** ns. 21, 42; 4.03[1][a]; 4.03[1][c]; 6.02[4]; 6.02[5]; **6** n.23; 9.02[2][a][ii][B]; **9** n.294; 16.02[1]; 16.05[1][b]; 19.01[2][a][iii]; 19.03; 19.03[3]; 19.04[1]; **19** n.221; 21.04[2]; 21.04[4]; 25.03
733(1) . . . . . . 7.02[3]; 7.02[4]; 11.05[2][b]; **11** n.618
733(2) . . . . .7.02[4]; 11.05[2][b]; 14.03[5]; S14.03[5]; 19.04[2]; 19.08[2][b]
734 . . . . . **1** ns. 45, 91, 196; S4.01[5][b][iii][C]; 9.02[3][k][ii]; 9.03[4][d]; 11.02[2][c][v]; S11.04[1][b][iv]; 14.04[8]; 16.02[1]; **17** n.31; **19** n.131; 20.05; 22.02[3]; **24** n.185; 25.01; 25.01[4]; 25.03
734(a) . . . . . . 1.03; **1** n.26; **6** n.1; 16.02[1][a]; 19.01[2][b][iii]; **19** n.55; 22.01[4][a]; 22.02[3]; **22** n.87; 25.01[1]; 25.01[1][a]; 25.01[1][b]; 25.01[2]; 25.01[2][a]; **25** ns. 6, 120

[Text references are to paragraphs; note references are to chapters (boldface numbers) and notes ("n."). References to the supplement are preceded by "S."]

IRC §

734(b) . . . . . **1** ns. 27, 186; 4.03[1][a]; 4.03[4]; 4.05[1]; **4** n.172; 6.03; **6** ns. 1, 12; 7.04[3][e]; 9.01[4][c][vii]; S9.02[3][c][i][B]; S9.02[3][c][i][C]; S9.02[3][c][i][J]; 9.02[3][k][i]; 9.02[3][k][ii][D]; S9.02[3][z][ii][E]; 9.03[1][a][vi]; **9** ns. 444, 455, 462; S11.02[2][c][iii]; 11.02[2][c][v]; S11.04[1][b][iv]; 11.04[4][d]; **11** ns. 189, 197, 200, 526; **S11** n.189; 12.03[1]; **13** n.135; 16.02[2][e]; 16.02[3][d]; 16.05[4]; 19.01[2][b][iii]; 19.02[5][a]; 19.02[5][b]; 19.07[1]; 19.07[2]; 19.08[4][b]; 19.10; **19** ns. 70, 131, 221; 20.05; **20** n.71; S21.01[2]; S21.01[6][a]; S21.01[6][c]; S21.01[6][d]; 21.03[5]; 21.06[2][a]; **21** ns. 71, 105, 122, 129; 22.01[4][a]; 22.02[3]; 22.02[4][c]; 22.02[4][d][i]; 22.02[5][a]; 22.06[1][a]; **22** n.22; 24.01[4]; 24.04[1][b]; 24.04[3][a]; 24.04[3][b]; 24.04[3][b][iii][B]; 24.09; 24.11[1]; 24.11[2]; 24.11[5]; **24** ns. 58, 219; 25.01[2]; 25.01[2][a]; 25.01[2][b]; 25.01[3]; 25.01[4]; 25.01[5]; 25.01[6]; 25.01[7]; S25.01[7]; 25.01[8]; S25.01[8]; 25.02; 25.02[1]; 25.02[1][a]; 25.02[1][b]; 25.02[2]; 25.02[3]; 25.02[4]; 25.02[5]; 25.02[6]; 25.02[7]; 25.02[8]; 25.03; 25.04; 25.05; 25.06; 25.07; 25.07[1]; 25.07[2]; **25** ns. 6–8, 21, 27, 30, 59, 70, 79, 83, 112, 116, 124; **S25** ns. 27, 122.1

734(b)(1) **4** n.172

734(b)(1)(A) . . . . 19.02[5][a]; 19.08[2][e]; 19.08[4][b]; **22** n.88; 25.01[2]; 25.01[2][a]; 25.03; **25** ns. 4, 101

734(b)(1)(B) . . . . 22.06[1][a]; 25.01[2]; 25.01[2][b]; 25.02[1][b]; 25.02[6]; 25.03; 25.05; 25.06; 25.07[2]; **25** n.20

734(b)(2) . . . . **21** n.86; 22.02[6]

734(b)(2)(A) . . . . 19.02[5][a]; 22.02[5][b]; 22.02[6]; 25.01[2]; 25.01[2][a]; S25.01[7]

734(b)(2)(B) . . . . . . 19.05; 22.02[6]; 25.01[2]; 25.01[2][b]; 25.01[3]; 25.01[4]; S25.01[7]; 25.02[2]; 25.04; 25.05; 25.07[2]; **25** n.102

734(d) . . . . **1** ns. 26, 99; 16.02[1][a]; 22.02[3]; 22.06[1][b]; 22.06[2][a]; **25** n.49

734(d)(1) **19** n.55

735 . . . . . . 1.04; **1** n.186; S4 n.199.1; 16.02[1]; 17.03[3]; **17** n.85; 21.01[1]

735(a) . . . . . . 1.01[3]; 4.02[3]; 4.05[6]; 17.03; 17.04[2]; 19.01[2][c][v]; **19** n.100; 20.02; 20.03[1]; **20** ns. 5, 14, 19; 21.01[1]; 21.01[2]; **21** ns. 2, 3, 9; 25.02[5]

735(a)(1) . . . . 17.03[3]; 22.06[2][b]

735(a)(2)   20.02; 21.04[2]; **21** ns. 19, 79, 109

735(b)   S13.05[2][f]; 16.02[3][b]; 16.02[3][d]; **16** n.19; 19.01[2][a][ii]; 19.03; 20.01; **20** ns. 42, 79

735(c)(1) **20** n.9

735(c)(2) **20** n.14

735(c)(2)(A) **20** n.14

735(c)(2)(B) **20** n.16

736 . . . 1.01[3]; 13.04[2]; 13.05[2][l]; 13.05[3]; 14.02[3][b][xi]; 14.02[4][c]; 16.02[1]; 16.02[2][a]; 16.02[2][b]; 16.02[3]; 16.02[3][a]; 16.02[3][b]; 16.02[3][e]; 16.07[1]; S16.08[7]; **16** n.60; 17.03[3]; 17.03[3][j]; 19.01[1]; 19.01[2][b][i]; 19.02[1]; 21.02[3][a]; 21.03[1]; **21** n.106; 22.01; 22.01[1]; 22.01[2]; 22.01[3]; 22.01[4]; 22.01[5]; 22.01[6]; 22.02[4][b]; 22.02[4][c]; 22.02[4][d][iv]; 22.04[2]; 22.06; 22.06[1]; 22.06[2][a]; 22.06[2][b]; 22.07; **22** ns. 6, 7, 9, 24, 35, 43, 48, 73, 123, 138; 23.04[3];23.07[7]

736(a) . . . . **1** n.31; 11.03[4][b]; 11.04[4][b][iii]; **13** n.142; 16.02[1]; 16.02[1][b]; 16.02[2][a]; 16.02[2][c]; 16.02[3]; 16.02[3][a]; **16** n.61; **17** n.63; 18.01[3]; 19.01[1]; 19.01[2][b][i]; 21.02[3][a]; 21.04[1]; 22.01; 22.01[4][b]; 22.01[5]; 22.02[2]; 22.03[1]; 22.03[2]; 22.03[2][b]; 22.04[1]; 22.04[2]; 22.04[3]; 22.05; 22.05[1]; 22.05[2]; 22.05[3]; 22.05[4]; 22.06[1][a]; 22.06[1][b]; 22.06[2][a]; 22.06[2][b]; 22.07; **22** ns. 1, 24, 30, 42, 49, 98, 122, 144; 23.02[2]; 23.02[2][a]; 23.02[2][b]; 23.05[2][a]; 23.06[2]; **23** ns. 6, 23; 24.08[1]

736(a)(1)   **9** n.608; 22.01; 22.01[4]; 22.01[6]; 22.03[2]; 22.03[2][b]; 22.06; 22.06[1]; 22.06[1][b]; 22.06; 22.06[2][a]; 22.06[3]; **22** ns. 26, 28, 107, 109

736(a)(2) . . . 11.02[2][c][i]; 11.08[2]; **14** n.279; **S14** n.249.1; **16** n.44; **18** n.26; 19.07[1]; **21** n.107; 22.01; 22.01[4]; 22.01[6]; 22.02[4][c]; 22.03[2]; 22.03[2][a]; 22.03[2][b]; 22.03[3]; 22.05[1]; 22.06[1]; 22.06[1][b]; 22.06[2]; 22.06[2][a]; 22.06[2][b]; **22** ns. 27, 28, 98, 100, 107, 126, 138

736(b) . . . . S9.03[4][a]; 11.08[2]; 16.02[1]; 16.02[1][a]; 16.02[1][b]; 16.02[2][a]; 16.02[2][b]; **16** n.39; 19.01[1]; 21.02[3][a]; 22.01; 22.01[4][a]; 22.01[4][b]; 22.01[5]; 22.01[6]; 22.02[1]; 22.02[2]; 22.02[3]; 22.02[4]; 22.02[4][a]; 22.02[4][b]; 22.02[4][c]; 22.02[4][d]; 22.02[4][d][i]; 22.02[4][d][ii]; 22.02[4][d][iii]; 22.02[5]; 22.02[5][a]; 22.02[5][b]; 22.03[2][a]; 22.04[1]; 22.04[2]; 22.04[3]; 22.05; 22.05[1]; 22.05[2]; 22.05[3]; 22.05[4]; 22.06; 22.06[1]; 22.06[1][a]; 22.06[1][b]; 22.06[2]; 22.06[2][a]; 22.06[2][b]; **22** ns. 1, 30, 42, 49, 58, 98, 126; 25.02[8]

736(b)(1) **1** n.30; **S9** n.831; 22.01

736(b)(2) . . . . . **1** n.29; 17.03; 23.02[2][a]

736(b)(2)(B) 22.01; **22** n.32

[Text references are to paragraphs; note references are to chapters (boldface numbers) and notes ("n."). References to the supplement are preceded by "S."]

IRC §

736(b)(3) .... **1** ns. 29, 186; 22.01; **22** ns. 32, 115

737....... 1.01[2]; **1** ns. 67, 186; 7.04[3][e]; 9.03[1][a][iv]; **S9** n.642; 11.04[1][a]; 11.04[4][b][vii]; S11.04[4][b][vii]; 11.04[4][b][x]; 11.04[4][d]; **S11** ns. 561.2−561.5, 561.7, 561.8; 13.05[2][c]; 13.06[1]; 13.06[2]; **13** ns. 176, 178; 14.02[3][b][ii]; **14** n.97; 16.02[1]; 16.02[1][a]; 18.03[11]; 19.01[1]; 19.01[2][a][i]; 19.01[2][b][i]; 19.01[2][c][i]; 19.02[1]; 19.03; 19.05; 19.07[1]; 19.08; S19.08; 19.08[1]; 19.08[2][b]; 19.08[2][c]; 19.08[2][d]; 19.08[2][e]; 19.08[2][f]; S19.08[2][f]; 19.08[3][a]; 19.08[3][b]; 19.08[3][c]; 19.08[3][d]; 19.08[4]; 19.08[4][a]; 19.08[4][b]; 19.08[5]; 19.08[6]; 19.08[7]; 19.09[4]; **19** ns. 130, 150, 167, 174, 185, 201, 206, 214, 246; 25.02[5]; **25** n.103

737(a) ...... 19.08[2][a]; 19.08[3]; S19.08[3]; 19.08[3][a]; 19.08[4][a]; **19** n.171; **S19** n.171

737(b) .... 11.04[4][b][vii]; 19.08[2][d]

737(c)(1) .... 19.08[2][b]; 19.08[4][a]

737(c)(2) .... 19.08[4][b]

737(d)(1) ... 19.08[3][a]; 19.08[3][b]; **19** n.174

741−743 ....1.01

741...... 1.01[4]; 1.02[4]; **1** n.41; 3.08[4]; **3** n.409; 4.03[1][a]; 4.03[1][c]; 4.05[6]; **4** ns. 130, 214, 217; **S4** n.199.1; 5.02[5]; 6.02[2]; **6** ns. 3, 4; S9.03[4][a]; 11.04[2]; 13.06[1]; 16.01[1]; 16.02[2][a]; 16.02[2][b]; 16.02[2][c]; 16.02[3]; 16.02[3][a]; 16.02[3][b]; 16.02[3][d]; 16.03; 16.03[1]; 16.04[1][b]; 16.04[2][b]; 16.05[1][b]; 16.06[3]; 16.07[1]; 16.08[1]; 16.08[3][b]; 16.08[4]; 16.08[6]; **16** ns. 61, 209, 221, 223, 237, 258, 284; 17.01; 17.01[1]; 17.01[2]; 17.02[1]; 17.02[2]; 17.02[3][a]; 17.02[3][b]; 17.03; 17.03[3]; 17.03[3][b]; 17.03[3][j]; 17.05[1]; **17** ns. 26, 33, 35; 19.02[1]; 19.02[4]; 19.02[5][a]; 19.03; 19.05; **20** n.7; 22.01[4]; 22.01[4][a]

742 .... 1.02[4]; **1** ns. 41, 42; **5** n.162; 6.02[1]; **6** n.11; S9.06[1][a]; 10.02[5]; **16** n.15; 23.02[2][b]; 24.08; **24** n.31

742(b)........................ **24** n.126

743............ **1** ns. 45, 91, 196; 2.02[3]; 9.02[3][k][ii]; 9.03[4][d]; 12.02[2][a]; 12.02[2][c]; 13.05[2][e]; 14.04[8]; 16.07[4]; S16.07[4]; S16.08[7]; **16** ns. 209, 280; **17** n.31; 23.05[2][b]; **23** n.67; 24.01; 24.01[4]; 24.02[1]; 24.03[2]; 24.03[4]; 24.05; 24.06; 24.07; 24.10; 24.11[6]; 25.07[2]; **26** n.15

743(a) ...... 1.03; **1** ns. 33, 41; 6.01; **6** n.1; 16.01[2]; **16** ns. 18, 306; **17** n.33; 23.05[2][a]; 24.01[1]; 24.01[2]; **25** n.6

IRC §

743(b) .... 1.02[3]; **1** n.34; 2.02[4][a]; S4.01[5][b][iii][E]; 4.05[9]; 5.03[5]; 6.02[3][d][ii]; **6** ns. 1, 12; S9.01[4][c][vii]; 9.02[2][a][ii][C]; S9.02[3][c][i][B]; S9.02[3][c][i][D]; S9.02[3][c][i][J]; 9.02[3][k][i]; 9.02[3][k][ii][A]; 9.02[3][k][ii][D]; 9.02[3][r]; 9.02[3][u]; S9.02[3][z][ii][E]; S9.02[5][e]; S9.03[1][a][ii][C]; 9.03[1][d][i]; 9.03[2]; 9.03[4][a]; S9.06[1][a]; **9** ns. 44, 163, 355, 442, 444, 462, 505, 677; **S9** ns. 355, 515, 551.53, 633.3f, 633.4a, 659.1; S11.02[2][c][ii]; 11.02[2][c][v]; 11.03[2][e]; S11.03[2][i]; 11.04[1][b]; S11.04[1][b][ii]; 11.04[3][a]; 11.04[4][c]; 11.05[2][c]; 11.08[3][b]; **11** ns. 190, 620; **S11** n.436.5a; 12.03[1]; **12** n.68; 13.05[2][e]; S13.06[1]; **13** ns. 99, 135, 165, 203; **S13** n.183.5; 16.01[2]; 16.02[2][c]; 16.02[2][e]; 16.05[4]; 16.07[1]; 16.07[2]; 16.07[3]; 16.08[1]; 16.08[3][a]; **16** ns. 83, 136, 197, 273, 306; **S16** n.269; 17.02[3][d]; 17.03[3]; 17.04[2]; **17** ns. 33, 45, 50, 51, 69, 94; 18.03[2]; 18.03[4]; **18** ns. 63, 79; 19.01[2][c][iii]; 19.08[2][e]; 19.09[1]; 20.05; **20** n.71; 21.01[2]; S21.01[6][b]; S21.01[6][c]; 21.03[5]; **21** ns. 25, 129; 22.02[1]; 22.02[5][c]; 22.02[6]; 23.03[2]; 23.05[2][b]; 23.07[5]; 24.01[2]; 24.01[3]; 24.01[4]; 24.01[5]; 24.02; 24.02[1]; 24.02[2]; 24.03; 24.03[1]; 24.03[2]; 24.03[3]; 24.03[4]; 24.04; 24.04[1]; 24.04[1][a]; 24.04[1][b]; 24.04[1][d]; 24.04[2]; 24.04[3][a]; 24.04[3][b]; 24.04[3][b][ii][B]; 24.04[3][b][iii][D]; 24.04[3][c]; 24.05; 24.06; 24.07; S24.07; 24.08; 24.08[1]; 24.08[2]; 24.09; 24.10; 24.11[1]; 24.11[2]; 24.11[5]; 24.11[6]; 24.11[7]; 24.12; **24** ns. 6, 7, 9, 29, 30, 45, 59, 60, 68, 70, 77, 125, 148, 173, 182, 196, 219; 25.01[2]; 25.01[2][a]; 25.01[3]; 25.01[4]; 25.01[7]; 25.02; 25.02[1]; 25.02[1][a]; 25.02[2]; 25.02[6]; 25.02[7]; 25.04; 25.05; 25.06; 25.07[1]; 25.07[2]; S25.07[2]; **25** ns. 6, 7, 19−21, 70, 106, 115, 128; **S25** n.121; 26.01; 26.01[1]; 26.01[2]; 26.02[1]; 26.03; **26** ns. 2, 36, 38

743(b)(2) .... 25.07[2]

743(d) .... **1** n.99; 24.01[4]

743(d)(1) ...... S13.06[1]; **16** n.18; **S16** n.18

743(d)(1)(A) .... 24.01[4]; **24** ns. 13, 221

743(d)(1)(B) 24.01[4]; 24.09; **24** ns. 13, 221, 222

743(d)(2) **24** n.19; **25** n.43

743(e) **16** n.18; **S16** n.18

743(e)(2) **24** n.23

743(e)(6) **24** n.22

743(f) **24** n.24

[Text references are to paragraphs; note references are to chapters (boldface numbers) and notes ("n."). References to the supplement are preceded by "S."]

[Text references are to paragraphs; note references are to chapters (boldface numbers) and notes ("n."). References to the supplement are preceded by "S."]

IRC §

751(c) . . . **1** n.103; 4.05[6]; S4.05[5][b]; **4** n.33; **S4** n.199.1; **7** n.192; S9.02[1][d][ii][B]; 9.03[1][d][i]; **9** n.714; 16.02[1]; 16.02[1][a]; 16.02[2][c]; **16** n.284; 17.01[3]; 17.03; 17.03[3]; 17.03[3][b]; 17.03[3][e]; 17.03[3][f]; 17.03[3][g]; 17.03[3][h]; 17.03[3][j]; 17.04[2]; 17.05[1]; **17** ns. 62, 68, 82, 86, 140; 19.02[4]; 19.04[1]; 19.05; S19.05; 19.06[1]; 19.06[2]; **19** ns. 126, 221; 20.03; 20.03[5]; **20** n.7; 21.01[5]; 21.02[3][a]; 21.03[1]; 21.04[4]; 21.05[1]; 21.05[3]; **21** ns. 2, 68; 22.01; 22.01[4]; 22.01[4][a]; 22.01[4][b]; 22.02[1]; 22.03[2][a]; **22** ns. 43, 55, 68; 24.04[1]; 24.04[3][b][ii][C]; 24.04[3][b][ii][D]; **24** ns. 100, 191; 25.01[2]; 25.02[6]
751(c)(2) . . . . 17.05[1]; **17** n.46
751(d) . . . . 4.05[6]; **4** n.199; 16.02[3][d]; 17.01[3]; 17.03[3]; 17.04; 17.04[2]; 19.02[4]; 19.04[1]; 19.05; S19.05; 19.06[1]; **19** n.221; 20.02; 21.03[1]; **21** ns. 2, 30, 54; 22.01[4]; **22** ns. 42, 55, 68; 25.01[2]
751(d)(1) . . . . **1** n.186; 17.01[2]; 17.04[1]; 17.05[1]; **17** ns. 127, 129; **18** n.58; 21.04[4]
751(d)(1) (former) . . . 21.01[4][a]; 21.01[4][b]; **21** n.26
751(d)(1)(B) **21** n.27
751(d)(2) . . . . **1** n.103; 4.05[6]; **4** n.199; 17.04[2]; **17** ns. 64, 130, 157; 21.04[4]; **21** n.55
751(d)(2)(B) . . . . 17.04[2]
751(d)(3) . . . 17.04[3]; 17.04[3][a]; 17.04[3][b]; 17.04[3][c]; **17** n.131
751(d)(3) (former) **17** n.143
751(d)(4) **9** n.70; **21** n.54
751(e) . . . . 17.03[3][f]
751(f) . . . **1** n.186; **4** n.201; 17.05[1]; 17.06; **24** n.191

IRC §

752 . . . . . 1.01[1]; 1.05[1][c]; 2.02[5]; **2** ns. 15, 35; 4.01[1][a]; S4.01[1][a]; 4.01[2][a]; S4.02[3]; 4.03[1][a]; 4.03[2]; S4.05[12]; **4** n.140; 5.02[3][f]; 6.02[5]; 6.04; **6** n.31; 7.01; 7.02; 7.02[3]; 7.02[6]; 7.03; 7.03[1]; 7.03[2]; 7.03[3]; 7.04[1]; 7.04[2]; 7.04[3]; 7.04[3][a]; 7.04[3][b]; 7.04[3][e]; 7.04[3][h]; 7.05; 7.05[1]; 7.05[2]; 7.06; 7.06[2]; 7.06[3]; 7.06[4]; 7.07; **7** ns. 22, 50, 60, 71, 72, 149, 163, 176, 193, 199; **S7** ns. 62, 68, 81.1; 8.01[1]; 8.02[1]; 8.02[2]; 8.02[3]; 8.02[4][b][i]; 8.02[4][b][iii][B]; 8.02[4][b][iv]; 8.02[4][b][v][A]; 8.02[4][b][v][E]; 8.02[4][c]; 8.02[5]; 8.02[6]; 8.02[7][a]; 8.02[7][b]; 8.02[9]; 8.02[10][a]; 8.03[1]; 8.03[3][a]; 8.03[3][b]; 8.03[4]; 8.03[5]; 8.04; **8** ns. 42, 45, 48, 72; 9.02[1][c][iv]; 9.02[2][a][ii][B]; 9.02[2][a][ii][C]; 9.02[3][c]; S9.02[3][c][i][F]; S9.02[3][c][ii]; 9.03[4][d]; S9.06[1][a]; **9** ns. 253, 295; S11.02[2][a][iv]; 11.02[2][c][x]; 11.02[4][e][vii]; 11.06[1]; 11.06[2][b]; **11** ns. 288, 636, 645; S13.06[1]; **13** n.168; S14.02[3][b][iv]; 14.02[3][b][v]; S14.02[3][b][v]; 14.02[3][b][vii]; S14.03[3][b][iv]; **14** ns. 108, 111; **S14** ns. 108, 108.1; 16.01[2]; 16.02[2][b]; 16.05[1]; 16.05[1][a]; 16.05[1][b]; 16.05[1][c]; 16.05[2][a]; **16** ns. 228, 261; **S16** ns. 261, 261.1; 19.04[2]; 19.05; 19.08[2][b]; 19.08[5]; **19** ns. 213, 237; **21** n.45; 22.02[4][b]; 22.02[4][d][iv]; **22** n.70; 24.01[4]; 24.04[3][b][ii][B]; 24.04[3][b][ii][D]; **24** n.31
752(a) . . . . . . 4.01[2][a]; 4.03[1][a]; 4.03[1][b]; 4.03[2]; 5.02[3][f]; 5.02[3][h]; 6.02[1]; 6.02[3][a]; **6** n.22; 7.02; 7.02[3]; 7.02[4]; 7.02[5]; 7.04[2]; 7.06[3]; 7.06[4]; 7.07; **7** ns. 17, 20, 130, 176, 186, 193; 8.01[1]; 9.02[1][c][iv]; 11.02[2][c][i]; 11.04[3][g]; **11** ns. 140, 142; 14.02[3][b][xi]; 16.05[1]; 16.05[1][c]; **16** n.216; **21** n.44; 22.02[4][b]; 22.02[4][c]; 22.03[2][a]; **22** n.106; 23.03[1][a]

[Text references are to paragraphs; note references are to chapters (boldface numbers) and notes ("n."). References to the supplement are preceded by "S."]

IRC §

752(b) . . . . S4.02[3]; 4.03[1][a]; 4.03[1][c];
4.03[2]; 4.03[3]; **4** ns. 143, 147;
5.02[3][f]; 5.02[3][h]; 6.02[5]; **6** n.31;
7.02; 7.02[3]; 7.02[4]; 7.02[5]; 7.04[2];
7.06[3]; 7.06[4]; 7.06[5]; 7.07; **7** ns. 35,
174, 176, 186; 8.01[1]; 8.02[4][b][v][E];
9.02[1][b]; 9.02[1][c][iii]; 9.02[1][c][iv];
9.02[2][a][ii][B]; **9** ns. 240, 294, 295; **10**
n.72; **S10** n.73; 11.02[2][c][i];
11.04[3][g]; **11** ns. 140, 142; S13.06[1];
13 n.33; 16.02[2][b]; 16.04[2][b];
16.05[1]; 16.05[1][b]; 16.05[1][c];
16.05[2][a]; 16.05[2][b]; 16.05[2][c];
16.05[4]; S16.06[2]; 16.06[3]; S16.07[1];
16 ns. 217, 223, 227, 237, 258; 19.02;
19.02[5][c]; 19.03[1]; 19.03[2]; **19** ns.
25, 78, 79, 81, 160; 21.02[1]; 21.02[2];
21.03[3]; 21.03[8]; 21.04[4]; **21** n.44;
22.01[1]; 22.02[2]; 22.02[4][b];
22.02[5][a]; 22.03[2][a]
752(c) . . . 7.02; 7.02[3]; 7.02[4]; 7.06; 7.06[1];
7.06[2]; 7.06[3]; 7.06[4]; 7.06[5];
7.06[6]; **7** ns. 18−20, 176, 182, 183,
186−188, 190, 192; 11.02[2][c][ii];
S11.02[2][c][ii]; **17** n.86
752(d) . . . . 7.02[6]; 7.06[2]; 7.06[4]; 7.06[5]; **7**
ns. 33, 176, 183; S9.03[4][a]; **13** n.33;
16.01[1]; 16.02[2][b]; 16.04[1][b];
16.05[1]; 16.05[1][a]; 16.05[1][b];
16.05[1][c]; 16.05[2][a]; 16.05[2][b];
16.05[2][c]; 16.05[4]; 16.07[1]; **16** ns.
209, 216, 217, 223, 227, 237; **S16** n.215;
17.02[3][a]; 23.05[2][a]
753 . . . . **1** n.32; 23.02[2][a]; 23.02[2][b];
24.08[1]

IRC §

754 . . . 1.01[4]; 1.02[4]; 1.05[3]; 1.05[4][b][vi];
1.05[4][d]; **1** ns. 67, 101; 2.02[4][a];
4.01[6]; 4.03[1][a]; 4.03[4]; 4.05[1]; **4**
ns. 149, 172; 5.03[5]; 6.02[3][d][i];
6.02[3][d][ii]; **6** ns. 12, 52; 7.04[1];
7.04[3][e]; **7** n.42; 9.01[7]; 9.01[8][d];
S9.02[3][c][i][B]; S9.02[3][c][i][J];
9.02[3][k][i]; 9.02[3][k][ii][B];
9.02[3][k][ii][D]; S9.02[5][e];
9.03[1][a][iv]; 9.03[1][a][ix]; 9.03[4][a];
9.06[1][a]; S9.06[1][a]; **9** ns. 166, 432,
435, 647, 727, 772; **S9** ns. 375.33,
659.1; 10.02[3]; S10.02[3]; **S10** n.77;
10A.02[3]; **10A** n.212; 11.02[2][c][v];
11.04[1][b]; S11.04[1][b][ii];
11.04[4][b][vii]; 11.04[4][d];
11.04[4][f][ii]; **11** ns. 188, 191, 197,
356, 573; 12.03[1]; 13.05[2][b];
13.05[2][e]; **13** ns. 72, 99, 165, 203;
16.01[2]; 16.02[1][a]; 16.02[2][a];
16.02[2][c]; 16.02[3][d]; 16.07[1];
16.07[2]; S16.08[7]; 17.03[3];
17.03[3][b]; **17** ns. 33, 46, 161; 18.03[2];
18.03[4]; **18** n.63; 19.01[2][b][iii];
19.02[5][a]; 19.02[5][b]; 19.05;
19.08[2][e]; 19.08[4][b]; 19.09[1]; **19**
n.131; 21.01[2]; S21.01[6][c];
S21.01[6][d]; 21.03[5]; 21.06[2][a]; **21**
ns. 86, 105, 122, 123; 22.01[4][a];
22.02[3]; 22.02[4][d][i]; 22.02[5];
22.02[5][a]; 22.02[5][b]; 22.02[5][c];
22.02[6]; 22.06[1][a]; 22.06[1][b];
22.06[2][a]; **22** n.121; 23.02[2][b];
23.03[2]; 23.05[2][a]; 23.05[2][b];
23.07[5]; **23** n.6; 24.01[2]; 24.01[3];
24.01[4]; 24.01[5]; 24.02[1]; 24.03[4];
24.04[1][c]; 24.04[3][b][ii][D]; 24.06;
24.07; 24.09; 24.11; 24.11[1]; 24.11[2];
24.11[3]; 24.11[4]; 24.11[5]; 24.11[6];
24 ns. 4, 5, 12, 29, 60, 70, 170, 183,
188, 202, 203, 219, 226; 25.01[2];
25.01[2][a]; 25.01[2][b]; 25.01[3];
25.01[4]; 25.01[6]; 25.01[7]; 25.01[8];
S25.01[8]; 25.02[1][a]; 25.03; 25.06;
25.07; 25.07[1]; S25.07[1]; 25.07[2]; **25**
ns. 3, 14, 16, 46, 48, 118, 120; **S25** ns.
121, 122.1; 26.01; 26.01[1]; 26.01[4];
26.02[1]; 26.03; **26** ns. 2, 3, 15, 27, 36,
39
754(a)(3) **1** n.93

[Text references are to paragraphs; note references are to chapters (boldface numbers) and notes ("n."). References to the supplement are preceded by "S."]

[Text references are to paragraphs; note references are to chapters (boldface numbers) and notes ("n."). References to the supplement are preceded by "S."]

[Text references are to paragraphs; note references are to chapters (boldface numbers) and notes ("n."). References to the supplement are preceded by "S."]

IRC §

1011–1023 . . . . **6** n.1
1011–1015 . . . . 1.01[4]
1011(b) . . . . 16.05[2][b]; 16.05[2][c]; **16** n.220
1012   **4** n.88; **6** ns. 16, 18; S9.02[3][z][ii][E];
        S9 n.551.11; 11.03[2][h]; 16.01[2];
        16.07[2]; 17.03[3]; 18.03[4]; 21.03[6][e];
                        22.02[3]; 25.03
1014 . . . . S9.02[3][z][ii][E]; 9.06[2][a];
        11.05[2][c]; 11.08[3][a]; 16.02[3][d];
        18.03[2]; 23.02[2][b]; 23.05[1];
        23.05[2][a]; **23** n.16; 24.01[3];
        24.04[3][b][ii][B]; 24.07; S24.07;
                24.08[1]; 24.11[7]; **24** n.182
1014(a) **2** n.23; **S2** n.23; **6** n.19; **S6** n.19;
        11.03[2][h]; 23.02[1]; 23.02[2][a];
        23.02[2][b]; 23.03[1][a]; 24.01[3];
        24.03[3]; 24.08; 24.08[1]; 24.08[2]; **24**
                                n.68
1014(b) **24** n.66
1014(b)(6) . . . . 24.03[3]; **24** n.68
1014(b)(9) . . . . 11.03[2][h]
1014(c)   23.02[1]; **23** n.57; 24.04[3][b][ii][B];
                                24 n.125
1014(f) **6** n.19
1015 . . . **6**.02[3][a]; **6** n.20; 9.06[2][a]; 16.01[2]
1015(a) **11** n.768
1015(d) . . . . 16.05[4]
1015(d)(6) . . . . 16.01[2]
1016(a)(2) . . . . S9.02[3][z][ii][E]
1016(a)(3) . . . . S9.02[3][z][ii][E]
1016(a)(20) . . . . 9.05[2]
1017 . . . . 9.02[2][a][i]; 9.02[2][a][ii][C]
1017(a) . . . . 9.02[2][a][ii][C]
1017(a)(2) **9** n.284
1017(b)(2) **9** n.275
1017(b)(3)(A) **9** n.284
1017(b)(3)(E) **9** n.279
1017(b)(3)(F) **9** n.284
1017(d) **9** n.275
1019 . . . . **6** n.32
1022 . . . . . . **23** n.16; **24** ns. 125, 177, 182
1023 (former) **24** n.66
1023(b)(1) (former) **24** n.66
1031 . . . . . . 1.02[1]; 3.05[5]; S3.05[5]; 3.08[3];
        S3.08[3]; **3** n.321; **S3** n.236.1;
        6.02[3][a]; 9.02[1][c]; S9.02[1][c];
        9.02[1][c][i]; S9.02[1][c][i];
        9.02[1][c][ii]; 9.02[1][c][iii];
        9.02[1][c][iv]; 9.02[1][c][v][A];
        9.02[1][c][v][B]; 9.02[1][c][vi];
        S9.02[1][c][vi]; 9.02[1][c][vi][A];
        S9.02[1][c][vi][A]; 9.02[1][c][vi][B];
        9.02[3][k][i]; S9.02[3][z][ii][E];
        9.03[1][a][iv]; **9** ns. 240, 265, 269, 270;
        S9 ns. 254.1, 269–271; S11.04[1][b][iii];
        11.04[4][e]; 11.08[3][a]; **13** n.38; **S13**
        n.93; 14.04[2][c]; **14** n.166; 16.02[3][b];
        16.02[3][d]; 16.04[2][a]; S16.04[2][a];
        16.04[2][b]; **16** ns. 86, 95, 203, 204; **S16**
                ns. 86, 203; 19.02[2]; 19.03[1]

IRC §

1031(a) . . . . 9.02[1][c][v]; S9.02[1][c][v];
        9.02[1][c][vi][A]; 9.02[1][c][vi][B];
        9.02[1][c][vi][C]; 9.02[3][k][i];
        S9.02[3][k][i]; **9** n.262; **S9** ns. 269,
        429.1; S16.04[2][a]; **19** n.46
1031(a)(1) . . . . 9.02[1][c][iii]; **9** n.246; **S9** ns.
                        235, 235.1; 16.04[2][a]
1031(a)(2) . . . . . 3.08[3]; S3.08[3]; **S3** n.403.1;
        9.02[1][c][i]; 9.02[1][c][v];
        S9.02[1][c][v]; **9** n.235; **S9** ns. 235,
                                235.1
1031(a)(2)(D) . . . . 3.08[3]; 9.02[1][c][i];
        9.02[1][c][v]; S9.02[1][c][v];
        9.02[1][c][v][B]; 9.02[1][c][vi][A]; **9** ns.
        235, 238, 269; **S9** ns. 235, 254.1, 269;
                                16.04[2][a]
1031(a)(3) **9** n.246; **19** n.82
1031(b) **9** n.234
1031(c) **9** n.234
1031(d) . . . . 9.02[3][k][i]; S9.02[3][k][i]
1031(e) . . . . . **S3** ns. 236.1, 403.1; **S9** n.235.1;
                                S16.04[2][a]
1031(f) . . . . 14.01[1][a]
1032 . . . 1.02[4]; 4.01[1][c]; 5.03[5]; 6.02[3][d];
        6.02[3][d][i]; 6.02[3][d][ii]; **6** ns. 52, 59;
        9.01[4][b]; 9.03[1][a][ix]; **11** n.466;
                18.01[4]; **19** n.101; **24** n.183
1033   **3** n.264; 6.02[3][a]; 9.01[7]; 9.02[1][b];
        9.02[1][c][iii]; S9.02[3][z][ii][E]; **9** ns.
        226, 227, 239, 257; **13** n.190; **16** n.111;
                        19.02[2]; 19.03[1]; 24.12
1033(a)(2)(A) **9** n.233
1033(a)(2)(C) . . . . **9** ns. 229, 230
1033(g) **9** n.233
1041 . . . . **4** n.249; 13.03[1][e]; **13** n.52;
                16.02[3][e]; **16** ns. 123, 217
1041(a) . . . . 11.03[2][h]
1041(a)(2) **16** n.114
1041(b) . . . . 16.02[3][e]; **16** n.114
1041(b)(1) **13** n.52
1042 . . . . 4.05[10]; 9.01[7]
1042(a) . . . . 4.05[10]
1042(a)(1) . . . . 4.05[10]
1042(c)(4) . . . . 4.05[10]
1042(d) . . . . 4.05[10]
1042(e)(1) . . . . 4.05[10]
1042(e)(3) . . . . 4.05[10]
1044 (repealed) 4.08; S4.08; **6** n.18;
                16.01[2]; S16.01[2]; **S16** ns. 17, 18
1044(b) **4** n.252
1044(c)(4) **4** n.253
1044(d) **6** n.18; **16** n.17; **S16** n.17.1
1045 . . . . . 9.02[3][u]; S9.02[3][u]; **S9** ns. 511,
                                514
1045(a) . . . . 9.02[3][u]; S9.02[3][u]
1056 . . . . 16.03[1]; 16.08[5]
1059 . . . . 1.05[6]; S6.02[3][c]; 9.01[8]
1059(g)(1) . . . . 1.05[6]
1060 . . . **1** n.162; 9.01[8][d]; **17** n.69; **22** n.123;
                        24.04[3][a]; 24.04[3][c]
1060(a) . . . . 24.04[3][a]

*[Text references are to paragraphs; note references are to chapters (boldface numbers)
and notes ("n."). References to the supplement are preceded by "S."]*

[Text references are to paragraphs; note references are to chapters (boldface numbers) and notes ("n."). References to the supplement are preceded by "S."]

[Text references are to paragraphs; note references are to chapters (boldface numbers) and notes ("n."). References to the supplement are preceded by "S."]

[Text references are to paragraphs; note references are to chapters (boldface numbers) and notes ("n."). References to the supplement are preceded by "S."]

IRC §		IRC §	
1563(e)	**9** n.352	6038(e)(3)(A)	**9** n.1074
1901(b)(1)(I)	**21** n.74	6038(e)(3)(B)	**9** n.1075
2032	**24** n.181	6038(e)(3)(C)	4.01[5]; S4.01[5][a]
2032A	23.07[6]; **24** n.181	6038B	4.01[5]; S4.01[5][a]; S4.01[5][b][i]; **4**
2032A(a)(2)	**23** n.99		n.45; **S4** n.46; 9.06[1][b]
2032A(a)(3)	**23** n.99	6038B(a)(1)	**4** n.46; **S4** n.47
2032A(b)(1)	23.07[6]	6038B(a)(1)(B)	4.01[5]; S4.01[5][a]
2032A(b)(2)	**23** n.101	6038B(b)(1)	4.01[5]; S4.01[5][a]
2032A(b)(3)(A)	**23** n.100	6038B(b)(2)	**4** n.47; **S4** n.48
2032A(b)(3)(B)	**23** n.104	6038B(c)(1)	**4** n.49; **S4** n.50
2032A(c)(1)	**23** n.111	6038B(c)(2)	**4** n.51; **S4** n.51.1
2032A(c)(2)	**23** n.112	6038B(c)(3)	**4** n.50; **S4** n.51
2032A(c)(5)	**23** n.113	6039C	9.03[4][b]
2032A(c)(6)	**23** n.111	6039C(a)	**9** n.838
2032A(c)(8)	**23** n.111	6039C(c)(3)(A)	**9** n.838
2032A(d)(1)	**23** n.110	6041	3.05[4][a]
2032A(d)(2)	23.07[6]	6045	17.07
2032A(e)(1)	**23** n.103	6046A	S4.01[5][a]; 9.06[1][b]
2032A(e)(2)	**23** n.102	6046A(c)	**9** n.1071
2032A(e)(6)	**23** n.106	6050K	17.07
2032A(e)(7)(A)	23.07[6]	6050K(a)	**17** n.179
2032A(e)(8)	23.07[6]	6063	**9** n.1055; **S9** n.1055
2032A(g)	**23** n.107	6072(b)	S9.06[1][a]
2033	**23** n.4	6073	**9** n.335
2042	23.06[1]	6103	**10** n.146
2042(1)	23.06[1]; 23.06[2]	6103(h)(4)	**10** n.146
2042(2)	23.06[1]; 23.06[2]; **23** n.72	6111	9.06[2][c]
2053(a)(4)	**23** n.100	6111 (former)	**9** n.1116
2503(b)	16.05[4]	6111(a)	**9** n.1111
2663(2)	**14** n.144	6111(b)(1)(A)	**9** n.1113
3402	**5** n.156	6111(b)(1)(B)	**9** n.1114
3403	**9** ns. 213, 890	6112	9.06[2][c]; **9** n.1121
3405(c)	**13** n.126	6112(a)	**9** n.1115
3797(a)(2) (1939 Code)	**1** n.186; **3** ns. 15,	6161(a)(2)	23.07[7]
	70; S3.00[1]	6166	**3** n.409; 23.07[7]; **23** ns. 117, 118,
4081	9.01[10]		126
4971	10.02[3]	6166(a)(2)	**23** n.125
4972	10.02[3]	6166(b)	23.07[6]
4972(a)	**2** n.75	6166(b)(1)	23.07[6]
4972(c)(4)	**2** n.75	6166(b)(1)(B)	23.07[6]; **23** n.117
4975	9.03[3][d]; 14.02[1]	6166(b)(1)(B)(i)	**23** n.119
4975(e)(2)(G)	**14** n.33	6166(b)(1)(B)(ii)	**23** n.120
4975(e)(5)	**14** n.34	6166(b)(2)(B)	**23** n.121
4975(e)(6)	**14** n.34	6166(b)(2)(C)	**23** n.122
4980(d)	**13** n.128	6166(b)(2)(D)	**23** n.123
4981	9.03[5]; **9** ns. 916, 921	6166(b)(5)	**23** n.115
4982	9.03[6]; **9** ns. 916, 921	6166(b)(9)	**23** n.116
6011	9.06[2][b]; **9** ns. 1082, 1096	6166(c)	**23** n.124
6011(e)(2)	**9** n.1050	6166(f)(1)	**23** n.114
6012(a)	9.02[2][d]	6166(g)(1)	23.07[7]
6013(e)	10.02[3]; 10.02[5]	6166(g)(1)(A)	23.07[7]
6015	**10** n.229	6166(g)(2)	**23** n.128
6020	10.06[1]	6166(g)(3)	**23** n.127
6031	S4.01[5][b][iii][F]; 9.01[1]; 10A.02[3]	6166A	**3** n.409; **23** n.117
6031(a)	3.05[4][a]; **9** n.6	6211–6216	9.06[1][a]; S10.07
6031(b)	9.06[1][a]; S9.06[1][a]; **S9** n.330	6212	S10.07; 10A.02[3]; 10A.11[3]
6031(c)	9.06[1][a]; **24** n.227	6213	**10** n.219
6037	9.06[3]	6213(b)(3)	**10** n.219
6037(a)	9.06[3]	6214	10.02[5]
6038	S4.01[5][a]; 9.06[1][c]	6214(a)	10.07
6038(a)(5)	**9** n.1076	6214(b)	10.02[5]; 10.06[1]; **10** n.289

[Text references are to paragraphs; note references are to chapters (boldface numbers) and notes ("n."). References to the supplement are preceded by "S."]

[Text references are to paragraphs; note references are to chapters (boldface numbers) and notes ("n."). References to the supplement are preceded by "S."]

[Text references are to paragraphs; note references are to chapters (boldface numbers) and notes ("n."). References to the supplement are preceded by "S."]

[Text references are to paragraphs; note references are to chapters (boldface numbers) and notes ("n."). References to the supplement are preceded by "S."]

Cumulative Table of Treasury Regulations

[Text references are to paragraphs; note references are to chapters (boldface numbers) and notes ("n."). References to the supplement are preceded by "S."]

[Text references are to paragraphs; note references are to chapters (boldface numbers) and notes ("n."). References to the supplement are preceded by "S."]

Reg. §	
1.52-1	9.02[4][i]; **9** n.593
1.53-3	**9** n.561
1.58-2(b)	**9** n.44
1.58-2(b)(2)	**9** n.44
1.58-2(b)(2)(i)	**9** n.362
1.58-2(b)(2)(ii)	**9** n.362
1.58-2(b)(2)(iii)	**9** n.362
1.59A-3(b)(2)(iii)	**S9** n.117.9a
1.59A-3(c)(6)	**S9** n.117.9k
1.59A-3(c)(6)(iii)	**S9** n.117.9l
1.59A-3(c)(6)(iv)(A)	**S9** n.117.9m
1.59A-3(c)(6)(iv)(B)	**S9** n.117.9n
1.59A-3(c)(6)(iv)(C)	**S9** n.117.9o
1.59A-7(c)	**S9** n.1047
1.59A-7(d)(1)	**S9** n.117.9b
1.59A-7(e)(1)	**S9** n.117.9b
1.59A-7(c)(5)(v)	**S9** n.117.9i
1.59A-7(g)(2)(i)	**S9** n.117.9c
1.59A-7(g)(2)(ii) Ex. 2	**S9** n.117.9d
1.59A-7(g)(2)(iii)	**S9** n.117.9e
1.59A-7(g)(2)(iv) Ex. 3	**S9** n.117.9e
1.59A-7(g)(2)(iv) Ex. 4	**S9** n.117.9e
1.59A-7(g)(2)(vi) Ex. 6	**S9** n.117.9f
1.59A-7(g)(2)(vii) Ex. 7	**S9** n.117.9g
1.59A-7(g)(2)(viii) Ex. 8	**S9** n.117.9h
1.59A-7(g)(2)(x) Ex. 10	**S9** n.117.9i
1.59A-9(b)(5)	**S9** n.117.9j
1.59A-9(b)(6)	**S9** n.117.9j
1.61-1(a)	**5** n.103
1.61-2(d)	**5** ns. 28, 120
1.61-2(d)(1)	**5** n.141
1.61-2(d)(2)	**5** n.141
1.61-2(d)(4)	**5** n.141
1.61-2(d)(6)	**5** ns. 6, 141
1.61-3(a)	**11** n.369
1.61-6(a)	16.01[1]; **24** n.92
1.61-12(a)	**19** n.62
1.67-2T(b)(1)	**9** n.63
1.67-2T(g)(3)(ii)	**11** n.529
1.67-2T(g)(3)(iii)	**11** n.487
1.79-0	**2** n.87
1.83-1(a)	**5** ns. 65, 80, 136
1.83-1(a)(1)	5.02[5]; **5** ns. 121, 135, 141
1.83-1(b)(2)	**5** ns. 26, 51
1.83-1(e)	**5** n.26
1.83-2(a)	5.02[3][h]; **5** ns. 25, 50
1.83-3(a)(1)	**5** n.127
1.83-3(a)(2)	5.03[1]
1.83-3(a)(4)	**5** n.128
1.83-3(a)(6)	**5** n.130
1.83-3(a)(6) Ex. (2)	**5** n.129
1.83-3(b)	5.02[3][b]; 5.04; **5** ns. 10, 68, 134, 137, 154
1.83-3(c)	**5** ns. 11, 69
1.83-3(c)(1)	**5** ns. 69, 153
1.83-3(d)	**5** ns. 12, 70
1.83-3(e)	5.02[3][b]; **5** ns. 13, 126
1.83-3(f)	**5** ns. 131, 132
1.83-3(h)	**5** ns. 147, 149, 150
1.83-3(i)	5.03[1]; **5** ns. 148, 151, 152
1.83-3(j)	**5** n.69

Reg. §	
1.83-3(k)	**5** n.69
1.83-5(a)	5.03[4]
1.83-5(b)(1)	**5** n.121
1.83-6	**14** ns. 226, 246
1.83-6(a)(1)	5.03[5]
1.83-6(a)(2)	**5** n.156
1.83-6(a)(3)	**5** n.158
1.83-6(a)(4)	5.03[5]; **5** n.157
1.83-6(b)	5.03[5]
1.83-6(c)	5.02[3][h]; 5.03[5]
1.83-7(a)	**5** n.121
1.83-8(b)(2)	**5** n.121
1.108-2(c)	**19** n.63
1.108-5(b)	**9** n.279
1.108-5(c)	**9** n.279
1.108-6(b)	**9** n.286
1.108-8	**S4** n.110.1
1.108-8(b)	**S4** n.110.2
1.108-8(b)(1)	**S4** n.110.3
1.108-8(b)(2)(ii)	**S4** n.110.4
1.108-9	**S9** n.311
1.108-9(b)	S9.02[2][a][ii][A]
1.108(i)-2	S4.02[3]
1.108(i)-2(a)	**S4** n.110.21
1.108(i)-2(b)(1)	**S4** ns. 110.12, 110.14
1.108(i)-2(b)(2)	**S4** n.110.22
1.108(i)-2(b)(2)(i)	**S4** n.110.15
1.108(i)-2(b)(2)(ii)	**S4** n.110.13
1.108(i)-2(b)(3)(i)	**S4** n.110.17
1.108(i)-2(b)(3)(ii)	**S4** n.110.18
1.108(i)-2(b)(3)(iv)	**S4** n.110.19
1.108(i)-2(b)(4)(i)	**S4** n.110.23
1.108(i)-2(b)(4)(ii)	**S4** n.110.24
1.108(i)-2(b)(6)	**S4** n.110.26
1.108(i)-2(b)(6)(iii)	**S4** n.110.27
1.108(i)-2(d)(2)	**S4** n.110.21
1.108(i)-2(d)(3)	**S4** n.110.20
1.111-1	**18** n.18
1.111-1(a)	**4** n.112; **9** n.320; **18** n.22
1.132-1(b)(1)	**2** n.100
1.132-1(b)(2)	**2** n.100
1.132-1(b)(3)	**2** n.100
1.132-1(b)(4)	**2** n.101
1.132-1(e)(5)	**2** n.104
1.132-5(q)	**2** n.105
1.132-6(f)	**2** n.105
1.132-8	**2** n.103
1.162-7	9.03[3][c][ii]
1.162-7(b)	**14** n.238
1.162-8	**14** n.238
1.162-33(c)(3)(ii)	**S9** n.361.1
1.162-33(c)(3)(iv)(C) Ex. 3	**S9** n.361.1
1.163-4(c)(1)	19.02[5][a]; **19** n.62
1.163-8T	**6** n.46; 9.02[3][m][ii]; **9** n.363; **S9** n.363; 11.02[4][f][vi]; **11** ns. 274, 725, 773, 794; S14.02[3][b][iii][C]; 14.02[3][b][iv][B]; 14.02[3][b][v]; 14.02[3][b][vii]; 14.02[3][b][xi]; **16** n.43
1.163-8T(j)(1)(iii)	**14** n.103
1.163-8T(m)(7)(ii)	9.02[3][m][ii]
1.163-9T(b)(2)	**9** n.129

[Text references are to paragraphs; note references are to chapters (boldface numbers) and notes ("n."). References to the supplement are preceded by "S."]

Reg. §

1.163-9T(b)(2)(i)(A)	**1** n.170; **9** n.129
1.163(j)-1(b)(17)	**S9** n.373
1.163(j)-1(b)(22)(iv)	**S9** n.375
1.163(j)-1(b)(22)(v)(E) Ex. 5	**S9** n.375.1
1.163(j)-1(b)(44)(ii)	**S9** n.375.21
1.163(j)-2(j)(1)	**S9** n.374
1.163(j)-2(j)(2)(ii) Ex. 2	**S9** n.374
1.163(j)-4(b)(1)	**S9** ns. 375.26, 375.27
1.163(j)-4(b)(3)	**S9** n.375.27
1.163(j)-4(b)(7)(ii) Ex. 2	**S9** n.375.27
1.163(j)-4(c)(3)	**S9** n.375.28
1.163(j)-6(b)(1)	**S9** n.375.17
1.163(j)-6(b)(6)	**S9** n.375.15
1.163(j)-6(c)(3)	**S9** ns. 370, 375.14
1.163(j)-6(d)(2)	**S9** n.375.4
1.163(j)-6(e)(2)	**S9** n.375.5; **S14** n.282
1.163(j)-6(e)(4)(ii)	**S9** n.370
1.163(j)-6(f)(2)	**S9** n.375.16
1.163(j)-6(f)(2)(vii)	**S9** n.375.18
1.163(j)-6(h)(3)	**S9** ns. 375.7, 375.10, 375.12, 375.13
1.163(j)-6(m)(1)	**S9** n.375.19
1.163(j)-6(m)(3)	**S9** n.375.20
1.163(j)-6(o) Exs. 18–21 . . .	S9.02[3][c][i][D]
1.163(j)-6(o)(6) Ex. 6(ii)	**S9** n.375.6
1.163(j)-6(o)(7) Ex. 7	**S9** n.375.13
1.163(j)-6(o)(13) Ex. 13	**S9** n.375.20
1.163(j)-6(o)(14) Ex. 14	**S9** n.375.20
1.163(j)-6(o)(15) Ex. 15	**S9** n.375.20
1.163(j)-6(o)(17) Ex. 17	S9.02[3][c][i][D]
1.163(j)-7(b) . . . . S9.02[3][c][i][K]; **S9** n.375.39
1.163(j)-9(d)(4)	**S9** n.375.22
1.163(j)-9(h)	**S9** n.375.22
1.163(j)-10(b)(4)(ii)	**S9** n.375.25
1.163(j)-10(b)(6)	**S9** n.375.27
1.163(j)-10(b)(7)(ii) Ex. 2	**S9** n.375.27
1.163(j)-10(c)(1)(i)	**S9** n.375.23
1.163(j)-10(c)(5)(ii)	**S9** n.375.24
1.167(a)-1(a)	**25** n.27
1.167(a)-11(a)(1)	**20** n.58; **25** n.27
1.167(a)-11(c)(2)(iv)(c)	**3** n.37
1.167(a)-11(c)(2)(iv)(d)	**3** n.37
1.167(a)-11(c)(2)(iv)(e)	**3** n.37
1.167(a)-11(e)(3)(ii)	**20** n.58; **25** n.27
1.167(c)-1(a)(6) **13** n.136; **20** n.58; **25** n.27
1.167(g)-1	**4** n.10
1.167(h)-1(c)	**23** n.28
1.168-5(d)(8)	**25** n.27
1.168(d)-1(b)(6)	**4** n.194; **9** n.385
1.168(d)-1(b)(7)	**12** n.47
1.168(d)-1(b)(7)(i)	**4** n.194; **20** n.59
1.168(d)-1(b)(7)(ii)	**4** ns. 194, 198; **S4** n.194; **20** ns. 59, 60
1.168(d)-1(b)(7)(iv) Ex. (ii)	**4** n.194; **20** n.59
1.168(d)-1(b)(7)(iv) Ex. (iii)	**4** n.194; **20** n.59
1.168(j)-1T **9** n.734, 737–739, 742, 743, 746–749, 752
1.168(k)-2	**S24** n.157.2
1.168(k)-2(a)(2)(iv)	**S24** n.157
1.168(k)-2(a)(3)(iv)(A)	**S11** n.519

1.168(k)-2(b)(3)(iv)(C)	**S25** n.27
1.168(k)-2(b)(3))(iv)(D)	**S24**.07
1.168(k)-2(g)(1)(i)	**S24** n.157.3
1.168(k)-2(g)(1)(iii)	**12** n.47
1.168(k)-2(h)(1)(i)	**S24** n.157.2
1.168(k)-2(h)(2)(i)	**S24** n.157.2
1.168(k)-2(h)(3)(i)	**S24** n.157.2
1.179-1(f)(1)	9.02[3][g]
1.179-1(f)(2)	**9** n.393
1.179-1(f)(3)	**9** n.394
1.179-1(h)	**9** ns. 45, 162, 388
1.179-2(c)(2)	**9** n.387; **11** n.377
1.179-2(c)(2)(ii)	**9** n.389
1.179-2(b)(3)	**9** n.391
1.179-2(b)(3)(iii)	**9** n.392
1.179-2(b)(3)(iv)	**9** n.389
1.179-2(c)(2)(v)	**9** n.390
1.179-3(f)(1)	**9** n.397
1.179-3(g)	**9** n.395
1.179-3(g)(2)	**9** n.396
1.179-3(g)(3)	**9** n.397
1.179-3(h)	**9** n.395
1.179-3(h)(1)	**9** n.396
1.179-3(h)(2)	**9** n.397
1.183-1(a)	**9** n.398
1.194-2(b)(5)(i)	**9** ns. 164, 414
1.195-1	**9** n.416
1.195-1(b)	**S9** n.416
1.195-2	**S13** n.147
1.195-2(a)	**S4** n.230
1.197-1(g)(4)(ii)	**24** n.57
1.197-1T	**9** n.462; **24** n.56
1.197-1T(b)(8)	**9** n.462
1.197-1T(c)(1)	**9** n.462
1.197-1T(c)(1)(iv)(A)	**9** n.462
1.197-1T(c)(1)(iv)(B)	**9** n.462
1.197-1T(c)(2)	**9** n.462
1.197-1T(c)(5)(ii)	**9** n.462
1.197-1T(c)(7)	**9** n.462
1.197-1T(c)(8) Ex. (1)	**9** n.462
1.197-2(c)	**9** n.425
1.197-2(d)	**9** n.423
1.197-2(d)(1)	**24** n.56
1.197-2(g)(2)(ii)	**9** n.426
1.197-2(g)(2)(ii)(B)	9.02[3][k][ii][D]; **9** n.444
1.197-2(g)(2)(iii)	**9** n.430
1.197-2(g)(2)(iv)(B)	**9** n.431; **13** n.151
1.197-2(g)(3) . . . **9** ns. 432, 436; **24** n.175; **25** n.32
1.197-2(g)(4)(i)	**9** n.427; **11**.04[3][f]
1.197-2(g)(4)(ii)	**9** n.428; **11**.04[3][f]
1.197-2(h)(1)(ii)	**9** n.437
1.197-2(h)(2)	**9** n.437
1.197-2(h)(6)	**9** n.438
1.197-2(h)(6)(ii)	**9** n.439
1.197-2(h)(6)(ii)(B)	**9** n.439
1.197-2(h)(9)	**9** n.438
1.197-2(h)(9)(iv)	**9** n.438
1.197-2(h)(10)	**4** n.207
1.197-2(h)(12)	**9** n.440

[Text references are to paragraphs; note references are to chapters (boldface numbers) and notes ("n."). References to the supplement are preceded by "S."]

Reg. §

1.197-2(h)(12)(i) **14** n.333; **25** n.33
1.197-2(h)(12)(ii) 20.05
1.197-2(h)(12)(ii)(A) . . . **9** n.445; **20** ns. 73, 74
1.197-2(h)(12)(ii)(A)(2) **9** n.452
1.197-2(h)(12)(ii)(B) **9** n.444
1.197-2(h)(12)(ii)(C) **9** n.447; 20.05
1.197-2(h)(12)(ii)(D) **20** n.72
1.197-2(h)(12)(ii)(E) **9** n.446
1.197-2(h)(12)(iii) . . . . **9** ns. 432, 443
1.197-2(h)(12)(iv) . . . . 25.01[6]
1.197-2(h)(12)(iv)(A) **9** n.450; **25** n.34
1.197-2(h)(12)(iv)(B) **9** n.449; **25** n.34
1.197-2(h)(12)(iv)(B)(2) **9** n.451
1.197-2(h)(12)(iv)(B)(3) **9** n.451
1.197-2(h)(12)(iv)(D) **25** n.35
1.197-2(h)(12)(iv)(D)(1) . . . . **9** n.448; 25.01[6]
1.197-2(h)(12)(iv)(E)(1) **9** n.453
1.197-2(h)(12)(iv)(F) **9** n.455; **25** n.36
1.197-2(h)(12)(v) . . . . **9** ns. 441, 442; **24** n.176
1.197-2(h)(12)(vi) . . . 9.02[3][k][ii][D]; **9** n.442
1.197-2(h)(12)(vii)(B) **9** n.428; **24** n.57
1.197-2(h)(12)(viii)(B) **11** n.534
1.197-2(j) **9** n.437
1.197-2(k) Ex. (14) **9** n.433
1.197-2(k) Ex. (15) **9** n.436
1.197-2(k) Ex. (16)(iii) **9** n.435
1.197-2(k) Ex. (16)(iv) **9** n.435
1.197-2(k) Ex. (17) **4** n.460
1.197-2(k) Ex. (18) **4** n.207; **9** n.459
1.197-2(k) Ex. (19) **4** n.208; **9** n.461
1.197-2(k) Ex. (27)(iii) **4** n.442
1.197-2(k) Ex. (28) **4** n.456
1.197-2(k) Ex. (29) **4** n.457
1.197-2(k) Ex. (29)(ii) **4** n.454
1.197-2(k) Ex. (30) **4** n.458
1.197-2(k) Ex. (31) **4** n.455; **25** n.38
1.199-1–1.199-9 . . . . 9.02[3][w]
1.199-1–1.199-8 . . . . . . 9.02[3][w]; **S9** n.539
1.199-2(e)(2) . . . .**S**9.02[3][w]
1.199-3T(i)(7) **S9** n.545
1.199-4(b) **S9** n.527
1.199-4(c) **S9** n.528
1.199-5 . . . .**9** n.528
1.199-5(a)(3) **S9** n.540
1.199-5(b)(1) . . . . **S9** ns. 535, 536
1.199-5(b)(2) **S9** n.537
1.199-5(b)(3) **S9** n.539
1.199-5(f) **S9** n.542
1.199-5(g) **S9** n.544
1.199-5T(b) **S9** n.529
1.199-5T(b)(3) **S9** n.529
1.199-8(i) . . . . .**9** ns. 531, 545, 547; **S9** n.532
1.199-8(i)(2) **9** n.539; **S9** n.543
1.199-9 . . . . 9.02[3][w]; **S**9.02[3][w]
1.199-9(b) **9** n.540; **S9** n.544
1.199-9(b)(1)(i) . . . **9** ns. 533, 534; **S9** ns. 535, 536
1.199-9(b)(2) **9** n.535; **S9** n.537
1.199-9(b)(3) **9** n.536; **S9** n.540
1.199-9(f) **9** n.537; **S9** n.542
1.199-9(g) **9** n.538; **S9** n.541

Reg. §

1.199-9(i) **9** n.541; **S9** n.545
1.199-9(j) **9** n.544
1.199-9(k) **9** n.550; **S9** n.533
1.199A-1(b)(4) **S9** n.551.15
1.199A-1(b)(5) **S9** n.550.2
1.199A-1(b)(7) **S9** n.550.4
1.199A-1(b)(8) **S9** n.550.3
1.199A-1(b)(9) . . . . . .**S9** ns. 551.18, 551.38
1.199A-1(b)(10) . . . . .**S9** ns. 551.10, 551.87
1.199A-1(b)(12) **S9** n.551.14
1.199A-1(b)(13) **S9** n.551.13
1.199A-1(b)(14) . . .**S9** ns. 551.3, 551.6, 551.7
1.199A-1(c) **S9** n.551
1.199A-1(c)(1) **S9** n.551.26
1.199A-1(c)(2) . . . . . .**S9** ns. 551.27, 551.73
1.199A-1(c)(3)(i) Ex. 1 . . . .**S9** n.551.26
1.199A-1(c)(3)(ii) Ex. 2 . . . .**S9** n.551.26
1.199A-1(c)(3)(iii) Ex. 3 . . . .**S9** n.551.26
1.199A-1(c)(3)(iv) Ex. 4 . . . . . .**S9** ns. 551.26, 551.73
1.199A-1(d) **S9** n.551
1.199A-1(d)(1) **S9** n.551.28
1.199A-1(d)(2)(i) . . . . . .**S9** ns. 551.19, 551.31
1.199A-1(d)(2)(ii) . . . . . .**S9** ns. 551.17, 551.33
1.199A-1(d)(2)(iii)(A) . . . .**S9** ns. 551.19, 551.34
1.199A-1(d)(2)(iii)(B) . . .**S9** ns. 551.20, 551.29, 551.35
1.199A-1(d)(2)(iv) . . . . . .**S**9.02[3][z][iii][A]; **S**9.02[3][z][iv]; **S9** n.551.18
1.199A-1(d)(2)(iv)(A) **S9** n.551.36
1.199A-1(d)(2)(iv)(B) **S9** n.551.37
1.199A-1(d)(3)(ii) . . . . .**S9** ns. 551.31, 551.43
1.199A-1(d)(3)(iii) . . . . .**S9** ns. 551.30, 551.44, 551.73
1.199A-1(d)(4) . . . .**S**9.02[3][z]
1.199A-1(d)(4)(ii) Ex. 2 . . . .**S9** n.551.39
1.199A-1(d)(4)(v) Ex. 5 . . . . . .**S9** ns. 551.37, 551.40
1.199A-1(d)(4)(vi) Ex. 6 . . . . . .**S9** ns. 551.37, 551.41
1.199A-1(d)(4)(vii) Ex. 7 . . . . . .**S9** n.551.77
1.199A-1(d)(4)(viii) Ex. 8 . . . . . .**S9** n.551.79
1.199A-1(d)(4)(ix) Ex. 9 . . . . . .**S9** ns. 551.19, 551.34, 551.78
1.199A-1(d)(4)(x) Ex. 10 . . . .**S9** n.551.35
1.199A-1(d)(4)(xi) Ex. 11 . . . . . .**S9** n.551.35
1.199A-1(d)(4)(xi)(A) Ex. 11(A) . . . . .**S9** ns. 551.20, 551.29
1.199A-1(d)(4)(xi)(B) Ex. 11(B) . . . . . .**S9** ns. 551.20, 551.29
1.199A-1(e)(1) **S6** n.24; **S9** n.551.11
1.199A-1(e)(2) . . . .**S9** ns. 551.9, 551.86
1.199A-1(e)(4) **S9** n.551.12
1.199A-2(a)(2) **S9** n.551.45
1.199A-2(b)(1) **S9** n.551.46
1.199A-2(b)(3) **S9** n.551.47
1.199A-2(b)(4) **S9** n.551.48
1.199A-2(c)(1)(i) **S9** n.551.51
1.199A-2(c)(1)(iv) **S9** n.551.51
1.199A-2(c)(2)(i) **S9** n.551.52
1.199A-2(c)(2)(ii) **S9** n.551.54

[Text references are to paragraphs; note references are to chapters (boldface numbers) and notes ("n."). References to the supplement are preceded by "S."]

[Text references are to paragraphs; note references are to chapters (boldface numbers) and notes ("n."). References to the supplement are preceded by "S."]

[Text references are to paragraphs; note references are to chapters (boldface numbers) and notes ("n."). References to the supplement are preceded by "S."]

Reg. §

1.409A-1(b)(7) **S14** n.202; **22** n.145	
1.416-1 . . . . **13** n.92	
1.421-6(d)(2)(ii) Ex. (2) **5** n.165	
1.441-1(d) . . . . 9.04[1][a]	
1.441-2(e)(1) **9** n.954	
1.441-2(e)(4) Ex. (2) **9** n.955	
1.442-1(b)(1) **9** n.950	
1.442-1(b)(2)(ii) **9** n.949	
1.442-1(c) **9** n.949	
1.443-1(a)(1) **9** n.951	
1.444-1T(a)(4)(i) **9** n.961	
1.444-1T(a)(4)(ii) **9** n.962	
1.444-1T(a)(5) **9** n.972	
1.444-1T(a)(5)(i) **9** n.972	
1.444-1T(a)(5)(iv) **9** n.972	
1.444-1T(b)(3) **9** n.959	
1.444-1T(d)(2) **9** n.959	
1.444-2T(b) **9** n.965	
1.444-2T(c)(2)(i) **9** n.968	
1.444-2T(c)(2)(ii) **9** n.969	
1.444-2T(c)(2)(iii) **9** n.967	
1.444-2T(c)(2)(iv) **9** n.969	
1.444-2T(c)(3) **9** n.970	
1.444-2T(d)(1) **9** n.971	
1.444-3T(b)(1) **9** n.973	
1.444-3T(b)(4) **9** n.974	
1.446-1(e)(2) **11** n.487	
1.446-1(e)(2)(i) **S11** n.487	
1.446-3 . . . . **S3** n.449	
1.448-1T(b) **9** n.146	
1.448-1T(b)(3) . . . . **9** ns. 147, 148	
1.448-1T(b)(4) **9** n.150	
1.448-1T(e) **9** n.142	
1.448-1(g) **9** n.144	
1.448-1(h) **9** n.144	
1.448-1(i) **9** n.144	
1.451-1(a) **5** n.15	
1.451-2(a) **5** n.15	
1.453-9(c)(2) . . . S4.02[3]; **4** n.66; **S4** n.66; **13**	
n.103; **S13** n.103; **19** n.136	
1.453C-2T(b)(1) **16** n.193	
1.460-4(k) . . . . 19.07[2]	
1.460-4(k)(2) . . . . . . 4.05[11]; 11.04[1][a]; **19**	
n.144; 21.01[5]	
1.460-4(k)(2)(ii) . . . . 19.07[2]; **19** n.145	
1.460-4(k)(2)(iii) **19** n.146	
1.460-4(k)(2)(iv) **21** n.35	
1.460-4(k)(2)(iv)(A) . . . . **19** ns. 143, 147	
1.460-4(k)(2)(iv)(B) **19** n.148	
1.460-4(k)(2)(iv)(C) **19** n.149	
1.460-4(k)(2)(iv)(E)(1) . . . . . 21.01[5]; **21** n.33	
1.460-4(k)(2)(iv)(E)(2) **21** n.34	
1.460-4(k)(3) . . . . 4.05[11]	
1.460-4(k)(3)(i)(I) **4** n.210	
1.460-4(k)(3)(i)(J) **4** n.211	
1.460-4(k)(3)(ii)(A) . . . . . 4.05[11]; 11.04[1][a]	
1.460-4(k)(3)(ii)(B) . . . . 4.05[11]	
1.460-4(k)(3)(iii) . . . . 4.05[11]	
1.460-4(k)(3)(iii)(A) . . . . 4.05[11]	
1.460-4(k)(3)(v)(A)(1) . . . . 11.04[1][a]	
1.460-4(k)(3)(v)(A)(3) **11** n.477	

1.465-1T **11** n.666	
1.465-8 . . . . **11** n.632	
1.465-8(a) . . . . **S11** ns. 631, 647	
1.465-8(b)(1) **11** n.632	
1.465-8(b)(2) **11** n.632	
1.465-27 . . . . 11.06[2][f]; **11** n.635	
1.465-27(b) **11** n.677	
1.465-27(b)(2)(i) **11** n.678	
1.465-27(b)(2)(ii) **11** n.680	
1.465-27(b)(4) **11** n.681	
1.465-27(b)(5) **11** n.681	
1.465-27(b)(6) Ex. 3 . . . . **11** n.681	
1.465-27(b)(6) Ex. 6 . . . . **11** n.681	
1.465-27(c) **11** n.682	
1.467-1(c) **4** n.190	
1.467-7 . . . . **4** n.189	
1.467-7(c)(3) **4** n.192	
1.467-7(c)(4) **4** n.192	
1.467-7(c)(7) **4** n.192; **17** n.126	
1.469-1(e)(2) **11** n.707	
1.469-1T(e)(3) . . . . 11.08[7]	
1.469-1T(e)(3)(i) **11** n.727	
1.469-1T(e)(3)(vii) **11** n.727	
1.469-1T(e)(4) **11** n.721	
1.469-1(e)(4)(iv) **11** n.722	
1.469-1T(e)(4)(v)(A) **11** n.723	
1.469-1T(e)(4)(v)(B) **11** n.723	
1.469-1T(e)(6) . . . . **11** ns. 708, 777	
1.469-1T(f)(2)(i)(A) **11** n.737	
1.469-1(f)(4) . . . . 11.08[7]; **11** n.736	
1.469-2(c)(2)(iii) . . . . **11** ns. 755, 762	
1.469-2(c)(6) **11** n.724	
1.469-2(d)(8) **11** n.739	
1.469-2(e)(2)(ii) . . . **11** n.715; **14** ns. 278, 279	
1.469-2(e)(2)(iii) **14** n.279; **22** n.38	
1.469-2(e)(2)(iii)(A) **11** n.717	
1.469-2(e)(2)(iii)(B) **11** n.716	
1.469-2(e)(3)(iii)(B) **11** n.764	
1.469-2(f)(5) . . . . **11** ns. 756, 784	
1.469-2(f)(5)(i)(B) **11** n.782	
1.469-2(f)(5)(ii) **11** n.783	
1.469-2(f)(6) **11** n.785	
1.469-2T(c)(2)(i)(A)(2) **11** n.752	
1.469-2T(c)(2)(i)(B) **23** n.39	
1.469-2T(c)(2)(i)(D) Ex. (2) **11** n.752	
1.469-2T(c)(2)(ii) . . . . . . **11** ns. 741, 753, 754	
1.469-2T(c)(3)(i) . . . **11** ns. 713, 769, 772, 775	
1.469-2T(c)(3)(ii) **11** n.769	
1.469-2T(c)(3)(ii)(A) **11** n.772	
1.469-2T(c)(3)(ii)(B) **11** n.772	
1.469-2T(c)(3)(ii)(D) **11** n.777	
1.469-2T(c)(3)(iii)(A) **11** n.777	
1.469-2T(c)(3)(iii)(B)(3) **11** n.770	
1.469-2T(c)(3)(iv) Ex. (2) **11** n.713	
1.469-2T(c)(4)(i) **9** n.326; **11** n.720; **14**	
n.280	
1.469-2T(c)(7)(i) **11** n.788	
1.469-2T(c)(7)(iii) **11** n.789	
1.469-2T(d)(1) **11** n.726	
1.469-2T(d)(2)(i) **11** n.771	

[Text references are to paragraphs; note references are to chapters (boldface numbers) and notes ("n."). References to the supplement are preceded by "S."]

[Text references are to paragraphs; note references are to chapters (boldface numbers) and notes ("n."). References to the supplement are preceded by "S."]

Reg. §

Reg. §	
1.514(c)-2(e)(4)	**9** ns. 776, 796
1.514(c)-2(e)(4)(i)	**9** n.799
1.514(c)-2(e)(5) Ex. (3)	**9** n.797
1.514(c)-2(e)(5) Ex. (3)(iv)	**9** n.808
1.514(c)-2(f)	**9** n.800
1.514(c)-2(g)	**9** n.801
1.514(c)-2(h)	**9** ns. 776, 802
1.514(c)-2(j)	**9** n.803; **S9** n.803
1.514(c)-2(j)(2)	**9** n.776
1.514(c)-2(k)(1)	**9** n.804
1.514(c)-2(k)(2)	**9** n.805
1.514(c)-2(k)(3)	**9** n.806
1.514(c)-2(k)(4)	**9** ns. 778, 807
1.514(c)-2(m)(1)	**9** n.809
1.514(c)-2(m)(1)(ii)	**9** n.776
1.514(c)-2(m)(2) Ex. (1)	**9** n.810
1.514(c)-2(m)(2) Ex. (2)	**9** n.811
1.514(c)-2(m)(2) Ex. (3)	**9** n.812
1.611-1(a)	**9** n.183
1.611-1(a)(1)	**9** n.501
1.611-1(c)(5)	**23** n.28
1.612-1(a)	**25** n.29
1.612-4(a)	**11** n.722
1.613A-3(e)	**6** n.41; **9** n.506; **11** n.403
1.613A-3(e)(1)	**9** n.183; **11** n.404
1.613A-3(e)(2)(ii)	**11** ns. 405, 406
1.613A-3(e)(3)(i)	**11** n.406
1.613A-3(e)(3)(ii)	**11** n.407
1.613A-3(e)(3)(iii)	**11** n.407
1.613A-3(e)(3)(iii)(A)	**11** n.409
1.613A-3(e)(3)(iv)	**11** n.408
1.613A-3(e)(6)(iv)	**24** n.171; **25** n.30
1.613A-3(e)(6)(v)	**25** n.30
1.613A-3(i)(2)(i)	**9** n.506
1.613A-3(i)(2)(v) Ex. (5)	**9** n.506
1.617-3(d)(4)	**20** n.47; **21** n.130
1.617-4(c)(3)	**4** n.174
1.643(f)-1	**S9** n.551.97
1.661(a)-2(f)(1)	**23** ns. 46, 47
1.663(a)-1	**23** n.45
1.663(a)-1(b)(2)	**23** n.45
1.691-1(b)	**23** n.3
1.691(c)-1(a)	**23** n.4
1.701-1(d) Ex. 6	**11** n.243
1.701-2	1.05[1]; **1** ns. 48, 100, 103, 107; **S1** n.69; 4.01[2][a]; **S9** n.642; 11.01[2]; **13** n.63; 14.03[6][i]; 19.06[2]; **19** n.101; **21** n.27; **26** n.31
1.701-2(a)	1.05[2]; **1** ns. 55, 81
1.701-2(a)(1)	1.05[2]; 1.05[3]; 1.05[4][b][vi]
1.701-2(a)(2)	1.05[2]
1.701-2(a)(3)	1.05[2]; **1** n.151
1.701-2(b)	1.05[4][e]; **1** ns. 54, 57, 79, 85, 164
1.701-2(c)	1.05[2]; 1.05[3]; 1.05[4][b][i]; **1** n.56
1.701-2(c)	**1** n.58
1.701-2(d)	**1** n.90
1.701-2(d) Exs.	1.05[3]; 1.05[4][a]; 1.05[4][d]; 1.05[4][e]; 1.05[5][b][i]; 1.05[5][b][ii]; 1.05[5][b][iii]; **1** ns. 45, 54, 58
1.701-2(d) Exs. (1)–(11)	1.05[1][a]
1.701-2(d) Exs. (1)–(4)	1.05[3]
1.701-2(d) Ex. (1)	1.05[3]
1.701-2(d) Ex. (2)	1.05[3]; 1.05[4][b][vi]; 1.05[4][c]; **1** n.149; **3** ns. 141, 378; 9.01[8][b]
1.701-2(d) Ex. (3)	1.05[3]
1.701-2(d) Ex. (4)	1.05[3]; 1.05[4][b][vi]; 1.05[4][c]; **3** ns. 140, 378
1.701-2(d) Ex. (5)	1.05[3]; **1** ns. 54, 58, 79
1.701-2(d) Ex. (6)	1.05[3]; 1.05[4][b][vi]; **1** ns. 54, 58, 79, 89, 94; **9** n.575
1.701-2(d) Ex. (7)	1.05[2]; 1.05[3]; 1.05[4][a]; 1.05[4][b][vi]; 1.05[4][c]; **1** ns. 86, 165
1.701-2(d) Exs. (8)–(11)	1.05[3]
1.701-2(d) Ex. (8)	1.05[1][a]; 1.05[3]; 1.05[4][a]; 1.05[4][b][vi]; 1.05[4][c]; **1** ns. 45, 70, 73, 91, 99, 165, 195; **9** n.461
1.701-2(d) Ex. (9)	1.05[3]; 1.05[4][b][vi]; **1** ns. 45, 91, 99
1.701-2(d) Ex. (10)	1.05[3]; 1.05[4][d]; **1** ns. 45, 91, 196
1.701-2(d) Ex. (11)	1.05[1][a]; 1.05[3]; 1.05[4][d]; **1** ns. 45, 91, 103, 165, 196
1.701-2(d) Ex. (11)(ii)	**19** n.129
1.701-2(e)	1.05[6]; **1** ns. 62, 203, 206; **S1** n.206; **6** ns. 3, 59
1.701-2(e) Exs.	1.05[6]
1.701-2(e)(1)	**1** n.43
1.701-2(e)(2)	**14** n.319
1.701-2(e)(2) Ex. (2)	**S6** n.46.2
1.701-2(f) Ex. (1)	1.05[6]
1.701-2(f) Ex. (2)	1.05[6]
1.701-2(f) Ex. (3)	1.05[6]
1.701-2(h)	**1** ns. 54, 58, 79
1.702-1(a)	**9** n.1
1.702-1(a)(1)	**9** n.21
1.702-1(a)(3)	**9** ns. 23, 24; **17** n.73
1.702-1(a)(4)	**9** n.27
1.702-1(a)(6)	**9** n.30
1.702-1(a)(8)(i)	9.01[3][b]; 9.01[8][a]; 9.02[3][q]; **9** ns. 75, 322, 338; **11** n.361
1.702-1(a)(8)(ii)	9.01[3][b]; 9.02[2][c]; 9.02[3][l]; **9** ns. 20, 39, 41–43, 51
1.702-1(c)(1)	9.02[2][d]; **9** n.333
1.702-1(c)(2)	9.02[2][d]; **9** n.348
1.702-1(d)	**11** n.17; **24** n.69
1.702-1(e)	**9** n.83
1.702-3T	**9** n.940
1.702-3T(a)	**9** n.976
1.703-1(a)(2)(iv)	**9** n.27
1.703-1(a)(2)(viii)	9.01[2]
1.703-1(b)(1)	**9** n.1044
1.703-1(b)(2)(i)	**9** ns. 30, 175
1.703-1(b)(2)(ii)	**9** ns. 176, 1042
1.703-1(b)(2)(iii)	**9** ns. 178, 833

[Text references are to paragraphs; note references are to chapters (boldface numbers) and notes ("n."). References to the supplement are preceded by "S."]

[Text references are to paragraphs; note references are to chapters (boldface numbers) and notes ("n."). References to the supplement are preceded by "S."]

Reg. §

1.704-1(b)(2)(iv)(j) **6** n.47; **S6** n.48;
          S9.02[4][h]; **S9** n.591; **11** n.239
1.704-1(b)(2)(iv)(k)(2) **11** n.203
1.704-1(b)(2)(iv)(*l*)   **11** ns. 49, 184, 186, 316;
          13.05[2][c]
1.704-1(b)(2)(iv)(m) **11** n.188
1.704-1(b)(2)(iv)(m)(2) ...... **11** ns. 190, 192
1.704-1(b)(2)(iv)(m)(3) **11** n.188
1.704-1(b)(2)(iv)(m)(4) **11** n.191
1.704-1(b)(2)(iv)(m)(5) ... **11** n.189; **S11** n.189
1.704-1(b)(2)(iv)(n) **11** n.150
1.704-1(b)(2)(iv)(o)   11.02[2][c][i]; **11** n.147;
          14 ns. 222, 257
1.704-1(b)(2)(iv)(p) **11** n.143
1.704-1(b)(2)(iv)(q) **S11** n.176.3
1.704-1(b)(2)(iv)(r) **6** n.113; **8** n.138;
          11.02[4][e][ii]; 11.02[4][f][ii]; **11** n.35
1.704-1(b)(2)(iv)(s) .... **S4** ns. 22, 51.35;
     10A.02[3]; S11.02[2][c][ii]; S11.02[4][g];
          S11 n.162
1.704-1(b)(2)(iv)(s)(1) ... S9.01[4][c][iii][D];
          S11 ns. 162, 179.3, 179.6, 357
1.704-1(b)(2)(iv)(s)(2) **S11** n.179.7
1.704-1(b)(2)(iv)(s)(3) ...... S11.02[2][c][ii];
          S11.02[4][g]; **S11** n.179.8
1.704-1(b)(3) .... **9** n.448; 11.02[1]; 11.02[2];
          11.02[2][a][i]; 11.02[2][a][ii][C];
          11.02[2][a][iii]; 11.02[2][c];
     11.02[2][c][vii]; 11.02[3]; 11.03[2][i];
     11.03[4][c]; **11** ns. 33, 55, 189; **S11** ns.
          33, 189
1.704-1(b)(3)(i) .... 11.02[3]; **11** ns. 215–219,
          230; **S11** n.230
1.704-1(b)(3)(ii) **11** n.223
1.704-1(b)(3)(ii)(C)(1)(i) ..... 8.02[4][b][v][A]
1.704-1(b)(3)(ii)(C)(1)(ii) .... 8.02[4][b][v][A]
1.704-1(b)(3)(ii)(C)(1)(iii) .... 8.02[4][b][v][A]
1.704-1(b)(3)(iii)   **S11** n.227; 11.02[3]; **11** ns.
          64, 225, 227
1.704-1(b)(3)(iii)(c) .... 11.02[2][b][iii]
1.704-1(b)(3)(iv)(f) .... 5.03[5]
1.704-1(b)(4) .... 11.02[1]; 11.02[2][c]; **11** ns.
          149, 185
1.704-1(b)(4)(i) ...... **5** n.74; 11.02[4][a]; **11**
          n.181; **21** ns. 110, 111; **22** n.70
1.704-1(b)(4)(ii) ... 9.02[4][d]; 11.02[4][b]; **11**
          n.240; **S11** ns. 240.2, 425, 426
1.704-1(b)(4)(iii)   11.02[4][c]; 11.03[2][e]; **11**
     ns. 245, 398, 402; **S11** n.132; **14** ns.
          276.1, 276.3
1.704-1(b)(4)(iv) .... 11.02[4][e]
1.704-1(b)(4)(iv) Ex. (20)(i) ... 11.02[4][e][ii];
          11.02[4][e][iv]
1.704-1(b)(4)(iv) Ex. (20)(iv) ... 11.02[4][e][v]
1.704-1(b)(4)(iv) Ex. (20)(v) ... 11.02[4][e][iii]
1.704-1(b)(4)(iv) Ex. (20)(vi) ... 11.02[4][e][iii]
1.704-1(b)(4)(iv) Ex. (20)(ix) ... 11.02[4][e][vii]
1.704-1(b)(4)(iv) Ex. (21) ..... 11.02[4][e][v]
1.704-1(b)(4)(iv) Ex. (22)(i) ... 11.02[4][e][iv]
1.704-1(b)(4)(iv) Ex. (22)(iii) ... 11.02[4][e][ii];
          11.02[4][e][v]

Reg. §

1.704-1(b)(4)(iv) Ex. (22)(iv) ... 11.02[4][e][iii]
1.704-1(b)(4)(iv) Ex. (23) ..... 11.02[4][e][ii]
1.704-1(b)(4)(iv) Ex. (23)(i) ... 11.02[4][e][iii]
1.704-1(b)(4)(iv)(c) **11** n.263
1.704-1(b)(4)(iv)(e) .... 11.02[4][e][i]
1.704-1(b)(4)(iv)(f) **11** n.265
1.704-1(b)(4)(iv)(g) **11** n.275
1.704-1(b)(4)(iv)(h) **11** n.275
1.704-1(b)(4)(iv)(h)(4) ...... **11** ns. 284, 285
1.704-1(b)(4)(iv)(h)(7) **11** n.282
1.704-1(b)(4)(v) ..... 11.02[4][e][i]; **11** n.247
1.704-1(b)(4)(vi) **11** n.34
1.704-1(b)(4)(vii) **11** n.380
1.704-1(b)(4)(viii)(a) .... S11.03[2][i]; **S11** ns.
          422, 423
1.704-1(b)(4)(viii)(b) **S11** n.429
1.704-1(b)(4)(viii)(c)(2)(i) **S11** n.434
1.704-1(b)(4)(viii)(c)(2)(iii)   **S11** ns. 431, 432
1.704-1(b)(4)(viii)(c)(3)(i) **S11** n.436.5a
1.704-1(b)(4)(viii)(c)(3)(ii) **S11** n.433
1.704-1(b)(4)(viii)(c)(4)(i) **S11** n.435
1.704-1(b)(4)(viii)(c)(4)(ii) **S11** n.436
1.704-1(b)(4)(viii)(c)(4)(iii) **S11** n.436.1
1.704-1(b)(4)(viii)(d)(1) **S11** n.436.2
1.704-1(b)(4)(ix) ..... S11.02[4][g]; **S11** n.357
1.704-1(b)(4)(x) .... **S4** n.22; S11.02[2][c][ii];
          S11 n.357
1.704-1(b)(5) .... 11.02[2][a][i]
1.704-1(b)(5) Ex. (1) .... 11.02[2][a][i]
1.704-1(b)(5) Ex. (1)(i) **11** n.231
1.704-1(b)(5) Ex. (1)(iv)   11.02[3]; **11** ns. 32,
          55
1.704-1(b)(5) Ex. (1)(v) **11** n.236
1.704-1(b)(5) Ex. (1)(vi) ... 11.02[2][a][i];
          11.02[2][a][ii][C]; **11** n.235
1.704-1(b)(5) Ex. (1)(viii) **11** n.83
1.704-1(b)(5) Ex. (1)(ix) ..... **11** ns. 85, 120
1.704-1(b)(5) Ex. (1)(x) **11** n.85
1.704-1(b)(5) Ex. (1)(xi) **1** n.94;
     11.02[2][b][iii]; **11** n.351; **S11** n.122
1.704-1(b)(5) Ex. (2) ...... 11.02[2][a][ii][C];
          11.02[2][b][iii]; 11.02[2][b][iv];
     11.02[2][b][v]; **11** ns. 118, 120; **S11**
          n.122
1.704-1(b)(5) Ex. (3) ..... 11.02[2][b][iii]; **11**
          n.120; **S11** n.122
1.704-1(b)(5) Ex. (4)(i) **11** n.232
1.704-1(b)(5) Ex. (4)(ii) **11** n.53
1.704-1(b)(5) Ex. (5) .... 11.02[2][b][iv];
     11.02[2][b][v]; S11.02[2][b][v]; **11** n.127;
          S11 ns. 120, 121
1.704-1(b)(5) Ex. (5)(i) **11** n.391; **S11** n.123
1.704-1(b)(5) Ex. (5)(ii)   S11.02[2][b][vi]; **11**
          n.229; **S11** n.125
1.704-1(b)(5) Ex. (6) .... 11.02[2][b][i];
     11.02[2][b][ii]; 11.02[2][b][v]; **11** ns. 96,
          120, 229; **S11** n.122
1.704-1(b)(5) Ex. (7) ...... 11.02[2][b][ii]; **11**
          n.120; **S11** n.122
1.704-1(b)(5) Ex. (7)(i) .... **11** ns. 97, 229

[Text references are to paragraphs; note references are to chapters (boldface numbers)
and notes ("n."). References to the supplement are preceded by "S."]

[Text references are to paragraphs; note references are to chapters (boldface numbers) and notes ("n."). References to the supplement are preceded by "S."]

Reg. §

1.704-1T(b)(4)(iv)(g)(3) . . . . . . 11.02[4][e][vi]
1.704-1T(b)(4)(iv)(g)(4) 1 n.274
1.704-1T(b)(4)(iv)(h) . . . . . **11** ns. 275, 276
1.704-1T(b)(4)(iv)(h)(1)(i) **11** n.279
1.704-1T(b)(4)(iv)(h)(2) **11** n.278
1.704-1T(b)(4)(iv)(h)(3) . . . . . **11** ns. 281–283
1.704-1T(b)(4)(iv)(h)(6) . . . 11.02[4][e][vii]; **11** n.280
1.704-1T(b)(4)(iv)(h)(7) **11** n.283
1.704-1T(b)(4)(iv)(j) **11** n.255
1.704-1T(b)(4)(iv)(k)(1) **11** n.276
1.704-1T(b)(4)(iv)(m)(1) **11** n.287
1.704-1T(b)(4)(xi) . . . . . **11** ns. 136, 422, 423
1.704-1T(b)(4)(xi)(a) . . . . .11.03[2][i]
1.704-1T(b)(4)(xi)(a)(2) **11** n.428
1.704-1T(b)(4)(xi)(b) . . . . **11** ns. 429, 430
1.704-1T(b)(4)(xi)(c) **11** n.431
1.704-1T(b)(5) Ex. (21)(ii) **11** n.266
1.704-1T(b)(5) Ex. (25) . . . . . S11.03[2][i]; **11** n.433
1.704-1T(b)(5) Ex. (26) **11** n.433
1.704-1T(b)(5) Ex. (27) **11** n.433
1.704-1T(b)(5) Ex. (28) . . . . . . 11.03[2][i]; **11** n.434
1.704-1T(b)(5) Ex. (31) . . . . . S11.02[2][c][ii]
1.704-1T(b)(5) Ex. (32) . . . . . S11.02[2][c][ii]
1.704-1T(b)(5) Ex. (33) . . . . . S11.02[2][c][ii]
1.704-2 . . . . 1.05[2]; 9.02[2][a][ii][C]; 11.02[4][f]; **11** n.305
1.704-2(a)(3) . . . . .1.05[4][d]
1.704-2(b)(1) **22** n.69
1.704-2(b)(2) S4 n.51.35; **11** n.323
1.704-2(b)(2)(ii)(d)(6) . . . . **11** ns. 324, 325
1.704-2(b)(2)(ii)(g) **11** n.51
1.704-2(b)(2)(iv)(m) **11** n.356
1.704-2(b)(3) . . . . **8** n.163; **11** ns. 305, 336
1.704-2(b)(4) **8** n.163
1.704-2(c) . . . . 11.02[4][f][ii]; **11** ns. 295, 299, 326
1.704-2(d) . . . 4.03[2]; **8** n.130; 11.02[4][f][iii]; **11** n.64; **22** n.69
1.704-2(d)(1) **11** n.305
1.704-2(d)(2) . . . . **11** ns. 305, 306
1.704-2(d)(3) . . . . **8** ns. 134, 155
1.704-2(d)(4) **11** n.303
1.704-2(d)(4)(i) **11** n.302
1.704-2(d)(4)(ii) **11** n.303
1.704-2(e) . . . . 11.02[4][f][v]; **11** n.293
1.704-2(e)(1)(ii) **11** n.250
1.704-2(e)(2) **11** n.305
1.704-2(f) . . . . 11.02[4][f][ix]; **11** n.307
1.704-2(f)(1) **11** n.312
1.704-2(f)(2) . . . . **11** ns. 290, 313
1.704-2(f)(3) **11** n.314
1.704-2(f)(4) **11** n.315
1.704-2(f)(5) **11** n.316
1.704-2(f)(6) . . . . . . **11** ns. 312, 321, 322; **S11** n.321
1.704-2(f)(7) Ex. (1) . . . **8** n.72; 11.02[4][f][v]; **S11** n.12
1.704-2(f)(7) Ex. (2) . . . . 11.02[4][f][v]

Reg. §

1.704-2(g) . . . . **8** n.133; **9** n.312; **22** ns. 65, 69
1.704-2(g)(1) . . . . . . **8** n.130; **11** ns. 308, 309
1.704-2(g)(1)(i) **11** n.327
1.704-2(g)(2) . . . . **11** ns. 304, 310, 311, 319
1.704-2(h) . . . . , . . . **11** n.354
1.704-2(h)(1) **11** n.329
1.704-2(h)(2) **11** n.328
1.704-2(h)(3) **11** n.331
1.704-2(h)(4) . . . . . . 11.02[4][f][vi]; **11** n.330
1.704-2(i) . . . . **11** ns. 332, 333
1.704-2(i)(1) **11** n.335
1.704-2(i)(2) **S4** n.51.35; **11** n.338
1.704-2(i)(3) **11** n.337
1.704-2(i)(4) **11** n.342
1.704-2(i)(5) . . . . .9.02[1][c][iii]
1.704-2(i)(6) . . . . **11** ns. 339, 340
1.704-2(j)(1) . . . . **11** ns. 338, 339
1.704-2(j)(1)(ii) . . . . **11** ns. 298, 299
1.704-2(j)(1)(ii)(A) **11** n.296
1.704-2(j)(1)(ii)(B) **11** n.297
1.704-2(j)(1)(iii) . . . . **11** ns. 301, 340
1.704-2(j)(2) **11** n.341
1.704-2(j)(2)(i) **11** n.321
1.704-2(j)(2)(iii) **11** n.322
1.704-2(k) **8** n.161
1.704-2(k)(1) **11** n.346
1.704-2(k)(2) **11** n.349
1.704-2(k)(3) **11** n.348
1.704-2(k)(4) **11** n.347
1.704-2(*l*) **11** n.291
1.704-2(*l*)(1) . . . . **11** ns. 287, 345
1.704-2(*l*)(1)(ii) **11** n.251
1.704-2(*l*)(1)(iii) **11** n.249
1.704-2(*l*)(2) **11** n.288
1.704-2(*l*)(3) **8** n.74; **11** n.289
1.704-2(*l*)(4) . . . . 11.02[4][e]; **11** n.252
1.704-2(m) Ex. (1) . . . . . 11.02[4][f][i]; **11** ns. 259, 292
1.704-2(m) Ex. (1)(i)–(1)(iii) . . . 11.02[4][f][i]
1.704-2(m) Ex. (1)(i) . . . . 11.02[4][f][ii]; 11.02[4][f][iv]; **14** n.112
1.704-2(m) Ex. (1)(ii) **14** n.112
1.704-2(m) Ex. (1)(iv) . . . . .11.02[4][f][v]
1.704-2(m) Ex. (1)(v) . . . . .11.02[4][f][iii]
1.704-2(m) Ex. (1)(vi) . . . . .11.02[4][f][vi]
1.704-2(m) Ex. (1)(vii) . . . .11.02[4][f][iii]; **S11** n.306.1
1.704-2(m) Ex. (1)(viii) . . . . . .11.02[4][f][vii]
1.704-2(m) Ex. (1)(ix) . . . . .11.02[4][f][vii]
1.704-2(m) Ex. (2) . . . . .11.02[4][f][v]
1.704-2(m) Ex. (2)(ii) **11** n.318
1.704-2(m) Ex. (3) . . . . 11.02[4][f][ii]
1.704-2(m) Ex. (3)(i) . . . . 11.02[4][f][iv]
1.704-2(m) Ex. (3)(ii) . . . . .11.02[4][f][ii]; 11.02[4][f][v]; **21** n.103
1.704-2(m) Ex. (3)(iii) . . . . .11.02[4][f][ii]
1.704-2(m) Ex. (3)(iv) . . . . .11.02[4][f][iii]
1.704-2(m) Ex. (3)(v) . . . . .11.02[4][f][v]
1.704-2(m) Ex. (4) . . . . 11.02[4][f][ii]; 11.02[4][f][iii]; **11** n.297
1.704-2(m) Ex. (4)(ii) . . . . . . 11.02[4][f][ii]

[Text references are to paragraphs; note references are to chapters (boldface numbers) and notes ("n."). References to the supplement are preceded by "S."]

[Text references are to paragraphs; note references are to chapters (boldface numbers) and notes ("n."). References to the supplement are preceded by "S."]

[Text references are to paragraphs; note references are to chapters (boldface numbers) and notes ("n."). References to the supplement are preceded by "S."]

[Text references are to paragraphs; note references are to chapters (boldface numbers) and notes ("n."). References to the supplement are preceded by "S."]

[Text references are to paragraphs; note references are to chapters (boldface numbers) and notes ("n."). References to the supplement are preceded by "S."]

[Text references are to paragraphs; note references are to chapters (boldface numbers) and notes ("n."). References to the supplement are preceded by "S."]

[Text references are to paragraphs; note references are to chapters (boldface numbers) and notes ("n."). References to the supplement are preceded by "S."]

[Text references are to paragraphs; note references are to chapters (boldface numbers) and notes ("n."). References to the supplement are preceded by "S."]

Reg. §

1.752-2(j)   8.02[4][b][i]; 8.02[6]; 8.02[10][a];
    14.02[3][b][vii]; **14** n.108; **S14** ns. 108,
    122.1
1.752-2(j)(1) . . . . . 8.02[5]; 8.02[10][a]; **8** n.112
1.752-2(j)(2) . . . . 80.2[10][a]; **8** n.44
1.752-2(j)(2)(ii) **8** n.47
1.752-2(j)(3) . . . . 8.02[4][b][i]; 8.02[5];
    8.02[10][a]; 8.02[10][b]; **8** ns. 20, 36,
    52; **11** n.82
1.752-2(j)(4) . . . . 8.02[10][b]
1.752-2(j)(4)(i) **8** n.14
1.752-2(k) . . . . 8.02[5]; 8.02[6]; 8.02[8];
    8.02[10][a]; **8** ns. 20, 36, 84, 89, 111,
    125; **S11** n.85.2
1.752-2(k)(1) . . . . **8** ns. 87, 113
1.752-2(k)(2) Ex. 1 . . . . **8** n.86
1.752-2(k)(2) Ex. 2 . . . . **8** n.86
1.752-2(k)(2)(i) **8** n.114
1.752-2(k)(2)(ii)−1.752-2(k)(2)(iv) **8** n.115
1.752-2(k)(3) . . . . 8.02[8]
1.752-2(k)(4) **8** n.116
1.752-2(k)(5) . . . . **8** ns. 118, 119
1.752-2(k)(6) Ex. (3) **8** n.117
1.752-2(k)(6) Ex. (4) **8** n.118
1.752-2(*l*) . . . . **8** ns. 4, 111
1.752-2(*l*)(1) **8** n.111
1.752-2(*l*)(2) . . . . **8** ns. 44, 77
1.752-3 . . . . **7** n.13; **11** n.636; **22** n.64
1.752-3(a) . . . . . . **4** n.143; 8.03[3][a]; 8.03[4]
1.752-3(a)(1) . . . . **8** ns. 75, 136; **22** n.65
1.752-3(a)(2)   **4** n.144; 8.03[3][a]; **8** ns. 137,
    145; **9** n.254; **11** n.305; **22** ns. 66, 70
1.752-3(a)(3)   **4** n.144; **7** n.15; 8.03[4]; **8** ns.
    148, 149, 151, 153, 157; **9** n.254; **11** ns.
    259, 292; S14.02[3][b][iv];
    S14.02[3][b][v]; **14** ns. 110−112; **S14**
    ns. 108.1, 112.1; **19** n.79; **22** n.67
1.752-3(b) **8** n.146
1.752-3(b)(1) **11** n.305
1.752-3(b)(2) **8** n.147
1.752-3(c) Ex. (3) **11** n.305
1.752-4(a) . . . . **8** ns. 120, 121, 158; **S14** n.106
1.752-4(b)   **8** ns. 19, 164; 11.02[4][f][vii]; **11**
    n.152; **S11** n.152
1.752-4T(b) **11** n.75
1.752-4(b)(1) 8.04; **8** n.165
1.752-4(b)(1)(i) 8.04
1.752-4(b)(2) 8.04; **11** n.334
1.752-4(b)(2)(i) . . . . **8** ns. 167, 168
1.752-4(b)(2)(ii) **8** n.170
1.752-4(b)(2)(iii) 8.04; **8** n.171; **S11** n.152
1.752-4(b)(2)(iv)(A) **8** n.174
1.752-4(b)(2)(iv)(B) **8** n.175
1.752-4(c) **7** n.6; **8** n.123
1.752-4(d) **6** n.25; **7** n.8
1.752-5 . . . . **11** n.286; **24** n.31
1.752-5(a) . . . . **8** ns. 146, 157
1.752-6 . . . . S7.03[2]; 7.04[1]; 7.04[2]; 7.04[3];
    S7.04[2]; **7** n.79; **S7** ns. 62, 67.2, 68, 79,
    81.1; 18.01[4]
1.752-6(a) . . . . 7.04[2]

Reg. §

1.752-6(b)(2) **7** n.148
1.752-6T **S7** n.62
1.752-7 . . . . 4.03[5]; **4** ns. 151, 155, 156; 7.03;
    7.04[1]; 7.04[2]; 7.04[3]; 7.04[3][a];
    7.04[3][b]; 7.04[3][c]; 7.04[3][d];
    7.04[3][e]; 7.04[3][f]; 7.04[3][g];
    7.04[3][h]; **7** ns. 2, 40, 83, 85, 89, 91,
    93, 101, 110, 114, 127, 132;
    11.02[2][c][x]; 11.04[3][g]; **11** ns. 212,
    213, 305, 494, 537; **S11** n.494; **S14**
    n.104; 18.01[4]; 24.01[4]
1.752-7(a) **4** n.155
1.752-7(a)(1) . . . . 7.04[3][d]
1.752-7(a)(3)(iii) Ex. **7** n.147
1.752-7(b)(1) **7** n.86
1.752-7(b)(2) **7** n.97
1.752-7(b)(3) **7** n.91; **11** n.212
1.752-7(b)(3)(i) **4** n.152
1.752-7(b)(3)(ii) **4** n.155; **7** n.88
1.752-7(b)(3)(iii) Ex. **7** n.90
1.752-7(b)(4)(ii) **7** n.87
1.752-7(b)(5) **7** n.92
1.752-7(b)(5)(ii)(A) **7** n.138
1.752-7(b)(5)(ii)(B) **7** n.142
1.752-7(b)(6) **7** n.94
1.752-7(b)(7) **7** n.96
1.752-7(b)(7)(i)(A) **7** n.97
1.752-7(b)(7)(ii) **7** n.114
1.752-7(c) . . . . **7** n.84; 11.02[2][c][x]; 18.01[4]
1.752-7(c)(1) . . . . 7.04[3][d]; **7** ns. 93, 95
1.752-7(c)(1)(i) . . . . . **7** ns. 101, 115; **11** n.537
1.752-7(c)(1)(ii) **7** n.103
1.752-7(c)(2) Ex. **4** n.159
1.752-7(d)(1) **7** n.101
1.752-7(d)(2) **7** n.101
1.752-7(d)(2)(i)(A) . . . . . 7.04[3][g]; 7.04[3][h]
1.752-7(e) . . . . . . **11** ns. 214, 494; **S11** n.494
1.752-7(e)(1)   7.04[3][g]; **7** ns. 98, 116−119,
    131, 133, 134
1.752-7(e)(2) Ex. 1(iii) **7** n.134
1.752-7(e)(2) Ex. 3 . . . . **7** n.134
1.752-7(e)(3) . . . . 7.04[3][g]; **7** n.98
1.752-7(e)(3)(i) **7** n.141
1.752-7(e)(3)(ii) Ex. 5 . . . . **7** ns. 143, 146
1.752-7(f) **7** n.99
1.752-7(f)(1) . . . . **7** ns. 120, 121, 1131, 133
1.752-7(g) . . . . 7.04[3][e]; **7** n.100
1.752-7(g)(1) **11** n.540
1.752-7(g)(2)   7.04[3][e]; **7** ns. 124, 131, 133
1.752-7(g)(3) **7** n.128
1.752-7(g)(4) . . . . **7** ns. 125−127
1.752-7(g)(5) Ex. **7** n.122
1.752-7(i)(1) . . . . **7** ns. 93, 110, 111
1.752-7(j)(1) . . . . **7** ns. 139, 145
1.752-7(j)(2) **7** n.144
1.752-7(j)(3) . . . . 7.04[3][g]; **7** n.140
1.752-7(j)(4)(i) . . . . 7.04[3][f]
1.752-7(j)(4)(i)(A) . . . . **7** ns. 135, 136
1.752-7(j)(4)(ii) **7** n.135
1.752-7(j)(5) Ex. (ii) **7** n.137
1.752-7(k)(2) **7** n.82

[Text references are to paragraphs; note references are to chapters (boldface numbers) and notes ("n."). References to the supplement are preceded by "S."]

Reg. §

1.753-1(a) . . . . 23.02[2][a]; **23** n.23
1.753-1(b) . . . . **S23** n.5; 24.08[1]
1.754-1(a) **24** n.202
1.754-1(b) . . . . **24** ns. 203, 205
1.754-1(b)(1) **24** n.207
1.754-1(c) . . . . 24.11[4]; **24** n.218
1.754-1(c)(2) **24** n.219
1.755-1 . . . . **24** n.7
1.755-1(a) . . . . . . 24.04[3][a]; 24.04[3][b];
    24.04[3][b][i]; 24.04[3][c]; **24** ns. 100,
    110, 137
1.755-1(a)(1) . . . . . 24.04[1]; **24** ns. 103, 191;
    25.02[1][b]; **25** ns. 52, 53, 71, 118
1.755-1(a)(1)(i) . . . . **24** ns. 98, 102
1.755-1(a)(1)(ii) . . **4** n.150; **24** n.104; **25** n.72
1.755-1(a)(1)(iii) . . **24** n.105; 25.02[2]; **25** n.73
1.755-1(a)(2) . . . **24** ns. 118, 120−122; **25** ns.
    70, 84
1.755-1(a)(4) . . . . 24.04[3][b][ii][A]
1.755-1(a)(4)(i)(A) . . . . 24.04[3][b][ii][B]
1.755-1(a)(4)(i)(B) . . . . 24.04[3][b][ii][B]
1.755-1(a)(4)(i)(C) . . . . 24.04[3][b][ii][B]
1.755-1(a)(4)(ii) . . . . 24.04[3][b][ii][B]
1.755-1(a)(4)(iii) . . . 24.04[3][b][ii][B]; **25** n.88
1.755-1(a)(5) . . . . . **17** n.46; 24.04[3][b][ii][A];
    24.04[3][b][ii][B]; **24** n.123
1.755-1(a)(5)(i) . . . 24.04[3][b][ii][C]; **25** ns. 85,
    87
1.755-1(a)(5)(ii) **25** n.86
1.755-1(a)(6) . . . . 24.04[3][b][ii][D]
1.755-1(a)(6) Ex. 1 . . . . . . 24.04[3][b][ii][D]
1.755-1(a)(6) Ex. 2 . . . . . . 24.04[3][b][ii][D]
1.755-1(a)(6) Ex. 3 . . . . . . 24.04[3][b][ii][D]
1.755-1(a)(6) Ex. 4 . . . . . . 24.04[3][b][ii][D]
1.755-1(a)(6) Ex. 5 . . . . **25** n.89
1.755-1(b) **S9** n.375.33; **24** n.98
1.755-1(b)(1) **24** n.77
1.755-1(b)(1)(i) . . . . . . **S4** n.211.6; 25.02[1][b]
1.755-1(b)(1)(ii) . . . . . **4** ns. 150, 172; **24** n.79
1.755-1(b)(2)−1.755-1(b)(4) . . . . . . **S4**.05[12];
    24.04[1][a]
1.755-1(b)(2) . . . . 24.04[1][a]; **24** ns. 101, 102
1.755-1(b)(2)(i) . . . . **24** ns. 80, 81
1.755-1(b)(2)(i)(B) . . . . **24** ns. 82−84
1.755-1(b)(2)(ii) Ex. (1) **24** n.77
1.755-1(b)(2)(ii) Ex. (2) **24** n.77
1.755-1(b)(3) **25** n.74
1.755-1(b)(3)(i)(A) **24** n.84
1.755-1(b)(3)(ii) **24** n.85
1.755-1(b)(3)(iii)(A) **24** n.85
1.755-1(b)(3)(iii)(B) **24** n.85
1.755-1(b)(3)(iv) Ex. (2) **24** n.86
1.755-1(b)(4) . . . . **24** ns. 87, 178; 25.02[2]; **25**
    n.75
1.755-1(b)(4)(ii) **24** n.125
1.755-1(b)(4)(ii) Ex. (ii) . . . . . **24** ns. 180, 182
1.755-1(b)(5) . . . **S4**.05[12]; 24.04[1][b]; 24.06;
    24 ns. 78, 88; **25** n.128
1.755-1(b)(5)(i) . . . . **24** ns. 78, 88
1.755-1(b)(5)(ii) **24** n.91; **25** n.129
1.755-1(b)(5)(iii)(A) **24** n.92

1.755-1(b)(5)(iii)(B) . . . . **24** ns. 93, 94
1.755-1(b)(5)(iii)(C) **24** n.93
1.755-1(b)(5)(iii)(D) **S21** n.35.4; **24** n.93
1.755-1(b)(5)(iv) Ex. (2) **24** n.111
1.755-1(c) . . . . . . **S11**.04[1][b][iv]; **S25**.01[8];
    25.04; **25** n.23
1.755-1(c) Ex. (1) **24** n.102
1.755-1(c) Ex. (2) **24** n.102; **25** n.71
1.755-1(c)(1) **24** n.137
1.755-1(c)(1)(i) . . . . 25.02[3]; **25** ns. 54, 57, 64
1.755-1(c)(1)(ii) . . . . **22** n.90; 25.02[4]; 25.02[5];
    25 n.58
1.755-1(c)(2) **25** n.55
1.755-1(c)(2)(i) . . . . 25.01[4]; **25** n.60
1.755-1(c)(2)(ii) **25** n.61
1.755-1(c)(3) . . . . **25** ns. 61, 91
1.755-1(c)(4) . . . . **S21** n.35.4; **24** n.140; **25** ns.
    65, 91
1.755-1(c)(6) . . . . 25.02[1][a]
1.755-1(e) **24** n.119
1.755-1(e)(2) **24** n.85
1.755-2 . . . . **24** n.126; **25** n.84
1.761-1(a) **3** n.268
1.761-1(a)(1) **3** n.165
1.761-1(c) . . . . **11** ns. 11, 13
1.761-1(d) . . . . **6** n.62; **7** n.25; 8.02[6];
    11.02[2][a][i]; **12** n.31; 19.02[3]; **19** ns.
    105, 114
1.761-1(e) . . . **13** ns. 107, 165, 203; **S13** n.203;
    23.05[2][b]; 24.11[6]
1.761-2(a)(1) **9** n.606
1.761-2(a)(2) . . . . 3.05[5]; **3** n.389
1.761-2(a)(2)(i) **16** n.203; **S16** n.203
1.761-2(a)(2)(iii) **3** n.231
1.761-2(a)(3) **3** n.393
1.761-2(a)(3)(i) **16** n.203; **S16** n.203
1.761-2(a)(3)(iii) **3** n.231
1.761-2(b) . . . . 3.08[2]
1.761-2(b)(2)(i) . . . . 3.08[2]
1.761-2(b)(2)(ii) . . . . **3** n.398; 9.06[1][a]
1.761-2(b)(3)(i) . . . . **3** ns. 396, 399
1.761-2(c) **3** n.400
1.761-2(d) **3** n.393
1.761-2(d)(2)(i) . . . . **3** ns. 394, 395
1.761-2(d)(3)(iv) **3** n.395
1.761-2(d)(4)(i) **3** n.394
1.761-3 . . . . **S3**.04[4]; S3.04[4][a][i]; S3.04[4][c];
    S3 ns. 180.1, 180.4, 180.8; **S4**.01[1][d];
    S11.02[2][c][ii]; S11.02[4][g]; **S11** ns.
    163, 166
1.761-3(a)(1)(i) **S3** n.180.5
1.761-3(a)(1)(ii) **S3** n.180.6
1.761-3(a)(2) **S3** n.180.7
1.761-3(b)(2) **S3** n.180.2
1.761-3(b)(3) **S3** n.180.3
1.761-3(c) **S3** n.180.4
1.761-3(d)(2)(ii)(A)(1) **S3** n.180.11
1.761-3(d)(2)(ii)(A)(2) **S3** n.180.12
1.761-3(d)(2)(ii)(B) **S3** n.180.12
1.761-3(d)(2)(ii)(C) **S3** n.180.10
1.761-3(d)(2)(ii)(D) **S3** n.180.13

[Text references are to paragraphs; note references are to chapters (boldface numbers) and notes ("n."). References to the supplement are preceded by "S."]

Reg. §

1.761-3(d)(3)(ii)	**S3** n.180.14
1.761-3(d)(3)(ii)(C)	**S3** n.180.15
1.761-3(d)(3)(iii)	**S3** n.180.16
1.761-3(e)(1)	**S3** n.180.18
1.761-3(e)(2)	**S3** n.180.17
1.856-3(g)	**9** n.910; **14** n.277
1.856-4	**3** n.451; **S3** n.451
1.861-2(a)(i)	**S9** n.360.2
1.861-2(a)(2)	**9** n.360
1.861-2(a)(2)(iii)	**S9** n.360.1
1.861-8	**S4**.01[5][b][iii][B]; **9** n.834; **S11**.03[2][i]
1.861-8T	**S4**.01[5][b][iii][B]; **S11**.03[2][i]
1.861-9 – 1.861-13T	**S11**.03[2][i]
1.861-9(b)(8)	**S9** n.360.3
1.861-9(e)(4)	**S9** n.508
1.861-9(e)(8)(ii)	**S9**.02[2][h]
1.861-9(e)(8)(v)	**S9**.02[2][h]
1.861-9(e)(9)	**S9**.02[2][h]
1.861-9(k)	**S9** n.508
1.861-9T	**9**.02[3][t]
1.861-9T(e)(1)	**9** n.507
1.861-9T(e)(4)	**9** n.508
1.861-17	**S11**.03[2][i]
1.861-17(f)	**9** n.61
1.861-20	**S11**.03[2][i]
1.863-1 – 1.863-3	**9**.02[2][g]
1.863-1(a)	**9** n.353
1.863-3(e)(5)	**S9** n.353
1.863-3(f)	**S9** n.353
1.863-3(f)(2)(i)	**S9** n.354
1.863-3(f)(2)(ii)	**S9** ns. 355, 356
1.863-3(f)(2)(iii)	**S9** n.355
1.863-3(f)(3) Ex. 1	**S9** n.357
1.863-3(f)(3) Ex. 2	**S9** n.358
1.863-3(f)(5)	**9** n.353
1.863-3(g)	**9** n.353
1.863-3(g)(2)(i)	**9** n.354
1.863-3(g)(2)(ii)	**9** ns. 355, 356
1.863-3(g)(2)(iii)	**9** n.355
1.863-3(g)(3) Ex. (1)	**9** n.357
1.863-3(g)(3) Ex. (2)	**9** n.358
1.864-4(c)	**S9** n.825
1.864(c)(8)-1	**S9** n.831.2a
1.871-10(d)(3)	**9** ns. 178, 833
1.871-14	**S9** n.822
1.881-2(a)(1)	**9** n.824
1.882-5(a)(1)(ii)(B)	**9** n.821
1.882-5(b)(2)(ii)(B)	**9** n.821
1.882-5(c)(2)(vi)	**9** n.821
1.882-5(d)(2)(vii)	**9** n.821
1.884-1(d)(3)	**9**.03[4][d]
1.884-1(d)(3)(i)	**9** n.901
1.884-1(d)(3)(ii)(A)	**9** n.893
1.884-1(d)(3)(ii)(B)	**9** n.894
1.884-1(d)(3)(ii)(C)	**9** n.895
1.884-1(d)(3)(iii)	**9** n.896
1.884-1(d)(3)(iv)(A)	**9** n.892
1.884-1(d)(3)(vi)	**9** n.897
1.892-2T	**3**.06[4][a]
1.892-5(a)(3)	**9** n.909

Reg. §

1.892-5T(a)	**9** n.909; **S9** n.909.1
1.892-5T(d)(3)	**S9** n.909.2
1.894-1(d)(1)	**9**.03[4][e]; **9** n.902
1.894-1(d)(2)	**9**.03[4][e]
1.894-1(d)(2)(ii)(A)	**9** n.904
1.894-1(d)(2)(ii)(B)	**9** n.906
1.894-1(d)(2)(ii)(B)(4)	**9** n.905
1.894-1(d)(3)(ii)(A)	**9** n.903
1.894-1(d)(3)(iii)	**9**.03[4][e]
1.894-1T(d)	**9** n.900
1.897-1(c)(2)(iv)	**9** ns. 835, 860
1.897-1(e)(2)	**9** n.835
1.897-2(e)(2)	**9** n.835
1.897-6T(a)(3)	**9** n.836
1.901-2(e)(5)(iv)	**S11** n.428
1.901-2(f)(4)	**S11** n.421.1a
1.904-4(n)(1)(i)	**S9** n.117.15
1.904-4(n)(1)(ii)	**S9** n.117.16
1.904-4(n)(3)	**S9** n.177.17
1.904-5T(o)(3)(ii)	**S9** n.201
1.904-6	**11**.03[2][i]
1.904(f)-2(d)(4)	**S16** n.206
1.904(f)-2(d)(5)(i)	**S16** n.206
1.904(f)-2(d)(5)(ii)	**S16** n.206
1.904(i)-1	**9** n.681
1.909-1(b)	**S11** n.425
1.909-2(b)(4)	**S11** n.426
1.911-3(b)(2)	**9** n.328; **15** n.15; **S15** n.15
1.911-3(b)(3)	**9**.02[2][c]
1.951A-1(e)(1)	**S9**.01[4][c]
1.951A-1(e)(2)	**S9** n.88.5
1.951A-1(e)(3)(ii) Ex. (2)	**S9** n.88.6
1.951A-3(g)(4)(ii)	**S9** n.88.2
1.952-1(g)	**9** ns. 102, 103
1.952-1(g)(1)	**9**.01[4][c][iii][C]
1.954-1(g)(2)	**9** ns. 107, 108
1.954-1(g)(2)(iii)	**9** n.114
1.954-1(g)(3) Ex. (3)	**9** n.109
1.954-1(g)(3) Ex. (4)	**9** n.109
1.954-2(a)(5)(ii)	**9** n.104
1.954-2(a)(5)(ii)(A)	**9** n.115
1.954-2(b)(4)(i)(B)	**9**.01[4][c][iii][A]; **S9**.01[4][c][v]
1.954-2(b)(5)(i)(B)	**9**.01[4][c][iii][A]; **S9**.01[4][c][v]
1.954-2(b)(6)	**9**.01[4][c][iv][C]; **9** n.117
1.954-2(e)(3)(iv)	**9** n.206
1.954-2T(a)(5)(ii)(C)	**9** n.105; **S9** n.105
1.954-2T(a)(5)(iii) Ex. (2)	**9** n.105; **S9** n.105
1.954-3(a)(4)	**9**.01[4][c][iii][B]
1.954-3(a)(6)	**9** n.106
1.954-4(b)(2)(iii)	**9** n.110
1.956-1(b)	**S9**.01[4][c][iii][D]
1.956-1(b)(1)(iii)	**S9** ns. 113.3, 113.4
1.956-1(b)(2)	**S9** n.113.3
1.956-1(b)(3)	**S9** n.113.5
1.956-1(g)(2)	**S9** n.113.6
1.956-2(a)(3)	**9** n.111; **S9** n.111
1.956-2(c)	**S9** n.113.8
1.956-4	**S9**.01[4][c][iii][D]
1.956-4(b)	**S9**.01[4][c][iii][D]

*[Text references are to paragraphs; note references are to chapters (boldface numbers)
and notes ("n."). References to the supplement are preceded by "S."]*

Reg. §

1.956-4(b)(1)	**S9** ns. 112, 113
1.956-4(b)(2)(i)(B)	**S9** n.113.1
1.956-4(b)(2)(ii)	**S9** n.113.2
1.956-4(c)	**S9** n.113.7
1.956-4(c)(3)(i)	**S9** n.113.9
1.956-4(c)(3)(ii)(A)	**S9** n.113.10
1.956-4(c)(3)(ii)(B)	**S9** n.113.11
1.956-4(e)	**S9** n.113.12
1.956-4(f)	**S9** n.113.9
1.956-4(f)(1)	**S9** n.113
1.961-1(b)(1)(ii)	**S6** n.40.2
1.987-1(b)(5)	**S9** n.548
1.987-2(c)(9)	**S9** n.548.1
1.987-7T(b)	**S9** n.548
1.987-12	**S9** n.548.1
1.995-4(a)(1)	**21** n.131
1.1001-1(e)	16.05[2][c]
1.1001-2	8.02[2]
1.1001-2(a)−1.1001-2(c) Ex. (3)	**7** n.33
1.1001-2(a)(1)	**16** ns. 214, 216
1.1001-2(a)(3)	**16** n.214
1.1001-2(a)(4)	**16** n.216
1.1001-2(a)(4)(i)	**16** n.214
1.1001-2(a)(4)(ii)	**16** n.214
1.1001-2(a)(4)(iii)	**16** n.214
1.1001-2(a)(4)(iv)	**13** n.34
1.1001-2(c) Ex. (3)	**16** n.216
1.1001-2(c) Ex. (4)	16.05[2][b]; **16** n.216
1.1001-2(c) Ex. (5)	**13** n.54
1.1012-1(c)	4.01[2][a]; **4** n.9; **6** n.6; 16.01[1]
1.1012-1(c)(3)	**11** n.541; **19** ns. 174, 234
1.1014-4(a)(3)	**23** n.47
1.1017-1(a)	**9** n.275
1.1017-1(c)	**9** ns. 279, 284
1.1017-1(c)(1)	**9** n.284
1.1017-1(g)(1)	**9** n.302
1.1017-1(g)(2)(i)	**9** ns. 291, 303, 304
1.1017-1(g)(2)(ii)(A)	**9** n.308
1.1017-1(g)(2)(ii)(B)	**9** n.309
1.1017-1(g)(2)(ii)(C)	**9** n.310
1.1017-1(g)(2)(iii)	**9** n.310
1.1017-1T(g)(2)(iii)(B)	**9** n.310
1.1017-1(g)(2)(iv)	**9** n.305
1.1017-1(g)(2)(v) Ex.	**9** n.307
1.1017-1(g)(2)(v)(B)	**9** n.306
1.1017-1(g)(2)(v)(C)	**9** n.306
1.1031(b)-1(c)	9.02[1][c][iii]
1.1031(k)-1(j)(2)	9.02[1][c][iii]
1.1032-1(a)	5.03[5]
1.1032-3	**4** n.12; 9.03[1][a][ix]; **9** n.707
1.1032-3 Ex. 3	**4** n.12
1.1032-3(b)(1)	**9** ns. 708, 709
1.1032-3(b)(2)	**9** n.709
1.1032-3(c)(4)	**9** n.706
1.1033(a)-2(c)(5)	**9** n.229
1.1041-1T	16.02[3][e]; **16** n.115
1.1041-2	**16** ns. 117, 124
1.1041-2(a)	**16** n.125
1.1041-2(a)(1)	16.02[3][e]
1.1041-2(b)	**16** n.125
1.1041-2(c)	**16** n.126

Reg. §

1.1041-2(e)	**16** n.126
1.1045-1(a)	**S9** n.512
1.1045-1(b)(1)	S9.02[3][u]; **S9** n.513
1.1045-1(b)(2)	**S9** n.515
1.1045-1(b)(3)(i)	S9.02[3][u]
1.1045-1(b)(3)(ii)	**S9** n.515
1.1045-1(b)(3)(ii)(A) . . .	S9.02[3][u]; **S9** n.516
1.1045-1(b)(4)	S9.02[3][u]
1.1045-1(c)(1)(i)	S9.02[3][u]
1.1045-1(c)(1)(ii)	S9.02[3][u]
1.1045-1(c)(1)(iii)(A)	S9.02[3][u]
1.1045-1(c)(1)(iii)(B)	S9.02[3][u]
1.1045-1(c)(5)	S9.02[3][u]
1.1045-1(h)	S9.02[3][u]
1.1060-1(a)(1)	**9** n.205; **24** n.114
1.1060-1(b)(2)	24.04[3][a]; 24.04[3][b];
	24.04[3][b][ii][A]; **24** n.115; 25.02[6]
1.1060-1T(b)(2)	**24** n.115
1.1092(d)-1	11.04[3][e]
1.1092(d)-1(a)	**19** n.223
1.1223-1(a)	**4** n.26
1.1223-3	S13.05[2][f]; **17** n.72
1.1223-3(a)(1)	**16** n.11
1.1223-3(b)(1) . . . **1** n.18; **4** n.31; 16.08[6]; **16**
	n.10
1.1223-3(b)(3)	4.01[2][a]
1.1223-3(b)(4)	**4** ns. 33, 34
1.1223-3(c)(1)	**4** n.35; 16.08[6]
1.1223-3(c)(2)(i)	**4** n.36
1.1223-3(d)(1)	**4** n.37
1.1223-3(d)(2)	**4** n.38
1.1223-3(e) Ex. 1	**4** n.32
1.1233-1(a)(1)	**7** n.61
1.1244(a)-1(b)	**18** n.75
1.1244(a)-1(b)(2)	**9** ns. 198, 199; **18** n.77
1.1244(a)-1(c) Ex. 2	**9** n.199
1.1245-1(a)(1)	**20** n.41
1.1245-1(e)	**17** n.98; **24** n.169
1.1245-1(e)(2) . . . 11.03[2][c]; **11** ns. 378−380;
	17 n.94
1.1245-1(e)(2)(i)	**11** n.382
1.1245-1(e)(2)(ii)(A)	**11** n.383
1.1245-1(e)(2)(ii)(B) **11** n.384; **17** n.100
1.1245-1(e)(2)(ii)(C)(1)	**11** n.385
1.1245-1(e)(2)(ii)(C)(2) . . . . 11.03[2][c]; **11**
	n.388; **17** n.94
1.1245-1(e)(2)(ii)(C)(3) . . . 11.03[2][c]; **17** n.94
1.1245-1(e)(2)(ii)(C)(4)	**11** n.389
1.1245-1(e)(2)(ii)(C)(5)	**11** n.390
1.1245-1(e)(2)(iii) Ex. 1	**11** n.386
1.1245-1(e)(2)(iii) Ex. 2	**11** n.387
1.1245-1(e)(2)(iv)	**11** n.381
1.1245-1(e)(3)	**17** ns. 90, 94, 99
1.1245-1(e)(3)(ii)	17.03[3]; **23** n.63; **24**
	n.169
1.1245-1(e)(4)	**17** n.94
1.1245-2(a)	11.03[2][c]
1.1245-2(c)(1)(iv)	**23** n.60
1.1245-2(c)(2)	**4** ns. 165, 169
1.1245-2(c)(6)(ii)	**21** ns. 68, 128
1.1245-4(c)	**18** n.8

[Text references are to paragraphs; note references are to chapters (boldface numbers) and notes ("n."). References to the supplement are preceded by "S."]

[Text references are to paragraphs; note references are to chapters (boldface numbers) and notes ("n."). References to the supplement are preceded by "S."]

[Text references are to paragraphs; note references are to chapters (boldface numbers) and notes ("n."). References to the supplement are preceded by "S."]

[Text references are to paragraphs; note references are to chapters (boldface numbers) and notes ("n."). References to the supplement are preceded by "S."]

Reg. §

15A.453-1(b)(2)(iv)	**16** ns. 182, 185
15A.453-1(b)(2)(v)	**16** n.184
15A.453-1(b)(3)(i)	**16** n.182
15A.453-1(b)(3)(iii)	**22** n.82
15A.453-1(b)(5) Ex. 2	**22** n.82
15A.453-1(b)(5) Ex. 3	**22** n.82
15A.453-1(d)(3)(i)	**9** n.163
16A.1255-2(c)(2)(vi)	**4** n.174
20.2031-1(b)	**5** n.142; **23** n.98
20.2031-2(f)	**23** ns. 77, 88
20.2031-2(h)	**23** ns. 78, 88
20.2031-3	23.07[1]; **23** ns. 87, 97
20.2032A-3	**23** n.106
20.2032A-3(b)(1)	**23** n.108
20.2032A-3(f)	**23** n.106
20.2042-1(c)(6)	**23** ns. 76, 82, 83
25.2701-3(d) Ex. (3)	**3** n.202
31.3401(c)-1	**2** n.87
31.3401(c)-1(e)	**2** n.87
301.6011-3	**9** n.1050
301.6011-3(b)	**9** n.1053
301.6011-3(d)(5)	**9** n.1051
301.6011-3(e) Ex. (3)	**9** n.1052
301.6109-1(b)(2)(v)	**3** n.342
301.6109-1(h)(1)	**3** n.341
301.6109-1(h)(2)(i)	**3** n.343
301.6111-2(b)(2)	14.03[6][i]
301.6112-1(b)(2)	14.03[6][i]
301.6112-1(e)(2)	**9** n.1117
301.6112-1(e)(3)(i)	**9** n.1118
301.6112-1(f)	**9** n.1121
301.6112-1(g)	**9** n.1122
301.6221-1	**S10** n.11; **10A** n.18
301.6221-1(c)	**10** ns. 88, 89, 224; **S10** n.89.6
301.6221-1(d)	**10** ns. 88, 89, 224
301.6221-1T(c)	S10.02[3]
301.6221-1T(d)	S10.02[3]
301.6221(b)-1(a)	**10A** ns. 46, 86
301.6221(b)-1(b)(2)(ii)	**10A** ns. 73, 79
301.6221(b)-1(b)(3)(i)	**10A** n.72
301.6221(b)-1(b)(3)(ii)	**10A** ns. 9, 74
301.6221(b)-1(b)(3)(iii)	**10A** ns. 72, 74
301.6221(b)-1(b)(3)(iv)	**10A** n.9
301.6221(b)-1(b)(3)(iv) Ex. 2	**10A** n.74
301.6221(b)-1(c)	**10A** n.75
301.6221(b)-1(d)	**10A** ns. 74, 87
301.6222-1(a)(1)	**10A** n.80
301.6222-1(a)(2)	**10A** n.87
301.6222-1(a)(3)	**10A** n.82
301.6222-1(a)(4)	**10A** n.80
301.6222-1(a)(5) Ex. 4	**10A** n.80
301.6222-1(a)(5) Ex. 6	**10A** n.87
301.6222-1(a)(5)(iv) Ex. 4	**10A** n.293
301.6222-1(b)	**10A** n.81
301.6222-1(b)(3)	**10A** n.88
301.6222-1(c)(1)	**10A** n.83
301.6222-1(c)(2)	**10A** n.83
301.6222-1(c)(4)(ii)	**10A** n.84
301.6222-1(c)(5)	**10A** ns. 83, 85, 333
301.6222-1(d)	**10A** n.80

Reg. §

301.6222(a)-1(a)	**10** n.137
301.6222(a)-1(b)	**10** n.140
301.6222(a)-1(c) Ex. (3)	**10** n.140
301.6222(a)-2(b)	**10** n.137
301.6222(a)-2(c)	**10** n.137
301.6222(b)-1	**10** n.138
301.6222(b)-2(a)	**10** ns. 137, 139
301.6222(b)-2(b)	**10** n.139
301.6222(b)-2(c)	**10** n.139
301.6222(b)-3(a)(1)	**10** n.140
301.6222(b)-3(b)	**10** n.140
301.6222(b)-3(b)(2)	**10** n.140
301.6223-1(b)(2)	**10A** n.89
301.6223-1(b)(3)	**10A** n.91
301.6223-1(b)(3)(ii)	**10A** n.92
301.6223-1(c)	**10A** n.89
301.6223-1(d)	**10A** ns. 89, 93
301.6223-1(e)	**10A** ns. 89, 93
301.6223-1(e)(2)	**10A** n.19
301.6223-1(f)	**10A** ns. 90, 93
301.6223-1(f)(5)	**10A** n.90
301.6223(a)-2(a)	**10** ns. 149, 150
301.6223(a)-2(b)	**10** n.151
301.6223(b)-1(a)	**10** ns. 170, 173
301.6223(b)-1(b)(2)	**10** n.174
301.6223(b)-1(b)(3)	**10** n.175
301.6223(b)-1(b)(4)	**10** n.176
301.6223(b)-1(b)(5)	**10** n.177
301.6223(b)-1(c)(1)	**10** n.178
301.6223(b)-1(c)(2)	**10** n.179
301.6223(b)-1(c)(3)	**10** n.180
301.6223(b)-1(c)(4)	**10** n.180
301.6223(b)-1(c)(5)	**10** n.181
301.6223(b)-1(c)(6)	**10** n.183
301.6223(b)-1(d)	**10** n.182
301.6223(b)-1(e)	**10** ns. 170, 239
301.6223(c)-1	**10** n.297
301.6223(c)-1(b)	**10** ns. 161, 189
301.6223(c)-1(b)(1)	**10** n.155
301.6223(c)-1(b)(2)	**10** n.157
301.6223(c)-1(b)(3)	**10** n.158
301.6223(c)-1(c)	**10** n.159
301.6223(c)-1(d)	**10** n.156
301.6223(c)-1(f)	**S10** n.154
301.6223(e)-1	**10** n.192
301.6223(e)-1(b)(2) Ex. (2)	**10** n.193
301.6223(e)-2(c)	**10** n.164
301.6223(e)-2(d)	**10** n.166; **S10** n.166
301.6223(e)-2(d)(2)	**10** n.165
301.6223(g)-1	**10** n.30
301.6223(g)-1(a)	**10** ns. 150, 186
301.6223(g)-1(a)(3)	**10** n.185
301.6223(g)-1(b)	**10** n.187
301.6223(g)-1(b)(1)(iv)	**10** n.203
301.6223(g)-1(b)(1)(vii)	**10** n.244
301.6223(h)-1	**10** n.191
301.6224(a)-1	**10** n.144
301.6224(b)-1	**10** n.145
301.6224(c)-1(a)	**10** n.198
301.6224(c)-1(b)	**10** n.198
301.6224(c)-2(a)(1)	**10** n.199

[Text references are to paragraphs; note references are to chapters (boldface numbers) and notes ("n."). References to the supplement are preceded by "S."]

Reg. §

301.6224(c)-2(b) **10** n.199
301.6224(c)-3(a) **10** n.209
301.6224(c)-3(b)(1) . . . . **10** ns. 206, 208, 209, 211
301.6224(c)-3(c) **10** n.201
301.6224(c)-3(c)(3) **10** n.202
301.6225-1(b)(1) . . . . 10A.06[1][a]; **10A** n.133
301.6225-1(b)(1)(v)(A) **10A** n.101
301.6225-1(b)(1)(v)(B) **10A** n.102
301.6225-1(b)(2) . . . . **10A** ns. 100, 110
301.6225-1(c) **10A** n.33
301.6225-1(c)(1) **10A** n.106
301.6225-1(c)(2) . . . . **10A** ns. 107, 326
301.6225-1(c)(2)(ii) **10A** n.109
301.6225-1(c)(3) **10A** n.112
301.6225-1(c)(4) **10A** n.112
301.6225-1(c)(5) **10A** n.108
301.6225-1(c)(5)(ii) **10A** n.330
301.6225-1(c)(6) **10A** n.113
301.6225-1(d)(1) **10A** n.115
301.6225-1(d)(2) **10A** ns. 103, 113, 225, 328
301.6225-1(d)(2)(ii) **10A** n.58
301.6225-1(d)(2)(iii) **10A** n.59
301.6225-1(d)(2)(iii)(B) **10A** n.330
301.6225-1(d)(3)(i) . . . . **10A** ns. 5, 116, 117
301.6225-1(d)(3)(ii) **10A** n.109
301.6225-1(d)(3)(ii)(A) **10A** n.118
301.6225-1(d)(3)(ii)(B) **10A** n.119
301.6225-1(d)(3)(iii)(A) **10A** n.119
301.6225-1(d)(3)(iv) **10A** n.120
301.6225-1(e)(1) **10A** n.125
301.6225-1(e)(2) . . . . **10A** ns. 125–128
301.6225-1(e)(3)(i) **10A** n.129
301.6225-1(e)(3)(ii) . . . . . . **10A** ns. 101, 102
301.6225-1(e)(3)(iii)(A) **10A** n.130
301.6225-1(f)(2) . . . . **10A** ns. 105, 111
301.6225-1(g) **10A** n.102
301.6225-1(h)(1) Ex. 1 . . . . 10A.06[1][c];
    10A.10[3]; **10A** ns. 122, 123, 126
301.6225-1(h)(2) Ex. 2 . . . . **10A** n.123
301.6225-1(h)(3) Ex. 3 . . . . **10A** n.115
301.6225-1(h)(4) Ex. 4 . . . . 10A.06; **10A** n.114
301.6225-1(h)(5) Ex. 5 . . . . **10A** n.128
301.6225-1(h)(6) Ex. 6 . . . . **10A** n.102
301.6225-1(h)(7) Ex. 7 . . . . 10A.02[3];
    10A.02[4]; 10A.10[3]; **10A** ns. 108, 331
301.6225-1(h)(8) Ex. 8 . . . . **10A** n.119
301.6225-1(h)(9) Ex. 9 . . . . **10A** n.119
301.6225-1(h)(10) Ex. 10 . . . . **10A** n.119
301.6225-1(h)(10) Ex. 10 . . . . **10A** n.119
301.6225-1(h)(11) Ex. 11 . . . . **10A** n.119
301.6225-1(h)(12) Ex. 12 . . . . 10A.06; **10A** ns. 109, 327
301.6225-2 . . . . 10A.06[2][a]; 10A.06[2][d][iii]; **10A** n.34
301.6225-2(a) . . . . 10A.06[2][b]
301.6225-2(b)(1) **10A** n.169
301.6225-2(b)(3)(i) **10A** n.150
301.6225-2(b)(3)(iii) **10A** n.150
301.6225-2(c)(3) . . . . . . **10A** ns. 137, 151, 346
301.6225-2(c)(3)(ii) **10A** n.151

Reg. §

301.6225-2(c)(3)(iii) **10A** n.151
301.6225-2(c)(4) **10A** n.139
301.6225-2(d)(2)   **10A** ns. 154, 155, 159, 166
301.6225-2(d)(2)(i) – 301.6225-2(d)(2)(ix) **10A** n.142
301.6225-2(d)(2)(ii)(B) **10A** n.153
301.6225-2(d)(2)(ii)(C) **10A** n.156
301.6225-2(d)(2)(iii) **10A** n.153
301.6225-2(d)(2)(iv) **10A** n.153
301.6225-2(d)(2)(v) **10A** n.186
301.6225-2(d)(2)(vi)(A) **10A** n.187
301.6225-2(d)(2)(vi)(B) **10A** n.188
301.6225-2(d)(2)(vii) . . . . . . 10A.06[2][d][iii]
301.6225-2(d)(2)(vii)(B) . . . . . 10A.06[2][d][iii]
301.6225-2(d)(2)(vii)(C) . . . . 10A.06[2][d][iii]; **10A** ns. 171, 193
301.6225-2(d)(2)(viii) **10A** n.162
301.6225-2(d)(2)(x) . . . . . . **10A** ns. 143, 157
301.6225-2(d)(2)(x)(A) . . . . . . 10A.06[2][e][i]
301.6225-2(d)(3) . . . . . **10A** ns. 144, 146, 174
301.6225-2(d)(4) . . . . . . **10A** ns. 145, 175, 177
301.6225-2(d)(6) . . . . . **10A** ns. 106, 149, 178
301.6225-2(d)(6)(ii) . . . . 10A.09[1]
301.6225-2(d)(7) . . . . **10A** ns. 147, 182
301.6225-2(d)(8) . . . . 10A.06[2][b]; 10A.09[1]; **10A** n.183
301.6225-2(d)(9) . . . . 10A.06[2][b]; **10A** n.184
301.6225-2(d)(10) . . . . . . 10A.09[1]; **10A** n.71
301.6225-2(f) **10A** n.159
301.6225-2(f)(1) Ex. 1 . . . . **10A** n.140
301.6225-2(f)(2) Ex. 2 . . . . . **10A** ns. 155, 166
301.6225-2(f)(3) Ex. 3 . . . . **10A** n.174
301.6225-2(f)(4) Ex. 4 . . . . **10A** n.174
301.6225-2(f)(6) Ex. 6 . . . . . **10A** ns. 155, 166
301.6225-2(f)(7) Ex. 7 . . . . . **10A** ns. 177, 178
301.6225-3 . . . 10A.06[1][b]; 10A.06[1][c]; **10A** ns. 105, 132, 206
301.6225-3(a) **10A** n.226
301.6225-3(b) . . . . **10A** ns. 28, 207, 322
301.6225-3(b)(1) **10A** n.227
301.6225-3(b)(2) **10A** n.228
301.6225-3(b)(3) **10A** n.229
301.6225-3(b)(4) . . . . **10A** ns. 230, 328
301.6225-3(b)(5) **10A** n.231
301.6225-3(b)(6) **10A** n.232
301.6225-3(b)(7) **10A** n.233
301.6225-3(d)(1) Ex. 1 . . . . **10A** n.228
301.6225-3(d)(2) Ex. 2 . . . . **10A** n.230
301.6226-1(a)(2) **10A** n.235
301.6226-1(b)(1) **10A** n.236
301.6226-1(b)(2) **10A** n.263
301.6226-1(c)(1) **10A** n.260
301.6226-1(c)(3)(i) **10A** n.257
301.6226-1(c)(3)(ii) **10A** n.258
301.6226-1(c)(3)(ii)(D) . . . . . **10A** ns. 179, 259
301.6226-1(d) . . . . **10A** ns. 261, 263
301.6226-1(e) . . . . 10A.08[2]; **10A** ns. 83, 253
301.6226-1(f) **10A** n.237
301.6226-2(a) . . . . **10A** ns. 263, 265
301.6226-2(b) **10A** n.264
301.6226-2(b)(1) . . . . **10A** ns. 243, 244

[Text references are to paragraphs; note references are to chapters (boldface numbers) and notes ("n."). References to the supplement are preceded by "S."]

Reg. §

301.6226-2(c) **10A** n.266
301.6226-2(d) **10A** n.262
301.6226-2(d)(1) **10A** n.243
301.6226-2(f) . . . . 10A.08[2]
301.6226-2(f)(1) **10A** n.270
301.6226-2(f)(1)(i) **10A** n.241
301.6226-2(f)(2) **10A** n.268
301.6226-3(a) . . . . 10A.09[2]
301.6226-3(b)(1) . . . . **10A** ns. 274, 279
301.6226-3(b)(2)(i) **10A** n.272
301.6226-3(b)(2)(ii) **10A** n.275
301.6226-3(b)(3) **10A** n.276
301.6226-3(b)(3)(i) **10A** n.273
301.6226-3(b)(3)(ii) **10A** n.252
301.6226-3(c)(1) . . . . **10A** ns. 277, 279
301.6226-3(c)(2) . . . . **10A** ns. 278
301.6226-3(c)(3) . . . . . 10A.09[2]; **10A** n.254
301.6226-3(d)(1) **10A** n.281
301.6226-3(d)(2) **10A** n.282
301.6226-3(d)(3) **10A** n.283
301.6226-3(e) **10A** n.284
301.6226-3(e)(2)(ii) **10A** n.290
301.6226-3(e)(3) . . . . **10A** ns. 287, 289
301.6226-3(e)(3)(i) **10A** n.288
301.6226-3(e)(3)(ii) **10A** n.287
301.6226-3(e)(3)(iv) . . . . . . **10A** ns. 285, 291
301.6226-3(e)(4)(iii) **10A** n.286
301.6226-3(e)(5) **10A** n.284
301.6226-3(g) **10A** n.284
301.6226(a)-1(a) **10** n.236
301.6226(b)-1 . . . . **10** n.239
301.6226(e)-1 . . . . **10** n.246
301.6226(e)-1(a) **10** n.247
301.6226(f)-1 . . . . **10** n.251
301.6227-1(a) . . . . **10A** ns. 292, 295, 300
301.6227-1(b) . . . . **10A** ns. 294, 296
301.6227-1(c)(2) **10A** n.299
301.6227-1(c)(2)(ii) **10A** n.306
301.6227-1(d) . . . . **10A** ns. 306, 312
301.6227-1(e) **10A** n.306
301.6227-1(f) . . . 10A.09[4]; **10A** ns. 297, 303
301.6227-2(a)(2)(i) **10A** n.303
301.6227-2(a)(2)(ii) **10A** n.303
301.6227-2(b) **10A** n.301
301.6227-2(b)(1) **10A** n.304
301.6227-2(b)(2) **10A** n.304
301.6227-2(b)(3) **10A** n.304
301.6227-2(c) **10A** n.302
301.6227-3 . . . . 10A.09
301.6227-3(a) **10A** n.311
301.6227-3(b)(1) . . . . **10A** ns. 307, 309, 313
301.6227-3(b)(2) **10A** n.308
301.6227-3(b)(2) Ex. 1 . . . . **10A** n.314
301.6227-3(b)(2) Ex. 2 . . . . **10A** n.314
301.6227-3(c) **10A** n.310
301.6227-3(c)(4) **10A** n.309
301.6227(c)-1(a) **10** n.261; **S10** n.261
301.6227(d)-1 . . . . **10** n.266
301.6227(d)-1(a) . . . . S10.05[2]
301.6229(b)-1 . . . . **10** n.286; **S10** n.286
301.6229(c)-1 . . . . **10** n.297

301.6229(c)(2)-1 . . . . **S10** n.292.2
301.6229(f)-1 . . . . **10** n.213
301.6230(b)-1 . . . . **10** n.232
301.6230(c)-1 . . . . **10** n.234
301.6230(e)-1 . . . . **10** n.29
301.6231-1(a) **10** n.165
301.6231(a)(1)-1(a)(1) **10** n.18
301.6231(a)(1)-1(a)(3) . . . . **10** ns. 18, 20, 21
301.6231(a)(1)-1(b)(3) **10** n.23
301.6231(a)(1)-1T(a)(3) **10** n.20
301.6231(a)(2)-1 . . . . **10** n.147
301.6231(a)(3)-1(a) . . . . S10.02[3]
301.6231(a)(3)-1(a)(1)(i)   **10** ns. 69, 134; **S10** n.69
301.6231(a)(3)-1(a)(1)(v) . . . . **S10** ns. 70, 73.1
301.6231(a)(3)-1(a)(1)(vi)(A) **10** n.134
301.6231(a)(3)-1(a)(1)(vi)(E) **10** n.73
301.6231(a)(3)-1(a)(2) **10** n.70; **S10** n.71
301.6231(a)(3)-1(a)(3) **10** n.71; **S10** n.72
301.6231(a)(3)-1(a)(4) **10** n.72; **S10** n.73
301.6231(a)(3)-1(b) **10** n.74; **S10** n.87.1
301.6231(a)(3)-1(c)(2) **10** n.72; **S10** n.73
301.6231(a)(3)-1(c)(2)(iv) **S10** n.87.2
301.6231(a)(5)-1 . . . . **10** n.226; **S10** n.226
301.6231(a)(5)-1(b) **10** n.113
301.6231(a)(5)-1T(b) . . . . 10.02[5]
301.6231(a)(5)-1(c) **10** n.113
301.6231(a)(5)-1(d) **10** n.113
301.6231(a)(5)-1(e)(2) **10** n.114
301.6231(a)(5)-1(e)(3) **10** n.115
301.6231(a)(5)-1(e)(4) Ex. (1) **10** n.114
301.6231(a)(6)-1 . . . . **10** n.226; **S10** n.226
301.6231(a)(6)-1(a) **10** n.65
301.6231(a)(6)-1(a)(3) **10** n.224
301.6231(a)(7)-1(b) **10** n.32
301.6231(a)(7)-1(c) **10** n.40
301.6231(a)(7)-1(d) **10** n.41
301.6231(a)(7)-1(e) **10** n.42
301.6231(a)(7)-1(f) **10** n.43
301.6231(a)(7)-1(g) **10** n.44
301.6231(a)(7)-1(k) **10** n.46
301.6231(a)(7)-1(*l*) . . . . **10** ns. 45, 51
301.6231(a)(7)-1(*l*)(1) **10** n.53
301.6231(a)(7)-1(*l*)(1)(iv) . . . . . . **10** ns. 47, 49
301.6231(a)(7)-1(m) **10** n.52
301.6231(a)(7)-1(m)(3) **10** n.54
301.6231(a)(7)-1(p)(2) **10** n.56
301.6231(a)(7)-1(r)(1) **10** n.56
301.6231(a)(7)-2(a) **10** n.60
301.6231(a)(7)-2(b)(3) **10** n.61
301.6231(a)(12)-1(a) **10** n.105
301.6231(a)(12)-1(a)(4) **10** n.107
301.6231(a)(12)-1(b)(1) **10** n.22
301.6231(a)(12)-1(c) **10** n.106
301.6231(c)-1(a) **10** n.219
301.6231(c)-1(c) **10** n.219
301.6231(c)-1(d) **10** n.219
301.6231(c)-1(d)(2)(ii) **10** n.219
301.6231(c)-3 . . . . **10** n.97
301.6231(c)-4 . . . . **10** n.98
301.6231(c)-5 . . . . **10** n.99

[Text references are to paragraphs; note references are to chapters (boldface numbers) and notes ("n."). References to the supplement are preceded by "S."]

[Text references are to paragraphs; note references are to chapters (boldface numbers) and notes ("n."). References to the supplement are preceded by "S."]

PROPOSED REGULATIONS

[Text references are to paragraphs; note references are to chapters (boldface numbers) and notes ("n."). References to the supplement are preceded by "S."]

Prop. Reg. §

1.168-5(b)(8) Ex. (3) (1984) **4** n.197; **13** n.137
1.168-5(b)(8) Ex. (7) (1984) **20** n.62
1.168-5(e)(7) (1984) . . . .! . .**9** n.157
1.168(i)-2(b)(2)(iv)(D) (2018) 24.07
1.168(k)-2(b)(3)(iii)(B)(5) (2019) **S24** n.157.1
1.199-4(b)(2) (2005) **9** n.527
1.199-4(f) (2005) . . . . 9.02[3][w]
1.199-5(a)(1) (2005) . . . . **9** ns. 533, 534
1.199-5(a)(2) (2005) **9** n.535
1.199-5(a)(3) (2005) **9** n.536
1.199-5(e) (2005) **9** n.537
1.199-5(f) (2005) **9** n.538; **S9** n.541
1.199-5(g) (2005) **9** n.540
1.199-5(h)(7) (2005) **9** n.541
1.199-5(h)(8) (2005) **9** n.544
1.199-8(g) (2005) **S9** n.531
1.263A-1(j)(2)(iii) (2020) **S9** n.467
1.280A-1(e)(3) (1980) **9** n.496
1.337(d)-3 (1992) . . . 4.02[7]; **S9** n.640; **19** ns. 30, 67
1.337(d)-3(a) (1992) **9** n.646
1.337(d)-3(c) (1992) **9** n.659
1.337(d)-3(c)(2) (2019) . . . . . . **S9** ns. 649, 650
1.337(d)-3(c)(2)(ii) (2019) **S9** n.650
1.337(d)-3(d)(1) (1992) **9** n.648
1.337(d)-3(d)(3) (1992) **9** n.649
1.337(d)-3(e)(1) (1992) **9** n.657
1.337(d)-3(f)(1) (1992) **9** n.658
1.337(d)-3(f)(2)(ii) (2019) **S9** n.659.10
1.337(d)-3(h) (1992) **9** n.651
1.337(d)-3(h) Ex. 1 (1992) . . . .**9** ns. 643, 650, 657
1.337(d)-3(h) Ex. 1(iii) (1992) . . . . 9.03[1][a][ii][B]; **9** n.652
1.337(d)-3(h) Ex. 2 (1992) **9** n.643
1.337(d)-3(h) Ex. 2(ii) (1992) **9** n.644
1.337(d)-3(h) Ex. 3(ii) (1992) **9** n.645
1.355-3 (2007) **S9** n.699
1.355-3(d)(2) Ex. (8) (2007) **S9** n.697.1
1.355-3(d)(2) Ex. (22) (2007) **S9** n.697.1
1.355-3(d)(2) Ex. (23) (2007) **S9** n.697.1
1.355-3(d)(2) Ex. (24) (2007) **S9** n.697.1
1.355-9 (2016) **S9** n.699
1.362-3(e) (2013) . . . . S18.01[4]
1.362-3(f) Ex. (5) (2013) **S18** n.10.1
1.409A-1(b)(7) (2005) **14** n.202
1.453B-1(c)(1)(i)(B) (2014) **S4** n.66
1.453B-1(c)(1)(ii) (2014)   **S4** n.66; **S13** n.103
1.460-3(b)(3)(ii)(C) (2020) **S9** n.352.1
1.465-1(a) (1979) **11** n.644
1.465-1(d) (1979) **11** n.628; **23** n.35
1.465-2(b) (1979) **11** n.641
1.465-3(a) (1979) **11** n.639
1.465-3(b) (1979) **11** n.640
1.465-5 (1979) **11** n.630
1.465-6 (1979) **11** n.634
1.465-12(b) (1979) **11** n.640
1.465-22(a) (1979) **11** n.654
1.465-22(b)(2) (1979) **11** n.639

Prop. Reg. §

1.465-24(a)(2) (1979) . . . . 11.06[2][b]
1.465-41 (1979) **11** n.646
1.465-41 Ex. (2) (1979) **11** n.640
1.465-66 (1979) **11** n.672
1.465-67 (1979) **11** n.672
1.465-69 (1979) **23** n.42
1.465-69(b) (1979) **23** n.43
1.469-5(e) (2011) . . . . S11.08[6]
1.469-5(e)(3)(i) (2011) **S11** n.818.1
1.469-5(e)(3)(ii) (2011) **S11** n.818.1
1.469-5(e)(4) (2011) **S11** n.818.2
1.514(c)-2(d)(2)(ii) (2016) . . . . . . **S9** ns. 780.1, 788.1
1.514(c)-2(d)(2)(iii) (2016) . . . . . **S9** ns. 780.1, 788.1
1.514(c)-2(e)(1)(vi) (2016) **S9** n.798.1
1.514(c)-2(e)(1)(vii) (2016) **S9** n.798.1
1.514(c)-2(e)(5) Ex. 5 (2016) **S9** n.798.1
1.514(c)-2(f)(4) (2016) **S9** n.800
1.514(c)-2(k)(1)(ii) (2016) **S9** n.806.1
1.514(c)-2(m)(2) Ex. 3(ii) (2016) . . . **S9** n.812.1
1.701-2(e) Ex. (3) (1994) **1** n.89
1.702-1(e) (1970) **9** n.44
1.704-1(b)(1)(ii) (2003) . . . **4** n.16; **11** ns. 162, 176, 357
1.704-1(b)(1)(viii)(b) (2018) **S10** n.349.5; **10A** n.203
1.704-1(b)(1)(viii)(b)(1) (2018) . . . **10A** n.205
1.704-1(b)(1)(viii)(b)(3) (2018) . . . **10A** n.204
1.704-1(b)(1)(viii)(f)(4) (2018) **S10** n.349.7
1.704-1(b)(2)(ii) (1983) **11** n.68
1.704-1(b)(2)(iii) (2005) **11** n.123
1.704-1(b)(2)(iii)(a) (2005) **S11** n.120
1.704-1(b)(2)(iii)(b) (1983) **11** n.92
1.704-1(b)(2)(iii)(a)(2)(ii) (2005)   **11** ns. 134, 135
1.704-1(b)(2)(iii)(f) (2018) . . . 10A.10[2]; **10A** ns. 13, 39, 141, 164, 305
1.704-1(b)(2)(iii)(f)(2) (2018) **S10** n.349.13; **10A** n.221
1.704-1(b)(2)(iii)(f)(4) (2018) . . . . **10A** ns. 210, 224
1.704-1(b)(2)(iv)(b)(1) (2005) **5** n.86
1.704-1(b)(2)(iv)(c)(1) (1983) **11** n.190
1.704-1(b)(2)(iv)(d)(4) (2003) **4** n.24; **11** n.167; **S11** n.170
1.704-1(b)(2)(iv)(f) (2014) **S11** n.176.2
1.704-1(b)(2)(iv)(f)(5)(iii) (2005) . . . . 5.02[3][g][i]; **5** n.88
1.704-1(b)(2)(iv)(f)(5)(v) (2014) **12** n.80
1.704-1(b)(2)(iv)(h)(2) (2003) **11** n.176
1.704-1(b)(2)(iv)(s) (2003) . . . .**4** n.24; 11.02[2][c][ii]; 11.02[4][g]; **11** n.359
1.704-1(b)(2)(iv)(s)(3) (2003) . . . 11.02[2][c][ii]; 11.02[4][g]
1.704-1(b)(2)(iv)(s)(4) (2003) **11** n.179
1.704-1(b)(4)(i) (2005) **5** n.74
1.704-1(b)(4)(ii) (2018) . . . . 10A.06[3][b][ii]
1.704-1(b)(4)(viii)(c)(4)(v) (2016) **S11** n.436.5a

[Text references are to paragraphs; note references are to chapters (boldface numbers) and notes ("n."). References to the supplement are preceded by "S."]

[Text references are to paragraphs; note references are to chapters (boldface numbers) and notes ("n."). References to the supplement are preceded by "S."]

Prop. Reg. §

1.707-2(d) Exs. 3–6 (2015) . . . . S14.02[4][d]
1.707-2(d) Ex. 3(ii) (2015) . . . **S14** ns. 206.10, 206.13
1.707-2(d) Ex. 3(iii) (2015) . . . . **S14** ns. 206.5, 206.11
1.707-2(d) Ex. 3(iv) (2015) **S14** n.206.11
1.707-2(d) Ex. 4(ii) (2015) **S14** n.206.10
1.707-2(d) Ex. 5 (2015) **S14** n.206.13
1.707-2(d) Ex. 5(iii) (2015) **S14** n.206.10
1.707-2(d) Ex. 6 (2015) . . . . . **S14** ns. 206.12, 206.13
1.707-2(d) Ex. 6(iii) (2015) **S14** n.206.10
1.707-3(a)(2) (1991) **14** n.60
1.707-3(d) (1991) **14** n.78
1.707-3(g) Ex. (9) (1991) **14** n.78
1.707-4(d)(2) (2014) **S14** n.93.2
1.707-4(d)(3) (2014) **S14** n.93.1
1.707-5 . . . . **S14** n.104
1.707-5(a)(3) **S14** n.113
1.707-5(a)(8) (2004) **14** n.133
1.707-5(f) (2014) **S14** n.119.1
1.707-6(c)(3) (2004) **14** n.134
1.707-7 (2004) . . . . **16** ns. 52, 60
1.707-7(a)(2)(ii)(A) (2004) . . . **14** ns. 160, 164
1.707-7(a)(2)(ii)(B) (2004) **14** n.161
1.707-7(a)(2)(ii)(C) (2004) **14** n.163
1.707-7(a)(2)(ii)(D) (2004) **14** n.169
1.707-7(a)(2)(ii)(E) (2004) **14** n.162
1.707-7(a)(3)(ii) (2004) **14** n.170
1.707-7(a)(4) (2004) **14** n.171
1.707-7(a)(5) (2004) **14** n.172
1.707-7(a)(6) (2004) **14** n.173
1.707-7(a)(7) (2004) **14** n.174
1.707-7(a)(8) (2004) **14** n.151
1.707-7(b)(1) (2004) **14** n.152; **16** n.53
1.707-7(b)(2) (2004) **14** n.153
1.707-7(b)(2)(iii) (2014) **S14** n.122
1.707-7(c) (2004) **14** n.147
1.707-7(d) (2004) **14** n.147
1.707-7(e) (2004) . . . **14** n.150; **16** ns. 54, 71, 88
1.707-7(f) (2004) **14** n.148
1.707-7(g) (2004) **14** n.149
1.707-7(i) Ex. (3) (2004) . . . . . 14.02[3][b][xi]
1.707-7(j)(1) (2004) . . . . . 14.02[3][b][xi]; **14** n.175
1.707-7(j)(2) (2004) . . . . . . 14.02[3][b][xi]; **14** n.175
1.707-7(j)(3) (2004) . . . . . . 14.02[3][b][xi]; **14** n.175
1.707-7(j)(5) (2004) **14** n.178
1.707-7(j)(6) (2004) . . . . **14** ns. 179, 180
1.707-7(j)(7) (2004) **14** n.181
1.707-7(j)(8) (2004) **14** n.182
1.707-7(l) (2004) **14** n.183
1.707-7(l) Ex. (4) (2004) **14** n.170
1.707-7(l) Ex. (5) (2004) **14** n.170
1.707-7(l) Ex. (6) (2004) . . . **16** ns. 55, 73, 88
1.707-8 (2004) **14** n.168
1.707-8(c) (2004) **14** n.135
1.707-9(a)(4) (2018) **S14** n.98.7

Prop. Reg. §

1.707-9(b) (2004) **14** n.136
1.721-1(b)(1) (1971) **5** n.122
1.721-1(b)(1) (2005) **5** n.59
1.721-1(b)(2) (2005) . . . . **1** n.20; **5** ns. 74, 95, 138
1.721-1(b)(2)(ii) (2005) **5** n.95
1.721-1(b)(3) (2005) . . . . **5** ns. 44, 55, 56, 75
1.721-1(b)(4) (2005) . . . . **5** ns. 67, 90
1.721-2(a) (2003) **4** n.20
1.721-2(b) (2003) **4** n.18
1.721-2(c) (2003) **4** n.19
1.721-2(d) (2003) **4** n.23; **11** n.165
1.721-2(e)(1) (2003) **4** n.22; **11** n.165
1.721-2(f) Ex. (2003) **4** n.24
1.721-2(g) (2003) . . . **4** n.16; **11** ns. 162, 176, 357
1.732-1(c)(2)(iii)–1.732-1(c)(2)(vi) (2014) . . . . **S21** ns. 35.14, 35.17
1.732-3 (2015) **S9** n.643
1.732-3(a) (2015) **S19** n.253
1.732-3(b) (2015) **S19** n.253
1.732-3(c) (2015) **S19** n.259.1
1.732-3(d) (2015) **S19** n.260
1.734-1(a)(2) (2014) **S25** n.43.1
1.734-1(d) (2014) . . . . . **S25** ns. 43.2, 43.4
1.734-1(f) (2014) **S25** n.43.3
1.734-1(f)(1) (2014) . . . . . . **S25** ns. 121, 122.1
1.734-2(c)(1) (2014) . . . . **S25.01[8]
1.734-2(c)(2) (2014) . . . **S11.04[1][b][iv]; S25** n.49.1
1.734-2(c)(3) Ex. 3 (2014) . . . . **S25.01[8]
1.734-2(c)(3) Ex. 4 (2014) . . . . **S25.01[8]
1.737-1(c)(3)(i) (2014) **S19** n.150
1.737-1(c)(3)(ii) (2014) . . . . **S13** ns. 100, 178; **S19** n.183
1.737-2(b) (2007) **S11** n.561.2; **S13** n.178
1.737-2(b)(1)(ii)(A) (2007) **S11** n.561.4
1.737-2(b)(1)(ii)(B) (2007) **S11** n.561.5
1.737-2(b)(1)(ii)(D) (2007) **S11** n.561.7
1.737-2(b)(1)(ii)(E) (2007) **S11** n.561.8
1.737-2(b)(2) (2007) . . . . **S11.04[4][b][vii]
1.743-1(a)(2)(ii) (2014) **24** n.15
1.743-1(a)(2)(iii)(A) (2014) **24** n.16
1.743-1(a)(2)(iii)(B) (2014) **24** n.17
1.743-1(f)(1) (2014) **24** n.147
1.743-1(f)(2) (2014) . . . . . . **24** ns. 96, 149, 153
1.743-1(f)(2) Ex. (2014) **24** n.150
1.743-1(f)(2) Ex. (ii) (2014) **24** n.151
1.743-1(f)(2) Ex. (iii) (2014) **24** n.96
1.743-1(k)(1)(iii)(B) (2014) **24** n.18
1.743-1(k)(2)(iv) (2014) **24** n.18
1.743-1(l) (2014) . . . . **24** ns. 184, 186, 187
1.743-1(l)(1) (2014) . . . . **24** ns. 170, 189
1.743-1(l)(2) Ex. (2014) **24** n.170
1.743-1(m) (2014) **24** n.20
1.743-1(n) (2014) **24** n.25
1.743-1(o) (2014) **24** n.26
1.743-1(p) (2014) **24** n.96
1.751-1(a)(2) (2014) **17** n.35
1.751-1(b)(2) (2014) . . . . . **S21.01[6][h]; S21** n.35.3

*[Text references are to paragraphs; note references are to chapters (boldface numbers)
and notes ("n."). References to the supplement are preceded by "S."]*

Prop. Reg. §

1.751-1(b)(2)(i) (2014) **S21** n.35.2
1.751-1(b)(2)(iv) (2014) **S21** n.35.5
1.751-1(b)(3) (2014) . . . . S21.01[6][h]
1.751-1(b)(3)(i) (2014) . . . . . S21.01[6][c]; **S21**
                                                    n.35.8
1.751-1(b)(3)(ii)(A) (2014) **S21** n.35.10
1.751-1(b)(4)(i) (2014) **S21** n.35.19
1.751-1(b)(4)(ii) (2014) **S21** n.35.20
1.751-1(b)(5) (2014) **S21** n.35.21
1.751-1(g) (2014)   S21.01[6][b]; **S21** n.35.11
1.751-1(g) Ex. 1 (2014) **17** n.35
1.751-1(g) Ex. 4 (2014) . . . . S21.01[6][b];
                        S21.01[6][c]; **S21** ns. 35.6, 35.9
1.751-1(g) Ex. 5 (2014) . . . . S21.01[6][c]; **S21**
                                                    n.35.12
1.751-1(g) Ex. 6 (2014) . . . . S21.01[6][c]
1.751-1(g) Ex. 7 (2014) . . . . S21.01[6][c]
1.751-1(g) Ex. 8 (2014) . . . . S21.01[6][c]
1.751-1(g) Ex. 9 (2014) . . . . S21.01[6][c];
                                                    S21.01[6][d]
1.752-2(a)(2) . . . . **8** ns. 70, 71
1.752-2(f) Ex. 9 . . . . **8** ns. 70, 71
1.752-2(i) . . . . **8** ns. 122, 124
1.752-2(k) (2004) . . . . **11** ns. 82, 342
1.752-2(*l*) (2014) . . . . . **8** ns. 70, 71, 122, 124
1.752-4(b)(1)(iv) (2013) 8.04
1.752-4(b)(2) (2013) **8** n.173
1.752-4(b)(3) (2013) 8.04
1.754-1(b)(1) (2017) **24** n.203
1.755-1(b)(5)(ii) (2014) **24** n.91
1.755-1(b)(5)(iii)(A) (2014) . . . . **24** ns. 92, 93
1.755-1(b)(5)(iii)(B) (2014) **24** n.93
1.755-1(b)(5)(iii)(C) (2014) **24** n.93
1.755-1(b)(5)(iii)(D) (2014) **24** n.94
1.755-1(c)(2)(iii)−1.755-1(c)(2)(vi) (2014) . . .
    . . . . **S21** n.35.13
1.755-1(c)(2)(iii)−1.755-1(c)(2)(v) (2014) . . . .
    . . . . **S21** n.35.16
1.755-1(c)(2)(vi) (2014) . . . . S21.01[6][d]; **S21**
                                        ns. 35.10, 35.16
1.755-1(c)(6) Ex. 2 (2014) **S21** n.35.15
1.755-1(e) (2014) **S19** n.263; **S25** n.68.1
1.755-1(f)(1) (2014) **S19** n.263; **S25** n.68.1
1.761-1(b) (2005) . . . . . . **5** ns. 2, 52, 78, 79
1.761-3 (2003) . . . . 4.01[1][d]; **4** n.17;
    11.02[2][c][ii]; 11.02[4][g]; **11** ns. 163,
                                                    166
1.761-3(b)(1) (2003) **4** n.21; **11** n.164
1.761-3(b)(2) (2003) **4** n.22; **11** n.165
1.761-3(c)(1)(iv) (2003) **S3** n.180.4
1.761-3(e) (2003) . . . **4** n.16; **11** ns. 162, 176,
                                        357, 358; **S11** n.358
1.882-5(c)(5) Ex. (4) (1996) **14** n.284
1.892-5(d)(5) (2011) **S9** n.909.3
1.892-5(d)(5)(ii) (2011) **S9** n.909.5
1.892-5(d)(5)(iii) (2011) **S9** n.909.4
1.905-4(b)(2)(ii) (2019) **10A** n.296
1.951-1(h) (2018) . . . . **S3** n.140.1; S9.01[4][c];
                                        S9.01[4][c][vi]
1.951-1(h)(2) (2019) . . . . S9.01[4][c][vi]
1.954-2(a)(5)(ii)(C) (2006) **9** n.105

Prop. Reg. §

1.954-2(a)(5)(iii) Ex. (2) (2006) **9** n.105
1.956-4(b)(2)(iii) (2016) **S9** n.113.2
1.958-1(d) (2019) . . . . . **S6** n.40.1; S9.01[4][c]
1.958-1(d)(4) (2019) **S9** n.88.7
1.1031(a)-3(a) (2020) . . . . . . **S9** ns. 235, 235.1
1.1031(b)-1(c) (1990) **9** n.266
1.1031(k)-1(g)(7)(iii) (2020) **S9** n.235.1
1.1045-1(a)(1) (2004) **9** n.513
1.1045-1(a)(2)(iii) (2004) **9** n.515
1.1045-1(b)(1) (2004) . . . . **9** ns. 516, 517
1.1045-1(b)(3) (2004) **9** n.518
1.1045-1(c)(1) (2004) **9** n.516
1.1045-1(c)(2) (2004) **9** n.519
1.1045-1(c)(3)(i) (2004) **9** n.519
1.1045-1(c)(3)(ii) (2004) **9** n.520
1.1045-1(d) (2004) **9** n.521
1.1045-1(e) (2004) **9** n.522
1.1045-1(g) Ex. (1) (2004) **9** n.514
1.1045-1(g) Ex. (7) (2004) **9** n.519
1.1061-1−1.1061-6 (2020) . . . . S9.02[1][d][ii]
1.1061-1 (2020) . . . . S9.02[1][d][ii]
1.1061-2 (2020) . . . . S9.02[1][d][ii]
1.1061-3 (2020) . . . . S9.02[1][d][ii];
                                        S9.02[1][d][ii][A]
1.1061-3(b)(2) (2020) **S9** n.271.9
1.1061-3(c)(3)(i) (2020) **S9** n.271.16
1.1061-3(c)(3)(iii)(A) (2020) **S9** n.271.18
1.1061-3(c)(4)(ii) (2020) **S9** n.271.19
1.1061-3(c)(5)(i) (2020) **S9** n.271.17
1.1061-3(c)(5)(ii) (2020) **S9** n.271.20
1.1061-3(c)(5)(iii) (2020) **S9** n.271.20
1.1061-3(c)(6)(ii)(A) (2020) **S9** n.271.22
1.1061-3(c)(6)(ii)(B) (2020) **S9** n.271.23
1.1061-3(c)(6)(ii)(D) (2020) **S9** n.271.24
1.1061-3(c)(7)(v) Ex. 5 (2020) **S9** n.271.25
1.1061-4 (2020) . . . . S9.02[1][d][ii];
                                        S9.02[1][d][ii][C]
1.1061-4(a)(1) (2020) **S9** n.271.27
1.1061-4(a)(2) (2020) **S9** n.271.28
1.1061-4(a)(3) (2020) **S9** n.271.31
1.1061-4(a)(3)(ii) (2020) **S9** n.271.32
1.1061-4(a)(4) (2020) . . . **S9** ns. 271.29, 271.30
1.1061-4(a)(4)(i)(B) (2020) **S9** n.271.26
1.1061-4(a)(4)(i)(C) (2020) **S9** n.271.30
1.1061-4(a)(4)(ii)(C) (2020) **S9** n.271.26
1.1061-4(b)(1) (2020) **S9** n.271.41
1.1061-4(b)(2) (2020) **S9** n.271.40
1.1061-4(b)(3) (2020) **S9** n.271.34
1.1061-4(b)(4) (2020) **S9** n.271.31
1.1061-4(b)(5) (2020) **S9** n.271.31
1.1061-4(b)(6) (2020) . . . . . . S9.02[1][d][ii][B]
1.1061-4(b)(6)(i)−1.1061-4(b)(6)(iv) (2020) . . .
    . . . . **S9** n.271.35
1.1061-4(b)(7)(ii) (2020) **S9** n.271.42
1.1061-4(b)(7)(iii)(A) (2020) **S9** n.271.43
1.1061-4(b)(7)(iii)(C) (2020) **S9** n.271.44
1.1061-4(b)(9) (2020) . . . S9.02[1][d][ii][B]; **S9**
                                                    n.271.37
1.1061-4(b)(9)(ii)(C) (2020) **S9** n.271.38
1.1061-4(c)(2)(i) (2020) **S9** n.271.39
1.1061-4(c)(2)(ii) (2020) **S9** n.271.39

[Text references are to paragraphs; note references are to chapters (boldface numbers) and notes ("n."). References to the supplement are preceded by "S."]

Cumulative Table of Revenue Rulings, Revenue Procedures, and Other IRS Releases

[Text references are to paragraphs; note references are to chapters (boldface numbers) and notes ("n."). References to the supplement are preceded by "S."]

REVENUE RULINGS

[Text references are to paragraphs; note references are to chapters (boldface numbers) and notes ("n."). References to the supplement are preceded by "S."]

Rev. Rul.

67-65	**9** n.257; **13** n.156; **16** ns. 19, 170; **18** n.66; **20** n.2
67-105	**14** n.308
67-158	**9** n.329; **11** ns. 98, 364; **14** ns. 8, 214, 215
67-188	**9** n.68
67-192	**18** n.8
67-406	**6** n.3; **9** n.330; **17** ns. 8, 9
67-466	**9** n.330
68-13	**16** ns. 186, 189; **17** ns. 167, 168, 173
68-48	**13** n.22
68-55	**18** n.8
68-79	**4** n.29; **9** ns. 22, 68; **S9** n.271.4a
68-139	**11** n.411
68-196	**15** n.70
68-215	**23** n.22
68-289	**13** ns. 160, 163
68-344	**3** ns. 160, 392
68-370	**9** n.53
68-629	**4** ns. 88, 138; **6** n.16; **19** n.110
69-24	**13** n.121
69-31	**5** n.109
69-40	**9** n.910
69-77	**7** n.169
69-144	**14** n.201
69-156	**4** n.84
69-172	**16** n.109; **19** n.40
69-180	**14** ns. 231, 236
69-184	**14** ns. 201, 258; **S14** n.258
69-493	**14** n.201
69-630	**11** n.456
70-45	**4** n.79
70-140	**16** n.145
70-144	**9** ns. 228, 257
70-239	**18** ns. 36, 49
70-409	**19**.02[5][b]; **19** n.66
70-411	**14**.02[4][b]; **14** n.200
70-430	**16** ns. 189, 289
70-626	**16** n.214
71-141	**9** ns. 30, 595, 664
71-271	**23** n.22
71-278	**9**.01[3][b]
71-301	**9**.02[2][a][ii][B]; **9** ns. 295, 300
71-455	**9** ns. 346, 719
71-502	**14** n.201
71-507	**23** n.23
71-564	**4** ns. 78, 84
72-73	**9** n.602
72-135	**7**.05[1]; **7** ns. 162–164
72-172	**16**.03[1]; **16** ns. 135, 312; **17** n.156; **18**.02[4]; **18** ns. 35, 36
72-320	**18** ns. 69, 78
72-350	**7** ns. 162, 164
72-352	**12** ns. 13, 18
72-504	**14** ns. 21, 37
73-24	**9** n.1152
73-300	**21** n.41
73-301	**6** ns. 31, 70; **7**.03[1]; **7**.03[2]; **7** ns. 44, 59; **11** ns. 460, 617, 618; **19** ns. 35, 53, 77, 87
73-360	**9** n.347

Rev. Rul.

73-391	**11** n.18
73-436	**16** n.190
73-437	**16** n.190
73-438	**16** n.190
74-40	**16** n.258
74-71	**9** n.51; **23** n.28
74-197	**9** n.770
74-231	**9** ns. 50, 330
75-19	**3**.07[3]; **3** n.379; **9** n.674
75-23	**9** n.825
75-43	**3** n.171
75-62	**16** n.290
75-86	**9** ns. 332, 341
75-113	**9** n.4; **16**.02[3][d]; **16** n.108; **19**.02[2]; **19** n.39; **26** n.28
75-154	**13** n.142; **22** n.112
75-194	**16**.05[2][b]; **16** ns. 214, 216, 235
75-214	**4** n.213; **14** n.236
75-245	**9** n.677; **16** n.301
75-291	**19** n.45
75-292	**9** n.268; **19** n.45
75-365	**23** n.117
75-367	**23** n.117
75-374	**3**.05[5]; **3** ns. 226, 228, 250
75-423	**13** n.34
75-451	**6** n.42
75-458	**11** ns. 175, 365; **S11** n.179.2
75-498	**14** n.245
75-523	**9** ns. 34, 466
75-525	**9** ns. 598, 601
76-83	**16** n.217
76-110	**16** n.186
76-163	**9** ns. 332, 341
76-189	**19** n.96
76-483	**16** ns. 176, 191, 192
76-528	**9** n.696; **19** n.137
77-37	**11** n.591
77-83	**11** n.456
77-110	**7** ns. 170, 188
77-137	**12** n.28; **24** n.64
77-176	**3** n.160
77-220	**1** n.149
77-257	**9** n.4
77-264	**9** n.630; **S9** n.629
77-304	**9** n.498
77-309	**8** n.120
77-311	**12** n.75
77-320	**9** n.399
77-321	**16**.03[1]; **16** ns. 143, 145
77-332	**24** n.65
77-337	**9** n.268; **19** n.45
77-398	**11** n.630
77-401	**4** n.139; **11** n.626
77-402	**13** n.54
77-403	**16** n.319
77-412	**21** ns. 146, 148
77-458	**13** ns. 160, 174
78-2	**24** n.183
78-22	**9** n.399
78-64	**9** n.327
78-135	**16** n.201

[Text references are to paragraphs; note references are to chapters (boldface numbers) and notes ("n."). References to the supplement are preceded by "S."]

Rev. Rul.

78-142 .... 3.05[3]; **3** ns. 146, 155, 202, 208
78-164 . . . . **16** n.253
78-175 . . . . **11** n.630
78-179 . . . . **9** n.949
78-268 . . . . **9** n.591; **S9** n.591.7
78-280 . . . . **4** n.114
78-306 . . . . **9** ns. 327, 330
78-321 . . . . **9** n.717
78-413 . . . . **11** n.630
79-20 . . . . **9** n.636
79-34 . . . . **9** n.608
79-51 . . . . **17** ns. 62, 68
79-84 . . . . **24** n.59
79-92 . . . . **9** n.163
79-124 . . . . **24** ns. 67, 70
79-127 . . . . **18** n.21
79-156 . . . . **9** n.711
79-205 . . . . **7** ns. 11, 27; **19** n.78
79-222 . . . . **9** ns. 345, 767
79-250 . . . . **1** n.84
79-288 . . . . **4** n.79
79-300 . . . . **9** n.412
79-301 . . . . 19.02[1]
80-96 . . . . **5** n.158
80-189 . . . . **4** n.156
80-198 . . . **4** n.102; **16** n.274; **18** ns. 13, 15, 25
80-219 . . . . **4** n.176; **9** n.591; **S9** n.591.7
80-234 . . . . **14** n.228
80-235 . . . . **4** ns. 88, 138; **6** n.15
80-323 . . . . **16** n.268
80-338 . . . . **9** n.130
81-38 . . . **12** n.8; **13** ns. 46, 73, 76; **16** ns. 267, 271; **S16** n.271
81-105 . . . . **9** n.53
81-150 . . . . **4** n.228; **9** n.416; **S9** n.416
81-153 . . . . **4** n.226
81-241 . . . **6** n.31; **7** n.59; **19** n.86; **21** n.41
81-242 . . . . . **6** n.31; 9.02[1][c][iii]; **9** ns. 231, 245, 249; 19.03[1]; **19** ns. 80, 81, 87
81-270 . . . . **9** n.1140
81-278 . . . . **4** n.137; **7** ns. 170, 188
81-300 . . . . S9.02[3][c][i][A]; **S9** n.375.2; 14.01[2]; **14** ns. 11, 15, 17, 187, 194, 217
81-301 . . . . **14** ns. 13, 184
82-61 . . . . **3** n.391
82-107 . . . . **18** n.73
82-150 . . . . **S3** n.180.8
82-213 . . . . **3** n.406; **24** n.173
82-225 . . . . **11** n.630
83-52 . . . . **13** n.127
83-129 . . . . **3** ns. 402, 411
83-147 . . . . 23.06[2]; **23** n.79
83-148 . . . . 23.06[2]; **23** n.80
83-155 . . . . **13** n.142; **18** n.26; **22** n.113
83-156 . . . **3** ns. 369, 378, 380; 9.03[1][a][viii]; **9** ns. 674, 692, 701; 18.01; **18** n.2
84-15 . . . . **4** n.147; **7** ns. 21, 27
84-52 . . . **9** n.255; **S9** n.255; **12** n.9; **13** ns. 36, 37; 16.04[2][b]; **16** ns. 204, 205, 208; **S16** n.206; **19** n.25

Rev. Rul.

84-53 . . . **4** ns. 9, 29, 30; **6** ns. 5, 6; 16.01[1]; **16** ns. 1, 6; **19** n.50
84-102 . . . **4** n.148; 21.02[2]; **21** ns. 43, 44, 103
84-111 . . . 16.03[3]; **16** ns. 146, 167, 172, 267; 18.03[1]; 18.03[10]; **18** ns. 7, 36, 50, 64, 83; **19** n.189
84-115 . . . . **4** n.102; **16** n.284
84-131 . . . . **9** ns. 46, 362
84-142 . . . . **9** n.165
84-158 . . . . **9** n.825
85-6 . . . . **13** n.127
85-32 . . . . **4** n.226; **13** n.144; **S13** n.144
85-60 . . . . **9** ns. 825, 828; **S9** n.828
85-61 . . . . **9** n.825
85-87 . . . . **S3** ns. 180.8, 180.9
85-134 . . . . **9** n.630; **S9** n.629
85-164 . . . . **4** ns. 9, 28; **18** n.8
85-179 . . . . **4** n.181; **13** n.111
86-23 . . . . **4** n.179
86-73 . . . . **13** n.104; **24** n.226; **26** n.3
86-101 . . . . **12** n.9
86-116 . . . . **4** n.179
86-138 . . . . **9** n.40
87-9 . . . . **4** n.238
87-50 . . . . 13.03[1][c]; **13** ns. 43, 115
87-51 . . . . 13.03[1][c]; **13** n.44
87-57 . . . . **9** n.945
87-110 . . . . **12** n.7; **13** n.47
87-111 . . . **4** ns. 216, 217; **13** ns. 145, 146, 148; **S13** n.149.2
87-115 . . . **6** n.58; **9** n.315; 24.09; **24** ns. 170, 183, 186, 188–190; **25** n.115
87-120 . . . . **7** ns. 27, 32; **19** n.78
88-4 . . . . **4** n.225
88-32 . . . . **4** n.249
88-42 . . . . **26** n.36
88-66 . . . . 9.03[1][a][iii]; **9** ns. 668, 670
88-77 . . . . 7.03[2]; 7.03[3]; **7** ns. 51, 54, 58
89-7 . . . . **9** ns. 388, 393
89-11 . . . . **4** n.216
89-17 . . . . **9** ns. 842, 845
89-33 . . . . **9** n.846
89-72 . . . . **9** ns. 41, 92
89-85 . . . . **16** n.136
89-87 . . . . **13** ns. 92, 120, 122, 123
89-108 . . . **16** ns. 138, 199; 17.05[1]; **17** n.164
90-17 . . . . **13** ns. 160, 165
90-27 . . . . . **S3.02[3]; 3.05[3]; **3** ns. 146, 155, 203; **S3** ns. 0.12, 68.8, 78.4
90-31 . . . . 17.03[3][f]; **17** n.114; **21** n.132
90-38 . . . . **11** n.487; **S11** n.487
90-60 . . . . **13** n.112
90-80 . . . . **9** n.827
90-112 . . . . **9** ns. 112, 200; **16** n.136
91-26 . . . . . **2** ns. 78, 79, 81; **14** ns. 266, 269
91-32 . . . . 9.03[4][a]; S9.03[4][a]; **9** ns. 829– 831; **S9** ns. 825, 829; **16** n.136
91-47 . . . . **14** n.144
92-15 . . . **13** n.40; **24** ns. 185, 186, 192; 25.07; 25.07[1]; **S25.07[1]; **25** ns. 114, 117– 119, 121, 126, 127; **S25** n.122.1

[Text references are to paragraphs; note references are to chapters (boldface numbers) and notes ("n."). References to the supplement are preceded by "S."]

Rev. Rul.

92-17 . . . . **9** n.697
92-27 . . . . 19.03[2]; **19** n.88.1
92-49 . . . . 3.05[4][a]; **3** n.215
92-97 . . . . 6.02[5]; **6** n.71; 9.02[2][a][ii][B]; **9** ns. 294, 297, 298; **11** ns. 58, 221; **19** ns. 81, 160
93-7 . . . . 19.02[5][b]; 19.02[5][c]; 19.02[5][d]; **19** ns. 56, 57, 59, 60, 68
93-13 . . . . 25.02[8]; **25** n.94
93-26 . . . . **9** n.716
93-80 . . . . **12** n.19; S16.06[2]; 16.06[3]; S16.06[3]; **16** ns. 256, 259; **S16** ns. 256.1, 256.3
93-90 . . . . **11** n.316
94-4 . . . 6.02[5]; **6** n.72; 9.02[1][b]; **9** ns. 232, 248; 19.03[2]; **19** ns. 81, 88.2, 160
94-40 . . . . 9.03[5]; 9.03[6]; **9** ns. 916, 921
94-40A . . . . **9** ns. 916, 921
94-43 . . . . **1** n.149; **3** n.378
94-71 . . . . **9** n.921
95-5 . . . . **11** n.757; **19** n.97
95-21 . . . . **9** ns. 295, 301
95-26 . . . . 7.03[2]; **7** ns. 56, 59; **S7** n.60
95-37 . . . . **13** ns. 1, 37; **16** n.206
95-41 . . . 8.03[3][a]; **8** ns. 135, 136, 140–143, 145, 150, 154
95-45 . . . . **7** n.57
95-55 . . . . **13** ns. 1, 37
95-69 . . . . 9.03[1][a][v]
95-71 . . . . **16** n.109
95-74 . . . . **7** n.73
96-10 . . . . **6** ns. 30, 43
96-11 . . **6** n.44; **S6** n.44; **10** n.110; S11.05[1]; **11** n.604; **S11** n.596.2
97-38 . . . . . 11.02[2][a][ii]; 11.02[2][a][ii][A]; 11.02[2][a][ii][B]; **11** ns. 60, 61
98-15 . . . . **9** n.817
98-37 . . . . **3** n.379; **9** n.674
99-5 . . . **3** n.352; **4** ns. 59, 61; **S4** ns. 51.5, 59; S9.01[4][c][vii]; S9.02[3][c][i][B]; **S11** n.541; 14.02[3][a]; S14.02[3][b][i]; **14** n.45; **S14** ns. 63.2–63.4; **S19** ns. 173.1, 234
99-6 . . . . **3** n.353; **9** ns. 228, 257, 258; **13** n.156; 16.02[3][b]; 16.02[3][e]; **16** ns. 19, 78, 83, 86, 116, 169; **S16** n.86; **18** n.66; **20** n.2; **S24** n.157.1
99-43 . . . . 11.02[2][b][i]; **11** ns. 93, 96
99-57 . . . . 1.02[4]; **1** ns. 44, 206; 4.01[1][c]; **4** ns. 12, 13; **6** n.50; 9.01[4][b]; 9.03[1][a][ix]; **9** ns. 79, 704; **11** n.466
2000-18 . . . . 4.05[10]; **4** n.209
2000-44 . . . . **14** ns. 95, 99, 100
2002-49 . . . . **9** n.699
2003-56 . . . . . . 9.02[1][c][iii]; **9** n.247; **19** n.83
2003-69 . . . . **10** n.18
2003-125 . . . . **3** n.356
2004-3 . . . . **9** n.827
2004-5 . . . . **9** n.26
2004-41 . . . . 9.01[10]; **9** n.216

Rev. Rul.

2004-43 . . . . 11.04[4][b][vii]; S11.04[4][b][vii]; **11** n.556; **13** n.178
2004-49 . . . . 11.04[3][f]; **11** n.535
2004-51 . . . . 9.03[3][e]; **9** n.819
2004-59 . . . . 18.03[1]; **18** n.51
2004-88 . . . . **10** ns. 8, 19, 32; **S10** n.17.1
2005-10 . . . **11** n.557; **S11** n.557; **13** n.178; **S13** n.178
2006-11 . . . . **S10** n.87.4
2007-30 . . . . S9.02[3][w]; **S9** n.545.1
2007-40 . . . . **S14** n.247.1
2007-42 . . . . **S9** ns. 697.1, 697.2
2008-12 . . . . **S9** n.363
2008-38 . . . . **S9** n.363
2008-39 . . . . **S9** ns. 68, 129; **S14** n.31
2009-15 . . . . **S18** n.71.1
2020-12 . . . . **10A** n.320

REVENUE PROCEDURES

Rev. Proc.

72-18 . . . . **9** ns. 58, 491
72-51 . . . . **9** n.934
75-21 . . . . 9.06[2][a]; **9** n.1103
77-1 . . . . **4** n.232
83-8 . . . . **10** n.2
84-35 . . . . 9.06[1][a]; **9** n.1058; **S9** n.1058
84-74 . . . . **9** ns. 144, 625, 629, 630
87-32 . . . . **9** n.962
87-35 . . . . **11** n.28
89-12 . . . . **3** n.172
89-31 . . . . **9** ns. 848, 865, 890, 891
92-66 . . . . **9** n.865
92-92 . . . . **9** n.288
93-27 . . . . **S3** ns. 78.1, 146.1; 5.02[1]; 5.02[2]; 5.02[3]; 5.02[3][e]; 5.02[5]; **5** ns. 1, 2, 5, 21, 23, 41–43, 45, 46, 48, 52, 53, 60, 62, 102, 123; **S9** n.271.1; S14.02[4][d]; **S14** n.206.1
94-46 . . . . **13** n.60
94-71 . . . . **9** n.916
94-75 . . . . **11** n.489
96-3 . . . . **4** n.231; **18** n.9
97-37 . . . . **13** ns. 89, 94
98-48 . . . . 9.02[3][u]; **9** n.511; **S9** n.511
2000-3 . . . . **4** n.231; **18** n.9
2001-3 . . . . **4** n.231
2001-28 . . . . **9** n.1103
2001-36 . . . . **11** n.487
2001-43 . . . 5.02[2]; 5.02[3]; 5.02[5]; **5** ns. 1, 2, 22, 23, 42, 47, 49, 52, 54, 102, 124; **S9** n.271.1
2002-15 . . . . 3.06[5][b]; **3** n.335
2002-16 . . . . **9** n.1006
2002-22 . . . 3.05[5]; **3** ns. 234, 235, 237, 238, 240–248, 250, 251, 253–257; **S3** n.258; **9** n.262
2002-38 . . . . **9** ns. 934, 947
2002-39 . . . . **9** ns. 934, 961

[Text references are to paragraphs; note references are to chapters (boldface numbers) and notes ("n."). References to the supplement are preceded by "S."]

Rev. Proc.

2002-68	**9** ns. 1001, 1003–1005
2003-3	**11** n.487
2003-32	**9** n.919
2003-64	**9** n.847; **S9** n.847
2003-65	9.03[5]; **9** n.917
2003-79	**9** n.934
2003-84	S3.02[3]; 3.02[4]; S3.02[4]; S3.04[3][a]; 3.05[3]; **3** ns. 86, 155, 205; **S3** ns. 0.11, 68.8, 78.4, 86, 88.1, 139.11, 205; **S9.**04[4]; **9** ns. 1001–1005
2004-21	**9** n.847
2004-66	**9** ns. 1092–1094
2004-67	9.06[2][a]; **9** n.1099
2005-3	**18** n.9
2005-20	**9** n.919
2006-3	**3** n.349; **15** n.14
2007-59	**S11** n.531
2007-65	**S3** ns. 35.1, 68.10; **S11** n.240.2
2009-37	**S4.**02[3]; **S4** n.110.28
2009-41	**S3** n.335
2010-32	**S3** n.343.11
2011-14	**S4** n.205; **S9** ns. 142, 625, 629, 630
2012-3	**S3** n.349
2012-28	**S3** n.449
2014-12	**S3** ns. 68.9, 68.11
2014-20	**S9** n.287
2014-47	**S9** n.847
2017-21	**S9** n.847
2019-3	**S3** n.349; **S11** n.487
2019-32	**10A** n.3
2020-23	**S9.**06[1][a]; **S9** n.1055.1; **10A** n.3
2020-50	**S24** n.157.1

PRIVATE LETTER RULINGS (Including TECHNICAL ADVICE MEMORANDA (TAM))

Priv. Ltr. Rul.

7107280880A	**13** n.160
7210270270A	**13** n.160
7730023	**16** n.144
7730029	**16** n.144
7743024	**9** n.233; **16** n.111; **19** n.47
7747002	**9** n.327
7747047	**18** n.7
7802043	**16** n.144
7803060	**9** n.233; **19** n.47
7804037	**11** n.643
7804038	**11** n.643
7804074	**16** n.144
7804118	**9** n.180
7806068	**14** n.237
7806070	**16** n.302
7808003	**9** ns. 62, 504
7808071	**22** n.12
7811008	**16** n.253

Priv. Ltr. Rul.

7813001	**14** ns. 187, 216
7813028	**16** n.111; **19** n.44
7814026	**22** n.107
7816073	**14** n.42
7823013	**21** ns. 21, 83, 84
7824062	**20** ns. 7, 22
7826096	**3** ns. 160, 229
7832007	**3** n.230; **9** n.226
7835016	**11** n.643; **14** n.237
7846031	**9** n.591; **S9** n.591.7
7901005	**13** ns. 89, 94
7902086	**12** n.30; **16** n.271; **S16** n.271
7903084	**1** n.143; **3** ns. 162, 229
7905032	**9** n.608
7905126	**11** n.371
7907001	**14** n.31; **S14** n.31
7913012	**13** n.97
7919065	**3** ns. 160, 230
7922083	**16** n.2
7924031	**19** n.136
7927062	**16** n.302
7933079	**9** n.257
7934096	**3** ns. 369, 380
7935005	**11** n.455
7938046	**3** n.402; **9** n.179
7938092	**16** n.217
7939005	**14** n.215
7941034	**19** n.136
7942094	**11** n.455
7948087	**9** n.231
7950002	**4** n.121
7951006	**3** ns. 229, 230
7951133	**16** n.302
7952057	**13** n.63
7952159	**12** ns. 15, 17
8002111	**3** n.230
8003010	**9** n.952
8006009	**14** n.32
8006092	**9** n.233
8007019	**13** n.89
8011040	**9** n.591; **S9** n.591.7
8015044	**9** n.226
8017007	**9** n.422
8017008	**9** n.422
8017013	**9** ns. 44, 925
8022005	**9** n.593
8022010	**9** ns. 4, 660
8026001	**3** n.39
8026071	**13** n.97
8030015	**15** n.32
8030064	**11** n.371
8032053	**22** n.17
8032119	**19** n.136
8035080	**13** n.163
8037024	**9** n.422
8038037	**4** n.119
8041035	**14** n.301
8041061	**9** n.233; **19** n.47
8042011	**3** n.409
8043098	**9** n.710
8044023	**9** n.767

[Text references are to paragraphs; note references are to chapters (boldface numbers) and notes ("n."). References to the supplement are preceded by "S."]

[Text references are to paragraphs; note references are to chapters (boldface numbers) and notes ("n."). References to the supplement are preceded by "S."]

Priv. Ltr. Rul.

9010027	13 n.37
9010042	18 n.69
9012024	4 n.247
9012063	23 n.70
9015016	13 n.193
9018005	4 n.108
9022044	9 n.733
9024056	4 n.108
9029019	13 ns. 37, 193
9029034	9 n.815
9032001	4 n.121
9034058	9 n.719
9035005	11 n.669
9035040	14 n.54; 21 n.146
9036013	11 n.645
9037027	16 n.43
9045053	4 n.249
9045064	4 n.249
9102018	23 n.16
9105015	3 n.453; S3 n.453
9105029	9 n.769
9106037	4 n.3; 9 ns. 702, 703; 18 n.3
9108015	13 n.193
9108025	1 n.143; 3 n.163
9109036	11 n.28
9110003	9 n.610
9118005	9 n.226
9122006	9 n.920
9124023	9 n.195
9130039	3 n.415; 9 n.920
9134003	14 n.197
9138043	18 n.7
9141041	3 n.164
9142026	3 n.37
9142032	9 n.830
9148041	13 n.70
9149008	11 n.251
9203008	9 n.920
9207027	11 ns. 50, 111
9209009	13 n.47
9214011	3 ns. 409, 410
9215043	4 n.108
9218003	10 n.80
9219002	14 n.187
9219003	11 n.440
9220043	9 n.718
9221006	9 n.922
9222040	23 n.126
9223028	23 n.117
9232022	26 ns. 3, 36
9233036	9 n.920
9233040	9 n.920
9235023	3 n.415; 9 n.920
9236042	9 n.700
9247003	11 n.727
9250031	13 n.52
9251003	11 n.708
9309021	6 n.30; 23 n.70
9309040	9 n.60
9310019	4 n.247
9311002	9.06[4]; 9 n.1133

Priv. Ltr. Rul.

9316003	9 ns. 14, 128; S9 n.14
9318029	9 n.920
9318031	9 n.920
9319044	9 ns. 769, 817; 14 n.72
9320004	14 n.20
9321047	13 n.37
9323030	9 n.769
9323035	9 n.816
9327011	11 n.169; S11 n.173
9327068	24 n.183
9328010	23 n.69
9328012	23 n.69
9328035	4 n.247
9329001	4 n.87
9330001	9 ns. 14, 128; S9 n.14
9330004	9 ns. 14, 128; S9 n.14
9330022	13 n.49
9330036	4 n.230
9332026	13 ns. 31, 45, 63
9332027	10 n.32
9335012	13 n.193
9338004	24 n.183
9338005	24 n.183
9338006	24 n.183
9338028	3 n.453; S3 n.453
9339014	3 n.453; S3 n.453
9340036	14 ns. 87, 103
9342022	9 n.769
9345047	4 n.250
9345057	9 n.817
9347016	23 n.70
9350013	9 n.149; 13 n.37
9350035	13 n.193; 14 n.122
9402013	9 n.168
9404021	4 n.56
9407022	9 n.817
9407030	9 n.149
9410039	23 n.70
9411006	9 n.719
9411034	9 n.719
9412030	9 n.149
9414004	3 n.398
9416024	14 n.90
9419015	18 n.26
9421022	18 n.69
9426006	9 ns. 291, 314, 315
9426037	13 n.37
9436032	13 n.13
9437007	13 n.193
9440017	13 n.63
9444004	14 ns. 93, 96, 103
9444013	4 n.193
9450012	13 n.13
9501007	4 n.221; S4 n.221
9501033	9 n.149
9504001	3 n.402
9507020	9.03[3][d]; 9 n.813
9508001	9 n.171
9510002	19 n.37
9514008	9 n.130
9525043	9 n.920; 16 n.290

[Text references are to paragraphs; note references are to chapters (boldface numbers) and notes ("n."). References to the supplement are preceded by "S."]

Priv. Ltr. Rul.	
9529037	**13** n.63
9534024	**9** n.719
9540034	**11** ns. 86, 102, 106, 203, 484
9606032	**4** n.108
9607005	**4** n.247
9607013	**3** n.196
9608011	**11** n.487
9609039	**9** n.719
9612017	**9** n.830
9616015	**11** n.466
9619002	**9** n.295
9619037	**11** n.529
9622014	**16** n.226
9623024	**23** n.79
9623028	**4** n.108
9640022	**19** n.130
9644003	**9** n.676
9644027	**S4** n.211.1
9644059	**3** ns. 369, 380
9645005	**16** n.107
9649007	**22** n.109
9651001	**9** n.770; **16** n.136
9701044	**3** n.420
9715008	**16** n.59
9722005	**9** n.1019
9734003	**26** n.39
9741010	**11** n.529
9743006	**3** n.449; **S3** n.449
9801016	**13** n.156
9801028	**9** n.580
9801057	**11** n.541; **19** n.234
9805017	**13** n.63
9807013	**3** n.321
9811022	**4** ns. 240, 249
9821015	**11** ns. 487, 529
9821017	**11** n.529
9821018	**11** n.529
9821051	**12** n.81
9822002	**9** n.704; **14** n.50
9822003	**1** n.44; **4** n.14
9822012	**9** n.523
9829016	**11** n.489
9829027	**14** n.93
9829045	**11** n.489
9829052	**3** n.414
9830018	**11** n.240
9831028	**4** n.230
9839002	**3** n.334
9840026	**9** n.303
9843035	**3** n.427
9844004	**3** n.427
9845012	**17** ns. 71, 135
9846005	**9** n.171
9846018	**3** n.334
9848033	**17** n.71
9851012	**11** n.529
9851020	**11** n.529
9853013	**19** n.136
9904027	**11** n.244
9906028	**11** n.244
9909025	**11** n.529

Priv. Ltr. Rul.	
9936019	**11** n.529
9936020	**11** n.529
9936021	**11** n.529
199901028	**4** n.250
199903013	**17** n.71
199903017	**11** n.679
199906025	**11** n.679
199907029	**9** ns. 226, 237
199908043	**13** n.190
199908057	**3** n.334
199909045	**4** ns. 243, 249
199910029	**17** n.71
199910033	**17** ns. 71, 135
199910056	**17** n.71
199915040	**4** n.85
199917049	**4** n.249; **19** n.239
199917050	**4** n.249; **19** n.239
199917051	**4** n.249; **19** n.239
199922014	**3**.05[1]; **3** n.189
199926032	**4** n.243; **19** n.239
199935065	**13** n.38
199943005	**4** n.133; **7** n.21.1
199943006	**4** n.133; **7** n.21.1
199943007	**7** n.21.1
200004036	**14** n.76
200006008	**4** n.250
200011022	**3** n.334
200012050	**3** n.334
200012072	**3** n.334
200014007	**9** n.287
200019020	**4** n.3
200021034	**9** n.555; **S9** n.555
200023036	**3** n.432
200033030	**13** n.112
200041005	**S11** n.487
200044040	**9** n.769
200046023	**9** n.555; **S9** n.555
200049031	**13** n.160
200050032	**8** n.10
200103032	**3** n.298
200111038	**23** n.79
200120020	**8** n.147
200123035	**4** n.203; **S4** n.211.9
200131014	**9** n.271; **S9** n.271
200133030	**14** n.317
200137038	**9** ns. 19, 713
200139005	**9** n.817
200142004	**9** n.608
200210047	**11** n.529
200211017	**4** n.244
200214016	**4** n.3
200222026	**19** n.117
200223036	**19** n.217
200224014	**9** n.804
200244013	**9** n.923
200301004	**14** n.144
200305025	**3** n.390
200310014	**9** ns. 911, 913
200313007	**9** n.207
200317011	**4** n.249
200322017	**9** n.250

[Text references are to paragraphs; note references are to chapters (boldface numbers) and notes ("n."). References to the supplement are preceded by "S."]

Priv. Ltr. Rul.

200327003	3 ns. 236, 253, 258; **S3** n.236
200332002	**3** n.431
200334037	**S16** n.79
200337005	**14** n.144
200340024	**8** n.147
200345007	**13** n.36; **16** n.206
200351032	**9** n.804
200403056	**9** n.608
200405026	**3** n.390
200411018	**3** n.449; **S3** n.449
200411044	**9** n.769
200414013	**13** n.37; **16** n.206
200420012	**9** n.827
200436011	**8** n.152; **11** ns. 259, 292; **14** n.112
200438029	**11** n.487
200445015	**13** n.112
200521002	**9** n.270; **S9** n.270
200530013	**11** n.484
200538005	**13** n.37; **16** n.206
200550039	**13** n.126
200606009	**4** n.3
200614002	**9** n.361
200626003	**24** n.216
200627013	**S19** n.239
200631014	**S11** n.555; **S13** n.178
200633019	**S11** n.530
200651023	**S19** n.227
200651030	**S9** n.271
200701030	**S9** n.207.2
200701032	**S3** n.26
200737006	**S16** n.79
200737013	**S16** n.79
200740010	**S3** n.453
200752002	**S9** n.743.1
200806002	**S13** n.98
200806003	**S13** n.98
200806004	**S13** n.98
200807005	**S9** n.254.2; **S16** n.86
200807015	**S1** n.87
200808013	**S13** n.98
200808014	**S13** n.98
200811019	**S9** n.825
200812012	**S9** n.271; **S13** n.93
200816029	**S9** n.549
200821021	**S3** n.453
200824005	**S11** n.541; **S19** ns. 173.1, 234
200824009	**S11** n.541; **S19** ns. 173.1, 234
200832024	**S3** n.153.1
200840018	**23** n.111
200841017	**S3** n.449
200845035	**S3** n.453
200848018	**S3** n.453
200851023	**S9** n.836
200852005	**S3** n.427
200919019	**S3** n.449
200921009	**S13** n.190
200921010	**S3** n.453
200927002	**S3** n.453
200931042	**S4** n.249
200939016	**S3** n.453

Priv. Ltr. Rul.

201005018	**S3** n.453
201027003	**S3** n.453
201027041	**S9** n.828
201028016	**S11** n.529
201028017	**S11** n.529
201032003	**S11** n.529
201043024	**S3** n.453
201103018	**S14** n.105
201129028	**S3** n.453
201206004	**S3** n.453
201208021	**S3** n.449
201213004	**S3** n.432
201241004	**S3** n.453
201244004	**S13** n.13
201305006	**S3** ns. 3, 99
201314004	**S19** n.53
201314005	**S9** n.347
201314025	**S3** n.445
201314029	**S3** n.453
201314038	**S3** n.453
201315008	**S3** n.449
201315015	**S3** n.453
201322024	**S3** n.453
201322034	**S3** n.453
201324002	**S3** n.453
201414002	**S3** n.453
201414004	**S3** n.453
201416003	**S3** n.453
201417005	**S3** n.453
201505001	**S16** n.86
201527039	**S3** n.420
201528007	**S16** n.79
201537002	**S19** n.180
201541008	**S3** n.453
201545002	**S3** n.453
201547003	**S4** n.241
201548013	**S3** n.453
201549013	**S3** n.451
201622008	**S3** n.258
201633028	**S4** n.241
201643016	**S13** ns. 183, 214
201710019	**S3** n.432
201929019	**S9** n.633.3f; **S13** ns. 183.2, 183.5
202016013	**S4** n.240
202017008	**S3** n.432

ACTIONS ON DECISION

AOD

2010-02	**S11** n.818

ANNOUNCEMENTS

Ann.

89-33	**9** n.633
92-70	**9** n.816

[Text references are to paragraphs; note references are to chapters (boldface numbers) and notes ("n."). References to the supplement are preceded by "S."]

Ann.

94-5	**9** n.972
94-87	**1** n.68
95-8	**1** ns. 54, 58, 79
97-5	**3** n.333
2000-101	**9** n.1053
2001-75	**9** n.1053
2003-2	**S10** n.89.3
2005-11	**14** ns. 96, 146
2007-112	**S3** ns. 35.1, 68.10
2008-65	**S9** n.363
2009-4	**S14** ns. 63.1, 132, 147
2009-69	**S3** ns. 35.1, 68.10; **S11** n.240.2
2013-30	**S9** n.861
2015-1	**S9** n.311

CHIEF COUNSEL ADVICE MEMORANDA

AM

2007-005	**S9** n.207.4
2011-003	**S4** n.95.1
2015-003	**S10** ns. 146, 162
2018-002	**S3** n.68.10

CHIEF COUNSEL ADVICE (including ILMs)

CCA

200002019	**11** n.37
200043003	**9** n.215
200127009	**9** n.215
200128053	**1** n.100
200245002	**10** n.286; **S10** n.286
200246014	**1** n.118; **8** ns. 127, 151; **14** n.108; **S14** n.108
200250013	**14** ns. 127, 144; **16** n.52; **19** ns. 227, 250
200513022	**8** n.152; **11** ns. 259, 292, 589; **14** ns. 66, 112
200613030	**9** n.3
200650014	**S1** n.84.1; **S19** n.74.1
200704028	**S1** n.97.1
200704030	**S1** ns. 68, 97.1
200722027	**S16** n.199
200728001	**S16** n.199
200749012	**S3** n.453
200812023	**S11** n.240.1
200816030	**S9** n.598
200907029	**S10** n.283.1
200909032	**S9** n.322
201016079	**S10** n.27
201017045	**S10** n.113
201139009	**S10** n.74
201308028	**S11** n.634
201312042	**S10** n.61
201312043	**S10** n.61

CCA

201315026	**S13** ns. 16, 17
201319024	**S10** n.94
201323015	**S3** ns. 24, 180
201324013	**S14** n.122.1
201326014	**S4** n.59
201423019	**S9** n.224
201425011	**S9** n.1055
201426013	**S9** n.765.1
201436049	**S9** ns. 624.1, 624.3
201517006	**S16** n.204
201534010	**S10** n.77
201606027	**8** n.42
20161101F	**S3** n.68.10
201726012	**S11** n.189; 24.01[5]; **24** ns. 29, 61
201729020	**S3** n.68.10
201741018	**S14** n.249.1
201818001	**S3** n.460
201917007	**S1** n.206
201945027	**S9** n.1055

CHIEF COUNSEL MEMORANDUM

CCM

20123903F	**S9** n.825
20124002F	**S3** n.68.6
20204201F	**S11** n.504.1

CHIEF COUNSEL NOTICE

CCN

2003-003	**9** n.212
2003-020	**1** n.71
2003-030	**1** n.98
2009-011	**S10** n.113
2009-027	**S10** ns. 68, 76, 77

FIELD ATTORNEY ADVICE

FFA

20132101F	**S13** n.16
20150801F	**S9** n.207.5

FIELD SERVICE ADVICE

FSA

563 (1992)	**S9** n.1055
1993-293	**8** n.40

[Text references are to paragraphs; note references are to chapters (boldface numbers) and notes ("n."). References to the supplement are preceded by "S."]

FSA

1995-12	**19** n.45
1998-6	**10** n.269
1998-28	**10** n.85
1998-158	**10** n.113
1998-161	**11** n.645
1998-162	**4** n.217
1998-314	**10** n.84; **S10** n.84
1998-316	**10** n.220
1998-318	**9** n.678
1998-325	**10** n.312
1998-330	**11** ns. 111, 442
1998-481	**4** n.84
1998-857	**10** n.196
1998-875	**10** n.196
1999-321	**10** n.110
1999-569	**14** n.58
1999-610	**10** ns. 110, 289
1999-613	**10** n.304
1999-738	**10** n.200
1999-744	**10** n.312
1999-829	**10** n.309; **S10** n.309
1999-864	**10** n.195
1999-869	**10** n.212
1999-883	**11** n.31
1999-930	**11** n.442
199901036	**10** n.219
199936007	**11** n.482; **S11** n.482
199936011	**14** n.144
199950007	**10** n.55
199952016	**10** n.55
200011025	**14** n.103
200018018	**9** n.146
200024001	**14** n.144; **16** n.87
200025011	**10** n.74
200025017	**24**.11[2]
200025018	**11** n.657
200026009	**1** n.206; **9** ns. 19, 713
200028019	**9** n.288
200049023	**10** n.72; **S10** n.73
200051016	**10** n.74
200102012	**11** ns. 20, 21, 23
200102043	**10** n.121
200108022	**10** n.195
200111001	**9** n.362
200112005	**10**.02[5]; **10** ns. 113, 122
200122023	**10** ns. 101, 109
200125014	**10** n.142
200128031	**11** n.22; **12** n.82
200131013	**13** n.191
200132009	**13** ns. 29, 96
200133003	**11** n.111
200134002	**1** n.101
200137059	**11** n.111
200140080	**9** n.26
200141021	**10** n.18
200149019	**4** n.80
200202022	**24** n.212
200203007	**10** ns. 101, 108

FSA

200205021	**1** ns. 203, 206
200216005	**3** n.390
200219008	**13** n.40; **19** n.227
200233018	**19** n.78
200234006	**24** n.226
200242004	**1** n.101

GENERAL COUNSEL MEMORANDA

GCM

34, TBR (1919)	**5** n.109
42, Sol. Op. (1920)	**5** n.109
10092	**4** n.1; **5** n.109
20251	**1** n.156
26379	**5** n.109; **6** n.3; **17** ns. 8, 9
32650	**14** ns. 274, 275
33774	**13**.06[2]; **13** ns. 17, 191; **14** n.49
33948	**7** n.45
34001	**14** n.195
34151	**14** ns. 274, 276.3
35117	**9** n.692
35921	**16** n.292
36072	**22** n.71
36329	**17** n.161; **24** n.4
36702	**9** n.375; **S9** n.375.53; **14** ns. 243, 254, 277
36960	**3** ns. 71, 151
37768	**7** n.190
38089	**7** n.177
38133	**9** n.375; **S9** n.375.53; **14** ns. 243, 254; **22** n.71
38186	**17** n.161; **24** n.4
38201	**14** n.31; **S14** n.31
39150	**9** n.692
39262	**16** n.284
39292	**9** n.678
39502	**26** ns. 3, 36
39673	**13** ns. 47, 48
39732	**9** ns. 815, 816
39749	**9**.03[1][a][iii]; **9** n.672
39781	**9** n.145
39862	**9** n.816

INCOME TAX UNIT RULINGS

IT

2286	**9** n.330
3845	**1** n.111
3924	**9** n.130
3930	**3** n.231
3948	**3** ns. 157, 231

[Text references are to paragraphs; note references are to chapters (boldface numbers) and notes ("n."). References to the supplement are preceded by "S."]

IRS NEWS RELEASES

IR

82-149 . . . . **9** n.1071

LITIGATION GUIDELINE MEMORANDA

LGM

TL-95 . . . . **10** n.110
199905040 . . . . . . **10** ns. 309, 312; **S10** n.309

MIMEOGRAPHS

Mim

3283 . . . . **9** n.330
6767 . . . . 1.05[4][a]; **1** ns. 116, 117; **3** n.75; **15** n.7

NOTICES

Notice

87-8 . . . . **11** n.752
88-20 . . . . **9** n.363; **S9** n.363; **16** n.20
88-37 . . . . **9** n.363; **S9** n.363; **11** n.773; **16** ns. 20, 21
88-72 . . . . **9** ns. 836, 837
88-75 . . . . . 3.09[6]; **3** ns. 424, 427, 434, 444
88-81 . . . . **9** n.633
88-85 . . . . **9** ns. 965, 993
88-87 . . . . **11** n.35
88-99 . . . 9.02[3][m][ii]; **9** ns. 471, 479, 483–489
89-35 . . . **9** n.363; **11** ns. 725, 773; **16** ns. 20, 43
89-37   **4** n.122; 9.03[1][a][ii]; S9.03[1][a][ii]; 9.03[1][a][ii][D]; **9** ns. 639, 640; **S9** n.639; **19** ns. 29, 67
89-39 . . . . **11** n.666
89-41 . . . . **9** n.995
92-46 . . . . **14** n.137
93-2 . . . . . 9.03[1][a][ii][C]; **9** ns. 653, 654; **S9** n.641
93-21 . . . . **4** n.123
94-41 . . . . **9** n.462
94-47 . . . . 3.05[3]; **3** n.200
96-39 . . . . **1** n.206; 9.01[4][c][ii]; **9** n.99
98-3 . . . . **6** n.45
98-35 . . . . **9** n.100
99-6 . . . . **9** n.217
99-57 . . . . **6** n.59
2000-44 . . . **S1** n.68; 7.04[2]; 7.04[3][h]; **7** ns. 68, 78, 79, 81.1, 148; **S7** ns. 77.1, 79
2001-4 . . . . **9** n.847

Notice

2001-18 . . . . 9.06[2][a]; **9** n.1102
2002-37 . . . . **11** n.476
2002-41 . . . . **9** n.847
2002-50 . . . . **1** n.206; **S1** n.68; **6** n.3; **16** n.310
2002-65 . . . . **S1** n.68
2003-41 . . . . **1** n.89
2003-47 . . . . **S1** n.68
2004-31 . . . . **1** n.96; **S1** n.68; **9** n.375; **S9** n.375.53; **11** n.111; 14.03[6][i]; **14** n.285
2004-67 . . . . **9** n.1084
2005-1 . . . . **14** ns. 204–206; 22.07; **22** n.144
2005-8 . . . . . **2** ns. 82, 83; **14** ns. 268, 269
2005-13 . . . . **9** n.755
2005-14 . . 9.02[3][w]; S9.02[3][w]; **9** ns. 529, 532, 533–537, 539, 551; **S9** ns. 530, 531, 535–537, 540, 542, 543
2005-15 . . . **11** n.555; **S11** n.555; **13** n.178; **S13** n.178
2005-29 . . . . **9** n.762; **S9** n.762
2005-32 . . . . **11** n.480; **24** ns. 14, 21
2005-43 . . . . . . 5.02[3]; 5.02[3][b]; 5.02[3][d]; 5.02[3][h]; 5.02[3][i]; **5** ns. 2, 52, 53, 60–63, 71, 73, 85, 100, 102, 140, 155
2006-2 . . . . **9** n.762; **S9** n.762
2006-6 . . . . **9** ns. 1096, 1107
2006-14 . . . S21.01[6][a]; 21.03[8]; **21** ns. 100, 115; **S21** n.35.1
2007-4 . . . . **S9** n.762
2007-9 . . . . **S9** n.117.3
2007-10 . . . . **S3** n.302.1
2007-78 . . . . **S14** n.206
2007-86 . . . . **S14** n.206
2008-80 . . . S3.04[3][a]; **S3** ns. 86, 155.1, 205; **S9** ns. 1005.1–1005.3
2009-7 . . . . **S3** n.140.1; S9.01[4][c][iv][C]; **S9** n.117.1
2009-70 . . . S11.04[4][b][vii]; **S11** n.561.9; **S13** n.178
2010-41 . . . . S9.01[4][c][iv][C]
2012-52 . . . . **S3** n.292
2015-54 . . . . **S4** n.51.2
2016-23 . . . . **S10** n.324
2017-71 . . . . **S9** n.1053.1
2018-8 . . . . **S9** n.831.3
2018-18 . . . . **S9** n.271.9
2018-67 . . . . **S9** n.768
2019-06 . . . . **10A** ns. 54, 73
2019-20 . . . . **S9** n.1062.7
2019-66 . . . . **S9** n.1062.7
2020-43 . . . . S9.06[1][a]; **S9** n.1062.8
2020-75 . . . . **S9** n.18.2

PROGRAM MANAGER'S TECHNICAL ADVICE

PMTA

2010-005 . . . . **S3** n.246

[Text references are to paragraphs; note references are to chapters (boldface numbers) and notes ("n."). References to the supplement are preceded by "S."]

SERVICE CENTER ADVICE

SCA

1998-030 . . . . **10** n.217

TREASURY DECISIONS

TD

6175 . . . . **7** n.176; **11** n.91; **24** n.205
7636 . . . . **11** n.412
7741 . . . . **16** n.216
8065 . . . . **S9** n.1062.1
8078 . . . . **9** n.1082
8080 . . . . **3** n.85
8175 . . . . **9** n.326; **11** ns. 720, 752
8205 . . . . **9** n.998
8224 . . . . **16** n.194
8237 . . . . **7** n.55; **8** n.1
8274 . . . . **8** n.2
8343 . . . . **9** n.267
8380 . . . . **8** ns. 3, 45, 48
8385 . . . . **11** n.305
8439 . . . . **14** ns. 61, 75, 79, 80, 131
8500 . . . . **11** ns. 489, 504
8501 . . . . **11** n.524
8531 . . . . **1** n.80
8569 . . . . **9** n.1013
8584 . . . . **9** n.472
8585 . . . . **11** n.524
8588 . . . . **1** ns. 53, 82, 102
8590 . . . . **1** n.88
8629 . . . . **3** n.423
8697 . . . . **3** n.460
8707 . . . . **S19** n.250.1
8717 . . . . **11** n.316; 13.05[2][k]; **13** ns. 42−44,
    93, 104, 112, 115, 130, 147; **S13** n.149.1
8730 . . . . **11** n.378
8808 . . . . **10** n.89
8827 . . . . **9** n.100
8847 . . . . **17** ns. 31, 47; **24** n.78; **26** ns. 13, 15
8875 . . . . **9** n.1082
8876 . . . . **9** n.1082
8877 . . . . **9** n.1082
8896 . . . . **9** n.1082
8902 . . . . **16** n.208; **S16** n.339.1
8906 . . . . **8** ns. 150, 156
8925 . . . . **13** ns. 164, 167, 168, 172, 194, 208,
    216, 217
8965 . . . . **10** n.245

TD

9008 . . . . **9** n.101
9035 . . . . **16** n.124
9046 . . . . **9** n.1082
9059 . . . . **25** n.84
9108 . . . . **9** ns. 1082, 1086
9121 . . . . **11** ns. 422, 423, 432
9137 . . . . **17** n.31
9207 . . . . . **7** ns. 2, 36, 79, 80, 93; **11** ns. 140,
    142, 212, 305, 494, 536; **S11** n.494
9240 . . . . **9** n.105
9289 . . . . **8** n.118
9292 . . . . **S11** n.436.3
9293 . . . . **S9** n.534
9321 . . . . **S14** ns. 202, 206
9398 . . . . **S11** ns. 121, 230.1
9485 . . . . **S11** n.501.1
9557 . . . . **S4** n.110.7
9607 . . . . **S11** n.134
9612 . . . . . . **S3** n.180.6; **S4** n.19; **S11** ns. 170,
    179.4, 179.5
9659 . . . . **5** n.15
9722 . . . . **S9** n.643
9728 . . . . **5** n.92
9759 . . . . **S4** n.211.8
9766 . . . . **S14** ns. 201.1, 258
9771 . . . . **S9** n.311
9773 . . . . **S9** n.1078.1
9780 . . . . **S10** n.326.2
9787 . . . . **S14** n.119.1
9788 . . . . **S14** n.104
9790 . . . . . **S9.03[1][a][x]; S9** ns. 709.1, 709.4
9800 . . . . **S11** n.436.5b
9811 . . . . **23** n.16; **24** ns. 125, 177
9814 . . . . **S4** ns. 51.2−51.4, 51.9, 51.13, 51.43
9817 . . . . **S3** n.454
9829 . . . . **10A** ns. 76, 78, 79
9833 . . . . **S9** ns. 643.1, 649, 650, 651.1
9839 . . . . **10A** n.19
9844 . . . . . **10A** ns. 53, 54, 56, 138, 160, 165,
    170, 172, 173, 246, 274, 334
9847 . . . . **S9** ns. 551.2, 551.4
9857 . . . . **S9** n.548
9866 . . . . **S9** ns. 88.2, 88.4
9871 . . . . S11.03[2][i]
9872 . . . . **S11** n.211
9877 . . . 8.02[5]; 8.02[10][a]; **8** ns. 76, 85, 126
9889 . . . . **S9** n.633.4a
9891 . . . . **S4** n.51.4a
9899 . . . . **S9** n.551.59
9916 . . . . **S24** n.157.1
9919 . . . . **S9** n.831.2b

Cumulative Table
of Cases

[Text references are to paragraphs; note references are to chapters (boldface numbers) and notes ("n."). References to the supplement are preceded by "S."]

[Text references are to paragraphs; note references are to chapters (boldface numbers) and notes ("n."). References to the supplement are preceded by "S."]

[Text references are to paragraphs; note references are to chapters (boldface numbers) and notes ("n."). References to the supplement are preceded by "S."]

[Text references are to paragraphs; note references are to chapters (boldface numbers) and notes ("n."). References to the supplement are preceded by "S."]

[Text references are to paragraphs; note references are to chapters (boldface numbers) and notes ("n."). References to the supplement are preceded by "S."]

[Text references are to paragraphs; note references are to chapters (boldface numbers) and notes ("n."). References to the supplement are preceded by "S."]

[Text references are to paragraphs; note references are to chapters (boldface numbers) and notes ("n."). References to the supplement are preceded by "S."]

[Text references are to paragraphs; note references are to chapters (boldface numbers) and notes ("n."). References to the supplement are preceded by "S."]

Foyt v. United States 3 n.212; 4 n.41
Frank, Isaac W., Trust 3 n.12
Frank v. Comm'r . . . 4 n.102; 15 ns. 17, 48, 49, 52–55
Frank, Hitchcock v. 14 n.294
Frank, Kuney v. . . . 15 ns. 34, 36, 37, 41, 52, 64
Frank, Maxwell v. 16 n.159
Frankel, E.J. . . . . 9.01[8][b]; 9 n.193
Frankfort, Jr., Fred 17 n.59; 22 n.100
Franklin, Charles T., Estate of . . . 7 ns. 170, 188
Frank Lyon Co. v. United States . . . .
    . . . . 1.05[4][b][i]; 1.05[4][b][ii]; 1 ns. 123, 136, 197; 14 n.283
Fraser, Robert D. 3 n.187
Frazell, Gene M. 3 n.39
Frazell, United States v. . . . 3 n.184; 4.02[1]; 4 ns. 68, 80; 5 n.27; 18 n.13
Frederick, Theodore A. . . . .
    . . . . 9.02[2][b]; 9 n.325
Fredericks, Fred L. 9 n.265
Fred H. Lenway & Co. 16 n.253
Freeland, Estate of v. Comm'r . . . . 9 ns. 67, 225; 17 n.133
Freesen, O. Robert 3 n.216
Fribourgh Navigation Co. v. Comm'r 13 n.141
Friedlander Corp. 3 n.367; 9 n.134; 11 n.441
Friedlander Corp. v. Comm'r . . . . 3 ns. 361, 362
Friednash v. Comm'r 3 n.181
Fritz v. Comm'r 14 n.49
Frye, Jon T. 16 n.97
Fuchs, Morton 9 n.226; 13 n.78; S13 n.78
Fuchs, Bert L., Estate of 23 n.71
Funai v. Comm'r . . . . 15 ns. 30, 39
Furstenberg v. United States . . . 16 n.111; 19 n.49

G

GAF Corp. 10 n.314; S10 n.226.1
Gail Vento, LLC v. United States . . . S10 ns. 248, 311
Gaines, Billy J. 4 n.212; 14 n.228
Galletti, United States v. . . . 9 n.212; S9 n.212
Gamma Farms v. United States 9 n.610
Gant v. Comm'r 3 n.192
Garcia, Joseph A. . . . . . 15 ns. 16, 34, 36, 75
Garcia, Richard E. 11 n.8
Gardner S10 n.24
Gardner, Samuel C. 16 n.258
Garnett, Paul D. S11 n.818
Gartling, Estate of 17 n.7
Gateway Hotel Partners, LLC (TCM 2014)
    . . . . S14 n.56.1
Gateway Hotel Partners, LLC (TCM 2009)
    . . . . S10 n.33.1
Gaudiano v. Comm'r 3 n.196

Gaughf v. Comm'r S10 n.297
GD Searle & Co. . . . . 1 n.154; 11 ns. 447, 450, 455, 457
Gefen, Sidney J. . . . . 1 n.140; 11.06[2][b]; 11 ns. 650, 651
Gemini Twin Fund III . . . 4 n.88; 6 n.15; 10 ns. 77, 79; S10 n.77; 11 n.153; S11 n.153
General Elec. Co. v. United States . . . 11 ns. 448, 450
General Mills, Inc. v. United States S10 n.233
General Shoe Corp., United States v. 14 n.245
General Utils. & Operating Co. v. Helvering
    . . . . 4.02[7]; 9.03[1][a][ii]; S9.03[1][a][ii]; S9.03[1][a][ii][A]; 9.03[5]; 9 n.640; S9 n.640
Generes, United States v. 14 n.29
Genesis Oil & Gas, Ltd. . . . . 10 ns. 238, 307
George Edward Quick Trust (8th Cir.) . . . . 9 n.350; 16 n.197; 23.02[2][b]; 23 ns. 9, 11-14; 24 n.179
Georgia RR & Banking Co., United States v.
    . . . . 16 n.24
Gerber & Assocs., Inc. 11 n.1
Gevirtz, Michael J. 9 n.12
Gibson Prods. Co.–Kell Blvd. v. United States . . . . . 7 ns. 72, 164, 187
Giffen v. Comm'r 15 n.28
Gilford, Almy 3 n.228
Gindes v. United States 24 n.209
Gingerich v. United States 10 n.298
Ginsberg v. Comm'r . . . . 15 ns. 44, 55, 64
Ginsburg, Alan H. S10 n.288
Ginsburg v. United States . . . 13.02; 13 n.12; 17 n.133
Giovanini v. United States 4 n.177
Girard Trust Co. v. United States . . . 13 n.4
Gitlitz v. Comm'r . . . . . 6 n.39; 16.03[1]; 16 n.141
Glazer, Herman 17 n.78
Glenn, Kaiser v. . . . . . 16 ns. 159, 161, 163
Glenshaw Glass, Comm'r v. 10A n.66
Glick v. United States 11 n.790
Glover Constr. Co., Andrus v. 1 n.177
Goddall, Robert A., Estate of 23 n.90
Goemans v. Comm'r . . . . . 15 ns. 36, 48, 52
Gold, Melvin L. 9 n.8; 11 n.5
Goldberg, Harry 16 n.318
Goldberg, Estate of v. Comm'r 16 n.295
Goldberger, Estate of, Comm'r v. 9 n.8; 11 n.5
Gold Coast Hotel & Casino 10 n.256
Goldfine, Morton S. . . . . 11 ns. 53, 462
Goldstein, Jerome K., Estate of . . . 3 n.264; 9 n.226
Goldstein v. Comm'r 1 n.129; 11 n.37
Golsen v. Comm'r . . . 1 n.130; 10 n.236; S14 n.56.1
G-1 Holdings, Inc., United States v. . . . . . . S9 n.336; S14.02[3][b][ii]; S14 ns. 71.1, 189

[Text references are to paragraphs; note references are to chapters (boldface numbers) and notes ("n."). References to the supplement are preceded by "S."]

H

[Text references are to paragraphs; note references are to chapters (boldface numbers) and notes ("n."). References to the supplement are preceded by "S."]

*[Text references are to paragraphs; note references are to chapters (boldface numbers)
and notes ("n."). References to the supplement are preceded by "S."]*

Klamath Strategic Inv. Fund, LLC v. United
   States (ED Tex. 2006) .... **7** ns. 81.1,
   81.2, 81.4
Klein, Frederick S. ... **4** n.162; **9** ns. 14, 128;
   S9 n.14; **11** n.2
Klein, Herman, Estate of **9** n.348
Klein v. United States **10** n.305
Kling, Frederick J. ...... 9.01[8][b]; **9** n.194
Knetsch v. United States (US) .... **1** ns. 126,
   197
Knetsch v. United States (Ct. Cl.) ... **1** n.133
Knipp, Frank H., Estate of .... **23** ns. 81, 92
Knott, Henry J. **23** n.95
Kobernat, Leonard J. **14** n.184
Koen, L.O., Estate of .... **3** ns. 170, 206
Kohn, David E. **10** n.63
Koppers Co. v. United States **4** n.212
Korff III, Edward F. .... **10** ns. 94, 194
Kornfeld v. Comm'r **16** n.24
Kornman & Assocs. v. United States **S7**
   ns. 62, 66, 68; **S16** n.215
Koshland v. Helvering **1** n.178
Kosonen, Matti **11** n.730
Kraasch, Otto H. .... 10.02[2]; **10** n.37
Kraatz & Craig Surveying, Inc. **S9** n.142
Krause, Adolph K. ..... **15** ns. 44, 52, 61, 77
Krause, Gary E. **9** n.1142
Krause, J. Winston v. United States **S10**
   n.89.6
Kreidle, In re **16** n.260; **S16** n.260
Kresser, Jean V. .... **11** ns. 13, 15, 35
Krist, Ed ...... **16** n.295; **17** ns. 5, 12, 132
Kuhl, Rupple v. **12** n.28
Kuney v. Frank .... **15** ns. 34, 36, 37, 41, 52,
   64
Kuney v. United States .... **15** ns. 36, 67
Kurzner v. United States .... **3** ns. 106, 272
Kynell, Ellen C. .... **15** ns. 37, 42, 43

L

Labrum & Doak, LLP v. Bechtle ... **11** n.15
Ladas, George D. **13** n.13
Laird, Mary A.B. DuPont **23** n.97
Lamas, Jose A. **S11** n.816
Lamb v. United States **9** n.1149
L&B Land Lease Group 82-4 ...... **3** n.39
Landreth, United States v. **17** n.7
Lane, In re **3** n.199
Lang, Edward D. .... 9.01[2]; **9** n.9
Lapin, Ron **16** n.245
Larson, Phillip G. **3** n.272
Larson, Thomas E. **5** n.122
LaRue, Joseph W. **16** n.258
Lazisky, Albert A. **16** n.315
LB&M Assocs., Inc. **10** n.77; **S10** n.77
Leahy, James B. **3** n.195
Leatherstocking 1983 P'ship **S10** n.286
Leavitt, Mark O. **18** n.27
LeBlanc, Jr. v. United States ... **S10** ns. 113,
   212; **S11** n.607

Lederer v. Parish .... **9** ns. 125, 127
Ledoux, John W. .... **17** ns. 60, 62
Leff v. Comm'r **17** n.10
Legallet, Paul ...... 23.06[1]; **23** ns. 75, 85
Lehman, Harry W. .... **5** ns. 27, 107
Lehman, Comm'r v. **4** n.29; **23** n.68
Leila G. Newhall Unitrust **9** n.769
Leland, In re **10** n.99
Lemmen, Gerrit B. **1** n.184
Lemons, Woody F. **11** n.593
Lenard L. Politte, MD, Inc. **9** n.925; **14**
   n.226
Lenney, John W. .... **17** ns. 5, 12, 132
LeSage v. Comm'r **12** n.27; **17** n.10
Lesher v. United States **9** n.213
Lessinger v. Comm'r ..... **4** ns. 88, 89, 108,
   138; **6** n.16; **16** n.270; **19** n.110
LeSuer, James E. .... **14** ns. 21, 37
Levasseur, United States v. .... **3** ns. 179, 180
Levine, Aaron, Estate of .... **3** n.228; **13** ns.
   13, 15; **S13** n.15; **16** n.214
Levy, Frank R. **1** n.136
Liberman, Meyer **9** n.122
Lidberg v. United States **9** n.1151
Lieber, Frank M. **4** n.221; **S4** n.221
Lieber, Marvin **1** n.130
Lieber v. United States .... **15** ns. 37, 49
Life Care Communities (TCM 2004) **11**
   n.47; **12** n.28
Life Care Communities of Am., Ltd. (TCM
   1997) **3** n.36; **10** n.86
Liflans Corp. v. United States **14** n.310
Lindsey, James **10** n.66
Linsmayer, Robert M. **9** n.924
Lipnick, William C. **S9** n.363
Lipscomb v. Ballard **3** n.39
Littriello v. United States (6th Cir.) **S3**
   n.274
Littriello v. United States (WD Ky.) ....
   .... 3.06[1]; **3** n.274
Livingston v. United States ... **9** ns. 213, 890
Lloyd, Augustine .... **5** ns. 105, 108; **14** n.208
Logan, Frank A. .... 17.05[2]; **17** ns. 28, 57,
   59, 61, 174–176
Logan, Burnet v. ..... 16.04[1]; **16** n.177; **19**
   n.106
Lomas Santa Fe, Inc. v. Comm'r **16** n.24
Lombardo, United States v. ... **10** n.284; **S10**
   n.284
Long, Arthur E. ....
   .... **6** n.89; **9** n.265; **16** n.201
Long, Marshall **7** n.72
Long v. Comm'r (5th Cir.) **6** n.3; **17** n.7
Long v. Comm'r (TCM) S3.03; **S3** n.101.1
Long v. United States **19** n.142
Long Term Capital Holdings v. United States
   .... **1** n.73; **S1** n.84.1; **S3** n.139.3; **11**
   n.494; **S11** n.494
Lopo, George J. ...... **4** n.161; **9** ns. 13, 127
Lorillard v. Pons **1** n.174
Lowenstein, Aaron, Estate of **9** n.26; **24**
   n.2
Lubken v. United States .... **17** ns. 168, 172

[Text references are to paragraphs; note references are to chapters (boldface numbers) and notes ("n."). References to the supplement are preceded by "S."]

Lucas v. Earl .... **3** ns. 51, 65, 74; **4** ns. 98, 102; **11** n.43; 15.01[3]; **15** n.10; **16** n.110; **19** n.41
Luckey, Clarence A. **20** n.10
Luna, Hubert M. ... 1.05[4][b][v]; **1** n.147; **3** ns. 168, 179, 181; **S3** ns. 24, 101.2, 180
Lusthaus v. Comm'r ... 3.02[2]; **3** ns. 9, 60, 74
Lutts v. United States **9** n.62
L.W. Tilden, Inc. v. Comm'r ..... **3** ns. 361, 363
Lynch, Michael Francis ... **7** n.35; **14** n.221

M

Maarten Investerings P'ship **10** n.248
MacConaughey, Harry E. **3** n.46
Macomber, Eisner v. ...... 9.03[1][a][iii]; **9** n.660
Maddock, Henry A., Estate of **23** n.91
Madison Gas & Elec. Co. (7th Cir.) .... 1.05[4][b][v]; **1** ns. 67, 146; S3.02[2A]; 3.04[3][a]; 3.08[4]; **3** ns. 160, 161, 229, 407, 409; **S3** ns. 68.7, 139.10; 9.02[3][j]; **9** n.422; **14** n.53
Madison Gas & Elec. Co. (TC) ... 3.08[4]; **3** n.408
Madison Recycling Assocs. (TCM) **10** n.286; **S10** n.286
Madison Recycling Assocs. v. Comm'r (2d Cir.) **10** n.251; **S10** n.286
Madorin, Bernard v. Comm'r ..... **3** ns. 71, 151; **13** n.54
Magneson, Norman J. **19** n.46
Magneson v. Comm'r **9** n.269; **S9** n.269
Magnolia Dev. Corp. **16** n.213
Magnolia Surf, Inc. v. Comm'r **16** n.315
Magruder, Chris H. **9** n.12
Maguire Partners—Master Invs., LLC v. United States .... **S7** ns. 68, 79
Mahoney v. United States .... **13** ns. 20, 68; **S13** n.20
Malat v. Riddell **1** n.80
Maletis v. United States **3** n.180
Mallary v. United States **9** n.504; **11** n.397; **14** n.274
Malone, Bernard P. **S10** n.137
Maloney, Bonny B. **9** n.269; **S9** n.269
Mammoth Lakes Project **11** n.223
Manchester Music Co. v. United States .... 3.05[4][a]; **3** n.214
Mangham, John W. ..... **11** n.462; **14** ns. 25, 223
Manspeaker, Demarest v. ..... **1** ns. 180, 181
Mantell, Alan M. **4** n.214
Manuel, Lizzie M. ...... **15** ns. 31, 49
Marathon Oil Co. v. Comm'r **3** n.115
Marcus, Frances **15** n.91
Marcus v. Comm'r **15** n.42
Margolis v. Comm'r **9** n.225

Marine Contractors & Supply, Inc. .... **4** ns. 212, 214
Markell Co. **S3** n.101.2; **S7** n.62
Marriott Int'l Resorts, LP (Fed. Cir. 2009) **S7** n.62
Marriott Int'l Resorts, LP v. United States (Fed. Cl. 2004) **S7** n.60
Marthinuss, Sharon H. ....**10** ns. 86, 129, 230
Martin, Phillip E. **11** n.14
Martin, Fahs v. **7** n.173
Martin v. United States **17** n.133
Martin, Candyce, 1999 Irrevocable Trust v. United States (9th Cir.) **S10** n.288
Martin, Candyce, 1999 Irrevocable Trust v. United States (ND Cal.) **S7** n.68
Martinez, Jose, Estate of **9** n.311
Martuccio, James V. **1** n.136
Martyr, Paul D. **4** n.225
Marx, Julius H. (Groucho) **16** n.320
Maryland Nat'l Bank v. United States ... **16** n.244
Mason, Miles H. **19** n.46
MAS One Ltd. P'ship v. United States **4** n.121
Masoni, John G. .... **3** ns. 361, 363
Masoni v. Comm'r **3** n.125
Mathia, Jean **S10** n.218
Maxcy, James G., Estate of .... **13** ns. 1, 77; **S13** n.77
Maxwell, Larry S. ..... 10.02[5]; **10** ns. 112, 116, 117, 119, 122, 130–135, 220, 314
Maxwell, Lester **15** n.61
Maxwell, Walter F. .... 3.07[2]; **3** n.368; **15** n.28
Maxwell v. Comm'r **10** n.112
Maxwell v. Frank **16** n.159
Mayer, Elizabeth **3** n.175
Mayerson, Manuel D. **7** n.169
Mayes v. United States **4** n.101; **9** n.124
Mayes, Jr., W.B. **4** n.101; **9** n.131
Mayhew, Lyle **3** n.181
Mayo Found. for Med. Research v. United States ... S1.05[5][b]; **S1** ns. 170, 192, 194; **S10** n.292.2
M. Buten & Sons **18** n.27
McAfee, James Wesley **16** n.152; **17** n.12
McBride v. United States **10** n.233
McCauslen, Edwin E. ... **9** n.257; **13** ns. 155, 156; 16.02[3][b]; **16** ns. 19, 81–83, 170; **18** ns. 36, 66; 20.01; **20** ns. 2, 3
McClellan v. Comm'r .... **17** ns. 4, 6
McClennen v. Comm'r **23** n.94
McCrory, Grant v. **12** n.29
McDaniel, R.D., Estate of .... **3** ns. 176, 182, 184, 262; **15** n.61
McDaniel, Robert S. .... 16.05[1][c]; **16** ns. 3, 231, 232
McDonald, Bill (9th Cir.) **11** n.13
McDonald, Bill (TCM) **11** n.230; **S11** n.230
McDonnell v. United States **9** n.129
McDonough, Bernard P. **9** n.493

[Text references are to paragraphs; note references are to chapters (boldface numbers) and notes ("n."). References to the supplement are preceded by "S."]

[Text references are to paragraphs; note references are to chapters (boldface numbers) and notes ("n."). References to the supplement are preceded by "S."]

[Text references are to paragraphs; note references are to chapters (boldface numbers) and notes ("n."). References to the supplement are preceded by "S."]

P

PAA Mgmt., Ltd. v. United States (ND Ill.) 10 n.168
PAA Mgmt., Ltd. v. United States (SDNY) 10 n.168
Pacific Nat'l Co. v. Welch S11 n.487
Pacific Transp. Co. v. Comm'r 17 n.18
PAE Enters. 10 n.55
Palda v. Comm'r 9 n.334
Palmer, Robert K. 10 n.80
Palmer v. Comm'r . . . . . . 18.02[1]; 18 n.16
Panero, Guy B., Estate of   12 n.4; 13 ns. 1, 77, 78; S13 ns. 77, 78
Papandon, United States v. 9 n.220
Papineau, George A. 14 n.197
Pappas, Peter N. 16 n.201
Parish, Lederer v. . . . . 9 ns. 125, 127
Park Cities Corp. v. Byrd 11 n.53
Parker, Robert W. S9 n.163
Parker v. Delaney 7 n.33; 16 n.212
Parker Props. Joint Venture 9 n.289
Park Realty Co. 14 n.93; S14 n.93
Parks v. United States . . . . . . 9 ns. 498, 500
Patterson, American Tobacco Co. v. 1 n.181
Patterson, Bolling v. 16 n.72
Patton v. Comm'r . . . . 14 ns. 238, 240
Paymer v. Comm'r 3 n.111
Payton v. United States . . . . . 15 ns. 17, 64
PCMG Trading Partners XX, LP S10 n.239
PDB Sports, Ltd.   16.03[1]; 16.08[5]; 16 ns. 130, 140, 323; 26 n.33
Peat Oil & Gas Assocs. (TC) . . . . 1.05[4][b][iv]; 1 ns. 137–139, 149; 9 n.401
Peat Oil & Gas Assocs. (TCM) 10 n.236
Peeler Realty Co. 16 n.112; 19 n.43
Peking Inv. Fund, LLC . . . . . . S3 ns. 101.2, 139.3; S10 n.286; S11 n.494
Peracchi v. Comm'r . . . . 4 ns. 88, 89; 6 n.16
Perry, Jr., Billy 3 n.160; 9 n.604
Perryman, Lawrence R. . . . . 11 ns. 448, 450
Petaluma FX Partners, LLC (TC 2008) . . . . S10.02[3]; S10 n.75.4
Petaluma FX Partners, LLC v. Comm'r (DC Cir.) . . . . . S10.02[3]; S10 ns. 68, 75.3
Peters, James 11 n.648; S11 n.648
Peters, Weldon T. . . . 3 ns. 36, 39; 11 n.650
Peterson v. Gray . . . . 15 ns. 66, 76
Petroleum Corp. of Tex., Inc. v. United States . . . 16.03[1]; 16 ns. 133, 134; 23 n.62
Pflugradt v. United States . . . . 3 n.73; 15 ns. 24, 61, 73
Phillips, Charles F. . . . 16 ns. 61, 76; 17 n.63
Phillips, Richard K. 10 n.99
Phinney, Armstrong v. . . . 2 n.84; 5 n.105; 14 ns. 197, 199, 262
Phinney v. Bank of Southwest NA 10 n.284; S10 n.284

Phipps v. United States (Ct. Cl. 1975) . . . . 9 ns. 490, 493
Phipps v. United States (Ct. Cl. 1969) 9 n.490; 11 n.222
Pickett, Elmer J. 16 n.316
Pierce, In re . . . . ; 9 n.1
Pietz, Edward H. . . . . . 19 n.96; 22 ns. 13, 48
Pilgrim's Pride Corp. v. Comm'r (5th Cir.) . . . . 12 n.20; S16.06[2]; S16 ns. 256.2, 256.4–256.7
Pilgrim's Pride Corp. v. Comm'r (TC) . . . . S16.06[2]
Piper v. Chris-Craft Indus., Inc. 1 n.181
Pittway Corp. v. United States 14 n.144
Plains Realty Co. 3 n.181
Plantation Patterns, Inc. v. Comm'r . . . . 14.02[3][b][xi]; 14 n.177
Pleasant Summit Land Corp. v. Comm'r 7 n.188
Plotkin, Martin G. S11 n.11; S14 n.8.1
PNRC Ltd. P'ship . . . . . 11 ns. 220, 222, 227
Podell, Hyman 3 n.46; 9 n.67
Poggetto v. United States . . . 3 ns. 166, 173; 15 ns. 9, 13, 17
Polakof, James 9 n.401
Polak's Frutal Works, Inc. . . . . 3 ns. 361, 364
Polin v. Comm'r 16 n.251
Pollack, Jr., H. Clinton 16 n.2; 19 n.96
Pons, Lorillard v. 1 n.174
Pope, W.W. 16 n.190
Pope & Talbot Inc. v. Comm'r . . . S16 n.144
Portland Golf Club v. Comm'r 1 n.135
Post, Troy V. 14 n.32
Pounds v. United States 3 n.187
Powell, Lulu Lung . . . . 3 ns. 228, 229
Poynor v. Comm'r 10 n.284; S10 n.284
Prati v. United States S10 n.82
Pratt, Edward T. . . . . 7 n.149; S9.02[3][c][i][A]; S9 n.375.3; 14 ns. 11, 12, 26, 216, 228
Pratt v. Comm'r . . . 5 n.114; 7 n.149; 14 ns. 11, 12, 27, 187, 216, 228
Prestop Holdings LLC v. United States . . . . S10 ns. 245, 246.1
Price, Chester L. 9 n.311
Pridgen v. United States 9 n.7
Primco Mgmt. Co. v. Comm'r . . . 10 ns. 8, 19
Principal Life Ins. Co. v. United States   S6 n.39
Pritchett, Jerry E. (9th Cir.) . . . . 11.06[2][b]; 11 n.655
Pritchett, Jerry E. (TCM) . . . . 11.06[2][b]; 11 ns. 659, 661
Pritchett, Richard H. 17 n.172
Pritired I, LLC v. United States S1 n.149.1; S3 n.156.1
Prizant, Jerome 9 n.199; 18 n.77
Prochorenko v. United States 10 n.197
Production House Ltd. P'ship C-23 . . . . . 10 n.35
Professional Equities, Inc. 4 n.137
Proulx v. United States 16 n.315
Prunier v. Comm'r 23 n.76

[Text references are to paragraphs; note references are to chapters (boldface numbers) and notes ("n."). References to the supplement are preceded by "S."]

[Text references are to paragraphs; note references are to chapters (boldface numbers) and notes ("n."). References to the supplement are preceded by "S."]

Runkle, Harry M. **4** n.28
Rupe v. United States **3** n.192
Rupple v. Kuhl **12** n.28
Russian Recovery Fund Ltd. v. United States
    (Fed. Cir. 2017) **S11** n.494
Russian Recovery Fund Ltd. v. United States
    (Fed. Cl. 2011) **S10** n.288
Russian Recovery Fund Ltd. v. United States
    (Fed. Cl. 2008) . . . . . **S10** ns. 119, 245
Ruth, Leonard T. **9** n.498
Ryza, Claire A. . . . .3 n.175; **S3** n.175; **11** ns.
    1, 13

S

Saba, William A. **9** n.29
Saba P'ship v. Comm'r   **1** n.129; 3.03[2]; **3**
   ns. 129, 132; **7** n.165; **S7** n.165
Sacks v. Comm'r **1** n.136
St. David's Health Care Sys., Inc. v. Comm'r
   (5th Cir. 2001) **10** n.237
St. David's Health Care Sys., Inc. v. United
   States (5th Cir. 2003) **9** n.817
Sala v. United States . . . **S7** ns. 79, 81.1, 81.3
Salina P'ship . . . 7.03[2]; **7** ns. 62, 64–66; **S7**
   n.62
Salman Ranch Ltd. v. Comm'r **S10**
   n.292.2
Salman Ranch Ltd. v. United States **S10**
   ns. 292.1, 292.2
Samford, Lester L. **3** n.41
Samueli, Henry F. **S10** n.278
S&M Plumbing Co. . . . 3.05[6]; **3** ns. 46, 260
Sandoval, Thomas C. **9** n.227
Sanford Homes, Inc. **20** n.4
San Gabriel Energy **10** n.54
Santa Fe Pac. Corp. v. Central States, South-
   east & Southwest Pension Areas Fund
   . . . . **1** n.80
Santa Monica Pictures, LLC   **1** ns. 70, 195;
   S3 n.139.3; **S10**.02[3]; **S10** n.89.1; **S11**
   n.494
Sarma, Raghunathan **S10** n.287.1
Sartin v. United States **11** n.373
Saso II, Martin **10** n.306
Scales, Riddell v. **9** n.225
Schlitz, Raymond W. . . . . **11** ns. 14, 364
Schmidt v. Comm'r **18** n.19
Schmitz, J. Leonard **16** n.316
Schmitz, Raymond W. . . . **3** ns. 170, 179; **22**
   n.17
Schneer, Stephen B. . . . . 9.01[5]; **9** n.126
Schreiber, Abe **15** n.22
Schulz v. Comm'r **16** n.316
Schumacher Trading Partners II v. United
   States . . . . **S10** ns. 308, 311
Schuster, Max **18** n.19
Schwalbach, Stephen **11** n.786
Schwartz, John W. **10** n.20
Schwartz, Murray **4** n.214
Scott, Sam E. **19** n.12

Sealy Power, Ltd. **10** n.119
Seaman, Jr., John W. **1** n.140
Seaview Trading, LLC v. Comm'r . . . **S10** ns.
   17.1, 283.1
Seay, Tym **14** n.25; **19** n.87
Securities-Intermountain, Inc. v. United
   States **17** n.64
Segall, Comm'r v. **12** n.27
Seismic Support Servs., LLC **S14** n.243
Sellers, Frank E. . . . . **11** ns. 11, 15
Sellers, Randy G. **S11** n.816
Sellers v. Comm'r . . . 3 n.362; **15** ns. 37, 43,
   61
Sellers v. United States **11** n.15
Seminole Flavor Co. v. Comm'r **3** n.125
Semmes, Bowen & Semmes v. United States
   . . . . **9** n.999
Seneca, Ltd. (9th Cir.) . . . . 10.02[2]; **10** n.49
Seneca, Ltd. (TC) . . . . . . 10.02[2]; **10** n.58
Sennett, William **11** n.616
Sente Inv. Club P'ship of Utah **10** n.8
September Partners, Ltd. **10** n.47
Service Bolt & Nut Co. Profit Sharing Trust
   . . . . **9** n.767
70 Acre Recognition Equip. P'ship . . **10** n.24
7050, Ltd. **S13** n.13
Seyburn, George D. . . . . **16** ns. 148, 151; **17**
   n.20
Shaheen, George A. **6** n.18; **16** n.15
Shapiro, Comm'r v. **16** n.156; **17** n.4
Shapiro, United States v. **17** n.7
Shasta Strategic Inv. Fund, LLC v. United
   States **S10** n.89.6
Sheldon, Steven R. . . . . . . 1.05[4][b][iii]; **1** ns.
   126, 128–130, 198
Shellabarger Grain Prods. Co. v. Comm'r
   . . . . **4** n.212
Shorthorn Genetic Eng'g 1982-2 Ltd. **10**
   n.195
Siben, Gary L. . . . . 9.06[3]; **9** ns. 1128, 1129
Sicard, Leon L. **14** n.228
Siegel, Charles H. **9** n.422
Sierra Design Research & Dev. Ltd. P'ship
   . . . . **10** n.52
Siller Bros.   9 n.698; **13** ns. 112, 175; **19** ns.
   141, 142
Silversmith v. United States **9** n.224
Simek v. United States **10** n.165
Simon v. Comm'r **16** n.213
Sirrine Bldg. No. 1 v. Comm'r . . . **10** n.218;
   13 n.13
6611, Ltd., Ricardo Garcia, Tax Matters
   Partner **S3** n.192; **S10** n.75.10
Sixty-Three Strategic Inv. Funds v. United
   States **S10** n.286
Skaggs, Ernest D., Estate of **13** n.82; **24**
   ns. 12, 209
Sloan, David B. **16** n.68
Slovacek v. United States (Fed. Cl. 1998) . . .
   . . . . **10** ns. 211, 303
Slovacek v. United States (Fed. Cl. 1996) . . .
   . . . . 10.02[3]; **10** ns. 82, 94
Slutsky, United States v. **9** n.3

[Text references are to paragraphs; note references are to chapters (boldface numbers) and notes ("n."). References to the supplement are preceded by "S."]

[Text references are to paragraphs; note references are to chapters (boldface numbers) and notes ("n."). References to the supplement are preceded by "S."]

[Text references are to paragraphs; note references are to chapters (boldface numbers) and notes ("n."). References to the supplement are preceded by "S."]

[Text references are to paragraphs; note references are to chapters (boldface numbers) and notes ("n."). References to the supplement are preceded by "S."]

Cumulative Index

[References are to paragraphs; references to the supplement are preceded by "S."]